THE APOCALYPSE
OF ST JOHN

THE APOCALYPSE OF ST JOHN

THE GREEK TEXT

WITH

INTRODUCTION NOTES AND INDICES

BY

HENRY BARCLAY SWETE, D.D.

HON. LITT.D. DUBLIN HON. D.D. GLASGOW
REGIUS PROFESSOR OF DIVINITY
AND FELLOW OF GONVILLE AND CAIUS COLLEGE, CAMBRIDGE
FELLOW OF THE BRITISH ACADEMY

Wipf and Stock Publishers
150 West Broadway • Eugene OR 97401

1998

ECCLESIAM TUAM, QUAESUMUS, DOMINE, BENIGNUS ILLUSTRA, UT BEATI IOHANNIS...ILLUMINATA DOCTRINIS AD DONA PERUENIAT SEMPITERNA. PER DOMINUM.

CONCEDE, QUAESUMUS, OMNIPOTENS DEUS, UT QUI...UNIGENITUM TUUM REDEMPTOREM NOSTRUM AD CAELOS ASCENDISSE CREDIMUS, IPSI QUOQUE MENTE IN CAELESTIBUS HABITEMUS. PER EUNDEM.

EXCITA, QUAESUMUS, DOMINE, POTENTIAM TUAM ET UENI, ET MAGNA NOBIS UIRTUTE SUCCURRE, UT AUXILIUM GRATIAE TUAE QUOD NOSTRA PECCATA PRAEPEDIUNT INDULGENTIA TUAE PROPITIATIONIS ACCELERET. QUI UIUIS.

The Apocalypse of St. John
The Greek Text with Introduction Notes and Indices
By Swete, Henry Barclay, D.D.

ISBN: 1-57910-218-2

Reprinted by *Wipf and Stock Publishers* 1999
150 West Broadway • Eugene OR 97401

Previously Published by Macmillan and Co., LTD., 1906

VIRO · ADMODVM · REVERENDO ·

FREDERICO · HENRICO · CHASE · S·T·P·

EPISCOPO · ELIENSI ·

APVD · CANTABRIGIENSES · NVPER · PROFESSORI · NORRISIANO ·

OBSERVANTIAE · ERGO · AMICITIAEQVE ·

STVDIA · HAEC · APOCALYPTICA · QVALIACVMQVE ·

DEDICO

PREFACE.

EIGHT years ago I was permitted to finish a commentary on the earliest of the four Gospels. As a sequel to it, I now offer a commentary on the Revelation of St John.

The Apocalypse discloses the heavenly life of our Lord, as the Gospels paint His life in Galilee and Jerusalem. In the Gospels, He is seen teaching and working in His mortal flesh; in the Apocalypse, He belongs to another and a higher order. But the ascended life is a continuation of the life in the flesh; the Person is *the same yesterday and to-day*, in Palestine and in Heaven.

Thus the Apocalypse carries forward the revelation of the Gospels. It carries it, however, into a region where the methods of the biographer and historian avail nothing. We are in the hands of a prophet, who sees and hears things that elude the eyes and ears of other men; the simple narrative of the Evangelist has given place to a symbolism which represents the struggle of the Apocalyptist to express ideas that lie in great part beyond the range of human thought. Yet the life which St John reveals is not less real than that which is depicted by St Mark, nor are its activities less amazing. No miracles meet us here, but we are in the presence of spiritual processes which are more wonderful than the healing of the sick or the raising of the dead: a supervision of all the Churches, which surpasses the powers of any earthly pastor; an ordering of nature and life, which bears witness to the investment of the risen Lord with *all authority in heaven and on earth*; a perfect knowledge of men, and a prescience which reads the issues of history. The revelation of the Lord's heavenly life becomes, as we proceed, a revelation of *the things which are and the things which shall come to pass hereafter*; we see the glorified life in its bearing upon the course of events, until the end has been attained and the whole creation has felt its renovating power.

To comment on this great prophecy is a harder task than to comment on a Gospel, and he who undertakes it exposes himself to the charge of presumption. I have been led to venture upon what I know to be dangerous ground by the conviction that the English student needs an edition of this book which shall endeavour to take account of the large accessions to knowledge made in recent years, and shall be drawn upon a scale commensurate with that of the larger commentaries on other books of the New Testament. More especially I have had in view the wants of the English clergy, who, scholars at heart by early education or by the instincts of a great tradition, are too often precluded from reaping the fruits of research through inability to procure or want of leisure to read a multitude of books. It is my belief, and the belief has grown in strength as my task has proceeded, that the Apocalypse offers to the pastors of the Church an unrivalled store of materials for Christian teaching, if only the book is approached with an assurance of its prophetic character, chastened by a frank acceptance of the light which the growth of knowledge has cast and will continue to cast upon it.

The Apocalypse is well-worked ground. It would not be difficult to construct a commentary which should be simply a catena of patristic and mediaeval expositions, or an attempt to compare and group the views of later writers. Such an undertaking would not be without interest or value, but it lies outside the scope of the present work. In this commentary, as in the commentary on St Mark, it has been my endeavour, in the first instance, to make an independent study of the text, turning to the commentaries afterwards for the purpose of correcting or supplementing my own conclusions. As a rule, the interpretations which are offered here are those which seemed to arise out of the writer's own words, viewed in connexion with the circumstances under which he wrote, and the general purpose of his work, without reference to the various schools of Apocalyptic exegesis. There are those to whom the results will appear bizarre, and a medley of heterogeneous elements; but the syncretism, if it be such, has been reached, not by the blending of divergent views, but through the guidance of definite principles, which are stated in the introduction. Here it may be briefly explained that I have sought to place each passage in the light of the conditions under which the book was composed, and to interpret accordingly; not forgetting, however, the power inherent in all true prophecy of fulfilling itself in circumstances remote from those which called it forth.

But, with this reservation, I have gladly used the labours of predecessors in the field, especially the pregnant remarks of the patristic writers. Of modern commentators, Bousset has helped me most, and though I differ profoundly from his general attitude towards the book, and from not a few of his interpretations, I gladly acknowledge that I have greatly benefited by the stores of knowledge with which his book abounds. The Jewish Apocalypses edited by Professor Charles, and other apocalyptic writings, Jewish and Christian, have been always at my side. For geographical and archaeological details I am deeply indebted to the works of Professor W. M. Ramsay, the article on Asia Minor by Dr Johannes Weiss in Hauck's recast of Herzog's *Realencyklopädie*, and the admirable monograph on Proconsular Asia contributed by Monsieur Victor Chapot to the *Bibliothèque de l'École des Hautes Études.*

During my preparations for the press, I have been unable to make a personal use of the University Library; and though my difficulty has been partly overcome in the past year through the kindness of the Syndics of the Library, the loss has been serious, and I fear that it will be felt by readers who look for fulness of detail and the use of the latest editions. From gross inaccuracies my work has been saved, as I trust, by the ready help of many friends. My warm thanks are due to the Rev. J. H. Srawley, of Gonville and Caius and Selwyn Colleges, and to the Rev. H. C. O. Lanchester, Fellow of Pembroke College, who have read the proofs of the introduction, text, and notes. Mr Srawley has verified nearly all the references in the notes; the indices and the Biblical references in the introduction have been corrected by the care of a relative. My colleagues, Professor Reid and Professor Ridgeway, have allowed me to submit to them the proofs of portions of my book in which I had occasion to enter upon ground which they have severally made their own. To the Rev. A. S. Walpole, editor of a volume of Latin Hymns which is shortly to appear in *Cambridge Patristic Texts*, I owe my knowledge of the splendid stanzas which precede the introduction.

Other debts of various kinds call for acknowledgement here. Messrs T. and T. Clark, of Edinburgh, with the ready consent of Professor Ramsay, have permitted me to adapt to my own use the map of Asia Minor which accompanies the article on *Roads and Travel* (*in the New Testament*) in the supplementary volume of Hastings' *Dictionary of the Bible.* The Rev. T. C. Fitzpatrick, President of Queens' College, supplied the negative from which the engraving of Patmos has been produced; and the specimen of MS. 186 came from a photograph of the entire MS. kindly taken for me by Professor Lake, of Oxford and Leyden. For the page of coins illustrating the life and worship of pagan Asia in the age of the Apocalypse I have to thank Dr M. R. James, Director of the Fitzwilliam Museum, who helped me to select them from Colonel Leake's famous collection, and his assistant, Mr H. A. Chapman, to whose skill the casts were due. Lastly, it is a pleasure once again to say how much I owe to the unfailing attention of the workmen and readers and the ready assistance of the officials of the University Press.

I part with the work which has occupied the leisure of some years under a keen sense of the shortcomings that are apparent even when it is judged by the standard of my own expectations, yet not without an assured hope that it may help some of my fellow-students to value and understand a book which is in some respects the crown of the New Testament canon. In letting it go from me, I can only repeat Augustine's prayer, which stood at the end of the preface to *St Mark*, and is even more necessary here. *Domine Deus...quaecumque dixi in hoc libro de tuo, agnoscant et tui; si qua de meo, et Tu ignosce et tui.*

H. B. S.

CAMBRIDGE,
F. of the Transfiguration, 1906.

CONTENTS.

IOHANNES APOCALYPTISTA

Caelum transit, veri rotam
solis uidit, ibi totam
mentis figens aciem :
speculator spiritalis
quasi seraphim sub alis
Dei uidit faciem.

audiit in gyro sedis
quid psallant cum citharoedis
quater seni proceres :
de sigillo Trinitatis
nostrae nummo ciuitatis
impressit characteres.

uolat auis sine meta
quo nec uates nec propheta
euolauit altius :
tam implenda quam impleta
numquam uidit tot secreta
purus homo purius.

I.

PROPHECY IN THE APOSTOLIC CHURCH.

1. The Christian era opened with a revival of Prophecy. In the Maccabean age and the times that followed it the prophetic order was believed to be dead, or in a state of suspended vitality; in matters pertaining to God men acted provisionally, "till there should arise a faithful prophet[1]" to interpret the Divine Will. Whether this impression was correct or not[2], it is certain that the Advent was marked by an outburst of prophetic utterance to which the two centuries before Christ can offer no parallel. Prophetic gifts were exercised by the priest Zacharias, by Simeon of Jerusalem, by Hannah of the tribe of Asher[3]. As for John, the son of Zacharias, he was not only universally accounted a prophet, but pronounced by Christ to be "much more," since the prophet who was the Lord's immediate forerunner had greater honour than those who from a distance foresaw His coming[4].

2. Christian prophecy begins with the Ministry of Christ. The crowds which hung upon His lips both in Galilee and at Jerusalem, and even the Samaritan woman who at first resented His teaching, recognized in Him a Prophet,—perhaps a *propheta redivivus*, a Jeremiah restored to life[5]. Nor did the Lord hesitate to accept this view of His mission[6]; if it was inadequate, yet it correctly described one side of His work. A Prophet Himself, He came to inaugurate a new line of prophets; He undertook to endow His new Israel with the prophetic Spirit which had been

[1] 1 Macc. iv. 46, ix. 27, xiv. 41; see also Ps. lxxiv. 9.

[2] See Harnack, *Mission u. Ausbreitung*, i. p. 240 f. (E. tr. i. p. 414 f.).

[3] Lc. i. 67, ii. 25, 36.

[4] Mt. xi. 9 ff., Mc. xi. 32, Lc. vii. 26 ff.

[5] Mt. xvi. 14, Mc. vi. 15, Jo. iv. 19, vi. 14, vii. 40, ix. 17.

[6] Mc. vi. 4, Jo. iv. 44; cf. Acts iii. 22, vii. 37.

the glory of the ancient people of God[1]. The Church was to possess not only "scribes," whose task it would be to interpret the Christian tradition, but inspired teachers, able through the Spirit to guide believers into new fields of thought and action[2].

3. The earliest history of the Church shews the fulfilment of these hopes and promises. On the Day of Pentecost, in a speech attributed to St Peter, the words of Joel are applied to the future Israel: *your sons and your daughters shall prophesy...yea and on my servants and on my handmaidens in those days will I pour forth of my Spirit, and they shall prophesy*[3]. How soon a recognized order of prophets arose in the Church of Jerusalem there is no evidence to shew, but about the year 43—4[4] Christian prophets from Jerusalem, Agabus and others, made their way to Antioch, and shortly afterwards resident prophets ministered there in the congregation[5]. After the conference at Jerusalem (A.D. 49) the hands of the Antiochian prophets were strengthened by the coming of two other prophets from the mother Church, Judas Barsabbas and Silas[6]. Seven years later, the daughters of Philip the Evangelist are found exercising prophetic gifts at Caesarea; and on the same occasion St Paul's arrest at Jerusalem is foretold by a prophet from Judaea, one Agabus[7], probably the same person who had predicted the Claudian famine. His prophecy came as no surprise to the Apostle, who had received similar warnings from Christian prophets in the cities through which he had passed on his way to Palestine[8]. Prophets were to be found everywhere in the Churches planted by St Paul.

4. From what has been said it appears that the new prophecy began at Jerusalem, and spread from Jerusalem to Antioch, and from Antioch to Asia Minor and Greece. The Epistles of St Paul bear witness to its presence at Thessalonica, at Corinth, at Ephesus,

[1] Lc. xi. 49, Jo. xvi. 12 ff.

[2] Mt. xiii. 52, xxiii. 34, Lc. xi. 49.

[3] Acts ii. 17 f. (Joel ii. 28 f.). On the probability that the Petrine speeches in the Acts substantially represent St Peter's words see Bp Chase, *Credibility of the Acts*, p. 117 ff.

[4] I follow Mr Turner's chronology (Hastings, *D.B.* i. p. 415 ff.).

[5] Acts xi. 27, xiii. 1 f.

[6] Acts xv. 22; cf. *ib.* 32 καὶ αὐτοὶ προφῆται ὄντες.

[7] Acts xxi. 10 ff.

[8] Acts xx. 23 τὸ πνεῦμα τὸ ἅγιον κατὰ πόλιν διαμαρτυρεῖταί. Cf. xxi. 4.

and at Rome[1]; and probably also in the Churches of South Galatia, at Lystra and Iconium[2]. To Rome as to Antioch the prophets may have come from Jerusalem; in the other Churches named above, prophecy was one of the fruits of St Paul's preaching. We are able to note the impression which the gift produced upon the Gentile converts. At Thessalonica there was a disposition to think light of it, and even at Corinth it was valued less highly than the gift of tongues. St Paul, while admitting the need of discrimination between the prophet and the pretender, or between worthy utterances and unworthy[3], insists that the true prophet was, after the apostle, the greatest of the gifts bestowed upon the Church by the ascended Christ[4]. The prophet's mission was to build up the Church which the apostle had founded; to edify, exhort, console believers[5]; to convict unbelievers, laying bare the secrets of their hearts and assuring them of the Divine Presence in the Christian brotherhood[6]. The ideal prophet knew all mysteries and all knowledge[7]. Yet prophecy was liable to abuse, and its exercise needed to be carefully regulated. At Corinth, where, when St Paul wrote his first Epistle (probably in 55), a strong tide of prophetic power had set in, it was necessary to enact that not more than two or three prophets should speak at the same meeting of the Church, and only one prophet at a time, and to remind the prophets themselves that they were responsible for the proper control of their gift; they were not automata in the hands of the Spirit, for *the spirits of the prophets are subject to the prophets*[8].

5. While the most remarkable display of prophetic powers of which we have any detailed account took place at Corinth, it was perhaps chiefly at Ephesus and in the other cities of Asia that the prophets took root as a recognized order. The Epistle to the Ephesians, probably an encyclical addressed to all the Asian Churches, not merely assigns to the prophetic order the same

[1] 1 Thess. v. 20, 1 Cor. xii. 28, xiii. 2, xiv. 3 ff., Eph. iii. 1 ff., iv. 7 ff., Rom. xii. 6.

[2] 1 Tim. iv. 14, 2 Tim. i. 6.

[3] 1 Th. v. 21, 1 Cor. xiv. 29. Contrast *Didache* 11.

[4] 1 Cor. xii. 28, Eph. iv. 11.

[5] 1 Cor. xiv. 3, 4.

[6] *Ib.* 23 ff.

[7] 1 Cor. xiii. 2.

[8] 1 Cor. xiv. 32.

place of honour which they receive in 1 Corinthians, but lays repeated stress on the greatness of their work; the local Church had been *built upon the foundation of the apostles and prophets*; the prophets, as well as the pastors and teachers, had been given *for the complete equipment of the saints for the work of service*[1].

It is from the prophetic circles in this group of Churches that the one great literary product of early Christian prophecy emanates. In St Paul's time the utterances of the prophets seem to have been exclusively oral; it is in the Apocalypse of John that prophecy under the New Covenant first takes a written form[2]. Both in the prologue and in the epilogue, the work of John lays claim to a prophetic character[3]; and in the heart of the book the writer represents himself as hearing a voice which warns him, *Thou must prophesy again*[4]. Moreover, it is clear that he is not a solitary prophet, but a member of an order which occupies a recognized and important position in the Christian societies of Asia. His 'brother-prophets' are mentioned[5], and they appear to form the most conspicuous circle in the local Churches. The Church, as viewed in the Apocalypse, consists of the Spirit and the Bride, the charismatic ministry and the great body of believers. No special place is assigned to local Church officers, whether bishops or presbyters or deacons[6]; unless they are also prophets, which may often have been the case, they take rank with ordinary members of the Church. We read of God's "servants the prophets," of "prophets and saints," of "saints, apostles, and prophets[7]"; but nowhere of "the saints with the bishops and deacons[8]," or even of "pastors and teachers" as distinct from prophets[9]. The Apocalyptist's standpoint in reference to the Christian ministry is not quite that of St Paul; indeed, he assigns to the apostles

[1] Eph. iv. 12 (see Dean Armitage Robinson's note *ad loc.*).

[2] Except in the case of prophecies which form part of an apostolic letter, or have been incorporated in the Gospels (e.g. 2 Thess. ii., Mc. xiii.).

[3] Cf. Apoc. i. 3, xxii. 7, 10, 18 f. It is scarcely necessary to say that this claim does not require us to expect direct predictions of future events. As Dr A. B. Davidson has well said (*O. T. Prophecy*, p. 119), "there is much prophecy, but there are few predictions, in the Apocalypse."

[4] Apoc. x. 11.

[5] Apoc. xxii. 9.

[6] For the probable meaning of the Angels of the Churches see the commentary on Apoc. i. 20.

[7] Apoc. x. 7, xvi. 6, xviii. 20, 24.

[8] Phil. i. 1 *τοῖς ἁγίοις...σὺν ἐπισκόποις καὶ διακόνοις*.

[9] Eph. iv. 11.

and prophets a position even more prominent than that which they hold in the *Didache*[1]. In the age of the Apocalypse, as in the lifetime of St Paul, the Asian Churches doubtless had their presbyters and deacons, but in the eyes of St John they were eclipsed by the greater lustre of the charismatic orders. Such a view of the ministry is not unnatural in a prophetic book, written by a prominent member of the prophetic order; but that it should have been presented frankly and without reserve to Churches so important and well organized as those of Ephesus, Smyrna, and Pergamum, is sufficient evidence of the high honour in which the Christian Prophet was held in Asia at that time. The prophets of the Church have contributed but one book to the canon of the New Testament; but it is a monument of the great position which they had attained before the end of the first century.

After the date of the Apocalypse the decline of the order in Asia must have been rapid and general[2]. Of pre-Montanistic prophets not named in the New Testament only two names have reached us —those of Ammia of Philadelphia and Quadratus (Eus. *H. E.* v. 17; cf. iii. 37[3]). It is significant also that in the letters of Ignatius, who magnifies the office of the bishop, "the prophets" are invariably those of the Old Testament canon (*Magn.* 8. 2, *Philad.* 5. 2, 9. 1, 2), and though Polycarp was remembered in his own Church as an "apostolic and prophetic teacher" (*mart. Polyc.* 16), in his letter to the Philippians he associates the Apostles with the old prophets, and not, as St Paul had done, with those of the New Testament (*Phil.* 6. 3 οἱ εὐαγγελισάμενοι ἡμᾶς ἀπόστολοι καὶ οἱ προφῆται οἱ προκηρύξαντες κτλ.). The Montanistic movement testifies to a reaction in favour of the prophets, which was at its strongest in Asia, but extended as far west as Gaul; cf. Iren. ii. 32, v. 6. 3. But the "new prophecy" produced no important literary work, for the 'catholic' Epistle of Themison (Eus. *H. E.* v. 18) does not appear to have had a prophetic character.

[1] The *Didache* shews some recovery in the position of the local officers; cf. § 15 ὑμῖν γὰρ λειτουργοῦσιν καὶ αὐτοὶ τὴν λειτουργίαν τῶν προφητῶν καὶ διδασκάλων. Yet the μὴ οὖν ὑπερίδητε αὐτούς which immediately follows proves that there were still those who held the prophet in the highest esteem, to the disparagement of the Church-officer. And the *Didache* itself (§ 13) says of the prophets: αὐτοὶ γάρ εἰσιν οἱ ἀρχιερεῖς ὑμῶν.

[2] It may have been due to the concurrence of several causes, such as persecution, which would fall on the prophets with special severity; the emergence of the monarchical episcopate; a decay of spiritual power in the prophetic order itself, and the seemingly not uncommon occurrence of ψευδοπροφῆται. Yet the Catholic Church was slow to abandon her hold on the gift; cf. Apollinarius *ap.* Eus. *H. E.* v. 17 δεῖν γὰρ εἶναι τὸ προφητικὸν χάρισμα ἐν πάσῃ τῇ ἐκκλησίᾳ μέχρι τῆς τελείας παρουσίας ὁ ἀπόστολος ἀξιοῖ, and see Harnack, *T. u. U.* ii. 1, p. 123.

[3] On these see Zahn, *Forschungen* vi. 1; Harnack, *Chronologie* i., p. 320 ff. Harnack places both under Hadrian.

II.

APOCALYPSES, JEWISH AND CHRISTIAN.

1. If the book which John addresses to the Churches of Asia is a 'prophecy,' a Divine message communicated by a member of the prophetic order, it is also an 'apocalypse,' a revelation of Divine mysteries. The title Ἀποκάλυψις, or Ἀποκάλυψις Ἰωάννου, may have found a place at the end of an early copy of the book, or on a label attached to the roll[1]; in any case it seems to have been familiar before the end of the second century[2]. The point is not material, since the author in the first words of his book describes it as an ἀποκάλυψις Ἰησοῦ Χριστοῦ, a revelation made by God to Jesus Christ, and by Christ through the ministry of an angel to John for transmission to the Churches. The word 'apocalypse' does not appear again in the book, but its position in the forefront of the prologue doubtless suggested the ancient title, and justifies our use of it.

2. The history of the verb ἀποκαλύπτειν and its derivative ἀποκάλυψις is sufficiently discussed in the commentary[3]. 'Revelation' is the converse of concealment[4], the process of casting aside the veil that hides a mystery. St Paul uses the noun in reference both to the gift of spiritual vision and to its results; the gift is a πνεῦμα ἀποκαλύψεως[5], and its exercise is an ἀποκάλυψις[6]. The

[1] See Gardthausen, *Griech. Palaeographie*, p. 53; Thompson, *Greek and Latin Palaeography*, p. 57 f.; Kenyon, *Pal. of Greek papyri*, p. 22.

[2] See *cc.* ix, x.

[3] See p. 5.

[4] See e.g. Mt. xi. 25 ἔκρυψας ταῦτα ἀπὸ σοφῶν καὶ συνετῶν, καὶ ἀπεκάλυψας αὐτὰ νηπίοις. Rom. xvi. 25 κατὰ ἀποκάλυψιν μυστηρίου χρόνοις αἰωνίοις σεσιγημένου. Eph. iii. 3 κατὰ ἀποκάλυψιν ἐγνωρίσθη μοι τὸ μυστήριον.

[5] Eph. i. 17.

[6] 1 Cor. xiv. 6, 26, 2 Cor. xii. 1 (where ἀποκαλύψεις are coupled with ὀπτασίαι), 7; the verb is similarly used in 1 Cor. xiv. 30.

gift of revelation took its place as an instrument of edification by the side of the gift of prophecy; it was in fact a particular manifestation of the prophetic Spirit, in which the spirit of the prophet seemed to be carried up into a higher sphere, endowed for the time with new powers of vision, and enabled to hear words which could not be reproduced in the terms of human thought, or could be reproduced only through the medium of symbolical imagery[1]. While the prophets normally dealt with human life in its relation to God, reading and interpreting the thoughts of men, and thus convicting, exhorting, or consoling them according to their several needs, he who 'had an apocalypse' strove to express his personal realization of the unseen or of the distant future.

3. The 'apocalypses' which in St Paul's day might be heard at times in the Christian assemblies were unpremeditated utterances, flashes of light which suddenly illumined the consciousness of the men who spoke, and as suddenly vanished[2]. Of these revelations no trace remains, nor were they ever, so far as we know, committed to writing. The Revelation of John is the only written apocalypse, as it is the only written prophecy of the Apostolic age. Yet it was not by any means the earliest literary product of the apocalyptic movement. A written apocalypse was no novelty in Jewish pre-Christian literature; there are examples of this class of writing within the canon of the Old Testament, and besides these, eight or nine extant apocalyptic works may be enumerated which are wholly or in part of Jewish provenance.

[1] 2 Cor. xii. 4 *ἡρπάγη εἰς τὸν παράδεισον καὶ ἤκουσεν ἄρρητα ῥήματα.* This was however no ordinary occasion; cf. *v.* 7 *τῇ ὑπερβολῇ τῶν ἀποκαλύψεων.* The anti-Montanist writer in Eus. *H. E.* v. 17 contends *μὴ δεῖν προφήτην ἐν ἐκστάσει λαλεῖν*, which agrees with St Paul's doctrine: *πνεύματα προφητῶν προφήταις ὑποτάσσεται.* Such an apocalypse, however, as that of John implies a state of 'ecstasy' at the time when it occurred (cf. e.g. i. 10 ff., iv. 1, and *passim*), although the message may well have been written afterwards.

[2] Tertullian describes the revelations which were heard in Montanist assemblies at Carthage in his own day; *de anima* 9 "nam quia spiritalia charismata agnoscimus, post Ioannem quoque prophetiam meruimus consequi. est hodie soror apud nos revelationum charismata sortita, quas in ecclesia inter dominica solemnia per ecstasin in spiritu patitur; conversatur cum angelis, aliquando etiam cum Domino, et videt et audit sacramenta et quorundam corda dinoscit," etc. The picture may be taken, *mutatis mutandis*, as descriptive of the *ἀποκαλύψεις* which broke the order of more primitive congregations at Corinth in St Paul's time.

Of these the greater number were earlier than the Apocalypse of John; a few were nearly contemporary with it.

Within the canon of the Old Testament apocalyptic passages occur even in the Pentateuch (Gen. xv., xlix., Num. xxiii., xxiv.) and historical books (1 Kings xxii.); in the Prophets they form a considerable element, especially in Isaiah (Isa. xiii. ff., xxiv. ff., lxv. f.), Ezekiel, Joel, and Zechariah; Ezekiel's prophecy in particular is almost wholly of an apocalyptic character[1]. But it is in the Book of Daniel that the later conception of the literary apocalypse is first realized. Though reckoned among the Kethubim of the Hebrew Bible, a class in which it usually stands eighth, ninth, or tenth of eleven writings[2], in the Greek Old Testament Daniel secured a place among the Prophets[3], doubtless because the second half of the book (*cc.* vii.—xii.) is of the nature of an apocalyptic prophecy[4]. Judging by its place in the Hebrew canon, and by historical and other considerations, this book seems to belong to the interval B.C. 168—165, the years during which the hand of Antiochus Epiphanes lay heavy on the Jewish people. The writer's purpose is to strengthen the religious section of the nation under this supreme test of their faith and loyalty. He is carried back in the Spirit to the days of the Exile, and identifies himself with Daniel, a Jewish captive at Babylon, who is represented as foreseeing in a series of great visions the course of events that culminated in the troubles of the Maccabean age. From the standpoint of the writer all events later than the age of Daniel are *ex hypothesi* future; but the book is not without actual predictions: the author, who writes while the persecution is still going on, foresees the issue with a confidence which comes from the sense of a Divine gift.

Next in importance to Daniel among Jewish apocalypses[5] is the Book of Enoch[6], a composite work of which the several portions are variously dated by scholars. It must suffice here to quote an eminent German and an eminent English authority. Schürer[7] regards *cc.* i.—xxxvi. and *cc.* lxxii.—cv. as belonging to the time of John Hyrcanus, and places the "Similitudes" (*cc.* xxxvii.—

[1] A. B. Davidson, *Ezekiel*, Introd. p. xxv.: "there are three things in particular which are characteristic of the Book: symbolical figures, symbolical actions, and visions."

[2] *Introduction to the O. T. in Greek*, p. 200.

[3] *Ib.* p. 201 ff.; cf. Mt. xxiv. 25 τὸ ῥηθὲν διὰ Δανιὴλ τοῦ προφήτου.

[4] Cf. Driver, *Daniel*, Introd. p. lxxvii.: "both the symbolism and the veiled predictions are characteristic of a species of literature which was now beginning to spring up, and which is known commonly by modern writers as *Apocalyptic literature.*"

[5] The following sketch of the non-canonical apocalypses is added for the sake of readers to whom this literature, much of which until recent years has been difficult of access, may be almost unknown. Further particulars may be found in Schürer, *Geschichte des jüd. Volkes*³ iii., p. 181 ff. [=E. T. II. iii., p. 54 ff.]; Kautzsch, *Die Apokryphen u. Pseudepigraphen des A. T.*; *Encyclopaedia Biblica*, art. "Apocalyptic Literature."

[6] Ed. Charles (Clarendon Press, 1893).

[7] *Geschichte*³ iii., p. 196 ff.

lxxi.) at the earliest in the reign of Herod the Great. According to Charles, *cc.* lxxxiii.—xc. are Maccabean (B.C. 166—161), and *cc.* i.—xxxvi. pre-Maccabean, "at latest before 170 B.C.[1]," while *cc.* xxxvii.—lxxi. belong to B.C. 94—79, or to B.C. 70—64. As the uncertainty which attends the dating of the sections indicates, allusions to events or persons are rare in Enoch; the book in all its parts is visionary and eschatological, dealing with angels and spirits, with the secrets of Nature and the mysteries of the unseen world and its rewards and punishments; and less often and in a vague and general way with the course of human history and its great issues. The apocalyptic imagery of Enoch anticipates the Apocalypse of John in not a few particulars; both books, e.g., know of the Tree of life and the Book of life; both represent heavenly beings as clothed in white; in both stars fall from heaven, horses wade through rivers of blood; the winds and the waters have their presiding spirits; a fiery abyss awaits notorious sinners[2].

The Book of the Secrets of Enoch[3], another survival of the pre-Christian Enoch literature, has been recently given to the world in an English translation by Professor Charles. According to its editor it belongs to the half century A.D. 1—50, but contains earlier fragments which have had a Hebrew original. In this attractive little book Enoch relates his travels into the unseen world; in the seventh heaven he sees the vision of God; he receives instructions from God, and is then sent back to the world for 30 days to teach his children, after which he is carried back by angels into the Divine Presence. As in the Book of Enoch, there are anticipations of the Johannine imagery. A great sea is above the clouds; in the third heaven there is a paradise stocked with fruit-trees bearing all manner of ripe fruits, and in the midst of it the Tree of Life. Faces are seen shining like the sun, and eyes as lamps of fire; there are angels set "over seasons and years...over rivers and the sea... over all the souls of men"; "six-winged creatures overshadow all the Throne...singing, Holy, Holy, Holy"; the world-week is of seven thousand years; Hades is a fortress whose keys are committed to safe keeping.

The Apocalypse of Baruch[4] is probably later than the fall of Jerusalem[5]. Like the book of Daniel its aim is to console and build up the Jewish people at a time of great depression. For this purpose the writer identifies himself with Baruch, the contemporary of Jeremiah, who is represented as foreseeing the coming troubles, and looking beyond them to their issue. He finds comfort in the prospect of the Messianic reign, and speaks of its glories in terms

[1] *Book of Enoch*, p. 25 ff. Cf. Dr Charles' articles in Hastings' *Dictionary of the Bible* and *Encycl. Biblica* ("Apocalyptic Literature").

[2] These coincidences are noted in the commentary as they occur. On the question of John's indebtedness to Enoch see *c.* xiii. in this introduction.

[3] Ed. Charles (Clarendon Press, 1896).

[4] Ed. Charles (A. & C. Black, 1896).

[5] So Schürer, *Geschichte*[3] iii., p. 227; Charles (*Apoc. Baruch*, p. vii.) prefers to say that it is "a composite work written in the latter half of the first century."

(*c.* xxix.) which stirred the enthusiasm of Christian millenarians, and were even attributed to our Lord[1]. He foresees also the fall of Rome (*c.* xxxix.), and the rise of a new Jerusalem (*c.* iv.). Thus the Apocalypse of Baruch approximates to the nearly contemporary Christian Apocalypse not merely in verbal coincidences and the use of similar imagery, but in some important lines of thought.

The Fourth Book of Esdras[2] contains (*cc.* iii.—xiv.) a Jewish apocalypse which is now generally recognized as a work of the time of Domitian[3], to whose reign the Apocalypse of St John, according to Irenaeus, also belongs. The Jewish portion of 4 Esdras is marked by a pessimism which contrasts strongly with the hopefulness of the older Jewish apocalypses, and of the contemporary Christian apocalypse. The writer, who personates Ezra, arranges his matter in seven visions; the first two (iii. 1—v. 20, v. 21—vi. 34) deal with the general problem of evil; the third vision (vi. 35—ix. 25) depicts the Messianic reign, the judgement, and the intermediate state; the fourth (ix. 26—x. 60) represents the mourning of Zion for the fallen city, and the building of a new Jerusalem, whose glories, however, are not revealed; in the fifth (xi. 1—xii. 39) Rome, represented by an eagle, receives its sentence from the Messiah, who appears under the form of a lion; the sixth (xiii. 1—58) shews the Messiah rising from the sea to destroy His enemies and gather the scattered tribes of Israel; the seventh (xiv. 1—47) has to do with Ezra's personal history. Even this bare summary is enough to reveal the strong contrasts which, amidst much that is similar, distinguish the Jewish from the Christian apocalypse.

Other Jewish books, which either in literary form or in their general purpose are further removed from the Apocalypse of John, can only be mentioned here. Such are the *Book of Jubilees*[4], an haggadic commentary on Genesis; the *Assumption of Moses*[5], which together with the oldest Enoch was used by the Christian writer of the Epistle of Jude; the *Martyrdom of Isaiah*, incorporated in the *Ascension of Isaiah* (*cc.* ii., iii., v.[6]); the *Psalms of Solomon*[7], written in the interests of the Pharisees between A.D. 70 and 40; the *Apocalypses of Adam, Elijah*, and *Zephaniah*; the *Testament of Abraham, Isaac, and Jacob*, and the more important *Testaments of the Twelve Patriarchs*[8], all of which have been more or less worked over by Christian hands. More serviceable than any of the above for illustrating St John's Apocalypse are the Sibylline Oracles[9]. Of the Jewish Sibyllines Bk iii. 97—829 is assigned to the time of Ptolemy Physcon (B.C. 145—117), while Bks iv. and v. are said to

[1] Cf. Iren. v. 33. 3.

[2] Ed. Bensly and James in *Texts and Studies* iii. 2 (Camb. University Press, 1895).

[3] For the grounds of this conclusion see Schürer, *Geschichte*[3] iii., p. 241 ff., and cf. Mr Thackeray's art. *Second Book of Esdras* in Hastings' *D. B.*

[4] Ed. Charles (A. & C. Black, 1902).

[5] Ed. Charles (1897).

[6] Ed. Charles (1900).

[7] Ed. Ryle and James (Camb. University Press, 1891).

[8] An account of these works with bibliographical materials is given in *Enc. Biblica*, s.vv. Apocalyptic literature, Apocrypha.

[9] Ed. A. Rzach (Vienna, 1891), and Geffcken (Leipzig, 1902).

belong severally to the reigns of Domitian and Hadrian. The points of contact between this strange conglomerate of Jewish and Christian oracles and the Apocalypse have been noted in the commentary as they occur.

4. The whole of this Jewish apocalyptic literature, it will be seen, belongs to times when prophecy in the stricter sense was believed to be in suspense. In no single instance do the non-canonical apocalyptists write in their own names; their message is delivered under the assumed personality of some one of the saintly or inspired teachers of the past. Moreover, their attitude differs from that of the Hebrew Prophets. The older prophecy had been concerned primarily with the moral and religious needs of the nation; it was a call to repentance and to faith in God. The prophet of the canon had been the authorized interpreter of the Divine Mind to a theocratic people; if he had foretold the future, it was "the prediction of dissatisfaction, the prediction of hope, of anticipation, of awakened thoughts, of human possibility and Divine nearness[1]," rather than a formal announcement of coming events. To this rôle the apocalyptists did not wholly succeed. With the Greek conquests a new order began which was unfavourable to prophecy of the older type. Relief from the pressure of heathen domination or from the distasteful presence of heathen surroundings was henceforth sought in efforts to pierce the veil of the future, and to discover behind it the coming triumphs of the righteous. The Pharisaic movement offered salvation to the Jewish race partly in the way of an exact observance of the Law, partly by opening wider hopes to those who obeyed, and painting in darker colours the doom of the transgressor; and the earlier non-canonical apocalypses gave literary expression to these new hopes and fears. Another cause contributed to the growth of apocalyptic literature. With the coming of the Romans and the subsequent rise of the Herodian dynasty, the political outlook changed, and a fresh impulse was given to the expectation of a Messianic reign. In the first century the habits of thought which produced apocalyptic writing

[1] Davidson, *O. T. Prophecy*, p. 90.

were so firmly rooted in the Jewish mind that even the destruction of the City and Temple did not at once eradicate them; unable any longer to connect a glorious future with the Herodian buildings, the writers of the apocalypses of Baruch and Ezra looked for a Messiah who should crush the enemies of Israel, restore the nation, and realize the vision of an ideal Jerusalem. Despondent as the writer of the Ezra-apocalypse manifestly is, he does not formally relinquish the national hope, though in his case it is indefinitely deferred.

5. The first Christian apocalypse came on the crest of this long wave of apocalyptic effort. Compositions more or less similar both in form and in substance to the work of St John had been in circulation among Palestinian and Alexandrian Jews for two centuries and a half before he took up his pen to write the "Revelation of Jesus Christ." It may be claimed for St Paul that he created the Epistle, as we find it in the New Testament[1]; and the "memoirs of the Apostles," which from Justin's time have been known as "Gospels," have no exact literary parallel in pre-Christian literature. This cannot be said of the writer of the New Testament Apocalypse; he had models to follow, and to some extent he followed them. The apocalyptic portions of Ezekiel, Zechariah, and Daniel are continually present to his mind; and though it is less certain that he made use of Enoch or any other post-canonical apocalypse[2], he could scarcely have been ignorant of their existence and general character. But while it cannot be claimed that the author of the Apocalypse originated a type of literature, he is far from being a mere imitator of previous apocalyptic writing. The Apocalypse of John is in many ways a new departure. (1) The Jewish apocalypses are without exception pseudepigraphic; the Christian apocalypse bears the author's name[3]. This abandonment of a long-established tradition is significant; by it John claims for himself the position of a prophet who, conscious that he draws his inspiration from Christ or His angel and not at second hand, has no need to seek shelter under the name of a Biblical

[1] See Ramsay, *Letters to the Seven Churches*, p. 24 f.

[2] See p. cliii.

[3] On this point see *c.* xv.

saint. (2) How hard it is to determine the date and provenance of Jewish apocalypses is clear from the wide differences which divide the best scholars on these points. The fictitious names under which they pose suggest dates which are no less fictitious, and any evidence which these books can be made to yield as to the conditions under which they were written is wrung from them, as it were, against the will of their authors. The Apocalypse of John, on the contrary, makes no secret of its origin and destination; it is the work of a Christian undergoing exile in one of the islands of the Aegean; and it is addressed to the Christian congregations in seven of the chief cities of the adjacent continent, under circumstances which practically determine its date. (3) But it is not only in regard to pseudonymity and other matters of literary form that our Apocalyptist differs from his Jewish predecessors; the cleavage goes deeper. Whatever view may be taken of his indebtedness to Jewish sources, there can be no doubt that he has produced a book which, taken as a whole, is profoundly Christian, and widely removed from the field in which Jewish apocalyptic occupied itself. The narrow sphere of Jewish national hopes has been exchanged for the life and aims of a society whose field is the world and whose goal is the conquest of the human race. The Jewish Messiah, an uncertain and unrealized idea, has given place to the historical, personal Christ, and the Christ of the Christian apocalypse is already victorious, ascended, and glorified. Thus the faith and the hope of the Church have diverted apocalyptic thought into new channels and provided it with ends worthy of its pursuit. The tone of St John's book presents a contrast to the Jewish apocalypses which is not less marked. It breathes a religious spirit which is not that of its predecessors; it is marked with the sign of the Cross, the note of patient suffering, unabashed faith, tender love of the brethren, hatred of evil, invincible hope; and, notwithstanding the strange forms which from time to time are seen to move across the stage, the book as a whole is pervaded by a sense of stern reality and a solemn purpose which forbid the approach of levity. The Apocalypse of John is differentiated from the Apocalypse of Baruch or of

Ezra just as the Book of Daniel is differentiated from the Book of Enoch. However the fact may be explained, the two canonical apocalypses possess the notes of insight and foresight which suggest inspiration; the attentive reader becomes conscious of something in them both which is better than the unchastened imaginings of the mere mystic who conceives himself to possess a key to the secrets of life. In the Apocalypse of John the presence of the Spirit of revelation is unmistakably felt, and the Christian student may be pardoned if he recognizes in this book a fulfilment of the promise of a Paraclete who *shall declare...the things that are to come.*

6. If it were asked with what subjects a Christian apocalyptist, writing towards the close of the Apostolic age, might be expected to occupy himself, it is not difficult to conjecture the answer. As the first century advanced, two topics filled the field of Christian thought when it turned its gaze on the unseen and the future. Behind the veil of phenomena the human life of Jesus Christ was believed to be enshrined in the glory of God. To reveal this hidden life, to represent to the imagination the splendour of the Divine Presence in which it exists, to translate into human words or symbols the worship of Heaven, to exhibit the ascended Christ in His relation to these unknown surroundings: this would be the first business of the Christian seer. But a second great theme is inseparable from it. With the life of the glorified Lord the life of His Body, the Church, was identified in primitive Christian belief. In the last years of the first century the Church, which had begun her course with the promise of a rapid success, was reeling under the blows dealt her by the world. The two empires, the Kingdom of God and the World-power, were already at open war[1]. Men were asking what the end would be; which of the two forces would prevail. A Christian in those days who was conscious of possessing the spirit of revelation could not but endeavour to read the signs of the times and, so far as it was given him, to disclose the course and outcome of

[1] On this subject see Bp Westcott's essay on the Church and the World (*Epistles of St John*).

the struggle which had begun between the Empire and the Church.

On some such lines we might have sought to reconstruct the Apocalypse of John, had only fragments of it survived, guided by what we knew of the beliefs and hopes of the Apostolic age and of the history of the last thirty years of the first century. As a matter of fact, these are the lines on which the book has been written. It is an apocalypse of the glory of the exalted Christ; it is also an apocalypse of the sufferings and the ultimate triumph of the militant Church.

Christian apocalypses later than the Apocalypse of John were for the most part either recensions of Jewish books, or original works issued under Old Testament names. In a few cases they claim to be the work of Apostles or other N.T. saints. Gnosticism produced an *Anabaticon Pauli*[1], and the Revelations of Stephen and Thomas, denounced as 'apocryphal' in the so-called Decree of Gelasius, were also probably of Gnostic origin. One apocalyptic pseudepigraphon of the second century, the Ἀποκάλυψις Πέτρου, seemed for a time about to find a place within the canon by the side of the Apocalypse of John; it is coupled with the latter in the Muratorian Fragment (l. 71 sqq. "apocalypse[s] etiam Iohanis et Petri tantum recipimus[2], quam quidam ex nostris legi in e[c]clesia nolunt"); it was quoted, apparently as a genuine work of St Peter, by Clement of Alexandria[3]; it is included in the early Claromontane list[4]. But as time went on, the book found its own level. Eusebius reckons it among the spurious, or at least the doubtful books (*H. E.* iii. 25, cf. *ib.* iii. 2); and though it retained its popularity and was even read in some Eastern churches in the time of Sozomen (*H. E.* vii. 19), in the later lists of scriptural books it is placed among the *antilegomena* or the *apocrypha*[5]. From the large fragment[6] of the Petrine Apocalypse recovered in 1892 it is easy to account for the difference of opinion which seems to have existed about the book from the first; on the one hand it appealed strongly to the uneducated imagination by its attempt to portray the joys of Paradise and the torments of Gehenna, while upon the other its tone and purpose were on a different level from those of the canonical Apocalypse.

[1] Epiph. *haer.* xxxviii. 2.

[2] Zahn (*Gesch. d. NTlichen Kanons*, ii. p. 105 ff.) would read "et Petri unam tantum recipimus epistulam; fertur enim altera quam" etc. But neither the emendation nor the reason which he gives for it can be regarded as convincing.

[3] Eus. *H. E.* vi. 14. 1; cf. *ecl. proph.* 41, 48 f.

[4] Zahn, *Gesch.* ii. p. 159.

[5] So the list of Sixty Books and the Stichometry of Nicephorus (Zahn, *ib.*, pp. 292, 299 ff.).

[6] Cf. Dr M. R. James, *Revelation of Peter*, p. 51 f.: "a fragment of sufficient length to give us a fair idea of the contents of the whole Apocalypse. As a fact, it does contain something like 140 out of the original 300 lines of which the book consisted."

The fourth century has given us an *Apocalypse of Paul*[1], an attempt to report the ἄρρητα ῥήματα which St Paul heard when he was caught up into Paradise (2 Cor. xii. 2 ff.), well characterized by Augustine as a work the folly of which is no less conspicuous than its presumption[2]. Later still, but of more importance to the student of the N.T. Apocalypse, is a spurious Greek *Apocalypse of John*[3], first mentioned in a scholion of cent. iv. The author supposes St John to be, after the Ascension, alone on Mt Tabor, whence he is carried up in a bright cloud to the door of Heaven. Several of the features of the story are obviously borrowed from the canonical book; e.g. the opened heaven (§ 2), the book with seven seals (§ 3), the sending of Enoch and Elijah to expose Antichrist and be slain by him (§ 8); the Lamb with seven eyes and seven horns who breaks the seven seals (§ 18). But the spurious Apocalypse is chiefly occupied with eschatological speculations, grotesque descriptions of Antichrist (§ 7), and answers to curious questions connected with the resurrection of the body, the intermediate state, the last things, and the final judgement (§ 9 ff.).

An interesting apocalypse[4] forms the prologue of the 'Church Order' known as *Testamentum Domini*, printed by Lagarde in his *Reliquiae...syriace*, and edited by Rahmani in 1899 and in an English translation by Cooper and Maclean in 1902; a Latin fragment which is "the literal equivalent of certain sections" of this apocalypse is given by Dr James in *Texts and Studies*, ii. 3, p. 151 ff. The same volume of *Texts and Studies* contains an *Apocalypse of Sedrach*, and a late *Apocalypse of the Virgin*.

A study of post-canonical Christian apocalypses serves only to accentuate the unique importance of the canonical book. Among apocalypses of Christian origin the N.T. Apocalypse alone stands in a real relation to the life of the age in which it was written, or attempts to reveal the meaning and issues of the events which the writer had witnessed or was able to foresee. The N.T. Apocalypse alone deserves the name, or is in any true sense a 'prophecy.'

[1] Edited by Tischendorf in *Apocalypses Apocryphae* (1866), pp. 34—69; an early Latin version (*Visio Pauli*) is printed by Dr James in *Texts and Studies*, ii. 3, pp. 11—42.

[2] Aug. *tr. in Joann.* 98 "qua occasione vani quidam Apocalypsim Pauli, quam sana non recipit ecclesia, nescio quibus fabulis plenam stultissima praesumptione finxerunt."

[3] Edited by Tischendorf in *Apocalypses Apocryphae* (1866), pp. 70—94.

[4] On this see Harnack, *Chron.* ii., p. 514 ff.

III.

CONTENTS AND PLAN OF THE APOCALYPSE OF JOHN.

1. In his treatise Περὶ ἐπαγγελιῶν Dionysius of Alexandria († 265) writes as if the Apocalypse were already divided into *κεφάλαια*[1]. But if he refers to a formal capitulation, no other trace of it remains. When preparing to comment upon the book in the sixth century, Andreas, Archbishop of Cappadocian Caesarea, devised a system for his own use, which he would scarcely have done if there had been one in existence dating from the third century. Andreas's method is conventional and arbitrary, after the fashion of his age; he breaks up the Apocalypse into 24 longer sections (λόγοι), corresponding with the number of the Elders in *c.* iv., and subdivides each of these into three chapters (*κεφάλαια*), an arrangement suggested, as he says, by the threefold nature of man[2]. His *κεφάλαια*, however, represent fairly well the natural subdivisions of the book, and are printed below as exhibiting the earliest known analysis.

Κεφάλαια τῆς Ἰωάννου τοῦ θεολόγου ἀποκαλύψεως.

α΄. προοίμιον τῆς ἀποκαλύψεως, καὶ ὅτι δι' ἀγγέλου αὐτῷ δέδοται (i. 1—8). β΄. ὀπτασία, ἐν ᾗ τὸν Ἰησοῦν ἐθεάσατο ἐν μέσῳ λυχνιῶν ἑπτά (i. 9—20). γ΄. τὰ γεγραμμένα πρὸς τὸν τῆς Ἐφεσίων ἐκκλησίας ἄγγελον (ii. 1—7). δ΄. τὰ δηλωθέντα τῷ ἐν τῇ Σμυρναίων ἐκκλησίᾳ ἀγγέλῳ (ii. 8—11). ε΄. τὰ σημανθέντα τῷ τῆς Περγαμηνῶν ἐκκλησίας ἀγγέλῳ (ii. 12—17). ϛ΄. τὰ γεγραμμένα τῷ τῆς Θυατείρων ἐκκλησίας ἀγγέλῳ (ii. 18—29). ζ΄. τὰ ἀπεσταλμένα τῷ ἀγγέλῳ τῆς ἐν Σάρδεσιν

[1] Eus. *H. E.* vii. 25. 1 (= Feltoe, p. 114), *τινὲς μὲν οὖν τῶν πρὸ ἡμῶν ἠθέτησαν καὶ ἀνεσκεύασαν πάντη τὸ βιβλίον καὶ καθ' ἕκαστον κεφάλαιον διευθύνοντες κτλ.* Cf. Gregory, *prolegg.*, p. 141.

[2] *prolegg. in comm.*, *διελόντες τὴν παροῦσαν πραγματείαν εἰς λόγους κδ΄ καὶ οβ΄ κεφάλαια, διὰ τὴν τριμερῆ τῶν κδ΄ ὑπόστασιν σώματος καὶ ψυχῆς καὶ πνεύματος.*

ἐκκλησίας (iii. 1—6). η′. τὰ γραφέντα πρὸς τὸν τῆς Φιλαδελφέων ἐκκλησίας ἄγγελον (iii. 7—13). θ′. τὰ δηλωθέντα πρὸς τὸν τῆς Λαοδικέων ἐκκλησίας ἄγγελον (iii. 14—22). ι′. περὶ τῆς ὁραθείσης αὐτῷ θύρας ἐν τῷ οὐρανῷ καὶ τοῦ θρόνου καὶ τῶν κδ′ πρεσβυτέρων καὶ τῶν ἑξῆς δειχθέντων (iv. 1—11). ια′. περὶ τῆς βίβλου τῆς ἐσφραγισμένης σφραγῖσιν ἑπτὰ τῆς ἐν τῇ χειρὶ τοῦ θεοῦ, ἣν οὐδεὶς ἀνοῖξαι δύναται τῆς κτιστῆς φύσεως (v. 1—5). ιβ′. περὶ τοῦ ἀρνίου τοῦ τὰ ἑπτὰ κέρατα ἔχοντος, ὅπως τὴν βίβλον ἀνέῳξεν (v. 6—14). ιγ′. λύσις τῆς πρώτης σφραγῖδος, τὴν ἀποστολικὴν διδαχὴν σημαίνουσα (vi. 1, 2). ιδ′. λύσις τῆς δευτέρας σφραγῖδος, δηλοῦσα τὸν τῶν ἀπίστων κατὰ τῶν πιστῶν πόλεμον (vi. 3, 4). ιε′. λύσις τῆς τρίτης σφραγῖδος, δηλοῦσα τῶν μὴ παγίως πεπιστευκότων Χριστῷ τὴν ἔκπτωσιν (vi. 5, 6). ις′. λύσις τῆς τετάρτης σφραγῖδος, ἐμφαίνουσα τὰς ἐπαγομένας παιδευτικὰς μάστιγας τοῖς δι' ἀνυπομονησίας ἀρνησαμένοις τὸν κύριον (vi. 7, 8). ιζ′. λύσις τῆς πέμπτης σφραγῖδος, τὴν τῶν ἁγίων ψυχων σημαίνουσα πρὸς Κύριον καταβόησιν ὥστε γενέσθαι συντέλειαν (vi. 9—11). ιη′. λύσις τῆς ἕκτης σφραγῖδος, τὰς ἐν τῇ συντελείᾳ ἐπαγομένας πληγὰς σημαίνουσα (vi. 12—17). ιθ′. περὶ τῶν σωζομένων ἐκ πληγῆς τῶν τεσσάρων ἀγγέλων χιλιάδων ρμδ′ (vii. 1—8). κ′. περὶ τοῦ ἀναριθμήτου ὄχλου τῶν ἐξ ἐθνῶν Χριστῷ συμβασιλευσάντων (vii. 9—17). κα′. λύσις τῆς ἑβδόμης σφραγῖδος, δηλοῦσα ἀγγελικὰς δυνάμεις προσάγειν θεῷ [τὰς] τῶν ἁγίων προσευχὰς ὡς θυμιάματα (viii. 1—6). κβ′. περὶ τῶν ἑπτὰ ἀγγέλων, ὧν τοῦ πρώτου σαλπίσαντος χάλαζα καὶ πῦρ καὶ αἷμα ἐπὶ τῆς γῆς φέρεται (viii. 7). κγ′. περὶ τοῦ δευτέρου ἀγγέλου, οὗ σαλπίσαντος τῶν ἐν [τῇ] θαλάσσῃ ἐμψύχων ἀπώλεια γίνεται (viii. 8, 9). κδ′. ὁ τρίτος ἄγγελος τὰ τῶν ποταμῶν πικραίνει ὕδατα (viii. 10, 11). κε′. ὁ τέταρτος ἄγγελος τὸ τρίτον τοῦ ἡλιακοῦ καὶ σεληνιακοῦ φωτὸς σκοτίζει (viii. 12, 13). κς′. περὶ τοῦ πέμπτου ἀγγέλου καὶ τῶν ἐκ γῆς ἀβύσσου ἀνερχομένων νοητῶν ἀκρίδων καὶ τοῦ ποικίλου τῆς μορφῆς αὐτῶν (ix. 1—12). κζ′. περὶ τοῦ ἕκτου ἀγγέλου καὶ τῶν ἐπὶ τῷ Εὐφράτῃ λυομένων ἀγγέλων ἐπίλυσις (ix. 13—21). κη′. περὶ ἀγγέλου περιβεβλημένου νεφέλην καὶ ἶριν καὶ τὸ κοινὸν τέλος προμηνύοντος (x. 1—9). κθ′. ὅπως τὸ βιβλαρίδιον ἐκ χειρὸς τοῦ ἀγγέλου ὁ εὐαγγελιστὴς εἴληφεν (x. 10—xi. 2). λ′. περὶ Ἐνὼχ καὶ Ἡλία διελέγχειν μελλόντων τὸν ἀντίχριστον (xi. 3—10). λα′. ὅπως ἀναιρεθέντες ὑπὸ τοῦ ἀντιχρίστου ἀναστήσονται, καὶ τοὺς ἠπατημένους ἐκπλήξουσιν (xi. 11—14). λβ′. περὶ τῆς ἑβδόμης σάλπιγγος καὶ τῶν ὑμνούντων τῷ θεῷ ἁγίων ἐπὶ τῇ μελλούσῃ κρίσει (xi. 15—18). λγ′. περὶ τῶν διωγμῶν τῆς ἐκκλησίας τῶν προτέρων καὶ τῶν ἐπὶ τοῦ ἀντιχρίστου (xi. 19—xii. 6). λδ′. περὶ τοῦ γενομένου πολέμου μεταξὺ τῶν ἁγίων ἀγγέλων καὶ τῶν πονηρῶν δυνάμεων καὶ τῆς καταπτώσεως τοῦ δράκοντος (xii. 7—12). λε′. ὅπως ὁ δράκων διώκων τὴν ἐκκλησίαν οὐ παύεται (xii. 13—17). λς′. περὶ τοῦ θηρίου τοῦ ἔχοντος κέρατα δέκα καὶ κεφαλὰς ἑπτά, ὧν μίαν ὡς ἐσφαγμένην ἔφη (xiii. 1—10). λζ′. περὶ ἑτέρου θηρίου δύο κέρατα ἔχοντος καὶ τῷ πρώτῳ τοὺς ἀνθρώπους προσάγοντος (xiii. 11—17). λη′. περὶ τοῦ ὀνόματος τοῦ θηρίου (xiii. 18). λθ′. περὶ τῶν ρμδ′ χιλιάδων τῶν σὺν [τῷ] ἀρνίῳ ἑστώτων ἐν ὄρει Σιών (xiv. 1—5). μ′. περὶ ἀγγέλου προαγορεύοντος τὴν ἐγγύτητα τῆς κρίσεως τῆς μελλούσης (xiv. 6, 7). μα′. περὶ δευτέρου ἀγγέλου τὴν πτῶσιν Βαβυλῶνος κηρύσσοντος (xiv. 8). μβ′. περὶ τρίτου ἀγγέλου ἀσφαλιζομένου τὸν τοῦ κυρίου λαὸν μὴ δέξασθαι τὸν ἀντίχριστον (xiv. 9—13). μγ′. ὅτι ὁ ἐν τῇ νεφέλῃ καθήμενος τῷ δρεπάνῳ συντελεῖ τὰ ἐκ τῆς γῆς βλαστάνοντα (xiv. 14—16). μδ′. περὶ ἑτέρου ἀγγέλου τρυγῶντος τὴν τῆς πικρίας ἄμπελον (xiv. 17—20). με′. περὶ τῶν ἑπτὰ ἀγγέλων τῶν ἐπαγόντων τοῖς ἀνθρώποις τὰς πληγὰς πρὸ τῆς συντελείας, καὶ περὶ τῆς ὑαλίνης θαλάσσης ἐν ᾗ τοὺς ἁγίους ἐθεάσατο (xv. 1—8). μϛ′. ὅπως τῆς πρώτης φιάλης ἐκχυθείσης ἕλκος κατὰ τῶν ἀποστατῶν γίνεται (xvi. 1, 2). μζ′. πληγὴ δευτέρα κατὰ τῶν ἐν θαλάσσῃ ἐπιτιμωμένων (xvi. 3). μη′. ὅπως διὰ τῆς τρίτης οἱ ποταμοὶ εἰς αἷμα μετακρινῶνται (xvi. 4—7). μθ′. ὅπως διὰ τῆς τετάρτης καυματίζονται οἱ ἄνθρωποι (xvi. 8, 9). ν′. ὅπως διὰ τῆς πέμπτης ἡ βασιλεία τοῦ θηρίου σκοτίζεται (xvi. 10, 11). να′. ὅπως διὰ τῆς ἕκτης ἡ ὁδὸς διὰ τοῦ Εὐφράτου τοῖς ἀπὸ ἀνατολῆς ἡλίου βασιλεῦσιν ἀνοίγεται (xvi. 12—16). νβ′. ὅπως διὰ τῆς ἑβδόμης χάλαζα καὶ σεισμὸς κατὰ τῶν ἀνθρώπων γίνεται (xvi. 17—21). νγ′. περὶ τοῦ ἑνὸς τῶν ἑπτὰ ἀγγέλων δεικνύντος τῷ εὐαγγελιστῇ τὴν τῆς πόρνης πόλεως καθαίρεσιν, καὶ περὶ τῶν ἑπτὰ κεφαλῶν καὶ τῶν δέκα κεράτων (xvii. 1—6). νδ′. ὅπως ὁ ἄγγελος τὸ ὁραθὲν αὐτῷ μυστήριον ἡρμήνευσεν (xvii. 7—18). νε′. περὶ ἑτέρου ἀγγέλου τὴν πτῶσιν Βαβυλῶνος δηλοῦντος, καὶ οὐρανίου φωνῆς τὴν ἐκ τῆς πόλεως φυγὴν ἐντελλομένης, καὶ τῆς ἀποβολῆς τῶν τερπνῶν ὧν τὸ πρὶν ἐκέκτη(ν)το (xviii. 1—24). νϛ′. περὶ τῆς τῶν ἁγίων ὑμνῳδίας καὶ τοῦ τριπλοῦ ἀλληλουϊὰ ὅπερ ἔψαλλον ἐπὶ τῇ καθαιρέσει Βαβυλῶνος (xix. 1—6). νζ′. περὶ τοῦ μυστικοῦ γάμου καὶ τοῦ δείπνου τοῦ ἀρνίου (xix. 7—10). νη′. πῶς τὸν χριστὸν ὁ εὐαγγελιστὴς ἔφιππον μετὰ δυνάμεων ἀγγελικῶν ἐθεάσατο σὺν φόβῳ (xix. 11—19). νθ′. περὶ τοῦ ἀντιχρίστου καὶ τῶν σὺν αὐτῷ βαλλομένων εἰς γέενναν (xix. 20, 21). ξ′. ὅπως ὁ σατανᾶς ἐδέθη ἀπὸ τῆς Χριστοῦ παρουσίας μέχρι τῆς συντελείας, καὶ περὶ τῶν χιλίων ἐτῶν (xx. 1—3). ξα′. περὶ τῶν ἡτοιμασμένων θρόνων τοῖς φυλάξασι τὴν Χριστοῦ ὁμολογίαν (xx. 4). ξβ′. τι ἐστὶν ἡ πρώτη ἀνάστασις, καὶ τίς ὁ δεύτερος θάνατος (xx. 5, 6). ξγ′. περὶ τοῦ Γὼγ καὶ Μαγώγ (xx. 7—10). ξδ′. περὶ τοῦ καθημένου ἐπὶ τοῦ θρόνου, καὶ τῆς κοινῆς ἀναστάσεως καὶ κρίσεως (xx. 11—15). ξε′. περὶ καινῶν οὐρανοῦ τε καὶ γῆς καὶ τῆς ἄνω Ἱερουσαλήμ (xxi. 1—4). ξϛ′. περὶ ὧν εἶπεν ὁ ἐν τῷ θρόνῳ καθήμενος καὶ ὁραθείς (xxi. 5—8). ξζ′. περὶ τοῦ ἀγγέλου δεικνύντος αὐτῷ τὴν τῶν ἁγίων πόλιν καὶ τὸ ταύτης τεῖχος σὺν τοῖς πυλῶσι διαμετροῦντος (xxi. 9—27). ξη′. περὶ τοῦ καθαροῦ ποταμοῦ τοῦ ὀπτανθέντος ἐκ τοῦ θρόνου πορεύεσθαι (xxii. 1—5). ξθ′. περὶ τοῦ ἀξιοπίστου τῶν τεθεαμένων τῷ ἀποστόλῳ (xxii. 6). ο′. ὅτι θεὸς τῶν προφητῶν ὁ χριστὸς καὶ δεσπότης τῶν ἁπάντων (xxii. 7—9). οα′. ὅπως ἐκελεύθη μὴ σφραγίσαι ἀλλὰ κηρύξαι τὴν ἀποκάλυψιν (xxii. 10—17). οβ′. ὅπως ἡ ἐκκλησία καὶ τὸ ἐν αὐτῇ πνεῦμα προσκαλοῦνται τὴν τοῦ χριστοῦ ἔνδοξον ἐπιφάνειαν, καὶ περὶ τῆς ἀρᾶς ᾗ ὑποβάλλονται οἱ τὴν βίβλον παραχαράττοντες ὡς ἄκυρον (xxii. 18—21).

The longer sections or λόγοι begin at i. 1, ii. 8, iii. 1, iv. 1, vi. 1, vi. 7, vii. 1, viii. 7, viii. 12, x. 1, xi. 11, xii. 7, xiii. 11, xiv. 6, xiv. 14, xvi. 2, xvi. 8, xvi. 17, xviii. 1, xix. 11, xx. 4, xx. 11, xxi. 9, xxii. 8. They shew less discrimination than the division into κεφάλαια, and it may be surmised that the latter was made first, and that the subsequent grouping into λόγοι was purely mechanical, based on the principle of trichotomy announced by its author.

2. The Latin authorities pursue an independent course in the matter of capitulation. The *recapitulatio* which follows the commentary of Primasius[1] divides the commentary into twenty heads, corresponding with Apoc. i. 1—iii. 22, iv. 1—11, v. 1—vi. 2, vi. 3—11, vi. 12—17, vii. 1—viii. 1, viii. 2—ix. 12, ix. 13—21, x. 1—xi. 2, xi. 3—14, xi. 15—xii. 17, xiii. 1—18, xiv. 1—13, xiv. 14—xvi. 21, xvii. 1—18, xviii. 1—xix. 10, xix. 11—xx. 10, xx. 11—xxii. 12, xxii. 13—15, xxii. 16—21—a distribution which shews a genuine desire to understand the plan of the book[2]. Moreover, each of the books of the commentary is preceded by a list of shorter *capitula*, 96 in all, which Haussleiter with much probability regards as due to a later hand[3]; as he points out, the number suggests a reference to the Elders and the ζῷα (96 = 24 × 4), which is of a piece with Andreas's fancy of connecting his κεφάλαια with the Elders and the human trichotomy (72 = 24 × 3). Haussleiter adds[4] a division into 48 *capitula* from cod. Vat. 4221 and cod. Monac. 17088 (a MS. of Haimo's commentary), and cod. Monac. 6230 (a MS. of the Vulgate); the chapters begin at i. 4, ii. 1, 8, 12, 18, iii. 1, 7, 14, iv. 1, v. 1, 6, 11, vi. 3, 9, 12, vii. 1, 9, 12, viii. 1, 7, 12, ix. 13, x. 1, xi. 1, 12, xii. 7, 12, 13, xiii. 1, 11, xiv. 1, 6, 13, xv. 1, xvi. 1, 12, xvii. 1, 7, xviii. 1, 21, xix. 1, 11, xx. 1, 11, xxi. 9, xxii. 1, 10. It will be observed that seventeen of these sections start where the modern chapters do[5]. Other systems of capitulation are found; cod. Amiatinus and cod. Fuldensis divide the Apocalypse into 25 chapters, while there are MSS. which give 22, 23, 24, 41, and 43[6].

[1] Haussleiter, *Die lateinische Apokalypse der alten africanischen Kirche*, p. 179 ff.

[2] Primasius himself thus explains the purpose of his compendium: "ut totius libri auctoritate decursa sic omnis series brevi recapitulatione iterum evolvatur insinuata per partes, ut omnium quisque librorum textus uno summatim loco clareat definitus, cum et partitionem recipit singulorum et plenitudinem videtur obtinere per totum."

[3] Haussleiter, pp. 184—193; see his remarks on pp. 193—4.

[4] *Ibid.*, p. 197 ff.

[5] The modern chapters are practically those of Stephen Langton († 1228); see von Soden, *Die Schriften d. N. T.*, p. 482. But in nearly every instance they were anticipated in the κεφάλαια of Andreas.

[6] See Gregory, *prolegg.* i., p. 161; *Textkritik*, ii., p. 879 f.

3. In the present edition the Greek text is divided into 42 minor sections (i. 1—3, 4—8, 9—20, ii. 1—7, 8—11, 12—17, 18—29, iii. 1—6, 7—12, 14—22, iv. 1—11, v. 1—14, vi. 1—17, vii. 1—8, 9—17, viii. 1—13, ix. 1—12, 13—21, x. 1—11, xi. 1—14, 15—19, xii. 1—18, xiii. 1—10, 11—18, xiv. 1—5, 6—13, 14—20, xv. 1—8, xvi. 1—21, xvii. 1—6, 7—18, xviii. 1—24, xix. 1—10, 11—16, 17—21, xx. 1—6, 7—10, 11—15, xxi. 1—8, 9—xxii. 5, xxii. 6—20, xxii. 21). The following table will shew the contents of the Book as thus arranged:

1. Prologue.
2. The writer's greeting to the Churches of Asia.
3. Vision of the risen and ascended Christ.

4—10. Messages to the Angels of the Seven Churches.

11. Vision of the Throne in Heaven.
12. The Sealed Book and the Lamb.
13. Opening of the first six Seals.
14. Sealing of the 144,000 from the Tribes of Israel.
15. Triumph of the Innumerable Multitude.
16. Opening of the seventh Seal; the half hour's silence in Heaven; the first four Trumpet-blasts.
17. The fifth Trumpet-blast, or first Woe.
18. The sixth Trumpet-blast, or second Woe.
19. Preparations for the seventh Trumpet-blast: the vision of the Angel with the open booklet.
20. Further preparations: measuring the Temple; the testimony of the Two Witnesses.
21. The seventh Trumpet-blast, or third Woe.
22. The Woman with child, and the Great blood-red Dragon.
23. The Wild Beast from the Sea.
24. The Wild Beast from the Earth.
25. Vision of the 144,000 on Mount Zion.
26. Three angelic proclamations, and a Voice from Heaven.
27. Vision of the Harvest and the Vintage of the Earth.
28. Preparation for the last Seven Plagues.
29. Pouring out of the Seven Bowls.

30. Vision of Babylon seated on the Beast.
31. Interpretation of the Vision of Babylon and the Beast.
32. Doom of Babylon.
33. Triumph in Heaven; two Hallelujah Psalms; an angelic message.
34. Vision of the Crowned Warrior.
35. Overthrow and end of the Beast and the False Prophet.
36. The Thousand Years of Satan's captivity and the Martyrs' Reign.
37. After the Thousand Years: release of Satan; war of Gog and Magog.
38. Vision of the General Resurrection and the Last Judgement.
39. Vision of a New Heaven and a New Earth.
40. Vision of the New Jerusalem.
41. Epilogue: Last words of the Angel, the Seer, and the Lord.
42. Final Benediction.

4. The whole book lies before us in this table of contents. It is found to consist of a succession of scenes and visions which are so easily distinguished that at this stage no serious difference of opinion can arise. Our difficulties begin when we attempt to group these sections into larger masses of apocalyptic matter, and by a process of synthesis to arrive at the plan upon which the author has constructed his work. The former of these operations is relatively simple. The first two sections and the last two form respectively the introduction and the conclusion of the Book; sections 3—10, 11—13, 16—18 (21), 22—24, 28—29, 30—33, 34—35, 36—38, 39—40 also form coherent groups, while 14—15, 19—20, 25—27 are episodes which can be seen to be in more or less definite relation with their surroundings. Thus our 42 sections are reduced to 14, which may be described as follows:

1. Prologue (i. 1—8).
2. Vision of Christ among the Churches, followed by messages to their Angels (i. 9—iii. 22).

3. Vision of Christ in Heaven, followed by the opening of the seven Seals of the sealed Book (iv. 1—vi. 17, viii. 1).
4. Episode, after the sixth Seal, of the 144,000 from the Tribes of Israel, and the countless multitude (vii. 1—17).
5. The seven Trumpet-blasts (viii. 2—ix. 21, xi. 15—19).
6. Episode, after the sixth Trumpet-blast, of the Angel with the open booklet, the measuring of the Temple, and the Two Witnesses (x. 1—xi. 14).
7. The Woman with child, the Dragon and the Two Wild Beasts (xii. 1—xiii. 18).
8. Episode of the 144,000 on Mt Zion, the angelic and celestial Voices, and the Harvest and Vintage of the world (xiv. 1—20).
9. Outpouring of the seven Bowls, containing the seven last plagues (xv. 1—xvi. 21).
10. Vision of Babylon the Great; her fall; the triumph of the Angels and the Church (xvii. 1—xix. 10).
11. Vision of the Royal Warrior, and overthrow of the Two Beasts (xix. 11—21).
12. The 1000 years, followed by the overthrow of the Dragon and the End (xx. 1—15).
13. The New World, and the New City (xxi. 1—xxii. 5).
14. Epilogue (xxii. 6—21).

5. As we look steadily at this scheme and study its connexion, we become conscious of a great cleavage, which practically divides the Book into two nearly equal parts (i. 9—xi. 14, xii. 1—xxii. 5). In the first half the Ascended Christ appears in two capacities, as the Head of the Church, and the Controller of the Destinies of the World. The antagonism between the two bodies comes into view; the Churches of Asia are already suffering persecution and have more to suffer; the World is ripe for judgements, which loom large in the visions of the Seal-openings and the Trumpet-blasts; the end is drawing on; the victory of righteousness and the final revelation of truth are foreseen. The first half—it might almost be called the first book—of the

Apocalypse is complete in itself, and had all our MSS. broken off at xi. 19, and no vestige of the last eleven chapters survived, it is conceivable that the loss might never have been suspected. In xii. 1 the author makes a fresh beginning, for which the reader had been prepared in x. 11. The theme of the second prophecy is the same on the whole as that of the first, but the subject is pursued into new regions of thought, and the leading characters and symbolical figures are almost wholly new. The Churches of Asia vanish[1], and their place is taken by the Church considered as a unity, which is represented by the Woman who is the Mother of Christ and the Saints. It is with her world-long struggle with the *κοσμοκράτορες τοῦ σκότους τούτου*, the spiritual forces which lie behind the antagonism of the World, that the second part of the Book chiefly deals. These forces are revealed under monstrous forms, the Great Red Dragon, the Beast from the Sea, the Beast from the Land, and they continue to operate until their final overthrow. But we lose sight of them, except in an occasional reference, from *c.* xiii. to *c.* xix. While they are working behind the scene, the apocalyptic history is occupied with mundane events—the judgements of the latter days which are now symbolized by seven bowls full of the last plagues; the greatness and the fall of the New Babylon, the Beast's mistress and representative. Beyond the fall of the World-empire the Seer can see in dim outline long days of comparative rest and triumph for the Church, and after them a temporary relapse, followed by the final destruction of the surviving powers of evil. This makes room for the manifestation of the Church as the Bride of Christ and City of God, and with a magnificent picture of the New Jerusalem, the antithesis of Babylon, the Apocalypse reaches its end.

Thus in its briefest form our scheme of the book will stand as follows:

Prologue (i. 1—8).

Part i. Vision of Christ in the midst of the Churches (i. 9—iii. 22).

[1] Until we reach *c.* xxii. 16, where the writer reverts to the ideas of *c.* i. 1, 4 ff.

Vision of Christ in Heaven (iv. 1—v. 14).
Preparations for the End (vi. 1—xi. 19).
Part ii. Vision of the Mother of Christ and her enemies (xii. 1—xiii. 18).
Preparations for the End (xiv. 1—xx. 15).
Vision of the Bride of Christ, arrayed for her husband (xxi. 1—xxii. 5).
Epilogue (xxii. 6—21).

6. Archbishop Benson relates that "in answer once to the question, 'What is the form the Book presents to you?' the reply of an intelligent and devout reader was, 'It is Chaos'[1]." If the above scheme is accepted, chaos will give place to something like cosmic order and progress. But the order and progress of apocalyptic writings must not be judged by the standards of ordinary literature. An apocalypse is neither a history nor a homily, though it may partake of the character of each; its methods are its own, and they must be learnt by a sympathetic study of the text.

The Apocalypse of John, in its literary setting, is an encyclical letter addressed to the Seven Churches of Asia[2]. If we detach the short prologue or preface (i. 1—3), it begins in the epistolary style familiar to readers of the letters of St Paul, and it ends, like the Pauline letters, with a benediction[3]. But this form is not maintained in the body of the work; it is exchanged in *c.* i. 9 for the apocalyptic manner, which continues almost to the end. The so-called 'Letters to the Churches' in *cc.* ii. iii. are no exception; they are in fact messages, and not true letters, and they form a sequel to the vision of *c.* i.[4]

The Apocalypse proper has been represented as a *quasi*-drama, divisible into acts and scenes, and interspersed with 'interludes'

[1] *Apocalypse*, p. 1.
[2] St Paul's Epistle 'πρὸς Ἐφεσίους' is probably an earlier example of a circular letter which starting with Ephesus made the tour of the Asian Churches: see WH., *Notes on Select Readings*, p. 123 f., and Hort, *Prolegomena to Romans and Ephesians*, p. 86 ff.

[3] See notes *ad loc.*
[4] The formula τῷ ἀγγέλῳ...γράψον Τάδε λέγει is not epistolary but prophetic; for γράψον cf. i. 11, 19, xiv. 13, xix. 9, xxi. 5. Τάδε λέγει announces a prophetic message, as frequently in the LXX.

and 'choric songs[1].' A similar view is advocated by an American writer[2], who, however, regards "the proper action of the Apocalyptic drama" as beginning with *c.* iv. But while there are points of resemblance between the Greek drama and the Jewish-Christian Apocalypse, the latter refuses to be bound by the laws of the Western stage. The order of the Apocalypse is rather that of a series of visions arranging themselves under two great actions, of which the Work of the Ascended Christ and the Destinies of the Christian Church are the respective subjects. As to the progress of the Book, the two actions, from the nature of the case, are more or less synchronous, both belonging to the interval between the writer's own time and the end; but, while covering the same ground, they approach it from different points of view. Within each of the actions there is orderly movement, but this again is not tied to chronological succession; it is the movement of great spiritual forces rather than of historical persons and events.

7. It may be worth while to examine somewhat more at length the progress of the Apocalyptic visions in each part of the Book. (*a*) The opening vision, with its messages to the Asian Churches, whatever may be the teaching which it holds for other times and Churches, belongs, as to its primary purpose, exclusively to the Seer's own age. In the second vision a wider outlook begins; if the breaking of the first four Seals discloses only the conditions of contemporary society, the fifth anticipates the coming age of persecution, and the sixth carries us to the verge of the end. The opening of the seventh Seal is followed after a brief pause by a vision of trumpet-bearing Angels, which works out into detail the revelations of the fifth and sixth Seals, and brings us again to the end, now seen in the light of a final triumph for the Kingdom of God. Two large episodes which follow seem to break the movement of the prophecy, but in fact assist in its development; of

[1] Benson, *Apocalypse*, pp. 5, 37. The Archbishop says indeed in his preface (p. 67): "The Book is no Drama. The Action is carried on *per Facta, non Verba.*" But he adds: "Yet the Book is like the relating of a Drama, a narrative of Scenes and Acts which had passed before the eye of the Seer."

[2] F. Palmer, *The Drama of the Apocalypse* (N. Y., The Macmillan Co., 1903), p. 35 ff.

these the first (*c.* vii.) assures the Churches of safe-keeping in the coming troubles and anticipates the rest which will follow them; while the second (*c.* x. 1—xi. 14) prepares for the seventh Trumpet-blast, as the first (*c.* vii.) had prepared for the opening of the seventh Seal.

(*b*) The second action of the book begins, like the first, with contemporary history (*cc.* xii., xiii.). The Church is seen struggling with Satan and his agents, the World-power and its spiritual ally, afterwards described as the False Prophet. Another large episode follows (*c.* xiv.), consisting of a series of secondary visions[1], the purpose of which is to exhibit the safety and purity of the ideal Church, the judgements impending over her persecutors, and the impending end of all things—a set-off against the apparent triumph of evil, and a preparation for the great vision which is to follow. Then come the Seven Last Plagues, a series corresponding in this half of the book with the seven Seals and seven Trumpets of the first half. But the end is not yet; the world has its counter-manifestation to make, and the magnificence of its great City is described, though only to enhance the terrors of its downfall. The fall of the existing World-power does not, however, exhaust the resources of the Enemy; long after it the prophet foresees a recrudescence of evil, and a final conflict between Christ and the forces of Satan, which ends in the annihilation of Satan's power. So the last obstacle to the mystic marriage of the Lamb is removed, and with the glories of His Bride, seen in the light of the consummation, the Apocalypse ends.

There is order here, and there is progress. Each part of the Book fulfils its own purpose, and is complete within its own sphere; taken together, the two parts present a revelation of the whole ordering of the world from the Ascension to the Return. If more than once, when the end is nearly reached, the writer turns back to the beginning, he does this in order to gather up new views of life which could not be embraced by a single vision. If here and there the course of the prophecy is

[1] xiv. 1 *εἶδον καὶ ἰδού*, 6 *καὶ εἶδον*, 14 *καὶ εἶδον καὶ ἰδού*.

broken by a by-play which seems to be irrelevant, it is because the episode prepares for the issue which is at hand. The issue is postponed for a time that when it comes its real significance may be more clearly seen.

It may be convenient to add an outline of the systems of division adopted by some of the chief modern writers on the Apocalypse, (1) in England and (2) on the continent.

(1) ALFORD: i. 1—3, i. 4—iii. 22; iv. 1—11, v. 1—14, vi. 1—viii. 5, viii. 6—xi. 19, xii. 1—xiii. 18, xiv. 1—20, xv. 1—xvi. 21, xvii. 1—xviii. 24, xix. 1—xxii. 5, xxii. 6—21. LEE: i. 1—iii. 22; iv. 1—v. 14, vi. 1—viii. 1, viii. 2—xi. 19, xii. 1—xiii. 18, xiv. 1—20, xv. 1—xvi. 21, xvii. 1—xxii. 5; xxii. 6—21. SIMCOX: i. 1—3; i. 4—iii. 22; iv. 1—v. 14, vi. 1—viii. 1, viii. 2—xi. 19, xii. 1—xiv. 13, xiv. 14—20, xv. 1—xvi. 21, xvii. 1—xviii. 24, xix. 1—21, xx. 1—6, xx. 7—10, xx. 11—15, xxi. 1—xxii. 9; xxii. 10—21. ANDERSON SCOTT: i. 1—8, 9—20, ii. 1—iii. 22, iv. 1—v. 14, vi. 1—viii. 1, viii. 2—xi. 19, xii. 1—xiv. 20, xv. 1—xvi. 21, xvii. 1—xix. 10, xix. 11—xx. 15, xxi. 1—xxii. 5, xxii. 6—17, 18—21. MOFFATT: i. 1—8; i. 9—iii. 22; iv. 1—vi. 17 (vii. 1—18, viii. 1); viii. 2—ix. 21 (x. 1—xi. 13, 14—19, xii. 1—17, xiii. 1—18, xiv. 1—5, 6—20); xv. 1—xvi. 21, xvii. 1—xx. 10; xx. 11—xxii. 5, xxii. 6—21.

(2) BENGEL: i. 1—3, 4—6, 7—8, 9—20, ii. 1—iii. 22; iv. 1—v. 14, v. 15—vi. 17, vii. 1—17, viii. 1—6, 7—12, viii. 13—ix. 21, x. 1—xi. 19, xii. 1—12, 13—17, xiii. 1—18, xiv. [1—5], 6—13, 14—20, xv. 1—xvi. 21, xvii. 1—18, xviii. 1—xix. 18, xix. 19—21, xx. 1, 2, 3, 4—6, 7—10, 11—15, xxi. 1—xxii. 5; xxii. 6—21. DE WETTE: i. 1—3, 4—8, 9—20, ii. 1—iii. 22; iv. 1—11, v. 1—14, vi. 1—8, 9—17, vii. 1—8, 9—17, viii. 1—6, 7—12 (13), ix. 1—11 (12), 13—21, x. 1—7, 8—11, xi. 1—13 (14), 15—19; xii. 1—6, 7—12, 13—17, 18—xiii. 10, xiii. 11—18, xiv. 1—5, 6—13, 14—20; xv. 1—xvi. 1, xvi. 2—11, 12—16, 17—21, xvii. 1—18, xviii. 1—24, xix. 1—8, 9, 10, 11—16, 17—21, xx. 1—3, 4—6, 7—10, 11—15, xxi. 1—xxii. 5, xxii. 6—21. EWALD: i. 1—3, 4—8, 9—20; ii. 1—iii. 21; iv. 1, 2—11, v. 1—14, vi. 1—8, 9—11, 12—17, vii. 1—8, 9—17; viii. 1, 2—6, 7—13, ix. 1—12, 13—21, x. 1—11, xi. 1—14; xi. 15—19, xii. 1—17, 18—xiii. 10, xiii. 11—18, xiv. 1—5, 6—13, 14—20; xv. 1—4, 5—xvi. 1, xvi. 2—9, 10, 11, 12—21, xvii. 1—18, xviii. 1—24; xix. 1—10, 11—16, 17—xx. 6, xx. 7—10, 11—15, xxi. 1—8, 9—xxii. 5, xxii. 6—9, 10—17, 18—20, 21. HOLTZMANN: i. 1—3, 4—8, 9—20, ii. 1—iii. 22, iv. 1—v. 14, vi. 1—17, vii. 1—17, viii. 1—5, 6—ix. 21, x. 1—xi. 14, xi. 15—19, xii. 1—xiv. 5, xiv. 6—20, xv. 1—xvi. 1, xvi. 2—21, xvii. 1—xix. 10, xix. 11—xxii. 5, xxii. 6—21. ZAHN: i. 1—9; 10—iii. 22; iv. 1—viii. 1, viii. 2—xi. 18, xi. 19—xiv. 20, xv. 1—xvi. 17, xvii. 1—xviii. 24, xix. 11—xxi. 8, xxi. 9—xxii. 5; xxii. 10—21.

It is more interesting to observe the methods of grouping adopted by the several authorities. Most of the English commentators break up the book, after the introduction and conclusion have been removed, into two unequal parts (i. 4—iii. 22, iv. 1—xxii. 5), a modification of the scheme of Bengel, who divides the whole book into (i) *introitus* (i. 1—iii. 22), (ii) *ostensio* (iv. 1—xxii. 5), (iii) *conclusio* (xxii. 6—21). In his *Historical N. T.* Mr Moffatt has departed from this tradition, seeing in the Apocalypse four heptads (seven letters, seven seals, seven trumpets, seven vials), followed by two visions, a vision of doom and a vision of the end. Of the Germans, De Wette makes the second part of the book begin at xii. 1, while Volkmar places the break at the end of *c.* ix.; Ewald adopts a sevenfold division (i. 1—20 + xxii. 1—21, ii.—iii., iv.—vii., viii.—xi. 4, xi. 15—xiv. 20, xv.—xviii., xix. 1—xxii. 5); Holtzmann has seventeen sections, placing in the right-hand column vii. 1—17, x. 1—xi. 14, xii. 1—xiv. 5, xvii. 1—xix. 10, xxi. 1—xxii. 5 which largely coincide with the portions of the book which have been thought to be of Jewish origin; while Zahn, who believes in the unity of the Apocalypse, is attracted by the theory that the body of the work falls into eight successive visions.

The division of the book at the end of *c.* xi. into two nearly equal sections, which is suggested in this chapter, recommended itself in the sixteenth century to the Spanish Jesuit Alcasar, but in connexion with a widely different system of interpretation[1]; to the present writer it has occurred independently, upon a study of the facts.

[1] See *c.* xviii.

IV.

UNITY OF THE APOCALYPSE.

In the attempt which has been made to establish the existence of a definite plan in the Apocalypse it is assumed that the book is a literary unity. This point, however, has been and still is hotly disputed by scholars of the first rank, and it demands a separate and somewhat prolonged examination.

1. The book creates a *prima facie* impression that it proceeds from one author or editor. The first and last chapters claim to be written by the same person (i. 1, 4, 9, xxii. 8); and that the first three chapters and the last two or three have come from the same hand may be shewn by simply placing in parallel columns the ideas and phraseology which they have in common.

i. 1.	xxii. 6.
δείξας τοῖς δούλοις αὐτοῦ ἃ δεῖ γενέσθαι ἐν τάχει.	δεῖξαι τοῖς δούλοις αὐτοῦ ἃ δεῖ γενέσθαι ἐν τάχει.
i. 3.	xxii. 7.
μακάριος ὁ ἀναγινώσκων καὶ οἱ ἀκούοντες τοὺς λόγους τῆς προφητείας καὶ τηροῦντες κτλ.	μακάριος ὁ τηρῶν τοὺς λόγους τῆς προφητείας τοῦ βιβλίου τούτου.
i. 3.	xxii. 10.
ὁ γὰρ καιρὸς ἐγγύς.	ὁ καιρὸς γὰρ ἐγγύς ἐστιν.
i. 8.	xxi. 6, xxii. 12.
ἐγώ εἰμι τὸ ἄλφα καὶ τὸ ὦ.	ἐγὼ τὸ ἄλφα καὶ τὸ ὦ.
i. 17.	xxii. 13.
ἐγώ εἰμι ὁ πρῶτος καὶ ὁ ἔσχατος.	ὁ πρῶτος καὶ ὁ ἔσχατος.
ii. 7.	xxii. 17.
τὸ πνεῦμα λέγει.	τὸ πνεῦμα καὶ ἡ νύμφη λέγουσιν.

ii. 7.	xxi. 7.
τῷ νικῶντι δώσω κτλ. (cf. ii. 11, 17, 26, iii. 5, 12, 21).	ὁ νικῶν κληρονομήσει ταῦτα.
ii. 11.	xx. 6.
οὐ μὴ ἀδικηθῇ ἐκ τοῦ θανάτου τοῦ δευτέρου.	ἐπὶ τούτων ὁ δεύτερος θάνατος οὐκ ἔχει ἐξουσίαν (cf. *v.* 14, xxi. 8).
ii. 28.	xxii. 16.
δώσω αὐτῷ τὸν ἀστέρα τὸν πρωϊνόν.	ἐγώ εἰμι...ὁ ἀστὴρ...ὁ πρωϊνός.
iii. 11.	xxii. 12.
ἔρχομαι ταχύ.	ἰδοὺ ἔρχομαι ταχύ.
iii. 12.	xxi. 2.
τῆς καινῆς Ἰερουσαλὴμ ἡ καταβαίνουσα ἐκ τοῦ οὐρανοῦ ἀπὸ τοῦ θεοῦ μου.	τὴν πόλιν τὴν ἁγίαν Ἰερουσαλὴμ καινὴν εἶδον καταβαίνουσαν ἐκ τοῦ οὐρανοῦ ἀπὸ τοῦ θεοῦ.

2. Such coincidences leave no doubt that the same writer has been at work in *cc.* i.—iii., xx.—xxii. But though they are most numerous in the beginning and end of the book, these traces of literary unity are not wanting elsewhere, as the following examples will shew.

iv. 1.	i. 1.
δείξω σοι ἃ δεῖ γενέσθαι.	δεῖξαι...ἃ δεῖ γενέσθαι.
iv. 2.	i. 10.
ἐγενόμην ἐν πνεύματι.	ἐγενόμην ἐν πνεύματι.
iv. 6.	xv. 2.
ὡς θάλασσα ὑαλίνη.	εἶδον ὡς θάλασσαν ὑαλίνην.
v. 5.	xxii. 16.
ἡ ῥίζα Δαυείδ.	ἡ ῥίζα καὶ τὸ γένος Δαυείδ.
v. 10.	i. 6.
ἐποίησας αὐτοὺς τῷ θεῷ ἡμῶν βασιλείαν καὶ ἱερεῖς.	ἐποίησεν ἡμᾶς βασιλείαν, ἱερεῖς τῷ θεῷ.
ix. 1.	xx. 1.
ἡ κλεὶς τοῦ φρέατος τῆς ἀβύσσου.	τὴν κλεῖν τῆς ἀβύσσου.
x. 1.	i. 14 f.
τὸ πρόσωπον αὐτοῦ ὡς ὁ ἥλιος, καὶ οἱ πόδες αὐτοῦ ὡς στύλοι πυρός.	οἱ πόδες αὐτοῦ ὅμοιοι χαλκολιβάνῳ ὡς ἐν καμίνῳ πεπυρωμένης ...καὶ ἡ ὄψις αὐτοῦ ὡς ὁ ἥλιος κτλ.

xi. 1.	xxi. 15.
ἐδόθη μοι κάλαμος...λέγων Ἔγειρε καὶ μέτρησον τὸν ναόν.	εἶχεν μέτρον κάλαμον χρυσοῦν ἵνα μετρήσῃ τὴν πόλιν...
xi. 7.	xvii. 8.
τὸ θηρίον τὸ ἀναβαῖνον ἐκ τῆς ἀβύσσου.	μέλλει ἀναβαίνειν ἐκ τῆς ἀβύσσου.
xii. 9.	xx. 2.
ὁ δρακὼν ὁ μέγας ὁ ὄφις ὁ ἀρχαῖος, ὁ καλούμενος διάβολος καὶ ὁ σατανᾶς.	ὁ ὄφις ὁ ἀρχαῖος, ὅς ἐστιν διάβολος καὶ ὁ σατανᾶς.
xiv. 13.	ii. 7 etc.
λέγει τὸ πνεῦμα.	τὸ πνεῦμα λέγει.
xiv. 14.	i. 13.
ὅμοιον υἱὸν ἀνθρώπου.	ὅμοιον υἱὸν ἀνθρώπου.
xv. 6.	i. 13.
περιεζωσμένοι περὶ τὰ στήθη ζώνας χρυσᾶς.	περιεζωσμένον πρὸς τοῖς μαστοῖς ζώνην χρυσᾶν.
xvi. 15.	iii. 3.
ἔρχομαι ὡς κλέπτης.	ἥξω ὡς κλέπτης.
xvii. 1.	xxi. 9.
ἐλάλησεν μετ' ἐμοῦ λέγων Δεῦρο δείξω σοι τὸ κρίμα τῆς πόρνης.	ἐλάλησεν μετ' ἐμοῦ λέγων Δεῦρο δείξω σοι τὴν νύμφην.
xix. 12.	i. 14.
οἱ ὀφθαλμοὶ αὐτοῦ φλὸξ πυρός.	οἱ ὀφθαλμοὶ αὐτοῦ ὡς φλὸξ πυρός.

3. It is clear from these instances, which might be multiplied, that the hand of the man who wrote *cc.* i.—iii., xx.—xxii., has been busy throughout the book. This in itself may not mean more than that he has acted as editor of the whole. But there are other indications of unity, running through large sections of the book, which carry us some steps further. Certain symbolical figures reappear at intervals in contexts which deal with widely different subjects. Though, as we have seen, the eleventh and twelfth chapters are separated by a marked cleavage, the Lamb and the Beast appear on both sides of it; the Lamb occurs in *cc.* v., vi., vii., xii., xiv., xv., xvii., xix., xxi., xxii., i.e. practically throughout

the book from *c.* v. onwards, and the Beast in *c.* xi. as well as in *cc.* xiii., xiv., xv., xvi., xvii., xix., xx. The figure of Hades as a companion of Death occurs in *cc.* i., vi., xx. There are certain unusual words and forms which are common to every part of the Apocalypse, or are found throughout great sections or in passages which are widely separated; e.g. *ἄβυσσος* (*cc.* ix., xi., xvii., xx.), *ἀδικεῖν* to hurt (ii., vi., vii., ix., xi., xxii.), *βασανισμός* (ix., xiv., xviii.), *διάδημα* (xii., xiii., xix.), *δράκων* (xii., xiii., xvi., xx.), *εὐαγγελίζειν* active (x., xiv.), *θρόνος* (i., ii., iii., iv., v., vi., vii., viii., xi., xii., xiii., xiv., xvi., xix., xx., xxi., xxii.), *καῦμα* (vii., xvi.), *κρύσταλλος* (iv., xxii.), *μεγιστάν* (vi., xviii.), *μεσουράνημα* (viii., xiv., xix.), *μολύνειν* (iii., xiv.), *οἰκουμένη* (iii., xii., xvi.), *παντοκράτωρ* (i., iv., xi., xv., xvi., xix., xxi.), *συνκοινωνεῖν*, *-νός* (i., xviii.), *σφάζειν* (v., vi., xiii., xviii.), *φαρμακία*, *φάρμακον*, *φαρμακός* (ix., xviii., xxi., xxii.), *φιάλη* (v., xv., xvi., xvii., xxi.), *χάραγμα* (xiii., xiv., xvi., xix., xx.). Still more striking as an indication of an underlying unity is the resumption in *c.* xv. of the series of sevenfold visitations which began in *c.* vi.; as there were seven seal-openings and seven trumpet-blasts in the first half of the Book, so the second has its seven bowls full of the seven last plagues. The cumulative force of this evidence is sufficient to create a strong presumption that the writer who announces his name in the prologue has been at work throughout the book. The impress of his peculiar style is to be seen in every part of it.

4. These considerations have not deterred modern scholars from regarding the Apocalypse as a composite work and attempting in some cases to resolve it into its sources.

Suggestions in this direction were hazarded in the seventeenth century by Grotius (1644)[1] and Hammond (1653)[2], and early in the nineteenth century by Vogel (1811—16)[3] and Bleek (1822)[4]. Weizsäcker (1882)[5] reopened the question with a theory that the author, although his hand may be seen throughout, made free use of older material. In the same year his pupil Völter[6]

[1] *Annotationes ad N.T.*

[2] *Paraphrases and Annotations upon the N.T.*

[3] *Commentationes vii de Apoc. Ioannis.*

[4] In the Berlin *Th. Zeitschrift*, ii., p. 240 ff. Bleek afterwards revoked his view.

[5] In *Th. Litteraturzeitung*, 1882, p. 78 f.

[6] In *Die Entstehung der Apok.* (1882–5). Völter has recently published a recast of his theory (*Die Offenbarung Johannis neu untersucht u. erläutert*,

started a more ambitious theory, according to which Apoc. i. 4—6, iv. 1—v. 10, vi. 1—17, vii. 1—8, viii. 1—13, ix. 1—21, xi. 14—19, xiv. 1, 3, 6, 7, 14—20, xviii. 1—24, xix. 1—10, make up the original Apocalypse, which Völter would assign to A.D. 62; *cc.* x. 1—xi. 13, xiv. 8, xvii. 1—18 were added in A.D. 68—70, and the rest of the book was contributed by successive editors in the time of Trajan and Hadrian; three such later redactions are distinguished, viz. (1) *cc.* xii. 1—17, xix. 11—xxi. 8; (2) v. 11—14, vii. 9—17, xii. 11, xiii., xiv. 1, 5, 9—12, xv.—xvi., xvii. 1 a, xix. 20 f., xx. 1, 20, xxi. 9—xxii. 5, 6—19; (3) i. 1—3, 7, 8, 9—iii. 22, v. 6 b, xiv. 13, xvi. 15, xix. 10 b, 13 b, xxii. 7 a, 12, 13, 16, 17, 20—21. In 1886 a new vein was struck by a pupil of Harnack, Eberhard Vischer[1], who set to work on the hypothesis that the Apocalypse of John is a Christian adaptation of a Jewish original; the specifically Christian portions of the book are i.—iii., v. 9—14, vii. 9—17, xiii. 9 f., xiv. 1—5, 12, 13, xv. 3, xvi. 15, xvii. 14, xix. 9 ff., 13, xx. 4—6, xxi. 5 b—8, xxii. 6—21, together with a few words interpolated in ix. 11, xi. 8, 15, xv. 3, xvii. 6, xx. 4, xxi. 14, 23. The year 1886 produced the theory of Weyland[2], which assumed two Jewish sources, one (א) written under Nero, and a second (ב) under Titus. To א Weyland attributes i. 10, 12—17, 19, iv.—vi., vii. 1—17, viii. —ix., xi. 14—18, xiv. 14—20, xv. 5, xvi. 17 b—20, xvii.—xviii., xix. 1—6, xxi. 9—27, xxii. 1—11, 14 f.; to ב x. 1—xi. 13, xii. 1—10, 12—18, xiii., xiv. 6—11, xv. 2—4, xvi. 13, 14, 16, xix. 11—21, xx., xxi. 1—8; to the Christian redactor he leaves i.—iii., v. 6—14, xi. 19, xii. 11, 17 c, xiv. 1—5, 12—13, xv. 1, 6—8, xvi. 1—17 a, 21, xix. 7—10, 13 b, xxii. 12, 13, 16—21. Other theories based on the assumption of a Jewish source or sources are those of Holtzmann[3], who assumes a Jewish *Grundschrift* of the age of Nero, in which was incorporated an older Jewish apocalypse written under Caligula; and Sabatier[4], who regards the Apocalypse as a Christian book embodying Jewish fragments (xi. 1—13, xii., xiii., xiv. 1—20, xvii. 1—xix. 2, xix. 11—xx. 10, xxi. 9—xxii. 5). Spitta[5] distinguishes three sources answering to the three series of sevenfold judgements—a Seal source, which is Christian (*c.* A.D. 60), a Trumpet and a Vial source, which are Jewish; the present form of the book being ascribed to a Christian redactor. Erbes[6], on the other hand, believing the book to be entirely of Christian origin, finds in it three Christian sources belonging respectively to the reigns of Caligula, Nero, and Domitian.

5. To the present writer it appears that most of the hypotheses which exercised the ingenuity of Germany during the ten years

1904), in which he distinguishes (1) an Apocalypse of John A.D. 65, (2) an Apocalypse of Cerinthus, A.D. 70, and (3) the work of a redactor of the time of Trajan.

[1] *Texte u. Untersuchungen*, II. 3 (1886).

[2] *Th. Tydschrift*, 1886, p. 454 ff.

[3] *Gesch. d. Volkes Israel* ii. 2, p. 658 ff.

[4] *Les origines littéraires et la composition de l'Apoc.* (Paris, 1887).

[5] *Die Offenbarung Johannis* (1884).

[6] *Die Off. Joh.* (1891).

that followed Weizsäcker's first pronouncement ignored the fundamental conditions of the problem. No theory with regard to the sources of the Apocalypse can be satisfactory which overlooks the internal evidence of its essential unity (§§ 1—3). The book has clearly passed through the hands of an individual who has left his mark on every part of it; if he has used old materials freely, they have been worked up into a form which is permeated by his own personality. This has been so far recognized by more recent criticism that less drastic methods are now being used to account for the literary phenomena of the work.

In 1886, after the completion of Völter's theory, Weizsäcker suggested that the apparent lack of cohesion in certain passages is due to the interpolation of fragments which are not from the author's pen, specifying *cc.* viii. 1—8, xii. 1—10, xiii., xvii., which he assigned to the reigns of Nero, Vespasian, and Domitian. An entirely new view was propounded by Gunkel in his epoch-making *Schöpfung und Chaos* (1894). Breaking loose at once from the prevalent view of the Apocalypse as a mere interpretation of local contemporary history, and from the tendency to frame elaborate schemes for its division into 'sources,' he saw in the book the outcome of a long course of apocalyptic traditions which in some cases went back to the Creation-myths of Babylonia. Gunkel's *Chaos* was followed in the next year by Bousset's *Antichrist*[1], a book succeeded in 1896 by its author's important commentary on the Apocalypse[2]. Bousset, while recognizing the essential unity of the Apocalypse, believes with Weizsäcker that certain contexts in it are fragments of older works, and with Gunkel finds traces of apocalyptic traditions in the writer's own work. Still more recently a contribution has been made to the subject by Professor Johannes Weiss of Marburg[3]. According to his view, the original Apocalypse of John was written before 70, and included i. 4—6, 9—19, ii., iii., iv., v., vi., vii., ix., xii. 7—12, xiii. 11—18, xiv. 14—20, xx. 1—10, 11—15, xxi. 1—4, xxii. 3—5; in its present form the book was issued at the end of the reign of Domitian by an editor who was not the original Apocalyptist.

6. It is impossible to contemplate the flood of literature on the composition of the Apocalypse which the last quarter of a century has called forth without asking the question whether there is any solid ground for the assumption which underlies it

[1] *Der Antichrist in der Ueberlieferung des Judenthums, des N.T. u. der alten Kirche* (1895).

[2] *Die Offenbarung Johannis neu bearbeitet* (1896).

[3] *Die Offenbarung des Johannis: ein Beitrag zur Literatur- u. Religionsgeschichte* (1904).

all. It is taken for granted by some recent authorities[1] that the Apocalypse is a composite work. But does this conviction rest on more than the reiterated assertion of writers who have found in the analysis of the book a fascinating field for intellectual exercise? When the enquirer investigates the grounds on which the hypothesis of compilation rests, they are found to be such as the following: (*a*) the presence of well defined breaks in the thread of the movement, as e.g. after iii. 22, vii. 17, ix. 21, xi. 19, xiii. 18, xiv. 20, xvi. 21; (*b*) the treatment of the same idea more than once under different points of view; thus the 144,000 of vii. 4 ff. reappear under another aspect in xiv. 1 ff., and the Beast of xiii. 1 in *c.* xvii.; the New Jerusalem of xxi. 9 does not altogether correspond to the New Jerusalem of xxi. 2; (*c*) the representation of the Last Judgement at two widely separated stages in the development of the book, i.e. in xiv. 14 ff., and xx. 11 ff.; (*d*) the different aspects of Christian thought revealed by the descriptions of Christ in i. 13 ff., v. 6, xiv. 14, and of the Church in xii. 1 ff., xvii. 7, xxi. 2; (*e*) the different dates which seem to be postulated by *cc.* xi. 1 f., xiii. 18, xvii. 10 f. Such a list of seeming inconsistencies is formidable until it is taken to pieces and examined in detail. But when this has been done, it will be found that the weight of the objections is greatly diminished. The phenomena which suggest diversity of authorship admit for the most part of another explanation; they may well be due to the method of the author or the necessities of his plan. Indeed the last head is the only one which demands serious consideration from those who advocate the unity of the book. If *c.* xi. 1 implies that the Temple at Jerusalem was still standing, and xvii. 10 that Vespasian's reign had not yet ended, while the general tenor of the book points to the reign of Domitian, it is clear that as far as these passages are concerned the Apocalypse must be admitted to contain fragments of an older work; but a reference to the commentary will shew, it is hoped, that even in these contexts the inference is far from being certain.

[1] E.g. by Bousset in *Encycl. Biblica* i. 205: "it seems to be settled that the Apocalypse can no longer be regarded as a literary unity."

7. That the author of the Apocalypse made free use of any materials to which he had access and which were available for his purpose, is highly probable. But did he transfer large masses of earlier apocalyptic writing to his own work, in such a manner as to make his book a compilation or to detract from its unity? Was this his method of dealing with the works of older apocalyptists? It so happens that we are in a position to give a definite answer to the second of these questions. The writer of the N. T. Apocalypse has made large use of the apocalyptic portions of the Old Testament. He refers to the Book of Daniel in some forty-five places (Apoc. i. 1, 7, 13, 14, 17, 19, 20, ii. 10, 18, iv. 1, 10, v. 11, vii. 14, ix. 20, x. 4 ff., xi. 2, 7, 13, 15, 18, xii. 3, 7 f., 14, xiii. 1 f., 5, 7, 8, 15, xiv. 14, xvi. 11, 18 f., xvii. 3, 5, 8, 12, xviii. 2, 20, xix. 6, 12, xx. 4, 11 f., 15, xxi. 27, xxii. 5 f., 10), and the Books of Isaiah, Ezekiel, and Zechariah are used with almost equal frequency, while the other Prophets, the Psalter, and the Pentateuch are often in view[1]. No book in the New Testament is so thoroughly steeped in the thought and imagery of the Hebrew Scriptures. Yet the writer has not once quoted the Old Testament, and rarely uses its *ipsissima verba.* Seldom does he borrow from it a scene or the suggestion of a vision without modifying the details, departing from his original with the utmost freedom, or combining features which have been brought together from different contexts. This method of using Old Testament materials runs through the whole of the Apocalypse, and is characteristic of the book. Whether the writer is indebted to non-canonical apocalypses is less certain, but if he is, he has followed the same principle. There is no evidence that any one of them has served him as a 'source'; coincidences between the work of John and the extant Jewish books are nearly limited to minor points connected with the imagery and diction[2]. Under the circumstances it is more than precarious to postulate sources of which nothing is known.

For these reasons it has been assumed in this edition that the Apocalypse of John is a literary unity. It may be added that, as

[1] See p. cxlviii. [2] See *cc.* ii, xiii.

the work has progressed, this assumption has grown into a conviction. Everywhere the presence of the same creative mind has made itself felt, and features which at first sight appeared to be foreign to the writer's purpose were found on nearer view to be necessary to the development of his plan. It is impossible to justify in this place an impression which depends upon the examination of the text, but in the commentary the reader will find the details on which it rests, and he is asked to reserve his judgement until he has completed his study of the book[1].

[1] It is not the intention of these remarks to deny that the Apocalypse, as we have received it, may be a reissue by the writer of the original work in an enlarged or amended form; such a view does not militate against the essential unity of the book. On the other hand the theory proposed by Prof. J. Weiss (*supra*, p. xlvii) presents difficulties which to the present writer seem to be greater than those which it seeks to remove.

V.

DESTINATION.

1. The Apocalypse of John professes to be an encyclical addressed to the Christian societies in seven of the cities of Asia (Apoc. i. 4 Ἰωάννης ταῖς ἑπτὰ ἐκκλησίαις ταῖς ἐν τῇ Ἀσίᾳ; *ib.* 11 ὃ βλέπεις γράψον εἰς βιβλίον καὶ πέμψον ταῖς ἑπτὰ ἐκκλησίαις, εἰς Ἔφεσον καὶ εἰς Σμύρναν καὶ εἰς Πέργαμον καὶ εἰς Θυάτειραν καὶ εἰς Σάρδεις καὶ εἰς Φιλαδελφίαν καὶ εἰς Λαοδικίαν).

2. At the end of the first century the peninsula known as Asia Minor[1] seems to have embraced six provinces, Asia, Bithynia (including Pontus), Galatia, Cappadocia, Cilicia, Lycia (including Pamphylia)[2]. The Province of Asia had been created as far back as the year B.C. 129[3] out of the domains bequeathed to the Senate by Attalus III., the last king of Pergamum. Ultimately it included Mysia, Lydia, and Caria, and the three Phrygian *dioeceses* of Cibyra, Apamea, and Synnada, besides certain islands in the Aegean Sea off the western coast[4]. Thus constituted, the province was bounded on the north by Bithynia, on the east by Galatia, and on the south by Lycia; on the west it was washed by the Aegean; inland, it reached a distance from the coast of about 300 English miles, while its greatest length was about 260[5]. In the region which falls under our consideration four rivers, the Caicus, the Hermus, the Cayster, and the Maeander, descended to the sea from the highlands of the interior, and three

[1] On the history of this term see Hort, *First Epistle of St Peter*, p. 165.

[2] For the last three see Hort, *op. cit.*, p. 158 f.

[3] Marquardt, *Röm. Staats-Verwaltung* i. p. 177.

[4] On these see V. Chapot, *La province romaine proconsulaire d'Asie*, p. 82 ff.

[5] The frontier is carefully defined by Chapot, p. 85.

considerable ranges of hills, Sipylus, Tmolus, and Messogis, mounted up to the highlands from the coast.

3. In the Greek Old Testament Asia is mentioned only by the writers of the Books of the Maccabees, who use it to represent the dominions of the Seleucid dynasty (1 Macc. viii. 6, xi. 13, xii. 39, xiii. 32; 2 Macc. iii. 3, x. 24; 3 Macc. iii. 14; 4 Macc. iii. 20). But in the New Testament, under the Empire, the case is different. Asia is named by St Luke, St Paul, St Peter, and St John (Acts ii. 9, vi. 9, xvi. 6, xix. 10, 22, 26 f., xx. 4, 16, 18, xxi. 27, xxiv. 18, xxvii. 2; Rom. xvi. 5; 1 Cor. xvi. 19; 2 Cor. i. 8; 2 Tim. i. 15; 1 Pet. i. 1; Apoc. i. 4), and by all in the sense familiar at the time. "Asia in the New Testament," wrote Dr Lightfoot in 1865, "is always Proconsular Asia"[1]; and his *dictum* has not been seriously shaken by the researches of the last forty years. In Acts ii. 9 f., indeed, Phrygia is distinguished from Asia and linked to Pamphylia; but by Phrygia in that place is probably meant the non-Asian region of Phrygia, as in Acts xvi. 6, xviii. 23[2]. But whatever may be the practice of St Luke or St Paul in reference to the use of the name 'Asia,' it is certain that the province of Asia is contemplated by St Peter in 1 Pet. i. 1 (παρεπιδήμοις διασπορᾶς Πόντου, Γαλατίας, Καππαδοκίας, Ἀσίας, καὶ Βιθυνίας), where, as Dr Hort says, "the five names coincide precisely with the five names that make up the titles of the four provinces of the Roman Empire into which Asia Minor, the southern littoral eventually excepted, was divided in and after the reign of Tiberius; and it would need strong positive evidence to refute the consequent presumption that the territory denoted... was the territory of these four Roman provinces[3]." In Apoc. i. 4 the inclusion of Western Phrygia in 'Asia' is implied by the enumeration among Asian cities of Laodicea on the Lycus, which belonged to the *dioecesis Cibyratica*.

4. If the Apocalypse was directed to the Churches of Roman Asia, it was natural that it should be sent in the first instance to

[1] *Galatians*, p. 19, n. 6. The province was assigned to the Senate by Augustus, A.D. 27, and was from that date to the time of Diocletian administered by a Proconsul (ἀνθύπατος).

[2] Blass (comm. on Acts, pp. 52, 176) contends that in these passages Asia = Western Asia Minor; but see Ramsay in Hastings, *D.B.* iii. 177.

[3] *First Epistle of St Peter*, p. 157.

the greater cities of the province. Asia was remarkable for the number and wealth of its cities. Pliny (*H. N.* v. 29) mentions nine which were distinguished by being the centres of a *conventus*: viz. Adramyttium, Alabanda, Apamea, Ephesus, Laodicea on the Lycus, Pergamum, Sardis, Smyrna, Synnada; and to these Cyzicus, Philomelium, and Tralles should be added[1]. A long list might be made of less important but yet considerable towns, such as Colossae, Dorylaeum, Eumenia, Hierapolis, Magnesia on the Maeander, Miletus, Philadelphia, Priene, Thyatira; the total number of townships in the province is stated by contemporary writers to have been 500, or even 1000[2]. "No province," writes Aristides of Smyrna in the second century, "has so many cities, nor are even the greatest cities of other provinces comparable for size to the cities of Asia[3]." Between the larger towns there was a keen though friendly rivalry, as the local coins and inscriptions testify. If Ephesus proclaims herself *ἡ πρώτη καὶ μεγίστη μητρόπολις τῆς Ἀσίας*[4], Smyrna, not to be outdone by her neighbour, claims to be both a *μητρόπολις*, and *πρώτη τῆς Ἀσίας κάλλει καὶ μεγέθει, καὶ λαμπροτάτη*[5]; while Pergamum, the old capital, is, like Ephesus and Smyrna, a *πρώτη μητρόπολις*. The title *μητρόπολις* is also assumed by Cyzicus, Laodicea on the Lycus, Sardis, Synnada, and Tralles[6]. Magnesia on the Maeander, though it cannot rise to this dignity, is described on coins as the seventh city of Asia[7].

5. In the light of these facts it is not at first sight easy to explain the principle on which the Apocalyptic list of seven has been formed. Why does it include two comparatively small towns, Thyatira and Philadelphia, while Tralles and Magnesia, Hierapolis and Colossae, Alexandria Troas and Adramyttium,

[1] Marquardt, *op. cit.* p. 185.

[2] Marquardt, p. 182, J. Weiss, art. *Kleinasien* in Herzog-Hauck, x. 543.

[3] Aristides of Smyrna xlii. (=xxiii. ed. Keil, p. 34) *οὔτε γὰρ πόλεις τοσαύτας οὐδεμία ἄλλη τῶν πασῶν παρέχεται, οὔτε δὴ τάς γε μεγίστας τοιαύτας*; see also Diod. xvii. 5, and Seneca, *Ep.* 102, 21. Cf. Mommsen, *Provinces*, i. p. 354. According to Beloch (*Zur Bevölkerungsgeschichte des Alterthums*, cited by Dobschütz (*Christian Life*, E. Tr., p. 382), both Ephesus and Smyrna had in the time of Augustus a population of 200,000, and Pergamum in the middle of the second century contained from 120,000 to 180,000 souls.

[4] CIG 2992.

[5] CIG 3179, 3205; Dittenberger, *Orient. Gr. inscriptiones select.* ii. p. 159 f.

[6] Ruggiero, *Dizionario epigrafico di Antichità Romane*, i. p. 731.

[7] Mommsen, *Provinces*, p. 329.

Miletus and Halicarnassus, Dorylaeum and Synnada, are passed by? Some at least of these cities had Christian communities before the end of the first century; under Trajan, Ignatius of Antioch addressed letters to Churches at Tralles and Magnesia; under Nero, St Paul spent the first day of the week with brethren at Troas[1], and recognized a "Church of the Laodiceans" and the presence of Christians at Hierapolis[2].

It is true that the first three cities in St John's list were by common consent πρῶται τῆς Ἀσίας, and they stand in the order which would naturally be followed, at least by a resident at Ephesus. Moreover Ephesus, Smyrna, and Pergamum were in direct communication with one another by the great road which the Romans had constructed shortly after their occupation of Asia. So far then both the selection of the names and their order are easy to understand. But why should not the Apocalyptic messenger have been sent on from Pergamum to Cyzicus or to Troas? why was his course at this point diverted to the inland towns of Thyatira, Sardis and Philadelphia, and brought to an end in the valley of the Lycus? The true answer is doubtless that which is given by Professor Ramsay: "all the Seven Cities stand on the great circular road that bound together the most populous, wealthy, and influential part of the Province, the west-central region[3]." "They were the best points on the circuit to serve as centres of communication with seven districts: Pergamum for the north...; Thyatira for an inland district on the north-east and east; Sardis for the wide middle valley of the Hermus; Philadelphia for Upper Lydia...; Laodicea for the Lycus Valley and for Central Phrygia...; Ephesus for the Cayster and lower Maeander Valleys and coasts; Smyrna for the lower Hermus Valley and the North Ionian coasts[4]." Planted at these seven centres, the Apocalypse would spread through their neighbourhoods, and from thence to the rest of the province. A Roman road led from Pergamum to Adramyttium and Troas, and another direct to Cyzicus; other roads connected Philadelphia with Dorylaeum, and Laodicea with

[1] Acts xx. 7 ff.
[2] Col. ii. 1, iv. 13, 16.
[3] *Letters*, p. 183.
[4] *Ib.* p. 191.

Apamea and Synnada, and with Cibyra. From Ephesus a great road passed through Magnesia, Tralles and Laodicea, and crossing Galatia and Cappadocia ultimately reached the Euphrates[1]; a branch road entered Syria through the 'Cilician Gates.' Thus the route prescribed in the Apocalypse provided for the circulation of the book throughout the churches of the entire province and beyond it.

6. Some account of the cities to which the book was originally sent is given in the notes to *cc.* ii. iii., and much more may be gathered from so accessible a book as Professor Ramsay's *Letters to the Seven Churches*[2]. Here it may suffice to place before the student the general conditions of the life into which Christianity entered when it established itself in the cities of Asia.

(i) At Ephesus by custom the Proconsul landed at his entry into the Province[3], and the city was regarded as the seat of the provincial government. But it retained at least the forms of municipal independence, and its civic life was full and many-sided. During the Roman period the population was divided into six tribes (φυλαί), which were again divided into thousands (χιλιαστύες). Local affairs were in the hands of three assemblies, a council (βουλή), which in A.D. 104 consisted of 450 members probably elected in equal numbers from each of the tribes; a senate (γερουσία), which seems to have been charged with the finance of public worship or perhaps with municipal finance in general, and the care of public monuments; and the popular assembly which bore the familiar name of *ecclesia*[4]. Each assembly had its γραμματεύς, and the γραμματεὺς τοῦ δήμου possessed an authority which as we learn from the Acts (xix. 25) could make itself respected even by an angry mob.

In the life of Ephesus commerce occupied no less important a place than local politics. The silting up of the harbour had indeed begun to threaten the city's command of the seas, but Strabo was able to report that in every other respect it was grow-

[1] Ramsay, *Hist. Geogr. of Asia Minor*, p. 164 ff. See also M. Chapot's chapter on the public roads of Asia (p. 358—368).

[2] Pp. 210—430.

[3] Bergmann, *De Asia*, p. 30.

[4] For the details see Hicks, *Ancient Greek Inscriptions*, iii. p. 68 ff.; Chapot, pp. 194—230.

ing in prosperity day by day, and that Asia within the Taurus had no market that could vie with it[1]. Foreign trade brought it into communication with Greece, Egypt, and Spain, and on the other hand with the Euphrates and the East. Among its local specialities were marble, vermilion, oils and essences, and the handicraft of workers in gold, silver and copper[2]. Its slaves fetched fabulous prices in the Roman market[3]. Nor were the intellectual interests of the place less keen or varied. In the first century the city of Heracleitus abounded with persons who followed the profession of the philosopher or the *rhetor*, and added to its reputation as a seat of learning[4]. It will not be forgotten that according to Eusebius[5] Ephesus is the scene of Justin's dialogue with Trypho, and probably also of his initiation into the Stoic, Peripatetic, and Platonist philosophies[6]. Nor was art neglected in Ephesus; the city was a famous school of sculpture and architecture; the great theatre remains to witness to the passion of its citizens for the drama[7]. But religion was the paramount power at Ephesus, as perhaps in all the Asian cities. The worship of the Ephesian Artemis was an inheritance from pre-Hellenic times, and possessed all the attractions which bind a people to a traditional or localized cult. The Artemision did not indeed dominate the city as the Parthenon dominated Athens; it lay in fact, as was demonstrated by Mr Wood's discovery on the last day of 1869, on the plain outside the Magnesian gate of Ephesus. Nevertheless it was the chief glory of the place, and life in Ephesus was at every point brought into contact with the great presiding deity of the city—the Πρωτοθρονία, as according to Pausanias (x. 38. 3) she was locally called. It was by the priestly college at the Artemision, known as the Essênes,

[1] Strabo xiv. 24 ἡ δὲ πόλις τῇ πρὸς τὰ ἄλλα εὐκαιρίᾳ τῶν τόπων αὔξεται καθ' ἑκάστην ἡμέραν, ἐμπόριον οὖσα μέγιστον τῶν κατὰ τὴν Ἀσίαν τὴν ἐντὸς τοῦ Ταύρου.

[2] Cf. Acts xix. 24, 2 Tim. iv. 14.

[3] See Zimmermann, *Ephesos im ersten christlichen Jahrhundert*, p. 50 ff.

[4] Apollonius of Tyana *ap*. Philostrat. *vit. Ap*. viii. 7, 8 (cited by Zimmermann, p. 65): Ἔφεσος μεστὴ φροντισμάτων φιλοσόφων τε καὶ ῥητορικῶν ὑφ' ὧν ἡ πόλις ἰσχύει σοφίαν ἐπαινοῦσα.

[5] *H.E*. iv. 28.

[6] *Dial*. 2 νεωστὶ ἐπιδημήσαντι τῇ ἡμετέρᾳ πόλει συνετῷ ἀνδρὶ καὶ προὔχοντι ἐν τοῖς Πλατωνικοῖς συνδιέτριβον. Cicero *De nat. deorum* 2 mentions a Peripatetic school at Ephesus.

[7] Zimmermann, p. 73.

that the lot was cast by which a new citizen was admitted to his tribe and thousand. In the Ephesian calendar the month of the spring equinox was named after Artemis (ὁ Ἀρτεμισιών), and during that month the city celebrated a yearly festival in honour of the goddess (τὰ Ἀρτεμίσια)[1]. On great festivals a sacred carriage (ἡ ἱερὰ ἀπήνη) carried the image of Artemis through the streets of the city. The great temple employed an army of officials; it had its wardens (νεωποῖαι), its guards (φύλακες), its hierophants and choirmen (θεολόγοι, ὑμνῳδοί), its crowd of ἱερόδουλοι, its priests and priestesses[2]. Private beneficence added to the splendours of the goddess; a great inscription of the year A.D. 104 records the munificent bequest of a citizen for the maintenance of the worship of Artemis, "marking," in the judgement of Canon Hicks, "a reaction against Christianity," which from the first had been felt to be a serious rival of the Ephesian cult. It is worthy of remark that the worship of the Emperors[3] did not present itself to the people of Ephesus in this light, and was even regarded as an ally of the local religion; a statue of Augustus was set up in the precinct of the Artemision[4], and Ephesus was proud to be the νεωκόρος of the Emperor as well as of her own goddess Artemis[5]. Indeed, there is abundance of evidence that in the cities of Asia generally the Caesar-worship was a welcome adjunct to the worship of the local deities[6].

Ex una disce omnes; the surroundings of the Church in Ephesus were more or less repeated in the other Asian cities. But each city had its special features, and something must be added in reference to these.

(ii) Smyrna, the new city of the Diadochi, claimed, as we have seen, a primacy of beauty[7]. Approached by a long gulf which

[1] Hicks, pp. 83, 117 ff.

[2] The inscriptions mention also ἱεροκήρυκες, ἱεροσαλπιγκταί, σπονδοποιοί: cf. J. Menadier, *Qua condicione Ephesii usi sunt*, p. 105 f.

[3] On this see *c.* vii.

[4] Hicks, p. 37; Ramsay, *Letters*, p. 231.

[5] Thus νεωκόρων δὶς (or τρὶς) καὶ τῆς Ἀρτέμιδος is found on Ephesian coins; see B. V. Head, *Greek coins of Lydia*, p. cvii.

[6] See Chapot, p. 424 ff.

[7] See p. liii; and Aristides of Smyrna, xli. (=xix. ed. Keil): Σμύρνα τὸ τῆς Ἀσίας ἄγαλμα, τῆς δὲ ὑμετέρας ἐγκαλλώπισμα ἡγεμονίας. Cf. the Life of Polycarp by Pionius, where the citizens are addressed as ἄνδρες οἱ τῆσδε τῆς περικαλλοῦς πόλεως κάτοικοι (Lightfoot, *Ignatius*, iii. p. 462).

opened into a noble harbour, and crowned by an acropolis[1], its natural advantages were in some respects superior to those of Ephesus. The city was worthy of its surroundings; its streets were straight and well paved; public buildings were numerous, including a library, an odeum, a stadium, a theatre, a temple of Homer (*τὸ Ὁμήρειον*) with a portico attached to it, and other large two-storied porticoes[2]. The relations of Smyrna with Rome were excellent, and its loyalty received due recognition; it was an *urbs libera* and the centre of a *conventus*, and from A.D. 26 the proud possessor of an Augusteum erected in honour of Tiberius, a privilege which Ephesus at the time coveted in vain[3]. If Smyrna did not claim, like Ephesus, a special cult, it could boast a number of temples, conspicuous among which were those of the Sipylene Cybele and the local Zeus. The public games of Smyrna[4] were noted for their magnificence, and it was one of the cities where periodical festivals were held under the authority of the *Commune Asiae* in honour of the Augusti[5]. On such occasions Christian citizens were doubtless placed in a position of peculiar peril, but at no season would they be regarded with favourable eyes by a population immersed in business and pleasure, devoted to the local cults, and proud of its loyalty to Rome and the Emperor[6].

(iii) Pergamum, the old capital of the Attalids, still claimed an hegemony, in right of its ancient glories[7]. The place possessed natural advantages which fitted it to sustain the character of leadership. "Beyond all other sites in Asia Minor it gives the traveller the impression of a royal city, the home of authority; the rocky hill on which it stands is so huge, and dominates the broad plain of the Caicus so proudly and boldly[8]." The plain was one of the richest in Mysia[9], and supplied the markets of the city; the local trade in skins (*διφθέραι*) prepared for the use of writers was so brisk that the material received its name from Pergamum[10]. But the fame of Pergamum rested chiefly on its religious pre-eminence. A tetrad of local deities, Zeus Soter, Athena Nicephoros, Dionysius Kathegemon, Asklepios Soter[11], presided over the city; the temple

[1] See the description in Aristides, xv. (=xvii. ed. Keil).

[2] Strabo, xiv. 37 (646).

[3] A second neocorate was adjudged to Smyrna under Hadrian and a third under Sept. Severus (Head, *Greek Coins of Ionia*, p. 263). Cf. CIG 3266 *τοῖς ἐν Σμύρνῃ νεοῖς τῶν Σεβαστῶν*, CIG 3205 *γʹ νεωκόρος κατὰ τὰ δόγματα τῆς ἱερωτάτης συνκλήτου*, CIG 3386 *ἀποτίσει μητρὶ θεῶν Σιπυληνῇ δηνάρια δισχίλια πεντακόσια.*

[4] Cf. Pausan. vi. 14. 1.

[5] Lightfoot, *Ignatius*, iii. p. 405.

[6] The coins shew that this loyalty suffered no decrease under Domitian; see Head, p. 273.

[7] Strabo, xiii. 4 (623) *ἔχει δέ τινα ἡγεμονίαν πρὸς τοὺς τόπους τούτους τὸ Πέργαμον, ἐπιφανὴς πόλις καὶ πολὺν συνευτυχήσασα χρόνον τοῖς Ἀτταλικοῖς βασιλεῦσι.*

[8] Ramsay, *Letters*, p. 281.

[9] Strabo *l.c.* *σφόδρα εὐδαίμονα γῆν... σχεδὸν δέ τι τὴν ἀρίστην τῆς Μυσίας.*

[10] *Membrana Pergamena*, 'parchment': see Gardthausen, *Gr. Palaeographie*, p. 39 f., or Maunde Thompson, *Handbook of Greek and Latin Palaeography*, p. 35 f.

[11] The legends ΑΘΗΝΑϹ ΝΙΚΗΦΟΡΟΥ, ΑϹΚΛΗΠΙΟΥ ϹΩΤΗΡΟϹ are frequent on coins of Pergamum; see Wroth, *Greek Coins of Mysia*, p. 128 ff.

of Athena almost crowned the acropolis, and beneath it, on the slope of the hill and visible from the agora, stood a great *al fresco* altar of the Pergamene Zeus. Still more celebrated was the Pergamene cult of Asklepios, to whose temple there was attached a school of medicine which attracted sufferers from all quarters. But in Roman times the city prided itself above all upon its devotion to the worship of the Emperors. From the time of Augustus Pergamene coins bear the inscriptions ΘΕΟΝ CYΓΚΛΗΤΟΝ, ΘΕΑΝ ΡΩΜΗΝ, ΘΕΟΝ CEBACTON[1]. Inscriptions proclaim the dignity of the city as the first in Asia to erect a temple to Augustus[2]; and as it was the first, so it continued to be the chief Asian seat of the Emperor-cult. In the time of Hadrian it was already δὶς νεωκόρος, and an inscription of the reign of Trajan mentions the ὑμνῳδοὶ θεοῦ Σεβαστοῦ καὶ θεᾶς Ῥώμης; the local priest of Zeus was proud to style himself also priest of the divine Augustus. In St John's eyes this new cult was the crowning sin of Pergamum; the city which had introduced the worship of the Augusti into Asia was the dwelling place, the very throne of Satan, who reigned from its acropolis; and the Church which resided in it must expect to find itself in the forefront of the battle about to be fought between Christ and Antichrist.

(iv) Thyatira "lies in an open, smiling vale, bordered by gently sloping hills," and "possesses no proper acropolis[3]." The contrast to Pergamum thus suggested is maintained when the two cities are compared in other particulars. Thyatira had no history reaching back beyond the Seleucids, who raised the obscure township into a Macedonian colony. It was distinguished by no famous cult; the Thyatiran coins and inscriptions mention only the local hero Tyrimnus, or his deified counterpart the Tyrimnaean Apollo, and an Artemis who bears the surname 'Boritene[4].' There is no evidence that Thyatira was as yet a νεωκόρος of the Augusti. Outside the city a Sibyl of Eastern origin known as Sambethe or Sambatha had her cell (τὸ Σαμβαθεῖον)[5]; and it has been suggested[6], though with little probability, that this person is to be identified with the prophetess Jezebel of Apoc. ii. 20. But the most outstanding feature in Thyatiran life was probably the institution of trade-guilds[7]. In certain of the Asian cities these guilds may have filled the place of the 'thousands' into which the 'tribes' were divided[8], and Thyatira is one of these. At Thyatira there were guilds of bakers, potters, workers in brass, tanners, leather-

[1] Wroth, *op. cit.* p. 134 ff. E.g. CIG 3548 ἡ βουλὴ καὶ ὁ δῆμος τῶν πρώτων νεωκόρων Περγαμηνῶν.

[2] Herzog-Hauck, x. p. 551. CIG 3569 ὁ ἱερεὺς τοῦ Σεβαστοῦ θεοῦ Καίσαρος, ὁ δὲ αὐτὸς...ἱερεὺς τοῦ Διός.

[3] Ramsay, *Letters*, p. 318.

[4] B. V. Head, *Greek Coins of Lydia*, p. 294 [T]YP[IM]NOC, *ib.* p. 295 BOPEITHNH.

[5] CIG 3509.

[6] Schürer[3], iii. p. 428.

[7] At Thyatira they were known as ἐργασίαι; other names were συμβιώσεις, συνεργασίαι, συστήματα: see Chapot, p. 167.

[8] Ramsay, *Cities and Bishoprics of Phrygia*, p. 105.

cutters, workers in wool and flax, clothiers, dyers[1]; the workers in wool and the dyers were probably the most numerous, for the manufacture and dyeing of woollen goods was a Lydian speciality, in which Thyatira excelled[2]. To these guilds many of the Thyatirene Christians would have belonged, and their connexion with them would raise questions of much difficulty. One of the inscriptions records an honour voted by the guild of dyers to the priest of the ancestral hero Tyrimnus[3]; in such circumstances what course ought the Christian members of the guild to follow? Such a problem might seldom arise, and when it arose, the Church might agree upon the answer; but there was another of frequent occurrence upon which Christians differed among themselves. From time to time the members of a guild partook together of a common meal which had a sacrificial character and moreover too often ended in revelry and licentiousness. At Thyatira, through circumstances which will appear further on, the question whether Christians might or might not take part in such guild-feasts became acute, and the Apocalyptic message to Thyatira turns upon it.

(v) Sardis, the capital of the old Lydian kingdom, and in Persian times the seat of a satrap, retained under the Romans the shadow of its ancient greatness[4]; commanding the great Valley of the Hermus, and standing at a point to which roads converged from Thyatira, Smyrna and Laodicea and the Lycus, it could not sink into neglect. The town was shattered by the great earthquake of A.D. 17, but with the liberal help of Tiberius it rose from its ruins. Its gratitude was shewn in a special devotion to the Emperor; in A.D. 26 it contended with Pergamum, Smyrna, and Ephesus for the privilege of erecting an Augusteum, and though it failed on that occasion, eventually it could claim a second and even a third neocorate. The chief local cult was that of Koré, but the name of the Lydian Zeus appears also on the coins[5]; Dionysus, too, Athena, Aphrodite, and the local heroes Tmolus and Hermus, were honoured at Sardis. The Church perhaps encountered in Sardis no special danger to her peace; but the atmosphere of an old pagan city, heavy with the immoral traditions of eight centuries, was unfavourable to the growth of her spiritual life.

(vi) Philadelphia has received a characteristic treatment from Bishop Lightfoot[6], to which little need be added here. "A city full of earthquakes" is Strabo's significant comment upon it; he adds that in his time the town had been largely forsaken by its inhabitants, who lived on the rich lands which surrounded it[7]. With Sardis, at the time of the earthquake, Philadelphia partook

[1] M. Clerc, *de rebus Thyatirenorum*, p. 92 (quoted by Ramsay *l.c.*). Chapot (p. 168 ff.) gives a complete list of the trades of Asia so far as they are mentioned in the inscriptions.

[2] Acts xvi. 14 *πορφυρόπωλος πόλεως Θυατείρων*. Cf. CIG 26, 3924.

[3] CIG 349 *τὸν ἱερέα τοῦ προπάτορος θεοῦ Τυρίμνου οἱ βαφεῖς.*

[4] Strabo xiii. 4 (625) *αἱ δὲ Σάρδεις πόλις ἐστὶ μεγάλη...ὑπέρκειται δὲ τῶν Σάρδεων ὁ Τμῶλος...ὑπόκειται δὲ τῇ πόλει τό τε Σαρδιανῶν πεδίον...καὶ τὸ τοῦ Ἕρμου.*

[5] Head, p. 246 ff.; cf. p. cvii.

[6] *St Ignatius*, ii. pp. 237—241.

[7] Strabo xiii. 10 (628).

of the bounty of the Emperor, and was duly grateful; though it did not acquire the neocorate until the beginning of the third century, its special loyalty was shewn by the titles assumed on its coins; under Caligula and Claudius it styled itself Neocaesarea, and under the Flavian Emperors Flavia[1]. It is more important for our purpose to notice the situation of Philadelphia in reference to Central Asia Minor. The city lay on the direct route from Smyrna to the highlands and plateau of Central Asia Minor. Thus the Church in Philadelphia had unusual opportunities of spreading the Gospel in the interior, and she seems to have availed herself of the open door[2].

(vii) Laodicea has been exhaustively described by Professor Ramsay in *Cities and Bishoprics of Phrygia*[3]. The student of the Apocalypse will take special note of the specialities in wool and in eyesalve produced in the neighbourhood of this city, to which reference seems to be made in the message to Laodicea; and of the prosperity of the Laodicenes as a banking and trading community, and the singular spirit of independence indicated by their rejection of imperial help after the earthquake of A.D. 60[4]. It is evident that the Christians of Laodicea shared the self-sufficiency of their fellow-townsmen, and carried it into the sphere of their relations with God and Christ. The commercial pre-occupations of the place saved them from persecution, but at the cost, as at Sardis, of the life of the Spirit. Of this decline of the Christian life in the Churches of the Lycus valley (for the message to Laodicea was doubtless intended also for Hierapolis and Colossae), the neighbourhood yielded a forcible illustration, which the Apocalyptist was not slow to use. The hot springs of Hierapolis, in their course over the platform on which the city was built, lose their heat, and the traveller who drinks of the water finds it intolerable to the palate. So, St John teaches, the Christ will reject the lukewarm profession of faith from which the fire of love has departed.

[1] Head, pp. lxxxv. 195 ff.

[2] Ramsay, *Letters*, c. xxviii.

[3] i. pp. 32—83.

[4] Cf. Lightfoot, *Colossians*, p. 44: "in all other cases of earthquake which Tacitus records as happening in these Asiatic cities...he mentions the fact of their obtaining relief from the Senate or the Emperor."

VI.

CHRISTIANITY IN THE PROVINCE OF ASIA DURING THE FIRST CENTURY.

1. The permanent interest of apocalyptic literature consists largely in its intimate connexion with the needs and sufferings, the hopes and fears, of the age and communities which produced it. From Daniel onwards the Jewish apocalypses reflect, with more or less distinctness, the conditions under which they were written, and the expectations which consoled or invigorated the Jews under Syrian, Hasmonaean, Herodian, or Roman rule, throwing side-lights, lurid but instructive, on contemporary life and history. The great Christian apocalypse is no exception to this rule. But whereas it is left to the critical student to elicit as he can the age and circumstances of the Jewish apocalyptists, the Christian writer makes no secret of the conditions under which he worked. The Apocalypse of John is clearly a product of Asian Christianity, and the purpose of the book cannot be understood without an effort to realize the position of Christianity in the cities of Asia during the first century of our era.

2. Long before the Christian era the Jews had formed a considerable factor in the population of the Asian cities[1]. There was a synagogue at Ephesus (Acts xviii. 19) and, it may be assumed, in almost every one of the great towns. But the Jew was the unconscious or, if ever he attained to a consciousness of the fact, the reluctant *avant-coureur* of Christianity. Christianity

[1] Cf. Philo, *leg. ad Cai.* 33 Ἰουδαῖοι καθ᾽ ἑκάστην πόλιν εἰσὶ παμπλήθεις Ἀσίας. *In Flacc.* 7 τὰς πλείστας καὶ εὐδαιμονεστάτας τῶν ἐν...Ἀσίᾳ...ἐκνέμονται. On the Jews in the Asian Cities see Ramsay, *Letters to the Seven Churches*, c. xii., and *infra*, p. lxxxviii f.

was doubtless discussed by Jewish circles in the cities of Asia as soon as the Asian Jews who had visited Jerusalem at the Passover or Pentecost of A.D. 29 returned to their homes in the Province. Even if the narrative of Acts ii. is not regarded as historical, it is clear that the story of the Crucifixion and the Resurrection could not fail to have been repeated everywhere. The same story came a little later across the sea from Rome and Alexandria[1], or by the great trade-roads from Syrian Antioch; or it might have been brought down to the sea coast by men who had heard St Paul tell it in the synagogues of the province of Galatia, at Pisidian Antioch or at Iconium, or of the Lycaonian towns, Lystra and Derbe. Yet there is no sign of any Christian movement in Asia before the arrival of St Paul at Ephesus[2], and to Ephesus his personal ministry seems to have been nearly limited.

3. Few things are more perplexing in connexion with the development of St Paul's evangelistic work than the long delay of its extension to Asia. At Antioch in Pisidia in the summer of 48 the Apostle stood literally at the parting of the ways; if he had turned to the west, he would have reached the Lycus valley and Ephesus; instead of this he turned his face eastwards, and his destination was the Lycaonian towns. On the next occasion a westward mission was in his mind, probably from the first, certainly when at Derbe or Lystra he took Timothy for his partner in a new work[3], and with his two colleagues 'went through' the 'Phrygo-Galatic region'[4], i.e. the Phrygian part of Galatia, which lay on the border of Asia. If he did not cross the border, he would have done so, had not a hand which was upon his spirit held him back. This mysterious check was repeated when he had got to the confines of Mysia, and wished to enter the great province of Bithynia and Pontus[5]. Both Asia and Bithynia were to become headquarters of Christian influence[6], but their time was not yet;

[1] Cf. Acts xviii. 18, 24 ff.

[2] Acts xix. 1. The brief previous visit (xviii. 19 f.) scarcely counts.

[3] Acts xvi. 2 τοῦτον ἠθέλησεν ὁ Παῦλος σὺν αὐτῷ ἐξελθεῖν.

[4] *Ib.* 6 διῆλθον δὲ τὴν Φρυγίαν καὶ Γαλατικὴν χώραν.

[5] *Ib.* 7 ἐλθόντες δὲ κατὰ τὴν Μυσίαν ἐπείραζον εἰς τὴν Βιθυνίαν πορευθῆναι.

[6] Cf. 1 Pet. i. 1 with Dr Hort's note *ad loc.*, and Additional Note on p. 157 f. As to Bithynia we have the testimony of the younger Pliny (A.D. 111): "multi enim omnis aetatis, omnis ordinis, utriusque sexus etiam, vocantur in periculum."

Macedonia and Achaia must receive their call first, and Asia must wait a while. The turn of Ephesus came in A.D. 52—3, when St Paul began a residence of more than two years in that city.

4. The Apostle reached Ephesus at the end of a progress through the "upper parts[1]," i.e. not by the direct route from Galatia (Acts xviii. 23) through the Lycus valley, but over the higher ground of the interior, possibly by way of Philadelphia, Sardis, and Smyrna, or by Philadelphia, Sardis, Thyatira, Pergamum, and thence down the coast. The purpose of this détour was apparently evangelistic[2], and it creates a suspicion that Ephesus was not the only or even the first Church in Asia which received the Gospel from St Paul's own lips. The outworks were carried before the citadel was attacked; in any case, the gradual approach to Ephesus is of a piece with the previous delays, and emphasizes the great importance of the city as a centre of Christian work. Meanwhile, at Ephesus itself forerunners had been at work—the Alexandrian Jew, Apollonius or Apollos[3]; a party of twelve men or thereabouts (ὡσεὶ δώδεκα), who had received John's baptism; and the Roman Christians Aquila and Priscilla, who had crossed with the Apostle from Corinth in the previous spring. The Apostle's own work began as usual in the synagogue. But as at Corinth (Acts xviii. 6, xix. 9), when his preaching was resented by the Jewish residents, he parted company with them, and thenceforth his teaching was carried on in one of the philosophical schools of the city[4]. This went on for two years, so that Ephesus had unusual opportunities of hearing a great Christian teacher; and though St Paul himself does not seem to have left the place, visitors from other parts of Asia carried back a report of his teaching to their own towns, and the evangelization of Asia, begun during his journey to Ephesus, was at length fairly complete (Acts xix. 10, 26). At Ephesus a Church

[1] Acts xix. 1 διελθόντα τὰ ἀνωτερικὰ μέρη.

[2] Compare the use of διέρχεσθαι in viii. 40, xi. 19, xiv. 24, etc.

[3] On the relation of Apollos to Christian teaching at this time see J. H. A. Hart, *J. T. S.*, Oct. 1905.

[4] The Western text says that he discoursed there daily ἀπὸ ὥρας πέμπτης ἕως δεκάτης, from 11 a.m. to 4 p.m.; i.e., as Ramsay (*St Paul*, p. 271) points out, he began after the usual work of the lecture room was over.

began to take shape during the biennium. Disciples had gathered round the Apostle before he left the synagogue (xix. 9), and after the separation the number grew, and gave satisfactory evidence of their sincerity (*ib.* 18 ff.); there were to be found men who had filled the office of Asiarch, and yet were well disposed towards the Christian cause or its leader (*ib.* 31). When the crash came in A.D. 55, St Paul was able to feel that his work in Ephesus had been practically accomplished, and that he might go elsewhere without danger to Asian Christianity (xix. 21, xx. 1)[1].

5. In the spring of 56, when St Paul landed at Miletus on his way to his last Pentecost at Jerusalem, the Church of Ephesus already had its college of elders[2]. In Asia as in Galatia and Lycaonia[3] the Apostle had instituted the presbyterate; although the order is mentioned only in connexion with Ephesus, it doubtless found a place in the other Asian Churches[4] which owed their origin to St Paul. Two pairs of letters, which if they are not the work of St Paul, certainly proceed from his school, supply further materials for the history of the Churches of Asia during the years that followed. (1) *Colossians, Ephesians.* The letter to Colossae deals chiefly with the conditions of the Church in that Phrygian city and other Churches in the Lycus valley. But *Ephesians*, as is generally recognized, was a circular letter intended for the cities of Asia generally[5]—a Pauline precursor in this respect of St John's Apocalypse—and it illumines the general situation in Asia about A.D. 60. From this point of view it is interesting to note the repeated reference in this Epistle to a charismatic ministry (Eph. ii. 20, iv. 11 f.); the stress laid on the reconciliation of the Jew and Gentile in Christ (ii. 11 ff.); the conception of the *ecclesia* as an ideal unity (iv. 1 ff.); the conception of the Christian life as bound up with the risen and ascended life of the Lord, and working itself out into a life of actual participation in

[1] His departure was perhaps slightly hastened in consequence of the riot: but he had not intended to stay beyond the Pentecost of 55 (1 Cor. xvi. 8).

[2] Acts xx. 17 ff.; on xx. 28, see Hort, *Ecclesia*, p. 99 f.

[3] Cf. xiv. 23.

[4] Cf. 1 Cor. xvi. 19 *αἱ ἐκκλησίαι τῆς Ἀσίας.*

[5] On this see Westcott-Hort[2], *Notes on select readings*, p. 123 ff.

His glory (ii. 6 ff.)—ideas which reappear in the Apocalypse of John. (2) 1, 2 *Timothy*. According to 1 Timothy, St Paul, after his release from the Roman captivity of Acts xxviii. 30, visited Ephesus again. He found that the fears which he had expressed in the address at Miletus were already realized in part. Unwholesome speculations, probably of Jewish origin[1], occupied the attention of the Ephesian Church, to the neglect of practical Christianity. Other evils were rife in the Christian society, such as eagerness for office, unseemly disputes in the Church assemblies, gossip and slander if not worse sins among the women, even those who as widows were pensioners and servants of the Church. There were Christians who attempted to make a gain of their religion, and others of the wealthier class who prided themselves on their wealth, and needed to be urged to share it with their poorer brethren. The whole picture is far from hopeful, and in the Second Epistle it becomes depressing. All Asia had turned away from its father in the faith (i. 15)—an exaggeration, it may be, but one which suggests at least an anti-Pauline movement in the churches of the province; two of the ringleaders—Phygellus and Hermogenes—are mentioned by name; a certain Onesiphorus is warmly commended, as if he were almost a solitary exception to the general apostasy. St Paul despatched to Ephesus (iv. 12) one of his few remaining friends, Tychicus of Asia[2], perhaps in the hope that a native of the province might succeed in recalling Asia to its allegiance. So the curtain falls upon the Apostle's relations with the Asian Churches.

6. It was probably after the death of St Paul that St Peter wrote his circular letter to the Churches of Asia Minor[3]. The letter makes no special reference to the affairs of the province of Asia, but its account of the condition of Christians in Asia Minor must be taken to apply to provincial Asia, which was one of the four provinces addressed[4]. In the first place it is remarkable that while St Paul himself is not mentioned, the Apostle of the

[1] Hort, *Judaistic Christianity*, p. 131 ff.

[2] Acts xx. 4 Ἀσιανοὶ δὲ Τύχικος καὶ Τρόφιμος. Cf. Eph. vi. 21.

[3] See *St Mark*², p. xxii.

[4] Not however the first province to receive the letter, which, to judge from the order of the names, entered Asia Minor by way of the Euxine, possibly at Sinope; cf. Hort, *First Ep. of St Peter*, pp. 17, 176 ff.

Circumcision not only associates himself in this letter with two of St Paul's companions, Silvanus and Mark (iv. 12 f.), but makes considerable use of St Paul's Epistles, and among them of the encyclical Πρὸς Ἐφεσίους. The fact has been used as an indication of date, but it may serve also to shew the delicate care with which St Peter endeavours to maintain the continuity of Christian teaching in churches which had been to some extent estranged from their founder, and without such an intimation might have been led to regard Peter in the light of a rival to whom they were invited to transfer their allegiance. But for our purpose it is more important to take note of the relations which existed at the time between the Christian communities and their pagan neighbours. Christians were spoken against as evil-doers (ii. 12); their reasons were demanded with a rudeness which called for the exercise of meekness (iii. 15); there was always a chance that any one of them might be called to suffer as a Christian; already they had been tried by fire, and were learning to bear their share in the sufferings of Christ (iv. 12 ff.). Yet the persecution was as yet unofficial. The Apostle presses on the Churches the duty of absolute loyalty to the Emperor and the Proconsul (ii. 13 ff.). Rome, indeed, is already 'Babylon' (v. 13), but Nero, if he is still living, exercises a power which is of God, and while God is alone to be feared, the Emperor must be held in honour (ii. 17). The troubles of the Asian Christians came as yet from their neighbours rather than from the State; their refusal to share in the revelries and impurities of heathenism brought upon them the illwill and abuse and, as far as the civil power permitted, the maltreatment of relatives or fellowcitizens (iv. 3 ff.). The trial fell with especial weight upon Christian slaves, who had no protection against the cruelty of pagan masters, and who formed a large proportion of the early Christian societies.

7. In the Apocalypse of John the field is narrowed again to Proconsular Asia. The opening chapters of the book take the reader on tour through a great part of the Province; he accompanies the bearer of the Apocalyptic circular from Ephesus to

Smyrna, and thence passes inland to Mysian Pergamum, Lydian Thyatira, Sardis, and Philadelphia, and Phrygian Laodicea. Each of the seven cities had its Christian society, and in some cases at least this society was associated with neighbouring churches to which it would transmit the Apocalypse or a copy. Thus Pergamum was within easy reach of Adramyttium and Troas (Acts xx. 5 ff., 2 Cor. ii. 12), Laodicea of Hierapolis and Colossae (Col. ii. 1, iv. 13), and Ephesus itself of Miletus, Magnesia and Tralles; so that the route indicated secured the distribution of St John's encyclical among all the Christian brotherhoods in Asia[1].

St John, like St Peter, makes no mention of St Paul. The founder of the Asian Churches seems to have disappeared altogether from their field of sight. If we are to believe a considerable school of modern critics, the Apocalypse not only ignores St Paul, but bitterly and repeatedly attacks those who still claimed to follow his teaching. In the opinion of these scholars the Nicolaitans of *c.* ii. are the Pauline Christians of the age of St John[2]. It is possible that this remarkable theory holds an element of truth. The advocates of laxity may have sheltered themselves under the great authority of St Paul, quoting detached sentences from his epistles[3] in support of their tenets; they may have represented the rôle of the Apostle of the Uncircumcision as that of a deliverer of Gentile Christendom from the yoke which the older Apostles and the mother Church had sought to impose by the decree of A.D. 49; it is even barely possible that behind the enigmatic name which they bore there may lie some reference to the spiritual victories won by the man whom they claimed as the author of their policy. Against pseudo-Paulinists such as these John takes his stand, as St Paul himself would certainly have done; but against Paul[4] or his teaching there is not a word. No doubt it is strange that so great a figure as that of St Paul should have been forgotten or eclipsed in the country which had been the earliest

[1] See above, *c.* v.

[2] See the commentary on *c.* ii. 13.

[3] E.g. 1 Cor. x. 19 *τί οὖν φημί; ὅτι εἰδωλόθυτόν τί ἐστιν;* ib. 23 *πάντα ἔξεστιν.* Tit. i. 15 *πάντα καθαρὰ τοῖς καθαροῖς.* That the Apostle's words were wrested after this manner we know from Rom. iii. 8; cf. 2 Pet. iii. 16.

[4] On the slight said to be intended in xxi. 14, see comm. *ad loc.*

and principal scene of his evangelistic work. But account must be taken of several circumstances. More than a generation had passed away since his residence at Ephesus, and the other Asian cities had never seen him in the flesh[1], or had known him only as an itinerant evangelist[2]. The rapid movements of life which played over the surface of Ionian civilization in the years between the beginning of Nero's reign and the end of Domitian's; the transit over Asia of many of the greater 'lights' of the Church on their way from Palestine westwards, and the settlement of some of them in the province[3]; the presence in Asia of men who had known the Lord in the days of His flesh or had conversed with those who knew Him[4]—these things all tended to wipe out the memory of St Paul from the minds of the Asian Christians. John himself as the *ἐπιστήθιος*, whether we regard him as the Apostle or the Elder, may well have excited throughout the province a sentiment of veneration such as had never been felt for the *ἔκτρωμα*[5] of the Apostolic body. It is not surprising that St John is seen to fill and more than fill the place once occupied by St Paul, or that so few traces are left of the great Apostle's work in the Churches of Asia when they emerge to sight again at the end of the first century.

8. That Christianity in Asia was, in the time of the Apocalyptist, a force with which paganism had to reckon is evident from the new attitude which its enemies were beginning to assume towards it—a point to which we shall presently recur. In the larger cities the Christians probably formed an appreciable fraction of the population; Ignatius, some fifteen or twenty years after the date of the Apocalypse, can speak of the *πολυπλήθεια* of the Ephesian Church[6]. Asia Minor was destined to become the stronghold of Christianity, and in no other province of the Empire was the faith so widely disseminated or represented by so many

[1] Cf. Col. ii. 1.

[2] See p. lxiv.

[3] Polycrates ap. Eus. *H.E.* iii. 31 *καὶ γὰρ καὶ κατὰ τὴν Ἀσίαν μεγάλα στοιχεῖα κεκοίμηται,...Φίλιππον τῶν δώδεκα ἀποστόλων ὃς κεκοίμηται ἐν Ἱεραπόλει καὶ δύο θυγατέρες αὐτοῦ γεγηρακυῖαι παρθένοι καὶ ἡ ἑτέρα αὐτοῦ θυγατὴρ ἐν ἁγίῳ πνεύματι πολιτευσαμένη ἐν Ἐφέσῳ ἀναπαύεται· ἔτι δὲ καὶ Ἰωάννης...*

[4] *Ib.* iii. 39.

[5] 1 Cor. xv. 8.

[6] Ign. *Eph.* i. 3, cf. Lightfoot's note *ad loc.*

societies[1] as in the province of Asia. Nevertheless, Asian Christianity, as represented by St John in the Apocalypse, does not create a wholly satisfactory impression. The Churches pass before us, and each is separately reviewed, with varying judgements. If good work is being done at Ephesus, it is not the work of the first days (ii. 4 f.). At Pergamum and Thyatira there is much to be commended, but also something to be censured; in each of these Churches there is a 'Nicolaitan' circle, and at Thyatira its ends are promoted by a local prophetess who is tolerated by the Church (ii. 15, 20). At Sardis Christianity is in danger of becoming an empty profession (iii. 1); at Laodicea, the self-satisfaction of commercial prosperity is eating out the heart of Christian humility and love (iii. 15 ff.). Only Smyrna and Philadelphia deserve unmixed praise, and in each case it has been earned under the discipline of suffering (ii. 9 ff., iii. 10). Only at Philadelphia do we seem to hear of progress; before this Church an open door had been set in the great trade-route which connected the town with the highlands of Phrygia, and some attempt had perhaps been made to take advantage of it for missionary work[2].

Yet as a whole the Asian Church as seen in the Apocalypse is still holding its own; the notes of faith, love, service, perseverance are to be found everywhere except at Laodicea, and to Laodicea itself a *locus poenitentiae* is still afforded. The Nicolaitan party has not as yet made great progress; at Ephesus its practices are regarded by the great body of the Church with detestation (ii. 6 *μισεῖς τὰ ἔργα τῶν Νικολαϊτῶν*); at Pergamum it seems to be a small minority (ii. 15 *ἔχεις καὶ σὺ κρατοῦντας κτλ.*); at Thyatira the Nicolaitan prophetess is merely suffered (ii. 20 *ἀφεῖς*). As for Judaism, the purity of the faith was no longer in danger from that cause; the open and bitter antagonism of the Synagogue had opened the eyes of the Christians, and worked for the good of the Church.

[1] Cf. A. Harnack, *Die Mission u. Ausbreitung d. Christentums*, p. 461: "Kleinasien ... ist das christliche Land *κατ' ἐξοχήν* in vorkonstantinischer Zeit gewesen"; ib. p. 484: "Die Provinz Asien ist...die christliche Hauptprovinz in Kleinasien geworden." (E. Tr., pp. 326, 364.)

[2] See Ramsay, *Letters*, p. 404 f.

9. The Nicolaitan minority calls for separate consideration. As represented by the Apocalyptist, the party—for it was still perhaps a party rather than a sect—taught Christians (τοὺς ἐμοὺς δούλους) to commit fornication and to eat food offered in sacrifice to idols (ii. 14, 20); it did the work of Balaam, whose counsels brought on Israel the disaster of Baal-peor; the prophetess who pushed its claims at Thyatira was a second Jezebel, pressing upon the people of God the immoralities of a heathen society. It may be assumed that the Nicolaitans themselves disclaimed any immoral object. Their purpose, it has been pleaded, was "to effect a reasonable compromise with the established usages of Graeco-Roman society"; they taught that Christians ought to remain members of the pagan clubs[1], and that they might do so without disloyalty to their faith. Such a course involved nothing worse than the abandonment of an obsolete decree. The Jerusalem decree had been issued at the first beginning of Gentile Christianity; it had been circulated by St Paul in Pamphylia and Lycaonia (Acts xvi. 4), and doubtless had reached Ephesus. But St Paul himself had permitted at Corinth some modification of the ban against εἰδωλόθυτα, recognizing the liberty of Christians to partake without question of meat which was sold in the markets or set before them at a friend's table, while he insisted that charity to weaker brethren should preclude them from eating an εἰδωλόθυτον which had been declared to be such or from taking part in a banquet held in a pagan temple (1 Cor. viii. 10, x. 25 ff.). It may be presumed that a similar compromise had been reached at Ephesus, and throughout the Pauline Churches. But the minority was dissatisfied. The existing rule excluded members of the Church not only from the public festivals which were the pride of the Ionian cities[2], but from the private clubs which connected their common meals with sacrificial rites, and met in buildings dedicated to a pagan deity. Those who desired to participate in gatherings of the latter kind might have had much to urge in their defence; it was only by such wise concessions that Christianity

[1] Ramsay, *Letters*, pp. 299, 335 ff., 346.

[2] For the Ephesian festivals see Hicks, *Ephesus*, p. 79 f.

could hope to leaven the life of these Greek cities; to stand aloof from all social reunions was to incur suspicion and dislike, and such conduct would end in a general uprising against the Church, perhaps in its suppression throughout Asia. These arguments might have been used by the party with more or less of sincerity, but they did not succeed in deceiving the Seer of the Apocalypse. He saw in the Nicolaitan proposals not the mere abandonment of a primitive Church order, not only the adoption of a weak concordat with the pagan society by which the Church was environed, but an indirect attack upon the sanctities of the Christian life. The Jerusalem conference had in its decree brought into juxtaposition the eating of *εἰδωλόθυτα* and indulgence in sexual impurity[1] (Acts xv. 20, 27), and John had not lived in a Greek city without becoming aware that the two things were in fact closely bound up together. Pagan festivities were too often occasions of immoralities from which Gentile converts had been rescued with the greatest difficulty. If words meant anything to the writer of the Apocalypse, he regarded the question raised by the Nicolaitans as vital, and the danger as imminent. From participation in a pagan guild-feast to licentiousness was but a step; yet the guilds were bound up with the life of the cities, and to repudiate them was a serious matter for Christians who were engaged in the local trades[2]. When even Christian prophecy, in the person of the Thyatiran Jezebel, was advocating Nicolaitan principles, it was time for the prophet of the Apocalypse to speak with no uncertain voice; and his words (ii. 22 f.) are not more severe than the occasion demanded.

10. The Nicolaitan controversy raises the whole question of the relation of Christianity in Asia to Paganism at the moment when St John wrote. In no part of the Empire was paganism more strenuous or resourceful, and in none, so far as we can judge, was the conflict between the old religion and the new so

[1] Πορνεῦσαι, πορνεία (Apoc. ii. 14, 20 f.) cannot be interpreted otherwise without doing violence to the plain meaning of the words, nor can the language used in ii. 6, 23 be justified if the Nicolaitan surrender was merely a well-meant attempt to live at peace with pagan neighbours.

[2] On this point see Ramsay, *Letters*, p. 352. He is speaking of Thyatira, where "Jezebel" was at work.

nearly brought to a head. At Ephesus in 54–5 the cry was already raised of Christ or Artemis, and the city of the Artemision had been lashed to a fine fury by the prospect of their great goddess, the worship of Asia and the Empire, being abandoned at the bidding of a Jew. What Artemis was to Ephesus, such was Asklepios to Pergamum; indeed, each of the cities had its local cult of one or more deities, Hellenic in name, but more or less Asiatic in origin and character. These cults were intimately connected with the interests of the local tradesmen and artizans[1], as well as of the municipalities and of those in authority; anyone who attacked the religion of an Asian city brought upon himself the illwill of the whole population. The Jews from the time of the Seleucids had been free to follow their own faith and even to make proselytes where they could, and it may have been their policy to preserve the *status quo*, by shutting their eyes to much that their consciences disapproved. But the new religion was content with nothing less than an active crusade against idolatry[2]; if St Paul and his friends were not *ἱερόσυλοι*, they were scarcely free, as the *grammateus* of Ephesus maintained, from the charge of speaking ill of the local deity; whatever Alexander the Jew may have had to say in his defence (Acts xix. 38), the Christian Apostle could scarcely have urged this plea. What happened at Ephesus in St Paul's time must have happened, *mutatis mutandis*, in all Asian cities where Christianity gained an entrance. Everywhere in Asia it found itself opposed to a religious system which was deeply rooted in the affections and supported by the interests of the citizens, and which entered into every department of social and commercial life. Sooner or later an open conflict was inevitable. When the Apocalypse was written the conflict had begun all along the line.

[1] Cf. Acts xix. 23, 25, 27.

[2] See Westcott, *Epp. of St John*, p. 264, and cf. Acts xix. 26.

VII.

ANTICHRIST IN THE PROVINCE OF ASIA DURING THE FIRST CENTURY.

1. The conflict which in the days of the Apocalyptist lay before the Christians of Asia was more than an encounter with the prejudices or the interests of their fellow-townsmen, due to an attempt to substitute a new religion for a long-established cult. Two empires[1] were about to meet in mortal combat: the Kingdom of God represented by the Church, the World-power represented by Rome. As the struggle revealed itself to the eyes of the Seer, it was a war of the Christ with the Antichrist.

Within the limits of the New Testament, the word 'Antichrist' occurs only in the Epistles of St John; cf. 1 Jo. ii. 18 καθὼς ἠκούσατε ὅτι Ἀντίχριστος ἔρχεται, καὶ νῦν ἀντίχριστοι πολλοὶ γεγόνασιν; *ib.* 22 οὗτός ἐστιν ὁ ἀντίχριστος, ὁ ἀρνούμενος τὸν πατέρα καὶ τὸν υἱόν; iv. 3 τοῦτο [*sc.* πᾶν πνεῦμα ὃ μὴ ὁμολογεῖ τὸν Ἰησοῦν] ἐστὶν τὸ τοῦ ἀντιχρίστου, ὃ ἀκηκόατε ὅτι ἔρχεται, καὶ νῦν ἐν τῷ κόσμῳ ἐστὶν ἤδη; 2 Jo. 7 οὗτος [*sc.* ὁ μὴ ὁμολογῶν Ἰησοῦν Χριστὸν ἐρχόμενον ἐν σαρκί] ἐστὶν ὁ πλάνος καὶ ὁ ἀντίχριστος. Here the expected coming of Antichrist is represented as finding a fulfilment in the docetic views of the person of Christ which were prevalent in St John's time, and 1 Jo. iv. 3 is accordingly quoted against the docetic schools of the second century by Polycarp (*Phil.* 7) and Irenaeus (iii. 16. 6, 8). Irenaeus, however, uses the name 'Antichrist' in connexion with eschatological speculations based on 2 Thess. ii. (Iren. iii. 7. 1, v. 25. 1) and on the Apocalypse (Iren. v. 26. 1 ff.), and from Irenaeus this use of the word descended to Hippolytus, whose tract Περὶ τοῦ σωτῆρος ἡμῶν Ἰησοῦ Χριστοῦ καὶ περὶ τοῦ ἀντιχρίστου is in our hands.

[1] The expression is borrowed from Bp Westcott's great Essay in *Epp. of St John*, p. 250 ff.

2. It is remarkable that a word so "characteristic of the School of St John[1]" does not appear in the Apocalypse, where it might have served the writer's purpose in more than one passage. That the conception of a personal Antichrist existed among the Christians of Asia in the first century is certain from 1 John ii. 18. Doubtless they had 'heard' it from the prophets, and the prophets had inherited the idea if not the word from the Synagogue. Whether the germ of the idea is to be found with Gunkel in the Babylonian myth of Marduk and Tiâmat, or in Daniel's presentation of Antiochus Epiphanes[2], Jewish apocalypses of the first century shew that the Messianic hope of the time rested on a dark background of forebodings aroused by the expectation of an anti-Messiah[3]. A corresponding development of the doctrine of Antichrist is to be found in Christian circles during the Apostolic age.

The *locus classicus* in the Epistles is 2 Thess. ii. 3 ff. Here the final antagonist of the Christ is described as ὁ ἄνθρωπος τῆς ἀνομίας or ὁ ἄνομος, ὁ ἀντικείμενος καὶ ὑπεραιρόμενος ἐπὶ πάντα λεγόμενον θεὸν ἢ σέβασμα[4]. His παρουσία stands in strong contrast with that of the Christ; it is κατ' ἐνέργειαν τοῦ σατανᾶ, not τοῦ θεοῦ; it is ἐν πάσῃ δυνάμει καὶ σημείοις καὶ τέρασι ψεύδους, not of truth. But his doom is sure; the Christ will prevail; the 'Lawless One' is destined to perish (ὁ υἱὸς τῆς ἀπωλείας) at the Coming of the Lord (ὃν ὁ κύριος Ἰησοῦς ἀνελεῖ τῷ πνεύματι τοῦ στόματος αὐτοῦ[5] καὶ καταργήσει τῇ ἐπιφανείᾳ τῆς παρουσίας αὐτοῦ). The revelation of this person (for such he certainly seems to be) is delayed by some restraining force (τὸ κατέχον, ὁ κατέχων), the nature of which had apparently been explained by the Apostle when he was at Thessalonica (τὸ κατέχον οἴδατε), though for some good reason he is unwilling to commit it to writing. Meanwhile, the principle of ἀνομία is already at work.

Assuming that 2 Thess. is a genuine work of St Paul, it is one of his earlier Epistles, and may be placed in the last years of Claudius (48—49, Harnack; 53, Zahn). Ὁ κατέχων is perhaps the reigning Emperor, and τὸ κατέχον his policy. As for the ἄνομος, the conception is based partly on the O.T., and partly it is suggested by the memory of the late Emperor Gaius, and his mad attempt to set up a statue of himself in the Temple at Jerusalem. When Claudius was gone, a new Emperor might return to Caligula's folly

[1] Westcott, *Epp. of St John*, p. 70.

[2] Cf. Dan. xi. 36.

[3] Cf. *Apoc. Baruch* xxxv. ff. *Asc. of Isaiah* 4, 4 Esdr. 5 ff.

[4] Cf. Dan. *l.c.*

[5] Cf. Isa. xi. 4, a passage which the Targum applies to Armillus.

or surpass it, and prove himself a very Antichrist. But there is nothing in the Apostle's words which compels the belief that Nero was in his thoughts, or even that he consciously connected the Antichrist with a future Emperor. All that he definitely foretells is the advent of a great antichristian power after the removal of the existing bar, and before the second Advent of the Lord.

An earlier Christian apocalypse, based on the teaching of Christ and now embodied in the Synoptic Gospels (Mc. xiii. = Mt. xxiv. = Lc. xxi.), may have been already in circulation when 2 Thess. was written. It speaks of the 'Abomination of Desolation' "standing (ἑστηκότα) where he ought not" (Mc.) or "standing (ἑστός) in a holy place" (Mt.)[1]. St Luke substitutes for this the paraphrase, "When ye see Jerusalem compassed with armies, then know that her desolation is at hand," i.e., writing after the fall of the city, he interprets the prophecy as fulfilled in the investment of Jerusalem by Titus. But whatever may be intended by the βδέλυγμα τῆς ἐρημώσεως, it is difficult to overlook the general resemblance between St Mark's ἑστηκότα ὅπου οὐ δεῖ = ἐν τόπῳ ἁγίῳ (Mt.), and St Paul's ὥστε αὐτὸν εἰς τὸν ναὸν τοῦ θεοῦ καθίσαι. The βδέλυγμα had been almost realized under Caligula, and the Apostle looked forward to its full realization, perhaps in the near future; to St Luke, who outlived St Paul, the day seemed to have come when the city was invested by the Roman general.

3. In the Apocalypse another stage is reached. Assuming that the book in its present form belongs, as Irenaeus states, to the end of Domitian's reign, the follies of Caligula, the atrocities of Nero, and the victory of Titus[2] belong to the past; a quarter of a century separates the fall of Jerusalem from the vision of Patmos. New developments call for new conceptions of the antichristian power, and to St John, guided by his recollections of the Book of Daniel, it assumes the form of a Wild Beast. Two Wild Beasts are mentioned in *c.* xiii., but the second does not retain the name; he reappears in a later chapter as the False Prophet; from *c.* xiii. 11 the first Wild Beast, whose prophet he is, receives the title τὸ θηρίον to the exclusion of his subordinate, and if we may use a word which the writer of the Apocalypse perhaps intentionally lays aside, this first Wild Beast is the Antichrist of St John's vision. To him belongs the mystic number 666; it is

[1] Mt. adds, τὸ ῥηθὲν διὰ Δανιὴλ τοῦ προφήτου. Cf. Dan. ix. 27, xi. 24, xii. 11.

[2] Both βδέλυγμα and ἐρημοῦν occur in the Apocalypse, but in reference not to Jerusalem but to Babylon (xvii. 4 f., xviii. 16, 19).

he who like St Paul's ἄνομος[1] is worshipped by the world, and sets his mark on his worshippers; it is on him that the new Babylon reposes; it is he who is at last seized and cast with his prophet into the lake of fire. In one important particular, however, St John has made an advance upon St Paul. The Apocalyptic Beast vanishes before the final *parousia*; a long interval appears to intervene between his disappearance and the end, during which the forces of evil muster round Satan himself, who is thus the ultimate antagonist of Christ and of the Church.

4. Who or what is the Beast of the Apocalypse? Sometimes he seems to be regarded as personal (e.g. xvii. 8, 11); at other times we appear to be dealing with an impersonal abstraction (xiii. 1 ff., xvii. 3, 7 f.). The same phenomenon has been observed in the Synoptic apocalypse and in St Paul's prophecy of the Man of Sin, and the obvious explanation is that in each case the writer means to represent a principle which finds its illustration and works itself out in individuals. If the line of interpretation adopted in the present commentary be accepted, the Apocalypse refers in terms which are necessarily obscure to Nero and Domitian as successive embodiments of the Beast; the Beast itself is properly the hostile World-power which was identified with the Roman Empire, and personified in the first two persecuting Emperors.

"Two Empires, two social organizations, designed to embrace the whole world, started together in the first century....In principle, in mode of action, in sanctions, in scope, in history they offer an absolute contrast....The history of the Roman Empire is from the first the history of a decline and fall...the history of the Christian Empire is from the first the history of a victorious progress[2]." The antithesis which is set forth in these eloquent words may not have been observed at first; it does not appear in our Lord's attitude towards the Roman rule in Judaea, or in the teaching of St Paul upon the duty of Christians towards civil rulers, or even in St Paul's prophecy, where the Empire and the Emperor are viewed in the light of a protecting rather

[1] Both descriptions rest ultimately on Daniel vii. 8, xi. 36.

[2] Westcott, *Epp. of St John*, p. 253.

than a hostile force. St Peter's Epistle is probably later than the outbreak of the Neronian persecution, but it reinforces St Paul's appeal for loyalty. There was obviously no ground for the charge of disloyalty which the Jews brought against our Lord before Pilate (Jo. xix. 12), and against Paul and Silas before the Thessalonian politarchs (Acts xvii. 5 ff.). It was not on the side of the Church that the quarrel began[1]; in all probability it would never have begun had not Rome provoked it by aggressive measures which the Church could not but resent.

5. Nero opened hostilities in 64, initiating a policy of persecution which was not formally abandoned during the rest of the century. The circumstances are thus described by Tacitus[2] and Suetonius:

> Tac. *Ann.* xv. 44 non ope humana, non largitionibus principis aut deum placamentis decedebat infamia, quin iussum incendium crederetur. ergo abolendo rumori Nero subdidit reos, et quaesitissimis poenis affecit quos per flagitia invisos vulgus Christianos appellabat. ...igitur primum correpti qui fatebantur[3], deinde indicio eorum multitudo ingens, haud perinde in crimine incendii quam odio humani generis coniuncti (*corr.* convicti) sunt. et pereuntibus addita ludibria, ut ferarum tergis contecti laniatu canum interirent, aut crucibus affixi, aut flammandi, atque ubi defecisset dies in usum nocturni luminis urerentur. hortos suos ei spectaculo Nero obtulerat et circense ludicrum edebat, habitu aurigae permixtus plebi vel curriculo insistens. unde quamquam adversus sontes et novissima exempla meritos miseratio oriebatur, tamquam non utilitate publica sed in saevitiam unius absumerentur." Suet. *Nero* 16 "multa sub eo et animadversa severe et coercita...afflicti suppliciis Christiani, genus hominum superstitionis novae ac maleficae."

It is evident that Tacitus, who certainly holds no brief for the Christian faith, represents Nero as the real author of the outrage. It took the form of a police measure, as Suetonius says, but in the first instance it was simply a device for screening his own infamy. Christians already had a bad name with the Roman populace, but no attack would have been made upon their lives had not Nero sacrificed them to save himself. When he proceeded to offer the use of the Vatican Gardens for the executions

[1] How little disposed the Church was to make difficulties on her part may be gathered (e.g.) from St Luke's readiness to use the title Σεβαστός (Acts xxv. 21, 25).

[2] On the trustworthiness of Tacitus see Lightfoot, *Ignatius*, i. pp. 9 f., 725.

[3] Either their Christian Faith or their guilt as incendiaries.

NERO.

From a bust in the British Museum.

and to mix with the spectators, even the Roman mob recognized the brutality (*saevitiam*) of his conduct.

6. Even if Nero had desired to abandon the policy of persecution, it would have been difficult for him to do so. The words of Suetonius suggest that notwithstanding the reaction brought about by the Emperor's callousness, repressive measures continued in force. Severus Sulpicius, who wrote in the fourth century, may be confusing later times with those of Nero when he writes (*chron.* ii. 29) in reference to the latter: "post etiam datis legibus religio vetabatur, palamque edictis propositis Christianum esse non licebat[1]," but he is certainly right in adding with regard to the atrocities of 64, "hoc initio in Christianos saeviri coeptum"; and, as Lightfoot points out, when once persecution had begun the Roman Jews, with Poppaea Sabina at their back, would scarcely have been content to let it cease altogether. The martyrdoms of St Peter and St Paul are connected with Nero by Tertullian (*scorp.* 15) and Origen (*ap.* Eus. *H. E.* iii. 1), and those Apostles were but the leaders of a great army of martyrs[2]. The horrors of that first onslaught on the Roman Christians must have made a lasting impression on the Churches throughout the Empire; and the man who had exhausted every form of cruelty in his sudden attack upon an innocent community and had revelled in the agonies of his victims may well have become among Christians everywhere the symbol of brute force triumphing over righteousness and truth, of the World-power standing in direct antithesis to the Kingdom of God—in a word, of Antichrist, or to use St John's image, of the Beast.

7. So strong was the impression made by the personality of Nero upon the Roman world that after his violent death in 68 there were many who believed or professed to believe that he was still alive. While some of his friends year after year strewed his tomb with the flowers of spring and summer, others issued edicts in his name and professed that he would shortly return to the con-

[1] So Ramsay, *Church in the Roman Empire*, p. 244; but see Lightfoot, *Ignatius*, i. p. 10 f.; Sanday, in *Exp.* IV. vii., p. 408.

[2] Cf. Clem. 1 Cor. 6 πολὺ πλῆθος ἐκλεκτῶν οἵτινες πολλαῖς αἰκίαις καὶ βασάνοις διὰ ζῆλος παθόντες ὑπόδειγμα κάλλιστον ἐγένοντο ὑμῖν.

fusion of his enemies[1]. More than one pretender claimed to be a Nero returned from his wanderings, or even restored to life[2]. There were those who whispered that the great Emperor was hiding in Parthia, and would some day cross the borders at the head of a Parthian host. The Christian prophet would not, of course, give credit to these stories, but they served to supply some of the features of his symbolism. The Beast is represented as simulating the Resurrection and Return of the Christ; his deadly wound has been healed (xiii. 3); he is coming again[3]. Nero is doubly an Antichrist; the historical Nero persecuted the Church, the Nero of popular myth caricatured[4] the faith. The legend, indeed, was not without a counterpart of historical fact. When the Apocalypse was written, Nero had in truth returned in the person of Domitian (xvii. 11).

8. The brief reigns of Galba, Otho, and Vitellius are of no interest to the student of the struggle between the Empire and the Church and may be left out of his reckoning, as St John leaves them out in Apoc. xvii. 10, where Vespasian follows immediately after Nero. With Vespasian the Flavian house[5] enters on a spell of power which lasted for more than a quarter of a century. Its policy, in the belief of Professor Ramsay, was strongly anti-christian. Attention is called to a passage in Severus Sulpicius, probably derived from the lost *Histories* of Tacitus[6], in which the chronicler describing a council of war held after the fall of Jerusalem says (ii. 30): "alii et Titus ipse evertendum in primis templum censebant quo plenius Judaeorum et Christianorum religio tollatur...Christianos ex Judaeis extitisse; radice sublata stirpem facile perituram." This, if trustworthy, assigns a reason for a Flavian policy adverse to the Church, and the hint dropt by Hilary (*c. Arian.* 3) that Vespasian was among the Imperial per-

[1] Suet. *Nero* 57, cf. Lightfoot, *Clement*, ii. p. 511.

[2] Cf. Renan, *L'Antéchrist*, pp. 317 ff., 351 ff.

[3] Apoc. xvii. 8 *πάρεσται*. Cf. 2 Thess. ii. 9 *οὗ ἐστὶν ἡ παρουσία κατ' ἐνέργειαν τοῦ σατανᾶ*.

[4] The *ἀντίχριστος* is not a mere *ἀντίδικος* or *ἀντικείμενος*, but an adversary who consciously or not simulates the character of the Christ. Compare *ἀντίκαισαρ* (representative of the Emperor), a word which passed into Aramaic (Dalman, *Wörterbuch*, s.v.).

[5] Vespasian 69—79, Titus 79—81, Domitian 81—96.

[6] Ramsay, *Church in the R. Empire*, pp. 253, 256. Cf. Lightfoot, *Ignatius*, i. p. 15.

secutors makes in the same direction[1]. But neither statement carries us far. It is only when we reach the third and last of the Flavian Emperors that there is indubitable evidence of a revival on a large scale of Nero's attitude towards the Christians.

Lightfoot has collected a catena of passages which justify the belief that Domitian was the second great persecutor[2]. One reference to his persecuting policy is contemporary: Clement of Rome speaks of *τὰς αἰφνιδίους καὶ ἐπαλλήλους γενομένας ἡμῖν συμφορὰς καὶ περιπτώσεις*—words which, as Lightfoot shews, accurately describe the capricious and reiterated attacks which distinguished this Emperor's policy in reference to the Church[3]. It is perhaps due to the feline stealthiness and rapidity with which Domitian dealt his blows that so few details remain. The names of two of his victims at Rome are preserved, and the facts are significant. T. Flavius Clemens, a cousin of the Emperor, had but just quitted the consulship, in which he had been Domitian's colleague, when he was arrested and put to death; while his wife Domitilla, Domitian's niece, was banished to one of the islands off the coast of Campania—Pontia or Pandataria—where political prisoners were detained. Suetonius[4] contents himself with saying that Flavius Clemens, whom he designates *contemptissimae inertiae*, was put to death *repente, ex tenuissima suspicione*, but from Dio Cassius[5] we learn that the charge brought against both husband and wife was one of 'atheism' (*ἀθεότητος*); he adds: *ὑφ' ἧς καὶ ἄλλοι ἐς τὰ τῶν Ἰουδαίων ἔθη ἐξοκέλλοντες πολλοὶ κατεδικάσθησαν, καὶ οἱ μὲν ἀπέθανον*. Putting the data together, it is natural to infer that Fl. Clemens and his wife suffered for their Christian faith, and that they were by no means the only victims of Domitian's hostility to 'Jewish' ways[6]. But this attack on the members of the Roman

[1] As to objections to this statement of Hilary founded on the silence of Melito (Eus. *H.E.* iv. 26) and a counter-statement of Tertullian (*Apol.* 5) see Lightfoot, *op. cit.* p. 16.

[2] *St Clement*, i. p. 104.

[3] *Op. cit.* i. p. 7 f.

[4] *Domitianus*, 15.

[5] *Hist. Rom.* lxvii. 14. 1 sq. The whole passage may be seen in Preuschen, *Analecta* p. 13 f.

[6] All Jews must have been severely tried by Vespasian's order that the half shekel payable to the support of the Temple at Jerusalem should be still collected and applied to the use of the Capitoline Jupiter. This order in the hands of Domitian became a pretext for harsh measures being directed against recusant Jews. (Suet. *Dom.* 2; see Lightfoot *Ignatius* i. p. 12.) But it could not affect the Emperor's relatives or other

Church, which seems to have been limited to a few leaders of Roman society, does not fully explain the position which Domitian holds in Christian tradition among Imperial persecutors of the faith. It is not only from Rome that the evidence comes, but from Sardis, whose bishop Melito writes to the Emperor Antoninus (Eus. *H. E.* iv. 26): *μόνοι πάντων ἀναπεισθέντες ὑπό τινων βασκάνων ἀνθρώπων τὸν καθ' ἡμᾶς ἐν διαβολῇ καταστῆσαι λόγον ἠθέλησαν Νέρων καὶ Δομετιανός*). Nero's persecution of the Roman Church was notorious, but was Melito likely to have coupled Domitian with him as a persecutor if the latter Emperor's actions had been limited to a few arrests and executions at Rome near the end of his reign? Is it not probable that the Asian Churches felt his hand, perhaps some years earlier? And do not the words suggest a cause for Domitian's antichristian policy in Asia which is entirely in accord with the conditions described in the Apocalypse?

9. It is known that Domitian went beyond his predecessor in asserting his own divinity: "cum procuratorum suorum nomine formalem dictaret epistulam sic coepit: *Dominus et Deus noster hoc fieri iubet*[1]." The history of this extraordinary claim is instructive, and must be given here as briefly as may be; for fuller details reference may be made to G. Boissier, *La religion romaine* (Paris, 1900), i. pp. 109—186; G. Wissowa, *Religion u. Kultus der Römer* (Munich, 1902), pp. 71—78, 280—289; V. Chapot, *op. cit.*, p. 419 ff.

As early as the second century before Christ a complimentary cult of the genius of Rome or the *dea Roma* had begun in the provinces; there was a *templum urbis Romae* at Smyrna in B.C. 195; a *βωμὸς τῆς Ῥώμης* occurs in 105; a priest of Rome is mentioned by name in a compact between Sardis and Ephesus about B.C. 98[2]. A new development of this cult sprang up with the rise of the Empire, when the majesty of Rome took a concrete form in the person of the *princeps*. After the apotheosis of Julius Caesar (29 B.C.) a temple of *Dea Roma* and *Divus Julius* was erected

non-Jewish Christians; against these the charge was one of 'atheism' simply, i.e. of rejecting the religion of Rome.

[1] Suet. *Domitian.* 13.

[2] Tac. *ann.* iv. 56. See Wissowa, *Religion u. Kultus der Römer*, p. 281 ff.

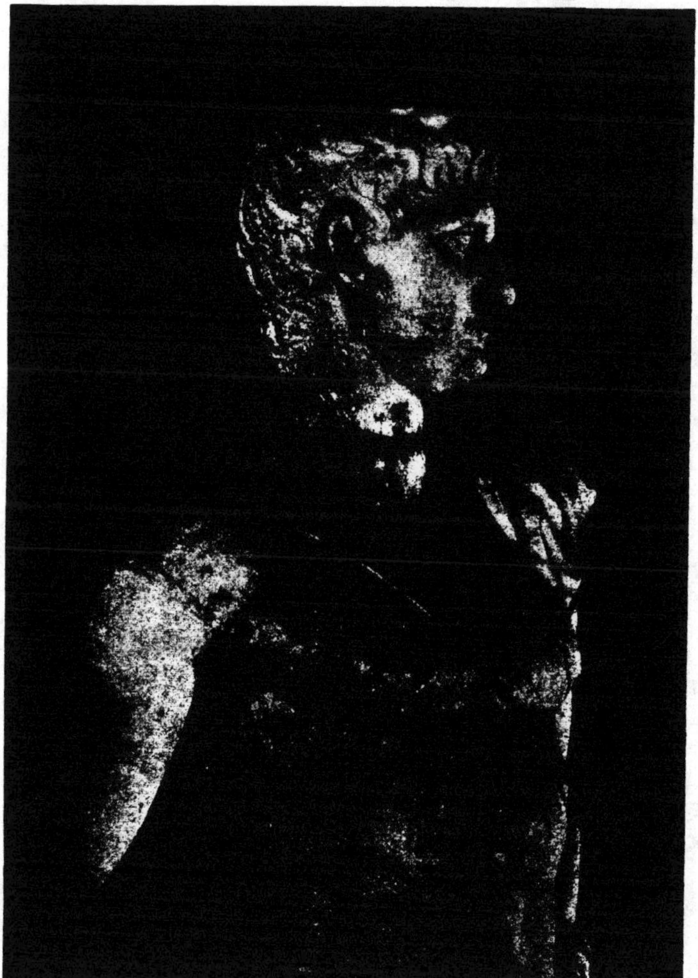

DOMITIAN.
From the Statue in Munich
(after Dr J. J. Bernoulli).

at Ephesus[1]. Augustus had no need to wait for an apotheosis; during his lifetime temples were erected under the dedication θεᾶς Ῥώμης καὶ Σεβαστοῦ Καίσαρος[2]. When the Pergamenes wished to build one in honour of Tiberius, the example of Augustus was quoted (Tac. *ann.* iv. 37 "cum divus Augustus sibi atque urbi Romae templum apud Pergamum sisti non prohibuisset"). Both Augustus and Tiberius kept the new cult within limits; at Rome no temple was dedicated to either Emperor within his lifetime: Tiberius allowed only one Augusteum to be erected in his honour within the province of Asia, and refused to permit Spain to follow the example of the Asian cities. Gaius, who succeeded him, was a man of another and a weaker type; epileptic, often on the verge of insanity, incapable of self-control, he had in early life imbibed from Herod Agrippa[3] a vicious taste for Oriental magnificence. The precedent sparingly allowed by his predecessors offered this prince a welcome opportunity of self-aggrandisement; as a god he could surround himself with more than royal display[4]. Gaius carried his pretensions to a point at which they became at once ridiculous and dangerous; he removed the heads of famous statues and substituted his own: he attempted to erect a statue of himself in the Holy of holies at Jerusalem. The Alexandrian Jews were forced to admit the Emperor's image into their synagogues, and if the Church did not suffer, it was probably because she had as yet no buildings set apart for worship, and was not sufficiently powerful to attract attention. The "furious Caligula," as Gibbon rightly designates him, might have gone to even greater lengths, had not his reign been cut short by assassination (41). Claudius, if no better than Gaius, was saner, and during his reign there was no fresh attempt to force the Emperor-worship on the Jews, unless indeed something of this kind, in which the Roman Christians were also involved, is suggested by the well-known words of Suetonius[5]: "Iudaeos impulsore Chresto assidue tumultu-

[1] Dio Cassius, li. 20.

[2] Dittenberger, *Or. Gr. inscr. select.* ii. p. 11.

[3] Wissowa, p. 284; Westcott, *Epp. of St John*, p. 274.

[4] Suet. *C. Caligula* 22, "admonitus et principum et regum se excessisse fastigium, divinam ex eo maiestatem asserere sibi coepit."

[5] *Divus Claudius*, 25.

antes Roma expulit." It is not clear why the Roman Jews or Jewish Christians should have given trouble on any other ground. Yet if the Imperial cult went on under Claudius, there is no evidence that it was encouraged by him. We read of a temple erected in honour of Claudius at Camelodunum in Britain, which was regarded as indicating that the Romans had come to stay and to rule[1]. After death Claudius received his apotheosis[2] amidst shouts of ridicule which are voiced in the *Apotheosis* of Seneca. Nero, on the other hand, might easily have made good a claim of this kind. No Emperor on the whole made so deep an impression, a circumstance due to the dramatic power and consciousness of something approaching to genius which remained with him to the last; *qualis artifex pereo!* Quite early in his life in an Egyptian inscription he is called *ὁ ἀγαθὸς δαίμων τῆς οἰκουμένης*. But he was not tempted like his predecessors to imagine himself divine, preferring to gain credit for brilliant endowments of a human type. He shrank from the title of *Divus* and the erection of temples in his honour, because they seemed to forebode the approach of death, and Nero loved life better than a shadowy immortality[3]. No such feelings held back Domitian from pressing his claims to Divine honours. He found a gloomy and perhaps a cynical pleasure in the shouts which greeted his arrival at the amphitheatre with Domitia; *domino et dominae feliciter*[4]. Unable to rouse enthusiasm or admiration, he could insist on being regarded as a god[5].

10. The province of Asia accepted with acclamation the new cult of Rome and the Emperor. For more than 200 years Rome had been mistress in Asia, and on the whole she had contributed to the prosperity of her great province; but the provincials had suffered from the extortions of greedy officials, and from the days

[1] Tac. *ann.* xiv. 31, "quasi arx aeternae dominationis aspiciebatur."

[2] Suet. *D. Claudius*, 45 "in numerum deorum relatus." Cf. Dittenberger, *Or. Gr. inscr.* ii. p. 397, ὁ θεὸς Κλαύδιος.

[3] Tac. *ann.* xv. 74, "nam deum honor principi non ante habetur quam agere inter homines desierit."

[4] Suet. *Domitian.* 13.

[5] Cf. the form of oath quoted by Wissowa, p. 71: "per Iovem et divom Augustum...et genium imperatoris Caesaris Domitiani Augusti deosque penates."

of Augustus the *principatus* had been hailed by the Asian towns as their salvation[1]. Inscription after inscription testifies to the loyalty of the cities towards the Empire. At Ephesus, at Smyrna, at Pergamum, and indeed throughout the province the Church was confronted by an imperialism which was popular and patriotic, and bore the character of a religion. Nowhere was the Caesar-cult more popular than in Asia[2]. The Augusteum (Σεβαστεῖον), or Temple of Rome[3] and the Augusti, had long taken its place among the public buildings of the greater cities. Augustus, as we have seen, refused Divine honours at Rome, but permitted a temple to be dedicated to *dea Roma* and himself at Pergamum. The other Asian cities followed the precedent set by the old capital. In A.D. 26 they vied with each other for the honour of building a temple to Tiberius, when Smyrna gained the coveted distinction over the head of Ephesus, on the ground that the latter already possessed the Artemision[4]. Ephesus, not to be outdone by her neighbour, erected an Augusteum, probably to Claudius, and thus acquired the title of νεωκόρος[5] of the Imperial worship. These local temples were not of merely local interest; their affairs were managed by the provincial league known as the *Commune Asiae* (τὸ κοινὸν τῆς Ἀσίας), whose president was styled Asiarch, and perhaps also ἀρχιερεὺς τοῦ κοινοῦ τῆς Ἀσίας[6]. It belonged to the Asiarch to direct the worship of the Augusti throughout the province, and to preside at games which were held quinquennially in the cities where Augustea had been erected[7]. Such festivals are known to have been celebrated from time to time at five of the

[1] Ramsay, *Letters*, p. 114 f.; Chapot, *La province Romaine proconsulaire d'Asie*, p. 62 ff. Cf. an inscription of Halicarnassus cited by Zimmerman, *Ephesos*, p. 52 f., which describes Octavian as εὐεργέτην τῶν ἀνθρώπων γένους, ὅς μεγίστας ἐλπίδας οὐκ ἐπλήρωσε μόνον ἀλλὰ καὶ ὑπερέβαλλεν, ἀσφαλὴς μὲν γὰρ γῆ καὶ θάλασσα, πόλεις δὲ ἀνθοῦσιν ἐν εἰρήνῃ καὶ ὁμονοίᾳ καὶ εὐετηρίᾳ.

[2] Mommsen, *Provinces* (E. Tr.), p. 345.

[3] In Asia the cult of Rome was older than the province itself; a temple was raised to Rome at Smyrna in B.C. 193 (Tac. *Ann.* iv. 56).

[4] Tac. *ann.* iv. 55.

[5] M. Chapot (p. 450) gives a useful list of the towns of Asia which possessed the neocorate, with the reigns or dates when it was received.

[6] On these titles see Lightfoot, *Ignatius*, iii. p. 404 ff.; Chapot, pp. 454—482; Pauly-Wissowa, s.vv.

[7] Each of the cities had its local high priest of the Augustan cult, who seems also to have had the style of 'Asiarch,' though he was supreme only in the local Augusteum. See Lightfoot, p. 415; Hicks, p. 87.

seven cities addressed in the Apocalypse, namely, at Ephesus, Smyrna, Pergamum, Sardis, and Philadelphia[1].

A system such as this, it is obvious, supplied machinery which could at any time be used against the Church with fatal facility. To refuse worship to Artemis or Asklepios was to decline a local cult; to refuse it to the statue of the Emperor at a time when the whole city was taking part in festivities organized by the *Commune*, was to expose oneself to the charge of disloyalty both to the provincial authorities and to the Emperor. Our only wonder is that this charge had not been laid against the Christians of Asia in the time of Claudius or of Nero[2]; perhaps there is a trace of such an anti-Christian movement in the reference to the days when Antipas suffered at Pergamum[3], the earliest centre of the Caesar-worship, but of any general persecution under Nero there is no evidence[4]. Yet it is easy to understand that when Domitian's desire for Divine honours became known in Asia, the zealous provincials would resent more keenly than before the abstention of Christian citizens from the games instituted in honour of the Augusti, and the situation would become threatening. It is just this position of affairs which the Apocalypse represents; the Beast of whom Christians spoke with bated breath as 'number 666' had returned; already the markets were closed against buyers and sellers who did not bear his mark (xiii. 17), and there were rumours in the air of an approaching massacre (*ib.* 15). For this the Apocalypse is, it is true, our only authority, and its witness is given in an enigmatic form which cannot always be interpreted with certainty; but the main features of its story are plain enough,

[1] Even the calendar shewed traces of the new cult. "César a son mois, son jour comme Aphrodite; l'époque de sa venue au monde inaugura l'année. Ce sont des commencements qui préparent le vrai culte" (Chapot, p. 394).

[2] This seems to follow not only from the silence of St Luke, but from St Paul's friendship with Asiarchs.

[3] It is significant that while Antipas was martyred at Pergamum, it was at Smyrna, the second centre of the Augustan cult, that trouble was imminent when St John wrote (ii. 10).

[4] Dr Hort indeed writes (*First Ep. of St Peter*, p. 2): "It is only likely that what was begun at Rome in connexion with the fire spread through the provinces till it culminated in the state of things implied in the Apocalypse." "The Apocalypse...proves the existence of persecutions in Asia Minor, and implies that they were on a wide scale." But there is nothing to shew that the martyrs mentioned in the Apocalypse, Antipas excepted, were Asiatics; the sufferings of the Roman Christians may have been in the writer's mind.

and they accord with what is known of life in Asia during the first century, and of Domitian's general policy.

11. With the Beast from the sea, the hostile World-power represented by Nero and Domitian, St John associates a Beast from the land, a power no less hostile to the Church, which has its origin and home in Asia itself. This second Beast allies itself with the first, especially in the matter of the worship of the Augusti; indeed the first Beast is represented as leaving the affairs of the Emperor-cult entirely in the hands of the second. The Beast from the land works miracles[1] in support of the new cult, calling down fire from heaven, and causing the statues of the Emperor to speak (xiii. 13, 15); he is the 'false prophet' of the Imperial religion, and imposes on the credulity of the populace, whom he sets against the Christian recusants (*ib.* 12, 14 ff., 17, xix. 20). By the second Beast Professor Ramsay[2] understands "the Province of Asia in its double aspect of civil and religious administration, the Proconsul and the Commune"; in this commentary the Beast from the land is identified with the False Prophet, and regarded as the religious power represented by the Asiarch and the priesthood of the Asian temples of the Augusti; while in the *σημεῖα* which he works we recognize the use of the magical arts for which Asia and Ephesus in particular were notorious. The magic formulae known as Ἐφέσια γράμματα[3] had a worldwide reputation, and one of the earliest conquests which the Gospel achieved at Ephesus was the destruction of costly books which contained them[4]. It is noteworthy that *φαρμακία* is named immediately after *εἰδωλολατρεία* in the Epistle to the Galatians (v. 20)[5], while the Apocalypse (xxi. 8, cf. xxii. 15) places *φαρμακοί*, the professors of magic, between *πόρνοι* and *εἰδωλολάτραι*.

Christianity, it is evident, set its face against magic from the first; paganism, on the other hand, had no serious quarrel with it; the cultivated Roman gentlemen who administered the provinces of

[1] Cf. 2 Thess. ii. 9 f.

[2] *Letters*, p. 97.

[3] Cf. Clem. Al. *strom.* v. 8. § 46 τὰ Ἐφέσια καλούμενα γράμματα ἐν πολλοῖς δὴ πολυθρύλητα ὄντα. Plutarch *symp.* vii. 5. 4 οἱ μάγοι τοὺς δαιμονιζομένους κελεύουσι τὰ Ἐφέσια γράμματα πρὸς αὐτοὺς καταλέγειν καὶ ὀνομάζειν. See Schürer, *Gesch.*[3] iii. p. 296 f.

[4] Acts xix. 19 f.

[5] See Lightfoot's note, and cf. Ign. *Eph.* 19, *Philad.* 5.

the Empire did not always scorn the attentions of the professional *magus*[1]; even Emperors were credited with dabbling in their secrets[2]. In Lucian's sarcastic sketch Ἀλέξανδρος ἢ Ψευδόμαντις, we see one of these conjurors on tour, and though St John's ψευδοπροφήτης is probably not an individual, but a class or system, it may be assumed that such travelling mountebanks were used to negotiate the wonders described in Apoc. xiii.[3] At Ephesus there were fourteen θεσμῳδοί[4] attached to the temple of the Augusti, who are supposed by Canon Hicks to correspond with the ὑμνῳδοί or choirmen of the Artemision; their official name admits of this explanation, but it may also mean 'oracle-chanters,'—a name under which dealers in magic might well have been concealed. But however this may have been, it is obvious that the Church was hard pressed in Asia by the magic-mongers, and it is easy to imagine the effect of their lying wonders on an excitable population already predisposed to the Imperial cult and impatient of Christianity. Nothing was needed to light the fires of persecution but a word from the Emperor or the Proconsul, and when they were kindled, it would be long, as the Prophet of the Apocalypse foresaw, before the peace of the Church was restored in Asia or in the Roman world.

12. One more force which made against the Kingdom of Christ in Asia must be mentioned here. The Jews of Asia Minor had been numerous from the days when Antiochus III sent 2000 families of the eastern Dispersion to settle in Lydia and Phrygia[5]. In Cicero's time tribute went to the Temple at Jerusalem from Jews in Adramyttium, Pergamum, Laodicea, and Apamea, and there is evidence from other quarters that in the first century there were Jews resident also at Smyrna, Magnesia, Tralles, Sardis, and Thyatira[6]. In the year of the Crucifixion worshippers came to Jerusalem at the feast of Pentecost from

[1] Acts xiii. 6 ff.

[2] *Orac. Sibyll.* viii. 52 ff. ἔσσετ' ἄναξ πολιόκρανος ἔχων πέλας οὔνομα πόντου (Hadrian)...καὶ μαγικῶν ἀδύτων μυστήρια πάντα μεθέξει.

[3] Apollonius of Tyana, to whom Prof. Ramsay refers (*Letters*, p. 102), was a strong opponent of the prevalent jugglery; see Dill, *Roman Society*, p. 400.

[4] *Inscr.* 481. 7 (A.D. 104): θεσμῳδοῖς ναοῦ τῶν Σεβαστῶν ἐν Ἐφέσῳ κοινοῦ τῆς Ἀσίας.

[5] Joseph. *Ant.* xii. 3 f.; cf. Philo *in Flacc.* 7. See p. lxii, note 1.

[6] Schürer, *Geschichte*[3], iii. p. 11 f.; art. *Diaspora* in Hastings, *D. B.* v. 93 ff. Chapot, p. 182 ff.

Cappadocia, Pontus, Asia, Phrygia, and Pamphylia[1]. At Salamis in Cyprus, at Antioch in Pisidia, at Iconium, at Ephesus, St Paul found synagogues, and in these synagogues he began his work. But the Asiatic Jews did not assimilate the new teaching; its popularity with Gentiles and proselytes aroused their suspicion and, as the writer of the Acts suggests, their jealousy[2]. In the Apocalypse the breach between the Synagogue and the Church is seen to be complete; the churches of Smyrna and Philadelphia have to bear the blasphemies of those who "affirm themselves to be Jews and are not," a synagogue which is not God's but "Satan's[3]." The Jews were protected by special privilege from molestation in the exercise of their faith[4]. Under Caligula indeed they had suffered severely for their opposition to the Caesar-cult[5], but the persecution ended with the death of the Emperor; under Domitian no attempt was made to enforce a worship which neither compulsion nor persuasion would have brought them to accept. Nevertheless, they had no scruple in turning the attention of the populace and the authorities to the resistance which the less favoured Christians offered to the Imperial religion. At the martyrdom of Polycarp it was noticed that the Jews of Smyrna not only made common cause with the heathen but outdid them in efforts to prepare fuel for the stake, and the *Martyrdom* notes that this was their wont[6]. Yet Polycarp was condemned for refusing to swear by the genius (τύχη) of Caesar[7], an act which the Jews should have been able to appreciate. This was in the year 165, but the attitude of the Asian Jew towards Christianity had been determined at least seventy years before. The Synagogue of Satan played the rôle of the great Adversary; it not only rejected Christ, but did its best by slander and delation and, when the opportunity was afforded, by cooperation with the pagan mob, to bring about the destruction of the Asian Church.

[1] Acts ii. 9.

[2] Acts xiii. 45 ἐπλήσθησαν ζήλου. Cf. 1 Thess. ii. 16.

[3] Apoc. ii. 9, iii. 9.

[4] On the privileges possessed by the Jews in Asia see Chapot, p. 182 f.

[5] Schürer, i. II. p. 91, ii. II. p. 266 ff., ii. III. p. 349 ff.

[6] *Polyc. mart.* 13 μάλιστα Ἰουδαίων προθύμως, ὡς ἔθος αὐτοῖς, εἰς ταῦτα ὑπουργούντων. Cf. § 12 ἅπαν τὸ πλῆθος ἐθνῶν τε καὶ Ἰουδαίων.

[7] Ib. 9 f.; cf. Lightfoot's note, and Westcott, *Epp. of St John*, p. 279.

VIII.

PURPOSE OF THE APOCALYPSE.

1. The Apocalypse of John is the letter of an exiled prophet to the Christian congregations to which he has ministered. He writes under the conviction that he has a message for them from the Supreme Prophet and Pastor of the Church, and his primary purpose is to deliver this message. It has come to him in the way of revelation, and under the form of a succession of visions, and he delivers it as it was given; his letter consists entirely of *visions and revelations of the Lord*, which he has been not only permitted but commanded to transmit[1]. But, as the style proclaims aloud, it is not, like some of the later apocalypses, a literary effort, appealing to readers generally without regard to special circumstances. It is a genuine outcome of the time, written with a view to the special needs of a particular group of Christian societies; it portrays the life of those societies, and ministers to their spiritual necessities. In form it is an epistle, containing an apocalyptic prophecy; in spirit and inner purpose, it is a pastoral.

2. Each of the Churches of Asia had difficulties peculiar to itself, and these problems are treated first. The first three chapters, which have seemed to some critics to have no real coherence with the rest of the book, are in fact occupied with this preliminary task. The glorified Head of Christendom is revealed as visiting the Churches, and taking note of their several conditions; and the so-called 'letters to the Churches' record the results of His inspection. Nothing in the book is more remarkable than the precision with which these separate messages differentiate be-

[1] On the one exception (x. 4) see the note *ad loc.*

tween Church and Church, as the searchlight of the Spirit[1] is turned upon each in succession. Only two of the Churches escape reproof: the strenuous commercial life and the material prosperity of the Asian cities have had their natural effect upon the Christian minorities, which were in the sight of the Bishop of souls suffering from this cause even more severely than from the slanders of the Jews or the menaces of the heathen. At Ephesus the standard of Christian life, though still high, had been sensibly lowered; at Laodicea the Church was lukewarm and supercilious, at Sardis it was spiritually dead. And not only is the spiritual condition of each society diagnosed, but the circumstances are carefully distinguished. At Smyrna and Philadelphia the Jews are specially hostile; at Pergamum and Thyatira trouble has been caused by the Nicolaitans. At every turn the messages to the Churches shew local knowledge; some of the allusions which have not yet received a satisfactory explanation will doubtless yield their secret to a fuller knowledge of the history and antiquities of Asia. The business of the prophet is with the particular Church to which for the moment attention is called, and which would recognize at once the force of his words. It is enough for the general reader if he grasps the spiritual lesson which is to be found in these messages by everyone who has an ear to hear it.

3. After *c.* iii. the separate interests of the Churches pass out of sight. The visions which follow open wider fields of view that embrace the whole Church and the whole of human history, reaching to the consummation and the Coming of the Lord. But the Asian Churches are not forgotten, even if they are not mentioned again till near the end (xxii. 16, 21). Their spiritual dangers are probably in view throughout the book, but especially in passages where the vices of heathenism are condemned and the faithful are warned against participation in them[2], or reminded of their obligation to keep themselves pure[3]. And the whole

[1] Apoc. ii. 7, 11, 17, 29, iii. 6, 13, 22.

[2] As e.g. in ix. 20 f., xviii. 9 f., xx. 8, xxii. 11, 15.

[3] As in vii. 14, xiv. 4 f., xvi. 15, xxii. 14.

series of visions which begins with *c.* iv. is in effect an answer to the forebodings by which the faithful in Asia were harassed in view of the gathering forces of Antichrist. The Churches of Asia knew themselves to be on the brink of an encounter with the greatest power the world had seen. The subject of *cc.* iv.—xxii. is the course and issue of the struggle, and the purpose of these chapters is to strengthen faith and kindle hope in the hearts of the faithful. In the light of the revelation vouchsafed to him the prophet John sees clearly that an age of persecution is beginning, and that it will affect not only the Churches of Asia, but the Church throughout the Roman world. How long it will last he does not say; in the earlier visions it seems to run on to the consummation, but in the later great reaches of time are seen to intervene between the end of the pagan power and the end of the existing order. The light grows as the Seer looks, and the issue becomes more and more distinct; Babylon falls, the Beast and the False Prophet receive their doom, Satan himself is finally consigned to destruction, and the City of God descends from heaven, idealized and glorious, as becomes the Bride of the glorified Christ. The final outcome of the struggle between the Church and the World, the Christ and the Antichrist, is postponed to the last two chapters, but there are anticipations of it all along the course of the book: in the promises with which each of the seven messages to the Churches ends; in the vision of the innumerable multitude before the Throne of God; in the vision of the 144,000 virgin-souls upon Mount Zion. The whole book is a *Sursum corda,* inviting the Churches to seek strength in the faith of a triumphant and returning Christ. In vain the Ancient Enemy stirs up trouble; in vain the Beast from the sea sets up his image, and the Beast from the land compels men under pain of outlawry or death to worship it. The *seal of the living God* secures those who refuse *the mark of the Beast*; the martyrs are conquerors, and shall *not be hurt of the Second Death*; their *names are in the Book of Life. Blessed are the dead which die in the Lord from henceforth,*... they *rest from their labours, for their works follow with them*; after the fall of their great enemy they *lived and reigned with Christ a thousand years*; they shall *enter through the gates into the City*; *the Lord God shall give them light*; *they shall reign for ever and ever*.

4. Of the immediate effect of the Apocalypse upon the Asian Churches we cannot judge; certainly they weathered the storm, for in the next Christian writing which comes to us from Asia, the Letters of Ignatius, they are represented as large and flourishing communities. The storm itself passed within two or three years after the date which Irenaeus assigns to the Apocalypse; Domitian was assassinated Sept. 18, 96, and the accession of Nerva probably gave peace to the Asian Churches. Trajan, who succeeded in the January of 98, seems to have taken no active measures before A.D. 112, when his attention was directed by the younger Pliny to the extraordinary progress of Christianity in Bithynia. Perhaps it may be safely inferred that in the interval between 96 and 112 the danger threatened by the Caesar-worship ceased to be pressing, and for the moment the need of comfort such as the Apocalypse offered was less keenly felt. But what St John had written in the Spirit for the times of Domitian and the Churches of Asia remained as a heritage for all suffering Churches throughout the Empire. An early example of the helpfulness of the book to Christians under persecution has survived in the Epistle of the Churches of Vienne and Lyons, written in 177 to their brethren in Asia and Phrygia, which bears many signs of the use of the Apocalypse by the Christian societies of South Gaul during the troubles in the reign of Marcus Aurelius. It quotes or alludes to Apoc. i. 5, iii. 14, xiv. 4, xxii. 11[1]. It is impossible to doubt that the roll which contained St John's great letter to the parent Churches in Asia was often in the hands of the daughter Churches in Gaul, and perhaps accompanied the confessors to the prisons where they awaited the martyr's crown.

5. There is some reason for believing that the writer of the Apocalypse, before his work was ended, realized that the book might find a larger field of service than the Churches of Asia or even the Churches of the Empire could offer. In the early chapters

[1] Eus. *H. E.* v. 1. 10, 57; 2. 3.

it is clear that St John writes with a view to his message being read aloud in the local Church assemblies: *blessed is he that readeth and they that hear the words of this prophecy; he that hath an ear, let him hear what the Spirit saith unto the Churches*[1]. Beyond the transmission of the letter for reading in neighbouring Churches, the prophet contemplates no circulation of his book; his message is to the Churches of Asia, and he is content to be the means of conveying it to them. But when he reaches the end a presentiment seems to enter his mind that the book will live: *I testify unto every man that heareth the words of the prophecy of this book, If any man shall add unto them, God shall add unto him the plagues which are written in this book; and if any man shall take away...God shall take away his part from the tree of life*[2]. The primary destination of the Apocalypse is still kept in view: it is to the hearer rather than the reader that the Apocalyptist makes his final appeal. Yet the appeal seems to imply an expectation that the book will be copied and circulated for wider reading. The words are based on two passages in Deuteronomy, and they practically place the Apocalypse on a level with the Torah and anticipate for it a place among the Scriptures of the Church. St John knew himself to be a prophet, and his writing to be a prophecy; that he was commanded to consign his visions to a book was an assurance to him that their purpose would not be fulfilled in one generation or in two. He sees the book going down to posterity, and like the Deuteronomist he endeavours to guard it against interpolation and excision. As he writes the last words upon the papyrus roll that lies upon his knee, the conviction dawns upon him that the *Revelation of Jesus Christ* was given for the warning and comfort of the whole Church to the end of time.

[1] Apoc. i. 3, ii. 7 etc. [2] Apoc. xxii. 18 f.

IX.

DATE.

1. Early Christian tradition is practically unanimous in assigning the Apocalypse to the last years of Domitian.

The following are the chief authorities. Iren. v. 30. 3 *ap.* Eus. *H. E.* iii. 18, iv. 8 εἰ γὰρ ἔδει ἀναφανδὸν τῷ νῦν καιρῷ κηρύττεσθαι τοὔνομα αὐτοῦ [*sc.* τοῦ ἀντιχρίστου], δι' ἐκείνου ἂν ἐρρέθη τοῦ καὶ τὴν Ἀποκάλυψιν ἑωρακότος· οὐδὲ γὰρ πρὸ πολλοῦ χρόνου ἑωράθη, ἀλλὰ σχεδὸν ἐπὶ τῆς ἡμετέρας γενεᾶς, πρὸς τῷ τέλει τῆς Δομετιανοῦ ἀρχῆς[1]. Clem. Alex. *quis dives* § 42 τοῦ τυράννου τελευτήσαντος ἀπὸ τῆς Πάτμου τῆς νήσου μετῆλθεν ἐπὶ τὴν Ἔφεσον. Origen, *in Mt.* tom. xvi. 6 ὁ δὲ Ῥωμαίων βασιλεύς, ὡς ἡ παράδοσις διδάσκει, κατεδίκασε τὸν Ἰωάννην μαρτυροῦντα διὰ τὸν τῆς ἀληθείας λόγον εἰς Πάτμον τὴν νῆσον[2]. Victorinus *in Apoc.* (x. 11) "hoc dicit propterea quod quando haec Ioannes vidit, erat in insula Patmos, in metallum damnatus a Domitiano Caesare. ibi ergo vidit Apocalypsin. et cum iam senior putaret se per passionem accepturum receptionem, interfecto Domitiano, omnia iudicio eius soluta sunt. et Ioannes, de metallo dimissus, sic postea tradidit hanc eandem quam acceperat a Deo Apocalypsin"; *ib.* in xvii. 10 "intellegi oportet tempus quo scripta Apocalypsis edita est, quoniam tunc erat Caesar Domitianus... unus exstat sub quo scripta est Apocalypsis, Domitianus scilicet." Euseb. *H.E.* iii. 18 ἐν τούτῳ [*sc.* in the time of Domitian] κατέχει λόγος τὸν ἀπόστολον ἅμα καὶ εὐαγγελιστὴν Ἰωάννην ἔτι τῷ βίῳ ἐκδιατρίβοντα τῆς εἰς τὸν θεῖον λόγον ἕνεκεν μαρτυρίας Πάτμον οἰκεῖν καταδικασθῆναι τὴν νῆσον: *ib.* 20 τότε δὴ οὖν [on the accession of Nerva] καὶ τὸν ἀπόστολον Ἰωάννην ἀπὸ τῆς κατὰ τὴν νῆσον φυγῆς τὴν ἐπὶ τῆς Ἐφέσου διατριβὴν ἀπειληφέναι ὁ τῶν παρ' ἡμῖν ἀρχαίων παραδίδωσι λόγος: *ib.* 23 Ἰωάννης τὰς αὐτόθι διεῖπεν ἐκκλησίας, ἀπὸ τῆς κατὰ τὴν νῆσον μετὰ τὴν Δομετιανοῦ τελευτὴν ἐπανελθὼν φυγῆς. Hieron. *de virr. illustr.* 9 "quarto decimo anno secundam post Neronem

[1] According to Dionysius Barsalibi, Hippolytus followed Irenaeus in assigning the Apocalypse to the reign of Domitian (Gwynn, in *Hermathena*, vii. 137).

[2] It will be seen that the Alexandrian testimony is not explicit; the Emperor who banished John is not named either by Clement or Origen. But in the absence of evidence to the contrary they may be presumed to have followed the tradition of South Gaul and Asia Minor.

persecutionem movente Domitiano in Patmon insulam relegatus scripsit Apocalypsin...interfecto autem Domitiano et actis eius ob nimiam crudelitatem a senatu rescissis sub Nerva principe redit Ephesum."

2. According to other ancient but not early authorities the book was written under Claudius, Nero, or Trajan.

Thus the title prefixed to both the Syriac versions of the Apocalypse assigns the banishment of St John to the reign of Nero (ܕܐܬܕܚܝ ܠܗ ܡܢ ܢܪܘܢ ܩܣܪ)[1]. Epiphanius places both the exile and the return under Claudius (*haer.* li. 12 μετὰ τὴν αὐτοῦ ἀπὸ τῆς Πάτμου ἐπάνοδον τὴν ἐπὶ Κλαυδίου γενομένην Καίσαρος: *ib.* 32 αὐτοῦ δὲ προφητεύσαντος ἐν χρόνοις Κλαυδίου Καίσαρος ἀνωτάτω ὅτε εἰς τὴν Πάτμον νῆσον ὑπῆρξεν κτλ.). The *Synopsis de vita et morte prophetarum* attributed to Dorotheus goes to the opposite extreme, placing the exile in the time of Trajan: ὑπὸ δὲ Τραϊανοῦ βασιλέως ἐξωρίσθη ἐν τῇ νήσῳ Πάτμῳ...μετὰ δὲ τὴν τελευτὴν Τραϊανοῦ ἐπάνεισιν ἀπὸ τῆς νήσου, adding however: εἰσὶ δὲ οἳ λέγουσιν μὴ ἐπὶ Τραϊανοῦ αὐτὸν ἐξορισθῆναι ἐν Πάτμῳ, ἀλλὰ ἐπὶ Δομετιανοῦ. Similarly Theophylact on Mt. xx. 22 Ἰωάννην δὲ Τραϊανὸς κατεδίκασε μαρτυροῦντα τῷ λόγῳ τῆς ἀληθείας (compare the extract from Origen in § 1). The reference to Trajan has perhaps been suggested by Iren. ii. 22. 5 παρέμεινε γὰρ αὐτοῖς [ὁ Ἰωάννης] μέχρι τῶν Τραϊανοῦ χρόνων.

3. The general situation presupposed by the book is consistent, as we have seen, with the early tradition which represents it as a work of the last years of Domitian. The evidence may be briefly summarized here. (*a*) The condition of the Asian Churches, as it is described in *cc.* ii., iii., is that of a period considerably later than the death of Nero. Their inner life has undergone many changes since St Paul's ministry at Ephesus, and even since the writing of the Epistles to the Ephesians and Colossians[2] and the two Epistles to Timothy. Deterioration has

[1] So Theophylact, *praef. in Ioann.*, but speaking of the fourth Gospel: ὃ καὶ συνέγραψεν ἐν Πάτμῳ τῇ νήσῳ ἐξόριστος διατελῶν μετὰ τριακονταδύο ἔτη τῆς τοῦ χριστοῦ ἀναλήψεως. Tertullian (*scorp.* 15) does not definitely say that the exile to Patmos took place under Nero, though he is credited by Jerome (*adv. Jovin.* i. 26) with doing so, and his words admit of that construction.

[2] Lightfoot, indeed, assuming the earlier date of the Apocalypse writes (*Colossians*, p. 41): "the message communicated by St John to Laodicea prolongs the note which was struck by St Paul in the letter to Colossae. An interval of a very few years has not materially altered the character of these Churches. Obviously the same temper prevails, the same errors are rife, the same correction must be supplied." But the examples which he gives (pp. 41—44) shew only that the same general tendencies were at work in the Lycus valley, as when St Paul wrote, and this might well have been so even after an interval of more than 30 years.

set in at Ephesus, and at Sardis and Laodicea faith is dying or dead. The Nicolaitan party, of which there is no certain trace in the Epistles of St Paul, is now widely distributed and firmly rooted. The external relations of the Churches shew a similar advance. In past days Pergamum had witnessed a single martyrdom: now a storm of persecution was about to break on the Churches, and the faithful might expect to suffer imprisonment and death. (*b*) The prevalence of the Imperial cult, and the pressure which was being put upon recusant Christians by the Asiarchs, are suggestive of the time of Domitian rather than of Nero or Vespasian[1]. Later than Domitian's reign this precise situation could not have arisen; Nerva did not maintain the aggressive policy of Domitian[2], and when Trajan's rescript began to do its work, the petty persecution described in Apoc. xiii. would give place to formal indictment before the Proconsul. Thus the death of Domitian (Sept. 18, 96) is our *terminus ad quem*; a *terminus a quo* is supplied by the date of his accession (Sept. 13, 81), but the superior limit may with great probability be pushed forward to A.D. 90 or even further, since Domitian's jealous insistence on his claims to Divine honours and his encouragement of the *delatores* belong to the later years of his reign.

4. There are other indications of date which are more definite, and point in the same direction. (*a*) It is impossible to doubt that the legend of *Nero redivivus* is in full view of the Apocalyptist in more than one passage (xiii. 3, 12, 14, xvii. 8).

Archbishop Benson, indeed, seeks to impale those who hold this theory on the horns of a dilemma[3]. If St John referred to the legend, either he believed it or he did not. If he believed it, "he believed not only what was not true, but what decently-informed and reasonable heathen never believed." If he did not believe it,

[1] Dr Hort (1 Peter, p. 2) maintains that "in Asia Minor, the special home of the Emperor-worship, we have no right to assume that it was only under an Emperor like Domitian...that Christians were likely to have it forced upon them." This no doubt is true, but the probability remains that the great outbreak of persecution, which was imminent when the Apocalypse was written, belongs to the later rather than to the earlier epoch; see *c*. vii. of this introduction.

[2] Cf. Dio Cassius, lxviii. 1 *μίσει δὲ Δομετιανοῦ αἱ εἰκόνες αὐτοῦ...συνεχωνεύθησαν...καὶ ὁ Νερούας τούς τε κρινομένους ἐπ' ἀσεβείᾳ ἀφῆκε, καὶ τοὺς φυγόντας κατήγαγεν.* See also Eus. *H.E.* iii. 20.

[3] *Apocalypse*, p. 173 f.

he was guilty of a grave political offence in using for his own ends a story which was "hostile to the peace of the district where it existed," and moreover was aimed against the reigning Emperor. The second alternative has been assumed in the following commentary, but the inference which Dr Benson draws is not admitted. No one who appreciates the greatness of our author will suppose that he gave credit to the wild legends which were afloat about Nero's return. But the conditions of apocalyptic writing did not preclude him from working mere legend into his symbolism, nor was there any appreciable danger in the use of this legend in a book addressed to Christians only. The reference to the reigning Emperor was not likely to be intelligible to any non-Christian into whose hands the book might fall, and to Christians it suggested nothing which was not already notorious.

In Asia the story of Nero's recovery was common talk as early as A.D. 69 (Tac. *hist.* ii. 8 "Achaia atque Asia falso exterritae velut Nero adventaret vario super exitu eius rumore, eoque pluribus vivere eum fingentibus credentibusque"); but pretenders continued to arise, and even under Trajan the belief that he was yet living was still general (Dio Chrysostom, *or.* xxi., *καὶ νῦν ἔτι πάντες ἐπιθυμοῦσι ζῆν, οἱ δὲ πλεῖστοι καὶ οἴονται*[1]). (*b*) In *cc.* xiii., xvii. Domitian is described in terms as plain as the circumstances allowed. Nero is dead, but *the stroke of his death is healed* (xiii. 3, 12). He is *the Beast*—he impersonates the brutal strength of the persecuting World-power, and he *was, and is not, and is about to ascend out of the Abyss* (xvii. 8). Nero himself was the fifth Emperor, and he has fallen; but the Beast which *was and is not* reappears in an eighth Emperor, who is *of the seven*, inasmuch as he recalls to men's minds the fifth, and plays his part over again, till he too *goeth into perdition* (xvii. 11 f.)[2].

5. Notwithstanding the external and internal evidence which supports the Domitianic date, the great Cambridge theologians of the last century were unanimous in regarding the Apocalypse as a work of the reign of Nero, or of the years which immediately

[1] Nero was born in A.D. 37, so that, had he lived till A.D. 100, he would have been not more than 63.

[2] See the commentary *ad locos*. It may be added that St John appears to refer (xvi. 12) to the dread of a Parthian invasion, which was connected with the expectation of Nero's return: cf. Tac. *hist.* i. 2; *Orac. Sibyll.* iv. 137 ff.

followed his death. Bishop Lightfoot seems to have accepted "the view which assigns it to the close of Nero's reign or thereabouts[1]." Bishop Westcott placed it "before the destruction of Jerusalem[2]." Dr Hort in his posthumous commentary on 1 Peter[3] writes: "there are strong reasons for placing [the Apocalypse] not long after Nero's death." Such a threefold cord of scholarly opinion is not quickly broken, and the reasons on which it was founded deserve the most careful consideration. In the partition of the New Testament between the three, the Apocalypse, unhappily, was "not finally assigned[4]," and their published writings contain but incidental references to the question of its date. From these it would appear that they were guided in their judgement on this point partly by the relation which they believed the Book to occupy with reference to the Fall of Jerusalem, partly by the contrast which it presents to the Fourth Gospel. Thus Dr Hort writes: "The day of the Lord which the writer to the Hebrews saw drawing nigh had already begun to break in blood and fire, when St John sent his Apocalypse to the Gentile Churches of Asia[5]." And Dr Lightfoot: "It marks the close of what we may call the *Hebraic* period of St John's life, *i.e.* the period which...he had spent chiefly in the East and among Aramaic-speaking peoples[6]." But perhaps the fullest treatment of the subject is to be found in Dr Westcott's introduction to the Gospel of St John: "Of the two books (he says) the Apocalypse is the earlier. It is less developed both in thought and style.... The crisis of the Fall of Jerusalem explains the relation of the Apocalypse to the Gospel. In the Apocalypse that 'coming' of Christ was expected, and painted in figures; in the Gospel the 'coming' is interpreted[7]."

It is clear that these arguments for placing the Apocalypse

[1] *Biblical Essays*, p. 52; cf. *Supernatural Religion*, p. 132.

[2] *St John*, Intr. p. lxxxvii.

[3] P. 2; cf. Hulsean Lectures, p. 140f., *Judaistic Christianity*, p. 160.

[4] See Bp Westcott's prefatory note to Dr Hort's 1 Peter (p. vii).

[5] *Jud. Christianity*, p. 160.

[6] *Supernatural Religion*, p. 132. Dr Lightfoot appears to be in general agreement here with his antagonist, who placed the Apocalypse "about A.D. 68, 69."

[7] *St John*, p. lxxxvi. f.

under Nero or Vespasian rest on more than one presupposition. The unity of the Book is assumed, and it is held to be the work of the author of the Fourth Gospel. But the latter hypothesis is open, and perhaps will always be open to doubt; and the former cannot be pressed so far as to exclude the possibility that the extant book is a second edition of an earlier work, or that it incorporates earlier materials, and either hypothesis would sufficiently account for the few indications of a Neronic or Vespasianic date which have been found in it[1]. When it is added that the great scholars who have been named dealt with the question incidentally and not in connexion with a special study of the Apocalypse, it seems permissible to attach less importance to their judgement on this point than on others to which their attention had been more directly turned.

6. With all due deference, therefore, to the great authority of Westcott, Lightfoot, and Hort, and of the foreign scholars[2] who have supported an earlier date, adhesion has been given in this edition to the view that the Apocalypse, at least in its present form, belongs, as Irenaeus believed, to the reign of Domitian and to the last years of that reign (90—96). This date appears to be consistent with the general character and purpose of the book. The Apocalypse as a whole presupposes a period when in Asia at least the Church was compelled to choose between Christ and Caesar. And the prophet foresees that this is no local or passing storm, but one which will spread over the whole Empire, and run a long course, ending only with the fall of paganism and of Rome. The Coming of the Lord is no longer connected with the Fall of Jerusalem, which is viewed as an event of past history[3]. A new Jerusalem has taken the place of the old city of God, and the Apocalyptist can already see its ideal glories revealed. But for the moment Babylon is in the foreground of the picture, and

[1] E.g. the cryptic representation of Nero's name in xiii. 18, and the apparent reference to Vespasian as the reigning Emperor in *c.* xvii. 10.

[2] E.g. Baur, Hilgenfeld, Beyschlag, who assign the book to the reign of Nero, and Weiss, Dusterdiek, and Mommsen, who place it under Vespasian; see C. Anderson Scott, *Revelation*, p. 48, note 1.

[3] On *c.* xi. 1 ff. see the commentary *ad l.*

Babylon must fall before the end, and after Babylon the Beast and the False Prophet. Even the triumph that follows on their destruction is not final, for the Dragon remains to be overcome. So the Coming is postponed indefinitely, though the old watchword, Ἰδοὺ ταχὺ ἔρχομαι, still rings in our ears. The whole standpoint is that of the closing years of the first century, when the Church knew herself to be entering upon a struggle of which she could not foresee the end, although of the victorious issue she entertained no doubt.

X.

CIRCULATION AND RECEPTION IN THE CHURCH.

1. Assuming that the Apocalypse was addressed by a person of influence or authority to seven of the leading Churches of Asia between the years 90 and 96, it is reasonable to suppose that it was copied and circulated to some extent before the beginning of the second century. As the encyclical was brought round by the author's messenger, each of the Churches addressed would transcribe it for its own use, and send a copy to the Churches in the immediate neighbourhood[1], and these in their turn would repeat the process. Within a few years the circulation of such a document would overstep the limits of the province, whether through the spontaneous action of the Asian societies[2], or in answer to the appeal of foreign Churches[3], or through the agency of individual Christians upon their travels. In one or all of these ways the great Christian apocalypse would have passed from Church to Church and from province to province, and wherever it went it could not fail to excite the interest of Christian readers.

2. Thus it is not incredible that Ignatius (110—117[4]) may shew some knowledge of the Apocalypse of John in more than one of

[1] Cf. Col. iv. 16 *ὅταν ἀναγνωσθῇ παρ' ὑμῖν ἡ ἐπιστολή, ποιήσατε ἵνα καὶ ἐν τῇ Λαοδικέων ἐκκλησίᾳ ἀναγνωσθῇ, καὶ τὴν ἐκ Λαοδικίας ἵνα καὶ ὑμεῖς ἀναγνῶτε.* On the method of transmission see Ramsay, *Letters to the Seven Churches*, *cc.* ii., iii.

[2] See *Mart. Polyc.* 20 *καὶ τοῖς ἐπέκεινα ἀδελφοῖς τὴν ἐπιστολὴν διαπέμψασθε.*

[3] Polyc. *Phil.* 13 *τὰς ἐπιστολὰς Ἰγνατίου τὰς πεμφθείσας ἡμῖν παρ' αὐτοῦ, καὶ ἄλλας ὅσας εἴχομεν παρ' ἡμῖν, ἐπέμψαμεν ὑμῖν καθὼς ἐνετείλασθε.*

[4] On Clem. R. *Cor.* 34. 3, see *N.T. in the Apostolic Fathers*, p. 58. Lightfoot, who placed the Apocalypse under Nero or Vespasian, was inclined to see in Clem. *l. c.* a reference to Apoc. xxii. 12; see his note *ad l.*

his letters to the Asian Churches (*Eph.* 15. 3 *ἵνα ὦμεν αὐτοῦ ναοί, καὶ αὐτὸς ἐν ἡμῖν θεός* [Apoc. xxi. 3]; Philad. vi. 1, *στηλαί εἰσιν καὶ τάφοι νεκρῶν, ἐφ' οἷς γέγραπται μόνον ὀνόματα ἀνθρώπων* [Apoc. iii. 12]), though the coincidences are not such as to justify a definite conclusion. In the Epistle of Barnabas[1], again, there are one or two passages which may allude to St John's work (Barn. 6. 13 *λέγει δὲ Κύριος Ἰδοὺ ποιῶ τὰ ἔσχατα ὡς τὰ πρῶτα* [Apoc. xxi. 3]; *ib.* 21. 3 *ἐγγὺς ὁ κύριος καὶ ὁ μισθὸς αὐτοῦ* [Apoc. xxii. 10 f.]); but the balance of probability is in each instance against the reference[2]. There is however abundant evidence that the Apocalypse was in circulation during the second half of the second century, not only in Asia, but in the West.

(1) Eusebius does not mention the Apocalypse among N.T. books known to Papias (*H. E.* iii. 39), unless this is implied in his attribution of Papias's chiliasm to a misunderstanding of certain statements made by Apostolic authority[3]. But against the silence of Eusebius we have to set the express statement of Andreas, who in the prologue to his commentary writes: περὶ μέντοι τοῦ θεοπνεύστου τῆς βίβλου περιττὸν μηκύνειν τὸν λόγον ἡγούμεθα, τῶν μακαρίων Γρηγορίου φημὶ τοῦ θεολόγου καὶ Κυρίλλου, προσέτι τε καὶ τῶν ἀρχαιοτέρων Παπίου, Εἰρηναίου, Μεθοδίου, καὶ Ἱππολύτου προσμαρτυρούντων τὸ ἀξιόπιστον. Andreas, moreover, quotes a remark of Papias upon Apoc. xii. 7 ff. Papias, it will be remembered, was according to Irenaeus (v. 33) an ἀκουστὴς Ἰωάννου and an ἀρχαῖος ἀνήρ, whose *floruit* is likely to be nearer to the beginning than to the middle of the century[4]. (2) About A.D. 180 Irenaeus knew of copies of the Apocalypse already 'ancient,' and of witness borne to the text of the book by persons who had seen the writer (v. 30 = Eus. *H.E.* v. 8)[5], and who, if not Papias and Polycarp, presumably belonged to their generation[6]. (3) Justin, who lived at Ephesus[7] before he went to Rome, speaks of the Apocalypse as a recognized Christian book, and identifies its author with the Apostle John: *apol.* i. 28 ὄφις καλεῖται καὶ σατανᾶς καὶ διάβολος, ὡς ἐκ τῶν ἡμετέρων συγγραμμάτων ἐρευνήσαντες μαθεῖν δύνασθε[8]; *dial.* 81 παρ' ἡμῖν ἀνήρ τις ᾧ ὄνομα Ἰωάννης, εἷς τῶν ἀποστόλων τοῦ χριστοῦ, ἐν ἀποκαλύψει γενομένῃ αὐτῷ, χίλια ἔτη ποιή-

[1] A.D. 130–1 (Harnack).

[2] See *N. T. in the Apostolic Fathers*, p. 16 f.

[3] ἃ καὶ ἡγοῦμαι τὰς ἀποστολικὰς παρεκδεξάμενον διηγήσεις ὑπολαβεῖν, τὰ ἐν ὑποδείγμασι πρὸς αὐτῶν μυστικῶς εἰρημένα μὴ συνεωρακότα. Cf. Lightfoot, *Supernatural Religion*, p. 214, note 4.

[4] See Sanday, *Criticism of the Fourth Gospel*, p. 250 f.; Lightfoot, *S.R.* p. 150: "we may say that Papias was probably born about A.D. 60—70."

[5] The words will be found on p. 172 (note to Apoc. xiii. 18).

[6] Lightfoot, *S.R.* p. 218.

[7] Harnack places the Ephesian residence of Justin *c.* A.D. 135.

[8] Cf. Apoc. xii. 9, xx. 2.

σειν ἐν Ἰερουσαλὴμ τοὺς τῷ ἡμετέρῳ χριστῷ πιστεύσαντας προεφήτευσε[1]. (4) Eusebius (*H.E.* iv. 26) mentions among the works of Melito, Bishop of Sardis (? *c.* 165), *τὰ περὶ τοῦ διαβόλου καὶ τῆς Ἀποκαλύψεως Ἰωάννου*[2]. The work, whatever its nature may have been, has perished[3], but the title shews that the Apocalypse was accepted at this time in one of the Churches to which it was originally sent—a Church, moreover, which had little cause to pride itself upon the character it receives from the Apocalyptist. In the wreck of the Montanistic[4] and anti-Montanistic literature which perplexed the Churches of Asia at this time, we have probably lost many similar references to the book; but we know, on the authority of Eusebius (*H.E.* v. 18), that it was quoted by the anti-Montanist Apollonius (*κέχρηται δὲ καὶ μαρτυρίαις ἀπὸ τῆς Ἰωάννου Ἀποκαλύψεως*)[5]. Later, but before the end of the century, Theophilus, Bishop of Antioch, cites the Apocalypse against the teaching of Hermogenes (Eus. *H.E.* iv. 24 *ἄλλο* [*σύγγραμμα τοῦ Θεοφίλου*] *πρὸς τὴν αἵρεσιν Ἑρμογένους τὴν ἐπιγραφὴν ἔχει, ἐν ᾧ ἐκ τῆς Ἀποκαλύψεως Ἰωάννου κέχρηται μαρτυρίαις*); in Asia Minor and in Western Syria the book had clearly become a court of appeal to which Christians of opposite schools could submit their differences. (5) In South Gaul about the same time the Apocalypse was held in equal regard. The Epistle of the Churches of Vienne and Lyons, addressed in 177 to the region from which the book emanated[6], cites or refers to it some five times[7], and one of the quotations is introduced by the N.T. formula for the citation of canonical Scripture (*ἵνα ἡ γραφὴ πληρωθῇ*). With Irenaeus, Bishop of Lyons, a few years later, quotations from the Apocalypse are frequent, and they are usually introduced by the words "John (or "John the disciple of the Lord") says in the Apocalypse" (Iren. iv. 14. 1, 17. 6, 18. 6, 20. 11, 21. 3; v. 26. 1, 28. 2, 34. 2, 35. 1); once we have "the Apocalypse of John" (i. 26. 3), and once "the Apocalypse," without the author's name (v. 20. 2)[8]. Such is the

[1] The allusion to Apoc. xxi. in Tatian's *λόγος πρὸς Ἕλληνας* to which reference is made by Westcott (*Canon*, p. 320), is too obscure to be used for the purpose of this chapter.

[2] Two separate books, according to Jerome (*de virr. illustr.* 9 "de diabolo librum unum, de Apocalypsi Ioannis librum unum").

[3] On the commentary of the pseudo-Melito see Harnack, *Gesch. d. altchr. Litteratur*, i. 254, and the chapter of this introduction on Apocalyptic commentaries (*c.* xvii).

[4] For some instances of a Montanistic use of the Apocalypse see Zahn, *Gesch. d. NTlichen Kanons*, i. p. 205 f.

[5] There is a possible allusion to Apoc. xxii. 18 f. in the anonymous anti-Montanistic writing quoted by Eusebius in *H. E.* v. 16. The same verses may be in the mind of Dionysius of Corinth, when he writes (*ap.* Eus. *H.E.* iv. 23): *ἃ μὲν ἐξαιροῦντες, ἃ δὲ προστιθέντες. οἷς τὸ οὐαὶ κεῖται.*

[6] Eus. *H.E.* v. 1 *τοῖς κατὰ τὴν Ἀσίαν καὶ Φρυγίαν...ἀδελφοῖς.*

[7] The passages to which reference is made are Apoc. xiv. 4 (*ἀκολουθῶν τῷ ἀρνίῳ ὅπου ἂν ὑπάγῃ*), xii. 1, xiv. 4 (*τῇ παρθένῳ μητρί*), xix. 9 (*ὡς εἰς νυμφικὸν δεῖπνον κεκλημένοι*), xxii. 11 (*ὁ ἄνομος ἀνομησάτω ἔτι, καὶ ὁ δίκαιος δικαιωθήτω ἔτι*).

[8] See Zahn, *Gesch. d. NTlichen Kanons*, i. 202, note 2. Quotations from the fourth Gospel are similarly announced, with the substitution of *in Evangelio* for *in Apocalypsi*, cf. Iren. i. 6. 5, iii. 21. 2, iv. 25. 1, v. 18. 2. On the title "disciple of the Lord" see *c.* xv. of this introduction.

authority of the book that when it is silent on a point Irenaeus permits himself to write (v. 30. 1), "dignum non est praeconari a Spiritu sancto." (6) At Rome, there is some reason to think, the Apocalypse was known even before the coming of Justin. The *Shepherd* of Hermas twice (*Vis.* ii. 2. 7, iv. 3. 1) uses the remarkable phrase ἡ θλίψις ἡ μεγάλη, which occurs in Apoc. vii. 14; moreover, it is hardly too bold to say with Bishop Westcott that "the symbolism of the Apocalypse reappears in the *Shepherd*[1]." Certainly there is a marked affinity between the two books, which shews itself in the use of similar imagery; in both the Church is a woman, and her adversary a wild beast; in both we read of the Book of Life, and of conquerors distinguished by their white robes and palms and crowns; if the Apocalypse describes the New Jerusalem as lying four-square within walls on whose foundation stones are the names of the Apostolic college, the *Shepherd* describes a tower which is in building, the bright squared stones of which are the Apostles and other teachers of the Church[2]. That these coincidences are not purely accidental is rendered probable by the circumstance that the Muratorian fragment on the Canon, which refers to the *Shepherd* as written "nuperrime temporibus nostris in urbe Roma," seems to intimate that the Apocalypse of John was universally recognized at Rome, in contrast to the Apocalypse of Peter which some refused to acknowledge ("Apocalypse[s] etiam Iohannis et Petri tantum recipimus, quam [?*sc.* Apocalypsim Petri] quidam ex nostris legi in ec[c]lesia nolunt[3]"). (7) At Carthage, the daughter of Rome, the Johannine Apocalypse was known and accepted at the end of the second century or in the early years of the third. Tertullian quotes from eighteen out of the twenty-two chapters of the book[4], and cites it as Scripture (*de res. carn.* 27 "habemus etiam vestimentorum in scripturis mentionem ad spem carnis allegorizare, quia et Apocalypsis Iohannis *Hi sunt*, ait, *qui vestimenta sua non coinquinaverunt*"); it is the work of the Apostle John (*Marc.* iii. 14, 24), the *instrumentum Ioannis* (*ib.* 38), and part and parcel of the *instrumentum*[5] *apostolicum* (*pud.* 12 sqq.)[6]. The Acts of Perpetua and Felicitas abound in imagery which is modelled on that of the Apocalypse (e.g. § 4 "circumstantes candidati milia multa"; § 12 "introeuntes vestierunt stolas candidas, et introivimus, et audivimus vocem unitam dicentem Agios agios agios sine cessatione...et vidimus in eodem loco sedentem quasi hominem canum...et in dextra

[1] *Canon*, p. 201, note 2. Cf. Lardner, *Works*, ii. p. 69: "it is very probable that Hermas had read the book of St John's Revelation and imitated it."

[2] *Vis.* ii. 4, iii. 5, iv. 2; *Sim.* viii. 2.

[3] That the *Apocalypsis Johannis* is identical with our book is clear by what precedes: "et Iohannes enim in Apocalypsi, licet septem ecclesiis scribat, tamen omnibus dicit"—an early and interesting appreciation of the wider purpose of the book.

[4] The quotations are most numerous in his Montanistic books, but they occur also in the earlier works, e.g. *orat.* 3, 5, *paen.* 8.

[5] Cf. *apol.* 18 "instrumentum litteraturae"; *ib.* 21 "Iudaeorum instrumenta"; *res. carn.* 40 "instrumenta divina." Cf. Zahn, *Gesch.* i. p. 107 ff.

[6] Zahn, *Gesch.* i. p. 204.

et in sinistra seniores quattuor...et introeuntes cum admiratione stetimus ante thronum." As in the case of the *Shepherd*, there is no direct quotation here, but the influence of the Apocalypse is scarcely doubtful. (8) At Alexandria about the same time the Apocalypse was known, and recognized as the work of St John. Clement, who cites it several times (*paed.* i. 6 § 36, ii. 10 § 108, 12 § 119; *strom.* iii. 18 § 106, vi. 13 § 116) with the formula ὥς φησιν ἐν τῇ ἀποκαλύψει Ἰωάννης, 16 § 141), regards it as Scripture (*paed.* ii. 12 § 119 τὸ συμβολικὸν τῶν γραφῶν), and the work of an Apostle (*quis dives* § 42)[1].

3. From two quarters in the second century there comes a protest against the general acceptance of the Apocalypse of John. (*a*) "Apocalypsin eius Marcion respuit[2]," as we learn from Tertullian (*adv. Marc.* iv. 5); and on Marcion's principles it would have been impossible to accept a book so saturated with the thought and imagery of the Old Testament. Whether he rejected at the same time the attribution of the book to the Apostle John which is already to be found in Justin, there is not sufficient evidence to shew; in any case it formed no part of his *apostolicum*; he did not recognize John as a writer of canonical Scripture[3]. (*b*) Far more significant is the attitude of the so-called Alogi. Irenaeus (iii. 11. 9), after referring to Marcion's attitude toward the Gospels, says: "alii vero, ut donum Spiritus frustrentur quod in novissimis temporibus secundum placitum Patris effusum est in humanum genus, illam speciem non admittunt quae est secundum Ioannis evangelium in qua paracletum se missurum dominus promisit, sed simul et evangelium et propheticum repellunt Spiritum." Epiphanius represents a nameless party which he calls the Alogi as rejecting both the Gospel and the Apocalypse (*haer.* li. 3 τί φάσκουσι τοίνυν οἱ Ἄλογοι—ταύτην

[1] If the *Judicium Petri*, printed by Hilgenfeld in *N.T. extra canon. recept.*, may be regarded as an Egyptian writing of the second century, its witness must be added here: § 2 εἴκοσι γὰρ καὶ τέσσαρές εἰσιν πρεσβύτεροι, δώδεκα ἐκ δεξιῶν καὶ δώδεκα ἐξ εὐωνύμων—a reference to Apoc. iv. 4.

[2] According to Pseudo-Tert. *adv. omn. haer.* 6 he was preceded here by Cerdon: "Cerdon...Acta apostolorum et Apocalypsim quasi falsa reicit."

[3] Tert. *op. cit.* iii. 14 "Ioannem agnitum non vis." Some of the Gnostic sects knew and used the Apocalypse, as the Marcosian Ὦ καὶ Ἄ (Iren. i. 14. 6, 15. 1) and Justin the Gnostic's aeon 'Amen' (Hipp. *phil.* v. 26) suggest; see Westcott, *Canon*, pp. 284, 311. Zahn (*Gesch.* i. 761) goes so far as to say: "wenigstens für die Valentinianer des Orients und insbesondere für Marcus in Kleinasien die Apokalypse ein Buch von nicht geringerem Ansehn als die Evv. war."

γὰρ αὐτοῖς τίθημι τὴν ἐπωνυμίαν...οὔτε τὸ τοῦ Ἰωάννου εὐαγγέλιον δέχονται οὔτε τὴν αὐτοῦ Ἀποκάλυψιν...λέγουσι γὰρ μὴ εἶναι αὐτὰ Ἰωάννου ἀλλὰ Κηρίνθου, καὶ οὐκ ἄξια αὐτά φασιν εἶναι ἐν ἐκκλησίᾳ[1]). Against the genuineness of the Apocalypse they urged (1) that the symbolism of the book was unedifying (*ib.* 32 *τί με, φησίν, ὠφελεῖ ἡ Ἀποκάλυψις Ἰωάννου, λέγουσά μοι περὶ ἑπτὰ ἀγγέλων καὶ ἑπτὰ σαλπίγγων;*), and (2) that it contained errors in matters of fact (*ib.* 33 *εἶπε πάλιν Γράψον τῷ ἀγγέλῳ τῆς ἐκκλησίας τῷ ἐν Θυατείροις, καὶ οὐκ ἔνι ἐκεῖ ἐκκλησία Χριστιανῶν ἐν Θυατείρῃ· πῶς οὖν ἔγραφε τῇ μὴ οὔσῃ;*[2]). It is not improbable that Epiphanius was indebted for this information to a lost work of Hippolytus[3], and that we have here a nearly contemporaneous account of the first impugners of the Apocalypse. If they are identical, as seems likely, with the party mentioned by Irenaeus, they may have been originally an Asiatic school of extreme anti-Montanists who felt that both the Gospel and the Apocalypse of John savoured too strongly of the principles of the New Prophecy to allow of their attribution to the Apostle John. The assignment of the Fourth Gospel to Cerinthus is absurd enough, as Epiphanius points out (*op. cit.* 4 *πῶς γὰρ ἔσται Κηρίνθου τὰ κατὰ Κηρίνθου λέγοντα;*); but the Vision of the Thousand Years in Apoc. xx. lent some colour to the suggestion that the Apocalypse was the work of that heretic. Possibly the idea of Cerinthian authorship was first broached in reference to the Revelation, and afterwards extended to the Gospel[4].

4. Like other Asiatic parties, the anti-Montanistic opponents of St John's writings made their way to Rome. At all events the controversy, so far as the Apocalypse is concerned, finds its centre in Rome at the beginning of the third century. Eusebius quotes

[1] The Latin writers on the heresies copy Epiphanius, or repeat what their predecessors had gleaned from him; see Philastr. 60, Aug. 30, Praedest. 30, Isid. 26, Paul. 7, Honor. 41.

[2] On this singular statement and Epiphanius's explanation see Stanton, *Gospels as historical documents*, p. 209.

[3] The *πρὸς ἁπάσας τὰς αἱρέσεις*, or possibly the *ὑπὲρ τοῦ κατὰ Ἰωάννου εὐαγγελίου καὶ ἀποκαλύψεως*, or both of these works. See Dr Stanton's note (p. 200).

[4] Dr Sanday (*Criticism of the Fourth Gospel*, p. 61) calls the attribution of the Fourth Gospel to Cerinthus "a piece of sheer bravado," and such indeed it was, if the Alogi began with the Gospel; but the other course seems more natural.

from Gaius, a Roman churchman, who lived in the days of Bishop Zephyrinus (202—219) and wrote against the Montanist Bishop Proclus[1], a statement that Cerinthus forged 'apocalypses' in the name of 'a great Apostle':

> Eus. *H.E.* iii. 28 ἀλλὰ καὶ Κήρινθος ὁ δι' ἀποκαλύψεων [Rufinus: *per revelationes quasdam*] ὡς ὑπὸ ἀποστόλου μεγάλου γεγραμμένων τερατολογίας ἡμῖν ὡς δι' ἀγγέλων αὐτῷ δεδειγμένας ψευδόμενος ἐπεισάγει, λέγων μετὰ τὴν ἀνάστασιν ἐπίγειον εἶναι τὸ βασίλειον τοῦ χριστοῦ, καὶ πάλιν ἐπιθυμίαις καὶ ἡδοναῖς ἐν Ἰερουσαλὴμ τὴν σάρκα πολιτευομένην δουλεύειν. καὶ ἐχθρὸς ὑπάρχων ταῖς γραφαῖς τοῦ θεοῦ ἀριθμὸν χιλιονταετίας ἐν γάμῳ ἑορτῆς, θέλων πλανᾷν, λέγει γίνεσθαι.

The words in spaced letters come very near to the terms of our Apocalypse, but until 1888 it was competent for scholars to suppose that Gaius referred to a book or books written by Cerinthus in which he imitated or travestied the work of St John[2]. In that year Dr Gwynn, of Dublin, published in the *Hermathena* (vi. p. 397 ff.) five Syriac scholia from Dionysius Barsalibi on the Apocalypse, consisting of extracts from "the heretic Gaius" in which Gaius comments on the Apocalypse in terms which shew that he did not admit the authority of the book. Gaius, therefore, was more or less in sympathy with the Alogi, and it is not improbable that, in his zeal against Montanism, he adopted the Cerinthian attribution. In any case it is to Gaius and his school[3] rather than to the Eastern 'Alogi' that Dionysius of Alexandria refers when he writes fifty years after:

> Eus. *H. E.* vii. 25 τινὲς μὲν οὖν τῶν πρὸ ἡμῶν ἠθέτησαν καὶ ἀνεσκεύασαν [Rufinus, *a canone scripturarum abiciendum putarunt*] πάντῃ τὸ βιβλίον, καθ' ἕκαστον κεφάλαιον διευθύνοντες ἄγνωστόν τε καὶ ἀσυλλόγιστον ἀποφαίνοντες, ψεύδεσθαί τε τὴν ἐπιγραφήν. Ἰωάννου γὰρ οὐκ εἶναι λέγουσιν, ἀλλ' οὐδὲ ἀποκάλυψιν εἶναι, τὴν σφοδρῷ καὶ παχεῖ κεκαλυμμένην τῷ τῆς ἀγνοίας παραπετάσματι· καὶ οὐχ ὅπως τῶν ἀποστόλων τινὰ ἀλλ' οὐδ' ὅλως τῶν ἁγίων ἢ τῶν ἀπὸ τῆς ἐκκλησίας τούτου γεγονέναι ποιητὴν τοῦ συγγράμματος, Κήρινθον δέ...τοῦτο γὰρ εἶναι τῆς διδασκαλίας αὐτοῦ τὸ δόγμα, ἐπίγειον ἔσεσθαι τὴν τοῦ χριστοῦ βασιλείαν, καὶ ὧν αὐτὸς ὠρέγετο φιλοσώματος ὢν καὶ πάνυ σαρκικός, ἐν τούτοις ὀνειροπολεῖν ἔσεσθαι...γάμοις καὶ...ἑορταῖς.

[1] Eus. *H.E.* ii. 25, vi. 20; cf. Lightfoot, *St Clement*, ii. p. 377 ff.

[2] See Westcott, *Canon*[6], p. 278, note 2: "I may express my decided belief that Caius is not speaking of the Apocalypse of St John."

[3] It will be observed that Dionysius in describing the Chiliastic views of Cerinthus uses language which comes very near to that of Gaius.

5. Neither the 'Alogi' of Asia Minor nor the party of Gaius at Rome proved dangerous to the general acceptance of the Apocalypse. At Rome Gaius was answered by Hippolytus. On the back of the chair which holds the seated figure of the Bishop of Portus, a list of his works is graved, and among them is one entitled ΥΠΕΡ ΤΟΥ ΚΑΤΑ ΙΩΑΝΝΗΝ ΕΥΑΓΓΕΛΙΟΥ ΚΑΙ ΑΠΟΚΑΛΥΨΕΩΣ[1]. The coupling of the Fourth Gospel and the Apocalypse suggests that this book was directed against the 'Alogi,' probably the Roman Alogi' represented by Gaius[2]. The same book may be intended by the *Heads against Gaius*, which Ebedjesu attributes to Hippolytus[3], and from which Dr Gwynn's fragments have been drawn. In his extant works and fragments Hippolytus repeatedly asserts his belief in the Johannine authorship of the Apocalypse (*e.g.* Lagarde, p. 48 *οὕτως γὰρ Ἰωάννης εἶπεν Ὁ ὢν καὶ ὁ ἦν καὶ ὁ ἐρχόμενος*: p. 159 *ὁ ἀνοίγων καὶ οὐδεὶς κλείει, ὡς Ἰωάννης λέγει*), and he identifies John the disciple of the Lord with the Apostle (*ib.* p. 17 *λέγε μοι, μακάριε Ἰωάννη, ἀπόστολε καὶ μαθητὰ τοῦ κυρίου, τί εἶδες καὶ ἤκουσας περὶ Βαβυλῶνος*). During the remainder of the first half of the third century we hear no more of the counter-movement. At Carthage Cyprian uses the Apocalypse freely, both in the *Testimonia*[4] and in his treatises and letters; at Alexandria Origen entertains no doubt as to the authenticity of the book (e.g. *in Ioann.* t. i. 14 *φησὶν οὖν ἐν τῇ Ἀποκαλύψει ὁ τοῦ Ζεβεδαίου Ἰωάννης*: *ap.* Eus. vi. 25 *τί δεῖ περὶ τοῦ ἀναπεσόντος ἐπὶ τὸ στῆθος λέγειν τοῦ Ἰησοῦ Ἰωάννου, ὃς εὐαγγέλιον ἓν καταλέλοιπεν...ἔγραψε δὲ καὶ τὴν Ἀποκάλυψιν*). Circumstances led, however, to the reopening of the question by Origen's pupil and successor, Dionysius, during the years when the latter was Bishop of Alexandria (247—265). The facts are given in the large fragments of a treatise by Dionysius Περὶ ἐπαγγελιῶν preserved by Eusebius *H. E.* vii. 24 f.[5]

[1] Lightfoot, *St Clement*, ii. pp. 394, 420.

[2] Dr Stanton, however (*Gospels as historical documents*, p. 230 ff.), after discussing the attitude of Gaius towards the Fourth Gospel, comes to the conclusion that there is at present no sufficient evidence to shew that he rejected it.

[3] Cf. Assemani, *bibl. orient.* iii. p. 15 (ܡܦܩܢܘܬܗ ܕܥܠ ܓܠܝܢܐ ܘܣܒܪܘܬܐ ܕܝܘܚܢܢ).

[4] It is quoted 27 times in the *Testimonia* alone.

[5] The fragments are edited by Dr Feltoe in *Letters and other remains of Dionysius of Alexandria*, pp. 106—125.

It appears that on the occasion of a visit to Arsinoe, where Chiliasm had long disturbed the peace of the Church, Dionysius found himself confronted by an Ἔλεγχος περὶ ἀλληγοριστῶν, written by Nepos, an Egyptian Bishop, in which, according to Eusebius, Nepos 'taught that the promises made in the Holy Scriptures to the saints will be fulfilled in a Jewish sense (Ἰουδαϊκώτερον), and held that there will be a millennium of bodily enjoyment on this earth.' A three days' conference followed which brought the Arsenoites back to a healthier view. But the incident led the critical mind of Dionysius to examine afresh for himself the grounds on which the Apocalypse was held to be the work of the Apostle John, and the results of his enquiry are given in the third, fourth, and fifth of the fragments of his answer to Nepos.

Dionysius refuses to follow the party who ascribed the Apocalypse to Cerinthus[1]. He cannot venture to reject a book which is held in high esteem by so many members of the Church (ἐγὼ δὲ ἀθετῆσαι οὐκ ἂν τολμήσαιμι τὸ βιβλίον, πολλῶν αὐτὸ διὰ σπουδῆς ἐχόντων ἀδελφῶν); with the modesty of the true scholar he is ready to attribute the difficulties which it presents to the limitations of his own understanding (εἰ μὴ συνίημι, ἀλλ' ὑπονοῶ γε νοῦν τινὰ βαθύτερον ἐγκεῖσθαι τοῖς ῥήμασιν). But while he does not presume to challenge the inspiration of the Apocalypse or its claim to be the work of a John, he declines to accept it as the work of the Apostle, to whom he attributes the fourth Gospel and "the Catholic Epistle" (i.e. 1 John). He is led to this conclusion by comparing (1) the character of the writer of the Apocalypse with that of the writer of the Gospel, (2) the thought and style of the writings, and (3) their linguistic differences (τεκμαίρομαι γὰρ ἔκ τε τοῦ ἤθους ἑκατέρων καὶ τοῦ τῶν λόγων εἴδους καὶ τῆς τοῦ βιβλίου διεξαγωγῆς)[2]. John the Evangelist abstains from mentioning his own name, but John the Apocalyptist names himself more than once at the very outset of his book, and again near the end. Doubtless there were many who bore the name of John in the early Christian communities; we read, for instance, of "John whose surname was Mark," and there may have been a second John in Asia, since at Ephesus, we are told, there were two tombs said to be John's (δύο φασὶν ἐν Ἐφέσῳ γενέσθαι μνήματα, καὶ ἑκάτερον Ἰωάννου λέγεσθαι). Again, while the Gospel and Epistle of John shew marks of agreement which suggest a common authorship, the Apocalypse differs widely from both in its ideas and in its way of expressing them; we miss in it (e.g.) the frequent references to 'life,' 'light,' 'truth,' 'grace,' and 'love' which are characteristic of the Apostle, and find ourselves in a totally different region of thought (ἀλλοιοτάτη δὲ καὶ ξένη παρὰ ταῦτα ἡ ἀποκάλυψις, μήτε ἐφαπτομένη μήτε γειτνιῶσα τούτων μηδένι, σχεδὸν ὡς εἰπεῖν μηδὲ συλλαβὴν πρὸς αὐτὰ κοινὴν ἔχουσα). Lastly, the linguistic eccentricities of the Apocalypse bar the way against an acceptance of the book as the work of the Evangelist. The Gospel and first Epistle are written in correct and flowing Greek,

[1] See above, p. cvi f.

[2] See Dr Feltoe's note *ad l.*

and there is not a barbarism, a solecism, or a provincialism in them; whereas the Greek of the Apocalypse is inaccurate, disfigured by unusual or foreign words, and even at times solecistic (γλῶσσαν οὐκ ἀκριβῶς ἑλληνίζουσαν αὐτοῦ βλέπω, ἀλλ' ἰδιώμασί τε βαρβαρικοῖς χρώμενον, καί που καὶ σολοικίζοντα).

6. This criticism, not the less trenchant because carefully guarded against the imputation of levity or irreverence[1], and proceeding from so distinguished a Bishop as Dionysius 'the Great[2],' could not fail to carry weight in Egypt and in the Greek-speaking East, shaking the faith of many in the apostolical authorship of the Apocalypse, and therefore in its canonical authority. In the fourth century Eusebius is unable to speak positively as to its canonicity (*H.E.* iii. 25 τῆς δὲ Ἀποκαλύψεως ἐφ' ἑκάτερον ἔτι νῦν παρὰ πολλοῖς περιέλκεται ἡ δόξα. *Ib.* 25 ἐπὶ τούτοις [the canonical books] τακτέον, εἴ γε φανείη, τὴν Ἀποκάλυψιν Ἰωάννου...ἥν τινες, ὡς ἔφην, ἀθετοῦσιν, ἕτεροι δὲ ἐγκρίνουσι τοῖς ὁμολογουμένοις). Cyril of Jerusalem, a few years later, not only omits the Apocalypse from his list of canonical books, but seems definitely to exclude it from private as well as public use (*Catech.* iv. 31 τὰ δὲ λοιπὰ πάντα ἐν δευτέρῳ κείσθω, καὶ ὅσα μὲν ἐν ἐκκλησίαις μὴ ἀναγινώσκεται, ταῦτα μηδὲ κατὰ σαυτὸν ἀναγίνωσκε). It is more remarkable that Asia Minor should have ignored the book even in formal canons; it finds no place in the Laodicean list of 363, or in that of Gregory of Nazianzus; while Amphilochius of Iconium expressly says: τὴν δ' Ἀποκάλυψιν τὴν Ἰωάννου πάλιν | τινὲς μὲν ἐγκρίνουσιν, οἱ πλείους δέ γε | νόθον λέγουσι. In Eastern Syria the Apocalypse was either still unknown or it was ignored; it formed no part of the Peshitta New Testament[3]. Junilius, who represents the Biblical criticism of the school of Nisibis in the sixth century, is silent about the book; Ebedjesu, a Nestorian Bishop in the first year of the fourteenth century, still passes it over without notice in his list of New Testament books. Western Syria, as repre-

[1] Fragment 5, e.g. ends: οὐδὲ γὰρ ἐπισκώπτων, μή τις νομίσῃ, ταῦτα εἶπον, ἀλλὰ μόνον τὴν ἀνομοιότητα διευθύνων τῶν γραφῶν. As Dr Westcott points out, *Canon*, p. 369, note 4, Dionysius "quoted the Apocalypse with respect: Eus. *H.E.* vii. 10."

[2] Cf. Feltoe, p. xi.

[3] Gwynn, *Apocalypse*, pp. xiii, ciii f.; cf. Zahn, *Gesch.* i. p. 374 f.

sented by the School of Antioch, looked with little favour on the most mystical of early Christian writings. Neither Theodore, Chrysostom, or Theodoret is known to have quoted the Apocalypse[1]. Constantinople inherited the traditions of Antioch in this respect as in others, and the Apocalypse is omitted altogether in the *Synopsis scripturae sacrae* which is found among the work of Chrysostom, nor has it any place in the catalogue of "the Sixty books" or in either of its supplementary lists. As late as the beginning of the ninth century Nicephorus places it among the *antilegomena* with the Apocalypse of Peter. It is significant of the slow progress made by the circulation or acceptance of the book in eastern lands that no Greek commentary seems to have been written upon it before the fifth or sixth century[2]. Several causes may have concurred to cause this delay. There may have been in some minds a lingering dread of Montanism, and in many others a doubt as to the inspiration or the apostolical authority of the Apocalyptist. Moreover, the Apocalypse may have been known in the East only to a few. From the first perhaps the book went west rather than east; traders from Smyrna and Ephesus carried it to Italy and Gaul, to North Africa and Egypt; few copies seem to have penetrated to Antioch, and fewer or none to Edessa and Nisibis.

7. In the West, on the contrary, the Apocalypse, which had won acceptance in the second century, held its own notwithstanding the strictures of Gaius at Rome, and the rejection of its apostolic authorship by Dionysius at Alexandria. Alexandria

[1] Suidas, indeed, remarks: *δέχεται δὲ ὁ Χρυσόστομος...τὴν Ἀποκάλυψιν.* "If this is true," Dr Westcott writes, not without a touch of humour, "it is a singular proof of the inconclusiveness of the casual evidence of quotation" (*Canon*, p. 442, note 3).

[2] It is to be noted, also, that Greek MSS. of the Apocalypse, uncial or cursive, are relatively few; that *ὑποθέσεις* to this book are rare (von Soden, *Die Schriften d. N. T.*, p. 360); and that no Greek MS. shews a stichometry (Tischendorf, ii. 1044), though the stichi were counted—according to Nicephorus they were 1400, according to the Claromontane list, 1200, and according to Mommsen's list, 1800; see Zahn, *Gesch.* ii. p. 397. The Apocalypse holds the last place in nearly all Greek MSS. of the N.T.; the exceptions will be found in Gregory, *prolegg.* p. 136. In the Latin lists and the MSS. of the Vulgate other arrangements are less rare, e.g. the Claromontane list places Apoc. after the Catholic Epistles but before the Acts, while in the Mommsen list and the 'Decree of Gelasius' it finds a place before the Catholic Epistles; see Zahn, *Gesch.* ii. p. 383, or Preuschen, *Analecta*, pp. 139—149.

soon returned to its allegiance; in his Festal Epistles (*Ep.* 39), Athanasius ends his list of the canon with the words *καὶ πάλιν Ἰωάννου Ἀποκάλυψις*, adding: *ταῦτα πηγαὶ τοῦ σωτηρίου... μηδεὶς τούτοις ἐπιβαλλέτω μηδὲ τούτων ἀφαιρείσθω τι.* In the pseudo-Athanasian Synopsis the Apocalypse forms the eighth and last book of the New Testament, and later Alexandrian writers accept it without hesitation[1]. The Latin West was from the time of Gaius practically unanimous in its favour[2]. It was there that the book found its earliest interpreters, Victorinus of Pettau, Tyconius, Primasius. It takes its place in all Western lists of the canonical Scriptures: in Mommsen's canon, in those of Codex Claromontanus and the Carthaginian Council of 397, in the 'Decree of Gelasius.' The authority of the great Latin fathers confirmed the general verdict of the Church; Ambrose, Jerome, Rufinus, Augustine, Innocent, accepted the Apocalypse as the work of the Apostle John.

The Eastern Church has long followed the example of the West. Although the Quinisextine Council endorsed without remark the Laodicean Canon which omits the Apocalypse, the commentaries of Oecumenius, Andreas, and Arethas must have gone far to secure a favourable hearing for the book. Even the Syrian Church in the seventh century possessed two versions, one connected with the work of Thomas of Harkel, emanating perhaps from Alexandria, and another of a Philoxenian type[3].

No book in the New Testament with so good a record was so long in gaining general acceptance. The reasons for this are well summarized in a scholion to one of the MSS. of the Apocalypse[4]: *ἢ διὰ τὸ μερικῶς μὴ ἐκτίθεσθαι αὐτήν, ἢ διὰ τὸ ἀσαφὲς αὐτῆς καὶ δυσέφικτον καὶ ὀλίγοις διαλαμβανόμενον καὶ νοούμενον, ἄλλως τε οἶμαι διὰ τὸ μηδὲ συμφέρον εἶναι τοῖς πολλοῖς τὰ ἐν αὐτῇ ἐρευνᾷν μηδὲ λυσιτελές.* The key to the interpretation disappeared with

[1] On the Coptic canon see p. cxci.

[2] There is an apparent exception in the *liber ecclesiasticorum dogmatum* attributed to Gennadius (§ 6 "erit resurrectio mortuorum hominum, sed una et in semel; non prima iustorum et secunda peccatorum, ut fabulat somniator"). But the author is probably an Eastern; see Mr. C. H. Turner in *J.T.S.* vii. 25, p. 88.

[3] See p. cxc.

[4] Cod. 24.

the generation to which the book was addressed, perhaps even with the relief which the Asian Churches experienced upon the death of Domitian, and apart from any clue to its immediate reference, it was little else but a maze of inexplicable mysteries. "Apocalypsis Ioannis," exclaims Jerome, "tot habet sacramenta quot verba[1]." It was not everyone who was able to meet the situation with the patient modesty of the great Dionysius, and in the circumstances we can only recognize with thankfulness the Providence which has preserved for us a treasure of which the full value is even now scarcely realized.

[1] *Ad Paulin.*, *ep.* liii. 8.

XI.

VOCABULARY, GRAMMAR, AND STYLE.

1. A complete vocabulary of the Apocalypse will be found at the end of this volume. Here it will suffice to point out some of the results which may be gleaned from it.

The Apocalypse contains 913 distinct words, or, excluding the names of persons and places, 871. Of these 871 words, 108 are not used elsewhere in the New Testament, and 98 are used elsewhere in the New Testament but once, or by but one other writer. It may be useful to the reader to have these relatively uncommon words placed before him in separate lists.

(*a*) Words in the Apocalypse which occur in no other N.T. writing[1].

Ἀβαδδών, †ἀκμάζειν, †ἄκρατος, †ἀλληλουϊά, ἄλφα, †ἀμέθυστος, ἄμωμον, **Ἀπολλύων**, **Ἁρ Μαγεδών**, ἄψινθος, †βασανισμός, †βάτραχος, †βήρυλλος, **βιβλαρίδιον**, †βότρυς, †βύσσινος, †διάδημα, διαυγής, διπλοῦν (verb), δισμυριάς, †δράκων, †δωδέκατος, Ἑλληνικός, †ἐμεῖν, ἐνδώμησις, †ἑξακόσιοι, ζεστός, ζηλεύειν, **ἡμίωρον**, θειώδης, θύϊνον, †ἴασπις, †ἱππικός, †ἶρις, **κατάθεμα**, †κατασφραγίζειν, **κατήγωρ**, †καῦμα, †κεραμικός, †κεραννύναι, †κέρας, κιθαρῳδός, †κιννάμωμον, †κλέμμα, †κολλούριον, †κριθή, κρυσταλλίζειν, †κρύσταλλος, †κυκλόθεν, †λιβανωτός, †λιπαρός, †μάρμαρος, †μασᾶσθαι, μεσουράνημα, †μέτωπον, †μηρός, †μουσικός, †μυκᾶσθαι, μύλινος, †νεφρός, **Νικολαΐτης**, †ὄλυνθος, †ὀπώρα, †ὅρμημα, †ὄρνεον, †οὐρά, †πάρδαλις, πελεκίζειν, †πέμπτος, †πέτεσθαι, †πλήσσειν, †ποδήρης, **ποταμοφόρητος**, †πρωϊνός, †πύρινος, †πυρρός, †ῥαίνειν, ῥέδη, ῥυπαίνεσθαι, σαλπιστής, †σάπφειρος, †σάρδιον, σαρδόνυξ, †σεμίδαλις, †σίδηρος, σιρικός, †σμάραγδος, †στρῆνος, ταλαντιαῖος, †τετράγωνος, τιμιότης, †τόξον, †τοπάζιον, †τρίχινος, †ὑάκινθος, †ὑακίνθινος, ὑάλινος, †ὕαλος, †φαρμακός, †φιάλη, †χάλαζα, χαλκηδών, **χαλκολίβανος**, χλιαρός, †χοῖνιξ, †χρυσόλιθος, χρυσόπρασος, †χρυσοῦν.

[1] Words to which a dagger is prefixed occur in the Greek O. T.; those printed in thick type appear to be ἅπαξ λεγόμενα.

(*b*) Words in the Apocalypse used elsewhere in the N.T. but once, or by one other writer[1].

†ᾄδειν (P$^{\text{e col}}$), †ἀδίκημα (L^{a}), †αἰχμαλωσία (P^{e}), †ἀποχωρίζεσθαι (L^{a}), †ἅρμα (L^{a}), †ἀρνίον (J^{ev}), †ἀσχημοσύνη (P^{r}), αὐλητής (Mt), †βδελύσσεσθαι (P^{r}), †βορρᾶς (L^{ev}), †γλυκύς (Jac), †γόμος (L^{a}), †γυμνότης (P$^{\text{r cor}}$), †δίστομος (H), †δρέπανον (Mc), Ἑβραϊστί (J^{ev}), εἰδωλολάτρης (P$^{\text{cor e}}$), †ἐκκεντεῖν (J^{ev}), ἐλ[ε]εινός (P^{cor}), †ἑλίσσειν (H), †ἕλκος (L^{ev}), †ἔμπορος (Mt), †ἔμφοβος (L$^{\text{ev, a}}$), †ἐνδέκατος (Mt), †ἔριον (H), †θαῦμα (P^{cor}), †θεῖον (L^{ev}), †θεραπεία (L^{ev}), †θυμίαμα (L^{ev}), †θώραξ (P$^{\text{e th}}$), †ἵππος (Jac), †κάμινος (Mt), †καπνός (L^{a}), †κατοικητήριον (P^{e}), †κιθάρα (P^{cor}), †κιθαρίζειν (P^{cor}), †κυβερνήτης (L^{a}), †κυκλεύειν (J^{ev}), †κυριακός (P^{cor}), †λευκαίνειν (Mc), †ληνός (Mt), †λίβανος (Mt), †λίμνη (L^{ev}), †λίνον (Mt), †μαστός (L^{ev}), †μεγιστάν (Mc), †μῆκος (P^{e}), †μολύνειν (P^{cor}), ναύτης (L^{a}), †νῆσος (L^{a}), †ξύλινος (P^{tim}), †ὁμοίωμα (P$^{\text{r php}}$), †ὀξύς (P^{r}), †ὅρασις (L^{a}), ὁσάκις (P^{cor}), †ὄφελον (P$^{\text{cor g}}$), †ὄψις (J^{ev}), †παντοκράτωρ (P^{cor}), †πατεῖν (Lc), †πένθος (Jac), †πικραίνειν (P^{col}), †πλάτος (P^{e}), †πλύνειν (L^{ev}), πνευματικῶς (P^{cor}), †πολεμεῖν (Jac), †πόνος (P^{col}), †πορφύρεος (Jo^{ev}), †προφῆτις (L^{ev}), †πτωχεία (P^{cor}), †πύρωσις (Pet), †ῥομφαία (L^{ev}), †ῥυπαρός (Jac), †σιγή (L^{a}), †σιδήρεος (L^{a}), †σκηνοῦν (Jo^{ev}), †σκορπίος (L^{ev}), †σκοτοῦσθαι (P^{e}), συνκοινωνεῖν (P$^{\text{e php}}$), συνκοινωνός (P$^{\text{r cor php}}$), †σφάζειν (Jo^{ep}), †ταλαίπωρος (P^{r}), †τέχνη (L^{a}), †τρυγᾶν (L^{ev}), †φαρμακία (P^{g}), †φοῖνιξ (J^{ev}), †φωστήρ (P^{php}), †χαλινός (Jac), †χάραγμα (L^{a}), †χίλιοι (Pet), †χιών (Mt), †χλωρός (Mc), †χοῦς (Mc), †ψευδής (L^{a}), †ψηφίζειν (L^{ev}), †ψῆφος (L^{a}), †ψυχρός (Mt), †ᾠδή (P$^{\text{e col}}$), †ὠδίνειν (P^{g}).

2. An examination of these tables leads to some interesting facts. Relatively to its length the Apocalypse has an unusual number of words peculiar to itself. While the Second Gospel shews 80 such words in 2000 *stichi*, the Apocalypse has more than 100 in 1400[2]; one in eight of its words is used by no other N.T. writer, whereas in St Mark the ratio is about one in sixteen[3]. But it is to be remembered that whereas the simple narrative of the Evangelist demands for the most part only the commonest words of daily life, the Apocalyptist deals with a great variety of subjects, some of which call for a liberal use of special terms. Thus, e.g., the enumeration of articles of merchandize in Apoc. xviii. 11—13 is responsible for twelve of the words peculiar to this book, and the list of precious stones in *c.* xxi. 19 f. for ten more. Most of the Apocalyptic words which are not found

[1] The letters in brackets which follow the words in this list indicate the other N. T. writer and work in which the words are found; e.g. L^{a} = St Luke in Acts, P^{r} St Paul in Romans, J^{ev} St John in the Gospel, J^{ep} St John in the Epistles.

[2] The number of *stichi* is given in each case according to the stichometry of Nicephorus.

[3] See *St Mark*[2], p. xlvii.

or are found but rarely in other N. T. writings belong to the language of common or commercial life, which would be familiar to one who had been for many years resident in Ephesus. Further, it will be observed that two-thirds of the words in the first list ($\frac{72}{108}$), and nearly eleven-twelfths in the second ($\frac{89}{98}$), had been previously used in the Greek Old Testament. In the second list, the student will find it worth his while to notice the distribution of the words amongst other N. T. writers. St Paul, it will be seen, has 33, St Luke 30, St Matthew 9, St John 8, St James 6, St Mark 5, the author of Hebrews 3, and St Peter 2. The great preponderance of Pauline and Lucan words is remarkable, but perhaps it is sufficiently explained by the circumstance that both St Paul and St Luke wrote under conditions not altogether unlike those of the author of the Apocalypse. Their lives, like his, had been largely spent among Greek-speaking peoples, and in intercourse with Greek-speaking Churches.

The true *ἅπαξ λεγόμενα* of the Apocalypse are few. Some are name-forms (*'Αβαδδών*, *'Απολλύων*, *Ἃρ Μαγεδών*, *Νικολαΐτης*), which are perhaps in every case due to the writer. Others (*βιβλαρίδιον*, *ποταμοφόρητος*, *χαλκολίβανος*) are probably words current in Asia, although hitherto they have not been detected in any other Greek writing. *Κατήγωρ* and *κατάθεμα* seem to be of Jewish-Greek origin; *ἡμίωρον* is either a slip, or an alternative form of *ἡμιώριον*. The MSS. of the Apocalypse shew a considerable number of orthographical peculiarities, chiefly affecting the terminations of nouns and verbs, such as *χρυσᾶν* (i. 13), *χρυσέων* (ii. 1), *κεκοπίακες* (ii. 3), *πέπτωκες* (ii. 5), *βαθέα* (ii. 24), *εἶχαν* (ix. 8), *ἀπῆλθα* (x. 9), *πέπωκαν* (xviii. 3), *ἔβαλαν* (xviii. 19), *γέγοναν* (xxi. 6), and some of these are so well supported that they claim a place in the text. But there are comparatively few lexical eccentricities, and if we are reminded by an occasional transliteration that the author was a Jew by birth and education, it is clear that he had lived long enough in the Greek cities of Asia to have ready to his hand all the Greek words that he needed for the purpose of his book. The Greek vocabulary of the Apocalypse does not suggest that the writer was crippled by a want of appropriate words. His store is ample for his needs, and it seems to have been chosen with care.

3. When we pass from vocabulary to grammar, the case is different. Dionysius, as we have seen, with the acumen of an Alexandrian scholar, was struck by the many departures from the rules of syntax which mark the Apocalypse, and charges its author with writing incorrect Greek and even occasional solecisms. His criticism is courageous, but not unjust. Fortunately no systematic attempt was made in Egypt or elsewhere to bring the book up to the standard of literary orthodoxy, and in the best MSS. it has come down to us with many at least of the writer's grammatical peculiarities untouched.

Nothing like a grammar of the Apocalypse[1] can be attempted here, but some of the more striking features of its peculiar style are collected below.

(1) The 'solecisms' of the book consist largely of various forms of *anacoluthon*, shewing a singular indifference to the laws of concord. They may be roughly classed as follows. (*a*) Nominatives are placed in apposition to other cases: i. 5 ἀπὸ Ἰησοῦ Χριστοῦ, ὁ μάρτυς ὁ πιστός. ii. 20 τὴν γυναῖκα Ἰεζάβελ, ἡ λέγουσα ἑαυτὴν προφῆτιν. iii. 12 τῆς καινῆς Ἰερουσαλήμ, ἡ καταβαίνουσα ἐκ τοῦ οὐρανοῦ. viii. 9 ἀπέθανεν τὸ τρίτον τῶν κτισμάτων τῶν ἐν τῇ θαλάσσῃ, τὰ ἔχοντα ψυχάς. Other examples may be found in xiv. 12, xvi. 14, xx. 2, xxi. 11. (*b*) The participle λέγων—occasionally ἔχων—follows irregularly after the announcement of a fresh voice or *persona dramatis*: iv. 1 ἡ φωνὴ...ὡς σάλπιγγος...λέγων. ix. 13 ἤκουσα φωνὴν μίαν...λέγοντα. xi. 15 ἐγένοντο φωναὶ μεγάλαι...λέγοντες. xiv. 6 εἶδον ἄλλον ἄγγελον πετόμενον...ἔχοντα...λέγων. *Ib.* 14 εἶδον καὶ ἰδοὺ νεφέλη λευκή, καὶ ἐπὶ τὴν νεφέλην καθήμενον...ἔχων. (*c*) The construction is broken by a parenthetic clause, after which the sentence may or may not return to its original course: i. 5 f. τῷ ἀγαπῶντι ἡμᾶς καὶ λύσαντι.. καὶ ἐποίησεν...αὐτῷ ἡ δόξα. x. 1 f. εἶδον ἄλλον ἄγγελον ἰσχυρὸν καταβαίνοντα...καὶ τὸ πρόσωπον αὐτοῦ ὡς ὁ ἥλιος καὶ οἱ πόδες αὐτοῦ ὡς στύλοι πυρός, καὶ ἔχων... (*d*) The grammar is disturbed by the otiose addition of a personal pronoun or an adverb

[1] The subject has been treated more or less fully by Vögel (*Comm.*, p. 5 ff.), Winer (*Exeg. Studien*, i. p. 144 ff.), Ewald (prol. to Comm. § 6), Hitzig (*Über Johannes Marcus*, p. 65 ff.), Lücke, *Versuch einer vollständigen Einleitung*, i. p. 448 ff., Bousset (intr. to Comm. p. 183 ff.), and in England by S. Davidson (*Intr. to N. T.* iii. p. 552 ff.), Archd. Lee (intr. to Comm. p. 454 ff.). A *Johannine Grammar* has been recently published by Dr E. A. Abbott as a sequel to his *Johannine Vocabulary* (1905), but it deals with the Gospel only. A thorough monograph on the grammar of the Apocalypse is still to be desired.

of place after a relative or participial clause: ii. 7 τῷ νικῶντι (or, as in *v.* 26, ὁ νικῶν) δώσω αὐτῷ...iii. 12 ὁ νικῶν, ποιήσω αὐτόν...vi. 4 τῷ καθημένῳ...ἐδόθη αὐτῷ λαβεῖν τὴν εἰρήνην ἐκ τῆς γῆς...καὶ ἐδόθη αὐτῷ μάχαιρα. xii. 6 ὅπου ἔχει ἐκεῖ. xiii. 8 οὗ οὐ γέγραπται τὸ ὄνομα αὐτοῦ. (*e*) Genders, numbers, or cases are at fault: vii. 9 εἶδον, καὶ ἰδοὺ ὄχλος πολὺς...ἑστῶτες...περιβεβλημένους. viii. 9 τὸ τρίτον τῶν πλοίων διεφθάρησαν. xi. 4 οὗτοί εἰσιν αἱ δύο ἐλαῖαι καὶ αἱ δύο λυχνίαι αἱ...ἑστῶτες. xii. 5 ἔτεκεν υἱόν, ἄρσεν. xiv. 19 τὴν ληνὸν τοῦ θυμοῦ τοῦ θεοῦ τὸν μέγαν. xvii. 3 θηρίον...γέμοντα...ἔχον[τα]. xxi. 14 τὸ τεῖχος...ἔχων.

(2) Besides 'solecisms' the Apocalypse has, to borrow another term from Dionysius, a large number of 'idiotisms.' The idiosyncrasy of the writer shews itself sometimes in a startling phrase such as i. 4 ἀπὸ ὁ ὢν καὶ ὁ ἦν καὶ ὁ ἐρχόμενος, or i. 8 ἐγώ εἰμι τὸ ἄλφα καὶ τὸ ὦ, or ix. 12 and xi. 14 ἡ οὐαὶ ἡ μία, ἡ δευτέρα, ἡ τρίτη; sometimes in grammatical peculiarities, some of which frequently recur, such as the following: (*a*) Different tenses and moods are joined by a copula without any clear reason for the change: ii. 2 f. ἐπείρασας... ἔχεις...ἐβάστασας...κεκοπίακες. iii. 3 εἴληφας καὶ ἤκουσας. *Ib.* 9 ποιήσω αὐτοὺς ἵνα ἥξουσιν καὶ προσκυνήσουσιν...καὶ γνῶσιν. v. 7 f. ἦλθεν καὶ εἴληφεν...καὶ ὅτε ἔλαβεν. vii. 13 f. ἀπεκρίθη...καὶ εἴρηκα...καὶ εἶπεν. viii. 5 εἴληφεν...καὶ ἐγέμισεν...καὶ ἔβαλεν. ix. 5 ἐδόθη αὐτοῖς ἵνα μὴ ἀποκτείνωσιν αὐτούς, ἀλλ' ἵνα βασανισθήσονται. xxi. 24 ff. περιπατήσουσιν...φέρουσιν...οὐ μὴ κλεισθῶσιν...οἴσουσιν...οὐ μὴ εἰσέλθῃ. (*b*) Adjectives and verbs are made to govern cases other than those required by usage; i. 13, xiv. 14 ὅμοιον υἱὸν ἀνθρώπου. ii. 14 ἐδίδασκεν τῷ Βαλάκ. viii. 13 οὐαὶ τοὺς κατοικοῦντας ἐπὶ τῆς γῆς. xii. 12 οὐαὶ τὴν γῆν καὶ τὴν θάλασσαν. xix. 5 αἰνεῖτε τῷ θεῷ ἡμῶν. (*c*) Other unusual constructions abound, such as: iv. 9 f. ὅταν δώσουσιν...πεσοῦνται. viii. 4 ἀνέβη ὁ καπνὸς...ταῖς προσευχαῖς. ix. 4 ἐρρέθη αὐταῖς ἵνα μὴ ἀδικήσουσιν. xi. 3 δώσω...καὶ προφητεύσουσιν. *Ib.* 5 εἴ τις θελήσῃ. xii. 7 ἐγένετο πόλεμος...ὁ Μιχαὴλ καὶ οἱ ἄγγελοι αὐτοῦ τοῦ πολεμῆσαι. xviii. 20 ἔκρινεν ὁ θεὸς τὸ κρίμα ὑμῶν ἐξ αὐτῆς. xxii. 14 μακάριος...ἵνα ἔσται...καὶ...εἰσέλθωσιν.

Many attempts have been made to minimize the grammatical irregularities of the Apocalypse. In the most recent of these, a chapter of Archbishop Benson's *Apocalypse* which bears the characteristic heading "A Grammar of Ungrammar[1]," the instances are classified with the view of shewing that in most of them the Apocalyptist had a definite reason for his departure from usage. Whatever may be thought of the explanations which are offered in his defence, it is evident that he has not erred in all cases through ignorance[2], and it is possible that he has not done so

[1] Essay v. p. 131 ff.

[2] E.g. if he has twice permitted himself to write ὅμοιον υἱόν, in eighteen other passages ὅμοιος governs the dative.

in any instance. His eccentricities of syntax are probably due to more than one cause: some to the habit which he may have retained from early years of thinking in a Semitic language[1]; some to the desire of giving movement and vivid reality to his visions, which leads him to report them after the manner of shorthand notes, jotted down at the time; some to the circumstances in which the book was written. But from whatever cause or concurrence of causes, it cannot be denied that the Apocalypse of John stands alone among Greek literary writings in its disregard of the ordinary rules of syntax, and the success with which syntax is set aside without loss of perspicuity or even of literary power. The book seems openly and deliberately to defy the grammarian, and yet, even as literature, it is in its own field unsurpassed. No judge who compared it with any other Greek apocalyptic work would hesitate to give the palm to the canonical Apocalypse.

4. Apart from solecisms and other idiosyncrasies, the style of the Apocalypse is distinguished by a number of characteristic phrases and turns of expression which give it individuality.

Some of these recur with slight variations throughout the book. Thus i. 2 ἐμαρτύρησεν τὸν λόγον τοῦ θεοῦ καὶ τὴν μαρτυρίαν Ἰησοῦ Χριστοῦ starts a note which is heard again *ib.* 9 διὰ τὸν λόγον τοῦ θεοῦ καὶ τὴν μαρτυρίαν Ἰησοῦ, vi. 9 διὰ τὸν λόγον τοῦ θεοῦ καὶ διὰ τὴν μαρτυρίαν ἣν εἶχον, xx. 4 διὰ τὴν μαρτυρίαν Ἰησοῦ καὶ διὰ τὸν λόγον τοῦ θεοῦ. The reader meets again and again the phrase οἱ κατοικοῦντες ἐπὶ τὴν γῆν, or ἐπὶ τῆς γῆς, or τὴν γῆν (iii. 10, vi. 10, viii. 13,

[1] The present writer, while welcoming all the light that can be thrown on the vocabulary and syntax of the N.T. by a study of the Graeco-Egyptian papyri, and in particular the researches of Professor Deissmann, Professor Thumb, and Dr J. H. Moulton, deprecates the induction which, as it seems to him, is being somewhat hastily based upon them, that the Greek of the N.T. has been but slightly influenced by the familiarity of the writers with Hebrew and Aramaic. "Even the Greek of the Apocalypse," Dr Moulton writes (*Grammar of N.T. Greek*, prolegg. p. 8f.), "does not seem to owe any of its blunders to 'Hebraisms'...Apart from places where he [the author] may be definitely translating a Semitic document, there is no reason to believe that his grammar would have been materially different had he been a native of Oxyrhynchus, assuming the extent of Greek education the same." But the facts seem at present insufficient to warrant this conclusion. It is precarious to compare a literary document with a collection of personal and business letters, accounts, and other ephemeral writings; slips in word-formation or in syntax which are to be expected in the latter, are phenomenal in the former, and if they find a place there, can only be attributed to lifelong habits of thought. Moreover, it remains to be considered how far the quasi-Semitic colloquialisms of the papyri are themselves due to the influence of the large Greek-speaking Jewish population of the Delta.

xi. 10, xiii. 8, 12, 14, xvii. 2, 8), the combination πιστὸς καὶ ἀληθινός (iii. 14, xix. 11, xxi. 5, xxii. 6), the refrain ὁ ἔχων οὖς ἀκουσάτω (ii. 7, 11, 17, 29, iii. 6, 13, 22, and with a slight difference, xiii. 9). Μετὰ ταῦτα εἶδον, καὶ ἰδού, ὁ καθήμενος ἐπὶ τὸν θρόνον (τοῦ θρόνου, τῷ θρόνῳ) are other examples. Further, the writer has a habit of repeating the article or a governing clause before every member of a series when the same subject or class of subjects is in view, e.g. ix. 20 τὰ εἴδωλα τὰ χρυσᾶ καὶ τὰ ἀργυρᾶ καὶ τὰ χαλκᾶ καὶ τὰ λίθινα καὶ τὰ ξύλινα. xv. 2 τοὺς νικῶντας ἐκ τοῦ θηρίου καὶ ἐκ τῆς εἰκόνος αὐτοῦ καὶ ἐκ τοῦ ἀριθμοῦ τοῦ ὀνόματος αὐτοῦ. xvi. 13 ἐκ τοῦ στόματος τοῦ δράκοντος καὶ ἐκ τοῦ στόματος τοῦ θηρίου καὶ ἐκ τοῦ στόματος τοῦ ψευδοπροφήτου. xvii. 6 μεθύουσαν ἐκ τοῦ αἵματος τῶν ἁγίων καὶ ἐκ τοῦ αἵματος τῶν μαρτύρων Ἰησοῦ. There are many minor singularities, such as the frequent use of the instrumental dative preceded by ἐν, e.g. ἐν ῥομφαίᾳ (ii. 16), ἐν ῥάβδῳ (ii. 27, xii. 5, xix. 15), ἐν φωνῇ (v. 2, xiv. 7), ἐν ταῖς κιθάραις (xiv. 2), ἐν πυρί (xvi. 8, xvii. 16); the nearly constant omission of the article before proper names, not excluding Ἰησοῦς; the employment of εἷς as almost equivalent to an indefinite article (viii. 13 ἑνὸς ἀετοῦ, xviii. 21 εἷς ἄγγελος); the peculiar use of ὧδε in such clauses as xiii. 10, 18 (xiv. 12) ὧδέ ἐστιν ἡ ὑπομονή, ὧδε ἡ σοφία ἐστιν, xvii. 9 ὧδε ὁ νοῦς ὁ ἔχων σοφίαν; the recurrence of the formula ἐδόθη αὐτῷ (αὐτοῖς) followed by a noun, an infinitive, or a subjunctive with ἵνα; the partiality shewn for the perfect tense, especially in the case of εἴληφα (ii. 27, iii. 3, v. 7, viii. 5, xi. 17) and εἴρηκα (vii. 14, xix. 3); the many beatitudes interspersed among the visions (i. 3, xiv. 13, xvi. 15, xix. 9, xx. 6, xxii. 7, 14). Lastly, a considerable number of ordinary words occur with remarkable frequency, catching the eye again and again as the book is turned; a few may be specified here: ἄγγελος, ἅγιος, αἷμα, ἀκούειν, ἀμήν, ἀνοίγειν, ἀποθνήσκειν, ἀστήρ (never ἄστρον), βάλλειν, βασιλεύς, βιβλίον, βλέπειν, βροντή, γῆ, γράφειν, δεικνύειν, δόξα, δύναμις, ἔθνος, ἐκκλησία, ἐνώπιον, ἐξουσία, ἔργον, ἑτοιμάζειν, εὐφραίνεσθαι, ζωή, ἥλιος, θάλασσα, θάνατος, θρόνος, θυσιαστήριον, ἰδεῖν, ἰδού, καθῆσθαι, καταβαίνειν, κεφαλή, κράζειν, κρίνειν, λαμβάνειν, λευκός, λόγος, μέγας, ναός, νεκρός, νικᾶν, οἰκουμένη, ὅμοιος, ὄνομα, οὐρανός, ὀφθαλμός, παντοκράτωρ, πέμπειν, περιβάλλεσθαι, πίπτειν, πλανᾶν, πληγή, πόλις, προσκυνεῖν, πρόσωπον, προφήτης and its cognates, πῦρ, ῥομφαία, σημεῖον, στέφανος, στόμα, σφάζειν, σφραγίς, τελεῖσθαι, ὕδωρ, ὑπομονή, φοβεῖσθαι, φωνή, χείρ, χρύσεος, ᾠδή. This list will be found a suggestive one; in most cases the subject of the book or the circumstances of the author sufficiently account for the more or less frequent recurrence of the words; in some the reason lies deeper. But however their repetition may be explained, it goes far to impart to the Apocalypse the colouring which marks its style.

5. It is of interest to compare the vocabulary, grammar, and style of the Apocalypse with those of other New Testament writings traditionally assigned to St John, and especially with those

of the Fourth Gospel. (1) Vocabulary. Of the 913 words used in the Apocalypse 416 are found also in the Gospel, but the words common to both books are either of the most ordinary type, or are shared by other N.T. writers. The eight words *ἀρνίον*, *Ἑβραϊστί*, *ἐκκεντεῖν*, *κυκλεύειν*, *ὄψις*, *πορφύρεος*, *σκηνοῦν*, *φοῖνιξ*, which occur only in these two books, do not supply a sufficient basis for induction. *Ἀρνίον*, used 29 times in the Apocalypse, is used but once in the Gospel, and then with a different reference; the form *κυκλεύειν* in Jo. x. 24 and Apoc. xx. 9 is found in the Gospel only in Cod. B; *ὄψις*, *πορφύρεος*, and *φοῖνιξ* are fairly well established in the Greek of the O.T.; on the other hand, *Ἑβραϊστί* is somewhat markedly Johannine, occurring five times in the Gospel, which uses also *Ῥωμαϊστί* and *Ἑλληνιστί*; *σκηνοῦν* is strongly characteristic of the teaching of the fourth Gospel, though it occurs there but once[1], and the use of *ἐξεκέντησαν* for דָּקָרוּ in Zech. xii. 10, both in Jo. xix. 37 and Apoc. i. 7, is certainly noteworthy and probably more than a coincidence[2]. If we extend our examination to words which, though not exclusively used in these books, are prominent in them or in one of them, the evidence is similarly divided. On the one hand there are not a few points in which the diction of the Apocalypse differs notably from that of the Gospel: the conjunctions *ἀλλά*, *γάρ*, *οὖν*, which continually meet the reader of the Gospel, are comparatively rare in the Apocalypse[3]; *ἐνώπιον*, a characteristic preposition in the Apocalypse, occurs but once in the Gospel; the Evangelist invariably writes *Ἰεροσόλυμα*, the Apocalyptist *Ἰερουσαλήμ*[4]; the one chooses *ἀμνός* when he is speaking of the Lamb of God, the other *ἀρνίον*; to the one the Eternal Son is simply *ὁ λόγος*, to the other the glorified Christ is *ὁ λόγος τοῦ θεοῦ*. The

[1] St Paul has *ἐπισκηνοῦν* in a similar sense (2 Cor. xii. 9).

[2] See p. cl.

[3] *Ἀλλά* occurs 101 times in J^{ev}, 13 times in Apoc.; *γάρ* 65 times in J^{ev}, 16 in Apoc. *Οὖν* which is the favourite mark of transition in the Gospel is used but 6 times in the Apocalypse, and only in *cc.* i.—iii. But *οὖν* is wholly absent from the first Epistle of St John, and *γάρ* occurs there but thrice (Westcott, *Epistles of St John*, p. xl.).

[4] The exclusively local use of the name in the Gospel does not altogether account for this difference. *Ἰερουσαλήμ* is used freely in speaking of the locality by St Luke and St Paul; with Mt., Mc., J^{ev}, on the other hand, the use of *Ἰεροσόλυμα* is habitual, though Mt. once writes *Ἰερουσαλήμ* (xxiii. 37).

Apocalyptist uses the Synoptic and Pauline terms *εὐαγγέλιον*, *εὐαγγελίζειν*, *κηρύσσειν*, *κληρονομεῖν*, *μετανοεῖν*, *μυστήριον*, *ἡ οἰκουμένη*, *συνκοινωνεῖν*, from which the Evangelist seems to refrain; while on the other hand, as Dionysius long ago pointed out, of many of the key-words of the Gospel he shews no knowledge. On the other hand the two books have in common a fair number of characteristic words and phrases, such as *ἀληθινός*, *ἐξουσία*, *μαρτυρεῖν*, *νικᾷν*, *ὁδηγεῖν*, *οἶδα*, *σημαίνειν*, *τηρεῖν* (*λόγον*, *ἐντολήν*), *ὑπάγειν*. It is still more significant, that both attach a special meaning to certain words; both use Ἰουδαῖος of the Jew considered as hostile to Christ or the Church, and in both such words as *ζωή*, *θάνατος*, *διψᾷν*, *πεινᾷν*, *νύμφη*, *δόξα*, bear more or less exclusively a spiritual sense—a remark which applies also to several of the words mentioned above (e.g. *νικᾷν*, *ὁδηγεῖν*).

(2) Thus on the question of the literary affinity of the Fourth Gospel and the Apocalypse the vocabulary speaks with an uncertain sound, though the balance of the evidence is perhaps in favour of some such relationship between the two writings. This probability is increased when we compare them from the point of view of their grammatical tendencies. While the solecistic anacolutha of the Apocalypse have no parallel on any large scale in the Gospel, there is a considerable number of unusual constructions which are common to the two books. Some may be mentioned here. (*a*) The partitive *ἐκ* with its dependent noun or pronoun is used in both as the object or subject of a verb: e.g. Jo. xvi. 17 *εἶπαν οὖν ἐκ τῶν μαθητῶν αὐτοῦ*; Apoc. ii. 10 *μέλλει βαλεῖν ἐξ ὑμῶν*, iii. 9 *διδῶ ἐκ τῆς συναγωγῆς*, xi. 9 *βλέπουσιν ἐκ τῶν λαῶν*. (*b*) Both books place *μετά* after *λαλεῖν* (Jo. iv. 27 *bis*, ix. 37; Apoc. i. 12, iv. 1, x. 8, xvii. 1, xxi. 9, 15), and *περιπατεῖν* (Jo. vi. 66; Apoc. iii. 4), and *ἐκ* after *σῴζειν* or *τηρεῖν* (Jo. xii. 27 *σῶσόν με ἐκ τῆς ὥρας ταύτης*, Apoc. iii. 10 *σε τηρήσω ἐκ τῆς ὥρας τοῦ πειρασμοῦ*). (*c*) Both use *ἵνα* in an unusual sense (Jo. viii. 56 *ἠγαλλιάσατο ἵνα ἴδῃ*, ix. 2 *τίς ἥμαρτεν ...ἵνα τυφλὸς γεννηθῇ*; xi. 15 *χαίρω...ἵνα πιστεύσητε*: Apoc. xiv. 13, xxii. 14).

(3) Coming to the style of the books, a comparison will lead to results very similar to those which were obtained by examining their vocabularies. The general effect of the style of the Gospel is as far as possible from the effect which the Apocalypse produces on the mind of the reader: "it is free from solecisms, because it avoids all idiomatic expressions[1]." The book flows along smoothly from the prologue to the end; there is no startling phrase, no defiance of syntax; if it is obviously the work of one who was more familiar with the construction of the Semitic than of the Greek sentence[2], yet the author seldom or never offends against definite laws. In these respects he not only differs from the Apocalyptist, but stands at the opposite pole to the eccentricities, the roughnesses, the audacities, of the latter. Yet it is also true that he has many points of resemblance with the writer of the Apocalypse, both in regard to sentence-formation and to the phrasing of his thoughts. As to the former, the following points have been noticed amongst others. (i) Both the Evangelist and the Apocalyptist fall in places into parallelisms; cf. Jo. i. 4 f. *ὃ γέγονεν ἐν αὐτῷ ζωὴ ἦν,* | *καὶ ἡ ζωὴ ἦν τὸ φῶς τῶν ἀνθρώπων·* ‖ *καὶ τὸ φῶς ἐν τῇ σκοτίᾳ φαίνει,* | *καὶ ἡ σκοτία αὐτὸ οὐ κατέλαβεν.* Apoc. xxi. 23 *ἡ πόλις οὐ χρείαν ἔχει τοῦ ἡλίου* | *οὐδὲ τῆς σελήνης, ἵνα φαίνωσιν αὐτῇ·* ‖ *ἡ γὰρ δόξα τοῦ θεοῦ ἐφώτισεν αὐτήν,* | *καὶ ὁ λύχνος αὐτῆς τὸ ἀρνίον.* (ii) Both are partial to the form of antithesis which presents first the positive and then the negative side of a statement or direction; e.g. Jo. i. 3 *πάντα δι' αὐτοῦ ἐγένετο, καὶ χωρὶς αὐτοῦ ἐγένετο οὐδὲ ἕν.* x. 12 f. *ὁ μισθωτὸς καὶ οὐκ ὢν ποιμήν...μισθωτός ἐστιν καὶ οὐ μέλει αὐτῷ περὶ τῶν προβάτων.* Apoc. iii. 3 *ἥξω ὡς κλέπτης, καὶ οὐ μὴ γνῷς ποίαν ὥραν ἥξω*; *ib.* 16 *χλιαρὸς εἶ, καὶ οὔτε ζεστὸς οὔτε ψυχρός.* x. 4 *σφράγισον ἃ ἐλάλησαν αἱ ἑπτὰ βρονταί, καὶ μὴ αὐτὰ γράψῃς.* (iii) Both repeat the article for the sake of emphasis: Jo. i. 9 *τὸ φῶς τὸ ἀληθινόν*, vi. 32 *τὸν ἄρτον...τὸν ἀληθινόν*, xv. 1 *ἡ ἄμπελος ἡ ἀληθινή*, x. 11 *ὁ ποιμὴν ὁ καλός*; Apoc. i. 5 *ὁ μάρτυς ὁ πιστός*, ii. 11 *τοῦ θανάτου τοῦ δευτέρου*,

[1] Westcott, *St John*, p. l.

[2] Cf. Sanday, *Authorship and Historical Character of the Fourth Gospel*, p. 28 f.

ib. 12 τὴν ῥομφαίαν τὴν δίστομον τὴν ὀξεῖαν, xviii. 10 ἡ πόλις ἡ μεγάλη...ἡ ἰσχυρά, xxi. 10 τὴν πόλιν τὴν ἁγίαν. (iv) Both add parenthetic explanations for the sake of circumstantial fulness: cf. Jo. vi. 22 f., xi. 1 ff., xviii. 13 f.; Apoc. xii. 9 (xix. 2), xiv. 11 (xix. 20), xx. 14 (xxi. 8). (v) Similar or identical phrases occur in both, e.g. ποιεῖν ἀλήθειαν (Jo. iii. 21), ποιεῖν ψεῦδος (Apoc. xxii. 15); ποιεῖν σημεῖον (Jo. ii. 11, 23, iv. 54, etc., Apoc. xiii. 13 f., xix. 20); μέρος ἔχειν (Jo. xiii. 8, Apoc. xx. 6); ὄνομα αὐτῷ (Jo. i. 6, iii. 1, xviii. 10, Apoc. vi. 8, ix. 11). Even more remarkable are the following coincidences of language: Jo. i. 14 ὁ λόγος ... ἐσκήνωσεν ἐν ἡμῖν, Apoc. vii. 15 ὁ καθήμενος ἐπὶ τὸν θρόνον σκηνώσει ἐπ' αὐτούς; Jo. iv. 6 κεκοπιακὼς ἐκ τῆς ὁδοιπορίας, Apoc. ii. 3 οὐ κεκοπίακες; Jo. vii. 37 ἐάν τις διψᾷ ἐρχέσθω πρός μὲ καὶ πινέτω, Apoc. xxii. 17 ὁ διψῶν ἐρχέσθω; Jo. x. 18 ταύτην τὴν ἐντολὴν ἔλαβον παρὰ τοῦ πατρός μου, Apoc. ii. 28 ὡς κἀγὼ εἴληφα παρὰ τοῦ πατρός μου; Jo. xvi. 12 οὐ δύνασθε βαστάζειν, Apoc. ii. 2 οὐ δύνῃ βαστάσαι; Jo. xx. 12, Apoc. iii. 4 ἐν λευκοῖς. The bearing of this evidence on the question of authorship will be discussed in a later chapter[1]; meanwhile we may observe that it creates a strong presumption of affinity between the Fourth Gospel and the Apocalypse, notwithstanding their great diversity both in language and in thought.

[1] c. xv.

XII.

SYMBOLISM.

1. The Apocalypse of John shares with other apocalyptic writings a partiality for symbolical imagery and the symbolical use of numbers. Teaching by the use of symbols is found in every part of the Old Testament, but it becomes especially noticeable in the later prophecies, and in the book of Daniel. The visions of which these books largely consist present a succession of strange and sometimes weird or even monstrous shapes, designed to suggest ideas that could not be expressed in words, or persons or forces that the writer preferred to leave unnamed. This habit was adopted by the non-canonical apocalyptists, from Enoch onwards, and it receives illustration in every page of St John's book.

2. The imagery of the Apocalypse lays under contribution all the departments of nature and life. The animal kingdom lends its *ζῷα* and its *θηρία*—horses white, red, black and pale, the lamb and the calf, the lion, the leopard and the bear, the locust, the scorpion and the frog, the eagle and the vulture, the birds of the air and the fishes of the sea; the vegetable kingdom, its trees and herbs and grass. Earth, sea, and sky bring their tribute. Agricultural operations such as harvest and vintage, the life and trade of great cities, the march and clash of great armies, are all depicted on its canvas. A sea of glass is spread before the Throne in Heaven: a river flows through the Holy City. The sky yields its stars, now shining in the firmament, now falling to the earth, now forming a cluster in the hand of the Christ, or

a coronet on the head of the Mother of Christ and Christendom. Across the heavens there sweeps from time to time a more than tropical storm of thunder, lightning, and hail, followed by earthquake. Human life supplies an abundance of imagery. We see the mother and her child, the harlot and her lovers, the bride arrayed for her husband. Crowned heads wear the *στέφανος* or the *διάδημα*; warriors carry the two-edged sword; the shepherd appears with his iron-tipped staff, the reaper with his sickle, the herald with his trumpet, the builder with his measuring rod, the holiday-keeper with flute and harp, the reveller with golden cup, the king with his roll, written within and on the back with the secrets of State and sealed. Figures move across the stage attired in the long girdled robe of kingly or priestly dignity, or in the shining white of *byssus*; two are dressed in sackcloth; one wears purple and scarlet, and is decked with gold and precious stones and pearls.

3. (*a*) A large proportion of this imagery is drawn, as a previous section will have shewn, from the Old Testament. Places, persons, and objects which occur in the historical books reappear in the Apocalypse as symbols of facts in the life of the Church or of the new world to which the Church points and which lies behind the visible order. Familiar place-names meet us here and there—the Euphrates, Egypt, Sodom, the Hill of Megiddo, Babylon, Jerusalem. The seven-branched candlestick of the Tabernacle suggests the golden *λυχνίαι* which represent the Churches of Asia; Balaam finds his analogue in the Nicolaitans, and Jezebel in a Thyatiran prophetess. The new Israel is confronted by a new Babylon, and the Bride of Christ is a new Jerusalem. The Elders round the Throne answer to the elders of Israel; the Two Witnesses exercise powers which remind the reader of the miracles of Moses and Elijah. Tabernacle and Temple, altar and censer and ark, recall the religious glories of ancient Israel. A holy place not made with hands is seen in the heavenly places; the manna laid up before God finds its counterpart in the future life of the victorious Christian. (*b*) In other instances the N.T. Apocalypse adopts in part or in whole the

symbolism of the O.T. writers, as when it speaks of the Tree of Life, the Book of Life, the Water of Life; or the metaphors of the O.T. become the symbols of the new prophecy, as when our Lord is designated the Lamb and the Lion of the Tribe of Judah, or the Root of David; or again, a whole system of O.T. symbolism is more or less fully pressed into the service of the book, as in the case of the High Priest's breastplate, and of Ezekiel's scheme of a restored Jerusalem.

4. The Apocalyptist, however, does not limit himself to O.T. imagery, but has much that is his own, or that belongs to the common stock of the later apocalyptic. The Woman with Child has no parallel in the O.T., and in spite of Gunkel's efforts to find the genesis of this fine conception in Babylonian folklore, it may be confidently regarded as essentially a creation of the writer's own mind, under the influence of the Spirit of Christ. The description of the Harlot Babylon, seated on the scarlet Beast, has points of contact with passages in the Hebrew Prophets; but as a whole it is new and original. A like verdict may be passed upon the three great sevenfold visions, the Seal Openings, the Trumpet Blasts, and the Outpouring of the Bowls; their partial indebtedness to the Old Testament does not take from the freshness and vigour of St John's symbolism. The idea of a millennium was in the air when St John wrote, but no writer had used it as the symbol of a spiritual triumph, or worked it into a scheme of the Divine ordering of history.

5. Much of the imagery of the Apocalypse is doubtless not symbolism, but merely designed to heighten the colouring of the great picture, and to add vividness and movement to its scenes. Such secondary details, like many of the minor features in the Parables of our Lord, must not be pressed into the service of a spiritual interpretation, or indeed of any specific interpretation whatever, their purpose being simply to contribute to the general effect of the context where they occur. These non-symbolical images are sometimes taken from the life of the times, as when the writer recounts the imports that found their way to the new Babylon, many of which he may himself have seen shipped off

to Ostia from the port of Ephesus; or they belong to the common stock of the eschatological language of apocalyptic writing (e.g. vi. 12 ff.); or they are due to the inspired imagination of the Apocalyptist himself, forming part of the picture which is present to his mind as he writes.

6. But there is also much which is directly symbolical. In not a few cases the writer stops to interpret the symbol (e.g. in *cc.* i. 20, iv. 5, v. 6, xii. 9, xvii. 9 f., 12, 15). In others the symbolical meaning is only half veiled; thus it is impossible to mistake the import of the standing Figure in i. 13 ff., or of the seated Figure in *c.* iv. 2, or of the Lamb, or the Lamb's Wife. There remain, however, a certain number of symbolic forms as to which there is room for diversity of judgement even among interpreters who follow the same general method of interpretation. Thus in *c.* vi. 2 the rider on the white horse is by some commentators identified with the Divine Rider of *c.* xix. 11, while others regard the former as symbolizing either the Roman or the Parthian conqueror. In *c.* vii. the 144,000 are by some understood to represent, like the countless multitude, the whole body of the Church, though under a different aspect or at another stage of its history, whereas others take the two visions to set forth respectively the Jewish and Gentile Christians, or the Jewish Church and the Christian Church. In *c.* xi. 8 interpreters are divided as to the meaning of "the great city"; in xvii. 12 there is considerable difference of opinion as to the identity of the "ten kings." Many other such ambiguities perplex the student of the Apocalypse, and though he may be able to arrive at conclusions with regard to them which satisfy his own judgement, it is impossible to offer such convincing reasons for them as will compel assent. But the uncertainty which thus besets apocalyptic interpretation does not seriously detract from the general value of the book. Nor can it be laid to the charge of the author that he is unnecessarily obscure. It is of the nature of apocalyptic literature to be involved in some measure of obscurity; and this is not the least valuable of its characteristics, for it affords scope for the exercise of the Christian judgement:

ὧδε ἡ σοφία ἐστίν· ὧδε ὁ νοῦς ὁ ἔχων σοφίαν (xiii. 18, xvii. 9). In the elasticity of symbolical language the Apocalypse has its chief advantage over the more exact and didactic, but less inspiring and suggestive style of ordinary prophecy.

7. No reader of our Apocalypse can have failed to notice the frequent recurrence of numbers which appear to carry with them a certain symbolical meaning[1].

The following are the numbers that are met with in the book: 2, 3, 3½, 4, 5, 6, 7, 10, 12, 24, 42, 144, 666 (or according to another reading, 616), 1000, 1260, 1600, 7000, 12000, 144,000, 100,000,000, 200,000,000. The predominant number is *seven*, which occurs fifty-four times. The book is addressed to seven Churches represented by seven lampstands, while their 'angels' are seven stars. There are seven Spirits of God, symbolized by seven lamps. The Book in the Hand of God is sealed with seven seals; the Lamb before the Throne has seven eyes and seven horns. Seven angels blow seven trumpet-blasts; seven other angels pour out the contents of seven bowls full of the seven last plagues. Seven thunders utter voices which the Seer is bidden not to write. Seven thousand are killed in the great earthquake which follows the ascension of the Two Witnesses. The Dragon has seven heads, and upon them seven diadems; the Wild Beast from the Sea has seven heads on which are "names of blasphemy"; the Scarlet Beast on which Babylon sits has likewise seven heads, variously interpreted by the writer as seven mountains, or seven kings. Next in frequency to the heptad is the dodecad. The new Israel, like its predecessor, consists of twelve tribes; the Mother of Christ is crowned with twelve stars; the new Jerusalem has twelve portals, and the wall that girdles it rests on twelve foundation stones on which are engraved the names of the twelve Apostles; the Tree of Life in the new Paradise bears twelve manner of fruits, after the number of the months. Multiples of twelve, also, are common. Each of the tribes of the new Israel contains 12,000, making a total of 144,000; and 144,000 is also the number of the virgin souls which in the second part of the book are seen surrounding

[1] On the symbolism of numbers see Tyconius *reg.* v (ed. Burkitt).

the Lamb on Mount Zion. The Elders round the Throne are twenty-four, and they are seated on as many subordinate thrones. Each side of the Holy City is 12,000 stades in length, and the wall which surrounds it is 144 cubits in height.

Ten is another favourite number. The time of pressure which is coming on the Churches of Asia will last ten days. Both the Dragon and the first of the two Wild Beasts have ten horns; and so has the Scarlet Beast, whose horns are interpreted as "ten kings." As a multiple *ten* enters into most of the higher numbers in the book. *Four*, again, occurs frequently. The *ζῷα* are four; four angels stand at the four corners of the earth, charged with the control of the four winds of heaven; four angels are bound at the Euphrates, until the moment comes for the execution of their work of slaughter. The Holy City lies four-square, and forms a perfect cube. *Three* is somewhat less prominent, but the last three Trumpets constitute a triad of "Woes," and under the earlier Trumpets a third part of everything which has been attacked is smitten (viii. 7–12; cp. ix. 15, xii. 4). The "great city" is rent by an earthquake into three parts; each side of the square which forms the new Jerusalem is entered by three portals. There are other numbers which are used symbolically but once. The wings of the *ζῷα* are *six*; there are *five* months during which the world is tortured by the locusts of the Abyss; the Witnesses who are slain and rise again and ascend to heaven are *two*.

8. The recurrence of some of these numbers, notably of seven[1], twelve, ten and four, can scarcely be accidental. The writer's partiality for them is due in some measure to his Semitic habits of thought. To the Hebrew mind *seven* denotes completion, as we gather from countless passages of the Old Testament[2]. An apocalyptist would find a special attraction in a number which had already played a great part in Jewish apocalypses from Daniel onwards.

[1] Dr Abbott points out (*Grammar*, § 2624) that the Fourth Gospel is "permeated structurally with the idea" of sevenfoldness.

[2] The genesis of the idea is well stated by Philo *legg. alleg.* I. 4 χαίρει δὲ ἡ φύσις ἑβδομάδι· πλανῆτές τε γὰρ ἑπτὰ γεγόνασιν...καὶ ἄρκτος ἑπτὰ ἄστροις συμπληροῦται...καὶ τροπαὶ δὲ σελήνης ἑβδομάσι γίνονται.

It would fall in with this tendency of his own mind if, as has been thought, the most prominent of the Churches of Asia were as a matter of fact seven in number, so that as the phrase *αἱ ἑπτὰ ἐκκλησίαι αἱ ἐν τῇ Ἀσίᾳ* (i. 4) suggests, they were probably known as the Seven Churches in Asia even before they were so addressed by St John[1]. But in any case the selection of Seven Churches as the recipients of the Apocalypse strikes a keynote which rings through the earlier chapters, and determines the number of the lampstands, the Angel-stars, the Spirits of God, and the Eyes of the Lamb. In the second part of the book the seven heads of the Dragon and the Wild Beast are perhaps suggested by the seven hills of Rome and the seven Augusti who preceded Domitian. But though local circumstances chimed in with the traditional use of this number, its O.T. associations doubtless drew the writer to it, and it is used in conformity with O.T. practice. Each series of seven is complete in itself, and each suggests the perfection which belongs to the Divine, or that which is claimed by the Antichrist.

Of other numbers which appear to be symbolically used in the Apocalypse *three* and *four* occur in connexion with memorable incidents or contexts of the Old Testament (Gen. xviii. 2, Ex xxiii. 14, Deut. iv. 41, Dan. vi. 10; Gen. ii. 10, Ez. i. 5, Dan. vii. 2, viii. 8). *Three* seems to denote limited plurality; *four*, as the number of the winds and the quarters of the sky, is a fitting symbol for the visible creation. *Ten*, also, has a recognised meaning; as the round number, it is suggestive at once of indefiniteness and of magnitude; in a thousand both these features are magnified, and a thousand years thus represents a great period of time stretching over many generations, but of unknown length. The uncertainty which results from such a use of numbers would be fatal to the value of a historical document, but it is admirably adapted to the purpose of an apocalypse, where the veil is lifted only so far as to disclose the dim outline of great issues.

9. Two of the Apocalyptic numbers call for separate treatment. (*a*) Three and a half days are given as the interval

[1] So Ramsay, *Letters to the Seven Churches*, p. 178. But this is perhaps to build too much upon the article.

between the death and resurrection of the Two Witnesses (xi. 9, 11). This period corresponds with the "time, times and a half" of *c.* xii. 14, which is taken over from Dan. vii. 25, xii. 7. In Daniel this expression probably represents the three and a half years during which Jerusalem was in the hands of the Syrian oppressor, and the Apocalypse accordingly uses it or its equivalents (42 months, 1260 days) to signify the age of persecution, whatever its duration might be. Other explanations are less probable. Gunkel thinks of the $3\frac{1}{2}$ months which intervened between the winter solstice and the Babylonian festival of Marduk[1]. Others, again, identifying the time, times, and a half of Dan. vii. 25 with the half-week (חֲצִי הַשָּׁבוּעַ) of Dan. ix. 27, regard the Apocalyptic $3\frac{1}{2}$ in the light of a 'broken seven,' a symbol of the interruption of the Divine order by the malice of Satan and evil men.

(*b*) If the number 666 in Apoc. xiii. 18 is to be regarded as a symbol, there is verisimilitude in Dr Briggs' suggestion that a number which in every digit falls short by one of the completeness and perfection of the mystic seven, fitly represents the failure of Antichrist to reach the goal to which he aspires. But (1) this conception might have been conveyed with equal effect by 66, or 6666; (2) it leaves the alternative reading (616) wholly unexplained; and (3) from the time of Irenæus tradition has fixed on another and a more natural explanation. The number, whether we read χξϛ', or with some contemporaries of Irenaeus χιϛ', is probably a cryptogram, and not a true symbol. It is possible that the Number of the Beast holds its secret still. Although the challenge ὁ ἔχων νοῦν ψηφισάτω τὸν ἀριθμόν has been accepted by the scholars of many generations, no solution hitherto offered commands general assent.

10. In this chapter a Semitic origin has been claimed for the symbolism of the Apocalypse. The force of local circumstances is not, indeed, to be overlooked. In the words of Professor W. M. Ramsay[2], "such ideas and symbolic forms were in the atmosphere and in the minds of men at the time; and the ideas with which he [St John] was familiar moulded the imagery of

[1] *Schöpfung u. Chaos*, p. 309 ff.

[2] *Letters to the Seven Churches*, p. 59.

his visions, unconsciously to himself." But apart from influences of this kind, it must not be forgotten that it was necessary to provide the Church with a make-weight against the power which heathenism exerted over the Asian cities through its abundant use of symbolism in literature and in art. In art Christianity could as yet do nothing to counteract this hostile force. The Apostolic age was necessarily opposed to the Art of the time[1], which was pagan to the core; the Church of the first century had not either the power or the desire to emulate the splendours of the heathen temples. She could not erect statues to the Glorified Christ, or stamp His image and superscription on the currency, or institute public festivals in His honour. But if she might not avail herself as yet of the help of Art, there was abundant precedent in the Hebrew Scriptures for the literary representation of the unseen world. It was permissible to assist the faith of the suffering Churches by symbolical visions of the majesty of their Divine Lord, now walking in their midst, now standing before the celestial Throne, now riding forth to victory with the armies of Heaven under His command. It was not less permissible to paint in glowing colours the moral glory of the Christian Society, and her magnificent destiny, or to place in contrast with them the abominable vices, the paltry display, and the certain doom of Rome. Yet in this legitimate appeal to the Christian imagination the Apocalyptist is careful to avoid representations which could be placed before the eye by the painter's art. No scene in the great Christian Apocalypse can be successfully reproduced upon canvas; "the imagery...is symbolic and not pictorial[2]."

[1] Westcott, *Epp. of St John*, p. 339 (App. on the relation of Christianity to Art).

[2] Westcott, *op. cit.* p. 335.

XIII.

USE OF THE OLD TESTAMENT AND OTHER LITERATURE.

1. The Apocalyptist's use of the Old Testament is by no means limited to its symbolical imagery and numbers; its thoughts and its very words appear in every part of his book. It is true that the Apocalypse is marked by an entire absence of the formal quotations which are to be found in other parts of the New Testament[1]; the nature of the work precluded the author from a direct appeal to his source. Yet no writer of the Apostolic age makes larger use of his predecessors. From the list of "quotations from the Old Testament" with which the appendix to Westcott and Hort's second volume ends, it appears that of the 404 verses of the Apocalypse there are 278 which contain references to the Jewish Scriptures. The following table is not exhaustive, but it will suffice to shew the extent of St John's debt to the Old Testament, and his method of using it.

Apocalypse.	Greek versions of the Old Testament[2].
i. 1 (iv. 1, xxii. 6) ἃ δεῖ γενέσθαι.	Dan. ii. 28 ἃ δεῖ γενέσθαι.
i. 4 (i. 8, iv. 8, xi. 17, xvi. 5) ὁ ὤν.	Ex. iii. 14 ὁ ὤν.
i. 5ᵃ (ii. 13, iii. 14) ὁ μάρτυς ὁ πιστός.	Ps. lxxxviii. (lxxxix.) 38 ὁ μάρτυς ἐν οὐρανῷ πιστός.
i. 5ᵇ ὁ πρωτότοκος τῶν νεκρῶν καὶ ὁ ἄρχων τῶν βασιλέων τῆς γῆς.	Ps. lxxxviii. (lxxxix.) 28 κἀγὼ πρωτότοκον θήσομαι αὐτόν, ὑψηλὸν παρὰ τοῖς βασιλεῦσιν τῆς γῆς. (σ′ ἀνώτατον τῶν βασιλέων τῆς γῆς.)

[1] See *Introduction to the O. T. in Greek*, p. 381 ff.

[2] ο′ = LXX., α′ = Aquila, θ′ = Theodotion, σ′ = Symmachus, οἱ λ̥ = οἱ λοιποί. Where the version is not specified it is that of the LXX.

i. 5^{c} λύσαντι ἡμᾶς ἐκ τῶν ἁμαρτιῶν ἡμῶν. — Isa. xl. 2 λέλυται αὐτῆς ἡ ἁμαρτία.

i. 6 (v. 10, xx. 6) ἐποίησεν ἡμᾶς βασιλείαν, ἱερεῖς τῷ θεῷ. — Ex. xix. 6 ὑμεῖς δὲ ἔσεσθέ μοι βασίλειον ἱεράτευμα (מַמְלֶכֶת כֹּהֲנִים). Cf. Isa. lxi. 6 ὑμεῖς δὲ ἱερεῖς Κυρίου κληθήσεσθε.

i. 7^{a} ἔρχεται μετὰ τῶν νεφελῶν. — Dan. vii. 13 ἐπὶ (θ′ μετὰ) τῶν νεφελῶν...ἤρχετο (θ′ ἐρχόμενος).

i. 7^{b} ὄψεται αὐτὸν πᾶς ὀφθαλμὸς καὶ οἵτινες αὐτὸν ἐξεκέντησαν, καὶ κόψονται ἐπ᾿ αὐτὸν πᾶσαι αἱ φυλαὶ τῆς γῆς. — Zech. xii. 10 ff. ἐπιβλέψονται πρὸς μὲ ἀνθ᾿ ὧν κατωρχήσαντο (θ′ εἰς ὃν ἐξεκέντησαν), καὶ κόψονται ἐπ᾿ αὐτὸν...καὶ κόψεται ἡ γῆ κατὰ φυλὰς φυλάς...πᾶσαι αἱ ὑπολελιμμέναι φυλαί.

i. 8 ὁ παντοκράτωρ. — Am. iv. 13 ὁ παντοκράτωρ.

i. 13 (xiv. 14) ὅμοιον υἱὸν ἀνθρώπου. — Dan. vii. 13 ὡς υἱὸς ἀνθρώπου. Cf. Dan. x. 16 θ′ ὡς ὁμοίωσις υἱοῦ ἀνθρώπου. Ez. i. 26 ὁμοίωμα ὡς εἶδος ἀνθρώπου: viii. 2 ὁμοίωμα ἀνδρός.

i. 13^{b} ἐνδεδυμένον ποδήρη καὶ περιεζωσμένον πρὸς τοῖς μαστοῖς ζωνὴν χρυσᾶν. — Ez. ix. 11 ὁ ἐνδεδυκὼς τὸν ποδήρη καὶ ἐζωσμένος τῇ ζώνῃ τὴν ὀσφὺν αὐτοῦ. Cf. Dan. x. 5 ἐνδεδυμένος βύσσινα καὶ τὴν ὀσφὺν περιεζωσμένος βυσσίνῳ.

i. 14 αἱ τρίχες λευκαὶ ὡς ἔριον λευκόν, ὡς χιών[1], καὶ οἱ ὀφθαλμοὶ αὐτοῦ ὡς φλὸξ πυρός (cf. ii. 18, xix. 12). — Dan. vii. 9 τὸ τρίχωμα τῆς κεφαλῆς αὐτοῦ ὡσεὶ ἔριον λευκὸν καθαρόν (θ′ ἡ θρὶξ τ. κ. α. ὡσεὶ ἔριον καθαρόν)[1]: x. 6 οἱ ὀφθαλμοὶ αὐτοῦ ὡσεὶ λαμπάδες πυρός.

i. 15 (xiv. 2, xix. 6) ἡ φωνὴ αὐτοῦ ὡς φωνὴ ὑδάτων πολλῶν. — Ez. i. 24 ὡς φωνὴν ὕδατος πολλοῦ: xliii. 2 ὡς φωνὴ διπλασιαζόντων (ὁ Ἑβρ. καὶ ὁ Σύρος, ὑδάτων = M.T. מַיִם) πολλῶν. Cf. Dan. x. 6 φωνὴ λαλιᾶς αὐτοῦ ὡσεὶ φωνὴ θορύβου (θ′ ὄχλου).

i. 16^{a} (ii. 12) ἐκ τοῦ στόματος αὐτοῦ ῥομφαία δίστομος ὀξεῖα. — Isa. xlix. 2 ἔθηκεν τὸ στόμα μου ὡς μάχαιραν ὀξεῖαν.

i. 16^{b} (cf. x. 1) ὡς ὁ ἥλιος φαίνει ἐν τῇ δυνάμει αὐτοῦ. — Jud. v. 31 (B) ὡς ἔξοδος ἡλίου ἐν δυνάμει αὐτοῦ.

i. 17^{a} ἔπεσα πρὸς τοὺς πόδας αὐτοῦ, καὶ ἔθηκεν...λέγων Μὴ φοβοῦ. — Dan. x. 9, 12 ἤμην πεπτωκὼς... καὶ ἰδοὺ χεῖρα προσήγαγέ μοι...καὶ εἶπεν πρὸς μέ Μὴ φοβοῦ.

i. 17^{b} (ii. 8, xxii. 13) ἐγώ εἰμι ὁ πρῶτος καὶ ὁ ἔσχατος. — Isa. xliv. 6 ἐγὼ πρῶτος καὶ ἐγὼ μετὰ ταῦτα (אַחֲרוֹן): xlviii. 12 ἐγώ εἰμι πρῶτος καὶ ἐγώ εἰμι εἰς τὸν αἰῶνα (אַחֲרוֹן; οἱ λοιποί, ἔσχατος).

[1] Both LXX. and Th. have ὡσεὶ χιόνα (χιών) just before, in reference to the clothing.

i. 18 (vi. 8, xx. 13 f.) τοῦ θανάτου καὶ τοῦ ᾅδου.	Hos. xiii. 14 ἐκ χειρὸς ᾅδου ῥύσομαι καὶ ἐκ θανάτου λυτρώσομαι αὐτούς· ποῦ ἡ δίκη σου, θάνατε; ποῦ τὸ κέντρον σου, ᾅδη;
i. 19 ἃ μέλλει γίνεσθαι μετὰ ταῦτα.	Isa. xlviii. 6 ἃ μέλλει γίνεσθαι.
i. 20 τὸ μυστήριον.	Dan. ii. 29 ἀνακαλύπτων μυστήρια ἐδήλωσέ σοι ἃ δεῖ γενέσθαι.
ii. 7 (xxii. 2, 14, 19) ἐκ τοῦ ξύλου τῆς ζωῆς, ὅ ἐστιν ἐν τῷ παραδείσῳ τοῦ θεοῦ.	Gen. ii. 9 τὸ ξύλον τῆς ζωῆς ἐν μέσῳ τῷ παραδείσῳ (cf. iii. 22 f., Ez. xxxi. 8).
ii. 10 ἔχητε θλίψιν ἡμερῶν δέκα.	Dan. i. (12), 14 ἐπείρασεν αὐτοὺς ἡμέρας δέκα.
ii. 14 ἐδίδασκεν...φαγεῖν εἰδωλόθυτα καὶ πορνεῦσαι (cf. ii. 20).	Num. xxv. 1 f. ἐβεβηλώθη ὁ λαὸς ἐκπορνεῦσαι...καὶ ἔφαγεν ὁ λαὸς τῶν θυσιῶν αὐτῶν; cf. xxxi. 16 τοῖς υἱοῖς Ἰσραήλ.
ii. 17ᵃ δώσω αὐτῷ τοῦ μάννα.	Ps. lxxvii. (lxxviii.) 24 ἔβρεξεν αὐτοῖς μάννα φαγεῖν, καὶ ἄρτον οὐρανοῦ ἔδωκεν αὐτοῖς.
ii. 17ᵇ (iii. 12) ὄνομα καινόν.	Isa. lxii. 2 τὸ ὄνομα τὸ καινόν (cf. lxv. 15).
ii. 20 τὴν γυναῖκα Ἰεζάβελ.	3 Regn. xx. (xxi.) 25 Ἰεζάβελ ἡ γυνὴ αὐτοῦ.
ii. 23ᵃ ἐγώ εἰμι ὁ ἐραυνῶν νεφροὺς καὶ καρδίας.	Jer. xvii. 10 ἐγὼ Κύριος ἐτάζων καρδίας καὶ δοκιμάζων νεφρούς (cf. xi. 20, xx. 12; Ps. vii. 10, xxv. (xxvi.) 2).
ii. 23ᵇ (xxii. 12) δώσω ὑμῖν ἑκάστῳ κατὰ τὰ ἔργα ὑμῶν.	Ps. lxi. (lxii.) 13 ἀποδώσεις ἑκάστῳ κατὰ τὰ ἔργα αὐτοῦ.
ii. 26 (xii. 5, xix. 15) δώσω αὐτῷ ἐξουσίαν ἐπὶ τῶν ἐθνῶν, καὶ ποιμανεῖ αὐτοὺς ἐν ῥάβδῳ σιδηρᾷ, ὡς τὰ σκεύη τὰ κεραμικὰ συντρίβεται.	Ps. ii. 8 f. δώσω σοι ἔθνη τὴν κληρονομίαν σου· ποιμανεῖς αὐτοὺς ἐν ῥάβδῳ σιδηρᾷ, ὡς σκεῦος κεραμέως συντρίψεις αὐτούς.
iii. 5 (xiii. 8, xvii. 8, xx. 12, 15, xxi. 27) οὐ μὴ ἐξαλείψω τὸ ὄνομα αὐτοῦ ἐκ τῆς βίβλου τῆς ζωῆς.	Ex. xxxii. 32 f. ἐξάλειψόν με ἐκ τῆς βίβλου σου ἧς ἔγραψας: Isa. iv. 3 οἱ γραφέντες εἰς ζωήν (cf. Ps. cxxxviii. (cxxxix.) 16, Mal. iii. 16, Dan. xii. 1).
iii. 7 ὁ ἔχων τὴν κλεῖν Δαυείδ, ὁ ἀνοίγων καὶ οὐδεὶς κλείσει, καὶ κλείει καὶ οὐδεὶς ἀνοίξει.	Isa. xxii. 22 (B) δώσω τὴν δόξαν (α′ θ′ κλεῖδα) Δαυεὶδ αὐτῷ, καὶ ἄρξει καὶ οὐκ ἔσται ὁ ἀντιλέγων (α′ θ′ ἀνοίξει καὶ οὐκ ἔ. ὁ ἀποκλείων), καὶ κλείσει καὶ οὐκ ἔσται ὁ ἀνοίγων.
iii. 9ᵃ ἥξουσιν καὶ προσκυνήσουσιν ἐνώπιον τῶν ποδῶν σου.	Isa. xlv. 14 διαβήσονται πρὸς σὲ καὶ προσκυνήσουσίν σοι (cf. xlix. 23, lx. 14).

iii. 9^b ἐγὼ ἠγάπησά σε.	Isa. xliii. 4 ἐγώ σε ἠγάπησα.
iii. 12^a τὸ ὄνομα τῆς πόλεως.	Ez. xlviii. 35 τὸ ὄνομα τῆς πόλεως.
iii. 14^b ἡ ἀρχὴ τῆς κτίσεως τοῦ θεοῦ.	Prov. viii. 22 Κύριος ἔκτισέν με ἀρχὴν ὁδῶν αὐτοῦ εἰς τὰ ἔργα αὐτοῦ.
iii. 17 λέγεις ὅτι Πλούσιός εἰμι καὶ πεπλούτηκα.	Hos. xii. 8 εἶπεν Ἐφράιμ Πλὴν πεπλούτηκα (cf. Zech. xii. 5).
iii. 19 ἐγὼ ὅσους ἐὰν φιλῶ ἐλέγχω καὶ παιδεύω.	Prov. iii. 12 ὃν γὰρ ἀγαπᾷ Κύριος ἐλέγχει (ℵA, παιδεύει), μαστιγοῖ (οἱ λοιποί, ἐλέγχει) δὲ πάντα υἱὸν ὃν παραδέχεται.
iii. 20 ἰδοὺ ἕστηκα ἐπὶ τὴν θύραν καὶ κρούω· ἐάν τις...ἀνοίξῃ τὴν θύραν...	Cant. v. 2 κρούει ἐπὶ τὴν θύραν Ἄνοιξόν μοι.
iv. 1 ἡ φωνὴ...ὡς σάλπιγγος.	Ex. xix. 16 φωνὴ τῆς σάλπιγγος.
iv. 2 ἰδοὺ θρόνος ἔκειτο ἐν τῷ οὐρανῷ καὶ ἐπὶ τὸν θρόνον καθήμενος.	3 Regn. xxii. 19 εἶδον θεὸν Ἰσραὴλ καθήμενον ἐπὶ θρόνον αὐτοῦ (cf. Isa. vi. 1, Ps. xlvi. (xlvii.) 9).
iv. 3 ἶρις κυκλόθεν τοῦ θρόνου.	Ez. i. 28 ὡς ὅρασις τόξου... οὕτως...κυκλόθεν.
iv. 5 (cf. viii. 5, xi. 15, 19, xvi. 18) ἐκ τοῦ θρόνου ἐκπορεύονται ἀστραπαὶ καὶ φωναὶ καὶ βρονταί.	Ex. xix. 16 ἐγίνοντο φωναὶ καὶ ἀστραπαί. Ez. i. 13 ἐκ τοῦ πυρὸς ἐξεπορεύετο ἀστραπή.
iv. 6^a (cf. xv. 2) θάλασσα...ὁμοία κρυστάλλῳ.	Ez. i. 22 ὁμοίωμα...ὡσεὶ στερέωμα, ὡς ὅρασις κρυστάλλου.
iv. 6^b ἐν μέσῳ...τέσσερα ζῷα γέμοντα ὀφθαλμῶν ἔμπροσθεν καὶ ὄπισθεν (cf. 8).	Ez. i. 5 ἐν τῷ μέσῳ ὡς ὁμοίωμα τεσσάρων ζῴων, *ib.* 18 οἱ νῶτοι αὐτῶν πλήρεις ὀφθαλμῶν κυκλόθεν τοῖς τέσσαρσιν.
iv. 7 ὅμοιον λέοντι...μόσχῳ...τὸ πρόσωπον ὡς ἀνθρώπου...ὅμοιον ἀετῷ.	Ez. i. 10 πρόσωπον ἀνθρώπου... λέοντος...μόσχου...ἀετοῦ (cf. x. 14, α'θ').
iv. 8^a ἓν καθ' ἓν αὐτῶν ἔχων ἀνὰ πτέρυγας ἕξ.	Isa. vi. 2 ἓξ πτέρυγες τῷ ἑνὶ καὶ ἓξ πτέρυγες τῷ ἑνί.
iv. 8^b λέγοντες Ἅγιος ἅγιος ἅγιος Κύριος ὁ θεὸς ὁ παντοκράτωρ.	*ib.* 3 ἔλεγον Ἅγιος ἅγιος ἅγιος Κύριος σαβαώθ.
iv. 10 τῷ ζῶντι εἰς τοὺς αἰῶνας τῶν αἰώνων.	Dan. iv. 31 (34) θ' τῷ ζῶντι εἰς τὸν αἰῶνα (cf. vi. 26 (27), xii. 7).
v. 1 ἐπὶ τὴν δεξιὰν...βιβλίον γεγραμμένον ἔσωθεν καὶ ὄπισθεν, κατεσφραγισμένον.	Ez. ii. 9 f. χείρ...καὶ ἐν αὐτῇ κεφαλὶς βιβλίου...ἐν αὐτῇ γεγραμμένα ἦν τὰ ἔμπροσθεν καὶ τὰ ὀπίσω. Isa. xxix. 11 ὡς οἱ λόγοι τοῦ βιβλίου τοῦ ἐσφραγισμένου...οὐ δύναμαι ἀναγνῶναι, ἐσφράγισται γάρ.
v. 5 (xxii. 16) ὁ λέων ὁ ἐκ τῆς φυλῆς Ἰούδα, ἡ ῥίζα Δαυείδ.	Gen. xlix. 9 σκύμνος λέοντος, Ἰούδα...ὡς λέων. Isa. xi. 1, 10 ἐξελεύσεται ῥάβδος ἐκ τῆς ῥίζης Ἰεσσαί...ἔσται ἐν τῇ ἡμέρᾳ ἐκείνῃ

	ἡ ῥίζα τοῦ Ἰεσσαί (cf. Jer. xxiii. 5, Zech. iii. 8, vi. 12).
v. 6^{a} (12, xiii. 8) ἀρνίον...ὡς ἐσφαγμένον.	Ex. xii. 5 f. ἀπὸ τῶν ἀρνῶν λήμψεσθε...καὶ σφάξουσιν αὐτό (cf. Lev. i. 10 f.). Isa. liii. 7 ὡς πρόβατον ἐπὶ σφαγὴν ἤχθη, καὶ ὡς ἀμνός... Jer. xi. 19 ἐγὼ δὲ ὡς ἀρνίον (α´ σ´ ὡς ἀμνός) ἄκακον ἀγόμενον τοῦ θύεσθαι (α´ σ´ εἰς σφαγήν).
v. 6^{b} ὀφθαλμοὺς ἑπτὰ...εἰς πᾶσαν τὴν γῆν.	Zech. iv. 10 ἑπτὰ οὗτοι ὀφθαλμοί εἰσιν οἱ ἐπιβλέποντες ἐπὶ πᾶσαν τὴν γῆν.
v. 8 (viii. 3^{b}) θυμιαμάτων αἵ εἰσιν αἱ προσευχαί.	Ps. cxl. (cxli.) 2 ἡ προσευχή μου ὡς θυμίαμα.
v. 9 (xiv. 3) ᾄδουσιν ᾠδὴν καινήν.	Ps. cxliii. (cxliv.) 9 ᾠδὴν καινὴν ᾄσομαί σοι.
v. 11 μυριάδες μυριάδων καὶ χιλιάδες χιλιάδων.	Dan. vii. 10 χίλιαι χιλιάδες... καὶ μύριαι μυριάδες.
vi. 2 ff. ἵππος λευκός...πυρρός... μέλας...χλωρός.	Zech. i. 8 ἵπποι πυρροὶ καὶ ψαροὶ καὶ ποικίλοι καὶ λευκοί. vi. 2 ff. ἵπποι πυρροί...μέλανες... λευκοί...ποικίλοι ψαροί.
vi. 8 ἀποκτεῖναι ἐν ῥομφαίᾳ... ἐν λιμῷ...ἐν θανάτῳ...ὑπὸ τῶν θηρίων.	Jer. xiv. 12 ἐν μαχαίρᾳ καὶ ἐν λιμῷ καὶ ἐν θανάτῳ ἐγὼ συντελέσω αὐτούς. Ez. xiv. 21 ῥομφαίαν καὶ λιμὸν καὶ θηρία πονηρὰ καὶ θάνατον (cf. Jer. xxi. 7, Ez. v. 12, 17, xxix. 5, xxxiii. 27, xxxiv. 28).
vi. 10 ἕως πότε...οὐ κρίνεις καὶ ἐκδικεῖς τὸ αἷμα ἡμῶν ἐκ τῶν κατοικούντων ἐπὶ τῆς γῆς; (cf. xix. 2).	Zech. i. 12 ἕως τίνος οὐ μὴ ἐλεήσῃς; Deut. xxxii. 43^{b} τὸ αἷμα τῶν υἱῶν αὐτοῦ ἐκδικᾶται. Hos. iv. 1 κρίσις τῷ κυρίῳ πρὸς τοὺς κατοικοῦντας τὴν γῆν.
vi. 12 ὁ ἥλιος ἐγένετο μέλας... καὶ ἡ σελήνη ὅλη ἐγένετο ὡς αἷμα.	Joel ii. 31 ὁ ἥλιος μεταστραφήσεται εἰς σκότος καὶ ἡ σελήνη εἰς αἷμα.
vi. 13 οἱ ἀστέρες...ἔπεσαν εἰς τὴν γῆν, ὡς συκῆ βάλλει τοὺς ὀλύνθους αὐτῆς.	Isa. xxxiv. 4 πάντα τὰ ἄστρα πεσεῖται...ὡς πίπτει φύλλα ἀπὸ συκῆς.
vi. 14 ὁ οὐρανὸς...ὡς βιβλίον ἑλισσόμενον.	Isa. xxxiv. 4 ἑλιγήσεται ὡς βιβλίον ὁ οὐρανός.
vi. 15^{a} οἱ βασιλεῖς τῆς γῆς.	Ps. ii. 2 οἱ βασιλεῖς τῆς γῆς (xlvii. (xlviii.) 5, A : Isa. xxiv. 21, xxxiv. 12).
vi. 15^{b}, 16 ἔκρυψαν ἑαυτοὺς εἰς τὰ σπήλαια καὶ εἰς τὰς πέτρας τῶν ὀρέων...ἀπὸ προσώπου τοῦ καθημένου...	Isa. ii. 10, 19 εἰσέλθετε εἰς τὰς πέτρας καὶ κρύπτεσθε...ἀπὸ προσώπου τοῦ φόβου Κυρίου ..εἰσενέγκαντες εἰς τὰ σπήλαια (cf. Jer. iv. 29).

vi. 17 ἦλθεν ἡ ἡμέρα ἡ μεγάλη τῆς ὀργῆς αὐτῶν, καὶ τίς δύναται σταθῆναι;	Joel ii. 11 μεγάλη ἡμέρα τοῦ κυρίου...καὶ τίς ἔσται ἱκανὸς αὐτῇ; Zeph. i. 14 f., 18 ἐγγὺς ἡμέρα Κυρίου ἡ μεγάλη...ἡμέρα ὀργῆς ἡ ἡμέρα ἐκείνη ... ἐν ἡμέρᾳ ὀργῆς Κυρίου. Nah. i. 6 τίς ἀντιστήσεται; (cf. Ps. lxxv. (lxxvi.) 8, Mal. iii. 2).
vii. 1 (xx. 8) ἐπὶ τὰς τέσσαρας γωνίας τῆς γῆς.	Ez. vii. 2 ἐπὶ τὰς τέσσαρας πτέρυγας τῆς γῆς.
vii. 3 (ix. 4, xiv. 1, xxii. 4) ἄχρι σφραγίσωμεν...ἐπὶ τῶν μετώπων.	Ez. ix. 4 δὸς σημεῖον ἐπὶ τὰ μέτωπα.
vii. 14^a τῆς θλίψεως τῆς μεγάλης.	Dan. xii. 1 ἐκείνη ἡ ἡμέρα θλίψεως οἵα οὐκ ἐγενήθη.
vii. 14^b (xxii. 14) ἔπλυναν τὰς στολὰς αὐτῶν...ἐν τῷ αἵματι τοῦ ἀρνίου.	Gen. xlix. 11 πλυνεῖ...τὴν στολὴν αὐτοῦ...ἐν αἵματι.
vii. 16 f. οὐ πεινάσουσιν ἔτι οὐδὲ διψήσουσιν ἔτι, οὐδὲ μὴ πέσῃ ἐπ' αὐτοὺς ὁ ἥλιος οὐδὲ πᾶν καῦμα... ὁδηγήσει αὐτοὺς ἐπὶ ζωῆς πηγὰς ὑδάτων.	Isa. xlix. 10 οὐ πεινάσουσιν οὐδὲ διψάσουσιν, οὐδὲ πατάξει αὐτοὺς καύσων οὐδὲ ὁ ἥλιος...διὰ πηγῶν ὑδάτων ἄξει αὐτούς (cf. Jer. ii. 13).
vii. 17^b (xxi. 4) ἐξαλείψει ὁ θεὸς πᾶν δάκρυον ἐκ τῶν ὀφθαλμῶν αὐτῶν.	Isa. xxv. 8 ἀφεῖλεν (σ' ἐξαλείψει) Κύριος ὁ θεὸς πᾶν δάκρυον ἀπὸ παντὸς προσώπου.
viii. 3^a ἐστάθη ἐπὶ τοῦ θυσιαστηρίου.	Am. ix. 1 ἐφεστῶτα ἐπὶ τοῦ θυσιαστηρίου.
viii. 5 εἴληφεν...τὸν λιβανωτόν, καὶ ἐγέμισεν αὐτὸν ἐκ τοῦ πυρὸς τοῦ θυσιαστηρίου.	Lev. xvi. 12 λήμψεται τὸ πυρεῖον πλῆρες ἀνθράκων πυρὸς ἀπὸ τοῦ θυσιαστηρίου.
viii. 7 ἐγένετο χάλαζα καὶ πῦρ μεμιγμένα ἐν αἵματι.	Ex. ix. 24 ἦν δὲ ἡ χάλαζα καὶ τὸ πῦρ φλογίζον ἐν τῇ χαλάζῃ. Ez. xxxviii. 22 κρινῶ αὐτὸν... αἵματι ... καὶ λίθοις χαλάζης, καὶ πῦρ...βρέξω ἐπ' αὐτόν. Joel ii. 30 ἐπὶ τῆς γῆς αἷμα καὶ πῦρ.
viii. 8^a ὄρος μέγα πυρὶ καιόμενον.	Jer. xxviii. (li.) 25 ὡς ὄρος ἐμπεπυρισμένον.
viii. 8^b (xvi. 3) ἐγένετο τὸ τρίτον τῆς θαλάσσης αἷμα.	Ex. vii. 19 f. ἐγένετο αἷμα... μετέβαλεν πᾶν τὸ ὕδωρ τὸ ἐν τῷ ποταμῷ εἰς αἷμα.
viii. 10 (ix. 1) ἔπεσεν ἐκ τοῦ οὐρανοῦ ἀστὴρ μέγας.	Isa. xiv. 12 ἐξέπεσεν ἐκ τοῦ οὐρανοῦ ὁ ἑωσφόρος.
ix. 2 ἀνέβη καπνὸς...ὡς καπνὸς καμίνου.	Gen. xix. 28 ἀνέβαινεν φλὸξ (M. T., קִיטֹר) τῆς γῆς ὡσεὶ ἀτμὶς (קִיטֹר) καμίνου. Ex. xix. 18 ἀνέβαινεν ὁ καπνὸς ὡς καπνὸς καμίνου.

ix. 3 f. ἐξῆλθον ἀκρίδες εἰς τὴν γῆν κτλ.	Ex. x. 12 ff. ἀναβήτω ἀκρὶς ἐπὶ τὴν γῆν κτλ.
ix. 6 ζητήσουσιν τὸν θάνατον καὶ οὐ μὴ εὑρήσουσιν αὐτόν.	Job iii. 21 ὁμείρονται τοῦ θανάτου καὶ οὐ τυγχάνουσιν.
ix. 7 τὰ ὁμοιώματα...ὅμοια ἵπποις.	Joel ii. 4 ὡς ὅρασις ἵππων ἡ ὅρασις αὐτῶν.
ix. 8 οἱ ὀδόντες αὐτῶν ὡς λεόντων ἦσαν.	Joel i. 6 οἱ ὀδόντες αὐτοῦ ὀδόντες λέοντος.
ix. 9 ἡ φωνὴ τῶν πτερύγων...ὡς φωνὴ ἁρμάτων ἵππων...εἰς πόλεμον.	Joel ii. 5 ὡς φωνὴ ἁρμάτων... εἰς πόλεμον.
ix. 14 ἐπὶ τῷ ποταμῷ τῷ μεγάλῳ Εὐφράτῃ (cf. xvi. 12).	Gen. xv. 18 ἕως τοῦ ποταμοῦ τοῦ μεγάλου Εὐφράτου (Deut. i. 7, Jos. i. 4).
ix. 20^{a} τῶν ἔργων τῶν χειρῶν αὐτῶν.	Isa. xvii. 8 τοῖς ἔργοις τῶν χειρῶν αὐτῶν.
ix. 20^{b} ἵνα μὴ προσκυνήσουσιν τὰ δαιμόνια.	Deut. xxxii. 17 ἔθυσαν δαιμονίοις καὶ οὐ θεῷ.
ix. 20^{c} καὶ τὰ εἴδωλα τὰ χρυσᾶ καὶ τὰ ἀργυρᾶ καὶ τὰ χαλκᾶ καὶ τὰ λίθινα καὶ τὰ ξύλινα.	Dan. v. 23 ᾐνέσατε πάντα τὰ εἴδωλα (θʹ τοὺς θεοὺς τοὺς χρυσοῦς καὶ ἀργυροῦς καὶ σιδηροῦς καὶ ξυλίνους καὶ λιθίνους); cf. v. 3 θʹ.
ix. 20^{d} ἃ οὔτε βλέπειν δύνανται οὔτε ἀκούειν οὔτε περιπατεῖν.	Ps. cxiii. 13 ff. (cxv. 5 ff.) ...οὐ λαλοῦσιν...οὐκ ὄψονται...οὐκ ἀκούσονται...οὐ περιπατήσουσιν.
ix. 21 τῶν φαρμακιῶν... τῆς πορνείας.	4 Regn. ix. 22 αἱ πορνεῖαι Ἰεζάβελ...καὶ τὰ φάρμακα αὐτῆς.
x. 3 ὥσπερ λέων μυκᾶται.	Hos. xi. 10 ὡς λέων ἐρεύξεται.
x. 4 (xxii. 10) σφράγισον ἃ ἐλάλησαν....	Dan. viii. 26 πεφραγμένον (Θʹ σφράγισον) τὸ ὅραμα. xii. 4 σφράγισαι (θʹ σφράγισον) τὸ βιβλίον.
x. 5 f. ἦρεν τὴν χεῖρα αὐτοῦ τὴν δεξιὰν εἰς τὸν οὐρανόν, καὶ ὤμοσεν ἐν τῷ ζῶντι εἰς τοὺς αἰῶνας τῶν αἰώνων, ὃς ἔκτισεν τὸν οὐρανὸν καὶ τὰ ἐν αὐτῷ κτλ.	Gen. xiv. 22 ἐκτενῶ τὴν χεῖρά μου πρὸς τὸν θεὸν τὸν ὕψιστον ὃς ἔκτισεν τὸν οὐρανὸν καὶ τὴν γῆν. Dan. xii. 7 θʹ ὕψωσεν τὴν δεξιὰν αὐτοῦ...εἰς τὸν οὐρανὸν καὶ ὤμοσεν ἐν τῷ ζῶντι (οʹ τὸν ζῶντα εἰς) τὸν αἰῶνα. Deut. xxxii. 40 ἀρῶ εἰς τὸν οὐρανὸν τὴν χεῖρά μου, καὶ ὀμοῦμαι τὴν δεξιάν μου καὶ ἐρῶ Ζῶ ἐγὼ εἰς τὸν αἰῶνα. Ex. xx. 11 τὸν οὐρανὸν καὶ τὴν γῆν καὶ πάντα τὰ ἐν αὐτοῖς (cf. Ps. cxlv. (cxlvi.) 6, 2 Esdr. xix. 6).
x. 7 ὡς εὐηγγέλισεν τοὺς ἑαυτοῦ δούλους τοὺς προφήτας.	Am. iii. 7 ἐὰν μὴ ἀποκαλύψῃ παιδείαν (סוֹדוֹ, θʹ τὴν βουλὴν αὐτοῦ) πρὸς τοὺς δούλους αὐτοῦ τοὺς προφήτας (cf. Dan. ix. 6, 10, Zech. i. 6).

x. 10 ἔλαβον τὸ βιβλαρίδιον... καὶ κατέφαγον αὐτό, καὶ ἦν ἐν τῷ στόματί μου ὡς μέλι γλυκύ.	Ez. iii. 1, 3 εἶπεν πρὸς μέ... κατάφαγε τὴν κεφαλίδα ταύτην... καὶ ἔφαγον αὐτήν, καὶ ἐγένετο ἐν τῷ στόματί μου ὡς μέλι γλυκάζον.
x. 11 δεῖ σε πάλιν προφητεῦσαι ἐπὶ λαοῖς καὶ ἔθνεσιν καὶ γλώσσαις καὶ βασιλεῦσιν πολλοῖς.	Jer. i. 10 καθέστακά σε σήμερον ἐπὶ ἔθνη καὶ βασιλείας (cf. Dan. iii. 4, vii. 14).
xi. 1 κάλαμος ὅμοιος ῥάβδῳ... μέτρησον τὸν ναόν (cf. xxi. 15 ff.).	Ez. xl. 3 f. κάλαμος μέτρον. Zech. ii. 1 (5) f. σχοινίον γεωμετρικόν...διαμετρῆσαι τὴν Ἰερουσαλήμ.
xi. 2 ἐδόθη τοῖς ἔθνεσιν καὶ τὴν πόλιν τὴν ἁγίαν πατήσουσιν.	Zech. xii. 3 θήσομαι τὴν Ἰερουσαλὴμ λίθον καταπατουμένην πᾶσιν τοῖς ἔθνεσιν.
xi. 4 αἱ δύο ἐλαῖαι καὶ αἱ δύο λυχνίαι αἱ ἐνώπιον τοῦ κυρίου τῆς γῆς ἑστῶτες.	Zech. iv. 2 ff., 14 λυχνία χρυσῆ... καὶ δύο ἐλαῖαι...αἱ δύο ἐλαῖαι... παρεστήκασιν κυρίῳ πάσης τῆς γῆς.
xi. 5 πῦρ ἐκπορεύεται ἐκ τοῦ στόματος αὐτῶν, καὶ κατεσθίει τοὺς ἐχθροὺς αὐτῶν.	2 Regn. xxii. 9 πῦρ ἐκ τοῦ στόματος αὐτοῦ κατέδεται. 4 Regn. i. 10 κατέβη πῦρ...καὶ κατέφαγεν αὐτόν.
xi. 7 τὸ θηρίον τὸ ἀναβαῖνον ἐκ τῆς ἀβύσσου (xvii. 8, cf. xiii. 1) ποιήσει μετ' αὐτῶν πόλεμον.	Dan. vii. 3, τέσσαρα θηρία ἀνέβαινον ἐκ τῆς θαλάσσης. *ib.* 21 πόλεμον συνιστάμενον πρὸς τοὺς ἁγίους (θ' ἐποίει πολ. μετὰ τῶν ἁγίων).
xi. 8 καλεῖται πνευματικῶς Σόδομα.	Isa. i. 10 ἄρχοντες Σοδόμων.
xi. 10 εὐφραίνονται, καὶ δῶρα πέμψουσιν ἀλλήλοις.	Ps. civ. (cv.) 38 εὐφράνθη Αἴγυπτος. 2 Esdr. xviii. 12 ἀποστέλλειν μερίδας καὶ ποιῆσαι εὐφροσύνην.
xi. 11[a] πνεῦμα ζωῆς ἐκ τοῦ θεοῦ εἰσῆλθεν ἐν αὐτοῖς καὶ ἔστησαν ἐπὶ τοὺς πόδας αὐτῶν.	Ez. xxxvii. 5, 10 φέρω εἰς ὑμᾶς πνεῦμα ζωῆς...καὶ εἰσῆλθεν εἰς αὐτοὺς τὸ πνεῦμα καὶ ἔζησαν, καὶ ἔστησαν ἐπὶ τῶν ποδῶν αὐτῶν.
xi. 11[b] φόβος μέγας ἐπέπεσεν ἐπί...	Ps. *l.c.* ἐπέπεσεν ὁ φόβος αὐτῶν ἐπ' αὐτούς.
xi. 12 f. ἀνέβησαν εἰς τὸν οὐρανὸν ἐν τῇ νεφελῇ...καὶ...ἐγένετο σεισμὸς μέγας.	4 Regn. ii. 11 ἀνελήμφθη Ἠλειοὺ ἐν συνσεισμῷ ὡς εἰς τὸν οὐρανόν.
xi. 13 τῷ θεῷ τοῦ οὐρανοῦ.	Dan. ii. 44 ὁ θεὸς τοῦ οὐρανοῦ.
xi. 15 ἐγένετο ἡ βασιλεία...τοῦ κυρίου ἡμῶν καὶ τοῦ χριστοῦ αὐτοῦ, καὶ βασιλεύσει εἰς τοὺς αἰῶνας τῶν αἰώνων.	Ps. ii. 2 τοῦ κυρίου καὶ...τοῦ χριστοῦ αὐτοῦ (cf. 1 Regn. xii. 3), ix. 37 (x. 16) βασιλεύσει Κύριος εἰς τὸν αἰῶνα κτλ. (cf. Ex. xv. 18).
xi. 17 f. ἐβασίλευσας· καὶ τὰ ἔθνη ὠργίσθησαν.	Ps. xcviii. (xcix.) 1 Κύριος ἐβασίλευσεν· ὀργιζέσθωσαν λαοί (cf. ii. 5, 12).

xi. 18 τοῖς φοβουμένοις τὸ ὄνομά σου, τοὺς μικροὺς καὶ τοὺς μεγάλους.	Ps. cxiii. 21 (cxv. 13) τοὺς φοβουμένους τὸν κύριον, τοὺς μικροὺς μετὰ τῶν μεγάλων.
xii. 2, 5 ὠδίνουσα...τεκεῖν... ἔτεκεν υἱόν, ἄρσεν.	Isa. lxvi. 6 f. πρὶν τὴν ὠδίνουσαν τεκεῖν...ἔτεκεν ἄρσεν.
xii. 3 ἔχων...κέρατα δέκα.	Dan. vii. 7 εἶχε δὲ κέρατα δέκα (θ′ κ. δ. αὐτῷ).
xii. 7 ὁ Μιχαὴλ...τοῦ πολεμῆσαι.	Dan. x. 13 Μιχαὴλ...ἐπῆλθε βοηθῆσαί μοι (*ib.* 20 θ′ τοῦ πολεμῆσαι).
xii. 8 (xx. 11) οὐδὲ τόπος εὑρέθη αὐτῶν.	Dan. ii. 35 θ′ καὶ τόπος οὐχ εὑρέθη αὐτοῖς.
xii. 9ᵃ ὁ ὄφις ὁ ἀρχαῖος...ὁ πλανῶν.	Gen. iii. 13 ὁ ὄφις ἠπάτησέν με.
xii. 9ᵇ (xx. 12) ὁ καλούμενος Διάβολος καὶ ὁ σατανᾶς.	Job i. 6 (Zech. iii. 1) ὁ διάβολος (הַשָּׂטָן, α′ Σατάν) θ′ ὁ ἀντικείμενος.
xii. 12 εὐφραίνεσθε, οὐρανοί.	Isa. xliv. 23 εὐφράνθητε (xlix. 13 εὐφραίνεσθε), οὐρανοί.
xii. 14 καιρὸν καὶ καιροὺς καὶ ἥμισυ καιροῦ.	Dan. vii. 25 ἕως καιροῦ καὶ καιρῶν καὶ ἕως ἡμίσους καιροῦ (θ′ καί γε ἥμισυ καιροῦ), xii. 7 εἰς καιρὸν καὶ καιροὺς καὶ ἥμισυ καιροῦ.
xiii. 2 τὸ θηρίον...ἦν ὅμοιον παρδάλει...ὡς ἄρκου...ὡς..λέοντος.	Dan. vii. 6 θηρίον...ὡσεὶ πάρδαλιν. 16 ἄρκου, 4 ὡσεὶ λέαινα.
xiii. 4 τίς ὅμοιος τῷ θηρίῳ;	Ex. xv. 11 τίς ὅμοιός σοι; (Ps. xxxiv. (xxxv.) 10, lxx. (lxxi.) 19), cf. Isa. xiv. 4.
xiii. 5 στόμα λαλοῦν μεγάλα.	Dan. vii. 20 στόμα λαλοῦν μεγάλα.
xiii. 7 ποιῆσαι πόλεμον μετὰ τῶν ἁγίων, καὶ νικῆσαι αὐτούς.	Dan. vii. 21 θ′ ἐποίει πόλεμον μετὰ τῶν ἁγίων, καὶ ἰσχύσει πρὸς αὐτούς.
xiii. 10 εἴ τις εἰς αἰχμαλωσίαν, εἰς αἰχμαλωσίαν ὑπάγει κτλ.	Jer. xv. 2 ὅσοι εἰς μάχαιραν, εἰς μάχαιραν...καὶ ὅσοι εἰς αἰχμαλωσίαν, εἰς αἰχμαλωσίαν.
xiii. 15 ἵνα ὅσοι ἐὰν μὴ προσκυνήσωσιν τῇ εἰκόνι τοῦ θηρίου ἀποκτανθῶσιν.	Dan. iii. 6 πᾶς ὃς ἂν μὴ πεσὼν προσκυνήσῃ [τῇ εἰκόνι] κτλ.
xiv. 5 ἐν τῷ στόματι αὐτῶν οὐχ εὑρέθη ψεῦδος.	Isa. liii. 9 οὐδὲ δόλον ἐν τῷ στόματι αὐτοῦ (Zeph. iii. 13).
xiv. 7 τῷ ποιήσαντι τὸν οὐρανὸν καὶ τὴν γῆν καὶ τὴν θάλασσαν.	Ex. xx. 11 ἐποίησεν...τὸν οὐρανὸν καὶ τὴν γῆν [+ καὶ τὴν θάλασσαν B^ab AF].
xiv. 8 ἔπεσεν ἔπεσεν Βαβυλὼν ἡ μεγάλη (xvi. 19, xvii. 5, xviii. 2, 10, 21).	Isa. xxi. 9 πέπτωκεν πέπτωκεν Βαβυλών. Jer. xxviii. (li.) 8 ἄφνω ἔπεσεν B. Dan. iv. 27 B. ἡ μεγάλη.
xiv. 10ᵃ πίεται ἐκ τοῦ οἴνου τοῦ	Isa. li. 17 ἡ πιοῦσα ἐκ χειρὸς

k 2

θυμοῦ τοῦ θεοῦ τοῦ κεκερασμένου ἀκράτου.	Κυρίου τὸ ποτήριον τοῦ θυμοῦ αὐτοῦ (cf. Ps. lxxiv. (lxxv.) 8 ποτήριον ἐν χειρὶ Κυρίου οἴνου ἀκράτου πλῆρες κεράσματος).
xiv. 10b ἐν πυρὶ καὶ θείῳ.	Gen. xix. 24 θεῖον καὶ πῦρ (Ez. xxxviii. 22). *ib.* 28 ἀνέβαινεν φλὸξ τῆς γῆς.
xiv. 11 ὁ καπνὸς τοῦ βασανισμοῦ αὐτῶν εἰς αἰῶνας αἰώνων ἀναβαίνει ἡμέρας καὶ νυκτός (cp. xix. 3, xx. 10).	Isa. xxxiv. 10 νυκτὸς καὶ ἡμέρας, καὶ οὐ σβεσθήσεται εἰς τὸν αἰῶνα χρόνον, καὶ ἀναβήσεται ὁ καπνὸς αὐτῆς ἄνω.
xiv. 15, 18 πέμψον τὸ δρέπανόν σου καὶ θέρισον, ὅτι ἦλθεν ἡ ὥρα θερίσαι...καὶ τρύγησον κτλ.	Joel iii. (iv.) 13 ἐξαποστείλατε δρέπανα, ὅτι παρέστηκεν τρυγητός... διότι πλήρης ὁ ληνός.
xiv. 19 f. ἔβαλεν εἰς τὴν ληνὸν τοῦ θυμοῦ τοῦ θεοῦ τὸν μέγαν. καὶ ἐπατήθη ἡ ληνός.	Isa. lxiii. 6 κατεπάτησα αὐτοὺς τῇ ὀργῇ μου. Thren. i. 15 ληνὸν ἐπάτησεν Κύριος.
xv. 1 πληγὰς ἑπτά.	Lev. xxvi. 21 πληγὰς ἑπτά.
xv. 3a ᾄδουσιν τὴν ᾠδὴν Μωυσέως τοῦ δούλου τοῦ θεοῦ.	Ex. xv. 1 τότε ᾖσεν Μωυσῆς... τὴν ᾠδὴν ταύτην. Deut. xxxi. 30 ἐλάλησεν Μωυσῆς...τὰ ῥήματα τῆς ᾠδῆς ταύτης. Jos. xiv. 7 M. ὁ παῖς τοῦ θεοῦ.
xv. 3b μεγάλα καὶ θαυμαστὰ τὰ ἔργα σου, Κύριε.	Ps. cx. (cxi.) 2 μεγάλα τὰ ἔργα Κυρίου. cxxxviii. (cxxxix.) 14 θαυμάσια τὰ ἔργα σου.
xv. 3c δίκαιαι καὶ ἀληθιναὶ αἱ ὁδοί σου.	Deut. xxxii. 4 θεός, ἀληθινὰ τὰ ἔργα αὐτοῦ, καὶ πᾶσαι αἱ ὁδοὶ αὐτοῦ κρίσεις.
xv. 4 ὁ βασιλεὺς τῶν ἐθνῶν· τίς οὐ μὴ φοβηθῇ...καὶ δοξάσει τὸ ὄνομά σου;	Jer. x. 7 (M.T.) θ′ τίς οὐ μὴ φοβηθήσεται, βασιλεῦ τῶν ἐθνῶν; Ps. lxxxv. (lxxxvi.) 9 καὶ δοξάσουσιν τὸ ὄνομά σου.
xv. 8a ἐγεμίσθη ὁ ναὸς καπνοῦ ἐκ τῆς δόξης τοῦ θεοῦ.	Isa. vi. 4 ὁ οἶκος ἐνεπλήσθη καπνοῦ. Ex. xl. 28 (34) δόξης Κυρίου ἐνεπλήσθη ἡ σκηνή.
xv. 8b οὐδεὶς ἐδύνατο εἰσελθεῖν εἰς τὸν ναόν.	Ex. xl. 29 οὐκ ἠδυνάσθη Μωσῆς εἰσελθεῖν εἰς τὴν σκηνήν.
xvi. 1 ἐκχέετε τὰς ἑπτὰ φιάλας τοῦ θυμοῦ τοῦ θεοῦ εἰς τὴν γῆν.	Ps. lxviii. (lxix.) 25 ἔκχεον ἐπ᾽ αὐτοὺς τὴν ὀργήν σου (Jer. x. 25, Zeph. iii. 8).
xvi. 2 ἐγένετο ἕλκος κακὸν καὶ πονηρόν.	Ex. ix. 10 ἐγένετο ἕλκη. Deut. xxviii. 35 ἐν ἕλκει πονηρῷ.
xvi. 3 πᾶσα ψυχὴ ζωῆς ἀπέθανεν, τὰ ἐν τῇ θαλάσσῃ.	Ex. vii. 21 οἱ ἰχθύες οἱ ἐν τῷ ποταμῷ ἐτελεύτησαν.
xvi. 4 ἐξέχεεν...εἰς τοὺς ποταμούς...καὶ ἐγένετο αἷμα.	Ps. lxxvii. (lxxviii.) 44 μετέστρεψεν εἰς αἷμα τοὺς ποταμοὺς αὐτῶν (cf. Ex. vii. 20).
xvi. 5 δίκαιος εἶ...ὁ ὅσιος.	Ps. cxliv. (cxlv.) 17 δίκαιος Κύριος...καὶ ὅσιος.

xvi. 6 αἷμα αὐτοῖς δέδωκας πεῖν.	Ps. lxxviii. (lxxix.) 3 ἐξέχεαν τὸ αἷμα αὐτῶν ὡς ὕδωρ. Isa. xlix. 26 πίονται...τὸ αἷμα αὐτῶν.
xvi. 7 δίκαιαι αἱ κρίσεις σου.	Ps. cxviii. (cxix.) 137 δίκαιος εἶ, Κύριε· καὶ εὐθὴς ἡ κρίσις σου.
xvi. 10 ἐγένετο ἡ βασιλεία αὐτοῦ ἐσκοτωμένη.	Ex. x. 21 γενηθήτω σκότος ἐπὶ γῆν Αἰγύπτου.
xvi. 12 ἐξηράνθη τὸ ὕδωρ αὐτοῦ.	Isa. xliv. 27 τοὺς ποταμούς σου ξηρανῶ. Jer. xxvii. (l.) 38 (Heb. Hex.).
xvi. 13 ὡς βάτραχοι.	Ex. viii. 3 (vii. 28) ἐξερεύξεται ὁ ποταμὸς βατράχους.
xvi. 16 εἰς τὸν τόπον τὸν καλούμενον Ἑβραϊστὶ Ἅρ Μαγεδών.	Zech. xii. 11 ἐν πεδίῳ ἐκκοπτομένου (*v.l.* Μαγεδδών).
xvi. 18 οἷος οὐκ ἐγένετο ἀφ' οὗ ἄνθρωπος ἐγένετο ἐπὶ τῆς γῆς.	Dan. xii. 1 οἵα οὐκ ἐγενήθη ἀφ' οὗ ἐγενήθησαν (θ' γεγένηται ἔθνος ἐν τῇ γῇ (*v.l.* ἐπὶ τῆς γῆς)).
xvii. 1 τῆς καθημένης ἐπὶ ὑδάτων πολλῶν.	Jer. xxviii. (li.) 13 κατασκηνοῦντας (-νοῦσα Q) ἐφ' ὕδασι πολλοῖς.
xvii. 2 μεθ' ἧς ἐπόρνευσαν οἱ βασιλεῖς τῆς γῆς, καὶ ἐμεθύσθησαν ...ἐκ τοῦ οἴνου τῆς πορνείας αὐτῆς.	Isa. xxiii. 17 ἔσται ἐμπόριον (זָנְתָה) πάσαις ταῖς βασιλείαις τῆς οἰκουμένης. Jer. xxviii. (li.) 7 μεθύσκον πᾶσαν τὴν γῆν.
xvii. 14 (xix. 16) κύριος κυρίων ἐστὶν καὶ βασιλεὺς βασιλέων.	Deut. x. 17 θεὸς τῶν θεῶν καὶ κύριος τῶν κυρίων. Dan. ii. 47 θεὸς τῶν θεῶν καὶ κύριος τῶν βασιλέων (cf. iv. 34).
xviii. 2 κατοικητήριον δαιμονίων κτλ.	Isa. xiii. 21 f. ἀναπαύσονται ἐκεῖ σειρῆνες, καὶ δαιμόνια ἐκεῖ ὀρχήσονται, καὶ ὀνοκένταυροι ἐκεῖ κατοικήσουσιν (cf. xxxiv. 14). Jer. ix. 11 κατοικητήριον δρακόντων.
xviii. 4 ἐξέλθατε, ὁ λαός μου, ἐξ αὐτῆς.	Jer. xxviii. (li.) 45 θ' (?) ἐξέλθετε ἐκ μέσου αὐτῆς, λαός μου.
xviii. 6 ἀπόδοτε αὐτῇ ὡς καὶ αὐτὴ ἀπέδωκεν.	Ps. cxxxvi. (cxxxvii.) 8 μακάριος ὃς ἀνταποδώσει σοι τὸ ἀνταπόδομά σου ὃ ἀνταπέδωκας ἡμῖν (cf. Jer. xxvii. (l.) 29).
xviii. 7 ἐν τῇ καρδίᾳ αὐτῆς λέγει Κάθημαι βασίλισσα, καὶ χήρα οὐκ εἰμί.	Isa. xlvii. 7 f. εἶπας Εἰς τὸν αἰῶνα ἔσομαι ἄρχουσα...ἡ καθημένη...ἡ λέγουσα ἐν καρδίᾳ αὐτῆς... οὐ καθιῶ χήρα.
xviii. 8 ἰσχυρὸς Κύριος ὁ θεὸς ὁ κρίνας αὐτήν.	Jer. xxvii. (l.) 34 ἰσχυρός, Κύριος...κρίσιν κρινεῖ.
xviii. 9—19.	Ez. xxvi., xxvii. *passim*.
xviii. 21 λίθον...ἔβαλεν...λέγων	Jer. xxviii. (li.) 63 f. λίθον...

Οὕτως... βληθήσεται Βαβυλὼν... καὶ οὐ μὴ εὑρεθῇ ἔτι.	ῥίψεις... καὶ ἐρεῖς Οὕτως καταδύσεται Βαβυλὼν... καὶ οὐ μὴ ἀναστῇ.
xviii. 22 φωνὴ... μουσικῶν οὐ μὴ ἀκουσθῇ ἐν σοὶ ἔτι.	Ez. xxvi. 13 τῶν μουσικῶν σου ...ἡ φωνὴ οὐ μὴ ἀκουσθῇ ἔτι.
xviii. 23ᵃ φωνὴ μύλου... φῶς λύχνου... φωνὴ νυμφίου καὶ νύμφης.	Jer. xxv. 10 φωνὴν νυμφίου καὶ φωνὴν νύμφης, ὀσμὴν μύρου (Heb. קוֹל רֵחַיִם, LXX., codd. Syro-hex., φωνὴν μύλου) καὶ φῶς λύχνου.
xviii. 23ᵇ οἱ ἔμποροί σου ἦσαν οἱ μεγιστᾶνες τῆς γῆς.	Isa. xxiii. 8 οἱ ἔμποροι αὐτῆς ἔνδοξοι, ἄρχοντες τῆς γῆς.
xix. 1 ff. ἀλληλουϊά.	Ps. civ. (cv.), al., tit. ἀλληλουϊά.
xix. 3 ὁ καπνὸς αὐτῆς ἀναβαίνει εἰς τοὺς αἰῶνας.	Isa. xxxiv. 10 εἰς τὸν αἰῶνα χρόνον.. ἀναβήσεται ὁ καπνὸς αὐτῆς ἄνω.
xix. 6 f. ὡς φωνὴν ὄχλου... ἐβασίλευσεν Κύριος... ἀγαλλιῶμεν.	Dan. x. 6 θ′ ὡς φωνὴ ὄχλου. Ps. xcvi. (xcvii.) 1 ὁ κύριος ἐβασίλευσεν, ἀγαλλιάσεται ἡ γῆ.
xix. 11 εἶδον τὸν οὐρανὸν ἠνεῳγμένον, καὶ ἰδού....	Ez. i. 1 ἠνοίχθησαν οἱ οὐρανοί, καὶ εἶδον....
xix. 17 f. ἔκραξεν... λέγων πᾶσιν τοῖς ὀρνέοις... Δεῦτε συνάχθητε εἰς τὸ δεῖπνον τὸ μέγα τοῦ θεοῦ ἵνα φάγητε σάρκας.	Ez. xxxix. 17 εἰπὸν παντὶ ὀρνέῳ ...Συνάχθητε... ἐπὶ τὴν θυσίαν μου ...θυσίαν μεγάλην... καὶ φάγεσθε κρέα.
xix. 21 πάντα τὰ ὄρνεα ἐχορτάσθησαν ἐκ τῶν σαρκῶν αὐτῶν.	*ib.* 20 ἐμπλησθήσεσθε ἐπὶ τῆς τραπέζης μου.
xx. 4 εἶδον θρόνους καὶ ἐκάθισαν ἐπ' αὐτούς, καὶ κρίμα ἐδόθη αὐτοῖς.	Dan. vii. 9, 22 ἐθεώρουν ἕως ὅτε θρόνοι ἐτέθησαν, καὶ παλαιὸς ἡμερῶν ἐκάθητο... καὶ τὴν κρίσιν (θ′ τὸ κρίμα) ἔδωκε τοῖς ἁγίοις.
xx. 8 τὸν Γὼγ καὶ Μαγώγ, συναγαγεῖν αὐτούς.	Ez. xxxviii. 1, 4 ἐπὶ Γὼγ καὶ τὴν γῆν τοῦ Μαγώγ... καὶ συνάξω σε.
xx. 9 ἐπὶ τὸ πλάτος τῆς γῆς.	Hab. i. 6 ἐπὶ τὰ πλάτη (A, τὸ πλάτος) τῆς γῆς.
xx. 9ᵇ τὴν ἠγαπημένην.	Jer. xi. 15 ἡ ἠγαπημένη (cf. Ps. lxxxvi. (lxxxvii.) 1).
xx. 9ᶜ κατέβη πῦρ ἐκ τοῦ οὐρανοῦ καὶ κατέφαγεν αὐτούς.	4 Regn. i. 10 κατέβη πῦρ ἐκ τοῦ οὐρανοῦ καὶ κατέφαγεν αὐτόν.
xx. 11 οὗ ἀπὸ τοῦ προσώπου ἔφυγεν ἡ γῆ, καὶ τόπος οὐχ εὑρέθη αὐτοῖς.	Ps. cxiii. (cxiv.) 3, 7 ἡ θάλασσα εἶδεν καὶ ἔφυγεν... ἀπὸ προσώπου Κυρίου ἐσαλεύθη ἡ γῆ. Dan. ii. 35 θ′ καὶ τόπος οὐχ εὑρέθη αὐτοῖς.
xx. 12 βιβλία ἠνοίχθησαν.	Dan. vii. 10 βίβλοι ἠνεῴχθησαν.
xx. 15 εἴ τις οὐχ εὑρέθη ἐν τῇ βίβλῳ τῆς ζωῆς γεγραμμένος.	Dan. xii. 1 ὃς ἂν εὑρεθῇ ἐγγεγραμμένος ἐν τῷ βιβλίῳ (θ′ γεγρ. ἐν τῇ βίβλῳ) (cf. Ps. lxviii. (lxix.) 29).
xxi. 1 οὐρανὸν καινὸν καὶ γῆν καινήν.	Isa. lxv. 17 ἔσται γὰρ ὁ οὐρανὸς καινὸς καὶ ἡ γῆ καινή (lxvi. 22).

xxi. 2^{a} τὴν πόλιν τὴν ἁγίαν Ἰερουσαλήμ.	Isa. lii. 1 Ἰερουσαλήμ, πόλις ἡ ἁγία.
xxi. 2^{b} ὡς νύμφην κεκοσμημένην τῷ ἀνδρὶ αὐτῆς.	Isa. lxi. 10 ὡς νύμφην κατεκόσμησέν με.
xxi. 3 ἡ σκηνὴ τοῦ θεοῦ μετὰ τῶν ἀνθρώπων, καὶ σκηνώσει μετ' αὐτῶν, καὶ αὐτοὶ λαοὶ αὐτοῦ ἔσονται.	Ez. xxxvii. 27 ἔσται ἡ κατασκήνωσίς μου ἐν αὐτοῖς, καὶ ἔσομαι αὐτοῖς θεός, καὶ αὐτοί μου ἔσονται λαός (cf. Zech. ii. 10 (14)).
xxi. 5 ἰδοὺ καινὰ ποιῶ πάντα.	Isa. xliii. 19 ἰδοὺ ἐγὼ ποιῶ καινά.
xxi. 6 τῷ διψῶντι δώσω...δωρεάν.	Isa. lv. 1 οἱ διψῶντες, πορεύεσθε ἐφ' ὕδωρ...ἄνευ ἀργυρίου καὶ τιμῆς.
xxi. 7 ἔσομαι αὐτῷ θεός, καὶ αὐτὸς ἔσται μοι υἱός.	2 Regn. vii. 14 ἐγὼ ἔσομαι αὐτῷ εἰς πατέρα, καὶ αὐτὸς ἔσται μοι εἰς υἱόν (cf. Ps. lxxxviii. (lxxxix.) 29 f.).
xxi. 10 ἀπήνεγκέν με ἐν πνεύματι ἐπὶ ὄρος...ὑψηλόν.	Ez. xl. 1 f. ἤγαγέν με ἐν ὁράσει θεοῦ...ἐπ' ὄρος ὑψηλόν.
xxi. 11 ἔχουσαν τὴν δόξαν τοῦ θεοῦ.	Isa. lviii. 8 ἡ δόξα τοῦ θεοῦ περιστελεῖ σε (cf. lx. 1 f.).
xxi. 12 f. ἔχουσα πυλῶνας...ἀπὸ ἀνατολῆς...ἀπὸ βορρᾶ...ἀπὸ νότου ...ἀπὸ δυσμῶν.	Ez. xlviii. 31 ff. πύλαι πρὸς βορρᾶν...τὰ πρὸς ἀνατολάς...τὰ πρὸς νότον...τὰ πρὸς θάλασσαν.
xxi. 16 τετράγωνος κεῖται.	Ez. xliii. 16 τετράγωνον ἐπὶ τὰ τέσσερα μέρη αὐτοῦ.
xxi. 18 ἡ ἐνδώμησις τοῦ τείχους αὐτῆς ἴασπις.	Isa. liv. 12 θήσω τὰς ἐπάλξεις σου ἴασπιν.
xxi. 19 ὁ θεμέλιος...ὁ δεύτερος σάπφειρος.	*ib.* 11 ἑτοιμάζω...τὰ θεμέλιά σου σάπφειρον.
xxi. 23 (xxii. 5) ἡ πόλις οὐ χρείαν ἔχει τοῦ ἡλίου οὐδὲ τῆς σελήνης κτλ.	Isa. lx. 19 οὐκ ἔσται σοι ἔτι ὁ ἥλιος εἰς φῶς κτλ.
xxi. 24 (26) περιπατήσουσιν τὰ ἔθνη διὰ τοῦ φωτὸς αὐτῆς, καὶ οἱ βασιλεῖς τῆς γῆς φέρουσιν τὴν δόξαν αὐτῶν εἰς αὐτήν.	Isa. lx. 3 πορεύσονται βασιλεῖς τῷ φωτί σου καὶ ἔθνη τῇ λαμπρότητί σου (cf. 11^{b}). Ps. lxxi. (lxxii.) 10 βασιλεῖς...δῶρα προσοίσουσιν.
xxi. 25 οἱ πυλῶνες αὐτῆς οὐ μὴ κλεισθῶσιν ἡμέρας· νὺξ γὰρ οὐκ ἔσται ἐκεῖ.	Isa. lx. 11 ἀνοιχθήσονται αἱ πύλαι σου διὰ παντός, ἡμέρας καὶ νυκτὸς οὐ κλεισθήσονται.
xxi. 27 οὐ μὴ εἰσέλθῃ εἰς αὐτὴν πᾶν κοινόν.	Isa. lii. 1 οὐκέτι προστεθήσεται διελθεῖν διὰ σοῦ...ἀκάθαρτος.
xxii. 1 ποταμὸν...ἐκπορευόμενον ἐκ τοῦ θρόνου.	Ez. xlvii. 1 ἰδοὺ ὕδωρ ἐξεπορεύετο ὑποκάτωθεν τοῦ αἰθρίου.
xxii. 2 ἐντεῦθεν καὶ ἐκεῖθεν ξύλον ζωῆς ποιοῦν καρποὺς δώδεκα, κατὰ μῆνα ἕκαστον...καὶ τὰ φύλλα τοῦ ξύλου εἰς θεραπείαν τῶν ἐθνῶν.	Ez. xlvii. 12 ἔνθεν καὶ ἔνθεν πᾶν ξύλον βρώσιμον...οὐδὲ μὴ ἐκλίπῃ ὁ καρπὸς αὐτοῦ...καὶ ἀνάβασις (עָלֵהוּ; LXX., *al. lect.* ἀνάδοσις) αὐτῶν εἰς ὑγίειαν.
xxii. 3 πᾶν κατάθεμα οὐκ ἔσται ἔτι.	Zech. xiv. 11 ἀνάθεμα οὐκ ἔσται ἔτι.

xxii. 4 ὄψονται τὸ πρόσωπον αὐτοῦ.	Ps. xvi. (xvii.) 15 ὀφθήσομαι τῷ προσώπῳ σου.
xxii. 5 βασιλεύσουσιν εἰς τοὺς αἰῶνας τῶν αἰώνων.	Dan. vii. 18 καθέξουσι τὴν βασιλείαν ἕως τοῦ αἰῶνος τῶν αἰώνων.
xxii. 13 ὁ μισθός μου μετ' ἐμοῦ.	Isa. xl. 10 ὁ μισθὸς αὐτοῦ μετ' αὐτοῦ.
xxii. 18 f. ἐάν τις ἐπιθῇ ἐπ' αὐτά, ἐπιθήσει ὁ θεός...καὶ ἐάν τις ἀφέλῃ...ἀφελεῖ...	Deut. iv. 2 οὐ προσθήσεσθε πρὸς τὸ ῥῆμα...καὶ οὐκ ἀφελεῖτε ἀπ' αὐτοῦ (xii. 32 = xiii. 1).
xxii. 19 τῶν γεγραμμένων ἐν τῷ βιβλίῳ τούτῳ.	Deut. xxix. 20 (19) αἱ γεγραμμέναι ἐν τῷ βιβλίῳ τούτῳ.

2. An examination of this table brings to light some instructive facts. (*a*) The writer of the Apocalypse refers to each of the three great divisions of the Hebrew canon, and to most of the books. He lays under contribution each of the books of the Law, the Book of Judges, the four Books of Kingdoms, the Psalms, the Proverbs, the Song, the Book of Job, all the major and seven of the minor Prophets. But there are certain books which he uses with especial frequency; more than half his references to the Old Testament belong to the Psalms, the prophecies of Isaiah and Ezekiel, and the Book of Daniel, and in proportion to its length the Book of Daniel yields by far the greatest number[1]. The preponderance of these four books is easily explained; they are those which most abound in mystical and apocalyptic elements. (*b*) The references are of two kinds. One, which is to be found in every page of the Apocalypse, consists of Old Testament words and phrases, used with no special allusion to particular contexts. If GOD is frequently described as *He that sitteth on the throne*, and the saints as *they which are written in the book of life*, while the Roman Emperors or their vassals are *the kings of the earth*, and the pagan inhabitants of the Empire *they that dwell on the earth*, the recurrence of these and similar terms is sufficiently explained by the writer's lifelong familiarity with Old Testament language. But there are other references in which it is clear that he has in view certain books and passages, and is practically

[1] The numbers in our list are: Psalms, 27; Isaiah, 46; Ezekiel, 29; Daniel, 31; after these come Genesis, Exodus, Deuteronomy, Jeremiah, Joel, and Zechariah. See, however, p. xlix; and cf. p. cxxxv.

quoting from them, although no formula of quotation is used. These occur chiefly in the visions of the Apocalypse, which are based in almost every case on the histories or the prophecies of the Old Testament. Thus the vision of the Glorified Christ walking in the midst of the Churches (i. 13—16) rests on Ezekiel and Daniel; the vision of the Court of Heaven (iv. 2—8) on Isaiah and Ezekiel and Zechariah; the four horses of c. vi. are from Zechariah; Isaiah supplies much of the description of the bliss of the redeemed in c. vii.; the vision of the seven last plagues in c. xvi. is suggested by the Plagues of Exodus, and the dirge of Babylon the Great by the doom pronounced upon Tyre and the older Babylon; the vision of the New Jerusalem is inspired by the patriotic hopes of Isaiah and Ezekiel. (*c*) In many cases, indeed in most, the Apocalyptist blends two or more Old Testament contexts, whether from different books or from different parts of the same book. The result has been described as a 'mosaic,' but the word is not altogether apt as an illustration of his method. It suggests the work of a cunning artist who has formed a design out of the fragments which were at his disposal. But the Apocalyptist's use of his Old Testament materials is artless and natural; it is the work of a memory which is so charged with Old Testament words and thoughts that they arrange themselves in his visions like the changing patterns of a kaleidoscope, without conscious effort on his own part. (*d*) There is not a single instance in which the Christian prophet of the Apocalypse has contented himself with a mere compilation or combination of Old Testament ideas. His handling of these materials is always original and independent, and he does not allow his Old Testament author to carry him a step beyond the point at which the guidance ceases to lend itself to the purpose of his book. Thus in the first vision of the Apocalypse, while nearly every feature is drawn from Ezekiel or Daniel, and the words *ὅμοιον υἱὸν ἀνθρώπου* point beyond doubt to a direct use of the latter book, the conception of the Glorified Christ as a whole has no parallel in the Old Testament. If the vision of c. iv. owes much to Isaiah, Ezekiel and Zechariah, no mere compiler could have produced it; and the same may be said with absolute conviction of every other vision throughout the book. Though in constant relation to the older apocalyptic, St John's pictures of the unseen and the future are truly creations, the work of the Spirit of prophecy upon a mind full of the lore of the earlier revelation and yet free to carry its reminiscences into new and wider fields of spiritual illumination.

3. An inspection of the table further shews that the Apocalyptist generally availed himself of the Alexandrian version of the Old Testament. The familiar phraseology of the LXX. meets us everywhere, and here and there we observe its peculiar renderings; e.g. in xi. 17 *ὠργίσθησαν* is a scarcely doubtful recollection of the LXX. *ὀργιζέσθωσαν* (Heb. יִרְגְּזוּ, Aq. *κλονείσθωσαν*, Symm. *φοβείσθωσαν*). On the other hand many of the references depart widely from the LXX. in particular words, where the writer of the Apocalypse has either rendered independently, or has used another version, or possibly a text of the LXX. different from that which is found in our MSS.; e.g. i. 6 *βασιλείαν, ἱερεῖς* (θ′ σ′)[1], i. 17 *ἔσχατος* (οἱ λ̥), ii. 23 *ἐραυνῶν* (cf. Rom. viii. 27), iii. 7 *τὴν κλεῖν Δαυείδ* (α′ θ′), vii. 1 *γωνίας*, x. 3 *μυκᾶται*, xii. 9 *πλανῶν*, xiv. 5 *ψεῦδος*, xv. 8 *ναός* (θ′ σ′), xviii. 22 *φωνὴ μύλου* (so some MSS. of the LXX.), xxi. 12 f. *πυλῶνες*, xxii. 2 *ἐντεῦθεν καὶ ἐκεῖθεν*, *ib.* *τὰ φύλλα*, xxii. 3 *κατάθεμα*. Now and then the Apocalyptist seems to adopt a conflation of two versions, e.g. iii. 19 *ἐλέγχω καὶ παιδεύω*, xvi. 2 *κακὸν καὶ πονηρόν*; more often he has brought together readings from two separate contexts, as when in iv. 8 he substitutes *παντοκράτωρ* for the *σαβαώθ* of the Greek Isaiah.

The references in the Apocalypse to Daniel demand separate notice. Dr Salmon (*Introduction to the N.T.*[7], p. 548 ff.) calls attention to the affinity between these references and the version of Theodotion. He finds "no clear evidence that St John had ever seen the so-called LXX. version" of Daniel[2]; if in two passages (i. 14 f., xix. 16), the writer may be thought to follow the

[1] On the remarkable rendering of Zech. xii. 12 in Apoc. i. 7 see the note in the commentary *ad loc.*, and cf. Deissmann, *Die Septuaginta-papyri der Heidelberger Papyrus-sammlung* (Heidelberg, 1905), p. 66 ff.

[2] i. e. the version in the unique Chigi MS.

LXX. against Theodotion, there are seven (ix. 20, x. 6, xii. 7, xiii. 7, xix. 6, xx. 4, 11) in which he supports Theodotion against the LXX. The evidence at any rate shews that Theodotion has preserved a considerable number of readings which were current in the first century, and that the Greek text of Daniel known to the Apocalyptist came nearer to the Theodotionic than to the Chigi text.

If it be asked whether there are traces in the Apocalypse of a direct use of the Hebrew Old Testament, the answer must be that the departures from the LXX. may perhaps in every instance be otherwise explained. But the forms Ἀβαδδών (ix. 11) and Ἅρ Μαγεδών (xvi. 16) seem to imply acquaintance on the writer's part with Hebrew or Aramaic, and this inference is supported, as we have seen, by the style and manner of his work.

4. If we accept the later date of the Apocalypse, it may be assumed that the Churches of Asia were already in possession of some of the earlier books of the New Testament. Certain of the Pauline Epistles, and if not one or more of our present Gospels, some collection or collections of the sayings of the Lord were probably in their hands, and familiar to our author. Such documents would not be regarded as possessing canonical authority, like the writings of the Old Testament, but they could not fail to influence a Christian writer who was acquainted with them. If the earlier Epistle of St Peter uses Ephesians and Romans[1], and the contemporary Epistle of Clement of Rome refers to Hebrews and some evangelical collection[2], we may reasonably look for similar traces of Apostolic writings in the Apocalypse of John.

This expectation is to some extent borne out by an examination of the book. (*a*) The Apocalypse contains distinct reminiscences of some known sayings of Christ. Perhaps the most remarkable instance is the formula ὁ ἔχων οὖς ἀκουσάτω which recurs toward the end of each of the messages addressed by the Spirit of Christ to the Churches. The following parallels also are fairly certain:

[1] See Hort, *Romans and Ephesians*, p. 168 f.

[2] *N. T. in the Apostolic Fathers*, pp. 38, 46, 61 f.

Apoc. iii. 3 ἐὰν οὖν μὴ γρηγορήσῃς, ἥξω ὡς κλέπτης, καὶ οὐ μὴ γνῷς ποίαν ὥραν ἥξω ἐπὶ σέ.

Mt. xxiv. 43 εἰ ᾔδει ὁ οἰκοδεσπότης ποίᾳ φυλακῇ (Lc. ὥρᾳ) ὁ κλέπτης ἔρχεται, ἐγρηγόρησεν ἄν.

Apoc. iii. 5 ὁμολογήσω τὸ ὄνομα αὐτοῦ ἐνώπιον τοῦ πατρός μου καὶ ἐνώπιον τῶν ἀγγέλων αὐτοῦ.

Mt. x. 32 ὁμολογήσω κἀγὼ ἐν αὐτῷ ἔμπροσθεν τοῦ πατρός μου (Lc. ἔμπροσθεν τῶν ἀγγέλων τοῦ θεοῦ).

Apoc. xiii. 10 εἴ τις ἐν μαχαίρῃ ἀποκτενεῖ, δεῖ αὐτὸν ἐν μαχαίρῃ ἀποκτανθῆναι.

Mt. xxvi. 52 πάντες γὰρ οἱ λαβόντες μάχαιραν ἐν μαχαίρῃ ἀπολοῦνται.

Apoc. xxi. 6 ἐγὼ τῷ διψῶντι δώσω ἐκ τῆς πηγῆς τοῦ ὕδατος τῆς ζωῆς δωρεάν. xxii. 17 ὁ διψῶν ἐρχέσθω· ὁ θέλων λαβέτω ὕδωρ ζωῆς δωρεάν.

Jo. iv. 10 εἰ ᾔδεις τὴν δωρεὰν τοῦ θεοῦ καὶ τίς ἐστιν ὁ λέγων σοι Δός μοι πεῖν, σὺ ἂν ᾔτησας αὐτόν, καὶ ἔδωκεν ἄν σοι ὕδωρ ζῶν. vii. 37 ἐάν τις διψᾷ, ἐρχέσθω πρός μέ, καὶ πινέτω.

There is also in the Apocalypse a considerable number of probable allusions to the teaching of Christ, such as ii. 17 *δώσω αὐτῷ τοῦ μάννα*, iii. 14 *ὁ ἀμήν*, iii. 17 *εἶ...τυφλός* (in an ethical sense), iii. 21 *ἐνίκησα* (cf. v. 5), xii. 10 *ἡ ἐξουσία τοῦ χριστοῦ αὐτοῦ*, xiv. 12 *ἡ ὑπομονὴ τῶν ἁγίων*, xvii. 14 *κλητοὶ καὶ ἐκλεκτοί*, xix. 9 *οἱ εἰς τὸ δεῖπνον τοῦ γάμου τοῦ ἀρνίου κεκλημένοι*.

(*b*) There are no such close parallels between the Apocalypse and the Apostolic Epistles[1], yet there is much in the Apocalypse which suggests that its writer was acquainted with some of them. Bishop Lightfoot has pointed out[2] that "the message communicated by St John to Laodicea prolongs the note which was struck by St Paul in the letter to Colossae." Here and there even the phraseology of the book reminds us of the Pauline letters to Asian Churches; thus Apoc. i. 5 *ὁ πρωτότοκος τῶν νεκρῶν* recalls Col. i. 18 *πρωτότοκος ἐκ τῶν νεκρῶν*, and Apoc. iii. 14 *ἡ ἀρχὴ τῆς κτίσεως τοῦ θεοῦ* has affinities with Col. i. 15 *πρωτότοκος πάσης κτίσεως κτλ.*; while echoes of Eph. ii. 19 ff. *συνπολῖται τῶν ἁγίων... ἐποικοδομηθέντες ἐπὶ τῷ θεμελίῳ τῶν ἀποστόλων καὶ προφήτων... ...εἰς ἅγιον ναὸν ἐν Κυρίῳ* may be heard by those who 'have an ear' in Apoc. iii. 12, xxi. 14. Points of contact have also been

[1] The saying in Apoc. ii. 14 *οὐ βάλλω ἐφ' ὑμᾶς ἄλλο βάρος* has probably been suggested by the letter of the council of Apostles and elders held at Jerusalem; cf. Acts xv. 28 *ἔδοξεν γὰρ τῷ πνεύματι τῷ ἁγίῳ καὶ ἡμῖν μηδὲν πλέον ἐπιτίθεσθαι ὑμῖν βάρος πλὴν κτλ.*

[2] *Colossians*, p. 41 ff.

found between the Apocalypse and the Epistle of James[1] and the first Epistle of Peter[2], and it has occasional resemblances to the Epistle to the Hebrews[3]. Yet on the whole, except in the case of our Lord's sayings, which may or may not have been known to him in a written form, there is no convincing evidence that our author was indebted to the Christian writers who preceded him.

5. Can a better case be made out for the Apocalyptist's use of non-canonical Jewish writings? Dr Charles pronounces the "writer or writers" of the Apocalypse to be "steeped in Jewish apocalyptic literature." The details may be seen in his editions of Enoch and other Jewish apocalypses, and most of them are briefly enumerated in *c.* ii of this introduction[4] and quoted in the commentary, where the parallels occur. Here it is enough to say that while they shew the writer of the Christian Apocalypse to have been familiar with the apocalyptic ideas of his age, they afford little or no clear evidence of his dependence on Jewish sources other than the books of the Old Testament. Certainly he does not use these sources with anything like the distinctness with which he refers to Isaiah, Ezekiel, or Daniel, or to sayings of Christ which are in our present Gospels. The most that can be safely affirmed is that he shared with the Jewish apocalyptists the stock of apocalyptic imagery and mystical and eschatological thought which was the common property of an age nurtured in the Old Testament and hard pressed by the troubles and dangers of the times.

This consideration does not encourage the view which regards the Apocalypse of John as a composite work largely made up of extracts from unknown non-Christian apocalypses. If it cannot be shewn that the author availed himself to any extent of sources still extant, including the well-known Book of Enoch, it is certainly precarious to build theories upon the hypothesis that he was indebted to lost works of which not a trace remains.

[1] Mayor, *St James*, p. cii.

[2] Bigg, 1 *Peter*, p. 22. He adds however: "There is nothing to show that the one book was known to the author of the other."

[3] Cf. e.g. Apoc. xxi. with Heb. xii. 22.

[4] pp. xxi ff.

XIV.

DOCTRINE.

1. No one who comes to the Apocalypse fresh from the study of the Gospels and Epistles can fail to recognize that he has passed into another atmosphere. The great objects of faith are the same, but they are seen in new lights, and the general impression differs from that which is left on the mind by the teaching of our Lord or of St Paul. Nor is it only in the region of eschatology that the book takes its own course; its views of the Person of Christ, of the Holy Spirit, of Redemption, and of the Church, are its own; even its doctrine of God has no exact parallel in the rest of the New Testament.

2. The Apocalypse takes its stand on a monotheism which is Jewish in the sharpness of its opposition to polytheistic systems of every kind. Its God is the God of the Old Testament, the *I am* of Exodus, the *Holy, Holy, Holy* of Isaiah, the *Lord God* of Ezekiel, the *God of heaven* of Daniel[1]. The writer adopts the titles which the Greek translators found to express the glories of the God of Israel: God is ὁ ὤν, ὁ ζῶν, ὁ παντοκράτωρ: He is ἅγιος, ὅσιος, ἀληθινός, ἰσχυρός, ὁ πρῶτος καὶ ὁ ἔσχατος[2], while later Jewish use contributes a designation for His unique eternity: He is *the Alpha and the Omega, the Beginning and the End*[3]. The God of the Church is the Supreme King Whose Throne is in heaven, the Master and Lord of all[4]; He is the

[1] i. 4; iv. 8; i. 8, xxii. 5; xi. 13, xvi. 11.

[2] i. 4, iv. 9 f.; i. 8, vi. 10, xv. 4, xviii. 8, i. 17.

[3] i. 8, xxi. 6.

[4] iv. 2, vi. 10, xi. 4, 15, xv. 3.

Creator of earth and sea and sky, and of all that is in them[1], the Judge of mankind, the Avenger of the wrongs that are done on the earth, to be feared and worshipped by all[2]. But of His love no express mention is made, although there is frequent reference to His wrath[3]. He is nowhere represented as the Father of men, even of the righteous; His righteousness and truth are magnified, but there is no proportionate exhibition of His goodness and beneficence. The picture inspires awe, but it wants the magnetic power of our Lord's doctrine of the Divine Fatherhood. In fact it serves another purpose. Like the solemn descriptions of God-head in the Hebrew Prophets, it is an answer to the inanities of heathenism rather than a call to fellowship with the Living God. A revelation of the "severity of God" was needed by Churches which were hard pressed by the laxity of pagan life and the claims to Divine honours made by the masters of the Empire. The Apocalyptist meets the immoralities and blasphemies of heathendom by a fresh setting forth of the majesty of the One God and a restatement of His sole right to the worship of men. Thus he represents a view of the Divine Character which, apart from his book, would be nearly wanting in the New Testament, and supplies a necessary complement to the gentler teaching of the Gospels and Epistles.

3. The doctrine of God maintained in the Apocalypse cannot be rightly understood apart from its Christology. Our author's revelation of the Father is supplemented by his revelation of the Son. The Christ of the Apocalypse is the Christ of the Gospels, but a change has passed over Him which is beyond words. He is still 'like a son of man[4],' but the weaknesses and limitations of His humanity have finally passed away. He *was dead*, but now He is *alive for evermore*[5]. He was slain as a victim, but only the splendid results of His Sacrifice remain[6]. The Woman's Son has been *caught up unto God, and unto His Throne*[7]; He sits and reigns with His Father[8]. All this had been taught by

[1] iv. 11, x. 6.
[2] xiv. 7, xv. 4; vi. 10, xix. 2.
[3] xiv. 10, 19, xv. 1, etc.
[4] i. 13, xiv. 14.
[5] i. 18.
[6] v. 6 ὡς ἐσφαγμένον.
[7] xii. 5.
[8] iii. 21.

St Peter, St Paul, and the writer to the Hebrews; but it was left for the Apocalyptist to describe the glorified life. In the Apocalypse the veil is lifted, and we see the extent of the change wrought by the Resurrection and Ascension. Even the Lord's human form is idealized; the face shines as the noonday sun, the eyes flash, the hair is white as snow, the feet glow like metal in a furnace, the voice is like the thunder of the waterfall; at the sight of the glorified humanity the Seer swoons, as Daniel before the angel[1]. Other appearances of the ascended Christ are not less overwhelming; whether He sits on the white cloud, crowned, and carrying the sharp sickle with which He will presently reap the harvest of the world[2], or comes forth from the open heavens as the Warrior-King, followed by the armies of Heaven, His head encircled by the diadems of many empires, His *paludamentum* inscribed with the title *King of kings and lord of lords,* all is transcendental and on a scale which surpasses human imagination[3]. But these three great symbolical visions do not by any means exhaust the wealth of St John's conception of the glorified Christ. He depicts with great fulness His relations to the Church, to the world, and to God. (*a*) To the members of His Church the ascended Christ is all in all. He loves them, He redeemed them, and He has made them what they are, a new Israel, a kingdom of priests[4]. His ascension has not separated Him from them; He is in their midst, regulating all the affairs of the Churches[5]; removing, punishing, guarding, giving victory, as He sees fit[6]. From Him are to be obtained all spiritual gifts and helps[7]; from Him are to be expected the final rewards[8]. The martyrs are his witnesses, the saints His servants[9]. He penetrates the inner life of the faithful; He leads them on, and they follow Him[10]. They keep the faith of Jesus, as they keep the commandments of God; they share His sufferings, and expect His kingdom[11]. (*b*) In the creation Jesus Christ holds the foremost

[1] i. 14—17.
[2] xiv. 14 ff.
[3] xix. 11 ff.
[4] i. 5, 6 (Exod. xix. 6).
[5] i. 13, ii. 1, xiv. 1.
[6] ii. 5, 25 ff., iii. 9, 10.
[7] iii. 18.
[8] ii. 7 etc., 23.
[9] ii. 13, 20, xi. 18.
[10] iii. 20, vii. 17, xiv. 4.
[11] xiv. 12, i. 9.

place. He is its Beginning and its goal[1]; He receives its tribute of praise[2]. In human history He is supreme: He alone is able to open, one after another, all the seals of the Book of Destiny[3]; He is the *Ruler of the kings of the earth*[4]; He was born to rule the nations with the iron-tipped rod of the universal Pastor of men[5]; the greatest of Emperors is His vassal[6], and the day will come when the Augustus and the meanest slave in his empire will tremble alike before His victorious wrath[7]. The Apocalyptist foresees an empire more truly oecumenical than that of Rome, in which Christ shall reign with God[8]. (*c*) What is the relation of Christ, in His glorified state, to God? (i) He has the prerogatives of God. He searches men's hearts[9]; He can kill and restore to life[10]; He receives a worship which is rendered without distinction to God[11]; His priests are also priests of God[12]; He occupies one throne with God[13], and shares one sovereignty[14]. (ii) Christ receives the titles of God. He is the Living One[15], the Holy and the True[16], the Alpha and the Omega, the First and the Last, the Beginning and the End[17]. (iii) Passages which in the Old Testament relate to God are without hesitation applied to Christ, e.g. Deut. x. 17 (Apoc. xvii. 14), Prov. iii. 12 (Apoc. iii. 19), Dan. vii. 9 (Apoc. i. 14), Zech. iv. 10 (Apoc. v. 6). Thus the writer seems either to coordinate or to identify Christ with God. Yet he is certainly not conscious of any tendency to ditheism, for his book, as has been said, is rigidly monotheistic; nor, on the other hand, is he guilty of confusing the two Persons. The name of God is nowhere given to Christ in the Apocalypse; He is the *Son of God*[18], the *Word of God*[19]; but the Apocalyptist does not add, with the fourth Evangelist, "the Word was God," nor does he say that the Father and the Son are

[1] iii. 14, xxii. 13.
[2] v. 13.
[3] v. 5, vi. 1 ff.
[4] i. 5.
[5] xii. 5.
[6] xvii. 14.
[7] vi. 15 ff.
[8] xi. 15; cf. xii. 10.
[9] ii. 23.
[10] i. 18, ii. 23.
[11] v. 13.
[12] xx. 6.
[13] xxii. 1, 3.
[14] xi. 15.
[15] i. 18.
[16] iii. 7.
[17] xxii. 13.
[18] ii. 18.
[19] xix. 13.

one. He is careful to identify the ascended Christ with the Christ of the humiliation; He is the *firstborn of the dead*[1], the *root and the offspring of David*[2], the *Lion of the tribe of Judah*[3]; He can call God His God. The enigma meets us everywhere in the New Testament, but in no book is it so perplexing to those who reject the Catholic doctrine of our Lord's Person as in the Apocalypse of John. It has been urged that "the point of view of the Seer is continually changing. He conceives of Jesus now as the highest of the creatures, now as the eternal beginning and end of all things...to us each of these is a definite and separate conception, while to him such definiteness and separation did not exist[4]." But this explanation is doubly unsatisfactory. The Seer's consciousness of the gulf which parts the creature from the Uncreated was far from indefinite; twice he represents an angel as flatly refusing divine honours—*see thou do it not...worship God*[5]: the assumption or acceptance of divine names by the Roman Emperors was in his judgement the damning sin of the Empire. Nor is it quite fair to charge him with shifting his ground from time to time; from the first his Christ is a complex conception in which human and Divine characteristics coexist. On the other hand we should doubtless err if we read into the Seer's visions the precision of the Nicene or the Chalcedonian Christology. An intuitive faith carries him beyond the point reached by the understanding; he knows that the identification of the ascended Christ with the Almighty Father is not inconsistent with strict monotheism, but he does not stop to ask himself how this can be. Some of his words point to the preexistence of the Son, others represent His exalted condition as the reward of victory. The reconciliation of these points of view is not necessary to the purpose of the book; it is enough that the Head of the Church is master of the situation which had arisen in Asia and of every similar situation that can arise to the world's end. The John of the Apocalypse is less of the theologian than St Paul, and less of

[1] i. 5, 18.
[2] v. 5, xxii. 16.
[3] v. 5.
[4] R. Palmer, *Drama of the Apocalypse*, p. 105.
[5] xix. 10, xxii. 9.

the mystic than the author of the fourth Gospel, but he surpasses both in his revelation of the unbounded power of the exalted Christ. Nowhere else in the New Testament are the personal activities of Jesus Christ present in His Church, the glories of His heavenly life, or the possibilities of His future manifestation so magnificently set forth. The Christology of the Apocalypse may evade analysis, but it meets the need of the Church in times of storm and stress. It is the New Testament counterpart of the Old Testament hymns of anticipated triumph: *God is our refuge and strength, a very present help in trouble; therefore will we not fear.... God is in the midst of her; she shall not be moved.* However the fact may be explained, Christ is in the Apocalypse the power of God and the wisdom of God present with the Church, while in His exalted life He is in the midst of the Throne.

4. Of the Spirit we expect to hear much in the one prophetical book of the New Testament, and we are not altogether disappointed, though there is less on the surface of the book than we might have looked for. It is *in the Spirit* that the Seer receives his first and second visions[1]; in the Spirit, again, he is carried into the wilderness where he sees the harlot Babylon, and to the mountain from whence can be descried the new Jerusalem[2]; and doubtless we are to understand that the same condition of spiritual exaltation accompanied the other visions of the Apocalypse. The *Spirit of prophecy* speaks everywhere, bearing witness to Jesus[3], exhorting the Churches in His Name[4], conveying the *revelation of Jesus Christ* to the Seer, and through him to the readers and hearers. It is the Spirit of prophecy who answers to the voice from heaven[5]; who identifies Himself with the Churches in their call for the Lord to *come*[6]. But the book recognizes other and wider manifestations of the Spirit of God. When the writer desires *grace and peace* for the Churches of Asia from the *seven Spirits which are before His Throne* it is probable that he is thinking of the One Spirit in the variety and completeness of

[1] i. 10, iv. 2.
[2] xvii. 3, xxi. 10.
[3] xix. 10.
[4] ii. 1, 7 etc.
[5] xiv. 13.
[6] xxii. 17.

His gifts. The phrase might in itself mean only the seven Angels of the Presence[1], and this interpretation receives some support from *c.* iv. 5, but it does not accord either with the trinitarian character of *c.* i. 4 f.[2], or with *c.* v. 6. The seven Spirits which blaze like torches before the Throne, are in the last passage the eyes of the sacrificed Lamb, i.e. they are the organs of supernatural vision which illuminate the humanity of our Lord, and which He sends forth into the world. It is impossible not to recognize here the mission of the Paraclete, Who is at once the Spirit of Christ, and the Spirit sent by Him from the Father to the Church. And on looking back to *c.* i. 4 we see the fitness of the number seven; each of the seven Churches has its own *μερισμός* of the Spirit; only to the Christ and to the whole body of the Church considered in its unity belongs the fulness of spiritual powers and gifts, the *septiformis Spiritus* Who is in His essence indivisible. Thus the Apocalypse extends the teaching of the Epistles. Diversities of gifts mark the work of the Spirit in the Churches as in their individual members; to each is given the manifestation of the Spirit. Yet the individual is not overlooked. The action of the Spirit on the personal life is shewn in the symbolism which points to the water of life. *The Lamb... shall guide them unto fountains of waters of life. I will give unto him that is athirst of the fountain of the water of life freely. He shewed me a river of water of life,...proceeding out of the throne of God and of the Lamb. He that is athirst, let him come; he that will, let him take the water of life freely*[3]. These passages are remarkable for the width of their outlook: they carry us from the beginnings of the spiritual life to its maturity, from the first gift of the water of life to the state in which access is given to the fountain-head. There is no stage in the progressive development of the new life at which the human spirit is not dependent on the Divine; the water of life which satisfies the first thirst, is not less necessary to the ultimate perfection of the Saints. On the essential nature of the Spirit the Apocalypse has nothing

[1] viii. 2.

[2] Cf. such contexts as 1 Cor. xii. 4 ff., 2 Cor. xiii. 14, Eph. iv. 4 ff.

[3] vii. 17, xxi. 6, xxii. 1, 17.

to add to the teaching of other New Testament books. But in its symbolism we catch glimpses of His relation to the Father and the Son. Jesus Christ *hath the seven Spirits of God*; they are *the eyes of the Lamb*, and are *sent forth* by Him *into all the earth*. The River of the water of life issues from the Throne of God and of the Lamb. There are echoes here of the teaching both of Christ and of St Paul. The Spirit of God is also the Spirit of Christ, and the outpouring of the Spirit which began on the day of Pentecost was a direct consequence of the Ascension; the Paraclete was sent by the Ascended Lord from the Father, and by the Father in the name of the Son. The temporal mission of the Spirit is here in view, but behind it there may be also the eternal procession from the Father through the Son of which the Creed speaks. But the latter does not come within the express scope of the Apocalyptist's words.

5. His treatment of the doctrine of the Church is not less interesting. Like St Paul's Epistle to the Galatians and perhaps also the Epistle to the Ephesians, the Apocalypse is addressed to a plurality of Churches; seven are named, but after the first chapter the number is dropped, and the writer speaks simply of *αἱ ἐκκλησίαι*[1], or once of *πᾶσαι αἱ ἐκκλησίαι*[2]. The singular *ἡ ἐκκλησία* is used of each of the local Christian societies, but not of the Churches in the aggregate, or of the ideal unity of the Christian body. Each society is symbolized by a separate *λυχνία*, and each has its own presiding spirit, its star or angel. There is no spiritual counterpart to the *κοινὸν τῆς Ἀσίας*, no provincial Church or representative council, though the seven Churches may be taken as in a sense representative of the Churches of Asia in general. Yet, as the book proceeds, the conception of an universal Christian society, a catholic Church, appears under more than one symbolical figure. We have first the 144,000 *sealed out of every tribe of the children of Israel*[3], changing, as the Seer watches, into an innumerable company before the Divine Throne, and afterwards seen again as 144,000, surrounding the Lamb on

[1] ii. 7, 11, 17, 29; iii. 6, 13, 22; xxii. 16.

[2] ii. 23.

[3] *cc.* vii., xiv.

Mount Zion. Then *a great sign* appears *in heaven, a woman arrayed with the sun, and the moon under her feet, and upon her head a crown of twelve stars,* who becomes the Mother of the Christ and His Saints[1]. Lastly, in sharp contrast with the Harlot Babylon, we see the Bride of Christ arrayed for her marriage day, and presently transfigured into a new Jerusalem, *coming down out of heaven from God*[2]. In the first of these visions the Church appears as a collection of units, making up the whole number of the elect; in the second and third she is seen in the unity of her common life, first as militant against the evil of the world, her life hid in God, herself imperishable but suffering in the persons of her members; and then, in the final picture, as reaching her ideal in the presence of God and of Christ. There are side-lights, also, in this great series of pictures which deserve attention; in the first, the reconciliation of Divine foreknowledge with the freedom of the human will; in the second, the relation of the Church of the Old Testament to the Church of the New, and of both to the individual; in the third, the social aspect of the Christian life, as set forth in the order and beauty of the City of God.

On the local ministry in the Churches the Apocalyptist preserves a complete silence; he speaks of the itinerant, charismatic, ministry of Apostles and Prophets, but not of the bishops or presbyters and deacons who were doubtless to be found in the Christian communities of Asia. The prophetic order, from his point of view, eclipses the officers of the Church. But it does not take from the lustre of the Church herself. She is a kingdom and a priesthood; all her members have been made by the sacrifice of the Cross kings and priests unto God and to the Lamb[3]. The Augustus and the Caesars, the Asiarchs and high-priests of the Augustea, are of little account in comparison with the despised and persecuted members of the Christian brotherhoods.

6. The soteriology of the Apocalypse demands attention. Thrice in the book[4] "Salvation" (ἡ σωτηρία) is ascribed to God,

[1] c. xii.
[2] c. xxi.
[3] i. 6, v. 10, xx. 6.
[4] vii. 10, xii. 10, xix. 1.

or to God and Christ. The phrase is perhaps suggested by the free use of *σωτήρ* on coins and in inscriptions in reference to certain of the heathen deities (e.g. Zeus, Asklepios), and to the Emperors. John recalls the word from these unworthy uses and claims it for the Ultimate Source of health and life. But in this attribution he includes Jesus Christ[1]; *Salvation unto our God... and unto the Lamb.* It is by the Sacrifice of the Lamb that the salvation of men has become possible[2]: *thou wast slain and didst purchase unto God with thy blood men of every tribe; unto him that loved us and loosed us from our sins by his blood...to him be the glory;* the Saints *washed their robes, and made them white in the blood of the Lamb: they overcame* the accuser *because of the blood of the Lamb.* Whatever may be the exact meaning of these words, it is clear from them that the writer attached the greatest importance to the death of Christ; His sacrificed life was the price of man's redemption from sin to the service of God. The idea is St Paul's, who twice in one epistle writes: "ye were bought with a price[3]," and lays emphasis on the virtue of the sacrificial blood[4]; and the latter point was present to the mind of our Lord Himself when He spoke of His Blood as *shed for many unto remission of sins*[5]. The writer of the Apocalypse took over the familiar figures by which the Churches had long expressed the mystery of the Atonement. But there are new features in his use of them. Redemption is a liberation from the sins of the past life, which have hitherto "tied and bound" the sinner with their chains; it is a purchase for God, its purpose being to transfer the sinner from the service of sin to the service of God[6]. But its end is not attained without the concurrence of the human will. The redeemed cooperate with the Redeemer; they wash their robes and make them white, they fight and overcome. Neither action would have been possible without our Lord's sacrifice, but the sacrifice would have been ineffectual without

[1] vii. 10.

[2] i. 5, v. 9, vii. 14, xii. 11.

[3] 1 Cor. vi. 20 ἠγοράσθητε γὰρ τιμῆς, vii. 23 τιμῆς ἠγοράσθητε.

[4] Acts xx. 28; Rom. iii. 25, v. 9; Eph. i. 7, ii. 13; Col. i. 20. Cf. 1 Pet. i. 2, 19; 1 Jo. i. 7.

[5] Mt. xxvi. 28; Mc. xiv. 24; 1 Cor. xi. 25.

[6] There is a partial parallel in Rom. vi. 15 ff.

repentance and faith on their part. *Blessed are they that wash their robes, that they may have the right to come to the tree of life, and may enter in by the gates into the city*[1]. In accordance with the importance thus attached to human effort, the Apocalyptist dwells more frequently on "works" than on "faith." *I know thy works* stands in the forefront of five of the seven messages addressed to the Churches[2]. *Repent and do the first works; I will give unto each one of you according to your works; I have found no works of thine fulfilled before my God; the dead were judged... according to their works; my reward is with me to render to each man according as his work is*[3]—are examples of the insistence on practical religion which marks the book. To represent this as a return to a Jewish standpoint is arbitrary[4], but it cannot be denied that the frequent occurrence of such sayings is a distinguishing note of the Apocalypse. Faith is rarely named in the book[5], and when it is, it does not appear as the primary necessity of the Christian life; the decisive place is given to works; the fair linen which decks the Saints is woven out of their righteous acts[6]. Salvation is the fruit of the Lord's victory, but the faith which appropriates it overcomes the world as He overcame it.

7. The Angelology of the Apocalypse is abundant. Beyond any other book either in the Old Testament or in the New, it occupies itself with the inhabitants of the unseen order; even of apocalyptic writings the Enoch literature alone perhaps is more fruitful in revelations of this kind. The Apocalypse of John, however, is singularly free from the wild speculations of Jewish angelology. If angels frequently appear in its visions, they belong to the scenes which the visions reveal, and are there because the supermundane events which are in progress demand their intervention. They are seen engaged in the activities of their manifold ministries, now as worshipping before the Throne[7],

[1] xxii. 14.

[2] ii. 2 (Ephesus), 19 (Thyatira), iii. 1 (Sardis), 8 (Philadelphia), 15 (Laodicea).

[3] ii. 5, 23, iii. 2, xx. 12 f., xxii. 12.

[4] The present writer is unable to discover here or elsewhere in the Apocalypse the "unadulterated Judaism" which has been ascribed to it (Charles, *Eschatology*, p. 347).

[5] Only in ii. 13, 19, xiii. 10, xiv. 12.

[6] xix. 8.

[7] vii. 11.

now as bearing messages to the world[1], or as stationed in some place of trust, restraining elemental forces[2], or themselves under restraint until the moment for action has arrived[3], or as presiding over great departments of Nature[4]. Sometimes their ministries are cosmic; they are entrusted with the execution of worldwide judgements[5], or they form the rank and file of the *armies of heaven*, who fight God's battles with evil, whether diabolical or human[6]; the Abyss is under their custody[7]. Sometimes an angel is employed in the service of the Church, offering the prayers of the Saints, or presiding over the destinies of a local brotherhood or ministering to an individual brother, e.g. to the Seer himself[8]. No charge seems to be too great for an angel to undertake, and none too ordinary; throughout the book the angels are represented as ready to fill any place and do any work to which they are sent. Little light is thrown on such a speculative topic as the distribution of the angelic host into orders or ranks. The greater angels are distinguished by their superior strength or more splendid surroundings. Only one angel receives a name, and it is borrowed from the Book of Daniel[9]; there is but a passing allusion to the seven angels of the Presence, of whom Enoch has so much to say[10].

The Apocalypse is comparatively silent as to fallen angels and evil spirits. The Dragon of *c.* xii. is identified with Satan or the Devil of the Old Testament; in the celestial war of xii. 7 ff. he is followed by his "angels" who fight his battles[11]. Idolatry is regarded as demonolatry[12]: heathen magic is due to *spirits of demons, working signs*. Babylon becomes *a habitation of demons, and a hold of every unclean spirit*[13]. The Seer is able to foresee the course of Satanic activity from his own age to the end. Failing to dethrone the ascended Christ, Satan turns his attention to the Church which is left on earth[14]. He finds ready allies in

[1] i. 1, xxii. 6.
[2] vii. 1.
[3] ix. 15.
[4] xvi. 1 ff.
[5] viii. 6 ff., xix. 14.
[6] xii. 7, xix. 14.
[7] ix. 11, xx. 1.
[8] viii. 3 f., ii. 1 etc., xvii. 1, xxi. 9.
[9] xii. 7; cf. Dan. x. 21.
[10] viii. 2; cf. Enoch xx.
[11] xii. 9.
[12] ix. 20.
[13] xviii. 2.
[14] xii. 7 ff., 13 ff.

the persecuting Emperors and the heathen priesthood[1], backed by the power of the new Babylon on the Tiber[2]. Babylon falls at last[3], and for a long period Satan is bound, and the Church dominant[4]. Then a reaction follows, and the whole world is persuaded to attack the Church[5]. But her hour of greatest peril ushers in the final victory. Fire falls from heaven upon the enemy, and Satan himself is consigned to the burning morass from which there is no escape. The fate of his "angels" is not described, but it may be assumed that they perish with their leader[6], for from this point all superhuman forces of evil disappear.

8. Eschatology, in the widest sense, forms one of the main subjects of this book, which from *c.* iv. deals chiefly with *the things which must come to pass hereafter*[7]. Here our discussion of the subject must be limited to the "last things" in the narrower use of the phrase, i.e. to the Coming of the Lord, the Judgement, and the new world beyond them. No mention is made of the *παρουσία*[8] or *ἐπιφάνεια*[9] of the Lord, and though *ἔρχομαι* and the response *ἔρχου* are watchwords in this book, the "coming" intended, in some instances at least, is not the final Advent, but the visitation of a Church or an individual[10]. Moreover, there is no one vision which answers altogether to the conception of the Return, as it is presented in our Lord's teaching and in the Epistles. We look for such an appearance immediately before the general resurrection and judgement (xx. 11 ff.), or in connexion with the descent of the Bride, but it is absent. Perhaps the Reaper on the white cloud[11], or the crowned Warrior on the white horse[12], may describe, each in its own way, the Last Coming, but neither of these visions exhausts the conception, or occupies the position which the Parousia might have been expected to fill.

1 xiii. 1 ff., 11 ff.
2 *c.* xvii.
3 *c.* xviii.
4 xx. 1 ff.
5 *Ib.* 8 ff.
6 Cf. Mt. xxv. 41.
7 iv. 1; cf. i. 19.
8 Mt. xxiv. 3 ff.; 1 Cor. xv. 23; 1 Th. ii. 19, iii. 13, iv. 15, v. 23; Jac. v. 7 f.; 2 Pet. iii. 4; 1 Jo. ii. 28.
9 1 Tim. vi. 14; 2 Tim. i. 10, iv. 1, 8; Tit. ii. 12.
10 E.g. ii. 5, 16, and perhaps also iii. 11, xvi. 15.
11 xiv. 14.
12 xix. 11.

Yet the book starts with a clear reference to the Advent, which is represented as visible to the whole world: *behold, he cometh with the clouds, and every eye shall see him*[1]; and it ends with the solemn witness, *Yea, I come quickly.* The hope of a visible Coming, and that a speedy one, has not vanished, though it is clear that ταχύ must be interpreted relatively, in the light of a prophecy which interposes between the Seer's time and the Return an age of persecution of unknown length and a subsequent millennium of dominant Christianity. The Lord's *quickly* is His final answer to the rising impatience of the Church[2], now on the verge of the second century; measured by the standard of His endless life, *the time is at hand.*

The final Reign of Christ and of His Saints is connected with the hope of His return. His own Reign began with the Ascension, and it is spiritually shared by the Church, even in an age of persecution; the Saints *reign upon the earth*[3], though a Nero or a Domitian may be on the throne. The Apocalyptist dimly foresees the conversion of the Empire, when *the kingdom of the world* became *the kingdom of our Lord and of His Christ,* and the Church entered on a long period of triumph, reigning with Christ for a thousand years[4]. But he also anticipates a future kingdom of the Saints which will fulfil its ideal, and to which no period can be put: *they shall reign for ever and ever*[5].

The General Resurrection and the Judgement belong to the same series of events. If the interpretation of the Thousand Years which is given in this commentary[6] is correct, the "first resurrection" of *c.* xx. 5 is, like the resurrection of the Two Witnesses in *c.* xi., a symbol of the revival and extension of the Church which would follow the age of persecution. No "second resurrection" is mentioned, but a resurrection of the body is implied in *c.* xx. 12 and the glory of the risen Saints is perhaps symbolized in *c.* xxi. 11. The former of these passages clearly

[1] i. 7.
[2] Cf. 2 Pet. iii. 9.
[3] v. 10, reading βασιλεύουσιν.
[4] xi. 15, xx. 6.
[5] xxii. 5.
[6] P. 260 ff.

teaches the doctrine of a general Judgement. But the Judge seems to be not the Incarnate Son, but the Almighty Father: the Apocalyptist does not appear to recognize with the Evangelist that all judgement has been given to the Son[1].

The vision of the Last Judgement is followed by a vision of the new world and the new City of God. Perhaps it will always be a matter of dispute whether the final vision of the Apocalypse is an idealistic picture of the Church as she now is, or a realistic picture of the Church as she will be hereafter. There is in fact an element of truth in each of these views, for the best ideals of the present are the realities of the future. The position of the vision points to the future, for though the succession of the Apocalyptic visions is not chronological, there is in it a certain sequence which accords with the orderly development of the Divine purpose. And no stretch of the imagination can discover in any period of the Church's lengthening history the full counterpart of the glories described by St John. The Bride of Christ has not yet made herself ready; the City of God is not free from the presence of the unclean and the false: night still falls upon her streets, alternating with periods of daylight[2]. But the future holds the perfection of the present; in the imperfect life of the Asian brotherhoods the Seer can find the earnest of a maturity which, when extended to the race, will leave no part of God's great plan for the reconstruction of human society unrealized.

9. It is not the purpose of the Apocalypse to teach Christian doctrine, but to inspire Christian hope. But incidentally it instructs, and its teaching, so far as it goes, is fresh, strenuous, and suggestive. While it has points of contact with the sayings of our Lord in the Synoptic Gospels, with the doctrine of St Paul and his school, and with the Gospel and the First Epistle of St John, there are features in the doctrine of the Apocalypse which are peculiar to itself; nor is the proportion in which

[1] Jo. v. 22; cf. Mt. xxv. 31 ff. It may be noted that St Paul speaks indifferently of the βῆμα τοῦ θεοῦ (Rom. xiv. 10) and the β. τοῦ χριστοῦ (2 Cor. v. 10); the Father judges in the person of the Son.

[2] xxi. 2, 25, 27, xxii. 5.

it presents the aspects of Christian truth quite that which is to be found in other books of the New Testament. Without the Apocalypse, so far as we can judge, our knowledge of the teaching of the Apostolic age would have been imperfect; in this respect the book is complementary to the Gospels and Epistles, and fulfils the important work of preserving the balance of truth. This is not the least of the reasons for which it deserves careful study, and may in itself be held to justify the felicitation: *blessed is he that readeth, and they that hear the words of this prophecy.*

XV.

AUTHORSHIP.

1. At the beginning of the book, and again at the end[1], the Apocalypse professes to be the work of John. The author further states that he is a servant of Jesus Christ, a brother of the Churches of Asia, and a partaker in their sufferings, and that at the time when he received the revelation he was in the island of Patmos *for the word of God and the testimony of Jesus*[2]. By the "testimony of Jesus" he appears to mean the witness which he had borne to our Lord in his capacity as a member of a brotherhood of Christian prophets[3]. The intimate knowledge which he shews of the circumstances of the Churches in Asia, and the unhesitating tone of authority in which he addresses them, leave no doubt that he had resided in the province, and had exercised his office in the Christian societies there.

It is scarcely possible that the book can be pseudonymous. The Jewish pseudepigrapha bear the names of Old Testament patriarchs, kings, or prophets; and a Christian apocalypse, if pseudonymous, would naturally have been attributed to an Apostle. But in that case the writer would assuredly have proclaimed his identity with the son of Zebedee. The apocryphal apocalypse of Paul begins: ἀποκάλυψις τοῦ ἁγίου ἀποστόλου Παύλου, and the apocryphal apocalypse of John: ἀποκάλυψις τοῦ ἁγίου Ἰωάννου τοῦ θεολόγου[4]. These are later documents, but even in a first century apocryphon we should have expected some such note of identification as ὁ τοῦ

[1] i. 1, 4, 9, xxii. 8.

[2] i. 9.

[3] xix. 10, xxii. 9.

[4] Tischendorf, *Apocalypses apocryphae*, pp. 34, 70. The opening of the earlier Apocalypse of Peter has not been recovered, but in the Petrine Gospel the identification is explicit: § 14 ἐγὼ δὲ Σίμων Πέτρος καὶ Ἀνδρέας ὁ ἀδελφός μου.

Ζεβεδαίου, ὁ ἐπὶ τὸ στῆθος, or at least ὁ μαθητὴς τοῦ κυρίου or ὁ πρεσβύτερος. But there is not only an entire absence of such appellatives; the indications, so far as they go, are unfavourable to the hypothesis that the writer meant to pose as an Apostle. The John of the Apocalypse is simply a "brother," and the only office which he claims is that of prophet. This does not indeed disprove his identity with the Apostle[1], but it is not what might have been expected from a writer who wished to pass as one of the Twelve.

2. The name Johanan[2] was by no means uncommon in Jewish history from the time of the Captivity onwards. Some fifteen persons of this name are mentioned in the books of Chronicles, Ezra, and Nehemiah, and five more in the books of the Maccabees. Josephus refers to seventeen Johns[3]; in the New Testament there are at least five—the son of Zacharias, and the son of Zebedee, the father of St Peter[4], John whose surname was Mark, and a John who was of the kindred of the High Priest[5]. Of these, John the son of Zebedee was from an early time identified with the author of the Apocalypse.

The witness of Justin has been given already[6]. Irenaeus calls the author of the fourth Gospel and the Apocalypse ὁ μαθητὴς Κυρίου, *domini discipulus* (iii. 11. 1 ff., iv. 20. 11), but the title, as he uses it, does not exclude Apostleship; cf. ii. 22. 5, where, immediately after mentioning "John, the disciple of the Lord," he proceeds: "non solum Ioannem, sed et alios apostolos." Hippolytus expressly calls the writer of the Apocalypse "Apostle" as well as "disciple[7]," and Tertullian is no less explicit[8]. Origen, again, entertains no doubt that both the Gospel and the Apocalypse proceeded from the son of Zebedee[9]. The earliest suggestion that the Apocalypse was the work of a second John, not of apostolic rank, came from Alexandria after Origen's death[10]; earlier opponents of the apostolic authorship regarded the book as pseudonymous[11].

3. As an alternative to John the son of Zebedee, Dionysius of Alexandria mentions the name of John Mark, but dismisses it on the ground that Mark did not accompany St Paul to Asia.

[1] Even in 2 Peter St Paul is ὁ ἀγαπητὸς ἡμῶν ἀδελφός (iii. 15).

[2] Ἰωάννης, or Ἰωάνης as WH., following cod. ℵ, write the name in *c.* i., is a Hellenized form of Ἰωανάν (= יְהוֹחָנָן, or יוֹחָנָן) which occurs in the LXX. and in Lc. iii. 27. As to the doubled ν see Dalman, *Gr.* p. 142.

[3] See Niese's index, p. 46.

[4] Jo. xxi. 15 ff. Σίμων Ἰωάν[ν]ου.

[5] Acts iv. 6 Ἰωάννης...καὶ ὅσοι ἦσαν ἐκ γένους ἀρχιερατικοῦ.

[6] P. ciii f.

[7] P. cix.

[8] P. cv.

[9] P. cix.

[10] P. cx.

[11] P. cvi. ff.

Apart from this objection, the hypothesis of Marcan authorship has little to recommend it; the style of the second Gospel has no marked affinity with that of the Apocalypse, and its author shews none of the characteristics of the prophet or the mystic: he is graphic and can draw a telling picture, but he is not a visionary and has no eye for the transcendental. The John of the Apocalypse, if not the son of Zebedee, must be, Dionysius concludes, some otherwise unknown John who visited Asia[1], and he finds some support for this view in the story he has heard (*φασίν*) that there were at Ephesus two monuments which passed as the tomb of John. To this Eusebius adds that Papias also seems to speak of two Johns who were both disciples of the Lord, and putting the facts together he infers that if the Apocalypse is not to be ascribed to the Apostle, it was probably the work of the second John who is known to Papias as the Elder[2].

The following are the words of Papias as reported by Eusebius: *τοὺς τῶν πρεσβυτέρων ἀνέκρινον λόγους· τί Ἀνδρέας ἢ τί Πέτρος εἶπεν... ἢ τί Ἰωάννης ἢ Ματθαῖος ἤ τις ἕτερος τῶν τοῦ κυρίου μαθητῶν· ἅ τε Ἀριστίων καὶ ὁ πρεσβύτερος Ἰωάννης οἱ τοῦ κυρίου μαθηταὶ λέγουσιν.* Eusebius' comment is: *ἔνθα καὶ ἐπιστῆσαι ἄξιον δὶς καταριθμοῦντι αὐτῷ τὸ Ἰωάννου ὄνομα...εἰκὸς γὰρ τὸν δεύτερον* (i.e. the Elder), *εἰ μή τις ἐθέλοι τὸν πρῶτον, τὴν ἐπ' ὀνόματος φερομένην Ἰωάννου Ἀποκάλυψιν ἑωρακέναι.*

4. Perhaps no conjecture hazarded by an ancient writer has been so widely adopted in modern times. A conjecture it still remains, for no fresh light has been thrown on the enigmatic figure of John the Elder. But this circumstance has not prevented scholars from confidently attributing to him one or more of the Johannine group of writings. Even in Jerome's time it was usual to identify the Elder of 2 and 3 John with the second John of Papias.

Hieron. *de virr. ill.* 9 "Iohannis presbyteri adseruntur, cuius hodie alterum sepulcrum apud Ephesum ostenditur." In *c.* 18 he speaks of the "opinionem qua a plerisque rettulimus traditum duas posteriores epistulas Iohannis non apostoli esse sed presbyteri." On the other hand he holds that both the Gospel and the Apocalypse were written by the Apostle (*c.* 9).

[1] *ap.* Eus. *H. E.* vii. 25. [2] *H. E.* iii. 39.

PATMOS.
From a photograph taken in 1887 by Rev. T. C. Fitzpatrick.

The Apocalypse is now ascribed to the Elder by perhaps a majority of critics. But recent criticism goes further, and transfers to the Elder nearly all that has been hitherto given to the Apostle. There were two Johns in the Apostolic age, but only one of them was a resident in Asia, and he was the Elder and not the son of Zebedee. It was the Elder and not the Apostle who was the disciple that Jesus loved, who gave his name to the Johannine books of the New Testament, and claims to be the writer of the Apocalypse.

At this point it will be convenient to collect the traditions which relate to the residence of John in Asia and his exile to Patmos. (1) *Residence in Asia.* Iren. ii. 22. 5 (*ap.* Eus. *H.E.* iii. 23): πάντες οἱ πρεσβύτεροι μαρτυροῦσιν, οἱ κατὰ τὴν Ἀσίαν Ἰωάννῃ τῷ τοῦ κυρίου μαθητῇ συμβεβληκότες, παραδεδωκέναι [ταῦτα] τὸν Ἰωάννην· παρέμεινε γὰρ αὐτοῖς μέχρι τῶν Τραϊανοῦ χρόνων. *Ib.* iii. 3. 4 (*ap.* Eus. *H. E.* iv. 14): καὶ εἰσὶν οἱ ἀκηκοότες αὐτοῦ [*sc.* τοῦ Πολυκάρπου], ὅτι Ἰωάννης ὁ τοῦ κυρίου μαθητὴς ἐν τῇ Ἐφέσῳ πορευθείς κτλ. *Ib.* (*ap.* Eus. *H. E.* iii. 23): ἀλλὰ καὶ ἡ ἐν Ἐφέσῳ ἐκκλησία ὑπὸ Παύλου μὲν τεθεμελιωμένη, Ἰωάννου δὲ παραμείναντος αὐτοῖς μέχρι τῶν Τραϊανοῦ χρόνων, μάρτυς ἀληθής ἐστι τῆς τῶν ἀποστόλων παραδόσεως. *Ib. Ep. ad Florin.* (*ap.* Eus. *H. E.* v. 20): εἶδον γάρ σε, παῖς ὢν ἔτι, ἐν τῇ κάτω Ἀσίᾳ παρὰ τῷ Πολυκάρπῳ...ὥστε με δύνασθαι εἰπεῖν καὶ τὸν τόπον ἐν ᾧ καθεζόμενος διελέγετο ὁ μακάριος Πολύκαρπος...καὶ τὰς διαλέξεις ἃς ἐποιεῖτο πρὸς τὸ πλῆθος, καὶ τὴν μετὰ Ἰωάννου συναναστροφὴν ὡς ἀπήγγελλε, καὶ τὴν μετὰ τῶν λοιπῶν τῶν ἑωρακότων τὸν κύριον. Polycrates (*ap.* Eus. *H. E.* iii. 31, v. 24): ἔτι δὲ καὶ Ἰωάννης ὁ ἐπὶ τὸ στῆθος τοῦ κυρίου ἀναπεσών, ὃς ἐγενήθη ἱερεύς, τὸ πέταλον πεφορεκώς, καὶ μάρτυς καὶ διδάσκαλος, οὗτος ἐν Ἐφέσῳ κεκοίμηται. Of Apollonius (A.D. 196–7, Harnack) Eusebius writes (*H. E.* v. 18): κέχρηται δὲ καὶ μαρτυρίαις ἀπὸ τῆς Ἰωάννου Ἀποκαλύψεως· καὶ νεκρὸν δὲ δυνάμει θείᾳ πρὸς αὐτοῦ Ἰωάννου ἐν τῇ Ἐφέσῳ ἐγηγέρθαι ἱστορεῖ. (2) *Exile to Patmos.* Clem. Al. *quis dives* 42 ἄκουσον μῦθον, οὐ μῦθον ἀλλὰ ὄντα λόγον, περὶ Ἰωάννου τοῦ ἀποστόλου...τοῦ τυράννου τελευτήσαντος ἀπὸ τῆς Πάτμου τῆς νήσου μετῆλθεν ἐπὶ τὴν Ἔφεσον. Origen, *in Matt.* xvi. 6 ὁ δὲ Ῥωμαίων βασιλεύς, ὡς ἡ παράδοσις διδάσκει, κατεδίκασε τὸν Ἰωάννην μαρτυροῦντα διὰ τὸν τῆς ἀληθείας λόγον εἰς Πάτμον τὴν νῆσον. Tertullian, *praescr.* 36: "habes Romam...ubi apostolus Ioannes, posteaquam in oleum igneum demersus nihil passus est, in insulam relegatur." *Act. Iohann.* 14 ἀπέπλευσεν ὁ Ἰωάννης εἰς Πάτμον, ὅπου καὶ ἠξιώθη τὴν τῆς συντελείας ἰδεῖν ἀποκάλυψιν, *ib.* 88 ἔρχεται πρός με καὶ τὸν ἀδελφόν μου Ἰάκωβον. Victorinus *in Apoc.* x. 11 "quando haec Ioannes vidit erat in insula Patmos, in metallum damnatus[1] a

[1] "Down the middle of the island run a succession of hills; in one of them, in the northern half of the island, there are quarries. This, perhaps, is the explanation of the statement that St John was 'damnatus in metallum,' as there do not appear to have been any mines, properly so called. The rock is

Domitiano Caesare. ibi ergo vidit Apocalypsin...et cum iam senior putaret se per passionem accepturum receptionem, interfecto Domitiano, omnia eius iudicia soluta sunt, et Ioannes de metallo dimissus sic postea tradidit hanc eandem quam acceperat a Deo Apocalypsin."

6. Read cursorily, this evidence may seem to establish the identity of John the Apostle with the resident in Asia and the exile of Patmos. But a more careful examination suggests caution. The witness of Irenaeus shews beyond a doubt that a John who had been a disciple of the Lord resided in Asia within the lifetime of Polycarp Bishop of Smyrna, who was born (Harnack) in A.D. 69. A bishop of Ephesus at the end of the second century asserts that the John who lay on the Lord's breast was buried at Ephesus; and another Asian writer of the same period speaks of a miracle which John the author of the Apocalypse performed in that city. No second century testimony, except that of the Leucian Acts, excludes the hypothesis that the John who lived in Asia and wrote the Apocalypse was the Elder, or compels us to believe that John the Apostle ever resided in Asia. Moreover it is certainly remarkable that in so many of the earliest references to him John of Asia is called "the disciple," and not, expressly at least, the Apostle[1]. Nor is the evidence for the Apostle's exile to Patmos quite conclusive. It begins with Clement of Alexandria, and it is chiefly western; Irenaeus does not mention the exile; from residents in Asia, where the event would have made the deepest impression, no reference to it is forthcoming. We cannot overlook the possibility that the tradition rests ultimately on Apoc. i. 9, though against this we must set the apparent independence of the witnesses, and certain amplifications of the traditional story, for which the Apocalypse offers no support.

On the whole it may be said that if early Christian tradition favours the identification of John of Ephesus with the Apostle, it does not exclude the opposite hypothesis, whether in the Eusebian form or in that which is now advocated.

chiefly volcanic." T. C. Fitzpatrick, *A visit to Patmos* (in Christ's College Magazine, 1887).

[1] See Bousset, *Die Offenbarung*, p. 41 f., and in *Encycl. Bibl.*, i., col. 198.

7. It would materially assist us in arriving at a decision if we could ascertain the length of the Apostle's life. Irenaeus, as we have seen, represents John, the disciple of the Lord, as having lived to the time of Trajan, i.e. to the year 98 at least. That the Apostle lived to old age is assumed by ancient writers, e.g. by Clement of Alexandria in his *Quis dives*[1], and by Jerome in his commentary on Galatians. There is, however, some evidence to be set on the other side. A MS. of Georgius Hamartolus (cent. IX.) alleges the authority of Papias, in the second book of his work, for the statement that John the son of Zebedee was martyred by the Jews[2], and the reference to Papias is now supported by an extract printed by Dr C. De Boor from an Oxford MS. of the 7th or 8th century[3], an epitome probably based upon the Chronicle of Philip of Side (cent. V.).

The Coislin MS. of Georgius adds at *Chron.* iii. 134: ['Ιωάννης] μαρτυρίου κατηξίωται· Παπίας γὰρ ὁ Ἱεραπόλεως ἐπίσκοπος, αὐτόπτης τούτου γενόμενος, ἐν τῷ δευτέρῳ λόγῳ τῶν Κυριακῶν λογίων φάσκει ὅτι ὑπὸ Ἰουδαίων ἀνῃρέθη, πληρώσας δηλαδὴ μετὰ τοῦ ἀδελφοῦ τὴν τοῦ χριστοῦ περὶ αὐτῶν πρόρρησιν. De Boor's fragment runs: Παπίας ἐν τῷ δευτέρῳ λόγῳ λέγει ὅτι Ἰωάννης ὁ θεολόγος[4] καὶ Ἰάκωβος ὁ ἀδελφὸς αὐτοῦ ὑπὸ Ἰουδαίων ἀνῃρέθησαν.

With this testimony before us it is not easy to doubt that Papias made some such statement, for the suggestion of a lacuna, offered by Bishop Lightfoot in 1875[5], is now scarcely tenable, though it has been lately revived by Harnack[6]. But if Papias made it, the question remains whether he made it under some misapprehension, or merely by way of expressing his conviction that the prophecy of Mc. x. 39 had found a literal fulfilment. Neither explanation is very probable in view of the early date of Papias[7]. He does not, however, affirm that the brothers

[1] Ap. Eus. *H.E.* iii. 24, ὁ πρεσβύτης... τὸν γέροντα.

[2] See Nolte in *Th. Quartalschrift*, 1862, p. 466.

[3] In *Texte u. Untersuchungen* (v. 2, p. 170, 1888).

[4] Ὁ θεολόγος, as Dr Sanday points out (*Criticism of the Fourth Gospel*, p. 251), "may quite well have been due to the fragmentist."

[5] *Supernatural Religion*, p. 212: "the sentence may have run in the original somewhat in this way, Παπίας...φάσκει ὅτι Ἰωάννης [μὲν ὑπὸ τοῦ Ῥωμαίων βασιλέως κατεδικάσθη, Ἰάκωβος δὲ] ὑπὸ Ἰουδαίων ἀνῃρέθη."

[6] *Chronologie*, i. p. 665 f.

[7] Dr Sanday (*Criticism*, p. 251) writes: "The natural date for the extracts in this chapter [Eus. *H.E.* iii. 39] seems to me to be *circa* 100."

suffered at the same time: the martyrdom of John at the hand of the Jews might have taken place at any date before the last days of Jerusalem. But even if we postpone it to the year 69, and accept the earlier date of the Apocalypse, the book can hardly have come from the hand of the son of Zebedee.

8. Thus, if the statement of Papias is to be allowed to enter into our calculations, it becomes a very important factor, for it disposes of the Apostolic authorship of the Apocalypse[1]. If we believe it, we shall be compelled to attribute the book to an unknown John, who will probably be the second of the two who are named in the Eusebian fragment of Papias. To John the Elder we shall then ascribe the residence in Ephesus and the exile to Patmos which from the time of Clement of Alexandria it has been usual to ascribe to John the Apostle. The Elder will also be, as it seems, the "disciple whom Jesus loved," whose personality is felt throughout the Johannine literature. If an unverifiable reference to a lost book seems too narrow a basis for so large a superstructure, there is still the chance of a primary error, a confusion between the Apostle and the Elder, which may have existed even in the mind of Irenaeus, and have perpetuated itself in the writings of his successors. On this supposition, again, the Apocalypse is not the work of the son of Zebedee and probably comes from the disciple who was not of the Twelve.

9. But there is something to be said on the other side. The Synoptists have preserved some characteristic recollections of John the son of Zebedee, from which the reader of the Gospels may gain an impression of the man. He was one of the three who formed the inner circle of the Apostolic college, and had shared with Peter and James opportunities which were denied to the other nine. He was one of the two brethren who received from the Lord the great name of Boanerges, a word which, whatever its exact history, seems to indicate a strenuous nature[2]. It was John the son of Zebedee who confessed that he forbade one who did not follow our Lord in the company of His disciples

[1] Unless we follow Epiphanius, who places the exile and the visions of the Apocalypse under Claudius; see above, p. xcvi.

[2] *St Mark*[2], p. 60.

to use His name for the working of miracles. It was John and his brother who would have called down fire from heaven upon the Samaritan villages which refused to receive the Master on His way to Jerusalem. It was for John and his brother that their mother sought the nearest places to the Messiah in the glory of His Kingdom. In all these respects the Apocalyptist shews some affinity to the John of the Synoptic Gospels. He is a son of thunder; he calls down fire from heaven; his aversion to the enemies of the Christ and His Church is whole-hearted. The hostile Jews of Smyrna and Philadelphia are the *synagogue of Satan*; Nero, Domitian, the Empire itself so far as it adopts their policy, is *the Beast*; Rome is *Babylon, the mother of the harlots and of the abominations of the earth.* The tone of the book when it lashes the persecutor, the idolater, the unclean, is almost truculent; the Seer's righteous wrath reaches a white heat. The conception of the Christ is one which might seem impossible for the ἐπιστήθιος, though not for the son of Zebedee as he appears in the Synoptists. The Christ of the Apocalypse is infinitely majestic and august, but His predominant characteristic is unbounded power shewing itself in a just severity. As the Shepherd, He rules with a rod of iron; as the Lamb, He is terrible in His anger; as the King, He treads the winepress of the wrath of God. Only once or twice does the tenderness of our Lord's compassion, or the intimacy of His fellowship with men make itself felt in this book. There are few echoes in the Apocalypse of the intense sympathy for the suffering and for sinners which the Gospels associate with the human life of our Lord. The Ascension and Exaltation account for the power and glory with which He is invested by the Apocalyptist, but they do not wholly explain the changed point of view; we feel that the *Revelation of Jesus Christ* has passed through a mind which has coloured it with its own severity, and the colouring is not unlike that which the John of the Synoptic Gospels might have been expected to impart. This fact, though far from being decisive, may well lead us to hesitate before we definitely reject the attribution of the Apocalypse to the Apostle John.

10. The subject must not be dismissed without an attempt to consider, however briefly, the literary relation between the Apocalypse and the fourth Gospel. Some of the evidence has been collected in an earlier chapter of this introduction[1]. It appears to shew that there is an affinity between the two books, extending occasionally to minute resemblances, but counterbalanced by differences so profound that the doubt raised by Dionysius remains unsolved.

(*a*) The difference of style and language has been explained as due in part to a "difference in the scope of the books[2]," and in part to their relative dates. (i) Dr Lightfoot calls attention to the peculiar style of the apocalyptic passages in the Epistles to the Thessalonians and in 2 Peter; "we seem," he writes, "to have stumbled on a passage out of the Hebrew prophets," adding that this "explains also to a great extent the marked difference in style between the Revelation of St John and his other writings[3]." But the analogy of apocalyptic passages in other books of the New Testament goes only a little way towards explaining the stylistic eccentricities of the author of the Apocalypse. Even the LXX. version of the Prophets, uncouth and unintelligible as it often is, can shew no succession of anomalies comparable to those of the Revelation of St John. The argument from analogy would be convincing if the style of the Revelation differed from the style of the Gospel in the same or nearly the same degree as the apocalyptic passages in St Paul differ from the rest of his writings. But in the former case the difference is in truth not one of degree, but of kind. It is incredible that the writer of the Gospel could have written the Apocalypse without a conscious effort savouring of literary artifice. (ii) Is this difficulty removed if we suppose that the Apocalypse was written twenty or five-and-twenty years before the Gospel? Dr Westcott (*l.c.*), arguing for the priority of the Apocalypse, says that it is "very difficult to suppose that the language of the writer of the Gospel could pass at a later time in a Greek-speaking country into the language of the Apocalypse," but on the other hand he thinks that "intercourse with a Greek-speaking people would in a short time naturally reduce the style of the author of the Apocalypse to that of the author of the Gospel." To the present writer the latter hypothesis is at least as difficult as the former. The writer of the Apocalypse may not have been either more or less of a Greek scholar than the writer of the Gospel; but in their general attitude towards the use of language they differ fundamentally. The difference is due to personal character rather than to relative familiarity with Greek. And when style expresses individual character it undergoes little material change even in a long life of literary

[1] *C.* xi.; see especially p. cxxi. ff.

[2] Westcott, *St John*, p. lxxxvi.

[3] *Notes on the Epp. of St Paul*, p. 72 f.

activity, especially after the age which St John must have reached in A.D. 69 or 70.

(*b*) The differences of thought which distinguish the two books have never been more successfully delineated than by Dr Westcott in his introduction to the Gospel of St John[1]. Of these, too, he finds a sufficient explanation in the priority of the Apocalypse[2]: "the differences," in conception as in language, "answer to differences in situation, and are not inconsistent with identity of authorship." "Of the two books the Apocalypse is the earlier. It is less developed both in thought and style...to go back from the teaching of the Gospel to that of the Apocalypse...to reduce the full expression of truth to its rudimentary beginnings, seems to involve a moral miracle." But, even conceding the priority of the Apocalypse, can we explain the difference of standpoint by developement? Is the relation of the Apocalyptic to the Evangelical teaching that which exists between rudimentary knowledge and the maturity of thought? And is it to be maintained that St John's conceptions of Christian truths were still rudimentary forty years after the Ascension, and reached maturity only in extreme old age?

11. But how are we to explain the affinities of the two books—the characteristic phrases and ideas which they have in common? It is usual to account for these by saying that all the Johannine books proceed from the same school, the school of John of Ephesus, whether the Apostle or the Presbyter. Perhaps it is possible to advance a step further. While the Apocalypse definitely claims to be the work of John, no such claim is put forth in the Gospel; for such passages as Jo. xix. 35, xx. 30 f., do not assert more than that the book contains the testimony of John, and xxi. 24 *οὗτός ἐστιν ὁ μαθητὴς...ὁ γράψας ταῦτα* is an editorial note which must not be pressed too closely. On the other hand early tradition explicitly states that the Gospel was written from dictation, and underwent some kind of revision at the hands of those who received it.

The Muratorian fragment thus describes the genesis of the fourth Gospel: "quartum[3] euangeliorum Iohannis ex discipulis. cohortantibus condiscipulis et episcopis suis dixit: Conieiunate mihi hodie triduo et quid cuique fuerit reuelatum alterutrum nobis enarremus. eadem nocte reuelatum Andreae ex apostolis ut recognoscentibus cunctis Iohannes suo nomine cuncta describeret." With

[1] P. lxxxv. f.

[2] On this question see *c*. ix. of this introduction.

[3] Cod. *quarti*. The MSS. have been tacitly corrected in this extract and the next.

this should be compared the singular statement of a Latin prologue to the Gospel, printed in Wordsworth-White (*N. T. Latine*, i. 490 f.): "hoc igitur evangelium post apocalypsin scriptum[1] manifestum, et datum est ecclesiis in Asia a Iohanne adhuc in corpore constituto, sicut Papias nomine Hierapolitanus episcopus, discipulus Iohannis et carus, in exotericis[2] suis, id est, in extremis quinque libris, retulit, qui hoc evangelium Iohanne sub dictante conscripsit[3]." An anonymous Greek writer in the catena of Corderius tells the same story: Ἰωάννης...πάνυ γηραλέου αὐτοῦ γενομένου, ὡς παρέδοσαν ἡμῖν ὅ τε Εἰρηναῖος καὶ Εὐσέβιος καὶ ἄλλοι πιστοὶ κατὰ διαδοχὴν γεγονότες ἱστορικοί,...ὑπηγόρευσε τὸ εὐαγγέλιον τῷ ἑαυτοῦ μαθητῇ Παπίᾳ.

The first of these statements deserves especial attention. It belongs to the second century, and proceeds from the Church of Rome, which was in frequent communication with the Churches of Asia Minor, and had recently been visited by Polycarp: it may even have originated with Polycarp. If its main points are true, the fourth Gospel was not written by the hand of John, but dictated—a word which may be interpreted with some laxity; and it underwent much editorial revision (*recognoscentibus cunctis*). In these circumstances it is possible to conceive of the writer of the Apocalypse being the author of the Gospel, in the sense of having supplied the materials from which it was written.

12. But the question of the authorship of the Apocalypse must not be complicated by considerations connected with the still more vexed question of the authorship of the fourth Gospel. The issue which lies before the student of the Apocalypse is in fact independent of the decision at which the critics of the Gospel may ultimately arrive. Was the John who wrote the Apocalypse the Synoptic son of Zebedee? Was it John the son of Zebedee who lived in Asia, and was exiled to Patmos, or was it the mysterious Elder, who is distinguished by Papias from the Apostle of the same name? A fair case may be made for either view. On the one hand the general character of the book accords

[1] This is the order usually alleged; see e.g. the passages collected by Corssen, *Monarch. Prologe*, p. 801 (in *T. u. U.* xv. 1).

[2] On this word see Lightfoot, *Biblical Essays*, p. 69, n. 5; *Supernatural Religion*, p. 210 ff.

[3] So Cod. Toletanus; Cod. reg. Suet. ends: descripsit vero evangelium, dictante Johanne recte. (The spelling of the MSS. has been conformed to the usual orthography.)

with what the Synoptists relate with regard to the Apostle John, and the main current of Christian tradition favours this conclusion. On the other hand, there is some uncertainty as to the length of the Apostle's life, and some reason to suspect that the Apostle and the disciple are confused in our earliest authorities. While inclining to the traditional view which holds that the author of the Apocalypse was the Apostle John, the present writer desires to keep an open mind upon the question. Fresh evidence may at any time be produced which will turn the scale in favour of the Elder. There are those whom this indecision will disappoint, but it is best frankly to confess the uncertainty which besets the present state of our knowledge. We cannot yet with safety go far beyond the dictum of Dionysius: *ὅτι μὲν οὖν Ἰωάννης ἐστὶν ὁ ταῦτα γράφων, αὐτῷ λέγοντι πιστευτέον· ποῖος δὲ οὗτος, ἄδηλον.*

XVI.

TEXT.

1. The following Uncial MSS. contain the Greek text of the Apocalypse, or a part of it.

ℵ. Cod. Sinaiticus (IV.). Ed. Tischendorf, 1862.

A. Cod. Alexandrinus (V.). Ed. E. M. Thompson, 1879.

C. Cod. Ephraemi Parisiensis (V.). Ed. Tischendorf, 1843. Contains Apoc. i. 1—iii. 19, v. 14—vii. 14, vii. 17—viii. 5, ix. 16—x. 10, xi. 3—xiii. 13, xviii. 2—xix. 5.

P. Cod. Porfirianus Chiavensis (IX.). Ed. Tischendorf (in *mon. sacra ined.* vi.), 1869. Contains Apoc. i. 1—xvi. 12, xvii. 1—xix. 21, xx. 9—xxii. 6.

Q (= B_2). Cod. Vaticanus Gr. 2066, olim Basiliensis 105 (VIII.). Ed. Tischendorf (*in app. N. T. Vatic.*), 1867.

ℷ. Cod. Kosinitsanus (IX. or X.): see Scrivener-Miller, ii., p. 377; Gregory, *Textkritik des N.T.*, i., p. 96; Kenyon, *Handbook to the textual criticism of the N.T.*, p. 104. Von Soden, *Die Schriften des N.T.*, I. i. p. 104, locates it at Drama. Not yet edited or collated.

2. Thus at present there are available only three complete and two imperfect uncials of the Apocalypse. The minuscules also are comparatively few; while we have 1725 MSS. of the Gospels, 520 of the Acts and Catholic Epistles, and 619 of Paul, those of the Apocalypse do not reach 230[1]. The following list is based on Dr C. R. Gregory's *Prolegomena* to Tischendorf and *Textkritik*.

[1] The numbers are von Soden's (1902).

1. Maihingen, Libr. of the Prince of Öttingen-Wallerstein (XII. or XIII.). The only MS. used by Erasmus in 1516 for the Apocalypse[1]. Rediscovered by Delitzsch in 1861: collated by Tregelles in 1862.
2. Paris, Bibl. Nat. Gr. 237 (X.) = Acts 10, Paul 12.
[3. A MS. cited by Stephen: otherwise unknown.]
4. Paris, Bibl. Nat. Gr. 219 (XI.) = Acts 12, Paul 16.
[5. Readings cited by Laurentius Valla a. 1440.]
6. Oxford, Bodl. Barocc. 3 (XI.) = Acts 23, Paul 28.
7. London, Brit. Mus., Harl. 5537 (A.D. 1087) = Acts 25, Paul 31.
8. London, Brit. Mus., Harl. 5778 (XII.) = Acts 28, Paul 34.
9. Oxford, Bodl. Misc. Gr. 74 (XI.) = Acts 30, Paul 36.
10. Cambridge, Univ. Dd. ix. 69 (XV.) = Ev. 60.
[11. Petavius 2 = Acts 39, Paul 45, has disappeared.]
12. Rome, Vat. Reg. Gr. 179 (XV.) = Acts 40, Paul 46.
13. Frankfort on Oder, Lyceum (XI.) = Paul 48.
14. Leicester, Libr. of the Town Council (XV.) = Ev. 69, Acts 31, Paul 37.
15. Basle, Univ. A.N. iii. 12 (?): annexed to Cod. E of the Gospels, but in a later hand; contains only Apoc. iii. 3—iv. 8.
16. Hamburg, City Libr. (XV.) = Acts 45, Paul 52.
17. Paris, Bibl. Nat., Coisl. Gr. 199 (XI.) = Ev. 35, Acts 14, Paul 18.
18. Paris, Bibl. Nat., Coisl. Gr. 202 (XII.) = Acts 18, Paul 22.
19. Paris, Bibl. Nat., Coisl. Gr. 205 (X.) = Acts 17, Paul 21.
20. Rome, Vat. Libr., Gr. 2080 (X. or XI.) = Ev. 175, Acts 41, Paul 194.
21. Rome, Vallicelli D. 20 (XV.).
22. Rome, Vallicelli B. 86 (XIV.) = Acts 166, Paul 204.
23. Florence, Laur. Conv. Soppr. 53 (A.D. 1331) = Ev. 367, Acts 146, Paul 182.
24. Rome, Vat. Gr. 2062 (X. or XI.) = Acts 160, Paul 193.
25. Rome, Vat. Palat. Gr. 171 (XV.) = Ev. 149, Acts 77, Paul 88.
26. Oxford, Christ Ch. Wake 12 (XI. or XII.) = Ev. 506, Acts 199, Paul 256.
27. Oxford, Christ Ch. Wake 34 (XI. or XII.) = Ev. 517, Acts 190, Paul 244.
28. Oxford, Bodl. Barocc. 48 (XV.): ends at xvii. 5.

[1] On the text of Erasmus see Hort, introd. to WH., § 346.

29. London, Brit. Mus. Harl. 5613 (A.D. 1407) = Acts 60, Paul 63.
30. Wolfenbüttel, xvi. 7 (XIV.) = Acts 69.
31. London, Brit. Mus. Harl. 5678 (XV.).
32. Dresden, Reg. A 124 (XV.).
33. Vienna, Imp. Gr. th. 23 (XIII.) = Ev. 218, Acts 65, Paul 57: wants xiii. 5—xiv. 8, xv. 7—xvii. 2, xviii. 10—xix. 15, xx. 7—xxii. 21.
34. Vienna, Imp. Gr. th. 302 (XI.) = Acts 66, Paul 67; wants xv. 6—xvii. 3, xviii. 10—xix. 9, xx. 8—xxii. 21.
35. Vienna, Imp. Gr. th. 307 (XIV.).
36. Vienna, Imp. Libr. suppl. Gr. 93 (XIII.).
37. Rome, Vat. Gr. 366 (XV.) = Acts 72, Paul 79.
38. Rome, Vat. Gr. 579 (XV.).
39. Rome, Vat. Gr. 1136 a (XIV.) = Paul 85; wants i. 1—3, 17; vi. 18—xiii. 11.
40. Rome, Vat. Gr. 1160 (XIII. or XIV.) = Ev. 141, Acts 75, Paul 86.
41. Rome, Vat. Reg. Gr. 68 (XV.).
42. Rome, Vat. Pius II Gr. 50 (XII.) = Acts 80, Paul 91.
43. Rome, Barb. iv. 56 (XIV.). Contains Apoc. xiv. 17—xviii. 20.
44. Rome, Propag. L. vi. 19 (XIV.) = Ev. 180, Acts 82, Paul 92.
45. Florence, Laur. iv. 32 (A.D. 1092) = Acts 89, Paul 99.
46. Venice, St Mark's 10 (XV.) = Ev. 209, Acts 95, Paul 108.
47. Dresden, Reg. A 172 (XI.) = Ev. 241, Acts 104, Paul 120.
48. Moscow, Syn. 380 (XII.) = Ev. 242, Acts 105, Paul 121.
49. Moscow, Syn. 67 (XV.).
50. Moscow, Syn. 206 (XV.).
51. Paris, Nat. Gr. 47 (A.D. 1364) = Ev. 18, Acts 113, Paul 132.
52. Paris, Nat. Gr. 56 (XII.) = Acts 51, Paul 133.
53. Paris, Nat. Gr. 59 (XV.) = Acts 116, Paul 136.
[54. Vacant.]
55. Paris, Nat. Gr. 101 (XIII.) = Acts 118, Paul 138.
56. Paris, Nat. Gr. 102 (XIII. or XIV.) = Acts 119, Paul 139.
57. Paris, Nat. Gr. 124 (XVI.) = Ev. 296, Acts 124, Paul 149.
58. Paris, Nat. Gr. 19 (XV. or XVI.).
59. Paris, Nat. Suppl. Gr. 99 (XV. or XVI.).
[60. Vacant.]
61. Paris, Nat. Gr. 491 (XIII. or XIV.); contains i. 1—xxii. 8.
62. Paris, Nat. Gr. 239 (A.D. 1422).

63. Paris, Nat. Gr. 241 (XVI.).
64. Paris, Nat. Gr. 224 (XI.) = Paul 159.
65. Moscow, Univ. 25 (XII.); contains xvi. 20—xxii. 21.
[66. Vacant.]
67. Rome, Vat. Gr. 1743 (A.D. 1301).
68. Rome, Vat. Gr. 1904 (XI. or XII.). Contains Apoc. i. 11—ii. 20, iii. 16—vi. 9, vii. 17—ix. 5, xxi. 18—xxii. 21.
69. Rome, Vat. Ottob. 258 (XIV.) = Acts 161, Paul 198; a Graeco-Latin text. Wants xviii. 22—xxii. 21.
70. Rome, Vat. Ottob. 66 (XIV.) = Ev. 386, Acts 151, Paul 199.
[71. Vacant.]
72. Rome, Chigi R. iv. 8 (XVI.).
73. Rome, Corsini 41 E. 37 (XV.).
74. Venice, St Mark's 546 (XI.) = Acts 140, Paul 215.
75. Florence, Laur. iv. 30 (X.) = Acts 86, Paul 96.
[76. Vacant; = 75.]
77. Florence, Laur. vii. 9 (XVI.).
78. Rome, Vat. Ottob. Gr. 176 (XV.) = Paul 197.
79. Rome, Vat. Gr. 656 (XIV.).
79 a. Munich, Reg. Gr. 248 (XVI.).
80. Munich, Reg. Gr. 544 (XIV.).
81. Munich, Reg. Gr. 23 (XVI.).
82. Munich, Reg. 211 (XI.) = Acts 179, Paul 128.
83. Turin, Univ. B. v. 8 (302) (XIII.) = Ev. 339, Acts 135, Paul 170.
84. Florence, Riccardi 84 (XV.) = Ev. 368, Acts 150.
85. Jerusalem, Holy Sep. 9 (XIII.) = Acts 184, Paul 232.
86. St Saba 10 (XIV.) = Ev. 462, Acts 187, Paul 235.
87. Berlin, Reg. Phillipps 1461 (XIV. and XV.) = Acts 178, Paul 242; wants xiv. 4—14, xxi. 12—xxii. 21.
88. Venice, St Mark's 5 (XV.) = Ev. 205, Acts 93, Paul 106.
89. St Saba 20 (XIII.) = Ev. 466, Acts 189, Paul 237.
90. Dresden, Reg. A. 95 (XII.).
91. Rome, Vat. Gr. 1209 (XV.) = Paul 293.
92. Dublin, Trin. A. 4. 21 (XVI.) = Ev. 61, Acts 34, Paul 40.
93. London, Lambeth 1186 (XI.) = Paul 290; wants xiv. 16—xv. 7; xix. 4—xxii. 21.
94. London, Brit. Mus. Add. 11837 (A.D. 1357) = Ev. 201, Acts 91, Paul 104.
95. Parham, Curzon 82. 17 (XI. or XII.).
96. Parham, Curzon 93. 28? (XIV.).

97. London, Brit. Mus. Add. 17469 (XIV.) = Ev. 498, Acts 198, Paul 255.
98. Oxford, Bodl. Canon. gr. 34 (A.D. 1515) = Ev. 522, Acts 200, Paul 257; wants ii. 11—23.
99. Naples, Nat. ii. Aa. 7 (XII.) = Acts 83, Paul 93.
100. Naples, Nat. ii. Aa. 10 (XIV. or XV.).
101. Petersburg, Muralt 129 (XV.).
102. Paris, Nat. Armen. 9 (XI.) = Acts 301, Paul 259; wants xix. 16—xxii. 21.
103. Ferrara, Univ. 188 NA. 7 (A.D. 1334) = Ev. 582, Acts 206, Paul 262.
104. St Saba 20 (XI.) = Acts 243, Paul 287.
105. Athens, Nat. (43), Sakk. 94 (XII.) = Acts 307, Paul 469; Ap. xxi. 27—xxii. 21 in a later hand.
106. Zittau, Town Libr. A. 1 (XV.) = Ev. 664, Acts 253, Paul 303.
107. Cheltenham, 7682 (XI.) = Ev. 680, Acts 255, Paul 305.
108. Highgate, Burdett-Coutts ii. 4 (XI.) = Ev. 699, Acts 256, Paul 306.
109. Venice, St Mark's 6 (XV. or XVI.) = Ev. 206, Acts 94, Paul 107.
110. Athens, Nat. th. 12, Sakk. 150 (XIII. or XIV.) = Ev. 757, Acts 260, Paul 309.
111. Athens, Nat. 67[M], Sakk. 107 (XIII.) = Ev. 792.
112. Athens, Mamouka (XII.) = Ev. 808, Acts 265, Paul 314.
113. Grottaferrata A'. a'. 1 (XIV.) = Ev. 824, Acts 267, Paul 316.
114. Rome, Vat. Gr. 1882 (XIV.) = Ev. 866. Contains Apoc. vi. 17—xiii. 2 in Greek and Latin.
115. Rome, Vat. Reg. Gr. 6 (A.D. 1454) = Ev. 886, Acts 268, Paul 317.
116. Athos, Greg. 3 (A.D. 1116) = Ev. 922, Acts 270, Paul 320.
117. Athos, Esphigm. 186 (XIV.) = Ev. 986, Acts 277, Paul 326.
118. Athos, Laur. (XIV.) = Ev. 1072, Acts 284, Paul 333.
119. Athos, Laur. (XIV.) = Ev. 1075, Acts 286, Paul 334.
120. Athos, Panteleem. xxix. (XIV.) = Ev. 1094, Acts 287, Paul 335.
121. Paris, Nat. Coisl. 224 (XI.) = Acts 250, Paul 299.
122. Athens, Nat. th. 217, Sakk. 490 (XIV.) = Acts 251, Paul 301.
123. Paris, Nat. Suppl. Gr. 159 (XIV.) = Ev. 743, Acts 259.
124. Athens, Nat. (64), Sakk. 91 (XII.) = Acts 309, Paul 300; wants xviii. 22—xxii. 21.
125. Escurial, Ψ. iii. 6 (XI.) = Acts 235.
126. Escurial, Ψ. iii. 18 (X.) = Acts 236.

127. Lesbos, τοῦ λειμῶνος 55 (IX. or X.) = Acts 323, Paul 429.
128. Venice, St Mark's ii. 114 (A.D. 1069) = Acts 332, Paul 434.
129. Linköping, Dioc. Libr. 14. 35 (X. or XI.) = Acts 334, Paul 436.
130. Athos, Iveron 25 (XI.) = Acts 359, Paul 452 [see p. cxcii.].
131. Athos, Iveron 60 (XIII.) = Acts 362, Paul 455.
132. Athos, Paul 2 (IX.) = Acts 374, Paul 463.
133. Chalcis, schol. 26 (X.) = Acts 384, Paul 355.
134. Chalcis, schol. 96 (XII.) = Acts 386, Paul 357.
135. Sinai, 279 (XV.) = Acts 399, Paul 367; contains i. 1—xiii. 8.
136. Vienna, Imp. Gr. th. 69 (A.D. 1507).
137. Vienna, Imp. Gr. th. 163 (XV.).
138. Vienna, Imp. Gr. th. 220 (XV.).
139. Paris, Nat. Gr. 240 (A.D. 1543).
140. Paris, Nat. Coisl. Gr. 256 (XI. or XII.).
141. Athens, τῆς βουλῆς (XVI.).
142. Escurial, T. iii. 17 (X.).
143. Escurial, X. iii. 6 (A.D. 1107).
144. Madrid, O. 19, no. 7 (XVI.).
145. Florence, Laur. vii. 29 (XVI.); contains i. 1—vii. 5.
146. Messina, Univ. 99 (XIII.).
147. Modena, Este iii. E. 1 (XV. or XVI.).
148. Modena, Este iii. F. 12 (XV.).
149. Rome, Angel. A. 4. 1 (XIV. or XV.).
150. Rome, Angel. B. 5. 15 (XV.).
151. Rome, Chigi R.V. 33 (XIV.).
152. Rome, Vat. Gr. 370 (XI.).
153. Rome, Vat. Gr. 542 (A.D. 1331).
154. Rome, Vat. Gr. 1190 (XV. or XVI.).
155. Rome, Vat. Gr. 1426 (XIII.).
156. Milan, Ambr. H. 104. sup. (A.D. 1434) = Acts 139, Paul 174.
157. Rome, Vat. Gr. 1976 (XVI.).
158. Rome, Vat. Gr. 2129 (XVI.).
159. Rome, Vat. Ottob. Gr. 154 (XV.).
160. Rome, Vat. Ottob. Gr. 283 (A.D. 1574).
161. Rome, Vat. Palat. Gr. 346 (XV.).
162. Venice, St Mark's i. 40 (XVI.).
163. Venice, St Mark's ii. 54 (XV. or XVI.).
164. Athos, Anna 11 (A.D. 1356).
165. Athos, Vatoped. 90.

166. Athos, Vatoped. 90 (2) (?).
167. Athos, Dionys. 163 (A.D. 1622) = Evst. 642, Apost. 170.
168. Athos, Docheiar. 81 (A.D. 1798).
169. Athos, Iveron 34 (XIV.).
170. Athos, Iveron 379 (X.).
171. Athos, Iveron 546 (XIV.).
172. Athos, Iveron 594 (XVII.).
173. Athos, Iveron 605 (A.D. 1601).
174. Athos, Iveron 644 (A.D. 1685).
175. Athos, Iveron 661 (A.D. 1562).
176. Athos, Konstamon. 29 (XVI.).
177. Athos, Konstamon. 107 (XIII.).
178. Patmos, St John 12 (XIV.) = Apost. 161.
179. Patmos, St John 64 (XII.).
180. Florence, Laur. Conv. Soppr. 150 (XII.) = Acts 149, Paul 349: Graeco-Latin.
181. London, Brit. Mus. Add. 28816 (A.D. 1111) = Acts 205, Paul 477.
182. Dresden, Reg. A. 187 (XVI.).
183. Saloniki, ἑλληνικοῦ γυμνασίου 10 (X.) = Apost. 163.
184. Leyden, Univ. Isaac Voss Gr. 48 (A.D. 1560).
185. Cambridge, Univ. (XI. or XII.) = Ev. 1277, Acts 418, Paul 484.
186. Athos, Pantocr. 44 (X.); contains xii. 4—xxii. 21 [see p. cxcii.].
187. [Greg. 495.] Jerusalem, Patr. 38 (XI.) = Acts (Paul) 495.
188. [Greg. 500.] Jerusalem, Patr. Saba 665 (XI.) = Acts (Paul) 500.
189. [Greg. 501.] Jerusalem, Patr. Saba 676 (XII.) = Acts (Paul) 501.
190. [Greg. 504.] Jerusalem, Patr. Staur. 57 (XII.—XIII.) = Acts 504, Evl. 991 b.
191. [Greg. 506.] Constantinople, Holy Sep. 303. 2 (XIV.).
192. [Greg. 511.] Athens, Nat. Sakk. 142 (XV.).
193. [Greg. 1328.] Jerusalem, Patr. Saba 101 (XIV.) = Ev. 1328.
194. [Greg. 1380.] Athos, Greg. 3 (A.D. 1112) = Ev. (Acts, Paul) 1380.
195. [Greg. 1384.] Andros, Παναχράντου 13 (XI.) = Ev. (Acts, Paul) 1384.

Von Soden (*Die Schriften des N.T.* I. i. p. 289) raises the number of Apocalypse MSS. to 229, of which 223 are cursives.

Of the cursive texts, so far as they are known, the following are perhaps specially noteworthy: 1, 6, 7, 12, 14, 31, 36, 38, 91, 92, 93, 95, 130, 152, 170, 186. An appreciation of the available uncials is given by Dr Hort in his introduction to *The N.T. in the original Greek*, § 344.

3. The ancient Versions of the Apocalypse are as follows:

I. *Latin* (latt.).

(*a*) Old Latin (lat^{vt})[1].

g. Cod. Holmiensis (XIII.), known as Gigas, from its size; a Bohemian MS. now at Stockholm. Ed. Belsheim, 1878. The text of the Apocalypse is "late European" (WH., Intr. § 116); "scheint italienischer Art zu sein" (Gregory, *Tk.* p. 608).

h (or reg). Cod. Floriacensis (VII.), formerly at Fleury, now at Paris. Ed. Berger, 1889. Offers, according to WH., *l.c.*, a "a purely African text." Contains only Apoc. i. 1—24, viii. 7—ix. 12, xi. 16—xii. 5, xii. 6—14, xiv. 15—xvi. 5.

m. Text of the Apocalypse in the *Speculum* (a Pseudo-Augustinian treatise *de divinis scripturis*). The book is edited by Weihrich in the Vienna *Corpus scr. eccl. lat.*, vol. xii. p. 296 ff. (1887). The fragments of the N. T. text are collected by Belsheim (1899). Hort (Gregory, *Tk.* p. 606) was disposed to regard the N. T. text of the *Speculum* as Spanish, or a recension parallel to the European text.

Prim. Text of the Apocalypse in the commentary of Primasius (VI.). Ed. Haussleiter, 1891 (in Zahn's *Forschungen*, IV.).

(*β*) Vulgate (lat^{vg}).

am. Cod. Amiatinus (*c.* A.D. 700).
demid. Cod. Demidovianus (XII.).
fuld. Cod. Fuldensis (VI.).
harl. Cod. Harleianus (IX.).
lipss.$^{4,5,6.}$ Codd. Lipsienses (XIV., XV.).
tol. Cod. Toletanus (VIII.).
vg.$^{cle.}$ Edition of the Vulgate issued by Clement VIII. in 1592 (Vercellone, *Biblia sacra vulgatae editionis Sixti V. et Clementis VIII. iussu recognita atque edita.* Romae, 1861).

[1] On the Old Latin version (or versions) of the Apocalypse see H. Linke, *Studien zur Itala*, i.; Breslau, 1889.

II. *Syriac* (syrr).

(*a*) Supplement to the Vulgate Syriac or Peshitta (syr., Gwynn's Σ). Ed. Leusden and Schaaf, Leyden 1708, 1717. The "canon of the true Peshitta did not contain the Apocalypse" (above, p. cxi.), and the version of this book printed in Schaaf's edition and originally published by De Dieu in 1629 is closely akin to the Harkleian version, "if not actually the work of Thomas of Harkel [VII.]...it cannot be placed earlier—or (probably) much if at all later—than his time[1]." Only one known MS. is older than cent. XVI.

(*β*) A version printed in 1897 by Dr Gwynn[2], Regius Professor of Divinity in the University of Dublin ($syr^{gw.}$, Gwynn's S), from a MS. (XII) in the library of the Earl of Crawford and Balcarres. As Dr Gwynn shews[3], $syr^{gw.}$ is prior to *syr.*, and is probably "the work of Polycarpus, and belongs to his version of the whole New Testament into Syriac, the Philoxenian proper of A.D. 508."

Thus our extant Syriac texts of the Apocalypse correspond in character with the Philoxenian and Harkleian versions respectively. The book was not included in the canon of the Peshitta.

III. *Armenian* (arm).

On the editions of the Armenian N. T. see *St Mark*, p. ci. Zohrab held that the Apocalypse was not translated into Armenian before the eighth century, and Goussen (*Studia theologica*, ii.), while printing a version of the Apocalypse which he calls *antiquissima* and regards as based on a copy of extraordinary age (*mirae vetustatis exemplar habuisse videtur fontem*), pronounces the ordinary Armenian Apocalypse to be a work of cent. XII.[4] Cf. F. C. Conybeare in Hastings, *D. B.* i. p. 154: "the Apocalypse was not read in church before the 12th century, when Nerses of Lampron issued a much changed recension of the old version[5]."

IV. *Egyptian* (aegg).

(*a*) Memphitic or Bohairic (me). Ed. D. Wilkins, 1717; G. Horner, 1898—1905. Mr Horner prints the text of the Apocalypse from the Curzon MS. 128, with the variants of ten other MSS.[6]

(*β*) Thebaic or Sahidic (the). Large fragments of the Sahidic Apocalypse are known to have survived, including *cc.* i. 13—ix. 21, x. 6—xvi. 18, xvii. 2—xviii. 2, xviii. 12—23,

[1] Gwynn, *Apocalypse of St John in Syriac*, p. xv.; cf. p. xcii.

[2] His edition was preceded by a memoir in the *Transactions of the Royal Irish Academy* for 1891.

[3] Gwynn, *Apocalypse*, pp. xciii., xcvii.

[4] Gregory, *Tk.* ii. p. 368.

[5] Mr Conybeare, who will shortly publish an edition, informs me that the Armenian text is ultimately traceable to about A.D. 440.

[6] Mr Horner's edition did not appear in time to be used in the *apparatus criticus*.

xviii. 25—xix. 2, xix. 7—xxi. 9, xxi. 25—xxii. 21[1]. Some of these have been collected by Amélineau (*Zeitschrift f. Aeg. Sprache*, xxvi. 1888), and Goussen (*Apocalypsis S. Iohannis Apostoli*, Leipzig, 1895)[2].

The Apocalypse seems to have formed no part of the original Bohairic or Sahidic N. T., or at any rate it was held to be of inferior authority; for with few exceptions it is written separately from the rest of the N. T., and it is not represented in the Copto-arabic vocabularies[3].

V. *Ethiopic* (aeth).

Roman edition, 1548—9. Ed. Platt, 1826—1830 (1874). Cf. Dr Charles in Hastings, *D. B.* i. p. 791.

VI. *Arabic* (ar).

Ed. Erpe, Leyden, 1616; Paris polyglott, 1645; Roman edition of 1703. Cf. Prof. Burkitt in Hastings, *D. B.* i. p. 136 ff.

The Arabic versions of the Apocalypse are said to "vary greatly," and to shew the influence of the Coptic and Syriac[4].

In their *L'Apocalypse en Français*, MM. Paul Meyer and Delisle have printed a twelfth century version of which the earliest MSS. are written in the Anglo-Norman dialect. English versions of the French Apocalypse were current in the fourteenth century, and on one of these the later Wycliffite version was based. An interesting account of the early English Apocalypse is given by Miss A. C. Paues, Fellow of Newnham College, Ph. D., Upsala, in her degree thesis: *A fourteenth century English Biblical Version* (Cambridge, 1902). Miss Paues, to whom this information is due, is preparing for publication a fuller description of these versions.

4. The patristic evidence for the text of the Apocalypse, if not so extensive as in the case of some of the other books of the New Testament, is both early and important. The book is cited, sometimes in large contexts, by Irenaeus, Hippolytus, Origen, and Methodius, and, among Latin fathers of the Ante-Nicene period, by Tertullian, Cyprian, and Augustine. But the most important witness under this head is Primasius, whose commentary retains its original text, and has secured for the Apocalypse "the unique advantage of having been preserved in a Latin text at once continuous and purely African[5]." The African text of Tyconius also is represented, probably with fair accuracy, in the pseudo-Augustinian

[1] I owe this information to the kindness of Mr Horner. Cf. Gregory, *prolegg.* p. 865; *Tk.* ii. p. 337. A specimen of a British Museum fragment is given by Dr Kenyon (p. 160).

[2] F. Robinson in Hastings, *D. B.*, p. 669; Gregory, *Tk.* ii. p. 537.

[3] Scrivener-Miller, ii. p. 123; Gregory *prolegg.* 861, 864, *Tk.* ii. pp. 531, 534; Horner, iii. p. x. See above, p. cxiii.

[4] Burkitt, *l.c.* Scrivener-Miller, ii. p. 162 f.; Gregory, *prolegg.* p. 929 f.

[5] Hort (introduction to WH., § 117).

homilies[1] which embody much of his commentary. On the commentary of Victorinus some doubt still rests, and his text, as printed, is largely Vulgate in character. In the MSS. of the commentary of Andreas the Greek text of the Apocalypse varies considerably[2]; its evidence has been used in the apparatus of this edition only where the MSS. agree.

5. The grouping of the authorities for the text of the Apocalypse is a task of more than ordinary difficulty, for, as Dr Hort remarks, "historical landmarks are obscure, and familiar documents assume a new position[3]." Since Dr Hort's Introduction was written, much has been done to bring the problem nearer to a solution, and the student of the text will find help in various directions from the following writers: Weiss, *Die Johannes-Apokalypse* (in *Texte und Untersuchungen* VII. 1, 1891); Bousset, *Zur Textkritik der Apokalypse* (in *T. u. U.* XI. 4, 1894); Bousset, *Die Offenbarung Johannis,* 1896; Haussleiter, *Die lateinische Apokalypse der alten afrikanischen Kirche* (in Zahn's *Forschungen* IV., 1891); Gwynn, *The Apocalypse of St John, in a Syriac Version* (1897).

The text of the present edition will be found to differ only in a few places[4] from that of Westcott and Hort, although the editor has held himself free in each case to follow to the best of his own judgement the leading of the evidence. In the apparatus he has used the materials collected in Tischendorf's *editio octava critica maior* (1872), as amended in Gregory's *prolegomena* iii. (1894)[5], and he has added to them the evidence of Dr Gwynn's Syriac, and of two early Athos minuscules (130, 186[6]), which were kindly photographed for his use by Professor Lake, of Oxford and Leyden. It is hoped that an apparatus thus constructed will be sufficient to provide the student of the Apocalypse with opportunities of testing for himself the principles of criticism which the works enumerated above will suggest.

[1] Migne *P. L.* xxxv. Cf. the citations in the *Regulae* of Tyconius (ed. Burkitt, pp. 3, 50, 59, 60 f., 71, 82).

[2] For those used by Tischendorf see Gregory *prolegg.* p. 1160.

[3] Introduction to WH., § 344.

[4] The more important of these are discussed in the commentary.

[5] Pp. 1298—1302.

[6] On these MSS. see Lambros, *Catalogue of the Greek MSS. on Mt Athos*, i. p. 97, ii. p. 3. It may be added that a fresh collation has been made of cod. A, from the London photograph.

XVII.

COMMENTARIES[1].

The literature of the Apocalypse is immense, but it is unequally distributed in regard both to time and to place of origin. From the Greek-speaking East, which produced the book, no exposition has reached us which is earlier than the sixth century, and none of any importance which is later than the tenth. The West, on the other hand, began to comment upon St John's prophecy in the time of Diocletian, and has occupied itself with Apocalyptic problems from the days of Irenaeus to our own.

The following list is fairly complete so far as regards the patristic period, but from the age of Charlemagne to the end of the Middle Ages it has been thought sufficient to notice the more important commentaries. Since the invention of printing the output of books upon the Apocalypse has steadily increased, and a bare enumeration of them would occupy more space than we can afford. Only those have been mentioned which possess some permanent value, or are representative of the several schools of Apocalyptic interpretation.

A. Greek commentaries.

MELITO, Bishop of Sardis, who flourished under Marcus Aurelius, wrote, according to Eusebius, *H.E.* iv. 26, περὶ τοῦ

[1] For a detailed account of commentaries on the Apocalypse see Lücke, *Versuch einer vollständigen Einleitung in die Offenbarung des Iohannes* (Bonn, 1852), pp. 951—1070; and Bousset, *Die Offenbarung Iohannis neu bearbeitet* (Göttingen, 1896), pp. 51—141. Lücke refers to Stosch, *Catalogus rariorum in Apoc. Ioannis commentariorum*, a book which I have not been able to consult. Elliott (*Horae Apocalypticae*, iv. pp. 275—528) is especially full on the post-Reformation period, but must be used with caution; his zeal for the anti-papal interpretation leads him at times to do scant justice to writers, whether Roman Catholic or Protestant, who take another view.

διαβόλου καὶ τῆς ἀποκαλύψεως Ἰωάννου—probably a treatise on the Devil in which certain passages in the Apocalypse (e.g. *cc.* xii., xx.) came under discussion. A fragment of this work may survive[1] in Origen, *in Ps.* iii. tit.: Μελίτων γοῦν ὁ ἐν τῇ Ἀσίᾳ φησὶν αὐτὸν [sc. τὸν Ἀβεσσαλὼμ] εἶναι τύπον τοῦ διαβόλου ἐπαναστάντος τῇ Χριστοῦ βασιλείᾳ, καὶ τούτου μόνου μνησθεὶς οὐκ ἐπεξεργάσατο τὸν τόπον. On a Pseudo-Melito *super Apocalypsin* see Harnack, *Gesch.* I. p. 254.

IRENAEUS (ii.). A MS. found at Altenberg by Martène and Durand[2] bore the title *Herenei Lugdunensis episcopi in Apocalypsin*, but it proved to contain extracts from later writers as well as from Irenaeus. The statement of Jerome, *de virr. illustr.* ii. 9, "Apocalypsin, quam interpretantur Iustinus martyr et Hirenaeus," is satisfied by the expositions of certain Apocalyptic passages which are found in their works (cf. Harnack, *Gesch.* i. p. 272).

HIPPOLYTUS (ii.—iii.). Jerome (*op. cit.* 61) says of this profuse writer: "scripsit nonnullos in scripturas commentarios, e quibus haec repperi...*De Apocalypsi.*" The exact title of this work is given on the back of the Chair as ΥΠΕΡ ΤΟΥ ΚΑΤΑ ΙΩΑΝΗΝ Ε[ΥΑ]ΓΓΕΛΙΟΥ ΚΑΙ ΑΠΟΚΑΛΥΨΕΩϹ, on which Lightfoot (*Clement* ii. p. 374; cf. p. 420) remarks: "from the preposition (ὑπέρ, not περί), and from the association of the two words together, it is a safe inference that this was an apologetic work directed against those persons who objected to both works alike," i.e. the so-called Alogi. Harnack, on the other hand, writes (*Gesch.* ii. p. 642): "*De Apocalypsi* ist wahrscheinlich...als besonderes Werk zu betrachten...welches wahrscheinlich auch Andreas für seinen Commentar benutzt hat (zu *c.* 13. 1 und 17. 10)."

CLEMENT of Alexandria (ii.—iii.), according to Eusebius, *H.E.* vi. 14, commented in his Ὑποτυπώσεις on all the canonical books not excepting the *antilegomena*[3].

ORIGEN (iii.), it is known, intended to expound the Apocalypse; cf. *in Matt.* § 49 (Lommatzsch): "omnia haec exponere singillatim ...non est temporis huius; exponentur autem tempore suo in Revelatione Ioannis...horum autem principales expositiones atque probationes oportet fieri cum ipse liber propositus fuerit nobis ad exponendum." But the commentary on Matthew was probably one of his later works, belonging to his sixtieth year (A.D. 246[4]), and, as his death followed in 253, it must be feared that he did not succeed in reaching the Apocalypse; certainly no fragments of homilies or a commentary on that book from his pen have been produced.

OECUMENIUS (vi.), Bishop of Tricca in Thessaly. A complete commentary under this name has been discovered in a Messina MS. (cod. S. Salvatore 99, xii.)[5] by Dr F. Diekamp, who described it in

[1] Harnack, *Geschichte*, i. p. 248.

[2] See their *Voyages Litteraires*, ii. p. 260, cited by Harnack, *Gesch.* i. p. 264.

[3] Cf. Zahn, *Forschungen*, iii. p. 154 ff.

[4] Westcott in Smith and Wace's *D.C.B.* iv. p. 111.

[5] The work is also found, but in a shorter form, in a Turin MS. (cod. gr. 84) and the Roman MSS. Vat. gr. 1426, Ottob. gr. 126—8.

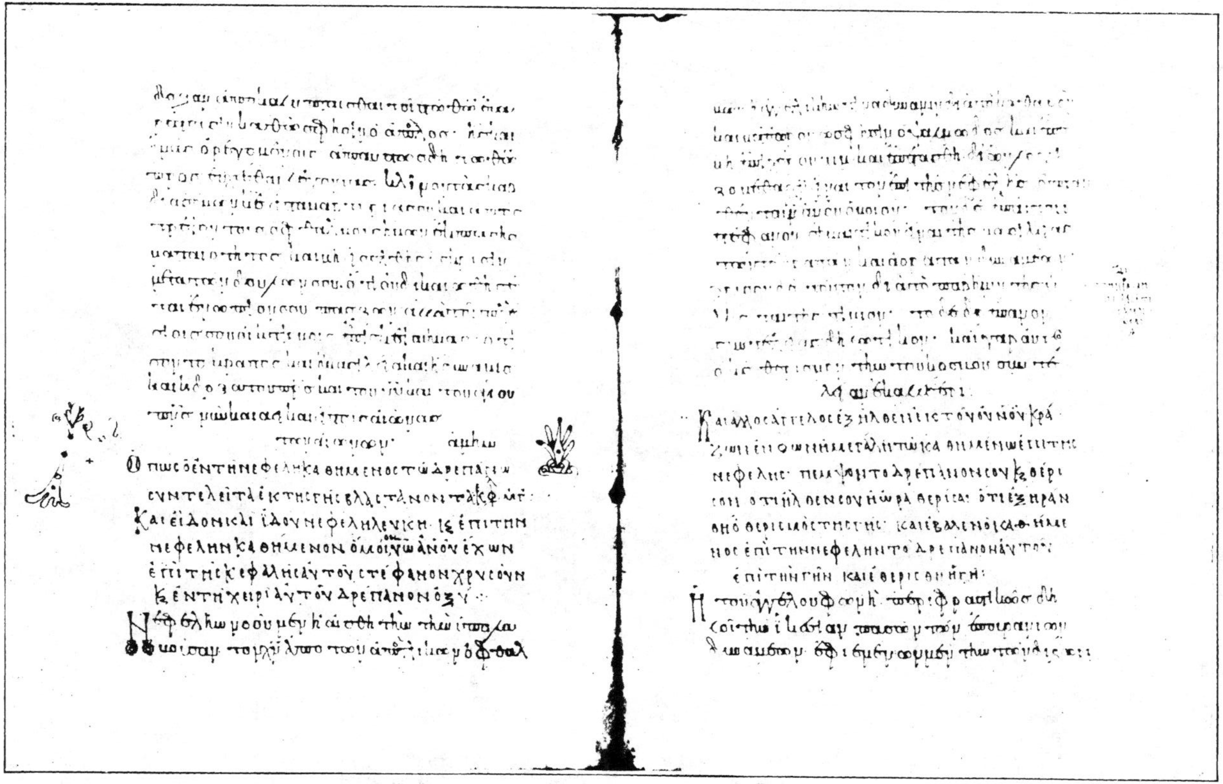

COD. APOC. 186 (ATHOS, PANTOCRATOR 44).
Commentary of Andreas on Apoc. xiv. 13—16.

the Berlin *Sitzungsberichte der kön. preuss. Akademie der Wissenschaften* for 1901 (p. 1046 ff.)[1]. The commentary is entitled Ἑρμηνεία τῆς Ἀποκαλύψεως τοῦ θεσπεσίου καὶ εὐαγγελιστοῦ καὶ θεολόγου Ἰωάννου ἡ συγγραφεῖσα παρὰ Οἰκουμενίου. It claims to have been written more than 500 years after the Apocalypse (cf. i. 2 ἤδη πλείστου δεδραμηκότος χρόνου...ἐτῶν πλειόνων ἢ πεντακοσίων), but there are indications which mark the work as not much if at all later than A.D. 600. The discoverer proceeds to shew that Oecumenius has been used by Andreas, and must therefore in future take precedence of him and stand first in the short list of extant Greek commentators upon the Apocalypse.

ANDREAS[2], metropolitan of Cappadocian Caesarea has left us a Ἑρμηνεία εἰς τὴν Ἀποκάλυψιν which may be assigned to the second half of the sixth century. He quotes patristic authorities from Papias to Cyril of Alexandria, and refers (on xx. 7 f.) to the invasion of the Empire by barbaric hordes ἃ καλοῦμεν Οὐννικά, and to Dionysius the Areopagite, who is styled ὁ μακάριος. While the work of Andreas takes account of earlier writers and occasionally quotes them, yet, as the preface leads the reader to expect, it is in no sense a catena, but an independent effort to interpret the book. The interpretation is on Origenistic lines, but though it allegorizes to some extent, an attempt is made from time to time to find historical fulfilments of the Apocalyptic visions. Such a work naturally attracted attention in the Greek-speaking East, and from the ninth century onwards the commentary of Andreas was widely transcribed: nearly a third of the known minuscule MSS. of the Apocalypse contain it, viz. codd. 1, 18, 21, 35, 36, 43, 49, 59, 62, 63, 67, 68, 70a, 72, 73, 77, 79, 79a, 80, 81, 100, 101, 123, 136, 137, 138, 139, 144, 145, 147, 148, 149, 151, 152, 153, 157, 158, 159, 160, 161, 163, 164, 167, 168, 169, 170, 171, 174, 175, 179, 184, 186[3], 192, and seven more which have not received a number.

The *editio princeps* of Andreas is that of Sylburg (1596). The commentary was also printed in the *Bibliothecae Patrum* of 1589, 1618, 1644 and 1677[4]; in the present volume it is quoted from Migne, *P. G.* cvi.

ARETHAS, a successor of Andreas in the see of Caesarea (ix.—x.), occupied himself with a compilation in which his predecessor holds a large place; the title is Συλλογὴ ἐξηγήσεως ἐκ διαφόρων ἁγίων ἀνδρῶν, or, according to another MS., Ἐκ τῶν Ἀνδρέα...πεπονημένων σύνοψις σχολική, παρατεθεῖσα ὑπὸ Ἀρέθα. His date is now given as c. A.D. 900[5].

[1] I owe this reference to Mr C. H. Turner's article *Patristic Commentaries*, in Hastings' *D.B.* v. p. 523.

[2] On Andreas (Andrew) of Caesarea see Fabricius-Harles, viii. p. 696 ff.; Smith and Wace, *D.C.B.* i. p. 154 f.; Herzog-Hauck, i. p. 514 ff.; Bousset, comm. p. 68 f.; Gregory, *prolegg.* p. 1159; von Soden, pp. 284 ff., 702 f.

[3] Of this MS. a photograph is shewn opposite. Cod. 186 = Athos, Pantocrator 44, was photographed for the writer by Mr (now Professor) Lake in 1901–2, and a collation of its text of the Apocalypse has been made for this edition.

[4] Ittig, *De bibliothecis et catenis patrum*, pp. 52, 109, 426, 492.

[5] See Harnack in *T. u. U.* i. 1, pp. 39 ff., 43 f.

Arethas is printed in the Cologne and Lyons *Bibliothecae Patrum*[1], in Cramer's *Catena*, viii. pp. 181—496, and in Migne *P. G.* cvi.; the quotations in the notes of this volume are from Migne. A critical edition of Andreas and Arethas is still a *desideratum*.

Besides the commentary of Andreas and the compilation of Arethas we have in print (Cramer, viii. pp. 497—582, from MS. Coisl. 224, f. 333 v., sqq.) a briefer exposition of which Diekamp truly says that it is "nichts Anderes als der etwas verkürzte Commentar des Andreas[2]." Cramer himself represents it as Oecumenian (*ib.* p. vi.), for what reason it does not appear; Montfaucon (*Biblioth. Coislin.*, p. 275) mentions no name in connexion with it, though Oecumenius is named in the heading to the previous item (p. 330 v.).

B. Syriac commentaries.

"The chief Nestorian commentator, Isho'-dād of Merw (fl. A.D. 850), covers both Testaments in his exegetical works, but passes over the four shorter Catholic Epistles and the Apocalypse, which were not included in the canon of the Peshitta. The Jacobite Barhebraeus († A.D. 1286) in his *Auṣar Rāzē* has the same range and the same exceptions as Isho'-dād. The known Syriac commentaries on the Apocalypse seem to be no more than three, and they are unpublished. (1) An anonymous commentary of unknown date accompanies the text in Brit. Mus. Add. 17127; an extract from the comment on *c.* iii. is given in Wright's Catalogue of Syriac MSS., part ii. p. 1020 f. (2) The second commentary is that of JACOB (Dionysius) BARṢALIBI († A.D. 1171), preserved in Brit. Mus. Rich. 7185; extracts are given by Dr Gwynn in *Hermathena* vi., vii. (3) The third is found in Cambr. Univ. Lib. Add. 1970, a Nestorian MS. of the eighteenth century. An extract from it is given in the *Catalogue of Syriac MSS.* in the Library of the University of Cambridge, vol. i. p. 44 f. It is apparently a recent production, not much earlier in date than the MS.[3]"

C. Latin commentaries from the third century to the sixteenth.

VICTORINUS, Bishop[4] of Pettau, in Pannonia (iii.)[5]. Of this earliest of Latin interpreters of the Apocalypse Jerome, himself a Pannonian, writes (*de virr. ill.* 74): "Victorinus, Pitabionensis episcopus, non aeque Latine ut Graece noverat. unde opera eius grandia sensibus viliora videntur compositione verborum. sunt autem haec: commentarii in Genesim, in Exodum...in Apocalypsim Iohannis." Elsewhere he says of Victorinus (*ep.* 58): "quod intellegit eloqui non potest," and again (*ep.* 70): "licet desit eruditio, non tamen deest eruditionis voluntas." According to the same authority,

[1] Ittig, *op. cit.* pp. 438, 504.

[2] Similarly Bousset, *Comm.* p. 70.

[3] I owe this account of the Syriac commentaries on the Apocalypse to the kindness of my colleague, Dr W. Emery Barnes, Hulsean Professor of Divinity.

[4] "Ex oratore episcopus," according to Cassiodorius (*De inst. div. libr.* 5).

[5] On Victorinus and his commentary on the Apocalypse see Harnack, *Gesch.* i. p. 371 ff., and Kattenbusch, *Der Apost. Symbol*, p. 212.

Victorinus was a chiliast (*de virr. ill.* 18: "Tertullianus...et Victorinus Pitabionensis et Lactantius hac opinione ducuntur"), and in his expository methods a follower of Origen (*ep.* 62: "taceo de Victorino Pitabionensi et ceteris qui Origenem in explanatione dumtaxat scripturarum secuti sunt"). His exact date is not known, but he suffered martyrdom (*de virr. ill.* 74: "ad extremum martyrio coronatus est"), probably during the last persecution—an epoch when the Apocalypse may well have recovered in the eyes of Christians much of the freshness of its original interest.

A commentary on the Apocalypse bearing the name of Victorinus is extant in two forms—a shorter form printed in De la Bigne's *Bibliotheca Patrum*, t. vi. (Paris, 1575)[1], and a longer which appears in Gallandi, t. iv., and in Migne, *P. L.* v. In the *Zeitschrift f. kirchl. Wissenschaft u. kirchl. Leben* for 1886 Haussleiter maintained that neither form represents the original work as it came from the pen of Victorinus. The shorter form is a revision of Victorinus by Jerome, who used also the commentary of Tyconius, and the longer is based on a later recension of the shorter. Since this theory was broached Haussleiter has been engaged in preparing an edition of Victorinus for the Vienna Corpus, and his researches have convinced him that the text presented by Cod. Vat. Ottob. Lat. 3288 A approaches more nearly to the original than either of the printed texts, and in particular that it contains the chiliastic end of the commentary, which Jerome removed[2]. In the notes of the present volume 'Victorinus' stands for the longer form of the Jerome-Victorinus commentary, which is quoted from Migne's reprint.

Tyconius (? Tichonius, Ticonius[3]), African and Donatist, followed Victorinus after an interval of about a century; his *floruit* is usually given as *c.* A.D. 390. According to Gennadius of Marseilles he was "in Divinis litteris eruditus iuxta historiam sufficienter, in saecularibus non ignarus." His exposition differed widely from his predecessor's: "exposuit et Apocalypsin Iohannis ex integro, nihil in ea carnale sed totum intellegens spiritale...mille quoque annorum regni in terra iustorum post resurrectionem futuri suspicionem tulit...neque duas in carne resurrectiones mortuorum futuras, unam iustorum et alteram iniustorum, sed unam et tunc semel omnium."

Donatist as he was, Tyconius wins high praise for his exposition of the Apocalypse from one who was no mean judge of the interpreter's art. Bede writes of him: "[Apocalypsin] et vivaciter intellexit, et veridice satisque catholice disseruit, praeter ea duntaxat loca in quibus suae partis schisma defendere nisus, perse-

[1] Ittig, p. 52. It had been previously edited in an appendix to Theophylact on St Paul by Jo. Lornicerus in 1543.

[2] See *Th. Litteraturblatt*, Apr. 26, 1895; and cf. J. H. Harris, in *Expositor*, v. I. p. 448, and A. Ehrard, *Die altchr. Litteratur, von* 1884–1900, i. p. 484 ff.

[3] On the spelling of this name see Burkitt in *Texts and Studies*, iii. I. p. 103. On Tyconius himself and his commentary see *D.C.B.* iv. 1025 ff., Haussleiter in *Zeitschrift f. kirchl. Wissenschaft* etc., vii. (1886), p. 239 ff., and in Zahn's *Forschungen*, iv. (1891); Tr. Hahn, *Tyconius-Studien* in Bonwetsch and Seeberg's *Studien*, vi. 2 (1900); and Prof. Burkitt's edition of the *Regulae*, already named.

cutiones quas ipsi...pertulerunt...in eadem gloriatur Apocalypsi fuisse praedictas[1]." That this judgement is just is shewn by the free use which was made of Tyconius not only by Bede himself, but by a succession of Catholic writers—Primasius, Beatus, the author of the homilies on the Apocalypse printed in the appendix to the third volume of the Benedictine Augustine and in Migne, *P. L.* xxix.[2], and the commentary published by Dom Amelli in the *Spicilegium Casinense* (iii. pp. 263—331)[3]. The work of Tyconius as a whole is perhaps no longer extant, but it can be largely reconstructed from those Catholic expositors who followed in his steps.

In the apparatus to the text of the present commentary 'Tyc.' is used, after the example of Tischendorf, as a synonym for 'anon$^{\text{Aug.}}$,' i.e. the Apocalyptic text of the Pseudo-Augustine.

PRIMASIUS, of Hadrumetum in Byzacena[4], another African, but a Catholic Bishop, wrote on the Apocalypse before 543–4, when his commentary is mentioned by Cassiodorius (*de inst. div. libr.* 9: "nostris quoque temporibus Apocalypsis...Primasii antistitis Africani studio...quinque libris exposita est"). It was thus an early work, completed before Primasius was embroiled in the controversy raised in Africa by the 'Three Chapters.' With regard to its character it possesses, as Haussleiter remarks, only a secondary value, being largely made up of Tyconius and Augustine. Augustine is in places (e.g. in the comment on Apoc. xx.) transferred almost bodily to the pages of Primasius; Tyconius is a "preciosa in stercore gemma," which the Bishop picks out of the mire to adorn his pages.

The commentary of Primasius has come down to us entire. The *editio princeps* was that of Cervicornus (Hirschhorn), Cologne, 1535. This was followed by editions in the Cologne, Paris, and Lyons *bibliothecae* of 1618, 1644, and 1677[5]; the Paris edition is followed generally in Migne, *P. L.* lxviii., whose reprint is quoted in the present volume. The African Latin text of the Apocalypse, which happily has been preserved in the commentary of Primasius, is cited from Haussleiter's admirable edition in Zahn's *Forschungen*. It is in this text that the value of Primasius to the modern student chiefly lies: see above, p. cxci.

APRINGIUS (vi.) Bishop of Pax (whether Pax Julia = Béja, in Portugal, or P. Augusta = Badajoz, in Spain), under Theudis, King of the Visigoths (A.D. 531—548), was working upon the Apocalypse nearly about the time when Primasius wrote his commentary. So we learn from Isidore of Seville (*de virr. ill.* 30: "Apringius, ecclesiae Pacensis Hispaniarum episcopus...claruit temporibus Theudis

[1] Migne, *P. L.* xciii. col.

[2] See Haussleiter, *Zeitschrift*, p. 240. In a St John's (Cambridge) MS. this commentary is strangely entitled: "tractatus Gennadii presbiteri Massiliae de mille annis et de Apocalypsi"; see Dr M. R. James in *Class. Review*, iii. p. 222.

[3] See H. L. Ramsay, *Commentaire de l'Apocalypse par Beatus*, p. 17 f.

[4] On Primasius see Haussleiter in Zahn, and in Herzog-Hauck, xvi. p. 55 ff., as well as his earlier 'programm,' *Leben u. Werke des Bischofs Primasius* (Erlangen, 1887); and cf. Kihn, *Theodor v. Mopsuestia*, p. 248 ff.

[5] Ittig, pp. 109, 439, 505.

principis Gothorum"). The commentary of Apringius was published at Paris in 1900 by Dom Féroten from a MS. belonging to the University of Copenhagen. Unfortunately the MS. gives the work of Apringius only so far as regards Apoc. i. 1—v. 7, and xviii. 6—xxii. 21, the lacuna v. 8—xviii. 5 being filled with scholia from Jerome-Victorinus.

According to Isidore, Apringius expounded the Apocalypse "subtili sensu atque illustri sermone, melius pene quam veteres ecclesiastici viri exposuisse videntur." A few specimens from M. Féroten's edition have been given in the notes of this commentary.

CASSIODORIUS, probably after his retirement to Viviers (A.D. 540), wrote brief notes (*complexiones*) on the Acts, Epistles, and Apocalypse, which were first published by Maffei in 1721, and are reprinted in Migne, *P. L.* lxx. In the Apocalypse he refers his readers to Tyconius, and shews also the influence of Victorinus and Augustine.

BAEDA of Wearmouth and Jarrow (A.D. 672—735) comes next in order of time among Latin commentators on the Apocalypse. In his *explanatio Apocalypsis*, as in his other expository works, Bede freely recognizes the secondary character of his expositions; in the Apocalypse, while drawing on the Fathers generally, he makes especial use of earlier Western commentators on the book, especially of Primasius and Tyconius; the latter is not seldom quoted by name. Yet Bede is no mere compiler, and not the least valuable of his remarks are those where the personality of the Northumbrian saint reveals itself. Bede's work on the Apocalypse is quoted in this volume from Migne, *P. L.* xcv.

AMBROSIUS AUSBERTUS (or Autpertus)[1], a Benedictine monk of French origin who died as Abbot of an Italian monastery, composed his *commentarii in Apocalypsim* during the pontificate of Paul I. (A.D. 757—767), and dedicated them to Paul's successor, Stephen IV. (A.D. 768—772). He makes use of Jerome-Victorinus, Tyconius, and even of Bede, but especially of Primasius, who supplies the staple of his expositions. The work is printed in the Cologne and Lyons *Bibliothecae Patrum*, but does not appear in Migne's Latin Patrology.

BEATUS of Liebana (Libana), the Spanish Benedictine who in A.D. 785 joined Etherius Bishop of Osma in a work against Elipandus of Toledo on the Adoptianist question. His commentary on the Apocalypse[2], which is dedicated to Etherius, is, like Bede's, professedly based to a great extent on the works of his predecessors, among whom he specifies Jerome (i.e. Victorinus in Jerome's recension), Augustine, Tyconius, and Apringius. Tyconius, in particular, has been largely used, although it is possible to exaggerate the debt

[1] See Fabricius-Harles, *Bibl. Lat.* i. p. 77; Smith and Wace, *D. C. B.* i. p. 232; Herzog-Hauck, ii. p. 308 f.

[2] On the Commentary of Beatus and its MSS. see two articles by Dom H. L. Ramsay, of Downside Abbey, reprinted from the *Revue d'histoire et de littérature religieuses*, t. vii. (1902), kindly communicated to me by Dom E. C. Butler, and Haussleiter's article already mentioned.

which Beatus owes to him. The conclusion at which Dom Ramsay arrives is probably not far from the truth: "je crois que partout où Beatus, Primasius, et le Pseudo-Augustine exploitent un fonds commun, ce fonds est celui de Tyconius (sinon de Victorinus)[1]."

The MSS. of Beatus have long been famous for their illuminations, which supply rich materials for the study of early Spanish art[2]. But there is only one printed text[3], and the book is so rare that no copy is to be found at the British Museum or in the Cambridge University Library[4].

Of Latin writers on the Apocalypse from the beginning of the ninth century to the sixteenth the following deserve to be specially mentioned:

Cent. ix. ALCUIN (Migne *P. L.* c.). BERENGAUDUS (Migne xvii.). HAYMO (Migne cxviii.). WALAFRID STRABO (?) (Migne cxiv.).

Cent. xii. ANSELM of Havilberg (D'Achéry, *Spicilegium*, i.). ANSELM of Laon (Migne clxiii.). BRUNO of Aste (Migne clxv.). JOACHIM of Calabria (Venice, 1519 and 1527). RICHARD of St Victor (Migne xcvi.). RUPERT of Deutz (Migne clxix.).

Cent. xiii. ALBERTUS MAGNUS (*Opera*, t. xii., Lyons, 1651). HUGO DE S. CARO (*postilla* vii., Cologne, 1620). PETER JOHN OLIVA (*postilla* in *Apocalypsin*). PSEUDO-AQUINAS (*Opera S. Thomae Aq.*, t. xxiii., Parma, 1869).

Cent. xiv. NICOLAS DE GORHAM (Antwerp, 1617—20). NICOLAS OF LYRA (Rome, 1471—2).

Cent. xv. DIONYSIUS CARTHUSIANUS (Paris, 1530).

Most of these mediaeval expositors follow their predecessors more or less closely, and satisfy themselves with a spiritualizing exegesis. But there are exceptions, especially Berengaud, Rupert of Deutz, and Joachim; the last-named has left a work which is a landmark in the history of Apocalyptic interpretation.

D. Commentaries, and other books bearing upon the interpretation of the Apocalypse, from the beginning of the sixteenth century to the present time.

D. Erasmus. *Annotationes in N. T.* Basle, 1516.

F. Lambertus. *Exegeseos in Apoc. libri vii.* Marburg, 1528.

H. Bullinger. *In Apoc. conciones c.* Basle, 1557.

T. Bibliander. *Commentarius in Apoc.* Basle, 1569.

J. Foxe. *Meditations on the Apoc.* London, 1587.

J. Winckelmann. *Commentarius in Apoc.* Frankfort, 1590.

F. Ribeira. *Commentarius in sacram b. Ioannis Apoc.* Salamanca, 1591.

J. Napier. *A plain discovery of the whole Revelation.* Edinburgh, 1593.

[1] *Le Commentaire de Beatus*, p. 18.

[2] H. L. Ramsay, *The MSS. of Beatus*, p. 1 ff.

[3] The edition of Florez (Madrid, 1770).

[4] Burkitt, *Tyconius*, p. xiii. I owe my quotations to the kindness of Prof. Burkitt, who left in my hands for some weeks a copy which had come into his possession.

L. ab Alcasar. *Vestigatio arcani sensus in Apoc.* Antwerp, 1614.

A. Salmeron. *In Iohannis Apoc. praeludia.* Cologne, 1614.

T. Brightman. *The Revelation of St John illustrated.* London, 1616.

D. Paraeus. *Commentarius in Apoc.* Heidelberg, 1618.

Cornelius a Lapide. *Commentaria in...Apoc.* Antwerp and Lyons, 1627.

J. Mede. *Clavis Apocalypseos...una cum Commentario.* Cambridge, 1627.

J. Gerhard. *Annotationes in Apoc.* Jena, 1643.

H. Grotius. *Annotationes in Apoc.* Paris, 1644.

L. de Dieu. *Animadversiones in Apoc.* Leyden, 1646.

H. Hammond. *Paraphrase and Annotations upon the N. T.* London, 1653.

J. B. Bossuet. *L'Apocalypse avec une explication.* Paris, 1660.

J. Cocceius. *Cogitationes in Apoc.* Amsterdam, 1673.

D. Hervé. *Apocalypsis explicatio historica.* Lyons, 1684.

P. Jurien. *L'accomplissement des prophéties.* Rotterdam, 1686.

C. Vitringa. Ἀνάκρισις *Apocalypsios.* Franeker, 1705.

W. Whiston. *Essay on the Revelation of St John.* Cambridge, 1706.

J. J. Schlurmann. *Die Offenbarung Iohannis.* Lippstadt, 1722.

F. Abauzit. *Essai sur l'Apocalypse.* Geneva, 1730.

I. Newton. *Observations upon the prophecies of Daniel and the Apoc.* London, 1732.

J. A. Bengel. *Erklärte Offenbarung Johannis.* Stuttgart, 1740.

J. J. Wetstein. *N. T. Graecum* (ii.). Amsterdam, 1752.

J. Gill. *Exposition of the Revelation.* London, 1776.

J. G. von Herder. Μαρὰν ἀθά. Riga, 1779.

J. S. Herrenschneider. *Tentamen Apocalypseos.* Strassburg, 1786.

I. G. Eichhorn. *Commentarius in Apoc.* Göttingen, 1791.

P. J. S. Vogel. *Commentationes vii. de Apocalypsi.* Erlangen, 1811—16.

G. H. A. Ewald. *Commentarius in Apoc.* Göttingen, 1828.

A. L. Matthäi. *Die Offenbarung Johannis.* Göttingen, 1828.

Edw. Irving. *Lectures on the Book of Revelation.* London, 1829.

J. Croly. *The Apocalypse of John.* London, 1838.

C. F. J. Züllig. *Die Offenbarung Johannis erklärt.* Stuttgart, 1834—40.

W. De Burgh. *An Exposition of the Book of Revelation.* Dublin, 1845.

M. Stuart. *Commentary on the Apocalypse.* London, 1845.

W. M. L. de Wette. *Kurze Erklärung der Offenbarung.* Leipzig, 1848.

E. W. Hengstenberg. *Die Offenbarung...erläutert.* Berlin, 1849—51.

E. H. Elliott. *Horae Apocalypticae.* London, 1851.

F. Düsterdieck. *Handbuch ü. d. Offenbarung.* Göttingen, 1852.

I. Williams. *The Apocalypse.* London, 1852.

J. H. E. Ebrard. *Die Offenbarung Johannis.* Königsberg, 1853.

C. A. Auberlen. *Der Prophet Daniel u. die Offenbarung.* Basle, 1854.

C. Stern. *Commentar ü. die Offenbarung.* Schaffhausen, 1854.

F. Bleek. *Vorlesungen ü. die Apocalypse.* Berlin, 1859.

H. Alford. *The Greek Testament*, vol. iv. Cambridge, 1861.

H. Ewald. *Die Johanneischen Schriften...erklärt.* Göttingen, 1861.

F. D. Maurice. *Lectures on the Apocalypse.* Cambridge, 1861.

R. C. Trench. *Commentary on the Epistles to the Seven Churches.* London, 1861.

G. Volkmar. *Commentar zur Offenbarung.* Zürich, 1862.

C. Wordsworth. *The New Testament*, vol. ii. London, 1864.

A. Cerese. *L'apocalysse o Revelatione*, 1869—71.

C. J. Vaughan. *The Revelation of St John.* London, 1870.

E. Renan. *L'Antichrist.* Paris, 1871.

J. C. A. Hofmann. *Die Offenbarung Johannis.* 1874.

A. Bisping. *Erklärung der Apocalypse.* Münster, 1876.

C. H. A. Burger. *Die Offenbarung Johannis.* 1877.

E. Reuss. *L'Apocalypse.* Paris, 1878.

S. Lee. *The Revelation of St John.* London, 1881.

Th. Zahn. *Apokalyptische Studien* (in *Z. f. kirchl. Wissenschaft u. k. Leben*), 1885—6; *Einleitung*, ii. 1899.

H. J. Holtzmann. *Die Offenbarung Johannis.* Freiburg i. B., 1891.

W. Milligan. *The Book of Revelation.* London, 1889.

W. H. Simcox. *The Revelation of St John.* Cambridge, 1893.

W. Bousset. *Die Offenbarung Johannis.* Göttingen, 1896.

E. W. Benson. *The Apocalypse: an introductory study.* London, 1900.

L. Prager. *Die Offenbarung Johannis.* Leipzig, 1901.

C. Anderson Scott. *Revelation* (*in the Century Bible*). Edinburgh (n. d.).

F. C. Porter. *Messages of the Apocalyptical writers.* London, 1905.

A volume on the Apocalypse by Prof. R. H. Charles is announced by Messrs. T. and T. Clark, in connexion with the *International Critical Commentary.*

XVIII.

HISTORY AND METHODS OF INTERPRETATION.

1. More than once[1] the Apocalypse appeals to the intelligence of the Christian student, inviting him to unravel its meaning if he can. *Here is wisdom. He that hath understanding, let him count the number of the Beast. Here is the mind which hath wisdom.* The challenge was accepted almost from the first, but with results which shew by their wide divergence the difficulties of the task. Schools of Apocalyptic interpretation have arisen, varying not only in detail, but in principle. It is the purpose of the present chapter to sketch[2] the progress of this movement from the second century to our own time, and then to indicate the lines which have been followed in the present exposition.

2. The Ante-Nicene Church, although she seems to have produced but one exposition of the book, was certainly not indifferent to the chief problems which it raises. Two of these, in particular—the questions connected with the coming of Antichrist and the hope of the Thousand Years—excited the liveliest interest during the age of persecution. Justin, as we have seen[3], found support for his chiliastic views in Apoc. xx. Irenaeus[4] bases upon Apoc. xxi., amongst other prophecies, his expectation of a terrestrial kingdom and a restored Jerusalem. He identifies the first of St John's Wild Beasts with St Paul's Man of Sin, and gives as one reading of the Number of the Beast the word Λατεινός, adding:

[1] Apoc. xiii. 18, xvii. 9.

[2] Details must be sought in Lücke and Bousset.

[3] P. ciii. f.

[4] *Haer.* v. 35. 2 (cf. Eus. *H. E.* iii. 39).

"Latini enim sunt qui nunc regnant[1]." From Apoc. xvii. 12 ff. he gathers that the Empire would be broken up into ten kingdoms, and Babylon (? Rome) be reduced to ashes[2]. Hippolytus, especially in his tract *On Christ and Antichrist*, carries the interpretation of Irenaeus some steps further. The first Beast is the Empire, which will be wounded to death, but restored by Antichrist; the Second Beast, the ten kingdoms that are to take the place of the Empire[3]. The Woman with child is the Church[4]; Babylon is Rome[5]; the Two Witnesses are Enoch and Elijah, the πρόδρομοι of the Second Coming[6]. In common with Justin and Irenaeus, Hippolytus entertains millennarian hopes, which he grounds on Apoc. xx.[7]

In Justin and Irenaeus—probably also in Hippolytus—we seem to catch a glimpse of the interpretation which prevailed in Asia in the early decades of the second century. The Alexandrians, who were without such guidance, interpreted the Apocalypse spiritually. Thus Clement sees in the four and twenty Elders a symbol of the equality of Jew and Gentile within the Christian Church[8]; in the tails of the locusts of the Abyss, the mischievous influence of immoral teachers[9]: in the many-coloured foundation stones of the City of God, the manifold grace of Apostolic teaching[10]. Origen repudiates as "Jewish[11]" the literal interpretation which the chiliasts gave to the closing chapters of the book; and his incidental references to the Apocalypse savour of an arbitrary though often noble and helpful mysticism. Thus he takes the sealed roll to be Scripture, to which Christ alone has the key[12]: the vision of the open heaven, from which the Word of God issues forth on a white horse, suggests to him the opening of heaven by the Divine Word through the white light of knowledge which He imparts to believers[13]. Methodius must on the whole

[1] v. 28. 3, 30.
[2] v. 26. 1.
[3] Ed. Lagarde, p. 24 ff.
[4] Lag. p. 31 f. τὴν μὲν οὖν γυναῖκα σαφέστατα τὴν ἐκκλησίαν ἐδήλωσεν.
[5] Lag. p. 17 καὶ γὰρ αὐτή σε [e.g. τὸν Ἰωάννην] ἐξώρισεν.
[6] Lag. p. 26.
[7] Lag. p. 153 τὸ σάββατον τύπος ἐστὶ καὶ εἰκὼν τῆς μελλούσης βασιλείας τῶν ἁγίων, ὡς Ἰωάννης ἐν τῇ ἀποκαλύψει διηγεῖται.
[8] *strom.* vi. 13, § 107.
[9] *strom.* iii. 18, § 106.
[10] *paed.* ii. 12, § 109.
[11] *de princ.* ii. 11. 12.
[12] *philoc.* v. 5.
[13] *in Ioann.* t. ii. 6.

be ranked with the Alexandrians, in regard to his method of interpreting the Apocalypse. In his exposition of Apoc. xii.[1] he finds in the Woman's child not Christ Himself but the baptized soul in which Christ is born. The seven heads of the Dragon are the greater sins[2]; his ten horns are contrasted with the Ten Commandments of the Decalogue. The Beast appears to be regarded as a symbol of fleshly lust[3].

The Latin fathers of the first three centuries, on the other hand, carry on the line of interpretation started by Irenaeus and Hippolytus. Thus Tertullian regards Babylon as an image of Rome, "ut proinde magnae et regno superbae et sanctorum Dei debellatricis[4]." The Beast from the sea is Antichrist, who with his False Prophet will wage war against the Church[5]. A kingdom of the Saints is expected which will have its seat on earth, though it belongs to another order, and will be preceded by a resurrection of the body[6]. An orderly plan runs through St John's work, though the order must not be pressed so far as to include chronological details[7].

Of the commentary of Victorinus in general it is impossible to speak with confidence until it is before us in the form in which it came from his pen[8]. But the extract published by Haussleiter[9] from what appears to be the original work confirms the statement that Victorinus held firmly by the chiliastic interpretation of Apoc. xx.

A few sentences will sufficiently illustrate his attitude. "In hac eadem prima resurrectione et civitas futura et sponsa per hanc scripturam expressa est...quotquot ergo non anticipaverint surgere in prima resurrectione et regnare cum Christo super orbem...surgent in novissima tuba post annos mille...In regno ergo et in prima resurrectione exhibetur civitas sancta, quam vidit descensuram de caelo quadratam, differentem a vice mortuositatis et doloris et genesis...ostendit scriptura adferri ibi munera regum serviturorum novissimorum...et civitatum."

3. A new stage of Apocalyptic interpretation is reached at the end of the fourth century, when Tyconius wrote his epoch-

[1] *Symp.* viii. 4 ff.
[2] Cf. Origen, *in Mt.* xxiv. 29.
[3] *Ib.* 13.
[4] *adv. Marc.* iii. 13.
[5] *de resurr. carnis*, 25.
[6] *adv. Marc.* iii. 24.
[7] *de res.*, *l.c.* "in Apocalypsi Ioannis ordo temporum sternitur."
[8] See *c.* xvii., p. cxcvii.
[9] In *Theologisches Literaturblatt*, 26 Apr. 1905, col. 192 ff.

making commentary. Though the work has not survived as a whole, its line of interpretation and many of its details can be recovered from later expositions[1]. It is abundantly clear that Tyconius trod in the steps of Origen rather than of Victorinus; he inclined to a mystical exegesis, even if he did not altogether exclude literal or historical fulfilments. But his method was largely new, and his own, as may be gathered from his *liber regularum*. His fourth 'rule' reveals the principle with which he approached his task: "loquimur secundum mysteria caelestis sapientiae magisterio Sancti Spiritus, qui cum veritatis pretium fidem constituerit mysteriis narravit in speciem genus abscondens...dum enim speciem narrat, ita in genus transit ut transitus non statim liquido appareat[2]." The expositor of the Apocalypse, on this principle, would pass insensibly from a name which suggested a particular object to the universal fact which it symbolized; e.g. from Jerusalem to the Church, or from Babylon to the hostile world[3]. By this means Tyconius was enabled to pass lightly over the references to Rome and the persecuting Emperors, which since the conversion of the Empire had ceased to be of special interest, and to fix the attention of the reader upon the world-long struggle between good and evil; while on the other hand his 'rule' did not prevent him from finding a crucial instance of that struggle in the fight which his own party were making at the time in Africa against the Catholic Church, identified in his judgement with the evil of the world.

So far as his principle of interpretation is concerned Tyconius had many Catholic followers, who made no secret of their indebtedness to the great Donatist. In his interpretation of Apoc. xx.[4] Augustine agrees in the main with Tyconius. Primasius, Cassiodorius, Apringius, Bede, Beatus, and most of the writers on the Apocalypse who followed them in the earlier centuries of the Middle Ages, were content with a mystical exegesis which varied in its details according to the fancy of the individual expositor or the needs or ideas of his time.

[1] P. cxcvii f.
[2] Burkitt, pp. xv, 31.
[3] Burkitt, pp. 31, 50.
[4] *de civitate*, xx. 7 ff.

4. While Primasius and others were popularizing the method of Tyconius in the Latin West, the Greek East made its first and only serious attempt to expound the Apocalypse. Of Oecumenius nothing can be said until his commentary finds an editor. But Andreas is perhaps the best known of ancient expositors of the Apocalypse, and certainly none of them is more edifying or, in his own way, more attractive. Entering on his work with the conviction that Scripture holds a threefold sense[1], he agrees with the Alexandrians in attaching especial importance to the spiritual interpretation of a book, which beyond other books in the New Testament lends itself to such treatment. But he does not depart so entirely from the earlier school of Irenaeus and Hippolytus as his Western contemporaries did; side by side with mystical exposition he places suggestions of a historical fulfilment. If he regards Babylon as the world considered as the standing enemy of the Church, in the seven kings he sees successive embodiments of the World-power, of which the sixth was Rome and the seventh Constantinople. On the other hand the millennium is explained as it is by Augustine and the other followers of Tyconius. Thus the greatest of the Greek commentaries on the Apocalypse is a syncretism, blending the methods of Irenaeus, Origen, and Tyconius, while at the same time the writer feels his way towards the later system of interpretation which discovers in St John's prophecy anticipations of the course of history.

5. In the West at long intervals one or two expositors succeeded in breaking loose from the tradition started by Tyconius. Berengaud, a ninth century writer whose commentary has found a place in the appendix to the works of St Ambrose, combines the mystical with the historical interpretation, and endeavours to make the Apocalypse cover the whole course of human events. The first six seals carry the history of the world from Adam to the fall of Jerusalem; the first six trumpets represent the preaching of the word from the age of the patriarchs to the age of the Christian martyrs. The Two Witnesses are Enoch and Elijah,

[1] *prol.*: πᾶσα θεόπνευστος γραφή, ἅτε τριμερεῖ τῷ ἀνθρώπῳ ὑπάρχοντι, τριμερὴς ἐκ τῆς θείας δεδώρηται χάριτος.

whose coming will precede the second Coming of the Lord. The first Beast is Antichrist, and his seven heads are the seven deadly sins[1]; the second Beast is a follower of Antichrist, or those who preach him taken collectively; as for the number of the Beast, Berengaud is afraid to inquire into it, lest it may correspond with the letters of his own name. Babylon is Pagan Rome, but Rome regarded as representing the "civitas Diaboli"; the ten horns of the Beast on which she sits are the successive incursions of barbarians which broke up the Roman Empire. The Thousand Years reach from the Ascension to the end of the world; the first resurrection is the condition of the Saints in the present life. A more remarkable departure from the older interpretations is made in the *Enchiridion in Apocalypsim* of Joachim († 1202), founder of the Ordo Florensis. Joachim's work is an attempt to find correspondences between the Apocalypse and the events and expectations of the twelfth century. The Beast from the sea is Islam, wounded to the death by the Crusades; the False Prophet is identified with the heretical sects of the age; Babylon is Rome, no longer pagan, but worldly and vice-ridden nevertheless. Of the seven heads of the Beast the fifth is the Emperor Frederick I., and the sixth Saladin; the seventh is Antichrist; the destruction of Antichrist will be followed by the millennium, which thus recovers its place as a hope of the future.

Of Joachim's personal loyalty to the Roman Church there can be no doubt. But his method was speedily turned against the Church by indiscreet followers. Under the year 1257 Matthew Paris relates that certain Franciscans of Paris "quaedam nova praedicabant...deliramenta quae de libro Ioachim Abbatis...extraxerunt, et quendam librum composuerunt quem sic eis intitulare complacuit *Incipit Evangelium aeternum*[2]"; the Pope, he adds, commanded the book to be burnt, "et alia quae de Ioachim corruptela dicuntur emanasse." But the movement continued, and early in the fourteenth century the fate of the *Evangelium*

[1] See p. ccv.

[2] See note on Apoc. xiv. 6. The author of the *Introductorius in Aeternum Evangelium* was a friar named Gerhard; see Giesler (E. Tr.), iii. p. 257 n.

aeternum was shared by the *postilla super Apocalypsim* of Peter John Oliva, another Franciscan; nor can we wonder when among the scanty extracts of Oliva's work which escaped the flames we read: "Per sedem bestiae principaliter designatus carnalis clerus ...in quo quidem bestialis vita...regnat...longe plus quam in laicis."..."Mulier stat hic pro Romana gente et imperio, tam prout fuit quondam in statu paganismi quam prout postmodum fuit in fide Christi."..."Quidam putant quod tam Antichristus mysticus quam proprius et magnus erit pseudo-papa." When such things were written within the Church, it is not matter for surprise that the sects took the further step of identifying Antichrist with the Papacy or the occupants of the Papal See, or that this became a commonplace of Apocalyptic interpretation among reforming sects and Churches.

On the papal side a counter-attempt to interpret the Apocalypse in the light of history was made by Nicolas of Lyra (†1340). He finds in it a forecast of the course of events from the time of Domitian to his own. In Lyra's judgement the millennium began with the founding of the Mendicant orders, which had bound Satan, as he thinks, for a considerable period of time.

6. With the Reformation of the sixteenth century a new era of Apocalyptic exegesis begins. Each side in the great controversy found inspiration in this book. The reforming party inherited the method of Joachim and the Franciscans: the equation 'the Pope, or the Papacy, is Antichrist' was the cornerstone of their interpretation. On the papal side, under the stress of the Protestant attack, new methods arose, which at a later time found followers among the reformed. Their authors were Spaniards and members of the Society of Jesus. Francis Ribeira († 1601), a professor at Salamanca, came to his task equipped with a knowledge of both the Greek and Latin commentators of the patristic period, but with an open mind which refused to be bound by their exegesis. He took his stand on the principle that the Apocalyptist foresaw only the nearer future and the last things, and offered no anticipations of intermediate history. Thus he was able to relegate Antichrist to the time

of the end, and though with the majority of interpreters he identified Babylon with Rome, he could contend that the city which St John saw upon the Beast was not, as some said, Rome under papal rule, but the degenerate Rome of a future age. Ribeira has been described as a futurist, but the designation is inaccurate if it overlooks his real appreciation of the historical groundwork of the Revelation. His brother-Jesuit, Alcasar (†1613), on the other hand, was a thorough-going 'preterist.' In his judgement the body of St John's prophecy falls into two great portions, *c.* iv.—xi., and *c.* xii.—xix., answering severally to the conflict of the Church with Judaism and her conflict with paganism; while the closing chapters (xx.—xxii.) describe her present triumph and predominance. Both Alcasar and Ribeira wrote in the interests of a party, and neither of the schemes which they propose is free from manifest difficulties; yet both works mark an advance upon earlier interpretations in so far as they approach the book from the standpoint of the writer and his time, and abstain from reading into it the events or ideas of a widely different period.

7. The seventeenth and eighteenth centuries were busy with the work of Apocalyptic exposition. In England Joseph Mede and two eminent Cambridge mathematicians, Sir Isaac Newton and William Whiston, found minute fulfilments of St John's prophecy from the days of Domitian to their own[1]; on the continent the same general system of interpretation was adopted, with varying results, by two no less eminent authorities, Vitringa and Bengel. On the other hand Grotius and Hammond trod generally in the steps of Alcasar, while on the papal side the great Bossuet suggested the division of the prophecy into three historical periods, the age of persecution (*cc.* v.—xix.), the triumph of the Church (*c.* xx. 1—10), and the epoch of final conflict and victory (*cc.* xx. 11—xxii. 13). At the end of the eighteenth century Eichhorn struck a note which has been taken up again quite recently. The Apocalypse is in his view a great poem, or

[1] "'While I write,' says Mede, 'news is brought of a Prince from the North (meaning Gustavus Adolphus) gaining victories over the Emperor in defence of the German afflicted Protestants'." (Elliott, *H.A.* iv. p. 474.)

rather a drama, which may be broken up into acts and scenes—the drama of the progress and victory of the Christian faith.

8. While inheriting the methods of its predecessors, the nineteenth century found itself in possession of new data by which it was enabled to correct or extend their application. The progress of events shifted the point of view from which the advocates of the continuously historical interpretation regarded St John's visions; room had to be made, for instance, for the French Revolution and all the disturbing tendencies which it represented or set going[1]. Among expositors who revolted from a system which was under the necessity of revising its results with the progress of events some, like S. R. Maitland and Isaac Williams in England, and Stern, Bisping, and others on the continent, revived and carried to greater lengths the 'futurist' views of Ribeira; while others, like Auberlen, fell back upon the position that the Apocalypse revealed a philosophy of history and anticipated persons or events only when they were "solitary examples of a principle[2]." In Germany a new attitude towards the interpretation of the book was created by the endeavour to investigate its sources. If the Apocalypse of John is a Jewish work adapted for reading in Christian congregations, or a compilation from non-canonical apocalypses, it is difficult to regard the book as more than a storehouse of first-century eschatology, or a historical monument which throws light on an obscure age. In that case it is undoubtedly of first-rate importance to the student of history, but its claims to be regarded as a prophecy in any true sense of the word can no longer be taken seriously. In Germany this estimate of the Apocalypse is still dominant, and it has revolutionized the interpretation of the book. In England there are signs of a desire to assimilate all that may be of permanent value in the results of research, without abandoning belief in the canonical authority or prophetical character of St John's work. Examples of this attitude may be found in Professor W. M. Ramsay's *Letters to the Seven Churches*, and in the most recent of English commentaries on the Revelation, the brief but

[1] See, e.g., Elliott, *H.A.* iii. 309 ff.

[2] Auberlen, cited by Archbp. Benson, *Apocalypse*, p. 48.

suggestive contribution made to Professor Adeney's *Century Bible* by Mr Anderson Scott.

9. It remains to state the principles of interpretation by which the following exposition has been guided.

The interpretation of an ancient book, especially of a book such as the Apocalypse, must depend in great part on the view which the interpreter is led to take of its literary character, purpose, destination, and date. These points have been discussed in the earlier chapters of the introduction, and it is only necessary here to shew how the judgements which have been formed upon them affect the writer's attitude toward the problems and the general significance of the book.

(1) This commentary has been written under the conviction that the author of the Apocalypse was, what he claimed to be, an inspired prophet. He belongs to the order which in older days produced the books of Isaiah, Ezekiel, and Zechariah. He is a medium of communication between God and Christ on the one hand, and the Church on the other. His mind has been lifted into a sphere above its natural powers by the Divine Spirit, which has enabled him to assimilate a message from the invisible world. His rendering of this message into human thought and speech must be interpreted as we interpret the prophecies of the Old Testament canon; it will possess the same Divine elevation that we find in them, and be liable to the same human limitations. The student who approaches the Apocalypse from this point of view will not expect to find in it express predictions of persons and actions which in St John's day were yet hidden in the womb of a remote future; nor will he look for exact chronological order in its successive visions, or for a sense of the distances which part great epochs from one another. But on the other hand he will expect and, it is firmly believed, will find that the prophet of the New Testament is not less able than the prophets of the Old Testament to read the secrets of God's general purpose in the evolution of events, to detect the greater forces which are at work in human life under all its vicissitudes, and to indicate the issues towards which history tends.

(2) As the title suggests, the prophecy of this book possesses a special character of which the interpreter must not fail to take note. The Divine message came to John in a series of visions; it is an apocalypse, and it uses the ideas, the symbols, and the forms of speech which were characteristic of apocalyptic literature. Thus St John's work challenges comparison with the apocalyptic portions of the Old Testament, more especially with the Book of Daniel; and further, with the non-canonical Jewish apocalypses, to which ready access can now be had through the labours of Professor Charles and Dr M. R. James. It is possible to exaggerate the influence which these Jewish books exerted over the mind of the Christian Apocalyptist, and it may be questioned whether he has made direct use of any of them; but they establish the existence of a common stock of apocalyptic imagery on which St John evidently drew. The modern interpreter of the Apocalypse is bound to take into account the presence in St John's book of the conventional language of apocalyptic literature, and to refrain from pressing it into the service of his own line of interpretation. Phrases and imagery which fall under this category must generally be held to belong to the scenery of the book rather than to the essence of the revelation. A recognition of this canon of interpretation will save the student from adopting the naïve and sometimes grotesque attempts which have been made to interpret every detail in a book which, like all writings of its class, defies treatment of this kind.

(3) Another important landmark for the guidance of the interpreter is to be found in the purpose of the book and the historical surroundings of its origin. The Apocalypse is cast in the form of a letter to certain Christian societies, and it opens with a detailed account of their conditions and circumstances. Only the most perverse ingenuity can treat the messages to the seven Churches as directly prophetical. The book starts with a well-defined historical situation, to which reference is made again at the end, and the intermediate visions which form the body of the work cannot on any reasonable

theory be dissociated from their historical setting. The prophecy arises out of local and contemporary circumstances; it is, in the first instance at least, the answer of the Spirit to the fears and perils of the Asian Christians toward the end of the first century. Hence all that can throw light on the Asia of A.D. 70—100, and upon Christian life in Asia during that period, is of primary importance to the student of the Apocalypse, not only in view of the local allusions in *cc.* ii.—iii., but as helping to determine the aim and drift of the entire work. No one who realizes that the prophecy is an answer to the crying needs of the seven Churches will dream of treating it as a detailed forecast of the course of mediaeval and modern history in Western Europe. So far as the Apocalyptist reveals the future, he reveals it not with the view of exercising the ingenuity of remote generations, but for the practical purpose of inculcating those great lessons of trust in God, loyalty to the Christ-King, confidence in the ultimate triumph of righteousness, patience under adversity, and hope in the prospect of death, which were urgently needed by the Asian Churches, and will never be without meaning and importance so long as the world lasts.

It will be seen that an interpretation conducted upon these lines will have points of contact with each of the chief systems of Apocalyptic exegesis, without identifying itself with any one of them as a whole. With the 'preterists' it will take its stand on the circumstances of the age and locality to which the book belongs, and will connect the greater part of the prophecy with the destinies of the Empire under which the prophet lived; with the 'futurists' it will look for fulfilments of St John's pregnant words in times yet to come. With the school of Auberlen and Benson it will find in the Apocalypse a Christian philosophy of history; with the 'continuous-historical' school it can see in the progress of events ever new illustrations of the working of the great principles which are revealed. And while it maintains, against the majority of recent continental scholars, the essential unity of the book and its prophetic inspiration, it will gladly accept all that research and discovery can yield for the better understanding of the conditions under which the book was written. Indeed it is from this quarter that it will look most confidently for further light.

No attempt to solve the problems of this most enigmatic of canonical books can be more than provisional; even if the principles on which it rests are sound, their application must often be attended with uncertainty through the interpreter's lack of knowledge, or through his liability to err in his judgements upon the facts which are known to him. The present writer expects no immunity from this law; he has stated his conclusions without reserve, but he is far from desiring to claim for them a finality which perhaps will never be attained. Nor has he gone to his work with any preconceptions beyond the general principles just indicated. His purpose has not been to add a system of interpretation to those which are already in the field, but simply to contribute whatever a personal study, conducted in the light shed upon the Apocalypse by many explorers, may be able to offer towards a true appreciation of this great Christian prophecy.

The following are a few of the least obvious abbreviations employed in the footnotes:

Ar. Arethas.

BDB. Brown Driver and Briggs, *Hebrew and English Lexicon of the O.T.* (Oxford, 1892—1906).

Blass, *Gr.* F. Blass, *Grammar of N.T. Greek.* Translated by H. St J. Thackeray (London, 1898).

Burton. E. de W. Burton, *Syntax of the Moods and Tenses in N.T. Greek* (Edinburgh, 1894).

C. I. G. *Corpus inscriptionum graecarum.*

Enc. Bibl. T. K. Cheyne and J. S. Black, *Encyclopaedia Biblica* (London, 1899—1903).

Ev. Petr. The Gospel of Peter (cited from the writer's edition).

Exp. The *Expositor.*

Hastings, *D.B.* J. Hastings, *Dictionary of the Bible* (Edinburgh, 1898—1904).

J. Th. St. The *Journal of Theological Studies.*

SH. Sanday and Headlam, *Commentary on the Epistle to the Romans* (Edinburgh, 1895).

St Mark. The writer's edition.

Tyc. Tyconius (see p. cxcviii.).

Vg. The Latin Vulgate.

Vict. Victorinus (see p. cxcvii.).

WH. Westcott and Hort, *N.T. in Greek* (Cambridge, 1891); WH.², second edition (1896).

WM. Winer-Moulton, *Grammar of N.T. Greek*, 8th Engl. ed. (Edinburgh, 1877).

WSchm. Winer-Schmiedel, *Grammatik d. NTlichen Sprachidioms* (Göttingen, 1894—).

Zahn, *Einl.* Th. Zahn, *Einleitung in das N.T.* (Leipzig, 1897—9).

ΑΠΟΚΑΛΥΨΙΣ ΙΩΑΝΝΟΥ

ΑΠΟΚΑΛΥΨΙϹ Ἰησοῦ Χριστοῦ, ἣν ἔδωκεν αὐτῷ ὁ 1 I.

αποκαλυψις Ιωαννου (Ιωανου ℵ) ℵC (cf. A in subscr) 2 8 82 93 (95) (130) Ir Or Eus Hier] απ. Ι. του θεολογου 14 17 91 97 απ. του αγιου Ι. του θεολ. 1 25 28 31 (37) 38 (49) 51 90 94 απ. Ι. του θεολ. και ευαγγελιστου Q 12 η απ. του αποστολου Ι. και ευαγγελιστου P 42 (cf. vg^ed syr)

I 1 αυτω] αυτη Q

Title. Ἀποκάλυψις or Ἀ. Ἰωάννου was the title of the book in the second century, cf. Iren. v. 30. 3 τοῦ καὶ τὴν ἀποκάλυψιν ἑωρακότος: *can. Murat.* l. 71 sq. "apocalypse[s] etiam Iohannis et Petri tantum recipimus": Tert. *adv. Marc.* iv. 5 "apocalypsin eius Marcion respuit." Τοῦ ἀποστόλου καὶ εὐαγγελιστοῦ, τοῦ θεολόγου etc. are manifestly due to later transcribers. Ὁ θεολόγος as a distinctive title of St John is perhaps not earlier than the end of cent. iv. (see exx. in Suicer, *s.v.*); in Eus. *praep. ev.* xi. 19 the Evangelist θεολογεῖ, but the writer of Hebrews is ἄλλος θεολόγος.

I. 1—3. Superscription.

1. ἀποκάλυψις Ἰησοῦ Χριστοῦ] Ἀποκάλυψις occurs here only in this book. The noun is rare in literary Greek, but Jerome's dictum (*in Gal.* i. 11 sq.) "verbum ipsum ἀποκαλύψεως...proprie scripturarum est et a nullo sapientum saeculi apud Graecos usurpatum" is too sweeping, for it is found in Plutarch *mor.* 70 F. In the LXX. ἀποκαλύπτειν is far more frequent than ἀνακαλύπτειν, and the noun is used euphemistically for עֶרְוָה in 1 Regn. xx. 30, and metaphorically in Sirach (xi. 27, xxii. 22, xlii. 1); in the N.T. ἀποκάλυψις in a metaphorical sense is fairly common (Lc.[1], Paul[14], Pet.[3], Apoc.[1]). The Epistles use it in reference to (1) the revelation of God (Rom. ii. 5), of Christ (1 Cor. i. 7, 2 Th. i. 7, 1 Pet. i. 7, 13, iv. 13), and of the Saints (Rom. viii. 19), which is to be made at the Parousia; and (2) any revelation now made to the Church (Rom. xvi. 25, 1 Cor. xiv. 6, 26, 2 Cor. xii. 1, 7, Gal. i. 12, ii. 2, Eph. iii. 3) through the Spirit as a πνεῦμα ἀποκαλύψεως (Eph. i. 17). The corresponding χάρισμα was exercised not only by Apostles (2 Cor. xii. 7, Gal. ii. 2), but at times as it appears by ordinary believers in the congregation (cf. 1 Cor. xiv. 26 ὅταν συνέρχησθε ἕκαστος...ἀποκάλυψιν ἔχει). In this sense ἀποκάλυψις is coupled with other gifts, such as γνῶσις, προφητεία, διδαχή (1 Cor. xiv. 6), ψαλμός, γλῶσσα, ἑρμηνεία (*ib.* 26), ὀπτασία (2 Cor. xii. 1), σοφία (Eph. i. 17).

Here the exact meaning depends upon the interpretation of the genitive. Is Ἰησοῦ Χριστοῦ the gen. of object or of subject? Dr Hort (on 1 Pet. i. 7) inclines to the former, but the next words, ἣν ἔδωκεν κτλ., seem to be decisive. The book is a Divine revelation of which Jesus Christ was the giver; cf. Gal. i. 12, where δι' ἀποκαλύψεως Ἰ. Χ. means 'by revelation from J. C.' (Lightfoot), in contrast with teaching received παρὰ ἀνθρώπου. The title might have been Ἀποκάλυψις Ἰησοῦ, though the instinct of the

θεὸς δεῖξαι τοῖς δούλοις αὐτοῦ ἃ δεῖ γενέσθαι ἐν
τάχει, καὶ ἐσήμανεν ἀποστείλας διὰ τοῦ ἀγγέλου
§ C 2 αὐτοῦ τῷ δούλῳ αὐτοῦ Ἰωάννῃ, §² ὃς ἐμαρτύρησεν τὸν

1 δουλοις] αγιοις ℵ* (δ. ℵ$^{c.a}$) | τω δουλω αυτ.] του δουλου αυτ. A om 130 | Ιωανει ℵ* (Ιωαννη ℵ$^{c.a}$)

Church has rightly substituted the name of the disciple through whom the message was delivered.

ἣν ἔδωκεν αὐτῷ ὁ θεός κτλ.] Arethas: δέδοται μὲν παρὰ τοῦ πατρὸς τῷ υἱῷ, δέδοται δὲ παρὰ τοῦ υἱοῦ ἡμῖν τοῖς δούλοις αὐτοῦ. The Father is the ultimate Revealer (Mt. xi. 25 ἀπεκάλυψας), the Son the medium through Whom the revelation passes to men (*ib.* 27 ᾧ ἐὰν βούληται ὁ υἱὸς ἀποκαλύψαι, cf. Jo. i. 18 μονογενὴς θεὸς...ἐκεῖνος ἐξηγήσατο). That the Son receives what He is and has from the Father is the constant teaching of the Gospel of St John (iii. 35, v. 20 ff., 26, vii. 16, viii. 28, xii. 49, xvi. 15, xvii. 2 ff.; cf. Bede: "Iohannes more suo filii gloriam ad patrem referens"); for a statement of the doctrine in its relation to the Christology of the Creeds see Hooker *E. P.* v. 54 ff. The particular revelation now about to be made was given to Jesus Christ that it might be communicated (δεῖξαι = ἵνα δείξῃ, *palam facere*) to the servants of God (αὐτοῦ = τοῦ θεοῦ, cf. xxii. 6), i.e., primarily the Christian prophets (see Amos iii. 7 οὐ μὴ ποιήσει Κύριος ὁ θεὸς πρᾶγμα ἐὰν μὴ ἀποκαλύψῃ παιδείαν πρὸς τοὺς δούλους αὐτοῦ τοὺς προφήτας, and Apoc. x. 7, xi. 18, xxii. 6), but not to the exclusion of the other members of the Church; in vii. 3 οἱ δοῦλοι τοῦ θεοῦ ἡμῶν are the whole company of the sealed, and the reading of ℵ* (ἁγίοις) is doubtless a true gloss in this place.

ἃ δεῖ γενέσθαι ἐν τάχει, the contents of the Apocalypse. Δεῖ γενέσθαι is from Dan. ii. 28, see Mc. xiii. 7, note; δεῖ denotes not the necessity of a blind εἱμαρμένη, but the sure fulfilment of the purpose of God revealed by the Prophets; cf. Mc. viii. 31, ix. 11, xiii. 10, Lc. xxiv. 26, Jo. xii. 34. To this the keen hope of primitive Christianity adds ἐν τάχει (Lc. xviii. 8, Rom. xvi. 20, Apoc. xxii. 6), another O.T. phrase (Deut.^{5}, Jos.^{2}, 1 Regn.^{1}, Ps.^{1}, Sir.^{1}, Bar.^{3}, Ez.^{1}), which must be interpreted here and in xxii. 6 relatively to Divine measurements of time (Arethas, παραμετρῶν τὰ ἀνθρώπινα τοῖς θείοις).

καὶ ἐσήμανεν ἀποστείλας, sc. Ἰησοῦς Χριστός. The Latin *significavit nuntianda* seems to imply a reading ἀποστεῖλαι, with ὁ θεός as the subject. With ἐσήμανεν compare the use of the verb in Jo. xii. 33, xviii. 32, xxi. 19, and in Acts xi. 28 ἐσήμαινεν διὰ τοῦ πνεύματος. Here the message is sent by Christ διὰ τοῦ ἀγγέλου αὐτοῦ, cf. Beatus: "non cogitatione concepta res est, non aliquibus scripturarum carminibus; sed per angelum, id est, puritatis suae nuntium...Ioanni directa est"; see Mt. xiii. 41, Mc. xiii. 27, Apoc. xxii. 16. Ἀποστέλλειν διά (= שָׁלַח בְּיַד, Exod. iv. 13, 2 Sam. xi. 14, xii. 25, xv. 36), cf. Mt. xi. 2 πέμψας διὰ τῶν μαθητῶν αὐτοῦ, Acts xi. 30 ἀποστείλαντες...διὰ χειρὸς Βαρνάβα καὶ Σαύλου. For τῷ δούλῳ αὐτοῦ Ἰωάννῃ see Rom. i. 1, Jas. i. 1, Jude 1. John is named again in i. 4, 9 and xxii. 8; the question of his identity with the Apostle is discussed in the Introduction.

The genesis of the Apocalypse has now been traced from its origin in the Mind of God to the moment when it reached its human interpreter.

2. ὃς ἐμαρτύρησεν τὸν λόγον κτλ.] Μάρτυς, μαρτυρεῖν, μαρτυρία, are frequent in the Apocalypse, as in other Johannine books; the verb is usually

λόγον τοῦ θεοῦ καὶ τὴν μαρτυρίαν Ἰησοῦ Χριστοῦ,
ὅσα εἶδεν. ³μακάριος ὁ ἀναγινώσκων καὶ οἱ ἀκούοντες 3
τοὺς λόγους τῆς προφητείας καὶ τηροῦντες τὰ ἐν
αὐτῇ γεγραμμένα· ὁ γὰρ καιρὸς ἐγγύς.

2 Ιησου Χριστου] om Χριστου 12 αυτου Dion | οσα]+τε 1 al^nonn arm^codd Ar | ειδεν (ιδεν ℵAQ 7 98)]+και ατινα εισι και α(τινα) χρη γενεσθαι μετα ταυτα 1 7 12 28 37 38 46 49 al^sat mu arm (cod ap Ar)   3 τους λογους ACP al^pl vg me syrr Vict Prim Andr Ar]+τουτους C τον λογον ℵQ 100 aeth | της προφητειας (-τιας ℵC)]+ταυτης 7 16 9 vg^cle am dem fu harl me syrr arm^codd Vict Prim

followed by περί or ὅτι, but the cognate acc. occurs again in 1 Jo. v. 10, Apoc. xxii. 16, 20.

Τὸν λόγον...τὴν μαρτυρίαν, i.e. the revelation imparted by God and attested by Christ; the phrase occurs again, with some modifications in form or meaning, in i. 9, vi. 9, xii. 17, xx. 4. This word and witness reached John in a vision (ὅσα εἶδεν: the reading ὅσα τε εἶδεν has arisen from a misunderstanding). Εἶδεν strikes a note which is heard repeatedly throughout the book (cf. i. 12, 17, 19 f., iv. 1, v. 1 f., etc.) and indicates its general character, which is that of a prophetic vision (cf. Isa. i. 1). The aorist ἐμαρτύρησεν is epistolary; from the reader's point of view John's testimony was borne at the time when the book was written.

3. μακάριος ὁ ἀναγινώσκων κτλ.] Felicitation of the reader and hearers of the vision. Ὁ ἀναγινώσκων is not the private student (cf. Mc. xiii. 14, note), but, as οἱ ἀκ. shews, the person who reads aloud in the congregation. The Church inherited the Jewish practice of reading in the congregation (cf. Exod. xxiv. 7, Neh. viii. 2, Lc. iv. 16, Acts xiii. 15, xv. 21, 2 Cor. iii. 15), and extended it to such Christian documents as Apostolic letters (Col. iv. 16, 1 Th. v. 27, and see also Justin *ap.* i. 67, Dionys. Cor. ap. Eus. *H. E.* iv. 23); and the writer of the Apocalypse clearly desires to encourage this public use of his book. The reader (ἀναγνώστης, *lector*), soon acquired an official position, and became a member of the *clerus* (Tert. *de praescr.* 41; see Wordsworth, *Ministry of Grace*, p. 187 f.). But no such character was attributed to him in the first century; in the Apostolic Church as in the Synagogue the reading of the Scriptures was probably deputed by the presbyters or the president to any member of the congregation who was able and willing to perform it.

The μακαρισμός of the reader (μακάριος = אַשְׁרֵי as in Deut. xxxiii. 29, Ps. i. 1) is extended to the hearers if they keep what they have heard. There is here a scarcely doubtful reference to our Lord's saying in Lc. xi. 28 μακάριοι οἱ ἀκούοντες τὸν λόγον τοῦ θεοῦ καὶ φυλάσσοντες, though the Johannine τηρεῖν (Jo. viii. 51 f., xiv. 23, xv. 20, xvii. 6, 1 Jo. ii. 5, etc.) takes the place of φυλάσσειν. The thought is worked out by St James (i. 22 f.)

Τῆς προφητείας: the Apocalyptist claims for his book that it shall take rank with the prophetic books of the O.T.; cf. 2 Chr. xxxii. 32 ἐν τῇ προφητείᾳ Ἠσαίου, Sir. *prol.* 15 αἱ προφητεῖαι. The claim is repeated in Apoc. xxii. 7, 10, 18 f.

Ὁ γὰρ καιρὸς ἐγγύς: a motive for hearing and keeping: the season (cf. xi. 18, xxii. 10; Acts i. 7) for the fulfilment of the vision is at hand; the hopes and fears which it arouses belong to the near future; cf. Beatus: "perficientibus enim non longum tempus remunerationis facit." The words, like ἐν τάχει (*v.* 1), are repeated in xxii. 10. They rest ultimately on such sayings

4 [4] Ἰωάννης ταῖς ἑπτὰ ἐκκλησίαις ταῖς ἐν τῇ Ἀσίᾳ·
χάρις ὑμῖν καὶ εἰρήνη ἀπὸ ὁ ὢν καὶ ὁ ἦν καὶ ὁ ἐρχό-

4 Ιωανης ℵ | απο ο ων ℵACP 1 2 5 6 7 10 38 91 al[sat mu] *g h* vg syrr] απο του ο ων 30 92[mg] Ar[ed] απο θεου ο ων Q 36 95 130 al[fere 40] arm[codd] Vict Prim

of Christ as Mc. xiii. 28 f. and are among the commonplaces of primitive Christianity; cf. Rom. xiii. 11, 1 Cor. vii. 29, Phil. iv. 5 (where see Lightfoot's note).

4—8. THE WRITER'S GREETING TO THE CHURCHES ADDRESSED.

4. Ἰωάννης ταῖς ἑπτὰ ἐκκλησίαις κτλ.] The customary form for beginning a letter; cf. Gal. i. 1 Παῦλος...ταῖς ἐκκλησίαις τῆς Γαλατίας, 1 Th. i. 1, II. τῇ ἐκκλησίᾳ Θεσσαλονικέων, 1 Cor. i. 1, 2 Cor. i. 1, Ign. *Eph.* 1 etc. The Apocalypse is in fact a letter from i. 4 onwards, though we are not reminded of the fact till we reach the closing benediction (xxii. 21); it might have borne the title Πρὸς τὰς ζ' ἐκκλησίας, or Πρὸς Ἀσιανούς.

Ἡ Ἀσία in the Books of Maccabees (1 Macc. viii. 6, xi. 13, xii. 39, xiii. 32; 2 Macc. iii. 3, x. 24; 3 Macc. iii. 14; 4 Macc. iii. 20) is conterminous with the empire of the Seleucids. But before N.T. times it had acquired another meaning. The Romans identified Asia with the Pergamene kingdom, and when in B.C. 129 the possessions of Attalus III. passed into their hands, they gave the name to the new province. The province of Asia at first included only the western sea-board of Asia Minor, but after B.C. 49 two *dioeceses* of Phrygia were added to it; see Cic. *pro Flacco* 27 "Asia vestra constat ex Phrygia Mysia Caria Lycia." In the N.T. ἡ Ἀσία is always Proconsular Asia, with the possible exception of Acts ii. 9, where Phrygia appears to be definitely excluded. In addition to the cities named below in *v.* 11, there were Christian communities at Troas (Acts xx. 5 ff., 2 Cor. ii. 12), Hierapolis and Colossae (Col. i. 1, ii. 1, iv. 13), possibly also at Magnesia and Tralles; and the question arises why John addresses only the seven churches which are specified (ταῖς ἑπτὰ ἐκκλησίαις). The selection may partly be explained by circumstances; Troas lay far off the road which the messenger would naturally follow, while Hierapolis and Colossae were so near to Laodicea and Magnesia and Tralles to Ephesus that they might be disregarded. The seven Churches addressed were fairly representative of Asiatic Christianity; and as Ramsay points out (*Exp.* 1904, i. p. 29), the "seven cities were the best points of communication with seven districts." Yet the repeated occurrence of the number seven in this book (i. 4[b], 12, 16, iv. 5, v. 1, 6, viii. 2, x. 3, xi. 13, xii. 3, xiii. 1, xiv. 6 f.) suggests a further reason for the limitation. Seven, the number of the days of the week, presented to the Semitic mind the idea of completeness (Adrian *Isagoge* 83 ἡ γραφὴ...τὸν ἑπτὰ ἀριθμὸν ...λέγει...ἐπὶ τελειοῦ ἀριθμοῦ) Thus "the seven Churches" may represent to us not only the Churches of Asia as a whole, but (*can. Murat.* 57 f.) all the Churches of Christ; and Andreas is probably not altogether wide of the mark when he writes: διὰ τοῦ ἑβδοματικοῦ ἀριθμοῦ τὸ μυστικὸν τῶν ἁπανταχῇ ἐκκλησιῶν σημαίνων. Cf. Primasius: "id est, uni ecclesiae septiformi; septenario numero saepe universitas figuratur"; and Rupert of Deutz: "idem nobis sit ac si dixerit 'Ioannes omnibus ecclesiis quae sunt in mundo'"; cf. Beatus: "quid sibi Asianus populus esse videtur ut solus suscipere revelationem apostolicam mereatur?" But any such application of ταῖς ἑπτὰ ἐκκλησίαις is only in the background of the words; as they stand, they have a definite reference from which they must not be diverted to mystical uses.

Χάρις ὑμῖν καὶ εἰρήνη. So all the Pauline Epistles open except 1, 2

μενος, καὶ ἀπὸ τῶν ἑπτὰ πνευμάτων ἃ ἐνώπιον τοῦ

4 *α ενωπιον* CQ 6 14 93 95 al^{fere 40} syrr^{vid}] *α εστιν εν.* P 1 38 49 *α εισιν εν.* 36 *των εν.* ℵA 47 79 99 om 80

Tim., where and in 2 Jo. we find *χάρις ἔλεος εἰρήνη*. The same salutation is used in 1, 2 Peter; St James prefers the classical *χαίρειν* (Acts xv. 23, Jac. i. 1). Ἀπὸ ὁ ὢν καὶ ὁ ἦν καὶ ὁ ἐρχόμενος i.e. *ἀπὸ θεοῦ πατρός* (Rom. i. 7, 1 Cor. i. 3 etc.). That this is the true interpretation appears from *καὶ ἀπὸ* Ἰ. Χ. which follows; the view of Andreas (*ἀπὸ τῆς τρισυποστάτου θεότητος*), and that of Primasius ("ad personam tamen filii hic proprie redigendus est locus") are equally excluded by the context. As to the phrase itself, *ὁ ὢν* is the LXX. rendering of אֲשֶׁר אֶהְיֶה in Exod. iii. 14; cf. Philo *de Abr.* 24 *ἐν ταῖς ἱεραῖς γραφαῖς κυρίῳ ὀνόματι καλεῖται* Ὁ ὤν. Aquila, however, followed by Theodotion, translated, אֶהְיֶה אֲשֶׁר אֶהְיֶה by *ἔσομαι* [*ὃς*] *ἔσομαι*, and the Targums read into the words a reference to the infinite past and future of God's eternal 'now'; thus the Jerusalem Targum interprets "qui fuit est et erit," and the T. of Jonathan on Deut. xxxii. 39 renders אֲנִי אֲנִי הוּא "ego ille qui est et qui fuit et qui erit." Similar descriptions of the Divine Life are cited from Greek poetry, e.g. the oracle in Paus. x. 12 *Ζεὺς ἦν, Ζεὺς ἔστι, Ζεὺς ἔσσεται*, and the Orphic lines *Ζεὺς πρῶτος γένετο, Ζεὺς ὕστατος ἀρχικέραυνος· | Ζεὺς κεφαλή, Ζεὺς μέσος*. Thus the Apocalyptist strikes a note familiar both to Jewish and Greek ears. But he expresses his thought *more suo*: *ὁ ἦν* (Benson: 'the Was') is a characteristically bold attempt to supply the want of a past part. of *εἰμί*, while *ὁ ἐρχόμενος* is perhaps preferred to *ὁ ἐσόμενος* because it adumbrates at the outset the general purpose of the book, which is to exhibit the comings of God in human history; if *ἔρχεσθαι* is used elsewhere chiefly of the Son, the Father also may be said to come when He reveals Himself in His workings; cf. e.g. Jo. xiv. 23 [*ἐγὼ καὶ*] *ὁ πατήρ μου...ἐλευσόμεθα*. As a whole the phrase exhibits the Divine Life under the categories into which it falls when it becomes the subject of human thought, which can conceive of the eternal only in the terms of time. Such a title of the Eternal Father stands fitly among the first words of a book which reveals the present in the light both of the past and of the future.

The construction *ἀπὸ ὁ ὢν κτλ.* must be explained by regarding the whole phrase as an indeclinable noun (Viteau, *Étude*, ii. pp. 12, 126); a more exact writer would perhaps have said *ἀπὸ τοῦ* Ὁ ὢν *κτλ.* (cf. WM. p. 79 f.).

καὶ ἀπὸ τῶν ἑπτὰ πνευμάτων κτλ.] Cf. iii. 1, iv. 5, v. 6, where after *πν.* the writer adds *τοῦ θεοῦ*. Jewish angelology recognised seven angels of the Presence (Tob. xii. 15, Enoch xx. 7, xc. 21; cf. Targum Jon. on Gen. xi. 7: "dixit Deus vii angelis qui stant coram illo"). Seven angels are mentioned in Apoc. viii. 2 ff., xv. 1 ff.; and some early interpreters were disposed to identify the "seven spirits of God" with such a group of angelic beings. Thus Andreas: *ἑπτὰ δὲ πνεύματα τοὺς ἑπτὰ ἀγγέλους νοεῖν δυνατόν*, and Arethas more confidently: *δοκιμώτερον δὲ ἀγγέλους ταῦτα νοεῖν*, urging that *ἃ ἐστιν ἐνώπιον τοῦ θρόνου* implies *τὴν οἰκετικὴν τάξιν, οὐ τὴν ἰσότιμον*. But against this view must be set (1) the description of the 'seven spirits' in *c.* v. 6, with obvious reference to Zech. iv. 10; and (2) the apparent coordination of the spirits in this place with the Father and the Son. Bousset finds a parallel to this in Justin, *ap.* i. 6, but Justin's Christology is less consistent than that of

5 θρόνου αὐτοῦ, [5]καὶ ἀπὸ Ἰησοῦ Χριστοῦ, ὁ μάρτυς ὁ

the Apocalypse, where Christ is distinguished from the angels (see upon this the notes to *c.* xxii. 8 f., 16). Moreover the N. T. rarely uses πνεύματα of angels; Heb. i. 7, 14 is based on a quotation, and in Apoc. xvi. 13 f. πνεύματα is qualified by ἀκάθαρτα or δαιμονίων, which removes all ambiguity. On the whole, therefore, it is safer to accept the alternative followed by the best Latin commentators, Victorinus, Primasius, Apringius, Beatus ("sanctus scilicet Spiritus unus in nomine, virtutibus septiformis") and offered by Andreas (ἴσως δὲ καὶ ἑτέρως τοῦτο νοηθήσεται...διὰ...τῶν ἑπτὰ πνευμάτων τῶν ἐνεργειῶν τοῦ ἁγίου Πνεύματος [σημαινομένων]). We may compare Heb. ii. 4 πνεύματος ἁγίου μερισμοῖς, 1 Cor. xii. 10 διακρίσεις πνευμάτων, ib. xiv. 32 πνεύματα προφητῶν, Apoc. xxii. 6 ὁ θεὸς τῶν πνευμάτων τῶν προφητῶν. Here the 'spirits' are seven, because the Churches in which they operate are seven. An early interpretation connected them with the aspects of the רוּחַ יְהוָֹה enumerated in Isa. xi. 2 LXX.; cf. Justin, *dial.* 87, and Ps.-Hippolytus (ed. Lagarde, p. 198), where the passage in Isaiah is quoted in the form ἀναπαύσεται ἐπ' αὐτὸν ἑπτὰ πνεύματα τοῦ θεοῦ. Hence the *Spiritus septiformis* of Latin devotional theology. But there is nothing to shew that the writer of the Apocalypse had Isa. *l. c.* in his thoughts; moreover the septenary number appears there only in the LXX., to which comparatively little weight is assigned in this book.

ἃ ἐνώπιον τοῦ θρόνου αὐτοῦ anticipates the vision of iv. 2, 5, *q.v.* The readings τῶν, ἅ ἐστιν (εἰσιν), are grammatical corrections for the rougher ἅ: for the omission of the verb cf. *c.* v. 13 πᾶν κτίσμα ὃ ἐν κτλ. Nestle (*Text. Crit.* p. 331) suggests that the original reading was τά.

5. καὶ ἀπὸ Ἰ. Χρ., ὁ μάρτυς ὁ πιστός] Grace and peace come also from the Person who received and communicated the revelation. Ἀπὸ Ἰ. Χρ., as in the Pauline form of salutation from Rom. i. 7 onwards; St John (2 Jo. 3) has παρά in the same sense. Since our Lord is the medium rather than the source of the Divine favour we might have expected διά, as in Jo. i. 17 ἡ χάρις καὶ ἡ ἀλήθεια διὰ Ἰ. Χρ. ἐγένετο. But the Son in His oneness with the Father may also be regarded as the source of the gifts which He communicates. From this point the full title Ἰησοῦς Χριστός disappears, unless we read it in the closing benediction (xxii. 21); elsewhere throughout the Apoc. Ἰησοῦς stands alone (i. 9 bis, xii. 17, xiv. 12, xvii. 6, xix. 10 bis, xx. 4, xxii. 16, 20)—a use elsewhere limited with few exceptions to the Gospels and the Ep. to the Hebrews. It may be the purpose of the writer to emphasize in this way the humanity of the glorified Christ, and His identity with the historical Person who lived and suffered.

Ὁ μάρτυς ὁ πιστός, and the other nominatives which follow, are the first examples of an anomaly which is common in the Apoc.; cf. ii. 13, 20, iii. 12 etc. Such irregularities may be partly attributable to Semitic habits of thought—a Greek could scarcely have permitted himself to use them; but they are partly due to the character of the book and perhaps are parenthetic rather than solecistic. See Archbp. Benson's remark, *Apocalypse*, p. 143 ff.: "the seeming Ungrammar of the Apocalypse is [sometimes] no such thing." Μάρτυς looks back to *v.* 2 τὴν μαρτυρίαν Ἰησοῦ, but the phrase ὁ μ. ὁ πιστός has a wider reference; cf. Jo. iii. 11, 32 f., viii. 14 f., xviii. 37, 1 Tim. vi. 13; so Victorinus: "in homine suscepto perhibuit testimonium in mundo"; we are reminded also of Prov. xiv. 5

πιστός, ὁ πρωτότοκος τῶν νεκρῶν καὶ ὁ ἄρχων τῶν βασιλέων τῆς γῆς. τῷ ἀγαπῶντι ἡμᾶς καὶ λύσαντι ἡμᾶς ἐκ τῶν ἁμαρτιῶν ἡμῶν ἐν τῷ αἵματι αὐτοῦ,

5 *των νεκρων*] pr *εκ* 1 91 96 al arm[codd] | *βασιλειων* ℵ* (-*λεων* ℵ[1 vid]) | *αγαπωντι* ℵACQ 6 7 14 38 95 al[sat mu]] *αγαπησαντι* P 1 28 36 79 91 92[mg] 96 99 Andr Ar | *λυσαντι* ℵAC 1 6 12* 28 36 38 69 79 99 (syrr) arm Prim] *λουσαντι* PQ min[pl] vg me aeth Andr Ar | om *ημας* 2° ℵ* (hab ℵ[c.a]) | *εκ* ℵAC 1 12 28* 36 38 79 92[mg] 99 *g* arm Prim] *απο* PQ min[pl] vg me aeth Ar | om *ημων* A 1 12 16 Prim[vid]

עֵד אֱמוּנִים, Isa. lv. 4 עֵד לְאוּמִּים נְתַתִּיו. It occurs again in *c.* iii. 14 (*q.v.*), where it is amplified (ὁ Ἀμήν, ὁ μάρτυς ὁ π. καὶ ἀληθινός).

ὁ πρωτότοκος τῶν νεκρῶν] So St Paul in Col. i. 18 ὅς ἐστιν ἡ ἀρχή, πρωτότοκος ἐκ τῶν νεκρῶν, and 1 Cor. xv. 20 ἐγήγερται ἐκ νεκρῶν, ἀπαρχὴ τῶν κεκοιμημένων. Though others had risen, those e.g. who were raised by Him, yet as Alcuin (quoted by Trench) well observes, "nullus ante ipsum non moriturus surrexit." In His capacity of 'firstborn' Jesus is also ὁ ἄρχων τῶν βασιλέων τῆς γῆς. Here John follows another line of thought, suggested by Ps. lxxxviii. (lxxxix.) 28 κἀγὼ πρωτότοκον (בְּכוֹר) θήσομαι αὐτόν, ὑψηλὸν παρὰ (עֶלְיוֹן לְ) τοῖς βασιλεῦσιν τῆς γῆς. The Resurrection carried with it a potential lordship over all humanity (Rom. xiv. 9), not only over the Church (Col. *l.c.*). The Lord won by His Death what the Tempter had offered Him as the reward of sin (Mt. iv. 8 f.); He rose and ascended to receive universal empire; cf. *c.* xix. 12, 16 ἐπὶ τὴν κεφαλὴν αὐτοῦ διαδήματα πολλά...ἔχει...ὄνομα γεγραμμένον Βασιλεὺς βασιλέων. The words ὁ ἄρχων τ. β. τῆς γῆς, *imperator regum terrae*, stand appropriately at the head of a book which represents the glorified Christ as presiding over the destinies of nations.

The threefold title μάρτυς...πρωτότοκος...ἄρχων answers to the threefold purpose of the Apocalypse, which is at once a Divine testimony, a revelation of the Risen Lord, and a forecast of the issues of history.

τῷ ἀγαπῶντι ἡμᾶς κτλ.] The first of the many doxologies of the book (iv. 11, v. 9, 12 f., vii. 10, 12 etc.) is offered to Jesus Christ. "To Him that loves us and—the crucial instance of His love—loosed us from our sins at the cost of His blood." The reading ἀγαπήσαντι, though it represents a fact (Jo. xiii. 1, 34, xv. 9, Rom. viii. 37, Apoc. iii. 9) misses the contrast between the abiding ἀγάπη and the completed act of redemption. Between λύσαντι and λούσαντι it is not so easy to decide. Λύειν ἁμαρτίαν is Biblical, see Job xlii. 9 (LXX.), and the construction λύειν ἀπό occurs in Lc. xiii. 16, 1 Cor. vii. 27; cf. Apoc. xx. 7 λυθήσεται ἐκ τῆς φυλακῆς. On the other hand λούσαντι yields a good sense, and presents a more usual metaphor; cf. Ps. l. (li.) 4, Isa. i. 16, 18, 1 Cor. vi. 11, Eph. v. 26, Tit. iii. 5, Heb. x. 22; but it rests on inferior authority and may be "due to failure to understand the Hebraic use of ἐν to denote a price...and a natural misapplication of vii. 14" (WH.[2], *Notes*, p. 136; cf. Nestle, *Textual Criticism*, p. 332). It is interesting to find Plato by a play upon the words bringing together the two verbs in a very similar connexion: *Crat.* 405 B οὐκοῦν ὁ καθαίρων θεὸς καὶ ὁ ἀπολύων τε καὶ ἀπολούων τῶν τοιούτων κακῶν αἴτιος ἂν εἴη; Such a passage serves at least to account for the vacillation of the scribes; cf. Arethas: δισσογραφεῖται ταῦτα πρὸς διάφορον

6 ^{6}καὶ ἐποίησεν ἡμᾶς βασιλείαν, ἱερεῖς τῷ θεῷ καὶ

6 εποιησεν ℵACP min^{pl} syrr] ποιησαντι Q 7 13 14 16 25 29 36 43 55 92^{txt} | ημας ℵPQ al^{pl} syrr Vict Prim Andr Ar] ημιν A 13 23 27 31 38 55 76 ημων C vg$^{\text{am fu harl tol}}$ (*nostrum regnum*) | βασιλειαν ιερεις] βασιλειαν και ιερεις ℵ$^{\text{c.a}}$ 99 vg^{cod} Tert Vict Prim βασιλεις και ιερεις P 1 28 36 79 80 81 161 βασιλειον ιερεις Q βασιλειον ιερατευμα (9) 13 14 23 27 55 92^{txt} 130 βασιλειαν ιεραν syr$^{\text{gw vid}}$

ἔννοιαν. Ἐν τῷ αἵματι: the blood, emblem of the sacrificed life, was the λύτρον (Mc. x. 45, note; cf. Rom. v. 9, 1 Pet. i. 19, 1 Jo. i. 7); for ἐν 'at the price of' (=בְּ) see 1 Chron. xxi. 24, Jer. xxxix. (xxxii.) 44, Apoc. v. 9 ἠγόρασας τῷ θεῷ ἐν τῷ αἵματί σου. The gift of ἄφεσις ἁμαρτιῶν bestowed upon the Church on the very day of the Resurrection (Jo. xx. 23) was an immediate result of the 'loosing' effected by the Cross; cf. Jo. xi. 44 λύσατε αὐτὸν καὶ ἄφετε, and Aug. *ad loc.*

6. καὶ ἐποίησεν ἡμᾶς βασιλείαν, ἱερεῖς κτλ.] Beatus: "quia pro nobis passus est et resurrexit a mortuis, nostrum regnum ipse construxit." The construction of the sentence requires καὶ ποιήσαντι, but the writer *more suo* (see on *v.* 5, ὁ μάρτυς) suffers the new thought that rises in his mind to take the form of a parenthesis. As the apparatus criticus testifies, early students of the book were driven to despair by the words which follow. They rest on Exod. xix. 6 "ye shall be to Me a kingdom of priests" (מַמְלֶכֶת כֹּהֲנִים, LXX. βασίλειον ἱεράτευμα, Aq. βασιλεία ἱερέων, Symm., Th. βασιλεία ἱερεῖς, Vg. *regnum sacerdotale*). Exod. *l.c.* is quoted also in 1 Pet. ii. 9 (where see Hort's note), Apoc. v. 9 (βασιλείαν καὶ ἱερεῖς), *Jubilees* xvi. 13 (ed. Charles, p. 116 note). As Dr Hort has shewn, the LXX. probably read מַמְלָכָה, and the same reading is represented by Th. and in the Apoc. (on the frequent agreement of the latter with Th. see Salmon, *Introd. to the N.T.*[7], p. 548 ff., and the writer's *Introd. to the O.T. in Greek*, p. 48). It is a further question whether βασιλεία in this passage means a nation under the government of a king, or a nation of kings; for the latter interpretation see the Jer. Targum cited by Charles *l.c.* (מלכין וכהנים). But, as Hort observes, "in Exodus 'Kingdom' is little more than a synonym of 'people' or nation, with the idea of government by a king added"; and this sense suits the present context. The Apoc. is largely a protest against the Caesar-cult and the attitude of the Empire towards the Church, and it sets the Divine Kingdom in sharp contrast to the imperial power. As Israel when set free from Egypt acquired a national life under its Divine King, so the Church, redeemed by the Blood of Christ, constituted a holy nation, a new theocracy.

Ἱερεῖς stands in apposition to βασιλείαν; ἱεράν (Syrr., ܟܗܢܘܬܐ), καὶ ἱερεῖς are needless attempts to save the grammar. The members of the Church, a Kingdom in their corporate life, are individually priests; as Bede truly says: "nemo sanctorum est qui spiritualiter sacerdotii officio careat, cum sit membrum aeterni Sacerdotis." Baptism inaugurates this priestly service (Eph. v. 26, Heb. x. 22, Tit. iii. 5), which is fulfilled by the offering of living, reasonable, and spiritual sacrifices (Rom. xii. 1, Heb. xiii. 15 f., 1 Pet. ii. 5). These are presented to the God and Father of Jesus Christ. Αὐτοῦ should probably be taken with τῷ θεῷ as well as with τῷ πατρί (Jo. xx. 17, Apoc. iii. 12); if the Incarnate Son is not ashamed to call men His brethren (Heb. ii. 11), neither is He ashamed to call the Father His God. From another point of view the Christian priesthood is exercised to-

πατρὶ αὐτοῦ, αὐτῷ ἡ δόξα καὶ τὸ κράτος εἰς τοὺς
αἰῶνας [τῶν αἰώνων·] ἀμήν. [7]ἰδοὺ ἔρχεται μετὰ 7
τῶν νεφελῶν, καὶ ὄψεται αὐτὸν πᾶς ὀφθαλμὸς καὶ

6 τον αιωνα ℵ* (τους αιωνας ℵ$^{c.a}$) syr^{gw} | om των αιωνων AP 9 28 79 97 99 me | om αμην 33 vg^{tol} 7 μετα] επι C | οψονται ℵ 1 12 152 me syrr | om αυτον 1° 1 46 88

wards both the Father and the Son, see *c.* xx. 6 ἔσονται ἱερεῖς τοῦ θεοῦ καὶ τοῦ χριστοῦ. Thus the Church, like Israel, is a great sacerdotal society. That there are special ministries within the body which belong to an ordained *clerus*, an ἱερουργία τοῦ εὐαγγελίου committed to Apostles and their successors (Rom. xv. 16), in no way conflicts with the reality of the priesthood which is the privilege of every baptized member of Christ.

αὐτῷ ἡ δόξα καὶ τὸ κράτος κτλ.] Sc. τῷ ἀγαπῶντι ἡμᾶς καὶ λύσαντι κτλ. i.e. to Jesus Christ. The Apoc. freely associates Christ with the Father in doxologies; cf. v. 13 f., vii. 10. An equally unequivocal instance is to be found in 2 Pet. iii. 18; others which are cited from the Apostolic writings (1 Pet. iv. 11, Rom. xvi. 27, Heb. xiii. 21, 2 Tim. iv. 18) are for various reasons open to doubt. The simple formula ἡ δόξα εἰς τοὺς αἰῶνας [τῶν αἰώνων] is found in 4 Macc. xviii. 24, Rom. *l.c.*, Gal. i. 5, etc.; καὶ τὸ κράτος is added in 1 Pet. *l.c.*, and other amplifications occur (cf. Mt. vi. 13, T.R., 1 Tim. i. 17, vi. 16, Jude 25, Apoc. v. 13, vii. 12); for further details see Chase, *Lord's Prayer in the Early Church*, p. 168 ff. Ἀμήν is well supported at the end of nearly all the N.T. doxologies; it had taken its place at once in the worship of the Church as the ἐπευφήμησις of the private members to the prayer or thanksgiving of the presiding Apostle prophet or presbyter (1 Cor. xiv. 16; Justin, *ap.* i. 65).

7. ἰδοὺ ἔρχεται μετὰ τῶν νεφελῶν] To the doxology the writer adds a forecast of the coming of the Lord, to which he points as if it were already in sight. The words are from Dan. vii. 13 Th. ἐθεώρουν...καὶ ἰδοὺ μετὰ (LXX. ἐπί) τῶν νεφελῶν τοῦ οὐρανοῦ ὡς υἱὸς ἀνθρώπου ἐρχόμενος (cf. Mc. xiii. 26, xiv. 62, notes; Acts i. 9 ff., 1 Thess. iv. 17). The note thus sounded at the outset of the book is repeated more than once at the end (xxii. 7, 12, 20).

καὶ ὄψεται αὐτὸν πᾶς ὀφθαλμός κτλ.] With Dan. *l.c.* the Apocalyptist combines Zech. xii. 10. His reminiscence of Zech. agrees with the form which the words take in Jo. xix. 37 ὄψονται εἰς ὃν ἐξεκέντησαν (דקרו), against the LXX. ἐπιβλέψονται πρὸς μὲ ἀνθ' ὧν κατωρχήσαντο (רקדו). Zahn (*Einleitung*, ii. p. 563) argues that St John translated direct from the Hebrew, using a text which read as M.T.; but as ἐξεκέντησαν appears also in Aq. and Th., and in an independent quotation by Justin, *dial.* 32, it is more probable that both Gospel and Apocalypse were indebted to a Greek version of the prophecy other than the LXX., perhaps to some collection of prophetic testimonies. With ὄψεται αὐτὸν πᾶς ὀφθ. comp. *Didache* xvi. 7 τότε ὄψεται ὁ κόσμος τὸν κύριον ἐρχόμενον. Καὶ οἵτινες specifies a class already included in πᾶς ὀφθ. (cf. Mc. i. 5, note); οἵτινες is generic (WM., p. 209), pointing not so much to the original crucifiers as to those who in every age share the indifference or hostility which lay behind the act. Καὶ κόψονται ἐπ' αὐτὸν ('at Him,' Vulg. *super eum*; cf. xviii. 9) πᾶσαι αἱ φυλαὶ τῆς γῆς; the first three words are from Zech. xii. 12 καὶ κόψεται ἡ γῆ κατὰ φυλὰς φυλάς. Mt., who also (xxiv. 30) blends Dan. vii. 13 with Zech. xii. 10, turns the sentence precisely as John does—a

οἵτινες αὐτὸν ἐξεκέντησαν, καὶ κόψονται ἐπ' αὐτὸν
πᾶσαι αἱ φυλαὶ τῆς γῆς. ναί, ἀμήν.
8 [8]Ἐγώ εἰμι τὸ ἄλφα καὶ τὸ ὦ, λέγει Κύριος ὁ

7 om *αυτον* 2° ℵ* (hab $ℵ^{c.a}$) | om *επ* ℵ* (hab $ℵ^{c.a}$) | om *επ αυτον* 1 | *ναι* bis scr syr^{gw} 8 *αλφα*] *α* 1 29 33 47 49 90 99 100 al^{mu} | *και το ω*] pr *και εγω* ℵ* (om $ℵ^{c.a}$) + (*η*) *αρχη και* (*το*) *τελος* ℵ* 1 (28) 35 (36, 49, 79, 80) 92^{mg} 99 130 al$^{mu\ vid}$ vg me

circumstance which increases the probability that the quotation came as it stands from a book of excerpts. Prim. renders: "et videbit eum omnis terra talem"; other Latin texts give "omnis caro terrae" or "omnes tribus terrae." Did they read ὄψονται αὐτόν and add *talem* (i. q. ἐκκεντηθέντα) to relieve the monotony of the repeated ὄψονται?

Hippolytus (ed. Lag. p. 117) interprets too narrowly: θεάσονται ὁ τῶν Ἑβραίων δῆμος καὶ κόψονται. Πᾶσαι αἱ φυλαί strikes quite another note.

Ναί, ἀμήν unites the Greek and Hebrew forms of affirmation, as Andreas remarks: τὸν αὐτὸν νοῦν τῇ τε Ἑλληνίδι τῇ τε Ἑβραϊκῇ γλώττῃ ἐσήμανεν. A somewhat similar combination is the ἀββὰ ὁ πατήρ of Mc. xiv. 36, where see note. The words ναί, ἀμήν, however, are not quite synonymous; from its associations ἀμήν possesses a religious character, which gives it greater solemnity; cf. 2 Cor. i. 20 ὅσαι γὰρ ἐπαγγελίαι θεοῦ, ἐν αὐτῷ τὸ ναί· διὸ καὶ δι' αὐτοῦ τὸ ἀμήν. Christ is Himself ὁ ἀμήν (iii. 14); ὁ ναί would be felt to be unbecoming. Elsewhere in the book (xiv. 13, xvi. 7, xxii. 20) the writer contents himself with the simple affirmation which sufficed for Christians in their ordinary intercourse (Mt. v. 37, Jas. v. 12); but in this extremely solemn announcement of the coming Parousia the double asseveration is in place.

8. ἐγώ εἰμι τὸ ἄλφα καὶ τὸ ὦ κτλ.] The solemn opening of the book reaches its climax here with words ascribed to the Eternal and Almighty Father.

Τὸ ἄλφα καὶ τὸ ὦ is interpreted by ἡ ἀρχὴ καὶ τὸ τέλος (xxi. 6), ὁ πρῶτος καὶ ὁ ἔσχατος (xxii. 13); cf. Isa. xli. 4, xliii. 10, xliv. 6, xlviii. 12. The book being for Greek readers, the first and last letters of the Greek alphabet are used, but there is doubtless a reference to the Jewish employment of א, ת; cf. e.g. *Jalkut Rab.* f. 17. 4 "Adamus totam legem transgressus est ab Aleph usque ad Tau" (מא' ועד ת'); *ib.* f. 48. 4, where the contrary is said of Abraham. The symbol את was regarded as including the intermediate letters, and stood for totality; and thus it fitly represented the Shekinah (Schoettgen, i. p. 1086). Early Christian writers enter at large into the mystical import of ΑΩ, e.g. Tertullian, *de monog.* "duas Graecas litteras, summam et ultimam...sibi induit Dominus, uti...ostenderet in se esse initii decursum ad finem, et finis recursum ad initium; ut omnis dispositio in eum desinens per quem coepta est...proinde desinat quemadmodum et coepit." So Clement of Alexandria, *strom.* iv. 25 § 158 sq. ὡς πάντα ἓν ἔνθεν καὶ πάντα· κύκλος γὰρ ὁ αὐτὸς πασῶν τῶν δυνάμεων εἰς ἓν εἰλουμένων καὶ ἑνουμένων. διὰ τοῦτο ἄλφα καὶ ὦ ὁ λόγος εἴρηται, οὗ μόνον τὸ τέλος ἀρχὴ γίνεται καὶ τελευτᾷ πάλιν ἐπὶ τὴν ἄνωθεν ἀρχήν, οὐδαμοῦ διάστασιν λαβών. See also Origen *in Joann.* t. i. 31. The phrase is seen to express not eternity only, but infinitude, the boundless life which embraces all while it transcends all, "fons et clausula omnium quae sunt" (Prudentius, *cathem.* ix. 10 ff.). In xxi. 6, xxii. 13, where it occurs again, it is applied to Christ, and this reference is assumed by the

θεός, ὁ ὢν καὶ ὁ ἦν καὶ ὁ ἐρχόμενος, ὁ παντοκράτωρ.

9 Ἐγὼ Ἰωάννης, ὁ ἀδελφὸς ὑμῶν καὶ συνκοινωνὸς 9
ἐν τῇ θλίψει καὶ βασιλείᾳ καὶ ὑπομονῇ ἐν Ἰησοῦ,

8 ο παντοκρατωρ] om ο Q pr ο θεος Hipp^noet 9 Ιωανης ℵ* | κοινωνος 6 7 8 Ar | και βασιλεια] και εν τη β. P 1 7 49 al^nonn om syrr aeth | εν Ιησου] εν Χριστω A 25 εν Χρ. Ιησου Q min^50 syr arm Prim Ar εν Ι. Χρ. ℵ^c.c syr Ιησου Χριστου 1 28 79 130 al^nonn

ancient interpreters in the present case (cf. Hippolytus *adv. Noet.* (ed. Lag. p. 48) εἶπεν παντοκράτορα Χριστόν, Clem. Al. *strom.* iv. 25 § 159, Orig. *de princ.* i. 2, 10 "qui enim venturus est, quis est alius nisi Christus?" Andreas: ὁ χριστὸς ἐνταῦθα δηλοῦται, and the passages cited above), but incorrectly, as the next words shew.

λέγει Κύριος ὁ θεός = אָמַר אֲדֹנָי יֱהוִֹה, a phrase specially common in Ezekiel (vi. 3, 11, vii. 2 etc.) with whom and the rest of the O.T. prophets the Christian prophet of the Apocalypse associates himself by his use of it. Ὁ ὢν κτλ., see *v.* 4, note. Ὁ παντοκράτωρ, which in other books of the N. T. is found but once and then in a quotation (2 Cor. vi. 18), occurs again in Apoc. iv. 8, xi. 17, xv. 3, xvi. 7, 14, xix. 6, 15, xxi. 22. Like Κ. ὁ θεός, ὁ παντοκράτωρ is from the O.T., where the LXX. use it for שַׁדַּי in Job and in the other books for צְבָאוֹת. Κ. ὁ θεὸς ὁ π. occurs in Hos. xii. 5 (6), and in Amos *passim*; in 2, 3 Macc. ὁ π. often stands alone. Ὁ παντοκράτωρ = ὁ πάντων κρατῶν, ὁ πάντων ἐξουσιάζων (Cyril. Hier. *catech.* viii. 3), the All-Ruler rather than the Almighty (ὁ παντοδύναμος, Sap. vii. 23, xi. 17, xviii. 15); see Suicer *ad v.*, and Kattenbusch, *Das apost. Symbol*, ii. p. 533 f.

9—20. VISION OF THE RISEN AND GLORIFIED CHRIST.

9. ἐγὼ Ἰωάννης, ὁ ἀδελφὸς ὑμῶν κτλ.] From the ecstatic utterances of *vv.* 7, 8 the writer returns to his address to the Churches. Ἐγὼ Ἰ. identifies him with the John of *vv.* 2, 4, and is after the manner of the apocalyptic prophets when they relate their visions; cf. Dan. vii. 28, viii. 1 ἐγὼ Δανιήλ, Enoch xii. 3 ἑστὼς ἤμην Ἑνώχ, 4 Esdr. ii. 33 "ego Esdras accepi praeceptum," Apoc. xxii. 8 κἀγὼ Ἰ. ὁ ἀκούων. Ὁ ἀδελφὸς ὑμῶν, while not claiming for John an official character, does not exclude it; cf. 2 Pet. iii. 15 ὁ ἀγαπητὸς ἡμῶν ἀδελφὸς Παῦλος. His purpose being to establish a community of interests with the Churches, he is content with the title which Apostles and presbyters shared with other Christians (cf. Acts xv. 23 οἱ ἀπόστολοι καὶ οἱ πρεσβύτεροι ἀδελφοὶ τοῖς...ἀδελφοῖς...χαίρειν). Καὶ συνκοινωνός κτλ.: κοινωνεῖν (-νία, -νός, -νικός) συνκοινωνεῖν (-νός) are Pauline words, but not exclusively so: cf. 1 Pet. iv. 13, v. 1, 1 Jo. i. 3, Apoc. xviii. 4; for the construction with ἐν cf. Mt. xxiii. 30. The thought of a κοινωνία in suffering belongs to the stock of primitive Christian ideas; see 1 Pet. *l. c.*, 2 Cor. i. 7, Phil. iii. 10, iv. 14 συνκοινωνήσαντές μου τῇ θλίψει. Θλίψει... βασιλείᾳ...ὑπομονῇ: for θλίψις see Mc. iv. 17, note, xiii. 19, Jo. xvi. 33; for βασιλεία, Lc. xii. 32, xxii. 29, Jas. ii. 5, 1 Th. ii. 12, 2 Th. i. 5; ὑπομονή is not less constantly connected with the Christian life (Lc. viii. 15, xxi. 19, Rom. v. 3 ἡ θλίψις ὑπομονὴν κατεργάζεται, viii. 25 f., Apoc. ii. 2 f., 19, iii. 10, xiii. 10, xiv. 12), and with the coming Kingdom (2 Tim. ii. 12 εἰ ὑπομένομεν καὶ συμβασιλεύσομεν). The

ἐγενόμην ἐν τῇ νήσῳ τῇ καλουμένῃ Πάτμῳ διὰ τὸν λόγον τοῦ θεοῦ καὶ τὴν μαρτυρίαν Ἰησοῦ. 10 ἐγενόμην

9 την μαρτυριαν] pr δια ℵPQ min^pl syrr arm | Ιησου]+Χριστου ℵ^c.a Q al^pl me syrr arm aeth Prim 10 εγενομην] pr εγω A

obvious order is θλίψις, ὑπομονή, βασιλεία; but that which is adopted here has the advantage of leaving on the reader's mind the thought of the struggle which still remains before the kingdom is attained. The juxtaposition of θλίψις and βασιλεία (Beatus: "retributionem tribulationis regnum") is quite usual, cf. Acts xiv. 22 διὰ πολλῶν θλίψεων δεῖ ἡμᾶς εἰσελθεῖν εἰς τὴν βασιλείαν τοῦ θεοῦ. Ἐν Ἰησοῦ, equivalent to the Pauline ἐν Χριστῷ, ἐν Χριστῷ Ἰησοῦ: on the use of the personal name in the Apoc. see *v.* 5, note. The whole life of a Christian, whether he suffers or reigns or waits, is in union with the life of the Incarnate Son.

ἐγενόμην ἐν τῇ νήσῳ τῇ καλ. Πάτμῳ κτλ.] Patmos, *Patino*, one of the Sporades, though seldom mentioned by ancient writers (Thuc. iii. 33, Strab. x. 5, 13, Plin. *H. N.* iv. 23), finds a place in the inscriptions (*CIG* 2261, 2262 etc.), and its safe harbourage must have made it a place of some importance to navigators; see Renan, *L'Antechrist*, p. 372f., who remarks: "on a tort de la représenter comme un écueil, comme un désert. Patmos fut et redeviendra peut-être une des stations maritimes les plus importantes de l'Archipel." Lying in the Icarian Sea between Icaria and Leros, about 40 miles S.W. by W. from Miletus, it was "the first or last stopping-place for the traveller on his way from Ephesus to Rome or from Rome to Ephesus." The island forms a crescent with its horns facing eastward (H. F. Tozer, *Islands of the Aegean*, p. 179); the traditional scene of the Apocalypse (τὸ σπήλαιον τῆς ἀποκαλύψεως) and the monastery of St John are towards the southern horn. The locality has doubtless shaped to some extent the scenery of the Apocalypse, into which the mountains and the sea enter largely; see Stanley, *Sermons in the East*, p. 230. John found himself (ἐγενόμην, *v.* 10) in Patmos, not as a traveller or a visitor, but διὰ τὸν λόγον τοῦ θεοῦ καὶ τὴν μαρτυρίαν Ἰησοῦ. For the phrase as a whole see *v.* 2, note; ἡ μαρτ. Ἰ., 'the witness borne by Jesus,' occurs again xii. 17, xix. 10, xx. 4. Here "the word of God and the witness of Jesus" are not as in *v.* 2 the Apocalypse itself, but the preaching of the Gospel: for ὁ λ. τ. θ. in this sense cf. 1 Jo. ii. 7, 1 Th. ii. 13, 2 Tim. ii. 9, and for ἡ μ. τ. Ἰ., Jo. viii. 13 f. The meaning may be either that John had gone to the island to carry the Gospel thither, or that he was sent to Patmos as an exile (cf. Pliny, *l. c.*) because of his preaching. The latter view is confirmed (*a*) by the use of διά in vi. 9, xx. 4; (*b*) by συνκοινωνὸς ἐν τῇ θλίψει, which suggests that the writer has in view his own sufferings ἐν Ἰησοῦ; (*c*) by an early and practically unanimous tradition of the Church: cf. Tert. *de praescr.* 36 "apostolus Ioannes...in insulam relegatus," Clem. Al. *quis dives* 42 τοῦ τυράννου τελευτήσαντος ἀπὸ τῆς Πάτμου τῆς νήσου μετῆλθεν ἐπὶ τὴν Ἔφεσον, Orig. *in Mt.* t. xvi. 6 ὁ δὲ Ῥωμαίων βασιλεύς, ὡς ἡ παράδοσις διδάσκει, κατεδίκασε τὸν Ἰωάννην μαρτυροῦντα διὰ τὸν τῆς ἀληθείας λόγον εἰς Πάτμον τὴν νῆσον. See also Eus. *H. E.* iii. 18; Hieron. *de virr. ill.* 10.

10. ἐγενόμην ἐν πνεύματι κτλ.] Εἶναι ἐν πνεύματι is the normal condition of Christians, in contrast with εἶναι ἐν σαρκί (Rom. viii. 9); γενέσθαι ἐν πν. denotes the exaltation of the prophet

ἐν πνεύματι ἐν τῇ κυριακῇ ἡμέρᾳ, καὶ ἤκουσα ὀπίσω
μου φωνὴν μεγάλην ὡς σάλπιγγος [11]*λεγούσης* ˹Ὃ 11
βλέπεις γράψον εἰς βιβλίον καὶ πέμψον ταῖς ἑπτὰ

10 *οπισω μου φ. μεγ.* ℵCP min^{pl}] *φ. οπισω μου μεγαλη* Q 2 7 8 13 14 al$^{fere\ 40}$ *φ. μεγ. οπισθεν μου* A 38 aeth | *σαλπιγγα* *h* syr^{gw} Prim   11 *λεγουσης*] *λεγουσαν* ℵ$^{c.c}$ *h* syr^{gw} Prim om 7 + *μοι* 130 | *ο βλεπεις*] pr *εγω αλφα και το ω ο πρωτος και ο εσχατος* (*και*) P 7 pr *εγω ειμι το α και το ω ο πρ. και ο εσχατος και* 1 36 38 69 al | *ο*] *α* 34 35 38 72 87 syr^{gw} me Prim | *βιβλιον*] pr *το* ℵ

under inspiration; see Ez. iii. 12, 14, xxxvii. 1, and cf. Acts xxii. 17 *ἐγένετο... γενέσθαι με ἐν ἐκστάσει*—the return to a non-ecstatic state being described as *ἐν ἑαυτῷ γ.* (Acts xii. 11). The phrase *ἐγ. ἐν πν.* is repeated *c.* iv. 2 *q.v.* Ἐν *τῇ κυριακῇ ἡμέρᾳ*: the second *ἐν* dates the revelation; it was vouchsafed on the Lord's Day; on the dative of time, with or without a preceding *ἐν*, see Blass, *Gr.* p. 119 f. Ἡ *κυριακὴ ἡμέρα*, the day consecrated to the Lord; cf. 1 Cor. xi. 20 *οὐκ ἔστιν κυριακὸν δεῖπνον φαγεῖν* 'it is not to eat a Supper of the Lord.' 'The Lord's day,' according to the analogy of writings some of which are but a few decades later than the Apoc., is the first day of the week, the day of the Lord's Resurrection; cf. *Didache* 14 *κατὰ κυριακὴν δὲ Κυρίου συναχθέντες κλάσατε ἄρτον*, Ign. *Magn.* 9 *κατὰ κυριακὴν ζῶντες* (see Lightfoot's note), *Ev. Petri* 9 *ἐπέφωσκεν ἡ κυριακή*, ib. 11 *ὄρθρου δὲ τῆς κυριακῆς*; Melito of Sardis wrote *περὶ κυριακῆς* (Eus. *H. E.* iv. 26). Since all the early examples are from Asia Minor, it is not improbable that the term arose in Asiatic circles; but before the end of the second century it was used generally, cf. Dionysius of Corinth *ap.* Eus. *H. E.* iv. 23 *τὴν σήμερον οὖν κυριακὴν ἁγίαν ἡμέραν διηγάγομεν*, Clem. Al. *strom.* vii. 12, Tert. *cor.* 3, *orat.* 23, *anim.* 9 (*dies dominicus*, or *dominicae resurrectionis, dominica sollemnia*). To interpret *ἐν τῇ κυριακῇ ἡμ.* here as = *ἐν τῇ παρουσίᾳ* is contrary to usage, besides introducing a thought foreign to the context; it is not Christ at His coming who is revealed, but Christ present with the Church on earth. The exile of Patmos, shut out from the weekly Breaking of the Bread in the Christian assembly at Ephesus, finds the Lord's Presence in his solitude. Bede: "congruum quoque spirituali visioni tempus indicat."

καὶ ἤκουσα ὀπίσω μου φωνήν κτλ.] The Seer follows Ez. iii. 12 *καὶ ἀνέλαβέν με πνεῦμα, καὶ ἤκουσα κατόπισθέν μου καὶ ἤκουσα φωνήν*. Cf. Plutarch, *Lyc.* 23, cited by Wetstein: *ἀκοῦσαι δὲ φωνὴν ὥσπερ ἀνθρώπου τινὸς ἐξόπισθεν ἐπιτιμῶντος αὐτῷ*. The Voice comes with startling suddenness as from one who, approaching from behind, is unobserved until he speaks. Ὄπισθεν is a correction for the less exact *ὀπίσω*: for *ὀπίσω* 'behind' cf. xii. 15. Μεγάλην: cf. v. 22; *ὡς σάλπιγγος* looks back to the theophany of Sinai (Exod. xix. 16 *φωνὴ τῆς σάλπιγγος ἤχει μέγα*: cf. Heb. xii. 19 *σάλπιγγος ἤχῳ καὶ φωνῇ ῥημάτων*), but the trumpet blast had already acquired Christian associations (Mt. xxiv. 31, 1 Th. iv. 16). Here it is probably the voice of Christ's Angel (*v.* 1) rather than of Christ Himself, whose utterance is otherwise described (*v.* 15); see Benson, *Apocalypse* p. 95 n. Λεγούσης for *λέγουσαν*, by hypallage; the true antecedent is not *σάλπιγγος* but *φωνὴν μεγάλην*.

11. *ὃ βλέπεις γράψον εἰς βιβλίον*] The vision was not for John's personal benefit only, but for transmission to the Church; cf. Mc. iv. 22, note. It brought with it to the Seer the responsibility of witnessing to what he had seen (*v.* 2), and the witness must be borne in a literary form (*v.* 19).

ἐκκλησίαις, εἰς Ἔφεσον καὶ εἰς Σμύρναν καὶ εἰς
Πέργαμον καὶ εἰς Θυάτειραν καὶ εἰς Σάρδεις καὶ εἰς
12 Φιλαδελφίαν καὶ εἰς Λαοδικίαν. [12]καὶ ἐπέστρεψα
βλέπειν τὴν φωνὴν ἥτις ἐλάλει μετ' ἐμοῦ· καὶ

11 om και 2° ℵ* (hab ℵ$^{c.a}$) | Ζμυρναν ℵ vg$^{am\ fu\ (harl)}$ syr^{gw} | εις Θυατειραν (AC)(Q) 6 8 11 14 34 35 87 91 130 latt (*in Thyatiram, Thyatirae*)] εις Θυατειρα ℵ 7 38 91 99 al^{pl} Andr Ar εν Θυατειροις P 12 36 46 88 | om και εις Σαρδεις ℵ* (hab post Λαοδ. ℵ$^{c.a}$) | Φιλαδελφειαν min^{pl} | Λαοδικειαν PQ min^{pl} Andr Ar 12 και 1°]+εκει Q 7 91 95 al$^{fere\ 40}$ | επεστρεψα βλεπειν] επιστρ. επι 130 *conversus respexi ut viderem...et vidi* (quasi επιστρεψας εβλεψα...και ειδον) *g* Cypr Prim | ελαλει] λαλει A ελαλησεν P 1 7 al^{mu} syrr

Βιβλίον (cf. v. 1 ff., x. 2, 8), a papyrus roll, as distinguished from a parchment book; cf. 2 Tim. iv. 13 τὰ βιβλία, μάλιστα τὰς μεμβράνας. The Apocalypse formed a μονόβιβλον, the length of which "may be estimated at 15 feet" (Kenyon, *Text. Crit.* p. 30); on the length to which such rolls sometimes ran see the same writer's *Palaeography of Greek papyri*, p. 17 f.

καὶ πέμψον ταῖς ἑπτὰ ἐκκλησίαις κτλ.] Cf. *v.* 4, note. The messenger would carry the roll to each of the Churches in turn, and by each it would be read and probably copied; cf. Col. iv. 16, Polyc. *Phil.* 13. His route is indicated by the order in which the Churches are named. Starting from Ephesus, he is to proceed northward to Smyrna and Pergamum, and from Pergamum in a south-easterly direction to Thyatira, Sardis, Philadelphia, and Laodicea, doubtless making his way back to Ephesus along the valley of the Maeander; the reverse order (Ephesus, Laodicea, Philadelphia, Sardis, Thyatira, Pergamum, and Smyrna) would have been less natural in view of the importance of Smyrna and Pergamum. As to the roads which connected the seven cities see Ramsay, *History of the Geography of Asia Minor*, p. 164 ff.; and his art. on *Roads and Travel in N.T. times*, in Hastings' *D.B.* v. Starting from Ephesus the Cyzican road conducted the traveller to Pergamum, whence another road led through Thyatira Sardis and Philadelphia to the valley of the Lycus.

The book is sent to the several cities (εἰς Ἔφεσον κτλ.; on the directive sense of εἰς see Blass, *Gr.* p. 122, and cf. Acts xxi. 1), for the use of the Christian communities in them (ταῖς ἐκκλησίαις: cf. Gal. i. 2). On the localities see the notes to ii. 1, 8, 12, 18, iii. 1, 7, 14.

12. καὶ ἐπέστρεψα βλέπειν τὴν φωνήν κτλ.] For ἐπιστρέφειν *convertere se* cf. Acts xv. 36, xvi. 18, and for λαλεῖν μετά (= דִּבֶּר עִם, Gen. xxxi. 24, 29) see Mc. vi. 50 (note), Jo. iv. 27, ix. 37, xiv. 30, Apoc. iv. 1, x. 8, xvii. 1, xxi. 9, 15. Ἥτις ἐλάλει, i.e. τίς ἦν ὁ λαλῶν. On turning, John's attention was at first arrested by seven golden lampstands (cf. Mc. iv. 21, note; Arethas *ad l.*: λυχνίας δὲ αὐτὰς ὠνόμασεν οὐ λύχνους, ὡς τῆς λυχνίας οἰκεῖον φῶς οὐκ ἐχούσης, ἀλλ' ὄχημα μόνον οὔσης τοῦ λύχνου). In the LXX. λυχνία answers to מְנוֹרָה, the candelabrum bearing seven lamps (λύχνοι, נֵרוֹת), which according to P in Exod. xxv. 36 ff. were placed in the Tabernacle outside the second veil (cf. Heb. ix. 2). Solomon's Temple had five λυχνίαι on the right side and five on the left before the oracle (1 Kings vii. 49 = 35 LXX.), but in Zechariah's vision (iv. 2) the one λυχνία reappears with its seven λύχνοι; see also 1 Macc. iv. 49 f., 2 Macc. i. 8, x. 3; Joseph. *B. J.* vii. 5. 5, and comp. the representation on the Arch of

ἐπιστρέψας εἶδον ἑπτὰ λυχνίας χρυσᾶς, [13]καὶ ἐν 13
μέσῳ τῶν λυχνιῶν ὅμοιον υἱὸν ἀνθρώπου, ἐνδεδυμένον

12 ιδον א$^{c.a}$CQ al   13 εν μεσω (εμμ. AC)] μεσον א | λυχνιων] pr επτα אQ min^{pl} vg$^{am\,mg\,fu\,harl\,al}$ Ar + των χρυσων 34 35 49 87 | ομοιον] ομοιωμα A *similitudinem* vg^{harl} ομοιος 130 | υιον אQ 1 7 8 11 14 17 28 31 33 41 82 87 92^{txt} 94 100 al$^{fere\,30}$ vg^{am*} Prim^{sem}] υιω ACP 10 12 36 38 49 80 81 91 95 96 130 Cypr Ar | ενδεδυμενος...περιεζωσμενος 130

Titus (W. Knight, *Arch of T.*, p. 109 ff.). Our writer, *more suo*, takes from each source the features which lend themselves to his conception—the septenary number from Exodus and Zechariah, the row of separate λυχνίαι from Kings. On the meaning of the symbol see *v.* 20.

13. καὶ ἐν μέσῳ τῶν λυχνιῶν ὅμοιον υἱὸν ἀνθρώπου] A second glance shewed a human form in the middle of the row, either behind the fourth λυχνία, or moving freely from one to another (ii. 1). Ὅμοιον υἱὸν ἀνθρ. is doubtless, both here and in xiv. 14, from Dan. vii. 13 כְּבַר אֱנָשׁ LXX. Th. ὡς υἱὸς ἀνθρ.; the recurrence of ὅμοιον υἱὸν in xiv. 14 (where it is supported by A) suggests that this strange defiance of grammar is due to the translation employed by our writer, who elsewhere consistently uses the dative after ὅμοιος (see i. 15, ii. 18, iv. 3 *bis*, etc., 20 times in all). Υἱὸς ἀνθρώπου, 'a son of man,' a human being, with allusion perhaps to our Lord's application of Daniel *l. c.* to Himself (Mc. xiii. 26); yet not to be taken as equivalent to ὁ υἱὸς τοῦ ἀνθρώπου, which outside the Gospels appears only in Acts vii. 56. The glorified Christ is human, but transfigured: Victorinus: "*similem* dicit post mortem devictam, cum ascendisset in caelos." Irenaeus, who (iv. 20. 11) quotes the passage at length, well says that John sees in it "sacerdotalem et gloriosum regni eius adventum"; the form is at once priestly and royal.

ἐνδεδυμένον ποδήρη καὶ περιεζωσμένον κτλ.] The clothing is first described. Ποδήρης (sc. χιτών), *poderis*, O.L. and Vulg., cf. Roensch, *Itala u. V.*, p. 245, ἅπ. λεγ. in the N.T., but used in the LXX. of Exodus for various priestly garments, as the breastplate (חֹשֶׁן, *cc.* xxv. 6 (7), xxxv. 8 (9)), the ephod (xxviii. 27 (31), the robe of the ephod (מְעִיל, xxviii. 4, xxix. 5); cf. Jos. *antt.* iii. 7. 4 ὁ δὲ ἀρχιερεὺς κοσμεῖται μὲν καὶ ταύτῃ... ἐπενδυσάμενος δ' ἐξ ὑακίνθου πεποιημένον χιτῶνα, ποδήρης δέ ἐστι καὶ οὗτος· μεεὶρ καλεῖται κατὰ τὴν ἡμετέραν γλῶσσαν, ζώνῃ περισφίγγεται κτλ. But perhaps the reference is rather to the Prophets, e.g. Zech. iii. 4, where ὁ ποδήρης = מַחֲלָצוֹת, the High Priest's robes of state, or Ez. ix. 2 f., 11 where it = בַּדִּים, the linen vesture of the man with the inkhorn; cf. Dan. x. 5 Th. ἀνὴρ εἷς ἐνδεδυμένος βαδδείν. The ποδήρης is thus seen to denote dignity or high office, usually but not necessarily the office of High Priest (cf. Sap. xviii. 24, Sir. xlv. 8); the ancient commentators are perhaps too positive on this point, e.g. Irenaeus (iv. 20. 11) "aliquid vero sacerdotale, ut podere"; Victorinus: "*in veste talari*, id est sacerdotali; Arethas: ὡς ἀρχιερέα τὸν ἄνω κατὰ τὴν τάξιν Μελχισέδεκ. Nor does the ζώνη χρυσᾶ quite determine the highpriestly character of the costume: the High Priest's girdle was of linen richly embroidered (Exod. xxxix. 29 = xxxvi. 37 LXX.), with a liberal use of gold thread (Jos. *antt.* *l. c.*, χρυσοῦ συνυφασμένου); the golden girdle points rather to Daniel's vision (x. 5 Th. ἡ ὀσφὺς αὐτοῦ περιεζωσμένη ἐν χρυσίῳ Ὠφάζ. In 1 Macc. x. 89 a golden clasp (πόρπη) is a royal distinction. Χρυσᾶν is characterised by Blass (*Gr.*, p. 24) as a gross blunder; more probably it is a colloquialism to which the writer was accustomed—that it is

ποδήρη καὶ περιεζωσμένον πρὸς τοῖς μαστοῖς ζώνην
14 χρυσᾶν· [14]ἡ δὲ κεφαλὴ αὐτοῦ καὶ αἱ τρίχες λευκαὶ
ὡς ἔριον λευκόν, ὡς χιών, καὶ οἱ ὀφθαλμοὶ αὐτοῦ ὡς
15 φλὸξ πυρός, [15]καὶ οἱ πόδες αὐτοῦ ὅμοιοι χαλκολιβάνῳ

13 ποδηρην A 11 | προς] εν 35 38 87 | μαστοις CPQ min^{pl}] μασθοις ℵ 7 29 46 88 97 100 μαζοις A 10 17 28 37 49 80* 91 96 | χρυσην ℵ^{c}PQ 130   14 ως 1° ℵAQ min$^{sat\ mu}$] ωσει CP 1 28 49 79 91 96 100 130 al Andr ωσπερ 46 48 pr και Q min^{20} | om λευκαι *h* Prim | λευκον]+και 36 vg arm aeth Vict και 8 *h* syr^{gw} Prim   15 om και 1° Prim | χαλκολιβανω] χαλκω λιβανω P 7 32 100 *chalcolibano* Ir^{int} *aurichalco* Cypr Vict vg *aur. Libano* Prim *aes Libani* syrr aeth

from his pen its retention in ℵ* A C leaves little doubt.

Πρὸς τοῖς μαστοῖς. High girding is said to have been usual when the ποδήρης was worn: Jos. *antt.* vii. 2 ἔστι δὲ τοῦτο τὸ ἔνδυμα ποδήρης χιτών ...ὃν ἐπιζώννυνται κατὰ στῆθος ὀλίγον τῆς μασχάλης ὑπεράνω. Cf. Apoc. xv. 6 where beings of angelic rank are περιεζωσμένοι περὶ τὰ στήθη ζώνας χρυσᾶς. For πρός with the dat. cf. Mc. v. 11 note, Jo. xx. 11, see Blass, *Gr.* p. 140. The MSS. vary (see app. crit.) between μαστοῖς, μασθοῖς, μαζοῖς; cf. W. Schm., p. 59, Blass, *Gr.* p. 24. The lexicographers endeavour to distinguish the forms (e.g. Suidas: μαζὸς κυρίως ἐπὶ ἀνδρός...μασθὸς καὶ μαστὸς κυρίως ἐπὶ γυναικός), but the distinction does not seem to have been commonly observed.

14. ἡ δὲ κεφαλὴ αὐτοῦ...ὡς χιών] From the costume the Seer proceeds to describe the person of the Central Figure. He has in view the *locus classicus* Dan. vii. 9 (Th. τὸ ἔνδυμα αὐτοῦ ὡς χιὼν λευκόν, καὶ ἡ θρὶξ τῆς κεφαλῆς αὐτοῦ ὡσεὶ ἔριον καθαρόν), where however the white hair belongs to the Ancient of Days. The transfer of this feature to the Son of Man is the more striking since Enoch (xlvi. 1, ed. Charles, p. 127) adheres strictly to Daniel's account. Our writer's Christology leads him frequently to attribute to the glorified Christ attributes and titles which belong to the Father, e.g. in i. 18, ii. 8, v. 12, xxii. 13. Ancient expositors find in the hair white as snow a symbol of the eternal preexistence of the Son; e.g. Andreas: εἰ γὰρ καὶ πρόσφατος δι' ἡμᾶς, ἀλλὰ καὶ ἀρχαῖος, μᾶλλον δὲ προαιώνιος, and this view seems to be justified by Daniel's עַתִּיק יוֹמִין. Yet the figure cannot be pressed; white hair suggests decay, whereas Jesus Christ is unchangeable (Heb. xiii. 8); cf. *ad Diogn.* 11 οὗτος ὁ ἀπ' ἀρχῆς, ὁ καινὸς φανεὶς καὶ παλαιὸς εὑρεθεὶς καὶ πάντοτε νέος...ὁ ἀεί. Ὡς χιών perhaps adds the thought of His sinlessness (Ps. l. (li.) 9, Isa. i. 18, Mt. xxviii. 3).

καὶ οἱ ὀφθαλμοὶ αὐτοῦ ὡς φλὸξ πυρός] Cf. ii. 18, xix. 12. In Dan. vii. 9 it is the throne of the Ancient of Days which is φλὸξ πυρός, but in x. 6 the man clothed in linen has eyes ὡσεὶ λαμπάδες πυρός, and the latter passage is perhaps in view here. The metaphor is common, as Wetstein shews, in Greek and Roman authors (e.g. Homer, *Il.* xiii. 474 ὀφθαλμοὶ δ' ἄρα οἱ πυρὶ λάμπετον, Verg. *Aen.* xii. 102 "oculis micat acribus ignis"), and indeed in descriptive writings of every age and country. The penetrating glance (Apringius: "inevitabile lumen oculorum"), which flashed with quick intelligence, and when need arose with righteous wrath, was noticed by those who were with our Lord in the days of His Flesh (Mc. iii. 5, 34, v. 32, x. 21, 23, xi. 11, notes, Lc. xxii. 61), and finds its counterpart, as the Seer now learns, in the Risen and Ascended Life.

15. καὶ οἱ πόδες αὐτοῦ ὅμοιοι χαλκολιβάνῳ κτλ.] Cf. Dan. x. 6 Th. τὰ

ὡς ἐν καμίνῳ πεπυρωμένης, καὶ ἡ φωνὴ αὐτοῦ ὡς

15 πεπυρωμενης AC] πεπυρωμενω ℵ 16 46 69 88 *h* vg aegg syrr^vid aeth Ir^int Cypr Vict Prim πεπυρωμενοι PQ min^pl Andr Ar (om ως εν κ. πεπυρ. 97)

σκέλη ὡς ὅρασις χαλκοῦ στίλβοντος, LXX. οἱ πόδες ὡσεὶ χαλκὸς ἐξαστράπτων (כְּעֵין נְחֹשֶׁת קָלָל); the expression is due ultimately to Ez. i. 7, where the same Heb. is similarly rendered by the LXX. See also Ez. viii. 2 ἰδοὺ ὁμοίωμα ἀνδρός...ἀπὸ τῆς ὀσφύος αὐτοῦ ὑπεράνω ὡς ὅρασις ἠλέκτρου (כְּעֵין הַחַשְׁמַלָה). Χαλκολίβανος (here and *c.* ii. 18 only) is a word of unusual difficulty. Suidas defines it as εἶδος ἠλέκτρου τιμιώτερον χρυσοῦ, adding: ἔστι δὲ τὸ ἤλεκτρον ἀλλότυπον χρυσίον μεμιγμένον ὑελῷ καὶ λιθείᾳ (cf. Plin. *H. N.* 33. 4 where ἤλεκτρον is a mixture of gold and silver). A somewhat similar sense is yielded by the Latin versions, which render χαλκολιβάνῳ by *aurichalco* or *orichalco* (so, with or without the addition of *Libani*, Cypr. *test.* ii. 26, Victorinus, Primasius, Beatus, etc.), a word which seems to have meant a mixture of metals similar to brass or bronze; cf. Verg. *Aen.* xii. 87 "auro squalentem alboque orichalco ...loricam," on which Servius remarks: "apud maiores orichalcum pretiosius metallis omnibus fuit." A precious metal, bright and flashing, would suit the present context well, but the explanation leaves the form χαλκολίβανος unexplained. Arethas offers the alternatives: εἴτε τὸν ἐν τῷ Λιβάνῳ τῷ ὄρει μεταλλευόμενον...φησίν, εἴτε καὶ τὸν χαλκοειδῆ λίβανον νοητέον ὃν ἰατρῶν παῖδες ἄρρενα καλοῦσιν. The former conjecture is unsupported, and seems to require λιβανοχάλκῳ; the latter finds some confirmation in a fragment of Ausonius, cited by Salmasius *exercit.* 810 ὁ λίβανος ἔχει τρία εἴδη δένδρων, καὶ ὁ μὲν ἄρρην ἐπονομάζεται χαλκολίβανος, ἡλιοειδὴς καὶ πυρρὸς ἤγουν ξανθός. But 'brass-coloured frankincense' is not a very apposite metaphor, notwithstanding the efforts of the Greek interpreters to educe a mystical meaning from it. The etymology proposed by Bochart (χαλκός, לָבָן, brass at a white heat) is even less tolerable. On the whole, with our present knowledge, it is best to follow the guidance of Suidas and the Latin versions and regard χαλκολ. as the name of a mixed metal of great brilliance, leaving the etymology uncertain.

Feet of brass represent strength and stability (contrast Dan. ii. 33, 41); such a mystical interpretation as that of Andreas (πόδες τοῦ χριστοῦ οἱ ἀπόστολοι) is unnecessary and improbable.

The reading ὡς ἐν καμίνῳ πεπυρωμένης (sc. τῆς χαλκολιβάνου), is recommended by its difficulty. If πεπυρωμένῳ is preferred, the reference must still be to χαλκολιβάνῳ, for κάμινος seems to be invariably fem. (cf. Mt. xiii. 42, 50, Apoc. ix. 2); πεπυρωμένοι is probably a correction intended to bring the part. into line with οἱ πόδες ...ὅμοιοι. For πυροῦσθαι used of a glowing metal see Eph. vi. 16 τὰ βέλη ...τὰ πεπυρωμένα σβέσαι, with Dean Robinson's note. In Apoc. iii. 18, χρυσίον πεπυρωμένον, the sense clearly is 'refined by having passed through the fire,' and R.V. adopts this meaning here; but 'glowing' suits the context better; the metal is not only of the finest and brightest, but it is aglow as if still in the crucible.

καὶ ἡ φωνὴ αὐτοῦ ὡς φ. ὑδάτων πολλῶν] Cf. Ez. xliii. 2, where the voice of the God of Israel is כְּקוֹל מַיִם רַבִּים. In Dan. x. 6, from which many of the details of this description are taken, the voice of the Angel is כְּקוֹל הָמוֹן, like the confused roar of a great multitude; but at Patmos it is the

16 φωνὴ ὑδάτων πολλῶν, [16]καὶ ἔχων ἐν τῇ δεξιᾷ χειρὶ
αὐτοῦ ἀστέρας ἑπτά, καὶ ἐκ τοῦ στόματος αὐτοῦ
ῥομφαία δίστομος ὀξεῖα ἐκπορευομένη, καὶ ἡ ὄψις
αὐτοῦ ὡς ὁ ἥλιος φαίνει ἐν τῇ δυνάμει αὐτοῦ.

16 *και εχων* ℵCPQ (me) Ar] *και ειχεν* ℵ* 34 35 36 87 *g h* vg arm Cypr Vict Prim (*et habebat*) om *και* 130 | *χειρι αυτου τη δεξια* Q *δ. αυτου χ.* 1 38 100 al^{pauc} om *χειρι* 10 28 95 vg arm Prim al | *αστερες* A 41 aeth | om *οξεια* 46 48 | *ο ηλιος*] om *ο* 37 46 47 69 88 97 100 | *φαινει* pon ante *ως* ℵ *h* Cypr Prim

roar of the Aegean which is in the ear of the Seer. It is instructive to contrast 3 Regn. xix. 12 *φωνὴ αὔρας λεπτῆς*: the Divine Voice can be of the gentlest or the most appalling as occasion requires. Irenaeus (iv. 14. 2) finds a mystical sense in *ὑδάτων πολλῶν*: "vere enim aquae multae Spiritus."

16. *καὶ ἔχων ἐν τῇ δεξιᾷ χειρὶ αὐτοῦ ἀστέρας ἑπτά*] To the Semitic mind the stars of heaven were in the Hand of God (cf. Job xxxviii. 31 f., Isa. xl. 12), and would fall (Mc. xiii. 25, Apoc. vi. 13) if the support were withdrawn. No particular constellation or group of planets can be intended by the anarthrous *ἑπτὰ ἀστέρας*; the number is determined by the requirements of the symbolism (*v.* 20).

καὶ ἐκ τοῦ στόματος αὐτοῦ ῥομφαία δίστομος] The elements of this bold conception are as usual from the O.T.; see Isa. xi. 4 *πατάξει γῆν τῷ λόγῳ τοῦ στόματος αὐτοῦ*, xlix. 2 *ἔθηκεν τὸ στόμα μου ὡς μάχαιραν ὀξεῖαν*: cf. Eph. vi. 17 *τὴν μάχαιραν τοῦ πνεύματος ὅ ἐστιν ῥῆμα θεοῦ*, Heb. iv. 12 *ὁ λόγος τοῦ θεοῦ...τομώτερος ὑπὲρ πᾶσαν μάχαιραν δίστομον*. The image is repeated in Apoc. xix. 15 in the description of the armed and militant 'Word of God.' There is a fine parallel in Sap. xviii. 15 *ὁ παντοδύναμός σου λόγος ἀπ' οὐρανῶν...ἀπότομος πολεμιστὴς ... ἥλατο ... ξίφος ὀξὺ τὴν ἀνυπόκριτον ἐπιταγήν σου φέρων*. For *ῥομφαία δίστομος* see Ps. cxlix. 6, Sir. xxi. 3. *Ῥομφαία*, used in N.T. in the Apoc. only, except Lc. ii. 35, occurs frequently throughout the LXX. from Gen. iii. 24 onwards as a synonym of *μάχαιρα*, both words being used to translate חֶרֶב; in strictness, it was a large blade of Thracian origin (for a full account see Hastings *D.B.* iv. p. 634). *Δίστομος* answers to the Heb. שְׁנֵי פֵּיוֹת or פִּיפִיּוֹת but it is used in connexion with the sword even by the Greek poets (e.g. Eur. *Hel.* 983 *δίστομον ξίφος*). The sword is regarded as proceeding, like the spoken word, from the mouth; "this last image is not so strange as appears at first sight, for the short Roman sword was tongue-like in shape" (Hastings, *l. c.*). With *ἐκπορευομένη* cf. Eph. iv. 29, Apoc. ix. 17 f., xi. 5.

καὶ ἡ ὄψις αὐτοῦ ὡς ὁ ἥλιος κτλ.] Cf. Jud. v. 31 *οἱ ἀγαπῶντες αὐτὸν ὡς ἔξοδος (ἀνατολή*, A) *ἡλίου ἐν δυνάμει αὐτοῦ*, Mt. xiii. 43 *οἱ δίκαιοι ἐκλάμψουσιν ὡς ὁ ἥλιος*, Apoc. x. 1 *τὸ πρόσωπον αὐτοῦ ὡς ὁ ἥλιος*. Slav. Enoch i. 5, ed. Charles, p. 2, "their faces shone like the sun." If the John of the Apocalypse is the son of Zebedee, he could scarcely have failed to think of the Transfiguration which anticipated the glory of the ascended Christ, when *ἔλαμψεν τὸ πρόσωπον αὐτοῦ ὡς ὁ ἥλιος* (Mt. xvii. 2). Andreas refers to Mal. iv. 2: *ἥλιος γάρ ἐστι δικαιοσύνης*. *Ὄψις* = *πρόσωπον*, though fairly common in the LXX., occurs in the N.T. only here and in Jo. xi. 44 (cf. vii. 24). *Ὡς φαίνει*, a *constructio praegnans*: 'as the sun shines [when he shines] in his might."

[17]καὶ ὅτε εἶδον αὐτόν, ἔπεσα πρὸς τοὺς πόδας αὐτοῦ 17
ὡς νεκρός· καὶ ἔθηκεν τὴν δεξιὰν αὐτοῦ ἐπ' ἐμὲ λέγων
Μὴ φοβοῦ· ἐγώ εἰμι ὁ πρῶτος καὶ ὁ ἔσχατος [18]καὶ 18
ὁ ζῶν, καὶ ἐγενόμην νεκρὸς καὶ ἰδοὺ ζῶν εἰμι εἰς

17 ιδον CQ 7 | επεσον min^satmu Ar | προς] εις ℵ 13 επι 72 syr^gw | ως] ωσει ℵ^(*)c.a om 130 | εθηκεν] επεθηκεν ℵ 1 28 49 79 93^mg al^nonn | την δεξιαν αυτου] + χειρα 1 28 91 92 96 al^nonn syrr Andr την χειρα αυτου 130 | om μη φοβου ℵ* (hab ℵ^c.a) | πρωτος] πρωτοτοκος A 18 om και 1° ℵ* (hab ℵ^c.a)

17. *καὶ ὅτε εἶδον αὐτόν, ἔπεσα κτλ.*] Cf. Isa. vi. 5, Ez. i. 28, Dan. viii. 17, x. 9, 11, Enoch xiv. 14, 24, Lc. v. 8. Beatus: "fragilitatis suae et humilitatis et subiectionis pavore perterritus corruit." As a whole the passage is moulded on Dan. x. 8 f. LXX. ἰδοὺ πνεῦμα ἐπεστράφη ἐπ' ἐμὲ εἰς φθοράν, καὶ οὐ κατίσχυσα...ἐγὼ ἤμην πεπτωκὼς ἐπὶ πρόσωπόν μου ἐπὶ τὴν γῆν. καὶ ἰδοὺ χεῖρα προσήγαγέ μοι (Th. χεὶρ ἁπτομένη μου), καὶ ἤγειρέν με. That the right hand holds seven stars does not hinder it from being laid on the Seer, for the whole representation is symbol and not art. The Hand which sustains Nature and the Churches at the same time quickens and raises individual lives. With ἔθηκεν τὴν δεξιὰν αὐτοῦ κτλ., cf. Mt. xvii. 7 προσῆλθεν ὁ Ἰησοῦς καὶ ἁψάμενος αὐτῶν εἶπεν Ἐγέρθητε καὶ μὴ φοβεῖσθε—another point of contact between this vision and the history of the Transfiguration. Irenaeus (iv. 20. 11) reminds us that the awful Form which John saw was that of Him on whose breast he had lain at the Last Supper.

μὴ φοβοῦ· ἐγώ εἰμι κτλ.] The words recall another scene in the Gospels (Mc. vi. 50); both μὴ φοβοῦ and ἐγώ εἰμι were familiar sounds to the ear of an Apostle. On the other hand ὁ πρῶτος καὶ ὁ ἔσχατος go back to Isa. xliv. 6 (אֲנִי רִאשׁוֹן וַאֲנִי אַחֲרוֹן), xlviii. 12, a title of the God of Israel ascribed, according to the writer's habitual practice, to the exalted Christ (cf. *vv.* 5 f., 8 notes). It is given to Him again with enlargements which leave no doubt as to its significance, *c.* xxii. 13 ἐγώ εἰμι τὸ ἄλφα καὶ τὸ ὦ, ὁ πρ. καὶ ὁ ἔ., ἡ ἀρχὴ καὶ τὸ τέλος; see note *ad l.* The reading of A here and in ii. 8 is probably a mere reminiscence of i. 5.

18. *καὶ ὁ ζῶν, καὶ ἐγενόμην νεκρός κτλ.*] Ὁ ζῶν is another Divine title based on the O.T., cf. θεὸς ζῶν (אֵל חַי) in Jos. iii. 10, Ps. xli. (xlii.) 3, lxxxiii. (lxxxiv.) 3, Hos. i. 10 (ii. 1), and the formulae ζῇ Κύριος, ζῶ ἐγώ (חַי יְהוָֹה, חַי אָנִי) in Deut. xxxii. 40, Isa. xlix. 18, Jer. v. 2, Dan. xii. 7. In the N.T. θεὸς ζῶν or ὁ θεὸς ὁ ζ. is used freely (Mt. xvi. 16, xxvi. 63, Acts xiv. 15, Rom. ix. 26, 2 Cor. iii. 3, vi. 16, 1 Th. i. 9, 1 Tim. iii. 15, iv. 10, Heb. iii. 12, ix. 14, x. 31, 1 Pet. i. 23. A fuller phrase is ὁ ζῶν εἰς τὸν αἰῶνα (Sir. xviii. 1) or εἰς τοὺς αἰῶνας τῶν αἰώνων (Apoc. iv. 9 f., x. 6, xv. 7). On ὁ ζῶν as applied to Christ we have a comment in words ascribed to Christ Himself, Jo. v. 26: ὥσπερ γὰρ ὁ πατὴρ ἔχει ζωὴν ἐν ἑαυτῷ, οὕτως καὶ τῷ υἱῷ ἔδωκεν ζωὴν ἔχειν ἐν ἑαυτῷ. According to the Johannine Christology, the Son is ὁ ζῶν by the communication of the Father's Life.

As a title of the God of Israel and of the Church ὁ ζῶν places Him in sharp contrast with the dead gods of heathenism. Here, in its reference to Christ, it draws another contrast scarcely less pointed: ἐγώ εἰμι...ὁ ζῶν, καὶ ἐγενόμην νεκρός. The antithesis is twofold; ἐγενόμην is opposed to εἰμί as in Jo. i. 1, 14, viii. 58, and νεκρός to ζῶν (Orig. *in Joann.* t. i. 31 (34)), cf. Phil. ii. 5 ἐν μορφῇ θεοῦ ὑπάρχων

τοὺς αἰῶνας τῶν αἰώνων, καὶ ἔχω τὰς κλεῖς τοῦ
19 θανάτου καὶ τοῦ ᾅδου. [19]γράψον οὖν ἃ εἶδες καὶ

18 om *των αιωνων* vg me aeth Ir[int] Cypr | *αιωνων*]+*αμην* ℵ[c]Q min[pl] syrr arm[ed] Andr Ar | *κλεις* ℵACP min[pl] Andr Ar[txt]] *κλειδας* Q min[plq 30] | *του αδου και του θανατου* 1 28 36 99 al   19 om *ουν* 1 38 97 al[nonn] arm Ar | *ειδες* ℵCP min[pl]] *ιδες* AQ 7

...*γενόμενος ὑπήκοος μέχρι θανάτου*, where however the shock of the contrast is broken by the intervening clause *σχήματι εὑρεθεὶς ὡς ἄνθρωπος*. *Νεκρός* takes up *ὡς νεκρός* of *v.* 17; the Lord Who says *Μὴ φοβοῦ*, had experience, not of the semblance of death, but of its reality. *Καὶ ἰδοὺ ζῶν εἰμι* (Burton, § 409); not *ὁ ζῶν*, for it is the restored human life which is now in view, not the essential life of Godhead; nor again *ζῶν ἐγενόμην* or *ἔζησα* (Rom. xiv. 9), for attention is directed to the life which the Lord still lives, and not to the historical fact of His resurrection. The risen life of Jesus Christ is henceforth conterminous with His Divine life, *εἰς τοὺς αἰῶνας τῶν αἰώνων*; cf. Rom. vi. 9 *ἐγερθεὶς ἐκ νεκρῶν οὐκέτι ἀποθνήσκει*.

καὶ ἔχω τὰς κλεῖς τοῦ θανάτου καὶ τοῦ ᾅδου] Death and Hades are joined again in vi. 8, xx. 13 f.; the conception fluctuates between two localities (xx. 13), and two personalities (vi. 8); here it is difficult to determine which view is uppermost. Other instances of quasi-personification of Death and Hades (שְׁאוֹל) are Ps. xlviii. (xlix.) 15, Hos. xiii. 14 (cited 1 Cor. xv. 54 f.). The 'gates of Death' appear in Ps. ix. 14, cvi. (cvii.) 18, and the 'gates of Hades' in Isa. xxxviii. 10, Sap. xvi. 13, Mt. xvi. 18; see also Job xxxviii. 17 *πυλωροὶ δὲ ᾅδου ἰδόντες σε ἔπτηξαν*, a passage connected by Christian interpreters with the *descensus ad inferos*. To "have the keys of Death and of Hades" is to possess authority over their domain; cf. Mt. xvi. 19, Apoc. iii. 7, ix. 1, xx. 1 (notes). According to Rabbinical teaching, this is the sole prerogative of God; see *Targ. Jon.* on Deut. xxviii. 12 "quatuor sunt claves in manu Domini, clavis vitae et sepulchrorum et ciborum et pluviae." *Sanhedrin* f. 113. 1 "Elias petiit ut daretur sibi clavis pluviae, petiit ut daretur sibi clavis resurrectionis mortuorum; dixerunt ipsi: 'tres claves in manum legati non dantur, clavis partus, pluviarum, et resurrectionis mortuorum.'" The claim to possess potentially the keys of death is made by Christ Himself in Jo. v. 28; the Apoc. connects the actual possession of the keys with His victory over death; they are from that moment in His keeping (*ἔχω*). For *κλεῖς* = *κλεῖδας* see Blass, *Gr.* p. 26; *κλεῖν* is beyond dispute in iii. 7, xx. 1. In the Gospels, on the other hand *κλεῖδα*, *κλεῖδας* are well supported (Mt. xvi. 19, Lc. xi. 52), though there also cod. D gives the shorter form.

19. *γράψον οὖν ἃ εἶδες κτλ.*] *Οὖν* resumes (Blass, *Gr.* p. 273) the directions given in *v.* 11, enforcing it with the authority of One Who has declared Himself conqueror of Death: cf. Mt. xxviii. 18 *ἐδόθη μοι πᾶσα ἐξουσία... πορευθέντες οὖν κτλ.* *Ἃ εἶδες*, i.e. the vision of the Glorified Christ. Besides this the book contains a revelation of the present state of the Church and the world (*ἅ εἰσίν*), and a revelation of the future (*ἃ μέλλει γίνεσθαι μετὰ ταῦτα*). The former is chiefly contained in *cc.* ii, iii; the latter begins at *c.* iv. 1 *δείξω σοι ἃ δεῖ γενέσθαι μετὰ ταῦτα*. But the division is rough and superficial; *cc.* ii, iii look forward to the future, while *cc.* iv—xxii are by no means limited to it. On *εἰσίν*, *μέλλει* see WM. p. 645 f.; things present are seen distinctly and separately, while things future are blended

ἃ εἰσὶν καὶ ἃ μέλλει γίνεσθαι μετὰ ταῦτα. 20 τὸ 20
μυστήριον τῶν ἑπτὰ ἀστέρων οὓς εἶδες ἐπὶ τῆς δεξιᾶς
μου, καὶ τὰς ἑπτὰ λυχνίας τὰς χρυσᾶς· οἱ ἑπτὰ

19 μελλει] δει μελλει(ν) ℵ*(C) | γινεσθαι ℵ^{c.a}A 1 17 38 al^{pl} Ar] γενεσθαι ℵ*CPQ min^{nonn} 20 ους] ων Q 6 7 14 38 91 al^{pl} Andr Ar | ιδες Q 7 36 | επι της δεξιας ℵCPQ syrr Andr Ar min^{omn vid}] εν τη δεξια A vg Prim (*in dextera*) | om τας χρ. 97 syr^{gw}

in a more or less confused whole. For μέλλει followed by a pres. inf. see Blass, *Gr.* pp. 197, 202.

20. τὸ μυστήριον τῶν ἑπτὰ ἀστέρων κτλ.] On μυστήριον in Biblical Greek see the note to Mc. iv. 11. Here τὸ μυστ. is the inner meaning of a symbolical vision, as in Dan. ii. 47; cf. Apoc. xvii. 7 ἐγὼ ἐρῶ σοι τὸ μυστήριον τῆς γυναικός. The grammar presents some difficulty. Τὸ μυστήριον...τὰς λυχνίας are not governed by γράψον or in apposition to ἃ...γίνεσθαι (WM. p. 290), for the secret about to be revealed relates only to certain points of interpretation. A new sentence begins with *v.* 20, yet the verse opens with two accusatives without a verb. There are partial parallels in Rom. viii. 3 τὸ γὰρ ἀδύνατον τοῦ νόμου...ὁ θεός κτλ. (see SH. *ad l.*), and 2 Cor. vi. 13 τὴν δὲ αὐτὴν ἀντιμισθίαν... πλατύνθητε, where the acc. anticipates the contents of the sentence which it opens. In the present instance the construction is further complicated by a second accusative; for τὰς ἑ. λυχνίας we expect τῶν ἑ. λυχνιῶν. Translate: 'As for the secret of the seven stars... and as for [the secret of] the seven lampstands.' Ἐπὶ τῆς δεξιᾶς interprets ἐν τῇ δεξιᾷ χειρί (*v.* 16); the stars rested on the open palm; cf. v. 1 ἐπὶ τὴν δεξιὰν...βιβλίον.

οἱ ἑπτὰ ἀστέρες ἄγγελοι τῶν ἑ. ἐκκλησιῶν εἰσιν] The usage of the N.T. permits us to translate ἄγγελοι as 'messengers'; cf. Mt. xi. 10, Lc. vii. 24, ix. 52, Jac. ii. 25. The seven stars then may represent certain delegates from the Asiatic Churches (cf. 2 Cor. viii. 23 ἀπόστολοι ἐκκλησιῶν), presumably delegates sent to Patmos who were returning with the book of the Apocalypse. Or we may accept the interpretation of Primasius (followed by Bede): "angeli ecclesiarum hic intellegendi sunt rectores populi," i.e. either the Bishops, or if the monarchical episcopate had not yet established itself in Asia, the presbyteral colleges, in the several cities. In support of the latter view it has been usual to quote Mal. ii. 7 ἄγγελος Κυρίου (מַלְאַךְ יְהוָֹה) Παντοκράτορός ἐστιν [ὁ ἱερεύς], or to refer to the title שְׁלִיחַ צִבּוּר borne by the messenger of the Synagogue; this person however was in no sense a Church-ruler, and offers no true analogy (see Schürer[3], ii. p. 442, and cf. Lightfoot, *Philippians*, p. 199 note). And tempting as it is to discover in these ἄγγελοι an allusion to the rising order of the Episcopate, the invariable practice of our writer forbids such an interpretation. The Apocalypse uses ἄγγελος some sixty times, excluding those in which it is followed by τῆς ἐκκλησίας or τῶν ἐκκλησιῶν, and always in the technical sense of a superhuman being employed in the service of God or of Satan. There is therefore a strong presumption that the ἄγγελοι τῶν ἐκκλησιῶν are 'angels' in the sense which the word bears elsewhere throughout the book. In Dan. x. 13, xii. 1 a προστασία over particular nations is ascribed to certain angelic beings, and a like relation to individuals is implied in Mt. xviii. 10 οἱ ἄγγελοι αὐτῶν (sc. τῶν μικρῶν τούτων), Acts xii. 15 ὁ ἄγγελός ἐστιν αὐτοῦ. That John should have extended this conception to Churches (Andreas:

ἀστέρες ἄγγελοι τῶν ἑπτὰ ἐκκλησιῶν εἰσιν, καὶ αἱ
λυχνίαι αἱ ἑπτὰ ἑπτὰ ἐκκλησίαι εἰσίν.

II. 1 [1] Τῷ ἀγγέλῳ τῷ ἐν Ἐφέσῳ ἐκκλησίας γράψον

20 om εισιν 1° ℵ* (hab ℵ[c]) | και αι λυχνιαι αι επτα] και (αι) επτα λ. ℵ[(*)c.a] 38 91 130 al[pl] om αι επτα *h* Prim + ας ειδες P 1 14[mg] 79 91 92[mg] 93 al[mu vid] me syr[gw]

II 1 τω 2° AC (36) 130 syr[gw]] της ℵPQ min[rell] | εν Εφεσω] Εφεσου 16 syr[gw] Prim Εφεσιων 1 28 arm Or[int]

τούτων δὲ ἑκάστῃ ἄγγελος φύλαξ ἐφέστηκε) is not surprising, especially in view of the highly developed angelology of the book; cf. *Ascension of Isaiah* iii. 15, "the descent of the angel of the Christian Church, which is in the heavens." The objection that the angel is in that case unduly credited with the praise or blame which belongs to his Church had occurred to Origen, who however was not deterred by it; *hom. in Num.* xx. 3 "admiratione permoveor quod in tantum Deo cura de nobis sit ut etiam angelos suos culpari pro nobis et confutari patiatur." As a παιδαγωγός is blamed if his pupils go wrong, so, he adds (§ 4), "venient enim angeli ad iudicium nobiscum... ne forte minus erga nos operis et laboris expenderint quo nos a peccatorum labe revocarint." But in this symbolical book the angel of a Church may be simply an expression for its prevailing spirit, and thus be identified with the Church itself (Beatus: "ecclesias et angelos earum intellegas unum esse"). An interesting parallel to this idea is presented by the *fravashis* of Zoroastrianism: cf. Hastings' *D.B.* iv. p. 991, *J. Th. St.* iii. p. 521.

αἱ λυχνίαι αἱ ἑπτὰ ἑ. ἐκκλησίαι εἰσίν] If the angels of the Churches are represented by stars, the Churches themselves are lampstands, both giving light in their own measure and degree; cf. Lightfoot, *Philippians l.c.*: "[the] contrast between the heavenly and the earthly fires...cannot be devoid of meaning. The star is the suprasensual counterpart, the heavenly representative; the lamp, the earthly realisation, the outward embodiment." For the use of stars as symbols of angelic beings see Enoch lxxxvi. 1 ff., and cf. Ramsay, *Exp.*, 1904, i. p. 164 ff. On ἑπτά (2°) cf. WH.[2] *Notes*, p. 156.

II. 1—7. THE MESSAGE TO THE ANGEL OF THE CHURCH IN EPHESUS.

1. τῷ ἀγγέλῳ...γράψον] A formula repeated at the head of each address. The MSS. fluctuate between τῷ ἐκκλ. and τῆς ἐκκλ.; the former has the best support in ii. 1, and is found in ii. 8, 18, iii. 1, 7, but is without MS. authority in ii. 12, iii. 14. WH., who (*Notes*, p. 136 f.) believe τῷ to be the original reading in all the seven occurrences of the phrase, compare the title of the highpriests of the Augustan cult (ἀρχιερεὺς τῆς Ἀσίας ναοῦ τοῦ ἐν [Ἐφέσῳ]), where ναοῦ is anarthrous as ἐκκλησίας in the form τῷ ἀγγ. τῷ ἐν...ἐκκλ. κτλ.

τῷ ἐν Ἐφέσῳ ἐκκλησίας] In primitive Christian letters to Churches this is the usual mode of locating a Church, e.g. 1 Cor. i. 2 τῇ ἐκκλησίᾳ τοῦ θεοῦ τῇ οὔσῃ ἐν Κορίνθῳ, Phil. i. 1 τοῖς ἁγίοις...τοῖς οὖσιν ἐν Φιλίπποις, Ign. Eph. *ad init.* τῇ ἐκκλησίᾳ...τῇ οὔσῃ ἐν Ἐφέσῳ: less frequent forms are to be found in Gal. i. 2 ταῖς ἐκκλησίαις τῆς Γαλατίας, 1 (2) Thess. i. 1 τῇ ἐκκλησίᾳ τῶν Θεσσαλονικέων, Clem. R. *Cor. ad init.* τῇ ἐκκλησίᾳ τοῦ θεοῦ τῇ παροικούσῃ Κόρινθον. The Christian communities had as yet no territorial settlements; there was a 'Church in Ephesus,' but no *ecclesia Ephesina* in the stricter sense.

Ephesus stands first among the cities to which addresses are sent.

Τάδε λέγει ὁ κρατῶν τοὺς ἑπτὰ ἀστέρας ἐν τῇ δεξιᾷ αὐτοῦ, ὁ περιπατῶν ἐν μέσῳ τῶν ἑπτὰ λυχνιῶν τῶν

1 *δεξια αυτου*] + *χειρι* ℵ* (35 87) arm | *εν μεσω* (*εμμ.* AC)] *επι* 1 | om *επτα* 38 66 97 syr^{gw} arm

Thither the messenger from Patmos would sail by an easy course of 60 miles. Moreover on many grounds this city took first rank. In a series of inscriptions found at Ayasaluk, the modern Ephesus, it receives the proud title *ἡ πρώτη καὶ μεγίστη μητρόπολις τῆς Ἀσίας* (Hicks, *Inscriptions* III. ii, dxli, dxlvii, dli, dlv, dlxiii). A *libera urbs*, with its own *βουλή* and *γερουσία*, and the head of a *conventus*—an assize town,—Ephesus was also a seat of proconsular government (Acts xix. 38). Its commercial prosperity kept pace with its political importance; cf. Strabo *c.* 641 *ἐμπόριον οὖσα μεγίστη τοῦ κατὰ τὴν Ἀσίαν τὴν ἐντὸς τοῦ Ταύρου.* The great road which brought the trade of the East from the Euphrates to the Aegean reached the sea at Ephesus; and though the port of Ephesus suffered from the silting up of the mouth of the Cayster, this process had been arrested for a time by works undertaken in A.D. 65. Ephesus was not less conspicuous as a centre of religious life. It was proud to be known as Warden (*νεωκόρος*) of the Temple of Artemis, a shrine of worldwide reputation (Acts xix. 27, 35). Further it was the headquarters of the magical arts which at this time were widely practised in Asia Minor (cf. Acts xix. 19); the *Ἐφέσια γράμματα* were famous everywhere. The city was a hotbed of cults and superstitions, a meeting-place of East and West, where Greeks Romans and Asiatics jostled one another in the streets.

The founder of the Ephesian Church was the Apostle Paul. As early as A.D. 50 (? 51, ? 52) he made an ineffectual effort to reach the province of Asia (Acts xvi. 6), and his first visit to Ephesus (xviii. 19 ff.) was too brief to bear permanent fruit. But he realized the importance of the place as a field of Christian work, and in 53 (? 54, ? 55) returned to spend over two years there (xix. 8, 10). Though he does not seem to have visited any other city in Asia, his Ephesian residence was the occasion of a general evangelization of the province (*l. c.* *ὥστε πάντας τοὺς κατοικοῦντας τὴν Ἀσίαν ἀκοῦσαι τὸν λόγον τοῦ κυρίου*). St Paul's work at Ephesus was carried on by Timothy (1 Tim. i. 3) and, after the Apostle's death and the withdrawal of Timothy, by St John, if we may believe the traditions of the second century; see Iren. iii. 1. 1, 3. 4; Polycrates *ap.* Eus. *H. E.* iii. 31, v. 24, and cf. the Introduction to this commentary.

γράψον Τάδε λέγει] Another part of the introductory formula which is common to all the messages. It is followed in each case by a description of the Speaker, in which He is characterised by one or more of the features in the vision of ch. i. (ii. 1, 12, 18, iii. 1, 7), or by one or more of His titles (ii. 8, iii. 7, 14); the features or titles selected appear to correspond with the circumstances of the church which is addressed. With *τάδε λέγει* cf. *λέγει Ἰησοῦς*, with which each of the Oxyrhynchus Sayings begins. The seven so-called letters are not 'epistles of Christ,' but rather utterances, pronouncements, judgements passed upon the churches as they pass in succession under the eye of the supreme *Ἐπίσκοπος*. See p. 64 f., *infra*.

ὁ κρατῶν...ὁ περιπατῶν κτλ. recalls i. 13, 16 *ἐν μέσῳ τῶν λυχνιῶν...ἔχων ἐν τῇ δεξιᾷ χειρὶ αὐτοῦ ἀστέρας ἑπτά* but

2 χρυσέων. 2 οἶδα τὰ ἔργα σου καὶ τὸν κόπον καὶ τὴν
ὑπομονήν σου, καὶ ὅτι οὐ δύνῃ βαστάσαι κακούς, καὶ

1 χρυσεων AC] χρυσων ℵPQ min$^{\text{omn vid}}$ 2 τον κοπον] + σου ℵQ min^{pl} me syr^{gw} aeth Andr Ar | υπομ. σου] om σου Prim | και οτι] om και A me | βασταξαι P 1 38 81

in a stronger form; ἔχων has become κρατῶν, and ἐν μέσῳ is qualified by περιπατῶν. Κρατεῖν is to hold in one's grip (e.g. Mt. xxvi. 4, Acts ii. 24), whether for the purpose of retaining (Jo. xx. 23) or of restraining (Apoc. vii. 1); here the former meaning is evidently in view, as in ii. 13 ff., 25, iii. 11; the acc. follows, because the Church as a whole is thus firmly grasped, and not only a part of it (cf. Blass, *Gr.* p. 101). As the Enemy περιπατεῖ ζητῶν καταπιεῖν (1 Pet. v. 8, cf. Job i. 7), so the Lord patrols the ground, is ever on the spot when He is needed; His Presence is not localized, but coextensive with the Church (Mt. xviii. 20, xxviii. 20, 2 Cor. vi. 16 ff.); cf. Arethas: ἐν μέσῳ ὁ ἐνοικεῖν αὐτοῖς καὶ ἐμπεριπατεῖν ἐπαγγειλάμενος Κύριος. The two images are complementary, representing the security which comes from strength and vigilance.

To the Church in Ephesus, the mother of the Churches of Asia, the Lord writes under titles which express His relation to the Churches generally. As Ephesus represented the Province (cf. Ἀσία ἡ Ἔφεσος, cited by Ramsay, *Exp.*, 1904, i. p. 173), so the Ephesian Church stands here for the seven. Yet the message shews the special need which the Ephesian Church had both of a firm grasp and a watchful safeguarding.

2. οἶδα τὰ ἔργα σου] Οἶδα is a note often struck in these letters (cf. ii. 9, 13, 19, iii. 1, 8, 15). The Apostles were deeply impressed by the Master's knowledge of men; see Jo. ii. 25, xxi. 15 ff., Acts i. 24. The Apocalypse does not use γινώσκω of Christ; οἶδα emphasizes better the absolute clearness of mental vision which photographs all the facts of life as they pass. The distinction is well seen in Jo. xxi. 17 Κύριε, πάντα σὺ οἶδας· σὺ γινώσκεις ὅτι φιλῶ σε, where the universal knowledge passes into the field of special observation. Οἶδα τὰ ἔ. σου is in itself neither praise nor blame, for 'works' may be either good (καλά, ἀγαθά, Mt. v. 16, Jo. x. 32, Acts ix. 36, Eph. ii. 10) or bad (πονηρά, ἄκαρπα, τοῦ διαβόλου, τῆς σαρκός, Jo. iii. 19, viii. 41, Gal. v. 19, Eph. v. 11); blame is conveyed by it in iii. 1, 15, but praise in iii. 8; here and in ii. 19, while praise predominates, it is not unmixed. The spirit, the ἦθος of each Church, represented as its 'angel,' is judged by its results, according to Christ's invariable rule (Mt. vii. 16 f., Apoc. ii. 23, xxii. 12).

καὶ τὸν κόπον καὶ τὴν ὑπομονήν σου] The single pronoun after ὑπομ. links κόπος and ὑπομονή together, as indicating the character of the ἔργα; they were signalized by two notes of excellence, self-denying labour and perseverance. Compare (with Lightfoot's note) 1 Th. i. 3 μνημονεύοντες ὑμῶν τοῦ ἔργου τῆς πίστεως καὶ τοῦ κόπου τῆς ἀγάπης καὶ τῆς ὑπομονῆς τῆς ἐλπίδος, where however ἔργον, κόπος, and ὑπομονή are strictly coordinated. Κόπος, often found with μόχθος (2 Cor. xi. 27, 1 Th. ii. 9, 2 Th. iii. 8), is with its cognate κοπιᾶν almost a technical word for Christian work; cf. Rom. xvi. 6, 12, 1 Cor. iii. 8, xv. 10, 58, xvi. 16, 2 Cor. vi. 5, xi. 23; Gal. iv. 11, Phil. ii. 16, Col. i. 29, 1 Th. v. 12, 1 Tim. v. 17, Apoc. xiv. 13. On ὑπομονή see i. 9, note, and cf. Lc. viii. 15 καρποφοροῦσιν ἐν ὑπομονῇ.

καὶ ὅτι οὐ δύνῃ βαστάσαι κακούς] Another good thing which has not escaped the eye of Christ. The

ἐπείρασας τοὺς λέγοντας ἑαυτοὺς ἀποστόλους, καὶ
οὐκ εἰσίν, καὶ εὗρες αὐτοὺς ψευδεῖς· [3]καὶ ὑπομονὴν 3
ἔχεις, καὶ ἐβάστασας διὰ τὸ ὄνομά μου, καὶ οὐ

2 αποστολους] + ειναι ℵ$^{c.c}$Q min$^{fere\ 50}$ vg syr* syr^{gw} Vict Prim Andr Ar 3 και υπομονην...μου] και εβαστασας (με) και υπομ. εχεις (P) (7 16) 28 38 (45 46) 49 79 (88) 91 om και υπομ. εχεις 33 34 35 om και εβαστασας 37 Vict | και ου κεκοπιακες (-κας 51) AC 51] και ουκ εκοπιασας ℵPQ min$^{fere\ 50}$ και κεκοπιακας (1) 16 37 38 39 69 arm

ὑπομονή of the Ephesians did not imply indifference to sin; they could not bear the company of bad men; cf. Ps. cxxxix. 21 f., Rom. xii. 9, 2 Jo. 10 f., and the story of St John's attitude towards Cerinthus (Iren. iii. 3. 4). These κακοί (cf. Phil. iii. 2 τοὺς κακοὺς ἐργάτας) who tried the patience of the Ephesians were not their pagan neighbours (Eph. iv. 17 ff.), but the false brethren mentioned in the next clause; cf. Ign. *Eph.* 9 οὓς οὐκ εἰάσατε σπεῖραι [τὴν κακὴν διδαχὴν] εἰς ὑμᾶς, βύσαντες τὰ ὦτα εἰς τὸ μὴ παραδέξασθαι τὰ σπειρόμενα ὑπ' αὐτῶν. Βαστάζειν is to carry a burden (βάρος, Mt. xx. 12; σταυρόν, Lc. xiv. 27, Jo. xix. 17; φορτίον, Gal. vi. 5). The form δύνῃ = δύνασαι, condemned by Phrynichus, occurs also in Mc. ix. 22 f., Lc. xvi. 2 (Blass, *Gr.* p. 49).

καὶ ἐπείρασας τοὺς λέγοντας κτλ.] The λύκοι βαρεῖς foreseen by St Paul (Acts xx. 29) had come, and in sheep's clothing (Mt. vii. 15); cf. 2 Cor. xi. 13 οἱ γὰρ τοιοῦτοι ψευδαπόστολοι, ἐργάται δόλιοι, μετασχηματιζόμενοι εἰς ἀποστόλους Χριστοῦ. The false teachers claimed to be ἀπόστολοι in the wider sense, itinerant teachers with a mission which placed them on a higher level than the local elders (1 Cor. xii. 28, Eph. iv. 11; cf. Lightfoot, *Galatians*, 'The name and office of an Apostle,' Harnack, *Die Lehre der zwölf Apostel*, p. 93 ff.). When such itinerants, whether 'Apostles' or 'Prophets,' visited a church where they were unknown, unless they brought 'commendatory letters' (2 Cor. iii. 1), it was necessary to test their claims (1 Th. v. 20 f., 1 Jo. iv. 1). A strangely superficial test, such as that enjoined in *Didache* c. 11 (πᾶς δὲ ἀπόστολος ἐρχόμενος πρὸς ὑμᾶς δεχθήτω ὡς Κύριος ...τρεῖς δὲ ἐὰν μείνῃ [ἡμέρας], ψευδοπροφήτης ἐστίν), is not to be thought of here; ἐπείρασας (= ἐδοκίμασας, as in 2 Cor. xiii. 5 ἑαυτοὺς πειράζετε εἰ ἐστὲ ἐν τῇ πίστει) doubtless refers to such a probation as the Lord prescribes in Mt. vii. 16 ἀπὸ τῶν καρπῶν αὐτῶν γνώσεσθε αὐτούς, and the *Didache* itself regards as the ultimate test (*infra*, ἐὰν ἔχῃ τοὺς τρόπους Κυρίου. ἀπὸ οὖν τῶν τρόπων γνωσθήσεται).

With τοὺς λέγοντας ἑαυτοὺς ἀπ. cf. ii. 20 ἡ λέγουσα ἑαυτὴν προφῆτιν; the full form appears in ii. 9 τῶν λεγόντων Ἰουδαίους εἶναι ἑαυτούς. Καὶ οὐκ εἰσίν, a parenthesis = καὶ οὐκ ὄντας: cf. i. 6, ii. 9, iii. 9.

καὶ εὗρες αὐτοὺς ψευδεῖς: not merely false apostles, for such might be self-deceived, but deceivers; for this use of ψευδής, cf. xxi. 8 πᾶσι τοῖς ψευδέσι.

3. καὶ ὑπομονὴν ἔχεις, καὶ ἐβάστασας κτλ.] With ὑπομ. ἔχεις cf. *v.* 6 τοῦτο ἔχεις, ὅτι κτλ., iii. 11 κράτει ὃ ἔχεις. Endurance was one of the best assets of the Ephesian angel. Unable to bear the society of the deceivers, the faithful at Ephesus had for the sake of Christ (διὰ τὸ ὄνομα, cf. Mc. xiii. 13, note) patiently borne the labour of resisting them or enduring their taunts (Arethas), and had not grown weary of the task. The play in *vv.* 2, 3 on βαστάζειν and κοπιᾶν (οὐ δύνῃ βαστάσαι...ἐβάστασας, οἶδα τὸν κόπον σου...οὐ κεκοπίακες) has perplexed the scribes; see app. crit. Καὶ οὐ κέκμηκας of the T. R. appears to rest on no better authority than a conjecture of Erasmus, but it gives the sense; for

4 κεκοπίακες. ^{4}ἀλλ' ἔχω κατὰ σοῦ ὅτι τὴν ἀγάπην
5 σου τὴν πρώτην ἀφῆκες. ^{5}μνημόνευε οὖν πόθεν
πέπτωκες, καὶ μετανόησον καὶ τὰ πρῶτα ἔργα

4 αλλα ℵQ min^{13} | την πρωτην σου αγαπην A | αφηκες ℵ$^{*c.a}$C] αφηκας ℵ$^{c.c}$APQ min$^{omn\ vid}$ 5 μνημονευσον 38 130 | om ουν syr^{gw} Prim | πεπτωκες ℵ (-κας ACQ min$^{plq\ 40}$)] εκπεπτωκας P 1 7 28 49 79 91 96 al *g* vg syr^{gw}

κοπιᾶν, to be weary, cf. Mt. xi. 28, Jo. iv. 6, and for the form κεκοπίακες see W. Schm. p. 113, note 16, and cf. ἀφῆκες, πέπτωκες (*vv.* 4, 5). Ἔχεις ...ἐβάστασας...κεκοπ.: such combinations are frequent in the Apoc. (e.g. v. 7, vii. 13 f., viii. 5) and not always easy to explain; here the perf. κεκοπ. indicates a condition which continued when the endurance (ἐβάστασας) was at an end.

4. ἀλλ' ἔχω κατὰ σοῦ ὅτι κτλ.] Yet on the other hand (ἀλλά) there is ground for complaint; for ἔχειν (τι) κατά τινος cf. Job xxxi. 35 (LXX.), Mt. v. 23, Mc. xi. 25, note, and below, *vv.* 14, 20. Patience and unremitting toil in His cause are not all that Christ requires, and indeed are of little value, if the spirit of love is absent. But at Ephesus love was waning, perhaps as the result of the controversies through which the Church had passed. Τὴν ἀγάπην σου τὴν πρώτην: the adj. in this position limits and corrects: 'thou hast left thy love, at least the love of the first days,' i.e. the days of St Paul's ministry at Ephesus; how fervent it was appears from Acts xix. 20, xx. 37, cf. Eph. i. 3 ff. Another generation has taken the place of the first converts; the loyalty and activity of the Church have been well maintained, but there is some falling off in the greatest of Christian gifts (cf. Mt. xxiv. 12 ψυγήσεται ἡ ἀγάπη τῶν πολλῶν), shewn perhaps, as the Greek commentators suggest, by a comparative indifference to the necessities of the poorer brethren. The phrase τὴν ἀγ. τ. πρ. ἀφῆκες is probably a reminiscence of Jer. ii. 2, Ez. xvi. 8 ff. The new Israel had begun too soon to follow the example of the ancient people of God.

5. μνημόνευε οὖν πόθεν πέπτωκες κτλ.] Comp. iii. 3 μνημόνευε οὖν πῶς εἴληφας καὶ ἤκουσας. The commentators contrast Cic. *ad Attic.* iv. 16 "non recordor unde ceciderim sed unde resurrexerim," a fine sentiment which is not really in conflict with the call to remember 'unde cecideris' as a motive to repentance. St Paul's τὰ μὲν ὀπίσω ἐπιλανθανόμενος (Phil. iii. 14) refers to past successes which must be disregarded in view of τὰ ἔμπροσθεν—an entirely different case from that which is contemplated by this 'Remember.' Μνημόνευε, μετανόησον, ποίησον answer to three stages in the history of conversion; the pres. imper. perhaps represents the first as continuous or habitual, but it is noteworthy that while μνημόνευε occurs seven times in the N.T., there is no well-supported instance of μνημόνευσον.

For πίπτειν in reference to a moral fall, cf. Rom. xi. 11, 1 Cor. x. 12, and the use of παραπίπτειν, παράπτωμα in Ps. xviii. (xix.) 13, Sap. x. 1, xii. 2, Mt. vi. 14 f., Heb. vi. 6. Ποίησον τὰ πρῶτα ἔργα: the Lord does not say ἀγάπησον τὴν πρώτην ἀγάπην, a precept which perhaps could not have been fulfilled; the last may be better or worse than the first, but never can be the same.

This verse is frequently quoted by Cyprian when he urges repentance upon those who had lapsed in the Decian persecution (*de laps.* 16, *epp.* 19. 1, 34. 1, 55. 22); and with other passages from the Apoc. it became a commonplace in the Novatianist controversy (*ad Novatian.* 13).

ποίησον· εἰ δὲ μή, ἔρχομαί σοι καὶ κινήσω τὴν
λυχνίαν σου ἐκ τοῦ τόπου αὐτῆς, ἐὰν μὴ μετανοήσῃς.
6 ἀλλὰ τοῦτο ἔχεις, ὅτι μισεῖς τὰ ἔργα τῶν Νικο- 6

5 σοι] + ταχυ Q min$^{\text{fere omn}}$ vg$^{\text{harl*}}$ syr arm Prim | om εκ του τοπου αυτης syr^{gw}

εἰ δὲ μή, ἔρχομαί σοι] Εἰ δὲ μή, i.e. ἐὰν δὲ μὴ μετανοήσῃς, as the phrase is written in full just below; on the elliptical form (='otherwise'), see WM. pp. 729, 757; Burton, § 275. Ἔρχομαι refers to a special coming or visitation, affecting a Church or an individual, as in *v.* 16, iii. 11; throughout the Apoc. the present of this verb is used in a quasi-future sense; cf. Blass, *Gr.* p. 189. Σοί is a *dativus incommodi* (WM. p. 265); for another view, see Blass, *Gr.* p. 113.

Καὶ κινήσω τὴν λυχνίαν σου, i.e. thy church. Since the λυχνίαι are separate and do not form a single candelabrum, any one of them can be removed at pleasure. Κινεῖν (cf. vi. 14) is preferred to ἀφαιρεῖν, perhaps as indicating deliberation and judicial calmness; there would be no sudden uprooting as in anger, but a movement which would end in the loss of the place that the Church had been called to fill; unless there came a change for the better, the first of the seven lamps of Asia must disappear; its place must be filled by another (cf. Apoc. iii. 11, Mt. xxi. 43). This warning seems to have been taken to heart, since in the next generation Ignatius (*Eph.* prol. 1) could pronounce the 'church in Ephesus' to be ἀξιομακάριστος, and speak of its πολυαγάπητον ὄνομα. But though deferred, the visitation came at last. The Greek commentators mention the curious fancy that the removal of the candlestick from Ephesus had its fulfilment in the rise of the See of Constantinople, which eclipsed the glory of the older Church. But the Church and See of Ephesus lived on for centuries after the creation of the patriarchate of Constantinople. After the eleventh century however the line of Ephesian Bishops seems to have become extinct (Gams, *series episc.* p. 443), and in 1308 the place was finally surrendered to the Turks (Murray, *Handbook*, p. 280). The little railway station and hotel and few poor dwelling-houses of Ayasaluk (Ἅγιος Θεολόγος), which now command the ruins of the city, are eloquent of the doom which has overtaken both Ephesus and its church.

6. *ἀλλὰ τοῦτο ἔχεις, ὅτι μισεῖς κτλ.*] This second ἀλλά modifies the ἀλλά of *v.* 4. If the loss of her first love was a heavy charge against the Church in Ephesus, there must be set against it and in her favour her hatred of deeds which Christ hated.

Irenaeus (i. 26. 3, iii. 10. 7), followed by Hippolytus (*philos.* vii. 36), asserts that the Nicolaitans of the Apocalypse were founded by Nicolaus the proselyte of Antioch who was one of the Seven (Acts vi. 5): ἀποστὰς τῆς κατ' εὐθεῖαν διδασκαλίας ἐδίδασκεν ἀδιαφορίαν βίου τε καὶ βρώσεως (Hipp. *l. c.*). There was a sect which bore the name at the end of the second century, but its identity with the Νικολαῖται of the Apoc. cannot be assumed (Tert. *de praescr.* 33 "sunt et nunc alii Nicolaitae") and its claim to be spiritually descended from Nicolaus of Antioch was questioned (Clem. Al. *strom.* ii. 20, § 118 φάσκοντες ἑαυτοὺς Νικολάῳ ἕπεσθαι, ἀπομνημόνευμά τι τἀνδρὸς φέροντες: cf. ib. iii. 4, § 25; Eus. *H. E.* iii. 29; *Constitutions* vi. 8 οἱ νῦν ψευδώνυμοι Νικολαῖται, with which cf. the interpolated Ignatius, *Trall.* 11, *Philad.* 6; Victorinus *ad l.* "ficti homines et pestiferi qui sub nomine Nicolai ministri fecerunt sibi haeresim"). A modern conjecture (due to C. A. Heumann, 1712) takes Νικολαῖται

7 λαϊτῶν, ἃ κἀγὼ μισῶ. 7ὁ ἔχων οὖς ἀκουσάτω τί
τὸ πνεῦμα λέγει ταῖς ἐκκλησίαις. τῷ νικῶντι δώσω

6 om ἃ A *sicut* aeth Prim | καγω] εγω syr[gw] 7 ους] *aures* vg[codd] Prim | εκκλησιαις] pr επτα A + ταις επτα C | νικουντι A

in Apoc. ii. 6, 15 as = Βαλααμῖται (cf. *v.* 14), בלעם being derived either from בלע עם or בעל עם. But (1) a play upon the etymology of Greek and Hebrew words is perhaps too subtle for the genius of the writer, and (2) no etymology has been suggested which makes Νικόλαος a true equivalent of בִּלְעָם. On the whole it seems best to fall back upon the supposition that a party bearing this name existed in Asia when the Apoc. was written, whether it owed its origin to Nicolaus of Antioch, which is not improbable (see Lightfoot, *Galatians*, p. 297, n.), or to some other false teacher of that name. According to Ps.-Dorotheus he was a Samaritan Christian who joined the party of Simon Magus, but the statement lacks confirmation. On the teaching of this sect see *v.* 14, note.

Ἃ κἀγὼ μισῶ. Hatred of evil deeds (ἅ, not οὕς; contrast Ps. cxxxix. 21 f.) is a true counterpart of the love of good, and both are Divine; cf. Isa. lxi. 8, Zech. viii. 17. There is a μῖσος as well as an ὀργή (Mc. iii. 5, Apoc. vi. 16 f.) which can be predicated of Christ. To share His hatred of evil is to manifest an affinity of character with Him, which is a sign of grace in Churches and in individuals.

7. ὁ ἔχων οὖς ἀκουσάτω κτλ.] Another formula common to the seven messages preceding the promise to the conqueror in the first three, and following it in the last four. It recalls a familiar saying of Christ which is found in the three Synoptists (Mt. xi. 15, xiii. 9, 43; Mc. iv. 9, 23; Lc. viii. 8, xiv. 35), but not in the Gospel of St John. On variations in the form of the saying see Mc. iv. 9, note; the consistent use of οὖς for ὦτα in the Apoc., even in xiii. 9, shews independence; yet see Mt. x. 27, Lc. xii. 3. At the end of each of these instructions ὁ ἔχων οὖς is an individualizing note, calling upon each of the hearers of the book (i. 3) to appropriate the warnings and promises addressed to the Churches. Ταῖς ἐκκλησίαις, not τῇ ἐκκλησίᾳ: cf. Primasius: "Si quae singulis partiliter ecclesiis praedicat universam generaliter convenire dicatur ecclesiam. neque enim dicit 'Quid spiritus dicat ecclesiae' sed 'ecclesiis.'" Bede: "quae singulis scribit universis se dicere demonstrat ecclesiis."

Τὸ πνεῦμα λέγει, cf. Acts viii. 29, xiii. 2, Apoc. xiv. 13, xxii. 17. According to the opening formula (ii. 1) the Speaker is Christ; but the Spirit of Christ in the prophet is the interpreter of Christ's voice.

τῷ νικῶντι δώσω αὐτῷ φαγεῖν κτλ.] In τῷ νικ. there is a possible allusion to Νικολαϊτῶν, but νικᾶν is a characteristically Johannine word (Jo. xvi. 33, 1 Jo. ii. 13 f., iv. 4, v. 4 f.), and specially frequent in the Apoc. (ii. 7, 11, 17, 26, iii. 5, 12, 21, v. 5, xii. 11, xv. 2, xvii. 14, xxi. 7); the book is a record and a prophecy of victories won by Christ and the Church. The note of victory is dominant in St John, as that of faith in St Paul; or rather, faith presents itself to St John in the light of a victory (1 Jo. v. 4). Τῷ νικῶντι: so or with ὁ νικῶν the promise at the end of each utterance begins, not τῷ νικήσαντι or τῷ νενικηκότι. The pres. part. here is timeless, like ὁ βαπτίζων, ὁ πειράζων (Mc. i. 4 note, Mt. iv. 3); ὁ νικῶν (*vincens, qui vicerit*) is 'the conqueror,' the victorious member of the Church, as such, apart from all consideration of the circumstances; cf. Tert. *scorp.* 12 "victori cuique promittit nunc arborem vitae."

αὐτῷ φαγεῖν ἐκ τοῦ ξύλου τῆς ζωῆς, ὅ ἐστιν ἐν τῷ παραδείσῳ τοῦ θεοῦ.

8 Καὶ τῷ ἀγγέλῳ τῷ ἐν Cμύρνῃ ἐκκλησίας γράψον 8

7 om αυτω ℵ 10 17 46 49 88 91 96 *g* vg[cle harl lipss] syr[gw] | εν τω παραδεισω] εν μεσω τω π. ℵ[c.c]P εν μεσω του παραδεισου 1 28 35 36 49 79 91 92[mg] 96 al me arm Andr | του θεου] + μου Q min[plq 45] *g* vg me syr aeth Or[int] Cypr Prim al 8 τω 2° A] της ℵCPQ rell | εν Σμυρνη (Ζμ. ℵ) εκκλησιας] εκκλ. Σμυρναιων 1 (28 79) arm της εκκλησιας Σμυρνης (s. Ζμυρνης) vg me syr[gw] Prim

Δώσω is another Apocalyptic word (ii. 10, 17, 23, 26, 28, iii. 21, xxi. 6). There is here nothing inconsistent with Mc. x. 40 οὐκ ἔστιν ἐμὸν δοῦναι; Christ gives it as Judge to those for whom it has been prepared by the Father; see Mt. xxv. 34, 2 Tim. iv. 8, and cf. Rom. vi. 23 τὸ δὲ χάρισμα τοῦ θεοῦ ζωὴ αἰώνιος ἐν Χριστῷ Ἰησοῦ. The hands of the ascended Christ are full of gifts (cf. Eph. iv. 7 ff.). With the promise δώσω αὐτῷ φαγεῖν κτλ., cf. xxii. 14 ἵνα ἔσται ἡ ἐξουσία αὐτῶν ἐπὶ τὸ ξύλον τ. ζ. and *Test. xii patr.*, Levi 18 δώσει τοῖς ἁγίοις φαγεῖν ἐκ τοῦ ξύλου τ. ζ.; for the construction see vi. 4 ἐδόθη αὐτῷ λαβεῖν, vii. 2, xiii. 7, 14, xvi. 8. Τὸ ξύλον τῆς ζωῆς κτλ. (cf. xxii. 2, 14, 19) is of course from Gen. ii. 9; on ξύλον = δένδρον see WM., p. 23. In the LXX. παράδεισος represents either גַּן (Gen. ii., iii. *passim*), or פַּרְדֵּס a pleasaunce (2 Esdr. xii. 8, Eccl. ii. 5, Cant. iv. 13) "from the old Persian *pairidaêza*," (*Encycl. Bibl.* s.v.); and once עֵדֶן (Isa. li. 3); τοῦ θεοῦ has been added from Gen. xiii. 10 or Ez. xxviii. 13, xxxi. 8. The Rabbinical writers use the word of the heavenly גַּן עֵדֶן which is the opposite state to their גֵּי הִנֹּם; see Weber, *Jüd. Theol.* p. 344 ff. Of the idealized Tree of Life we read already in Prov. iii. 18 (cf. Isa. lxv. 22, LXX., 4 Macc. xviii. 16), but its first appearance in a vision of the celestial Paradise is in *Enoch* xxiv. f. τὰ φύλλα αὐτῆς καὶ τὸ ἄνθος καὶ τὸ δένδρον οὐ φθίνει εἰς τὸν αἰῶνα...καὶ οὐδεμία σὰρξ ἐξουσίαν ἔχει ἅψασθαι αὐτοῦ μέχρι τῆς μεγάλης κρίσεως...τότε δικαίοις καὶ ὁσίοις δοθήσεται ὁ καρπὸς αὐτῶν; cf. Slavonic Enoch 8, and Ps. Sol. xiv. 3. In the N.T. 'Paradise' is either the state of the blessed dead (Lc. xxiii. 43), or a supra-mundane sphere identified with the third heaven into which men pass in an ecstasy (2 Cor. xii. 2 f.); or, as here, the final joy of the saints in the presence of God and of Christ. On the history of the subject generally see Tennant, *Sources of the Doctrine of the Fall and of Original Sin*, passim.

The general sense of the promise δώσω κτλ. is clear. Man's exclusion from the Tree of Life (Gen. iii. 22 f.) is repealed by Christ on condition of a personal victory over evil. To eat of the Tree is to enjoy all that the life of the world to come has in store for redeemed humanity. Apringius: "pomum ligni vitae aeternitatem immarcescibilem subministrat." Bede: "lignum vitae Christus est, cuius in caelesti paradiso visione sanctae reficiuntur animae."

8—11. THE MESSAGE TO THE ANGEL OF THE CHURCH IN SMYRNA.

8. τῷ ἐν Σμύρνῃ] The road from Ephesus—a distance of about 35 miles—entered Smyrna by the 'Ephesian Gate.' The city, which had been rebuilt by Lysimachus, was now the finest of the Asiatic towns (Strabo, 646), and boasted of being τὸ τῆς Ἀσίας ἄγαλμα. Situated at the head of a well protected gulf, with an ample harbour, it possessed an export trade second only to that of Ephesus, while like Ephesus it was the terminus of a great road, which tapped the rich valley of the Hermus and penetrated to the interior. As far back as the reign of

Τάδε λέγει ὁ πρῶτος καὶ ὁ ἔσχατος, ὃς ἐγένετο
9 *νεκρὸς καὶ ἔζησεν.* [9]*οἶδά σου τὴν θλίψιν καὶ τὴν*
πτωχίαν, ἀλλὰ πλούσιος εἶ, καὶ τὴν βλασφημίαν

8 *πρωτος*] *πρωτοτοκος* A | om *ος* min[20] 9 *την θλιψιν*] pr *τα εργα σου και* ℵQ min[pl] syr arm Andr[txt] Ar | *πτωχιαν* ℵAC 11 97] *πτωχειαν* PQ min[fere omn] + *σου* *g* vg syr[gw]

Tiberius the loyalty of Smyrna to Rome procured for it the privilege of erecting a temple to the Emperor, and the city henceforth claimed the title of *νεωκόρος* of the new cult. She disputed with her neighbour Ephesus the honour of being styled *πρώτη τῆς Ἀσίας* and *μητρόπολις*. But the writer of the Apocalypse follows an order to which Ephesus itself would have assented, when he assigns to Smyrna the second place among the seven.

The N.T. throws no light on the origin of the Church in Smyrna beyond the general statement as to the evangelization of Asia in Acts xix. 10; see Lightfoot, *Ignatius*, i. p. 462. But according to *Vita Polycarpi* 2 St Paul visited Smyrna on his way to Ephesus (cf. Acts xix. 1 *διελθόντα τὰ ἀνωτερικὰ μέρη*), and found disciples there, as he did at Ephesus. The Church is still strong at Smyrna; out of a population of perhaps 250,000 more than half are Christians, while the *Εὐαγγελικὴ Σχολή* with its fine library witnesses to the vigour and intelligence of the Orthodox community.

On the form *Ζμύρνα* see WH.[2], *Notes*, p. 155; Blass, *Gr.* p. 10. It occurs on coins of the period and in inscriptions (see e.g. *CIG* iii. 3276 ff.).

τάδε λέγει ὁ πρῶτος καὶ ὁ ἔσχατος κτλ.] These titles (from i. 17 f.) are chosen with the view of inspiring confidence into a Church threatened with suffering and death; cf. Bede: "apta praefatio patientiam suasuro." Ramsay (*Exp.*, 1904, i. p. 321 f.) finds a reference also to the early struggles of the city (Strabo, 646 *ἀνήγειρεν αὐτὴν Ἀντίγονος*). *Ἔζησεν* takes the place of *ζῶν εἰμι*, the purpose being to fix attention upon the fact of the Resurrection. As the Lord rose, so will His martyrs triumph over death; cf. 2 Tim. ii. 8 *μνημόνευε Ἰησοῦν Χριστὸν ἐγηγερμένον ἐκ νεκρῶν.* The parallel in Apoc. xiii. 14 is instructive: *τῷ θηρίῳ ὃς ἔχει τὴν πληγὴν τῆς μαχαίρης καὶ ἔζησεν* (see note *ad l.*).

9. *οἶδά σου τὴν θλίψιν κτλ.*] The Church in Smyrna was characterized by its endurance of suffering and poverty in the cause of the Gospel. With the paradox *οἶδά σου...τὴν πτωχείαν, ἀλλὰ πλούσιος εἶ* comp. Jac. ii. 5 *οὐχ ὁ θεὸς ἐξελέξατο τοὺς πτωχοὺς τῷ κόσμῳ πλουσίους ἐν πίστει*, 2 Cor. vi. 10 *ὡς πτωχοί, πολλοὺς δὲ πλουτίζοντες*, and contrast Apoc. iii. 17 *λέγεις ὅτι Πλούσιός εἰμι καὶ πεπλούτηκα ...καὶ οὐκ οἶδας ὅτι σὺ εἶ ὁ...πτωχός.* The nature of the wealth possessed by the Church in Smyrna but lacking to the Church in Laodicea is well shewn in Lc. xii. 21 *εἰς θεὸν πλουτῶν*, 1 Tim. vi. 18 *πλουτεῖν ἐν ἔργοις καλοῖς.* The poverty (*πτωχία*, not merely *πενία*; cf. Mc. xii. 42, note) of the Apostolic Churches, even in so rich a city as Smyrna, is remarkable; it may have been due partly to the fact that the converts were drawn chiefly from the poorer classes (Jac. *l. c.*, 1 Cor. i. 26), partly to the demands made upon them by their faith (cf. 2 Cor. viii. 2 *ἡ κατὰ βάθους πτωχεία αὐτῶν ἐπερίσσευσεν εἰς τὸ πλοῦτος τῆς ἁπλότητος αὐτῶν*); but also in some cases to the pillage of their property by a Jewish or pagan mob (Heb. x. 34 *τὴν ἁρπαγὴν τῶν ὑπαρχόντων ὑμῶν μετὰ χαρᾶς προσεδέξασθε*). The context suggests that the poverty of the Smyrnaean Church was at least aggravated by the last of these causes.

καὶ τὴν βλασφημίαν κτλ.] Andreas: *κατὰ κοινοῦ δὲ τὸ οἶδα καὶ τὴν βλασ-*

ἐκ τῶν λεγόντων Ἰουδαίους εἶναι ἑαυτούς, καὶ οὐκ
εἰσίν, ἀλλὰ συναγωγὴ τοῦ σατανᾶ. [10]μὴ φοβοῦ 10
ἃ μέλλεις πάσχειν. ἰδοὺ μέλλει βάλλειν ὁ διάβολος
ἐξ ὑμῶν εἰς φυλακήν, ἵνα πειρασθῆτε καὶ ἔχητε

9 εκ] om P 1 28 36 49 79 91 96 130 al arm aeth Andr pr την ℵ syrr | Ιουδαιων ℵ* (-ους ℵ$^{c.a}$) CP | σατανα]+εισιν ℵ$^{c.c}$ 10 μη ACQ 1 38 49] μηδεν ℵP min^{pl} vg syrr | πασχειν] παθειν Q min$^{fere\ 35}$ Ar | ιδου]+δη Q min^{30} Ar | βαλλειν] βαλειν Q min^{pl} Ar (βαλλειν βαλιν ℵ* βαλλειν ℵ$^{c.a}$) | εξ] αφ 130 | εχητε A 36 130 Prim] εχετε CP 1 11 12 εξετε ℵQ min^{pl} syrr vg Ar

φημίαν...φησίν, ἐπίσταμαι. The Jews at Smyrna were both numerous and aggressively hostile; see Lightfoot, *Ignatius*, i. p. 468 f., Schürer, *Geschichte*³, iii. pp. 11, 29, 34. In the martyrdom of Polycarp they took a leading part, even surpassing the heathen in their zeal, and this, it is added, was their wont: Polyc. *mart.* 13 f. μάλιστα Ἰουδαίων προθύμως, ὡς ἔθος αὐτοῖς, εἰς ταῦτα ὑπουργούντων. At present they contented themselves with blaspheming, railing at Christ and Christians (cf. Vg. "et blasphemaris ab his"), as they had done from the first days of St Paul's synagogue preaching in Asia Minor (Acts xiii. 45). Against their sharp tongues the Christians are fortified by the reflexion that these blasphemers are Jews in name only. They called themselves Jews (for the constr. see *v.* 2, note), but were not so in truth; comp. Rom. ii. 28 οὐ γὰρ ὁ ἐν τῷ φανερῷ Ἰουδαῖός ἐστιν...ἀλλ' ὁ ἐν τῷ κρυπτῷ Ἰουδαῖος, καὶ περιτομὴ καρδίας ἐν πνεύματι οὐ γράμματι, Gal. vi. 15 f. οὔτε γὰρ περιτομή τι ἔστιν οὔτε ἀκροβυστία, ἀλλὰ καινὴ κτίσις...εἰρήνη ἐπ' αὐτοὺς καὶ ἔλεος, καὶ ἐπὶ τὸν Ἰσραὴλ τοῦ θεοῦ. So far from being ἀληθῶς Ἰσραηλεῖται (Jo. i. 47), such men were a συναγωγὴ τοῦ Σατανᾶ (Jo. viii. 44 ὑμεῖς ἐκ τοῦ πατρὸς τοῦ διαβόλου ἐστέ), not a συναγωγὴ Κυρίου (Num. xvi. 3, 24, xxvi. 9, xxxi. 16). On συναγωγή in its relation to ἐκκλησία see Hort, *Ecclesia*, p. 4 ff. Ἡ συναγωγὴ τοῦ Σατανᾶ occurs again in iii. 9; comp. ii. 13 ὁ θρόνος τοῦ Σ., ii. 24 τὰ βαθέα τοῦ Σ.

The commentators refer to an inscription of the time of Hadrian which has been thought to mention Jewish renegades (*CIG* 3148 οἵ ποτε Ἰουδαῖοι, cf. Lightfoot, *Ignatius*, i. p. 470; see however Ramsay in Hastings, *D.B.* iv. p. 555 for another view of the words, and cf. *Exp.*, 1904, i. p. 324). But the 'synagogue of Satan' at Smyrna professed Judaism and perhaps sincerely, though their hostility may have been partly due to a desire to curry favour with the pagan mob or the Imperial authorities.

10. μὴ φοβοῦ ἃ μέλλεις πάσχειν κτλ.] There were worse things in store than πτωχεία or even βλασφημία; imprisonment, perhaps death might await the faithful at Smyrna. Behind the 'synagogue of Satan' was the Devil himself (ὁ διάβολος = ὁ κατήγωρ τῶν ἀδελφῶν, xii. 10 = ὁ Σατανᾶς, xii. 9, xx. 2), who by means of false charges laid before the magistrates would cast certain members of the Church (ἐξ ὑμῶν) into prison. His purpose was to try the faith of the whole body (ἵνα πειρασθῆτε): cf. Lc. xxii. 31 ὁ Σατανᾶς ἐξῃτήσατο ὑμᾶς τοῦ σινιάσαι ὡς τὸν σῖτον. That its Jewish and pagan adversaries were prompted by Satan was the firm belief of the early Church; cf. *e.g.* Polyc. *mart.* 2 πολλὰ γὰρ ἐμηχανᾶτο κατ' αὐτῶν ὁ διάβολος, Eus. *H.E.* v. 1 ἑτέρας μηχανὰς ὁ διάβολος ἐπενόει, τὰς κατὰ τὴν εἱρκτὴν ἐν τῷ σκότει καὶ τῷ χαλεπωτάτῳ χωρίῳ συγκλείσεις κτλ.

καὶ ἔχητε θλίψιν ἡμερῶν δέκα] "And that ye may have affliction for ('during,'

θλίψιν ἡμερῶν δέκα. γίνου πιστὸς ἄχρι θανάτου,
11 καὶ δώσω σοι τὸν στέφανον τῆς ζωῆς. ¹¹ὁ ἔχων
οὖς ἀκουσάτω τί τὸ πνεῦμα λέγει ταῖς ἐκκλησίαις.
ὁ νικῶν οὐ μὴ ἀδικηθῇ ἐκ τοῦ θανάτου τοῦ δευτέρου.

10 ημερας Q min$^{\text{fere 40}}$ *g* vg syrr Ar | om γινου ℵ* (hab ℵ$^{\text{c.a}}$) 11 ους] *aures* vg$^{\text{codd nonn}}$ Prim | om του δευτερου 130

the temporal gen., see Blass, *Gr.* p. 109) ten days." A further disclosure of Satan's plans; it was his purpose to prolong the persecution if the faithful did not yield at once. This point is missed by ἕξετε, doubtless a correction made in the interests of the sense. Δέκα is perhaps suggested by Dan. i. 14 ἐπείρασεν αὐτοὺς δέκα ἡμέρας; cf. Gen. xxiv. 55, Num. xi. 19, xiv. 22, Job xix. 3. Beatus thinks of the 'ten persecutions,' but it is unnecessary to seek for any historical fulfilment. Equally wide of the mark is the interpretation preferred by Bede: "totum tempus significat in quo Decalogi sunt memoriae mandata." The number ten is probably chosen because, while it is sufficient to suggest continued suffering, it points to an approaching end. Ten days of suffering and suspense might seem an eternity while they lasted, yet in the retrospect they would be but a moment (2 Cor. iv. 17 τὸ παραύτικα ἐλαφρὸν τῆς θλίψεως: cf. Arethas: ἐφήμερος ἡ ἐπιφορά, καὶ ὅσον εἰ καὶ ἡμερῶν δέκα ἐξισουμένη). The trial might be prolonged, but it had a limit known to God.

γίνου πιστὸς ἄχρι θανάτου κτλ.] 'Prove thyself loyal and true, to the extent of being ready to die for My sake.' Γίνου π., cf. iii. 2 γίνου γρηγορῶν, Jo. xx. 27 μὴ γίνου ἄπιστος ἀλλὰ πιστός. Here πιστός is 'trustworthy' rather than 'believing,' as in Mt. xxv. 21, 23, Lc. xvi. 10 f., Apoc. ii. 13, iii. 14. Ἄχρι θανάτου hints that the supreme trial of martyrdom may follow; comp. Phil. ii. 8 γενόμενος ὑπήκοος μέχρι θ., and contrast Heb. xii. 4 οὔπω μέχρις αἵματος ἀντικατέστητε. Ἄχρι occurs in this book eleven times, μέχρι not once; the other Johannine writings, as it happens, have neither, but in the rest of the N.T. the proportion is a little over 2 to 1.

καὶ δώσω σοι τὸν στέφανον τῆς ζωῆς] 'And so,' the consecutive καί which is "specially found after imperatives" (Blass, *Gr.* p. 262). Ζωῆς stands in sharp contrast with θανάτου, and τ. στέφανον comes naturally after the prophecy of a coming struggle. The exact phrase ὁ στέφανος τ. ζ. occurs in the very similar passage, Jac. i. 12 μακάριος ἀνὴρ ὃς ὑπομένει πειρασμόν, ὅτι δόκιμος γενόμενος λήμψεται τὸν στ. τ. ζ., ὃν ἐπηγγείλατο τοῖς ἀγαπῶσιν αὐτόν: elsewhere we have ὁ στ. τῆς ἐλπίδος (Isa. xxviii. 5), τῆς καυχήσεως (Ez. xvi. 12, xxiii. 42, 1 Th. ii. 19), τῆς δικαιοσύνης (2 Tim. iv. 8), τῆς δόξης (1 Pet. v. 4), τῆς ἀφθαρσίας (Polyc. *mart.* 17, 19, Eus. *H.E.* v. 1). So familiar a metaphor need not have been suggested by local circumstances, yet it is noteworthy that Smyrna was famous for its games (Paus. vi. 14. 3, cited in *Enc. Bibl.*, 4662) in which the prize was a garland. There may be a reference to this, or again, as Ramsay thinks (Hastings, *D.B.* iv. p. 555 ff.) the writer may have in his mind the garlands worn in the service of the pagan temples. In any case the στέφανος is not a royal diadem, but an emblem of festivity: cf. Mc. xv. 17, note. Τῆς ζωῆς is epexegetical: the crown consists of life, so that the promise is practically equivalent to that of *v.* 7, though it is presented under another aspect.

11. ὁ νικῶν οὐ μὴ ἀδικηθῇ κτλ.] The special promise of the second message, appropriate to a Church which

[12] Καὶ τῷ ἀγγέλῳ τῆς ἐν Περγάμῳ ἐκκλησίας 12
γράψον Τάδε λέγει ὁ ἔχων τὴν ῥομφαίαν τὴν
δίστομον τὴν ὀξεῖαν. [13] οἶδα ποῦ κατοικεῖς, ὅπου 13

12 της] τω syr^{gw} | εν Περγαμω] Περγαμου vg syr^{gw} Or^{int} Prim al   13 που κατοικεις] pr τα εργα σου και Q min$^{fere\ omn}$ syr arm Andr Ar

may presently be called to martyrdom. He who conquers by proving himself faithful unto death shall possess immunity from the second death. Ὁ δεύτερος θάνατος occurs again in *c.* xx. 6, 14, xxi. 8, where it is defined as ἡ λίμνη τοῦ πυρός; see notes *ad l.* The conception is partly anticipated in Dan. xii. 3 and Jo. v. 29, and yet more distinctly by Philo, *de praem. et poen.* ii. 419 θανάτου γὰρ διττὸν εἶδος, τὸ μὲν κατὰ τὸ τεθνάναι...τὸ δὲ μετὰ τὸ ἀποθνήσκειν, ὃ δὴ κακὸν πάντως. But the exact expression was probably current in Jewish circles, for it occurs frequently in the Targums; cf. e.g. *Targ. Hieros.* on Deut. xxxiii. 6 "vivat Reuben in hoc saeculo et non moriatur morte secunda"; other exx. may be seen in Wetstein. Οὐ μὴ ἀδικηθῇ, 'shall in no wise be hurt'; see Blass, *Gr.* p. 209 f. For ἀδικεῖν in this sense see Isa. x. 20, Apoc. vi. 6, vii. 2 f., ix. 4, 10, 19, xi. 5 bis. The attempt to retain in these contexts the etymological meaning of ἀδικεῖν (Benson, *Apocalypse*, pp. xvi. f., 73 *n.*) cannot be regarded as successful; in usage ἀδικεῖν, like our 'injure,' has acquired a weaker sense and is nearly a synonym of βλάπτειν (cf. Thuc. ii. 71, Xen. *de re equ.* vi. 3).

12—17. THE MESSAGE TO THE ANGEL OF THE CHURCH IN PERGAMUM.

12. τῆς ἐν Περγάμῳ] After leaving Smyrna the road from Ephesus followed the coast for about 40 miles and then struck N.E. up the valley of the Caicus, for a further distance of 15 miles, when it reached Pergamum. Pergamum in Mysia, on the Caicus (ἡ Πέργαμος in Xenophon, Pausanias and Dion Cassius, but τὸ Πέργαμον in Strabo and Polybius and most other writers and in the inscriptions; the termination is left uncertain in Apoc. i. 11, ii. 12), now Bergama, the capital of the Attalid Kingdom (B.C. 241—133), held a similar position in Roman Asia (Plin. *H. N.* v. 30 "longe clarissimum Asiae") until its place was taken by Ephesus. If Pergamum had no Artemision, it was richer in temples and cults than Ephesus. Zeus Soter, Athena Polias, Dionysos, Asklepios were the chief local deities; the temple of Athena crowned the steep hill of the Acropolis, and beneath it on the height was a great altar of Zeus. Beside these, the city possessed as early as A.D. 29 a temple dedicated to Rome and Augustus (Tac. *ann.* iii. 37); a second temple was erected in the time of Trajan, when Pergamum acquired the title of δὶς νεωκόρος. At so strong a centre of paganism the Church was confronted with unusual difficulties, and to these the message to Pergamum refers (*v.* 13 f.).

Τάδε λέγει ὁ ἔχων τὴν ῥομφαίαν: the ῥομφαία of *c.* i. 16, where see note. To what use it is to be put at Pergamum appears below, *v.* 16.

13. οἶδα ποῦ κατοικεῖς κτλ.] The special point in the life of the Church at Pergamum which the Lord singles out for notice. She resided in a city which was also Satan's residence (ὅπου ὁ Σατανᾶς κατοικεῖ), nay more, where he had set his throne. Θρόνος in the N.T. is always the seat of office or chair of state, whether of a Judge (Mt. xix. 28), or a King (Lc. i. 32, 52), or of God or Christ (Mt. v. 34, xxv. 31); in the Apoc. the word occurs 45 times in this sense. At Pergamum Satan was enthroned and held his court.

ὁ θρόνος τοῦ σατανᾶ· καὶ κρατεῖς τὸ ὄνομά μου, καὶ οὐκ ἠρνήσω τὴν πίστιν μου καὶ ἐν ταῖς ἡμέραις

13 *μου* 1°] *σου* ℵ* (*μ.* ℵ$^{c.c}$) | om *και* 3° ℵPQ min$^{fere\ 30}$ vg^{dem} arm aeth Prim Andr Ar (hab AC 91 vg^{rell} me) | *ημεραις*] + *αις* Q 6 14 29 31 36 38 41 47 51 82 92^{txt} al$^{fere\ 25}$ vg^{dem} syr aeth + *εν αις* ℵ^{c} (*εν ταις* ℵ*) P (1) 7 10 12^{fort} 16 17 28 34 35 36 37 45^{fort} 46^{fort} 79 80 81 87 91 96 121 130 161 *g* vg$^{am\ fu\ harl\ tol\ al}$ arm

The question arises what there was at Pergamum to gain for it this character. The Nicolaitans were there, but they were also at Ephesus; the Jews, who at Smyrna formed a 'synagogue of Satan,' are not mentioned in the Pergamene message. It remains to seek a justification of the phrase in some peculiarly dangerous form of pagan worship. Pergamum was the chief seat in Asia of the worship of Asklepios (cf. Philostratus, *Vit. Apollon.* iv. 34 ἡ Ἀσία εἰς τὸ Πέργαμον...ξυνεφοίτα, Herodian, iv. 4. 8 ἠπείχθη εἰς Π. τῆς Ἀσίας χρήσασθαι βουλόμενος θεραπείας τοῦ Ἀσκληπίου, Mart. ix. 1 "Aesculapius Pergamensis deus": according to Galen a common form of oath was μὰ τὸν ἐν Περγάμῳ Ἀσκλήπιον), and the serpent which was the symbol of the god (Paus. *Cor.* 27 κάθηται δ' ἐπὶ θρόνου βακτηρίαν κρατῶν τήν τε ἑτέραν τῶν χειρῶν ὑπὲρ κεφαλῆς ἔχει τοῦ δράκοντος) is in this book (xii. 9) the symbol of Satan. But attractive as this explanation is, it does not altogether satisfy; the Aesculapian cult, with its therapeutic aims, could scarcely have presented special difficulties to the Christian brotherhood. It is better to find in 'Satan's throne' an allusion to the rampant paganism of Pergamum (Arethas: ὡς κατείδωλον οὖσαν ὑπὲρ τὴν Ἀσίαν πᾶσαν), symbolized by the great altar which seemed to dominate the place from its platform cut in the Acropolis rock, but chiefly perhaps to the new Caesar-worship in which Pergamum was preeminent and which above all other pagan rites menaced the existence of the Church. The insidious plea Τί κακόν ἐστιν εἰπεῖν 'Κύριος Καῖσαρ,' καὶ ἐπιθεῖναι καὶ τὰ τούτοις ἀκόλουθα, καὶ διασώζεσθαι (*mart. Polyc.* 8), must have appealed to many Christians who would have stood firm against the grosser idolatries of heathenism. If the worship of the Emperor is in view, ὁ θρόνος τοῦ Σατανᾶ may be an occult reference to the agents of this false Imperialism, as συναγωγὴ τ. Σ. to the hostile Jews.

For ποῦ = ὅπου see WM. p. 640. Κατοικεῖς, κατοικεῖ, point to settled residence. There was no possibility of escaping from the situation; the local Church could not migrate in a body, and Satan would not quit his vantage ground. From another point of view even the residents in any place are, from the Christian standpoint, 'strangers and pilgrims,' and such words as παροικεῖν, πάροικος, παρεπίδημος are usually preferred in describing the relations of the Church to the locality where she is placed; see 1 Pet. i. 1 (with Hort's note), 17; ii. 11, Heb. xi. 9, and the opening words of Clem. R. *Cor.* cited in the note to *v.* 1.

καὶ κρατεῖς τὸ ὄνομά μου κτλ.] The Church in Pergamum maintained her Κύριος Ἰησοῦς (1 Cor. xii. 3), and refused to say Κύριος Καῖσαρ and to revile her Master; cf. *mart. Polyc.* 9. For κρατεῖν see ii. 1 note, and for οὐκ ἀρνεῖσθαι cf. Jo. i. 20 ὡμολόγησεν καὶ οὐκ ἠρνήσατο. Τὴν πίστιν μου, 'thy faith in Me'; μου is the gen. of the object as in Mc. xi. 22 ἔχετε πίστιν θεοῦ, Apoc. xiv. 12 οἱ τηροῦντες...τὴν πίστιν Ἰησοῦ.

Καὶ ἐν ταῖς ἡμέραις Ἀντίπα: 'even in the days of Antipas.' The reading Ἀντείπας (ἀντεῖπας) must be ascribed to itacism, while the proposal to treat

†Ἀντίπα†, ὁ μάρτυς μου ὁ πιστός μου, ὃς ἀπεκτάνθη

13 Αντιπας ℵ*CPQ min[pl] vg Prim Αντειπας (αντ.) ℵ[c.c]A 2 9 13 19 23 41 42 50[corr] 97 al ut vid me syrr + και 68 87 syr[gw] | μου 3°] om ℵPQ min[pl] vg me syr[gw] aeth Prim Andr Ar + οτι πας μαρτυς μου πιστος (152) syr[gw] | om ος 6 31 87 vg[dem] syr[gw] aeth

Ἀντίπας as a *nom de plume* (ἀντί, πᾶς, cf. ἀντίχριστος, a primitive *Athanasius contra mundum*) can scarcely be taken seriously. The name is an abbreviated form of Ἀντίπατρος, as Κλεόπας of Κλεόπατρος, and occurs frequently in Josephus (e.g. *antt.* xix. 1. 3 οὗτος τοινῦν ὁ Ἀντίπατρος Ἀντίπας τὸ πρῶτον ἐκαλεῖτο). There is little to be gleaned about this primitive martyr from post-canonical writings. Tertullian's allusion to him (*Scorp.* 12 "de Antipa fidelissimo martyre, interfecto in habitatione Satanae") shews no independent knowledge. Andreas had read his 'acts' (οὗπερ ἀνέγνων τὸ μαρτύριον) and there are acts under his name printed by the Bollandists (April 11), according to which he was burnt to death in a brazen bull in the reign of Domitian. But the date at least is probably wrong, for ἐν ταῖς ἡμ. Ἀ. throws the time of the martyrdom back some years before the writing of the Apocalypse; cf. Lc. i. 5, Acts v. 37. Other martyrs connected with Pergamum in the first two centuries were Carpus, Papylus, and Agathonice, mentioned by Eusebius (*H.E.* iv. 15); Attalus, the 'pillar and ground' of the persecuted Viennese, was Περγαμηνὸς τῷ γένει (*H.E.* v. 1). Yet, as Ramsay observes (Hastings, *D.B.* iii. 75 f.), it is not certain that Antipas was a member of the Pergamene Church; he suffered at Pergamum, but may have been brought thither from one of the smaller towns.

Ἀντίπας is indeclinable, if we accept the reading of the best MSS. WH., however (*Notes*, p. 137), are disposed to favour Lachmann's conjecture that the final c arose from an accidental doubling of the following o, while Nestle (*Text. Crit.* p. 331) thinks that Ἀντίπα was conformed to ὁ μάρτυς. The anomaly, however it may have arisen, has misled the scribes, who have sought to save the grammar by inserting αἷς or omitting ὅς: see *app. crit.* For ὁ μάρτυς μου cf. Acts i. 8 ἔσεσθέ μου μάρτυρες, xxii. 20 ἐξεχύννετο τὸ αἷμα Στεφάνου τοῦ μάρτυρός σου, Apoc. xvii. 6 μεθύουσαν...ἐκ τοῦ αἵματος τῶν μαρτύρων Ἰησοῦ. It is tempting to translate μάρτυς by 'martyr' in the last two passages, and even R.V. yields to the temptation in Apoc. *l. c.*, though it is content to call Stephen and Antipas 'witnesses.' But it may be doubted whether the word had acquired a technical sense at the end of the first century; Clem. *Cor.* 5 μαρτυρήσας ἐπορεύθη εἰς τὸν ὀφειλόμενον τόπον τῆς δόξης is not decisive. Even in the second half of the second century the title could be given to confessors at Lyons and Vienne, though it is significant that they disclaimed it as due only to the Lord (Apoc. i. 5) and to those who had died for Him. By that time the technical sense had nearly established itself (see Lightfoot's note on Clem. *l.c.*, and Benson's *Cyprian*, p. 90 f.); but in the N.T. this stage has not been reached, though the course of events was leading up to it. The Lord gives Antipas His own title, ὁ μάρτυς ὁ πιστός (i. 5, iii. 14), qualifying it by a double μου, 'my witness, my faithful one'; Antipas bore witness to Christ, was loyal to Christ even unto death, as Christ to the Father (1 Tim. vi. 13 τοῦ μαρτυρήσαντος ἐπὶ Ποντίου Πειλάτου τὴν καλὴν ὁμολογίαν). Ἀπεκτάνθη, see Mc. viii. 31 note; in Attic Greek ἀπέθανεν would have been preferred, cf. Blass, *Gr.* pp. 44, 55. Παρ' ὑμῖν...κατοικεῖ recalls at the end of the sentence the solemn fact with which it began: the home of this Church was also the residence of Satan.

14 παρ' ὑμῖν, ὅπου ὁ σατανᾶς κατοικεῖ. [14]ἀλλ' ἔχω
κατὰ σοῦ ὀλίγα, ὅτι ἔχεις ἐκεῖ κρατοῦντας τὴν
διδαχὴν Βαλαάμ, ὃς ἐδίδασκεν τῷ Βαλὰκ βαλεῖν
σκάνδαλον ἐνώπιον τῶν υἱῶν Ἰσραήλ, φαγεῖν εἰδωλό-
15 θυτα καὶ πορνεῦσαι. [15]οὕτως ἔχεις καὶ σὺ κρατοῦντας

13 *υμων* 95 syr^gw^ | om *οπου...κατοικει* 38 syr^gw^ 14 *αλλα* Q min^plq 10^ Ar | om *κατα σου* ℵ* (hab ℵ^c.a^) | om *οτι* C 130 vg^am fu harl* al^ me syr Prim | *εδιδαξε* Q min^plq 44^ me syrr arm Or^int^ Ar | *τω Βαλακ* A(C) 11] *εν τω Βαλακ* 1 18 92^mg^ *εν τω Βαλααμ τον Βαλακ* P Andr^comm^ *Βαλαακ* Q (ita et C 95** 130) om ℵ* *τον Βαλακ* ℵ^c.a^ 95 al^pl^ | *βαλειν*] *βαλλειν* ℵ^c.a^ *βασιλει* A | *φαγειν*] pr *και* Q min^fere 30^ Ar | om *ειδωλοθυτα* vg *ειδωλοθυτον* 130

14. *ἀλλ' ἔχω κατὰ σοῦ ὀλίγα*] At Ephesus the attitude of the Church towards the Nicolaitans was matter for praise, but at Pergamum it invited censure; contrast *ἔχω κατὰ σοῦ* with *v.* 6 *τοῦτο ἔχεις*. The Church which could resist Satan in the form of the Emperor-cult was not equally proof against an insidious heresy.

ὅτι ἔχεις ἐκεῖ κρατοῦντας τὴν διδαχὴν Βαλαάμ, κτλ.] A party in the Church at Pergamum (*ἐκεῖ* = *παρ' ὑμῖν*) taught as Balaam had done. Balaam made it his aim to teach (*ἐδίδασκεν*) Balak how to beguile Israel into the double sin of idolatry and fornication. The reference is to Num. xxxi. 16, where the sin of Peor is traced to Balaam's suggestion (cf. Philo, *vit. Moys.* i. 54, Jos. *antt.* ix. 6. 6, Origen *in Num. hom.* xx.). Modern O.T. scholars (e.g. Driver, *Introd.* p. 62 f., F. H. Woods in Hastings, *D.B.* i. 233) point out that the story of Balaam blends two accounts, Num. xxii. 1—xxv. 5 belonging to JE, while Num. xxv. 6 ff. is from P; in the former Balaam after blessing Israel returns to Pethor (Num. xxiv. 25), in the latter he is the author of Balak's later policy and eventually is slain by Israel in battle (Num. xxxi. 8, cf. Josh. xiii. 22). Josephus *l.c.* reconciles the two stories by supposing that Balaam on reaching the Euphrates sent for Balak and imparted his scheme; some such addition to the history was doubtless in the mind of the writer of the Apoc. There is an interesting parallel in the stratagem suggested by Achior in Judith v. 20, xi. 11 ff.

The construction *ἐδίδ. τῷ Βαλάκ* is perhaps a Hebraism (cf. Job xxi. 22 הַלְאֵל יְלַמֶּד דָּעַת), but more probably a colloquialism; see WM. p. 279. *Βαλεῖν σκάνδαλον*, cf. *τιθέναι σκ.* in Ps. xlix. (l.) 20, Judith v. 1, Hos. iv. 17, Rom. xiv. 13. A *σκάνδαλον* (Att. *σκανδάληθρον*) is any object that is apt to trip up one who is walking carelessly; see Hort on 1 Pet. ii. 8, and Carr, *Hor. Bibl.*, p. 58 ff. The women of Moab were deliberately thrown in the way of unsuspecting Israel, in the hope of bringing about the downfall of the latter. The order *φαγεῖν...καὶ πορνεῦσαι* is the opposite of that in Num. xxv. 1 ff., which is followed below, *v.* 20; but it doubtless answers to the experience of the Church at Pergamum, where the mixed company at pagan feasts was the occasion of the greater evil. *Εἰδωλόθυτον*, see 4 Macc. v. 2, Acts xv. 29, xxi. 25, 1 Cor. viii. 1 ff.; cf. *ἱερόθυτον* in 1 Cor. x. 28.

15. *οὕτως...ὁμοίως*] *Ἔχεις* takes up the thread of *v.* 14 (*ἔχεις ἐκεῖ κρατοῦντας κτλ.*), while *οὕτως καὶ σύ* compares the situation at Pergamum with that of Israel exposed to the wiles of Balaam; *ὁμοίως* at the end of the sentence emphasizes *οὕτως*, and keeps the parallel still in view. The general sense of *vv.* 14, 15 would have been clearer if the Apocalyptist had

τὴν διδαχὴν Νικολαϊτῶν ὁμοίως. [16]μετανόησον οὖν· 16
εἰ δὲ μή, ἔρχομαί σοι ταχύ, καὶ πολεμήσω μετ'

15 Νικολαιτων] pr των ℵP 1 7 28 38 91 al Andr Ar | ομοιως] ο μισω 1 92^{mg} arm + ο μισω P 12 13 17 vg^{cod} om aeth ομως 130 16 om ουν ℵP 1 14 28 36 49 76 91 92 96 al vg syr Prim (hab ACQ $min^{fere\,45}$ me syr^{gw} arm aeth Ar)

written: ὥσπερ γὰρ Βαλαὰμ ἐδίδασκεν ...οὕτως ἔχεις καὶ σύ, κτλ.; or ἔχεις ἐκεῖ κρατοῦντας...ἔχεις γὰρ κρατοῦντας τὴν διδαχὴν Νικολαϊτῶν.

For the Nicolaitans see note on *v.* 6. As to their teaching, it is clear that they disregarded the restriction imposed upon the Gentile Churches by the Apostolic council held at Jerusalem in 49—50 (Acts xv. 29 ἀπέχεσθαι εἰδωλοθύτων, cf. 20 ἀπ. τῶν ἀλισγημάτων τῶν εἰδώλων) with the practical result that they encouraged a return to pagan laxity of morals (cf. *v.* 6). Writing to Corinth some fifteen years after the council St Paul had occasion to argue with Christians who regarded the eating of εἰδωλόθυτα as a thing indifferent; and though he does not take his stand on the Jerusalem decree, he opposes the practice on the ground that it gave offence to weak brethren (1 Cor. viii. 4, 9 f.), and also because of the connexion which he regarded as existing between idol-worship and unclean spirits (1 Cor. x. 20 ἃ θύουσιν τὰ ἔθνη δαιμονίοις καὶ οὐ θεῷ θύουσιν, οὐ θέλω δὲ ὑμᾶς κοινωνοὺς τῶν δαιμονίων γίνεσθαι); to partake of the 'table of unclean spirits' (*ib.* 21 τραπέζης δαιμονίων) was inconsistent with participation in the Eucharist. In the face of these facts a perverse theory, originating with the Tübingen school, identifies the Nicolaitans with the followers of St Paul; cf. Renan, *Saint Paul*, p. 303 f.: "on s'habitue à désigner l'apôtre des gentils par le sobriquet de Nicolas...ses disciples du même coup furent appelés nicolaïtes"; and see van Manen's art. *Nicolaitans* in *Enc. Bibl.* 3410 f. It would be nearer to the truth to say that they were the spiritual descendants of the libertines who perverted the Pauline doctrine and against whom St Paul strongly protests. In the next century these views were embraced by certain Gnostic teachers; see Justin, *dial.* 35 χριστιανοὺς ἑαυτοὺς λέγουσιν...καὶ ἀνόμοις καὶ ἀθέοις τελεταῖς κοινωνοῦσιν· καὶ εἰσὶν αὐτῶν οἱ μέν τινες καλούμενοι Μαρκιανοί, οἱ δὲ Οὐαλεντινιανοί κτλ. Iren. i. 6. 3 καὶ γὰρ εἰδωλόθυτα ἀδιαφόρως ἐσθίουσι, μηδὲ μολύνεσθαι ὑπ' αὐτῶν ἡγούμενοι...οἱ δὲ καὶ ταῖς τῆς σαρκὸς ἡδοναῖς κατακόρως δουλεύοντες κτλ. The Nicolaitans of the next century were of this class, cf. Iren. iii. 1. 3 "indiscrete vivunt"; Hippol. *philos.* vii. 36 Νικόλαος...ἐδίδασκεν ἀδιαφορίαν βίου τε καὶ βρώσεως; Tert. *adv. Marc.* i. 29 "aliqui Nicolaitae assertores libidinis atque luxuriae." According to Clement Alex. *strom.* iii. 4 they quoted a saying of their founder, ὅτι παραχρήσασθαι τῇ σαρκὶ δεῖ, and acted upon it: ἐκπορνεύουσιν ἀναίδην οἱ τὴν αἵρεσιν αὐτοῦ μετιόντες. It is noteworthy that the party was strong at Ephesus and Pergamum; they had established themselves at the two most important centres in Asia, the 'metropolis,' and the ancient and perhaps still official capital.

16. μετανόησον οὖν] There was occasion not only for vigilance, but for an act of repentance (on μετανόησον see *v.* 5). The Church was already compromised by undue tolerance of the Nicolaitans; she had not purged herself of complicity with them as the Church at Ephesus had done; (contrast *v.* 6 μισεῖς with *v.* 15 ἔχεις).

εἰ δὲ μή, ἔρχομαί σοι ταχὺ κτλ.] For εἰ δὲ μή (= ἐὰν δὲ μὴ μετανοήσῃ) see *v.* 5 note; ταχύ is now added, for the matter would brook no delay. Yet

17 αὐτῶν ἐν τῇ ῥομφαίᾳ τοῦ στόματός μου. [17]ὁ ἔχων
οὖς ἀκουσάτω τί τὸ πνεῦμα λέγει ταῖς ἐκκλησίαις.
τῷ νικῶντι δώσω αὐτῷ τοῦ μάννα τοῦ κεκρυμμένου,

17 ους] *aures* vg^{dem} Amb Prim | νικουντι AC | αυτω (om ℵ 92 *g* vg^{cle} syr^{gw})] + (του) φαγειν P 1 7 (13 14) 28 (35) 49 79 (87) 91 92^{mg} 96 al arm syrr | του μαννα AC min$^{fere\ 32}$ Ar] εκ του μαννα ℵ 36 39 me syrr arm Prim (*de manna*) το μ. Q Vict Amb απο του μαννα 1 7 28 79 96 al απο του ξυλου P

the Lord does not say πολεμήσω μετὰ σοῦ, but μετ᾽ αὐτῶν, i.e. μετὰ τῶν κρατούντων τὴν διδαχὴν τῶν Νικολαϊτῶν; if the Church had tolerated the Nicolaitans, and some of her members had listened to their teaching, yet she had not as a whole identified herself with the party; cf. Andreas: ἐν τῇ ἀπειλῇ δὲ ἡ φιλανθρωπία· οὐ γὰρ 'μετὰ σοῦ' φησιν, ἀλλὰ 'μετ᾽ ἐκείνων,' τῶν νοσούντων ἀνίατα. Πολεμεῖν μετά τινος, frequent in the LXX., is used in the N.T. only by the Apocalyptist (ii. 16, xii. 7, xiii. 4, xvii. 14), and the verb itself outside the Apoc. only in Jac. iv. 2. The glorified Christ is in this book a Warrior, who fights with the sharp sword of the word; cf. i. 16, xix. 13 ff., and see Eph. vi. 17, Heb. iv. 12. The idea of a Divine Warrior, which appears first in the Song of Miriam (Exod. xv. 3 יְהוָה אִישׁ מִלְחָמָה, equivocally rendered by the LXX. Κύριος συντρίβων πολέμους) is associated with the Logos in Sap. xviii. 15 ὁ παντοδύναμός σου λόγος ἀπ᾽ οὐρανοῦ ἐκ θρόνων βασιλείων ἀπότομος πολεμιστὴς ...ἥλατο. The ἀποτομία of the Divine Word is directed especially against those who "turn the grace of God into lasciviousness," as the Nicolaitans did. Possibly, as in *v.* 14, there is an allusion to the story of Balaam (Num. xxii. 23, xxxi. 8).

17. τῷ νικῶντι δώσω αὐτῷ τοῦ μάννα κτλ.] On τῷ νικ. δ. αὐτῷ see *v.* 7, note. Τοῦ μάννα is the partitive genitive, WM. p. 247; Blass, against the documentary evidence, discounts this solitary instance of the gen. after φαγεῖν as "not authentic" (*Gr.* p. 100, note 3). Μάννα (מָן, Aram. מַנָּא, LXX. μάν in Exod. xvi. 31 ff., μάννα elsewhere) has passed from the LXX. into the N.T. (Jo. vi. 31, 49, Heb. ix. 4) and Josephus (*antt.* iii. i. 6). Τοῦ κεκρυμμένου refers no doubt to the golden pot "laid up before God" (Exod. xvi. 23), i.e. in the Ark (Heb. ix. 4); the Ark itself was believed to have been hidden by Jeremiah in a place where it would not be discovered until Israel was restored (2 Macc. ii. 5 ff.; cf. the Rabbinical traditions in Abarbanel on 1 Sam. iv. 4 "haec arca futuro tempore adveniente Messia nostro manifestabitur"; Tanchuma, 83. 2 "Elias Israelitis restituit...urnam mannae"; other passages may be seen in Wetstein). The Apoc. of Baruch has the story in *c.* vi. 7 ff. and adds in xxix. 8 (ed. Charles): "at that self-same time [when the Messiah is revealed] the treasury of manna will again descend from on high, and they will eat of it in those years"; cf. *Orac. Sibyll.* vii. 148 f. κλήματα δ᾽ οὐκ ἔσται οὐδὲ στάχυς, ἀλλ᾽ ἅμα πάντες | μάννην τὴν δροσερὴν λευκοῖσιν ὀδοῦσι φάγονται. As for the interpretation of the promise, its full meaning is hardly covered by St Paul's θεοῦ σοφία ἐν μυστηρίῳ, ἡ ἀποκεκρυμμένη (1 Cor. ii. 7), or by Origen's "intellectus verbi Dei subtilis et dulcis" (*hom.* on Exod. ix. 4); rather by τὸ μάννα τὸ κεκρυμμένον must be understood the life-sustaining power of the Sacred Humanity now "hid with Christ in God" (Col. iii. 3), of which the faithful find a foretaste in the Eucharist but which can be fully known only to the conqueror (Jo. vi. 31 f., 54 ff.). Victorinus: "*manna absconditum* immortalitas est." Pri-

καὶ δώσω αὐτῷ ψῆφον λευκήν, καὶ ἐπὶ τὴν ψῆφον ὄνομα καινὸν γεγραμμένον, ὃ οὐδεὶς οἶδεν εἰ μὴ ὁ λαμβάνων.

17 om *δωσω αυτω* 2° ℵ 38 | *ο ουδεις οιδεν*] om *ο* ℵ* (hab ℵ[c.a])

masius, followed by Bede: "panis invisibilis qui de caelo descendit." Arethas points out the fitness of this reference to the heavenly food at the end of a message which condemns participation in heathen feasts: *τῷ νικῶντι δοθῆναι φαγεῖν τοῦ μάννα ἀντὶ τῆς ἀκαθάρτου βρώσεως* [sc. *τῶν εἰδωλοθύτων*] *ὑπέσχετο.*

καὶ δώσω αὐτῷ ψῆφον λευκήν κτλ.] *Ψῆφος* is a rare word in Biblical Greek (LXX.[6], N.T.[3]), where it is used to denote (1) a piece of rock (צֹר. Exod. iv. 25; חָצָץ, Lam. iii. 16, cf. Sir. xviii. 10); (2) a counter or voting pebble, *calculus* (4 Regn. xii. 4(5) A, Eccl. vii. 26, 4 Macc. xv. 26, Acts xxvi. 10). Here it is to be noted that the *ψῆφος* is white, and that it bears a mystical name which only the possessor can read. Few of the solutions hitherto proposed satisfy these conditions. The Rabbinical tradition that precious stones fell with the manna (*Joma* 8) may have suggested the collocation of the manna and the *ψῆφος*, but it carries us no further. Züllig's theory, adopted by Trench, that there is an allusion to the Urim (Exod. xxviii. 30), supposed to have been a diamond engraved with the Tetragrammaton, is too purely conjectural to be satisfactory, even if it were not open to other objections. If we turn to the Greek surroundings of the Asiatic Churches, which must not be excluded, as Trench maintains, from the field of Apocalyptic hermeneutics, there is a larger choice of interpretations. *Ψῆφος* may refer to the ballot thrown into the voting urn (Ovid, *met.* xv. 41 "mos erat antiquis niveis atrisque lapillis, | his damnare reos, illis absolvere culpa") or to the counters used for calculation (cf. Apoc. xiii. 18 *ψηφισάτω τὸν ἀριθμόν*); or the *ψῆφος* *λευκή* might be the symbol of a good time (Plin. *ep.* vi. 4. 3 "o diem notandum candidissimo calculo"), or of victory (Andreas, *τουτέστι νικῶσαν*; Arethas, *τὴν ἀπὸ τῶν ἐν τοῖς θεάτροις καὶ τοῖς σταδίοις ἀγωνιζομένων γνώριμον οὖσαν, τοῖς νικῶσι παρεχομένην*). Or there may be a reference to the tickets which were sometimes distributed to the populace and entitled the holders to free entertainment or amusement (cf. Xiphilin. *epit.* 228 *σφαίρια γὰρ ξύλινα μικρὰ ἄνωθεν εἰς τὸ θέατρον ἐρρίπτει σύμβολον ἔχοντα τὸ μὲν ἐδωδίμου τινός...ἁρπάσαντάς τινας ἔδει πρὸς τοὺς δοτῆρας αὐτῶν ἀπενεγκεῖν καὶ λαβεῖν τὸ ἐπιγεγραμμένον*), or to the *tessera frumentaria* or the *t. hospitalis* of Roman life (cf. Plaut. *Poen.* v. 1. 8). Each of these explanations, however, leaves something to be desired; either the *ψῆφος* is not inscribed or it is not necessarily white. Prof. Ramsay (Hastings, *D.B.* iii. 751) supposes a contrast with the parchment which took its name (*charta Pergamena*) from the city, and interprets: "the name is written not on white parchment such as Pergamum boasts of, but on an imperishable white *tessera*." "The white stone," he writes elsewhere (*Exp.*, 1904, i. p. 411) "was, doubtless, a *tessera*." But the *tessera* does not suggest imperishableness. Possibly *ψῆφος λευκή* may refer to the engraved stones which were employed for magical purposes and bore mystic names; see King, *Engraved Gems*, p. 97 ff.: *Gnostics and their remains*, passim. Magic in all its forms entered largely into the life of the great cities of Asia; for its prevalence at Ephesus see Acts xix. 19. The Divine magic which inscribes on the human character and life the Name of God and of

18 [18]Καὶ τῷ ἀγγέλῳ τῷ ἐν Θυατείροις ἐκκλησίας

18 τω 2° A syrr Prim] της ℵPQ min[omn vid] om C | Θυατειροις (-τεροις AC -τηροις P)] Θυατηρα P 79 Θυατειρη 1 7 8 9 16 19 23 al Θυατιρη (-ρα) Q *g* vg Prim (*Thyatirae*) me | om εκκλησιας A

Christ is placed in contrast with the poor imitations that enthralled pagan society.

It may be that the precise reference will be ascertained in the course of explorations which are still in progress in Asia Minor and in particular at Pergamum. Meanwhile the general sense is fairly clear. The white stone is the pledge of the Divine favour which carries with it such intimate knowledge of God and of Christ as only the possessor can comprehend: cf. iii. 12 ὁ νικῶν...γράψω ἐπ' αὐτὸν τὸ ὄνομα τοῦ θεοῦ μου...καὶ τὸ ὄνομά μου τὸ καινόν, and on this knowledge as the gift of Christ see Mt. xi. 27. The alternative is to regard the ὄνομα καινόν as the symbol of the new life and relations into which moral victory transports the conqueror, an interpretation supported by Isa. lxii. 2 καλέσει σε τὸ ὄνομα τὸ καινὸν ὃ ὁ κύριος ὀνομάσει αὐτό, lxv. 15 τοῖς δὲ δουλεύουσί μοι κληθήσεται ὄνομα καινόν, and suggesting a reference to the mysteries and the prevalent magical rites (Ramsay, *Exp.*, 1904, i. p. 414; see also his reference to a σύνθημα received by Aristides of Smyrna from Asklepios, *ib.* p. 419 f.). If this view be accepted—and it is perhaps the more probable—the victorious disciple is represented as resembling in his measure the victorious Master; cf. xix. 12 ἔχων ὄνομα γεγραμμένον ὃ οὐδεὶς οἶδεν εἰ μὴ αὐτός. The 'new name' is one of a series of καινά which belong to the Church (καινὸς ἄνθρωπος, καινὴ διαθήκη, διδαχή, ἐντολή, Ἰερουσαλήμ, κτίσις, ᾠδή, καινὸς οὐρανὸς καὶ καινὴ γῆ); cf. 2 Cor. v. 17, Apoc. xxi. 5. Νέος is used in this connexion only in Heb. xii. 24; it is not the recent origin of the Gospel—its νεότης, but its καινότης, its unfailing freshness, to which attention is called. The Christian 'name,' i.e. the character or inner life which the Gospel inspires, possesses the property of eternal youth, never losing its power or its joy.

18—29. Message to the Angel of the Church in Thyatira.

18. τῷ ἐν Θυατείροις] Some 40 miles S.E. of Pergamum lay Thyatira (τὰ Θυάτειρα), a Lydian city on the borders of Mysia and sometimes claimed by the latter (Strabo, 625 βαδίζουσιν ἐπὶ Σάρδεων πόλις ἐστὶν ἐν ἀριστερᾷ Θυάτειρα...ἣν Μυσῶν ἐσχάτην τινὲς φασίν). It was founded by the Seleucidae, but since B.C. 190 it had been in the hands of the Romans, and was included in the province of Asia. Though not the equal of Ephesus, Smyrna, or Pergamum (Pliny, *H. N.* v. 33 "Thyatireni aliaeque inhonorae civitates"), Thyatira was a thriving centre of trade (Ramsay, *Exp.*, 1904, ii. 40); the inscriptions shew that the city was remarkable even among Asiatic towns for the number of its guilds (Ramsay, *Cities and Bishoprics*, i. p. 105), among which may be mentioned the ἀρτοκόποι, βαφεῖς, βυρσεῖς, ἱματευόμενοι (clothiers), κεραμεῖς, λανάριοι, λινουργοί, σκυτοτόμοι, χαλκεῖς, χαλκοτύποι; to the βαφεῖς there is a reference in Acts xvi. 14 γυνὴ ὀνόματι Λυδία (was she so called as coming from a Lydian town?), πορφυρόπωλις πόλεως Θυατείρων. There were temples of Apollo (Ramsay, *Exp.*, *l.c.* 42) and Artemis in the city, and near it the shrine of Sambathe (τὸ Σαμβαθεῖον), an Oriental (Chaldean or Persian) Sibyl; but Thyatira had no temple dedicated to the Emperors. The Church in Th. was probably small, even relatively to the population; according to Epiphanius (*haer.* li. 33) the Alogi towards the end of the second century asserted that no Church was then to be found there. Its dangers arose

γράψον Τάδε λέγει ὁ υἱὸς τοῦ θεοῦ, ὁ ἔχων τοὺς
ὀφθαλμοὺς αὐτοῦ ὡς φλόγα πυρός, καὶ οἱ πόδες
αὐτοῦ ὅμοιοι χαλκολιβάνῳ. ¹⁹οἶδά σου τὰ ἔργα καὶ 19
τὴν ἀγάπην καὶ τὴν πίστιν καὶ τὴν διακονίαν καὶ
τὴν ὑπομονήν σου, καὶ τὰ ἔργα σου τὰ ἔσχατα
πλείονα τῶν πρώτων. ²⁰ἀλλ' ἔχω κατὰ σοῦ ὅτι 20

18 om *αυτου* 1° A 36 38 syr^{gw} vg Prim | *φλογα*] *φλοξ* ℵ vg^{fu} *λαμπαδας* 130 | *χαλκω λιβανω* P^{vid} 7 *aeramento Tyrino* Quaest^{102} 19 *κ. τ. αγαπην κ. τ. πιστιν κ. τ. διακονιαν* ℵ$^{(*)(c.a)c.c}$ ACPQ 6 7 8 24 28 29 31 36 (38) 48 49 87 al$^{fere 25}$ vg$^{am\ fu\ al}$ (me) syrr arm aeth Or^{int} Prim Andr Ar] *και την πιστιν κ. τ. αγαπην κ. τ. διακονιαν* 32 51 90 95 *κ. τ. αγαπην κ. τ. διακονιαν κ. τ. πιστιν* 1 | om *σου* 2° ℵ 49 vg^{codd} Or^{int} Quaest^{102} Prim | *τα εσχατα*] pr *και* 1 20 *αλλ* ℵCP 6 7 14 28 29 31 38 80 al] *αλλα* AQ 8 13 18 19 30 33 35 36 al | *κατα σου*] + *πολυ* ℵ 12 17 36 43 81 *g* syr^{gw} + *πολλα* 28 79 80 arm Cypr Prim + *ολιγα* 1 vg$^{codd\ clo}$

from within rather than from Jews or pagans. Epiphanius (*l. c.*) represents the place as having become at a later date a stronghold of Montanism.

τάδε λέγει ὁ υἱὸς τοῦ θεοῦ κτλ.] Ὁ *υἱὸς τ. θ.* occurs here only in the Apoc., but the title is implied in i. 6, ii. 27, iii. 5, 21, xiv. 1; on its import see Dr Sanday's art. *Son of God* in Hastings' *D. B.* iv. 570 ff. In this place it adds solemnity to the quasi-human features which are recited from the vision of ch. i. For *ὁ ἔχων τοὺς ὀφθαλμοὺς...καὶ οἱ πόδες κτλ.*, see the notes on i. 14 f. This mention of the eyes that flash with righteous indignation and the feet that can stamp down the enemies of the truth prepares the reader for the severe tone of the utterance which follows.

19. *οἶδά σου τὰ ἔργα καί κτλ.*] A fuller and ampler tribute of praise than that awarded to the Church in Ephesus (*v.* 2): *τὴν ἀγάπην καὶ τὴν πίστιν καὶ τὴν διακονίαν* enumerates the motive forces of Christian activity and their most characteristic result. Love is characteristically placed first in a Johannine book, though faith is not overlooked (cf. ii. 13, xiii. 10, xiv. 12); the Pauline order is the reverse (1 Th. iii. 6, v. 8; 1 Tim. i. 14, ii. 15, vi. 11; 2 Tim. i. 13, ii. 22; Tit. ii. 2; the only exception is Philem. 5). The scribes, as the apparatus shews, have endeavoured to conform St John's order to St Paul's. What kind of 'service' is intended by *διακονία* may be gathered from Rom. xv. 25, 31, 1 Cor. xvi. 15, 2 Cor. viii. 4, ix. 1, Heb. vi. 10. The acts of service had shewn no tendency to diminish, as at Ephesus (cf. *vv.* 4, 5); on the contrary they were still increasing in number, "the last more than the first." It is noteworthy that in these addresses praise is more liberally given, if it can be given with justice, when blame is to follow; more is said of the good deeds of the Ephesians and Thyatirans than of those of the Smyrnaeans and Philadelphians, with whom no fault is found.

20. *ἀλλ' ἔχω κατὰ σοῦ ὅτι ἀφεῖς τὴν γυναῖκα Ἰεζάβελ κτλ.*] Like the Pergamenes, the Thyatiran Christians were harbouring an enemy of Christ, but their guilt seems to have been greater, since *ἀφεῖς* implies a tolerance of evil which is not suggested by *ἔχεις* (*v.* 14); and their attitude was certainly the very opposite of that of the Ephesians towards the Nicolaitans; cf. *vv.* 2, 6 *οὐ δύνῃ βαστάσαι, μισεῖς.* On the form *ἀφεῖς* see WH.², *Notes*, p. 174, W. Schm. p. 123; it occurs already in Exod. xxxii. 32 LXX. Jezebel (אִיזֶבֶל,

ἀφεῖς τὴν γυναῖκα Ἰεζάβελ, ἡ λέγουσα ἑαυτὴν προφῆτιν, καὶ διδάσκει καὶ πλανᾷ τοὺς ἐμοὺς δούλους

20 αφεις] αφηκας ℵ[c.a] 26 36 syrr arm Cypr[cd] | την γυναικα] + σου AQ min[40] syrr Ar Cypr Prim (om ℵCP 1 7 36 38 95 al vg me arm aeth Tert Quaest[102]) | η λεγουσα ℵ*AC] η λεγει Q min[45] Andr Ar την λεγουσαν ℵ[c.a]P 1 36 38 130 al | εαυτην ACP min[pl] syr[gw] Prim] αυτην ℵQ 7 16 40 69 | προφητιν (-τειαν ℵ* -την PQ 7 36 87 96*)] + ειναι ℵ*[c.a] syr[gw] | και διδασκει και πλανα ℵACPQ min[plq50] syrr (me) aeth Andr] διδασκειν και πλαναν vg Cypr Prim Ar

LXX. Ἰεζάβελ, Josephus Ἰεζαβέλη, *Isabel*), the Phoenician wife of Ahab (1 Kings xvi. 31), who sought to force upon the northern kingdom the worship of Baal and Astarte and (2 Kings ix. 22) the immoralities and magical practices connected with it, doubtless represents some person or party at Thyatira in whose doings the writer saw a resemblance to those of Ahab's wife; cf. his use of the name Balaam in *v.* 14. But while 'Balaam' is identified by the context with the Nicolaitans, there is no such clue to the meaning of 'Jezebel.' There is much to be said for Schürer's suggestion (in *Th. Abh. Weizsäcker gewidmet*, 1892), that the Thyatiran Jezebel is the Sibyl of the Σαμβαθεῖον (see *v.* 18, note). Her shrine was situated in the 'Chaldean' quarter (*CIG* 3509 πρὸ τῆς πόλεως πρὸς τῷ Σαμβαθείῳ ἐν τῷ Χαλδαίων περιβόλῳ) and she is variously described as Chaldean, Hebrew, Egyptian, Persian, and Babylonian (Paus. x. 12. 9 γυνὴ χρησμολόγος, ὄνομα δὲ αὐτῇ Σάββη...οἱ δὲ αὐτὴν Βαβυλωνίαν, ἕτεροι δὲ Σίβυλλαν καλοῦσιν Αἰγυπτίαν: cf. Suidas *s.v.* Σίβυλλα; Σ. Χαλδαία, ἡ καὶ πρός τινῶν Ἑβραία ὀνομαζομένη ἢ καὶ Περσίς). But it is difficult to believe that this person, even if of Semitic origin, could have gained admission to the Church under the guise of a Christian prophetess (ἡ λέγουσα ἑαυτὴν προφῆτιν). More probably her success as a χρησμολόγος was emulated by some female member of the Church who claimed the gift of prophecy and exercised it in the interests of the Nicolaitan party (*vv.* 14 f.); cf. Tert. *de pudic.* 19, "haereticam feminam quae quod didicerat a Nicolaitis docere susceperat." Notwithstanding St Paul's rule (1 Cor. xiv. 34 αἱ γυναῖκες ἐν ταῖς ἐκκλησίαις σιγάτωσαν, οὐ γὰρ ἐπιτρέπεται αὐταῖς λαλεῖν, 1 Tim. ii. 12 διδάσκειν δὲ γυναικὶ οὐκ ἐπιτρέπω), female prophets were not unknown in the early Church; cf. Acts xxi. 9, and the cases of Priscilla and Maximilla (Eus. *H. E.* v. 14) and Ammia (*ib.* 17); in the O.T. prophetesses are not infrequent; προφῆτις occurs in Exod. xv. 20 (Miriam), Jud. iv. 4 (Deborah), 4 Regn. xxii. 14 (Huldah), Isa. viii. 3 (Isaiah's wife); cf. Lc. ii. 36 ἦν Ἄννα προφῆτις. This Jezebel of the Thyatiran brotherhood was still teaching when the Apocalypse was written (διδάσκει), and making converts to her immoral creed; with πλανᾷ τοὺς ἐμοὺς δούλους comp. Mc. xiii. 22 ἐγερθήσονται γὰρ...ψευδοπροφῆται...πρὸς τὸ ἀποπλανᾶν εἰ δυνατὸν τοὺς ἐκλεκτούς. Πορνεῦσαι is here perhaps significantly placed before φαγεῖν εἰδωλόθυτα, as justifying the use of the name Jezebel; cf. 4 Regn. ix. 22 αἱ πορνεῖαι Ἰεζάβελ. The well supported reading τὴν γυναῖκά σου (Vg. *uxorem tuam*) was perhaps suggested by 3 Regn. xix. 1, xx. (xxi.) 5, 7, 26; the Angel of the Church is regarded as the weak Ahab who allows himself to be the tool of a new Jezebel. Grotius, who accepted this reading and believed the Angels of the Churches to be their Bishops, was driven to the strange but logical conclusion that the false prophetess was the wife of the Bishop of the Church at Thyatira.

πορνεῦσαι καὶ φαγεῖν εἰδωλόθυτα. [21]καὶ ἔδωκα αὐτῇ 21
χρόνον ἵνα μετανοήσῃ, καὶ οὐ θέλει μετανοῆσαι ἐκ
τῆς πορνείας αὐτῆς. [22]ἰδοὺ βάλλω αὐτὴν εἰς κλίνην, 22
καὶ τοὺς μοιχεύοντας μετ᾽ αὐτῆς εἰς θλίψιν μεγάλην,
ἐὰν μὴ μετανοήσουσιν ἐκ τῶν ἔργων αὐτῆς· [23]καὶ τὰ 23

21 αυτη] αυτοις arm | και ου θελει...αυτης] εκ της πορνειας αυτης και ου μετενοησεν 1 (arm) | θελει] ηθελησεν A Prim | πορνιας ℵA | αυτης] ταυτης ℵ 22 ιδου] + εγω 1 arm | βαλλω AC 1 al^pl syrr vg^am fu al Cypr Prim Andr Ar] βαλω ℵ^c.a (καλω ℵ*) PQ 38 vg^cle (*mittam*) Tert (*dabo*) | κλινην] φυλακην A καμινον (?) arm *luctum* 'alia transl' ap Prim | μετανοησουσιν ℵA] μετανοησωσιν CPQ min omn^vid | αυτης] αυτων A 1 12 36 49* 79 92^mg al vg^cle am dem harl**lipss 4, 6 me syr^gw arm aeth Cypr Prim Andr 23 om και 1° A me

21. *καὶ ἔδωκα αὐτῇ χρόνον κτλ.*] Arethas: *ἐγώ, φησίν, ὁ μὴ θέλων τὸν θάνατον τοῦ ἁμαρτωλοῦ ἀλλὰ τὴν ἐπιστροφὴν ζητῶν, ἔδωκα αὐτῇ μετανοίας καιρόν.* On this use of *ἵνα* cf. Jo. xii. 23 *ἐλήλυθεν ἡ ὥρα ἵνα δοξασθῇ*, xvi. 32. The evil had been going on for some time (cf. *v.* 13, note), not necessarily, however, at Thyatira, since the prophets were itinerant, though they might settle in a locality where the Church was willing to provide for them; see *Didache* 11 f. 'Jezebel,' who was prospering at Thyatira, had up to the present moment shewn no disposition to change her course (*οὐ θέλει μετανοῆσαι*, cf. Mt. xxiii. 37 *οὐκ ἠθελήσατε*). *Μετανοεῖν ἐκ* is the usual construction in this book (cf. ii. 22, ix. 20 f., xvi. 11); elsewhere we find *μετανοεῖν ἀπό* Jer. viii. 6, Acts viii. 22.

22. *ἰδοὺ βάλλω αὐτὴν εἰς κλίνην κτλ.*] The time for repentance having expired, judgement follows; *βάλλω* is preferred to *βαλῶ*, since the event is regarded as imminent (cf. *v.* 5, note). *Κλίνη* may be either a bed (Mt. ix. 2, 6, Mc. vii. 30), or the couch of a *triclinium*. Ramsay (*Exp.* 1901, p. 99 ff. and in Hastings' *D. B.* iv. 759), and J. H. Moulton (*Exp.* 1903, ii. p. 431) adopt the latter meaning here, supposing the writer to refer to the guild-feasts at which the *εἰδωλόθυτα* were consumed. In the latter case there is a sharp contrast between the luxurious couch where the sin was committed and the bed of pain (Ps. xl. (xli.) 4 *ἐπὶ κλίνης ὀδύνης αὐτοῦ*) which the parallelism *εἰς θλίψιν μεγάλην* obviously suggests; cf. Sap. xi. 16 *δι᾽ ὧν τις ἁμαρτάνει, διὰ τούτων κολάζεται.* *Βάλλω* does not imply violence, but merely the prostration of sickness, cf. Mt. *l.c.* *παραλυτικὸν ἐπὶ κλίνης βεβλημένον.* *Καὶ τοὺς μοιχεύοντας μετ᾽ αὐτῆς*: cf. xvii. 2, xviii. 3. *Μοιχεύοντες* suggests a reference to the charges of unfaithfulness laid against Israel by the O.T. prophets (see Hosea ii. 2 (4), Ezek. xvi. 17 f., 32). Members of the Church who were led into pagan vices by the teaching of 'Jezebel' were guilty of spiritual adultery (cf. 2 Cor. xi. 2). *Ἐὰν μὴ μετανοήσουσιν ἐκ τῶν ἔργων αὐτῆς* leaves a door of hope open still for the dupes of the false prophetess; for the fut. after *ἐὰν μή*, see Blass, *Gr.* p. 215. *Αὐτῆς* is doubtless right, for *πορνεία* and *μοιχεία* are Jezebel's works, not those of the members of Christ (Gal. v. 19, Eph. v. 3 ff.).

23. *καὶ τὰ τέκνα αὐτῆς ἀποκτενῶ ἐν θανάτῳ*] Her children, i.e. her spiritual progeny, as distinguished from those who have been misled for a time; the *σπέρμα μοιχῶν καὶ πόρνης* (Isa. lvii. 3), who inherit the parent's character and habits; contrast Gal. iv. 19 f. The children of the Thyatiran Jezebel are doomed like those of Ahab (2 Kings x. 7). *Ἀποκτενῶ ἐν θανάτῳ* is an O.T. phrase; cf. Ez.

τέκνα αὐτῆς ἀποκτενῶ ἐν θανάτῳ· καὶ γνώσονται
πᾶσαι αἱ ἐκκλησίαι ὅτι ἐγώ εἰμι ὁ ἐραυνῶν νεφροὺς
καὶ καρδίας, καὶ δώσω ὑμῖν ἑκάστῳ κατὰ τὰ ἔργα
24 ὑμῶν. [24]ὑμῖν δὲ λέγω τοῖς λοιποῖς τοῖς ἐν Θυατεί-
ροις, ὅσοι οὐκ ἔχουσιν τὴν διδαχὴν ταύτην, οἵτινες
οὐκ ἔγνωσαν τὰ βαθέα τοῦ σατανᾶ, ὡς λέγουσιν·

23 *αυτης*] *αυτων* 46 88 arm | *εραυνων* AC] *ερευνων* ℵPQ min^{omn} | *καρδιαν* syr^{gw} Prim | *τα εργα*] om *τα* C | *υμων* ℵ$^{c.a}$ ACP min^{pl} vg$^{am\ fu\ al}$ syrr aeth Prim Andr Ar] *αυτου* Q 38 vg$^{cle\ codd\ nonn}$ me arm Cypr Quaest^{102} Prim om ℵ* 24 *τοις λοιποις* (*τους εν λ.* ℵ*)] *και λοιπ.* 92^{mg} vg$^{cle\ harl\ tol}$ Quaest^{102} Ar *λοιποις* 2 3 17 18 96 al^{fort} om arm | *Θυατειροις* (-*τεροις* AC -*τηροις* P) ℵ*$^{c.c}$ ACP] *Θυατειραις* 14 92 (-*τηραις* Q) *Θυατειρη* ℵ$^{c.a}$ *Thyatirae* vg Prim | *βαθεα* ACQ min$^{fere\ 50}$ syrr Ar^{txt}] *βαθη* ℵP 1 28 36 79 Andr^{comm} Ar^{comm}

xxxiii. 27 *θανάτῳ* (בַּדֶּבֶר) *ἀποκτενῶ*. *Θάνατος* is probably 'pestilence,' as in vi. 8 f., where see note.

καὶ γνώσονται πᾶσαι αἱ ἐκκλησίαι κτλ.] Remote as Thyatira was from the greater cities of Asia, the news would spread through the province, and reach "all the churches." The phrase *γνώσονται κτλ.* is from the O.T. (cf. e.g. Exod. vii. 5 *καὶ γν. πάντες οἱ Αἰγύπτιοι ὅτι ἐγώ εἰμι Κύριος*), and the same is true of *ὁ ἐραυνῶν νεφροὺς καὶ καρδίας* (cf. Ps. vii. 10 *ἐτάζων καρδίας καὶ νεφροὺς ὁ θεός*: Jer. xvii. 10 *ἐγὼ Κύριος ἐτάζων καρδίας καὶ δοκιμάζων νεφρούς, τοῦ δοῦναι ἑκάστῳ κατὰ τὰς ὁδοὺς αὐτοῦ*: *ib.* xi. 20, xx. 12). By *νεφροί* (*renes*, 'reins,' i.e. the kidneys, כְּלָיוֹת) are denoted the movements of the will and affections, and by *καρδία* the thoughts; see Delitzsch, *Biblical Psychology*, p. 317. Both are subject to the scrutiny of Him Whose eyes are as a flame of fire (*v.* 18), the *καρδιογνώστης* of the Church; cf. Jo. xxi. 17, Acts i. 24, xv. 8. *Ἐραυνᾶν* is said to be an Alexandrian form (Blass, *Gr.* p. 21; cf. *Oxyrhynchus Papyri*, i. 67. 18, ii. 294. 9 f.); for its use in the N.T. see WH.[2], *Notes*, p. 157. *Ὁ ἐραυνῶν τὰς κ.* occurs also in Rom. viii. 27, cf. 1 Cor. ii. 10; the LXX. use *ἐτάζειν* or *ἐξετάζειν* in this connexion.

δώσω ὑμῖν ἑκάστῳ κτλ.] Not *σοί*, the Angel, i.e. the Church collectively, but *ὑμῖν*: 'to you, members of the Church, even to each individual.' Another Divine prerogative (Ps. lxi. (lxii.) 13 *σὺ ἀποδώσεις ἑκάστῳ κατὰ τὰ ἔργα αὐτοῦ*, Jer. *l. c.*), but one which was claimed by the Lord even in the days of His Flesh; see Mt. xvi. 27 *ὁ υἱὸς τοῦ ἀνθρώπου...ἀποδώσει ἑκάστῳ κατὰ τὴν πρᾶξιν αὐτοῦ*.

24. *ὑμῖν δὲ λέγω τοῖς λοιποῖς κτλ.*] 'The rest,' i.e. the members of the Church who had not been deceived by 'Jezebel,' not necessarily a minority; see 1 Thess. iv. 13, where *οἱ λ.* are the heathen world; Apoc. ix. 20, where they are two-thirds of the whole, and xix. 21, where they are contrasted with *οἱ δύο*. *Τὴν διδαχὴν ταύτην*, i.e. the teaching of the prophetess, whether professedly Nicolaitan or not; cf. *v.* 20 with *vv.* 14 f. The age was one in which *διδαχαὶ ποικίλαι καὶ ξέναι* abounded (Heb. xiii. 9). 'Doctrine' is an unfortunate rendering, suggestive of a logical system rather than a heterogeneous mass of wild speculations and loose views of life.

οἵτινες οὐκ ἔγνωσαν τὰ βαθέα του σατανᾶ] A definition of the faithful borrowed from the taunts of the Jezebelites; they were such as (cf. i. 7, note) "knew not the deep things," were lacking in the intuition which pene-

οὐ βάλλω ἐφ' ὑμᾶς ἄλλο βάρος, 25πλὴν ὃ ἔχετε 25
κρατήσατε ἄχρι οὗ ἂν ἥξω. 26καὶ ὁ νικῶν καὶ ὁ 26
τηρῶν ἄχρι τέλους τὰ ἔργα μου, δώσω αὐτῷ ἐξουσίαν

24 βαλλω ACP min$^{plq 40}$ syr Andr Ar Vict (*mitto*)] βαλω ℵQ (1) 10 14 28 33 37 47 49 82 91 92 96 vg syr^{gw} me Prim 25 αχρι ℵC 14 15 82 (αχρις PQ min^{pl} Andr Ar)] εως A 47 | αν ηξω] ανοιξω Q 2 8 13 14 29 82 93 al *miserear* aeth 26 om και 1° 7 16 38 69 98

trated below the surface of things, and reached the deeper mysteries of the Nicolaitan creed: depths, the writer adds, not of God (1 Cor. ii. 10 τὰ βάθη τοῦ θεοῦ) but of Satan (cf. ii. 9, 13, iii. 9). Ὡς λέγουσιν, sc. οἱ κρατοῦντες τὴν διδαχὴν ταύτην: "'the deep things,' as they speak" or "as they call them." The term, perhaps taken over from St Paul (see 1 Cor. *l. c.*, Rom. xi. 33, Eph. iii. 18) was used by more than one Gnostic sect in the second century; cf. Iren. ii. 21. 2 "profunda Bythi adinvenisse se dicunt"; 22. 3 "profunda Dei adinvenisse se dicentes." Hippol. *philos.* v. 6 ἐπεκάλεσαν [οἱ Νaασσηνοὶ] ἑαυτοὺς γνωστικούς, φάσκοντες μόνοι τὰ βάθη γινώσκειν. Tert. *adv. Valent.* 1 "nihil magis curant quam occultare quod praedicant (si tamen praedicant qui occultant)...si bona fide quaeras, concreto vultu, suspenso supercilio, 'Altum est' aiunt." They professed to commiserate those who remained in ignorance of their secret: Tert. *de res. carn.* 19 "vae qui non dum in hac carne est cognoverit arcana haeretica."

οὐ βάλλω ἐφ' ὑμᾶς ἄλλο βάρος] A scarcely doubtful reference to the Apostolic decree in Acts xv. 28 ἔδοξεν ...μηδὲν πλέον ἐπιτίθεσθαι ὑμῖν βάρος πλὴν τούτων τῶν ἐπάναγκες, ἀπέχεσθαι εἰδωλοθύτων...καὶ πορνείας. The rest of the prohibitions imposed in the year 49–50 (ἀπέχεσθαι...αἵματος καὶ πνικτῶν) are not reimposed. Contrast this wise concession with the exacting spirit of the Pharisees, Mt. xxiii. 4 δεσμεύουσιν δὲ φορτία βαρέα καὶ ἐπιτιθέασιν ἐπὶ τοὺς ὤμους τῶν ἀνθρώπων.

25. πλὴν ὃ ἔχετε κρατήσατε κτλ.] After οὐ βάλλω...ἄλλο βάρος the reader expects πλήν followed by the genitive (Gen. xxxix. 6, 9, Mc. xii. 32, Acts, *l. c.*); but ἄλλο is left standing by itself, and πλήν begins a new sentence as a conj. ('howbeit'). Neither ὃ ἔχετε nor κρατήσατε can well refer to burdens already being borne; rather they point back to *v.* 19 τὰ ἔργα καὶ τὴν ἀγάπην κτλ.: cf. iii. 11 κράτει ὃ ἔχεις: a single decisive effort seems to be indicated by κρατήσατε. Ἥξω may be either the future ind. or the conj. of the aor. ἦξα (cf. W. Schm. p. 109, n. 10); on the use of the fut. conj. in the N.T. see WH.[2] *Notes*, p. 179, W. Schm. p. 107.

26 f. καὶ ὁ νικῶν καὶ ὁ τηρῶν κτλ.] Primasius rightly: *et qui vicerit et qui servaverit.* He who conquers is he who keeps, but the art. is repeated to emphasize the two conditions of success. At Thyatira the battle was to be won by resolute adherence to the 'works of Christ,' i.e. to the purity of the Christian life, as opposed to the 'works of Jezebel' (*v.* 22 τὰ ἔργα αὐτῆς). Τηρεῖν (a Johannine word, Ev.[18], Ep. 1[7], Apoc.[11]) is usually followed by τὸν λόγον or τὰς ἐντολάς: τὰ ἔργα presents the same thought in a concrete form (cf. Jo. vi. 28 τὰ ἔργα τοῦ θεοῦ). 'Works' are in these addresses to the Churches constantly used as the test of character; cf. ii. 2, 5 f., 19, 22 f., iii. 1 f., 8, 15. Ἄχρι τέλους corresponds with ἄχρι οὗ ἂν ἥξω, *v.* 25; cf. Mc. xiii. 7, note.

δώσω αὐτῷ ἐξουσίαν κτλ.] The construction reverts to that of *vv.* 7, 17, as if the sentence had begun τῷ νικῶντι καὶ τῷ τηροῦντι: comp. the

27 ἐπὶ τῶν ἐθνῶν, [27] καὶ ποιμανεῖ αὐτοὺς ἐν ῥάβδῳ
σιδηρᾷ, ὡς τὰ σκεύη τὰ κεραμικὰ συντρίβεται, ὡς
28 κἀγὼ εἴληφα παρὰ τοῦ πατρός μου· [28] καὶ δώσω
29 αὐτῷ τὸν ἀστέρα τὸν πρωϊνόν. [29] ὁ ἔχων οὖς
ἀκουσάτω τί τὸ πνεῦμα λέγει ταῖς ἐκκλησίαις.

26 om επι ℵ* (hab $ℵ^{c.a}$) 27 και ποιμανει...ως] ινα ποιμανει...και ως syr^{gw} | ποιμαινειν 130 | συντριβεται ℵAC 17 36 38 40 51 80 81 130 *g* syr^{gw}] συντριβησεται PQ $min^{fere\ 50}$ vg me syr aeth Prim Ar

similar anacoluthon in iii. 12, 21. The promise is based on Ps. ii. 8 f. *δώσω σοι ἔθνη τὴν κληρονομίαν σου...ποιμανεῖς αὐτοὺς ἐν ῥάβδῳ σιδηρᾷ, ὡς σκεῦος κεραμέως συντρίψεις αὐτούς*, where the LXX. read תרעם as תְּרְעֵם (*ποιμανεῖς*), while M. T. has תְּרֹעֵם (Symm. *συντρίψεις s. συνθλάσεις*). Cf. Apoc. xii. 5, xix. 15. Ποιμανεῖ, Prim. *pascet*, Vulg. *reget*, 'will do the part of the *ποιμήν*,' whether in the way of feeding (*βόσκειν*, Jo. xxi. 15 ff.) or of ruling ("pastoraliter reges," as Hilary on Ps. ii. 9 well expresses it). Here the second point is emphasized by *ἐν* (instrumental) *ῥάβδῳ σιδηρᾷ*. The "rod of iron" (שֵׁבֶט בַּרְזֶל) is "the shepherd's oaken club, developed on the one hand into the sceptre (Gen. xlix. 10), and on the other into the formidable weapon" (Cheyne, *Psalms*, p. 6; cf. Hastings' *D. B.* iv. p. 291); in the latter case it would be capped with iron, and capable of inflicting severe punishment. Such is its character in the Psalm, *l. c.*; the Gentile nations are to be shattered like pottery by the Divine Shepherd of Israel. Τὰ *σκεύη τὰ κεραμικά*, i.e. *τοῦ κεραμέως*, cf. Vg. *vas figuli*; for *κεραμικός* cf. Dan. ii. 41, LXX. Ὡς *κἀγὼ εἴληφα παρὰ τοῦ πατρός μου* carries on the reference to Ps. ii. (cf. *v.* 7 *Κύριος εἶπεν πρός μέ Υἱός μου εἶ σύ, ἐγὼ σήμερον γεγέννηκά σε*). The Only Begotten Son imparts to His brethren, in so far as their sonship has been confirmed by victory, His own power over the nations; cf. Mt. xxv. 21, 28, 1 Cor. vi. 2, Apoc. xx. 4, xxi. 5. On the contrast between this promise and the outward conditions of life at Thyatira see Ramsay, *Exp.* 1904, ii. 40 f. Historically the promise fulfils itself in the Church's influence upon the world; no other voluntary Society can be compared with her as a factor in the shaping of national character and life: and the individual disciple, in proportion as he is loyal, bears his share in the subjugation of the world to Christ; cf. Rom. xv. 18 *κατειργάσατο Χριστὸς δι' ἐμοῦ εἰς ὑπακοὴν ἐθνῶν*. But the deeper fulfilment of this promise as of the rest of the series awaits the Parousia; cf. Lc. xix. 15 ff. *ἐγένετο ἐν τῷ ἐπανελθεῖν αὐτὸν λαβόντα τὴν βασιλείαν καὶ εἶπεν φωνηθῆναι αὐτῷ τοὺς δούλους...καὶ εἶπεν...Ἴσθι ἐξουσίαν ἔχων ἐπάνω δέκα (πέντε) πόλεων*. The new order must be preceded by the breaking up of the old (*συντρίβεται*), but the purpose of the Potter is to reconstruct; out of the fragments of the old life there will rise under the Hand of Christ and of the Church new and better types of social and national organization.

28. *καὶ δώσω αὐτῷ τὸν ἀστέρα τὸν πρωϊνόν*] The conqueror is not only to share Christ's activities; he is to possess Christ. The ancient expositors offer a choice of interpretations; the morning star is "the first resurrection" (Victorinus), or it is the fallen Lucifer put under the feet of the saints (Andreas, citing Isa. xiv. 12 *πῶς ἐξέπεσεν ἐκ τοῦ οὐρανοῦ ὁ ἑωσφόρος*, and adding *ὃν δώσειν ὑπὸ τοὺς πόδας τῶν πιστῶν ἐπήγγελται*); or it is Christ Himself (Beatus: "id

[1] Καὶ τῷ ἀγγέλῳ τῆς ἐν Σάρδεσιν ἐκκλησίας 1 III.
γράψον Τάδε λέγει ὁ ἔχων τὰ ἑπτὰ πνεύματα τοῦ θεοῦ καὶ τοὺς ἑπτὰ ἀστέρας. οἶδά σου τὰ ἔργα, ὅτι

III 1 της] τω syrr Prim | om εκκλησιας syr | οτι] και Q 6 8 14 29 92^{txt} 95 al Ar και οτι syr^{gw} Prim

est, Dominum Jesum Christum quem numquam suscepit vesper, sed lux sempiterna est, et ipse super in luce est"; and Bede: "Christus est stella matutina qui nocte saeculi transacta lucem vitae sanctis promittit et pandet aeternam"). The last explanation is surely right, on the evidence of the Apocalypse itself; see xxii. 16 ἐγώ εἰμι...ὁ ἀστὴρ ὁ λαμπρὸς ὁ πρωϊνός. If the Churches are λυχνίαι and their angels ἀστέρες, the Head of the Church may fitly be the ἀστὴρ ὁ πρωϊνός, the brightest of stars, whose advent ushers in the day; cf. 2 Pet. i. 19 ἕως οὗ ἡμέρα διαυγάσῃ καὶ φωσφόρος ἀνατείλῃ ἐν ταῖς καρδίαις ὑμῶν. Thus the promise points to the Parousia, and yet does not exclude the foretastes which are given to the faithful in the growing illumination of the mind and the occasional flashings upon it of the yet distant light of "the perfect day" (Prov. iv. 18).

III. 1—6. The Address to the Angel of the Church in Sardis.

1. τῆς ἐν Σάρδεσιν] A little over 30 miles S.E.S. of Thyatira the messenger would reach Sardis (Σάρδιες, Σάρδεις, Σάρδις, *Sardis*), now Sart (cf. Ramsay, *Exp.* 1904, ii. 167), the old capital of Lydia, lying at the foot of Mount Tmolus. Under Roman rule it recovered some of its ancient importance, becoming head of the local *conventus* (Ramsay, *Hist. Geogr.* p. 120); and though in A.D. 17 it suffered severely from an earthquake, through the liberality of Tiberius (Tac. *ann.* ii. 47) Sardis rose rapidly from its ruins, so that Strabo (625) is able to characterize it as πόλις μεγάλη. Like Thyatira, it was famous for its woollen manufactures and dyeing industry (cf. Smith, *D. B.* p. 1140), and the ancient system of roads of which it was a meeting-point secured for it the trade of central Asia (cf. Ramsay, *Hist. Geogr.* p. 42 ff., *Encycl. Bibl.* 4286). The chief cult of Sardis was that of Cybele, two columns of whose temple are still visible (Murray, *Turkey in Asia*, p. 305). The inhabitants bore a bad name in antiquity for luxury and loose living, as indeed did the Lydians generally (Herod. i. 59, Aesch. *Pers.* 41). The Church of Sardis lingered to the fourteenth century, but did not play a distinguished part in Christian history; among its early Bishops, however, appears the name of Melito (fl. 165—195: Eus. *H. E.* iv. 13, 26; v. 24), the earliest interpreter of the Apocalypse.

τάδε λέγει ὁ ἔχων κτλ.] Cf. ii. 1 τ. λ. ὁ κρατῶν τοὺς ἑπτὰ ἀστέρας. Here ἔχων is preferred to κρατῶν because τὰ ἑπτὰ πνεύματα precedes. Not only are the churches in the hand of Christ, but the spirits also belong to Him; it is His to guide or withhold the powers of the πνεῦμα ζωοποιόν, on which the life of the Churches depends. The Ascended Christ 'has' the spirits of God in virtue of His exaltation, cf. Acts ii. 33 ὑψωθεὶς τήν τε ἐπαγγελίαν τοῦ πνεύματος τοῦ ἁγίου λαβὼν παρὰ τοῦ πατρὸς ἐξέχεεν τοῦτο, Eph. iv. 7 f. ἑνὶ δὲ ἑκάστῳ ἡμῶν ἐδόθη ἡ χάρις κατὰ τὸ μέτρον τῆς δωρεᾶς τοῦ χριστοῦ κτλ. A further view of the relation of the seven Spirits to the glorified Christ is given in *c.* v. 6, where see notes.

οἶδά σου τὰ ἔργα, ὅτι κτλ.] On οἶδά σ. τ. ἔ. see ii. 2 note. Here the words introduce almost unqualified censure: the Church at Sardis presented to the

2 ὄνομα ἔχεις ὅτι ζῇς, καὶ νεκρὸς εἶ. ²γίνου γρηγορῶν,
καὶ στήρισον τὰ λοιπὰ ἃ ἔμελλον ἀποθανεῖν· οὐ γὰρ

2 γενου 130 | στηρισον ACP 93* 95 96^{corr} al (-ξον ℵQ 1 14 37^{fort} 80 al)] τηρησον 9 13 25 27 28 29 30 al syr^{sch} | τους λοιπους οι syr | εμελλον ℵACP $min^{fere 8}$ (-λλεν 1 2 (7) 16 vg me syr Vict Prim Ar -λλες Q (ημ.) 2 6 8 14 19 91 (94 97) $al^{plq 20}$ syr^{gw}) | αποθανειν ℵACP 1^{mg} 7 38 al^{mu} vg me syrr arm aeth (-θνησκειν 28 36 79 Ar)] αποβαλλειν Q 2 6 8 14 (91) 95 $al^{plq 20}$ (-βαλειν 17 49 91 96)

eye of Christ the paradox of death under the name of life. For the constr. ὄνομα ἔχεις ὅτι ζῇς cf. Herod. vii. 138 οὔνομα εἶχε ὡς ἐπ' Ἀθήνας ἐλαύνει, and for the general sense 2 Tim. iii. 5 ἔχοντες μόρφωσιν εὐσεβείας τὴν δὲ δύναμιν αὐτῆς ἠρνημένοι. Καὶ νεκρὸς εἶ: cf. Mt. viii. 22 ἄφες τοὺς νεκροὺς θάψαι τοὺς ἑαυτῶν νεκρούς, Lc. xv. 24 οὗτος ὁ υἱός μου νεκρὸς ἦν καὶ ἀνέζησεν, Jo. v. 25 ἔρχεται ὥρα καὶ νῦν ἐστὶν ὅτε οἱ νεκροὶ... ζήσουσιν, Rom. vi. 13 ὡσεὶ ἐκ νεκρῶν ζῶντας. Sardis, while retaining the Christian name, had relapsed into the state of spiritual death from which Christ had raised her (Eph. ii. 1, 5; Col. ii. 13). Victorinus: "non satis est Christianum dici et Christum confiteri, ipsum vero in opere non habere."

2. γίνου γρηγορῶν, καὶ στήρισον κτλ.] After νεκρὸς εἶ we expect the call ἀνάστα ἐκ τῶν νεκρῶν (Eph. v. 14). But amid the general reign of spiritual death Christ detected vestiges of life, though they were on the point of becoming extinct (τὰ λοιπὰ ἃ ἔμελλον ἀποθανεῖν). There was therefore still room for a final appeal. For γίνου γρ. ($Syr.^{gw}$ ܗܘܝ ܥܝܪܐ) see ii. 10 note: an effort must be made to restore vigilance, and to maintain it when restored; on γρηγορεῖν cf. Mc. xiii. 34 note. The word is frequently on the lips of Christ in the Synoptic narrative of the last days of His intercourse with the Twelve. It has been pointed out that it is specially suitable in an address to the Church at Sardis; twice during the history of that city the acropolis had fallen into the hands of an enemy through want of vigilance on the part of its citizens (viz. in B.C. 549, 218; see Hastings' *D. B.* iv. 49; Ramsay, *Exp.* 1904, ii. 87 ff.); and a similar disaster now threatened the Church of Sardis from a similar cause. But more than vigilance was needed; the Church must set herself to work for the establishment of any faith, love, or works of piety that were left: cf. Ez. xxxiv. 4, 16 τὸ ἠσθενηκὸς οὐκ ἐνισχύσατε...τὸ ἐκλιπὸν ἐνισχύσω κτλ. Τὰ λοιπά = τὰ λελειμμένα, not = τοὺς λοιπούς (*v.* 4), but more generally, whatever remained at Sardis out of the wreck of Christian life, whether persons or institutions: all must be preserved and set on a firmer basis—a principle of reconstruction worthy of the notice of Christian teachers who are called to deal with corrupt or decaying branches of the Church. Στηρίζειν, like βεβαιοῦν and θεμελιοῦν, is a technical word in primitive *pastoralia*; cf. Acts xviii. 23, Rom. i. 11, xvi. 25, 1 Th. iii. 2, 13, 2 Th. ii. 17, iii. 3, Jac. v. 8, 1 Pet. v. 10, 2 Pet. i. 12. This frequent reference to the need of στηριγμός in Christian communities planted in the heart of a heathen population will readily explain itself to those who are familiar with the history of Missions.

On the form στήρισον see WH.² *Notes*, p. 177; W. Schm. p. 105, Blass, *Gr.* pp. 40, 42. Ἃ ἔμελλον ἀποθανεῖν: the imperfect looks back from the standpoint of the reader to the time when the vision was seen, and at the same time with a delicate optimism it expresses the conviction of the writer that the worst would soon be past; for another explanation see Burton § 28. The plural is used because the things that remain are

εὕρηκά σου ἔργα πεπληρωμένα ἐνώπιον τοῦ θεοῦ
μου· ³μνημόνευε οὖν πῶς εἴληφας καὶ ἤκουσας, καὶ 3
τήρει καὶ μετανόησον. ἐὰν οὖν μὴ γρηγορήσῃς, ἥξω
ὡς κλέπτης, καὶ οὐ μὴ γνῷς ποίαν ὥραν ἥξω ἐπὶ σέ.

2 ευρηκαν Q | εργα AC 1^{mg}] pr τα ℵPQ min$^{fere\,omn}$ Andr Ar | om μου 1 81 161 syr^{gw} arm Prim   3 μνημονευσον 130 | om ουν 1° ℵ 14 syr^{gw} aeth Prim Ar | ηκουσας και ειληφας syr^{gw} | om και τηρει Q 2 6 14 49 al$^{sat\,mu}$ aeth^{utr} Ar | ουν 2°] δε 36 syr^{gw} Prim | γρηγορησης] μετανοησης ℵ* (γρ. ℵ$^{c.a}$) Prim μεταν. και μη γρηγ. me^{vid} | ηξω] + επι σε ℵQ min^{pl} vg$^{am\,al}$ syrr Ar | γνως ACP 1 10 28 31 32 36 37 48 49 51 80 81 91 96 161 Ar] γνωση ℵQ 2 7 8 14 29 35 38 al vg (*nescies*) Prim (*non scies*) | ποιαν] οιαν ℵ | ηξα 95

regarded as living realities; on the augment see W. Schm. p. 99, and on the aor. inf. after μέλλω, Blass, *Gr.* p. 197.

οὐ γὰρ εὕρηκά σου ἔργα κτλ.] Cf. Dan. v. 27 Th. ἐστάθη ἐν ζυγῷ καὶ εὑρέθη ὑστεροῦσα. Works were not wanting to this Church, but they lacked the πλήρωμα which makes human actions acceptable in the sight of God; in some unexplained way they were 'deficient.' Cf. the use of πληροῦσθαι in Col. ii. 10 ἐστὲ ἐν αὐτῷ πεπληρωμένοι, and the Johannine phrase ἵνα ἡ χαρὰ ὑμῶν ᾖ πεπληρωμένη (Jo. xvi. 24, 1 Jo. i. 4, 2 Jo. 12); 'works' are πεπληρωμένα only when they are animated by the Spirit of life. Οὐχ εὕρηκα recalls Mc. xi. 13 ἦλθεν εἰ ἄρα τι εὑρήσει ἐν αὐτῇ, καὶ... οὐδὲν εὗρεν εἰ μὴ φύλλα, Lc. xiii. 7 ἔρχομαι ζητῶν καρπὸν...καὶ οὐχ εὑρίσκω: the perf. implies that at Sardis the search was not yet ended. Σου ἔργα, 'works of thine,' i.e. 'any of thy works'; a more sweeping censure than σ. τὰ ἔ., 'thy works as a whole.' Τοῦ θεοῦ μου: cf. Mc. xv. 34, Jo. xx. 17, Eph. i. 17, Heb. i. 9, and the phrase ὁ θεὸς καὶ πατὴρ τοῦ κυρίου ἡμῶν 'I. X. (Rom. xv. 6, etc.; see Hort on 1 Pet. i. 3). The Son of God (ii. 18) does not forget that He is also Son of Man, and as such stands in a creaturely relation to God. Yet this relation is in some sense unique, as μου shews (not ἡμῶν); cf. Jo. *l. c.* θεόν μου καὶ θεὸν ὑμῶν.

3. μνημόνευε οὖν πῶς εἴληφας κτλ.] Οὖν resumes and coordinates, as often in the Fourth Gospel (Blass, *Gr.* p. 272 f.) and in the Apoc. (i. 19, ii. 5, 16, iii. 19). In order to stimulate the Church in her work of self-recovery, her thoughts are sent back to the first days; cf. the appeal to the Church at Ephesus, ii. 5 μν. οὖν πόθεν πέπτωκες. Εἴληφας represents the faith as a trust; cf. Mt. xxv. 20 ff. ὁ τὰ πέντε τάλαντα λαβών...ὁ τὰ δύο... ὁ τὸ ἓν τάλαντον εἰληφώς: 1 Cor. iv. 7 τί δὲ ἔχεις ὃ οὐκ ἔλαβες; Even the Son confesses (ii. 28), Εἴληφα παρὰ τοῦ πατρός μου. Εἴληφας καὶ ἤκουσας: the aor. looks back to the moment when faith came by hearing (Rom. x. 17, cf. 1 Th. i. 5 f., ii. 13); the perf. calls attention to the abiding responsibility of the trust then received. Τήρει καὶ μετανόησον: 'keep that which thou hast received, and promptly turn from thy past neglect.'

ἐὰν οὖν μὴ γρηγορήσῃς κτλ.] Οὖν is again resumptive, looking back to *v.* 2 γίνου γρηγορῶν, to which the succeeding imperatives (στήρισον, μνημόνευε etc.) are subordinate. Ἥξω ὡς κλέπτης, not speedily only (ταχύ, ii. 16), but stealthily, at an unexpected moment. For the figure cf. Mt. xxiv. 43, Lc. xii. 39, 1 Th. v. 2, 2 Pet. iii. 10, Apoc. xvi. 15. Κλέπτης is doubtless preferred to the less ignoble λῃστής, because the point of comparison is the stealthiness of the thief's approach. In His relation to the faithful the Lord is the opposite of both (Jo. x. 1, 7).

4 [4]ἀλλὰ ἔχεις ὀλίγα ὀνόματα ἐν Σάρδεσιν ἃ οὐκ
ἐμόλυναν τὰ ἱμάτια αὐτῶν, καὶ περιπατήσουσιν μετ'
5 ἐμοῦ ἐν λευκοῖς, ὅτι ἄξιοί εἰσιν. [5]ὁ νικῶν, οὕτως

4 αλλα] αλλ PQ min^{pl} om 1 al^{vid} arm | εν Σαρδεσιν] pr και 1 Prim | α] οι 1 17 28 37 38 46 79 80 81 88 161 vg me arm Tert Prim Ar | αυτων] εαυτων C + *cum mulieribus* me aeth | om μετ εμου arm   5 ουτως ℵ*AC min^{20} vg me syrr arm aeth Prim] ουτος ℵ$^{c.a}$PQ 1 6 7 8 14 (16) 28 29 31 34 36 38 47 48 50 al

καὶ οὐ μὴ γνῷς κτλ.] On οὐ μὴ γνῷς see Blass, *Gr.* p. 209 f.; γνώσῃ (ℵQ) is a grammatical correction. The whole sentence is another echo of the Synoptic tradition; cf. Mc. xiii. 35 οὐκ οἴδατε γὰρ πότε ὁ κύριος τῆς οἰκίας ἔρχεται, Lc. xii. 39 εἰ ᾔδει...ποίᾳ ὥρᾳ ὁ κλέπτης ἔρχεται, ἐγρηγόρησεν ἄν. Ποίαν ὥραν (Prim., Vulg. *qua hora*), strictly 'during what hour'; but the acc. is used occasionally even in classical Greek in answer to πότε; see Blass, *Gr.* p. 94.

4. ἀλλὰ ἔχεις ὀλίγα ὀνόματα ἐν Σάρδεσιν κτλ.] Beatus: "notandum est quod Dominus ait: *Multi sunt vocati, sed pauci electi;* et *pusillus* est *grex* cui compromittit dare hereditatem." Bede: "*proprias* enim *oves vocat nominatim.*" For ὀνόματα = 'persons,' see Acts i. 15 ὄχλος ὀνομάτων, Apoc. xi. 13 ἀπεκτάνθησαν... ὀνόματα ἀνθρώπων. Deissmann (*Bible Studies*, p. 196 f.) shews that ἕκαστον ὄνομα was freely used in papyri of the second century B.C. in the sense of 'each individual.' Οἵ is a needless correction; the sense is clear from the context (ἐμόλυναν, ἄξιοί εἰσιν). Οὐκ ἐμόλυναν τὰ ἱμάτια αὐτῶν: even in days of general defilement they remained pure. Μολύνειν differs from μιαίνειν as *inquinare* from *maculare* (Trench); in the LXX., while μιαίνειν usually represents legal defilement (טמא), μολύνειν (טבל, גאל) stands for actual pollution as with blood (Gen. xxxvii. 31, Isa. lix. 3, Thren. iv. 14) or with pitch (Sir. xiii. 1). Here the reference is doubtless to heathen impurities into which the Sardians had plunged, spiritual deadness having issued in indifference to moral evil. For the metaphor μ. τὰ ἱμάτια see Jude 23 μισοῦντες καὶ τὸν ἀπὸ τῆς σαρκὸς ἐσπιλωμένον χιτῶνα, Apoc. vii. 14, xxii. 14; the ἱμάτια of the Christian life are the professions made in Baptism (Gal. iii. 27) which at Sardis had been besmirched by too many in the mire of the streets. The few who had kept them clean and white (cf. Tob. iii. 15 οὐκ ἐμόλυνα τὸ ὄνομά μου...ἐν τῇ γῇ τῆς αἰχμαλωσίας μου) should be suitably rewarded: περιπατήσουσιν μετ' ἐμοῦ ἐν λευκοῖς (sc. ἱματίοις, cf. Mt. xi. 8 ἐν μαλακοῖς, and see *vv.* 5, 18, iv. 4; Latt. *in albis*). For the general sense of the promise see note on the next verse. In περιπατήσουσιν there may be a reference to the story of Enoch (Gen. v. 22 וַיִּתְהַלֵּךְ חֲנוֹךְ אֶת־הָאֱלֹהִים, LXX. εὐηρέστησεν δὲ Ἐνὼχ τῷ θεῷ, but Aq. περιεπάτει σὺν τ. θ.), but more probably the writer has in view the peripatetic ministry in Galilee (Jo. vi. 66), and the call δεῦρο ἀκολούθει μοι. Cf. vii. 17, xiv. 1, 4.

Ἄξιοί εἰσιν: contrast *c.* xvi. 6. Ἀξιότης in the good sense is elsewhere in this book attributed only to God and Christ (e.g. iv. 11, v. 9): but a relative 'worthiness' is predicated of the saints in Lc. xx. 35, Eph. iv. 1, Phil. i. 27, Col. i. 10, 1 Th. ii. 12, 2 Th. i. 5.

5. ὁ νικῶν, οὕτως περιβαλεῖται κτλ.] The promise of *v.* 4 repeated in general terms, corresponding with those of the promises appended to the other messages to the Churches.

περιβαλεῖται ἐν ἱματίοις λευκοῖς, καὶ οὐ μὴ ἐξαλείψω τὸ ὄνομα αὐτοῦ ἐκ τῆς βίβλου τῆς ζωῆς, καὶ ὁμολογήσω τὸ ὄνομα αὐτοῦ ἐνώπιον τοῦ πατρός μου
καὶ ἐνώπιον τῶν ἀγγέλων αὐτοῦ. [6]ὁ ἔχων οὖς 6
ἀκουσάτω τί τὸ πνεῦμα λέγει ταῖς ἐκκλησίαις.

5 περιβαλλεται C syrr | ενωπιον 1°] εμπροσθεν ℵ

'The conqueror, whoever he may be, shall be clad after the manner aforesaid (for this use of οὕτως cf. xi. 5, οὕτως δεῖ αὐτὸν ἀποκτανθῆναι: Jo. iv. 6, ἐκαθέζετο οὕτως, is not apposite, nor is there any need to read οὗτος for οὕτως), i.e. clad in white garments.' On the Roman use of the white *toga* see Ramsay, *Exp.*, 1904, ii. 164. In Scripture white apparel denotes (*a*) festivity (Eccl. ix. 8 ἐν παντὶ καιρῷ ἔστωσαν ἱμάτιά σου λευκά i.e. 'be always gay'), (*b*) victory (2 Macc. xi. 8 ἐφάνη προηγούμενος αὐτῶν ἔφιππος ἐν λευκῇ ἐσθῆτι κτλ.), (*c*) purity (Apoc. vii. 9 ff.); (*d*) the heavenly state, Dan. vii. 9 Th. τὸ ἔνδυμα αὐτοῦ ὡσεὶ χιὼν λευκόν; so Apoc. iv. 4, vi. 11, xix. 11, 14). All these associations meet here: the promise is that of a life free from pollution, bright with celestial gladness, crowned with final victory. The glory of the risen body may enter into the conception; see Mt. xiii. 43, 1 Cor. xv. 43, 49, 54, 2 Cor. v. 2, Phil. iii. 21, Enoch lxii. 15 f., xc. 32.

Περιβάλλεσθαι occurs again with a dat. but without ἐν in *c.* iv. 4; for the construction περιβ. τι see vii. 9, 13, x. 1, xi. 3, xii. 1, xvii. 4, xviii. 16, xix. 8, 13.

καὶ οὐ μὴ ἐξαλείψω τὸ ὄνομα αὐτοῦ κτλ.] A Divine register of men is mentioned first in Ex. xxxii. 32 f. ἐξάλειψόν με ἐκ τῆς βίβλου σου ἧς ἔγραψας. As a civic register contains only the names of living citizens, so this Book of God is a βίβλος ζώντων (Ps. lxviii. (lxix.) 29), the 'living' being in this case the righteous (Mal. iii. 16, Dan. xii. 1). The conception established itself in Jewish thought (1 Sam. xxv. 29, Ps. lxviii. 29, cxxxviii. 16, Neh. xii. 22 f., Isa. xlviii. 19, Jer. xxii. 30, Ez. xiii. 9, Enoch xlvii. 3 (where see Charles' note), *Pirqe Aboth* 2, Targ. on Ez. *l. c.*), and appears in the N.T. (Lc. x. 20 τὰ ὀνόματα ὑμῶν ἐνγέγραπται ἐν τοῖς οὐρανοῖς, Phil. iv. 3 ὧν τὰ ὀνόματα ἐν βίβλῳ ζωῆς, Apoc. xiii. 8, xx. 15, xxi. 27). The blotting out of names from the Book of Life is frequently referred to; beside the passages cited above see Deut. ix. 14, xxv. 19, xxix. 20. Οὐκ ἐξαλείψω implies that the book is in the hands of Christ; cf. xiii. 8, xxi. 27 ἐν τῷ βιβλίῳ τῆς ζωῆς τοῦ ἀρνίου.

This promise is singularly appropriate at the end of the present message. The 'few names' in Sardis which are distinguished by resisting the prevailing torpor of spiritual death find their reward in finally retaining their place among the living in the City of God.

καὶ ὁμολογήσω τὸ ὄνομα αὐτοῦ κτλ.] A further grant to the conqueror. Not only shall his name be found in the register of the living; it shall be acknowledged before God and His Angels. Another reminiscence of the sayings of the Ministry (Mt. x. 32, Lc. xii. 8); ὁ νικῶν here answers to ὅστις (ὃς ἂν) ὁμολογήσει ἐν ἐμοί (Mt., Lc.). The reverse of the picture, ὁ δὲ ἀρνησάμενός με...ἀπαρνηθήσεται, is mercifully withheld; even in the message to Sardis the last note is one of unmixed encouragement and hope. Ἐνώπιον τοῦ πατρός μου: cf. *v.* 2 ἐν. τ. θεοῦ μου.

7—13. The Message to the Angel of the Church in Philadelphia.

7 [7] Καὶ τῷ ἀγγέλῳ τῆς ἐν Φιλαδελφίᾳ ἐκκλησίας
γράψον Τάδε λέγει ὁ ἅγιος, ὁ ἀληθινός, ὁ ἔχων τὴν
κλεῖν Δαυείδ, ὁ ἀνοίγων καὶ οὐδεὶς κλείσει, καὶ κλείων

7 της] τω Prim | εν Φιλαδελφια ℵCPQ (-φεια min^{pl})] *Philadelphiae* *g* vg syr^{gw} Prim | εκκλησια A | ο αγιος ο αληθινος CPQ min$^{fere\ omn}$ vg me syrr arm aeth Prim Ar] ο αληθινος ο αγιος ℵA | την κλειν (om την ℵ*)] την κλειδα 1 al^{mu} | Δαυειδ] αδου 7* 16 33 45 codd ap Andr et Ar pr του ℵPQ min$^{fere\ omn}$ Andr Ar | ο ανοιγων] και αν. ℵ Or $\frac{1}{1}$ | κλεισει] κλειει 1 6 31 36 49 92^{mg} al vg (me) syrr arm Prim + αυτην Q min^{35} + ει μη ο ανοιγων Q 7 14 91 93 94 95 al | om και 3° ℵ^{corr}A vg | κλειων] κλειει C 31 92^{mg} al *g* vg syr arm Tyc

7. τῆς ἐν Φιλαδελφίᾳ] After a run of a little less than 30 miles from Sart the railway from Smyrna reaches Ala Shehr, 'the white city,' the modern representative of Philadelphia. The ancient city, founded by Attalus II. (Philadelphus) who died in B.C. 138, commanded the trade of the rich volcanic region lying to the N. and N.E. and known as the Katakekaumene (Burntland), from the cinders and *scoriae* with which the ground was strewn. Philadelphia itself was subject to frequent shocks of earthquake (Strabo, 628 πόλις Φιλαδέλφεια σεισμῶν πλήρης); like Sardis it was rebuilt by Tiberius after the great earthquake of A.D. 17 (Tac. *ann.* ii. 47) and subsequently it bore on coins for a time the name of Neo-Caesarea, but the old name reasserted itself or perhaps never went out of common use. The city was not a large one, the fear of earthquakes driving most of the inhabitants into the surrounding country (Strabo, *l. c.*), and the Church was probably proportionately small, at least within the walls. As was natural in a vine-growing district, the worship of Dionysos was the chief pagan cult; but the difficulties of this Church arose from Jewish rather than pagan antagonists, and the message contains no reference to direct persecution from without or to heresy within the brotherhood. It offers a strong contrast to the Sardian utterance which precedes it; for the Church at Philadelphia the Lord has no censure and scarcely a word of warning. It is interesting to note that the modern city has its resident Bishop, five churches, and about 1000 Christian inhabitants.

τάδε λέγει ὁ ἅγιος, ὁ ἀληθινός] 'The Holy, the True,' Vg. *Sanctus et Verus*; not, as Arethas, ὁ ἀληθινὸς ἅγιος, 'the True Saint.' Cf. vi. 10 ὁ δεσπότης ὁ ἅγιος καὶ ἀληθινός. Ὁ ἅγιος, a Divine title (Hab. iii. 3, Isa. xl. 25), is applied to Christ with the qualifying words τοῦ θεοῦ or παῖς τ. θ. in Mc. i. 24, Jo. vi. 69, Acts iv. 27, 30, and here absolutely. Ὁ ἀληθινός is used of Him again in iii. 14 ὁ πιστὸς καὶ ἀληθινός, xix. 11 πιστὸς καλούμενος καὶ ἀληθινός. Ἀληθινός is *verus* as distinguished from *verax* (ἀληθής); cf. Orig. *in Joann.* t. ii. 6 πρὸς ἀντιδιαστολὴν σκιᾶς καὶ τύπου καὶ εἰκόνος, i.e. the ideal, contrasted with all imperfect representations or approximations; see Jo. iv. 37, vii. 28, viii. 16, and see Lightfoot on 1 Th. i. 9, Westcott on Heb. x. 22, and Trench, *syn.* 8. The Head of the Church is characterised at once by absolute sanctity (Heb. vii. 26 τοιοῦτος γὰρ ἡμῖν ἔπρεπεν ἀρχιερεύς, ὅσιος ἄκακος ἀμίαντος κεχωρισμένος ἀπὸ τῶν ἁμαρτωλῶν), and by absolute truth; He is all that He claims to be, fulfilling the ideals which He holds forth and the hopes which He inspires.

ὁ ἔχων τὴν κλεῖν Δαυείδ κτλ.] Cf. Isa. xxii. 22, where it is said of Hezekiah's faithful vizier (2 K. xviii. 18 ff.), Eliakim the son of Hilkiah: δώσω τὴν κλεῖδα

καὶ οὐδεὶς ἀνοίγει. [8] οἶδά σου τὰ ἔργα· ἰδοὺ δέδωκα 8
ἐνώπιόν σου θύραν ἀνεῳγμένην, ἣν οὐδεὶς δύναται
κλεῖσαι αὐτήν· ὅτι μικρὰν ἔχεις δύναμιν, καὶ ἐτήρησάς

7 ανοιγει] ανοιξει (א)Q min[40] me Ar 8 δεδωκα] + σοι 130 | ανεωγμενην ACQ min[pl]] ηνεωγμενην אP 31 35 38 87 | ην] και 1 92[mg] al[pauc] om א 49 vg | om αυτην א 49 vg | μικραν] pr ου 38 μακραν 14

οἴκου Δαυεὶδ ἐπὶ τοῦ ὤμου αὐτοῦ, καὶ ἀνοίξει καὶ οὐκ ἔσται ὁ ἀποκλείων καὶ κλείσει καὶ οὐκ ἔσται ὁ ἀνοίγων (codd. QΓ, with M.T.). Eliakim, with his key of office (Andreas, σύμβολον τῆς ἐξουσίας) slung over his shoulder, is the antitype of the exalted Christ, set over the House of God (Eph. i. 22, Heb. iii. 6), and exercising all authority in heaven and on earth (Mt. xxviii. 18), and even in Hades (Apoc. i. 18, cf. Rom. xiv. 9, Phil. ii. 9 ff.). Τὴν κλεῖν Δαυείδ, cf. v. 5 ἡ ῥίζα Δ., xxii. 16 ἡ ῥ. καὶ τὸ γένος Δ.; the reference to David recalls the long series of prophetic hopes now fulfilled in the exaltation of the Christ. Compare Mt. xvi. 19 δώσω σοι τὰς κλεῖδας τῆς βασιλείας τῶν οὐρανῶν. The grant to the Church in the person of St Peter is less comprehensive, for the keys of the Kingdom unlock but one of the great areas of the House of God; moreover it is significant that the Lord does not say to him ὃ ἐὰν κλείσῃς...κλεισθήσεται· ὃ ἐὰν ἀνοίξῃς ἀνοιχθήσεται, but ὃ ἐὰν δήσῃς, ὃ ἐὰν λύσῃς, changing the metaphor; the supreme power of shutting and opening is kept in His own hands (cf. Mt. xxv. 10 f., and comp. the *Te Deum*: "tu devicto mortis aculeo aperuisti credentibus regna caelorum"). The ancient interpreters blend the present passage with *c.* v. 5 ff., and thus unduly limit the meaning of this power: cf. Hippolytus (Lag. 159): τὰ μὲν οὖν πάλαι ἐσφραγισμένα νῦν διὰ τῆς χάριτος τοῦ κυρίου πάντα τοῖς ἁγίοις ἠνέῳγεν· αὐτὸς γὰρ ἦν ἡ τελεία σφραγὶς καὶ κλεὶς ἡ ἐκκλησία [? τῇ ἐκκλησίᾳ], ὁ ἀνοίγων καὶ οὐδεὶς κλείει...ὡς Ἰωάννης λέγει· καὶ πάλιν ὁ αὐτός φησι Καὶ εἶδον ... βιβλίον ... ἐσφραγισμένον. On κλεῖν = κλεῖδα see i. 18 note; the *v.l.* ᾅδου for Δαυείδ is from the same passage.

8. οἶδά σου τὰ ἔργα] No description follows as in ii. 2, 19, iii. 1. The Lord's οἶδα is here one of unqualified approval (Andreas: τουτέστιν, ἀποδέχομαι), needing no specification, since there are no deductions to be made. This tacit witness is the more remarkable in view of His claim to be ὁ ἅγιος, ὁ ἀληθινός.

ἰδοὺ δέδωκα ἐν. σ. θύραν ἀνεῳγμένην κτλ.] The 'key of David' has already unlocked a door, which now stands open before the Church. Cf. Isa. xlv. 1 f. ἀνοίξω ἔμπροσθεν αὐτοῦ θύρας, καὶ πόλεις οὐ συνκλεισθήσονται ... θύρας χαλκᾶς συντρίψω καὶ μοχλοὺς σιδηροῦς συνκλάσω. The metaphor of the 'open door' was familiar to the Apostolic age: cf. Acts xiv. 27 (the door of faith), 1 Cor. xvi. 9, 2 Cor. ii. 12, Col. iv. 3 (the door of speech and preaching); see Lightfoot on Col. *l. c.* The latter is here probably in view (Arethas: ἡ τοῦ διδασκαλικοῦ κηρύγματος εἴσοδος); the faithfulness of the Philadelphian Church found its reward in fresh opportunities of service, on the principle of the Lord's familiar saying ὃς ἔχει δοθήσεται αὐτῷ. The position of Philadelphia on the borders of Mysia, Lydia and Phrygia, and "on the threshold of the eastern country" (Ramsay, in Hastings iii. p. 831; cf. *Exp.*, 1904, ii. 344 f.), gave this Church peculiar opportunities for spreading the Gospel. If she had already availed herself of these, the 'open door' would readily explain itself; her opportunities were to be regarded as Christ's gift (δέδωκα) and she was assured of its continuance (οὐδεὶς δύναται κλεῖσαι αὐτήν).

Ὅτι μικρὰν ἔχεις δύναμιν resumes the thread broken by the parenthetic clause ἰδοὺ δέδωκα...κλεῖσαι αὐτήν. "I

9 *μου τὸν λόγον καὶ οὐκ ἠρνήσω τὸ ὄνομά μου.* [9]*ἰδοὺ*
διδῶ ἐκ τῆς συναγωγῆς τοῦ σατανᾶ, τῶν λεγόντων
ἑαυτοὺς Ἰουδαίους εἶναι, καὶ οὐκ εἰσὶν ἀλλὰ ψεύ-
δονται—ἰδοὺ ποιήσω αὐτοὺς ἵνα ἥξουσιν καὶ προσκυ-
νήσουσιν ἐνώπιον τῶν ποδῶν σου, καὶ γνῶσιν ὅτι

9 *διδω* AC] *διδωμι* PQ min^omn vid *δεδωκα* ℵ *dabo* vg Prim | *ηξωσι* Q min^pl Andr Ar *ηξω* 1 | *προσκυνησωσιν* Q 7 14 38 91 95 130 al Andr Ar | *γνωσιν* ACPQ 1 6 7 38 91 95 al^pl syr arm aeth Andr Ar] *γνωσονται* 15 36 syr^gw vid *γνωση* ℵ 14 Prim

know thy works...that thou hast" etc.; cf. *οἶδα...ὅτι* in ii. 2, iii. 1, 15. The Church had little influence in Philadelphia; her members were probably drawn from the servile and commercial classes; cf. 1 Cor. i. 26 *οὐ πολλοὶ δυνατοί*. And under these circumstances (for the slightly adversative force of *καί* see WM. p. 545, Blass, *Gr.* p. 261), the words of Christ had been kept (cf. ii. 26, iii. 3), and there had been no backwardness in confessing His name (for *οὐκ ἀρνεῖσθαι* see ii. 13). *Ἐτήρησας, οὐκ ἠρνήσω*, point to some period of trial, now for the moment gone by; its character may be conjectured from the next verse.

9. *ἰδοὺ διδῶ ἐκ τῆς συναγωγῆς κτλ.*] Andreas: *ἕξεις, φησί, μισθὸν τῆς ὁμολογίας τοῦ ἐμοῦ ὀνόματος τὴν τῶν Ἰουδαίων ἐπιστροφήν τε καὶ μετάνοιαν*. The opposition implied in *ἐτήρησας καὶ οὐκ ἠρνήσω* came at Philadelphia, as at Smyrna, from the Jews; cf. ii. 9 *οἶδα...τὴν βλασφημίαν ἐκ τῶν λεγόντων Ἰουδαίους εἶναι ἑαυτούς, καὶ οὐκ εἰσίν, ἀλλὰ συναγωγὴ τοῦ σατανᾶ*, a description repeated here with the addition of *ἀλλὰ ψεύδονται*, which contrasts the Philadelphian Jews with *ὁ ἀληθινός* (*v.* 7): they are *ψευδώνυμοι*, and their claim is a sin against truth. The construction is broken by the explanatory clauses *τῶν λεγόντων κτλ.*, but starts afresh with *ἰδοὺ ποιήσω αὐτούς*. For *διδόναι* and *ποιεῖν* in this sense see Blass, *Gr.* p. 226, and for the form *διδῶ*, WH. *Notes*, p. 174.

Ἵνα ἥξουσιν καὶ προσκυνήσουσιν κτλ. is a phrase borrowed from Isaiah (xlv. 14, xlix 23, lx. 14, cf. Zech. viii. 20 ff.); the prophet's anticipations of the submission of the Gentile nations to Israel will find a fulfilment in the submission of members of the synagogue (on *ἐκ τ. σ.* see ii. 9, note) to the Church, the Israel of God. *Προσκυνεῖν ἐνώπιον τῶν ποδῶν* describes the cringing attitude of a beaten foe, familiar to us through the Assyrian sculptures; in what sense the picture was realised in the conversion of Jews and pagans may be gathered from 1 Cor. xiv. 24, where an *ἄπιστος* entering a Christian assembly *ἐλέγχεται ὑπὸ πάντων ... καὶ οὕτως πεσὼν ἐπὶ πρόσωπον προσκυνήσει τῷ θεῷ, ἀπαγγέλλων ὅτι Ὄντως ὁ θεὸς ἐν ὑμῖν ἐστίν*. It is noteworthy that twenty years later the Philadelphian Church was more in danger from Judaizing Christians than from Jews (Ign. *Philad.* 6 *ἐὰν δέ τις ἰουδαϊσμὸν ἑρμηνεύῃ ὑμῖν μὴ ἀκούετε αὐτοῦ· ἄμεινον γάρ ἐστιν παρὰ ἀνδρὸς περιτομὴν ἔχοντος χριστιανισμὸν ἀκούειν ἢ παρὰ ἀκροβύστου ἰουδαϊσμόν*. Was this the result of a large influx of converts from Judaism in the previous generation?

For other instances of the fut. ind. after *ἵνα* in the Apoc. see vi. 4, 11, viii. 3, ix. 4 f., xiii. 12, xiv. 13, xxii. 14; and cf. Blass, *Gr.* p. 211 f.

καὶ γνῶσιν ὅτι ἐγὼ ἠγάπησά σε] The change to the aor. conj. perhaps indicates that the purpose of the whole action now comes into view. Both the phrase *ἵνα...γνῶσιν* and the words *ἐγὼ ἠγάπησά σε* are from Isaiah; for the former see Isa. xxxvii. 20, xlv. 3, *et passim*; for the latter Isa. xliii. 4. The aor. (contrast i. 5 *τῷ ἀγαπῶντι*)

ἐγὼ ἠγάπησά σε. ¹⁰ὅτι ἐτήρησας τὸν λόγον τῆς 10
ὑπομονῆς μου, κἀγώ σε τηρήσω ἐκ τῆς ὥρας τοῦ
πειρασμοῦ τῆς μελλούσης ἔρχεσθαι ἐπὶ τῆς οἰκουμένης
ὅλης, πειράσαι τοὺς κατοικοῦντας ἐπὶ τῆς γῆς.
¹¹ἔρχομαι ταχύ· κράτει ὃ ἔχεις, ἵνα μηδεὶς λάβῃ 11

9 om εγω Q min^{35} Prim Ar   10 οτι] και A pr και 33 | om τηρησω ℵ
11 ερχομαι] pr ιδου 28 36 79 al vg$^{\text{fu dem harl lipss}}$ arm aeth | ινα μηδεις λαβη] ινα μη λαβη τις ταχυ 7 16 45

carries the love of Christ for the Church back into an indefinite past; cf. Jo. xiii. 1, 34, 1 Jo. iv. 10, where see Westcott's note.

10. *ὅτι ἐτήρησας τὸν λόγον τῆς ὑπομονῆς μου*] Not 'my word of patience,' i.e. my commandment to exercise patience, but 'the word of my patience,' i.e. the teaching which found its central point in the patience of Christ; cf. 2 Th. iii. 5 τὴν ὑπομονὴν τοῦ χριστοῦ, Heb. xii. 1 f. δι' ὑπομονῆς τρέχωμεν...ἀφορῶντες εἰς...'Ιησοῦν...ὃς ὑπέμεινεν σταυρόν, Ign. *Rom.* 10 ἔρρωσθε εἰς τέλος ἐν ὑπομονῇ 'Ιησοῦ Χριστοῦ. The ὑπομονὴ τῶν ἁγίων (Apoc. xiii. 10, xiv. 12) is the echo of the λόγος τῆς ὑπομονῆς τοῦ χριστοῦ. Κἀγώ σε τηρήσω: by the *benigna talio* of the Kingdom of God (as Trench observes) one τήρησις is followed by another; Christ on His part (the καί of reciprocal action, as in Mt. x. 32 ὁμολογήσω κἀγὼ ἐν αὐτῷ) pledges Himself to keep those who have kept His word. Cf. Jo. xvii. 6, 11 τὸν λόγον σου τετήρηκαν...πάτερ ἅγιε, τήρησον αὐτούς. The promise, as Bede says, is "non quidem ut non tenteris, sed ut non vincaris [ab] adversis." 'Εκ τῆς ὥρας τοῦ πειρασμοῦ τῆς μελλούσης ἔρχεσθαι: 'from that season (cf. Sir. xviii. 20 ὥ. ἐπισκοπῆς, Dan. xi. 40 ὥ. συντελείας, Apoc. xiv. 7 ἡ ὥ. τῆς κρίσεως) of trial which is coming upon the whole habitable earth'; i.e. the troublous times which precede the Parousia. In the foreshortened view of the future which was taken by the Apostolic age this final sifting of mankind was near at hand, not clearly differentiated from the imperial persecution which had already begun. Cf. Andreas: τὴν ὥραν δὲ τοῦ πειρασμοῦ· εἴτε ὡς αὐτίκα παρεσομένην τὴν τῶν ἀσεβῶν τῆς 'Ρώμης τὸ τηνικαῦτα βασιλευσάντων κατὰ Χριστιανῶν δίωξιν εἴρηκεν...ἢ τὴν ἐπὶ συντελείᾳ τοῦ αἰῶνος παγκόσμιον κατὰ τῶν πιστῶν τοῦ ἀντιχρίστου κίνησιν λέγει. To the Philadelphian Church the promise was an assurance of safekeeping in any trial that might supervene—an appropriate promise, see Ramsay, *Exp.*, 1904, ii. 348. It is at least an interesting coincidence that in the struggle with the Turk Philadelphia held out longer than any of her neighbours, and that she still possesses a flourishing Christian community; see note on *v.* 1.

The phrase οἱ κατοικοῦντες ἐπὶ τῆς γῆς (in LXX. = יֹשְׁבֵי הָאָרֶץ) occurs again in vi. 10, viii. 13, xi. 10, xiii. 8, 14, xvii. 8, and always, as it seems, means either the pagan world or the world in contrast with the heavenly state. Cf. Enoch xxxvii. 5, with Charles' note.

11. *ἔρχομαι ταχύ*] The great πειρασμός will be followed by the Parousia, and the Parousia is near (cf. ii. 16, xxii. 7, 12, 20). The shortness of the interval is urged as a motive for persevering: the Advent is the limit of the Church's ὑπομονή.

κράτει ὃ ἔχεις κτλ.] The promise of safekeeping (*v.* 10) brings with it the responsibility of continual effort (κράτει). Each Church has its own inheritance (ὃ ἔχεις), which it is called to guard on pain of losing its proper

12 τὸν στέφανόν σου. [12] ὁ νικῶν, ποιήσω αὐτὸν στύλον
ἐν τῷ ναῷ τοῦ θεοῦ μου, καὶ ἔξω οὐ μὴ ἐξέλθῃ ἔτι·
καὶ γράψω ἐπ' αὐτὸν τὸ ὄνομα τοῦ θεοῦ μου καὶ τὸ
ὄνομα τῆς πόλεως τοῦ θεοῦ μου, τῆς καινῆς Ἰερου-

12 αυτον 1°] αυτω ℵ* (-τον ℵ^c.a) | om εν ℵ* (hab ℵ^c.a) | om μου 1° 11 29 36 syr^gw | om ετι ℵ | om επ αυτον C 28 | om του θεου μου και το ονομα Q | om και το ονομα της πολεως του θεου μου 1 12 syr^sch

crown (τὸν στέφανόν σου: cf. 2 Tim. iv. 8 ἀπόκειταί μοι ὁ τῆς δικαιοσύνης στέφανος—on στέφανος see ii. 10 note), which may be taken from it and given to another; cf. Mt. xxv. 28 ἄρατε οὖν ἀπ' αὐτοῦ τὸ τάλαντον καὶ δότε τῷ ἔχοντι τὰ δέκα τάλαντα. Λάβῃ, Prim. *accipiat*, not ἀφέληται or ἀφαρπάσῃ; the picture is not that of a thief snatching away what is feebly held, but rather of a competitor receiving a prize which has been forfeited. The vacant room left by the lapse of a Church may be filled by the rise of another; cf. Rom. xi. 17 f.

12. ὁ νικῶν, ποιήσω αὐτὸν στύλον] The discourse turns, as at the end of each address, to the individual member of the Church. Ὁ νικῶν...αὐτόν, cf. ii. 26, iii. 21; the anacoluthon may in this case be "very awkward" from the grammarian's point of view (Blass, *Gr.* p. 283), but it adds to the movement of the sentence; it is only necessary to write τὸν νικῶντα ποιήσω στύλον in order to see what we have gained by the boldness of the Apocalyptist. In στύλον ἐν τῷ ναῷ a reference has been found to the brazen pillars 'Jachin' and 'Boaz' which stood before the sanctuary in Solomon's temple (1 K. vii. 15, 21, 2 Chr. iii. 15 ff.); or to the porticoes of the Temple of Herod, or even to the magnificent colonnades which surrounded the Artemision at Ephesus. All these, however, are excluded by ἐν τῷ ναῷ, for they were external to the sanctuary. It is better therefore to start with the metaphorical use of the word in Scripture and in Jewish and early Christian literature. In Prov. ix. 1 we read: ἡ σοφία οἰκοδόμησεν ἑαυτῇ οἶκον, καὶ ὑπήρεισεν στύλους ἑπτά (cf. Jud. xvi. 29 τοὺς δύο κιόνας τοῦ οἴκου ἐφ' οὓς ὁ οἶκος ἱστήκει). In the N.T. the word is used as a pure metaphor, see 1 Tim. iii. 15 ἐκκλησία...στύλος καὶ ἑδραίωμα τῆς ἀληθείας, Gal. ii. 9 Ἰάκωβος καὶ Κηφᾶς καὶ Ἰωάνης, οἱ δοκοῦντες στύλοι εἶναι; cf. Clem. R. *Cor.* 5 οἱ μέγιστοι καὶ δικαιότατοι στύλοι. The personal use is common in Rabbinical writers, by whom a great Rabbi is described as עַמּוּד עוֹלָם (Schöttgen on Gal. *l. c.*). There is a double fitness in this metaphor; while a pillar gives stability to the building which rests upon it, it is itself firmly and permanently fixed; and this side of the conception often comes into view (cf. Isa. xxii. 23, lvi. 5, Sap. iii. 14 δοθήσεται γὰρ αὐτῷ...κλῆρος ἐν ναῷ Κυρίου), and is paramount here. With ἐν τῷ ναῷ cf. vii. 15, xxi. 22, notes, and for τοῦ θεοῦ μου see iii. 2, note.

Ἔξω οὐ μὴ ἐξέλθῃ ἔτι: contrast xxi. 27, xxii. 15. As the pillar cannot be moved out of its place while the house stands, so a lapse from goodness will be impossible for a character which has been fixed by the final victory. A λυχνία may be removed (ii. 6), but not a στύλος.

καὶ γράψω ἐπ' αὐτὸν τὸ ὄνομα κτλ.] Each pillar in the sanctuary (Arethas: ἐπὶ τὸν νοητὸν στύλον) is to be inscribed by the hand of Christ with three names, the Name of God, the name of the new Jerusalem, and the new name of Christ. (1) The Name of God was 'put on' every Israelite in the priestly blessing (Num. vi. 27

σαλήμ, ἡ καταβαίνουσα ἐκ τοῦ οὐρανοῦ ἀπὸ τοῦ
θεοῦ μου, καὶ τὸ ὄνομά μου τὸ καινόν. [13]ὁ ἔχων οὖς 13
ἀκουσάτω τί τὸ πνεῦμα λέγει ταῖς ἐκκλησίαις.
[14]Καὶ τῷ ἀγγέλῳ τῆς ἐν Λαοδικίᾳ ἐκκλησίας 14

12 *η καταβαινουσα* ℵ*AC(P) 1 12 15 25 28 37 40 45 51 130] *η καταβαινει* Q min[pl] Andr Ar *της καταβαινουσης* ℵ[c.a] | *εκ*] *απο* 2 6 7 16 29 31 35 al Ar om 7 | om *μου* 5° Q 6 7 14 38 95 130 al[pl] vg[fu] arm 13 *ους*] *aures* vg[fu dem] al 14 *της εν Λαοδικια εκκλ.* ℵAC (PQ *-κεια*) 7 94 al Andr Ar] *της εκκλ. Λαοδικεων* 1 *eccl. Laodiciae* vg me syr[gw] arm aeth (Prim)

ἐπιθήσουσιν το ὄνομά μου ἐπὶ τοὺς υἱοὺς Ἰσραήλ); on members of the Israel of God it is to be inscribed by the Spirit of the great High Priest (cf. 2 Cor. iii. 3 *ἐστὲ ἐπιστολὴ Χριστοῦ...ἐνγεγραμμένη...πνεύματι θεοῦ ζῶντος*), i.e. their lives and characters are to be dominated by the sense of their consecration to the service of God as He is revealed in Christ. (2) The name of the new Jerusalem (cf. xxi. 2 *τὴν πόλιν τὴν ἁγίαν εἶδον Ἰερουσαλὴμ καινήν*), the successor of the old Jerusalem which was already of the past, not however a *νέα* Ἰ. like Hadrian's Aelia, but a *καινή*, instinct with the powers of an endless life (cf. ii. 17, note), and like Christ Himself of heavenly origin (*ἡ καταβαίνουσα κτλ.*, cf. xxi. 2, and see Jo. vi. 33; the idea is found already in Gal. iv. 26 *ἡ ἄνω Ἰερουσαλήμ*, Heb. xii. 22 *προσεληλύθατε Ἰ. ἐπουρανίῳ*). To bear the name of the City of God is to be openly acknowledged as one of her citizens, a privilege already potentially belonging to the members of the Church (Gal. *l. c.* *ἥτις ἐστὶν μήτηρ ἡμῶν*, Phil. iii. 20 *ἡμῶν γὰρ τὸ πολίτευμα ἐν οὐρανοῖς ὑπάρχει*, Heb. *l. c.*), but not as yet confirmed or proclaimed. (3) Christ's new name—*τὸ ὄνομα τὸ καινόν* emphasizes the *καινότης*—can scarcely be one of the names or titles familiar to the Church from the first (Jesus, Christ, Son of God, the Lord, etc.); if any such designation were meant here, it would rather be the Johannine title *Λόγος*; cf. xix. 12 *ἔχων ὄνομα γεγραμμένον ὃ οὐδεὶς οἶδεν εἰ μὴ αὐτός...καὶ κέκληται τὸ ὄνομα αὐτοῦ Ὁ λόγος τοῦ θεοῦ*. But the 'new name' of Christ is more probably a symbol for the fuller glories of His Person and Character which await revelation at His Coming (Andreas: *τὸ ἐν τοῖς ἁγίοις ἐν τῷ μέλλοντι αἰῶνι γνωριζόμενον*); cf. ii. 17 *δώσω αὐτῷ ὄνομα καινόν*. Both the victorious Christian and the victorious Christ will receive a new name, i.e. sustain a new character and appear in a new light; cf. Col. iii. 4, 1 Jo. iii. 2. There are interesting parallels in the Rabbinical writers; cf. *Baba Bathra*, f. 75. 2 "tres appellari nomine Dei, iustos, Messiam, et Hierosolyma"; *Bereshith Rabba* in Gen. xviii. 17 "Abrahamus etiam novit nomen novum quo appellanda erat Hierosolyma." Ignatius (*Philad.* 5) draws a picture which presents a striking contrast to this: *ἐὰν δὲ...περὶ Ἰησοῦ Χριστοῦ μὴ λαλῶσιν, οὗτοι ἐμοὶ στῆλαί εἰσιν καὶ τάφοι νεκρῶν ἐφ' οἷς γέγραπται μόνον ὀνόματα ἀνθρώπων*.

Ἰερουσαλήμ: so the name is written in the Apoc. (iii. 12, xxi. 2, 10); the Gospel of St John has uniformly *Ἰεροσόλυμα*.

Ramsay (*Exp.*, 1904, ii. 349 f.) finds in *v.* 12 a reference to the name Neocaesarea assumed by Philadelphia in honour of Tiberius.

14—22. The Message to the Church in Laodicea.

14. *τῆς ἐν Λαοδικίᾳ*] Forty miles S.E. of Philadelphia the road from Sardis reached Laodicea-on-the-Lycus.

γράψον Τάδε λέγει ὁ ἀμήν, ὁ μάρτυς ὁ πιστὸς καὶ ἀληθινός, ἡ ἀρχὴ τῆς κτίσεως τοῦ θεοῦ.
[15]οἶδά

14 ο μαρτυς] pr και ℵ* (om ℵ^{c.a}) | και αληθινος APQ min^{pl} vg me syr^{gw} arm aeth Prim Ar] και ο αληθ. ℵC 2 ο αληθ. 7 14 16 28 45 79 80 syr | η αρχη] pr και ℵ syr^{gw} | κτισεως] εκκλησιας ℵ* (κτ. ℵ^{c.a}) πιστεως 94

The valley of the Lycus has been described by Lightfoot (*Colossians*, p. 1 ff.), and more recently and in some respects more fully by Ramsay (*Cities and Bishoprics of Phrygia*, p. 1 ff.; there is a useful map in his *Church in the Roman Empire*, pp. 472—3). Laodicea (Λαοδίκεια in literature and inscriptions, but in MSS. of the N.T. Λαοδικία is well supported at each occurrence of the name; Lat. *Laodicea*, and in the N.T. also *Laodicia, Laudicia*) was founded about the middle of the 3rd cent. B.C. by Antiochus II., and named in honour of his wife, Laodice. Under Roman rule the city flourished, and became a centre of commercial activity. Cicero repaired to it for monetary transactions (*ad fam.* iii. 5, *ad Att.* v. 15); and the neighbourhood was noted for the manufacture of woollen carpets and clothing (Ramsay, *Cities*, p. 40 ff.). So opulent were the Laodiceans under the earlier Emperors that after the great earthquake which overthrew the town in A.D. 60–1, it rose from its ruins without being compelled to accept an Imperial subsidy (Tac. *ann.* xiv. 29 "tremore terrae prolapsa nullo a nobis remedio propriis viribus revaluit"). The Church in Laodicea was perhaps founded by Epaphras of Colossae (Col. i. 7, iv. 12 f.). St Paul had not visited the Lycus valley down to the time of his first Roman imprisonment (Col. ii. 1), but brethren at Laodicea were known to him by name (Col. iv. 15), and he had addressed a letter to the Church there (*ib.* 16 τὴν ἐκ Λαοδικίας, unless the circular now entitled Πρὸς Ἐφεσίους is intended; for the apocryphal letter *Ad Laodicenses* see Lightfoot, *Colossians*, p. 393 ff.). The ruins which strew the site of Laodicea are known as *Eski Hissar*; it is now without inhabitant, but a Bishop of Laodicea is mentioned as late as A.D. 1450 (Ramsay, *Cities and Bishoprics*, p. 79).

τάδε λέγει ὁ ἀμὴν κτλ.] The personal *Amen*, whose character and nature are in themselves a guarantee for the truth of His testimony. The commentators refer to Isa. lxv. 16 בֵּאלֹהֵי אָמֵן, LXX. τὸν θεὸν τὸν ἀληθινόν, Symm. apparently, τὸν θεὸν ἀμήν. But it is simpler to explain ὁ ἀμήν as referring to our Lord's repeated use of the formula ἀμὴν ἀμὴν λέγω ὑμῖν, coupled with His assurance ἐγώ εἰμι...ἡ ἀλήθεια—ἡ αὐτοαλήθεια, or ἡ οὐσιώδης ἀλήθεια, as the Greek fathers express it. Cf. ii. 16, note. Ὁ μάρτυς ὁ πιστός looks back to *c.* i. 5; for ὁ ἀληθινός see iii. 7; ὁ μ. ὁ ἀληθινός is the witness who fulfils his ideal, whose testimony never falls short of the truth.

ἡ ἀρχὴ τῆς κτίσεως τοῦ θεοῦ: cf. Col. i. 15, 18 πρωτότοκος πάσης κτίσεως ...ὅς ἐστιν ἡ ἀρχή—a passage doubtless familiar to the Church of Laodicea (cf. Col. iv. 15). This title of Christ rests on Prov. viii. 22, LXX. Κύριος ἔκτισέν με [sc. τὴν σοφίαν] ἀρχὴν ὁδῶν αὐτοῦ εἰς ἔργα αὐτοῦ, but readjusts the conception; He is not, as the Arians inferred, ἓν τῶν κτισμάτων, but the ἀρχὴ τῆς κτίσεως (Andreas: ἡ προκαταρκτικὴ αἰτία καὶ ἄκτιστος), the uncreated principle of creation, from whom it took its origin—the *principium principians*, not the *principium principatum*. The whole tendency of the Johannine writings and of the Apocalypse itself forbids the interpretation 'the first of crea-

σου τὰ ἔργα, ὅτι οὔτε ψυχρὸς εἶ οὔτε ζεστός.
ὄφελον ψυχρὸς ἦς ἢ ζεστός. [16]οὔτως ὅτι χλιαρὸς 16

15 om *οτι* 28 152 syr[gw] | om *ψυχρος ει ουτε* syr[sch] | om *ει* ℵ* (hab ℵ[c.a]) | *ωφελον* PQ | om *οφελον...ζεστος* A 1 47 | *ης*] *εις* (*sic*) Q 16 32 16 *ουτως οτι*] *οτι ουτως* ℵ om *ουτως* 130 syr[gw] om *ουτ. οτι* arm | *χλιερος* ℵ* (*χλιαρ.* ℵ[c.a]) 130: cf. W. Schm. p. 50

tures.' 'Η *ἀρχή* is applied to our Lord again in *c.* xxi. 6 *ἐγὼ τὸ ἄλφα καὶ τὸ ὦ, ἡ ἀρχὴ καὶ τὸ τέλος*: cf. xxii. 13 which adds *ὁ πρῶτος καὶ ὁ ἔσχατος*. In its present connexion *ἡ ἀρχή* perhaps carries the further thought of preeminence, cf. Gen. xlix. 3 *'Ρουβὴν πρωτότοκός μου, σὺ ἰσχύς μου καὶ ἀρχὴ τέκνων μου*, the head of the family as well as the first in point of time. The Creation is subjected (Heb. ii. 8) to the Eternal Word with Whom it began. *Τοῦ θεοῦ* reserves the supreme proprietorship for the Father; cf. 1 Cor. viii. 6 *ὁ πατήρ, ἐξ οὗ τὰ πάντα*, Eph. iv. 6 *εἷς θεὸς καὶ πατὴρ πάντων, ὁ ἐπὶ πάντων*. Elsewhere *ἡ κτίσις* stands by itself, e.g. Rom. viii. 19 f.

15. *οἶδά σου τὰ ἔργα, ὅτι κτλ.*] The Amen, the Head of the whole Creation, bears witness to the condition of the last of the Seven Churches. The solemnity of the title prepares for a searching and severe criticism. From the faults of the Churches at Ephesus, Pergamum, Thyatira, and Sardis the Laodicean angel seems to have been free. No Nicolaitans, no Jezebel, infested Laodicea. But his error, if less patent, was even more vital. Judged by his works he was neither frigid (*ψυχρός*, icy cold: cf. Sir. xliii. 20 *ψυχρὸς ἄνεμος βορέης πνεύσει καὶ παγήσεται κρύσταλλος ἀφ' ὕδατος*; Mt. x. 42 *ποτήριον ψυχροῦ*), nor at boiling heat (*ζεστός, ἅπ. λεγ.* in Biblical Greek, 'boiled' i.e. boiling hot, Syr. ܪܬܝܚܐ). I.e. the Church was neither wholly indifferent, nor on the other hand 'fervent in spirit' (cf. Acts xviii. 25, Rom. xii. 11 *τῷ πνεύματι ζέοντες*), but held an intermediate position between the two extremes. Cf. *Sohar*, Gen. f. 83 "tres dantur classes hominum, sunt enim vel iusti perfecti, vel impii imperfecti, vel intermedii."

ὄφελον ψυχρὸς ἦς ἢ ζεστός] For *ὄφελον* (= *ὤφελον*), *utinam*, used as a particle and followed by a verb in the ind., see 1 Cor. iv 8, 2 Cor. xi. 1, Gal. v. 12, and in the LXX., Exod. xvi. 3, Job xiv. 13 (= מִי יִתֵּן), Num. xiv. 2, xx. 3 (= לוּ), 4 Regn. v. 3, Ps. cxviii. (cxix.) 5 (= אַחֲלַי); and cf. Blass, *Gr.* p. 206 f., and W. Schm. p. 102, note. Andreas (citing Greg. Naz.): *ὁ μὲν γὰρ ψυχρὸς καὶ τῆς ζεούσης πίστεως ἄγευστος ἐν ἐλπίδι πολλάκις ἔσται τοῦ τυχεῖν αὐτῆς*. Cf. Gregory the Great, *reg. past.* iii. 34 "qui vero post conversionem tepuit, et spem quae esse potuit de peccatore subtraxit. aut calidus ergo quisquis esse aut frigidus quaeritur, ne tepidus evomatur." *Χλιαρός* is neither boiling nor cold, 'tepid'; like *ζεστός*, the word is a *ἅπ. λεγ.* in Biblical Greek. The *χλιαρός* is the Christian who is without enthusiasm (Arethas: *ὃς μετουσίας ἔλαβε πνεύματος ἁγίου διὰ τοῦ βαπτίσματος, ἔσβεσε δὲ τὸ χάρισμα*).

16. *οὔτως ὅτι χλιαρὸς εἶ κτλ.*] A draught of tepid water provokes nausea, and a tepid Christianity is nauseous to Christ (*μέλλω σὲ ἐμέσαι ἐκ τοῦ στ. μου*); He prefers the frigid indifference which the Divine Love has not begun to thaw. There is probably an allusion to the hot springs of Hierapolis, which in their way over the plateau become lukewarm, and in this condition discharge themselves over the cliff right opposite to Laodicea; cf. Strabo, 903 *καταντικρὺ Λαοδικείας 'Ιεράπολις, ὅπου τὰ θερμὰ ὕδατα*. It is but six miles across the valley from one city to the other, and the

εἶ, καὶ οὔτε ζεστὸς οὔτε ψυχρός, μέλλω σε ἐμέσαι
17 ἐκ τοῦ στόματός μου. [17]ὅτι λέγεις ὅτι Πλούσιός
εἰμι καὶ πεπλούτηκα καὶ οὐδὲν χρείαν ἔχω, καὶ οὐκ
οἶδας ὅτι σὺ εἶ ὁ ταλαίπωρος καὶ ἐλεινὸς καὶ πτωχὸς
18 καὶ τυφλὸς καὶ γυμνός, [18]συμβουλεύω σοι ἀγοράσαι

16 *ουτε* 1°] *ου* min$^{\text{fere 32}}$ syrr^{vid} | *ζεστος ουτε ψυχρος* ℵCQ min$^{\text{fere 40}}$ me syr^{gw} arm Andr Ar] *ψ. ουτε ζ.* AP 17 18 (19) vg syr^{gw} om 10 vg$^{\text{harl*}}$ aeth Amb Ambrst Prim | *ψυχρος*] + *ει* ℵ$^{*(\text{c.a})}$ | *μελλω σε εμεσαι* (*εμιν* ℵ$^{\text{c.a}}$) *εκ τ. στ. μου*] *παυσαι τ. στ. μ.* ℵ* 17 om *οτι* 2° ℵPQ min$^{\text{fere 35}}$ vg^{ed} syr arm aeth (hab AC 1 6 17 28 31 al *g* vg^{codd} syr^{gw}) | *ουδεν* AC 12] *ουδενος* ℵPQ min^{pl} Ar | *συ ει ο ταλαιπωρος*] *ταλ. ει* ℵ* | *ελεινος* (*ελεειν.* ℵPQ min^{pl} Andr Ar)] pr *ο* AQ min$^{\text{fere 30}}$ Ar *αληθινος* 130

cliff over which the *χλιαρὸν ὕδωρ* tumbles is visible for a great distance, owing to the white incrustation of lime which has been deposited upon it in the course of ages. Moreover, the letter for Laodicea was practically addressed to the other Churches of the Lycus valley, to the Church of Hierapolis as well as to Laodicea and Colossae. On the hot springs of Hierapolis see Ramsay, *Cities*, ii. p. 85 f.

17. *ὅτι λέγεις ὅτι Πλούσιός εἰμι κτλ.*] The Laodicene Church was not only tepid; it was contented to be so, and thought highly of its own condition. External circumstances were favourable to this state of feeling; the city was one of the most prosperous of the Asiatic towns (Ramsay, *Cities*, i. p. 38 f.). The Christian community carried the pride of wealth into its spiritual life, "I am rich," it boasted, "and have gotten riches (*πεπλούτηκα*)," i.e. my wealth is due to my own exertions. Cf. Hos. xii. 8 (9), *εἶπεν Ἐφράιμ Πλὴν πεπλούτηκα, εὕρηκα ἀναψυχὴν ἐμαυτῷ*, Zech. xi. 5 *εὐλογητὸς Κύριος, καὶ πεπλουτήκαμεν*, 1 Cor. iv. 8 *ἤδη κεκορεσμένοι ἐστέ; ἤδη ἐπλουτήσατε*; In *οὐδὲν χρείαν ἔχω*, *οὐδὲν* is the acc. of reference (cf. Blass, *Gr.* p. 94) or of content (*ib.* p. 91, where however the note should be cancelled); *οὐδενός* is an obvious correction, cf. 1 Th. iv. 12. The Church brags like a *nouveau riche*, but in complete ignorance of the true condition of affairs.

οὐκ οἶδας ὅτι σὺ εἶ ὁ ταλαίπωρος κτλ.] Contrast Christ's *οἶδα* (*v.* 15). *Σύ* is emphatic, 'thou that boastest,' and the article that precedes the predicates (cf. Blass, *Gr.* p. 157) strengthens the picture: 'it is thou that art the (conspicuously, pre-eminently) wretched' etc. For *ταλαίπωρος* cf. Rom. vii. 24, and for *ἐλεεινός* 'pitiable' see Dan. ix. 23, x. 11, 19 (LXX.), 1 Cor. xv. 19 *ἐλεεινότεροι πάντων ἀνθρώπων ἐσμέν*: the form *ἐλεινός*, given by AC, is perhaps to be preferred here; see however Blass, *Gr.* p. 23. The next three adjectives state the grounds for commiseration; a blind beggar (cf. Mc. x. 46), barely clad (Matt. xxv. 36 ff., Jac. ii. 2, 5; for this sense of *γυμνός* cf. Jo. xxi. 7), was not more deserving of pity than this rich and self-satisfied Church. On *πτωχός* see ii. 9, Mc. xii. 43, note; the *πτωχός* is the direct opposite of the *πλούσιος*, cf. Lc. xvi. 19 f., 2 Cor. vi. 10. It is possible that each of the epithets alludes to some local subject of self-complacency. On other local allusions see the next note.

18. *συμβουλεύω σοι ἀγοράσαι κτλ.*] *Συμβουλεύειν* (*τινί*) is to give counsel (Exod. xviii. 19, Num. xxiv. 14, 2 Regn. xvii. 11, 15, Jo. xviii. 14); *συμβουλεύεσθαι* to take counsel together (Sir. ix. 14, Isa. xl. 14, Mt. xxvi. 4, Acts ix. 23).

παρ' ἐμοῦ χρυσίον πεπυρωμένον ἐκ πυρὸς ἵνα πλουτήσῃς, καὶ ἱμάτια λευκὰ ἵνα περιβάλῃ καὶ μὴ φανερωθῇ ἡ αἰσχύνη τῆς γυμνότητός σου, καὶ κολλούριον ἐγχρῖσαι τοὺς ὀφθαλμούς σου ἵνα

18 παρ εμου χρ. ℵACP 1 28 36 49 79 al^mu vid^ *g* vg syrr] χρ. παρ εμου Q 6 7 8 14 29 38 al^fere 30^ me Ar om παρ εμου 31 34 35 87 97 Prim | εκ πυρας Q | περιβαλλη 13 14 28 79* 80 87 92 Ar | αισχυνη] ασχημοσυνη P 1 36 | κολλουριον AP 10 17 30 32 36 49 51 81 91 (130)] κολ(λ)υριον ℵC(Q) 2 6 7 8 14 31 35 (38) 82 87 92^txt^ al^fere 20^ Ar al κουλ(λ)ουριον (1) 28 29 79 (80?) | εγχρισαι ℵ (ενχρ.) AC 7 16 18 28 36 45 syr^gw^] εγχρισον P 1 49 79 91 92^mg^ 96 130 al Andr ινα εγχριση Q (-σει) min^plq 35^ Ar | om τους οφθ. σου syr^gw^

There is perhaps a reference to Isa. lv. 1 ὅσοι μὴ ἔχετε ἀργύριον...ἀγοράσατε...ἄνευ ἀργυρίου καὶ τιμῆς: for ἀγοράσαι παρ' ἐμοῦ cf. 2 Esdr. xx. 31 οὐκ ἀγορῶμεν παρ' αὐτῶν, and for ἀγοράζειν in this metaphorical sense, Mt. xxv. 9 f. The allusions to local conditions are here even more distinct. Χρυσίον presents a contrast to the wealth of the Laodicene τραπεζῖται; ἱμάτια λευκά, to the black fabric for which the neighbourhood was famous (Ramsay, *Cities and Bishoprics*, p. 40 "a fine kind of wool, soft in texture and glossy black in colour, grew on the Laodicene sheep...a kind of small cheap cloak...was manufactured at Laodicea and called *Laodicia*, or ἁπλᾶ ἱμάτια"); while κολλούριον probably refers to the school of medicine attached to the neighbouring temple of Asklepios, and the eye-powder (τέφρα Φρυγία) used by its physicians (Ramsay, p. 52). It is possible to make too much of these coincidences, which may be in part accidental, but at least they are interesting and suggestive.

As to details. With πεπυρωμένον ἐκ πυρός, cf. Ps. xvii. (xviii.) 31 τὰ λόγια Κυρίου πεπυρωμένα, Prov. xxiv. 28 (xxx. 5); the thought is of purity attained by removing dross (cf. Ps. lxv. (lxvi.) 10 ἐπύρωσας ἡμᾶς ὡς πυροῦται τὸ ἀργύριον, Zach. xiii. 9, Isa. i. 25 πυρώσω [σὲ] εἰς καθαρόν), perhaps with reference to the fiery trial which attends the process (cf. 1 Pet. i. 7 τὸ δοκίμιον ὑμῶν τῆς πίστεως πολυτιμότερον χρυσίου...διὰ πυρὸς...δοκιμαζομένου). Ἐκ πυρός is nearly = ἀπὸ or ὑπὸ π., but hints at the metal coming out of the fire intact. Ἵνα μὴ φανερωθῇ κτλ.; an O.T. idea, cf. Exod. xx. 26, Nah. iii. 5, Ezek. xvi. 36; there is perhaps special reference to Ezek. xxiii. 29, LXX. Κολλούριον (or κολλύριον, *collyrium* Hor. *Sat.* i. 5. 30, the קִילוֹרִית of Jewish literature), a diminutive of κολλύρα, is (1) a small roll of bread (3 Regn. xii. 24 ff.), (2) from its roll-like shape, a kind of eye-salve made according to Celsus (vi. 7) from the poppy, the acacia, and other flowering plants; here possibly used with reference to the local powder already mentioned. For ἐγχρίειν of applications to the eyes see Tobit ii. 10 (ℵ), vi. 9, xi. 7; it is instructive to compare the construction of the verb in Tobit with that employed here; cf. Jo. ix. 6 (ἐπέχρισεν AD).

With regard to the interpretation, the gold which is to be acquired is doubtless faith with its accompanying works (Lc. xii. 21 εἰς θεὸν πλουτῶν, Jac. ii. 5 πλουσίους ἐν πίστει, 1 Pet. i. *l. c.*, 1 Tim. vi. 18 πλουτεῖν ἐν ἔργοις καλοῖς); the white raiment is a life in Christ unspotted by the world (Gal. iii. 27, Jac. i. 27), which alone can escape disgrace under the fierce light of the Parousia (2 Cor. v. 10); the eye-salve which stings while it heals is the ἐλεγμός of the Holy Spirit (Jo. xvi. 8 ff.), which destroys self-deception

19 βλέπῃς. ¹⁹ἐγὼ ὅσους ἐὰν φιλῶ ἐλέγχω καὶ παιδεύω·
¶C 20 ζήλευε οὖν καὶ μετανόησον.¶ ²⁰ἰδοὺ ἕστηκα ἐπὶ τὴν

19 οσους] ους vg syr^{gw} Prim | εαν] αν ℵ 36 | ζηλευε ACQ min$^{pl\,30}$ Ar] ζηλωσον ℵP 1 al$^{sat\,mu}$ Andr ζηλου 6 11 31 ζητησον 91 | om ουν 7 12 16 28

and restores spiritual vision. To buy these from Christ is to seek His gifts at the cost of personal ease or self-esteem: cf. Phil. iii. 7 ἅτινα ἦν μοι κέρδη, ταῦτα ἥγημαι διὰ τὸν χριστὸν ζημίαν.

19. ἐγὼ ὅσους ἐὰν φιλῶ κτλ.] The plain speaking of this letter was not to be attributed to aversion on the part of Christ, notwithstanding His μέλλω σε ἐμέσαι; rather it was evidence of friendship and love. Φιλῶ (Bengel: "Philadelphiensem ἠγάπησεν, Laodicensem φιλεῖ") is perhaps deliberately preferred to the less emotional and less human ἀγαπῶ (i. 5, iii. 9; cf. Jo. xi. 3, 36, xvi. 27, xx. 2, xxi. 15 ff.), notwithstanding the use of the latter in Prov. iii. 12 (LXX. ὃν γὰρ ἀγαπᾷ Κύριος ἐλέγχει) which supplies the groundwork of the thought. Ἐλέγχω καὶ παιδεύω: two stages in one process; ἔλεγξις aims at effecting by words or thoughts what παιδεία accomplishes, where ἔλεγξις fails, by act; παιδεία is ἔλεγξις brought about through external means. The two verbs are perhaps a double rendering of יוֹכִיחַ in Prov. *l. c.*, where ἐλέγχει is read by B but παιδεύει by ℵA; or παιδεύω (and the reading παιδεύει) may have been suggested by the preceding verse in Prov. (υἱέ, μὴ ὀλιγώρει παιδείας Κυρίου). For ἐλέγχειν it is instructive to compare Eph. v. 13, 2 Tim. iv. 2, and St John's use of the verb in Jo. iii. 20, viii. 46, xvi. 8; on παιδεύειν a good note will be found in Westcott, *Hebrews*, ad loc.; cf. H. A. A. Kennedy, *Sources*, p. 101. Perhaps the deplorable condition of the Laodicene Church was due to lack of chastisement; there is no word of any trials hitherto undergone by this Church. The needed discipline came under Marcus Aurelius, when Sagaris, the Bishop of Laodicea, was martyred (Eus. *H. E.* iv. 26, v. 24).

ζήλευε οὖν καὶ μετανόησον] Cf. ii. 5, iii. 3 μνημόνευε οὖν...καὶ μετανόησον. In the present case not memory but enthusiasm was at fault. Ζηλεύειν is a late and rare form for ζηλοῦν, as κυκλεύειν (xx. 9) for κυκλοῦν (WH. *Notes*, p. 178), but with the sense 'be zealous'; for other exx. of late verbs in -εύειν see WM., p. 114, Kennedy, *Sources*, p. 43, *Introd. to the O. T. in Gk*, p. 503. Ζήλευε looks back to ζεστός (*v.* 15 f.; Bengel: "et ζεστός et ζῆλος est ex ζέω"), dwelling upon its ethical meaning: 'prove thyself to possess (pres. imper.) a whole-hearted devotion for the Master." So doing, the Laodicean Church would arrive at a better mind (μετανόησον), and be no longer 'tepid' but 'fervent in spirit.'

20. ἰδοὺ ἕστηκα ἐπὶ τὴν θύραν κτλ.] Arethas: ἀβίαστος, φησίν, ἡ ἐμὴ παρουσία. The voice is that of a friend (*v.* 19); there is perhaps a reference to Cant. v. 2 φωνὴ ἀδελφιδοῦ μου, κρούει ἐπὶ τὴν θύραν· ἄνοιξόν μοι, ἀδελφή μου, ἡ πλησίον μου. In this light the homiletic use of the passage, which sees in it a picture of our Lord knocking at the hearts of men, and which Holman Hunt's great painting has made familiar, finds its justification. But as they stand in this context, the words are eschatological (cf. Mt. xxiv. 33 ἐγγύς ἐστιν ἐπὶ θύραις, Jac. v. 9 ὁ κριτὴς πρὸ τῶν θυρῶν ἕστηκεν); the opening of the door is the joyful response of the Church to the last call, cf. Lc. xii. 36 ὑμεῖς ὅμοιοι ἀνθρώποις προσδεχομένοις τὸν κύριον ἑαυτῶν... ἵνα ἐλθόντος καὶ κρούσαντος εὐθέως ἀνοίξωσιν αὐτῷ. The picture is exactly reversed in Lc. xiii. 25, where

θύραν καὶ κρούω· ἐάν τις ἀκούσῃ τῆς φωνῆς μου καὶ
ἀνοίξῃ τὴν θύραν, εἰσελεύσομαι πρὸς αὐτὸν καὶ
δειπνήσω μετ' αὐτοῦ καὶ αὐτὸς μετ' ἐμοῦ. [21]ὁ νικῶν, 21
δώσω αὐτῷ καθίσαι μετ' ἐμοῦ ἐν τῷ θρόνῳ μου, ὡς
κἀγὼ ἐνίκησα καὶ ἐκάθισα μετὰ τοῦ πατρός μου ἐν

20 om ακουσῃ της φωνης μου και Or Hil | ανοιξῃ] ανοιξω ℵ ανοιξει syr^{gw} | εισελευσομαι] pr και ℵQ min$^{fere\ 35}$ syr^{gw} Prim (om AP 1 6 13 17 18 19 28 36 37 38 79 80 81 161 vg syr me arm aeth Or Hil Ar)

the Master shuts the door and the servants knock in vain; cf. Mt. xxv. 10 f.

ἐάν τις ἀκούσῃ τῆς φωνῆς μου κτλ.] If any Church (or individual) gives heed to the call of Christ (cf. Jo. x. 3 τὰ πρόβατα φωνῆς αὐτοῦ ἀκούει, 16 f., xviii. 37 πᾶς ὁ ὢν ἐκ τῆς ἀληθείας ἀκούει μου τῆς φωνῆς) and opens the door, Christ will enter that dwelling (Jo. xiv. 23 πρὸς αὐτὸν ἐλευσόμεθα καὶ μονὴν παρ' αὐτῷ ποιησόμεθα, Eph. iii. 17 κατοικῆσαι τὸν χριστὸν διὰ τῆς πίστεως ἐν ταῖς καρδίαις ὑμῶν ἐν ἀγάπῃ), and exchange with such an one the fellowship of intimate communion (cf. Jo. vi. 56 ὁ τρώγων μου τὴν σάρκα καὶ πίνων μου τὸ αἷμα ἐν ἐμοὶ μένει κἀγὼ ἐν αὐτῷ) in that endless feast of Love of which the Eucharist is the earnest (Mt. xxvi. 29 ἕως τῆς ἡμέρας ἐκείνης ὅταν αὐτὸ πίνω μεθ' ὑμῶν καινὸν ἐν τῇ βασιλείᾳ τοῦ πατρός μου).

Εἰσέρχεσθαι πρός τινα, to enter a man's house, Mc. xv. 43, Acts xi. 3. Δειπνήσω is preferred to ἀριστήσω partly because the δεῖπνον came at the end of the day and was the principal meal and the usual occasion for hospitality, but perhaps chiefly with reference to the κυριακὸν δεῖπνον. Origen's οὐ γὰρ δεῖται εἰσαγωγῆς καὶ πρώτων μαθημάτων (*in Joann.* t. xxxii. 2) is ingenious but far-fetched.

21. ὁ νικῶν, δώσω αὐτῷ καθίσαι μετ' ἐμοῦ κτλ.] An extension of the promise made to the Twelve in Mt. xix. 28 ὅταν καθίσῃ ὁ υἱὸς τοῦ ἀνθρώπου ἐπὶ θρόνου δόξης αὐτοῦ, καθήσεσθε καὶ ὑμεῖς ἐπὶ δώδεκα θρόνους: cf. Lc. xxii. 29 f. κἀγὼ διατίθεμαι ὑμῖν, καθὼς διέθετό μοι ὁ πατήρ μου βασιλείαν, ἵνα ἔσθητε καὶ πίνητε ἐπὶ τῆς τραπέζης μου ἐν τῇ βασιλείᾳ μου, καὶ καθῆσθε ἐπὶ θρόνων τὰς δώδεκα φυλὰς κρίνοντες τοῦ Ἰσραήλ, where, as here, the enthronement follows immediately after the mention of the heavenly feast. The θρόνοι however (cf. ii. 13, note) are not places on the *triclinium*, but thrones of dignity and judicial power, cf. 1 Cor. vi. 2 f. οὐκ οἴδατε ὅτι οἱ ἅγιοι τὸν κόσμον κρινοῦσιν;...οὐκ οἴδατε ὅτι ἀγγέλους κρινοῦμεν; The Apocalyptic promise adds that the conqueror shall not merely be enthroned like Christ, but be His σύνθρονος. Μετ' ἐμοῦ might imply association only, but ἐν τῷ θρόνῳ μου implies a share in the same throne, i.e. in the glory and powers of Christ's own triumphant humanity.

ὡς κἀγὼ ἐνίκησα κτλ.] Cf. Jo. xvi. 33 ἐγὼ νενίκηκα τὸν κόσμον, 1 Jo. v. 4 αὕτη ἐστὶν ἡ νίκη ἡ νικήσασα τὸν κόσμον, ἡ πίστις ἡμῶν. Here ἐνίκησα looks back upon the historical fact of the Lord's victory as past and complete; νενίκηκα in Jo. *l. c.* regards the victory, as abiding in its effects. The rewards of victory are not the same in the case of Christ as in the case of the disciple; the disciple becomes σύνθρονος with Christ in Christ's throne, whereas the Lord is σύνθρονος with the Father; cf. ii. 27 f. δώσω αὐτῷ...ὡς κἀγὼ εἴληφα παρὰ τοῦ πατρός μου. Ἐκάθισα like ἐνίκησα is the historical aorist; the session followed at the moment of the Ascension,

22 τῷ θρόνῳ αὐτοῦ. ²²ὁ ἔχων οὖς ἀκουσάτω τί τὸ
πνεῦμα λέγει ταῖς ἐκκλησίαις.

22 ους] *aures* vg[fu al] Prim

whilst the victory was achieved by the Resurrection; see Mc. xvi. 19, Eph. i. 20, Heb. i. 3, viii. 1, xii. 2. The ultimate source of the conception is Ps. cx. 1; on its meaning see Apringius *ad l.*: "quid est in throno Dei sedere, nisi quiescere et gloriari cum Deo et eius adsistere tribunalibus beatis, atque immensa praesentiae illius felicitate gaudere?" With the parallel ὡς κἀγὼ κτλ. cf. Jo. xv. 10, xvii. 18, xx. 21, Apoc. ii. 28.

Looking back over the seven λόγοι (ii. 1—iii. 22), it is easy to see that widely as their contents differ, they are constructed upon a common plan. Each begins with the formula Τῷ ἀγγέλῳ τῷ (τῆς) ἐν...ἐκκλησίας γράψον Τάδε λέγει ὁ..., and ends with the call Ὁ ἔχων οὖς κτλ. followed (1—3) or preceded (4—7) by a promise to the Christian victor (τῷ νικῶντι δώσω αὐτῷ (1, 3), or ὁ νικῶν...δώσω αὐτῷ (4, 7), or ὁ νικῶν ποιήσω αὐτόν (6) or ὁ νικῶν followed by a verb expressing the reward (2, 5)).

Even in the contents of the several messages a certain uniformity may be detected. After the opening words each λόγος begins with οἶδα—οἶδά σου τὰ ἔργα (1, 4—7), οἶδά σου τὴν θλίψιν (2), or οἶδα ποῦ κατοικεῖς (3); i.e. each is based on the Speaker's knowledge of the conduct or circumstances of the several churches. The distinctive merits and faults of each community are then set forth, together with suitable encouragement and reproof. Lastly, advice is given as to the future: μνημόνευε οὖν...καὶ μετανόησον (1, 5), μετανόησον οὖν (3), ζήλευε οὖν καὶ μετανόησον (7), μὴ φοβοῦ...γίνου πιστὸς ἄχρι θανάτου (2), ὃ ἔχετε κρατήσατε or κράτει ὃ ἔχεις (4, 6).

Yet uniform as the λόγοι are in their general structure, they present a rich variety of detail. As each Church passes under review, it receives a judgement which is evidently based upon a full knowledge of its condition, both external and spiritual. Smyrna and Philadelphia gain unqualified approval; Ephesus, Pergamum, Thyatira, are commended, but with reservations (ἔχω κατὰ σοῦ [ὀλίγα] ὅτι...): for Laodicea there is only censure, and Sardis would fall under the same category, were it not for a few loyal Christians (ἔχεις ὀλίγα ὀνόματα κτλ.) whose fidelity is not overlooked. But the discrimination goes further. The Supreme Pastor descends into the minutest particulars which affect the well-being of the several brotherhoods: the decay of love at Ephesus, redeemed in part by hatred of Nicolaitan laxity; the fidelity of the Smyrnaeans under the bitter reproaches of the self-styled Jews; the concessions to Nicolaitanism which marred the zeal of the Pergamenes; the indulgence shewn at Thyatira to a prophetess who, like a new Jezebel, initiated her disciples into "deep things" of Satan; the deadness of the great majority of the members of the Church at Sardis; the patient efforts of the Philadelphians to spread the faith of Christ in the teeth of Jewish opposition; the tepid, nauseous Christianity of the prosperous and self-satisfied Laodiceans. Nothing has escaped the Eye of flame, which reads the secrets of men and of churches.

Even in the formulae with which the λόγοι are opened and closed there are variable elements, which shew the same discrimination. Each τάδε λέγει is followed by a title of the Speaker, usually borrowed from the vision of *c.* i., which has special significance

1 Μετὰ ταῦτα εἶδον, καὶ ἰδοὺ θύρα ἠνεῳγμένη ἐν τῷ 1 IV.
οὐρανῷ, καὶ ἡ φωνὴ ἡ πρώτη ἣν ἤκουσα ὡς σάλπιγγος
λαλούσης μετ' ἐμοῦ, λέγων Ἀνάβα ὧδε, καὶ δείξω

IV 1 ειδον P min^{pl} Ar] ιδον ℵAQ 7 14 92 | ανεωγμενη Q min^{satmu} | και 2°] + ιδου ℵ Prim | om η πρωτη syr^{gw} | σαλπιγγα syrr | λαλουσης] λαλουσαν ℵ Prim ελαλησεν syr^{gw} | λεγων ℵ*AQ min^{plq30}] λεγουσα ℵ$^{c.a}$P 1 38 49 79 91 130 al^{satmu} και λεγουσα μοι 36 και λεγουσης 7 16 om P Prim | αναβηθι A

when we consider the circumstances of the Church addressed. Each promise to the victor places the final reward in a light which gives it special attractiveness under the circumstances in which the local Church is placed. Thus the Ephesian Christian, tempted to participate in pagan banquets, is promised, if he conquers, to eat of the fruit of the Tree of Life; the Smyrnaean, called to face martyrdom, is assured that he shall not be hurt of the Second Death; the Pergamene, if he rejects the εἰδωλόθυτα, shall taste of the Hidden Manna. If it is not always easy to discover the appropriateness of the form which the victor's prize assumes, there is reason to believe that the problem would be solved were our knowledge of the special circumstances less incomplete.

IV. 1—11. THE VISION OF THE THRONE IN HEAVEN.

1. μετὰ ταῦτα εἶδον] This formula, which occurs again vii. 1 (μ. τοῦτο), 9, xv. 5, xviii. 1, serves to introduce a new vision of special importance, καὶ εἶδον (v. 1 etc.) being used in other cases. Here μετὰ ταῦτα refers to the vision of i. 12 ff. (καὶ ἐπιστρέψας εἶδον κτλ.) which, with the messages to the Churches arising out of it, has occupied the first three chapters. The vision of the glorified Christ walking among the Churches on earth is followed by a vision of the Court of Heaven.

θύρα ἠνεῳγμένη ἐν τῷ οὐρανῷ] Not as in iii. 8 the door of opportunity, or as in iii. 20 the door of the heart, but the door of revelation; cf. Enoch xiv. 13 καὶ ἰδοὺ ἄλλη θύρα ἀνεῳγμένη κατέναντί μου. The conception of the opened heavens occurs first in Ezek. i. 1 ἠνοίχθησαν οἱ οὐρανοὶ καὶ εἶδον ὁράσεις θεοῦ: cf. Mc. i. 10 εἶδεν σχιζομένους τοὺς οὐρανούς, Jo. i. 51 ὄψεσθε τὸν οὐρανὸν ἀνεῳγότα. In this vision a door only is opened (cf. *Test. xii patr.*, Levi 5), and not heaven as a whole, i.e. the vision is limited to the Seer; only one who has been lifted up into the heavenly places can see what is passing within. The perf. part. ἠνεῳγμένη implies that the door stood open, ready for the Seer's coming.

καὶ ἡ φωνὴ ἡ πρώτη ἣν ἤκουσα κτλ.] "The first voice which I heard" is apparently the voice of i. 10 ἤκουσα...φωνὴν μεγάλην ὡς σάλπιγγος, where see note; cf. Victorinus: "id est spiritus quem paulo ante quam filium hominis...se vidisse fatetur"; Bede: "similis utique priori voci quae dixerat *Quae vides scribe in libro.*" Now it comes again to prepare John for the second great vision, and calls him up to the height where the Angel stands. Λέγων, a *constructio ad sensum*; behind the trumpet voice there is a personality who speaks. Ἀνάβα (= ἀνάβηθι W. Schm., p. 115, cf. κατάβα Ar. *Ran.* 35, *Vesp.* 979; μετάβα, Mt. xvii. 20) recalls the summons at the Lawgiving, Exod. xix. 24 f.; for ὧδε, 'hither' (Blass, *Gr.* p. 58 f.), cf. Jo. vi. 25, xx. 27. For δείξω, the Hierophant's (Benson, *Apocalypse*, p. 15) offer of guidance, see i. 1, xvii. 1, xxi. 9 f., xxii. 1, 6; ἃ δεῖ γενέσθαι (i. 1, xxii. 6) comes from Dan. ii. 28 f., 45. The vision that follows is an anticipation

2 σοι ἃ δεῖ γενέσθαι μετὰ ταῦτα. [2]εὐθέως ἐγενόμην
ἐν πνεύματι· καὶ ἰδοὺ θρόνος ἔκειτο ἐν τῷ οὐρανῷ,
3 καὶ ἐπὶ τὸν θρόνον καθήμενος, [3]καὶ ὁ καθήμενος ὅμοιος

1 α] οσα A ο syr^{gw} 2 ευθεως] pr και P 1 7 130 al$^{sat\,mu}$ me syr^{gw} arm aeth | επι] pr ο ℵ* | τον θρονον] του θρονου P 1 28 36 77 91 96 3 om και ο καθημενος 1 6 8 14 31 38 130 al me syr^{gw} arm aeth Vict Andr Ar | om ομοιος 1°...του θρονου ℵ* | λιθου vg syrr

of a future which is yet to find its accomplishment (*μετὰ ταῦτα*). WH. connect *μετὰ ταῦτα* (2°) with *εὐθέως*, but the analogy of i. 10 and Dan. *l.c.* (Th.) seems to be decisive in favour of the usual punctuation.

2. *εὐθέως ἐγενόμην ἐν πνεύματι*] 'At once,' as the words were spoken, 'I found myself in the Spirit.' The state of spiritual exaltation which preceded the first vision (i. 10 note) has returned, but in greater force; then it gave the Seer ears to hear and eyes to see; now it lifts him up and places him by the Angel at the open door.

καὶ ἰδοὺ θρόνος ἔκειτο ἐν τῷ οὐρανῷ κτλ.] When he looked in, the first Object that met his eyes was a throne and One seated on it. The Person is identified by *v.* 8 with the God of Israel (i. 4, 8), Who is represented in the O.T. sometimes as making the heaven His throne (Isa. lxvi. 1; cf. Mt. v. 34 f., xxiii. 22), sometimes as enthroned in heaven (Ps. x. (xi.) 4 *Κύριος, ἐν οὐρανῷ ὁ θρόνος αὐτοῦ*; cf. Enoch xiv. 18 ff. *ἐθεώρουν δὲ καὶ εἶδον θρόνον ὑψηλόν κτλ.*). The imagery of the Apocalypse requires the latter symbolism in which the Throne is distinguished from the sphere which it occupies.

ἔκειτο = *ἐτέθη* (cf. Dan. vii. 9), 'stood,' rather than 'was set up,' a rendering which permits the English reader to suppose that the placing of the throne entered into the vision. For *κεῖσθαι* in this sense cf. Jo. ii. 6, xix. 29, xxi. 9, and see Blass, *Gr.* p. 51. In this book *ἐπὶ τὸν θρόνον* can scarcely be distinguished from the more exact *ἐπὶ τοῦ θρόνου* or *τῷ θρόνῳ*; for the gen. see iv. 9 ff., v. 1, 7, 13, vi. 16, vii. 15; for the dat., vii. 10, xix. 4, xxi. 5; for the acc., iv. 4, vi. 2, 4 f., xi. 16, xx. 4.

3. *καὶ ὁ καθήμενος κτλ.*] The description rigorously shuns anthropomorphic details. The Seer's eye is arrested by the flashing of gemlike colours, but he sees no form: cf. Exod. xxiv. 10 *εἶδον τὸν τόπον οὗ ἱστήκει ὁ θεὸς τοῦ Ἰσραήλ* (Heb. simply אֵת אֱלֹהֵי יִשְׂרָאֵל), *καὶ τὰ ὑπὸ τοὺς πόδας αὐτοῦ ὡσεὶ ἔργον πλίνθου σαπφείρου, καὶ ὥσπερ εἶδος στερεώματος τοῦ οὐρανοῦ τῇ καθαριότητι.* Less reserve is manifested in Ezek. i. 26 *ὡς εἶδος ἀνθρώπου*, Dan. vii. 9 *παλαιὸς ἡμερῶν ἐκάθητο...ἡ θρὶξ τῆς κεφαλῆς αὐτοῦ ὡσεὶ ἔριον καθαρόν*; cf. Enoch xlvi. 1, lxxi. 10. In the great Christian Apocalypse there is no need for anthropomorphic descriptions of Deity; one like a Son of Man is always at hand to whom they are naturally transferred (see i. 14, note); cf. Andreas: *ἐπειδὴ δὲ τὸν πατέρα τὸν ὁραθέντα ἐνταῦθα παρίστησι, σωματικὸν αὐτῷ χαρακτῆρα οὐ περιτίθησιν ὥσπερ ἐν τῇ προτεραίᾳ τοῦ υἱοῦ ὀπτασίᾳ.*

The Enthroned Majesty was like in appearance (*ὁράσει* = לְמַרְאֵה, ܚܙܘܐ) to the light of two precious stones, the *λίθος ἴασπις* and the *σάρδιον*, and their brilliance was relieved by a circle of emerald green. The three stones are named together as samples of their kind by Plato (*Phaed.* 110 E *σάρδια καὶ ἰάσπιδας καὶ σμαράγδους καὶ πάντα τὰ τοιαῦτα*), and hold an honourable place in Biblical lists of gems; thus, acc. to Exod. xxviii. 17 ff., the *σάρδιον* and the emerald stand in the first row of stones in the High Priest's breastplate, and the *ἴασπις* in the

ὁράσει λίθῳ ἰάσπιδι καὶ σαρδίῳ, καὶ ἶρις κυκλόθεν
τοῦ θρόνου ὅμοιος ὁράσει σμαραγδίνῳ. ⁴καὶ κυκλόθεν 4
τοῦ θρόνου θρόνους εἴκοσι τέσσαρες, καὶ ἐπὶ τοὺς

3 ιασπιδι] + και σμαραγδω Q 13 26 41 42 44 130 (sed om και σαρδιω) | σαρδινω P 1 36 al | ιρις] ιερεις ℵ*A 28 79 arm aeth | κυκλοθεν] κυκλω 36 38 47 | ομοιος 2°] AP 1 6 7 11 12 30 36 79 vg me syr Prim ομοιως ℵ$^{\text{c.a}}$Q min$^{\text{sat mu}}$ Ar ομοια 7 10 14 16 17 18 31 47 al | ορασει σμαραγδινω] ορασις σμαραγδινων Q min^{nonn} ορασει σμαραγδων 14 syrr ως ορασις σμαραγδου 38 47 4 om και 1° Q min^{nonn} syr | θρονους 1° ℵA 34 35 87 121] θρονοι PQ min^{pl} Andr Ar syr^{vid}

second: among the precious stones which adorn the person of the King of Tyre (Ezek. xxviii. 13) the same three stones stand first, third, and sixth respectively; and of the twelve foundation stones of Apoc. xxi. 19 the ἴασπις is first, the emerald fourth, and the σάρδιον sixth. The ἴασπις (יָשְׁפֵה, said to be a Persian word, B. D. B. *s. v.*) appears to have been translucent like glass or rock-crystal (Apoc. xxi. 11 κρυσταλλίζοντι, Pliny, *H. N.* xxxvii. 115 "semper translucent"), whereas the modern jasper is opaque; the opal has been suggested (*Enc. Bibl. s. v.*), but it is excluded by the same consideration. The σάρδιον (אֹדֶם, 'redness,' cf. Epiph. *de gemmis* πυρωπὸς τῷ εἴδει καὶ αἱματοειδής) is perhaps the carnelian, or other red stone (see Hastings, *D. B. s. v.*); acc. to Pliny, *H. N. l. c.* it derived its name from Sardis, where it was found. Most of the engraved gems of antiquity were of 'sard,' see King, *Antique Gems*, p. 5.

In the vision the flashing lustre of the ἴασπις and the fiery red of the sard are relieved by the halo (ἶρις) of emerald which encircled the Throne (κυκλόθεν τοῦ θρόνου, cf. *vv.* 4, 8). From Homer downwards ἶρις is the rainbow; the LXX. however use τόξον in this sense (Gen. ix. 13, Ezek. i. 28), and ἶρις is perhaps preferred here and in x. 1 because it may also be used for a complete circle, e.g. a solar or lunar halo. The conception is borrowed from Ezek. *l. c.* ὡς ὅρασις τόξου, ὅταν ᾖ ἐν τῇ νεφέλῃ ἐν ἡμέραις ὑετοῦ, οὕτως ἡ στάσις τοῦ φέγγους κυκλόθεν. But the circle of light seen by the Apocalyptist was like (for ὅμοιος, used as an adj. of two terminations, cf. WM. p. 80, Blass, *Gr.* p. 33) in appearance (see *v.* 3) to an emerald (σμαραγδίνῳ *sc.* λίθῳ), μονοειδὴς σμαραγδίζουσα, as Arethas says. Σμαράγδινος seems to be ἅπ. λεγ., but σμαραγδίτης λίθος occurs in Esth. i. 6 A, and σμάραγδος λ. is used by Herod. ii. 44, iii. 41. Archbp. Benson translates 'like to a vision of emerald,' taking ὅμ. ὁράσει σμαρ. as if it = σμαραγδώδης, but ὁράσει in *v.* 3 does not lend itself easily to this construction; cf. however Vg. *similis aspectui lapidis iaspidis... similis visioni smaragdinae.* In Exod. xxxvi. 17 (xxxix. 10) σμάραγδος = בָּרֶקֶת, which suggests a brilliant like rock-crystal (see Hastings, *D. B.* iv. 620); on its identification with the emerald see King, *Antique Gems*, p. 27 ff. Since ἶρις is substituted for τόξον, it is precarious to press a reference to the rainbow of the covenant (Gen. ix. 12 ff.); but if the σμάραγδος was a green stone, it may perhaps represent the mercy which tempers the revelation of the Divine Majesty.

4. καὶ κυκλόθεν τοῦ θρόνου θρόνους εἴκοσι τέσσαρες] Sc. εἶδον, unless with WH. we read θρόνοι; see their note (p. 138). Τέσσαρες acc. is well supported, see WH. *Notes*, p. 157, Blass, *Gr.* p. 26.

Beyond the emerald halo there is another circle round the Throne, an environment of four and twenty other thrones on which are seated four and

θρόνους εἴκοσι τέσσαρας πρεσβυτέρους καθημένους
περιβεβλημένους ἱματίοις λευκοῖς, καὶ ἐπὶ τὰς κεφαλὰς
5 αὐτῶν στεφάνους χρυσοῦς. [5]καὶ ἐκ τοῦ θρόνου ἐκ-
πορεύονται ἀστραπαὶ καὶ φωναὶ καὶ βρονταί· καὶ
ἑπτὰ λαμπάδες πυρὸς καιόμεναι ἐνώπιον τοῦ θρόνου,

4 *θρονους* 2°] + *ειδον* 49 91 96 al^{vid} | *εικοσι τεσσ.* 2° ante *θρονους* pon A 17 18 19 pr *τους* Q 6 7 8 14 al^{mu} Ar | *τεσσερας* A | *ιματιοις λευκοις*] pr *εν* ℵQ min^{pl} om *ιμ.* ℵ *εν λευκοις* 130 (om *περιβεβλ.*) | *χρυσεους* ℵ 5 *του θρονου* 1°] *των θρονων* syr^{gw} | *βρονται και φωναι και αστραπαι* 1 29 38 95 *βρ. κ. αστρ. κ. φ.* syr^{gw} | om *πυρος* syr^{gw} | *του θρονου* 2°] + *αυτου* Q(*)^{corr} min^{mu} syrr

twenty Elders, white-robed and gold-crowned. The Elders are not *σύνθρονοι* (iii. 21), but *περιθρόνιοι* or *πάρεδροι*, forming the *γερουσία* of Heaven. There may be a reference to the Elders of Israel in Exod. xxiv. 11, who *ὤφθησαν ἐν τῷ τόπῳ τοῦ θεοῦ*, and to Isa. xxiv. 23 *βασιλεύσει Κύριος ..ἐνώπιον τῶν πρεσβυτέρων δοξασθήσεται.* But the number is at first sight perplexing. As a symbolical number 24 occurs in the Apocalypse only, and there only when these Elders are mentioned (iv. 4, 10, v. 8, xi. 16, xix. 4). It has been supposed to refer to the 24 courses of the sons of Aaron (1 Chron. xxiv. 1—19); but the Elders do not fulfil any special priesthood, though they take their part (iv. 10, v. 8) in the worship of Him who sits on the Throne. Gunkel suggests (*Schöpfung u. Chaos*, p. 302 ff.) that they answer to the 24 stars of the Babylonian astrology (cf. Diod. Sic. ii. 31 *μετὰ δὲ τὸν ζῳδιακὸν κύκλον εἴκοσιν καὶ τέτταρας ἀφορίζουσιν ἀστέρας, ὧν τοὺς μὲν ἡμίσεις ἐν τοῖς βορείοις μέρεσι τοὺς δὲ ἡμίσεις ἐν τοῖς νοτίοις τετάχθαι φασί· καὶ τούτων τοὺς μὲν ὁρωμένους τῶν ζώντων εἶναι καταριθμοῦσι, τοὺς δὲ ἀφανεῖς τοῖς τετελευτηκόσι προσωρίσθαι νομίζουσιν, οὓς δικαστὰς τῶν ὅλων προσαγορεύουσιν*); but the parallel is only partial, and the whole question of the Apocalyptist's indebtedness to Babylonian sources needs further investigation. Meanwhile a key which seems to fit the lock is supplied by the earliest Latin commentator on the Apocalypse, Victorinus, who sees in the 24 Elders "duodecim Apostoli, duodecim Patriarchae"; similarly Andreas and Arethas. The symbol appears to be based on the number of the tribes of Israel; the *δωδεκάφυλον* is represented by 24 Elders, two for each tribe, the double representation suggesting the two elements which coexisted in the new Israel, the Jewish and Gentile believers who were one in Christ. Thus the 24 Elders are the Church in its totality, but the Church idealized and therefore seen as already clad in white, crowned, and enthroned in the Divine Presence—a state yet future (*ἃ δεῖ γενέσθαι*), but already potentially realised in the Resurrection and Ascension of the Head; cf. Eph. ii. 6 *συνήγειρεν ἡμᾶς καὶ συνεκάθισεν αὐτῷ ἐν τοῖς ἐπουρανίοις.*

5. *καὶ ἐκ τοῦ θρόνου ἐκπορεύονται ἀστραπαί κτλ.*] The eye of the Seer returns to the central Throne. What he sees there reminds him of the Lawgiving; cf. Exod. xix. 16 *ἐγίνοντο φωναὶ καὶ ἀστραπαί*, and Ezek. i. 13 *ἐκ τοῦ πυρὸς ἐξεπορεύετο ἀστραπή.* The same imagery occurs again in xi. 19, xvi. 18, and (with the order *βρονταὶ καὶ φωναὶ καὶ ἀστραπαί*), in viii. 5. The thunderstorm is in Hebrew poetry a familiar symbol of the Divine power and glory: cf. e.g. 1 Sam. ii. 10, Ps. xviii. 9 ff., Job xxxvii. 4 f.

καὶ ἑπτὰ λαμπάδες πυρός κτλ.] Λαμ-

ἅ εἰσιν τὰ ἑπτὰ πνεύματα τοῦ θεοῦ. ⁶καὶ ἐνώπιον 6
τοῦ θρόνου ὡς θάλασσα ὑαλίνη ὁμοία κρυστάλλῳ,
καὶ ἐν μέσῳ τοῦ θρόνου καὶ κύκλῳ τοῦ θρόνου τέσσερα

5 *α εισιν* ℵ$^{c.a}$P 1 36 81 94 syr] *αι εισιν* Q min^{pl} syr^{gw} *g* vg^{am} *α εστιν* A *και εισιν* 130 *και* 14 92^{txt} | *τα επτα*] om *τα* Q min$^{sat\,mu}$ syrr^{vid} Andr Ar 6 *θρονου*] + *αυτου* 7 40 46 + *του θεου* me | om *ως* 1 80 94 161 al syr^{gw} arm aeth Prim | *υελινη* 9 10 35 38 al | *εμμεσω* A 130 | om *και κυκλω του θρονου* 28 29 30 98 vg^{harl*} me arm^{zoh} | *τεσσαρα* ℵPQ

πάδες occur also in Ezekiel's vision (*l.c.* *ὡς ὄψις λαμπάδων*); but whereas Ezekiel's torch-like lights flashed hither and thither (*συνστρεφομένων ἀνὰ μέσον τῶν ζῴων*), these burn steadily before the Throne, and they are seven in number, corresponding, as the Seer recognises, with the Seven Spirits of God (i. 4, iii. 1). They are *λαμπάδες*, not *λυχνίαι* as in i. 12, where the reference is different; the idea presented here is rather that of the *ἀστὴρ μέγας καιόμενος ὡς λαμπάς* (*c.* viii. 10), except that the torch-like star is seen falling across the sky, whereas these torches blaze perpetually before the Throne of God.

6. *καὶ ἐνώπιον τοῦ θρόνου ὡς θάλασσα κτλ.*] In Exod. xxiv. 10 the Elders see under the Feet of God *ὡσεὶ ἔργον πλίνθου σαπφείρου, καὶ ὥσπερ εἶδος στερεώματος τοῦ οὐρανοῦ τῇ καθαριότητι*, and this conception is reproduced in Ezekiel (i. 22, 26). But instead of the 'firmament,' the Seer of the Apocalypse sees a glassy Sea before the Throne. The idea of a celestial sea was current in Jewish circles, cf. Enoch xiv. 9, *Secrets of Enoch*, ed. Charles, p. 4; *Test. xii Patr.*, Levi 2, where a sea greater than any on earth is seen suspended between the first heaven and the second: cf. Gen. i. 7 *τοῦ ὕδατος τοῦ ἐπάνω τοῦ στερεώματος*, Ps. ciii. (civ.) 3. The Apocalyptic sea is *ὑαλίνη*, a pavement of glass resembling an expanse of water; comp. a legend in the Koran, *Sur.* 27, that the Queen of Sheba mistook for water a glass pavement in Solomon's palace. The Seer, still looking through the door, sees between himself and the Throne a vast surface which flashes back the light that falls upon it, like the Aegean when on summer days he looked upon it from the heights of Patmos; cf. xv. 2 *εἶδον ὡς θάλασσαν ὑαλίνην μεμιγμένην πυρί*. Though of glass, the sea was *ὁμοία κρυστάλλῳ*, not semi-opaque, like much ancient glass, but clear as rock-crystal. *Κρύσταλλος* may be 'ice,' both here and in Ezek. i. 22, but the mineral is more probably intended in a context which mentions precious stones; the metaphor occurs again in xxii. 1 *ποταμὸν...λαμπρὸν ὡς κρύσταλλον*. The costliness of glass in ancient days enhances the splendour of the conception; cf. Job xxviii. 17 LXX. *οὐκ ἰσωθήσεται αὐτῇ χρυσίον καὶ ὕαλος*. But the Sea of glass is not only a striking and splendid feature in the scene; it suggests the vast distance which, even in the case of one who stood at the door of heaven, intervened between himself and the Throne of God.

καὶ ἐν μέσῳ τοῦ θρόνου...τέσσερα ζῷα κτλ.] Cf. Enoch xl. 2, *Apoc. of Baruch* li. 11 (ed. Charles). The exact position assigned to the *ζῷα* is not easy to grasp. *Ἐν μέσῳ* is from Ezek. i. 5 *ἐν τῷ μέσῳ* (*τοῦ πυρὸς*) *ὡς ὁμοίωμα τεσσάρων ζῴων*, where some cursives and versions of the LXX. add *καὶ κύκλῳ τοῦ θρόνου*, but probably from the Apoc. But *ἐν τῷ μ.* in Ezekiel = מִתּוֹכָהּ i.e. 'out of the midst of the fire,' which has no parallel in the present passage. The words must therefore be interpreted independently. As they stand here, followed by

7 ζῷα γέμοντα ὀφθαλμῶν ἔμπροσθεν καὶ ὄπισθεν. ⁷καὶ
τὸ ζῷον τὸ πρῶτον ὅμοιον λέοντι, καὶ τὸ δεύτερον
ζῷον ὅμοιον μόσχῳ, καὶ τὸ τρίτον ζῷον ἔχων τὸ
πρόσωπον ὡς ἀνθρώπου, καὶ τὸ τέταρτον ζῷον ὅμοιον

6 *οφθαλμους* 16 28 36 | *ενπροσθεν* ℵAP   7 om *και* 1° syr^{gw} Prim | *εχων* AQ 7 28 30 32 33 34] *εχον* ℵP min^{pl} | *το προσωπον*] om *το* Q min$^{sat\ mu}$ arm Andr Ar | *ως ανθρωπου* A 11 13 36 vg syr^{gw} Ir Prim] *ως ομοιον ανθρωπω* ℵ *ανθρωπου* Q min$^{sat\ mu}$ *ως ανθρωπος* P 1 7 28 al syr | om *ζωον* 4° Q min$^{sat\ mu}$ (om *ζωον* quater aeth, ter Ir^{int} Vict)

καὶ κύκλῳ τ. θρ., they seem to imply that the figures are so placed that one of the *ζῷα* is always seen before the Throne, and the others on either side of it and behind, whether stationary or moving round in rapid gyration; the latter is suggested by Ezek. i. 12 f. *Ζῷα* (Syr.$^{gw.}$ ܢܦ̈ܫܐ) clearly answers to Ezekiel's חַיּוֹת, who in Ezek. ix. 3, x. 2 ff., 20 ff., are identified with the Cherubim. The Cherubim are previously mentioned in Scripture in connexion with (1) the story of the Fall (Gen. iii. 24), (2) the Ark (Exod. xxv. 18 etc.), (3) the inner chamber (דְּבִיר) of Solomon's Temple (1 Kings vi. 25 ff., etc.), (4) the Divine title 'He that sitteth upon the Cherubim' (Ps. lxxx. 1, xcix. 1, Isa. xxxvii. 16). The Ark and the Oracle had but two representations of cherubic figures; in Ezekiel they are four and yet one, and seem to symbolize the power which in its worldwide and manifold operations upholds and pervades while it transcends Creation. The Apocalyptist abandons the complexities of Ezekiel's imagery; the wheels and lightning-like movements of the *ζῷα* disappear, and so does their mysterious unity: the 'living creatures' of the Apocalypse are four distinct organisms. But in the main no doubt he presents the same idea; the *ζῷα* represent Creation and the Divine immanence in Nature. Cf. Andreas: *διὰ τῶν τεσσάρων προσώπων δηλοῦντα τὴν τῶν τεσσάρων στοιχείων τοῦ θεοῦ δημιουργίαν καὶ συντήρησιν.*

γέμοντα ὀφθαλμῶν ἔμπροσθεν καὶ ὄπισθεν] Cf. Ezek. i. 18 *οἱ νῶτοι αὐτῶν πλήρεις ὀφθαλμῶν κυκλόθεν τοῖς τέσσαρσιν*, x. 12 *καὶ οἱ νῶτοι αὐτῶν καὶ αἱ χεῖρες αὐτῶν καὶ αἱ πτέρυγες αὐτῶν καὶ οἱ τροχοὶ πλήρεις ὀφθαλμῶν κυκλόθεν τοῖς τέσσαρσιν τροχοῖς.* Again Ezekiel's description is simplified, while the main thought is preserved; the *ζῷα* are full of eyes before and behind and (*v.* 8) around and within. The symbolism sets forth the ceaseless vigilance of Nature, or rather of the immanent Power which works under visible forms. *Γέμειν*, a somewhat rare word in Biblical Gk. generally (LXX.[8], Mt.[2], Lc.[1], Paul[1]), occurs seven times in the Apoc. (iv. 6, 8, v. 8, xv. 7, xvii. 3 f., xxi. 9); on the construction, see Blass, *Gr.* p. 102.

7. *καὶ τὸ ζῷον τὸ πρῶτον ὅμοιον λέοντι κτλ.*] Cf. Ezek. i. 10 (x. 14) *καὶ ὁμοίωσις τῶν προσώπων αὐτῶν· πρόσωπον ἀνθρώπου ... λέοντος ... μόσχου ... ἀετοῦ*, where the forms are the same, but the order differs. The four forms represent whatever is noblest, strongest, wisest, and swiftest in animate Nature. Nature, including Man, is represented before the Throne, taking its part in the fulfilment of the Divine Will, and the worship of the Divine Majesty. On the early (Iren. iii. 11. 8) but unfortunate identification of the *ζῷα* with the *τετραευαγγέλιον*, see *St Mark*², p. xxxvi ff., and Zahn, *Forschungen*, ii. p. 257 ff. *Ἔχων τὸ πρόσωπον ὡς ἀνθρώπου*: see WM. p. 132.

ἀετῷ πετομένῳ. [8]καὶ τὰ τέσσερα ζῷα, ἓν καθ' ἓν 8
αὐτῶν ἔχων ἀνὰ πτέρυγας ἕξ, κυκλόθεν καὶ ἔσωθεν
γέμουσιν ὀφθαλμῶν· καὶ ἀνάπαυσιν οὐκ ἔχουσιν
ἡμέρας καὶ νυκτὸς λέγοντες

> Ἅγιος ἅγιος ἅγιος Κύριος ὁ θεὸς ὁ παντοκράτωρ,
> ὁ ἦν καὶ ὁ ὢν καὶ ὁ ἐρχόμενος.

7 *πετωμενου* 1 7 28 al^{pauc} 8 om *και* 1° syr^{gw} | *τα τεσσερα*] om *τα* Q 1 8 32 38 47 48 50 80 al^{pauc} Andr Ar | *εν καθ εν αυτων* AP min$^{sat\,mu}$] *εν εκαστον αυτων* ℵ 38 syrr *εν καθ εν* Q *εν καθ εαυτο* 1 92^{mg} + *εστως* 34 35 68 87 (syr^{gw}) | *εχων* A 1 2 7 13 16 30 al] *εχον* Q min$^{sat\,mu}$ *εχοντα* P 38 50 me *ειχον* ℵ 92^{mg} | *ανα*] *απο των ονυχων αυτου και επανω* syr$^{gw\,vid}$ | *πτερυγων* Q | *κυκλοθεν και εσωθεν*] *κυκλ. και εξωθεν* 91 *κυκλ. και εξωθεν και εσωθεν* Q min^{perpauc} *κυκλοθεν* 28 33 35 38 98 *ante se et retro* Prim *intus et foris* al tr ap Prim *in priora et retro* anon^{aug} | *γεμοντα* 1 38 Ar | *ουκ εχουσιν*] *ουκ εξοσαν* ℵ *non habebant g* vg$^{am\,dem\,lipss}$ Vict Tyc Prim | *λεγοντες*] *λεγοντα* 8 29 49** 93 96 | *αγιος* ter] *αγιος* octies ℵ* 29 novies Q min^{25} sexies 38 40 bis 12 51 | *ο θεος*] *σαβαωθ* 7 17* 28 36 39 79 | *ο παντοκρατωρ*] om *ο* ℵ 36 | *ο ην*] *ος ην* 130

8. ἓν καθ' ἓν αὐτῶν ἔχων ἀνὰ πτέρυγας ἕξ] 'Each one of them having severally six wings.' Ezekiel (i. 6) gives each of the ζῷα four wings; six is the number assigned to the Seraphim in Isa. vi. 2, a passage which the Apocalyptist, who does not identify his ζῷα with either the Cherubim or the Seraphim, has constantly in view. The wings, if our interpretation is right, represent the velocities of Nature, as the eyes represented its sleepless vigilance. For εἷς καθ' (κατὰ) εἷς see Mc. xiv. 19, note; and for ἀνά, used as a distributive adverb, WM. p. 496 f., Blass, *Gr.* p. 122. Ἔχων, not ἔχον, here and in *v.* 7, because the ζῷα are invested with intelligence, as the sequel shews; cf. v. 6, xxi. 14, and see WM. p. 660. The remarkable reading of Syr.^{gw} (ܡܢ ܛܦܪ̈ܗ ܘܠܥܠ) seems to have arisen from Ez. i. 27 (LXX.); see Gwynn *ad loc.*

κυκλόθεν καὶ ἔσωθεν γέμ. ὀφθ. It is tempting to connect κυκλ. with the previous clause, especially if we read with Q καὶ ἔξωθεν καὶ ἔσωθεν: cf. Vict. "habentes alas senas in circuitu et oculos intus et foris"; but Ezekiel i. 18 (x. 12) seems to decide in favour of the punctuation given in the text, and κυκλόθεν corresponds with ἔμπροσθεν κ. ὄπισθεν (iv. 6). Ἔσωθεν adds a new feature, pointing to the secret energies of Nature.

καὶ ἀνάπαυσιν οὐκ ἔχουσιν κτλ.] While man and the other animals divide the twenty-four hours between work and repose, and are allowed by the Creator one day in seven for rest (Exod. xvi. 23 ἀνάπαυσις ἁγία τῷ κυρίῳ), and the individual worker rests at length in the grave (Apoc. vi. 11, xiv. 13), the wheel of Nature (Jac. iii. 6 τὸν τροχὸν τῆς γενέσεως), i.e. the Divine activity immanent in Nature, pursues an unbroken course: cf. Jo. v. 17 ὁ πατήρ μου ἕως ἄρτι ἐργάζεται, κἀγὼ ἐργάζομαι. This ceaseless activity of Nature under the Hand of God is a ceaseless tribute of praise. Cf. Enoch xxxix. 12 "those who sleep not bless Thee"; lxxi. 7 "round about were Seraphim, Cherubim, and Ophanim; these are they who sleep not and guard the throne of His glory." Arethas well remarks: οὐ τὸ ἔγκοπον τὸ 'Ανάπαυσιν οὐκ ἔχουσιν παριστᾷ, ἀλλὰ τὸ περὶ θείαν ὑμνῳδίαν ἀνένδοτον.

λέγοντες Ἅγιος ἅγιος ἅγιος κτλ.]

9 [9]καὶ ὅταν δώσουσιν τὰ ζῷα δόξαν καὶ τιμὴν καὶ εὐχαριστίαν τῷ καθημένῳ ἐπὶ τῷ θρόνῳ τῷ ζῶντι εἰς

9 δωσουσιν AP (-σι) 1 28 36 38 79 al^sat mu] δωσωσιν ℵQ 7 12 14 16 32** 39 81 92 130 δωσι 2 6 9 29 31 35 49 87 91 al^sat mu syr^gw vid | τα τεσσερα ζωα 68 87 syr^gw | ευχαριστειας A | τω θρονω ℵA] του θρονου PQ min^omn vid Andr Ar

Another loan from Isaiah's description of the Seraphim (vi. 3 ἐκέκραγεν ἕτερος πρὸς τὸν ἕτερον καὶ ἔλεγον Ἅγιος ἅγιος ἅγιος Κύριος σαβαώθ); the Apocalyptist, as usual, does not tie himself to his source; he inserts ὁ θεός after Κύριος, changes σαβαώθ into παντοκράτωρ, and adds ὁ ἦν κτλ. from i. 8, dropping altogether Isaiah's πλήρης πᾶσα ἡ γῆ τῆς δόξης αὐτοῦ, as less appropriate in a tribute of praise which is offered in heaven. On παντοκράτωρ as a rendering of צְבָאוֹת see i. 8, note. The Liturgies retain the Isaianic form (Brightman, pp. 18 f., 50, 132, etc.; cf. Clem. R., *Cor.* 34), which has also found its way into the *Te Deum*; but they attribute the *Ter Sanctus* to "Cherubim and Seraphim," as if meaning to blend Isaiah's with Ezekiel's vision, after the manner of the Apocalypse. Ὁ ἐρχόμενος (God in His future self-manifestations) in the mouth of the ζῷα suggests the ἀποκαραδοκία of Creation (Rom. viii. 19 ff., Apoc. xxi. 1 ff.).

9. καὶ ὅταν δώσουσιν τὰ ζῷα δόξαν κτλ.] The difficult δώσουσιν, which is probably the true reading, is not without example, see WH.[2] *Notes*, p. 178, WM. p. 388, Burton, § 308; Viteau, *Étude*, i. pp. 125, 227 ff., and cf. Mc. viii. 35, note. Translate: "whensoever the living creatures shall give" (i.e. as often as they give) glory...the Four and twenty Elders shall fall" etc. The two actions are coordinated as simultaneous. Nature and the Church must ever unite in the praise of God; when one begins its anthem, it is the signal for the other to fall upon its knees before the Throne. The Seer states this fact, of which the vision made him cognisant, in the form of a law. This concurrence of the κόσμος and the ἐκκλησία in the worship of God was keenly realised by the Ancient Church; cf. e.g. the *Liturgy of St Mark* (Brightman, p. 132), πάντοτε μὲν πάντα σε ἁγιάζει, ἀλλὰ καὶ μετὰ πάντων τῶν σε ἁγιαζόντων δέξαι, δέσποτα Κύριε, καὶ τὸν ἡμέτερον ἁγιασμὸν σὺν αὐτοῖς ὑμνούντων κτλ. There is certainly not less cause for its recognition in an age which like our own is replete with new revelations of the wonders of the physical universe. Every fresh discovery of physical science should deepen the adoration of the faithful.

Δόξα καὶ τιμή (= כָּבוֹד וְהָדָר) is from the LXX. (Ps. viii. 6, xxviii. (xxix.) 1, xcv. (xcvi.) 7). The phrase is coupled in the N.T. with ἀφθαρσία (Rom. ii. 7), ἔπαινος (1 Pet. i. 7), δύναμις (Apoc. iv. 11, v. 12). Εὐχαριστία, a word which with its cognate verb is unknown to the canonical books of the LXX., occurs in a theological sense Paul[12], Apoc.[2], and in both the Apocalyptic passages is found in a doxology. While τιμή and δόξα have regard to the Divine perfections, εὐχαριστία refers to the Divine gifts in creation and redemption.

τῷ ζῶντι εἰς τοὺς αἰῶνας τῶν αἰώνων] The Living Creatures and the Elders offer their tribute to the Living God; created life adores the Uncreated. On ὁ ζῶν see i. 18; here it is evidently a title of the Father (ὁ καθήμενος ἐπὶ τοῦ θρόνου), though not to the exclusion of the Son, Who is the Father's σύνθρονος, or of the Spirit, Who is represented by the Seven Spirits before the Throne. With ζῆν εἰς τοὺς αἰῶνας cf. Deut. xxxii. 40, Dan. iv. 31 (34), Apoc. x. 6, xv. 7.

τοὺς αἰῶνας τῶν αἰώνων, [10]πεσοῦνται οἱ εἴκοσι τέσ- 10
σαρες πρεσβύτεροι ἐνώπιον τοῦ καθημένου ἐπὶ τοῦ
θρόνου, καὶ προσκυνήσουσιν τῷ ζῶντι εἰς τοὺς αἰῶνας
τῶν αἰώνων, καὶ βαλοῦσιν τοὺς στεφάνους αὐτῶν
ἐνώπιον τοῦ θρόνου, λέγοντες

[11]Ἄξιος εἶ, ὁ κύριος καὶ ὁ θεὸς ἡμῶν, λαβεῖν 11
τὴν δόξαν καὶ τὴν τιμὴν καὶ τὴν δύναμιν· ὅτι σὺ
ἔκτισας τὰ πάντα, καὶ διὰ τὸ θέλημά σου ἦσαν
καὶ ἐκτίσθησαν.

9 *των αιωνων* (om 130)] + *αμην* ℵ 32 95* syr^{gw} 10 *πεσουνται*] pr *και* ℵ | om *του καθημενου επι* Prim | *προσκυνησουσιν*] *adorabant* vg me Prim | *των αιωνων*] + *αμην* ℵ 32 syr^{gw} | *βαλουσιν*] *βαλλουσιν* ℵ*Q 1 12 17 28 30 130 al *mittebant* vg^{cle} me arm 11 *ο κυριος και ο θεος ημων* AQ min$^{fere\ 40}$ syrr arm Ar] *κυριε ο θεος ημων* P 7 14^{vid} 16 28 36 38 39 47 79 80 130 vg me aeth *κυριε ο κυριος κ. ο θ. ημ.* ℵ + *ο αγιος* Q min^{40} syr arm Ar | *την τιμην*] om *την* ℵ | *την δυναμιν*] om *την* A | *τα παντα* om *τα* Q Andr Ar | *δια θεληματι* (sic) A | *ησαν* ℵA min$^{fere\ 40}$ *g* vg me syrr aeth al tr ap Prim Ar] *ουκ ησαν* Q 14 38 51 *εισι* P 1 7 35 49 79 87 91 130 | om *ησαν και* 36 Prim | om *και εκτισθησαν* A

10. *πεσοῦνται οἱ εἴκοσι τέσσαρες πρεσβύτεροι κτλ.*] Hitherto the Elders have been silent assessors; now they rise from their thrones (*v.* 4), fall upon their knees, and prostrate themselves (*προσκυνήσουσιν*, cf. 1 Regn. xxv. 23) on the floor of heaven, laying their crowns of victory at the foot of the central Throne, in readiness to offer their tribute of praise. The last act is suggestive either of the homage paid to an overlord, or of the submission of a suppliant, seeking mercy from a conqueror. Cf. Plutarch, *Lucull.*, p. 522 Τιγράνης τὸ διάδημα τῆς κεφαλῆς ἀφελόμενος ἔθηκε πρὸ τῶν ποδῶν; Cicero, *pro Sext.* 27 "hunc Cn. Pompeius, cum in suis castris supplicem abjectumque vidisset, erexit, atque insigne regium, quod ille de suo capite abiecerat, reposuit"; Tac. *ann.* xv. 29 "ad quam [*sc.* effigiem Neronis] progressus Tiridates sublatum capite diadema imagini subiecit." In *Jabbuk*, 1 f. 55, Pharaoh and the Kings of the East are represented as taking off their crowns in the presence of Moses and Aaron. The 'crowns' of the Elders however were not *διαδήματα* but *στέφανοι*, symbols of victory and eternal life, and in their case the act is equivalent to an acknowledgment that their victory and their glory were from God, and were theirs only of His grace. Cf. Andreas: *σύ, φησί, Δέσποτα, τῶν στεφάνων τῆς νίκης αἴτιος καὶ χορηγὸς γέγονας.* Arethas: *τί ἂν ἄλλο ἢ τὴν κατὰ πάντων νίκην τῷ ἐπὶ πάντων ἀνατιθέασι θεῷ;*

11. *ἄξιος εἶ, ὁ κύριος κτλ.*] The *ζῷα* addressed the Creator simply as *ὁ θεὸς ὁ παντοκράτωρ.* The Elders recognise a relation to Him which the Creation as such cannot claim. He is (1) the Lord, the יהוה of revelation, and (2) their God (*ὁ θεὸς ἡμῶν*, cf. iii. 12 *ὁ θεός μου*). On the use of the nominatives *ὁ κύριος, ὁ θεός*, for the vocatives see Blass, *Gr.* p. 87. To the *δόξα* and *τιμή* which the *ζῷα* ascribe to God the Elders add *δύναμις*, cf. v. 12, vii. 12, xix. 1, and the doxologies in Mt. vi. 13, T.R., *Didache* 8. Glory, honour, and power are rightly ascribed to the Creator of the universe (*τὰ πάντα*), which owes its existence

V. 1 [1]Καὶ εἶδον ἐπὶ τὴν δεξιὰν τοῦ καθημένου ἐπὶ τοῦ
θρόνου βιβλίον γεγραμμένον ἔσωθεν καὶ ὄπισθεν,

V 1 ειδον ℵP min^{pl}] ιδον AQ 7 14 36 92 130: item ap v 2 | εσωθεν APQ min$^{\text{omn vid}}$] εμπροσθεν ℵ Or^{2} | οπισθεν ℵA 1 14 al syr] εξωθεν PQ min^{40} syr^{gw} me arm aeth Hipp^{dan} Andr Ar

to His will. Ἦσαν καὶ ἐκτίσθησαν is at first sight perplexing; we expect ἐκτίσθησαν καὶ εἰσίν, cf. Acts xvii. 28 ἐν αὐτῷ γὰρ ζῶμεν καὶ κινούμεθα καὶ ἐσμέν. Οὐκ ἦσαν (Q), 'they were not, and out of that state of non-existence were called into being by the act of creation,' is an ingenious correction. But the better supported ἦσαν also yields a good sense. It places the potential existence of the universe before its creation. The Divine Will had made the universe a fact in the scheme of things before the Divine Power gave material expression to the fact. Thus ἦσαν looks back to the eternal past, ἐκτίσθησαν to the genesis of Nature. Both are ascribed to the Father; His Will was the cause (διὰ τὸ θέλημά σου), as His Logos was the Agent of Creation: cf. 1 Cor. viii. 6 ἡμῖν εἷς θεὸς ὁ πατήρ, ἐξ οὗ τὰ πάντα...καὶ εἷς κύριος Ἰησοῦς Χριστός, δι' οὗ τὰ πάντα.

Of this chapter as a whole it may be well said with Tertullian *de coron.* 15 "si tales imagines in visione, quales veritates in repraesentatione?"

V. 1—14. The Sealed Book and the Lamb.

1. καὶ εἶδον ἐπὶ τὴν δεξιάν κτλ.] Looking again at the Majesty upon the central Throne the Seer sees a book-roll upon (ἐπί, acc., cf. xx. 1) the open palm of His right hand. Βιβλίον, a roll of papyrus (Maunde Thompson, *Palaeography*, p. 54 f.); cf. Ps. xxxix. (xl.) 8 ἐν κεφαλίδι βιβλίου, Lc. iv. 17, 20, and 2 Tim. iv. 13 where βιβλία are contrasted with μεμβρᾶναι. The present roll was 'sealed down' and made fast (κατεσφραγισμένον, cf. Isa. xxix. 11 οὐ δύναμαι ἀναγνῶναι, ἐσφράγισται γάρ, Sap. ii. 5 κατεσφραγίσθη, καὶ οὐδεὶς ἀναστρέφει) with seven seals, as if to ensure perfect security; cf. *Ev. Petr.* 8, where ἐπέχρισαν ἑπτὰ σφραγῖδας answers to Mt. xxvii. 66 ἠσφαλίσαντο τὸν τάφον σφραγίσαντες τὸν λίθον. But secret as the contents were, the roll was so full that they had overflowed to the *verso* of the papyrus, so that it was an ὀπισθόγραφον (see Maunde Thompson, p. 59, Hastings, iv. p. 946, and cf. Lucian, *vit. auct.* 9 ἡ πήρα... μεστὴ...ὀπισθογράφων βιβλίων, Juv. *Sat.* i. 6 "summi plena iam margine libri | scriptus et in tergo necdum finitus Orestes"). The description is based on Ezek. ii. 9 f. ἰδοὺ χεὶρ ἐκτεταμένη πρὸς μέ, καὶ ἐν αὐτῇ κεφαλὶς βιβλίου· καὶ ἀνείλησεν αὐτὴν ἐνώπιον ἐμοῦ, καὶ ἐν αὐτῇ γεγραμμένα ἦν τὰ ἔμπροσθεν καὶ τὰ ὀπίσω (פָּנִים וְאָחוֹר). But the Apocalyptic roll is sealed against inspection and not offered to the Seer to read. It contains no doubt the unknown future (i. 19 ἃ μέλλει γίνεσθαι); it is the Book of Destiny, to be unrolled and read only as the seals are opened by the course of events. The prevalent view of the ancient expositors, beginning with Hippolytus (ed. Lag. p. 159 ἔλαβεν οὖν τὸ βιβλίον καὶ ἔλυσεν, ἵνα τὰ πάλαι περὶ αὐτοῦ ἀποκρύφως λαλούμενα νῦν μετὰ παρρησίας ἐπὶ τῶν δωμάτων κηρυχθῇ), that the opening of the seals means the interpretation of the O.T. by the coming and teaching of Christ, or the allegorical interpretation of Scripture (Origen *philoc.* ii. 1, v. 5 ἡ γὰρ πᾶσα γραφή ἐστιν ἡ δηλουμένη διὰ τῆς βίβλου ἔμπροσθεν μὲν γεγραμμένη διὰ τὴν πρόχειρον αὐτῆς ἐκδοχήν, ὄπισθεν δὲ διὰ τὴν ἀνακεχωρηκυῖαν καὶ πνευματικήν) is inconsistent with the account of the process which is given in Apoc. vi. 1 ff. Apringius is nearer to the truth: "liber hic praesentis est mundi totius

κατεσφραγισμένον σφραγῖσιν ἑπτά. ²καὶ εἶδον ἄγ- 2
γελον ἰσχυρὸν κηρύσσοντα ἐν φωνῇ μεγάλῃ Τίς ἄξιος
ἀνοῖξαι τὸ βιβλίον καὶ λῦσαι τὰς σφραγῖδας αὐτοῦ;
³καὶ οὐδεὶς ἐδύνατο ἐν τῷ οὐρανῷ οὐδὲ ἐπὶ τῆς γῆς 3
οὐδὲ ὑποκάτω τῆς γῆς ἀνοῖξαι τὸ βιβλίον οὐδὲ
βλέπειν αὐτό. ⁴καὶ ἔκλαιον πολύ, ὅτι οὐδεὶς ἄξιος 4
εὑρέθη ἀνοῖξαι τὸ βιβλίον οὔτε βλέπειν αὐτό.
⁵καὶ εἷς ἐκ τῶν πρεσβυτέρων λέγει μοι Μὴ κλαῖε· 5

2 *αγγελον*] pr *αλλον* 35 87 syr^{gw} | *κηρυσσ. ισχυρον* ℵ 130 | om *εν* P 1 28 36 130 al vg arm Or | om *μεγαλη* 130 | *τις αξιος*] + *εστιν* Q min^{mu} *g* me syr Cypr Prim Andr Ar 3 *εδυνατο* ℵ min$^{fere\,25}$] *ηδυνατο* APQ min^{nonn} | *εν τω ουρανω*] + *ανω* Q 7 8 14 al$^{sat\,mu}$ syr | *ουδε* 1° AP min$^{fere\,33}$] *ουτε* ℵQ min^{mu} | *επι της γης*] *εν τη γη* syr$^{gw\,vid}$ | *ουδε* 2° P 1 6 7 28 49 79 91] *ουτε* Q min$^{sat\,mu}$ (om *ουδε υποκ. τ. γ.* ℵ 130) | *βιβλιον*] + *και λυσαι τας σφραγιδας αυτου* syr^{gw} Prim | *ουδε* 3° AP 1 6 7 28 49 79 91] *ουτε* ℵQ min$^{fere\,33}$ *και* syr^{gw} 4 totum vers om A 98 | *και* 1°] + *εγω* Q min^{pl} vg Prim Andr Ar | *πολυ*] *πολλοι* 1 arm^{codd} aeth *παντες* me^{vid} | *ευρεθησεται* ℵ* | *ανοιξαι*] + *και αναγνωναι* 1 36 49 91 | *ουτε βλεπειν αυτο*] *και λυσαι τας σφραγιδας αυτου* syr^{gw} Prim

creatura"; and better still is the comment of Andreas: *βιβλίον τὴν πάνσοφον τοῦ θεοῦ μνήμην νοοῦμεν...καὶ τῶν θείων κριμάτων τὴν ἄβυσσον.* Zahn (*Einl.* ii. p. 596) followed by Nestle (*Text. Crit.* p. 333) regards the *βιβλίον* as a papyrus in book-form, connecting *καὶ ὄπισθεν* with *κατεσφραγισμένον.* But his reasons are not convincing.

2. *καὶ εἶδον ἄγγελον ἰσχυρὸν κηρύσσοντα κτλ.*] A "strong angel" (x. 1, xviii. 21) is needed to be the herald of a challenge addressed to the whole creation. *Τίς ἄξιος;* cf. *τίς ἱκανός;* (2 Cor. ii. 16). The *ἄξιος* supports his claims on moral grounds; the *ἱκανός*, on grounds which prove him capable whether morally or otherwise. In the present case moral fitness is the only *ἱκανότης.* *'Ανοῖξαι καὶ λῦσαι*; the same order occurs in *v.* 5. The *hysteron proteron*, as in iv. 11 *ἦσαν καὶ ἐκτίσθησαν*, is apparent rather than real; to be able to open the book is the first necessity and therefore takes the first place in the order of thought.

3. *καὶ οὐδεὶς ἐδύνατο ἐν τῷ οὐρανῷ κτλ.*] The challenge is not taken up by any being in heaven, on earth, or in Hades. For this threefold division of created life see Phil. ii. 10 *ἐπουρανίων καὶ ἐπιγείων καὶ καταχθονίων*: an earlier grouping in Exod. xx. 4 has under the third head *ἐν τοῖς ὕδασιν ὑποκάτω τῆς γῆς*, or (*v.* 11) *τὴν θάλασσαν.* *Οὐδεὶς ... οὐδὲ ... οὐδέ* implies a quasi-ascensive scale, which has given trouble to the scribes, and the MSS. waver between *οὐδέ* and *οὔτε*; the point appears to be that as one after another of the three regions declined the challenge, the hope that it will be met approaches a vanishing point; cf. Primasius: *nec quisquam...neque ...neque...sed neque...*In *οὐδείς...οὔτε βλέπειν* (here and in *v.* 4) there is an implied *οὔτε* before *ἀνοῖξαι*, cf. WM. p. 66. For *ἀνοίγειν* in reference to a roll see Lc. iv. 17.

4 f. *καὶ ἔκλαιον πολύ, ὅτι κτλ.*] With the unrestrained emotion of one in a dream or ecstasy the Seer wept at the result, whether because of his own disappointment, or because of the failure of creation to open the roll. Its inability implied moral incapacity; *οὐδεὶς ἐδύνατο*, because *οὐδεὶς ἄξιος εὑρέθη.* His weeping continued (*ἔκλαιον*) until it was stopped by one

ἰδοὺ ἐνίκησεν ὁ λέων ὁ ἐκ τῆς φυλῆς Ἰούδα, ἡ ῥίζα
Δαυείδ, ἀνοῖξαι τὸ βιβλίον καὶ τὰς ἑπτὰ σφραγῖδας
6 αὐτοῦ. [6]καὶ εἶδον ἐν μέσῳ τοῦ θρόνου καὶ τῶν

5 ο λεων ο] om ο 2° ℵ 14 28** syr^{gw} + ων 1 | ανοιξαι] ο ανοιγων Q min$^{fere 40}$ ανοιξει 13 syrr | τας επτα σφραγιδας] pr λυσαι ℵ vg^{cle} syr^{gw} arm^{zoh} Or^{int} Cypr^{edd} Hier^{dan} om επτα 73 syr^{gw} 6 ειδον (ιδον 36 92 130 ιδων Q 9)] ιδου A + και ιδου 35 87 vg

of the Elders (εἷς ἐκ τῶν πρ.). Here and in vii. 13 the Elder is merely an interlocutor, as an Angel is on other occasions (xvii. 1, xxi. 9), and his intervention has no symbolical meaning. Μὴ κλαῖε occurs on the lips of Christ in Lc. vii. 13, viii. 52 etc., and τί κλαίετε in Jo. xx. 13 ff. Higher natures see that human grief is often needless, springing from insufficient knowledge.

ἰδοὺ ἐνίκησεν ὁ λέων κτλ.] Ἐνίκησεν may be either 'prevailed' (A.V.) = ἴσχυσεν as in Ps. l. (li.) 6 ὅπως ἂν ...νικήσῃς ἐν τῷ κρίνεσθαί σε, and see Ps. Sol. iv. 13 ἐνίκησεν σκορπίσαι; or 'overcame' (R.V.), as in iii. 21. But both the usage of the Johannine books, and the position of ἐνίκησεν, which is separated by a whole line from ἀνοῖξαι, are in favour of the latter rendering, which places in the forefront the great historical fact of the victory of the Christ; 'behold, a victory was won by Him Who is the Lion, etc....which gives Him the right to open the book.' Ὁ λέων ὁ ἐκ τῆς φυλῆς Ἰούδα refers to Gen. xlix. 9 σκύμνος λέοντος, Ἰούδα... ἀναπεσὼν ἐκοιμήθης ὡς λέων. In the Blessing of Jacob Judah is the lion of the tribes (cf. Prov. xxiv. 65 (xxx. 15) σκύμνος λέοντος ἰσχυρότερος κτηνῶν), as Dan is in the Blessing of Moses (Deut. xxxiii. 22); and the noblest son of the tribe of Judah is fitly styled the Lion of that tribe; cf. Hippolytus, ed. Lag., p. 4, διὰ τὸ βασιλικὸν καὶ ἔνδοξον ὡς λέοντος προκεκηρυγμένου. With ὁ ἐκ τῆς φ. Ἰ. comp. Heb. vii. 14 πρόδηλον γὰρ ὅτι ἐξ Ἰούδα ἀνατέταλκεν ὁ κύριος ἡμῶν. His Judaean origin was bound up in the primitive belief with His descent from David. Ἡ ῥίζα Δαυείδ looks back to Isa. xi. 1 ἐξελεύσεται ῥάβδος ἐκ τῆς ῥίζης (מִגֵּזַע) Ἰεσσαί, καὶ ἄνθος ἐκ τῆς ῥίζης (מִשָּׁרָשָׁיו) ἀναβήσεται, *ib.* 10 ἔσται ἐν τῇ ἡμέρᾳ ἐκείνῃ ἡ ῥίζα (שֹׁרֶשׁ) τοῦ Ἰεσσαί, καὶ ὁ ἀνιστάμενος ἄρχειν ἐθνῶν; the latter verse is quoted as Messianic in Rom. xv. 12. As the Prophet foresaw, the stump of the old tree of the House of David had sent forth a new David to rule the nations. The Apocalyptist evidently finds satisfaction in this title of Christ, for he repeats it in xxii. 16 ἐγὼ (Ἰησοῦς) εἰμὶ ἡ ῥίζα καὶ τὸ γένος Δαυείδ (where see note): cf. also *c.* iii. 7, note.

The Lion of Judah, the Son of David, conquered the world (Jo. xvi. 33, Apoc. i. 18, iii. 21), and one fruit of His victory is that it belongs to Him to open the seals of God's Book of Destiny, i.e. to carry history onward through successive stages to the final revelation.

6. καὶ εἶδον ἐν μέσῳ τοῦ θρόνου κτλ.] The Seer, roused from his dejection by the Elder's ἰδού, looks again, and sees, not a Lion but a Lamb (ἀρνίον). The conception is from Isa. liii. 7 ὡς πρόβατον ἐπὶ σφαγὴν ἤχθη, καὶ ὡς ἀμνὸς ἐναντίον τοῦ κείροντος ἄφωνος. Ἀμνός has passed from the LXX. into the other passages in the N.T. where Christ is described as the Lamb (Jo. i. 29, 36, Acts viii. 32, 1 Pet. i. 19), but does not occur in the Apocalypse, which uses τὸ ἀρνίον as a title of our Lord 29 times in 12 chapters. It is possible that the Apocalyptist has taken the latter word from a non-Septuagintal version of Isaiah, *l. c.*; or he may have had in view Jer. xi. 19 ὡς ἀρνίον ἄκακον ἀγόμενον τοῦ θύεσθαι. The diminutive must not be pressed, since ἀρνός has no nom., but the

τεσσάρων ζῴων καὶ ἐν μέσῳ τῶν πρεσβυτέρων ἀρνίον ἑστηκὸς ὡς ἐσφαγμένον, ἔχων κέρατα ἑπτὰ καὶ ὀφθαλμοὺς ἑπτά, οἵ εἰσιν τὰ ἑπτὰ πνεύματα τοῦ θεοῦ,

6 om *εν μεσω* (2°) syr[gw] ante *των τεσσ. ζωων* pon Prim | *εστηκος* APQ min[pl]] *εστηκως* ℵ 1 7 28 32 36 87 | om *ως* 31 50 95 arm Hipp[dan] | *εσφαγμενον*] *εσφραγισμενον* 7 31 32 38 | *εχων* ℵAQ 7 28 30 32 35] *εχον* P min[pl] | *οι εισιν* ℵA 1 38 51 87 al] *α εισιν* Q min[sat mu] | om *επτα* A 1 12 vg[am* fu]

contrast of the Lamb with the Lion is sufficiently striking in any case, directing attention to the unique combination of majesty and meekness which characterized the life of Jesus Christ. Cf. Victorinus: "ad devincendam mortem leo, ad patiendum vero pro hominibus tanquam agnus ad occisionem ductus est." Ἑστηκὸς ὡς ἐσφαγμένον: the sacrifice foreseen by Isaiah and Jeremiah has taken place and is yielding lasting fruits (perf.), and there are indications of the fact that it has been offered (ὡς ἐσφ.); yet the Lamb stands erect and alive in the sight of Heaven (cf. i. 18 ἐγενόμην νεκρὸς καὶ ἰδοὺ ζῶν εἰμι). The position which He occupies in the picture is not quite clear, for ἐν μέσῳ...καὶ ἐν μέσῳ may mean either 'between the Throne and the Four Living creatures on the one hand and the Elders on the other' (cf. Gen. i. 7 ἀνὰ μέσον...καὶ ἀνὰ μέσον = בֵּין...וּבֵין), or 'in the midst of all,' the Centrepiece of the whole *tableau*. But the relative positions of the Throne, the ζῷα, and the Elders (iv. 4, 6), seem to exclude the former interpretation, and the latter is wholly consistent with the general place assigned to the Lamb throughout the Apocalypse. With ἑστηκός cf. Acts vii. 56 θεωρῶ ... τὸν υἱὸν τοῦ ἀνθρώπου ἐκ δεξιῶν ἑστῶτα τοῦ θεοῦ, Apoc. xiv. 1 ἰδοὺ τὸ ἀρνίον ἑστὸς ἐπὶ τὸ ὄρος Σιών. The position is that of the Priest offering sacrifice (Heb. x. 11), and the Lamb is both Sacrifice and Priest. But perhaps ἑστ. denotes here no more than the restored life and activity of the Victim; cf. vii. 17, xiv. 1.

ἔχων κέρατα ἑπτὰ καὶ ὀφθαλμοὺς ἑπτά κτλ.] The horn as the symbol of strength is an old Hebrew metaphor which occurs first in Deut. xxxiii. 17, where Ephraim is said to have the horns of the רְאֵם, LXX. μονοκέρως (a species of wild ox); cf. 1 Regn. ii. 1, 10, 3 Regn. xxii. 11, Ps. xvii. (xviii.) 3, cxi. (cxii.) 9. In the later books of the O.T. the horn is a symbol of a dynastic force (Zech. i. 18 (ii. 1) ff., Dan. vii. 7 ff., viii. 3 ff.); and in this sense it is used in Apoc. xii. 3, xiii. 1, 11, xvii. 3 ff. (where see notes). The 'seven horns of the Lamb' symbolize the fulness of His power as the Victorious Christ; cf. Mt. xxviii. 18 ἐδόθη μοι πᾶσα ἐξουσία ἐν οὐρανῷ καὶ ἐπὶ γῆς, Jo. xvii. 1 ἔδωκας αὐτῷ ἐξουσίαν πάσης σαρκός. In Enoch xc. 37 f. the Messiah appears as a white רְאֵם with great black horns (see Charles, *ad l.*). With the fulness of strength the Lamb possesses also the fulness of vision, symbolized by seven eyes; cf. iv. 6, 8, where the ζῷα have eyes before and behind, around and within, yet do not possess the plenary illumination ascribed to the Lamb. The Apocalyptist has in view Zech. iii. 9 ἐπὶ τὸν λίθον τὸν ἕνα ἑπτὰ ὀφθαλμοί εἰσιν, iv. 10 ἑπτὰ οὗτοι ὀφθαλμοί εἰσιν [Κυρίου] οἱ ἐπιβλέποντες (מְשׁוֹטְטִים). He identifies the "seven eyes of the Lord," which are also the eyes of the Lamb, with the "seven Spirits of God." The eyes of Christ are ὡς φλὸξ πυρός (i. 14), and the seven Spirits (i. 4, note) blaze like torches before the Throne of God (iv. 5). But in their position before the Throne they are stationary, whilst, as the eyes of the Lamb, they have a mission to all

7 ἀπεσταλμένοι εἰς πᾶσαν τὴν γῆν. [7]καὶ ἦλθεν καὶ
εἴληφεν ἐκ τῆς δεξιᾶς τοῦ καθημένου ἐπὶ τοῦ θρόνου.
8 [8]καὶ ὅτε ἔλαβεν τὸ βιβλίον, τὰ τέσσερα ζῷα καὶ οἱ
εἴκοσι τέσσαρες πρεσβύτεροι ἔπεσαν ἐνώπιον τοῦ
ἀρνίου, ἔχοντες ἕκαστος κιθάραν καὶ φιάλας χρυσᾶς

6 απεσταλμενοι A] απεσταλμενα ℵ 38 49 130 τα απεσταλμ. 1 79 Hipp αποστελλομενα Q min$^{\text{sat mu}}$ τα αποστελλ. 7 8 9 13 16 syr$^{\text{gw vid}}$ 7 ειληφεν]+το βιβλιον 1$^{\text{**mg}}$ 7 36 (38) syr$^{\text{*}}$ syr^{gw} me Prim 8 ελαβεν] ειληφεν 130 | τεσσαρα PQ min$^{\text{omn vid}}$ | επεσον Q min^{pl} | εκαστος εχοντες ℵ εχ. εκαστος αυτων syr$^{\text{gw vid}}$ | κιθαρας 1 7 29 36 49 51 91 96 al vg | φιαλην χρυσην γεμουσαν syr^{gw} | χρυσεας ℵ

the earth. The reading is uncertain; we have to choose between ἀπεσταλμένα (ℵ), ἀποστελλόμενα (Q) and ἀπεσταλμένοι (A). The last agrees with Zech. *l. c.* (ὀφθ. οἱ ἐπιβλέποντες), and has the merit of being the harder reading. The sense in any case is materially the same; the eyes, that is the Spirits, are sent. Ἀποστέλλεσθαι, it can hardly be doubted, has been chosen with reference to the Mission of the Spirit (cf. Lc. xxiv. 49 ἰδοὺ ἐγὼ ἐξαποστέλλω τὴν ἐπαγγελίαν τοῦ πατρός μου ἐφ' ὑμᾶς, Gal. iv. 6 ἐξαπέστειλεν ὁ θεὸς τὸ πνεῦμα τοῦ υἱοῦ αὐτοῦ εἰς τὰς καρδίας ἡμῶν, though the Johannine Gospel uses πέμπειν in this connexion (xiv. 26, xv. 26, xvi. 7). The mission of the Spirit to the whole world carries us beyond the earlier conception of His work, yet see Jo. xvi. 8 f. As the Spirit of Jesus (Acts xvi. 7) and the "Eyes of the Lamb," His mission is oecumenical.

7. καὶ ἦλθεν καὶ εἴληφεν ἐκ τῆς δεξιᾶς κτλ.] 'And I saw Him go (aor.), and now He has taken [the book] out of the hand of Him who sits on the Throne.' Cf. iii. 3 εἴληφας καὶ ἤκουσας, viii. 5 εἴληφεν...καὶ ἐγέμισεν, xi. 17 εἴληφας καὶ ἐβασίλευσας; εἴρηκα is similarly joined with an aorist in vii. 13 f., xix. 3. WM. (p. 340) holds the perf. in v. 7, viii. 5, to be simply aoristic; cf. Blass, *Gr.* p. 200, who gives other exx. from the Pauline Epp., and from subapostolic literature. On the other hand see Benson, *Apocalypse*, p. 150 f., who makes a good case for retaining in the Apocalyptic instances a more or less distinct flavour of the sense of the perfect. Here εἴληφεν may point (Weiss, Bousset) to the abiding results of the action, or it may be simply realistic, as explained above. Realism also explains the absence of τὸ βιβλίον; the movement is so rapid that the subject is left to be understood.

8. καὶ ὅτε ἔλαβεν τὸ βιβλίον κτλ.] The aorist of ordinary narration is resumed. When the Lamb took the roll, the representatives of the animate creation and of the universal Church fell before Him. Προσκύνησις, though not mentioned as in iv. 10, is perhaps implied; cf. *v.* 14, where after their praise of God and of the Lamb the Elders ἔπεσαν καὶ προσεκύνησαν. Ἔχοντες ἕκαστος is probably to be referred to the Elders only, for though the masculines might include the ζῷα (cf. ἔχων, iv. 7 f.), the particulars which follow are not appropriate to the latter. Each Elder is now seen to carry a κιθάρα, i.e. a lyre or zithern (the כִּנּוֹר of the O.T., in Daniel קיתרס (*ḳ'ri* קַתְרֹס)), the traditional instrument of psalmody (cf. Ps. xxxii. (xxxiii.) 2, xcvii. (xcviii.) 5, cxlvi. (cxlvii.) 7, cl. 3); the word is used again by the Apocalyptist in another description of the celestial music (xiv. 2 ὡς κιθαρῳδῶν κιθαριζόντων ἐν ταῖς κιθάραις αὐτῶν, xv. 2 ἔχοντας κιθάρας τοῦ θεοῦ). Beside their lyres the Elders had golden bowls

γεμούσας θυμιαμάτων, αἵ εἰσιν αἱ προσευχαὶ τῶν
ἁγίων. ⁹καὶ ᾄδουσιν ᾠδὴν καινὴν λέγοντες 9
Ἄξιος εἶ λαβεῖν τὸ βιβλίον καὶ ἀνοῖξαι τὰς
σφραγῖδας αὐτοῦ, ὅτι ἐσφάγης καὶ ἠγόρασας
τῷ θεῷ ἐν τῷ αἵματί σου ἐκ πάσης φυλῆς καὶ

8 *αι εισιν* AP min^pl syrr Andr Ar] *α εισιν* ℵQ 36 | *αι προσευχαι*] om *αι* ℵ* 6 14 130 al^mu *προσευχων* 2 7 8 19 27 29 41 43 48 50 82 93 9 *και αδουσιν*] *αδοντες* syr^gw vid Prim | *ανοιξαι*] λυσαι syr^gw | om *εσφαγης και* 130 | *τω θεω* (om 1 vg^harl* me Cypr)] + *ημας* ℵPQ min^pl syrr

or saucers (*φιάλαι*, *paterae*, see xvii. 1), full of incense, such as according to Josephus were placed on the shewbread (*antt.* iv. 6. 6; in iii. 10. 7 he calls them *πίνακες*, plates). *Θυμιάματα*, pl., as usually in the LXX. (Gen. xxxvii. 25, 1 Chr. vi. 49, Jer. xvii. 26) and elsewhere in this book (Apoc. viii. 3 f., xviii. 13). *Αἵ* probably refers to *θυμ.* and not to *φιάλας*, deriving its gender by attraction (WM. p. 206 f.) from *προσευχαί*: *ἅ* (ℵQ) is the correction of a scribe who has felt the difficulty without realising the true solution. The prayers of the Church are symbolized by the incense (Ps. cxl. 2 *κατευθυνθήτω ἡ προσευχή μου ὡς θυμίαμα ἐνώπιόν σου*, Lc. i. 10 *πᾶν τὸ πλῆθος ἦν τοῦ λαοῦ προσευχόμενον ἔξω τῇ ὥρᾳ τοῦ θυμιάματος*), as its psalmody, already an important element in Church worship (1 Cor. xiv. 15, 26, Eph. v. 19, Col. iii. 16), is represented by the lyres. The Elders are fitly charged with both, since they represent the Church, and in the act which follows symbolize the Church's adoration of Christ. For *αἱ προσευχαί*, the normal, familiar, acts of prayer, individual or collective, see Acts ii. 42, Rom. i. 10, 1 Tim. ii. 1, v. 5, 1 Pet. iii. 7, and esp. Apoc. viii. 3 f.

9. *καὶ ᾄδουσιν ᾠδὴν καινήν*] A 'new song' (שִׁיר חָדָשׁ, *ᾠδὴ καινή*, *ᾆσμα καινόν*, *ὕμνος καινός*) is mentioned in Ps. xxxii. (xxxiii.) 3, xxxix. (xl.) 4, xcv. (xcvi.) 1, xcvii. (xcviii.) 1, cxliii. (cxliv.) 9, cxlix. 1, Isa. xlii. 10. Originally denoting only a fresh song of praise, the phrase lent itself especially to songs composed for great occasions; e.g. in Isa. *l. c.* the new song springs out of a prophecy of the new order which is to be inaugurated by the Servant of Jehovah; and similarly Judith's paean over the death of Holofernes is a *ὕμνος καινός* (Judith xvi. 13). In the Apocalypse it is appropriately used for the Church's praise of Redemption (cf. xiv. 3); the *ᾠδὴ καινή* answers to the *ὄνομα καινόν* (ii. 17, iii. 12), the *Ἰερουσαλὴμ καινή* (iii. 12, xxi. 2), the *οὐρανὸς καινὸς καὶ γῆ καινή* (xxi. 1), the *καινὰ πάντα* (xxi. 5) of the great Christian prophecy.

ἄξιος εἶ λαβεῖν τὸ βιβλίον κτλ.] The Elders recognise in Christ the absolute moral worthiness which has qualified Him to take the Book of Destiny from the hand of God and open its seals (*ἀνοῖξαι τὰς σφρ.* = *ἀν. τὸ βιβλίον καὶ λῦσαι τὰς σφρ.*, *v.* 2). This *ἀξιότης* is based neither on His unique relation to God, nor on the perfection of His human life, but on the fact of His sacrifice (*ὅτι ἐσφάγης*, cf. *v.* 6 *ὡς ἐσφαγμένον*). *Σφάζεσθαι* is used to describe the Death of Christ only in this book (*vv.* 6, 9, 12, xiii. 8), where its use is due to Isa. liii. 7 *ὡς πρόβατον ἐπὶ σφαγὴν ἤχθη*; it is interesting to find it occurring also in references to the martyrdoms which were trying the faith of the Churches of Asia (vi. 9, xviii. 24). Other Apostolic writings speak of Christ as 'crucified' or 'sacrificed,' or simply as having 'died.' *Ἀγοράζειν*, a Pauline word

10 γλώσσης καὶ λαοῦ καὶ ἔθνους, [10]καὶ ἐποίησας
αὐτοὺς τῷ θεῷ ἡμῶν βασιλείαν καὶ ἱερεῖς, καὶ
βασιλεύουσιν ἐπὶ τῆς γῆς.

10 *αυτους*] *ημας* vg$^{\text{cle fu}}$ | *τω θεω ημων* om A | *βασιλειαν* ℵA vg me Cypr Prim] *βασιλεις* Q min$^{\text{omn vid}}$ syr arm aeth Andr Ar *βασιλειαν και ιερεις και βασιλεις* syr^{gw} | *βασιλευουσιν* AQ 7 14 28 29 35 38 al syr] *βασιλευσουσιν* ℵP 1 2 4 5 6 8 30 31 32 36 130 al *g* vg$^{\text{am fu harl tol}}$ syr^{gw} me Cypr *βασιλευσομεν* vg$^{\text{cle dem}}$ Ar Prim^{vid} (*regnavimus*)

(1 Cor. vi. 20, vii. 23, and in the compound ἐξαγ., Gal. iii. 13, iv. 5), is used in this sense elsewhere only in Apoc. (here and xiv. 3 f.) and in 2 Peter (ii. 1); it rings with echoes of the Greek *ἀγοραί*, familiar both to St Paul and St John. The 'purchase' was made with the Blood of the slain Lamb (*ἐν τῷ αἵματί σου*, where *ἐν* denotes the price, as in i. 5 *λύσαντι ἡμᾶς ἐν τῷ αἵμ. αὐτοῦ*); see Acts xx. 28, 1 Cor. vi. 20, 1 Pet. i. 18 ff. It was made "for God," the thing purchased being destined for His service (Rom. vi. 22, 1 Cor. *l. c.*). In what it consisted, i.e., what was purchased, appears in the words that follow: *ἐκ πάσης φυλῆς κτλ.*, 'representatives of every nationality, without distinction of race or geographical or political distribution'; cf. vii. 9, xiv. 6 and the similar enumerations in x. 11, xi. 9, xiii. 7, xvii. 15. The origin of the phrase is perhaps to be sought in Dan. iii. 4, 7, v. 19, vi. 25: cf. also 4 Esdr. iii. 7 (16). The scope which it assigns to the redemptive virtue of the Cross is less wide than that which is contemplated in 1 Tim. ii. 3 f., 1 Jo. ii. 2; but the 'new song' refers only to those in whom Redemption has become effective by their incorporation in the Body of Christ. The oecumenical mission, however, of the Church is fully recognised; the Seer sees in it a worldwide Empire extending far beyond the shores of the Mediterranean and the sway of the Caesars.

10. *καὶ ἐποίησας αὐτοὺς τῷ θεῷ ἡμῶν κτλ.*] A further result of the Lamb's Sacrifice. Those whom He purchased He made a Kingdom and priests unto God. Cf. i. 6 *ἐποίησεν ἡμᾶς βασιλείαν, ἱερεῖς τῷ θεῷ καὶ πατρὶ αὐτοῦ*, xx. 6 *ἔσονται ἱερεῖς τοῦ θεοῦ καὶ τοῦ Χριστοῦ, καὶ βασιλεύσουσιν μετ' αὐτοῦ*, and see notes on both verses. The fact that this chord is struck thrice in the Apoc. seems to imply special familiarity on the part of both writer and readers with the words as well as the thought: possibly they entered into a primitive hymn which may have run: *ἐποίησας ἡμᾶς βασιλείαν* | *ἱερεῖς τῷ θεῷ καὶ πατρί σου* | *καὶ βασιλεύ[σ]ομεν ἐπὶ τῆς γῆς*. In the present passage the harder *βασιλεύουσιν* (AQ) is perhaps to be preferred; the reign of the Saints had begun in the life of the Spirit, though in the fuller sense it was yet future: cf. Mt. v. 3, 5 *αὐτῶν ἐστὶν ἡ βασιλεία...κληρονομήσουσι τὴν γῆν*, 1 Cor. iv. 8 *χωρὶς ἡμῶν ἐβασιλεύσατε; καὶ ὄφελόν γε ἐβασιλεύσατε, ἵνα καὶ ἡμεῖς ὑμῖν συμβασιλεύσωμεν.* For the future, see Apoc. xx. 6, xxii. 5.

The 'new song' vindicates for Jesus Christ the unique place which He has taken in the history of the world. By a supreme act of self-sacrifice He has purchased men of all races and nationalities for the service of God, founded a vast spiritual Empire, and converted human life into a priestly service and a royal dignity. He who has done this is worthy to have committed into His hands the keeping of the Book of Destiny, and to break its Seals and unroll its closely packed lengths; to preside over the whole course of events which connects His Ascension with His Return.

[11]καὶ εἶδον, καὶ ἤκουσα ὡς φωνὴν ἀγγέλων πολλῶν 11
κύκλῳ τοῦ θρόνου καὶ τῶν ζῴων καὶ τῶν πρεσβυτέ-
ρων, καὶ ἦν ὁ ἀριθμὸς αὐτῶν μυριάδες μυριάδων καὶ
χιλιάδες χιλιάδων, [12]λέγοντες φωνῇ μεγάλῃ 12

Ἄξιόν ἐστιν τὸ ἀρνίον τὸ ἐσφαγμένον
λαβεῖν τὴν δύναμιν καὶ πλοῦτον καὶ σοφίαν καὶ
ἰσχὺν καὶ τιμὴν καὶ δόξαν καὶ εὐλογίαν.

11 *ειδον* ℵP min^{pl}] *ιδον* AQ 7 14 92 | om *ως* APQ* 1 14 49 70 al vg me arm aeth Prim (hab ℵQ** min$^{\text{sat mu}}$ syr Andr Ar) | *κυκλοθεν* 1 | om *και των πρεσβυτερων...μυριαδων* 1 | *μυριας...χιλιας* syr^{gw} | om *και χιλ. χιλ.* 38 130   12 *λεγοντες*] *λεγοντων* 38 95 97 vg Prim pr *και* syr^{gw} | *αξιον* ℵQ min$^{\text{omn vid}}$ syr] *αξιος* A *αξιος ει* syr^{gw} | *εσφαγμενον*] *εσφραγισμενον* 58 | *πλουτον*] pr *τον* Q min$^{\text{sat mu}}$

11. *καὶ εἶδον, καὶ ἤκουσα ὡς φωνὴν ἀγγέλων πολλῶν κτλ.*] A new feature in the vision introduced by a fresh *καὶ εἶδον* (*v.* 1, 2, 6, vi. 1, 2, 5, 8, 9, 12 etc.; cf. iv. 1, note). Except the 'Hierophant' (iv. 1), and the Strong Angel of *v.* 2, this vision has been hitherto without angelic appearances; now at length the Angels are seen in their myriads, forming a vast ring around and therefore outside the Elders, who are themselves around the central Throne (cf. iv. 4). The Seer gives their numbers from Dan. vii. 10: *χίλιαι χιλιάδες ἐλειτούργουν αὐτῷ, καὶ μύριαι μυριάδες παριστήκεισαν αὐτῷ*: cf. Enoch xiv. 22 *κύκλῳ μύριαι μυριάδες ἑστήκασιν ἐνώπιον αὐτοῦ*; *ib.* xl. 1, lx. 1, lxxi. 8, and Heb. xii. 22 f. *προσεληλύθατε μυριάσιν ἀγγέλων*: the source of all these computations is probably Deut. xxxiii. 2 *κατέσπευσεν ἐξ ὄρους Φαρὰν σὺν μυριάσιν Κάδης* (מֵרִבְבֹת קֹדֶשׁ), *ἐκ δεξιῶν αὐτοῦ ἄγγελοι μετ' αὐτοῦ*: cf. Ps. lxvii. (lxviii.) 18. With the phrases *μυριάδες μυριάδων, χιλιάδες χιλιάδων* cf. Gen. xxiv. 60 *γίνου εἰς χιλιάδας μυριάδων*, Num. x. 36 *χιλιάδας μυριάδας*, Apoc. ix. 16 *δισμυριάδες μυριάδων*. The voice of this vast concourse—a *μεγάλη φωνή* indeed—is a shout rather than a song. There is no mention of *κιθάραι* or *ᾠδή* here; the Angels simply acclaim the Lamb as worthy.

12. *ἄξιόν ἐστιν τὸ ἀρνίον κτλ.*] Not *ἄξιος εἶ* as in *v.* 9. The terms, moreover, are more general—*τὸ ἐσφαγμένον* for *ὅτι ἐσφάγης*, and for *λαβεῖν τὸ βιβλίον* the usual *λ. τὴν δύναμιν κτλ.* (iv. 11). The Angels stand outside the mystery of Redemption, though they are far from being uninterested spectators (Eph. iii. 10, 1 Pet. i. 12), and recognise both the grandeur of the Lord's sacrificial act, and its infinite merit. The doxology which they offer to the Lamb is even fuller than that which in iv. 11 is offered by the Elders to the Creator, for to "glory, honour, and power" it adds riches, wisdom, strength, and blessing. *Πλοῦτος, σοφία, ἰσχύς, εὐλογία*, are specially appropriate in a doxology offered to Christ; cf. 2 Cor. viii. 9 *ἐπτώχευσεν πλούσιος ὤν*, 1 Cor. i. 24 *θεοῦ δύναμιν καὶ θεοῦ σοφίαν*, Lc. xi. 22 *ἐπὰν δὲ ἰσχυρότερος αὐτοῦ* [*τοῦ ἰσχυροῦ*] *ἐπελθὼν νικήσῃ αὐτόν*, Rom. xv. 29 *ἐν πληρώματι εὐλογίας Χριστοῦ*. For *πλοῦτος* and *ἰσχύς* in a doxology see 1 Chron. xxix. 11 f. The seven attributes form a heptad of praise which leaves nothing wanting in the Angels' acclamation of the Lamb. Arethas compares Mt. xxviii. 18 *ἐδόθη μοι πᾶσα ἐξουσία ἐν οὐρανῷ κτλ.*, and adds: *τῷ ἀρνίῳ ἡ ἐξουσία ὑπὲρ τοῦ ἐσφάχθαι δέδοται τῶν ἐπουρανίων καὶ ἐπιγείων καὶ καταχθονίων.*

13 [13]καὶ πᾶν κτίσμα ὃ ἐν τῷ οὐρανῷ καὶ ἐπὶ τῆς
γῆς καὶ ὑποκάτω τῆς γῆς καὶ ἐπὶ τῆς θαλάσσης
καὶ τὰ ἐν αὐτοῖς πάντα, ἤκουσα λέγοντας
Τῷ καθημένῳ ἐπὶ τῷ θρόνῳ καὶ τῷ ἀρνίῳ ἡ
εὐλογία καὶ ἡ τιμὴ καὶ ἡ δόξα καὶ τὸ κράτος εἰς
τοὺς αἰῶνας τῶν αἰώνων.

13 ο] + *εστιν* P 1 28 35 36 al$^{mu\,vid}$ vg syr Prim Andr (conj *το* Nestle) | *επι της γης*] *εν τη γη* 1 al$^{vix\,mu}$ syr^{gw} | om *και υποκατω της γης* ℵ 12 14 33 47 95 vg^{fu} me arm | *επι της θαλασσης*] *τα εν τη θαλασση* ℵ vg syrr me Prim + *εστιν* A 6 78 130 al + *α εστιν* PQ 1 30* 34 35 49 al vg + *ο εστιν* syr$^{gw\,vid}$ | *παντα ηκουσα λεγοντας* P 6 32 90 130] *παντα ηκ. λεγοντα* A 1 12 *παντας ηκ. λεγοντας* 2 7 8 al$^{sat\,mu}$ *παντα και ηκ. λεγοντας* ℵ 30 34 35 36 87 98 al syrr *παντα και παντας ηκ. λεγοντας* Q | *τω θρονω* AQ 2 6 7 8] *του θρονου* ℵP 1 al^{mu} Andr Ar | *και τω αρνιω*] om me om *και* ℵ$^{c.a}$ A syr | *η ευλογια*] om *η* P | *των αιωνων*] + *αμην* Q 1 al$^{sat\,mu}$ aeth^{utr} Andr Ar

13. *καὶ πᾶν κτίσμα ὃ ἐν τῷ οὐρανῷ κτλ.*] A still wider circle offers its doxology. The whole Creation is summoned from its four great fields of life (cf. *v.* 3); the Sea is now added explicitly. The gathering is no longer representative only, but exhaustive, not one created thing being omitted (*πᾶν κτίσμα, τὰ ἐν αὐτοῖς πάντα*). *Κτίσμα* occurs first in Sirach and Wisdom, where it seems to be distinguished from (*ἡ*) *κτίσις*; in the N.T. (Jac. i. 18, 1 Tim. iv. 4, Apoc. v. 13, viii. 9) it is invariably concrete, 'a creature,' 'a created thing.' The Seer does not himself see Creation rising in its innumerable forms of life to offer its doxology; this is no part of the vision which comes to him through the open door. But he hears the roar of the great acclamation as it rises to heaven, and it is heard also within the circle round the Throne, for the *ζῷα* respond (*v.* 14). John's nearness to the Throne, or (what is the same thing) the elevation of his spirit, enables him to voice the purpose of universal Nature; he becomes conscious that it exists only to glorify God and the Lamb.

τῷ καθημένῳ ἐπὶ τῷ θρόνῳ καὶ τῷ ἀρνίῳ] Cf. vii. 10. In xxii. 1, 3 the Throne belongs to God and to the Lamb conjointly (see iii. 21 note); but the offering of the doxology to Both in the same terms is scarcely less significant. While the Angels' doxology was sevenfold, the Creation's is fourfold, consisting of the last three points in the former, with the addition of *κράτος* which takes the place of *ἰσχύς*, active power being here in view rather than a reserve of secret strength (cf. Eph. i. 19, vi. 10). This fourfold attribution of praise agrees with the character of those who offer it, for four is the number of the creature; see Mc. xiii. 27, Apoc. iv. 6, vii. 1; Iren. iii. 11. 8 *τέσσαρα κλίματα τοῦ κόσμου ἐν ᾧ ἐσμέν εἰσι, καὶ τέσσαρα καθολικὰ πνεύματα.* It is perhaps not without meaning that each of the perfections named is separately emphasized by the article (*ἡ εὐλογία κ. ἡ τιμὴ κ. ἡ δόξα κ. τὸ κράτος*): contrast *v.* 12 *τὴν δύναμιν καὶ πλοῦτον κτλ.* *Εἰς τοὺς αἰῶνας τῶν αἰώνων* gives infinity to the whole; the exaltation of the Lamb is not temporary but enduring.

14. *καὶ τὰ τέσσερα ζῷα ἔλεγον Ἀμήν*] The heavenly representatives of animate creation confirm the doxology which rises from the earth. For *ἔλεγον Ἀμήν* cf. 1 Chron. xvi. 36

[14]καὶ τὰ τέσσερα ζῷα ἔλεγον Ἀμήν, καὶ οἱ πρεσ- 14
βύτεροι ἔπεσαν καὶ §προσεκύνησαν. §C
[1]Καὶ εἶδον ὅτε ἤνοιξεν τὸ ἀρνίον μίαν ἐκ τῶν ἑπτὰ 1 VI.
σφραγίδων, καὶ ἤκουσα ἑνὸς ἐκ τῶν τεσσάρων ζῴων

14 *τεσσαρα* ℵPQ | *ελεγον* 1 7 28 vg] *λεγοντα* Q $min^{sat\ mu}$ syr^{gw} me Ar | *αμην*] pr *το* Q $min^{fere\ 40}$ Ar | *πρεσβυτεροι*] pr *εικοσι τεσσαρες* vg^{cle} arm^{zoh} Prim | *επεσον* Q $min^{plq\ 40}$ Andr Ar | *και προσεκυνησαν*] + *viventem in saecula saeculorum* vg^{cle} Prim om 130

VI 1 *ειδον* CP min^{pl} Ar] *ιδον* ℵAQ 7 14 92 | *οτε*] *οτι* Q $min^{fere\ 40}$ arm $vg^{fu\ tol\ harl}$ Andr Ar | om *επτα* P 1 6 28 34 79 al me arm

καὶ ἐρεῖ πᾶς ὁ λαός Ἀμήν, 1 Cor. xiv. 16 πῶς ἐρεῖ τὸ Ἀμὴν ἐπὶ τῇ σῇ εὐχαριστίᾳ; Justin, *apol.* i. 65, 67. The words are probably suggested by the familiar 'Amen' with which at Ephesus and elsewhere in Asia the Seer's own Eucharistic thanksgiving had always been ended. The whole passage is highly suggestive of the devotional attitude of the Asiatic Church in the time of Domitian towards the Person of Christ. It confirms Pliny's report that Christians "carmen Christo quasi deo dicere secum invicem," and the statement in Euseb. *H. E.* v. 28 ψαλμοὶ δὲ ὅσοι καὶ ᾠδαὶ ἀδελφῶν ἀπ' ἀρχῆς ὑπὸ πιστῶν γραφεῖσαι τὸν λόγον τοῦ θεοῦ τὸν χριστὸν ὑμνοῦσι θεολογοῦντες.

καὶ οἱ πρεσβύτεροι ἔπεσαν καὶ προσεκύνησαν] The whole service of praise ends with a fresh act of homage on the part of the Church's representatives. Here as in iv. 10 it is the Elders who prostrate themselves. The deepest homage is due from the Church, which has been redeemed and made a royal priesthood unto God.

VI. 1—17. The Opening of the first six seals.

1. καὶ εἶδον κτλ.] The vision proceeds (on καὶ εἶδον see v. 1, 6, 11). The Lamb, who has already taken the roll (v. 7) now opens the seals one by one. The first four openings (*vv.* 1—8) form a series, marked by a common note; each is preceded by an utterance from one of the four ζῷα, and followed by the appearance of a horse and his rider, whose significance is partly explained.

For μίαν ἐκ, ἑνὸς ἐκ, see v. 5 note; ἐκ with a partitive genitive is especially frequent in the Apoc., cf. Blass, *Gr.* p. 96 f. The writer declines to say which seal was opened first, or which of the ζῷα began; neither point is material. Ὡς φωνῇ βροντῆς, cf. xiv. 2, xix. 6, and for the instrumental dative see v. 12, vi. 10; φωνήν (ℵ), φωνῆς (P), are corrections. It is unnecessary to create an irregularity by reading φωνή (with Tischendorf, Bousset, Nestle).

Each of the ζῷα in succession thunders out his ἔρχου (*vv.* 1, 3, 5, 7). The scribes have understood this as a call to the Seer, and many MSS. accordingly add καὶ ἴδε, or καὶ βλέπε; see *app. crit.* But (1) δεῦρο would have been the natural word to invite the approach of the Seer; and (2) no reason can be shewn why he should have been called within the door and across the Sea in order to witness the visions which follow. Many ancient interpreters, regarding the white horse as the "verbum praedicationis" (Victorinus, cf. Zahn, *Einl.* ii. p. 689), explain *Veni* as the summons to faith (*e.g.* Apringius: "*veni* dicitur invitatio ad fidem"). But throughout the Apoc. ἔρχεσθαι is used of the comings of God or of Christ (ὁ ἐρχόμενος, i. 4, 8, iv. 8; ἔρχομαι, ii. 5, 16, iii. 11, xvi. 15, xxii. 7, 12, 20; ἔρχεται, i. 7; ἔρχου, xxii. 17, 20). The last two references help to determine the meaning of

2 λέγοντος ὡς φωνὴ βροντῆς Ἔρχου. [2]καὶ εἶδον, καὶ
ἰδοὺ ἵππος λευκός, καὶ ὁ καθήμενος ἐπ' αὐτὸν ἔχων
τόξον, καὶ ἐδόθη αὐτῷ στέφανος, καὶ ἐξῆλθεν νικῶν
3 καὶ ἵνα νικήσῃ. [3]καὶ ὅτε ἤνοιξεν τὴν σφραγῖδα τὴν

1 λεγοντος] λεγουσαν ℵ syr post βροντης pon A 130 | φωνης P 1 6 31 φωνην ℵ 26 91 130 vg arm | βροντων syr$^{\text{gw vid}}$ | ερχου] + και ιδε ℵQ min$^{\text{fere 25}}$ + *et vide* vg$^{\text{cle fu}}$ syrr me aeth Vict Prim   2 και ειδ. ℵP 1 al$^{\text{sat mu}}$ (και ιδον AC 7 36)] om Q min$^{\text{fere 30}}$ vg$^{\text{fu dem harl* tol lips}}$ Vict Prim Ar pr και ηκουσα syr^{gw} | νικων] pr ο A arm | και ινα νικηση] και ενικησεν ℵ + και ενικ. 32 36 pr και ενικ. syr^{gw} 3 την σφραγιδα την δευτεραν] την δευτ. σφρ. Q min^{pl} Andr Ar

ἔρχου here; the 'Come' of the ζῷα corresponds to the 'Come' of the Spirit and the Bride, of the hearer and the writer of the book; Nature no less than the Spirit in redeemed Man calls for the coming of the Christ. Thus the fourfold ἔρχου of the ζῷα represents the ἀποκαραδοκία τῆς κτίσεως (Rom. viii. 19 ff.) which at each crisis in the preparatory process becomes vocal in the ear of the prophet.

2. καὶ εἶδον, καὶ ἰδοὺ ἵππος λευκός κτλ.] The vision of the four horsemen, distinguished by the colour of their horses, who follow successively the opening of the first four seals, has evidently been suggested by Zech. vi. 1 ff., ἰδοὺ τέσσαρα ἅρματα...ἐν τῷ ἅρματι τῷ πρώτῳ ἵπποι πυρροί, καὶ ἐν τῷ ἅρματι τῷ δευτέρῳ ἵπποι μέλανες, καὶ ἐν τῷ ἅρματι τῷ τρίτῳ ἵπποι λευκοί, καὶ ἐν τῷ ἅρματι τῷ τετάρτῳ ἵπποι ποικίλοι ψαροί (grizzled bay). Zechariah's four horses are "the four winds of heaven" (*v.* 5), and their mission is to execute judgement upon Babylon, Egypt, and the other heathen nations of the world. The Apocalyptist borrows only the symbol of the horses and their colours, and instead of yoking the horses to chariots he sets on each of them a rider in whom the interest of the vision is centred.

In the first vision the horse is white, the rider carries a bow and receives a conqueror's crown (στέφανος); he goes forth, it is noted, as a conqueror, and with the purpose of winning fresh conquests (ἵνα νικήσῃ, not ὡς νικήσων). It is tempting to identify him with the Rider on the white horse in xix. 11 ff., whose name is 'the Word of God'; cf. Iren. iv. 21. 3 "ad hoc enim nascebatur Dominus...de quo et Ioannes in Apocalypsi ait *Exivit vincens, ut vinceret.*" But the two riders have nothing in common beyond the white horse; the details are distinct; contrast e.g. the διαδήματα πολλά of xix. 12 with the single στέφανος here, and the ῥομφαία ὀξεῖα with the τόξον. A vision of the victorious Christ would be inappropriate at the opening of a series which symbolizes bloodshed, famine, and pestilence. Rather we have here a picture of triumphant militarism. The lust of conquest which makes great Empires, whether the Seer had in view the Empire of the Caesars or the Parthian power which menaced it, was the first and most momentous of the precursors of the final revelation.

White horses were used by the conqueror in Roman triumphant processions; cf. Verg. *Aen.* iii. 537 "quattuor hic, primum omen, equos in gramine vidi | tondentes campum late candore nivali"; on which Servius remarks, "hoc ad victoriae omen pertinet."

3 f. καὶ ὅτε ἤνοιξεν τὴν σφραγῖδα τὴν δευτέραν κτλ.] As the white horse and his rider vanish, bent on the career of conquest (ἵνα νικήσῃ), the Lamb opens the second seal, and there comes forth another horse, not white

δευτέραν, ἤκουσα τοῦ δευτέρου ζῴου λέγοντος Ἔρχου.
[4]καὶ ἐξῆλθεν ἄλλος ἵππος πυρρός, καὶ τῷ καθημένῳ ἐπ' 4
αὐτὸν ἐδόθη αὐτῷ λαβεῖν τὴν εἰρήνην ἐκ τῆς γῆς καὶ
ἵνα ἀλλήλους σφάξουσιν, καὶ ἐδόθη αὐτῷ μάχαιρα
μεγάλη. [5]καὶ ὅτε ἤνοιξεν τὴν σφραγῖδα τὴν τρί- 5
την, ἤκουσα τοῦ τρίτου ζῴου λέγοντος Ἔρχου. καὶ
εἶδον, καὶ ἰδοὺ ἵππος μέλας, καὶ ὁ καθήμενος ἐπ' αὐτὸν

3 ερχου] + και ιδε ℵ 34 35 38 39 al^{pauc} + *et vide* vg$^{\text{cle fu dem harl tol lips}}$ me (aeth) Vict Prim Andr 4 και εξηλθεν] και ιδον και ιδου εξ. (34 35) Andr | om αλλος 130 syr^{gw} | πυρρος] πυρος APQ 1 6 7 8 al$^{\text{fere 40}}$ me Andr | τω καθημενω] pr εν A | επ αυτον] επ αυτω 1 29 87 al | om αυτω ℵ$^{\text{c.a}}$A 31 | εκ της γης] om ℵ$^{\text{c.a}}$ om εκ A 7 16 39 46 απο τ. γ. 1 36 al | om και 3° Q min$^{\text{fere 40}}$ me syr^{gw} arm aeth Andr Ar | σφαξωσιν ℵPQ 1 al^{pl} Andr Ar | μεγαλη μαχαιρα A 5 ηνοιξεν την σφραγιδα την τριτην] ηνοιξεν την τρ. σφρ. 1 36 38 al ηνοιγη η σφραγις η τριτη 28 73 79 syr^{gw} | ερχου] + και ιδε ℵQ 6 8 9 al^{mu} Andr Ar + *et vide* vg$^{\text{cle dem harl tol lips al}}$ me syr Vict Prim al | και ειδ. ℵCP 28 47 49 al^{mu} (και ιδον A 1 7 36)] om Q min^{mu} *g* vg$^{\text{cle dem harl tol lips s al}}$ me syr^{gw} aeth Andr Ar | επ αυτον] επ αυτω 1 al^{nonn} | om αυτον 130

but πυρρός, 'blood red' (cf. 4 Regn. iii. 22 τὰ ὕδατα πυρρὰ (אֲדֻמִּים) ὡσεὶ αἷμα); the word is used of the red-brown of the heifer (Num. xix. 2), and here, as in Zech. i. 8, vi. 2, of the roan of the horse, not however without allusion to its proper meaning. The rider on the red horse has received (ἐδόθη αὐτῷ) a great sword, as a symbol of his mission. Μάχαιρα may be either a knife carried in a sheath at the girdle (Jo. xviii. 10), or a weapon for use in war (see Hastings' *D. B.* iv. 634); this one is clearly of the latter sort, and it is large of its kind (μεγάλη).

Together with the sword the second rider had received power to plunge the world into war; his sword was not the symbol of civil justice (Rom. xiii. 4) but of bloodshed. "It was given him to take Peace (τὴν εἰρήνην) from off the earth and (to cause men) to slay one another"—the negative and positive sides of warfare. The construction is rugged and broken, as if in sympathy with the subject (τῷ καθ. ἐδόθη αὐτῷ λαβεῖν ... καὶ ἵνα ἀλλ. σφάξουσιν, sc. οἱ κατοικοῦντες ἐπὶ τῆς γῆς). For ἵνα with the fut. ind. see WM. p. 360 f., Blass, *Gr.* p. 211 f.; other exx. may be found in Apoc. iii. 9, vi. 11, viii. 3, ix. 4 f., 20, xiii. 12, 16 (?), xiv. 13, xxii. 14.

If the first Seal has been interpreted rightly, there can be little difficulty in explaining the second. Victory, white-horsed and crowned, wears another aspect when viewed in the lurid light of the battlefield. Triumph spells much bloodshed and slaughter in the past, and the maintenance and extension of an Empire based on conquest demands more in the future.

5. καὶ ὅτε ἤνοιξεν τὴν σφραγῖδα τὴν τρίτην κτλ.] The breaking of the third seal lets loose a black horse. Bloodshed is not the only attendant upon conquest; Scarcity follows. The rider on the black horse is not named, but this description leaves no doubt who he is. He carries in his hand, not bow or sword, but the beam of a pair of scales. For the meaning of ζυγός cf. Prov. xvi. 11 ῥοπὴ ζυγοῦ δικαιοσύνη παρὰ Κυρίῳ, Ezek. v. 1 λήμψῃ ζυγὸν σταθμίων, xlv. 10 ζυγὸς δίκαιος καὶ μέτρον

6 ἔχων ζυγὸν ἐν τῇ χειρὶ αὐτοῦ. [6]καὶ ἤκουσα ὡς
φωνὴν ἐν μέσῳ τῶν τεσσάρων ζῴων λέγουσαν Χοῖνιξ
σίτου δηναρίου, καὶ τρεῖς χοίνικες κριθῶν δηναρίου·
7 καὶ τὸ ἔλαιον καὶ τὸν οἶνον μὴ ἀδικήσῃς. [7]καὶ ὅτε
ἤνοιξεν τὴν σφραγῖδα τὴν τετάρτην, ἤκουσα φωνὴν
8 τοῦ τετάρτου ζῴου λέγοντος Ἔρχου. [8]καὶ εἶδον, καὶ
ἰδοὺ ἵππος χλωρός, καὶ ὁ καθήμενος ἐπάνω αὐτοῦ,

6 om ως Q min^{pl} me syrr arm aeth Prim Andr Ar | εν μεσω (εμμ. AC)] εκ μεσου syr^{gw} | κριθης Q min^{pl} syr^{gw} Andr Ar | δηναριου 2°] pr του A | μη] + ου 130 | αδικησεις (P) min^{nonn} 7 την τεταρτην σφραγιδα 38 | om φωνην CPQ min$^{\text{40}}$ me syr (hab ℵA 1 28 36 49 79 91 vg$^{\text{cle am}}$ syr^{gw}) | του τεταρτου ζωου] om τεταρτου syr^{gw} το τεταρτον ζωον C | λεγουσαν 1 | ερχου] + και ιδε ℵQ min$^{\text{fere 35}}$ Andr Ar + *et vide* vg$^{\text{cle dem tol}}$ me syr^{sh} aeth Prim 8 και ειδ. P 1 49 79 91 al (και ιδον ℵAC 7 28 36 92)] om Q 6 14 38 al$^{\text{sat mu}}$ vg$^{\text{cle dem tol al}}$ aeth Andr Ar | om και ιδου syr^{gw} Prim | ιππον χλωρον syr^{gw} Prim | ο καθημενος] om ο C τον καθημενον syr^{gw} | επανω αυτου] om αυτου CP 1 12 vg$^{\text{dem harl}}$ επ αυτον 130

δίκαιον καὶ χοῖνιξ δικαία ἔστω ὑμῖν τοῦ μέτρου; the masc. is found also in the LXX. wherever the gender can be determined, and in Mt. xi. 29 f.

6. *καὶ ἤκουσα ὡς φωνὴν ἐν μέσῳ τῶν τεσσ. ζῴων*] Lest this rider should not be sufficiently identified by his equipment, there comes from the midst of the *ζῷα* what sounds like a voice (*ὡς*, cf. v. 11, vi. 1, xix. 1, 6), the protest of Nature against the horrors of famine.

λέγουσαν Χοῖνιξ κτλ.] The voice fixes a maximum price for the main foodstuffs. The denarius, the silver 'franc' of the Empire, was the daily wage (Mt. xx. 2), and a *choenix* of wheat the average daily consumption of the workman (Suidas: *ἡ γὰρ χοῖνιξ ἡμερήσιος τροφή*, cf. Athen. iii. 20). Barley was largely the food of the poor, as being relatively cheaper than wheat, cf. 4 Regn. vii. 18 *δίμετρον κριθῆς σίκλου καὶ μέτρον σεμιδάλεως σίκλου*: in N.T. times the proportionate cost was probably as three to one, as the Apocalyptist puts it here (*χοῖνιξ σίτου, τρεῖς χοίνικες κριθῶν*). *Χοῖνιξ* represents the Hebrew בַּת in Ezek. xlv. 10 f. LXX., i.e., 60—70 pints (Hastings, *D. B.* iv. 912); but the Greek measure in view was something under two pints; the Vg. renders *χοῖνιξ* here by *bilibris*. The proclamation, then, forbids famine prices, ensuring to the labourer a sufficiency of bread, and warning the world against such a rise in the price of cereals as would deprive men of the necessaries of life. A similar embargo is laid on any attempt to destroy the liquid food of the people—*τὸ ἔλαιον καὶ τὸν οἶνον μὴ ἀδικήσῃς*—the prohibition is addressed to the nameless rider who represents Dearth. The oliveyards and vineyards are not to suffer to such an extent as seriously to interfere with the supply. Wheat and barley, oil and wine, were the staple food both of Palestine and Asia Minor, and the voice from the midst of the *ζῷα* deprecates any heavy loss in these crops. Yet the very cry reveals the presence of relative hardships, and the danger of worse things; cf. Mc. xiii. 8 *ἔσονται λιμοί· ἀρχὴ ὠδίνων ταῦτα*. Cf. Hastings, *D. B.* iii. 432 *a*.

On *ἀδικεῖν* to 'injure,' hurt, see ii. 11, note.

7 f. *καὶ ὅτε ἤνοιξεν τὴν σφραγῖδα τὴν τετάρτην κτλ.*] At the opening of the fourth seal, after the call from the fourth *ζῷον*, another horse is seen,

*ὄνομα αὐτῷ ὁ θάνατος, καὶ ὁ ᾅδης ἠκολούθει μετ'
αὐτοῦ, καὶ ἐδόθη αὐτοῖς ἐξουσία ἐπὶ τὸ τέταρτον τῆς
γῆς, ἀποκτεῖναι ἐν ῥομφαίᾳ καὶ ἐν λιμῷ καὶ ἐν θανάτῳ
καὶ ὑπὸ τῶν θηρίων τῆς γῆς. ⁹καὶ ὅτε ἤνοιξεν τὴν* 9

8 *ο θανατος* (*αθανατος* A) PQ min[pl] Or Andr Ar] om *ο* ℵC 16* 37 49 95 96 | *ακολουθει* 1 28 49 79 91 96 al me Andr | *μετ αυτου* ACP min[pauc]] *αυτω* ℵQ min[fere 40] syr[gw] Ar | *αυτοις*] *αυτω* Q min[plq 40] vg syrr me arm aeth Prim | om *εν* 2°, 3° ℵ | *υπο των θηριων*] *το τεταρτον των θ.* A 9 *την σφραγιδα την πεμπτην* (ℵ*) 14 92 vg[cle]

described as *χλωρός*, which the Apocalyptist substitutes for Zechariah's *ποικίλος ψαρός*. In the LXX. and N.T. *χλωρός* is the usual epithet of *χόρτος*, *βοτάνη*, *ξύλον* (Gen. i. 30, 4 Regn. xix. 26, Ezek. xvii. 24, Mc. vi. 39, Apoc. viii. 7), and *πᾶν χλωρόν* is 'vegetation' generally (Gen. ii. 5, Apoc. ix. 4). But "equus viridis" (Tert. *pud.* 20) is scarcely tolerable, even in this book of unimaginable symbols; *χλωρός* must bear here its other meaning, 'of pale complexion'; the word is used especially in reference to the grey, ashen colour of a face bleached by fear (cf. *χλωρὸν δέος*, *Il.* vii. 479). The 'pale' horse is the symbol of Terror, and its rider a personification of Death (*ὁ θάνατος*, as in i. 18, ix. 6, xx. 13 f., xxi. 4; cf. 1 Cor. xv. 26, 54 f.), with whom follows—whether on the same or another horse or on foot the writer does not stop to say or even to think—his inseparable comrade, Hades (i. 16, note, xx. 13 f.).

καὶ ἐδόθη αὐτοῖς ἐξουσία κτλ.] Cf. *v.* 4. A far wider commission is given to the fourth rider than to the second; his authority extends over a fourth of the earth (cf. viii. 7 ff.), and his opportunities of exercising it are manifold. Τὸ *τέταρτον* shews that this is no mere commonplace of human mortality, but describes an unusual visitation, in which Death is busy in various forms. Ἐν *ῥομφαίᾳ...λιμῷ...θανάτῳ...ὑπὸ τῶν θηρίων*—the 'four sore judgements' of Ezekiel xiv. 21: *τὰς τέσσαρας ἐκδικήσεις μου τὰς πονηράς, ῥομφαίαν καὶ λιμὸν καὶ θηρία πονηρὰ καὶ θάνατον·* cf. Lev. xxvi. 23 ff., Jer. xxi. 7, Ezek. v. 12—17, xxix. 5, xxxiii. 27, xxxiv. 28. In these O.T. passages *ὁ θάνατος* is = הַדֶּבֶר, pestilence; and such is doubtless the meaning of *θανάτῳ* here, as distinguished from other causes of mortality. On *ῥομφαία* see Apoc. i. 16, note. The devastations caused by wild beasts are perhaps mentioned chiefly because they belong to Ezekiel's list of judgements. But they suggest the depopulation caused by war, dearth, and pestilence (cf. Deut. vii. 22), and so have a special fitness in this context.

The first group of seal-openings, now completed, describes the condition of the Empire as it revealed itself to the mind of the Seer. He saw a vast world-wide power, outwardly victorious and eager for fresh conquests, yet full of the elements of unrest, danger, and misery; war, scarcity, pestilence, mortality in all its forms, abroad or ready to shew themselves. This series of pictures repeats itself in history, and the militarism and lust of conquest, which it represents both in their attractive and repellent aspects, are among the forces set loose by the hand of Christ to prepare the way for His coming and the final publication of the secrets of the Sealed Book.

9. *καὶ ὅτε ἤνοιξεν τὴν πέμπτην σφραγῖδα*] The Lamb continues to open the seals, but no Ἔρχου comes from the *ζῷα*; the history of the world-wide Empire has been exhausted by the first four. With the fifth seal

πέμπτην σφραγῖδα, εἶδον ὑποκάτω τοῦ θυσιαστηρίου
τὰς ψυχὰς τῶν ἐσφαγμένων διὰ τὸν λόγον τοῦ θεοῦ
10 καὶ διὰ τὴν μαρτυρίαν ἣν εἶχον. [10]καὶ ἔκραξαν φωνῇ
μεγάλῃ λέγοντες Ἕως πότε, ὁ δεσπότης ὁ ἅγιος καὶ

9 ειδον ℵ[c.a] P min[pl] (ιδον ℵ*ACQ 7 (14) 32 (92))] + και C | των εσφαγμενων (εσφραγισμενων 7 16* 33 130 arm[zoh] μεμαρτυρηκοτων Clem-Al)] pr των ανθρωπων ℵP 1 10 al[nonn] me arm τας εσφαγμενας syr[gw] | om δια 2° A 130 vg[tol] me Cypr Prim | μαρτυριαν] + του αρνιου Q min[40] syr + Ιησου Χριστου 34 35 87 + Ιησου syr[gw] + αυτου arm aeth Cypr Prim | εσχον ℵ* 10 εκραζον P 1 31 36 38 79 130 *clamabant* vg syr | φωνην μεγαλην Q | om ο δεσποτης 130

the Church comes into sight, in its persecuted, suffering, state. While the Empire was pursuing its victorious course through bloodshed and death, the Church followed the steps of 'the Lamb that was slain.' The loosing of the fifth seal interprets the age of persecution, and shews its relation to the Divine plan of history.

εἶδον ὑποκάτω τοῦ θυσιαστηρίου κτλ.] An altar is mentioned also in viii. 3, 5, ix. 13, xi. 1, xiv. 18, xvi. 7, where see notes. Though no altar appears in the vision of *c.* iv., its existence is assumed by the article, perhaps on the ground that the heavenly worship which the Seer had witnessed is the ἀντίτυπον of the earthly; cf. Heb. viii. 5. The altar here in view is the counterpart of the Altar of burnt offering, and the victims which have been offered at it are the martyred members of the Church, who have followed their Head in the example of His sacrificial death (τῶν ἐσφαγμένων; cf. v. 6 ὡς ἐσφαγμένον). Their souls (ψυχάς) are seen "under the altar," because in the Levitical rite the blood, which is the ψυχή (Lev. xvii. 11 ἡ γὰρ ψυχὴ πάσης σαρκὸς αἷμα αὐτοῦ ἐστίν), was poured out at the foot of the altar of burnt offering (Lev. iv. 7 πᾶν τὸ αἷμα τοῦ μόσχου ἐκχεεῖ παρὰ τὴν βάσιν τοῦ θυσιαστηρίου: cf. *Pirqe Aboth* 26). They had been slain διὰ τὸν λόγον τοῦ θεοῦ καὶ διὰ τὴν μαρτυρίαν ἣν εἶχον—a phrase repeated with a slight change from i. 9, and found again with variations in xii. 11, 17, xix. 10, xx. 4. If the two causes of martyrdom are to be sharply distinguished, as the repeated διά seems to indicate, the first will be the martyrs' confession of the One Living and True God, as against polytheism and Caesarism, and the second their witness to Jesus Christ. In *mart. Polyc.* 9 the test offered to Polycarp is twofold: ὄμοσον [τὴν Καίσαρος τύχην], καὶ ἀπολύω σε· λοιδόρησον τὸν χριστόν. On εἶδον...τὰς ψυχάς see Tertullian *anim.* 8 "animae corpus invisibile carni, spiritui vero visibile est."

10. καὶ ἔκραξαν φωνῇ μεγάλῃ κτλ.] Beatus: "animarum verba ipsa sunt desideria"; cf. Bar. iii. 4. As the blood of Abel cried for vengeance on Cain (Gen. iv. 10 φωνὴ αἵματος...βοᾷ, cf. Heb. xii. 24), so in the ears of the Seer the souls of the martyrs (i.e. their sacrificed lives) called aloud for judgement on the pagan world. It was a *quousque tandem?* 'how long, Master Holy and True, dost thou not judge and avenge?' For ἕως πότε see Mc. ix. 19, and cf. Exod. xvi. 28 ἕως τίνος; 2 Esdr. xii. 16 ἕως τότε. Δεσπότης as a title of God (= אָדוֹן, אֲדֹנָי), in the LXX. usually occurs in the voc., whether alone or with Κύριος (Gen. xv. 2, 8, Jer. iv. 10, Dan. ix. 15); on ὁ δεσπότης = δέσποτα, see Blass, *Gr.* p. 87. Christ is ὁ μόνος δεσπότης καὶ κύριος ἡμῶν in Jude 4 (cf. 2 Pet. ii. 1), and receives the epithets ἅγιος, ἀληθινός in Apoc. iii.

ἀληθινός, οὐ κρίνεις καὶ ἐκδικεῖς τὸ αἷμα ἡμῶν ἐκ τῶν
κατοικούντων ἐπὶ τῆς γῆς; [11]καὶ ἐδόθη αὐτοῖς ἑκάστῳ 11
στολὴ λευκή, καὶ ἐρρέθη αὐτοῖς ἵνα ἀναπαύσονται

10 αληθινος] pr ο 1 30** 87 | εκδικησεις ℵ | εκ] απο P 1 7 28 35 49 11 εδοθησαν ...στολαι λευκαι vg arm aeth Cypr^bis Prim al | αυτοις εκαστω] εκαστω αυτων 28 73 syrr om εκαστω Q min^plq 25 om αυτοις min^pauc Clem-Al | ινα αναπαυσονται APQ 1 7 8 28 36 79 98 al] ινα αναπαυσωνται ℵC min^pl αναπαυσασθε 130

7; but in a passage so full of O.T. reminiscences as this is, the Person addressed as δεσπότης is probably the Father, as in Lc. ii. 29, Acts iv. 24. The martyrs being Christ's are also God's (1 Cor. iii. 23), and the holiness and truth of the Supreme Master demand the punishment of a world responsible for their deaths. The words only assert the principle of Divine retribution, which forbids the exercise of personal revenge (Rom. xii. 19 f. μὴ ἑαυτοὺς ἐκδικοῦντες...ἀλλὰ δότε τόπον τῇ ὀργῇ (sc. τοῦ θεοῦ), γέγραπται γάρ Ἐμοὶ ἐκδίκησις). But it was long before this was fully understood, and the Acts of the martyrs relate many instances in which the sufferers met their judges with threatenings of the coming wrath, not always free from the spirit of vindictiveness; even Polyc. *mart.* 11 shews something of this tendency. It is not however to be read into this *quousque*, as the fiery Tertullian more than once implies; cf. Bede: "non haec odio inimicorum, pro quibus in hoc saeculo rogaverunt, orant, sed amore aequitatis."

Οὐ κρίνεις καὶ ἐκδικεῖς: 'dost Thou refrain from pronouncing judgement and executing vengeance.' Cf. Lc. xviii. 7 f. ὁ δὲ θεὸς οὐ μὴ ποιήσῃ τὴν ἐκδίκησιν τῶν ἐκλεκτῶν αὐτοῦ τῶν βοώντων αὐτῷ...λέγω ὑμῖν ὅτι ποιήσει τὴν ἐκδίκησιν αὐτῶν ἐν τάχει—a passage which goes far to answer many questions in theodicy. Ἐκδικεῖν τὸ αἷμά τινος ἐκ occurs again in xix. 2; cf. ἐκδικεῖν (ἐκδικάζειν) τὸ αἷμα in Deut. xxxii. 41 A, 43, Hos. i. 4, Joel iii. 21 A, and ἐκδικεῖν ἐκ in Deut. xviii. 19; other combinations are ἐκδ. τινά, 1 Regn. xiv. 24; περί τινος, 1 Macc. xiii. 6; ἔν τινι, Jer. v. 9, 29; ἐπί τινα, Hos. ii. 13, iv. 9, Soph. i. 8, 12 ff.; ἀπό τινος, Lc. xviii. 3.

11. καὶ ἐδόθη αὐτοῖς ἑκάστῳ στολὴ λευκή] The present condition of the martyrs is revealed. (1) They have received a white robe (cf. iii. 4 f., iv. 4, vii. 9, 13, xix. 14; on στολή see Mc. xii. 38, note); the honours of victory have already been conferred upon them individually (ἑκάστῳ), though the general and public award is reserved for the Day of the Lord. The *Ascension of Isaiah* rightly represents the "white array" of the Saints as stored up for them in the seventh heaven, ready against the day when they will descend with Christ (iv. 16), after which all the righteous are seen "in their celestial apparel" (ix. 9 "existentes in stolis excelsis"). But the martyr's individual victory is assured as soon as he is 'with Christ'; he knows himself a conqueror, while on earth the Church recognises his victory by adding his name to her hagiographies.

καὶ ἐρρέθη αὐτοῖς ἵνα ἀναπαύσονται κτλ.] On the other hand (2) for their full reward, for the triumph which they will share with Christ, they must await the completion of the *martyrologion*. But their waiting is qualified by two considerations; (1) it is but "for a little while" (ἔτι μικρὸν χρόνον; cf. ἐν τάχει, ταχύ, i. 1, xxii. 6 f., 12, 20—the exact phrase occurs again in another connexion, xx. 3; cf. Heb. x. 37 μικρὸν ὅσον ὅσον); and (2) the waiting is a rest; they are not bidden simply to wait (ἵνα προσκαρτερήσω-

ἔτι χρόνον μικρόν, ἕως πληρωθῶσιν καὶ οἱ σύνδουλοι
αὐτῶν καὶ οἱ ἀδελφοὶ αὐτῶν οἱ μέλλοντες ἀποκτέν-
12 νεσθαι ὡς καὶ αὐτοί. [12] καὶ εἶδον ὅτε ἤνοιξεν τὴν
σφραγῖδα τὴν ἕκτην, καὶ σεισμὸς μέγας ἐγένετο, καὶ
ὁ ἥλιος ἐγένετο μέλας ὡς σάκκος τρίχινος, καὶ ἡ

11 ετι χρονον μικρον] χρ. ετι μ. A vg$^{\text{am fu tol}}$ ετι χρονον Q min$^{\text{fere 45}}$ Ar εως καιρου χρ. μ. syr^{gw} | εως] + ου 1 28 36 49 51 al | πληρωθωσιν AC 29 *g* vg$^{\text{lipss 5, 6}}$ syr^{gw} Cypr Prim] πληρωσωσιν ℵPQ 1 al$^{\text{fere 50}}$ Andr | om και ante οι συνδ. Q vg me arm Cypr | οι μελλοντες] pr και Q min^{30} Ar | αποκτεννεσθαι ℵAC 2 17 18 19 130 al] αποκτεινεσθαι PQ 1 6 14 30 38 91 92 + υπ αυτου ℵ* 12 12 ειδον ℵP 1 al^{pl} Andr Ar (ιδον ACQ 7 14 32 92)] om 18 29 30 40 90 93 95 aeth | οτε] pr και P 1 12 13 al vg^{am} Prim | σεισμος] pr ιδου A vg$^{\text{cle harl** lipss}}$ | om ολη P 1 35 49 81 91 96

σιν), but to enjoy repose (ἵνα ἀναπαύσωνται, cf. xiv. 13 ἵνα ἀναπαήσονται ἐκ τῶν κόπων αὐτῶν). The delay is itself a part of the reward; to the Church on earth it may be irksome, to the martyrs themselves it is an ἀνάπαυσις. Further, the cause of the delay is revealed. They are kept waiting ἕως πληρωθῶσιν οἱ σύνδουλοι αὐτῶν, till the number of their fellow-slaves is fully made up. For this use of πληροῦν, cf. Mt. xxiii. 32, 1 Thess. ii. 16; and for the idea see Baruch xxx. 2 "aperientur promptuaria in quibus custoditus erat numerus animarum iustarum"; and cf. the Anglican Order for the Burial of the Dead: "that it may please Thee...shortly to accomplish the number of Thine Elect, and to hasten Thy Kingdom." The harder reading πληρώσωσιν implies a scarcely tolerable ellipse of τὸν δρόμον (Acts xiii. 25, xx. 24, 2 Tim. iv. 7) or τὸν ἀριθμόν. Οἱ σύνδουλοι αὐτῶν are the rest of the saints (cf. Mt. xviii. 28 ff., Col. i. 7, iv. 7, Apoc. xix. 10, xxii. 9); οἱ ἀδελφοὶ αὐτῶν is limited by the participial clause which follows to the rest of the martyrs; καὶ...καί, both the saints in general, and the martyrs in particular. Οἱ μέλλοντες ἀποκτ.: the Apocalyptist foresees an age of persecution impending, cf. ii. 10, iii. 10. On the form ἀποκτέννεσθαι see WH.[2], *Notes*, p. 176, Blass, *Gr.* p. 41, 55.

12. καὶ εἶδον ὅτε ἤνοιξεν τὴν σφραγῖδα τὴν ἕκτην κτλ.] The first five openings had revealed the condition of the world and of the Church; the sixth opening looks on to the troubles which were expected to precede the end. The sufferings of the nations and of the Church were but an ἀρχὴ ὠδίνων (Mc. xiii. 8); with the opening of the sixth seal the cosmical disturbances of the last age begin; cf. Mc. xiii. 24 ff. ἐν ἐκείναις ταῖς ἡμέραις μετὰ τὴν θλίψιν ἐκείνην κτλ. First there is a great earthquake, not one of the σεισμοὶ κατὰ τόπους of which Asia had much experience in the first century, but the final upheaval of Hagg. ii. 6 (Heb. xii. 26 ff.): ἔτι ἅπαξ ἐγὼ σείσω τὸν οὐρανὸν καὶ τὴν γῆν καὶ τὴν θάλασσαν καὶ τὴν ξηράν, καὶ συνσείσω πάντα τὰ ἔθνη, where the last words supply the key to the meaning of the symbolism: racial and social revolutions are the σεισμοί which herald the approach of the end.

καὶ ὁ ἥλιος ἐγένετο μέλας ὡς σάκκος τρίχινος, κτλ.] The earthquake is followed by the celestial phenomena which find a place in all apocalyptic descriptions of the last day: cf. Joel ii. 31 (= iii. 4 Heb.): ὁ ἥλιος μεταστραφήσεται εἰς σκότος καὶ ἡ σελήνη εἰς αἷμα πρὶν ἐλθεῖν ἡμέραν Κυρίου, Isa. xiii. 10 σκοτισθήσεται τοῦ ἡλίου ἀνατέλλοντος, καὶ ἡ σελήνη οὐ δώσει τὸ

σελήνη ὅλη ἐγένετο ὡς αἷμα, [13]καὶ οἱ ἀστέρες τοῦ 13
οὐρανοῦ ἔπεσαν εἰς τὴν γῆν, ὡς συκῆ βάλλει τοὺς
ὀλύνθους αὐτῆς ὑπὸ ἀνέμου μεγάλου σειομένη, [14]καὶ 14
ὁ οὐρανὸς ἀπεχωρίσθη ὡς βιβλίον ἑλισσόμενον, καὶ
πᾶν ὄρος καὶ νῆσος ἐκ τῶν τόπων αὐτῶν ἐκινήθησαν.

13 *του ουρανου*] *του θεου* A | *επεσον* Q $\text{min}^{\text{plq 30}}$ | *εις*] *επι* ℵ 47 syr^{gw} | *βαλλει*] *βαλλουσα* ℵ 16 30 35 39 51 87 90 97 130 syrr *βαλουσα* 2 4 6 7 8 al | *υπο*] *απο* ℵ 14 31** syr^{gw} | *σειομενη*] *σαλευομενη* A 12 14 *ελισσομενον* (*ειλ.* P min^{nonn})] *ελισσομενος* ℵ 1 6 8 31 38 91 al Ar *ελισσονται* $\text{syr}^{\text{gw vid}}$ | *νησος*] *βουνος* ℵ *insulae* vg Vict Prim pr *πασα* syr^{gw} | om *αυτων* ℵ 26 31 | *εκινηθησαν*] *εκινησαν* ℵ* *απεκεινησαν* A

φῶς αὐτῆς (Mc. xiii. 24): *ib.* l. 3 *ἐνδύσω τὸν οὐρανὸν σκότος, καὶ ὡς σάκκον θήσω τὸ περιβόλαιον αὐτοῦ*, *Assumption of Moses*, 10. 5 f. "sol non dabit lumen et in tenebras convertet se; cornua lunae confringentur et tota convertet se in sanguinem." *Σάκκος τρίχινος*, Vg. *saccus cilicinus*, made of the hair of the black goat; cf. Isa. l. 3, and Sirach xxv. 17 *σκοτοῖ τὸ πρόσωπον αὐτῆς ὡς σάκκον*. *Ὡς αἷμα* well depicts the deep copper colour which the moon assumes when totally eclipsed; with *ἡ σελήνη ὅλη* contrast c. viii. 12 *ἐπλήγη...τὸ τρίτον τῆς σελήνης*. Eclipses and occultations of the heavenly bodies are treated in Eccl. xii. 2 as symbols of old age and failing strength: here they seem to represent the decay of society, such a period of collapse as followed the ruin of the Empire, and may yet be in store for civilization.

13. *καὶ οἱ ἀστέρες τοῦ οὐρανοῦ ἔπεσαν κτλ.*] The stars fell from the sky as unripe figs fall when the tree is swept by a gale. Cf. Isa. xxxiv. 4 *πάντα τὰ ἄστρα πεσεῖται ὡς φύλλα ἐξ ἀμπέλου, καὶ ὡς πίπτει φύλλα ἀπὸ συκῆς*, Mc. xiii. 25 *οἱ ἀστέρες ἔσονται ἐκ τοῦ οὐρανοῦ πίπτοντες*. The Seer saw the terrible vision realised (*ἔπεσαν*). *Ὄλυνθοι* are the green figs (*grossi*) which appear in winter and of which, while some ripen, many fall off in spring: cf. Cant. ii. 11 ff. *ὁ χειμὼν παρῆλθεν...ἡ συκῆ ἐξήνεγκεν ὀλύνθους αὐτῆς* (פַּגֶּיהָ). It will be remembered that during the Ministry the fig-tree supplied our Lord with a parable of the Last Things (Mc. xiii. 28). Its early greenness suggested the approaching end of the world's long winter, proclaiming *Ἐγγὺς τὸ θέρος ἐστίν*. *Ὑπὸ ἀνέμου μεγάλου σειομένη*: cf. Mt. xi. 7 *κάλαμον ὑπὸ ἀν. σαλευόμενον*.

14. *καὶ ὁ οὐρανὸς ἀπεχωρίσθη κτλ.*] 'The heaven was parted'; cf. Acts xv. 39 *ὥστε ἀποχωρισθῆναι αὐτοὺς ἀπ' ἀλλήλων*. Here the exact sense is determined by what follows: *ὡς βιβλίον ἑλισσόμενον* 'like a papyrus roll (v. 1) when it is being rolled up'; i.e. the expanse of heaven (הָרָקִיעַ, *τὸ στερέωμα*) was seen to crack and part, the divided portions curling up and forming a roll on either hand. The conception is borrowed from Isa. xxxiv. 4 *ἑλιγήσεται ὡς βιβλίον ὁ οὐρανός*, cf. Ps. ci. (cii.) 27 *ὡσεὶ περιβόλαιον ἑλίξεις αὐτούς*. The writer of 2 Peter explains the cause of the phenomenon (iii. 12 *οὐρανοὶ πυρούμενοι λυθήσονται καὶ στοιχεῖα καυσούμενα τήκεται*).

καὶ πᾶν ὄρος καὶ νῆσος κτλ.] Cf. xvi. 20 *πᾶσα νῆσος ἔφυγεν, καὶ ὄρη οὐχ εὑρέθησαν*: the source is perhaps Nahum i. 5 *τὰ ὄρη ἐσείσθησαν ἀπ' αὐτοῦ, καὶ οἱ βουνοὶ ἐσαλεύθησαν*, or Jer. iv. 24. But to 'move mountains' was a proverbial expression for attempting apparent impossibilities, cf. Mc. xi. 23, note, 1 Cor. xiii. 2; whilst

15 [15]*καὶ οἱ βασιλεῖς τῆς γῆς καὶ οἱ μεγιστᾶνες καὶ οἱ
χιλίαρχοι καὶ οἱ πλούσιοι καὶ οἱ ἰσχυροὶ καὶ πᾶς
δοῦλος καὶ ἐλεύθερος ἔκρυψαν ἑαυτοὺς εἰς τὰ σπήλαια*
16 *καὶ εἰς τὰς πέτρας τῶν ὀρέων,* [16]*καὶ λέγουσιν τοῖς
ὄρεσιν καὶ ταῖς πέτραις Πέσατε ἐφ' ἡμᾶς καὶ κρύψατε
ἡμᾶς ἀπὸ προσώπου τοῦ καθημένου ἐπὶ τοῦ θρόνου*

15 *και οι χιλ.*] om *και* A | *και οι ισχυροι*] om 1 12 36 aeth om *οι* ℵ 50 95 | *ελευθερος*] pr *πας* ℵ$^{c.a}$ P 1 al^{mu} me arm Andr | om *και ελ.* ℵ* | *πετρας*] *οπης* 130
16 *πεσατε* AP 7 28 79] *πεσετε* ℵCQ min^{pl} Andr Ar | *επι του θρονου* APC 1 al^{mu} Andr] *επι τω θρονω* ℵQ min^{plq25} Andr | om *του καθημενου...της οργης* syr^{gw}

the residence of the Seer in Patmos suggests a reference to the rocky islands of the Aegean. The last times held in store movements not less improbable than the upheaval of Mt Sipylos or Messogis or Cadmos, or the submerging of Patmos or Samos, or even the whole archipelago; movements, however, not disastrous in their ultimate results, but issuing in a higher order, cf. Arethas: *εἰλιγμόν τινα καὶ ἀλλαγὴν ἐπὶ τὸ βέλτιον. Πᾶν ὄρος καὶ νῆσος*, i.e. *πᾶν ὄ. καὶ πᾶσα ν.*; cf. WM. p. 661.

15. *καὶ οἱ βασιλεῖς τῆς γῆς κτλ.*] Seven conditions of life are named, covering the whole fabric of society from the Emperor down to the meanest slave. For *οἱ βασιλεῖς τῆς γῆς*, the heads of states hostile to the Christ, see Ps. ii. 2 ff., Acts iv. 26 ff.; the Caesars are in view here, but not exclusively; of the other persons in authority named the *μεγιστᾶνες* (*magistratus*) are the civil officials (e.g. the persecuting proconsuls), while the *χιλίαρχοι* (*tribuni*) are the military authorities (cf. Mc. vi. 21, note); the former word is frequently coupled with *βασιλεῖς* (Jon. iii. 7, Isa. xxxiv. 12, Jer. xxv. 18 (xlix. 38), xxxii. 5 (xxv. 19), Dan. v. 2 f. Th., vi. 17); *χιλίαρχος* is the LXX. equivalent of שַׂר אֶלֶף and in the N.T. (e.g., Acts xxi. 31 ff., xxii. 24 ff., xxiii. 10 ff., xxiv. 22) usually represents the Roman *tribunus militum* (see Blass on Acts *l. c.*); it is therefore not necessary to find an allusion in the use of the word to the Parthian as contrasted with the Roman authorities (Mommsen v. 343 f. cited by Bousset). Not officials only will be terror-struck by the signs of the approaching end, but all classes of society; wealth and physical strength will afford no security (for *οἱ ἰσχυροί* see Jer. xxvi. (xlvi.) 5 f., xxxi. (xlviii.) 14); slaves and free—the contrast indicates the deepest of class-distinctions in ancient life—will be huddled together in the frantic attempt to escape. *Ἔκρυψαν ἑαυτούς κτλ.* is based on Isa. ii. 10, 18 f.: *εἰσέλθετε εἰς τὰς πέτρας καὶ κρύπτεσθε εἰς τὴν γῆν...καὶ τὰ χειροποίητα πάντα κατακρύψουσιν, εἰσενέγκαντες εἰς τὰ σπήλαια καὶ εἰς τὰς σχισμὰς τῶν πετρῶν.*

16. *καὶ λέγουσιν τοῖς ὄρεσιν καὶ ταῖς πέτραις κτλ.*] From Hosea x. 8 *ἐροῦσιν τοῖς ὄρεσιν Καλύψατε ἡμᾶς, καὶ τοῖς βουνοῖς Πέσατε ἐφ' ἡμᾶς.* The words were quoted by our Lord on His way to the cross, Lc. xxiii. 30 *τότε ἄρξονται λέγειν τοῖς ὄρεσιν κτλ.* What sinners dread most is not death, but the revealed Presence of God. There is deep psychological truth in the remark of Gen. iii. 8 *ἐκρύβησαν ὅ τε Ἀδὰμ καὶ ἡ γυνὴ αὐτοῦ ἀπὸ προσώπου Κυρίου.* The Apocalyptist foresees the same shrinking from the sight of God in the last generation of mankind which

καὶ ἀπὸ τῆς ὀργῆς τοῦ ἀρνίου, [17]ὅτι ἦλθεν ἡ ἡμέρα ἡ 17
μεγάλη τῆς ὀργῆς αὐτῶν, καὶ τίς δύναται σταθῆναι;
[1]Μετὰ τοῦτο εἶδον τέσσαρας ἀγγέλους ἑστῶ- 1 VII.
τας ἐπὶ τὰς τέσσαρας γωνίας τῆς γῆς, κρατοῦντας

16 απο 2°] επι ℵ* | οργης] σχολης 130 17 αυτων ℵC 38 130 vg syrr] αυτου APQ min^fere omn me arm aeth Andr Ar Prim | σταθηναι] στηναι 34 35 36 σωθηναι 40 48 Ar

VII 1 μετα] pr και ℵPQ min^omn vid syrr arm aeth Andr Ar (om AC me vg Prim) | τουτο] ταυτα P 1 28 36 al vg syrr arm | ειδον P min^pl Ar] ιδον ℵACQ 7 14 32 92 | τεσσαρας] τεσσαρες 1° et 3° A, 2° P | om της γης 38 syr^gw arm | κρατουντας] pr και 28 73 97 syrr

Genesis attributes to the parents of the race. But there will be then a further source of terror: the end brings together with the revelation of God "the wrath of the Lamb." The words ἀπὸ τῆς ὀργῆς τοῦ ἀρνίου are pregnant with the grave irony which has already shewn itself in v. 5 f. ἰδοὺ...ὁ λέων... καὶ εἶδον...ἀρνίον. But the situation is now reversed. The Lion standing before the Throne is the Lamb; the Lamb in the great day of His appearing is once more the Lion, in the terribleness of His wrath. In the Gospels ὀργή is attributed to Christ once only (Mc. iii. 5, see note), but His scathing denunciations of the Pharisees (Mt. xxiii. 14 ff.) and His stern predictions of the doom of the impenitent make it evident that the Sacred Humanity is capable of a righteous anger which is the worst punishment that the ungodly have to fear, more insupportable even than the vision of the Divine Purity.

17. ὅτι ἦλθεν ἡ ἡμέρα ἡ μεγάλη τῆς ὀργῆς αὐτῶν] 'The great day' is a phrase borrowed from the Prophets (Joel ii. 11, 31, Zeph. i. 14; cf. Jude 6). Here it is combined with another prophetic phrase, 'the day of wrath' (Zeph. i. 15, 18, ii. 3; cf. Rom. ii. 5). The Great Day of the Lord is a *dies irae* to the world. Ἦλθεν, 'is already come' (i.e. it came when the signs of the end described in *vv.* 12—14 began). Fear anticipates the actual event, for there is another seal to be opened before the *parousia*. There have been epochs in history when the conscience of mankind has antedated the judgement and believed it imminent. Τῆς ὀργῆς αὐτῶν, sc. the wrath of God and of the Lamb: cf. v. 13, xxii. 1.

καὶ τίς δύναται σταθῆναι;] 'And who, that has to meet that wrath, can hold his ground?' Cf. Nah. i. 6 ἀπὸ προσώπου ὀργῆς αὐτοῦ τίς ὑποστήσεται; καὶ τίς ἀντιστήσεται ἐν ὀργῇ θυμοῦ αὐτοῦ; Mal. iii. 2 τίς ὑπομενεῖ ἡμέραν εἰσόδου αὐτοῦ; ἢ τίς ὑποστήσεται ἐν τῇ ὀπτασίᾳ αὐτοῦ; Ps. xxxv. (xxxvi.) 13 οὐ μὴ δύνωνται στῆναι. The only possible answer is given by Christ Himself in Lc. xxi. 36 ἀγρυπνεῖτε δὲ ἐν παντὶ καιρῷ δεόμενοι, ἵνα κατισχύσητε ... σταθῆναι ἔμπροσθεν τοῦ υἱοῦ τοῦ ἀνθρώπου.

VII. 1—8. THE SEALING OF 144,000 FROM THE TRIBES OF ISRAEL.

1. μετὰ τοῦτο εἶδον κτλ.] Cf. iv. 1, note. The reader expects καὶ ὅτε ἤνοιξεν τὴν σφραγῖδα τὴν ἑβδόμην (viii. 1). But two episodes, occupying the whole of *c.* vii., are introduced between the loosings of the sixth and seventh seals. A similar break follows the blowing of the sixth trumpet (x. 1—xi. 13). The purpose of the present pair of visions (1—8, 9—17) is to contrast the preparedness of the Church for the coming end with the panic of the unprepared world (vi. 15 ff.).

ἐπὶ τὰς τέσσαρας γωνίας τῆς γῆς. Cf. xx. 8. The earth is regarded as τετράγωνος, in view of the four quarters from which the winds blow—the כַּנְפוֹת הָאָרֶץ, LXX. οἱ πτέρυγες τῆς γῆς,

τοὺς τέσσαρας ἀνέμους τῆς γῆς, ἵνα μὴ πνέῃ ἄνεμος
ἐπὶ τῆς γῆς μήτε ἐπὶ τῆς θαλάσσης μήτε ἐπὶ πᾶν
2 δένδρον. [2]καὶ εἶδον ἄλλον ἄγγελον ἀναβαίνοντα ἀπὸ
ἀνατολῆς ἡλίου, ἔχοντα σφραγῖδα θεοῦ ζῶντος· καὶ

1 της γης 1°] om 38 syr^{gw} arm al | πνεη] πνευση ℵ 130 | ανεμος] pr ο C 14 26 92 93 95 98 | επι της γης] om A + Ισραηλ 130 | της θαλ.] om της A | επι παν δενδρον ℵ 1 10 17 28 al] επι τι δ. CQ min^{pl} επι δ. A me arm aeth 2 ειδον ℵP al^{pl}] ιδον ACQ 7 14 92 | αναβαντα 1 arm | ανατολων A 90 syr^{gw}

of Isa. xi. 12, Ezek. vii. 2. For *οἱ τέσσαρες ἄνεμοι* cf. Zech. ii. 6, vi. 5, Dan. vii. 2, viii. 8, xi. 4, Mc. xiii. 27; Enoch (lxxvi. 7) mentions twelve winds (E. S. W. N., and the intermediate points).

κρατοῦντας τοὺς τέσσαρας ἀνέμους κτλ.] At each of the quarters one of the four winds is held prisoner by an angel appointed to the task. For *κρατεῖν*, 'hold fast,' 'detain,' cf. Cant. iii. 4 *ἐκράτησα αὐτὸν καὶ οὐκ ἀφῆκα αὐτόν*, Jo. xx. 23 *ἄν τινων κρατῆτε* [*τὰς ἁμαρτίας*] *κεκράτηνται*. With these angel-custodians of the winds may be compared the angel *ὁ ἔχων ἐξουσίαν ἐπὶ τοῦ πυρός* (xiv. 18) and the "angel of the waters" (xvi. 5). The angels of the winds control their movements; it is their mission to prevent outbreaks of elemental fury. According to Jewish belief a terrific storm was to usher in the end, cf. *Orac. Sibyll.* viii. 204 f. *πολλῇ δέ τε λαίλαπι τυφῶν | γαῖαν ἐρημώσει· νεκρῶν δ' ἐπανάστασις ἔσται.* *Μήτε ἐπὶ πᾶν δένδρον*: the trees are specified, as suffering most severely from the violence of the winds. The change of case (*γῆς...θαλάσσης...δένδρον*) answers to a subtle difference in the force of *ἐπί*; the winds blow on land and sea, but the trees are singled out for a direct attack.

2. *καὶ εἶδον ἄλλον ἄγγελον ἀναβαίνοντα κτλ.*] A fifth angel is seen mounting up from the sunrising, i.e. from the Orient; *ἀπὸ ἀνατολῶν* is the usual LXX. phrase (Gen. xi. 2, Mt. ii. 1) or less frequently, *ἀπὸ ἀνατολῆς* (Num. iii. 38, B), but *ἡλίου* is sometimes expressed (Jos. i. 15, xiii. 5; Isa. xi. 11, 14, Apoc. xvi. 12). From the writer's point of view the East is the direction of Palestine and the countries beyond it; and it was fitting that the angel who is to seal the tribes of Israel should appear from that quarter. Or there may be a reference to Ezek. xliii. 2 *ἰδοὺ δόξα θεοῦ Ἰσραὴλ ἤρχετο κατὰ τὴν ὁδὸν τὴν πρὸς ἀνατολάς*, Mal. iv. 2 (iii. 20) *ἀνατελεῖ ὑμῖν...ἥλιος δικαιοσύνης*. The angel's ascent implies that he has been employed in some service on the earth, and now rises into the sky to deliver his message.

ἔχοντα σφραγῖδα θεοῦ ζῶντος] *Σφραγίς* is here the signet-ring = *δακτύλιος* (Gen. xli. 42, Esther iii. 10, viii. 2 ff., Dan. vi. 17, 1 Macc. vi. 15), which the Oriental monarch uses to give validity to official documents or to mark his property. The symbolism seems to be based on Ezek. ix. 4, where a man provided with an inkhorn is bidden to set a mark (תָּו, *σημεῖον*, i.e. the letter ת which in the older script was cruciform, see Hastings, *D. B.* i. p. 71) on the foreheads of the righteous in Jerusalem, with a view to their being spared in an impending massacre. But for a mark made by the pen of a scribe the Apocalyptist, who has lately had before him the vision of the sealed roll, substitutes the impression of the Divine signet-ring. The conception of a Divine sealing occurs freely in St Paul (2 Cor. i. 22 *ὁ καὶ σφραγισάμενος ἡμᾶς*, Eph. i. 13 *ἐσφραγίσθητε τῷ πνεύματι*, iv. 30 *τὸ πνεῦμα τὸ ἅγιον τοῦ θεοῦ, ἐν ᾧ ἐσφραγίσθητε εἰς ἡμέραν ἀπολυτρώσεως*), and once in the Fourth Gospel (Jo.

ἔκραξεν φωνῇ μεγάλῃ τοῖς τέσσαρσιν ἀγγέλοις οἷς
ἐδόθη αὐτοῖς ἀδικῆσαι τὴν γῆν καὶ τὴν θάλασσαν,
[3]λέγων Μὴ ἀδικήσητε τὴν γῆν μήτε τὴν θάλασσαν 3
μήτε τὰ δένδρα, ἄχρι σφραγίσωμεν τοὺς δούλους τοῦ
θεοῦ ἡμῶν ἐπὶ τῶν μετώπων αὐτῶν. [4]καὶ ἤκουσα 4
τὸν ἀριθμὸν τῶν ἐσφραγισμένων· ἑκατὸν τεσσερά-
κοντα τέσσαρες χιλιάδες ἐσφραγισμένοι ἐκ πάσης
φυλῆς υἱῶν Ἰσραήλ.

2 *εκραξεν* AP | *τοις τεσσαρας* א* | om *αυτοις* 16 17 28 49 79 80 3 *αδικησεται* א | *μητε* 1°] *μηδε* א 130 (item 2°) *και* A 37 38 41 42 vg | *αχρι*] *αχρις ου* Q min[pl] *αχρις αν* 18 28 79 80 4 om *και ηκουσα...εσφραγισμενων* A | *εσφραγισμενοι*] *εσφραγισμενων* Q 2 6 7 14 al om 130 syr[gw]

vi. 27 τοῦτον γὰρ ὁ πατὴρ ἐσφράγισεν ὁ θεός). In post-Apostolic writings 'the seal of the Lord' is either Baptism (Herm. *sim.* ix. 16 ἡ σφραγὶς οὖν τὸ ὕδωρ ἐστίν, Clem. Al. *quis div.* 42 τὸ τέλεον αὐτῷ φυλακτήριον ἐπιστήσας τὴν σφραγῖδα τοῦ κυρίου), or the chrism which followed it. Here the seal, being in the hands of an angel, can hardly be sacramental. The general sense is well given in 2 Tim. ii. 19 ὁ μέντοι στερεὸς θεμέλιος τοῦ θεοῦ ἕστηκεν, ἔχων τὴν σφραγῖδα ταύτην Ἔγνω κύριος τοὺς ὄντας αὐτοῦ κτλ. Cf. Orig. *in Joann.* t. i. 1 τίς οὖν ἄλλη εἴη ἡ σφραγὶς ἡ ἐπὶ τῶν μετώπων ἢ τὸ ὄνομα τοῦ ἀρνίου καὶ τὸ ὄνομα τοῦ πατρὸς αὐτοῦ; With θεοῦ ζῶντος cf. x. 6, xv. 7: the phrase, which is fairly common in the N.T. (Mt.[2], Acts[1], Paul[5], Heb.[4], Apoc.[3]), rests on the אֵל חַי of the O.T. (Jos. iii. 10, Ps. xli. 3 (xlii. 2), Hos. i. 10 (ii. 2)). In the Apoc. it suggests a contrast between the God of Christ and of Christians and the nonentities (1 Cor. viii. 4) of pagan worship.

καὶ ἔκραξεν φωνῇ μεγάλῃ κτλ.] The first care of the Angel with the Seal is to prohibit the angels of the winds from letting loose the elements until his work of sealing is done. For φωνῇ μεγ. see vi. 10. The angels of the winds are identified with the winds, as the angels of the Churches with the societies they represent (see i. 20, note); it is theirs to hurt or not as they will, unless withheld by a special prohibition (οἷς ἐδόθη αὐτοῖς ἀδικῆσαι ...μὴ ἀδικήσητε). The restraint which is put upon them represents the Divine postponement of the catastrophe until the Church is ready (xxi. 2).

For οἷς...αὐτοῖς see ii. 7, note; and for ἀδικεῖν = βλάπτειν, cf. ii. 11, note, vi. 6.

3. ἄχρι σφραγίσωμεν τοὺς δούλους κτλ.] Cf. Apoc. ix. 4, xiv. 1, xxii. 4; a mark (χάραγμα) of the opposite character is mentioned in xiii. 16, xiv. 9, xx. 4. On τ. δούλους τοῦ θεοῦ see Apoc. i. 1, ii. 20, xix. 2, 5, xxii. 3, 6. Ἡμῶν, addressed by an angel to angels, points to the bond of a common service which links angels with the saints: 'they are the servants of the God whom we also serve.'

4—8. καὶ ἤκουσα τὸν ἀριθμὸν κτλ.] The Seer does not witness the sealing, but he hears the number of the sealed announced, and who they are. Ἐσφραγισμένοι: the gender is determined by τοὺς δούλους (*v.* 3); WH. places a comma after χιλ., but perhaps unnecessarily. The sum is 12 × 12,000, and each of the tribes of Israel contributes an equal proportion. The tribes are named separately in the order: Judah, Reuben, Gad, Asher,

5 [5]ἐκ φυλῆς Ἰούδα δώδεκα χιλιάδες ἐσφραγισμένοι,
ἐκ φυλῆς Ῥουβὴν δώδεκα χιλιάδες,
ἐκ φυλῆς Γὰδ δώδεκα χιλιάδες,
6 [6]ἐκ φυλῆς Ἀσὴρ δώδεκα χιλιάδες,
ἐκ φυλῆς Νεφθαλεὶμ δώδεκα χιλιάδες,
ἐκ φυλῆς Μανασσὴ δώδεκα χιλιάδες,

5 *εσφραγισμενοι*] *εσφραγισμενων* min^{pauc} om syr^{gw} | *Ρουβημ*, *-βειμ*, *-βιμ* min^{nonn} | *-βειν* 130 | *Γαδ*] *Δαν* (1) 9 13 130 | om *εκ φυλης Γαδ δωδ. χιλ.* ℵ   6 *Νεφθαλειμ* P 1 7 28 29 31 32] *Νεφθαλιμ* AQ min^{pauc} *-λιν* C *-λι* ℵ syrr | *Μανασση*] *Μαννασση* A *Μανασση* Q syr^{gw} *Δαν* me

Naphtali, Manasseh, Simeon, Levi, Issachar, Zebulon, Joseph (i.e. Ephraim), Benjamin.

Lists of the patriarchs or of the tribes occur in Gen. xxxv. 22 ff., xlvi. 8 ff., xlix., Exod. i. 1 ff., Num. i., ii., xiii. 4 ff., xxvi., xxxiv., Deut. xxvii. 11 ff., xxxiii. 6 ff., Josh. xiii—xxii., Judg. v., 1 Chron. ii—viii., xii. 24 ff., xxvii. 16 ff., Ezek. xlviii.; a comparative table will be found in Hastings, *D. B.* iv. p. 811. The order differs more or less in every case. The Apocalyptic order starts with the tribe from which Christ came (cf. *c.* v. 5); and then proceeds to the tribe of the firstborn son of Jacob, which heads most of the O.T. lists; next come the tribes located in the North, broken by the mention of Simeon and Levi who in other lists usually follow Reuben or Judah, while Joseph and Benjamin bring up the rear. This arrangement seems to have been suggested partly by the birth-order of the patriarchs and partly by the geographical situation of the tribes; Christian associations have probably determined the place of Judah and of the Galilean tribes. Since Levi is counted in, it has been necessary to omit one of the other tribes; the omitted name is Dan, a tribe which perhaps is dropped also, together with Zebulun, in 1 Chron. ii. 3—viii., but see *Enc. Bibl.* i. p. 996, note 4. A mystical reason was given for the omission of Dan from the Apocalyptic list by Irenaeus v. 30. 2 "Hieremias...et tribum ex qua veniet [Antichristus] manifestavit dicens: *ex Dan audiemus vocem velocitatis equorum eius* (Jer. viii. 16)...et propter hoc non annumeratur tribus haec in Apocalypsi cum his quae salvantur." Cf. Hippolytus *de Antichristo* 14 *ὥσπερ γὰρ ἐκ τῆς Ἰούδα φυλῆς ὁ χριστὸς γεννᾶται, οὕτως ἐκ τῆς Δὰν φυλῆς ὁ ἀντίχριστος γεννηθήσεται.* So Arethas: *ἡ φυλὴ τοῦ Δὰν διὰ τὸ ἐξ αὐτῆς τὸν Ἀντίχριστον τίκτεσθαι ταῖς λοιπαῖς οὐ συντέτακται, ἀλλ' ἀντὶ αὐτῆς ἡ τοῦ Λευὶ ὡς ἱερατικὴ εἰς μερισμὸν ἐχομένη.* Either from a misunderstanding of Gen. xlix. 17 or from the story of Judges xviii. (cf. Targ. Jon. on Exod. xvii. 8), Dan is associated in Rabbinical lore with idolatry and apostasy (see *Shabbath* 66); the Testaments of the xii Patriarchs (*Dan* 5) seem to predict an alliance between Dan and Beliar. On the late Christian tradition which assigns Antichrist to this tribe, see Bousset *Antichrist*, p. 112 ff.; it may partly be due to Jewish sources, and partly have been suggested by the omission of Dan from the Apocalyptic list.

It is more important to enquire whether the Apocalyptist intends the 144,000 sealed Israelites to represent the elect of Israel (cf. Rom. xi. 5 *λίμμα κατ' ἐκλογὴν χάριτος*), the Jewish Christians (Victorinus), or the whole number of the faithful (Primasius: "omnis significatur ecclesia," and so Bede). The third of these views is supported by (*a*) the tendency of the Apocalypse to regard

7 ἐκ φυλῆς Συμεὼν δώδεκα χιλιάδες, 7
ἐκ φυλῆς Λευεὶ δώδεκα χιλιάδες,
ἐκ φυλῆς Ἰσσαχὰρ δώδεκα χιλιάδες,
8 ἐκ φυλῆς Ζαβουλὼν δώδεκα χιλιάδες, 8
ἐκ φυλῆς Ἰωσὴφ δώδεκα χιλιάδες,
ἐκ φυλῆς Βενιαμεὶν δώδεκα χιλιάδες ἐσφραγισμένοι.
9 Μετὰ ταῦτα εἶδον, καὶ ἰδοὺ ὄχλος πολύς, ὃν 9

7 om *εκ φυλης Συμεων δωδ. χιλ.* ℵ 87 | *Λευει* ℵ] *Λευι* ACPQ min^{omn} | *Ισσαχαρ* ℵAP] *Ισαχαρ* CQ syr^{gw} g vg^{fu} Prim 8 *Ιωσηφ* et *Βενιαμειν* transp ℵ 28 | *Βενιαμειν* AP 161] *Βενιαμιν* ℵCQ min^{pl} | *εσφραγισμεναι* Q min$^{plq 25}$ *εσφραγισμονων* 130 9 *μετα ταυτα*] pr *και* syr^{gw} | *ειδον* CP min^{pl}] *ιδον* ℵA(Q) 7 14 92 130 | om *και ιδου* A vg me syr^{gw} aeth Cypr^{bis} Prim al om *ιδου* C | *οχλον πολυν* A vg me syr^{gw} aeth Cypr Prim al | *ον*] *και* A

the Church as the true Israel (cf. e.g. ii. 9, iii. 9 ff.), (*b*) the use of the same number in xiv. 1 for the followers of the Lamb, whose foreheads bear the names of God and Christ, and (*c*) the circumstance that none are sealed but the 144,000 of Israel. Had it been the purpose of the Apocalyptist to distinguish between two bodies of the elect, he would surely have represented both as alike receiving the seal which was to mark the "servants of God"; but the sealing is expressly limited to the twelve tribes. It follows that the Israel of the first vision is coextensive with the whole Church (cf. Orig. *in Joann.* t. i. 1, Renan, *l'Antechrist*, p. 390), and the ὄχλος πολύς of *v.* 9 have been sealed already in their capacity of elect Israelites. The two visions depict the same body, under widely different conditions; in *vv.* 4—8 the true Israelites (Jo. i. 17, Rom. ii. 29, Gal. vi. 16) of a single generation are marshalled under the banners of their several tribes for the campaign which is yet before them, whereas in *vv.* 9—17 all the generations of the faithful appear in their countless numbers, no longer needing the safeguard of the Divine Seal, but triumphant and at rest. Cf. Beatus: "cxliv millia omnino ecclesia est; quid sit *ex omni tribu* exposuit dicens *ex omni gente.*

9—17. THE TRIUMPH OF THE INNUMERABLE MULTITUDE.

9. μετὰ ταῦτα εἶδον κτλ.] The second vision, introduced by a fresh μετὰ ταῦτα, presents a series of sharp contrasts when compared with the first. In the first, the concourse can be counted; in the second, it is incalculably great. In the first, it is drawn from the twelve tribes of Israel; in the second, from every nation. In the first, it is being prepared for imminent peril; in the second, it is victorious and secure.

καὶ ἰδοὺ ὄχλος πολὺς κτλ.] Cf. xix. 1, 6. The writer perhaps recalls the vast crowd that thronged our Lord during His ministry; see Mc. iv. 1, v. 21, 24, Lc. xii. 1, Jo. vi. 2, xii. 9, 12. Ὃν ἀριθμῆσαι αὐτὸν οὐδεὶς ἐδύνατο, in contrast with *v.* 4 ἤκουσα τὸν ἀριθμόν; possibly there is an allusion to Gen. xv. 5, xxxii. 12 (cf. Heb. xi. 12). In the Church, which is Abraham's seed, the promise of a countless progeny will at length be realised (Gal. iii. 7, 29). With ἐκ παντὸς ἔθνους κτλ. cf. Apoc. v. 9, xi. 9, xiii. 7, xiv. 6, xvii. 15; this favourite formula found a daily illustration in the polyglott cosmopolitan crowd who jostled one another in the agora or on the quays of the Asian seaport towns. Ἑστῶτες (a *constructio ad sensum*; the crowd is

ἀριθμῆσαι αὐτὸν οὐδεὶς ἐδύνατο, ἐκ παντὸς ἔθνους καὶ φυλῶν καὶ λαῶν καὶ γλωσσῶν, ἑστῶτες ἐνώπιον τοῦ θρόνου καὶ ἐνώπιον τοῦ ἀρνίου, περιβεβλημένους στολὰς λευκάς, καὶ φοίνικες ἐν ταῖς χερσὶν αὐτῶν·

9 om *αυτον* Q min^nonn et ut vid vg Cypr Prim | *ηδυνατο* P 1 14 28 al^mu | *εστωτας* Q min^plq 35 syr^gw vid *εστωτων* C 38 *εστωτα* 11 19 93 | *ενωπιον*] *επι* A | *περιβεβλημενους* ℵ*ACQ min^fere 35 Ar] *περιβεβλημενοι* ℵ^c.a P 1 28 36 49 91 130 pr *και* syr^gw | *φοινικες* ℵ^c.a ACP 1 7 35 36 38 87 130 Andr] *φοινικας* ℵ*Q min^sat mu Ar

in thought resolved into the plurality of its countless constituents) *ἐνώπιον τοῦ θρόνου κτλ.* Hitherto only the Elders, the *ζῷα*, and the Angels have had places assigned to them in the presence of God and of the Lamb, but in this prospective vision the presence-chamber is crowded with a vast assemblage of men; drawn from every nation upon earth and by some unexplained process transported to heaven. Perhaps no passage in the Apocalypse has had so wide an influence on popular eschatology. The symbolism must not however be pressed into the service of the fancy which places redeemed humanity in a localised abode of God and of Angels. Life "before the Throne of God" is life wherever spent, if it is dominated by a joyful consciousness of the Divine Presence and Glory. The present picture must be correlated with that of *cc.* xxi., xxii., where the future state is presented in the light of a City descending from Heaven, yet possessing within its walls the Throne of God.

The scene of vii. 9 ff. anticipates the final condition of redeemed humanity. Like the Transfiguration before the Passion, it prepares the Seer to face the evil which is yet to come.

περιβεβλημένους στολὰς λευκάς κτλ.] The construction is much broken, as if in sympathy with the rapture and *abandon* of the moment. (*ὄχλος ... ἑστῶτες ... περιβεβλημένους ... καὶ φοίνικες ... καὶ κράζουσιν*). The acc. *περιβεβλημένους* seems to presuppose an *εἶδον*, understood in *ἰδού* (WM. pp. 671, 724; Blass, *Gr.* p. 81); *περιβεβλημένοι* is an obvious correction. The whole company of the elect are now seen clad in the white robes which in vi. 11 distinguish the Martyrs; what the symbol here represents is explained below, *v.* 13 f., where see notes.

φοίνικες ἐν ταῖς χερσὶν αὐτῶν] *Φοίνικες*, palm branches (= *κάλλυνθρα φοινίκων* (Lev. xxiii. 40), *φύλλα φ.* (2 Esdr. xviii. (viii) 15) or *βαΐα φ.* (Jo. xii. 13)), as in 2 Macc. x. 7 *φοίνικας ἔχοντες ηὐχαρίστουν*; cf. Pollux i. 244 *τοῦ μέντοι φοίνικος καὶ ὁ κλάδος ὁμωνύμως φοῖνιξ καλεῖται.* They were carried at the Feast of Tabernacles, and used in constructing the shelters on the housetops required on that occasion (Lev. xxiii. 42, 2 Esdras *ll. cc.*); an allusion to these *σκηναί* may be latent in *v.* 15 *σκηνώσει ἐπ' αὐτούς.* But palm-branches were regarded as appropriate at any season of joy or triumph; the Triumphal Entry (Jo. *l. c.*) may be in view, or such a scene as that described in 1 Macc. xiii. 51 *εἰσῆλθεν εἰς αὐτὴν* [sc. *τὴν Ἰερουσαλήμ*]...*μετὰ αἰνέσεως καὶ βαΐων...ὅτι συνετρίβη ἐχθρὸς μέγας ἐξ Ἰσραήλ*, or in 2 Macc. *l.c.* Cf. Verg. *Aen.* v. 111 "palmae, pretium victoribus"; Pausanias, *Arcad.* 48 *εἰς δὲ τὴν δεξιάν ἐστι καὶ πανταχοῦ τῷ νικῶντι ἐπιτιθέμενος φοῖνιξ*; Tert. *scorp.* 12 "palmis victoriae insignes revelantur scilicet de Antichristo triumphantes"; Andreas: *τοὺς τῆς νίκης χαρακτηριστικοὺς κλάδους...φοινίκων ταῖς χερσὶν ἔχοντες.* Deissmann's suggestion (*Bible Studies*, p. 370) needs confirmation.

10 καὶ κράζουσιν φωνῇ μεγάλῃ λέγοντες 10
Ἡ σωτηρία τῷ θεῷ ἡμῶν τῷ καθημένῳ ἐπὶ
τῷ θρόνῳ καὶ τῷ ἀρνίῳ.
11 καὶ πάντες οἱ ἄγγελοι ἱστήκεισαν κύκλῳ τοῦ θρόνου 11
καὶ τῶν πρεσβυτέρων καὶ τῶν τεσσάρων ζῴων, καὶ
ἔπεσαν ἐνώπιον τοῦ θρόνου ἐπὶ τὰ πρόσωπα αὐτῶν
καὶ προσεκύνησαν τῷ θεῷ, 12 λέγοντες 12
Ἀμήν, ἡ εὐλογία καὶ δόξα καὶ ἡ σοφία καὶ
ἡ εὐχαριστία καὶ ἡ τιμὴ καὶ ἡ δύναμις καὶ
ἡ ἰσχὺς τῷ θεῷ ἡμῶν εἰς τοὺς αἰῶνας τῶν
αἰώνων· ἀμήν.

10 *κραζουσιν*] *εκραζον* vg Cypr Prim *κραζοντες* 1 me arm Ar | *του θεου* A 38 me | *τω καθημενω*] pr *και* syr^{gw} | *του θρονου* ℵ$^{c.a}$ Q 1 7 36 79 al | *του αρνιου* ℵ$^{c.a}$ + *εις τους αιωνας των αιωνων αμην* ℵ* 11 *ιστηκεισαν* ℵAP 36 130 (*ειστ.* Q)] *εστηκεισαν* (C) 51 | *επεσον* Q min^{pl} Andr Ar | *θρονου* 2°] + *αυτου* Q min$^{plq\,25}$ syr aeth Ar | *τα προσωπα*] *προσωπον* 1 48 me aeth | om *και προσεκυνησαν τω θεω* syr^{gw} 12 om *αμην* 1° me | *η δοξα και η ευλογια* 130 syr^{gw} | om *και η σοφια* A | om *αμην* 2° C 28 36 161 Prim

10. *καὶ κράζουσιν φωνῇ μεγάλῃ κτλ.*] The polyglott multitude (*ἐκ παντὸς ἔθνους...καὶ γλωσσῶν*, *v.* 9) shouts its praises as with one voice; for *φωνῇ μεγάλῃ* see vi. 10, vii. 2. The key note of the strain is *ἡ σωτηρία* (cf. xii. 10, xix. 1); those who raise it have all experienced the great deliverance (*v.* 14) which they ascribe to God and the Lamb: cf. Ps. iii. 9 *τοῦ κυρίου ἡ σωτηρία*. To cry Ἡ *σωτηρία τῷ θεῷ καὶ τῷ ἀρνίῳ* is equivalent to attributing to Both the title of *Σωτήρ*, so freely given by the loyal or pliant cities of Asia to the Emperors, but belonging in Christian eyes only to God and to His Christ. The Pastoral Epistles supply examples of both applications, (1) 1 Tim. i. 1 *θεοῦ σωτῆρος ἡμῶν*, ii. 3, Tit. i. 3, iii. 4 *τοῦ σωτῆρος ἡμ. θεοῦ*: (2) Tit. i. 4 *Χριστοῦ Ἰησοῦ τοῦ σωτῆρος ἡμῶν*, ii. 13 *τοῦ μεγάλου θεοῦ καὶ σωτῆρος ἡμ. Χριστοῦ Ἰησοῦ*, iii. 6 *διὰ Ἰησοῦ Χριστοῦ τοῦ σωτῆρος ἡμῶν*. For *ἡ σωτ.* compare Jo. iv. 22 *ἡ σ. ἐκ τῶν Ἰουδαίων ἐστίν*, Acts iv. 12 *οὐκ ἔστιν ἐν ἄλλῳ οὐδενὶ ἡ σ.*, Jude 3 *γράφειν... περὶ τῆς κοινῆς ἡμῶν σωτηρίας*. *Τῷ θεῷ ἡμῶν*: cf. *v.* 3, note. The elect of mankind claim God as their God, since He is the God of Christ (Jo. xx. 17, Apoc. iii. 12).

11. *καὶ πάντες οἱ ἄγγελοι ἱστήκεισαν κτλ.*] Ἰδοὺ (exclaims Andreas) *μία ἐκκλησία ἀγγέλων καὶ ἀνθρώπων*. The Angels endorse the ascription of praise, as in iv. 11 ff. They form, as there, a circle round the Throne, outside the Elders and the *ζῷα*; their position relatively to the *ὄχλος πολύς* is not stated, but the exigencies of the scene appear to require that they should stand nearer the Throne. For the *ὄχλος* it is sufficient to be *ἐνώπιον τοῦ θρόνου* (*vv.* 9, 15), seeing the God Whom they serve.

καὶ ἔπεσαν...ἐπὶ τὰ πρόσωπα αὐτῶν κτλ.] Cf. iv. 10, xi. 16; and for *ἀμήν*, i. 7, v. 14, xix. 4. The Angels, while adding their 'Amen' to the doxology of the Church, offer their own tribute in other words. It is addressed to the Majesty on the throne, Whom like the redeemed they call their God (*v.* 12); the Lamb is not included as in v. 13. The ascription is sevenfold,

13 [13]καὶ ἀπεκρίθη εἷς ἐκ τῶν πρεσβυτέρων λέγων μοι
Οὗτοι οἱ περιβεβλημένοι τὰς στολὰς τὰς λευκὰς
14 τίνες εἰσὶν καὶ πόθεν ἦλθον; [14]καὶ εἴρηκα αὐτῷ Κύριέ
¶ C μου, σὺ οἶδας. καὶ εἶπέν μοι Οὗτοί εἰσιν¶ οἱ ἐρχό-
μενοι ἐκ τῆς θλίψεως τῆς μεγάλης, καὶ ἔπλυναν τὰς

13 om εκ ℵ 91 130 14 ειρηκα] ειπον Q min[40] Ar | om μου A 1 vg[cdd] aeth[utr] arm Prim | om μοι ℵ | εκ της θλιψεως της μεγαλης] απο θλιψ. μεγ. A Cypr[cd] | επλυναν] επλατυναν 1 2 9 13* 29 30 41 42 50 93 94 95 97 98 130

as in v. 12, but it does not exactly agree with any of the previous doxologies, although each of its features has occurred in one or more of them; for εὐλογία cf. v. 12, 13; δόξα, i. 6, iv. 11, v. 12, 13; σοφία, v. 12; εὐχαριστία, iv. 9; τιμή, iv. 9, 11, v. 12, 13; δύναμις, iv. 11, v. 12; ἰσχύς, v. 12; see notes *ad ll.* As in v. 12, each word is emphasized by the article. The concluding ἀμήν is perhaps a liturgical addition, but it rests on good authority.

13. *καὶ ἀπεκρίθη εἷς ἐκ τῶν πρεσβυτέρων κτλ.*] An Elder intervenes, as in v. 5, to interpret the vision. For ἀπεκρίθη see Mc. ix. 5 note; for a similar use of ἀποκρίνεσθαι in the LXX. cf. Cant. ii. 10 ἀποκρίνεται ἀδελφιδός μου καὶ λέγει μοι Ἀνάστα, ἐλθέ. The Elder anticipates the questions which the Seer was ready to put (οὗτοι...τίνες εἰσίν; πόθεν ἦλθον;); Bede: "interrogat ut doceat." The vision was not a mere spectacular display, but a revelation; and its points must not be missed. Τὰς στολὰς τὰς λευκάς, the white robes which arrest attention: cf. στολὰς λευκάς, *v.* 9, note.

14. *καὶ εἴρηκα αὐτῷ κτλ.*] Cf. Zech. iv. 2, 5 καὶ εἶπεν πρὸς μέ Τί σὺ βλέπεις; ...καὶ εἶπεν...Οὐ γινώσκεις τί ἐστιν ταῦτα; καὶ εἶπα Οὐχί, κύριε. If the perfect (εἴρηκα) is to be pressed here, it must be explained as meaning that to the Seer's mind the whole scene was still fresh and vivid, that he seemed to himself to have but just spoken, as if the echoes of his voice were not yet silent. On the quasi-aoristic use of the perfect in this book, see v. 7, note. Κύριε, so the O.T. apocalyptic writers address a superhuman person; cf. Dan. x. 16 f., Zech. iv. 5, 13; or κύριε may be merely the 'sir' of courtesy, as in Jo. xx. 15, where it is addressed to one who is supposed to be a κηπουρός. Σὺ οἶδας is at once a confession of ignorance, and an appeal for information; cf. Ezek. xxxvii. 3 καὶ εἶπεν πρὸς μέ...Εἰ ζήσεται τὰ ὀστέα ταῦτα; καὶ εἶπα Κύριε, σὺ ἐπίστῃ ταῦτα. Contrast the σὺ οἶδας of Jo. xxi. 15 ff.

καὶ εἶπέν μοι Οὗτοί εἰσιν οἱ ἐρχόμενοι κτλ.] The answer covers both questions (τίνες, καὶ πόθεν;). 'These who wear the white robes are such as come (οἱ ἐρχόμενοι, timeless, cf. WM. p. 444) out of the Great Tribulation.' The reference is probably to Dan. xii. 1 Th. ἔσται καιρὸς θλίψεως, θλίψις οἵα οὐ γέγονεν ἀφ' ἧς γεγένηται ἔθνος; cf. Mc. xiii. 19. There is a θλίψις Ἰησοῦ which His servants share (i. 9, ii. 9 f.), but the Great Tribulation (ἡ θλ. ἡ μεγ., cf. Acts viii. 10 ἡ δύναμις ἡ θεοῦ ἡ καλουμένη μεγάλη) is the superlatively great crisis of trial through which all must pass (iii. 10), and from which the servants of God alone emerge unscathed. The present vision, which anticipates the issue of the final judgement, represents the latter as already delivered out of the evil to come.

καὶ ἔπλυναν τὰς στολὰς αὐτῶν κτλ.] The conception comes partly from

στολὰς αὐτῶν καὶ ἐλεύκαναν αὐτὰς ἐν τῷ αἵματι τοῦ
ἀρνίου. 15 διὰ τοῦτό εἰσιν ἐνώπιον τοῦ θρόνου τοῦ 15
θεοῦ, καὶ λατρεύουσιν αὐτῷ ἡμέρας καὶ νυκτὸς ἐν τῷ

14 om αυτας Q min^{plq30} arm aeth^{utr} Ar

Exod. xix. 10, 14, where the Israelites wash their clothes before the law-giving; partly from Gen. xlix. 11 πλυνεῖ ἐν οἴνῳ τὴν στολὴν αὐτοῦ, καὶ ἐν αἵματι σταφυλῆς τὴν περιβολὴν αὐτοῦ. The στολαί of the redeemed, however, are not ἐρυθραί (cf. Isa. lxiii. 1), but λευκαί. Hence ἔπλυναν is explained by ἐλεύκαναν (Tert. *candidaverunt*, Prim. *candidas fecerunt*, Vg. *dealbaverunt*); cf. Ps. l. (li.) 9, which may also be in view: πλυνεῖς με, καὶ ὑπὲρ χιόνα λευκανθήσομαι: cf. Isa. i. 18 ἐὰν ὦσιν αἱ ἁμαρτίαι ὑμῶν ὡς φοινικοῦν, ὡς χιόνα λευκανῶ, ἐὰν δὲ ὦσιν ὡς κόκκινον, ὡς ἔριον λευκανῶ. Λευκαίνειν is used in reference to the fuller's art, cf. Mc. ix. 3 τὰ ἱμάτια αὐτοῦ ἐγένετο στίλβοντα λευκὰ λίαν, οἷα γναφεὺς ἐπὶ τῆς γῆς οὐ δύναται οὕτως λευκᾶναι. The whiteness of the saints' robes is gained ἐν τῷ αἵματι τοῦ ἀρνίου; cf. i. 5, v. 9, parallels which ought to have saved some ancient writers (*e.g.* Tertullian, *scorp.* 12; Arethas: ἡ ὑπὲρ χριστοῦ ἔκχυσις) from the mistake of understanding the Blood of the Lamb here to mean the blood of martyrs shed for His sake; the *candidatus martyrum exercitus* itself owes its whiteness to the Great Sacrifice. Cf. Beatus: "*hi sunt qui venerunt* etc.: non ut aliqui putant martyres soli sunt, sed omnis ecclesia; non enim 'in sanguine suo' lavari dixit ... sed in *sanguine agni*." Τὸ αἷμα τοῦ ἀρνίου is the Sacrifice of the Cross, cf. 1 Pet. i. 2, 19, 1 Jo. i. 7, Rom. iii. 25, v. 9, Eph. i. 7, Col. i. 20, Heb. ix. 14; the paradox λευκαίνειν ἐν αἵματι is in accord with the manner of this book, where violent contrasts abound. The aorists ἔπλυναν, ἐλεύκαναν, look back to the life on earth when the cleansing was effected (Mc. ii. 10). The act is ascribed to the saints themselves, and not to Christ, as is the act of redemption (i. 5, τῷ λύσαντι, v. 9 ἠγόρασας); the saints are not passive recipients of redemption, but cooperate with the Divine grace by repentance and faith and the use of the Sacraments (Acts xxii. 16 βάπτισαι καὶ ἀπόλουσαι τὰς ἁμαρτίας σου: Mt. xxvi. 28 πίετε ἐξ αὐτοῦ πάντες, τοῦτο γάρ ἐστιν τὸ αἷμά μου τῆς διαθήκης τὸ περὶ πολλῶν ἐκχυννόμενον εἰς ἄφεσιν ἁμαρτιῶν), and by vigilance and victory over sin (*c.* xii. 11).

15. διὰ τοῦτό εἰσιν ἐνώπιον τοῦ θρόνου τοῦ θεοῦ] Διὰ τοῦτο refers to the whole of the preceding sentence (καὶ ἔπλυναν...τοῦ ἀρνίου). The purification of the conscience and character derived in their lifetime from faith in the Blood of Jesus Christ (Acts xv. 9, Heb. ix. 14) had fitted them for the Presence of God; cf. Mt. v. 8 μακάριοι οἱ καθαροὶ τῇ καρδίᾳ, ὅτι αὐτοὶ τὸν θεὸν ὄψονται. See Ephes. v. 26 f. for a picture of the Church in her final purity, fresh from the bath of a perfect absolution—μὴ ἔχουσα σπίλον ἢ ῥυτίδα ἤ τι τῶν τοιούτων, ἁγία καὶ ἄμωμος.

καὶ λατρεύουσιν αὐτῷ ἡμέρας καὶ νυκτὸς κτλ.] Cf. xxii. 3 οἱ δοῦλοι αὐτοῦ λατρεύσουσιν αὐτῷ. On λατρεύειν see Lightfoot, ***Philippians*** (iii. 3). In the LXX. (excepting Daniel) it is the normal equivalent of עָבַד, as distinguished from the priestly שֵׁרֵת which is usually represented by λειτουργεῖν. Since the members of the Church are 'priests unto God' (i. 6, v. 10, xx. 6) λειτουργεῖν might have been expected here and in xxii. 3 rather than λατρεύειν. But the conception is that of a vast worshipping congregation, and the use of λειτουργεῖν would rather have

ναῷ αὐτοῦ, καὶ ὁ καθήμενος ἐπὶ τοῦ θρόνου σκηνώσει
16 ἐπ' αὐτούς. [16]οὐ πεινάσουσιν ἔτι οὐδὲ διψήσουσιν
ἔτι, οὐδὲ μὴ πέσῃ ἐπ' αὐτοὺς ὁ ἥλιος οὐδὲ πᾶν καῦμα·

15 τω θρονω PQ min$^{\text{plq }30}$ syr^{gw} Ar | σκηνωσει επ αυτους] γινωσκει αυτ. ℵ* 16 om ετι 1° ℵ 36 vg me syrr arm aeth Cypr Prim | ουδε 1°] ουδε μη A 14 92 | διψησωσιν P 14 | om ετι 2° P 1 34 al^{8} *g* me syr^{gw} arm | ουδε μη] ουδ ου μη Q min$^{\text{fere }40}$ Andr Ar

suggested that of an exclusive priesthood admitted to the sanctuary, while the great majority were content to pray without (Lc. i. 10, 21). Ἐν τῷ ναῷ αὐτοῦ. The Israelite who was not a Priest or Levite did not proceed beyond the ἱερόν, one tribe alone having access to the ναός. But in the Eternal Temple the Seer sees the whole 'Israel of God' admitted to the ναός, and the occasion for the λειτουργία of a tribal or special priesthood has disappeared, all being priests and all serving in the Presence of God. The mention of a temple must be corrected by the later revelation in *c.* xxi. 22 καὶ ναὸν οὐκ εἶδον ἐν αὐτῇ, ὁ γὰρ κύριος...ναὸς αὐτῆς ἐστιν. The 'Temple' is here the Divine Presence, realized and enjoyed; ἐν τῷ ναῷ αὐτοῦ is equivalent to ἐνώπιον τοῦ θρόνου (*vv.* 9, 15).

The λατρεία of the Church is not interrupted by nightfall (for ἡμέρας καὶ νυκτός see Lc. xviii. 7, 1 Thess. v. 5, Apoc. iv. 8). Even the Temple had its night offices; see 1 Chron. ix. 33 ἡμέρα καὶ νὺξ ἐπ' αὐτοῖς (τοῖς ψαλτῳδοῖς) ἐν τοῖς ἔργοις, Ps. cxxxiii. (cxxxiv.) 2 ἐν ταῖς νυξὶν ἐπάρατε χεῖρας ὑμῶν εἰς τὰ ἅγια. The Church inherited the practice, and the stillness of the night was broken by the vigil services of the early times (Batiffol, *Bréviaire*, p. 2 ff.) and at a later date, in monastic communities, by the matin-lauds. But the vision of ceaseless worship is realized only when life itself is regarded as a service. The consecration of all life to the service of God is the goal to which our present worship points, and it is symbolized by the Apocalyptist's λατρεύουσιν ἡμέρας καὶ νυκτός. Here again the later vision of the closing chapter corrects the earlier: cf. Apoc. xxi. 25, xxii. 5 νὺξ οὐκ ἔσται ἔτι. Cf. Andreas: τὸ γὰρ ἡμέρας καὶ νύκτας ἐνταῦθα δηλοῖ τὸ ἀκατάπαυστον.

καὶ ὁ καθήμενος ἐπὶ τοῦ θρόνου σκηνώσει ἐπ' αὐτούς.] Perpetual service will find its stimulus and its reward in the perpetual vision of Him Who is served. Σκηνοῦν represents שָׁכַן in the LXX. (Jud. v. 17, viii. 11 (B), 3 Regn. viii. 14 (A)); in the N.T. its use is limited to the Johannine writings (Jo. i. 14, Apoc. vii. 15, xii. 12, xiii. 6, xxi. 3). The reference both here and in xxi. 3 is to the O.T. promise that God would 'walk' or 'dwell' in Israel (Lev. xxvi. 22 ἐνπεριπατήσω ἐν ὑμῖν, Zech. ii. 10 κατασκηνώσω ἐν μέσῳ σου, *ib.* viii. 3, 8, Ezek. xxxvii. 27 ἔσται ἡ κατασκήνωσίς μου ἐν αὐτοῖς). The assonance of σκηνοῦν, שָׁכַן, שְׁכִינָה, has probably suggested the use of σκηνοῦν both in Jo. *l. c.* (ὁ λόγος...ἐσκήνωσεν ἐν ἡμῖν) and in Apoc. vii., xxi. Σκηνώσει ἐπ' αὐτούς (here only: cf. xxi. 3 σκηνώσει μετ' αὐτῶν) brings in the further idea of God's Presence as a protection from all fear of evil, with reference perhaps to Isa. iv. 5 f., where the Pillar of the Exodus suggests the overshadowing of Israel by the Shechinah. An allusion to the σκηναί of the Feast of Tabernacles is also possible; see *v.* 9, note.

The Apocalyptist now passes from the present tense to the future (σκηνώσει, cf. *v.* 16 f.); the vision becomes a prediction.

16. οὐ πεινάσουσιν ἔτι κτλ.] Andreas: εἰκότως τὸν γὰρ ἄρτον τῶν οὐρανῶν καὶ τὸ ὕδωρ τῆς ζωῆς ἕξουσι.

[17]ὅτι τὸ ἀρνίον τὸ ἀνὰ μέσον τοῦ θρόνου ποιμανεῖ 17
αὐτοὺς καὶ ὁδηγήσει αὐτοὺς ἐπὶ ζωῆς πηγὰς ὑδάτων·
καὶ ἐξαλείψει ὁ θεὸς πᾶν § δάκρυον ἐκ τῶν ὀφθαλμῶν § C
αὐτῶν.

17 ποιμαινει 2 4 13 29 31 al fere 25 me | οδηγει 2 4 al plq 25 | ζωης] ζωσας 1 38 79 96 me syr ζωην και επι syr gw | om ο θεος syr gw | εκ] απο ℵ 28 al *g* vg cle lipss me

This verse, with part of the next, is borrowed from Isa. xlix. 10 where of Israel returning from exile we read: οὐ πεινάσουσιν οὐδὲ διψήσουσιν, οὐδὲ πατάξει αὐτοὺς καύσων οὐδὲ ὁ ἥλιος, ἀλλ' ὁ ἐλεῶν αὐτοὺς παρακαλέσει, καὶ διὰ πηγῶν ὑδάτων ἄξει αὐτούς. The changes which the Apocalyptist makes are interesting: καύσων (the sirocco, cf. Mt. xx. 12, Lc. xii. 55, Jac. i. 11) is changed into πᾶν καῦμα (Latt. *aestus*, scorching heat of any kind), παρακαλέσει (יְנַהֲגֵם) καὶ ἄξει into ποιμανεῖ καὶ ὁδηγήσει, while ὁ ἐλεῶν αὐτούς becomes τὸ ἀρνίον.

For the interpretation of οὐ πεινάσουσιν here see Jo. vi. 35, and for οὐ διψήσουσιν, Jo. iv. 14, vi. 35, vii. 37. With οὐδὲ πᾶν καῦμα contrast xvi. 9.

17. ὅτι τὸ ἀρνίον κτλ.] Τὸ ἀρνίον τὸ ἀνὰ μέσον τοῦ θρόνου looks back to c. v. 6 ἐν μέσῳ τ. θρ. ἀρνίον. Ἀνὰ μέσον (used here only in Apoc.) is usually 'between,' 'amongst' (cf. Mt. xiii. 25, Mc. vii. 31, 1 Cor. vi. 5), but it sometimes stands for ἐν μέσῳ (e.g. Jos. xix. 1, Sir. xxvii. 2, Mt. xiii. 25), and this must be its meaning here. Τὸ ἀρνίον...ποιμανεῖ is a bold mixture of two metaphors. Ποιμαίνειν has been used of Christ in ii. 27, where and in xii. 5, xix. 15, there is a reference to Ps. ii. 9; here the context guides us to Isa. xl. 11 ὡς ποιμὴν ποιμανεῖ τὸ ποίμνιον αὐτοῦ, or to Ezek. xxxiv. 23, but especially to Ps. xxii. (xxiii.) 1 ff. Κύριος ποιμαίνει με... ὡδήγησέν με, lxxix. (lxxx.) 1 ὁ ποιμαίνων τὸν Ἰσραὴλ...ὁ ὁδηγῶν ὡσεὶ πρόβατα. In Christ the Shepherd has taken the nature of the sheep; the ποιμὴν ὁ καλός is Himself of the fold (τὸ ἀρνίον). On ποιμαίνειν see ii. 27, note. Ὁδηγεῖν no less than ποιμαίνειν has an interesting history in Biblical Greek. It is used of the Divine guidance of Israel (Exod. xv. 13, Deut. i. 33), of the guidance of individual lives (Ps. v. 9, lxxxv. (lxxxvi.) 11, Sap. ix. 11); of the work of the Spirit of Christ (Jo. xvi. 13); and lastly, in this place, of the work of Christ Himself in the future order. The Divine shepherding and guidance of men belongs to the future as well as to the present life, and in the future only meets with a full response (cf. Jo. x. 4, Apoc. xiv. 4).

ἐπὶ ζωῆς πηγὰς ὑδάτων] The order emphasizes ζωῆς—'to life's water springs,' Vg. *ad vitae fontes aquarum*; Alford well compares 1 Pet. iii. 21 σαρκὸς ἀπόθεσις ῥύπου. Isa. *l. c.* עַל מַבּוּעֵי מַיִם supplies ἐπὶ π. ὑδ.; ζωῆς is perhaps from Jer. ii. 13 [ὁ λαός μου] ἐμὲ ἐνκατέλιπον, πηγὴν ὕδατος ζωῆς (מְקוֹר מַיִם חַיִּים). The change of order gives prominence to the mention of life. It is to God as the Fountain of life (Ps. xxxv. (xxxvi.) 10 παρά σοι πηγὴ ζωῆς) that the Lamb leads His sheep: cf. xxi. 6, xxii. 1, 17. The interpretation is again supplied by the Johannine Gospel; see Jo. iv. 12, 14; vii. 38 f. The plurals πηγὰς ὑδάτων are perhaps not to be pressed, being merely echoes of the Hebrew (cf. viii. 10, xiv. 7, xvi. 4); if they have any significance here, they point to the secondary sources which are replenished by the Fountain itself, or to the manifold energies of the one Christ-life (1 Cor. xii. 4 ff.), as the πνεύματα of i. 4 etc. represent the διαιρέσεις χαρισμάτων of the One Spirit.

καὶ ἐξαλείψει ὁ θεὸς πᾶν δάκρυον κτλ.] Yet another reference to the

VIII. 1 [1]Καὶ ὅταν ἤνοιξεν τὴν σφραγῖδα τὴν ἑβδόμην,
2 ἐγένετο σιγὴ ἐν τῷ οὐρανῷ ὡς ἡμίωρον. [2]καὶ εἶδον

VIII 1 οταν AC] οτε ℵPQ min$^{\text{omn vid}}$ Andr Ar | ημιωρον AC 91 97] ημιωριον ℵPQ min^{pl} Andr Ar 2 ειδον P 1 al^{pl} Andr Ar] ιδον ℵACQ 7 14 92 130

O.T.; cf. Isa. xxv. 8 where the LXX. have ἀφεῖλεν Κύριος ὁ θεὸς πᾶν δάκρυον ἀπὸ παντὸς προσώπου, but Symmachus, influenced perhaps by his recollections of this passage, renders וּמָחָה by καὶ ἐξάλειψεν. The sentence occurs again with verbal changes in *c.* xxi. 4; indeed, the whole of the episode *c.* vii. 9—17 finds echoes in the last two chapters of the book, where the climax here anticipated is fully described. On the main thought see Tertullian *de res. carn.* 58 *delebit deus omnem lacrimam ab oculis eorum*, utique ex iisdem oculis qui retro fleverant, quique adhuc flere potuissent, si non omnem lacrimae imbrem indulgentia divina siccaret...dolor et maeror et gemitus...quomodo auferentur, nisi cessaverint causae?...ubi casus adversi apud Deum, aut ubi incursus infesti apud Christum?... quae infirmitas post virtutem? quae imbecillitas post salutem?

Beati—so Bede sums up in the words of the second Beatitude—*qui lugent, quoniam ipsi consolabuntur.*

VIII. 1—13. THE OPENING OF THE SEVENTH SEAL; THE HALF-HOUR'S SILENCE: THE FIRST FOUR TRUMPET-BLASTS.

1. καὶ ὅταν ἤνοιξεν τὴν σφραγῖδα τὴν ἑβδόμην] The sequence broken by the two visions of *c.* vii. is resumed. The Lamb opens the last of the seals (cf. vi. 1, 3, 5, 7, 9, 12), and the book can now be unrolled and read. We expect the catastrophe, which had been foreboded by the signs and by the panic that followed the penultimate opening, at length to supervene. But all is still; there is neither sight nor sound to indicate the approach of the end.

Ὅταν is substituted for ὅτε, which is used on previous occurrences of the formula, perhaps with the view of emphasizing the uncertainty of the time of the end; cf. Mc. xi. 19, Apoc. iv. 9, where it implies the indefinite repetition of an act. Blass (*Gr.* p. 218) prefers to regard it simply as due to linguistic deterioration, urging that in late Greek ὅταν and ὅτε are indistinguishable. Ἤνοιξεν, sc. τὸ ἀρνίον, as in vi. 1.

ἐγένετο σιγὴ ἐν τῷ οὐρανῷ κτλ.] Heaven, hitherto resonant with voices, now holds its peace: neither Elder nor Angel offers a word of explanation (v. 5, vii. 13); there is neither chorus of praise nor cry of adoration (iv. 8, 11, v. 9 f., 12 f., vii. 10, 12); no ζῷον calls Ἔρχου (vi. 3 etc.); no thunders issue from the Throne (iv. 5). This silence does not spell a cessation of the Divine workings (Ign. *Eph.* 19 ἐν ἡσυχίᾳ θεοῦ ἐπράχθη, *Magn.* 8 λόγος ἀπὸ σιγῆς προελθών), but a temporary suspension of revelation; cf. Renan, *l'Antechrist*, p. 391 "le premier acte du mystère est terminé." There is a partial parallel in Apoc. x. 4 σφράγισον ἃ ἐλάλησαν αἱ ἑπτὰ βρονταί, καὶ μὴ αὐτὰ γράψῃς, but there the Seer hears though he may not impart; here the Seer himself is kept in ignorance.

The remark of Victorinus, "significatur initium quietis aeternae," is attractive, but exegetically irrelevant; σιγή is not characteristic of the heavenly rest. Nor is it more to the point to refer to such passages as Hab. ii. 20, Zeph. i. 7, Zech. ii. 13; the Apocalyptic silence is in heaven and not on earth.

ὡς ἡμίωρον, sc. χρόνον (Prim. *fere semihora*, Vg. *quasi media hora*), acc. of duration. The adjective is ἅπ. λεγ., ἡμιώριον being the usual form. For ὥρα, as the twelfth part of the

τοὺς ἑπτὰ ἀγγέλους οἳ ἐνώπιον τοῦ θεοῦ ἑστήκασιν,
καὶ ἐδόθησαν αὐτοῖς ἑπτὰ σάλπιγγες. ³καὶ ἄλλος 3
ἄγγελος ἦλθεν καὶ ἐστάθη ἐπὶ τοῦ θυσιαστηρίου

2 om *τους επτα* 1 26 | *θεου*] *θρονου* 130 | *ειστηκεισαν* 38 *g* syr[gw] | *εδοθη* A 35 87 93 95 96   3 om *αγγελος* syr[gw] | *εξηλθεν* 130 al[mu] | *του θυσιαστηριου* ℵCQ 6 7 14 28 29 31 35 38 al[nonn]] *το θυσιαστηριον* AP 1 36 49

natural day, see Jo. i. 40, iv. 6, xix. 14, Acts v. 7, x. 3.

Half-an-hour, though a relatively short time, is a long interval in a drama, and makes an impressive break between the Seals and the Trumpets.

2. *καὶ εἶδον τοὺς ἑπτὰ ἀγγέλους κτλ.*] Seven Angels are required by the situation, and the number finds a parallel in the 'seven Spirits of God' and other hebdomads in this book. The article seems to point to the well-known group of Angels first mentioned, as it seems, in Tobit xii. 15 *Ῥαφαὴλ εἷς ἐκ τῶν ἑπτὰ ἀγγέλων οἳ ...εἰσπορεύονται ἐνώπιον τῆς δόξης τοῦ Ἁγίου.* In Enoch xx. 7 (Gr.) they are styled 'archangels,' and their names are given as Uriel (4 Esdr. iv. 1), Raphael (Tob. *l. c.*) Raguel, Michael (Dan. x. 13, 21, xii. 1, Jude 9, Apoc. xii. 7), Sariel (Eth. Saraqâêl), Gabriel (Lc. i. 19, 26), Remiel (Hieremihel; 4 Esdr. iv. 36); cf. *ib.* lxxxi. 5, xc. 21 f. 'Angels of the Presence' are mentioned repeatedly in the Book of Jubilees (i. 27, 29; ii. 1 f., 18, xv. 27, xxxi. 14, where see Charles's note); the title comes from Isa. lxiii. 9 מַלְאַךְ פָּנָיו, and the idea from the practice of Oriental courts (cf. Gen. xlv. 1, 2 Esdr. vii. 24, Esth. i. 14, viii. 4, Job i. 6, Zech. iv. 14, vi. 5, Dan. vii. 10, 4 Macc. xvii. 18, Lc. i. 19). On the possible connexion of the later Jewish angelology with Parsism or Zoroastrianism, see Hastings, *D. B.* i. 96, iv. 991; Driver, *Daniel*, p. xcvi.; the evidence, so far as it has been produced, is interesting but scarcely conclusive. *Οἳ ἐνώπιον κτλ.*; cf. Lc. i. 19 *ἐγώ εἰμι Γαβριὴλ ὁ παρεστηκὼς ἐνώπιον τοῦ θεοῦ.*

καὶ ἐδόθησαν αὐτοῖς ἑπτὰ σάλπιγγες] Trumpets are assigned to Angels in Mt. xxiv. 31, 1 Cor. xv. 52, 1 Thess. iv. 16, Apoc. iv. 1, 4 Esdr. vi. 23, *Apoc. Mos.* 22; the conception rests ultimately on the scene of the Lawgiving (Exod. xix. 16 ff.), which Jewish thought connected with the ministry of Angels (Acts vii. 38, Gal. iii. 19). The Trumpets of the Seven are presently to break the silence which followed the opening of the last seal with fresh revelations of the Divine purpose. There is possibly an allusion to Jos. vi. 13 *οἱ ἑπτὰ ἱερεῖς οἱ φέροντες τὰς σάλπιγγας τὰς ἑπτά κτλ.*; cf. also Joel ii. 1 *σαλπίσατε σάλπιγγι ἐν Σειὼν ...διότι πάρεστιν ἡμέρα Κυρίου, ὅτι ἐγγύς.*

3. *καὶ ἄλλος ἄγγελος ἦλθεν κτλ.*] Another Angel, not one of the Seven (cf. vii. 2, x. 1, xiv. 6 ff., xviii. 1), came forward and took his place (*ἐστάθη*, cf. Lc. xviii. 11, 40, Acts v. 20, xvii. 22) over, i.e. before, the Altar, as in Amos ix. 1 *εἶδον τὸν κύριον ἐφεστῶτα ἐπὶ* (עַל) *τοῦ θυσιαστηρίου*, where the prep. denotes the position of one who stands (B.D.B., p. 756) "by (prop. leaning *over*) an altar or sacrifice." The celestial messenger takes the place of the priest, and offers the incense; contrast the position of Gabriel in Lc. i. 11 (*ἑστὼς ἐκ δεξιῶν τοῦ θυσιαστηρίου τοῦ θυμιάματος*). The altar is not as in vi. 9 the Altar of Burnt offering, but the Altar of Incense; *τὸ θ. τὸ χρυσοῦν τὸ ἐνώπιον τοῦ θρόνου* points to Exod. xl. 5 *θήσεις τὸ θυσιαστήριον τὸ χρυσοῦν...ἐναντίον τῆς κιβωτοῦ*, cf. Lev. iv. 7 *ἐναντίον Κυρίου*; it is the *θυσιασ-*

ἔχων λιβανωτὸν χρυσοῦν, καὶ ἐδόθη αὐτῷ θυμιάματα πολλά, ἵνα δώσει ταῖς προσευχαῖς τῶν ἁγίων πάντων ἐπὶ τὸ θυσιαστήριον τὸ χρυσοῦν τὸ ἐνώπιον τοῦ

3 λιβανωτον] λιβανον το C | ινα δωσει ℵAC 1 al[nonn]] ινα δωση PQ min[satmu] Ar ινα δω 6 9 14 36 om syr[gw] | om το χρυσουν syr[gw] | το ενωπιον] om το ℵ

τήριον τοῦ θυμιάματος of Lev. iv. 7, 18—the θυμιατήριον of Heb. ix. 4. Cf. Iren. iv. 18. 6 "est ergo altare in caelis, illuc enim preces nostrae et oblationes nostrae diriguntur."

ἔχων λιβανωτὸν χρυσοῦν κτλ.] Λιβανωτός is elsewhere 'frankincense'; the commentators quote the scholiast on Ar. *nub.* λίβανος...αὐτὸ τὸ δένδρον, λιβανωτὸς δὲ ὁ καρπὸς τοῦ δένδρου, and Ammonius: λίβανος γὰρ κοινῶς τὸ δένδρον καὶ τὸ θυμιώμενον, λιβανωτὸς δὲ μόνον θυμιώμενος. The latter is evidently the meaning of λιβανωτός in 1 Chron. ix. 29, 3 Macc. v. 2, as of λίβανος in Lev. ii. 1, Apoc. xviii. 13; but here and in *v.* 5 χρυσοῦν shews that a censer is intended; for 'censer' (מַחְתָּה, מִקְטֶרֶת) the LXX. use πυρεῖον (Exod. xxvii. 3, xxxviii. 23 (3), Num. xvi. 6 ff., Sir. l. 9), or θυίσκη (3 Regn. vii. 36 (50)), or θυμιατήριον (2 Chron. xxvi. 19, Ezek. viii. 11, 4 Macc. vii. 11); the later Greek has λιβανωτίς or λιβανωτρίς.

καὶ ἐδόθη...ἵνα δώσει κτλ.] The Angel received the incense for a particular purpose. Ἐδόθη, as ἐδόθησαν in *v.* 2 (cf. vi. 2, 4, 8, 11, vii. 2, *et passim*), does not describe an act which forms part of the vision, but is simply a recognition of the Divine ordering of all life; cf. 1 Cor. iv. 7 τί δὲ ἔχεις ὃ οὐκ ἔλαβες; On the future δώσει (ℵAC) see iii. 9, note; δώσῃ, δῷ, are probably corrections of the less usual form. Θυμιάματα, as in v. 8, where see note; but the metaphor is differently handled here, for while in *c.* v. the prayers of the saints are the incense or incense-bowls, in this place they are apparently the live coals on which the grains of incense fall (ἵνα δώσει ταῖς προσευχαῖς, Prim. *ut daret orationibus*, Vg. wrongly, *ut d. de orationibus*), the meeting of the incense and the hot coals producing the fragrant smoke cloud, the symbol of Divine acceptance. This change brings into sight the relation of Christ's sacrifice and intercession to the prayers of the Church; cf. Bede: "Christo Domino se hostiam suavitatis offerente compunctio cordis sanctorum acceptabilis facta est." Cf. Eph. v. 2 ὁ χριστὸς... παρέδωκεν ἑαυτὸν ὑπὲρ ὑμῶν προσφορὰν καὶ θυσίαν τῷ θεῷ εἰς ὀσμὴν εὐωδίας: the doctrine is substantially that of Jo. xiv. 16, xvi. 23 f., 1 Jo. ii. 1 f., Rom. viii. 34, Heb. xii. 25. Τῶν ἁγίων πάντων, not of the martyrs only (vi. 9 f.) but of all the faithful; cf. Eph. iii. 18. The Angel with the golden censer belongs perhaps to the scenery of the vision rather than to its teaching; at the same time it does not seem improbable that the λειτουργικὰ πνεύματα (Heb. i. 14) are concerned in some way with the ministry of prayer—an idea anticipated in Tob. xii. 15 εἷς τῶν ἑπτὰ ἁγίων ἀγγέλων οἳ προσαναφέρουσιν τὰς προσευχὰς τῶν ἁγίων, and frequent in Enoch (ix. 3, xv. 2, xl. 6, xlvii. 2, civ. 1). Ἐπὶ τὸ θυσιαστήριον, 'upon the altar (of incense)'; one sees the whole process depicted, the fire kindled on the altar, and then taken up into the censer where it receives the incense: see Lev. x. 1 λαβόντες...ἕκαστος τὸ πυρεῖον αὐτοῦ ἐπέθηκαν ἐπ' αὐτὸ πῦρ, καὶ ἐπέβαλον ἐπ' αὐτὸ θυμίαμα, xvi. 12 λήμψεται τὸ πυρεῖον πλῆρες ἀνθράκων πυρὸς ἀπὸ τοῦ θυσιαστηρίου, Num. xvi. 46 (xvii. 11) λάβε τὸ πυρεῖον καὶ ἐπίθες ἐπ' αὐτὸ πῦρ ἀπὸ τοῦ θυσιαστηρίου.

θρόνου. [4]καὶ ἀνέβη ὁ καπνὸς τῶν θυμιαμάτων ταῖς 4
προσευχαῖς τῶν ἁγίων ἐκ χειρὸς τοῦ ἀγγέλου ἐνώπιον
τοῦ θεοῦ.¶ [5]καὶ εἴληφεν ὁ ἄγγελος τὸν λιβανωτόν, 5 ¶ C
καὶ ἐγέμισεν αὐτὸν ἐκ τοῦ πυρὸς τοῦ θυσιαστηρίου
καὶ ἔβαλεν εἰς τὴν γῆν· καὶ ἐγένοντο βρονταὶ καὶ
φωναὶ καὶ ἀστραπαὶ καὶ σεισμός. [6]καὶ οἱ ἑπτὰ 6

4 *ταις προσευχαις*] *de orationibus* vg | *του θεου*] + *ημερας χιλιας διακοσιας εξηκοντα* C 5 *το λιβανωτον...αυτο* 7 33 34 36 40 50 | *του θυσιαστηριου*] *του επι του θυσ.* syr[gw] | *εβαλεν*] *ελαβον* A *εβαλλεν* P | *βρονται κ. φωναι κ. αστραπαι* ℵQ 6 8 14 29 31 35 87 vg syr[gw]] *βρ. κ. αστρ. κ. φωναι* A 16 38 me syr *φωναι κ. βρ. κ. αστρ.* P 1 al[mu] | om *και σεισμος* Ar

4. *καὶ ἀνέβη ὁ καπνός κτλ.*] I.e., from the censer in the Angel's hand; cf. Ezek. viii. 11 *ἕκαστος θυμιατήριον αὐτοῦ εἶχεν ἐν τῇ χειρί, καὶ ἡ ἀτμὶς τοῦ θυμιάματος ἀνέβαινεν. Ταῖς προσευχαῖς*, the *dat. commodi*, 'for the benefit of the prayers,' i.e. to help them (Blass, *Gr.* p. 111), or perhaps (WM. p. 270) the dative of reference; the incense-cloud stood in a certain relation to the prayers, as their symbol and representative; it was 'given to them' (*v.* 3). The symbolical meaning of the incense offered in the Temple was well understood in pre-Christian times, cf. Ps. cxl. (cxli.) 2 *κατευθυνθήτω ἡ πρὸσευχή μου ὡς θυμίαμα ἐνώπιόν σου.*

The words added by C (*app. crit.*) appear to be a gloss from *c.* xi. 3.

5. *καὶ εἴληφεν ὁ ἄγγελος τὸν λιβανωτόν κτλ.*] The Angel had laid aside the censer. But he takes it again (on *εἴληφεν* followed by *ἐγέμισεν* see v. 7 f., note) in order to fulfil another office; it is to be used now not for intercession but for judgement. The censer is again filled with fire from the altar: cf. Isa. vi. 6 *ἐν τῇ χειρὶ εἶχεν ἄνθρακα ὃν τῇ λαβίδι ἔλαβεν ἀπὸ τοῦ θυσιαστηρίου.* But now no incense is added, and no fragrant cloud goes up; the contents of the censer are poured upon the earth; the prayers of the saints return to the earth in wrath: cf. Ezek. x. 2 *πλῆσον τὰς δράκας σου ἀνθράκων πυρὸς...καὶ διασκορπίσεις ἐπὶ τὴν πόλιν.* There is perhaps an ultimate reference to the doom of Sodom (Gen. xix. 24).

This casting of fire on the earth (cf. Lc. xii. 49) is immediately followed by results (*ἐγένοντο βρονταὶ καὶ φωναὶ καὶ ἀστραπαὶ καὶ σεισμός*) premonitory of a great visitation; cf. iv. 5, vi. 12, xi. 19, notes, and for *σεισμός* see Ezek. iii. 12 *ἤκουσα φωνὴν σεισμοῦ μεγάλου Εὐλογημένη ἡ δόξα Κυρίου ἐκ τοῦ τόπου αὐτοῦ.* The whole scene in *vv.* 3—5 is a prelude to the Seven Trumpets, which now begin to sound.

6. *καὶ οἱ ἑπτὰ ἄγγελοι οἱ ἔχοντες κτλ.*] The Angels of the Presence who are charged with the Seven Trumpets know the signal, and make ready. They are seen to take their stand and to raise the trumpets to their mouths. *Σαλπίσωσιν*: *σαλπίσω* (*σαλπιῶ*, Num. x. 5 ff.), *ἐσάλπισα*, in Biblical Greek take the place of *σαλπίγξω*, *ἐσάλπιγξα* (W. Schm. p. 105); cf. *σαλπιστῶν*, Apoc. xviii. 22.

The first four Trumpet-blasts, like the first four Seal-openings, form a closely connected group. They describe the coming visitation as primarily affecting inanimate Nature; although animals and men are involved in the destruction which is caused (*vv.* 9, 11), direct judgements upon mankind are reserved for the last three. The imagery was perhaps in part suggested by the storms earthquakes and eclipses of the first century.

ἄγγελοι οἱ ἔχοντες τὰς ἑπτὰ σάλπιγγας ἡτοίμασαν
αὑτοὺς ἵνα σαλπίσωσιν.
7 ⁷Καὶ ὁ πρῶτος ἐσάλπισεν· καὶ ἐγένετο χάλαζα
καὶ πῦρ μεμιγμένα ἐν αἵματι, καὶ ἐβλήθη εἰς τὴν γῆν.
καὶ τὸ τρίτον τῆς γῆς κατεκάη, καὶ τὸ τρίτον τῶν
δένδρων κατεκάη, καὶ πᾶς χόρτος χλωρὸς κατεκάη.

6 *οι εχοντες*] om *οι* ℵ 36 | *αυτους* ℵ* A] *εαυτους* ℵ$^{c.a}$ PQ min$^{fere\ omn}$ syrr Andr Ar 7 *ο πρωτος*] + *αγγελος* 1 28 36 79 98 al^{nonn} vg me arm aeth Prim | *μεμιγμενα* AQ min^{pl} *g* vg syrr Prim Ar] *μεμιγμενον* ℵP 12 37 38 46 81 161 Tyc | *εν αιματι*] om *εν* 1 al vg$^{dem\ harl*}$ *εν υδατι* syr^{gw} | *εβληθησαν* 34 35 87 syr^{gw} | om *και το τριτον της γης κατεκαη* 1 35 130 me | om *και το τριτον των δενδρων κατεκαη* Q* al^{nonn} aeth | *χορτος*] + *της γης* syr$^{gw\ vid}$

7. **καὶ ὁ πρῶτος ἐσάλπισεν· καὶ ἐγένετο χάλαζα κτλ.**] The judgements ushered in by the first four Trumpets borrow many of their features from the Plagues of Egypt; cf. Iren. iv. 30. 4: the attentive reader "inveniet easdem plagas universaliter accipere gentes quas tunc particulatim accepit Aegyptus." Χάλαζα καὶ πῦρ recalls the seventh plague; Exod. ix. 24 ἦν δὲ ἡ χάλαζα καὶ τὸ πῦρ φλογίζον ἐν τῇ χαλάζῃ—a description of a semi-tropical thunderstorm which is heightened here by μεμιγμένα ἐν αἵματι. Μιγνύναι ἐν αἵματι 'to mix with blood,' cf. Ps. cv. (cvi.) 35 ἐμίγησαν ἐν (בְּ) τοῖς ἔθνεσιν: the usual construction is with μετά (Mt. xxvii. 34, Lc. xiii. 1), or the simple dative (Apoc. xv. 2 θάλασσαν ὑαλίνην μεμιγμένην πυρί). A rain of mingled fire and blood is mentioned also in the Sibyllines, v. 377 πῦρ γὰρ ἀπ' οὐρανίων βρέξει...πῦρ καὶ αἷμα. Blood-red rain is not unknown in nature; in the spring of 1901 the daily journals contained accounts of this phenomenon, which was then being witnessed in Italy and the South of Europe, the result, as it seemed, of the air being full of particles of fine red sand from the Sahara. The interpretation suggested to Andreas by passing events is interesting as a specimen of its kind: τὸ δὲ πῦρ σὺν τῷ αἵματι [ἐμφαίνει] τὰς ἐκ βαρβαρικῶν χειρῶν γενομένας πυρπολήσεις τε καὶ ἀνδροκτασίας ὁσημέραι.

The storm flung itself (ἐβλήθη, cf. *vv.* 5, 8, xii. 9 f., xx. 14 f.) on the earth, with the result that a third part of its surface and the whole of the verdure were devoured by the fire (κατεκάη = κατεκαύθη, cf. 1 Cor. iii. 15, 2 Pet. iii. 10 (A) κατακαήσεται—an early form which survives in late Gk., cf. W. Schm. p. 108). Τὸ τρίτον (sc. μέρος, cf. Num. xxviii. 14) appears again *vv.* 8 f., 11 f., ix. 15, 18, xii. 4. See Zech. xiii. 7 ff. τὰ δύο μέρη αὐτῆς [sc. τῆς γῆς] ἐξολεθρευθήσεται καὶ ἐκλείψει, τὸ δὲ τρίτον ὑπολειφθήσεται ἐν αὐτῇ, and compare the Rabbinical parallel cited by Schoettgen: "percussus est mundus, tertia nempe pars olearum, tertia pars tritici et tertia hordei." Τῆς γῆς, the land (=τῆς ξηρᾶς) as contrasted with the sea (*v.* 8) and other waters (*vv.* 10 f.). The fire destroyed the whole of the vegetation, which was scorched at once (cf. Jac. i. 12), and one-third of the trees and other perishable things. Two-thirds escaped everywhere, i.e. the visitation was partial, and not final; cf. vi. 8. Τῶν δένδρων: the fruit-trees especially, the olive, the fig, and the vine, on which the inhabitants of Palestine and Asia Minor depended so largely: cf. vii. 3 μὴ ἀδικήσητε ... τὰ δένδρα, a prohibition now partly withdrawn. For χόρτος χλωρός see Mc. vi. 39, note, and Apoc. ix. 4; cf. vi. 8, note.

[8]καὶ ὁ δεύτερος ἄγγελος ἐσάλπισεν· καὶ ὡς ὄρος 8
μέγα πυρὶ καιόμενον ἐβλήθη εἰς τὴν θάλασσαν· καὶ
ἐγένετο τὸ τρίτον τῆς θαλάσσης αἷμα, [9]καὶ ἀπέθανεν 9
τὸ τρίτον τῶν κτισμάτων τῶν ἐν τῇ θαλάσσῃ, τὰ
ἔχοντα ψυχάς, καὶ τὸ τρίτον τῶν πλοίων διεφθάρη-
σαν. [10]καὶ ὁ τρίτος ἄγγελος ἐσάλπισεν· καὶ ἔπεσεν 10

8 om αγγελος ℵ syr^{gw} (item in *vv.* 10, 12 et c. ix. 1 syr^{gw}) | om πυρι Q min$^{sat\,mu}$ syr^{gw} arm Ar | εβληθη] επεσεν syr^{gw} | εγενετο] εγενηθη ℵ   9 το τριτον 1°] + μερος ℵ 35 36 87 cf. *tertia pars* vg Prim | των κτισματων] + παντων syrr | των εν τη θαλασση] om των Q min^{nonn} Ar om omnia vg$^{am\,harl}$ post τα εχ. ψυχας pon vg$^{cle\,fu\,dem\,lipss\,tol}$ | τα εχοντα φυχας] τα εχ. ψυχην ℵ me aeth το εχον ψυχην syr^{gw} | διεφθαρη Q min^{pl} syr^{gw} Ar

8 f. καὶ ὁ δεύτερος ἄγγελος ἐσάλπισεν· καὶ ὡς ὄρος κτλ.] As at the first trumpet-blast the fiery hail was flung upon the earth, so at the second a burning mass falls into the sea. With ὄρος μέγα πυρὶ καιόμενον may perhaps be compared Jer. xxviii. (li.) 25, where Babylon is likened to an ὄρος ἐμπεπυρισμένον (הַר שְׂרֵפָה). But Babylon is not in view here, and ὡς ὄρος καιόμ. may be merely a figure of speech for a blazing mass. If a volcano is in the Apocalyptist's mind, the simile may have been suggested either by the eruption of Vesuvius which desolated the Bay of Naples in August, 79, or to some movements among the volcanic islands in the Aegean, of which Thera (Santorin) was the chief (cf. Tozer, *Islands of the Aegean*, p. 94 ff.); Strabo (i. 3. 16) reports an eruption in B.C. 196 which issued in the formation of a new island afterwards known as *Palaea Kaumene*. But volcanoes are not flung bodily into the sea, so that such phenomena were at most but remotely suggestive of the writer's bold conception. He is perhaps rather indebted to Enoch for the figure of the burning mountain; see En. xviii. 13 ἴδον ἑπτὰ ἀστέρας ὡς ὄρη μεγάλα καιόμενα, which is curiously close to ὡς ὄρος μέγα πυρὶ καιόμενον. The phrase seems to have been proverbial; cf. Plaut. *mercat.* iii. 4. 32 "montes tu quidem mali in me ardentes iamdudum iacis."

καὶ ἐγένετο τὸ τρίτον τῆς θαλάσσης αἷμα κτλ.] The sea is smitten, like the Nile in the first plague (Exod. vii. 20 μετέβαλεν πᾶν τὸ ὕδωρ τὸ ἐν τῷ ποταμῷ εἰς αἷμα); as the fish in the Nile died (*ib.* 21), so do the animate inhabitants of the stricken Aegean. With τῶν κτ. τῶν ἐν τῇ θαλάσσῃ cf. v. 13 πᾶν κτίσμα ὃ...ἐπὶ τῆς θαλάσσης, Ps. civ. 25; and for τὰ ἔχοντα ψυχάς, Vg. *quae habebant animas*, 'animate,' see Gen. i. 20 ἐξαγαγέτω τὰ ὕδατα ἑρπετὰ ψυχῶν ζωσῶν (נֶפֶשׁ חַיָּה). The illapse of the burning mass had a still more serious result; the ships in the waters disturbed by its fall were wrecked; for διαφθείρεσθαι of wrecked or disabled ships see Herod. i. 166 αἱ μὲν γὰρ τεσσεράκοντά σφι νῆες διεφθάρησαν. Yet in the case of the sea as in that of the dry land, the visitation was partial; two-thirds of the inhabitants of the sea and the ships on its surface were unhurt. The plural διεφθάρησαν (sc. τὰ πλοῖα, understood in τὸ τρίτον τῶν πλ.) attributes a quasi-personal life to the ships, in view of their human masters and crews.

10. καὶ ὁ τρίτος ἄγγελος ἐσάλπισεν· καὶ ἔπεσεν κτλ.] The fresh water supply is smitten next. At the third trumpet-blast there falls from heaven upon a third of the rivers and upon

ἐκ τοῦ οὐρανοῦ ἀστὴρ μέγας καιόμενος ὡς λαμπάς,
καὶ ἔπεσεν ἐπὶ τὸ τρίτον τῶν ποταμῶν καὶ ἐπὶ τὰς
11 πηγὰς τῶν ὑδάτων. [11]καὶ τὸ ὄνομα τοῦ ἀστέρος
λέγεται ὁ Ἄψινθος. καὶ ἐγένετο τὸ τρίτον τῶν
ὑδάτων εἰς ἄψινθον, καὶ πολλοὶ τῶν ἀνθρώπων ἀπέ-
12 θανον ἐκ τῶν ὑδάτων, ὅτι ἐπικράνθησαν. [12]καὶ ὁ
τέταρτος ἄγγελος ἐσάλπισεν· καὶ ἐπλήγη τὸ τρίτον

10 om vid και επεσεν 2° Prim | om και επι τας πηγας των υδατων A   11 ο αψινθος] om ο ℵ*c.a 1 7 14 36 38 al arm αψινθιον ℵ* syr[gw] *absinthium* vg[cle dem harl* tol al] me Prim *absinthius* vg[am (fu)] | εγενετο] γινεται 1 36 al | εις αψινθον] εις αψινθιον ℵ 7 8 16 28 49 79 Ar ως αψινθιον *h* syr[gw] Prim | εκ] επι A | απεθανον οτι επικρ. τα υδατα syr[gw]

the water-springs a great meteor (ἀστήρ, cf. Mt. ii. 2), flashing across the sky like a blazing torch (λαμπάς, cf. *c.* iv. 5); for ὡς λ. see *v.* 8 ὡς ὄρος. With ἔπεσεν...ἀστήρ cf. Isa. xiv. 12 ἐξέπεσεν ἐκ τοῦ οὐρανοῦ ὁ ἑωσφόρος, and Mc. xiii. 25, note; here the 'star' is merely a symbol of Divine visitation, like the burning mountain in *v.* 8. Αἱ πηγαὶ τῶν ὑδάτων = מַעְיְנֵי הַמַּיִם, a common phrase in the LXX. (cf. e.g. 3 Regn. xviii. 5, Ps. cxiii. (cxiv.) 8, Hos. xiii. 15.

11. καὶ τὸ ὄνομα τοῦ ἀστέρος λέγεται ὁ Ἄψινθος] Ἄψινθος, normally ἡ ἄψινθος or τὸ ἀψίνθιον but here assimilated in gender to ἀστήρ, does not occur elsewhere in the N.T. or the LXX., though it is used by Aquila in Prov. v. 4, Jer. ix. 15, xxiii. 15; the LXX. render לַעֲנָה, wormwood, variously by χολή, πικρία, ὀδύνη, ἀνάγκη. The Heb. word is employed in the O.T. as a metaphor for (1) the perversion of justice (Amos v. 7, vi. 12); (2) the bitter fruits of idolatry (Deut. xxix. 17); (3) Divine chastisements (Jer. ix. 14); see B.D.B. *s.v.* The genus *Artemisia*, to which wormwood (*A. absinthiaca*) belongs, is represented in the flora of Palestine by several species; see Tristram, *W.H.*, p. 493; Hastings, *D. B.*, iv. p. 941.

καὶ ἐγένετο τὸ τρίτον τῶν ὑδάτων εἰς ἄψινθον κτλ.] The reverse of the miracle at Marah (Exod. xv. 23). Wormwood water is more than once in the Prophets a symbol of suffering, e.g. Jer. ix. 15 (14) ποτιῶ αὐτοὺς ὕδωρ χολῆς, xxiii. 15; cf. 4 Esdr. v. 9 "in dulcibus aquis salsae invenientur." Wormwood mixed with water does not kill, but in the Apocalyptic vision the waters are not mixed with wormwood but changed into it (ἐγένετο εἰς ἄψινθον). As the creatures in the sea perished when it was smitten by the burning mass (*v.* 9), so the rivers and fountains converted into wormwood are destructive of human life. For ἀποθανεῖν ἐκ, 'to die of,' see WM. p. 460.

12. καὶ ὁ τέταρτος ἄγγελος ἐσάλπισεν· καὶ ἐπλήγη κτλ.] Visitations on land and water are followed by a visitation on the heavenly bodies, having for its object the further punishment of mankind. The conception is borrowed from the ninth of the Egyptian plagues (Exod. x. 21 γενηθήτω...ψηλαφητὸν σκότος...ἐγένετο σκότος, γνόφος, θύελλα, ἐπὶ πᾶσαν γῆν Αἰγύπτου τρεῖς ἡμέρας, cf. Am. viii. 9, Joel iii. (iv.) 4). To the Apocalyptic plague no time limit is fixed, but it is limited in its extent; only a third of the sun's and moon's disk is obscured, and a third of the stars suffer occultation. By this partial eclipse of the lights of heaven a partial darkness would obviously be produced, but not a shortening of the duration of daylight and moonlight and starlight such as the following

τοῦ ἡλίου καὶ τὸ τρίτον τῆς σελήνης καὶ τὸ τρίτον
τῶν ἀστέρων, ἵνα σκοτισθῇ τὸ τρίτον αὐτῶν καὶ ἡ
ἡμέρα μὴ φάνῃ τὸ τρίτον αὐτῆς, καὶ ἡ νὺξ ὁμοίως.
[13] Καὶ εἶδον, καὶ ἤκουσα ἑνὸς ἀετοῦ πετομένου ἐν 13
μεσουρανήματι λέγοντος φωνῇ μεγάλῃ Οὐαὶ οὐαὶ

12 τριτον 1°] τεταρτον 130 | ινα σκοτισθη] και εσκοτισθη 35 87 syr^{gw} arm aeth | και η ημερα μη φανη το τριτον (τεταρτον A) αυτης] και το τριτον αυτης (s. αυτου) μη φανη (η) ημερα Q min^{nonn} (multum hoc loco inter se variant tam codd min quam verss) | μη φανη] μη φαινη (P) 28 49 79 al Ar ουκ εφαινεν 35 87 syr^{gw} arm 13 om και ειδον syr^{gw} | ειδον ℵ min^{pl}] ιδον AQ 7 14 92 | om ενος ℵ me syrr arm | αετου ℵAQ min$^{fere\ 35}$ vg me syrr aeth Ar] αγγελου P 1 7 28 36 47 79 al arm Vict Andr αγγελου ως αετου 13 *unus ut aquilam* Prim | πετωμενου Q 1 6* 7* 32 130 al^{nonn} | om εν ℵ | εν μεσουρανηματι] εν μεσω ουραν αιματι εχοντος syr (et similiter c. xiv. 6) εν ουρανω syr^{gw} | φωνη μεγαλω syr^{gw} | ουαι bis tantum 1 syr aeth

words (ἵνα ἡ ἡμέρα μὴ φάνῃ τὸ τρίτον αὐτῆς) seem to suggest. There is an inconsistency here which shews the writer's independence of the ordinary laws of thought: he is content to produce a desired effect by heaping up symbolism without regard to the consistency of the details. Here his purpose is chiefly to emphasize the partial character of the visitation. Its purpose is the reformation and not the destruction of mankind; it is charged with serious warning, but not with final doom. Contrast Isa. xxx. 26 τὸ φῶς τοῦ ἡλίου ἔσται ἑπταπλάσιον, ἐν τῇ ἡμέρᾳ ὅταν ἰάσηται Κύριος τὸ σύντριμμα τοῦ λαοῦ αὐτοῦ. For ἐπλήγη see Isa. ix. 13, and for φάνῃ (not φανῇ) c. xviii. 23.

The first series of Trumpet-blasts is now complete. It has set loose the elemental forces of Nature and wrought havoc on a large scale. But the next verse warns the reader that worse things are to follow.

13. καὶ εἶδον, καὶ ἤκουσα ἑνὸς ἀετοῦ κτλ.] For εἶδον καὶ ἤκουσα, cf. v. 11, vi. 1; the scene which follows is one which arrests both eye and ear. Ἀγγέλου may be a correction for the harder ἀετοῦ, suggested by xiv. 6; or possibly it is due to the error of a scribe who read ΑΕΤΟΥ as ΑΓΓΕΛΟΥ; for ἀετὸς πετόμενος, see iv. 7, Job ix. 26, Prov. xxiv. 54 (xxx. 19). Had the Apocalyptist written ἀγγέλου, ἄλλου would probably have taken the place of ἑνός; cf. vii. 2, viii. 3. The eagle is chosen not only for his strength of wing (xii. 14), but as the emblem of coming judgement (Mt. xxiv. 28, *Apoc. Bar.* lxxvii. 19 ff.); ἑνός points perhaps to the solitary figure projected against the sky (cf. Mt. xxi. 19), but εἷς in such instances approaches in meaning to τις or the indefinite article, cf. ix. 13, xviii. 21, and see Blass, *Gr.* p. 144. Ἐν μεσουρανήματι, "in the meridian" or "the zenith"; that part of the sky where the sun is at noon-day; cf. xiv. 6, xix. 17. The eagle μεσουρανεῖ, i.e. he flies not near the horizon where he may pass unobserved, but overhead, where his course can be seen by all. The word is said to belong to Alexandrian Greek: Pollux iv. 157 μεσημβριάζειν ὑπὲρ κεφαλῆς ἑστάναι· τὸ γὰρ μεσουρανεῖν Αἰγυπτίων. Syr.$^{gw.}$ for μεσουρανήματι has simply ܒܫܡܝܐ.

λέγοντος φωνῇ μεγάλῃ Οὐαὶ οὐαὶ οὐαί κτλ.] The eagle is not only seen but heard. In Ezek. xvi. 23 (A), Apoc. xviii. 10, 16, 19, the double οὐαί is merely for emphasis; the triple οὐαί here has reference to the three remaining trumpet-blasts or rather the visitations that will follow them; see ix. 12 οὐαὶ ἡ μία ἀπῆλθεν· ἰδοὺ ἔρχεται ἔτι δύο οὐαί. Τοὺς κατοικοῦντας: the acc. after οὐαί is unusual, the

οὐαὶ τοὺς κατοικοῦντας ἐπὶ τῆς γῆς ἐκ τῶν λοιπῶν
φωνῶν τῆς σάλπιγγος τῶν τριῶν ἀγγέλων τῶν
μελλόντων σαλπίζειν.

IX. 1 [1] Καὶ ὁ πέμπτος ἄγγελος ἐσάλπισεν· καὶ εἶδον
ἀστέρα ἐκ τοῦ οὐρανοῦ πεπτωκότα εἰς τὴν γῆν,
καὶ ἐδόθη αὐτῷ ἡ κλεὶς τοῦ φρέατος τῆς ἀβύσσου.

13 τους κατοικουντας ℵQ 6 8 14 29 31 35 38 48 51 87 92 130 al^nonn] τοις κατοικουσιν AP 1 7 al^satmu Ar | εκ της φωνης των σαλπιγγων syr^gw

IX 1 ειδον ℵP min^pl] ιδον AQ 7 14 92 130 | αστερας...πεπτωκοτας ℵ* | επι της γης 38 97 syrr

dativus incommodi might rather have been expected, as in Lc. vi. 24 ff.; but cf. xii. 12 οὐαὶ τὴν γῆν καὶ τὴν θάλασσαν, and see Blass (*Gr.* p. 112), who compares *vae me*=*vae mihi*. The earth has suffered already from the first four Trumpets; the time has now come for her inhabitants to suffer yet more severely. Οἱ κατοικοῦντες ἐπὶ τῆς γῆς, the pagan or non-Christian population of the Empire, as in iii. 10, vi. 10, xi. 10, xiii. 8 ff., xvii. 2 ff.

ἐκ τῶν λοιπῶν φωνῶν τῆς σάλπιγγος, "by reason of the remaining trumpet-blasts." Τῆς σάλπιγγος modifies φωνῶν—the sound is that of the trumpet; τῶν σαλπίγγων is unnecessary, since the reader's attention is not called to the plurality of the trumpets but to the trumpet-like utterance which proceeds from each of the angels. On ἐκ in this sense see WM. p. 461.

IX. 1—12. The Fifth Trumpet, or the First Woe.

1. ὁ πέμπτος ἄγγελος ἐσάλπισεν, καὶ εἶδον ἀστέρα κτλ.] In viii. 8, 10 the Seer witnesses the fall of a star; now he sees only a star lying where it fell (πεπτωκότα). Cf. Isa. xiv. 12 πῶς ἐξέπεσεν ἐκ τοῦ οὐρανοῦ ὁ ἑωσφόρος; Lc. x. 18 ἐθεώρουν τὸν σατανᾶν ὡς ἀστραπὴν ἐκ τοῦ οὐρανοῦ πεσόντα. As the sequel shews, this fallen Star represents a person, possibly Satan, as a comparison of Lc. *l. c.* with Apoc. xii. 9 may suggest. For a personification of the stars comp. Jud. v. 20 ἐξ οὐρανοῦ παρετάξαντο οἱ ἀστέρες; for the image of the fallen star see Enoch lxxxviii. 1.

ἐδόθη αὐτῷ ἡ κλεὶς τοῦ φρέατος τῆς ἀβύσσου] Ἄβυσσος is the usual equivalent in the LXX. of תְּהוֹם, whether in the sense of 'deep waters' (Gen. i. 2, vii. 11, Ps. cv. (cvi.) 9, cvi. (cvii.) 26), or in reference to the depths of the earth (Ps. lxx. (lxxi.) 21 ἐκ τῶν ἀβύσσων τῆς γῆς πάλιν ἀνήγαγές με; cf. Deut. viii. 7). By an easy process of thought, it is applied to Sheol: Job xli. 22 f. ἀναζεῖ τὴν ἄβυσσον ὥσπερ χαλκεῖον...τὸν δὲ τάρταρον τῆς ἀβύσσου ὥσπερ αἰχμάλωτον, Rom. x. 7 τίς καταβήσεται εἰς τὴν ἄβυσσον; τοῦτ' ἔστιν Χριστὸν ἐκ νεκρῶν ἀναγαγεῖν. In Lc. viii. 31 (παρεκάλουν αὐτὸν ἵνα μὴ ἐπιτάξῃ αὐτοῖς εἰς τὴν ἄβυσσον ἀπελθεῖν) a lower depth is sounded, and it is this which is in view when ἄβυσσος is used in the Apoc. (ix. 1, 2, 11, xvii. 8, xx. 1, 3). The Enochic literature has much to say of this 'abyss' (Enoch xviii. f., xxi., xc.; Slavonic Enoch, xxviii. 3; cf. Charles, *Eschatology*, p. 198). The Apocalyptist represents it as entered by a shaft or well (φρέαρ, cf. Jo. iv. 11), the mouth of which is kept under lock and key; the key is in the custody of an angel (xx. 1) or, as here apparently, of Satan, i.e. he is authorised to open and shut the mouth of the abyss at his pleasure (for κλείς see Mt. xvi. 19, Apoc. i. 18, iii. 7; and on the idea, Slavonic Enoch, xlii. 1). This power however is exercised only by Divine permission (ἐδόθη αὐτῷ), and

[2]καὶ ἤνοιξεν τὸ φρέαρ τῆς ἀβύσσου· καὶ ἀνέβη καπνὸς 2
ἐκ τοῦ φρέατος ὡς καπνὸς καμίνου μεγάλης, καὶ ἐσκο-
τώθη ὁ ἥλιος καὶ ὁ ἀὴρ ἐκ τοῦ καπνοῦ τοῦ φρέατος.
[3]καὶ ἐκ τοῦ καπνοῦ ἐξῆλθον ἀκρίδες εἰς τὴν γῆν, καὶ 3
ἐδόθη αὐταῖς ἐξουσία ὡς ἔχουσιν ἐξουσίαν οἱ σκορ-
πίοι τῆς γῆς. [4]καὶ ἐρρέθη αὐταῖς ἵνα μὴ ἀδικήσουσιν 4

2 om *και ηνοιξεν το φρεαρ της αβυσσου* ℵQ min$^{plq\,30}$ vg$^{am\ harl*\ tol*}$ me syr^{gw} arm aeth^{utr} Ar | om *εκ του φρεατος ως καπνος* 1 35 41 87 | *μεγαλης*] *καιομενης* Q min$^{sat\,mu}$ syr Ar *μεγ. καιομενης* 36 37 38 40 41 42 (130) *g* syr^{gw} | *εσκοτωθη* A 12 14 92] *εσκοτισθη* ℵPQ min^{pl} Ar | om *εκ του καπνου του φρ.* ℵ* Prim 3 *αυταις* AP min^{pl} Andr Ar] *αυτοις* ℵQ 7 4 *ερρηθη* Q 35 50 87 130 | *αυταις* AP min^{pl} syr^{gw} Andr Ar] *αυτοις* ℵQ 14 87 90 92 | *αδικησουσιν* A 367] *αδικησωσιν* ℵPQ min$^{fere\ omn}$ Andr Ar

behind it is the omnipotent Hand which controls both the visible and the invisible order; cf. Prayer of Manasses 3 *ὁ κλείσας τὴν ἄβυσσον καὶ σφραγισάμενος τῷ φοβερῷ καὶ ἐνδόξῳ ὀνόματί σου.*

2. *καὶ ἤνοιξεν τὸ φρέαρ κτλ.*] The Fallen Star-spirit unlocks the mouth of the Abyss, and at once the sky is darkened by a volume of smoke which rises from it; cf. Gen. xix. 28 *ἀνέβαινεν φλὸξ τῆς γῆς ὡσεὶ ἀτμὶς καμίνου*, Exod. xix. 18 *ἀνέβαινεν ὁ καπνὸς ὡς καπνὸς καμίνου.* The sun's face is hidden (Joel ii. 20), and the atmosphere (*ὁ ἀήρ*, the region of the clouds, cf. 2 Regn. xxii. 12, Ps. xvii. (xviii.) 12, 1 Thess. iv. 17 f.), the air through which the birds fly (Sap. v. 11), and which men breathe (Sap. xv. 15), and in which evil spirits were thought to exercise a limited authority (Eph. ii. 2 *τὸν ἄρχοντα τῆς ἐξουσίας τοῦ ἀέρος*), is darkened by reason of (*ἐκ*, cf. viii. 11, 13) the smoke cloud emitted from the well as from the chimney of a furnace. On *σκοτοῦσθαι* see WH.[2], *Notes*, p. 178: the verb is used of an occultation of heavenly bodies in Job iii. 9 *σκοτωθείη τὰ ἄστρα τῆς νυκτὸς ἐκείνης.*

3. *καὶ ἐκ τοῦ καπνοῦ ἐξῆλθον ἀκρίδες κτλ.*] The smoke wrought worse evil than the darkening of the air; out of it came a swarm of hellish locusts; for *ἀκρίδες* see Mc. i. 6, note. There may be a reference both to Exod. x. 13 ff. and to Joel i. 4 ff. But these *ἀκρίδες τῆς ἀβύσσου* were entrusted with a power (*ἐδόθη αὐταῖς ἐξουσία*) wholly unlike that of the locust tribe, and akin to that of the common scorpion (*οἱ σκορπίοι τῆς γῆς*, in contrast with *αἱ ἀκρίδες τῆς ἀβύσσου*). The venomous stab of the scorpion is proverbial in both O. and N.T.; see e.g. 3 Regn. xii. 11 *παιδεύσω ὑμᾶς ἐν σκορπίοις*, Ezek. ii. 6 *ἐν μέσῳ σκορπίων σὺ κατοικεῖς*, Lc. xi. 12 *ἐπιδώσει αὐτῷ σκορπίον;* The scorpion takes its place with the snake and other creatures hostile to man, and with them symbolizes the forces of spiritual evil which are active in the world: cf. Sir. xxxix. 29 f. *πάντα ταῦτα εἰς ἐκδίκησιν ἔκτισται· θηρίων ὀδόντες καὶ σκορπίοι καὶ ἔχεις*, Lc. x. 19 *δέδωκα ὑμῖν τὴν ἐξουσίαν τοῦ πατεῖν ἐπάνω ὄφεων καὶ σκορπίων, καὶ ἐπὶ πᾶσαν τὴν δύναμιν τοῦ ἐχθροῦ.*

4. *καὶ ἐρρέθη αὐταῖς ἵνα μὴ ἀδική-σουσιν κτλ.*] Their mission, moreover, is not that of the locust tribe; they are, in fact, prohibited from devouring herbage and stripping trees; cf. Exod. x. 15 *κατέφαγεν [ἡ ἀκρὶς] πᾶσαν βοτάνην τῆς γῆς καὶ πάντα τὸν καρπὸν τῶν ξύλων*, cf. Joel ii. 3 *τὰ ὄπισθεν αὐτοῦ πεδίον ἀφανισμοῦ.* This had been done sufficiently by the hail which followed the first Trumpet (viii. 7);

τὸν χόρτον τῆς γῆς οὐδὲ πᾶν χλωρὸν οὐδὲ πᾶν δέν-
δρον, εἰ μὴ τοὺς ἀνθρώπους οἵτινες οὐκ ἔχουσιν τὴν
5 σφραγῖδα τοῦ θεοῦ ἐπὶ τῶν μετώπων. [5]καὶ ἐδόθη
αὐτοῖς ἵνα μὴ ἀποκτείνωσιν αὐτούς, ἀλλ' ἵνα βασα-
νισθήσονται μῆνας πέντε· καὶ ὁ βασανισμὸς αὐτῶν
ὡς βασανισμὸς σκορπίου, ὅταν παίσῃ ἄνθρωπον.

4 om *ουδε παν χλωρον* ℵ vg[harl*] arm Cassiod | *ουδε παν δενδρον*] *ουδε δενδρα* syr[gw] | *ανθρωπους*] + *μονους* 49 91 96 *tantum homines* vg | om *του θεου* 1 12 17 28 47 79 vg[harl*] arm | *μετωπων*] + *αυτων* Q min[pl] vg[cle fu dem lipss] syrr arm aeth Ar   5 *αυτοις* ℵA 1 7 12] *αυταις* PQ min[pl] Ar | om *ινα* 2° syr[gw] | *βασανισθησονται* ℵAP 1 12 36 38 (130)] *βασανισθωσιν* Q min[pl] Ar *βασανισωσιν* 7 *cruciaverint* latt similiter arm aeth | *πεντε*] *sex* Prim | *παιση* (*πεση* ℵAPQ 7 87 al[mu] *πεση επ* syr[gw]) *ανθρωπον*] *πληξη ανθρ.* 10 26 37 41 42 43 49 96[corr]

the produce left by the hail in Egypt was devoured by the locusts (Exod. *l. c.*), but the Apocalyptic locusts are bent on another errand; men and not mere food stuffs are their goal. For ἐρρέθη see vi. 11, note; on the future after ἵνα, iii. 9, note; and on ἀδικεῖν = βλάπτειν, ii. 11, note. Οὐδὲ πᾶν = 'nor any'; cf. Lc. i. 37 οὐκ ἀδυνατήσει ...πᾶν ῥῆμα; for οὐδέ after ἵνα μή, see WM. p. 602, note 3.

εἰ μὴ τοὺς ἀνθρώπους κτλ.] 'But only the men,' etc.; for this use of εἰ μή cf. WM. p. 789. The power to hurt men is limited to a particular class of men (τοὺς ἀνθρ. οἵτινες; on this use of ὅστις see Lightfoot on Gal. v. 19 and Blass, *Gr.* p. 173, and cf. Apoc. i. 7, ii. 24, xx. 4), viz. to those whose foreheads have not been marked by the Seal of God (vii. 3 ff.). As Israel in Egypt escaped the plagues which punished their neighbours, so the new Israel is exempted from the attack of the locusts of the Abyss.

5. καὶ ἐδόθη αὐτοῖς ἵνα μή κτλ.] I.e. the commission which they received ran Μὴ ἀποκτείνατε αὐτούς, ἀλλὰ βασανισθήτωσαν. The wound inflicted by the scorpion is not usually fatal, but it causes exquisite pain; and this is the point of resemblance between the scorpion and the Apocalyptic locusts; it was no part of their mission to kill, but rather to inflict suffering worse than death. Βασανίζειν, 'to apply the touchstone,' is used, from Thucydides downwards, of torture, and this is its meaning in the LXX. (1 Regn.[1], Sap.[4], Sir.[1], 2 Macc.[3], 4 Macc.[20], a significant distribution); and in the N.T. βασανίζειν, βασανισμός describe acute pain whether physical (Mt. viii. 6, Apoc. xii. 2), or mental (Mt. viii. 29, 2 Pet. ii. 8), or are employed metaphorically (Mt. xiv. 24, Mc. vi. 48); in the Apocalypse, written at a time of active persecution, the thought of punishment is again uppermost (ix. 5, xi. 10, xiv. 10 f., xviii. 7, 10, 15, xx. 10; xii. 2 is the only exception).

μῆνας πέντε] This limit of time has been supposed to be a reminiscence of the 150 days of the Flood (Gen. vii. 24) or to refer to the duration of locust life. But the number five is frequently used without any apparent purpose beyond that of giving definiteness to a picture, e.g. Mt. xxv. 15 πέντε τάλαντα, Lc. xii. 6, πέντε στρουθία, *ib.* 52 πέντε ἐν ἑνὶ οἴκῳ, xiv. 19 ζεύγη βοῶν πέντε, xvi. 28 πέντε ἀδελφούς, 1 Cor. xiv. 19 πέντε λόγους. If a further reason is to be sought for its employment here, πέντε may point to the incompleteness of the visitation; it lasted five-twelfths of the year, as the plagues of *c.* viii. affected a third of

[6]*καὶ ἐν ταῖς ἡμέραις ἐκείναις ζητήσουσιν οἱ ἄνθρωποι* 6
τὸν θάνατον καὶ οὐ μὴ εὑρήσουσιν αὐτόν, καὶ ἐπιθυ-
μήσουσιν ἀποθανεῖν καὶ φεύγει ὁ θάνατος ἀπ' αὐτῶν.
[7]*καὶ τὰ ὁμοιώματα τῶν ἀκρίδων ὅμοια ἵπποις ἡτοι-* 7
μασμένοις εἰς πόλεμον, καὶ ἐπὶ τὰς κεφαλὰς αὐτῶν
ὡς στέφανοι ὅμοιοι χρυσῷ, καὶ τὰ πρόσωπα αὐτῶν

6 *ζητησουσιν*] *ζητουσιν* 2 8 9 19 27 42 50 91 96 al vg^{harl*} | *ευρησουσιν* ℵQ 6 7 8 29 30 al^{mu} Ar *invenient* vg$^{(exc\ harl)}$ Ambr] *ευρησωσιν* 1 2 9 al *ευρωσιν* AP 12 17 28 34 35 46 49 79 87 130 *inveniant* vg^{harl*} | *φευγει* AP 1 12 17 36 38] *φυγη* ℵ *fugiat* vg^{harl*} *φευξεται* Q min^{pl} syrr Ar *fugiet* vg$^{(exc\ harl*)}$ Prim   7 *τα ομοιωματα*] *το ομοιωμα* *g* syrr | *ομοια* PQ min$^{omn\ vid}$ Andr Ar] *ομοιοι* ℵ *ομοιωματα* A | *ιππων ητοιμασμενων* 130 | *ομοιοι χρυσω* ℵAP 1 al vg syrr arm aeth Andr] *χρυσοι* Q min$^{fere\ 40}$ Ar

nature. There is a progress in the visitations, but the end is not yet.

ὅταν παίσῃ ἄνθρωπον: cf. Achill. Tat. ii. 7 *καί τις μέλιττα...ἐπάταξε τὴν χεῖρα.* For *παίειν*=*πατάσσειν* see Num. xxii. 28, 2 Regn. xiv. 6, Mc. xiv. 47 (comp. with Mt. xxvi. 51). The *ictus* is inflicted by the scorpion-like tails ascribed to the locusts in *v.* 10; cf. Plin. *h. n.* ii. 25 "semper cauda in ictu est, nulloque momento cessat ne quando desit occasioni." The reading of Syr.$^{gw.}$ *πέσῃ ἐπ' ἄνθρωπον* has probably arisen from *παίσῃ* written as *πέσῃ*; see *app. crit.*

6. *καὶ ἐν ταῖς ἡμέραις ἐκείναις ζητήσουσιν κτλ.*] During those terrible months (cf. Mc. i. 9, xiii. 19) men will prefer death to the agony of living. Cf. Job iii. 21 *ὁμείρονται τοῦ θανάτου καὶ οὐ τυγχάνουσιν κτλ.*, Jer. viii. 3 *εἵλοντο τὸν θάνατον ἢ τὴν ζωήν*: see Apoc. vi. 16, *Orac. Sibyll.* ii. 307 *καὶ καλέσουσι καλὸν τὸ θανεῖν καὶ φεύξετ' ἀπ' αὐτῶν.* The thought was familiar to the Greek and Roman poets: Soph. *Electr.* 1007 *οὐ γὰρ θανεῖν ἔχθιστον, ἀλλ' ὅταν θανεῖν | χρῄζων τις εἶτα μηδὲ τοῦτ' ἔχῃ λαβεῖν.* Ovid, *Ib.* 123 "desit tibi copia mortis, | optatam fugiat vita coacta necem." *Οὐ μὴ εὑρήσουσιν αὐτόν*: such a death as they desire, a death which will end their sufferings, is impossible; physical death is no remedy for the *βασανισμός* of an evil conscience. With *ἐπιθυμήσουσιν ἀποθανεῖν* Alford aptly contrasts Phil. i. 23 *τὴν ἐπιθυμίαν ἔχων εἰς τὸ ἀναλῦσαι καὶ σὺν Χριστῷ εἶναι*; under such circumstances death is a gain, but it is not sought, for life also has its compensations, in duty and in enjoyment. *Ζητεῖν, ἐπιθυμεῖν*, form a climax.

7 f. *καὶ τὰ ὁμοιώματα τῶν ἀκρίδων κτλ.*] Hitherto only the powers of the locusts have been in view; now they are described. Their shapes (*ὁμοίωμα*, a word "midway between *μορφή* and *σχῆμα*," Lightfoot on Phil. ii. 7, cf. Ezek. i. 16, x. 21 = דְּמוּת, Rom. i. 23) were like horses caparisoned for battle. The description is borrowed from Joel's account of a locust swarm (ii. 4 f. *ὡς ὅρασις ἵππων ἡ ὅρασις αὐτῶν, καὶ ὡς ἱππεῖς οὕτως καταδιώξονται...ὡς λαὸς παρατασσόμενος...εἰς πόλεμον*); a metaphor chosen "partly on account of their speed and compact array, but chiefly on account of a resemblance which has been often observed between the head of a locust and the head of a horse" (Driver, *ad loc.*, citing Theodoret: *εἰ γάρ τις ἀκριβῶς κατίδοι τὴν κεφαλὴν τῆς ἀκρίδος σφόδρα τῇ τοῦ ἵππου ἐοικυῖαν εὑρήσει· ἔστι δὲ ἰδεῖν καὶ πετομένην αὐτὴν κατ' οὐδὲν τῆς τοῦ ἵππου ταχύτητος ἐλαττουμένην*).

καὶ ἐπὶ τὰς κεφαλὰς αὐτῶν ὡς στέφανοι κτλ.] So far the picture might have been that of an ordinary swarm of locusts: the next two features are peculiar to the locusts of the Abyss.

8 ὡς πρόσωπα ἀνθρώπων· [8]καὶ εἶχαν τρίχας ὡς τρίχας
γυναικῶν, καὶ οἱ ὀδόντες αὐτῶν ὡς λεόντων ἦσαν,
9 [9]καὶ εἶχον θώρακας ὡς θώρακας σιδηροῦς, καὶ ἡ φωνὴ
τῶν πτερύγων αὐτῶν ὡς φωνὴ ἁρμάτων ἵππων πολ-
10 λῶν τρεχόντων εἰς πόλεμον. [10]καὶ ἔχουσιν οὐρὰς
ὁμοίας σκορπίοις καὶ κέντρα, καὶ ἐν ταῖς οὐραῖς αὐτῶν

8 ειχαν ℵA] ειχον PQ min$^{\text{omn vid}}$ Andr Ar 9 om των πτερυγων 130 10 ομοιας PQ min$^{\text{fere omn}}$ Andr Ar] ομοιοις ℵA 14 | σκορπιω syr^{gw} | και εν] ην εν vg$^{\text{cle fu dem harl** lipss}}$ εν 1 7 28 34 130 al vg$^{\text{am harl* tol}}$ syr^{gw} arm aeth Andr | αυτων 1°]+και 1 36 47 79 vg$^{\text{cle harl lipss}}$

(1) They are crowned like conquerors (cf. iv. 4, xiv. 14), as indeed they are so long as their power lasts. (2) Their faces are strangely human, suggesting the intelligence and capacity of man; their long hair resembles that of women (1 Cor. xi. 15). Perhaps it is unnecessary to take ἀνθρώπων here as = ἀνδρῶν, though some support for this view may be found in Esth. iv. 10 (πᾶς ἄνθρωπος ἢ γυνή), and 1 Cor. vii. 1 (καλὸν ἀνθρώπῳ γυναικὸς μὴ ἅπτεσθαι). Ὡς τρίχας may allude to the long *antennae* of the locust tribe, or, as some suppose, to the long hair worn by the Parthians (Suet. *Vesp.* 20). The ancient commentators for the most part regard the reference to women as symbolizing the abuse of the sexual relations; e.g. Bede, "in capillis mulierum fluxos et effeminatos mores." But it is safer not to press the details. As to the general sense, the locusts of the Abyss may be the memories of the past brought home at times of Divine visitation; they hurt by recalling forgotten sins; cf. 1 Kings xvii. 13. Καὶ οἱ ὀδόντες αὐτῶν κτλ. looks back to Joel i. 6 οἱ ὀδόντες αὐτοῦ ὀδόντες λέοντος. For εἶχαν see WH.[2], *Notes*, p. 172.

9. καὶ εἶχον θώρακας ὡς θ. σιδηροῦς] The scaly backs and flanks of the insects resembled coats of mail, whether the scale-armour worn by Goliath (1 Regn. xvii. 5 θώρακα ἁλυσιδωτόν; cf. Driver, *ad loc.*, "like the scales of a fish, plates overlapping each other and allowing free movement"), or a cuirass of "metal plates across the chest and long flexible bands of steel over the shoulders" (*Enc. Bibl.* i. 606, and see Dean Robinson's note on Eph. vi. 14). Σιδηροῦς points to the material of which such armour was ordinarily made, and at the same time indicates the hopelessness of any effort to destroy assailants who were so protected. The next feature is again from Joel (ii. 5 ὡς φωνὴ ἁρμάτων...ὡς λαὸς πολὺς καὶ ἰσχυρὸς παρατασσόμενος εἰς πόλεμον). In the onrush of the locust-swarms the Prophet heard the din of war chariots; the Seer adds ἵππων πολλῶν τρεχόντων, thinking of "the pransings of their strong ones" (Jud. v. 22) as well as of the clatter of the chariots and the rumbling of their wheels (Jer. xxix. = xlvii. 3); comp. 4 Regn. vii. 6 Κύριος ἀκουστὴν ἐποίησεν τὴν παρεμβολὴν Συρίας φωνὴν ἅρματος καὶ φωνὴν ἵππου, φωνὴν δυνάμεως μεγάλης. For the vast numbers of chariots employed in ancient warfare cf. 1 Sam. xiii. 5 (30,000), 1 Chron. xix. 7 (32,000); for the phrase ἅρματα ἵππων see 3 Regn. xii. 24 b ἦσαν αὐτῷ ἅρματα τριακόσια ἵππων.

10. καὶ ἔχουσιν οὐρὰς ὁμοίας σκορπίοις κτλ.] The body of the locust of the Abyss ended in a flexible tail (Clem. Al. *strom.* iii. 18 § 106 οὐραῖς... ἃς κέρκους Ἕλληνες καλοῦσιν) like the tail of the scorpion. Ὁμοίας σκορπίοις = ὁμ. ταῖς οὐραῖς τῶν σκορπίων, as in Mt. v. 20 πλεῖον τῶν γραμματέων = πλ. τῆς δικαιοσύνης τῶν γρ. (cf. WM. pp. 307, 377). The tails were armed with stings, in which resided the power of

ἡ ἐξουσία αὐτῶν ἀδικῆσαι τοὺς ἀνθρώπους μῆνας
πέντε. [11]ἔχουσιν ἐπ' αὐτῶν βασιλέα τὸν ἄγγελον 11
τῆς ἀβύσσου, ὄνομα αὐτῷ Ἑβραϊστὶ Ἀβαδδών, καὶ
ἐν τῇ Ἑλληνικῇ ὄνομα ἔχει Ἀπολλύων. [12]ἡ οὐαὶ 12

10 η εξουσια αυτων] εξουσιαν εχουσιν Q 6 8 14 al^{mu} syr Ar εξουσιαν εχουσαι 51 90 92 αι εξουσιαι αυτων 130 | αδικησαι] pr του Q min$^{fere\ 30}$ 11 εχουσιν] pr και P 1 al$^{sat\ mu}$ vg syrr arm aeth εχουσαι Q min$^{fere\ 35}$ Ar | εφ εαυτων τον βασιλεα ℵ 130 | τον αρχοντα της αβυσσου τον αγγελον A | τον αγγελον] om τον Q min$^{plq\ 30}$ Ar | ονομα αυτω] pr ω ℵ syrr *cui nomen* vg | Αβαδδων] Αβααδδων Q 27 30 93 al *Armageddon* Prim *Labbadon* Haym alia alii | και εν τη] εν δε τη Q min^{40} vg syr Prim Ar | Ελληνικη] Ελληνιδι ℵ | Απολλυων (cf. vg *latine habens nomen Exterminans*; anon^{aug} *cui nomen latine Perdens*)] Απολυων 49* 98 syr^{gw}

the locusts to hurt. Κέντρον is properly the goad used for oxen (Prov. xxvi. 3, Acts xxvi. 14), and in a secondary sense the sting of the bee (4 Macc. xiv. 19 μέλισσα...καθάπερ σιδηρῷ τῷ κέντρῳ πλήσσουσι) or other insect. With the symbolism cf. Hos. xiii. 14 ποῦ τὸ κέντρον σου, ᾅδη; 1 Cor. xv. 56 τὸ δὲ κέντρον τοῦ θανάτου ἡ ἁμαρτία. Πέντε μῆνας: see *v.* 5, note.

11. ἔχουσιν ἐπ' αὐτῶν βασιλέα κτλ.] In Prov. xxiv. 62 (xxx. 27) we read: ἀβασίλευτόν ἐστιν ἡ ἀκρίς. If the Apocalyptist remembered this statement, he found an exception to it in the locusts of the Abyss, which are in other respects quite abnormal; but for his comparative independence of the LXX. we might have supposed him to have been influenced by Amos vii. 1 ἰδοὺ ἐπιγονὴ ἀκρίδων ἐρχομένη ἑωθινή, καὶ ἰδοὺ βροῦχος εἷς Γὼγ (אֶחָד גּוֹג for M.T. אַחַר גִּזֵּי) ὁ βασιλεύς. For their king the locusts of the Abyss have the Angel who presides over it (*v.* 1), i.e. they obey his orders and do his work. The Seer knows the name of this angel; it is in Hebrew (Ἑβραϊστί, as in Jo. v. 2, xix. 13, 17, 20, xx. 16, Apoc. xvi. 16) *Abaddon*, and in the Greek (ἐν τῇ Ἑλληνικῇ, sc. γλώσσῃ = Ἑλληνιστί; for the latter see Jo. xix. 20, Acts xxi. 37), Ἀπολλύων, Destroyer; Vg., *Exterminans*; the rendering in Syr.$^{gw.}$ [illegible] rests upon the false reading Ἀπολύων (*app. crit.*). Abaddon, אֲבַדּוֹן, a word used almost exclusively in the Wisdom literature (Job xxvi. 6, xxviii. 22, xxxi. 12, Ps. lxxxviii. 11, Prov. xv. 11, xxvii. 20) is represented in the LXX. (exc. Job xxxi. 12) by ἀπώλεια, meaning either destruction generally (Job xxvi. 6, Esth. viii. 6) or destruction in Sheol. (*Emek hammelek*, f. 15. 3 "infimus gehennae locus est Abaddon, unde nemo emergit"). Here Destruction in the deeper sense is personified, and ἀπολλύων is therefore preferred to ἀπώλεια (cf. 1 Cor. x. 10 τοῦ ὀλοθρευτοῦ); the allusion to Ἀπολλών, suggested by some commentators, seems far-fetched, but it is not in this book impossible. The personification of Abaddon is known to the Talmud; see *Shabb.* f. 55 a, where six destroying Angels are mentioned, over whom preside מָוֶת and אֲבַדּוֹן; *ib.* f. 89. 1 אֲבַדּוֹן וּמָוֶת אָמְרוּ. It is unnecessary to enquire whether by Abaddon, the Destroyer, the Seer means Death or Satan; perhaps he does not consciously identify the personality, which belongs to the scenery of the vision. The Apollyon of *Pilgrim's Progress* is a more fully developed conception, and indeed in all but the name it is a creation of Bunyan. With the construction ὄνομα ἔχει Ἀπολλύων cf. xix. 16 ἔχει... ὄνομα γεγραμμένον Βασιλεύς, κτλ., and see WM. p. 226; on the form ἀπολλύειν see WH.[2], *Notes*, p. 175 f.

12. ἡ οὐαὶ ἡ μία ἀπῆλθεν κτλ.] "Woe the first is gone past; behold, there

ἡ μία ἀπῆλθεν· ἰδοὺ ἔρχεται ἔτι δύο οὐαὶ μετὰ
ταῦτα.
13 [13]Καὶ ὁ ἕκτος ἄγγελος ἐσάλπισεν· καὶ ἤκουσα
φωνὴν μίαν ἐκ τῶν κεράτων τοῦ θυσιαστηρίου τοῦ
14 χρυσοῦ τοῦ ἐνώπιον τοῦ θεοῦ, [14]λέγοντα τῷ ἕκτῳ
ἀγγέλῳ, ὁ ἔχων τὴν σάλπιγγα Λῦσον τοὺς τέσσα-

12 *απηλθεν*] *παρηλθεν* 28 79 80 | *ερχεται* ℵ*A 7 8 14 29 30 al$^{\text{plq 20}}$ syrr] *ερχονται* ℵ$^{\text{c.a}}$ PQ 1 28 32 35 36 al$^{\text{sat mu}}$ syr^{gw} Andr Ar | *ετι δυο*] om *ετι* 1 49 97 *δευτερα* 7 me | *μετα ταυτα* c. versu sequenti conjung ℵ (Q) 8 14 29 31 47 48 50 90 al^{mu} syr^{gw} 13 om *και* 1° ℵ me syr^{gw} | *φωνην μιαν*] *φωνης μιας* ℵ$^{\text{c.a}}$ *φωνην μεγαλην* 34 35 87 *φωνην* tantum ℵ* 38 me arm *vocem, unum* vg$^{\text{am fu etc.}}$ *unum* Cypr Prim anon^{aug} om 130 | om *εκ των κερατων* ℵ* (hab ℵ$^{\text{c.a}}$) 14 92 | *κερατων*] pr *τεσσαρων* PQ$^{\text{min fere omn}}$ vg$^{\text{cle dem lipss 4, 6}}$ syrr Cypr Prim Andr Ar (om ℵ$^{\text{c.a}}$ A 28 79 vg$^{\text{am fu harl lips 5 tol}}$ me syrr aeth) 14 *λεγοντα* ℵ*A] *λεγοντος* Q min$^{\text{fere 30}}$ Ar *λεγουσαν* P 1 7 28 35 36 38 al *λεγουσης* ℵ$^{\text{c.a}}$ | om *εκτω* A | *ο εχων*] *τω εχοντι* 34 35 87 (130) *ος ειχε* Ar *qui habebat* vg Cypr | *τεσσαρας*] *τεσσαρες* ℵ 87

come yet two Woes after this," i.e., the sixth and seventh Trumpets have yet to be blown (cf. viii. 13, note). Ἡ *οὐαί*, which occurs again in xi. 14 (*ἡ οὐαὶ ἡ δευτέρα, ἡ οὐαὶ ἡ τρίτη*), is not easy to explain: Blass (*Gr.* p. 32) seems to attribute the gender to the fact that the word *οὐαί* is here equivalent to *θλίψις*, but it is simpler to regard the three Woes in the light of female personages, the Erinnues or Eumenides of the Apocalypse, representing the avenging powers evoked by the last three Trumpets. Μία = *πρώτη*, a Hebraism which the LXX. takes over in Gen. i. 5, 8 *ἡμέρα μία*: cf. Mc. xvi. 2 *τῇ μιᾷ τῶν σαββάτων* with 'Mc.' xvi. 9 *πρώτῃ σαββάτου*, and see notes there. In *ἔρχεται δύο οὐαί* the personification seems to disappear, for the writer treats *οὐαί* as a neuter. For *οὐαί* as a noun see Prov. xxiii. 29, Ezek. vii. 26, 1 Cor. ix. 16.

13—21. THE SIXTH TRUMPET, OR SECOND WOE.

13. *καὶ ὁ ἕκτος ἄγγελος ἐσάλπισεν· καί κτλ.*] The sixth trumpet-blast is followed by a solitary voice (*μίαν φωνήν*, cf. viii. 13 *ἑνὸς ἀετοῦ*) which seems to proceed from (*ἐκ*) the horns of the Golden Altar mentioned in viii. 3. The voice may be that of the Angel who had been seen standing over the Altar with a golden censer; or it may represent the prayers of the Saints, which now have the effect of a command issued to the Angel of the sixth Trumpet. The general sense is the same in either case; the prayers of the Church, which initiated the entire series of visitations connected with the Trumpets, now bring about a greater catastrophe than the world has yet experienced. *Τῶν κεράτων τ. θυσ.* (Exod. xxvii. 1, 2) may be intended to point to the four corners of the earth (vii. 1) from which prayer ascends; the single voice interprets the desire of the 'Holy Church throughout all the world.'

14. *λέγοντα τῷ ἕκτῳ ἀγγέλῳ, ὁ ἔχων τὴν σ.*] Λέγοντα personifies the voice, as in iv. 1; *ὁ ἔχων τ. σ.* must be regarded as a parenthesis; the alternative of connecting the words with *λῦσον κτλ.* ('thou that hast the trumpet, loose,' etc.), is less in accordance with the manner of the Apocalypse. Similar constructions occur in iv. 1, xi. 15.

λῦσον τοὺς τέσσαρας ἀγγέλους τοὺς δεδεμένους κτλ.] Another quaternion (Acts xii. 4) of angels; cf. vii. 1 *εἶδον*

ρας ἀγγέλους τοὺς δεδεμένους ἐπὶ τῷ ποταμῷ τῷ
μεγάλῳ Εὐφράτῃ. [15]καὶ ἐλύθησαν οἱ τέσσαρες ἄγ- 15
γελοι οἱ ἡτοιμασμένοι εἰς τὴν ὥραν καὶ ἡμέραν καὶ
μῆνα καὶ ἐνιαυτόν, ἵνα ἀποκτείνωσιν τὸ τρίτον τῶν

14 *επι*] *εν* 7 19 37 *in flumine* vg | *τω μεγαλω*] + *ποταμω* P om *τω μεγ.* arm^{zoh} Cassiod 15 *ελυθησαν*] *ελυπηθησαν* A | *οι ητοιμασμενοι*] om *οι* ℵ 41 90 98 | *εις την ωραν και ημεραν και μηνα και ενιαυτον*] *εις τ. ημ. κ. εις τον μηνα κ. εις τον εν.* syr^{gw} | *και ημεραν*] om ℵ 1 *και εις την ημ.* Q min$^{plq\,20}$ Ar *και την ημ.* 28 38 49 79 91 96 | *το τριτον*] + *μερος* 28 37 79 80 *tertiam partem* vg

τέσσαρας ἀγγέλους. Those in *c.* vii. restrain the winds of heaven; these are themselves bound, for they are Angels of the Divine wrath which is not to be executed before the predestined time; cf. Mt. xiii. 41. They are held in readiness "at the great river Euphrates"; a phrase which sends the reader back to Gen. xv. 18, where the Land of promise is said to extend *ἀπὸ τοῦ ποταμοῦ Αἰγύπτου ἕως τοῦ ποταμοῦ τοῦ μεγάλου Εὐφράτου*, cf. Exod. xxiii. 31 (LXX.), Deut. i. 7, xi. 24, Josh. i. 4, 1 Kings iv. 21, Ps. lxxxii. The Euphrates was on the East "the ideal limit" of the land of Israel (Driver on Gen. *l. c.*). Beyond it lay the great heathen kingdoms of the East, Babylonia on the east bank of the river, the Assyrian Empire further to the N.E.; an invasion of Israel by these nations is likened to an overflow of the Great River (Isa. viii. 7 *Κύριος ἀνάγει ἐφ' ὑμᾶς τὸ ὕδωρ τοῦ ποταμοῦ τὸ ἰσχυρὸν καὶ τὸ πολύ, τὸν βασιλέα τῶν Ἀσσυρίων*). Thus the idea presented by the angels of vengeance bound on the banks of the Euphrates is that the day of vengeance was held back only till God's time has come. When at length they are loosed, the flood will burst its barriers, and ruin will follow. The Euphrates is mentioned again in connexion with the Sixth Bowl (xvi. 12, where see note). The ancient Latin commentators explained the Euphrates mystically, e.g. Bede: "Euphrates qui fluvius est Babyloniae mundani regni potentiam...indicat." Andreas satisfies himself by saying *ἴσως δὲ... δηλοῦται ἐκ τῶν μερῶν ἐκείνων ἐξιέναι τὸν ἀντίχριστον.* It is possible that the Apocalyptist had in mind the unknown and at the time greatly dreaded resources of the Parthian Empire.

15. *καὶ ἐλύθησαν κτλ.*] *Ἐλύθησαν* is the correlative of *ἐδέθησαν*, cf. Mt. xvi. 19, xviii. 18, Mc. xi. 4 f., Lc. xiii. 16, 1 Cor. vii. 27. The ministers of vengeance, now set free, at once enter on the work for which they had been prepared in the Divine foreknowledge. *Οἱ ἡτοιμασμένοι*, "who had been made ready"; for this quasi-pluperfect sense of the part. see Jo. ii. 9, Acts xviii. 2, Gal. ii. 11, Heb. ii. 9, and for *ἑτοιμάζειν* of Divine preparation, Mt. xxv. 34, 41, Mc. x. 40, Lc. ii. 31, 1 Cor. ii. 9, Apoc. xii. 6, xvi. 12. *Εἰς τ. ὥραν κτλ.*; the preparation had been made with a view to the result being attained at a definite time; for this use of *εἰς* cf. *v.* 7, and 2 Tim. ii. 20, and for a similar use of *πρός*, Tit. iii. 1, 1 Pet. iii. 15, 2 Pet. i. 3. The four notes of time are under one article, since the occasion is one and the same. The ascensive order (*ὥραν...ἐνιαυτόν*) is difficult to explain, but it occurs also in the O.T. (e.g. Num. i. 1, Zech. i. 7, Hagg. i. 15), and probably has in this place no special significance; perhaps it originated, as Primasius suggests, in the thought that "et horis gradatim dies et diebus menses et mensibus certum est annos impleri." The 'hour' and other 'times and seasons' are not revealed till they may be gathered from the event; cf. Mc. xiii. 32, Acts i. 7.

ἵνα ἀποκτείνωσιν τὸ τρίτον τῶν ἀνθρώ-

16 *ἀνθρώπων.* [16]*καὶ ὁ ἀριθμὸς τῶν στρατευμάτων τοῦ*
ἱππικοῦ δισμυριάδες μυριάδων· ἤκουσα τὸν ἀριθμὸν
§ C 17 *αὐτῶν.* §[17] *καὶ οὕτως εἶδον τοὺς ἵππους ἐν τῇ ὁράσει*

16 *του ιππικου*] *του ιππου* 2 8 9 13 16 24 35 49[txt] 51 91 al[plq 20] | *δισμυριαδες* (*dismyriades* Cypr)] *δυο μυριαδας* ℵ 1[corr] 28 79 syrr Ar *μυριαδες* Q min[fere 40] arm *ως μυρ.* 130 17 om *ουτως* 38 arm Prim anon[aug] | *ειδον* ℵP min[pl] Ar] *ιδον* AC(Q) 7 14 92 130 | *ιππους*] *ιππικους* Q 14

πων. If the fifth trumpet brought torture, the sixth brings death. But again the destruction is partial only; two-thirds remain unscathed, as in the lesser visitations heralded by the first four trumpets (viii. 7 ff.).

16. *καὶ ὁ ἀριθμὸς τῶν στρατευμάτων κτλ.*] The work of the destroying angels is done by the vast forces under their command. This new feature is introduced with strange abruptness, as if the Seer in his eagerness to describe it had forgotten to prepare the reader by some such connecting clause as *καὶ ἀπέκτειναν αὐτοὺς διὰ τῶν στρατευμάτων αὐτῶν*, or (as in xix. 14) *καὶ τὰ στρατεύματα αὐτῶν ἠκολούθει αὐτοῖς*. The hosts (for *στρατεύματα* see Judith xi. 8, 4 Macc. v. 1, Mt. xxii. 7, Lc. xxiii. 11, Apoc. ix. 16, xix. 14, 19) consisted of cavalry (cf. Herod. vii. 87 *Ἀράβιοι δὲ...ἔσχατοι ἐτετάχατο ἵνα μὴ φοβέοιτο τὸ ἱππικόν*), and the number, which was stated in the Seer's hearing (cf. vii. 4), was *δισμυριάδες μυριάδων* = 200,000,000. The figures rest ultimately on Ps. lxviii. 18: "the chariots of God are רִבֹּתַיִם אַלְפֵי שִׁנְאָן (LXX. *μυριοπλάσιον, χίλιοι*)"; cf. Deut. xxxiii. 2, Dan. vii. 10, Apoc. v. 11 note. *Δισμυριάδες* (not *δὶς μυριάδες*), cf. *τρισμύριοι* (Esth. i. 7), *δισμύριοι* (2 Macc. v. 24, viii. 9), *δισχίλιοι* (Mc. v. 13). These vast numbers forbid us to seek a literal fulfilment, and the description which follows supports this conclusion. On *ἀκούειν* with the acc. see Blass, *Gr.* p. 103. *Ἤκουσα τὸν ἀριθμὸν αὐτῶν*: cf. c. vii. 4 *ἤκ. τ. ἀριθμὸν τῶν ἐσφραγισμένων.*

17. *καὶ οὕτως εἶδον τοὺς ἵππους κτλ.*] A mixed construction which blends *κ. οὕτως εἶδον...εἶχον* with *κ. εἶδον...ἔχοντας.* The sentence is further complicated by the introduction of a second object, the riders (*τοὺς καθημένους ἐπ' αὐτῶν*, cf. vi. 4, xix. 11, 18 ff.); it is not clear whether *ἔχοντας* refers to *τοὺς ἵππους*, or to *τοὺς καθ.*, or to both. On the whole it is best perhaps to limit the participial clause to the riders; the horses are described in the sequel. The riders were armed in cuirasses whose colour suggested fire, smoke, and brimstone. *Πύρινος* is properly 'of fire,' while *πυρρός* (vi. 4, xii. 3) is 'flame-coloured': cf. Sir. xlviii. 9 [*Ἠλίας*] *ὁ ἀναλημφθεὶς... ἐν ἅρματι ἵππων πυρίνων*, with 4 Regn. ii. 11 *ἰδοὺ ἅρμα πυρὸς καὶ ἵππος πυρός.* The defensive armour of the warriors seemed to consist of fire; cf. Ps. ciii. (civ.) 4 *ὁ ποιῶν...τοὺς λειτουργοὺς αὐτοῦ πῦρ φλέγον.* *Ὑακίνθινος*, of *ὑάκινθος*, which in Apoc. xxi. 20 is a precious stone (cf. Syr.[gw.] ܡܪܟܕܢܐ i.e. *χαλκηδών*), but in the LXX. stands for a dye ('blue,' A.V., R.V.) which is combined with purple (Exod. xxv. 4, xxvii. 16), fine linen (Exod. xxvi. 1), and gold (Exod. xxviii. 8, Isa. iii. 23)—the equivalent of תְּכֵלֶת, probably the shell-fish *helix ianthina*, which yielded the famous Tyrian dye. The *ὑάκινθος* of classical Greek was a vegetable, perhaps the dark blue-flowering iris. Here *ὑακίνθινος* is doubtless meant to describe the blue smoke of a sulphurous flame (cf. infra, *πῦρ καὶ καπνὸς καὶ θεῖον*). The Latin version used by Primasius strangely rendered *ὑακ.* by *spineas*, "spineas significans vitas," as Primasius explains; but the rendering doubtless originated

καὶ τοὺς καθημένους ἐπ' αὐτῶν, ἔχοντας θώρακας
πυρίνους καὶ ὑακινθίνους καὶ θειώδεις· καὶ αἱ κεφαλαὶ
τῶν ἵππων ὡς κεφαλαὶ λεόντων, καὶ ἐκ τῶν στομά-
των αὐτῶν ἐκπορεύεται πῦρ καὶ καπνὸς καὶ θεῖον.
18 ἀπὸ τῶν τριῶν πληγῶν τούτων ἀπεκτάνθησαν τὸ 18
τρίτον τῶν ἀνθρώπων, ἐκ τοῦ πυρὸς καὶ τοῦ καπνοῦ
καὶ τοῦ θείου τοῦ ἐκπορευομένου ἐκ τῶν στομάτων
αὐτῶν. 19 ἡ γὰρ ἐξουσία τῶν ἵππων ἐν τῷ στόματι 19

17 επ] επανω א | υακινθινους] ακανθινους (*spineas*) Prim | θειωδεις] θυωδεις א* | των ιππων] + αυτων syr^{gw} | του στοματος syr^{gw} (item 18) 18 απο] υπο 1 5 | των τριων πληγων] om των C om τριων א arm om πληγων 1 38 | απεκτανθη 36 38 97 | εκ 1°] απο Q 7 14 $al^{fere\ 35}$ Ar | του καπνου] pr εκ CP 1 6 31 al $vg^{cle\ harl**\ lips4\ harl\ corr}$ syrr | του θειου] pr εκ P 1 6 31 79 al syrr arm 19 η γαρ εξουσια των ιππων (τοπων A)...εστιν] αι γαρ εξουσιαι αυτων...εισιν 1

in a confusion between ὑακινθίνους and ἀκανθίνους. With the colour of flame and smoke the cuirasses shewed also the pale yellow of brimstone. Θειώδης is ἅπ. λεγ. in Biblical Greek, but not unknown to postclassical writers. The description as a whole recalls the fate of the Cities of the Plain; Gen. xix. 24, 28 καὶ Κύριος ἔβρεξεν εἰς Σόδομα καὶ Γόμορρα θεῖον καὶ πῦρ...καὶ ἰδοὺ ἀνέβαινεν φλὸξ τῆς γῆς ὡσεὶ ἀτμὶς καμίνου (cf. Jude 7, 2 Pet. ii. 6).

καὶ αἱ κεφαλαὶ τῶν ἵππων ὡς κ. λεόντων κτλ.] Cf. *v.* 8 καὶ οἱ ὀδόντες αὐτῶν ὡς λεόντων ἦσαν. The horses in the vision seemed to unite the majestic mien of the lion with the swiftness of their own kind. Like their riders they were armed with fire, smoke, and brimstone; but while these formed the cuirasses of the horsemen, they proceeded from the lion-like jaws of the horses, which thus seemed to 'breathe threatening and slaughter' (Acts ix. 1). Cf. Job xli. 10 f. ἐκ στόματος αὐτοῦ ἐκπορεύονται λαμπάδες καιόμεναι ... ἐκ μυκτήρων αὐτοῦ ἐκπορεύεται καπνὸς καμίνου; and see Apoc. xi. 5, and Slavonic Enoch i. 5 "fire came forth from their lips." See also the description of the Chaldean cavalry in Hab. i. 8 ff.: possibly the Parthian cavalry are in the mind of the Seer.

18. ἀπὸ τῶν τριῶν πληγῶν τούτων ἀπεκτάνθησαν κτλ.] Πληγή, which in classical Greek scarcely goes beyond its etymological meaning, is used in the LXX. for the 'plagues' of Egypt (Exod. xi. 1 ff., cf. Num. xxv. 8 ff.), and this sense reappears frequently in the Apocalypse (ix. 18, 20, xi. 6, xiii. 3, 12, 14, xv. 1, 6, 8, xvi. 9, 21, xviii. 4, 8, xxi. 9, xxii. 18). The thought of the Egyptian plagues has been in the mind of the writer for some time, and he now uses the familiar LXX. word. The "three plagues" are the fire, smoke, and brimstone which proceed from the horses; the repeated article (τοῦ...τοῦ...τοῦ) indicates that they are regarded as distinct agencies. Ἀπό, ἐκ, 'arising from,' 'springing out of,' are here, as often in the N. T., practically indistinguishable; see Blass, *Gr.* p. 124 f. For ἐκπορεύεσθαι ἐκ, see xxii. 1; on ἀπεκτάνθησαν see ii. 13, note.

19. ἡ γὰρ ἐξουσία...ἐν ταῖς οὐραῖς αὐτῶν] Their power (ii. 26, vi. 8) resides in mouth and tail (cf. *v.* 10); if the one discharges fiery and noisome vapours, the other is armed with the poison of the snake. With ὅμοιαι ὄφεσιν, cf. *v.* 10 ἔχουσιν οὐρὰς ὁμοίας

αὐτῶν ἐστιν καὶ ἐν ταῖς οὐραῖς αὐτῶν· αἱ γὰρ οὐραὶ
αὐτῶν ὅμοιαι ὄφεσιν, ἔχουσαι κεφαλάς, καὶ ἐν αὐταῖς
20 ἀδικοῦσιν. ²⁰καὶ οἱ λοιποὶ τῶν ἀνθρώπων, οἳ οὐκ
ἀπεκτάνθησαν ἐν ταῖς πληγαῖς ταύταις, οὐδὲ μετε-
νόησαν ἐκ τῶν ἔργων τῶν χειρῶν αὐτῶν, ἵνα μὴ
προσκυνήσουσιν τὰ δαιμόνια καὶ τὰ εἴδωλα τὰ χρυσᾶ

19 om *και εν ταις ουραις αυτων* 1 36 aeth | *ομοιας* 130 | *οφεσιν*] *οφεων* Q min^{30} Ar *οφεως* 130 | *εχουσαις* ℵ$^{c.a}$ (-*σας* ℵ*) P 36 *habentibus* vg^{dem} *εχουσιν* C* | *αυταις*] *ταυταις* 130 | om *αι γαρ ουραι...αδικουσιν* syr^{gw} 20 *πληγαις*] + *αυτων* ℵ | *ουδε* ℵQ 14 38 92] *ουτε* AP 1 36 al$^{vix\ mu}$ | *του εργου* syr^{gw} | *προσκυνησουσιν* ℵAC 7* 36 42] *προσκυνησωσιν* PQ min^{pl} Andr Ar | *χρυσαια...χαλκεα* ℵ | *χρυσα*] pr *κωφα και* 130

σκορπίοις (note). As a picture *οὐραὶ... ἔχουσαι κεφαλάς* is intolerable, but, it serves to enhance the horror of the situation.

20. *καὶ οἱ λοιποὶ τῶν ἀνθρώπων κτλ.*] The two-thirds who escaped both the mouths and the tails of the horses might have been expected to take warning by the fate of their fellows, and to become servants of God and of Christ; but so far from doing this, they did not even (*οὐδέ*) repent of their idolatries. For *οὐδέ*, 'not even,' see Mc. vi. 31, 1 Cor. iii. 3, iv. 3 (*ἀλλ' οὐδέ*); for *μετανοεῖν ἐκ*, Apoc. ii. 21. *Τῶν ἔργων τῶν χειρῶν αὐτῶν* (Prim. wrongly *factorum suorum malorum*, Vg. *de operibus manuum suarum*) 'their idols,' an O.T. phrase = מַעֲשֵׂי יְדֵיהֶם, cf. e.g. Deut. iv. 28 *λατρεύσετε ἐκεῖ θεοῖς ἑτέροις, ἔργοις χειρῶν ἀνθρώπων, ξύλοις καὶ λίθοις*, Ps. cxxxiv. (cxxxv.) 15 *τὰ εἴδωλα τῶν ἐθνῶν ἀργύριον καὶ χρυσίον, ἔργα χειρῶν ἀνθρώπων*, Jer. i. 16 *ἔθυσαν θεοῖς ἀλλοτρίοις καὶ προσεκύνησαν τοῖς ἔργοις τῶν χειρῶν αὐτῶν*. That this is the true interpretation of the phrase here is clear from what follows.

ἵνα μὴ προσκυνήσουσιν κτλ.] Repentance would have led them to abandon the worship of unclean spirits and of the idols which represented them. Both in the O. and N. T. the heathen worship is regarded as paid to demons: cf. Deut. xxxii. 17 (where see Driver's note), Ps. cv. (cvi.) 37 *ἔθυσαν...δαιμονίοις* (שֵׁדִים), 1 Cor. x. 20 *ἃ θύουσιν* [*τὰ ἔθνη*], *δαιμονίοις καὶ οὐ θεῷ θύουσιν· οὐ θέλω δὲ ὑμᾶς κοινωνοὺς τῶν δαιμονίων γίνεσθαι*. Cf. Ps. xcv. (xcvi.) 5 *πάντες οἱ θεοὶ τῶν ἐθνῶν δαιμόνια* (אֱלִילִים). Of the two Hebrew words, the latter represents the deities of heathendom as non-existent, while the former points to the older belief that they were demigods, evil genii, or the like. In the Gospels the *δαιμόνια* are identified with *πνεύματα ἀκάθαρτα* (cf. Mc. v. 2 *ἄνθρωπος ἐν πνεύματι ἀκαθάρτῳ* = Mt. viii. 27 *δύο δαιμονιζόμενοι* = Lc. viii. 29 *ἀνήρ τις ἔχων δαιμόνια*), and this view was probably in the mind of St Paul and the Apocalyptist; it found its justification in the impurities associated with the Greek legends and the immorality too often promoted by the temples and their priesthood.

καὶ τὰ εἴδωλα τὰ χρυσᾶ κτλ.] Christianity rigorously maintained the old Hebrew protest against idol-worship. Though "an idol is nothing in the world" (1 Cor. viii. 4), has in itself no spiritual significance, yet it is a visible symbol of revolt from the Living God, and the *εἰδωλολάτρης* is excluded from the Divine Kingdom (1 Cor. vi. 9). The Seer goes to the O.T. for words to convey his scorn for this debasing worship: cf. Ps. cxiii. 12 ff. (cxv. 4) *τὰ εἴδωλα τῶν ἐθνῶν ἀργύριον καὶ χρυσίον, ἔργα χειρῶν ἀνθρώπων. στόμα ἔχουσιν καὶ οὐ λαλοῦσιν, ὀφθαλμοὺς ἔχουσιν καὶ οὐκ ὄψονται· ὦτα ἔχουσιν καὶ οὐκ ἀκούσονται...πόδας ἔχου-*

καὶ τὰ ἀργυρᾶ καὶ τὰ χαλκᾶ καὶ τὰ λίθινα καὶ τὰ
ξύλινα, ἃ οὔτε βλέπειν δύνανται οὔτε ἀκούειν οὔτε
περιπατεῖν· 21 καὶ οὐ μετενόησαν ἐκ τῶν φόνων αὐτῶν 21
οὔτε ἐκ τῶν φαρμακιῶν αὐτῶν οὔτε ἐκ τῆς πορνείας
αὐτῶν οὔτε ἐκ τῶν κλεμμάτων αὐτῶν. 1 καὶ εἶδον 1 X.
ἄλλον ἄγγελον ἰσχυρὸν καταβαίνοντα ἐκ τοῦ οὐ-

20 om και τα χαλκα 2 6 7 8 9 13 16 29 30 31 33 al Ar | ξυλινα...λιθινα ℵ syr^{gw} | δυναται Q$^{1\ vid}$ min^{pl} Ar 21 ουτε εκ bis] και εκ syr^{gw} | φαρμακιων APQ] φαρμακειων 1 al$^{sat\ mu}$ φαρμακων ℵC min^{25} Ar | πορνειας ℵ$^{c.a}$ CPQ min$^{omn\ vid}$ vg me syrr Andr Ar] πονηριας ℵ*A | om ουτε εκ των κλεμματων αυτων syr^{gw} Prim

X 1 ειδον ℵCP min^{pl}] ιδον AQ 7 14 92 130 | om αλλον PQ 1 al$^{plq\ 35}$ | om ισχυρον syr^{gw}

σιν καὶ οὐ περιπατήσουσιν, Dan. v. 23, Th. τοὺς θεοὺς τοὺς χρυσοῦς καὶ ἀργυροῦς καὶ χαλκοῦς καὶ σιδηροῦς καὶ ξυλίνους καὶ λιθίνους, οἳ οὐ βλέπουσιν καὶ οἳ οὐκ ἀκούουσιν καὶ οὐ γινώσκουσιν, ᾔνεσας. The theme is worked out *usque ad nauseam* in the Epistle of Jeremiah; see also Enoch xcix. 7, *Orac. Sibyll.* v. 80 ff.

21. καὶ οὐ μετενόησαν ἐκ τῶν φόνων αὐτῶν κτλ.] A further indictment as against the pagan world, closely connected with the first. They were no less unwilling to repent of their immoralities than of their idolatries. Murders, sorceries, fornication, thefts, appear in company in not a few lists of the vices of the time: cf. Mc. vii. 21 πορνεῖαι, κλοπαί, φόνοι (where see note), Gal. v. 20 πορνεία...εἰδωλολατρία, φαρμακία, Apoc. xxi. 8 φονεῦσι καὶ πόρνοις καὶ φαρμακοῖς καὶ εἰδωλολάτραις, xxii. 15 ἔξω ... οἱ φαρμακοὶ καὶ οἱ πόρνοι καὶ οἱ φονεῖς καὶ οἱ εἰδωλολάτραι. In three out of these contexts, it will be observed, idolatry is placed in close connexion with vice and crime. On φαρμακία see Lightfoot's note on Gal. *l.c.*, and cf. Exod. vii. 22, viii. 18 (14), 4 Regn. ix. 22, Mal. iii. 5, Isa. xlvii. 9, 12, Dan. ii. 2.

Primitive Christianity was a protest, not only against polytheism, but against the moral condition of the pagan world. The Seer voices this protest, and enforces it with a terrific description of the vengeance which threatened the world unless it should repent. Cf. Eph. v. 6 διὰ ταῦτα γὰρ ἔρχεται ἡ ὀργὴ τοῦ θεοῦ ἐπὶ τοὺς υἱοὺς τῆς ἀπειθείας.

X. 1—11. Preparations for the Seventh Trumpet-blast. (1) Vision of the strong Angel with the little Book.

1. καὶ εἶδον ἄλλον ἄγγελον ἰσχυρόν κτλ.] As the opening of the Seventh Seal was preceded by the two visions of *c.* vii., so the visions of *cc.* x., xi. are preparatory to the blowing of the last Trumpet. First the Seer sees an angel, not, as Primasius thinks, "Dominum Christum descendentem de caelo," but an "angel" in the technical sense which is maintained throughout the book; "another angel," not one of the Seven or of the Four (cf. vii. 2, xiv. 6, 15 ff.), remarkable for his strength (v. 2, xviii. 21) coming down from heaven (xx. 1), clad in a cloud, the vehicle in which heavenly beings descend and ascend (Ps. ciii. (civ.) 3, Dan. vii. 13, Acts i. 9 ff., 1 Thess. iv. 17, Apoc. i. 7, xi. 12, xiv. 14 ff.; for the acc. after περιβεβλ. see vii. 9, note). Upon his head is the rainbow (ἡ ἶρις), not the emerald bow of *c.* iv. 3 (Tert. *coron.* 15), but the ordinary bow of many colours connected with the cloud (Gen. ix. 13 τὸ τόξον μου τίθημι ἐν τῇ νεφέλῃ), and due in this

ρανοῦ, περιβεβλημένον νεφέλην, καὶ ἡ ἶρις ἐπὶ τὴν
κεφαλὴν αὐτοῦ, καὶ τὸ πρόσωπον αὐτοῦ ὡς ὁ ἥλιος,
2 καὶ οἱ πόδες αὐτοῦ ὡς στῦλοι πυρός, ²καὶ ἔχων ἐν τῇ
χειρὶ αὐτοῦ βιβλαρίδιον ἠνεῳγμένον. καὶ ἔθηκεν τὸν
πόδα αὐτοῦ τὸν δεξιὸν ἐπὶ τῆς θαλάσσης, τὸν δὲ
3 εὐώνυμον ἐπὶ τῆς γῆς, ³καὶ ἔκραξεν φωνῇ μεγάλῃ

1 η ιρις] om η P 1 7 32 36 38 98 al arm ιριν 28 79 80 Andr | την κεφαλην AC 9 12] της κεφαλης ℵPQ min[pl] Andr Ar | στυλος 38 vg[am fu dem tol lipss] syr arm aeth 2 εχων] ειχεν 1 7 28 35 36 47 al vg me arm Vict Prim Ar | βιβλαριδιον ℵ*AC[corr] P al Ar] βιβλιδαριον ℵ[c.a vid] C* 7 10 14 17 28 36 al βιβλιον Q min[35] | ηνεωγμενον ℵCP min[nonn]] ανεωγμενον Q min[pl] Ar om A me | om τον δεξιον C | την θαλασσαν...την γην 1 al[pauc vid]

instance to the sunshine of the Angel's face. Τὸ πρόσωπον αὐτοῦ ὡς ὁ ἥλιος recalls the description of the glorified Christ (i. 16), but does not serve to identify this angel with Him; cf. Mt. xiii. 43, Apoc. xviii. 1; nor can this be inferred from οἱ πόδες αὐτοῦ ὡς στῦλοι πυρός, notwithstanding that this description bears some resemblance to i. 15 οἱ πόδες αὐτοῦ ὅμοιοι χαλκολιβάνῳ, ὡς ἐν καμίνῳ πεπυρωμένης. In στῦλοι πυρός there is perhaps a reference to Exod. xiv. 19, 24 ἐξῆρεν δὲ ὁ ἄγγελος τοῦ θεοῦ, ἐξῆρεν δὲ καὶ ὁ στῦλος τῆς νεφέλης...ἐπέβλεψεν Κύριος...ἐν στύλῳ πυρὸς καὶ νεφέλης. The pillar-like extremities of the Angel's form accord with the posture ascribed to him in *v.* 2.

2. καὶ ἔχων ἐν τῇ χειρὶ αὐτοῦ βιβλαρίδιον ἠνεῳγμένον] The description is continued in the nom., as if the Seer had written ἰδοὺ ἄλλος ἄγγ. ἰσχ. καταβαίνων κτλ. The Angel's hand grasped a small papyrus roll which lay open—a double contrast to the βιβλίον κατεσφραγισμένον of c. v. 1. The little open roll contained but a fragment of the great purpose which was in the Hand of God, a fragment ripe for revelation. Βιβλαρίδιον is a diminutive of βιβλάριον, with which may be compared ὠτάριον (Mc. xiv. 47), παιδάριον (Jo. vi. 9), γυναικάριον (2 Tim. iii. 6); other forms are βιβλίδιον, βιβλιδάριον, cf. Pollux vii. 210: βίβλος, βιβλίον, βιβλάριον, παρὰ δὲ Ἀριστοφάνει βιβλιδάριον. Βιβλαρίδιον seems to be found here only, and, as the *app. crit.* shows, it has given the scribes trouble.

The Apocalyptist has in his mind Ezek. ii. 9 καὶ ἴδον, καὶ ἰδοὺ χεὶρ ἐκτεταμένη πρὸς μέ, καὶ ἐν αὐτῇ κεφαλὶς βιβλίου· καὶ ἀνείλησεν αὐτὴν ἐνώπιον ἐμοῦ.

καὶ ἔθηκεν τὸν πόδα αὐτοῦ τὸν δεξιὸν ἐπί κτλ.] The Angel's posture denotes both his colossal size and his mission to the world: 'sea and land' is an O.T. formula for the totality of terrestrial things (Exod. xx. 4, 11, Ps. lxviii. (lxix.) 35). Sea and land offer an equally firm foothold to the servants of God (Mc. vi. 48, note; Mt. xiv. 28 ff.); the Angel plants his right foot on the sea, as if to defy its instability. The sea is ever present to the mind of the Seer (v. 13, vii. 1 ff., viii. 8 f., etc.); to the exile in Patmos there must have been a peculiar attraction in the thought of the strong Angel to whom the Aegean was as solid ground.

3. καὶ ἔκραξεν φωνῇ μεγάλῃ κτλ.] Most things in the Apocalypse are on a great scale, and a φωνὴ μεγάλη is common (e.g. i. 10, v. 2, 12, vi. 10, vii. 2, 10, etc.); but the strength of this Angel's voice is emphasized by the added metaphor ὥσπερ λέων μυκᾶται. Μυκᾶσθαι, *mugire*, is used of a low deep sound like the lowing of the ox (Job vi. 5 LXX., and an anonymous translator in 1 Regn. vi. 12), or the growl of

ὥσπερ λέων μυκᾶται. καὶ ὅτε ἔκραξεν, ἐλάλησαν αἱ
ἑπτὰ βρονταὶ τὰς ἑαυτῶν φωνάς. [4]καὶ ὅτε ἐλάλη- 4
σαν αἱ ἑπτὰ βρονταί, ἤμελλον γράφειν· καὶ ἤκουσα
φωνὴν ἐκ τοῦ οὐρανοῦ λέγουσαν Σφράγισον ἃ ἐλά-
λησαν αἱ ἑπτὰ βρονταί, καὶ μὴ αὐτὰ γράψῃς. [5]καὶ 5

3 *αι επτα βρονται*] om *αι* ℵ* 1 4 7 18 arm | *ταις εαυτων φωναις* ℵ 7 *g* syr^gw arm aeth 4 *οτε*] *οσα* ℵ 37 79 *et quae* Prim | *βρονται*]+*τας φωνας εαυτων* vg^cle harl lipss Haym | *ημελλον* ACQ min^nonn] *εμελλον* ℵP min^pl Ar | *ουρανου*] pr *εβδομου* 130 syr^gw | *λεγουσαν*]+*μοι* vg^cle dem me | *α*] *οσα* ℵ | om *επτα* 2° C | *μη αυτα*] *μετα ταυτα* 1 10 12 17 37 49 79 91 96 Andr | *γραψης*] *γραψεις* 7 28 98 *γραφεις* 1 10 17 36 37 49 79 91 96+*αυτα* 130

thunder (Ar. *nub.* 291); cf. Arethas: οὐ προσφυῶς ἐπὶ λέοντος ἡ διὰ τοῦ μυκᾶσθαι φωνή, ἐπὶ βοῶν γὰρ μᾶλλον: the lion's roar is more exactly expressed by ὠρύεσθαι (LXX., 1 Pet. v. 8 ὡς λέων ὠρυόμενος περιπατεῖ) or ἐρεύγεσθαι (Hos. xi. 10, Am. iii. 4), or βρύχειν, βρυχᾶσθαι (Arethas, Phavorinus); but as Theocritus (xxvi. 21) has μύκημα λεαίνης, it is possible that μυκᾶσθαι was so employed in Alexandrian Greek. The word may have been preferred here, to indicate that the voice of the Angel had not only volume, but depth, at once compelling attention and inspiring awe. It was a signal rather than a message. No words were spoken, yet a reply was at once elicited.

ὅτε ἔκραξεν, ἐλάλησαν αἱ ἑπτὰ βρονταί] Αἱ ἑ. βρ., clearly a recognised group, like αἱ ἑπτὰ ἐκκλησίαι, τὰ ἑπτὰ πνεύματα, οἱ ἑπτὰ ἄγγελοι. But whereas other heptads are defined, the Seer does not stop to explain 'the Seven Thunders,' but assumes them to be known. No satisfactory explanation of the article has been given; unless (Züllig) it is to be found in the sevenfold קוֹל יְהוָה of Ps. xxix. which describes a thunderstorm upon the sea. The Thunders uttered their own (ἑαυτῶν) voices, distinct from the Angel's cry, and charged with a message intelligible (ἐλάλησαν) to those who had ears to hear; cf. Ps. xix. 1, and the remarkable parallel in Jo. xii. 28 ἦλθεν οὖν φωνὴ ἐκ τοῦ οὐρανοῦ... ὁ οὖν ὄχλος ὁ ἑστὼς καὶ ἀκούσας ἔλεγεν βροντὴν γεγονέναι· ἄλλοι ἔλεγον Ἄγγελος αὐτῷ λελάληκεν. In λαλεῖν φωνήν the acc. is that of 'content' (Blass, *Gr.* p. 90 f.); cf. xiii. 5 λαλοῦν μεγάλα, Heb. xii. 24 κρεῖττον λαλοῦντι.

4. καὶ ὅτε ἐλάλησαν...ἤμελλον γράφειν] The Seer in his vision seems to be engaged in taking notes of what he sees and hears (i. 11, 19, ii. 1, etc.). He has understood the special (ἑαυτῶν) utterance of the Thunders, and at once takes his papyrus-sheet and dips his reed pen into the inkhorn (2 Jo. 12, 3 Jo. 13), intending to write them down, when a voice from heaven (xiv. 2, 13, xviii. 4) bids him refrain. The form ἤμελλον occurs in Jo. iv. 47, xii. 33, xviii. 32, while on the other hand in Jo. vi. 6, Apoc. iii. 2, the best text has ἔμελλον; see WH.[2] *Notes*, p. 169. Ἐκ τοῦ οὐρανοῦ: Syr.^gw. adds ܕܫܒܝܥܝܐ =τοῦ ἑβδόμου apparently, and this interesting reading is now confirmed by the Athos MS. 130.

σφράγισον...μὴ αὐτὰ γράψῃς. Σφρ. is from Dan. xii. 4 καὶ σύ, Δανιήλ, σφράγισον τὸ βιβλίον ἕως καιροῦ συντελείας (cf. *ib.* viii. 26); but the application of the metaphor to unwritten utterances is a bold innovation. Μὴ αὐτὰ γράψῃς stands in sharp contrast with i. 19 γράψον οὖν ἃ εἶδες; the position of αὐτά is emphatic, cf. xi. 2 μὴ αὐτὴν μετρήσῃς. What the utterances were, or why they were not to be revealed, it is idle to enquire; but compare

ὁ ἄγγελος, ὃν εἶδον ἑστῶτα ἐπὶ τῆς θαλάσσης καὶ
ἐπὶ τῆς γῆς, ἦρεν τὴν χεῖρα αὐτοῦ τὴν δεξιὰν εἰς τὸν
6 οὐρανόν, [6]καὶ ὤμοσεν ἐν τῷ ζῶντι εἰς τοὺς αἰῶνας
τῶν αἰώνων, ὃς ἔκτισεν τὸν οὐρανὸν καὶ τὰ ἐν αὐτῷ
καὶ τὴν γῆν καὶ τὰ ἐν αὐτῇ καὶ τὴν θάλασσαν καὶ
7 τὰ ἐν αὐτῇ, ὅτι χρόνος οὐκέτι ἔσται· [7]ἀλλ᾽ ἐν ταῖς

5 ειδον ℵCP min^{pl} Andr Ar] ιδον AQ 7 14 (130) | om την δεξιαν A 1 36 vg syr^{gw} 6 om εν ℵ*Q min^{35} me | om των αιωνων 1 12 47 arm | om και την γην και τα εν αυτη A 1 12 | om και την θαλ. και τα εν αυτη ℵ* A 30 31 32 38 al syr^{gw} arm Prim | ουκετι εσται] ουκ εστιν ℵ* 40 me ουκ εσται ετι 1 79 *non erit amplius* vg^{cle}

2 Cor. xii. 4 ἤκουσεν ἄρρητα ῥήματα ἃ οὐκ ἐξὸν ἀνθρώπῳ λαλῆσαι. As Arethas says: γράφειν ἤτοι πρόδηλα ποιεῖν ἀνθρώποις—to be forbidden to write was to be forbidden to communicate to the Church what he had heard. The Seer's enforced reticence witnesses to the fragmentary character of even apocalyptic disclosures. The Seer himself received more than he was at liberty to communicate. He was conscious of having passed through experiences which he could not recall or express, and he rightly interpreted his inability to put them on paper as equivalent to a prohibition. Such a revelation was, for all practical purposes, a ῥῆμα ἄρρητον. Cf. Origen *in Joann.* t. xiii. 5: *c. Cels.* vi. 6.

5 f. καὶ ὁ ἄγγελος ὃν εἶδον ἑστῶτα κτλ.] See *v.* 1, notes. The angel now speaks (*v.* 3) and answers the Seven Thunders by a solemn oath. But first he lifts up his hand to heaven, a gesture which in the O.T. accompanies an adjuration; cf. Deut. xxxii. 40 ἀρῶ (אֶשָּׂא) εἰς τὸν οὐρανὸν τὴν χεῖρά μου, καὶ ὀμοῦμαι τὴν δεξιάν μου καὶ ἐρῶ Ζῶ ἐγὼ εἰς τὸν αἰῶνα (see Driver *ad loc.*). Ἐξαίρειν or ἐκτείνειν τὴν χεῖρα is in fact frequently a synonym of ὀμνύναι, see e.g. Gen. xiv. 22, Exod. vi. 8, Num. xiv. 30, Ez. xx. 15, 28. The passage in the Seer's mind is perhaps Dan. xii. 7 ὕψωσεν τὴν δεξιὰν αὐτοῦ καὶ τὴν ἀριστερὰν αὐτοῦ εἰς τὸν οὐρανόν, καὶ ὤμοσεν ἐν τῷ ζῶντι τὸν αἰῶνα. On ὀμνύειν ἐν Arethas remarks: δοκεῖ μὲν ἀνελλήνιστον εἶναι. ὀμνύειν γὰρ λέγεται 'κατά τινος,' οὐκ 'ἔν τινι.' The phrase ὁ ζῶν εἰς τοὺς αἰῶνας τῶν αἰώνων is frequent in the Apocalypse (i. 18, iv. 9 f., xv. 7). Ὃς ἔκτισεν τὸν οὐρανόν κτλ. is another familiar formula (Exod. xx. 11, Ps. cxlv. (cxlvi.) 6, 2 Esdr. ix. 6), which increases the solemnity of the oath by rehearsing the visible proofs of the almighty power of God; cf. Gen. xiv. 22. On ἔκτισεν see Deissmann, *Bible Studies*, p. 284.

ὅτι χρόνος οὐκέτι ἔσται] Ὀμνύειν is followed by (1) the object of the appeal in the acc. (Jac. v. 12) or governed by ἐν (Mt. v. 34, 36, xxiii. 16), εἰς (Mt. v. 35), or κατά (Heb. vi. 13, 16); (2) the contents of the oath, preceded by εἰ (Gen. xiv. 23, Ps. xciv. (xcv.) 11), or recited with or without ὅτι (Ps. cix. (cx.) 4, Mc. vi. 23, xiv. 71). The Angel's words were, Χρόνος οὐκέτι ἔσται: not 'Time shall be no more' (οὐκέτι ἔσται ὁ χρ.), as the ancient commentators for the most part interpret (e.g. Bede: "mutabilis saecularium temporum varietas...cessabit"), but 'there shall no more be any interval of time, any further delay': cf. Hab. ii. 3 (Heb. x. 37), ἐρχόμενος ἥξει καὶ οὐ μὴ χρονίσῃ, and contrast Apoc. vi. 11 ἐρρέθη αὐτοῖς ἵνα ἀναπαύσονται ἔτι χρόνον. There may be an allusion to Dan. xii. 7, which foretells a συντέλεια. But how neces-

ἡμέραις τῆς φωνῆς τοῦ ἑβδόμου ἀγγέλου, ὅταν μέλλῃ
σαλπίζειν, καὶ ἐτελέσθη τὸ μυστήριον τοῦ θεοῦ, ὡς
εὐηγγέλισεν τοὺς ἑαυτοῦ δούλους τοὺς προφήτας.
8 καὶ ἡ φωνὴ ἣν ἤκουσα ἐκ τοῦ οὐρανοῦ, πάλιν λαλοῦ- 8
σαν μετ' ἐμοῦ καὶ λέγουσαν Ὕπαγε λάβε τὸ βιβλίον
τὸ ἠνεῳγμένον ἐν τῇ χειρὶ τοῦ ἀγγέλου τοῦ ἑστῶτος

7 om της φωνης syr^{gw} | μελλει 7 28 30 31 35 36 51 79 87 91 98 | om και 10 17* 37 49 91 94 96 vg$^{cle\ fu\ dem\ tol}$ me arm Ar Prim Haym | ετελεσθη ℵACP min$^{fere\ 40}$ me syrr] τελεσθη (Q)˙ 1 (7) 28 36 48 79 91 96 τελεσθησεται Ar? *consummabitur* vg *finietur* Prim | ως] ο 10 28 37 49 79 91 96 syr^{gw} 130 | ευηγγελισατο 10 12 17 19 26 28 37 49 79 91 96 | τοις εαυτου δουλοις τοις προφηταις 1 28 79 97 Ar *per servos suos prophetas* vg (Prim) | τους προφητας] pr και ℵ 8 και η φωνη ην ηκουσα] και ηκουσα φωνην 7 vg^{cle} syr^{gw} | και η φωνη...λαλουσαν] και την φωνην ηκουσα παλιν του λαλουντος μετ εμου εκ τ. ουρ. λεγουσαν 130 | λαλουσα...λεγουσα 1 al^{pl} Ar | βιβλιον AC 6 14] βιβλαριδιον ℵP 1 al$^{vix\ mu}$ βιβλιδαριον Q min$^{fere\ 40}$ Ar | ανεωγμενον Q min$^{plq\ 30}$ Ar | εν τη χειρι] εκ χειρος 36 *de manu* vg Prim om C

sary so solemn an assurance became towards the end of the Apostolic age, when the early hopes of an immediate παρουσία had been dispersed, is clear from such a passage as 2 Pet. iii. 3 ff. ἐλεύσονται ἐπ' ἐσχάτων τῶν ἡμερῶν ἐμπαῖκται λέγοντες Ποῦ ἐστιν ἡ ἐπαγγελία τῆς παρουσίας αὐτοῦ; cf. Lc. xii. 45 ἐὰν δὲ εἴπῃ ὁ δοῦλος...Χρονίζει ὁ κύριός μου ἔρχεσθαι, κτλ.

7. ἀλλ' ἐν ταῖς ἡμέραις...τοῦ ἑβδόμου ἀγγέλου κτλ.] 'But, so far from further delays supervening, as soon as the days of the Seventh Trumpet have come, at the moment when the Seventh Angel is about to blow, then (for καί in apodosis, cf. WM. p. 546 f.) the Secret of God is finished.' The clause as a whole corrects the impression that χρόνος οὐκέτι ἔσται implies an immediate end. It will come in 'days' which though future are so distinctly present to the mind of the speaker that he writes ἐτελέσθη rather than τελεσθήσεται (the aor. of anticipation, WM. p. 346 f., cf. Burton, § 50).

Τὸ μυστήριον τοῦ θεοῦ: cf. the Synoptic phrase τὸ μ. τῆς βασιλείας τ. θ. (Mc. iv. 11, note), and St Paul's τὸ μ. τ. θ. (1 Cor. ii. 1, Col. ii. 2), or τοῦ χριστοῦ (Col. iv. 3). The mystery of which mention is made here is perhaps wider than these, including the whole purpose of God in the evolution of human history. The whole is now at length complete; with ἐτελέσθη cf. xv. 1 ἐτελέσθη ὁ θυμὸς τοῦ θεοῦ, xvii. 17 ἄχρι τελεσθήσονται οἱ λόγοι τοῦ θεοῦ. That a final and joyous clearing up of the problems of life should find a place in the last days was the Gospel of the prophets both Jewish and Christian (ὡς εὐηγγέλισεν [ὁ θεὸς] τοὺς ἑαυτοῦ δούλους τοὺς προφήτας). For the phrase 'His servants the prophets' see Am. iii. 7, Jer. vii. 25, xxv. 4, Apoc. i. 1, 3, xi. 18. The rare active εὐαγγελίζειν occurs also in 1 Regn. xxxi. 9, 2 Regn. xviii. 19, Apoc. xiv. 6; εὐαγγελίζεσθαί τινα is frequent in St Luke, and is found also in Gal. i. 9, 1 Pet. i. 12, but the usual construction is εὐαγγ. [εὐαγγέλιόν] τινι (Blass, *Gr.* p. 89 f.).

8. καὶ ἡ φωνὴ ἣν ἤκουσα κτλ.] Another example of mixed construction: normally, the sentence would run either ἡ φωνὴ ἣν ἤκουσα...πάλιν ἐλάλει...καὶ ἔλεγεν or τὴν φωνὴν τὴν ἐκ τοῦ οὐρανοῦ πάλιν ἤκουσα λαλοῦσαν κτλ. (cf. *app. crit.*). The sense is clear; the same heavenly voice, which had bidden

9 ἐπὶ τῆς θαλάσσης καὶ ἐπὶ τῆς γῆς. [9]καὶ ἀπῆλθα
πρὸς τὸν ἄγγελον, λέγων αὐτῷ δοῦναί μοι τὸ βιβλα-
ρίδιον. καὶ λέγει μοι Λάβε καὶ κατάφαγε αὐτό, καὶ
πικρανεῖ σου τὴν κοιλίαν, ἀλλ' ἐν τῷ στόματί σου
10 ἔσται γλυκὺ ὡς μέλι. [10]καὶ ἔλαβον τὸ βιβλαρίδιον
ἐκ τῆς χειρὸς τοῦ ἀγγέλου καὶ κατέφαγον αὐτό, καὶ
¶ C ἦν ἐν τῷ στόματί μου ὡς μέλι γλυκύ· καὶ ὅτε¶ ἔφα-

9 om *και απηλθα...λαβε* syr[gw] | *απηλθα* A] *απηλθον* ℵCPQ min[pl] Andr Ar | *δουναι*] *δος* P 1 28 36 38 49 51 79 91 96 me | *βιβλαριδιον* A[corr] CP 1 min[pl]] *βιβλαριον* A* *βιβλιδαριον* Q min[40] Ar *βιβλιον* ℵ 11 al[vid] | *κοιλιαν*] *καρδιαν* A | om *γλυκυ* syr[gw] 10 *βιβλαριδιον* ACP 1 al] *βιβλιον* ℵQ min[fere 30] Ar *βιβλιδαριον* 8 10 14 17 28 al | *ως μελι γλυκυ* ℵCP min[pl] vg syr] *γλυκυ ως μ.* AQ me om *γλυκυ* syr[gw] arm om *ως μελι* aeth

the Seer not to write the utterance of the Seven Thunders (*v.* 4), now bids him take the roll that lay open in the Angel's hand (*v.* 2). Cf. iv. 1, note.

9. *καὶ ἀπῆλθα πρὸς τὸν ἄγγελον κτλ.*] The Seer in his rapture quits his position at the door of heaven (iv. 1), and places himself before the great Angel whose feet rest on sea and land. On *ἀπῆλθα* see WH.[2], *Notes*, p. 171, W. Schm. p. 111. *Λέγων αὐτῷ δοῦναι* 'telling (bidding) him to give'; cf. Acts xxi. 21 *λέγων μὴ περιτέμνειν αὐτοὺς τὰ τέκνα.* The Angel does not give the book, but invites the Seer to take it, and thus to shew at once his fitness for the task before him (cf. v. 2 ff.), and his readiness to undertake it. The book did not need to be opened, like that which the Lamb had taken out of the Hand of God, nor were its contents to be read or published; it was to be consumed by the Seer (on *καταφαγεῖν* see Mc. iv. 4, note) i.e. taken in and digested mentally; cf. Primasius: "id est in secretis recondi visceribus," and Arethas: *καταφαγεῖν, τουτέστιν, ἐν πείρᾳ τοῦ πράγματος γενέσθαι.* There is a clear reference to Ez. iii. 1, 3 *καὶ εἶπεν πρὸς μέ Υἱὲ ἀνθρώπου, κατάφαγε τὴν κεφαλίδα ταύτην...ἡ κοιλία σου πλησθήσεται τῆς κεφαλίδος ταύτης τῆς δεδομένης εἰς σέ. καὶ ἔφαγον αὐτήν, καὶ ἐγένετο ἐν τῷ στόματί μου ὡς μέλι γλυκάζον.* The Seer adds: *καὶ πικρανεῖ σου τὴν κοιλίαν*, and (v. 10) *ἐπικράνθη ἡ κοιλία μου.* The sweetness of the roll reminds the reader of Ps. xviii. (xix.) 10, 11 *τὰ κρίματα Κυρίου ... γλυκύτερα ὑπὲρ μέλι καὶ κηρίον*, cxviii. (cxix.) 103 *ὡς γλυκέα τῷ λάρυγγί μου τὰ λόγιά σου, ὑπὲρ μέλι καὶ κ. τῷ στόματί μου.* The beauty of the revelation, the joy of insight and foresight which it afforded, the promise it held of greater joys to come, are well expressed by this metaphor: cf. Jer. xv. 16 *ἔσται ὁ λόγος σου ἐμοὶ εἰς εὐφροσύνην καὶ χαρὰν καρδίας μου.* But when the message has been digested, it has other and opposite effects—*πικρανεῖ σου τὴν κοιλίαν* (for this use of *κοιλία* cf. Jo. vii. 38 *ποταμοὶ ἐκ τῆς κοιλίας αὐτοῦ ῥεύσονται*). Every revelation of God's purposes, even though a mere fragment, a *βιβλαρίδιον*, is 'bitter-sweet,' disclosing judgement as well as mercy. The Seer, if he would be admitted into a part of God's secret, must be prepared for very mixed sensations; the first joy of fuller knowledge would be followed by sorrows deeper and more bitter than those of ordinary men. Cf. Orig. *philoc.* v. 6.

10. *καὶ ἔλαβον τὸ βιβλαρίδιον...καὶ κατέφαγον κτλ.*] The Seer obeys, and the result is as the Angel had said. There is however an instructive change of order: the Angel's words are *πικρα-*

γον αὐτό, ἐπικράνθη ἡ κοιλία μου. [11]καὶ λέγουσίν 11
μοι Δεῖ σε πάλιν προφητεῦσαι ἐπὶ λαοῖς καὶ ἔθνεσιν
καὶ γλώσσαις καὶ βασιλεῦσιν πολλοῖς. [1]καὶ ἐδόθη 1 XI.

10 επικρανθη] εγεμισθη ℵ 130 Prim | μου 2°]+πικριας ℵ$^{c.a}$ 130   11 λεγουσιν ℵAQ min^{30} vg$^{am* harl}$ Ar] λεγει P 1 7 28 31 38 47 49 51 79 91 96 130 vg$^{cleam** fu}$ me syrr arm aeth Prim | εθνεσιν] pr επι Q min^{plq30} syr Prim Ar

νεῖ σου τὴν κοιλίαν ἀλλ' ἐν τῷ στόματί σου ἔσται γλυκύ; the Seer relating his experience naturally places first the sensation which was first in order of time. The remarkable variant ἐγεμίσθη for ἐπικράνθη is best explained as the first word of a gloss ἐγεμίσθη πικρίας, accidentally transferred into the text from the margin or from a position over ἐπικράνθη; the gloss itself may have been suggested by Job xxxii. 19. Cf. *app. crit.*

11. καὶ λέγουσίν μοι Δεῖ σε πάλιν προφητεῦσαι κτλ.] Λέγουσιν is the plural of indefinite statement, nearly equivalent to ἐρρέθη; whether the words come from the heavenly voice (*vv.* 4, 8), or from the Angel (*v.* 9), or from some unknown source, is not obvious or material. Δεῖ σε κτλ. recalls the commission given to the prophets of Israel, especially to Jeremiah (i. 10 ἰδοὺ καθέστακά σε σήμερον ἐπὶ ἔθνη καὶ βασιλείας, ἐκριζοῦν καὶ κατασκάπτειν καὶ ἀπολλύειν καὶ ἀνοικοδομεῖν καὶ καταφυτεύειν) and Ezekiel (iv. 7 προφητεύσεις ἐπ' αὐτήν (*i.q.* Ἰερουσαλήμ), vi. 2, xi. 4 *et passim*). The Seer of the Apocalypse, full of the bitterness of the roll which he has devoured, is now bound (δεῖ) to prophesy again. After the Seventh Trumpet a second προφητεία will begin in which the destinies of nations and their rulers will be yet more fully revealed. The Seer is not sent to prophesy in their presence (ἐπί with gen., cf. Mc. xiii. 9 ἐπὶ ἡγεμόνων καὶ βασιλέων σταθήσεσθε), nor against them (ἐπί with acc., see Ez. *l. c.*), but simply with a view to their several cases (ἐπὶ λαοῖς κτλ.). Πολλοῖς emphasizes the greatness of the field. It is no one Empire or Emperor that is concerned in the prophecies of the second half of the Apocalypse; not merely Rome or Nero or Domitian, but a multitude of races kingdoms and crowned heads.

XI. 1—14. PREPARATION FOR THE SEVENTH TRUMPET. (2) MEASURING THE TEMPLE. THE HOLY CITY AND THE TWO WITNESSES.

1. καὶ ἐδόθη μοι κάλαμος κτλ.] The Seer is no longer a mere witness; the new inspiration imparted by the roll (x. 11) prompts him to take his place among the actors in the great drama. His part is to measure the Sanctuary, and for this end a reed is put into his hands. The conception is from Ezek. xl. 3, 6 ἰδοὺ ἀνήρ...καὶ ἐν τῇ χειρὶ αὐτοῦ ἦν σπαρτίον οἰκοδόμων καὶ κάλαμος μέτρον...καὶ διεμέτρησεν τὸ αἰλὰμ τῆς πύλης ἴσον τῷ καλάμῳ: cf. Zech. ii. 1 (5) ff.: ἰδοὺ ἀνὴρ καὶ ἐν τῇ χειρὶ αὐτοῦ σχοινίον γεωμετρικόν· καὶ εἶπα πρὸς αὐτόν Ποῦ σὺ πορεύῃ; καὶ εἶπεν πρὸς μέ Διαμετρῆσαι τὴν Ἰερουσαλήμ. Apoc. xxi. 15 καὶ ὁ λαλῶν μετ' ἐμοῦ εἶχεν μέτρον κάλαμον χρυσοῦν, ἵνα μετρήσῃ τὴν πόλιν. The κάλαμος (Ezekiel's קְנֵה הַמִּדָּה) is perhaps a cane of the *Arundo donax* which (Hastings iv. p. 212) grows in 'immense brakes' along the Jordan valley (cf. Mt. xi. 7), and often reaches the height of 15 or 20 feet. Such a reed would be in strength and straightness ὅμοιος ῥάβδῳ (Mc. vi. 8), but far longer and therefore better fitted to take the measurements of a great building. Ezekiel's reed was of six

μοι κάλαμος ὅμοιος ῥάβδῳ, λέγων Ἔγειρε καὶ μέτρη-
σον τὸν ναὸν τοῦ θεοῦ καὶ τὸ θυσιαστήριον καὶ τοὺς
2 προσκυνοῦντας ἐν αὐτῷ. [2]καὶ τὴν αὐλὴν τὴν ἔξωθεν
τοῦ ναοῦ ἔκβαλε ἔξωθεν καὶ μὴ αὐτὴν μετρήσῃς, ὅτι

XI 1 λεγων] pr και ειστηκει ο αγγελος א^{c.c*} Q 10 14 34 35 (36) 37 49 87 91 92 96 130 syr* syr^{gw} Vict | εγειραι 1 al^{plq20} Ar 2 εξωθεν 1°] εσωθεν א 1 12 35 80 87 syr^{gw} Vict | ναου] λαου א* | εκβαλε] pr και א* εκει βαλε 130 | εξωθεν 2°] εξω Q min^{pl} Ar εσω א* εσωθεν P

cubits, i.e. about 9 feet (xl. 5, see A. B. Davidson *ad loc.*).

λέγων Ἔγειρε καὶ μέτρησον κτλ.] On ἔγειρε intrans. see Mc. ii. 11, note. There is no need to ask with Andreas πῶς γὰρ ὁ κάλαμος ἄψυχος ὢν ἔλεγεν; or with Bp Chr. Wordsworth to understand by the reed the Canon of Holy Scripture regarded as the measure of human life. The speaker is the person who gave the reed, and whose presence is implied in ἐδόθη. A heavenly sanctuary has been mentioned in iii. 12, vii. 15; cf. xi. 19 ὁ ναὸς τοῦ θεοῦ ὁ ἐν οὐρανῷ. But the sanctuary which is now to be measured is evidently on earth (cf. *v.* 2), and its form is suggested by the Temple of Jerusalem; it has an 'outer court' and is in 'the Holy City.' At Jerusalem the Altar of Burnt-offering, which is probably meant by τὸ θυσιαστήριον, was in the Court of the Priests, while the worshippers filled the Court of the Israelites and the Court of the Women, so that the ναός here must be taken to include the ἱερόν, with the exception of the Court of the Gentiles. The Seer however has in view not the material Sanctuary, but the spiritual building of the Church; cf. 1 Cor. iii. 16 f., 2 Cor. vi. 16, Eph. ii. 21, 2 Thess. ii. 4. The measuring of the Sanctuary provides for its preservation from the general overthrow, and thus corresponds with the sealing of the 144,000, which preceded the seventh seal-opening as the measuring precedes the seventh trumpet-blast. Μέτρησον...τοὺς προσκυνοῦντας involves a *zeugma*; some such verb as καταρίθμησον must be mentally supplied (WM. p. 777).

2. καὶ τὴν αὐλὴν τὴν ἔξωθεν τοῦ ναοῦ ἔκβαλε κτλ.] The outer court is passed over and left to its fate. Solomon's Temple had two courts (3 Regn. vi. 34 (36) τὴν αὐλὴν τὴν ἐσωτάτην, Ezek. x. 5 ἕως τῆς αὐλῆς τῆς ἐξωτέρας; but see Hastings, iv. 702), and so had Ezekiel's (Ezek. xl. 17, 20); but in Herod's Temple the inner court was divided into three spaces, from the last of which the outer court was parted by a barrier (τὸ μεσότοιχον τοῦ φραγμοῦ, Eph. ii. 15, where see Dean Robinson's note) which might not be passed by a Gentile. The outer court was "given to the Gentiles" as an οἶκος προσευχῆς (Mc. xi. 17), and the Lord taught that its sanctity was not impaired by their admission; it was a true part of the ἱερόν. Now, however, the Seer is directed to 'cast it out' (ἔξωθεν = ἔξω, as in *c.* xiv. 20; cf. Blass, *Gr.* p. 59), i.e. to exclude it from the ναός, though the other courts are included. It is to be "given to the Gentiles" in another sense, to be profaned and, with the rest of the Holy City, trodden under foot. If the ναός represents the Church, the outer court is perhaps the rejected Synagogue; as in ii. 9, iii. 9, the tables are turned, and while the Church fills the court of Israelites and worships at the Altar of the Cross (Heb. xiii. 10), Israel after the flesh is cast out (Mt. viii. 12 οἱ δὲ υἱοὶ τῆς βασιλείας ἐκβληθήσονται) and delivered to the heathen. This interpretation of the outer court seems to have been in the mind of Andreas, though he obscures it by in-

*ἐδόθη τοῖς ἔθνεσιν, καὶ τὴν πόλιν τὴν ἁγίαν πατή-
σουσιν μῆνας τεσσεράκοντα [καὶ] δύο.* [3]*καὶ δώσω* 3
*τοῖς δυσὶν μάρτυσίν μου, καὶ προφητεύσουσιν ἡμέρας
§χιλίας διακοσίας ἑξήκοντα περιβεβλημένοι σάκκους.* § C

2 *τοις εθνεσιν*] pr *και* ℵ* | *πατησουσιν*] *μετρησουσιν* A | *τεσσαρακοντα* P min^pl | *και δυο* AQ 30 al] om *και* ℵP min^pl vg^cle am dem Prim 3 *και προφητευσουσιν*] *ινα προφητευσουσιν* syr^gw vid | *εξηκοντα*] + *πεντε* ℵ^c.c* (14) | *περιβεβλημενοι* ℵ^c.a C 1 min^pl vg syr^gw rell Vict Prim Andr Ar] *περιβεβλημενους* ℵ*APQ 4 7 28 48 79 96

cluding the pagan world: *ἡμεῖς δὲ νομίζομεν ναὸν θεὸν τὴν ἐκκλησίαν προσαγορεύεσθαι...αὐλὴν δὲ τὴν ἐξωτέραν τὴν τῶν ἀπίστων ἐθνῶν καὶ Ἰουδαίων συναγωγήν.*

καὶ τὴν πόλιν τὴν ἁγίαν πατήσουσιν κτλ.] A reminiscence of Zech. xii. 3 *καὶ ἔσται ἐν τῇ ἡμέρᾳ ἐκείνῃ θήσομαι τὴν Ἰερουσαλὴμ λίθον καταπατούμενον πᾶσιν τοῖς ἔθνεσιν.* Dan. viii. 13 Th. *ἕως πότε ...τὸ ἅγιον καὶ ἡ δύναμις συνπατηθήσεται;* Isa. lxiii. 18 (Aq.) *ὑπεναντίοι ἡμῶν κατεπάτησαν τὸ ἁγίασμά σου.* See also Ps. lxxix. 1, Ps. Sol. vii. 2, xvii. 25, 1 Macc. iii. 45, 51. There is a yet nearer parallel in Lc. xxi. 22 *Ἰερουσαλὴμ ἔσται πατουμένη ὑπὸ ἐθνῶν ἄχρις οὗ πληρωθῶσιν καιροὶ ἐθνῶν. Τὴν πόλιν τὴν ἁγίαν* comes perhaps from Dan. ix. 24 Th. (עִיר קָדְשֶׁךָ), but the phrase occurs also in 2 Esdr. xxi. 1, Isa. xlviii. 2, lii. 1, Mt. iv. 5, xxvii. 53. In Apoc. xxi. 2, xxii. 19 it is applied to the ideal City of God, but here, as the context shews, it stands for the Jewish polity, as the outer court of the Temple for the Jewish faith and worship.

μῆνας τεσσεράκοντα καὶ δύο] This limit of time is derived from Dan. vii. 25 Th., xii. 7 *ἕως καιροῦ καὶ καιρῶν καί γε ἥμισυ καιροῦ*, i.e. $3\frac{1}{2}$ years or 42 months, the duration of the sufferings of the Jews under Antiochus, whether we reckon from June 168 to Dec. 165, or from Dec. 168 to the middle of 164; see Driver *ad loc.* The same limit is given under various terms in Apoc. xi. 3, xii. 6 (1260 days), xii. 14 ("a time and times and half a time," as in Daniel), xi. 2, xiii. 5 (42 months). By comparing these passages with the present context we get the equation: the duration of the triumph of the Gentiles = the duration of the prophesying of the Two Witnesses, = the duration of the Woman's sojourn in the wilderness. The time-limit serves of course no further purpose than to synchronize the several periods, and to compare them with the greatest crisis through which the Jewish people passed between the Exile and the Fall of Jerusalem. In this place it suggests that as the Syrian domination yielded at last to the faith and courage of the Maccabees, so when the appointed time has come the Jewish people may be emancipated from Gentile oppression, and restored to the unity of the people of God. The words have a special interest in view of the recrudescence of Anti-Semitism.

3. *καὶ δώσω τοῖς δυσὶν μάρτυσίν μου κτλ.*] The Speaker is Christ (cf. ii. 13, xxi. 6) or His Angel-representative (xxii. 7, 12 ff.). *Δώσω ...καὶ προφητεύσουσιν = δώσω αὐτοῖς προφητεύειν* or *ἵνα προφητεύσωσιν* (Delitzsch, וְנָתַתִּי...וְנִבְּאוּ). Neither Moses and Elijah, nor Elijah and Elisha, nor Enoch and Elijah (Tert. *anim.* 50, Hipp., ed. Lag., p. 21; see Arethas, *ad loc.* *λόγος δὲ φέρεται ἐκ παραδόσεως φοιτῶν τῇ ἐκκλησίᾳ ἀπαρατρέπτως καὶ αὐτὸν* [sc. *τὸν Ἐνώχ*] *ἥξειν μετὰ Ἠλίου τοῦ Θεσβίτου*, and Thilo, *cod. apocr. N.T.*, p. 765 ff.; cf. Bousset, *Der Antichrist*, p. 134 ff.) can be intended by the two witnesses who prophesy through the whole period of Gentile domination, though, as the sequel shews (*vv.* 5, 6), the first pair at least

4 [4]οὗτοί εἰσιν αἱ δύο ἐλαῖαι καὶ αἱ δύο λυχνίαι αἱ
5 ἐνώπιον τοῦ κυρίου τῆς γῆς ἑστῶτες. [5]καὶ εἴ τις

4 ελαιαι] αυλαιαι A (αλαιαι C) | αι ενωπιον] om αι ℵ* 6 7 14 31 32 34 35 47 48 87 92 95 Ar | του κυριου] του θεου 1 28 36 79 al[vid] arm | της γης] pr πασης syr[gw] | εστωτες] εστωσαι ℵ[c.c] P 1 7 28 29 36 38 47 49 79 91 95 130 al[vid] Hipp

are in the mind of the writer, suggested doubtless by Mal. iv. 4, 6, and by the vision of the Transfiguration (Mc. ix. 4). Nor again can such allegorical interpretations as the Law and the Prophets, the Law and the Gospel, the Old Testament and the New, be maintained in view of all that follows. Rather the witnesses represent the Church in her function of witness-bearing (Acts i. 8 ἔσεσθέ μου μάρτυρες ...ἕως ἐσχάτου τῆς γῆς), and her testimony is symbolized by *two* witnesses, partly in reference to the well-known law of Deut. xix. 15 (ἐπὶ στόματος δύο μαρτύρων...στήσεται πᾶν ῥῆμα, cf. Jo. viii. 17 ἐν τῷ νόμῳ δὲ τῷ ὑμετέρῳ γέγραπται ὅτι δύο ἀνθρώπων ἡ μαρτυρία ἀληθής ἐστιν), partly in order to correspond with the imagery of Zechariah iv. 2 ff., about to be cited; or, as Primasius says, they may represent the Church in both stages of her career, "ecclesia duobus testamentis praedicans et prophetans." The witness of the Church, borne by her martyrs and confessors, her saints and doctors, and by the words and lives of all in whom Christ lives and speaks, is one continual prophecy (cf. xix. 10 ἡ γὰρ μαρτυρία τοῦ Ἰησοῦ ἐστιν τὸ πνεῦμα τῆς προφητείας) lasting throughout the 1260 days of the triumph of heathendom. Her witnesses are clad in sackcloth (for the construction see x. 1), a reference perhaps to the rough costume worn by ancient prophets; cf. 4 Regn. i. 8 ζώνην δερματίνην περιεζωσμένος, Zech. xiii. 4 ἐνδύσονται δέρριν τριχίνην, Isa. xx. 2 ἄφελε τὸν σάκκον ἀπὸ τῆς ὀσφύος σου, and see Mc. i. 6, note. But περιβεβλ. σάκκους has a special appropriateness in its present connexion, for the attitude of the Church during the prevalence of paganism was penitential and not triumphant; cf. Jonah iii. 6, 8 περιεβάλοντο σάκκους οἱ ἄνθρωποι, Mt. xi. 21 πάλαι ἂν ἐν σάκκῳ ...μετενόησαν. Cf. Bede: "*saccis amicti*, id est in exomologesi constituti." On the readings περιβεβλημένος, περιβεβλημένους, see WH²., *Notes*, p. 138.

4. οὗτοί εἰσιν αἱ δύο ἐλαῖαι κτλ.] After Zech. iv. 2 f., 14 ἰδοὺ λυχνία χρυσῆ ὅλη ...καὶ δύο ἐλαῖαι ἐπάνω αὐτῆς...οὗτοι οἱ δύο υἱοὶ τῆς πιότητος παρεστήκασιν Κυρίῳ πάσης τῆς γῆς. In Zechariah the λυχνία is Israel, and the two olive trees which feed it are either the priesthood and the royal house, represented by Joshua and Zerubbabel, or, as some suppose, certain heavenly ministries through which the Spirit was poured upon the nation. The Apocalyptist adopts so much of this as lends itself to his purpose. He has already likened the seven Churches to λυχνίαι (i. 12, 20); from another point of view the whole Church is a single λυχνία, fed by those of its members who are specially set apart to be Christ's witnesses. These, if faithful, carry with them the oil of the Spirit, which keeps alive the light of life (cf. Mt. xxv. 4, Rom. xi. 17). They stand before the Lord of the earth, living in His Presence, and ministering to Him by their confession of His Christ.

Αἱ...ἑστῶτες: in ἑστ. the thought of the writer goes back to οὗτοι, i.e. οἱ δύο μάρτυρες, and, full of his great conception, he is indifferent to the demands of grammar.

5. καὶ εἴ τις θελήσῃ αὐτοὺς ἀδικῆσαι κτλ.] To kill God's witnesses is impossible, so long as their witness is unfulfilled; those who attempt it bring destruction upon themselves. There

αὐτοὺς θέλει ἀδικῆσαι, πῦρ ἐκπορεύεται ἐκ τοῦ στό-
ματος αὐτῶν καὶ κατεσθίει τοὺς ἐχθροὺς αὐτῶν· καὶ
εἴ τις θελήσῃ αὐτοὺς ἀδικῆσαι, οὕτως δεῖ αὐτὸν ἀπο-
κτανθῆναι. [6]οὗτοι ἔχουσιν τὴν ἐξουσίαν κλεῖσαι τὸν 6
οὐρανόν, ἵνα μὴ ὑετὸς βρέχῃ τὰς ἡμέρας τῆς προφη-
τείας αὐτῶν, καὶ ἐξουσίαν ἔχουσιν ἐπὶ τῶν ὑδάτων

5 *θελει*] *θελη* 7 *θελησει* Hipp *voluerit* vg *vellet* Prim | *θελησῃ* ℵA] *θελησει* Hipp *θελει* CPQ min^{pl} syrr Andr Ar | *αδικησαι* 2°] *αποκτειναι* 28 36 37 43 79 | om *ουτως* A 6 *την εξουσιαν* ACP] om *την* ℵQ min$^{omn\ vid}$ Hipp Andr Ar | om *υετος* ut vid vg anon^{aug} | *τας ημερας*] *εν* (*ταις*) *ημεραις* 1 36^{vid} syr^{gw} (*in*) *diebus* vg^{fu} Prim anon^{aug}

is an allusion to Elijah's treatment of Ahaziah's messengers (2 Kings i. 10 ff. cf. Lc. ix. 54), but as usual the details are modified; the fire comes not from heaven but out of the mouths of the witnesses (cf. i. 16, ii. 16, ix. 17), i.e. the witnesses slay their enemies by the fire of the word which they utter; cf. Jer. v. 14 *δέδωκα τοὺς λόγους μου εἰς τὸ στόμα σου πῦρ καὶ τὸν λαὸν τοῦτον ξύλα, καὶ καταφάγεται αὐτούς.* Sir. xlviii. 1 *καὶ ἀνέστη Ἠλίας προφήτης ὡς πῦρ, καὶ ὁ λόγος αὐτοῦ ὡς λαμπὰς ἐκαίετο.* Victorinus rightly: "ignem...potestatem verbi dicit." Bede thinks of the Christian revenge inculcated in Rom. xii. 20 (*ἄνθρακας πυρὸς σωρεύσεις ἐπὶ τὴν κεφαλὴν αὐτοῦ*).

For *εἴ τις θελήσῃ* see WM. p. 368; Blass, *Gr.* p. 216; other exx. of *εἰ* with the subj. may be found in Lc. ix. 13, 1 Cor. xiv. 5. If *θελήσῃ* differs in meaning from *θέλει* (see *app. crit.*) the former must be held to state a hypothetical case, whilst the latter posits the *θέλησις* as a fact. For *θέλειν* 'to be minded' see the interesting parallel in Lc. xiii. 31 *Ἡρῴδης θέλει σε ἀποκτεῖναι. Οὕτως* (sc. *τῷ πυρὶ*) *δεῖ ἀποκτανθῆναι*, 'he is destined to be slain in this manner'; cf. xiii. 10 *δεῖ αὐτὸν ἐν μαχαίρῃ ἀποκτανθῆναι.* On *ἀδικεῖν* see ii. 11, note.

6. *οὗτοι ἔχουσιν τὴν ἐξουσίαν κτλ.*] Another reference to Elijah, the representative of O. T. prophecy. In 1 Kings xvii. 1 the drought proclaimed by Elijah is for 'these years' (הַשָּׁנִים הָאֵלֶּה, LXX. *τὰ ἔτη ταῦτα*), i.e. for an indefinite term of years beginning with the date of the prophecy. According to Menander, cited by Josephus (*antt.* viii. 13. 2) the period was actually one full year; see Burney *ad loc.* But a tradition adopted in Lc. iv. 25 (*ἐκλείσθη ὁ οὐρανὸς ἔτη τρία καὶ μῆνας ἕξ*) and Jac. v. 17 (*οὐκ ἔβρεξεν ἐπὶ τῆς γῆς ἐνιαυτοὺς τρεῖς καὶ μῆνας ἕξ*), made the length of the great drought correspond with that of the Syrian domination; and this agrees with the Apocalyptist's scheme of things, for according to *v.* 3 the days of the witnesses' prophesying are 1260, i.e. $3\frac{1}{2}$ years. *Τὴν ἐξουσίαν*, the power exercised by Elijah and now revived in the case of the two witnesses. *Κλείειν τὸν οὐρανόν* occurs elsewhere in this connexion only in Lc. *l.c.* *Ὑετὸς βρέχει* is unusual; the customary phrase is *ὁ θεὸς βρέχει ὑετόν* (Joel ii. 23), *ὁ θεὸς βρέχει* (Gen. ii. 5, Mt. v. 45), or simply *βρέχει* (Jac. *l.c.*). *Προφητεία* is here the execution of the prophetic office, as in 2 Esdr. vi. 13 *ἐν προφητείᾳ Ἀγγαίου τοῦ προφήτου καὶ Ζαχαρίου*; more usually the noun denotes either the gift of prophecy (1 Cor. xii. 10), or a particular prophecy or collection of prophecies (Apoc. i. 3, xxii. 7 ff.).

καὶ ἐξουσίαν ἔχουσιν ἐπὶ τῶν ὑδάτων] Reference is now made to Moses, the other prototype of the Church's witnesses. Like Moses in Egypt, they

στρέφειν αὐτὰ εἰς αἷμα καὶ πατάξαι τὴν γῆν ἐν
7 πάσῃ πληγῇ ὁσάκις ἐὰν θελήσωσιν. ⁷καὶ ὅταν
τελέσωσιν τὴν μαρτυρίαν αὐτῶν, τὸ θηρίον τὸ ἀνα-
βαῖνον ἐκ τῆς ἀβύσσου ποιήσει μετ' αὐτῶν πόλεμον

6 εν παση πληγη] om εν Q min[pauc vid] vg | εαν] αν C 38 130 | θελησουσιν C θελωσιν 14 36 97 7 το θηριον] + το τεταρτον A | αβυσσου] θαλασσης syr[gw]

can inflict plagues. The first of the Egyptian plagues has been already introduced into the scenery of the Third Trumpet (viii. 8), but less precisely; here *στρέφειν αὐτὰ* (sc. *τὰ ὕδατα*) *εἰς αἷμα* answers to Exod. vii. 20 וַיֵּהָפְכוּ כָּל־הַמַּיִם...לְדָם, cf. Ps. civ. (cv.) 29 *μετέστρεψεν τὰ ὕδατα αὐτῶν εἰς αἷμα.* Πατάξαι...ἐν πάσῃ πληγῇ comes from 1 Regn. iv. 8, where the Philistines exclaim, Οὗτοι οἱ θεοὶ οἱ πατάξαντες τὴν Αἴγυπτον ἐν πάσῃ πληγῇ. Ὁσάκις ἐὰν θελήσωσιν carries the power given to the Church far beyond that exercised by Moses, who received an express command before he inflicted a plague. The *ἐξουσία* committed to the witnesses of Christ has no bounds but those which are imposed by their own faith; cf. Mc. xi. 23, note; Jo. xv. 7 *ἐὰν μείνητε ἐν ἐμοὶ...ὃ ἐὰν θέλητε αἰτήσασθε καὶ γενήσεται ὑμῖν.* The general sense of the verse is well given in Jac. v. 17 *πολὺ ἰσχύει δέησις δικαίου ἐνεργουμένη.*

7. **καὶ ὅταν τελέσωσιν τὴν μαρτυρίαν αὐτῶν κτλ.**] The witnesses are immortal for so long a time only as their allotted term of office lasts; when they have delivered their message, their immunity from danger ceases, and they are at the mercy of their enemies. These are represented by *τὸ θηρίον τὸ ἀναβαῖνον ἐκ τῆς ἀβύσσου.* Of the Abyss we have heard in *c.* ix. 1 ff., but hitherto no mention has been made of a Wild Beast: there have been *ζῷα*, but there has been no *θηρίον*, nor is there any further reference to one until we reach *c.* xiii. 1. Yet the article (*τὸ θ.*) assumes that this Wild Beast which comes up from the Abyss is a figure already familiar to the reader. Perhaps it points back to Dan. vii. 3 Th. *τέσσερα θηρία μεγάλα ἀνέβαινεν ἐκ τῆς θαλάσσης*, the Apocalyptist mentally merging the four in one, or fixing his attention on the fourth (*ib.* 7 f., 20 f.), while for the sea he substitutes the Abyss (cf. Deut. xxx. 13 with Rom. x. 7, and the note on *c.* ix. 1). In Daniel the *θηρία* are earthly kingdoms or empires (Dan. vii. 17) which are contrasted with the Kingdom of the Saints (*vv.* 18, 27). A similar interpretation may be provisionally adopted here. This *θηρίον* from the Abyss is clearly a power of imperial magnitude and great strength which derives its origin from beneath, and opposes itself to Christ's witnesses. The ancient commentators identify this power with the Antichrist; (cf. Andreas: *τὸ θηρίον, δηλαδὴ ὁ ἀντίχριστος*, and so Arethas). For a fuller discussion of the symbol see notes on *cc.* xiii. 1, xvii. 8.

The Wild Beast prevails over the Witnesses; cf. Dan. vii. 21 Th. *τὸ κέρας ἐκεῖνο ἐποίει πόλεμον μετὰ* (עָבְדָא קְרָב עִם) *τῶν ἁγίων, καὶ ἴσχυσεν πρὸς αὐτούς.* The Seer anticipates a struggle between the Church and the whole power of the Roman Empire; he foresees that the troubles which began under Nero and Domitian will end in such a conflict as was actually brought about under Decius and in the last persecution under Diocletian. But his words cover in effect all the martyrdoms and massacres of history in which brute force has seemed to triumph over truth and righteousness.

καὶ νικήσει αὐτοὺς καὶ ἀποκτενεῖ αὐτούς. [8]καὶ τὸ 8
πτῶμα αὐτῶν ἐπὶ τῆς πλατείας τῆς πόλεως τῆς
μεγάλης, ἥτις καλεῖται πνευματικῶς Σόδομα καὶ Αἴ-
γυπτος, ὅπου καὶ ὁ κύριος αὐτῶν ἐσταυρώθη. [9]καὶ 9
βλέπουσιν ἐκ τῶν λαῶν καὶ φυλῶν καὶ γλωσσῶν καὶ

7 om και αποκτενει αυτους 1 12 36 41 87 97 syr[cdd] 8 το πτωμα ACQ min[35] me arm aeth Ar 'alia transl' ap Prim] τα πτωματα ℵP 1 35 36 38 49 79 87 91 130 al vg syrr Vict Prim Andr | επι της πλατειας] επι των πλατειων syr[gw] vg pr εσται ℵ[c.c*] 28 37 43 79 *iacebunt* vg *ponet* Prim *proicietur* 'al transl' ap Prim | οπου και] om και ℵ[c.a] 1 12 14 34 35 36 87 92 vg[lips 4] me syr[gw] | αυτων] ημων 1 om ℵ* 9 βλεψουσιν vg me arm aeth Prim

8. **καὶ τὸ πτῶμα αὐτῶν ἐπὶ τῆς πλατείας κτλ.]** 'Their corpses (for πτῶμα, *cadaver*, see Jud. xiv. 8, Ez. vi. 5 (A), Mc. vi. 29, xv. 45 (notes), and for the collective sing., cf. Gen. xlviii. 12, Lev. x. 6, Jud. xiii. 20, and see Blass, *Gr.* p. 83) lie on the open street (τῆς πλατείας, cf. *cc.* xxi. 21, xxii. 2) of the Great City.' With the sentiment of his race the Seer strongly resents the indignities offered to the bodies of the martyrs; cf. Ps. lxxix. 2 f., Tob. i. 18, ii. 3 ff.

The Great City is defined as "one which (ἥτις) in the language of mystery or of prophecy (πνευματικῶς, cf. 1 Cor. ii. 13 (B) πνευματικῶς πνευματικὰ συγκρίνοντες, x. 3 πνευματικὸν βρῶμα; contrast σαρκικῶς in Justin, *dial.* 14) is called 'Sodom' and 'Egypt'." The name of Sodom is given to Judah in its worst days (Isa. i. 9 f. ὡς Σόδομα ἂν ἐγενήθημεν...ἄρχοντες Σοδόμων...λαὸς Γομόρρας, cf. Ez. xvi. 46, 55 ἡ ἀδελφή σου...Σόδομα) and suggests at once moral degradation and utter ruin. Egypt, the 'house of bondage,' though not applied in the O. T. to Jerusalem or the Jewish people, is an obvious symbol of oppression and slavery. That Jerusalem is intended here seems to follow from ὅπου καὶ κτλ.; in the latter half of the book the 'Great City' is Babylon (xvi. 19, xvii. 18, xviii. 10 ff.), but the epithet ἡ μεγάλη is one which a Jew might not unnaturally give to the capital of his native land (cf. *Orac. Sibyll.* v. 154, 226, 413); even pagan writers extol its size (Appian, *Syr.* 50 μεγίστη πόλις Ἱεροσόλυμα). But if Jerusalem is in the Seer's thoughts, it is Jerusalem no longer regarded as the Holy City, but as given over to heathendom (v. 2), and thus for the time representing the world. The measured Sanctuary remains in its midst, an impregnable fortress, but the Witnesses go out into the street where the power of the Beast is supreme, and there, after a while, they meet their fate. In the ultimate meaning of the symbols, the City is doubtless not Jerusalem, but Rome, the persecutor of the Saints, the mystic Sodom and Egypt of the early centuries, where Christ was crucified afresh in His Saints. But this line of thought has not yet come into view; for the present Jerusalem, the city of the Crucifixion and of the earliest Christian martyrdoms, by a strange irony represents the antagonist of the *civitas Dei*.

Ὅπου καὶ ὁ κύριος αὐτῶν ἐσταυρώθη recalls the saying of Jo. xv. 20 οὐκ ἔστιν δοῦλος μείζων τοῦ κυρίου αὐτοῦ· εἰ ἐμὲ ἐδίωξαν, καὶ ὑμᾶς διώξουσιν.

9. **καὶ βλέπουσιν ἐκ τῶν λαῶν καὶ φυλῶν κτλ.]** Men of all races and nationalities (cf. v. 9, vii. 9; on the use of ἐκ see Blass, *Gr.* p. 97, who compares it with a similar use of מִן) gaze at the spectacle, which lasts $3\frac{1}{2}$ days—as many days as the years of the witnesses' prophesying—a short triumph,

ἐθνῶν τὸ πτῶμα αὐτῶν ἡμέρας τρεῖς καὶ ἥμισυ, καὶ
τὰ πτώματα αὐτῶν οὐκ ἀφίουσιν τεθῆναι εἰς μνῆμα.
10 [10]καὶ οἱ κατοικοῦντες ἐπὶ τῆς γῆς χαίρουσιν ἐπ' αὐτοῖς
καὶ εὐφραίνονται, καὶ δῶρα πέμψουσιν ἀλλήλοις, ὅτι
οὗτοι οἱ δύο προφῆται ἐβασάνισαν τοὺς κατοικοῦντας
11 ἐπὶ τῆς γῆς. [11]καὶ μετὰ [τὰς] τρεῖς ἡμέρας καὶ

9 *το πτωμα*] *τα πτωματα* P 1 28 36 38 49 79 91 95 96 al vg syrr Prim | *ημερας τρεις και ημισυ*] om *και* Q min[35] Andr Ar om omnia Prim anon[aug] | *αφιουσιν*] *αφησουσιν* Q min[pl] me syrr Ar *sinent* vg[cle am lipss 4,6] Prim | *μνηματα* ℵ[c.a] 98 al[pauc vid] vg syr[gw] arm aeth Prim 10 *χαιρουσιν*] *χαρησονται* 38 Ar *gaudebunt* vg syrr me aeth Prim | *ευφραινονται*] *ευφρανθησονται* Q 6 7 8 14 al[pl] vg syrr me Prim Ar | *πεμψουσιν* ℵ[c.a] AC 1 al[mu vid] vg[cle am fu] me syrr Prim] *πεμπουσιν* ℵ*P 28 36 79 80* vg[edd] arm *δωσουσιν* Q min[30] Ar | *οι προφηται οι δυο* ℵ 11 *μετα τας τρεις* ACQ Ar] om *τας* ℵP 1 14 28 35 36 37 38 40 49 91 96 130 syr[gw vid] arm

in point of fact, but long enough to bear the semblance of being complete and final. The delight of the spectators is represented as at once fiendish and childish; they not only leave the bodies without burial, but refuse to permit the friends of the martyrs to bury them (cf. Tobit i. 18 ff.). Further, they celebrate their victory by keeping holiday and exchanging gifts. The words depict the hatred entertained for the Christians by the pagan majority, and the joy with which the edicts against them were received.

Τὰ πτώματα: the plural is used in reference to the burial of the bodies, in which separate treatment would be necessary; contrast τὸ πτῶμα (*v.* 8, note). For the form ἀφίουσιν cf. Mc. i. 34, xi. 25; and for ἀφιέναι, *sinere*, see Jo. xi. 44, 48, xii. 7, xviii. 8.

10. **καὶ οἱ κατοικοῦντες ἐπὶ τῆς γῆς χαίρουσιν κτλ.**] The non-Christian world—an Apocalyptic formula, cf. iii. 10, vi. 10, viii. 13, xiii. 8, 12, 14, xvii. 2, 8—shew their joy at the overthrow of the Witnesses after the customary manner, keeping holiday (εὐφραίνεσθαι, specially of 'good cheer' and the mirth which it induces; cf. Lc. xii. 19 φάγε πίε εὐφραίνου, *ib.* xv. 23 ff., xvi 19), and sending portions from their own table to friends or to poorer neighbours (2 Esdr. xviii. 10 φάγετε...πίετε. .ἀποστείλατε μερίδα τοῖς μὴ ἔχουσιν, *ib.* 12 ἀποστέλλειν μερίδας καὶ ποιῆσαι εὐφροσύνην μεγάλην; Esth. ix. 22 ἐξαποστέλλοντας μερίδας τοῖς φίλοις καὶ τοῖς πτωχοῖς). The cause of joy was not so much the death of the Witnesses as the relief which the cessation of their testimony afforded; "the two prophets (cf. *v.* 3 προφητεύσουσιν) tortured" the world by setting men's consciences at work; cf. 1 Kings xviii. 17, xxi. 20, Mc. vi. 20, Apoc. ix. 5 f. note. Such a sense of relief is perhaps not seldom felt to-day by bad men when a preacher of righteousness or a signal example of goodness is removed, though good breeding prevents outward manifestation of joy; cf. Bede: "quoties affliguntur iusti exsultant iniusti." On βασανίζειν see *v.* ix. 5, note.

11. **καὶ μετὰ τὰς τρεῖς ἡμέρας καὶ ἥμισυ κτλ.**] The exultation of the pagan world will be shortened; when the $3\frac{1}{2}$ days are over, the Witnesses return to life. The Seer has in mind Ez. xxxvii. 10 καὶ εἰσῆλθεν εἰς αὐτοὺς τὸ πνεῦμα (A πν. ζωῆς) καὶ ἔζησαν, καὶ ἔστησαν ἐπὶ τῶν ποδῶν αὐτῶν: he sees the Church of the martyrs recovering herself from the effects of an age of persecution, as Ezekiel had seen new life

ἥμισυ πνεῦμα ζωῆς ἐκ τοῦ θεοῦ εἰσῆλθεν [ἐν] αὐτοῖς,
καὶ ἔστησαν ἐπὶ τοὺς πόδας αὐτῶν, καὶ φόβος μέγας
ἐπέπεσεν ἐπὶ τοὺς θεωροῦντας αὐτούς. [12]καὶ ἤκουσαν 12
φωνῆς μεγάλης ἐκ τοῦ οὐρανοῦ λεγούσης αὐτοῖς
Ἀνάβατε ὧδε· καὶ ἀνέβησαν εἰς τὸν οὐρανὸν ἐν τῇ
νεφέλῃ, καὶ ἐθεώρησαν αὐτοὺς οἱ ἐχθροὶ αὐτῶν. [13]καὶ 13
ἐν ἐκείνῃ τῇ ὥρᾳ ἐγένετο σεισμὸς μέγας, καὶ τὸ

11 *ημισυ*] pr *το* C | *εν αυτοις* A 18 28** 36 79 95] om *εν* CP 1 7 12 17 38 *εις αυτους* ℵQ min[30] Ar *in illis* vg Prim *επ αυτους* 49 53 91 96 | *επεπεσεν* ACP min[15]] *επεσεν* ℵQ min[pl] Ar | *τους θεωρουντας* ℵAQ min[fere omn] Andr Ar] *των θεωρουντων* CP 17* 12 *ηκουσαν*] *ηκουσα* ℵ[c.a] Q min[35] me Andr Ar *ακουσονται* 38 | *φωνην μεγαλην...λεγουσαν* AQ min[pl] Ar | om *αυτοις* A 28 anon[aug] | *αναβητε* Q min[pl] Andr Ar 13 om *και* 1° Q min[25] Ar | *ωρα*] *ημερα* Q min[fere 40] Ar | *και* 2°] *ωστε* C

infused into a dead Israel. Compare also 4 Regn. xiii. 21 *ἔζησεν καὶ ἀνέστη ἐπὶ τοὺς πόδας αὐτοῦ*. *Πνεῦμα ζωῆς*, רוּחַ חַיִּים (Gen. vi. 17, vii. 15, 22), the respiration of animal life, in this case proceeding directly 'from God.' With *εἰσῆλθεν ἐν αὐτοῖς* cf. Lc. ix. 46, and Blass, *Gr.* p. 130.

Καὶ φόβος μέγας ἐπέπεσεν ἐπὶ (Exod. xv. 16, Ps. liv. (lv.) 5, 2 Esdr. xvi. 16; in N.T., Lc. i. 12, Acts xix. 17) *τοὺς θεωροῦντας αὐτούς*: the spectators were panic-stricken. Each unexpected revival of the Church after an edict aimed at her extinction would strike dismay into the hearts of the persecutors, for it was manifestly *ἐκ τοῦ θεοῦ*.

12. *καὶ ἤκουσαν φωνῆς μεγάλης κτλ.*] The resurrection of the Witnesses is followed, as their Lord's (*v.* 8) had been, by an ascension into heaven in a cloud. But whereas none saw the Lord rise from the dead, and His Ascension was witnessed only by a few (Acts i. 9 *βλεπόντων αὐτῶν* sc. *τῶν ἀποστόλων*), His witnesses rise and ascend in full view of their enemies (*ἐθεώρησαν αὐτοὺς οἱ ἐχθροὶ αὐτῶν*, cf. *v.* 11 *τοὺς θεωροῦντας αὐτούς*); their triumph is celebrated openly. This public exaltation of the martyrs and saints will find its fulfilment in the rapture which St Paul foresees (1 Thess. iv. 17 *ἅμα σὺν αὐτοῖς ἁρπαγησόμεθα ἐν νεφέλαις εἰς ἀπάντησιν τοῦ κυρίου εἰς ἀέρα*). But meanwhile it has been partly anticipated in the sight of the world by the tribute paid to them, sometimes within a few years after their dishonour and death. Quite early in the history of the Church festivals were instituted in honour of the martyrs, *martyria* erected at their tombs, basilicas dedicated to their memory, their names were inserted in the diptychs and recited at the Christian sacrifice; and the later processes of canonization and invocation were at least an endeavour to do honour to those who had witnessed to Christ at the cost of their lives. In the popular esteem the Church's earlier witnesses were erected into a new Olympus; paganism saw the men it had hated and killed called up to heaven before its eyes. The vision of the Seer found a partial accomplishment before the age of persecution ceased, if its full and worthier realization is still in the future. For *ὧδε* 'hither' (Syr.[gw.] ܠܟܐ) cf. *c.* iv. 1. *Ἐν τῇ νεφέλῃ*: the cloud already associated with ascension into heaven in the Master's case (Acts i. 9). The Seer may also have in view the translation of Enoch and Elijah (Sir. xliv. 16, xlviii. 9, xlix. 14; cf. *c.* xi. 3, note).

13. *καὶ ἐν ἐκείνῃ τῇ ὥρᾳ ἐγένετο σεισμὸς μέγας κτλ.*] Earthquake (in

δέκατον τῆς πόλεως ἔπεσεν, καὶ ἀπεκτάνθησαν ἐν τῷ
σεισμῷ ὀνόματα ἀνθρώπων χιλιάδες ἑπτά, καὶ οἱ
λοιποὶ ἔμφοβοι ἐγένοντο καὶ ἔδωκαν δόξαν τῷ θεῷ
14 τοῦ οὐρανοῦ. [14]ἡ οὐαὶ ἡ δευτέρα ἀπῆλθεν· ἰδοὺ ἡ
οὐαὶ ἡ τρίτη ἔρχεται ταχύ.
15 [15]Καὶ ὁ ἕβδομος ἄγγελος ἐσάλπισεν· καὶ ἐγέ-
νοντο φωναὶ μεγάλαι ἐν τῷ οὐρανῷ, λέγοντες

13 δεκατον] τριτον Q me δωδεκατον 32 | επεσαν syr^{gw} | ανδρων 130 | εμφοβοι] εν φοβω ℵ 14 syr$^{gw\ vid}$ 14 η ουαι η δευτερα] ιδου αι ουαι αι δυο syr^{gw} | η ουαι 1°] om η ℵ$^{c.a}$ 28 79 | απηλθεν] παρηλθεν ℵ 28 79 | om ιδου 6 7 33 35 46 vg^{fu} | τριτη ουαι 130 15 ο εβδομος] om ο A | λεγοντες AQ 2 6 8 9 14 16 19 26 27 30 37 al] λεγουσαι ℵCP min^{pl} Andr Ar

the first century a too familiar experience of the Asiatic towns) is in the Prophets a constant symbol of great upheavals in the social or spiritual order; see Ez. xxxvii. 7, xxxviii. 19, Hagg. ii. 6 (cf. Heb. xii. 26 f.), Mc. xiii. 8, Apoc. xvi. 18. Here it seems to indicate the breaking up of the old pagan life which would follow the foreseen victory of the faith. The prophecy clothes itself in language borrowed from the well-known phenomena of a physical upheaval. Τὸ δέκατον, χιλιάδες ἑπτά, are conventional numbers like τὸ τρίτον in viii. 7—12, and the δώδεκα χιλιάδες of every tribe in Israel. But there is a studied moderation in the present figures; that but a tenth part of the great city should be overthrown and but 7000 souls should perish out of a population of at least 100,000 (cf. Jos. *c. Apion.* i. 22) indicates that the disaster was to be partial and ordinary.

Ὀνόματα ἀνθρώπων, i.e. ἄνθρωποι, 'persons': cf. iii. 4, note; to the examples of this use of ὄνομα given by Deissmann, *Bible Studies*, p. 196 f., may now be added those published by Grenfell and Hunt in the index to the *Tebtunis Papyri*. Ἔδωκαν δόξαν τῷ θεῷ τῶν οὐρανῶν: they glorified the True God by confessing their sin in having forsaken Him for idols; Jos. vii. 19 δὸς δόξαν σήμερον τῷ κυρίῳ θεῷ Ἰσραήλ, καὶ δὸς τὴν ἐξομολόγησιν. The phrase ὁ θεὸς τῶν οὐρανῶν (אֱלָהּ שְׁמַיָּא) is from Daniel (e.g. ii. 18 f., Th., iv. 28 (31) f., LXX.; see Driver, *Daniel*, p. 23), and reminds the reader that the Church was suffering, as Israel suffered during the Babylonian captivity, from predominant heathenism. The 'God of heaven' (2 Esdr. v. 12, vi. 10, xii. 4) is the invisible God of Jewish and Christian Monotheism, the "caeli numen" of Juv. xiv. 97, as contrasted with the 'gods many' whose images were to be seen in the pagan temples. In the end the Seer foresees a general movement towards Christianity, induced by fear or despair (οἱ λοιποὶ ἔμφοβοι ἐγένοντο, cf. Acts xxiv. 24 f.)—a prediction fulfilled more than once in ecclesiastical history.

14. ἡ οὐαὶ ἡ δευτέρα ἀπῆλθεν· ἰδοὺ κτλ.] See ix. 12, note. The Second Woe is the Sixth Trumpet, with the two episodes (x. 1—xi. 13) appended to it. The Seventh Trumpet—ἡ οὐαὶ ἡ τρίτη is now to follow without further delay. For ἔρχεσθαι ταχύ see ii. 16, iii. 11, xxii. 7, 12, 20; it seems always to refer, more or less directly, to the Parousia or to events leading up to it.

15—19. THE SEVENTH TRUMPET-BLAST OR THIRD WOE.

15. καὶ ὁ ἕβδομος ἄγγελος ἐσάλπισεν κτλ.] There is a marked contrast between the result of the opening of the Seventh Seal, and that of the blowing

Ἐγένετο ἡ βασιλεία τοῦ κόσμου τοῦ κυρίου
ἡμῶν καὶ τοῦ χριστοῦ αὐτοῦ, καὶ βασιλεύσει
εἰς τοὺς αἰῶνας τῶν αἰώνων.
16 καὶ οἱ εἴκοσι τέσσαρες πρεσβύτεροι, [οἱ] ἐνώπιον 16
τοῦ θεοῦ καθήμενοι ἐπὶ τοὺς θρόνους αὐτῶν, ἔπεσαν
ἐπὶ τὰ πρόσωπα αὐτῶν καὶ προσεκύνησαν τῷ θεῷ,

15 αι βασιλειαι 1 7 | κυριου] θεου 28 syr^{gw} Prim | βασιλευει 14 16 27 28 35 79 87 εβασιλευσεν vg^{am} syr^{gw} | αιωνων] + αμην ℵ 12 18 38 40 vg$^{dem\ tol}$ 16 οι εικοσι] om οι ℵ*A | οι ενωπιον] om οι AQ 1 7 12 14 46 92 95 | του θεου] pr του θρονου Q min$^{plq\ 25}$ syr Ar | καθημενοι AP 1 7 14 36 38 91 92 al me arm] καθηνται ℵ$^{c.a}$ C 2 95 syr^{gw} οι καθηνται ℵ* Q min$^{plq\ 35}$ syr Ar | επεσαν] επεσον Q min$^{fere\ 25}$ Ar pr και ℵ 95 al^{vid}

of the Seventh Trumpet. In the former case there was silence in Heaven; now there are 'great voices'; and the Seer can hear and write down what they say. The voices may be those of the ζῷα (cf. vi. 1, 3, 5, 7), who represent Creation and rejoice in the subjection of the cosmos to their Lord and His Christ. Λέγοντες, i.e. the persons or personifications from whom the voices come; cf. ix. 13, note. Φωναὶ...ἐν τῷ οὐρανῷ: "this knowledge at present is wholly in heaven...not manifested yet to the creation, but to be wrought out" (Benson).

ἐγένετο ἡ βασιλεία τοῦ κόσμου κτλ.] "The kingdom of the world has become (for the aor. cf. Lc. xix. 9) our Lord's and His Anointed's." The words suggest the vision of a world-empire, once dominated by an usurping power, which has now at length passed into the hands of its true Owner and Imperator; cf. Mt. iv. 8, 9, Jo. xiv. 30, Eph. ii. 2, vi. 12. The world-long struggle which will end in this transfer is described in Ps. ii. (cf. Acts iv. 26), which yields the phrase ὁ κύριος καὶ ὁ χριστὸς αὐτοῦ, Dan. vii. 13 ff., 22 ff.; and the magnificent issue is celebrated again in Apoc. xii. 10, xix. 6, 16. Ὁ κύριος ἡμῶν is here plainly not the Son, but the Father; the speakers are representatives of Creation, not of the Church, and the Lord of the Church is from their point of view not the Lord, but "the Lord's Christ" (Lc. ii. 26, ix. 20), an O.T. phrase for the anointed King of the theocracy. Καὶ βασιλεύσει εἰς τοὺς αἰῶνας τῶν αἰώνων: not βασιλεύσουσιν, for the rule of God and of Christ is one, and the Kingdom of the Son will ultimately be merged in the Reign of God (1 Cor. xv. 27). That Reign is perennial; no age will see its end (Dan. ii. 44, vii. 14, 28), and the Son's re-delivery of His mediatorial power to the Father does not exclude Him from sharing the Father's kingdom; against the perversion of the Pauline teaching by Marcellus the Church was able to cite Lc. i. 33 τῆς βασιλείας αὐτοῦ οὐκ ἔσται τέλος: see Robertson, *Regnum Dei*, p. 51 ff.

16. καὶ οἱ εἴκοσι τέσσαρες πρεσβύτεροι οἱ κτλ.] The Elders take up the witness of the ζῷα (if we may assume that they are the speakers in *v.* 15), as they do in iv. 9 ff. Ordinarily the Elders are seated (καθήμενοι) even in the Divine Presence on thrones which surround the central Throne (iv. 4), for the Church is the σύνθρονος of the Incarnate Son Who is the σύνθρονος of the Father (iii. 21); but they prostrate themselves at every act of adoration (iv. 10, v. 8, 14, xix. 4). With ἐπὶ τὰ πρόσωπα αὐτῶν cf. *c.* vii. 11, where the same prostration is ascribed to the Angels. The Angels and the Church, as creatures, share a common worship.

17 [17]λέγοντες
Εὐχαριστοῦμέν σοι, Κύριε ὁ θεὸς ὁ παντο-
κράτωρ, ὁ ὢν καὶ ὁ ἦν, ὅτι εἴληφας τὴν
δύναμίν σου τὴν μεγάλην καὶ ἐβασίλευσας·
18 [18]καὶ τὰ ἔθνη ὠργίσθησαν, καὶ ἦλθεν ἡ ὀργή
σου καὶ ὁ καιρὸς τῶν νεκρῶν κριθῆναι καὶ δοῦναι
τὸν μισθὸν τοῖς δούλοις σου τοῖς προφήταις καὶ

17 σοι] σε Q | κυριε] κυριος ℵ | ο παντοκρατωρ] om ο ℵ* | ο ην] + και ο ερχομενος 28 36 49 79 91 95 96 186 al vg^{cle lipss 4, 6*} me | οτι] pr και ℵ*C vg^{fu} | ειληφες C 18 ωργισθη ℵ* | καιρος] κληρος C

17. εὐχαριστοῦμέν σοι, Κύριε ὁ θεός κτλ.] The Elders represent the Church in her great function of εὐχαριστία. On Κύριε ὁ θ. ὁ παντοκράτωρ, "Lord God of Sabaoth," see *cc.* i. 8, iv. 8; and on ὁ ὢν καὶ ὁ ἦν, i. 4, 8, iv. 8. Here, and again in xvi. 5, ὁ ἐρχόμενος is omitted, since the future does not fall within the scope of the passage. Εἴληφας ... καὶ ἐβασίλευσας, "Thou hast assumed Thy power, and didst begin Thy reign"; with ἐβασίλευσας cf. *v.* 15 ἐγένετο ἡ βασιλεία. For this combination of tenses see iii. 3 εἴλ. καὶ ἤκουσας, v. 7 ἦλθεν καὶ εἴληφεν, viii. 5 εἴληφεν...καὶ ἐγέμισεν...καὶ ἔβαλεν; and with βασιλεύειν in this sense cf. 2 Regn. xv. 10 βεβασίλευκεν βασιλεὺς Ἀβεσσαλὼμ ἐν Χεβρών, Ps. xcii. (xciii.) 1 Κύριος ἐβασίλευσεν (מָלָךְ). Τὴν δύναμίν σου τὴν μεγάλην, not the normal exercise of the Divine power, but that final and overwhelming display to which all prophecy points. Compare and contrast Acts viii. 10 ἡ δύναμις τοῦ θεοῦ ἡ καλουμένη μεγάλη.

18. καὶ τὰ ἔθνη ὠργίσθησαν κτλ.] Ps. ii. is still in view, cf. *vv.* 1, 5 ἵνα τι ἐφρύαξαν (רָגְשׁוּ) ἔθνη, καὶ λαοὶ ἐμελέτησαν κενά; ...τότε λαλήσει πρὸς αὐτοὺς ἐν ὀργῇ αὐτοῦ: and xcviii. (xcix.) 1 Κύριος ἐβασίλευσεν, ὀργιζέσθωσαν λαοί. In Acts iv. 25 ff., Ps. ii. 1 f. is interpreted by the Church of Jerusalem in reference to the treatment of Christ by Antipas and Pontius Pilate (συνήχθησαν γὰρ ἐπ' ἀληθείας ἐν τῇ πόλει ταύτῃ ἐπὶ τὸν ἅγιον παῖδά σου Ἰησοῦν...Ἡρῴδης τε καὶ Πόντιος Πειλᾶτος σὺν ἔθνεσιν καὶ λαοῖς Ἰσραήλ): with a wider outlook the Seer of the Apocalypse sees in it the hostility of the world against the Church. Ὠργίσθησαν...ὀργή: the futile violence of men is answered by the effective judgements of God. Ἦλθεν ἡ ὀργή σου καὶ ὁ καιρός κτλ.; the *dies irae* is imagined as already come, and is seen to coincide with the Resurrection and the Judgement. With ὁ καιρὸς τῶν νεκρῶν cf. Mc. xi. 13 καιρὸς σύκων, Lc. xxi. 24 κ. ἐθνῶν. The dead will rise in their season, when all is ripe for the final award; cf. Mc. iv. 29, Apoc. xiv. 15 ff.; the scene is described in *c.* xx. ff. Οἱ νεκροί, good and bad, as in Jo. v. 25, Acts xxiv. 21.

The three infinitives, κριθῆναι ... δοῦναι...διαφθεῖραι, depend upon καιρός, as in Eccl. iii. 2 καιρὸς τοῦ ἀποθανεῖν or without the article, in Judith xiii. 5 καιρὸς ἀντιλαβέσθαι. But after κριθῆναι the construction is partly changed, and the writer proceeds as if he had begun ὁ καιρὸς τοὺς νεκροὺς κρῖναι.

δοῦναι τὸν μισθόν κτλ.] The μισθός to be given in the evening of the world to God's labourers (Mt. xx. 8) is with the Father (Mt. vi. 1) in heaven (Mt. v. 12), and will be dispensed by the Lord at His return (Apoc. xxii. 12); though essentially the same in all cases (Mt. *l. c.*), and though its payment is in all an act of grace on the

τοῖς ἁγίοις καὶ τοῖς φοβουμένοις τὸ ὄνομά σου,
τοὺς μικροὺς καὶ τοὺς μεγάλους, καὶ διαφθεῖραι
τοὺς διαφθείροντας τὴν γῆν.
19 καὶ ἠνοίγη ὁ ναὸς τοῦ θεοῦ ὁ ἐν τῷ οὐρανῷ, καὶ 19

18 *τοις αγιοις και* (om 130 186) *τοις* (om ℵ) *φοβουμενοις*] *τους αγιους και τους φοβουμενους* A | *τους μικρους και τους μεγαλους* ℵ*AC] *τοις μικροις κ. τοις μεγαλοις* ℵ$^{c.c}$ PQ min$^{omn\ vid}$ vg rell Cypr Prim Andr Ar *τοις μικροις μετα των μεγαλων* syr^{gw} | om *και* ult A | *διαφθειροντας* ℵAQ min^{pl} Ar] *φθειροντας* P 1 *διαφθειραντας* C 7 10 35 47 48 49 87 91 96 *qui corruperunt* vg Cypr Prim 19 *ηνοιγη*] *ηνοιχθη* Q min^{25} Ar | om *του θεου* syr^{gw} | *ο εν τω ουρανω*] om *ο* ℵPQ min^{pl} vg syr Prim Ar

part of God (Rom. iv. 4), it will vary in proportion to the work of the recipient (1 Cor. iii. 8). The prophet's *μισθός* is in some sense distinct from the *μισθὸς δικαίου* (Mt. x. 41), but no emphasis is laid here upon the difference (*δοῦναι τὸν μισθὸν...τοῖς προφήταις καὶ τοῖς ἁγίοις κτλ.*). "Thy servants the prophets" are the prophets of the Church, as in *cc.* i. 1, x. 7; "the saints" are, as always, the faithful in general. But who are "they that fear Thy Name"? In the Acts (xiii. 16, 43, 50) *οἱ φοβούμενοι* or *οἱ σεβόμενοι τὸν θεόν* are proselytes of the Synagogue; in the Apoc. (here and perhaps also in xix. 5) analogy suggests that they may be the unbaptized adherents of the Church, enquirers and catechumens. These too, if their desire to serve God be sincere, shall not lose their reward; though not *ἅγιοι* in the technical sense, they will receive the *μισθὸς δικαίου*. Small or great, the least in the Kingdom of Heaven (Mt. xi. 11), as well as those who stand in the highest rank of God's servants, the prophets of the New Covenant, are all remembered before Him. The acc. *τοὺς μικροὺς καὶ τοὺς μεγάλους* must be explained by supposing that the writer has forgotten that he started with *δοῦναι μισθόν*. The phrase (used also in *cc.* xiii. 16, xix. 5, 18, xx. 12; cf. Gen. xix. 11, Sap. vi. 7) includes all sorts and conditions of men, and witnesses to the *ἀπροσωποληψία* of the Judge. The meanest slave among the catechumens of the Church will receive the same consideration as an Imperial convert.

καὶ διαφθεῖραι τοὺς διαφθείροντας τὴν γῆν] Cf. xix. 2 *ἔκρινεν τὴν πόρνην τὴν μεγάλην ἥτις ἔφθειρεν τὴν γῆν ἐν τῇ πορνείᾳ αὐτῆς*. Here the reference is more general; by a Divine *ius talionis* (cf. Rom. i. 28 ff., ii. 5 ff.) destroyers of every kind shall be destroyed. *Διαφθεῖραι, διαφθείροντας* are perhaps preferred to the more usual *ἀπολέσαι, ἀπολλύοντας* (Jo. iii. 16, Rom. ii. 12, 2 Cor. ii. 15, 2 Thess. ii. 10), because of the double sense of *διαφθείρειν*. Paganism was 'destroying'—the lapse into the present is significant—'the earth' by corrupting the fountains of moral life, as well as by the physical horrors of the amphitheatre and the tyrannies of imperialism; and this moral reference is probably uppermost. All who helped to poison society were themselves *διεφθαρμένοι τὸν νοῦν* (1 Tim. vi. 5), and their true character would be recognised and fixed by the judgement of God.

19. *καὶ ἠνοίγη ὁ ναὸς τοῦ θεοῦ κτλ.*] The Sanctuary in heaven (iii. 12, vii. 15, xv. 5 ff., xxi. 22, cf. Iren. iv. 13. 6), as distinguished from the sanctuary on earth (xi. 1) was opened (*ἠνοίγη*, as in xv. 5; cf. Blass, *Gr.* p. 43); i.e. the Great Award is to be accompanied by a manifestation of the Divine glory; cf. Mc. viii. 38 *ὅταν ἔλθῃ ἐν τῇ δόξῃ τοῦ πατρὸς αὐτοῦ*. So Victorinus: "templum apertum manifestatio est

ὤφθη ἡ κιβωτὸς τῆς διαθήκης αὐτοῦ ἐν τῷ ναῷ αὐτοῦ, καὶ ἐγένοντο ἀστραπαὶ καὶ φωναὶ καὶ βρονταὶ καὶ σεισμὸς καὶ χάλαζα μεγάλη.

19 *ωφθη*] *εδοθη* C | *αυτου* 1°] (*του*) *κυριου* Q min$^{fere\,40}$ Vict Ar *του θεου* ℵ 94 om vg^{cd} me Prim | *αυτου* 2°] om syr^{gw} arm | *εγενοντο*] *εγενετο* ℵ* | *βρονται κ. φωναι* 14 28 al *g h* syrr | om *και σεισμος* Q min$^{plq\,30}$ Ar

Domini nostri." The vision apparently is but momentary, for the heavenly *ναός* is opened again in xv. 5; but the Seer has time to catch sight of (*ὤφθη*) the Ark of the Covenant which was within. On *ἠνοίγη* see Deissmann, *Bible Studies*, p. 189.

ἡ κιβωτὸς τῆς διαθήκης (אֲרוֹן הַבְּרִית), or as it is usually called in Exodus *ἡ κ. τοῦ μαρτυρίου* (א״ הָעֵדוּת), was within the sacred veil of the Tabernacle (Heb. ix. 4), and afterwards stood in the inner chamber of Solomon's Temple (1 Kings viii. 6). Probably it perished when Nebuchadrezzar burnt the Temple (2 Kings xxv. 9), for Jeremiah speaks of it as if it would shortly pass out of memory (Jer. iii. 16), and Tacitus (*hist.* v. 9) scoffs at the Jewish Sanctuary as "vacuam sedem et inania arcana." In Ezekiel's Temple the Ark does not appear, which renders its presence in the heavenly temple of the Apocalypse more remarkable. A legend related in 2 Macc. ii. 5 ff. represents Jeremiah as having hidden both the Ark and the Altar of Incense (which reappears in Apoc. viii. 3 ff.) in a cave against the day of Israel's restoration; it is added: *καὶ ἄγνωστος ὁ τόπος ἔσται ἕως ἂν συνάγῃ ὁ θεὸς ἐπισυναγωγὴν τοῦ λαοῦ...καὶ τότε ὁ κύριος ἀναδείξει ταῦτα καὶ ὀφθήσεται ἡ δόξα τοῦ κυρίου.* Other forms of the legend may be seen on p. 38, *supra*. This story in its earliest form may have been in the mind of the Seer, but he has his own reason for introducing the Ark at this point. In Christ God has made a new covenant with men (Heb. viii. 6 ff., ix. 15 ff.), and the appearance of the Ark of the Covenant through the opened doors of the heavenly temple, at the moment when the time has come for the faithful to receive their reward, indicates the restoration of perfect access to God through the Ascension of the Incarnate Son. Andreas: *διὰ τῆς ἀνοίξεως τοῦ οὐρανοῦ καὶ τῆς ὁράσεως τῆς κιβωτοῦ τῶν ἡτοιμασμένων ἀγαθῶν τοῖς ἀγαθοῖς δηλοῦται ἡ ἀποκάλυψις.*

καὶ ἐγένοντο ἀστραπαί κτλ. The usual symbols of majesty and power which attend manifestations of the Divine Presence, cf. (e.g.) Exod. xix. 16, Ps. xxix. 3 ff.—"the solemn salvos, so to speak, of the artillery of Heaven" (Alford). Of a "great hail" (Exod. ix. 18 ff.) we hear again in *c.* xvi. 21; lightning flashes across the sky in iv. 5, viii. 5, xvi. 18; earthquakes are felt in vi. 12, viii. 5, xi. 13, xvi. 18.

The second great section of the Book (iv. 1—xi. 19) ends, as it began, with a vision of the heavenly order. In iv. 1 ff. a door is set open in heaven, through which the Seer is able to discern the Throne of God and its surroundings; in xi. 19 the Temple of God in heaven is opened, and the Ark of the New Covenant is seen standing in the celestial Sanctuary. Moreover, the whole series of visions which intervenes between these two revelations is full of heavenly things and persons. Most of the scenes are laid in heaven; the rest, though on earth, are illuminated by the presence of superhuman agents. The seven Seals are opened by the Lamb Who is in the midst of the Throne; the seven Trumpets are blown by seven Angels. Angels are charged with the custody of the four winds; an Angel impresses on the elect the Seal of God; an Angel with one foot on the sea and the other on the dry land, makes solemn oath that the end is near.

Yet as a whole the section is concerned with movements which find their sphere on the earth. The purpose of the celestial scenery and the celestial agencies which are employed is not to take the attention of the reader from contemporary or coming events, but to lead him to connect these with the invisible powers by which they are controlled, and to let the light of heaven fall upon the earthly tragedy. The Throne and the Temple in the ἐπουράνια are seen to be the ultimate source of the energies by which human history is carried to its goal. But it is in human history that the interests of the prophecy are centred. In the events which follow the opening of the Seals, if they have been rightly interpreted in this commentary, the Seer depicts the conditions under which the Empire, as he knew it in Asia, was fulfilling its destiny, and passes from these to the great dynastic and social changes which must accompany or follow its collapse. In the scenes announced by the Trumpet-blasts, he works out at greater length the second of these topics; the revolutions which were in the lap of the future, the woes which it held in store for the unbelieving and impenitent world, are painted in a vivid symbolism borrowed partly from the Old Testament, partly from the apocalyptic thought of the time. These kaleidoscopic effects must be taken as a whole, and not pressed in detail, as if they were so many specific predictions; nevertheless they doubtless represent the impressions made upon the mind of the Seer, as in the Spirit he gazed into the future of the Empire and of the race. His sight does not reach as yet to the end; when the seventh Seal is opened, there is silence in heaven; when the seventh Trumpet is blown, he hears the acclamations of the invisible world, but the actual result is not revealed to him even under a symbolical disguise.

If the Seals and the Trumpets disclose the fortunes of the Roman Empire, and, in a foreshortened view, the troubles of the age which would follow its fall, the Seer is not left without a vision of the future of the great spiritual Power which was destined to outlive the rule of the Caesars. Both the seventh seal-opening and the seventh trumpet-blast are preceded by episodes which deal with the history of the Catholic Church. The churches of the province of Asia have vanished from the Seer's mind; he has now before him the thought of the world-wide Society. Each episode consists of two pictures. In the first pair the Church is represented as the Israel of God, marching in its tribal divisions to the inheritance of the Saints; and again as the universal brotherhood of all races and nations, seen in the glories of its ideal life. In the second, she appears in two aspects of her long struggle with the world; as the Sanctuary surrounded by the profanations of heathendom, and again as the Two Witnesses, the Enoch and Elijah or the Moses and Elijah of the new Covenant, to whom it is given to witness throughout the days of a militant paganism, dying for the faith, to rise again like the Master and ascend to heaven.

With the seventh trumpet-blast the Kingdom of God has come, and the general judgement is at hand. Thus the second section of the Apocalypse brings the course of history down to the verge of the Parousia. If the Book had ended here, it would have been within these limits complete. But the Seer pauses for a moment only to take up his rôle again with a fresh presentation of the future, in which the vision is to be carried to its issue. A new prophecy

XII. 1 [1]Καὶ σημεῖον μέγα ὤφθη ἐν τῷ οὐρανῷ· γυνὴ
περιβεβλημένη τὸν ἥλιον, καὶ ἡ σελήνη ὑποκάτω
τῶν ποδῶν αὐτῆς, καὶ ἐπὶ τῆς κεφαλῆς αὐτῆς
2 στέφανος ἀστέρων δώδεκα, [2]καὶ ἐν γαστρὶ ἔχουσα,

XII 1 περιβεβλημένη] περιβλεπομενη A | την σεληνην ℵ* | δωδεκα] δεκαδυο 1 12 Hipp

begins in *c.* xii, the contents of the open βιβλαρίδιον which the Seer had been directed to take from the hand of the Angel and consume. Impelled by this fresh gift of prophetic energy, he feels himself bound to prophesy again to a larger circle of hearers and with wider aims (x. 11); and this second message occupies the remainder of the Book.

XII. 1—18. The Woman with child, and the great blood-red Dragon.

1. σημεῖον μέγα ὤφθη ἐν τῷ οὐρανῷ] Hitherto a fresh vision has been announced by the formula [μετὰ ταῦτα] εἶδον καὶ ἰδού, or the simple εἶδον or ὤφθη (xi. 19). The present vision is the first characterised as a σημεῖον; others follow, cf. xiii. 3 ὤφθη ἄλλο σημεῖον ἐν τῷ οὐρανῷ, xv. 1 εἶδον ἄλλο σημ. ἐν τῷ οὐρ. μέγα καὶ θαυμαστόν. In the LXX. σημεῖον is usually the equivalent of אוֹת, and is used either of celestial phenomena, e.g. the heavenly bodies (Gen. i. 14), and the rainbow (Gen. ix. 12 ff.), or of tokens of God's presence or purpose given upon earth, e.g. the miracles in Egypt (Exod. vii. 3, etc.). In the N.T. the latter is the prevalent sense of σημεῖον; the word goes with τέρας (Jo. iv. 48) and δύναμις (Acts ii. 22), and it is thus used in this book (*cc.* xiii. 13 ff., xvi. 14, xix. 20), though only of wonders wrought by evil powers. But the Gospels speak also of σημεῖα ἀπὸ (ἐκ) τοῦ οὐρανοῦ (Mc. viii. 11, Mt. xvi. 1, and of a σημεῖον ἐν οὐρανῷ (Mt. xxiv. 3, 30), which is to attend the Parousia. Such signs, like the אוֹתוֹת of Gen. *ll. cc.*, would be visible in the skies to men upon earth, and this is probably the nature of the 'sign' now displayed to the Seer. It is not the interior of the heavenly world that he sees, as in iv. 1 ff., but its outer veil, the sky, on which the vision is depicted.

γυνὴ περιβεβλημένη τὸν ἥλιον κτλ.] The first 'sign in heaven' is a Woman—the earliest appearance of a female figure in the Apocalyptic vision. She is arrayed with the Sun; for the constr. see vii. 9, 13, x. 1, xi. 3, xvii. 4, xviii. 16, xix. 8, 13, and for the idea, cf. Ps. ciii. (civ.) 2 ἀναβαλλόμενος φῶς ὡς ἱμάτιον, and the partial parallels in Apoc. i. 16, x. 1, xix. 17. The moon is her ὑποπόδιον; the phrase ὑποκάτω τῶν ποδῶν may be borrowed from Ps. cix. (cx.) 1 (Mc. xii. 36) or from Ps. viii. 7 (Heb. ii. 8). The Seer perhaps has in mind Cant. vi. 9 (10) τίς αὕτη ἡ ἐκκύπτουσα ὡσεὶ ὄρθρος, καλὴ ὡς σελήνη, ἐκλεκτὴ ὡς ὁ ἥλιος; Further, this Woman in the sky is crowned with a wreath (*c.* ii. 10, note, of twelve stars, a coronet of celestial diamonds. The reader is reminded of Joseph's second dream (Gen. xxxvii. 9 ὁ ἥλιος καὶ ἡ σελήνη καὶ ἕνδεκα ἀστέρες προσεκύνουν με), and of *Test. xii. patr.* Napht. 5 ὁ Λευὶ ἐκράτησε τὸν ἥλιον καὶ ὁ Ἰούδας φθάσας ἐπίασε τὴν σελήνην, καὶ ὑψώθησαν ἀμφότεροι σὺν αὐτοῖς. καὶ ὄντος τοῦ Λευὶ ὡς ἡλίου...Ἰούδας ἦν λαμπρὸς ὡς ἡ σελήνη, καὶ ὑπὸ τοὺς πόδας αὐτοῦ ἦσαν δώδεκα ἀκτῖνες—passages which shew that Semitic fancy was apt to decorate ideal or representative persons with the heavenly bodies. The mention of twelve stars (δώδεκα, not οἱ δ. ἀστέρες) is

[καὶ] κράζει ὠδίνουσα καὶ βασανιζομένη τεκεῖν. ³καὶ 3

2 και 2°] om APQ min^{pl} vg$^{\text{cle lips 5}}$ me^{vid} syr arm Hipp Meth Andr Ar (hab ℵC 95 vg$^{\text{am fu dem lips 4, 6 tol}}$ syr^{gw} aeth Prim) | κραζει] εκραζεν C 7 8 31 38 87 al$^{\text{plq 20}}$ vg$^{\text{cle fu lips 4, 6}}$ Ar Prim εκραξεν Q min$^{\text{fere 12}}$ vg^{cod} syr arm κραζουσα syr$^{\text{gw vid}}$ Vict^{vid} | ωδινουσα] pr και syrr | om και ante βασ. 130

sufficiently explained as an allusion to the twelve tribes (Jac. i. 1, Apoc. xxi. 12) or possibly the twelve Apostles (xxi. 14), regarded as the crowning ornament of the Jewish Church; for the notion of the stars forming a wreath or circlet, cf. Sap. xiii. 2 κύκλον ἄστρων (*v. l.* ἀστέρων), and perhaps Apoc. i. 16.

2. καὶ ἐν γαστρὶ ἔχουσα κτλ.] The Woman is with child, and near to her delivery; in sharp contrast with the splendour of her attire the Seer places her cries of pain and the tortures (βασανιζομένη) of the birth-pangs. He can scarcely have failed to remember Isa. vii. 14 δώσει Κύριος αὐτὸς ὑμῖν σημεῖον· ἰδοὺ ἡ παρθένος ἐν γαστρὶ λήμψεται (Mt. i. 23 ἕξει), καὶ τέξεται υἱόν—a passage familiar to Christian thought towards the end of the Apostolic age, as its use by Mt., and apparently also by Lc. (i. 31), attests. But if so, he purposely substitutes γυνή for παρθένος, for the Virgin-Birth is not a point on which he wishes to insist; the ideal mother of the Lord is not the Virgin, but the Jewish Church (see below). Jerusalem is described in the Prophets as a travailing woman; cf. Mic. iv. 10 ὤδινε...θυγάτηρ Σειών, ὡς τίκτουσα, Isa. xxvi. 17 f. ὡς ἡ ὠδίνουσα...ἐπὶ τῇ ὠδῖνι αὐτῆς ἐκέκραξεν...ἐν γαστρὶ ἐλάβομεν καὶ ὠδινήσαμεν, *ib.* lxvi. 7 πρὶν τὴν ὠδίνουσαν τεκεῖν, πρὶν ἐλθεῖν τὸν πόνον τῶν ὠδίνων, ἐξέφυγεν καὶ ἔτεκεν ἄρσεν. The same metaphor is used by our Lord to characterize the anguish of the Apostles on the eve of the Passion (Jo. xvi. 21 ἡ γυνὴ ὅταν τίκτῃ λύπην ἔχει..καὶ ὑμεῖς οὖν νῦν μὲν λύπην ἔχετε), and by St Paul in reference to the spiritual travail of the guide of souls (Gal. iv. 19 τεκνία μου, οὓς πάλιν ὠδίνω μέχρις οὗ μορφωθῇ Χριστὸς ἐν ὑμῖν).

The reading is somewhat uncertain: ἔχουσα κράζει (ἔκραζεν, ἔκραξεν) is easier than ἔχουσα, καὶ κράζει, but the latter has on the whole better support and makes excellent sense; if it be accepted, καὶ ἐν γ. ἔχουσα will range with περιβεβλημένη κτλ., while καὶ κράζει begins a new clause.

The ancient expositors in general, beginning with Hippolytus and Methodius, understood the Woman with child to represent the Church, though some identified her with the Blessed Virgin. See Hipp. (ed. Lag. p. 31): τὴν μὲν οὖν γυναῖκα τὴν περιβεβλημένην τὸν ἥλιον σαφέστατα τὴν ἐκκλησίαν, ἐνδεδυμένην τὸν λόγον τὸν πατρῷον ὑπὲρ ἥλιον λάμποντα; Andreas: τινὲς μὲν δι' ὅλου τὴν θεοτόκον νενοήκασι.. ὁ δὲ μέγας Μεθόδιος [*conviv.* 6 ff.] εἰς τὴν ἁγίαν ἐκκλησίαν ἐξέλαβεν. The majority take the birth-pangs to symbolize the spiritual travail of the Church (Hipp. *l. c.*: οὐ παύσεται ἡ ἐκκλησία γεννῶσα ἐκ καρδίας τὸν λόγον τὸν ἐν κόσμῳ ὑπὸ ἀπίστων διωκόμενον; Ps. Aug.: "quotidie parit ecclesia." Andreas: ὠδίνειν δέ φαμεν τὴν ἐκκλησίαν καθ' ἕκαστον τῶν ἀναγεννωμένων δι' ὕδατος καὶ πνεύματος; Bede: "semper ecclesia, dracone licet adversante, Christum parit"). But the earliest Latin expositor of the Apocalypse, Victorinus, has grasped the meaning more precisely: "antiqua ecclesia est patrum et prophetarum et sanctorum et apostolorum; quae gemitus et tormenta desiderii sui habuit usquequo fructum ex plebe sua secundum carnem olim promissum sibi videret Christum ex ipsa gente corpus sumpsisse"—a comment which

ὤφθη ἄλλο σημεῖον ἐν τῷ οὐρανῷ, καὶ ἰδοὺ δράκων
μέγας πυρρός, ἔχων κεφαλὰς ἑπτὰ καὶ κέρατα δέκα
4 καὶ ἐπὶ τὰς κεφαλὰς αὐτοῦ ἑπτὰ διαδήματα, ⁴καὶ

3 μεγας πυρρος AP (1) 28 36 49 79 87 91 95 96 186 al vg syr^{gw} anon^{aug}] πυρρος μεγας ℵ(C)(Q) min^{35} me syr aeth Meth Ar Prim | πυρρος] πυρος CQ 1 130 al 30 | αυτου] αυτων A 87

Beatus repeats, adding: "semper enim haec mulier ante adventum Domini parturiebat in doloribus suis." Similarly Augustine *in Ps.* cxlii: "haec autem mulier antiqua est civitas Dei." The two views are not, however, wholly inconsistent. Doubtless the Church of the Old Testament was the Mother of whom Christ came after the flesh. But here, as everywhere in the Book, no sharp dividing line is drawn between the Church of the Old Testament and the Christian Society; the latter is viewed as the Jewish Church come to its maturity. Thus the woman who gave birth to the Christ is identical with her who after His departure suffered for her faith in Him (*v.* 13) and who is the mother of believers (*v.* 17, cf. Gal. iv. 27).

In βασανιζομένη τεκεῖν the infinitive is epexegetical (WM. p. 140), representing the issue, almost the purpose (Vg. *cruciabatur ut pariat*), of the torture endured. Burton, § 389, less simply explains it as "an object inf. governed by the idea of desire implied in the preceding participle." For βασανιζομένη see ix. 5 note.

3. καὶ ὤφθη ἄλλο σημεῖον κτλ.] A second *tableau*, following close upon the first and inseparable from it. The Dragon is the Serpent of Gen. iii. 1 ff., as the Apocalyptist himself tells us (*v.* 9). But the preference of δράκων (= תַּנִּין Job vii. 12, נָחָשׁ *ib.* xxvi. 13, לִוְיָתָן *ib.* xl. 20 (25)) to ὄφις, both in this context and in *cc.* xiii., xvi., xx., is significant. It is a mythical, symbolical, monster which is before us, whether suggested by the Babylonian Tiâmat (Gunkel, *Schöpfung u. Chaos*, p. 361, *Enc. Bibl.* 1131 ff.), or by Hebrew fancy (Ps. lxxiii. (lxxiv.) 13 σὺ συνέτριψας τὰς κεφαλὰς τῶν δρακόντων—cod. R, τοῦ δράκοντος τοῦ μεγάλου—ἐπὶ τοῦ ὕδατος: cf. Job xxvi. 13, Isa. xxvii. 1, Ez. xxix. 3). The Seer's Dragon is πυρρός, fiery red (Apoc. vi. 4, note; cf. Hom. *Il.* ii. 308 ἔνθ' ἐφάνη μέγα σῆμα, δράκων ἐπὶ νῶτα δαφοινός), the epithet denoting his murderous work (Andreas, διὰ τὸ φονικὸν αὐτοῦ, cf. Jo. viii. 44 ἀνθρωποκτόνος ἦν ἀπ' ἀρχῆς, 1 Jo. iii. 12 Κάιν ἐκ τοῦ πονηροῦ ἦν καὶ ἔσφαξεν τὸν ἀδελφὸν αὐτοῦ). He has seven heads (cf. xvii. 3, 7; *Kiddushim*, f. 29 *b*, "visus ei est daemon forma draconis septem habentis capita"; *Pistis Sophia*, p. 90 "basilisci serpentis, cui septem erant capita"), symbolical of a plenitude of power; and every head is crowned with the fillet which denotes sovereignty: for διάδημα as contrasted with στέφανος (*v.* 1) see 1 Esdr. iv. 30 ἀφαιροῦσαν τὸ διάδημα ἀπὸ τῆς κεφαλῆς τοῦ βασιλέως, Isa. lxii. 3 διάδημα βασιλείας, 1 Macc. xi. 13, xiii. 32 τὸ διάδημα τῆς Ἀσίας; and for the conception of a diadem-crowned serpent cf. Pliny, *H. N.* viii. 21. 33, where he describes the basilisk as "candida in capite macula ut quodam diademate insignem." The Beast of *c.* xiii. has ten diadems on his horns; the Divine Conqueror of *c.* xix. has on His head διαδήματα πολλά. The Dragon's ten diadems represent his power over the kingdoms of the world; cf. Lc. iv. 6 ἐμοὶ παραδέδοται, Jo. xii. 31, xiv. 30, xvi. 11 ὁ ἄρχων τοῦ κόσμου τούτου, and contrast Apoc. i. 5 ὁ ἄρχων τῶν βασιλέων τῆς γῆς. See xvii. 3, 7, 9 ff., notes.

4. καὶ ἡ οὐρὰ αὐτοῦ σύρει κτλ.] A

ἡ οὐρὰ αὐτοῦ σύρει τὸ τρίτον τῶν ἀστέρων τοῦ οὐρανοῦ, καὶ ἔβαλεν αὐτοὺς εἰς τὴν γῆν. καὶ ὁ δράκων ἕστηκεν ἐνώπιον τῆς γυναικὸς τῆς μελλούσης τεκεῖν, ἵνα ὅταν τέκῃ τὸ τέκνον αὐτῆς καταφάγῃ.

4 του ουρανου] των εν τω ουρανω syr[gw] | εστηκεν] εστηκει C syr[gw] εστη 14 92 | τεκειν] τικτειν 37 49 91 96 186 Hipp

reference to Dan. viii. 10 where it is said of the Little Horn: וַתִּגְדַּל עַד־ צְבָא הַשָּׁמָיִם וַתַּפֵּל אַרְצָה מִן־הַצָּבָא; τὸ τρίτον softens the hyperbole, as in *c.* viii. 7 ff. A similar incident occurs in the Babylonian myth of the conflict between Tiâmat and Marduk (Gunkel, *op. cit.* p. 387), but the Apocalyptist may well have had no other thought than to depict the colossal size and vast strength of the monster. Heaven (the sky) is too small to hold him; when he lashes his tail, it drags along (σύρει, Vg. *trahebat*, cf. Jo. xxi. 8, Acts xiv. 19, xvii. 6) a third of the stars, and dashes them to the earth: for the change of tense cf. ii. 3, note. Ἔβαλεν εἰς τὴν γῆν was frequently understood by the ancient interpreters in reference to the fall of the Angels (Jude 6 τοὺς μὴ τηρήσαντας τὴν ἑαυτῶν ἀρχὴν (see Dr Bigg's note); thus Arethas: συγκατέβαλε γὰρ ἑαυτῇ πλείστων ἀγγέλων μοῖραν συναποστατῆσαι πείσασα ἀπὸ θεοῦ. But other views obtained support; e.g., according to Bede, "Tyconius more suo tertiam partem stellarum quae cecidit falsos fratres interpretatur." Origen has a similar explanation *in Mt. comm.* (Lomm., iv. p. 306): "qui...peccatum...sequitur, trahitur a cauda draconis vadens post eum."

καὶ ὁ δράκων ἕστηκεν ἐνώπιον τῆς γυναικός κτλ.] The relation of the second σημεῖον to the first now becomes evident. The appearance of the Woman with Child has provoked a counter-manifestation on the part of the Dragon. His quarrel, however, is not immediately with the Woman, but with the Child, and he waits his time till the Child is born. For τῆς μελλούσης τεκεῖν cf. iii. 2, 16, note. Ἕστηκεν is at first sight a strange verb in connexion with the serpent, cf. Gen. iii. 14 ἐπὶ τῷ στήθει σου καὶ τῇ κοιλίᾳ πορεύσῃ. But the δράκων is a glorified ὄφις, which, as Pliny (*H. N.* viii. 21. 33) says, "nec flexu multiplici ut reliquae corpus impellit, sed celsus et erectus in medio incedens."

Ἵνα...καταφάγῃ: cf. Jer. xxviii. (li.) 34 κατέφαγέν με ... Ναβουχοδονόσορ βασιλεὺς Βαβυλῶνος κατέπιέν με, ὡς δράκων ἔπλησεν τὴν κοιλίαν αὐτοῦ ἀπὸ τῆς τρυφῆς μου. A greater sufferer than Jerusalem is here, and a greater foe than the King of Babylon. The Seer looks back over the long period of expectation which followed the original sentence on the Serpent (Gen. iii. 15; see Driver's remarks on this in *Genesis*, p. 57, and cf. Primasius: "in conspectu autem mulieris stetisse dicitur, quoniam *illa* (inquit) *observabit caput tuum*," etc.). Two figures dominate pre-Christian history—humanity, fallen but struggling to the birth of a higher life, and the hostile power of evil, watching (Gen. *l.c.*, LXX., τηρήσεις) its opportunity to defeat the realization of the hope; such tyrants as Pharaoh (Exod. i. 22, ii. 1 ff.) and Herod (Mt. ii. 7 ff.) may be in the Seer's mind, but his words cover the whole conflict which culminated in the Cross and its issue. On ὅταν τέκῃ see Burton, § 305.

5 [5]καὶ ἔτεκεν υἱόν, ἄρσεν, ὃς μέλλει ποιμαίνειν πάντα τὰ ἔθνη ἐν ῥάβδῳ σιδηρᾷ· καὶ ἡρπάσθη τὸ τέκνον αὐτῆς πρὸς τὸν θεὸν καὶ πρὸς τὸν θρόνον αὐτοῦ.

5 υιον] om Prim | αρσεν AC] αρσενα P 95 130 186 (sine υιον) Meth αρρενα ℵ(Q) 1 al[pl] Hipp Ar om Vict | εν ραβδω] om εν P 1 12 28 95 97 186 arm | ηρπασθη] ηρπαχθη Q ηρπαγη ℵ 10 29 31 37 47 49 91 95 96 Hipp Meth | om προς 2° 1 36[vid]

5. καὶ ἔτεκεν υἱόν, ἄρσεν, ὅς κτλ.] Either υἱόν or ἄρσεν seems to be redundant. Ἔτεκεν ἄρσεν is a familiar phrase in the LXX.; cf. Exod. i. 16 ff., ii. 2, Lev. xii. 2, 7, Num. iii. 40, Isa. lxvi. 7, Jer. xx. 15, xxxvii. (xxx.) 6, and would have sufficed here. On the other hand υἱόν, ἄρσεν or υἱὸν ἄρσενα may have been suggested by בֵּן זָכָר (Jer. xx. 15), or deliberately written instead of παιδίον ἄρσεν (cf. Ar. *Eccl.* 549) in order to call attention to the sex of the Child which υἱός by itself does not emphasize: cf. Hippolytus (ed. Lag., p. 32): τὸν ἄρρενα καὶ τέλειον Χριστόν; Andreas: ταῖς ἡδοναῖς ἀθήλυντος.

The 'man-child' is primarily the Son of Mary, with whom he is identified by ὃς μέλλει ποιμαίνειν κτλ.; cf. ii. 26 f., xix. 15, notes. The reference to Ps. ii. does not indeed exclude the thought of the members of Christ who are potentially interested in the promise, as ii. 26 shews (ὁ νικῶν... δώσω αὐτῷ ἐξουσίαν ἐπὶ τῶν ἐθνῶν, καὶ ποιμανεῖ αὐτοὺς ἐν ῥάβδῳ σιδηρᾷ); and the ancient interpreters lay the chief stress on this wider sense, cf. e.g. Primasius: "Christus in singulis membris dicitur nasci" and Bede, quoted above, p. 145 b. But it seems better in this place to limit the words to our Lord Himself, regarded as the offspring of the O.T. Church; the faithful (*v.* 17) are οἱ λοιποὶ τοῦ σπέρματος αὐτῆς.

καὶ ἡρπάσθη τὸ τέκνον αὐτῆς πρὸς τὸν θεόν κτλ.] The Seer foreshortens the Gospel history; for his present purpose the years between the Nativity and the Ascension are non-existent, and even the Passion finds no place in his summary. It is enough to point out that the Dragon's vigilance was futile; he failed to destroy the Woman's Son, and his failure was manifested by the Ascension. Interpreters who understand the whole passage in reference to the Church think here of the conglorification of the members with the Head; e.g. Primasius: "licet in capite Christo praecesserit...congruit tamen et corpori. hinc sunt illae voces Apostoli, *qui nos resuscitavit et consedere fecit in caelestibus*."

With ἡρπάσθη (Vg. *raptus est*, A.V., R.V., "was caught up") compare Acts viii. 39 πνεῦμα Κυρίου ἥρπασεν τὸν Φίλιππον, 2 Cor. xii. 2, 4 ἁρπαγέντα...ἕως τρίτου οὐρανοῦ...ἡρπάγη εἰς τὸν παράδεισον, 1 Th. iv. 17 ἁρπαγησόμεθα ἐν νεφέλαις. Here, if our interpretation is correct, it answers to ἀνελήμφθη in 4 Regn. ii. 11, Acts i. 2, 11, 22, 1 Tim. iii. 16, representing the Ascension as a 'rapture'—a graphic and true, if not exhaustive description. Πρός indicates the direction or goal, which was (1) God Himself (cf. Jo. xx. 17 ἀναβαίνω πρὸς τὸν πατέρα μου...καὶ θεόν μου), and (2) God's Throne. The Ascension involves the Session of the Sacred Humanity at the Right Hand of the Father (see 'Mc.' xvi. 19, Eph. i. 20, Heb. i. 3, Apoc. iii. 21), and not merely an elevation of spirit into the Divine Presence, which was never wanting to the Divine Son of Man.

6. καὶ ἡ γυνὴ ἔφυγεν εἰς τὴν ἔρημον κτλ.] The Mother of Christ, the Church (which has now become the larger Israel, the Christian Society) does not at once share the rapture

6 καὶ ἡ γυνὴ ἔφυγεν εἰς τὴν ἔρημον, ὅπου ἔχει ἐκεῖ 6
τόπον ἡτοιμασμένον ἀπὸ τοῦ θεοῦ, ἵνα ἐκεῖ τρέφωσιν
αὐτὴν ἡμέρας χιλίας διακοσίας ἑξήκοντα.

6 εχει] ειχεν 38 vg^cle fu lips 6 syr^gw | om εκει 1° C 1 14 36 38 186 al vg rell Prim al | απο] υπο Q min^plq 35 Meth Ar | om εκει 2° 130 186 syr^gw | τρεφουσιν AC 36 186 (εκτρεφουσιν 30 98) τρεφωσιν AP 1 al^mu Hipp Meth εκτρεφωσιν Q al^plq 25 Ar | διακοσιας] οκτακοσιας 130 | εξηκοντα] + πεντε ℵ^c.c*

of her Son, but is put beyond the reach of the Dragon's rage, so that his efforts to destroy are as unavailing in her case as in that of the Lord. A place of safety has been provided for her in the wilderness, and thither she flees after the Ascension. The Seer may have in his thoughts either the wanderings of Israel in the wilderness of Sinai (Deut. viii. 2 ff.), or Elijah's two withdrawals from Ahab and Jezebel (1 Kings xvii. 2 f., xix. 3 f.), or the flight of many devout Jews from Antiochus (1 Macc. ii. 29 κατέβησαν πολλοὶ ζητοῦντες δικαιοσύνην καὶ κρίμα εἰς τὴν ἔρημον), or the flight of Mary and Joseph with the Child into Egypt (Mt. ii. 13). But the event immediately in view is doubtless the escape of the Church of Jerusalem to Pella, alluded to in Mc. xiii. 14 οἱ ἐν τῇ Ἰουδαίᾳ φευγέτωσαν εἰς τὰ ὄρη (cf. Eus. *H.E.* iii. 5). In the wider sense the ἔρημος, as Primasius says, is the "solitudo huius vitae...in qua...ut *passer singularis* [Ps. cii. 7] vivit ecclesia"; and the figure is suggested either by the rocky wastes of the Sinaitic peninsula, or more probably by the "wide wild country of rolling hills and hollows" (Benson, *Apocalypse*, p. 32) which lay to the south of Jerusalem, or the high lands to the east of it on the further side of Jordan. Of this country the most striking feature is the absence of human habitations, and the mention of it suggests what was after all the heaviest trial of the Christian life in early times, the loneliness experienced by those who had cut themselves off from the sympathy of their neighbours and even of their nearest relatives. On the Lord's Day the brethren met for fellowship, but for the rest of the week the majority of them stood alone—in the world, but not of it. Yet in this solitude of her life the Church has a place of safety and repose prepared for her by God; for this use of ἑτοιμάζειν see Mt. xx. 23, xxv. 34, 41, Lc. ii. 31, 1 Cor. ii. 9, Heb. xi. 16, Apoc. ix. 15, and for ἑτοιμάζειν τόπον cf. 1 Chron. xv. 3, Jo. xiv. 2 f. What is meant by this τόπος ἡτοιμασμένος may be gathered from Ps. xxx. (xxxi.) 21 κατακρύψεις αὐτοὺς ἐν ἀποκρύφῳ τοῦ προσώπου σου, cf. Col. iii. 3 ἡ ζωὴ ὑμῶν κέκρυπται σὺν τῷ χριστῷ ἐν τῷ θεῷ. Fellowship with the Father and the Son in the Spirit (1 Jo. i. 3, 2 Cor. xiii. 13) is at once the Church's consolation and her safeguard.

For ὅπου...ἐκεῖ = אֲשֶׁר שָׁם see Blass, *Gr.* p. 175. Ἵνα ἐκεῖ τρέφωσιν αὐτὴν κτλ. The reference to Elijah is here apparent, cf. 3 Regn. xvii. 4 τοῖς κόραξιν ἐντελοῦμαι διατρέφειν σε ἐκεῖ, *ib.* xix. 5, 7; though the subject of τρέφωσιν is purposely left undefined. But the daily supply of manna during the Wanderings in the desert of Sinai may also be in view, as Bede supposes: "instar Israeliticae plebis, quae pane caelesti pasta [est] in eremo." The provision made for the Church in the wilderness of life is the spiritual food of the word of God (Mt. iv. 4) and the Flesh and Blood of the Lord (Jo. vi. 48 ff.). The supply lasts for 1260 days, or (*v.* 14) "a season seasons and a half," = $3\frac{1}{2}$ years; see Dan. vii. 25, and *c.* xi. 2, note; *i.e.* to the end of

7 [7] Καὶ ἐγένετο πόλεμος ἐν τῷ οὐρανῷ, ὁ Μιχαὴλ
καὶ οἱ ἄγγελοι αὐτοῦ τοῦ πολεμῆσαι μετὰ τοῦ δρά-

7 ο τε Μιχαηλ A syr | του πολεμησαι] om του ℵQ 1 6 7 8 14 130 al^{35} *praeliabantur* vg πολεμουντες syr^{gw} | μετα] κατα 1 94 al^{vid} *adversus* Ambrst

the age of persecution, and beyond it, to the end of the present order, or, as Primasius well says, "omnia Christianitatis tempora." Thus the story of the Woman in the wilderness synchronizes with the prophesying of the Two Witnesses (xi. 3); in fact the Woman and the Witnesses symbolize the one Catholic Church under different aspects.

The whole of this verse is anticipatory, and the symbolism is repeated in *v.* 12 f., where see notes.

7. καὶ ἐγένετο πόλεμος ἐν τῷ οὐρανῷ] Another *tableau*, not a σημεῖον (*vv.* 1, 3), but consequent upon the two σημεῖα which precede it. The birth and rapture of the Woman's Son issue in a war which invades the ἐπουράνια; for the conception cf. *Yalkut Rub.* f. 87. 2 (on Ex. xiv. 7): "bellum fecit grave in caelo." It is impossible to admit with Andreas that the original rebellion of Satan is intended, though Papias whom he quotes seems to have understood the passage so. Still less can we accept the interpretation of ἐν τῷ οὐρανῷ proposed by several of the Latin commentators, e.g. Bede: "caelum ecclesiam significat"—a view which throws the symbolism into hopeless confusion. The Seer sees an assault directed by the powers of evil against the Exalted Christ. As the Incarnation called forth a counter-manifestation of diabolic power on earth (Mc. i. 13, Lc. xxii. 3, 31, Jo. xii. 31, xiv. 30, xvi. 11), so after the Ascension the attack is supposed to be carried into Heaven.

Battles in the sky, suggested no doubt by the threatening phalanxes of clouds which forebode a storm, are familiar to the later Jewish writers (e.g. 2 Macc. v. 2 f. συνέβη...φαίνεσθαι διὰ τῶν ἀέρων τρέχοντας ἱππεῖς...τὰς προσβολὰς γινομένας, *Orac. Sibyll.* iii. 805 ἐν νεφέλῃ δ' ὄψεσθε μάχην πεζῶν τε καὶ ἱππέων. But in St John's vision the fighting occurs in Heaven itself; it is a πόλεμος ἐν τῷ οὐρανῷ and not a mere spectacle in the upper air. The words hint at nothing less than a supreme attempt on the part of the Dragon to unseat the Woman's Son, and to re-establish himself in the Presence of God.

ὁ Μιχαὴλ καὶ οἱ ἄγγελοι αὐτοῦ τοῦ πολεμῆσαι κτλ.] It is a war of Angels, in which one angelic host is led by the Archangel Michael, and the other by the Dragon. According to Daniel (x. 13, cf. Jude 9 ὁ ἀρχάγγελος, and see note on *c.* viii. 2) Michael is 'one of the chief princes,' and champion of the Jewish people (Dan. x. 21, xii. 1); and consistently with this position he now leads the armies of Heaven against the adversary of the Woman's Son. The construction is one of unusual difficulty; the inf. τοῦ πολεμῆσαι seems to require some such verb as ἐξῆλθον or ἀνέστησαν (cf. *v.* 2, note on βασ. τεκεῖν). But it is simpler to repeat ἐγένετο before ὁ Μιχαήλ: 'there arose war in heaven; [there arose] Michael...to make war. Blass's rendering (*Gr.* p. 236) 'it happened that there fought' (=ἐγένετο τοῦ πολεμῆσαι τὸν Μ.) involves an unnecessary solecism; Viteau's explanation (*Études*, i. p. 168) is better, but the plural (ἦσαν, or ἐγένοντο) is not required. Alford supposes a fusion of two sentences (ἐγένετο τοῦ τὸν Μ. καὶ τοὺς ἀγγέλους αὐτοῦ πολεμῆσαι, and ὁ Μ. καὶ οἱ ἄγγελοι αὐτοῦ ἐπολέμησαν). For πολεμεῖν μετά see ii. 16, note.

κοντος. καὶ ὁ δράκων ἐπολέμησεν καὶ οἱ ἄγγελοι
αὐτοῦ, [8]καὶ οὐκ ἴσχυσεν, οὐδὲ τόπος εὑρέθη αὐτῶν 8
ἔτι ἐν τῷ οὐρανῷ. [9]καὶ ἐβλήθη ὁ δράκων ὁ μέγας, 9
ὁ ὄφις ὁ ἀρχαῖος, ὁ καλούμενος Διάβολος καὶ ὁ
σατανᾶς, ὁ πλανῶν τὴν οἰκουμένην ὅλην· ἐβλήθη εἰς
τὴν γῆν, καὶ οἱ ἄγγελοι αὐτοῦ μετ' αὐτοῦ ἐβλήθησαν.

8 ισχυσεν A min$^{plq\,30}$ me aeth] ισχυσαν ℵCP 1 28 36 79 al^{mu} vg syrr arm Hier anon^{aug} Vict Prim Ar ισχυον Q 14 + προς αυτον ℵ | ουδε] ουτε P 1 36 al | αυτων] αυτοις ℵ$^{c.c}$ 17 36 syr^{gw} Hier (*eis*) αυτω 6 7 8 (29) 130 al$^{plq\,30}$ me aeth^{vid} | om ετι ℵ$^{c.c}$ 7 28 79 arm Hier 9 ο οφις] om ο ℵ 1 Prim^{vid} | διαβολος] *Beelzebul* arm | om και 2° ℵ | ο σατανας] om ο Q min$^{fere\,40}$ Ar | εβληθη 2°] pr και syr^{gw} | om μετ αυτου 1 186 | om εβληθησαν 26 28 49 79 anon^{aug} Hier

καὶ ὁ δράκων ἐπολέμησεν κτλ.] The Dragon also claims the rank of Archangel, and has angels under his command; cf. Mt. xxv. 41 τῷ διαβόλῳ καὶ τοῖς ἀγγέλοις αὐτοῦ.

8. καὶ οὐκ ἴσχυσεν, οὐδὲ τόπος κτλ.] The Dragon's supreme effort was not only a failure, but it resulted in his final expulsion from heaven. Ἔτι seems to imply that up to this moment Satan's claims had not been finally disallowed; compare Job i. 6 ἦλθον οἱ ἄγγελοι τοῦ θεοῦ, καὶ ὁ διάβολος ἦλθεν μετ' αὐτῶν, where he still takes his place in the council-chamber of God. The O.T. phrase τόπος οὐχ εὑρέθη (Dan. ii. 35 Th., cf. Zech. x. 10, Heb.) occurs again in *c.* xx. 11; on εὑρίσκεσθαι in this sense see WM. p. 769 f.

9. καὶ ἐβλήθη ὁ δράκων ὁ μέγας...εἰς τὴν γῆν] Cf. *Sohar Gen.* f. 27. 107 "proiecit Deus Sammaelem et catervam eius e loco sanctitatis ipsorum." A similar vision was present to the mind of our Lord, when the Seventy reported to him their successes; Lc. x. 18 ἐθεώρουν τὸν σατανᾶν ὡς ἀστραπὴν ἐκ τοῦ οὐρανοῦ πεσόντα; cf. Jo. xii. 31 νῦν ὁ ἄρχων τοῦ κόσμου τούτου ἐκβληθήσεται ἔξω. It is vain to attempt to grasp the nature of the spiritual fact which these visions symbolize, so far as it belongs to the celestial order. But the extraordinary progress of the Gospel and the Church during the first three decades and a half that followed the Ascension may well be the earthly counterpart of Satan's fall, while the outbreak of persecution in A.D. 64 shewed that the earth was still to be the field of his activities; see *v.* 13 note.

Ὁ μέγας looks back to *v.* 3 ἰδοὺ δράκων μέγας πυρρός. Ὁ ὄφις ὁ ἀρχαῖος, *serpens antiquus*, the Primaeval Serpent (so *Tanchuma*, f. 50. 2 הנחש הקדמוני, *Debarim Rabba*, f. 23. 3 הנחש הראשון; cf. Syr.$^{gw.}$ *ad loc.* ܪܫܐ = ἡ ἀρχή, and for this use of ἀρχαῖος see Acts xv. 7, 21, xxi. 16), identifies the Dragon with the serpent of Gen. iii. 1 ff., while ὁ καλούμενος Διάβολος καὶ ὁ σατανᾶς declares him to be the person so named in the later books of the O.T. and in Jewish literature. For (ὁ) διάβολος as a personal name = שׂטן see Job i. 6 f., Zech. iii. 1, Sap. ii. 24; though σατάν occurs in the sense of 'an adversary' in 3 Regn. xi. 14, 23, Σατάν or ὁ σατανᾶς (so written ἑλληνικώτερον, as Origen says (*c. Cels.* vi. 44)) is not found in the LXX., but the name had become familiar to the later Jews, and is used in the latter form in the Gospels (14), Acts (2), Pauline Epistles (10), and Apocalypse (8). Ὁ πλανῶν τὴν οἰκου-

10 [10]καὶ ἤκουσα φωνὴν μεγάλην ἐν τῷ οὐρανῷ λέγουσαν
Ἄρτι ἐγένετο ἡ σωτηρία καὶ ἡ δύναμις καὶ ἡ βασιλεία τοῦ θεοῦ ἡμῶν καὶ ἡ ἐξουσία τοῦ χριστοῦ αὐτοῦ, ὅτι ἐβλήθη ὁ κατήγωρ τῶν ἀδελφῶν ἡμῶν, ὁ κατηγορῶν αὐτοὺς ἐνώπιον

10 ηκουσαν 95 | σωτηρια κ. δυναμις κ. σωτηρια (sic) 130 | om και η εξ. του χριστου αυτου syr[gw] | χριστου] κυριου C | εβληθη] κατεβληθη 1 49 al[pauc vid] | κατηγωρ A] κατηγορος ℵCPQ al[omn vid] Or Andr Ar | om των αδελφων ημων syr[gw] | αυτους AP 1 28 36 79] αυτων ℵCQ al[pl]

μένην ὅλην: cf. xx. 3, 7. The earth was no new sphere of Satan's working: see Job i. 7 *περιελθὼν τὴν γῆν καὶ ἐμπεριπατήσας τὴν ὑπ' οὐρανὸν πάρειμι*. But he was henceforth to be limited to it, until the time came for him to fall yet lower.

10. *καὶ ἤκουσα φωνὴν μεγάλην ἐν τῷ οὐρανῷ λέγουσαν*] Cf. v. 11, x. 4, xi. 12, xiv. 2, 13, xviii. 4. No intimation is given as to the source from which the voice proceeds, but as *τῶν ἀδελφῶν ἡμῶν* seems to exclude both the Angels and the *ζῷα*—Bede's "congratulantur angeli saluti fratrum suorum" cannot be maintained in view of the usage of the Book—we are led to attribute it to one of the Elders, who represent the Church.

ἄρτι ἐγένετο ἡ σωτηρία κτλ.] Compare the outbreak of voices at the sounding of the Seventh Trumpet (xi. 15); for *ἡ σωτηρία* see vii. 10 note, xix. 1. Ἡ *βασιλεία* is not qualified by *τοῦ κόσμου* as in xi. 15; it is sovereignty, empire in the abstract, which is here in view. This is attributed to 'our God,' i.e. the Father; to the Son as His anointed (*τοῦ χριστοῦ αὐτοῦ* = מְשִׁיחוֹ, Ps. ii. 2) belongs *ἡ ἐξουσία*, the authority which He exercises by the Father's gift (Ps. ii. 8, Mt. xxviii. 18, Jo. xvii. 2).

The downfall of Satan manifests afresh (*ἐγένετο*) the saving and sovereign power of God, and its active exercise by the exalted Christ. The victory is not Michael's, but the Lord's.

ὅτι ἐβλήθη ὁ κατήγωρ κτλ.] The O.T. representation of Satan as the accuser of Job (Job i. 9) suggests that the Dragon similarly attacks the faithful under the New Covenant. There is perhaps a reference to the zeal of the *delatores* (cf. Juv. i. 33 with Mayor's notes), who abounded in Domitian's time, and were busy with their diabolical attacks on the Asian Christians. But the epithet must not be limited to one department of Satan's work; in Renan's words (*l'Antechrist*, p. 408), he is the "critique malveillant de la création"—the cynical libeller of all that God has made, but especially of His new creation, the Christian Church. *Ἐνώπιον τοῦ θεοῦ ἡμῶν* follows the lines of Job i. 6, while *ἡμέρας καὶ νυκτός* (cf. c. iv. 8) indicates the sleepless vigilance of evil when it seeks occasion against the good (1 Pet. v. 8).

The form *κατήγωρ*, though preserved only by cod. A, is probably right; a transliteration of the Aramaic קטיגור (Dalman, *Gr.* p. 147), it was perhaps preferred to the usual Greek *κατήγορος* (Acts xxiii. 30, 35; xxv. 16, 18) on account of its associations. In Rabbinical writings Satan or Sammael is the accuser of Israel, while Michael appears as its advocate (סניגור, *συνήγορος*); cf. *Shemoth Rabba*, f. 121. 2: "eo tempore quo Israelitae ex Aegypto egressi sunt, stetit Sammael angelus ad accusandum (לקטרג) eos"; *ib.* 129. 2: "si homo praecepta observat...tunc Satan stat et accusat eum (מקטרגו);

τοῦ θεοῦ ἡμῶν ἡμέρας καὶ νυκτός. [11]καὶ αὐτοὶ 11
ἐνίκησαν αὐτὸν διὰ τὸ αἷμα τοῦ ἀρνίου καὶ διὰ
τὸν λόγον τῆς μαρτυρίας αὐτῶν, καὶ οὐκ ἠγά-

10 om ημων ult 1 14 28 79 90 92 98 me arm aeth   11 αυτοι] ουτοι ℵ me | το αιμα] του αιματος 14 36 το ονομα 28 79 | τον λογον της μαρτυριας] την μαρτυριαν C *sanguinem testimonii* me | αυτων 1°] αυτου 43 47 87 me arm

sed advocati quoque ipsius stant iuxta ipsum"; *Vayyikra Rabba* f. 164. 3 "omnibus diebus anni Satanas homines accusat, sola die expiationis excepta." *Shemoth Rabba* f. 117. 3: "R. Jose dixit, Michael et Sammael similes sunt *συνηγόρῳ* et *κατηγόρῳ* (דומים לסניגור וקטיגור)...Satanas accusat, Michael vero merita Israelitarum proponit."

11. *καὶ αὐτοὶ ἐνίκησαν αὐτὸν διὰ τὸ αἷμα κτλ.*] The victory of the martyrs marks the failure of Satan's endeavours. Ἐνίκησεν is said of Christ Himself (v. 5, cf. iii. 21, and see Jo. xvi. 33); the normal condition of His members is progressive conquest (ii. 11, etc., and even xv. 2). But the martyrs' fight is over, and they are already victors, though their triumph is not yet. The Blood of the Lamb is here as in vii. 14 (where see note) the Sacrifice of the Cross, which is regarded as the primary cause (*διά*, *propter*, cf. WM. p. 498) of the martyrs' victory; His conquest of Satan rendered conquest possible for them (cf. Lc. xi. 21 f., Heb. ii. 18), while the loosing of sins which it effected (Apoc. i. 5) silences Satan's accusing voice. Thus the Lamb is the true *συνήγορος* of the new Israel, its *παράκλητος πρὸς τὸν πατέρα* (1 Jo. ii. 1). His Blood speaks of acceptance and not, as Abel's, of wrath (Heb. xii. 24). Yet the Sacrifice of the Death of Christ does not spell victory except for those who suffer with Him (Rom. viii. 17, 2 Tim. ii. 11 f.). Thus a secondary cause of the martyrs' victory is found in their personal labour and self-sacrifice; they overcame *διὰ τὸν λόγον τῆς μαρτυρίας αὐτῶν* (cf. vi. 9, xi. 7, xx. 4), i.e. because of their testimony to Jesus (ii. 13, note) and their indifference to life itself in comparison with loyalty to Him. *Καὶ οὐκ ἠγάπησαν* states the extent of this victory; for Christ's sake they overcame the natural love of life. There is here a clear reference to the Master's teaching in Jo. xii. 25 *ὁ φιλῶν τὴν ψυχὴν αὐτοῦ ἀπολλύει αὐτήν, καὶ ὁ μισῶν τὴν ψυχὴν αὐτοῦ ἐν τῷ κόσμῳ τούτῳ εἰς ζωὴν αἰώνιον φυλάξει αὐτήν*; other sayings of the same type occur in the Synoptic Gospels (Mt. x. 39, xvi. 25, Mc. viii. 35 f., Lc. ix. 24, xvii. 33). Compare St Paul's response in Acts xx. 24: *οὐδενὸς λόγου ποιοῦμαι τὴν ψυχὴν τιμίαν ἐμαυτῷ κτλ.*, and see also Acts xxi. 13, Phil. i. 20 ff. On *ψυχή* see Mc. viii. 35, note, and for *οὐκ ἠγάπησαν τὴν ψ. αὐτῶν* cf. M. Antoninus vii 46 *οὐ φιλοψυχητέον*. *Ἄχρι θανάτου* is elliptical: 'their non-attachment to life was carried to the extent of being ready to die for their faith'; cf. Phil. ii. 8 *ὑπήκοος μέχρι θανάτου*, 'obedient to the extent of surrendering life.' On *ἄχρι*, *μέχρι*, see c. ii. 10, note. On the whole verse Bede well remarks: "merito animas pro Christo contemnunt, qui per sanguinem Christi tantum vicerunt adversarium."

This reference to the martyrs is proleptic in the present context, for the fall of Satan precedes the age of persecution. But the age of persecution and the victory of the martyrs, which had begun some time before the Apocalypse was written (ii. 13), were consequent upon the expulsion

12 πησαν τὴν ψυχὴν αὐτῶν ἄχρι θανάτου. [12]διὰ
τοῦτο εὐφραίνεσθε, οὐρανοὶ καὶ οἱ ἐν αὐτοῖς
σκηνοῦντες· οὐαὶ τὴν γῆν καὶ τὴν θάλασσαν,
ὅτι κατέβη ὁ διάβολος πρὸς ὑμᾶς, ἔχων θυμὸν
μέγαν, εἰδὼς ὅτι ὀλίγον καιρὸν ἔχει.
13 [13]Καὶ ὅτε εἶδεν ὁ δράκων ὅτι ἐβλήθη εἰς τὴν γῆν,

11 την ψυχην] τας ψυχας 35 87 12 om δια τουτο 130 | ουρανοι] pr οι A 1 28 30** 36 47 49 79 91 95 186 al | σκηνουντες] κατασκηνουντες C κατοικουντες ℵ 26 29 30 31 98 | την γην (εις τ. γ. ℵ τ. αγαπην A) και την θαλασσαν] τη γη και τη θαλασση Q min[40] Ar τοις κατοικουσι την γην και την θαλασσαν 1 Andr[comm] | υμας] αυτους syr[gw] | om μεγαν ℵ 13 ειδεν ℵACP min[pl]] ιδεν Q 7 14 92 130 | οτι εβληθη ο δρακων ℵ[c.a]

of Satan from heaven, and are therefore anticipated in this acclamation of the Divine victory.

12. *διὰ τοῦτο εὐφραίνεσθε, οὐρανοί κτλ.*] The heavens (*οἱ οὐρανοί*, here only in Apoc.; cf. Dan. iii. 59 *εὐλογεῖτε, οὐρανοί, τὸν κύριον*) and their inhabitants might well keep high festival (cf. xi. 10, note, xviii. 20, for this sense of *εὐφραίνεσθαι*). Earth had cause to mourn, since it was henceforth the only field of his baleful energies. *Σκηνοῦντες* here and in xiii. 6 seems to be equivalent to *κατοικοῦντες*, and not to indicate brief or temporary residence, as in 2 Cor. v. 1, where *οἰκία τοῦ σκήνους* is opposed to *οἰκία αἰώνιος*. Perhaps *κατοικεῖν* is avoided because elsewhere in the Apocalypse it is used in reference to the pagan world (*c.* iii., note); and in *σκηνοῦν* there may be a reference to the Divine tabernacling of which mention is made in vii. 15 and xxi. 3. As God 'tabernacles' in Heaven 'with' or 'over' its inhabitants, so they are said to tabernacle there with Him or under His safe keeping. Earth and Sea are probably not to be explained allegorically (as by Andreas: *τοὺς τὰ γήϊνα φρονοῦντας καὶ τῇ θαλάσσῃ τοῦ βίου κλυδωνιζομένους*), but literally, of the world as the scene of Satan's future operations.

ὅτι κατέβη ὁ διάβολος πρὸς ὑμᾶς κτλ.] The Dragon's ignominious fall (*ἐβλήθη*) is euphemistically described as a descent (*κατέβη*). It has not impaired his strength, and he sets to work at once with redoubled zeal, goaded by his defeat (*ἔχων θυμὸν μέγαν*), and resolved to make the most of an opportunity which he now knows to be brief (*εἰδὼς ὅτι ὀλίγον καιρὸν ἔχει*). The participial clauses are parallel to one another, revealing the two motives which actuate Satan since the Ascension. With *εἰδώς κτλ.* Primasius acutely compares the cry of the 'Legion' in Mt. viii. 30 *ἦλθες ὧδε πρὸ καιροῦ βασανίσαι ἡμᾶς;* Cf. St Luke's comment (viii. 32): *παρεκάλουν αὐτὸν ἵνα μὴ ἐπιτάξῃ αὐτοῖς εἰς τὴν ἄβυσσον ἀπελθεῖν.* Earth is still the sphere of devilry in all its forms, but the abyss is its ultimate destination. *Ὀλίγον* is relative, like the *ταχύ* which accompanies announcements of the Parousia. In *vv.* 6, 14, the same interval of time is represented as $3\frac{1}{2}$ years.

13. *καὶ ὅτε εἶδεν ὁ δράκων ὅτι ἐβλήθη κτλ.*] The narrative of *v.* 9 is now resumed. The Dragon is too shrewd to ignore the fact that his expulsion from Heaven is final and irretrievable. But he recognises also that his position on the earth offers fresh opportunities. If he cannot directly attack the Woman's Son, he can hurt the Son through the Mother

ἐδίωξεν τὴν γυναῖκα ἥτις ἔτεκεν τὸν ἄρσενα. [14]καὶ 14
ἐδόθησαν τῇ γυναικὶ αἱ δύο πτέρυγες τοῦ ἀετοῦ τοῦ

13 εδιωκεν 130 | αρρενα (Q) min$^{\rm pl}$ Hipp Andr Ar 14 εδοθη ℵ$^{\rm c.a}$ syr$^{\rm gw}$ | αι δυο] om αι ℵQ min$^{\rm pl}$ syr$^{\rm gw}$ Hipp Ar | του αετου] om του ℵ arm

(cf. Mt. xxv. 45, Acts ix. 4). So he goes in pursuit of the Woman, who is identified with (ἥτις, acc. to Blass, *Gr.* p. 173, here nearly = ἥ) the Mother of the man-child. Ἐδίωξεν, while bearing its original sense 'pursue' (cf. Rom. ix. 30 f., xii. 13, Phil. iii. 12, 14), implies hostile pursuit, as in Mt. x. 23, xxiii. 34, Acts xxvi. 11, and thus approaches to the technical 'persecute' which is the prevalent meaning of διώκειν in the N.T. (Mt. v. 10 ff., 44, Acts vii. 52, ix. 4 f., Rom. xii. 14, 1 Cor. xv. 9, Phil. iii. 6). The historical moment in the Seer's mind is doubtless the dark day in A.D. 64 when Nero began the policy of persecution. From that time the Empire as such was more or less hostile to the Church, and in this hostility the Seer sees the hand of the great Adversary.

14. καὶ ἐδόθησαν τῇ γυναικὶ αἱ δύο πτέρυγες κτλ.] Ἀετός is probably here as in Mt. xxiv. 28, and elsewhere in this book, not the true eagle but the griffon (נֶשֶׁר, *gyps fulvus*), a great bird of the vulture type which abounds in Palestine (*Enc. Bibl.*, 1145); for τοῦ μεγάλου cf. Ez. xvii. 3 ἀετὸς ὁ μέγας ὁ μεγαλόπτερος, ὁ μακρὸς τῇ ἐκτάσει. Αἱ δύο πτέρυγες is pressed into the interpretation by Hippolytus (ed. Lag. p. 32: τοῦτ' ἐστὶν Ἰησοῦ Χριστοῦ...ὃς ἐκτείνας τὰς ἁγίας χεῖρας ἐν ἁγίῳ ξύλῳ ἥπλωσε δύο πτέρυγας: he adds a reference to Mt. xxiii. 37, Mal. iv. 2), Victorinus ("duo sunt prophetae"), and Primasius ("duobus utitur testamentis"), but perhaps unnecessarily. The figure as a whole is based on Exod. xix. 4 ἀνέλαβον ὑμᾶς ὡσεὶ ἐπὶ πτερύγων ἀετῶν, and Deut. xxxii. 11 ὡς ἀετὸς...διεὶς τὰς πτέρυγας αὐτοῦ ἐδέξατο αὐτούς [sc. Κύριος]; a still nearer parallel is Isa. xl. 31 πτεροφυήσουσιν ὡς ἀετοί, where the prophet transfers the eagle's wings to the men who are endowed with Divine strength. For ἐδόθησαν see *cc.* viii. 2, ix. 1, 3.

The escape of the Woman (*v.* 6) is now explained; even the Dragon is no match for God-given powers. Πέτεσθαι is used of the eagle's flight in iv. 7, viii. 13; cf. Job ix. 26 ἀετοῦ πετομένου ζητοῦντος βοράν, Prov. xxiv. 54 (xxx. 19) ἴχνη ἀετοῦ πετομένου. For εἰς τὴν ἔρημον κτλ. see *v.* 6, notes; a comparison of the two verses shews that τὸν τόπον αὐτῆς = τὸν τ. τὸν ἡτοιμασμένον αὐτῇ ἀπὸ τοῦ θεοῦ, and that the 1260 days and the 'season, seasons and a half' are strictly convertible expressions; see xi. 2 f., note. On the meaning of the time limit here see Hippolytus (ed. Lag. p. 32): αὗταί εἰσιν αἱ χίλιαι διακόσιαι ἑξήκοντα...ἃς κρατήσει τύραννος διώκων τὴν ἐκκλησίαν.

To some extent the solitary life is a necessity imposed upon Christians by their religion: to the end of the present order the Church dwells in the wilderness, and is a *vox clamantis in deserto*. But as an historical fact the withdrawal into the wilderness began with the outbreak of persecution. The Church was constrained to meet the policy of persecution by a policy of secrecy; she began to guard the mysteries from the sight of the heathen, to withhold the Creed and the Lord's Prayer from catechumens till the eve of baptism, to abstain from public amusements and from society, to substitute loyalty to the Christian brotherhood for an exclusive patriotism; cf. the interesting passage in *Ep. ad Diogn.* v. 4, 5 παράδοξον ἐνδείκνυνται τὴν κατάστασιν τῆς ἑαυτῶν πολιτείας· πατρίδας οἰκοῦσιν ἰδίας, ἀλλ'

μεγάλου, ἵνα πέτηται εἰς τὴν ἔρημον εἰς τὸν τόπον
αὐτῆς, ὅπου τρέφεται ἐκεῖ καιρὸν καὶ καιροὺς καὶ
15 ἥμισυ καιροῦ ἀπὸ προσώπου τοῦ ὄφεως. [15]καὶ ἔβαλεν
ὁ ὄφις ἐκ τοῦ στόματος αὐτοῦ ὀπίσω τῆς γυναικὸς
ὕδωρ ὡς ποταμόν, ἵνα αὐτὴν ποταμοφόρητον ποιήσῃ.
16 [16]καὶ ἐβοήθησεν ἡ γῆ τῇ γυναικί, καὶ ἤνοιξεν ἡ γῆ τὸ

14 *πεταται* Q*^{vid} 1 28 38 79 | om *εις* 1° 130 | *τον τοπον*] om *τον* א | *οπου*] *ινα* 130 | *τρεφηται* Q min^{35} Ar | om *και ημισυ καιρου* C   15 *αυτην*] *ταυτην* P 1 7 al | om *ινα...ποιηση* me *ut eam perderet* Prim   16 om *εβοηθη. η γη τη γυν.* me | om *η γη* 2° 34 35 40 41 42 al^{vid} anon^{aug}

ὡς πάροικοι...πᾶσα ξένη πατρίς ἐστιν αὐτῶν, καὶ πᾶσα πατρὶς ξένη.

Ἀπὸ προσώπου τοῦ ὄφεως = מִפְּנֵי־ הַנָּחָשׁ, cf. Jud. ix. 21 *ᾤκησεν ἐκεῖ ἀπὸ προσώπου Ἀβειμέλεκ* (מִפְּנֵי א״).

15. *καὶ ἔβαλεν ὁ ὄφις ἐκ τοῦ στόματος αὐτοῦ κτλ.*] The Serpent—*δράκων* is dropt here and in *v.* 14; the mind of the Seer glancing back at the *ὄφις ὁ ἀρχαῖος* of *v.* 9—unable to follow the Woman in her flight, seeks to intercept it by a flood of waters which he pours out from his mouth (contrast i. 16, ii. 16, xix. 15 ff.). The thought of the godly wrestling with a flood of evil is familiar to the Psalmist (Ps. xvii. (xviii.) 5) *χείμαρροι ἀνομίας ἐξετάραξάν με*, xxxi. (xxxii.) 6 *ἐν κατακλυσμῷ ὑδάτων πολλῶν πρὸς αὐτὸν οὐκ ἐγγιοῦσιν*, cxxiii. (cxxiv.) 4 f. *τὸ ὕδωρ κατεπόντισεν ἡμᾶς, χείμαρρον διῆλθεν ἡ ψυχὴ ἡμῶν...τὸ ὕδωρ τὸ ἀνυπόστατον* (הַמַּיִם הַזֵּידוֹנִים), and the Prophets (Isa. xliii. 2 *ἐὰν διαβαίνῃς δι' ὕδατος, μετὰ σοῦ εἰμι, καὶ ποταμοί οὐ συγκλύσουσίν σε*); it may have been suggested by the passage through the Red Sea and the Jordan, or possibly by the *χείμαρροι* of Palestinian wadys (cf. Mt. vii. 27).

Ps. Cyprian (*ad Novat.* 14) interprets the flood from the Dragon's mouth of the Decian edicts which led to the fall of many of the faithful; Victorinus sees in it the passions of the populace aroused against the Church: "aqua...populum qui persequatur eam significat," cf. Primasius: "impetum persecutorum aqua significat." Andreas offers a choice of explanations: *τοῦτ' ἐστίν, ἀθέων ἀνδρῶν ἢ πονηρῶν δαιμόνων ἢ ποικίλων πειρασμῶν πλῆθος.*

The torrent let loose by the Serpent is designed to sweep away the Woman. *Ποταμοφόρητος* is *ἅπ. λεγ.*, formed regularly after the example of *ἀνεμοφόρητος, ὑδατοφόρητος* (WM. p. 124); for *ποτ. ποιεῖν* cf. *ἠρημωμένην ποιεῖν καὶ γυμνήν* (xvii. 16)—the exact phrase is used by Hesychius in his note on *Il.* vi. 348 *ἀπόερσεν· ποταμοφόρητον ἐποίησεν.* The purpose which, consciously or not, animated Imperial persecutors was to destroy the Christian name. The Seer discovers it already in the work of Nero and Domitian; in the edicts of Decius and Diocletian it was openly avowed.

16. *καὶ ἐβοήθησεν ἡ γῆ τῇ γυναικί κτλ.*] Instances were known in Asia in which rivers or streams disappeared into the bowels of the earth; thus Herodotus had heard (vii. 30) that the Lycus flowed underground near Colossae, and the statement is confirmed by Strabo and Pliny (Ramsay, *Cities and Bishoprics of Phrygia*, i. p. 210 f.); at the present time the Chrysorrhoas, which flows from the hot springs of Hierapolis (cf. iii. 16, note), is said to bury itself in the plain between Hierapolis and Laodicea

στόμα αὐτῆς καὶ κατέπιεν τὸν ποταμὸν ὃν ἔβαλεν
ὁ δράκων ἐκ τοῦ στόματος αὐτοῦ. [17]*καὶ ὠργίσθη ὁ* 17
δράκων ἐπὶ τῇ γυναικί, καὶ ἀπῆλθεν ποιῆσαι πόλεμον
μετὰ τῶν λοιπῶν τοῦ σπέρματος αὐτῆς, τῶν τηρούν-

16 om *και κατεπιεν...στοματος αυτου* syr | *τον ποταμον ον*] *το υδωρ ο* A arm | *εβαλεν*] *ενεβαλεν* Q (14 92) 17 *οργισθη* Q 7 36 | om *επι* C Prim^{vid} (*mulieri*) | *των λοιπων*] *τ. επιλοιπων* ℵ *τ. αγιων* Hipp om 130

(Ramsay, *op. cit.* ii. p. 86, note 2). It is not easy to conjecture the exact meaning of the symbol here. But the general sense is clear: the Apocalyptist foresees the failure of any attempt, however virulent, to destroy the Church (cf. Mt. xvi. 18). Help would arise from unexpected quarters; the death of the persecuting Emperor, followed by a change of policy on the part of his successors, sudden revulsions of public feeling, or a fresh turn of events diverting public attention from the Church, would from time to time check or frustrate Satan's plans.

The phrase *ἤνοιξεν κτλ.* is from Num. xvi. 30 *ἀνοίξασα ἡ γῆ τὸ στόμα αὐτῆς καταπίεται αὐτούς*; cf. Num. xxvi. 10, Deut. xi. 6, Ps. cv. (cvi.) 17.

17. *καὶ ὠργίσθη ὁ δράκων ἐπὶ τῇ γυναικί κτλ.*] The Dragon, enraged at the escape of the Woman (for *ὀργίζεσθαι ἐπί* with dat. see Gen. xl. 2, Num. xxxi. 14; other constructions are *ὀργ. ἐπί* with acc., 4 Regn. xix. 28, Ps. lxxiii. (lxxiv.) 1, cv. (cvi.) 40; *ὀργ. εἰς* (Deut. vii. 4) or *ἐν* (Jud. ii. 20, iii. 8, x. 7); *ὀργ.* followed by dat. without preposition (Num. xxv. 3, Mt. v. 22)), seeks his revenge in other ways. If he can neither unseat the Throned Christ nor destroy the Church, yet individual Christians may enjoy no such immunity. In this hope he goes off (*ἀπῆλθεν*) to make war on "the rest of the Woman's seed"—a clear reference to Gen. iii. 15 *ἔχθραν θήσω ἀνὰ μέσον σοῦ καὶ ἀνὰ μέσον τῆς γυναικός, καὶ ἀνὰ μέσον τοῦ σπέρματός σου καὶ ἀνὰ μέσον τοῦ σπέρματος αὐτῆς.* That believers are (1) brethren of the Incarnate Son, and (2) children of the Church, is taught elsewhere in the N.T. (Rom. viii. 29 *εἰς τὸ εἶναι αὐτὸν πρωτότοκον ἐν πολλοῖς ἀδελφοῖς*, Gal. iv. 26 *ἡ δὲ ἄνω Ἰερουσαλὴμ ... ἐστὶν μήτηρ ἡμῶν*). From these two conceptions, combined with that of the Church as the Mother of Christ, it follows that the Seed of the Woman is not to be limited to the Messiah, but embraces all who are Christ's: compare St Paul's argument as to the Seed of Abraham (Gal. iii. 18, 29 *τῷ σπέρματι...ὅς ἐστιν Χριστός...εἰ δὲ ὑμεῖς Χριστοῦ, ἄρα τοῦ Ἀβραὰμ σπέρμα ἐστέ*). On *ποιεῖν πόλεμον μετά* see xi. 7, xiii. 7, xix. 19.

τῶν τηρούντων τὰς ἐντολὰς τοῦ θεοῦ κτλ.] The younger sons of the Mother of Christ are to be distinguished by two notes; they keep the commandments of God (xiv. 12), and they bear witness to Jesus (i. 9, vi. 9, xix. 10, xx. 4). The O.T. note of piety takes precedence, for the Apoc. comes from a Christian Jew, whose mind is steeped in the thought and language of the older Covenant; but it does not stand alone, for the writer sees that obedience to the Law does not constitute sonship without faith in Christ. It is those who possess both marks with whom the Devil is at war; as Bede well points out: "mandata Dei in fide Jesu Christi custodire, hoc est pugnare cum diabolo, et ipsum provocare in praelium." On *τηρεῖν* see i. 3, note.

των τὰς ἐντολὰς τοῦ θεοῦ καὶ ἐχόντων τὴν μαρτυρίαν
18 Ἰησοῦ· [18]καὶ ἐστάθη ἐπὶ τὴν ἄμμον τῆς θαλάσσης.
XIII. 1 [1]Καὶ εἶδον ἐκ τῆς θαλάσσης θηρίον ἀναβαῖνον,

17 Ιησου] του Ιησου Q** 1 7 8 Ιησου χριστου vg$^{\text{cle lips 4 tol}}$ Prim του θεου ℵ* θεου 98 | 18 εσταθη ℵAC 87 92 130 vg syr arm aeth^{utr} anon^{aug}] εσταθην PQ 186 me syr^{gw} Andr Ar
XIII 1 ειδον ℵP min^{pl} Andr Ar] ιδον ACQ 7 14 92

18. *καὶ ἐστάθη ἐπὶ τὴν ἄμμον τῆς θαλάσσης*] On his way to the war the Dragon comes to a halt (*ἐστάθη*, cf. viii. 3) by the seashore (*ἡ ἄμμος τῆς θαλ.*, חוֹל הַיָּם is found from Gen. xxxii. 12 (13) onwards: *ψάμμος* occurs only in Sap. vii. 9). Ἐστάθην is an attractive reading in view of the Seer's circumstances; nothing more natural for an exile in Patmos than to stand gazing out to sea, and in that position to receive one of his great inspirations. And, it may be added, nothing more easy than for ΕΣΤΑΘΗ̄ to lose its bar at an early stage in the transcription of the book, and degenerate into *ἐστάθη*. Nevertheless, the latter reading must be accepted, in view of the overwhelming support which it receives from the best MSS. (see *app. crit.*). Moreover it yields perhaps a more relevant if a less obvious sense. The picture of the Dragon halting on the seashore to call up his terrible ally is one of the highest interest, and forms a real feature in the revelation, whereas *ἐστάθην* is merely scenic. If *ἐστάθη* is read, the sentence clearly belongs to *c.* xii. (R.V.); if *ἐστάθην*, it must stand as in A.V. at the beginning of of *c.* xiii.

XIII. 1—10. The Wild Beast from the Sea.

1. *καὶ εἶδον ἐκ τῆς θαλάσσης θηρίον ἀναβαῖνον κτλ.*] The Seer has anticipated this vision in xi. 7 *τὸ θηρίον τὸ ἀναβαῖνον ἐκ τῆς ἀβύσσου*, where see note. The scene is suggested by Dan. vii. 2 f., Th. *ἐγὼ Δανιὴλ ἐθεώρουν, καὶ ἰδοὺ οἱ τέσσαρες ἄνεμοι τοῦ οὐρανοῦ προσέβαλλον εἰς τὴν θάλασσαν τὴν μεγάλην* (the Mediterranean), *καὶ τέσσερα θηρία μεγάλα ἀνέβαινεν ἐκ τῆς θαλάσσης*: cf. 4 Esdr. xi. 1 "ecce ascendebat de mari aquila." The Sea is an apt symbol of the agitated surface of unregenerate humanity (cf. Isa. lvii. 20), and especially of the seething caldron of national and social life, out of which the great historical movements of the world arise; cf. Isa. xvii. 12 *οὐαὶ πλῆθος ἐθνῶν πολλῶν· ὡς θάλασσα κυμαίνουσα, οὕτως ταραχθήσεσθε*; Apoc. xvii. 15 *τὰ ὕδατα ἃ εἶδες...λαοὶ καὶ ὄχλοι εἰσὶν καὶ ἔθνη καὶ γλῶσσαι*. The *θηρίον* which rises out of this troubled sea is, as in Dan. vii. 17, 23, some vast Empire, possessing a strength which is used in the interests of brute force. It is described at length, still after the manner of Daniel, but with independent details. Like the Dragon, it has ten horns and seven heads (cf. xii. 3), but in the case of the Beast it is the horns which are crowned and not the heads. The 'ten horns' come from Daniel's description of the Fourth Beast, in the interpretation of which they are explained as "ten kings" (Dan. vii. 24 Th. *τὰ δέκα κέρατα αὐτοῦ, δέκα βασιλεῖς ἀναστήσονται*, cf. Apoc. xvii. 12). Daniel's Fourth Beast is in all probability the Empire of Alexander, and its horns either the Kings of Antioch or the kingdoms of the Diadochi; see Bevan, *Daniel*, p. 122 f., and Driver, p. 98 f. The Seer has in view the great persecuting Power of his own age, the Empire of Rome; on its seven heads and ten horns see *c.* xvii. 9, 12, notes. An early interpretation, however, identified the Beast from the Sea with Antichrist, e.g. Irenaeus (v. 28. 2), who compares 2 Thess. ii. 10 ff.

ἔχον κέρατα δέκα καὶ κεφαλὰς ἑπτά, καὶ ἐπὶ τῶν
κεράτων αὐτοῦ δέκα διαδήματα, καὶ ἐπὶ τὰς κεφαλὰς
αὐτοῦ ὀνόματα βλασφημίας. [2]καὶ τὸ θηρίον ὃ εἶδον 2
ἦν ὅμοιον παρδάλει, καὶ οἱ πόδες αὐτοῦ ὡς ἄρκου, καὶ

1 *αυτου* 1°] *αυτων* ℵ* 7 | *δεκα διαδηματα*] *διαδ. δεκα* ℵ *διαδ. τεσσερα* me^{vid} om *δεκα* Prim | *ταις κεφαλαις* 130 | *ονοματα*] *ονομα* ℵCP 1 28 79 95 al vg $^{\text{fu dem lips 4 tol}}$ me syr^{gw} arm aeth Prim | om *βλασφημιας* me 2 *ειδον* ℵCP al^{pl} Andr Ar] *ιδον* AQ 14 92 130 | om *ην* 1 12 46 arm | *αρκτου* 29 30** 47 87* 90 91 92 94** 95 96 98 al Ar

καὶ ἐπὶ τὰς κεφαλὰς αὐτοῦ ὀνόματα βλασφημίας] His seven heads, if not crowned, wore titles (or, if we prefer the reading of ℵCP, a title), which were of the nature of blasphemy (cf. xvii. 3). What were the blasphemous titles assumed by the Heads of the Roman Empire in the first and second centuries may be learnt from the Imperial letters found by J. T. Wood among the inscriptions of Ephesus; see e.g. Hicks, *Ephesus*, p. 150 [αὐτο-κράτωρ] Καῖσαρ θεοῦ Τραϊανοῦ Παρθικοῦ υἱός | [θεοῦ Νερούα υ]ἱωνός, Τραϊανὸς Ἀδριανὸς Σεβαστός; *ib.* p. 154 αὐτο[κράτωρ Καῖσαρ θεοῦ Ἀδ]ριανοῦ | υἱός, θε[οῦ Τραϊανοῦ Παρθικοῦ υἱων]ός, | θεοῦ Νερ[ούα ἔκγονος, Τίτος Αἴλιος Ἀδρι]ανὸς | Ἀντωνῖνος Σεβαστός. How fully this language was reciprocated by the cities of Asia appears from other inscriptions which record honours decreed to the Emperor, e.g. Hicks, p. 162 [αὐ]τοκράτορι θεῷ Καίσαρι; *ib.* p. 169 θεοῖς Σεβαστοῖς. No Christian, none at least of Jewish origin, could have read such inscriptions day after day without a shock to his inbred monotheism. The use of Divine titles was a βλασφημία πρὸς τὸν θεόν (*v.* 6), and the very note of Antichrist; cf. 2 Thess. ii. 4 ff. Even apart from direct blasphemy, the pretensions of Rome were offensive to men who believed in the sovereignty of God; cf. Renan, *l'Antechrist*, p. 413, "la grandeur, l'orgueil de Rome, l'*imperium* qu'elle se décerne, sa divinité, objet d'un culte spécial et public, sont un blasphème perpétuel contre Dieu, seul souverain réel du monde."

2. *καὶ τὸ θηρίον ὃ εἶδον ἦν ὅμοιον παρδάλει κτλ.*] Daniel's first Beast was *ὡσεὶ λέαινα*, his second *ὅμοιον ἄρκῳ*, his third *ὡσεὶ πάρδαλις*. The Seer's Beast combined these features; whatever the Babylonian, Median and Persian Empires had of strength and brutality, was present in their latest successor, the Empire of Rome, as it was seen under Nero and Domitian. In the Seer's eyes Rome had the disposition of the leopard—the agility, the cat-like vigilance and craft, the fierce cruelty of that too familiar inhabitant of Palestine and the further East (Sir. xxviii. 23 (27) *ὡς πάρδαλις λυμανεῖται αὐτούς*, Hos. xiii. 7 *ἔσομαι αὐτοῖς ὡς πάρδαλις...κατὰ τὴν ὁδὸν Ἀσσυρίων*, Hab. i. 8 *ἐξαλοῦνται ὑπὲρ παρδάλεις*, Jer. v. 6 (*π. ἐγρηγόρησεν ἐπὶ τὰς πόλεις αὐτῶν*); the feet of the bear (*ἄρκος* rather than *ἄρκτος*, see W. Schm., p. 65, Blass, *Gr.*, p. 24), with their slow strength and power to crush (on the bear in Palestine see 1 Regn. xvii. 34, 4 Regn. ii. 24, Amos v. 19), and the roar of the on (also in ancient times a Palestinian beast, haunting the Judaean hills (1 Regn. *l.c.*), and the Jordan valley (Jer. xxvii. (l.) 17), and specially dreaded by the shepherd in charge of a flock (Zeph. iii. 3, Zech. xi. 3). The description, however impossible to realize as a picture, is surely admirable as a symbol of the character of the foe which the Church found in the Empire, blending massive strength with feline dexterity

τὸ στόμα αὐτοῦ ὡς στόμα λέοντος. καὶ ἔδωκεν
αὐτῷ ὁ δράκων τὴν δύναμιν αὐτοῦ καὶ τὸν θρόνον
3 αὐτοῦ καὶ ἐξουσίαν μεγάλην. ³καὶ μίαν ἐκ τῶν
κεφαλῶν αὐτοῦ ὡς ἐσφαγμένην εἰς θάνατον, καὶ ἡ

2 om *στομα* 2° 38 130 syr^gw^ arm aeth | *λεοντων* ℵ 14 92 syrr Vict | *ο δρακων*] om *ο* ℵ | *και εξουσιαν μεγαλην*] om 29 30 50 93 98 + *εδωκεν αυτω* A** 3 *και* 1°] + *ειδον* 95 vg^cle fu lipss dem^ anon^aug^ | om *εκ* Q* 1 36 me arm | *ως*] *ωσει* B min^plq 30^ Ar^txt^ om arm

following up a stealthy and perhaps unobserved policy of repression with the sudden terrors of a hostile edict. On *στόμα λέοντος* see 2 Tim. iv. 17, and cf. Victorinus: "ad sanguinem armatum os"; Primasius: "leoni [comparatur] propter...linguae superbiam."

καὶ ἔδωκεν αὐτῷ ὁ δράκων τὴν δύναμιν αὐτοῦ κτλ.] The Dragon works through the Beast as his agent; the war is of Satan's making, but the Empire is his tool for waging it. The Seer regards the persecuting Emperors as vassals of Satan; a great change has passed over the attitude of the Church in this respect since St Paul wrote to Roman Christians: *οὐ γὰρ ἔστιν ἐξουσία εἰ μὴ ὑπὸ θεοῦ, αἱ δὲ οὖσαι ὑπὸ θεοῦ τεταγμέναι εἰσίν* (Rom. xiii. 1). Even after persecution had begun, St Peter takes the same position (1 Pet. ii. 13). The Apocalyptist himself does not hint at resistance, and the Church of the first three centuries continued to be loyal under the greatest provocations. Nevertheless, it was clear that the new Imperial policy towards the Church was not of God. In some sense Satan was the source of power so abused; his claim (Mt. iv. 9 *ταῦτά σοι πάντα δώσω*, Lc. iv. 6 *ἐμοὶ παραδέδοται [ἡ ἐξουσία], καὶ ᾧ ἐὰν θέλω δίδωμι αὐτήν*) is admitted, so far as regards the persecuting Emperors: Nero, Domitian, were his vassals, and all the powers and authority of the *ἄρχων τοῦ κόσμου τούτου* were at their disposal. *Δύναμις...θρόνος* (ii. 13, note) ...*ἐξουσία*: "jedes Wort ist mit feierlichem Nachdruck gesetzt" (Bousset). With *τ. θρόνον* cf. ii. 13, note.

3. *καὶ μίαν ἐκ τῶν κεφαλῶν αὐτοῦ ὡς ἐσφαγμένην κτλ.*] *Μίαν...ὡς ἐσφαγμ.*, sc. *εἶδον*, which has been supplied by some MSS. (see *app. crit.*); *v.* 3 takes up the narrative of *v.* 1. *Ὡς ἐσφαγμένην* hints at a comparison between the Beast and the *ἀρνίον ὡς ἐσφαγμένον* (cf. Bede: "imitatione veri capitis nostri"). Like the Lamb, the Beast has sustained a mortal wound, a deathblow (*ἡ πληγὴ τοῦ θανάτου αὐτοῦ*, cf. WM. p. 297), which has fallen on one of his seven heads (cf. xvii. 8, 11). According to *c.* xvii. 9 the seven heads have a double meaning; they are seven mountains, but also seven kings, i.e. they represent seven Emperors who reigned over the city of the Seven Hills. If it be asked whether any of the earlier Roman Emperors received a death-blow from which he recovered or was supposed to have recovered, the answer is not far to seek. In June 68 Nero, pursued by the emissaries of the Senate, inflicted upon himself a wound of which he died. His remains received a public funeral, and were afterwards lodged in the mausoleum of Augustus. Nevertheless there grew up in the eastern provinces of the Empire a rumour that he was still alive, and in hiding. Pretenders who claimed to be Nero arose in 69 and 79, and even as late as 88 or 89 (Tac. *hist.* i. 78, ii. 8, Zonar. xi. 18, Suet. *Nero* 57). The legend of Nero's survival or resuscitation took root in the

πληγὴ τοῦ θανάτου αὐτοῦ ἐθεραπεύθη. καὶ ἐθαυ-
μάσθη ὅλη ἡ γῆ ὀπίσω τοῦ θηρίου, [4]καὶ προσεκύ- 4
νησαν τῷ δράκοντι, ὅτι ἔδωκεν τὴν ἐξουσίαν τῷ
θηρίῳ· καὶ προσεκύνησαν τῷ θηρίῳ λέγοντες Τίς

3 om αυτου 2° Q* | εθαυμασθη A 1 12 28 36 79 186 syr$^{gw\,vid}$] εθαυμαστωθη C εθαυμασεν ℵPQ min^{pl} Ar | ολη η γη] εν ολη τη γη 1 12 28 36 79 186 4 οτι εδωκεν] τω δεδωκοτι Q min$^{plq\,35}$ Ar τω δοντι 14 92 | om και προσεκ. τω θηριω 186 | τω θηριω 2°] το θηριον A 79 al$^{pauc\,vid}$ + τουτω syr^{gw}

popular imagination, and Dion Chrysostom (*orat.* xxi.) at the end of the century sneers at it as one of the follies of the time. Meanwhile the idea of Nero's return had begun to take its place in the creations of Jewish and Christian fancy, e.g. in the *Ascension of Isaiah* (ed. Charles, iv. 2 f.) we read that Beliar will descend ἐν εἴδει ἀνθρώπου βασιλέως ἀνόμου μητραλῴου, and in *Orac. Sibyll.* iv. 119 f. καὶ τότ' ἀπ' Ἰταλίης βασιλεὺς μέγας, οἷά τε δρήστης | φεύξετ' ἄφαντος ἄπυστος ὑπὲρ πόρον Εὐφρήταο; *ib.* 138 ἥξει καὶ Ῥώμης ὁ φυγάς, μέγα ἔγχος ἀείρας, | Εὐφρήτην διαβὰς πολλαῖς ἅμα μυριάδεσσιν (cf. *ib.* v. 143 ff., 362 ff.). The legend has been used by St John to represent the revival of Nero's persecuting policy by Domitian, "portio Neronis de crudelitate" (Tert. *apol.* 5); see more upon this point in *c.* xvii. 8 ff. That Nero is intended by the wounded but restored head of the Beast did not escape the earliest of the Latin commentators, though he failed to detect the reference to Domitian; on *c.* xvii. 16 Victorinus remarks: "unum autem de capitibus quasi occisum in mortem et plagam mortis eius curatam, Neronem dicit. constat enim dum insequeretur cum equitatus missus a senatu, ipsum sibi gulam succidisse. hunc ergo suscitatum Deus mittet."

καὶ ἐθαυμάσθη ὅλη ἡ γῆ ὀπίσω τοῦ θηρίου] Both for the use of θαυμάζεσθαι (cf. Blass, *Gr.* p. 44) and for the general sense see *c.* xvii. 8 θαυμασθήσονται οἱ κατοικοῦντες ἐπὶ τῆς γῆς...βλεπόντων τὸ θηρίον κτλ. The eyes of the whole earth—τῆς γῆς, not simply τῆς οἰκουμένης as in xii. 9—gaze with wonder after the Beast and his restored head. For the pregnant θαυμάζεσθαι ὀπίσω see Jo. xii. 19 ὀπίσω αὐτοῦ ἀπῆλθεν, Acts v. 37 ἀπέστησε λαὸν ὀπίσω αὐτοῦ, xx. 30 ἀποσπᾶν τοὺς μαθητὰς ὀπίσω ἑαυτῶν, 1 Tim. v. 15 ἐξετράπησαν ὀπίσω τοῦ σατανᾶ. Gunkel (*Schöpfung*, p. 358), postulating a Semitic original, believes ὀπίσω to be a rendering of מֵאַחֲרֵי read for מֵאַחֲרִית, but the conjecture is unnecessary, and not supported by evidence.

4. καὶ προσεκύνησαν τῷ δράκοντι κτλ.] In its worship of the Beast and the persecuting Emperors the admiring world worshipped in fact the evil Power which was behind them. Or the sense may be that the vices of the Emperors found ready imitators; the demoralizing effects of their example were apparent throughout the Empire. As for the direct worship of the Beast, toward the end of the first century it was already coordinated with the local cults; in Asia the cities vied with one another for the honour of erecting a temple to Rome and the Caesars and the neocorate attached to it. Such fragments as the following from the record of an 'Epigraphical Journey in Asia Minor' (*Papers of the American School at Athens*, vols. ii, iii) speak for themselves: [νεωκόρ]ου τῶν πατρίων | [θεῶν κα]ὶ τοῦ κυρίου | [αὐ]τοκράτορος...θύσαν[τα τοῖς] πατρίοις θ[εοῖς καὶ τοῖς Σε]βαστ[οῖς]...θεοῖς Σε-

ὅμοιος τῷ θηρίῳ, καὶ τίς δύναται πολεμῆσαι μετ'
5 αὐτοῦ; [5]καὶ ἐδόθη αὐτῷ στόμα λαλοῦν μεγάλα
καὶ βλασφημίας, καὶ ἐδόθη αὐτῷ ἐξουσία ποιῆσαι
6 μῆνας τεσσεράκοντα δύο. [6]καὶ ἤνοιξε[ν] τὸ στόμα
αὐτοῦ εἰς βλασφημίας πρὸς τὸν θεόν, βλασφημῆσαι
τὸ ὄνομα αὐτοῦ καὶ τὴν σκηνὴν αὐτοῦ, τοὺς ἐν τῷ

4 om *και* 3° 6 7 8 29 31 al$^{fere 20}$ Ar | *δυναται*] *δυνατος* Q min$^{fere 40}$ Ar 5 om *και εδοθη...βλασφ.* 1 31 32 Prim | *βλασφημιας*] *βλασφημιαν* PQ min^{35} syr^{gw} Ar *βλασφημα* A 12 28 34 35 al | om *εξουσια* ℵ* (hab ℵ$^{c.a}$) *η εξουσια* 130 | *ποιησαι*] + *ο θελει* ℵ (*signa quae voluit* aeth) *πολεμον ποιησαι* Q min^{pl} Ar *πολεμησαι* 14 92 me | *τεσσαρακοντα* P min^{pl} | *δυο*] pr *και* A 16 95 vg^{fu} syr Ir^{int} 6 *βλασφημιαν* PQ min^{pl} vg^{am} syrr arm Prim Ar | *το ονομα αυτου*] *αυτον* ℵ* | om *και την σκηνην αυτου* C vg^{tol} * | *τους εν τω ουρ. σκ.*] pr *και* ℵ$^{c.a}$ PQ* 1 al^{mu} vg me syr^{codd} arm Ir^{int} anon^{aug} Prim om *τους* 130 *των...σκηνουντων* syr^{gw}

βαστοῖς καὶ τῇ πατρίδι...ἀρχιερεὺς τῶν Σεβαστῶν. More upon this subject may be found in Renan, *Saint Paul*, p. 28 f., Ramsay, *Church in the Roman Empire*, *Letters to the Seven Churches*, passim.

Τίς ὅμοιος τῷ θηρίῳ;—an intentional parody of Exod. xv. 11 *τίς ὅμοιός σοι ἐν θεοῖς, Κύριε;* cf. Pss. lxxxii. (lxxxiii.) 1, lxxxviii. (lxxxix.) 6, cxiii. 5, Mic. vii. 18, Isa. xl. 25, xlvi. 5—perhaps not without reference to the name מִיכָאֵל. The worship of such a monster as Nero was indeed a travesty of the worship of God. *Τίς δύναται πολεμῆσαι μετ' αὐτοῦ;* points to the motive which prompted the worship of the Beast. It was not moral greatness but brute force which commanded the homage of the provinces. The invincible power of Rome won divine honours for the worst and meanest of men.

5. *καὶ ἐδόθη αὐτῷ στόμα λαλοῦν μεγάλα κτλ.*] The words *στ. λαλ. μεγάλα* are from Daniel's description of the Little Horn (Dan. vii. 8, 20). In their assumption of Divine titles (*v.* 1 note) the Emperors followed in the steps of Antiochus Epiphanes, who (1 Macc. i. 24, ℵV) *ἐλάλησεν ὑπερηφανίαν μεγάλην.* With *καὶ βλασφημίας* cf. Dan. vii. 25 *ῥήματα εἰς τὸν ὕψιστον λαλήσει.* In the repeated *ἐδόθη* there may be a reference to *ἔδωκεν αὐτῷ ὁ δράκων* of *v.* 2, cf. *v.* 4; but more probably, as elsewhere in the Apocalypse, *ἐδόθη* points to the ultimate Source of all power, without Whose permission Satan himself can do nothing.

For *ποιῆσαι μῆνας τεσσ. δύο* cf. xi. 2, xii. 6, 14, notes. *Ποιῆσαι* may be simply 'to do,' i.e. to carry on his work, as עָשָׂה in Dan. viii. 24, xi. 28; *μῆνας* will then be the accusative of duration. But perhaps it is better to understand *π.* here in the sense of 'passing time'; cf. Mt. xx. 12 *μίαν ὥραν ἐποίησαν*, Acts xx. 3 *ποιήσας τε μῆνας τρεῖς*, and the Latin *facere diem.* The Beast's power endures as long as the Woman's abode in the Wilderness, the prophesying of the Two Witnesses, and the Gentile profanation of the Holy City.

6. *καὶ ἤνοιξεν τὸ στόμα αὐτοῦ εἰς βλασφημίας πρὸς τὸν θεόν*] *Ἀνοίγειν τὸ στόμα* is used frequently, if not exclusively, of the beginning of a discourse or prolonged utterance; cf. Ps. xxi. (xxii.) 14, lxxvii. (lxviii.) 2, cviii. (cix.) 1; Sir. xv. 5; Mt. v. 2; Acts viii. 35. The Beast's blasphemy was not casual but sustained, when once his silence had been broken; the assumption of Divine Names in public

οὐρανῷ σκηνοῦντας. [7]καὶ ἐδόθη αὐτῷ ποιῆσαι πόλε- 7
μον μετὰ τῶν ἁγίων καὶ νικῆσαι αὐτούς, καὶ ἐδόθη
αὐτῷ ἐξουσία ἐπὶ πᾶσαν φυλὴν καὶ λαὸν καὶ γλῶσ-
σαν καὶ ἔθνος. [8]καὶ προσκυνήσουσιν αὐτὸν πάντες οἱ 8
κατοικοῦντες ἐπὶ τῆς γῆς, οὗ οὐ γέγραπται τὸ ὄνομα

7 *και εδοθη...νικησαι αυτους* om ACP 1* 12 14 92 arm^{zoh} Ir^{int} (? propter *ομοιοτελ.*) | *και λαον*] *κ. λαους* C om 1 36 49 91 186 al me arm 8 *αυτον* ACQ min$^{\text{plq 30}}$] *αυτω* ℵP 1 7 38 49 87 91 95 186 al^{vid} | *ου* 1°] *ων* ℵ$^{\text{c.a}}$ PQ min^{pl} vg me syr syr$^{\text{gw vid}}$ arm aeth Prim Andr Ar al | *ου* 2°] *ουτε* Q 8 29 al$^{\text{plq 10}}$ | *το ονομα*] *τα ονοματα* ℵP 1 28 79 95 vg arm aeth Prim Ar

documents and inscriptions was a standing and growing blasphemy. This blasphemy was aimed at the Divine *σκηνή*, i.e. as the Apocalyptist hastens to explain, *τοὺς ἐν τῷ οὐρανῷ σκηνοῦντας*; cf. xii. 12 *οὐρανοὶ καὶ οἱ ἐν αὐτοῖς σκηνοῦντες*. Primasius seems to have read *τοῦ...σκηνοῦντος* ("tabernaculum eius qui in caelo habitat"), though he interprets: "id est, adversus deum et ecclesiam quae in caelo habitat" (Haussleiter, p. 130); but the harder reading of the Greek text is to be preferred. *Τοὺς...σκηνοῦντας* either the 'company of Heaven,' or possibly the Church viewed as ideally installed in the *ἐπουράνια*; Andreas is perhaps on the right track when he says: *σκηνὴ δὲ τοῦ θεοῦ καὶ ἡ ἐν σαρκὶ τοῦ λόγου σκήνωσις...καὶ ἡ ἐν τοῖς ἁγίοις ἀνάπαυσις* (cf. Jo. i. 14, Apoc. vii. 15). Blasphemy against God was coupled with false accusations laid against His saints, the loyal members of the Church. The clause *βλασφημῆσαι...σκηνοῦντας* is epexegetical, developing *βλασφημίας πρὸς τὸν θεόν*.

7. *καὶ ἐδόθη αὐτῷ ποιῆσαι πόλεμον κτλ.*] Daniel's account of the Little Horn is still in view; cf. Dan. vii. 21 *ἐθεώρουν, καὶ τὸ κέρας ἐκεῖνο ἐποίει πόλεμον μετὰ τῶν ἁγίων καὶ ἴσχυσεν πρὸς αὐτούς*. The Beast, acting for the Dragon (xii. 17), makes war upon the Seed of the Woman, i.e. the faithful, and succeeds. Like the קַדִּישִׁין of Daniel's vision, i.e. the loyal defenders of Jerusalem against Antiochus, the citizens of the new Jerusalem must expect to fall before the persecuting Emperor. Wherever the Gospel was carried, Rome was there beforehand; the Beast's authority extended over all the nations and races which surrounded the Mediterranean (*ἐδόθη αὐτῷ ἐξουσία ἐπὶ πᾶσαν φυλήν κτλ.*). No escape from him was possible for the members of the Church, though, as the Seer has already foreseen (xii. 14 ff.), the Church herself, the Mother of the Saints, was beyond his reach. With *νικῆσαι* cf. *c.* vi. 2, note.

Καὶ ἐδόθη...νικῆσαι αὐτούς is omitted by the best uncials, but probably through *homoeoteleuton*, the eye of some early scribe having passed from *ἐδόθη* to *ἐδόθη*.

8. *καὶ προσκυνήσουσιν αὐτὸν πάντες οἱ κατοικοῦντες κτλ.*] Not only did the Roman Empire seem to the provincials a power of world-wide extent, but it had acquired a religious significance which rendered it yet more formidable (*v.* 4 note). The Caesars were not merely obeyed, they were worshipped by the whole world. The masc. *αὐτόν* points to the impersonation of the Beast in such Emperors as Nero or Domitian; for the acc. after *προσκυνεῖν* (the older construction), cf. Mt. iv. 10, Lc. iv. 8, Apoc. ix. 20, xiii. 12, xiv. 9, 11, xx. 4, and see Blass, *Gr.* p. 89. *Πάντες οἱ κατοικοῦντες ἐπὶ τῆς γῆς* is hyperbolical, even if the

αὐτοῦ ἐν τῷ βιβλίῳ τῆς ζωῆς τοῦ ἀρνίου τοῦ ἐσφαγ-
9 μένου ἀπὸ καταβολῆς κόσμου. ⁹εἴ τις ἔχει οὖς,
10 ἀκουσάτω. ¹⁰εἴ τις εἰς αἰχμαλωσίαν, εἰς αἰχμαλω-

8 αυτου] αυτων ℵ* 95 syr arm | εν] επι Q | τω (om ℵ*C) βιβλιω] τη βιβλω (ℵ*) 1 al^{nonn} 9 ους] *aures* Prim + *audiendi* vg$^{\text{lipss 4, 6**}}$ me 10 εις αιχμαλωσιαν 1°] + απαγει 33 130 (επ. 35 συν. Ar) vg$^{\text{cle dem lipss 4, 5, 6 tol}}$ me^{vid} syrr Ir^{int} Prim^{vid} εχει αιχμ. 6 8 29 31 91 93 94 96 97 98 186 | om εις αιχμ. (2°) ℵCPQ 186 (hab A vg$^{\text{am fu}}$)

Empire is viewed as co-extensive with the *orbis terrarum*; and the writer hastens to guard himself by adding: *οὗ οὐ γέγραπται κτλ.* There were those in the Roman world who, like Daniel and the three at the court of Babylon (Dan. iii. 16 f.), refused to worship the Caesars. Those who worshipped, though for the moment the immense majority, were only such as were not in the Book of Life. *Οὗ...αὐτοῦ* is unexpected after *πάντες*, but the purpose may be to minimize the significance of the general acceptance of the Caesar-cult, or possibly to call attention to the individual responsibility of the worshippers. Each Caesar-worshipper by his very act proclaimed himself to have no place among "the living in Jerusalem." On the 'Book of Life' see iii. 5, note; and compare with the present passage *cc.* xvii. 8, xx. 12, 15, xxi. 27. Here and in xxi. 27, the Divine Register is represented as belonging to "the Lamb that was slain," i.e. the crucified but now risen and exalted Christ, Who purchased the Church for God with His Blood (v. 9), and has authority to cancel the names of disloyal members (iii. 5). The reference of *ἀπὸ καταβολῆς κόσμου* is somewhat ambiguous; the order suggests that the words should be taken with *τοῦ ἐσφαγμένου*, in the sense indicated by 1 Pet. i. 18 f. *ἐλυτρώθητε...τιμίῳ αἵματι ὡς ἀμνοῦ... Χριστοῦ προεγνωσμένου μὲν πρὸ καταβολῆς κόσμου κτλ.*, but the close parallel in xvii. 8 (*θαυμασθήσονται οἱ κατοικοῦντες ἐπὶ τῆς γῆς, ὧν οὐ γέγραπται τὸ ὄνομα ἐπὶ τὸ βιβλίον τῆς ζωῆς ἀπὸ καταβολῆς κόσμου*) seems to be decisive in favour of connecting *ἀπὸ καταβ. κόσμου* with *γέγραπται* in this context also; and this is supported by such passages as Mt. xxv. 34 *ἡτοιμασμένην ὑμῖν βασιλείαν ἀπὸ καταβ. κόσμου*, Eph. i. 4 *ἐξελέξατο ἡμᾶς ἐν αὐτῷ πρὸ καταβ. κόσμου.* On the whole Arethas is right: *ἐν ὑπερβάτῳ ἀκουστέον τὸ Ὧν οὐ γέγραπται... τοῦ ἐσφαγμένου· ἐπεὶ ὧν γέγραπται, ἀπὸ καταβολῆς κόσμου γέγραπται. οὕτω γὰρ δεῖ νοεῖν, οὐχ ὡς ἡ γραφὴ ἔχει, ὅτι μηδὲ ἀπὸ καταβολῆς κόσμου ἡ τοῦ ἀρνίου σφαγή.*

As to the phrase *ἀπὸ (πρὸ) καταβολῆς κόσμου*, it is unknown to the LXX., though used by Mt. *l.c.* in a quotation from the Psalms, where it represents מִנִּי קֶדֶם (LXX., *ἀπ' ἀρχῆς*). The N.T. has it ten times (Mt.², Lc.¹, Jo.¹, Eph.¹, Heb.², 1 Pet.¹, Apoc.²). *Καταβολή* is the foundation of a house in 2 Macc. ii. 29, and *καταβάλλεσθαι θεμέλιον* occurs in Heb. vi. 1; the *καταβολὴ κόσμου* is doubtless 'the founding of the whole visible order,' the creation being represented as a vast building under the hands of the Divine Architect, as in Job xxxviii. 4 *ἐν τῷ θεμελιοῦν με τὴν γῆν*, and Heb. iii. 4 *ὁ δὲ πάντα κατασκευάσας θεός*: cf. Hort on 1 Peter *l.c.*, and Dalman, *Die Worte Jesu*, i. p. 136.

9. *εἴ τις ἔχει οὖς, ἀκουσάτω*] For the Apocalyptic form of this saying see ii. 7, note. It is a call to serious attention, and here, as in ii. 7, 11, 17, it is prospective and not retrospective, preparing the hearer for the proclamation which is to follow. 'Let every member of the Church who has

σίαν ὑπάγει· εἴ τις ἐν μαχαίρῃ ἀποκτενεῖ, δεῖ αὐτὸν
ἐν μαχαίρῃ ἀποκτανθῆναι. ὧδέ ἐστιν ἡ ὑπομονὴ καὶ
ἡ πίστις τῶν ἁγίων.
11 *Καὶ εἶδον ἄλλο θηρίον ἀναβαῖνον ἐκ τῆς γῆς,* 11

10 *μαχαιρα* bis ℵPQ min$^{\text{omn vid}}$ Andr Ar | *αποκτενει*] *αποκτεινει* ℵ 28 79 syr^{gw} *αποκτεννει* 35 95 130 *αποκταινει* 186 *αποκτανθηναι* A om 2 6 8 14 29 30 31 32 al$^{\text{plq 10}}$ | om *δει* A | om *εν μαχαιρη* (2°) 2 6 8 14 29 30 31 32 38 47 al$^{\text{plq 10}}$ | *η πιστις και η υπομονη* syr^{gw} | *πιστις*] *θλιψις* 38 97   11 *ειδον* ℵCP min^{pl} Andr Ar] *ιδον* AQ 7 14 32 130 186 om aeth

the power to comprehend it take to heart the warning now about to be given.'

10. *εἴ τις εἰς αἰχμαλωσίαν, εἰς αἰχμ. ὑπάγει κτλ.*] The epigrammatic style of this saying has perplexed the scribes (see *app. crit.*); some add a verb after the first *εἰς αἰχμαλωσίαν*, while others omit the second. Translate: "if any [is] for captivity, into captivity he goes; if any shall slay with the sword, he must with the sword be slain." The verse starts upon the lines of Jer. xv. 2 *ὅσοι εἰς θάνατον, εἰς θάνατον· καὶ ὅσοι εἰς μάχαιραν, εἰς μάχαιραν· καὶ ὅσοι εἰς λιμόν, εἰς λιμόν· καὶ ὅσοι εἰς αἰχμαλωσίαν, εἰς αἰχμαλωσίαν.* But after adopting the last clause of Jeremiah's proclamation, it goes off in quite another direction, referring to the saying of our Lord in Mt. xxvi. 52 *πάντες γὰρ οἱ λαβόντες μάχαιραν ἐν μαχαίρῃ ἀπολοῦνται.* Primasius conforms the first half of the verse to the last, translating: "qui captivum duxerit et ipse capietur," as if it had run: *εἴ τις αἰχμαλωτεύσει* (or *ἐάν τις αἰχμαλωτεύσῃ*), *αἰχμαλωτευθήσεται.* But no such change is necessary; the verse hangs together well enough as it stands in the best Greek text. The whole is a warning against any attempt on the part of the Church to resist its persecutors. If a Christian is condemned to exile, as St John had been, he is to regard exile as his allotted portion, and to go readily; if he is sentenced to death, he is not to lift his hand against the tyrant; to do so will be to deserve his punishment. For *ὧδέ ἐστιν κτλ.* see xiv. 12, note.

11—18. The Wild Beast from the Earth.

11. *καὶ εἶδον ἄλλο θηρίον ἀναβαῖνον ἐκ τῆς γῆς κτλ.*] A second Beast is seen in the act of rising, not as the first out of the sea, but out of the earth. In Daniel's visions four Beasts "came up from the sea" (Dan. vii. 3), but in the interpretation (*ib.* 17) and in the Gk. versions of both passages they "arise out of the earth." From this Bede infers the identity of the origin of the two Apocalyptic Beasts ("quod est autem mare, hoc, teste Daniele, est terra." But the cases are different; the Apocalyptist is not, like Daniel, interpreting his vision, but relating another, which he contrasts with the first. If the Beast from the sea denotes the world-wide Empire of the West, the Beast from the earth is of humbler pretensions, a native of the soil (cf. Arethas: *ἐκ τῆς γῆς...ὅθεν καὶ πᾶσιν ἀνθρώποις ἡ γένεσις*)—a product of the life of the Asian cities.

Early Christian opinion was divided upon the interpretation of the second Beast. Irenaeus (v. 28. 2), who identifies the first Beast with Antichrist, finds in the second Antichrist's 'armour-bearer' (cf. 1 Sam. xvii. 7), the false Prophet. Similarly Hippolytus (ed. Lag. p. 24): *τὸ μὲν οὖν θηρίον ἀναβαῖνον ἐκ τῆς γῆς τὴν βασιλείαν τὴν τοῦ ἀντιχρίστου ἐσομένην λέγει, τὰ δὲ δύο κέρατα καὶ τὸν μετ' αὐτὸν ψευδοπροφήτην.* Andreas mentions

καὶ εἶχεν κέρατα δύο ὅμοια ἀρνίῳ, καὶ ἐλάλει ὡς
12 δράκων. [12]καὶ τὴν ἐξουσίαν τοῦ πρώτου θηρίου
πᾶσαν ποιεῖ ἐνώπιον αὐτοῦ. καὶ ποιεῖ τὴν γῆν καὶ
τοὺς ἐν αὐτῇ κατοικοῦντας ἵνα προσκυνήσουσιν τὸ

11 δυο] δεκαδυο 12 om 2 6 8 13 29 31 32 al[fere 15] Ar | ομοια] ονομα C και ομοιον ην syr[gw]   12 ποιει 1°] εποιει 38 vg me syr arm aeth Ir[int] Hipp Prim ποιειται 186 | ποιει 2°] ποιησει 34 35 87 syr[gw] εποιει Q 6 7 8 14 29 31 38 49 al[plq 20] vg[cle am dem lipss] me syr arm aeth Hipp Ar | ινα προσκυνησουσιν AC 7 14 30* 36 98] ινα προσκυνησωσιν PQ min[pl] Hipp Ar και προσκ. syr[gw] προσκυνιν ℵ

other interpretations: *τὸ θηρίον τοῦτο οἱ μὲν τὸν ἀντίχριστόν φασιν, ἑτέροις δὲ ἔδοξε τὸν σατανᾶν εἶναι, καὶ τὰ δύο αὐτοῦ κέρατα τὸν ἀντίχριστον καὶ τὸν ψευδοπροφήτην.*

καὶ εἶχεν κέρατα δύο ὅμοια ἀρνίῳ κτλ.] The equipment of the second Beast was as unpretending as his origin. In sharp contrast to the first he had but one head furnished with two horns (cf. Dan. viii. 5), which were like those of a lamb. But if his appearance suggested innocence and even weakness, his voice was the roar of a dragon; cf. a fragment of Hermippus quoted by Wetstein: *τὸ πρόσωπον ἀρνίου ἔχειν δοκεῖς, τὰ δὲ ἔνδον οὐδὲν διαφέρεις δράκοντος.* Though both *ἀρνίῳ* and *δράκων* are anarthrous, they doubtless allude to the Lamb of *c.* v. 6 and the Dragon of *c.* xiii. 1. The second Beast is in some sense at once a Pseudochrist and an Antichrist: *ἐξομοιοῦσθαι μέλλει τῷ υἱῷ τοῦ θεοῦ, καὶ αὐτὸς ἑαυτὸν βασιλέα ἐπιδεικνύσιν* (Hippolytus); "agnum fingit, ut Agnum invadat" (Primasius).

The description recalls Mt. vii. 15 *προσέχετε ἀπὸ τῶν ψευδοπροφητῶν, οἵτινες ἔρχονται πρὸς ὑμᾶς ἐν ἐνδύμασιν προβάτων, ἔσωθεν δέ εἰσιν λύκοι ἅρπαγες.* Cf. Victorinus: "magnum falsumque prophetam dicit, qui facturus est signa et portenta." The second Beast is in fact in later chapters of the book called *ὁ ψευδοπροφήτης* (xvi. 13, xix. 20, xx. 10), while *τὸ ἄλλο θηρίον* or *τὸ θ. τὸ δεύτερον* does not appear; from this chapter onwards the only *θηρίον* mentioned is the first Beast, or the wounded head which is identified with him (xiv. 9, 11, xv. 2, xvi. 2, 10, 13, xvii. 3 ff., xix. 19, 20, xx. 4, 10). In the second Beast we have a religious, as in the first a civil, power; he is a *ψευδοπροφήτης* (xvi. 23, xix. 20, xx. 10), who claims a spiritual power which he does not possess, and misinterprets the Divine Will in the interests of the persecuting State. Some ancient interpreters saw in him the Christian ministry turned to unworthy uses; cf. Beatus: "bestia de terra praepositi mali sunt in ecclesia." Such men may be in the background of St John's thought, but the immediate reference is rather to the pagan priesthood of his own time; cf. iv. 14, 15, note.

12. *καὶ τὴν ἐξουσίαν τοῦ πρώτου θηρίου πᾶσαν ποιεῖ κτλ.*] The authority of the Dragon, which was delegated to the first Beast (xiii. 2), descends to the second; the first fights the Dragon's battles, the second supports the first by methods of his own, but with a strength which is derived ultimately from the Dragon. *Τὴν ἐξουσίαν...ἐνώπιον αὐτοῦ* is a pregnant sentence; written out at length it would be *τὴν ἐξουσίαν τ. πρ. θ. πᾶσαν λαβὼν ἕστηκεν ἐνώπιον αὐτοῦ ποιῶν τὸ θέλημα αὐτοῦ*, or to that effect. *Ἐνώπιον αὐτοῦ* recalls 3 Regn. xvii. 1 *ὁ θεὸς Ἰσραὴλ ᾧ παρέστην ἐνώπιον αὐτοῦ.* The true prophet lives in the presence of God, taking his orders from Him and doing His pleasure; the False Prophet stands before the Beast, whose interpreter and servant he is.

καὶ ποιεῖ τὴν γῆν καὶ τοὺς ἐν αὐτῇ κτλ.] It is the business of the second

θηρίον τὸ πρῶτον, οὗ ἐθεραπεύθη ἡ πληγὴ τοῦ θανά-
του αὐτοῦ. [13]καὶ ποιεῖ σημεῖα μεγάλα, ἵνα καὶ πῦρ 13
ποιῇ ἐκ τοῦ οὐρανοῦ καταβαίνειν εἰς τὴν γῆν ἐνώπιον
τῶν ἀνθρώπων. [14]καὶ πλανᾷ τοὺς κατοικοῦντας ἐπὶ 14
τῆς γῆς διὰ τὰ σημεῖα ἃ ἐδόθη αὐτῷ ποιῆσαι ἐνώπιον

12 το θηριον το πρωτον] τω θηριω τω πρωτω 6* 35 41 42 87 95 | om του θανατου A | om αυτου P 14 92 vg Prim al 13 ποιει] ποιησει 35 87 me syr^{gw} Ir^{int} anon^{aug} εποιει 31 Hipp vg$^{exc\,fu}$ (*fecit*) aeth Prim | και πυρ ινα Q min^{35} Ar | ποιη εκ τ. ουρ. καταβαινειν] π. εκ τ. ουρ. καταβηναι 130 εκ τ. ουρ. καταβαινη (Q) min$^{fere\,35}$ me Ar | εις] επι Q min$^{fere\,30}$ syr^{gw} 14 πλανησει syr^{gw} | τους κατοικουντας] pr τους εμους 2 6 8 29 30 31 32 49 186 al$^{fere\,30}$ Ar | om δια τα σημεια...επι της γης Q* 130 syr (propter ομοιοτελ.)

Beast to promote the worship of the first; for this end the False Prophet has been entrusted with his power. Ποιεῖ...ἵνα, 'causes to,' cf. Jo. xi. 37, Col. iv. 16, Apoc. iii. 9 (Blass, *Gr.* p. 225 f.). Τὴν γῆν καὶ τοὺς ἐν αὐτῇ κατοικοῦντας, cf. *vv.* 4, 8. Τὸ θηρίον... οὗ ἐθεραπεύθη κτλ. is repeated from *v.* 3, where see note.

13. καὶ ποιεῖ σημεῖα μεγάλα κτλ.] Being a false prophet the second Beast simulates the miracles wrought by true prophets; cf. Exod. vii. 11 f. (2 Tim. iii. 8), and see Deut. xiii. 1 ἐὰν δὲ ἀναστῇ ἐν σοὶ προφήτης...καὶ δῷ σοι σημεῖον ἢ τέρας κτλ. 'Great signs' were expected and believed to accompany the mission of the Church (cf. Jo. xiv. 12, 'Mc.' xvi. 20), but they were not to be limited to it; see Mc. xiii. 22 ἐγερθήσονται...ψευδοπροφῆται καὶ δώσουσιν σημεῖα καὶ τέρατα πρὸς τὸ ἀποπλανᾷν εἰ δυνατὸν τοὺς ἐκλεκτούς; 2 Thess. ii. 9 οὗ ἐστιν ἡ παρουσία κατ' ἐνέργειαν τοῦ σατανᾶ ἐν πάσῃ δυνάμει καὶ σημείοις καὶ τέρασιν ψευδοῦς. Calling down fire from heaven was one of the miracles attributed to Elijah (1 Kings xviii. 38, 2 Kings i. 10); if the writer of the Apocalypse was the son of Zebedee, he would not have forgotten that he had himself desired to imitate the O. T. prophet (Lc. ix. 54 Ἰάκωβος καὶ Ἰωάνης εἶπαν Κύριε, θέλεις εἴπωμεν πῦρ καταβῆναι ἀπὸ τοῦ οὐρανοῦ;). In the present case the sign of calling down fire would doubtless be exhibited in connexion with the worship of the Beast, for which it would seem to be a Divine guarantee. Ἵνα after ποιεῖ μ. σ. is scarcely distinguishable from ὥστε (Burton § 222); the Prophet's powers extend so far that he can even (καί) cause fire to descend from heaven, and that in the face of the world (ἐνώπιον τῶν ἀνθρώπων).

14. καὶ πλανᾷ τοὺς κατοικοῦντας ἐπὶ τῆς γῆς κτλ.] To deceive mankind is a characteristic power of Satan (xii. 9 ὁ πλανῶν τὴν οἰκουμένην ὅλην, where see note) and it has descended to the false Prophet; see reff. cited on *v.* 12. The success of the latter is due to the signs (διὰ τὰ σημεῖα) which he is empowered to work (*vv.* 13, 15). These are done 'before the Beast' (*v.* 12, note), i.e. in the presence and with the approval of the Imperial officers. It is hardly possible to misunderstand the Apocalyptist's meaning. The Caesar-worship was a State function at which the Proconsul and the other magistrates assisted, and the pagan priesthood wrought their σημεῖα before these representatives of the Empire; their jugglery addressed itself to persons in authority and not only to the ignorant populace.

τοῦ θηρίου, λέγων τοῖς κατοικοῦσιν ἐπὶ τῆς γῆς
ποιῆσαι εἰκόνα τῷ θηρίῳ, ὃς ἔχει τὴν πληγὴν τῆς
μαχαίρης καὶ ἔζησεν. 15 καὶ ἐδόθη αὐτῷ δοῦναι πνεῦμα
τῇ εἰκόνι τοῦ θηρίου, ἵνα καὶ λαλήσῃ ἡ εἰκὼν τοῦ

14 λεγων] λεγον B** 1 14 92 94 95 λεγοντος Q^{mg} | ποιησαι 2°] pr και ℵ | ος] ο ℵ 1 min^{pl} syr^{gw} Hipp Ar | εχει] ειχεν Q min$^{\text{plq 35}}$ syr Ar | την πληγην] om την (ℵ) Q 2 6 8 13 14 26 29 30 al^{10} | της μαχαιρης (-ρας PQ min$^{\text{omn vid}}$) και εζησεν] και εζησεν απο της μαχ. Q min$^{\text{plq 25}}$ Ar κ. εζ. απο της πληγης της μαχ. 16 39 15 αυτω ℵP**Q min$^{\text{omn vid}}$ Hipp Andr Ar] αυτη ACP*^{vid} | om δουναι C | om ινα και λαληση η εικων του θηριου C 14 16 28 31 99 130 me syrr

λέγων τοῖς κατοικοῦσιν...ποιῆσαι εἰκόνα τῷ θηρίῳ κτλ.] Yet the chief purpose of the *σημεῖα* wrought by the magic of the priests of the Augusti was to popularize the new cult, and promote its ends, by suggesting the religious use of the statue of the Emperor (on *λέγων*=*κελεύων* followed by the infinitive see Blass, *Gr.* pp. 232, 240). Any representation of the reigning Caesar which served to place him before the eyes of the provincials might be described as an *εἰκών* (see Lightfoot's note on Col. i. 15), whether it were merely the Emperor's head (*effigies*) upon a coin (Mc. xii. 16), or an *imago* painted or wrought upon a standard, or executed in metal or stone. The bust or statue, however, is doubtless intended here. Such *imagines* together with other symbols of the power of Rome had always received the highest honours from loyal subjects of the Empire; cf. Suetonius, *Tib.* 48 "largitus est...quaedam munera Syriacis legionibus, quod solae nullam Seiani imaginem inter signa coluissent" (i.e. because they alone had been loyal to himself; *ib.*, *Calig.* 14 "aquilas et signa Romana Caesarumque imagines adoravit)." When Christians were brought before Imperial officials an image of the reigning Emperor was produced by way of testing their Christianity. Cf. Pliny's famous letter (*ep.* 96, A.D. 112): "qui negabant esse se Christianos aut fuisse, cum praeeunte me deos appellarent et imagini tuae quam propter hoc iusseram cum simulacris numinum adferri ture ac vino supplicarent ...dimittendos esse putavi," and the appeal of the *εἰρήναρχος* to Polycarp (*Mart. P.* 8): *τί γὰρ κακόν ἐστιν εἰπεῖν 'Κύριος Καῖσαρ,' καὶ ἐπιθῦσαι* (i.e. to offer incense, see Lightfoot, *ad loc.*) *καὶ τούτοις ἀκόλουθα, καὶ διασώζεσθαι;* cf. Eus. *H. E.* vii. 15 *Χριστιανῷ γε ὄντι καὶ τοῖς βασιλεῦσι μὴ θύοντι.* But in the present passage the reference is rather to *imagines* set up in the *Σεβαστεῖα* or temples of Rome and the Augusti. The judicial use of the Emperor's 'image' was perhaps as yet unknown, but already, as it seems, the pagan priesthood had succeeded in securing for it religious worship with results disastrous to the Christian communities (*v.* 15).

Ὃς ἔχει τὴν πληγήν κτλ., as in *vv.* 3, 12, but with the addition of *μαχαίρης*—a new feature which makes for the identification of the wounded head with Nero—and with *ἔζησεν* substituted for *ἡ πληγὴ...ἐθεραπεύθη*. The Beast did not die with Nero; he lived on and reappeared in Domitian, who resumed Nero's policy of persecution (cf. note on xiii. 3).

15. *καὶ ἐδόθη αὐτῷ δοῦναι πνεῦμα τῇ εἰκόνι κτλ.*] Another *σημεῖον* wrought by the magic of the second Beast. That such tricks were employed in the *Σεβαστεῖα* is by no means improbable. As we are reminded by Andreas, it was the age of

θηρίου, καὶ ποιήσῃ [ἵνα] ὅσοι ἐὰν μὴ προσκυνήσωσιν
τῇ εἰκόνι τοῦ θηρίου ἀποκτανθῶσιν. ^{16}καὶ ποιεῖ 16

15 om και ποιηση...του θηριου C 28 | ποιησει ℵ 14 36 79 92 95 98 | om ινα ℵQ min^{32} vg^{am} Ir^{int} (hab AP 7 11 26 36 95 vg$^{\text{cle codd pl}}$ Hipp^{bis} Prim al) | προσκυνησουσιν ℵ 7* 14 31 36 42 130 186 | την εικονα A 1 al^{nonn} | αποκτανθωσιν] pr ινα 130 186
16 ποιει] ποιησει ℵ$^{\text{c.a}}$ vg syr^{gw} Hipp^{semel} ποιηση 130 *fecit* Prim

Apollonius of Tyana, whose legerdemain was freely attributed to the powers of evil: *ἱστόρηται πολλάκις γοητείαις λαλῆσαι δι' εἰκόνων καὶ ξοάνων καὶ δένδρων καὶ ὑδάτων διά τε Ἀπολλωνίου διά τε ἑτέρων δαίμονας.* In the Clementine Recognitions (iii. 47), Simon Magus is made to boast, "statuas moveri feci, animari exanima...haec non solum feci, sed et nunc facere possum," a claim doubtless suggested by the writer's experience of contemporary magic; as for calling down fire, see Apringius on *v.* 13: "haec magi per angelos refugas et hodie faciunt." It is not necessary to suppose that either Simon or Apollonius (Ramsay, *Exp.* 1904, ii. 4, p. 249 f., *Letters to the Seven Churches*, p. 101 ff.) is directly referred to; the second Beast is probably, like the first, a system rather than a person, though, as the first culminated in Nero, the second may well have been represented by the best known magician of the age. But that magic was used by the Caesar-priests is probable enough, as Ramsay has well pointed out (*ib.* p. 98 ff.), even if the Apocalypse is the only witness to the fact; nor is it impossible that they may have acted under the sanction of the officials, so that the Empire itself lent its weight to the proceeding. 'Magic' was not thought unworthy of a place in high quarters, as St Paul learnt at the outset of his missionary work; cf. Acts xiii. 6 *εὗρον ἄνδρα τινὰ μάγον ψευδοπροφήτην...ὃς ἦν σὺν τῷ ἀνθυπάτῳ.*

Thus in the immediate view of the Seer the second Beast represents the sorcery and superstition of the age engaged in a common attempt to impose the Caesar-cult upon the provinces, behind which there lay the Satanic purpose of bringing ruin upon the rising Christian brotherhoods. In its wider significance the symbol may well stand for any religious system which allies itself with the hostile forces of the world against the faith of Jesus Christ.

Πνεῦμα here = *πνεῦμα ζωῆς* (xi. 11), in the sense of breath or animation. *Ἵνα καὶ λαλήσῃ*: the vitalizing of the image went so far that it was even able to speak, an effect doubtless produced by the art of the *ἐγγαστρίμυθος*; of contemporary ventriloquism there is probably an instance in Acts xvi. 16, where see Knowling's note. The reading *ἐδόθη αὐτῇ* has good support (see *app. crit.*), but, as Dr Hort admits, it is unintelligible: "it is impossible either to account for the text [*αὐτῇ*] as a corruption of *αὐτῷ*, or to interpret it as it stands"; he suggests that "*τῇ γῇ* may have been lost after *αὐτῇ*, or have given place to it" (*Notes*, p. 138). But to bring in from *vv.* 11, 12 ff. "the conception of a spirit of the earth" seems artificial. Can *αὐτῇ* be an early or even primary error due to the mind of the writer having reverted to *εἰκόνα* (*v.* 14), or to his eye having been caught by *τῇ εἰκόνι*, which immediately follows?

Καὶ ποιήσῃ, sc. *ἡ εἰκών*. As they stand, the words can only mean that the ventriloquist used his opportunity to make the image suggest that all who refused worship to the image of Caesar should be put to death. But it is possible that *ποιήσῃ* is a slip on the part of the writer for *ποιῆσαι*.

16. *καὶ ποιεῖ πάντας, τοὺς μικροὺς κτλ.*] The False Prophet causes all

πάντας, τοὺς μικροὺς καὶ τοὺς μεγάλους, καὶ τοὺς πλουσίους καὶ τοὺς πτωχούς, καὶ τοὺς ἐλευθέρους καὶ τοὺς δούλους, ἵνα δῶσιν αὐτοῖς χάραγμα ἐπὶ τῆς χειρὸς αὐτῶν τῆς δεξιᾶς ἢ ἐπὶ τὸ μέτωπον αὐτῶν,

16 *τους μικρ. κ. τους μεγαλους* (om *τους* 2° ℵ)] *magnos et pusillos* Prim | *τους πλουσ. κ. τους πτωχους*] *τους πτωχους κ. τους πλουσ.* ℵ 79 | om *και τ. πτωχ. κ. τους ελευθ.* Prim | *ελευθερους*] *δεσποτας* syr[gw] | *δωσιν* ℵ* (*δωσι* ℵ[c.a]) ACPQ 6 10 12 13 14 17** 35 36 37 38 49 51 87 91 92 96] *δωσει* 1 *δωση* 186 Hipp[bis] *δωσουσιν* 4 18 29 31 40 46 94 *δωσωσιν* 2 7 16 28 30 32 79 93 97 98 al[10] *δοθη* syr[gw vid] *λαβωσι* (sine *αυτοις*) 26 95 *habere* (pro *ινα δ. αυτ.*) vg Prim al | *χαραγματα* Q min[fere 35] Ar | *το μετωπον*] *του μετωπου* C *των μετωπων* Q 1 28 130 186 al[mu] vg syr Prim

who accept the Caesar-cult to receive a mark of fealty. Τοὺς μικρούς, κτλ. (cf. xi. 18, xix. 5, 18, xx. 12) covers the entire population, from the Asiarch down to the meanest slave. The construction changes after the long string of accusatives: had the writer stopped to think of the formation of his sentence, he would naturally have written ποιεῖ ἵνα πάντες, οἱ μικροί κτλ., λάβωσιν, or ποιεῖ ἵνα πᾶσιν, τοῖς μικροῖς κτλ., δῶσιν αὐτοῖς or even ποιεῖ πάντας, τοὺς μικρούς κτλ., λαβεῖν or ἵνα λάβωσιν. The indefinite plural δῶσιν (*v. l.* δώσουσιν) finds a parallel in *cc.* x. 11 λέγουσιν, xvi. 15 βλέπωσιν. Dr Hort suggests (*Notes*, p. 139) that the original reading was δώσει, written by itacism ΔωCI. But δῶσιν, which is read by all our uncials, makes excellent sense; the second Beast worked through his ministers, the menials of the Augustan temples.

Χάραγμα may be either a work of art such as a graven image (Acts xvii. 29 χαράγματι τέχνης), or, as here and in *cc.* xiv., xvi., xix., xx., the impress made by a stamp; cf. the use of χαρακτήρ in Lev. xiii. 28 where the scar of a leprous spot is called χ. τοῦ κατακαύματος. To the procedure ascribed to the second Beast there is a striking parallel in 3 Macc. ii. 29, where Ptolemy Philopator I. (B.C. 217) orders such Jews as submitted to registration to be branded with the badge of the Dionysiac worship: τούς τε ἀπογραφομένους χαράσσεσθαι, καὶ διὰ πυρὸς εἰς τὸ σῶμα παρασήμῳ Διονύσῳ κισσοφύλλῳ. Deissmann (*Biblical Studies*, p. 242) shews that in Egypt under the Empire official documents were stamped with the name and year of the Emperor (e.g. L ιβʹ Αὐτοκράτορος Καίσαρος Νερούα Τραϊανοῦ Σεβαστοῦ Γερμανικοῦ Δακικοῦ), and that the stamp was known as a χάραγμα; but he produces no instance of persons being similarly marked. Others have thought of the branding of soldiers, slaves, and temple devotees; cf. Gal. vi. 17, with Lightfoot's note, and Philo *de monarch.*, p. 22 ἵενται πρὸς δουλείαν τῶν χειροκμήτων, γράμμασιν αὐτὴν ὁμολογοῦντες...ἐν τοῖς σώμασιν καταστίζοντες αὐτὴν σιδήρῳ πεπυρωμένῳ. But it is difficult to believe that such a mark was actually imposed on all the provincials who conformed. Ramsay (*op. cit.*, p. 110 f.) is disposed to think rather of some certificate, similar to the *libelli* of the Decian persecution, which was put into the hands of those who sacrificed, and to regard the mark on the forehead as merely "the apocalyptic description of a universal reputation for conspicuous devotion to the cult of the Emperor." This is hardly a satisfactory solution, and in our present ignorance it is perhaps better to be content with one which is suggested by the symbolism of the Book. As the servants of God receive on their foreheads (vii. 3) the impress of

[17][καὶ] ἵνα μή τις δύνηται ἀγοράσαι ἢ πωλῆσαι εἰ μὴ 17
ὁ ἔχων τὸ χάραγμα, τὸ ὄνομα τοῦ θηρίου ἢ τὸν
ἀριθμὸν τοῦ ὀνόματος αὐτοῦ. [18]ὧδε ἡ σοφία ἐστίν. 18

17 om *και* א*C 6 28 32 79 96 vg^{tol} me syrr Ir^{int} Hipp Prim al (hab א$^{\text{c.a}}$ APQ min^{pl} vg$^{\text{exc tol}}$ arm aeth Ar) | *μη τις*] *μηδεις* 130 | *δυναται* PQ 1 6 7 14 28 31 32 50 186 al^{10} | *το ονομα*] pr *η* א 36 38 vg$^{\text{cle dem lipss 4, 6}}$ anon^{aug} *του ονοματος* syr^{gw} | *η τον αριθμον*] pr *η τον αριθμον του θηριου* Q

the Divine Seal, so the servants of the Beast are marked with the 'stamp' of the Beast, "in fronte propter professionem, in manu propter operationem" (Ps. Aug.); the word *χάραγμα* being perhaps chosen (as Deissmann suggests) because it was the technical term for the Imperial stamp. For a partial parallel see Pss. Sol. xv. 8 ff. *τὸ σημεῖον τοῦ θεοῦ ἐπὶ δικαίους εἰς σωτηρίαν...καὶ οὐκ ἐκφεύξονται οἱ ποιοῦντες ἀνομίαν τὸ κρίμα Κυρίου...τὸ γὰρ σημεῖον τῆς ἀπωλείας ἐπὶ τοῦ μετώπου αὐτῶν.* That the Antichrist would seal his followers became a commonplace in the Christian legend; see Bousset, *Der Antichrist*, p. 132 ff.

17. *ἵνα μή τις δύνηται ἀγοράσαι ἢ πωλῆσαι κτλ.*] There is possibly a reference to 1 Macc. xiii. 49 *οἱ δὲ ἐκ τῆς ἄκρας ἐν Ἰερουσαλὴμ ἐκωλύοντο ἐκπορεύεσθαι εἰς τὴν χώραν καὶ ἀγοράζειν καὶ πωλεῖν.* But the cases differ materially. Here citizens who do not bear this mark are not prevented from entering the markets, but if they enter none will buy their goods or sell them the necessaries of life. Such a 'boycotting' of Christians might result partly from the unpopularity of their faith, partly from a dread of offending the dominant priesthood or their Roman supporters. If we ask whether the fear expressed by the Apocalyptist was realized, there is no certain answer. As Ramsay says (*op. cit.*, p. 107 f.), "how much of grim sarcasm...there lies in those words [*ἵνα μὴ δύνηται κτλ.*] it is impossible for us now to decide...but that there is an ideal truth in them, that they give a picture of the state of anxiety and apprehension, of fussy and over zealous profession of loyalty which the policy of Domitian was producing in the Roman world, is certain." Cf. Eus. *H.E.* v. 1 *ὥστε μὴ μόνον οἰκιῶν καὶ βαλανείων καὶ ἀγορᾶς εἴργεσθαι κτλ.*

Τὸ ὄνομα τοῦ θηρίου ἢ τὸν ἀριθμὸν τοῦ ὀνόματος αὐτοῦ is in apposition to *τὸ χάραγμα*; the stamp may bear the name or its number. The number of the name is probably the name itself written in numerals, according to a sort of *gematria* known to the Apocalyptist and his Asian readers, but not generally intelligible. The point of *ἢ τὸν ἀριθμόν* is not clear. According to Arethas, the name and the number are alternatives (*διττὴ δὲ τούτου ἡ γνῶσις ἢ διὰ παραφορᾶς αὐτοῦ τοῦ ὀνόματος ἢ διὰ ψήφου*). But as no *χάραγμα* would have borne the Christian cipher, it is better to treat *ἤ* here as practically equivalent to *τοῦτ' ἐστίν*—'the name, or, which is the same thing, the number.' Where the heathen provincial saw only the name of the reigning Emperor, the Christian detected a mystical number with its associations of vice and cruelty.

18. *ὧδε ἡ σοφία ἐστίν κτλ.*] A similar formula occurs in *c.* xvii. 9 *ὧδε ὁ νοῦς ὁ ἔχων σοφίαν.* Schoettgen compares the cabbalistic phrase רזא דחכמתא אית הכא. Ἡ *σοφία* is apparently the spiritual gift answering to the gift of *ἀποκάλυψις* (cf. Eph. i. 17 *πνεῦμα σοφίας καὶ ἀποκαλύψεως*)—the power of apprehending and interpreting mysteries. Here was an opportunity for the exercise of this power; let the hearer or

ὁ ἔχων νοῦν ψηφισάτω τὸν ἀριθμὸν τοῦ θηρίου, ἀριθμὸς γὰρ ἀνθρώπου ἐστίν· καὶ ὁ ἀριθμὸς αὐτοῦ ἑξακόσιοι ἑξήκοντα ἕξ.

18 ο εχων] pr και syr^{gw} | om και ℵ 6 7 8 14 29 31 al$^{plq\,20}$ syr^{gw} | ο αριθμος αυτου] om ℵ syr^{gw} + εστιν CP 1 10 18 28 37 38 49 79 91 95 96 vg$^{am\ fu\ lipss}$ syr arm Hipp^{bis} anon^{aug} | εξακοσιοι (-σιαι ℵ) εξηκοντα εξ (ℵ) AP(Q min^{mu} χξϛ')] εξακοσιοι (-σιαι C) δεκα εξ C (5 χιϛ') 11 quidam ap Ir anon^{aug}

reader interpret what is now about to be revealed. Ὁ *ἔχων νοῦν κτλ.*, 'let him who has intelligence—*ὁ νουνεχής*, a character not without its value in spiritual things; cf. Dan. xii. 10 *οὐ συνήσουσιν ἄνομοι, καὶ οἱ νοήμονες συνήσουσιν*; Mc. xii. 34 *ἰδὼν αὐτὸν ὅτι νουνεχῶς ἀπεκρίθη εἶπεν αὐτῷ Οὐ μακρὸν εἶ ἀπὸ τῆς βασιλείας τοῦ θεοῦ*—calculate (for *ψηφίζειν* cf. Lc. xiv. 28) [the meaning of] the Beast's number, for [beast though he is] his number is that of a man,' i.e. so far as the arithmetic goes, it is simple and intelligible, because it is human and not bestial; cf. xxi. 17 *μέτρον ἀνθρώπου, ὅ ἐστιν ἀγγέλου.*

καὶ ὁ ἀριθμὸς αὐτοῦ ἑξακόσιοι ἑξήκοντα ἕξ.] Within a century after the date of the Apocalypse the precise figures were uncertain. Irenaeus bears witness that while all good and old copies had *χξϛ'*, and this reading was attested by those who had seen St John, there were those who read *χιϛ'* (v. 30, 1 *ἐν πᾶσι τοῖς σπουδαίοις καὶ ἀρχαίοις ἀντιγράφοις τοῦ ἀριθμοῦ τούτου κειμένου, καὶ μαρτυρούντων αὐτῶν ἐκείνων τῶν κατ' ὄψιν τὸν Ἰωάννην ἑωρακότων... ἐσφάλησάν τινες ἐπακολουθήσαντες ἰδιωτισμῷ...ἀντὶ τῶν ἓξ δεκάδων μίαν δεκάδα βουλόμενοι εἶναι*), and attempted to interpret the cipher on these lines. The reading thus curtly dismissed gained so good a footing that it survives in one of our best uncials and in two cursives, and was adopted by a writer (?Tyconius) in the appendix to Augustine's works, who says *ad l.* "sexcenti et sexdecim graecis litteris sic faciunt *χιϛ*," and interprets accordingly. It can hardly therefore have originated in a simple confusion between *ξ* and *ι* (which indeed is itself unlikely, see Nestle, *Text. crit.* p. 334), and is probably a true though less widely received alternative for *χξϛ'*. With reference to the meaning of the cipher, Irenaeus speaks with far less confidence. If a clue had existed at first in the churches of Asia, it had been lost, probably because of the common belief that the second Beast directly represented Antichrist. Irenaeus's guesses (for they are obviously no more) are based on this hypothesis. The number, he says, is that of Noah's age at the time of the Flood (Gen. vii. 6), *plus* the height and breadth of the image set up by Nebuchadnezzar (*ὅλη γὰρ ἡ εἰκὼν ἐκείνη προτύπωσις ἦν τῆς τοῦ ἀντιχρίστου παρουσίας*); and it also alludes to the six *millennia* of the world's history (v. 29, § 2). When he comes to transform this number into a name for Antichrist, he mentions several guesses—the impossible word ΕΥΑΝΘΑϹ (= 5 + 400 + 1 + 50 + 9 + 1 + 200), ΛΑΤΕΙΝΟϹ (= 30 + 1 + 300 + 5 + 10 + 50 + 70 + 200), "Latini enim sunt qui nunc regnant," and ΤΕΙΤΑΝ (300 + 5 + 10 + 300 + 1 + 50); of these he thinks the last best, though he declines to decide (*ἡμεῖς οὖν οὐκ ἀποκινδυνεύομεν περὶ τοῦ ὀνόματος τοῦ ἀντιχρίστου*); urging that 'if the writer had wished us to know the name, he would have written it in full' (*ib.* 30, § 3). And this in the face of St John's *ὁ ἔχων νοῦν ψηφισάτω.*

Nor is Hippolytus more illuminat-

[1] Καὶ εἶδον, καὶ ἰδοὺ τὸ ἀρνίον ἑστὸς ἐπὶ τὸ ὄρος 1 XIV.

XIV 1 ειδον ℵP min[pl]] ιδον ACQ 7 14 36 92 130 186 | το αρνιον] om το P 1 28 35 36 49 91 96 130 al arm Andr | εστος ℵACP 79] εστως Q 1 al[plq10] Or Meth εστηκος 6 8 14 49 91 98 al[mu vid] Ar εστηκως 7 87 | το ορος Σιων] ορος C

ing. Regarding the stamp as bearing the number of the Beast, which like Irenaeus he reads as χξϛ', he sees in it the word ΑΡΝΟΥΜΕ = ἀρνοῦμαι (= 1 + 100 + 50 + 70 + 400 + 40 + 5), explaining: ἐπειδὴ καὶ πρώην...τοῖς μάρτυσι τοῦ χριστοῦ προέτρεπον οἱ ἄνομοι Ἄρνησαι, φησί, τὸν θεόν σου τὸν ἐσταυρωμένον (ed. Lag. p. 110 f.). Later patristic interpreters offer a large choice of conjectures, some of which are yet more improbable or even absurd. Such attempts to solve the enigma can only be regarded, as Andreas remarks, ἐν γυμνασίας λόγῳ, and bring us no nearer to the truth. Least probable of all are the attempts of many interpreters to find in the cipher 666 the name of one or another of the conspicuous characters of modern history; such guesses not only are inspired by personal antipathies, but betray ignorance of the real functions of Apocalyptic prophecy. Gunkel's theory (*Schöpfung*, p. 378) which finds in 666 the words תהום קדמוניה, 'primitive chaos,' i.e. Tiâmat, is not more convincing. If the number represents a name, the name is doubtless to be sought among the θηρία of the first century. It is interesting to find that the Greek letters of the style of Caligula (ΓΑΙΟϹ ΚΑΙϹΑΡ) represent numbers which added together make 616, while the Hebrew letters נרון קסר (Nero Caesar) make 666, or 616 if the first word is written as in Latin without the final *n*. Against this last explanation it has been urged that Caesar is written קיסר in the Talmud, a spelling which would bring the total to 676; but the abbreviated קסר is perhaps admissible in a cipher, and it is not without example (Renan, *l'Antechrist*, p. 415, note 4). Certainly Nero Caesar suits the context well; the Beast or persecuting world power might fitly be named after the Emperor who began the policy of persecution, and was himself an incarnation of its worst characteristics. Another line of interpretation may perhaps be combined with this. It has been pointed out (Briggs, *Messiah*, p. 324, Milligan, *Revelation*, p. 235) that in 666 every digit falls short by one of the perfect number—a mark of Antichrist. In *Orac. Sibyll.* i. 328, 888 represents Christ: ὀκτὼ γὰρ μονάδας, τόσσας δεκάδας δ' ἐπὶ ταύταις | ἠδ' ἑκατοντάδας ὀκτώ... | οὔνομα δηλώσει· σὺ δ' ἐνὶ φρεσὶ σῇσι νόησον | ἀθανάτοιο θεοῦ Χριστὸν παῖδ' ὑψίστοιο. The contrast is significant.

XIV. 1—5. The vision of the 144,000 on Mount Zion.

1. καὶ εἶδον, καὶ ἰδοὺ τὸ ἀρνίον ἑστὸς κτλ.] The vision of the two Beasts and their followers is fitly followed by a reassuring picture of the Lamb in the midst of His Church; "au milieu de flots de colère apparaît maintenant un îlot de verdure" (Renan). Cf. Primasius: "invicta quoque ecclesiae castra oportuit declarari, ne tam vehementi persecutionis impetu vel succubuisse vel periisse eandem ecclesiam infirmus animus aestimaret." Τὸ ἀρνίον looks back to v. 6 (where see note), vii. 17, xii. 11, xiii. 8, and stands in contrast with the anarthrous ἀρνίῳ in xiii. 11. On the other hand the ἑκατὸν τεσσεράκοντα τέσσαρες χιλιάδες, though doubtless alluding to the 144,000 of *c.* vii. (cf. Origen, *in Joann.* t. i. 1), are not directly identified with the latter (Arethas: ἢ γὰρ ἂν μετὰ τοῦ ἄρθρου προήνεγκεν, 'αἱ ρμδ' χιλιάδες' εἰπών). The distribution of the 12,000 among the tribes is no longer in view: the total number is used either as

Σιών, καὶ μετ' αὐτοῦ ἑκατὸν τεσσεράκοντα τέσσαρες
χιλιάδες ἔχουσαι τὸ ὄνομα αὐτοῦ καὶ τὸ ὄνομα τοῦ
πατρὸς αὐτοῦ γεγραμμένον ἐπὶ τῶν μετώπων αὐτῶν.
2 [2]καὶ ἤκουσα φωνὴν ἐκ τοῦ οὐρανοῦ ὡς φωνὴν ὑδάτων

1 *μετ αυτου*] + *αριθμος* Q min[25] syr Ar | *εκατον τεσσερακοντα* (*τεσσαρ.* P) *τεσσαρες*] *ρμδ'* Q min[pl] (item *v.* 3) Ar | om *αυτου και το ονομα* P 1 om *το ονομα* 7 16 38 | *γεγραμμενον*] *καιομενον* 1

that of a great but limited gathering, or possibly with reference to the "Twelve Apostles of the Lamb" (xxi. 14, cf. Andreas: *αἱ δὲ ρμδ' χιλιάδες...τὸ τοῦ ἀποστολικοῦ σπόρου πολυφόρον δηλοῦσι, τῆς ἐν ἑκάστῳ χάριτος δωδεκάκις χιλιοστὸν* (12 × 12 × 1000) *ἀπεργαζομένης*. But, as in vii. 4 ff., it is the living Church which is in the Seer's thought, not the *ἀναρίθμητος ὄχλος* of vii. 9; not, i.e., the Church in her final completed glory, but the faithful who are on earth at any given time.

ἐπὶ τὸ ὄρος Σιών] The site of the new City of God; cf. Heb. xii. 22, *προσεληλύθατε Σιὼν ὄρει*, where Westcott remarks: "Zion is distinctively the Acropolis...Mount Zion represents the strong Divine foundations of the new Order." For 'mount Zion' (הַר צִיּוֹן cf. xvi. 16, Ἁρ Μαγεδών) see Ps. ii. 6, xlvii. (xlviii.) 1 ff., lxxvii. (lxxviii.) 54, 68, lxxxvi. (lxxxvii.) 1, cxxiv. (cxxv.) 1, Mic. iv. 7, Obad. 17, 21, Isa. xxviii. 16, lix. 20; it is the O. T. symbol for the security and strength which belong to the people of God. Thus 'Mount Zion' is the counterpart to the *τόπος ἡτοιμασμένος* of *c.* xii. 6, 14; seen in the light of this new vision, the place where the Woman takes refuge is none other than the impregnable rock on which the Church reposes (Mt. xvi. 18). With the present passage cf. 4 Esdr. ii. 42, "ego Ezra vidi in monte Sion turbam magnam, quam numerare non potui, et omnes canticis conlaudabant Dominum"; *ib.* xiii. 35, 39, "ipse autem stabit super cacumen Montis Sion...et quoniam vidisti eum colligentem ad se aliam multitudinem pacificam," etc.

ἔχουσαι τὸ ὄνομα αὐτοῦ κτλ.] In *c.* vii. the 144,000 bear the imprint of the Divine Seal, which protects them against assault (cf. ix. 4). Here their foreheads are inscribed with the Name of the Lamb and that of His Father. (cf. iii. 12 *ὁ νικῶν...γράψω ἐπ' αὐτὸν τὸ ὄνομα τοῦ θεοῦ μου...καὶ τὸ ὄνομά μου τὸ καινόν*, xxii. 4 *τὸ ὄνομα αὐτοῦ* [*sc.* *τοῦ θεοῦ* or *τοῦ θ. καὶ τοῦ ἀρνίου*] *ἐπὶ τῶν μετώπων αὐτῶν*, and see notes *ad ll.*), a metaphor which supplies a more direct parallel to the methods of the Beast, whose servants are branded with the *χάραγμα* of his name (xiii. 17, xiv. 11). The Divine name on the forehead suggests at once the imparting of a character which corresponds with the Mind of God, and the consecration of life to His service.

2. *καὶ ἤκουσα φωνὴν ἐκ τοῦ οὐρανοῦ κτλ.*] Not, as the ancient commentators usually assume, the voice of the 144,000, but that of the 'company of Heaven' with whom the Church is closely united through the presence in her midst of the Lamb; cf. Heb. *l.c.* *προσεληλύθατε Σ. ὄρει...καὶ μυριάσιν ἀγγέλων πανηγύρει*, where see again Westcott's notes.

Much of the phraseology of this verse occurs elsewhere in the book: e.g. for *ἤκουσα φ. ἐκ τοῦ οὐρανοῦ* cf. x. 4, xiv. 15, xviii. 4; for *φωνὴν ὑδάτων πολλῶν*, i. 15 (4 Esdr. vi. 17); for *ὡς φ. βροντῆς*, vi. 1, xix. 6. On *κιθάρα* in connexion with celestial music see v. 8, xv. 2; *φωνὴ κιθαρῳδῶν* occurs again in xviii. 22, and *κιθαρίζειν* in Isa. xxiii. 16, 1 Cor. xiv. 7. On the meaning of *κιθάρα* see the note on v. 8.

πολλῶν καὶ ὡς φωνὴν βροντῆς μεγάλης, καὶ ἡ φωνὴ
ἣν ἤκουσα ὡς κιθαρῳδῶν κιθαριζόντων ἐν ταῖς κιθά-
ραις αὐτῶν. [3]καὶ ᾄδουσιν ὡς ᾠδὴν καινὴν ἐνώπιον 3
τοῦ θρόνου καὶ ἐνώπιον τῶν τεσσάρων ζῴων καὶ τῶν
πρεσβυτέρων· καὶ οὐδεὶς ἐδύνατο μαθεῖν τὴν ᾠδὴν εἰ
μὴ αἱ ἑκατὸν τεσσεράκοντα τέσσαρες χιλιάδες, οἱ

2 *η φωνη ην*] *φωνην* P 1 28 79 91 | om *ως* 3° 1 91 | om *κιθαρωδων* 130 | *κιθαρωδον κιθαριζοντα* syr^{gw} | *αυτων*] om C *αυτου* syr^{gw} 3 om *ως* ℵPQ min^{40} me syr arm aeth Or Meth Prim Ar (hab AC 1 28 36 79 95 al vg) | *καινην*] + *και ην* ℵ (*ην* sup lin ℵ^{1}) | om *και τ. πρεσβυτερων* C | *των πρεσβ.*] pr *ενωπιον* ℵ syr^{gw} arm | om *και* 4° 130 | *ουδεις*] *ουδε εις* Q 8 11 29 30 31 32 93 94 | *ηδυνατο* PQ min^{pl} | *αι εκατον*] om *αι* ℵ$^{c.a}$ 7 28 32* 93 | *τεσσαρακοντα* P min^{pl}

3. *καὶ ᾄδουσιν ὡς ᾠδὴν καινήν κτλ.*] On *καινὴ ᾠδή* in v. 9, notes. In *c.* v. the New Song is sung by the *ζῷα* and the Elders, representing Creation and the Church. Here it is sung before the *ζῷα* and the Elders, and therefore not by them, but apparently by the Angels, who are not themselves recipients of the benefits of Redemption. They are represented, however, in the N. T. as deeply interested in all that concerns the salvation of man (Lc. xv. 7, 10, Eph. iii. 10, 1 Pet. i. 12), and as joining in the praises of the Lamb (Apoc. v. 11 f.). Here they lead the Song, which the redeemed themselves have yet but imperfectly learnt. There is a feeling after the truth which lies behind this vision in more than one of the Prefaces that precede the *Sanctus* in the ancient liturgies; cf. e.g. the Liturgy of St James (Brightman, i. p. 50): *ὃν ὑμνοῦσιν...Ἰερουσαλὴμ ἡ ἐπουράνιος πανήγυρις, ἐκκλησία πρωτοτόκων...πνεύματα δικαίων...ψυχαὶ μαρτύρων ... ἄγγελοι, ἀρχάγγελοι ... χερουβὶμ...καὶ...σεραφὶμ ἃ...κέκραγεν... τὸν ἐπινίκιον ὕμνον...ᾄδοντα*, and the still more explicit form in the Roman Preface: "cum angelis et archangelis... hymnum gloriae tuae canimus," and our own: "with Angels and Archangels...we laud and magnify thy glorious Name."

καὶ οὐδεὶς ἐδύνατο μαθεῖν τὴν ᾠδήν κτλ.] Even the 144,000 have need to learn the Song; it does not come to them naturally, or without effort; every Eucharist, every thankful meditation on the Passion, is an exercise in the art. And only they can learn it; the music of the heart (Eph. v. 19, Col. iii. 16) cannot be acquired without a receptivity which is a Divine gift; cf. Jo. xiv. 17, *ὃ ὁ κόσμος οὐ δύναται λαβεῖν, ὅτι οὐ θεωρεῖ αὐτὸ οὐδὲ γινώσκει*, 1 Cor. ii. 14, *ψυχικὸς δὲ ἄνθρωπος οὐ δέχεται τὰ τοῦ πνεύματος τοῦ θεοῦ*. Commentators who interpret the 144,000 as an inner circle of saints, whether ascetics or others, and Mount Zion as belonging to the future order, are compelled to limit the New Song to a section of the redeemed: e.g. Andreas: *τὴν καινὴν ᾠδὴν διδάσκονται τὴν τοῖς πολλοῖς οὐ μόνον ἐν τῷ παρόντι βίῳ ἀλλὰ καὶ ἐν τῷ μέλλοντι αἰῶνι ἄγνωστον.*

Αἱ...χιλιάδες, οἱ ἠγορασμένοι ἀπὸ τῆς γῆς: 'the...thousands, namely, those who have been purchased [for God, by the Blood of the Lamb, cf. v. 9] from the earth' or (*v.* 4) 'from among men.' *Ἀπό* here denotes not 'separation,' but 'extraction,' as *ἐκ* in *v.* 9; see Blass, *Gr.* p. 125. The 144,000 are not taken away from the earth (Jo. xvii. 15), but while they are upon it they recognise their relation to God and to Christ.

4 ἠγορασμένοι ἀπὸ τῆς γῆς. [4]οὗτοί εἰσιν οἳ μετὰ
γυναικῶν οὐκ ἐμολύνθησαν, παρθένοι γάρ εἰσιν· οὗτοι
οἱ ἀκολουθοῦντες τῷ ἀρνίῳ ὅπου ἂν ὑπάγει. οὗτοι

3 τ. γης] + *Aegypti* aeth 4 om ουτοι εισιν A vg^{cod} $aeth^{utr}$ | ουτοι 2°] + εισιν Q min^{pl} vg^{fu} syr Meth Ar $Cypr^{bis}$ Prim | οι ακολ.] om οι ℵ | υπαγει AC 7 16 28 36 87] υπαγη ℵPQ min^{pl}

4. οὗτοί εἰσιν οἳ μετὰ γυναικῶν κτλ.] Cf. Tertullian, *res. carn.* 27 "virgines scilicet significans et qui semetipsos castraverunt propter regna caelorum." But if our interpretation is right, οἳ μ. γ. οὐκ ἐμολύνθησαν κτλ. must be taken metaphorically, as the symbolical character of the Book suggests. As Tyconius cited by Bede remarks, "virgines...castos dicit et pudicos"; they are the καθαροὶ τῇ καρδίᾳ of Mt. v. 8, the παρθένος ἁγνὴ ἑνὶ ἀνδρὶ ἡρμοσμένη of 2 Cor. xi. 2. No condemnation of marriage, no exclusion of the married from the highest blessings of the Christian life, finds a place in the N. T. Our Lord recognises abstinence as a Christian practice only in cases where men are able to receive it (Mt. xix. 12). If St Paul thinks of celibacy as the better state (1 Cor. vii. 1, 8), and moreover gives his reasons for doing so (*ib.* 32), yet he does not discourage marriage between Christians; indeed he not only allows (*ib.* 36) but in many cases recommends it (*ib.* 1, 8). The Epistle to the Hebrews even eulogizes "the honourable estate of matrimony" (xiii. 4, τίμιος ὁ γάμος ἐν πᾶσιν καὶ ἡ κοίτη ἀμίαντος). The Apocalyptist does not differ from the Pauline school, but he remembers the attitude of the Levitical ritual towards sexual intercourse (Exod. xix. 15, 1 Sam. xxi. 4), and transfers the μολυσμός which it involved in the eyes of the Law to the abuses of God's ordinance of which pagan society was full. That chastity should be chosen as the first distinctive virtue of the Christian brotherhood will not seem strange to those who reflect that pagan life was honeycombed with immorality of the grossest kind.

With the use of παρθένος masc. cf. the Apocryphal *Life of Asenath*, 3, ἐστὶν δὲ οὗτος ὁ Ἰωσὴφ ἀνὴρ θεοσεβὴς καὶ σώφρων καὶ παρθένος, *ib.* 6, ἄσπασον τὸν ἀδελφόν σου, διότι καὶ αὐτὸς παρθένος. The term is applied by Suidas to Abel and Melchizedek, and by Nonnus to St John, who was traditionally a celibate to his death. In Clement of Alexandria's *Hypotyposes* the first Epistle of St John is said to have been addressed "ad virgines (πρὸς παρθένους)," and an echo of this inscription probably survives in the headings of the Epistle in one of Sabatier's Latin MSS. (*Ad Sparthos*), as well as in the Πρὸς Παρθούς of a cursive Greek MS.; cf. Westcott, *Epp. of St John*, p. xxxii f., note 2.

οὗτοι οἱ ἀκολουθοῦντες τῷ ἀρνίῳ κτλ.] A reference to the Lord's familiar call ἀκολούθει μοι (Mc. ii. 14, x. 21, Lc. ix. 59, Jo. i. 43, xxi. 19), and to such sayings as those reported in Mc. viii. 34, Jo. viii. 12, x. 4, 27, xii. 26. The conception had rooted itself in the Christian imagination from the first; cf. 1 Pet. ii. 21, ὑμῖν ὑπολιμπάνων ὑπογραμμὸν ἵνα ἐπακολουθήσητε τοῖς ἴχνεσιν αὐτοῦ. As to its meaning, Augustine's "sequimini virginitate cordis...quid est enim sequi nisi imitari?" supplies the only answer: the Christian life is from first to last an *imitatio Agni*. Cf. Eus. *H. E.* v. 1, ἦν γὰρ καὶ ἔστι (Vettius Epagathus) γνήσιος Χριστοῦ μαθητής, ἀκολουθῶν τῷ ἀρνίῳ ὅπου ἂν ὑπάγῃ. Origen, *in Joann.* xi. 16 *fragm.* (ed. Brooke, ii.

ἠγοράσθησαν ἀπὸ τῶν ἀνθρώπων ἀπαρχὴ τῷ θεῷ καὶ
τῷ ἀρνίῳ, [5]καὶ ἐν τῷ στόματι αὐτῶν οὐχ εὑρέθη 5
ψεῦδος· ἄμωμοί εἰσιν.

4 ηγορασθησαν] pr υπο Ιησου Q 6 7 8 14 29 31 38 186 al[plq 30] syr Ar | om απο των ανθρωπων C | απαρχη ACPQ min[pl] vg me syr Or[bis] Meth Andr Ar] απ αρχης ℵ 16 39 aeth[vid] 5 ψευδος] δολος 1 al[pauc vid] | αμωμοι] αμωμητοι 7 + γαρ ℵQ min[fere omn] vg[cle am** dem harl* lips 6 tol] me syrr arm aeth Or[bis] Meth Andr Ar (om γαρ ACP 12 130 vg[am* fu harl** lips 4, 5]) pr οτι 186 | εισιν] + ενωπιον του θρονου του θεου vg[cle dem lipss] + ουτοι εισιν οι ακολουθουντες τω αρνιω 33 35 48 Ar

p. 289): εἶτα ὡς γνήσιος αὐτοῦ μαθητής (St Thomas), κρίνας αὐτῷ ἀκολουθεῖν ὅποι ποτ' ἂν ἀπίῃ, κτλ.

The reading ὅπου ἂν ὑπάγει, though rejected by Blass (*Gr.* p. 217) admits of explanation; ἄν qualifies ὅπου only; the direction is uncertain, but the movement (ὑπάγει) is actual. In all life Christ is leading, as a matter of fact; and the indicative emphasizes this point.

οὗτοι ἠγοράσθησαν...ἀπαρχὴ τῷ θεῷ καὶ τῷ ἀρνίῳ] This amplifies and interprets οἱ ἠγορασμένοι ἀπὸ τῆς γῆς. The 144,000 were purchased as an ἀπαρχή, the firstfruits of the harvest of the world; for this sense of ἀπαρχή cf. Rom. xvi. 5 ἀπαρχὴ τῆς Ἀσίας εἰς Χριστόν, 1 Cor. xvi. 15 ἀπαρχὴ τῆς Ἀχαίας. Here the ἀπαρχή is the generation of Christians who were living in the last years of the first century, and who, relatively to the company of the faithful in all future time, were as the firstfruits of the great θερισμός (Mt. ix. 37). An alternative but perhaps less probable interpretation regards ἀπαρχή as contrasting the contemporary Church with the mass of mankind (cf. 2 Thess. ii. 13 εἵλατο ὑμᾶς ὁ θεὸς ἀπαρχὴν—so BFGP, vg., Syr.[hcl.]—εἰς σωτηρίαν), or with creation in general (cf. Jac. i. 18 εἰς τὸ εἶναι ἡμᾶς ἀπαρχήν τινα τῶν αὐτοῦ κτισμάτων, where see Mayor's note).

But the ἀπαρχή is not only the first instalment of the human harvest; the word is connected by its O.T. associations with the service of God. The 144,000 are an ἀπ. τῷ θεῷ καὶ τῷ ἀρνίῳ (for the collocation see vii. 10, xxii. 1, 3), i.e. they are offered and consecrated to the Divine service: cf. the law of the firstfruits in Exod. xxii. 29 (28), Deut. xxvi. 2 ff.; the phrase προσφέρειν or ἀφορίζειν ἀπαρχὴν τῷ κυρίῳ occurs in Lev. ii. 12, Ez. xlv. 1, xlviii. 9. The new Israelite offers to God his own body (Rom. xii. 1), and the spiritual sacrifices of praise and thanksgiving (Heb. xiii. 15), of alms and offerings (ib. 16 f.), of heart and will (1 Pet. ii. 5).

5. καὶ ἐν τῷ στόματι αὐτῶν οὐχ εὑρέθη ψεῦδος] See Zeph. iii. 13 οἱ κατάλοιποι τοῦ Ἰσραὴλ...οὐ μὴ εὑρεθῇ ἐν τῷ στόματι αὐτῶν γλῶσσα δολία, and with the passage as a whole cf. Ps. xiv. 1 ff. τίς κατασκηνώσει ἐν τῷ ὄρει τῷ ἁγίῳ σου; πορευόμενος ἄμωμος ...λαλῶν ἀλήθειαν ἐν καρδίᾳ αὐτοῦ, ὃς οὐκ ἐδόλωσεν ἐν γλώσσῃ αὐτοῦ. After purity truthfulness was perhaps the most distinctive mark of the followers of Christ, when contrasted with their heathen neighbours; cf. Eph. iv. 20–25. The Lamb was characterized by the same trait: cf. Isa. liii. 9, as quoted in 1 Pet. ii. 23, οὐδὲ εὑρέθη δόλος ἐν τῷ στόματι αὐτοῦ. On οὐκ εὑρέθη (לֹא נִמְצָא) Tyconius cited by Bede remarks: "non dixit, 'non fuit...' sed *non est inventum*." The distinction, however, is in practice often slight: cf. WM. p. 769 f., &c., see *cc.* v. 4, xii. 8, xvi. 20, xviii. 21 ff., xx. 11.

Ἄμωμοί εἰσιν. Cf. Sir. xx. 24 μῶμος πονηρὸς ἐν ἀνθρώπῳ ψεῦδος. From this fatal blemish the followers of

6 [6]*Καὶ εἶδον ἄλλον ἄγγελον πετόμενον ἐν μεσου-*

6 *ειδον* ℵCP min[pl]] *ιδον* AQ 7 14 36 92 | om *αλλον* ℵ* Q 130 al[plq 35] Or Ar | *πετομενον* AC 14 29 31 35 38 79 91 186 al[20] Or Andr Ar] *πεταμενον* ℵ *πετωμενον* PQ 1 al[sat mu] | *μεσουρανηματι*] *μεσω ουρανηματι* ℵ* *μεσουρανισματι* 1 *ουρανω αιματι εχοντα* syr (cf. viii. 13)

Christ were free. Ἄμωμος is fairly frequent in the Epistles of the N.T.; cf. Eph. i. 4, v. 27, Col. i. 22, where it goes with ἅγιος or with ἅγιος and ἀνέγκλητος; Christ is ἀμνὸς ἄμωμος καὶ ἄσπιλος (1 Pet. i. 19), and Christians are τέκνα θεοῦ ἄμωμα (Phil. ii. 15, and cf. Jude 24). Behind all these uses of the word there lies the tradition of the Greek O.T., in which ἄμωμος is a Levitical term for sacrifices not vitiated by any flaw rendering them unfit to be offered. In this sense it is the regular equivalent of תָּמִים; for the history of this use see Dr Hort's interesting note on 1 Pet. *l. c.* Hence ἄμωμος in Biblical Greek is not 'blameless,' as the etymology would suggest, but 'unblemished,' sacrificially perfect. The 144,000 were such; their self-consecration was free from the insincerity which would have rendered it unacceptable in the sight of God. The interpretative gloss ἐνώπιον τοῦ θρόνου τοῦ θεοῦ (cf. *app. crit.*) is misleading; the scene is not laid in Heaven, but on Mount Sion; see *v.* 1, notes.

6—13. THREE ANGELIC PROCLAMATIONS, AND A VOICE FROM HEAVEN.

6. καὶ εἶδον ἄλλον ἄγγελον κτλ.] Each of the angels who now appear in succession is a new *persona dramatis* (ἄλλος, cf. vii. 2, viii. 3, x. 1, notes), to be distinguished from his predecessor. The first of the three is thus distinguished, as it seems, from the Seventh Angel of the Trumpets, the angelic being last mentioned (xi. 15). He appears flying in the meridian (for μεσουράνημα see viii. 13, xix. 17, notes), i.e., where he can be seen and heard by all whom his message concerns; and he carries (ἔχοντα, cf. i. 18, v. 8, vi. 2, al.) an announcement of good tidings to the world at large. On εὐαγγέλιον see Mc. i. 1, note; the noun is not used elsewhere in the Johannine writings, though the verb occurs here and in *c.* x. 7. The ancient interpreters (e.g. Primasius) compare Mt. xxiv. 14 κηρυχθήσεται τοῦτο τὸ εὐαγγέλιον τῆς βασιλείας...εἰς μαρτύριον πᾶσιν τοῖς ἔθνεσιν, καὶ τότε ἥξει τὸ τέλος, while Origen seems to think of a literal proclamation of the Gospel before the end by an angelic ministry (*in Joann.* t. i. 14 οὐ μίαν δὲ καὶ βραχεῖαν ἐκπιστεύονται διακονίαν εὐαγγελικὴν ἄγγελοι, οὐδὲ μόνην τὴν πρὸς τοὺς ποιμένας γεγενημένην· ἀλλὰ γὰρ ἐπὶ τέλει μετέωρος καὶ ἱπτάμενος ἄγγελος εὐαγγέλιον ἔχων εὐαγγελιεῖται πᾶν ἔθνος. But αἰώνιον εὐαγγέλιον cannot be rendered, as by A.V., "the everlasting Gospel"; the parallel cited from Rom. i. 1, εὐαγγέλιον θεοῦ, is not apposite, since εὐαγγέλιον is there sufficiently defined by the genitive which follows it (cf. WM. p. 155). Doubtless like ἀρνίῳ and δράκων in xiii. 11, and χιλιάδες in xiv. 1, this anarthrous εὐαγγέλιον alludes to that which answered to the name *par excellence*, but it is not synonymous with it. St John has in view not the Gospel as a whole, but rather a gospel which is a particular aspect of it, the gospel of the Parousia and the consummation which the Parousia will bring. Αἰώνιον, like εὐαγγέλιον, is ἅπ. λεγ. in the Apoc., though frequent in the Gospel and first Ep. of St John; and it is not easy to determine its import in this connexion. Origen supposed it to refer to a future revelation as compared with the Gospel which the Church preaches already; thus he writes (*in Rom.*, i. 4): "quod *aeternum* dicit Ioannes in Apocalypsi, quod tunc revelandum est cum umbra transierit

ῥανήματι, ἔχοντα εὐαγγέλιον αἰώνιον εὐαγγελίσαι
ἐπὶ τοὺς καθημένους ἐπὶ τῆς γῆς καὶ ἐπὶ πᾶν ἔθνος
καὶ φυλὴν καὶ γλῶσσαν καὶ λαόν, [7]λέγων ἐν φωνῇ 7
μεγάλῃ Φοβήθητε τὸν θεὸν καὶ δότε αὐτῷ δόξαν,
ὅτι ἦλθεν ἡ ὥρα τῆς κρίσεως αὐτοῦ, καὶ προσκυνή-
σατε τῷ ποιήσαντι τὸν οὐρανὸν καὶ τὴν γῆν καὶ

6 ευαγγελισαι] ευαγγελισασθαι ℵ 10 28 33 35 36 49 51 79 96 130 Or | om επι 1° Q min^{pl} Ar | *τους καθημενους* (*τοις καθημενοις* 38 97)] *τους κατοικουντας* A 14 28 79 92 186 al anon^{aug} *τους καθ. τους κατοικ.* 1 *τους καθ. και κατοικ.* 36 | om επι 3° 1 28 36 79 al me Ar   7 λεγων] λεγουσα 1 vg^{am} Or Cypr λεγοντα 186 om ℵ | om εν A | φοβηθητε] + *potius* Cypr Prim | *τον θεον*] *τον κυριον* Q min^{40} *g* vg$^{cle\ dem\ harl\ tol\ lipss}$ anon^{aug} Ar | *τω ποιησαντι*] (*αυτον*) *τον ποιησαντα* Q min^{30} (Or) Ar

et veritas venerit, et cum mors fuerit absorpta et aeternitas restituta"; but the contents of the Angel's message do not accord with his suggestion. The middle ages produced an *Evangelium aeternum* (c. A.D. 1254), and a book with the same title appeared in Germany as late as 1699, both works being founded, as it seems, upon a similar misapprehension; see Fabricius, *cod. apocr. N.T.* p. 337 ff.; Fabr.-Mansi, *Bibl. Lat. med. aet.*, iii. p. 397. In αἰώνιον εὐαγγέλιον the epithet may be either retrospective—'a gospel which has had an age-long history' (see Rom. xvi. 25 μυστηρίου χρόνοις αἰωνίοις σεσιγημένου), or, as is more probable, prospective,—'a gospel belonging to, stretching forward to, the eternal order' (cf. Mc. iii. 29, note)—αἰώνιον as contrasted with the πρόσκαιρα of the present life (2 Cor. iv. 18), a gospel which is a direct antithesis to the promises of brief indulgence with which the Empire excited the hopes of its subjects, the *panis et circenses* after which the Roman populace gaped (Juv. *sat.* x. 80).

εὐαγγελίσαι ἐπὶ τοὺς καθημένους ἐπὶ τῆς γῆς κτλ.] On the act. εὐαγγελίζειν see x. 7, note; the infinitive defines the purpose for which the εὐαγγέλιον was entrusted to the angel, and is nearly equivalent to ἵνα εὐαγγελίσῃ. The Angel's gospel was directed to (ἐπὶ τ. κ., cf. 1 Pet. i. 25 τὸ εὐαγγελισθὲν εἰς ὑμᾶς, Gal. i. 16 ἵνα εὐαγγελίζωμαι αὐτὸν ἐν τοῖς ἔθνεσιν, Apoc. x. 11 δεῖ σε πάλιν προφητεῦσαι ἐπὶ λαοῖς) the polyglott peoples who made up the Empire; for πᾶν ἔθνος κ. φυλὴ κ. γλῶσσα κ. λαός see v. 9, vii. 9, xi. 9, xiii. 7. The phrase καθῆσθαι ἐπὶ τῆς γῆς = κατοικεῖν ἐπὶ τῆς γῆς is Hebraic, cf. e.g. Jer. xxxii. (xxv.) 29 ἐπὶ τοὺς καθημένους ἐ. τ. γ. = עַל כָּל־יֹשְׁבֵי הָאָרֶץ; for other instances in the N.T. see Mt. iv. 16, Lc. xxi. 35, and cf. Apoc. xvii. 1.

7. λέγων ἐν φωνῇ μεγάλῃ Φοβήθητε κτλ.] The Angel's call seems to be the reverse of a gospel; it announces that judgement is imminent, and summons the pagan world to repentance. Like St Paul's speech at Lystra (Acts xiv. 15 ff.) it contains no reference to the Christian hope; the basis of the appeal is pure theism; the terms φοβεῖσθαι τὸν θεόν, δόξαν δοῦναι τῷ θεῷ (xi. 13), are O.T. phrases (Eccl. xii. 13, Josh. vii. 19), and no πιστεύετε ἐν τῷ εὐαγγελίῳ tempers the sternness of the cry (Mc. i. 14). It is an appeal to the conscience of untaught heathendom, incapable as yet of comprehending any other. Yet there is a gospel in the implied fact that repentance is still possible, and the very judgement that impends promises a new order

8 θάλασσαν καὶ πηγὰς ὑδάτων. ⁸καὶ ἄλλος δεύτερος
ἄγγελος ἠκολούθησεν λέγων Ἔπεσεν ἔπεσεν Βαβυ-
λὼν ἡ μεγάλη, ἣ ἐκ τοῦ οἴνου τοῦ θυμοῦ τῆς πορνείας

7 θαλασσαν] pr την ℵQ 1 130 186 al$^{\text{fere 40}}$ Or Andr Ar 8 αλλος δευτερος αγγελος ℵ* (sine αγγ.) AQ 1 al$^{\text{fere 30}}$ 95 et 130 (sine αγγ.)] αλλος αγγ. δευτερος ℵ$^{\text{c.a}}$ CP 6 9 10 17 18 28 36 (sine αλλος) 37 40 186 al^{5} me syr arm αλλος αγγελος 14 vg syr^{gw} aeth anon^{aug} | om επεσεν 2° ℵ$^{\text{c.a}}$ (transiliente ℵ*) CQ 130 al$^{\text{plq 30}}$ me aeth | η 2°] η μεγαλη] + πολις 130 οτι 1 36 Ar om ℵ$^{\text{c.a}}$ PQ 186 al$^{\text{plq 30}}$ me Prim | om του οινου syr^{gw} | om του θυμου 1 96 vg^{fu} Prim^{comm} | πορνιας ℵ$^{\text{c.a}}$ CQ

which is the hope both of the Church and of the world. Ἦλθεν ἡ ὥρα κτλ. Cf. Jo. xii. 23, xvi. 32, *infra v.* 15. Τῷ ποιήσαντι τὸν οὐρανὸν κτλ. is again from the O.T.; cf. Ps. cxlv. (cxlvi.) 6, and see Acts *l.c.*; the phrase sums up the claim of the Creator as such upon the allegiance of mankind, and the appeal of Nature can go no further. Πηγαὶ ὑδάτων, מַעְיְנֵי־מַיִם or עֵינוֹת, as in Exod. xv. 27, Lev. xi. 36; cf. *c.* viii. 10, xvi. 4.

8. καὶ ἄλλος δεύτερος ἄγγελος ἠκολούθησεν κτλ.] Another angel, a second, follows the first. His message interprets in part the "hour of judgement" of which the first had given warning: "fallen, fallen is Babylon the Great." Ἔπεσεν ἔπεσεν Β. is an echo of Isa. xxi. 9 נָפְלָה נָפְלָה בָּבֶל (LXX., πέπτωκεν πέπτωκεν Β.). As in xi. 7 (τὸ θηρίον), the writer assumes that the recipients of the book are familiar with a symbol which he has not hitherto used, and therefore partly anticipates what he has to say about it at a later stage. There is reason to think that in Jewish and Christian circles Babylon was already an accepted synonym for Rome; besides 1 Pet. v. 13 ἡ ἐν Βαβυλῶνι συνεκλεκτή, where most of the indications point to Rome, cf. *Orac. Sibyll.* v. (a pre-Christian Jewish book) 143 φεύξεται ἐκ Βαβυλῶνος ἄναξ φοβερὸς καὶ ἀναιδής, *ib.* 159 f. καὶ φλέξει πόντον τε βαθὺν καὐτὴν Βαβυλῶνα | Ἰταλίης γαῖάν θ', *ib.* 434 αἶ αἴ σοι, Βαβυλὼν χρυσόθρονε χρυσοπέδιλε, and the *Apoc. of Baruch* (contemporary with the N.T., Charles, p. xvi.) xi. 1. Early Christian interpretation supports the view that Babylon = Rome in 1 Peter and the Apoc.; cf. Eus. *H. E.* ii. 15 συντάξαι φασὶν [τὸν Μᾶρκον τὸ εὐαγγέλιον] ἐπ' αὐτῆς Ῥώμης, σημαίνειν τε τοῦτ' αὐτόν, τὴν πόλιν τροπικώτερον Βαβυλῶνα προσειπόντα (the information appears to be derived from Clement of Alexandria and perhaps ultimately from Papias of Hierapolis); Tertullian, *adv. Marc.* iii. 13 "Babylon etiam apud Ioannem nostrum Romanae urbis figura est, proinde magnae et regno superbae et sanctorum Dei debellatricis." The phrase Β. ἡ μεγάλη comes from Dan. iv. 27 בָּבֶל רַבְּתָא LXX. and Th.; the epithet is used wherever Babylon is mentioned in the Apocalypse (xiv. 8, xvi. 19, xvii. 5, xviii. 2, 10, 21), and emphasizes the Nebuchadnezzar-like self-importance of the rulers of Rome rather than the actual size or true greatness of the city; in the latter respect Jerusalem was in the eyes of a Jew ἡ πόλις ἡ μεγάλη (xi. 8, note).

But Rome was as dissolute as she was proud, and a source of moral infection to the world; ἣ ἐκ τοῦ οἴνου κτλ. justifies the doom pronounced by the second Angel upon her. Τοῦ οἴνου τοῦ θυμοῦ τῆς πορνείας αὐτῆς (here and in xviii. 3) brings together two phrases which occur separately elsewhere, viz. ἐκ τοῦ οἴνου τοῦ θυμοῦ τοῦ θεοῦ (xiv. 10), and ἐκ τοῦ οἴνου τῆς πορνείας αὐτῆς (xvii. 2). There is doubtless a reference to Jer. xxviii. (li.) 7 ποτήριον

αὐτῆς πεπότικεν πάντα τὰ ἔθνη. [9]καὶ ἄλλος ἄγ- 9
γελος τρίτος ἠκολούθησεν αὐτοῖς λέγων ἐν φωνῇ
μεγάλῃ Εἴ τις προσκυνεῖ τὸ θηρίον καὶ τὴν εἰκόνα
αὐτοῦ, καὶ λαμβάνει χάραγμα ἐπὶ τοῦ μετώπου
αὐτοῦ ἢ ἐπὶ τὴν χεῖρα αὐτοῦ, [10]καὶ αὐτὸς πίεται ἐκ 10

8 αυτης] ταυτης Q 2 7 29 al[15] | πεποτικεν] πεπτωκαν (vel -κεν) ℵ[c.a] (12) (130) me Prim 9 αλλος αγγελος τριτος ACPQ min[40] vg[am* fu tol vid] me syr arm Andr] τριτος αγγελος vg[cle dem] aeth Cypr Prim Ar αλλος αγγελος 1 14 92 αγγελος 12 | αυτοις] αυτω A Prim | το θηριον (τ. θυσιαστηριον A τ. ποτηριον 14)] τω θηριω C 95 | αυτου 1°] αυτων C | om και 3° C 14 | χαραγμα] pr το 28 35 36 37 79 95 130 + αυτου syr[gw] | τω μετωπω ℵ

χρυσοῦν Βαβυλὼν ἐν χειρὶ Κυρίου, μεθύσκον πᾶσαν τὴν γῆν· ἀπὸ τοῦ οἴνου αὐτῆς ἐπίοσαν ἔθνη; cf. also Hab. ii. 15, where the Chaldeans are in view: ὦ ὁ ποτίζων τὸν πλησίον αὐτοῦ ἀνατροπῇ θολερᾷ, and see *infra*, *c.* xvii. 4, note. The wine of Rome, as of Babylon, was the intoxicating influence of her vices and her wealth; but viewed from another point, it was the οἶνος τοῦ θυμοῦ, the wrath which overtakes sin; cf. Ps. lxxiv. (lxxv.) 9 ποτήριον ἐν χειρὶ Κυρίου, οἴνου ἀκράτου πλῆρες κεράσματος...καὶ πίονται πάντες οἱ ἁμαρτωλοὶ τῆς γῆς. Τῆς πορνείας αὐτῆς: the Seer ascribes to Rome a character which the Prophets of Israel had ascribed to more than one of the great pagan cities of antiquity; thus Nineveh (Nah. iii. 4) is a πόρνη καλὴ καὶ ἐπιχαρής...ἡ πωλοῦσα ἔθνη ἐν τῇ πορνείᾳ αὐτῆς, and Tyre (Isa. xxiii. 16 f.) a πόρνη ἐπιλελησμένη who, on her restoration to favour, ἔσται ἐμπόριον (וְזָנְתָה) πάσαις ταῖς βασιλείαις τῆς οἰκουμένης; even Zion had come to deserve the title (Isa. i. 21 πῶς ἐγένετο πόρνη πόλις πιστὴ Σειών;). While the charge of πορνεία might be amply justified by the moral condition of Rome under the Empire, it probably includes the utter venality of the capital, which was ready to sell both body and soul for a price; cf. Sallust, *Jug.* 35 "urbem venalem et mature perituram, si emptorem invenerit," and see Mayor's note on Juv. x. 77. As Delitzsch (*Isaiah*, i. p. 412 f.) truly says, "commercial activity" which, "thinking only of earthly advantage, does not recognise a God-appointed limit, and carries on a promiscuous traffic with all the world, is...a prostitution of the soul." On the πορνεία of Rome see xvii. 2, 4, xviii. 3, 9, notes. For ἥ...πεπότικεν Tyconius seems to have read ὅτι...πέπωκαν, as in xviii. 3, while the text of Primasius had πέπτωκαν for πέπωκαν (*a vino irae fornicationis suae ceciderunt universae civitates*).

9. καὶ ἄλλος ἄγγελος τρίτος ἠκολούθησεν κτλ.] The third of this succession of herald angels denounces the Caesar-worshippers; cf. xiii. 12 ff., notes. This is a counter proclamation to that which is put into the mouth of the Image of the Beast; if the supporters of the Caesar-worship threatened recusants with boycotting and even death (xiii. 15, 17), the angel seeks to deter them from yielding by the prospect of a worse doom.

On τὴν εἰκόνα αὐτοῦ see xiii. 15 note, and on χάραγμα xiii. 16, 17, notes.

10. καὶ αὐτὸς πίεται κτλ.] Not 'he too as well as Babylon' (Bousset), for Babylon is not represented as drinking of her own cup; but rather, 'he shall also drink,' where καὶ opens the apodosis (WM. p. 547, note 1), identifying the person who is to drink with him who has worshipped. The wrath of which he must drink is now defined;

τοῦ οἴνου τοῦ θυμοῦ τοῦ θεοῦ τοῦ κεκερασμένου
ἀκράτου ἐν τῷ ποτηρίῳ τῆς ὀργῆς αὐτοῦ, καὶ βασα-
νισθήσεται ἐν πυρὶ καὶ θείῳ ἐνώπιον ἀγγέλων ἁγίων
11 *καὶ ἐνώπιον τοῦ ἀρνίου.* [11]*καὶ ὁ καπνὸς τοῦ βασα-*
νισμοῦ αὐτῶν εἰς αἰῶνας αἰώνων ἀναβαίνει, καὶ οὐκ

10 *του θεου*] *του κυριου* syr^{gw} | *εν τω ποτηριω*] *εκ του ποτηριου* A 7 16 39 *εκ του θυμου* 130 | *της οργης*] *την οργην* A | *βασανισθησονται* A 8 14 36 92 | *αγγελων αγιων* ℵCP 38 92 95 vg$^{cle\ am\ fu\ tol\ lipss}$ syr] *των αγιων αγγελων* Q min^{pl} Cypr Prim Ar *των αγγελων* A 26 me aeth^{utr} (pr *αυτου*) *του θεου* arm | om *και εν. του αρνιου* 130 | *αρνιου*] *θρονου* syr 11 *αυτων*] *αυτου* 7 16 39 41 42 49 vg^{lipss} Ar | *εις αιωνας αιωνων* ℵ (c. *των αι.*) AQ 130 (c. *τους αι. των αι.*) al^{pl} syrr] *εις αιωνα αιωνος* (vel *αιωνων*) C(P) (1 7 14) 28 79 (92) (186) (Ar)

it is the wrath of God; the cup which holds it is the cup of His anger against sin. A Divine *ὀργή*, which is correlated with the Divine righteousness, is postulated throughout the N.T.; see esp. Rom. i. 18, iii. 5, xii. 19, Col. iii. 6, Apoc. vi. 17. Θυμὸς (or *ὀργὴ θυμοῦ*) *τοῦ θεοῦ*, the white heat of God's anger, is an O.T. phrase usually representing אַף יְהוָה (cf. Num. xii. 9, xxii. 22)—an anthropomorphic image, but one which covers a terrible reality; in the N.T. it occurs only in the second half of the Apocalypse, where it is frequent (xiv. 10, 19, xv. 1, 7, xvi. 1, 19, xix. 15). Τοῦ *κεκερασμένου ἀκράτου*: an *oxymoron* taken over perhaps from the LXX. of Ps. lxxv. 9 where *ἄκρατον κέρασμα* represents מֶסֶךְ, wine mixed with spices but not with water (see BDB., *s. v.*). Cf. also Jer. xxxii. 1 (xxv. 15) *τὸ ποτήριον τοῦ οἴνου τοῦ ἀκράτου τούτου* = כּוֹס הַיַּיִן הַחֵמָה, Pss. Sol. viii. 15 *διὰ τοῦτο ἐκέρασεν αὐτοῖς ὁ θεὸς πνεῦμα πλανήσεως· | ἐπότισεν αὐτοὺς ποτήριον οἴνου ἀκράτου εἰς μέθην.* Ἀκράτου emphasizes the strength of the intoxicant; or, as Andreas says, the meaning may be: *κοινωνήσει αὐτῷ τῆς τοῦ τιμωρητικοῦ ποτηρίου πόσεως, ἀκράτου μὲν καὶ ἀμιγοῦς θείων οἰκτιρμῶν, διὰ τὸ κρίσεως δίκαιον.*

καὶ βασανισθήσεται ἐν πυρὶ καὶ θείῳ κτλ.] For *βασανίζειν* see *c.* ix. 5, note, and for *πῦρ καὶ θεῖον*, *ib.* 17, note; compare also xix. 20, xx. 10, xxi. 8; the imagery looks back to Isa. xxx. 33, Ez. xxxviii. 22 and ultimately to Gen. xix. 24 (cf. 3 Macc. ii. 5). The punishment is aggravated by the presence of spectators. If Christians at the stake or in the amphitheatre suffered in the sight of a multitude of their fellowmen, those who deny their faith must suffer before a more august assembly, composed of the holy angels and the Lamb. There is a partial parallel in Lc. xii. 9 *ὁ δὲ ἀρνησάμενός με ἐνώπιον τῶν ἀνθρώπων ἀπαρνηθήσεται ἐνώπιον τῶν ἀγγέλων τοῦ θεοῦ*; but in the present passage not only angels are witnesses of the punishment; it is inflicted also in the presence of the Lamb. As in vi. 16, *τῆς ὀργῆς τοῦ ἀρνίου*, the name intensifies the horrors of the situation. The *βασανισμός* is aggravated by a consciousness of the pure spiritual beings which are around, but still more by the presence of the Lord Who died for the sins of men and has been denied and rejected by these sufferers.

11. *καὶ ὁ καπνὸς τοῦ βασανισμοῦ αὐτῶν εἰς αἰῶνας κτλ.*] The Seer is still thinking of the fate of Sodom and Gomorrah; cf. Gen. xix. 28 *ἰδοὺ ἀνέβαινεν φλὸξ τῆς γῆς ὡσεὶ ἀτμὶς καμίνου*; Isa. xxxiv. 9 f. *ἔσται ἡ γῆ αὐτῆς ὡς πίσσα καιομένη νυκτὸς καὶ ἡμέρας, καὶ οὐ μὴ σβεσθήσεται εἰς τὸν*

ἔχουσιν ἀνάπαυσιν ἡμέρας καὶ νυκτός, οἱ προσκυ-
νοῦντες τὸ θηρίον καὶ τὴν εἰκόνα αὐτοῦ, καὶ εἴ τις
λαμβάνει τὸ χάραγμα τοῦ ὀνόματος αὐτοῦ. [12]ὧδε 12
ἡ ὑπομονὴ τῶν ἁγίων ἐστίν, οἱ τηροῦντες τὰς ἐντολὰς
τοῦ θεοῦ καὶ τὴν πίστιν Ἰησοῦ. [13]καὶ ἤκουσα φωνῆς 13

11 το θηριον και την εικονα] τω θηριω κ. τη εικονι 36 95 τη εικονη 7 | το χαραγμα] om το A 12 οι τηρουντες] των τηρουντων ℵ 36 38 95 pr ωδε 1 7 49 79 91 186 | om του θεου 1 | Ιησου] pr του 37 49 91 96 186 + χριστου 28 71 13 φωνης] φωνην μεγαλην 130

αἰῶνα χρόνον, καὶ ἀναβήσεται ὁ καπνὸς αὐτῆς ἄνω. Contrast Apoc. ix. 5 βασανισθήσονται μῆνας πέντε. The partial punishments inflicted under the Trumpets have now given place to a judgement which is final and a sentence without time-limits. The denial of Christ by a Christian was a sin for which the Church knew no remedy, an αἰώνιον ἁμάρτημα which brought a corresponding recompense. Οὐκ ἔχουσιν ἀνάπαυσιν ἡμέρας καὶ νυκτός, sc. ἀπὸ τοῦ βασανισμοῦ; contrast iv. 8 ἀνάπαυσιν οὐκ ἔχουσιν ἡμέρας καὶ νυκτὸς λέγοντες Ἅγιος κτλ. Those who desert Christ for Caesar will be the victims of a remorse that never dies or sleeps. The passage is quoted by Cyprian (*ep.* 58. 7) in A.D. 252–3 to deter the African Churches from sacrificing: "grassatur et saevit inimicus, sed statim sequitur Dominus passiones nostras et vulnera vindicaturus...ille metuendus est cuius iram nemo poterit evadere, ipso praemonente et dicente: *ne timueritis eos qui occidunt corpus...qui amat animam suam perdet illam*...et Apocalypsis instruit et praemonet dicens: *si quis adorat bestiam* etc."

12. ὧδε ἡ ὑπομονὴ τῶν ἁγίων ἐστίν] A comment by the Seer, in a characteristic form; cf. xiii. 10 ὧδέ ἐστιν ἡ ὑπομονὴ καὶ ἡ πίστις τῶν ἁγίων, *ib.* 18 ὧδε ἡ σοφία ἐστίν, xvii. 9 ὧδε ὁ νοῦς ὁ ἔχων σοφίαν. Here, in this struggle with the Empire, lay the Church's opportunity of working out her salvation through patient endurance in well-doing. For ὑπομονή see i. 9, ii. 2 f., 19, iii. 10; and cf. Rom. v. 3 ἡ θλίψις ὑπομονὴν κατεργάζεται, ἡ δὲ ὑπομονὴ δοκιμήν, ἡ δὲ δοκιμὴ ἐλπίδα; Jac. i. 3 τὸ δοκίμιον ὑμῶν τῆς πίστεως κατεργάζεται ὑπομονήν. The Caesar-cult supplied the Saints with a test of loyalty which strengthened and matured those who were worthy of the name. Such were those who kept the commandments of God and the faith of Jesus—οἱ τηροῦντες defines τῶν ἁγίων, though the construction is broken, as if τίνες εἰσὶν οἱ ἅγιοι; had intervened—a phrase which combines the chief note of O.T. sainthood with the chief factor in the Christian life; cf. xii. 17, note. Τὴν πίστιν Ἰησοῦ, the faith which has Jesus for its Object; cf. Mc. xi. 22 πίστιν θεοῦ (note), Jac. ii. 1 τὴν πίστιν τοῦ κυρίου ἡμῶν Ἰ. Χ., Apoc. ii. 13 τὴν πίστιν μου.

13. καὶ ἤκουσα φωνῆς ἐκ τοῦ οὐρανοῦ λεγούσης Γράψον κτλ.] The Seer's meditation is broken by a Voice from heaven. His own insight had enabled him to see in the persecution which impended a call to ὑπομονή. But something further was needed for the comfort and guidance of the Asian Christians in the immediate future; and the Voice now imparts it. It is a message for the Churches, to be registered and communicated to them; for γράψον as a formula introducing such messages see i. 11, 19, ii. 1, 8 etc., iii. 1, 7 etc., xix. 9, xxi. 5, and contrast x. 4 μὴ γράψῃς.

ἐκ τοῦ οὐρανοῦ λεγούσης Γράψον Μακάριοι οἱ νεκροὶ οἱ ἐν Κυρίῳ ἀποθνήσκοντες ἀπ' ἄρτι. ναί, λέγει τὸ πνεῦμα, ἵνα ἀναπαήσονται ἐκ τῶν κόπων αὐτῶν· τὰ γὰρ ἔργα αὐτῶν ἀκολουθεῖ μετ' αὐτῶν.

13 λεγουσης]+μοι 1 28 36 38 49 79 91 96 186 vg$^{\text{cle dem tol}}$ arm Prim | εν κυριω ℵAQ min$^{\text{omn vid}}$ syr^{gw}] εν χριστω CP 130 *in deo* syr | αποθνησκοντες] *resurgentes* me | απ αρτι cum praeced coniung P 91 96 97 syrr Ar cum sequent Q 130$^{\text{al fere 30}}$ vg$^{\text{cle lips 5}}$ Prim non interpung ℵAC 186 | αναπαησονται ℵAC] αναπαυσονται Q 1 al$^{\text{plq 10}}$ αναπαυσωνται P min^{pl} αναπαυωνται 186 | εκ των κοπων] απο των κ. 130 απο των εργων 14 92 | om τα γαρ εργα...μετ αυτων syr^{gw} | γαρ ℵACP 18 26 38 95 vg syr Aug Prim] δε Q min^{pl} Andr Ar om me

Μακάριοι οἱ νεκροὶ οἱ ἐν Κυρίῳ ἀποθνήσκοντες is a new beatitude which needed a Voice from heaven to proclaim it. St Paul, speaking by revelation (ἐν λόγῳ Κυρίου), had taught that the dead in Christ (1 Cor. xv. 18 οἱ κοιμηθέντες ἐν Χριστῷ, 1 Th. iv. 14 τοὺς κοιμηθέντας διὰ τοῦ Ἰησοῦ, *ib.* 16 οἱ νεκροὶ ἐν Χριστῷ) were not to be the subjects of a hopeless grief, as if they were shut out from the glories of the Parousia (1 Th. iv. 15 ff.). St John (Apoc. vi. 9) had seen the souls of the martyrs under the Altar, crying, 'How long?' and had heard them bidden to rest awhile (ἵνα ἀναπαύσονται ἔτι χρόνον μικρόν). The Voice from heaven carries these revelations a stage further. Those who should die in the Lord henceforth, as the martyrs did, were to be felicitated for the rest on which they entered. Ἀπ' ἄρτι, 'from this time forth' (Jo. xiii. 19, xiv. 7), must be connected, as its position shews, not with μακάριοι but with οἱ ἀποθνήσκοντες; nothing is said with regard to the past, the purpose of the revelation being to bring comfort to those who in the coming persecutions would need a strong consolation. It is a message in the first instance for a particular age, and referred to those who were to be called to suffer for their faith. Yet in view of the quite general terms in which it is couched (οἱ ἀποθνήσκοντες ἐν Κυρίῳ), the later Church has felt herself at liberty to use it for the comfort of her mourners; *audivi vocem de caelo* found a place in the Sarum offices for the dead, and its English equivalent immediately follows the committal to the grave in our own Burial Service. Cf. Primasius: "universis pollicens felicitatem." But the limitation ἐν Κυρίῳ remains; as Andreas observes: ἡ ἐκ τοῦ οὐρανοῦ φωνὴ οὐ πάντας μακαρίζει τοὺς νεκρούς, ἀλλὰ τοὺς ἐν Κυρίῳ ἀποθνήσκοντας. Thus this Divine μακαρισμός differs widely from that which is sometimes indiscriminately pronounced on the dead by pagan writers (see exx. in Wetstein); a general μακάριοι οἱ νεκροί finds no justification here.

ναί, λέγει τὸ πνεῦμα, ἵνα ἀναπαήσονται κτλ.] The Spirit in the mind of the Seer responds to the Voice from above him 'Yea (cf. i. 7, xvi. 7, xxii. 20), they are blessed, to rest (as they shall) from their labours.' Ἵνα here passes into the meaning of ὅτι, 'in that' rather than 'in order that,' nearly as in Jo. viii. 56 ἠγαλλιάσατο ἵνα ἴδῃ, "he rejoiced to see." For the future after ἵνα cf. *cc.* vi. 4, ix. 5; and for the form ἀναπαήσονται see Blass, *Gr.* p. 44, and add to his exx. *Oxyrh. Papyri* iv. p. 4 [βασιλεύσας ἀναπα]ήσεται. Ἀναπαύεσθαι is more usually followed by ἀπό (2 Regn. vii. 11, Esth. ix. 16), but ἐκ occurs, e.g. Plat. *Crit.* 106 A ὡς ἐκ μακρᾶς ἀναπεπαυμένος ὁδοῦ. In the words that follow, κόπων, ἔργα are (ii. 2, note) antithetical; the 'labours

[14]Καὶ εἶδον, καὶ ἰδοὺ νεφέλη λευκή, καὶ ἐπὶ τὴν 14
νεφέλην καθήμενον ὅμοιον υἱὸν ἀνθρώπου, ἔχων ἐπὶ
τῆς κεφαλῆς αὐτοῦ στέφανον χρυσοῦν καὶ ἐν τῇ χειρὶ
αὐτοῦ δρέπανον ὀξύ. [15]καὶ ἄλλος ἄγγελος ἐξῆλθεν 15

14 om *και ειδον* ℵ 130 syr^{gw} | *ειδον* P min^{pl}] *ιδον* ACQ 7 14 92 | *καθημενος ομοιος* 1 7 49 91 al *καθημενος* 130 | *υιον* ℵAQ 2 8 9 11 13 14 27 (28) 30 31 32 al^{8}] *υιω* C 6 7 38 186 al$^{sat\ mu}$ Andr Ar *υιου* P 26 *υιος* 1 | *εχων*] *εχοντα* ℵ* 13 26 27 28 29 42** 79 95 *εχοντι* 38 | *της κεφαλης*] *την κεφαλην* A 8 28 29 30 38 40 51 79 93 94 98 130 | *επι την χειρα* syr^{gw}

of the saintly life end in the grave, but not its 'works'; its processes, methods, habits, results remain, and follow the saint into his new life; cf. *Pirke Aboth* vi. 9 (ed. Taylor[2], p. 103) "in the hour of a man's decease not silver nor gold nor precious stones and pearls accompany the man, but Thorah and good works alone." The contrast is latent in *γάρ*: 'they shall rest from their labours—I say not from their works, for their works go with them.' There is a further contrast between the sentence as a whole and the doom pronounced on the disloyal in *v.* 11 (*ἀνάπαυσιν οὐκ ἔχουσιν*); cf. Primasius: "e contrario illos impios dixit die ac nocte requiem non habere." Ἀκολουθεῖν μετά, cf. vi. 8; Blass, *Gr.* p. 113 f.

14—20. THE VISION OF THE HARVEST AND THE VINTAGE OF THE EARTH.

14. *καὶ εἶδον, καὶ ἰδοὺ νεφέλη λευκή κτλ.*] The revelations of the last section (*vv.* 8—13) now culminate in a vision of the Parousia, represented as a time of general ingathering of the fruits of life. First, the Seer sees 'One like a Son of Man' (for *ὅμοιον υἱόν* see i. 13, note), the same Person who had appeared in the first chapter of the Book, seated on a cloud (Dan. vii. 13 LXX. *ἰδοὺ ἐπὶ τῶν νεφελῶν τοῦ οὐρανοῦ ὡς υἱὸς ἀνθρώπου ἤρχετο*, cf. Mt. xxiv. 30, xxvi. 64, Acts i. 9, 11), the white cloud (cf. Mt. xvii. 5 *νεφέλη φωτινή*) which was so familiar an object to dwellers by the Mediterranean and Aegean; not the dark storm-cloud which to the Hebrew mind suggested the inscrutable mystery of unrevealed Deity (Ps. xcvi. (=xcvii.) 2 *νεφέλη καὶ γνόφος κύκλῳ αὐτοῦ*) but the symbol of light and blessing. Like the Elders in *c.* iv. 4 (cf. Tert. *de coron.* 15) the Figure on the Cloud is crowned with a victor's wreath wrought in gold, a *στέφανος χρυσοῦς*, contrasting sharply with the *στ. ἀκάνθινος* of the Passion (Mc. xv. 17), but not an imperial *διάδημα*; the crowned Christ is here the Conqueror rather than the King. He comes however not to conquer—this He has already done (iii. 21)—but to reap, and His hand carries not a sword but a sickle, sharp and ready for its work. It is instructive to compare this description with the vision of *c.* i. 13 ff. on the one hand, and with that of xix. 11 ff. on the other; in each case the ornaments and instruments are appropriate to the character sustained. In *c.* i. the royal Priesthood of Christ is the predominating thought; in *c.* xix. He appears as the true *Imperator*; here the writer's aim is to bring together the thought of Christ's victory over sin and death with the hope of His return to raise and judge mankind.

15. *καὶ ἄλλος ἄγγ. ἐξῆλθεν ἐκ τοῦ ναοῦ κράζων κτλ.*] Ἄλλος here looks back to *v.* 9, not to the human form on the cloud just described. Another angel—the fourth in this context—comes forth from the Sanctuary (cf. xi. 19, xiv. 17, xv. 5 ff., xvi. 1, 17), i.e. from the Presence of God, carrying to the Reaper the command of the Lord of

ἐκ τοῦ ναοῦ, κράζων ἐν φωνῇ μεγάλῃ τῷ καθημένῳ
ἐπὶ τῆς νεφέλης Πέμψον τὸ δρέπανόν σου καὶ θέ-
ρισον, ὅτι ἦλθεν ἡ ὥρα θερίσαι, ὅτι ἐξηράνθη ὁ
16 θερισμὸς τῆς γῆς. [16]καὶ ἔβαλεν ὁ καθήμενος ἐπὶ τῆς
νεφέλης τὸ δρέπανον αὐτοῦ ἐπὶ τὴν γῆν, καὶ ἐθερίσθη
17 ἡ γῆ. [17]καὶ ἄλλος ἄγγελος ἐξῆλθεν ἐκ τοῦ ναοῦ τοῦ

15 ναου] + αυτου ℵ aeth ουρανου 1 7 12 16 28 38 49 79 186 al arm | φωνη μεγαλη] φ. τη μεγαλη 1 me om Prim | ηλθεν] + σοι 7* al^{vid} + σου 1 12 17 36 186 | θερισαι] pr του 29 49 91 93 96 130 al του θερισμου ℵ 38 | om οτι εξηρανθη ο θερ. της γης syr^{gw} 16 της νεφελης ℵA 16* 36 38 47 97] την νεφελην CP min^{pl} Ar τη νεφελη Q 7 8 13 14 92 93 94 17 εξηλθεν] ηλθεν Q

the Harvest (Mt. ix. 38) to begin His work. Even the Son does not fix or even know the time, which it belongs to the Father to determine (Mc. xiii. 32, note; Acts i. 7). Ἐπὶ τῆς νεφέλης: cf. ἐπὶ τὴν νεφέλην in *v.* 14 and perhaps *v.* 16; there is no perceptible change of meaning.

Πέμψον τὸ δρέπανόν σου κτλ. echoes more than one passage in the Prophets, e.g. Joel iii. (iv.) 13 ἐξαποστείλατε δρέπανα (שִׁלְחוּ מַגָּל), ὅτι παρέστηκεν τρυγητός (קָצִיר), Jer. xxviii. (li.) 33 ἔτι μικρὸν καὶ ἥξει ὁ ἀμητὸς αὐτῆς (sc. Βαβυλῶνος). There are also parallels in our Lord's teaching, e.g. Mc. iv. 29 ὅταν δὲ παραδοῖ ὁ καρπός, εὐθὺς ἀποστέλλει τὸ δρέπανον, ὅτι παρέστηκεν ὁ θερισμός (where see notes); Mt. xiii. 39 ὁ δὲ θερισμὸς συντέλεια αἰῶνός ἐστιν. The harvest, however, is not here, as in Mt. *l. c.*, the whole produce of the world, the results, good and evil, of human history, but rather the wheat-harvest considered apart from the tares; the evil appear below (*v.* 18 ff.) under another metaphor. Ὅτι ἦλθεν ἡ ὥρα: the time, though in the Owner's Hands (Acts i. 7), does not depend on any arbitrary decree, but on the maturity of the crops, of which He alone can fully judge. Ἐξηράνθη, *aruit, arida est*, properly of the drying up of the juices of the wheat plant; in Joel i. 17 ἐξηράνθη σῖτος refers to premature desiccation, but here that which indicates perfect ripeness is probably intended. The R.V. 'overripe' is perhaps scarcely justified; the idea conveyed is rather that the precise moment has come for reaping, and there must be no further delay. On the aorists ἦλθεν, ἐξηράνθη see x. 7, xv. 1, notes.

16. καὶ ἔβαλεν ὁ καθήμενος κτλ.] Vg. rightly: *et misit...falcem suam in terram.* No violence is suggested by ἔβαλεν; cf. Mt. x. 34 οὐκ ἦλθον βαλεῖν εἰρήνην [ἐπὶ τὴν γῆν]. The Person on the cloud, at the Angel's call, sets His sickle to work, by casting it on the earth, and in due time the earth is reaped. There is no need to fill in the imagery; enough is said to emphasize the fact that the Son of Man is the Divinely commissioned Reaper (Jo. v. 27). He may use the ministry of men (Mt. ix. 37 f.) or of angels (Mt. xiii. 39, 41), but it belongs to Him to put in the sickle. It does not appear how the ingathering is to be effected, or how long the process will last. In the vision there is no interval between cause and effect (ἔβαλεν...ἐθερίσθη), but the completion of the work may occupy a generation or an age.

17. καὶ ἄλλος ἄγγελος ἐξῆλθεν ἐκ τοῦ ναοῦ κτλ.] Another—a fifth—angel issues from the Sanctuary, who like the Reaper on the cloud (καὶ αὐτός) is armed with a sharp sickle. A

ἐν τῷ οὐρανῷ, ἔχων καὶ αὐτὸς δρέπανον ὀξύ. [18]καὶ 18
ἄλλος ἄγγελος ἐξῆλθεν ἐκ τοῦ θυσιαστηρίου, [ὁ]
ἔχων ἐξουσίαν ἐπὶ τοῦ πυρός, καὶ ἐφώνησεν φωνῇ

17 *εν τω ουρανω*] om *τω* C   18 om *εξηλθεν* A vg$^{am\ fu}$ Prim | om *εκ του θυσιαστηριου* Prim | *ο εχων* AC vg (*qui habet*) syrr] om *ο* ℵPQ min$^{omn\ vid}$ | *εφωνησεν*]+*εν* 6 7 8 14 29 al^{mu} Ar | *φωνη*] *κραυγη* CP min^{pl} me Andr Ar

second ingathering will follow the first, as the vintage followed wheat-harvest (cf. Deut. xvi. 9 f., 13). In this second process the chief part is assigned to an angel, who gathers in the fruit of the Vine of the Earth, as the Son of Man had gathered in its wheat.

Both the wheat-harvest and the vintage are mentioned in Joel iv. 13 (בְּשַׁל קָצִיר...מָלְאָה גַּת), and the Seer follows the O.T. prophet, but with a difference; he treats the two harvests as distinct, placing them in their natural order, and using them as symbols of two separate spiritual ingatherings. In the Prophets the harvest, whether wheat-harvest or vintage, represents the overthrow of the enemies of Israel, who are ripe for their fall; in the Apocalypse, which like the Gospels identifies the wheat with the true 'children of the kingdom' (cf. Mt. xiii. 30, 38 τὸν δὲ σῖτον συνάγετε εἰς τὴν ἀποθήκην μου... τὸ δὲ καλὸν σπέρμα οὗτοί εἰσιν οἱ υἱοὶ τῆς βασιλείας, cf. Mc. iv. 29), the vintage, from its association with the 'wine of wrath' (xiv. 8, 10, notes), represents the evil, whether within the kingdom (Mt. *l.c.*) or outside it (Mt. xxv. 31 f.). Thus, by a new treatment of the old metaphor of a Divine harvesting of men, the Apocalyptist gives full expression to the Lord's teaching as to the great separation between man and man which is reserved for the Parousia. There is delicate beauty in the assignment of the ingathering of the Vintage to an angel, while the Son of Man Himself reaps the Wheat-harvest. The work of death is fitly left in the hands of a minister of justice; the Saviour of men appears εἰς σωτηρίαν (Heb. ix. 28). Cf. Arethas: οὔτε ὁ κύριος αὐτὸς ἀξιοῖ τὴν συλλογὴν ποιήσασθαι ὡς περὶ τῶν πρώτων, οὔτε τὸ μὲν εἰς τὰς ἀποθήκας τὸ δὲ εἰς τὸ ἀτελεύτητον παραπέμπει πῦρ, ἀλλά τις τῶν ἀγγέλων.

18. καὶ ἄλλος ἄγγελος ἐξῆλθεν ἐκ τοῦ θυσιαστηρίου κτλ.] Another angel—the sixth—brings to the Angel of vengeance a message similar to that which the angel in *v.* 15 had brought to the Son of Man—the Divine authority to begin the Vintage of the earth. The two messages closely correspond, *mutatis mutandis*; τὸ δρέπανον τὸ ὀξύ holds its place, the sickle being used in vine-culture and the vintage as well as in harvesting the grain (cf. Hesiod, *scut.* 292 οἱ δ' ἐτρύγων οἴνας, δρεπάνας ἐν χερσὶν ἔχοντες, Plat. *resp.* 333 D ὅταν δὴ δρέπανον δέῃ φυλάττειν, ἡ δικαιοσύνη χρήσιμος καὶ κοινῇ καὶ ἰδίᾳ· ὅταν δὲ χρῆσθαι, ἡ ἀμπελουργική); with τρύγησον τοὺς βότρυας cf. Lc. vi. 44 σταφυλὴν τρυγῶσιν, and the LXX. phrases τρυγᾶν ἀμπελῶνα (Deut. xxiv. 21), τρυγᾶν τρυγητόν (1 Regn. viii. 12); βότρυς is ἅπ. λεγ. in N.T., but fairly common in the LXX., with or without σταφυλῆς following. Ὅτι ἤκμασαν αἱ σταφυλαὶ αὐτῆς answers to ὅτι ἐξηράνθη ὁ θερισμός in *v.* 15. Ἀκμάζειν is used in 4 Macc. ii. 3, the only other instance in Biblical Greek of the use of the verb in the ordinary sense of adolescence, but the lexicons quote passages from Thucydides (ii. 19) and Xenophon (*Hell.* i. 2. 4) where it describes the ripening of corn. Σταφυλή

μεγάλῃ τῷ ἔχοντι τὸ δρέπανον τὸ ὀξὺ λέγων
Πέμψον σου τὸ δρέπανον τὸ ὀξὺ καὶ τρύγησον τοὺς
βότρυας τῆς ἀμπέλου τῆς γῆς, ὅτι ἤκμασαν αἱ στα-
19 φυλαὶ αὐτῆς. [19]καὶ ἔβαλεν ὁ ἄγγελος τὸ δρέπανον
αὐτοῦ εἰς τὴν γῆν, καὶ ἐτρύγησεν τὴν ἄμπελον τῆς
γῆς καὶ ἔβαλεν εἰς τὴν ληνὸν τοῦ θυμοῦ τοῦ θεοῦ τὸν

18 om λεγων 130 | βοτρυας] βοτρυς 28 79 βοτανας 94 | om της αμπελου 1 | ηκμασεν η σταφυλη Q min[30] Ar | αυτης] της γης Q 7 al[plq 30] syr Ar   19 εβαλεν 1°] εξεβαλεν 2 7 8 29 87 al[20] Ar | εις την γην] επι της γης ℵ 38 97 syr[gw] | την ληνον] τον ληνον 1 91 94 97 98 al τ. αλωναν C | τον μεγαν] την μεγαλην ℵ 7 28 35 79 95 130 syr[gw] om 12 34 Vict

is properly the ripe grape-cluster as opposed to ὄμφαξ, cf. Gen. xl. 10 *πέπειροι οἱ βότρυες σταφυλῆς*, Job xv. 33 *τρυγηθείη δὲ ὡς ὄμφαξ πρὸ ὥρας*; as contrasted with *βότρυς*, it describes the grapes rather than the cluster on which they grow.

The Angel-reaper of the Vintage proceeds from the Altar, where he is in charge of the fire; cf. xvi. 6, note. Earlier passages in the Book refer to the Altar of Burnt Offering (vi. 9, xi. 1), and the Altar of Incense (viii. 3, 5, ix. 13); here and in xvi. 7 there is nothing to shew which of the two is intended. If the former, we are reminded of the blood of the martyrs which cries for vengeance; if the latter, of the prayers of the saints by which the end is hastened. Ὁ ἔχων ἐξουσίαν ἐπὶ τοῦ πυρός is a suggestive description of the minister of wrath; cf. Arethas: *τοῦτον ἐπὶ τῆς κολάσεως νόει τῶν ἀσεβῶν τετάχθαι.*

19. *καὶ ἔβαλεν ὁ ἄγγελος τὸ δρέπανον αὐτοῦ κτλ.*] The ingatherer of the Vintage does as the Reaper of the Wheat-harvest had done; *εἰς τὴν γῆν* slightly varies the picture, but is practically = *ἐπὶ τ. γ.* in *v.* 16; while *ἐθερίσθη ἡ γῆ* is balanced by *ἐτρύγησεν τὴν ἄμπελον τῆς γῆς.* But the next clause, *καὶ ἔβαλεν εἰς τὴν ληνόν κτλ.*, enters upon a detail which has nothing to correspond with it in the former scene, and its object is to leave no doubt as to the symbolical meaning of the Vintage. It is the Vintage of the Vine of earth as contrasted with the 'Vine brought out of Egypt' (Arethas) and the "True Vine," whose branches bring forth fruit unto God; it is that part of the earth's produce, those results of human history and life, which must be trodden by the Feet of God; cf. Isa. lxiii. 2 *διὰ τί σου ἐρυθρὰ τὰ ἱμάτια, καὶ τὰ ἐνδύματά σου ὡς ἀπὸ πατητοῦ ληνοῦ;... κατεπάτησα αὐτοὺς ἐν θυμῷ μου.* Cf. Victorinus, "calcatio torcularis retributio est peccatoris"; Arethas: *ἡ τρύγησις τῶν σταφυλῶν τοὺς λίαν ἀνόμους αἰνίττεται.* On *ληνός* see Mc. xii. 1, note, and on *θυμός*, in relation to God, *v.* 8 *supra*, note. Τὸν μέγαν is explained by some of the Latin commentators as an acc. after *ἔβαλεν*: 'he cast the great into the wine press'; so Primasius: "*misit in torculari irae Dei magnum.* Superbum etiam *magnum* vocat...nam torcular, sicut Graeca exemplaria continent, feminini generis posuit"; and Beatus: "*misit in torcular irae Dei illum magnum*...id est unumquemque superbum." But *τὴν ληνὸν...τὸν μέγαν* is doubtless a solecism, which can only be excused on the ground of rapid writing, but finds a parallel in xxi. 14 *τὸ τεῖχος...ἔχων.* Ὁ ληνός, though used in class. Gk., receives no support from the best MSS. of the LXX. and N.T.; in Gen. xxx. 38,

μέγαν. ²⁰καὶ ἐπατήθη ἡ ληνὸς ἔξωθεν τῆς πόλεως, 20
καὶ ἐξῆλθεν αἷμα ἐκ τῆς ληνοῦ ἄχρι τῶν χαλινῶν
τῶν ἵππων, ἀπὸ σταδίων χιλίων ἑξακοσίων.

20 επατηθη] ετιθη 1 | η ληνος] ο λ. 16 36 38 91 97 98 | εξωθεν] εξω ℵ 1 28 38 79 al Ar^comm | της ληνου] του λ. 42 98 | χιλιων εξακοσιων (αχ′ Q 6 8 14 28 38 al)] χ. διακοσιων ℵ* 26 syr^gw δισχιλιων εξακοσιων 130 χ. εξακοσιων εξ (αχϛ′ 79) Andr^comm *decem et sex* aeth

adduced by Blass, the true reading is ἐν ταῖς ληνοῖς.

20. καὶ ἐπατήθη ἡ ληνὸς ἔξωθεν τῆς πόλεως] Apparently the scene is laid in sight of the city, though not within its walls. The city is doubtless the 'Holy City' of xi. 2, so long trodden down by the Gentiles, i.e. Jerusalem, but Jerusalem idealized as in *c.* xxi. At Jerusalem in the time of Zechariah (xiv. 10) the King's ὑπολήνια seems to have been on the slope of the Mount of Olives, the predicted battlefield on which the nations gathered against Jerusalem were to receive their final defeat (Joel iii. 12 ff., Zech. xiv. 2 ff., 12 ff.). Possibly there is an allusion here to these facts; but in any case the place of execution would naturally lie "outside the gate" (Heb. xiii. 12).

καὶ ἐξῆλθεν αἷμα ἐκ τῆς ληνοῦ κτλ.] The red blood of the 'Vine of the Earth' (cf. Gen. xlix. 11, Deut. xxxii. 14), bursting from the trodden σταφυλαί, overflowed and spread to a distance of 1600 stades, rising so high that riders or men in chariots (cf. xix. 11—15) passing through it would find it up to their horses' bridles; cf. Enoch c. 1, 3 (ed. Charles, p. 286 f.): "in those days the fathers together with their sons will be smitten in one place...until it streams with their blood like a river...and the horses will walk up to the breast in the blood of sinners, and the chariots will be submerged to its height." The conception rests ultimately on Isa. lxiii. 3, 6, but the metaphor is worked out with the exuberance of apocalyptic symbolism. Much difficulty has been found in explaining the distance named as the limit to which the overflow spreads. It has been supposed to answer to the length of Palestine, which is given by Jerome (cf. *ep.* 129, *ad Dard.*) as 160 Roman miles = 1280 stades (cf. the reading of ℵ Syr. ^gw.), and by Antoninus in the *itinerarium* as 1664 stades, measuring from Tyre to *El-Arish*. In this case ἀπὸ σταδίων χιλίων ἑξακοσίων is practically equivalent to the O.T. phrase ἀπὸ Δὰν καὶ ἕως Βηρσάβεε. But it is more in accordance with Apocalyptic arithmetic to regard 1600 ($=4 \times 400$) as symbolical of completeness; except within the walls of the City, the deluge of blood was everywhere; or as Victorinus explains, followed by Primasius and the later Latin commentators, it spread "per omnes mundi quattuor partes; quaternitas enim est conquaternata; quater enim quadragies mille sexcenti sunt." The point to be illustrated is the finality of the blow dealt to the enemies of the Israel of God; cf. Lactantius *instit.* vii. 19: "virtus angelorum tradet in manus iustorum multitudinem illam quae montem circumsederit...et fluet sanguis more torrentis."

According to Bede Tyconius wished to interpret the whole passage (*vv.* 14—20) as a prophecy of the benignant work of the Church after the conversion of the Empire: "messorem et vindemiatorem ecclesiam interpretatur post persecutionum flammas clarescentem et potestatem ligandi

XV. 1 [1] Καὶ εἶδον ἄλλο σημεῖον ἐν τῷ οὐρανῷ μέγα καὶ
θαυμαστόν, ἀγγέλους ἑπτὰ ἔχοντας πληγὰς ἑπτά,
τὰς ἐσχάτας, ὅτι ἐν αὐταῖς ἐτελέσθη ὁ θυμὸς τοῦ
2 θεοῦ. [2] καὶ εἶδον ὡς θάλασσαν ὑαλίνην μεμιγμένην

XV 1 ειδον P min^pl] ιδον ℵACQ 7 14 92 130 | om επτα 1° syr^gw 2 ειδον P min^pl] ιδον sicut in *v.* 1 | υαλινην 1°] υελινην 13 (29) 31 35 38 49 91 93 96 (97) 98 130

solvendique tenentem." But such a view is inconsistent with the general purpose of this chapter, which leads the reader on from the existing condition of the Church to her final triumph at the end of the present order.

XV. 1—8. Preparation for the Last Seven Plagues.

1. καὶ εἶδον ἄλλο σημεῖον ἐν τῷ οὐρανῷ κτλ.] Ἄλλο σημεῖον looks back to xii. 1, 3. This view of the appearances as 'signs' belongs exclusively to the second half of the Apocalypse, and serves to connect the present vision with the series which began with the Sign of the Sun-clad Woman. The Seven Bowls are usually classed with the Seven Seals (*c.* vi.) and the Seven Trumpets (*cc.* viii–xi.), and with the latter especially they have an obvious affinity; but their relation to the great section of the book which begins at xii. 1 is even closer; they belong to the drama of the long conflict between the Church and the World. Μέγα καὶ θαυμαστόν: cf. *v.* 3 μεγάλα καὶ θαυμαστὰ τὰ ἔργα σου, Κύριε; the phrase occurs in the later Greek writers, e.g. Dionysius of Halicarnassus and Diodorus Siculus (Wetstein *ad l.*).

Ἀγγέλους ἑπτὰ (cf. viii. 2) ἔχοντας πληγὰς ἑπτά, τὰς ἐσχάτας. Three πληγαί are named in ix. 18, and in xi. 6 the Witnesses are empowered to strike the earth ἐν πάσῃ πληγῇ; but the plagues now about to begin are distinguished from all that came before them as 'the last' (cf. xxi. 9), the final cycle of such visitations: the last, because, as the Seer hastens to explain, they complete the physical manifestations of the Divine Wrath. Ὅτι κτλ. explains and justifies the emphatic τὰς ἐσχάτας. But the explanation is not altogether easy to understand; the aor. can cause no difficulty in view of x. 7 ἐτελέσθη τὸ μυστήριον τοῦ θεοῦ (where see note), but is it possible to conceive of the wrath of God as burning itself out in any manifestations such as these? Must it not endure as long as evil endures? Ἐτελέσθη, then, can only be taken in a limited sense, as meaning that there will be no more similar displays of God's righteous displeasure against human sin; there may be reserves of wrath, but its cosmic effects will cease. With πληγὰς ἑπτά the commentators compare Lev. xxvi. 21, 24 ἐὰν μετὰ ταῦτα πορεύησθε πλάγιοι...προσθήσω ὑμῖν πληγὰς ἑπτὰ κατὰ τὰς ἁμαρτίας ὑμῶν...καὶ πατάξω ὑμᾶς κἀγὼ ἑπτάκις ἀντὶ τῶν ἁμαρτιῶν ὑμῶν. In the case of the Last Plagues the septenary number is peculiarly appropriate; cf. Victorinus: "septem plagis, id est, perfecte"; Primasius: "angelorum numero vel plagarum universitatem consummationis arbitror praesignari." It denotes at once the finality and the completeness of the visitation.

2. καὶ εἶδον ὡς θάλασσαν ὑαλίνην μεμιγμένην πυρί] A parenthesis follows (*vv.* 2—4), in which the Seer, after briefly introducing the Seven Angels, catches a view of the Martyrs in their bliss on which his eye rests for a moment before he proceeds with the terrors of the Last Plagues.

πυρί, καὶ τοὺς νικῶντας ἐκ τοῦ θηρίου καὶ ἐκ τῆς εἰκόνος αὐτοῦ καὶ ἐκ τοῦ ἀριθμοῦ τοῦ ὀνόματος αὐτοῦ

2 νικουντας C | εκ της εικονος και εκ του θηριου Q 2 4 6 8 13 14 26 27 29 31 33 39 40 92 95 al[25] | om εκ 2° ℵ 7 33 *h* Prim | και εκ του αριθμου] pr εκ του χαραγματος αυτου 1 17 35 36 39 79 80 161 186 al

In the Vision of Heaven, the distance between the spectator and the Throne is filled by a Sea of Glass (iv. 6 ὡς θάλασσα ὑαλίνη ὁμοία κρυστάλλῳ; see note *ad l.*), and this image is now recalled, though the writer, after his manner (xiii. 11, xiv. 1, notes) does not use the article to emphasize the identity of the Sea in this place with the Sea in *c.* iv. As he now sees it, the crystal light of the Sea of Glass is reddened as by fire; with μεμιγμένην πυρί, cf. Ex. ix. 24 τὸ πῦρ φλογίζον (מִתְלַקַּחַת) ἐν τῇ χαλάζῃ, and *c.* viii. 7 χάλαζα καὶ πῦρ μεμιγμένα ἐν αἵματι. The red glow on the Sea spoke of the fire through which the Martyrs passed, and yet more of the wrath about to fall on the world which had condemned them; cf. Mt. iii. 12 τὸ δὲ ἄχυρον κατακαύσει πυρὶ ἀσβέστῳ, and the *agraphon* ὁ ἐγγύς μου ἐγγὺς τοῦ πυρός; and see Heb. xii. 29 καὶ γὰρ ὁ θεὸς ἡμῶν πῦρ καταναλίσκον. The ζῷα and the Elders who are mentioned in *c.* iv., and again in xiv. 3, do not appear here, for the attention of the hearer or reader is concentrated upon another group with widely different associations. Τοὺς νικῶντας—not τ. νικήσαντας (cf. xii. 11), or even τ. νενικηκότας, though their struggle is at an end; for it is the abiding character of 'conqueror' on which emphasis is laid, and not the fact of conquest; cf. ὁ νικῶν in ii. 7, 11, 17, 26, iii. 5, 12, 21, xxi. 7. The words that follow define the field on which the victory was won and the character formed; the conquerors are martyrs who have suffered in the conflict with the promoters of the Caesar-cult (cf. *c.* xiii., notes), and have "come victorious from the Beast" (R.V., cf. Benson: "came conquering forth from the Wildbeast"); the construction is a pregnant one, 'by virtue of their victory they escaped out of the hand of the enemy.' Blass's suggestion "=τηρήσαντας ἑαυτοὺς ἐκ" is frigid, and the Latin phrase "victoriam ferre ex aliquo" usually quoted from Livy viii. 8 does not altogether meet the case. The all powerful Beast has been compelled after all to let them slip from his grasp; they, and not he, gained the day. The genuine Acts of the Martyrs shew them in the light of conquerors up to the moment of death, e.g. *Ep. Smyrn.* 19 διὰ τῆς ὑπομονῆς καταγωνισάμενος [ὁ Πολύκαρπος] τὸν ἄδικον ἄρχοντα καὶ οὕτως τὸν τῆς ἀφθαρσίας στέφανον ἀπολαβών; Eus. *H.E.* v. 1 ἡ δὲ μακαρία Βλανδίνα πάντων ἐσχάτη, καθάπερ μήτηρ εὐγενὴς (cf. 4 Macc. xvi. 14) παρορμήσασα τὰ τέκνα καὶ νικηφόρους προπέμψασα πρὸς τὸν βασιλέα...ἔσπευδε πρὸς αὐτοὺς χαίρουσα καὶ ἀγαλλιωμένη ἐπὶ τῇ ἐξόδῳ. *Passio S. Perpetuae* 18 "inluxit dies victoriae illorum, et processerunt de carcere in amphitheatrum quasi in caelum, hilares et vultu decori." But the Apocalyptist follows the victors into the life beyond, and sees them celebrating their victory in the Presence of God. It is a strangely different view of their condition from that presented by *c.* vi. 9 ff., but the announcement of xiv. 6 has partly prepared the reader for it; the present vision anticipates the final joy in which their rest will issue.

For τοῦ θηρίου, τῆς εἰκόνος, τοῦ ἀριθμοῦ see xiii. 1, 14, 17, xiv. 9, 11, xix. 20, xx. 4, and notes there.

ἑστῶτας ἐπὶ τὴν θάλασσαν τὴν ὑαλίνην, ἔχοντας
3 κιθάρας τοῦ θεοῦ. [3] καὶ ᾄδουσιν τὴν ᾠδὴν Μωυσέως
τοῦ δούλου τοῦ θεοῦ καὶ τὴν ᾠδὴν τοῦ ἀρνίου,
λέγοντες

2 υαλινην 2°] υελινην 7 13 (29) 35 38 49 91 95 96 (97) 98 130 | κιθαρας] pr τας Q 2 7 8 13 16 26 27 29 35 38 43 87 94 97 al^{pauc} Ar κιθαραν 130 | του θεου] pr κυριου ℵ 3 om αδουσιν...του θεου C | αδουσιν] αδοντας ℵ Ps-Cypr Prim | Μωσεως P 28 81 al^{mu} Μωυση 130 | του δουλου] om του Q al^{pl} Ar | om την ωδην (2°) 130

ἑστῶτας ἐπὶ τὴν θάλασσαν τὴν ὑαλίνην] Not on the shore of the Sea, like Israel in Ex. xiv. 30, but on the Sea itself which forms the solid pavement (cf. Mt. xiv. 25 ff.) of the final approach to the Throne (iv. 6). Their exodus from the spiritual Egypt (xi. 8) has led them through the Red Sea of Martyrdom, which is now exchanged for the Crystal Sea of Heaven. Like the Elders in v. 8, and the 144,000 in xiv. 2, they carry zitherns—*κιθάρας τοῦ θεοῦ*, not merely of unusual sweetness and power (cf. Ps. lxxix. (lxxx.) 11 *τὰς κέδρους τοῦ θεοῦ*), but dedicated to the service of God (cf. 1 Chron. xvi. 42 כְּלֵי שִׁיר הָאֱלֹהִים, *ὄργανα τῶν ᾠδῶν τοῦ θεοῦ*, 1 Th. iv. 16 *ἐν σάλπιγγι θεοῦ*). The symbolism is well explained by the ancient commentators, e.g. Primasius: "laudibus corda dicata"; Andreas: *τὴν ἐμμελῆ ζωὴν ἐν συμφωνίᾳ τῶν ἀρετῶν, κρουομένην τῷ πλήκτρῳ τοῦ θείου πνεύματος*.

3. *καὶ ᾄδουσιν τὴν ᾠδὴν Μωυσέως τοῦ δούλου τοῦ θεοῦ*] The allusion to the Exodus, hitherto latent, now becomes evident; cf. Ex. xv. 1 *τότε ᾖσεν Μωυσῆς καὶ οἱ υἱοὶ Ἰσραὴλ τὴν ᾠδὴν ταύτην τῷ θεῷ*. There is indeed another *ᾠδὴ Μωυσέως* in Deut. xxxii. which was used as a Sabbath hymn in the Jewish liturgy (Wolff, *curae*, v. p. 563); and the two songs are placed together among the *ᾠδαί* of the Church in the liturgical Psalter of cod. A (*α΄ ᾠδὴ Μ. ἐν τῇ Ἐξόδῳ, β΄ ᾠ. Μ. ἐν τῷ Δευτερονομίῳ*), and both find a place among the Canticles both of Eastern and Western Christendom (*Intr. to the O.T. in Greek*, p. 253 f.); but it is surely the song of victory which is in view here rather than the swan-like song ascribed to the dying Lawgiver. Moses is *ὁ δοῦλος τοῦ θεοῦ*, an O.T. title = עֶבֶד יְהוָֹה, where עֶבֶד is variously rendered in the LXX. by *θεράπων* (Ex. xiv. 31, Num. xii. 7), *δοῦλος* (3 Regn. viii. 53, 56, Ps. civ. (cv.) 26), or *παῖς* (Isa. xlii. 1). The contrast drawn in Heb. iii. 5 between Moses the Servant and Christ the Son (*Μωυσῆς μὲν πιστὸς... ὡς θεράπων...Χριστὸς δὲ ὡς υἱός*) is latent here also, for *τοῦ δούλου* is followed immediately by *τοῦ ἀρνίου*, the exalted Person who throughout the Book is associated with God.

Καὶ τὴν ᾠδὴν τοῦ ἀρνίου. The song of the martyrs is not only the song of Moses, triumphant over Pharaoh and Egypt; it is also the song of the Glorified Christ, the conqueror of the world (Jo. xvi. 33) and of Death (*c.* i. 18). The martyrs have not only overcome Domitian and the power of Rome; they share the victory of Christ (*c.* iii. 21). St John does not write *τὴν ᾠδὴν Μωυσέως καὶ τοῦ ἀρνίου*, for the notes are distinct though they form a harmony. As throughout the Book, the Apocalyptist places together, without confounding, the experiences of the two dispensations, bringing out of his treasure things

Μεγάλα καὶ θαυμαστὰ τὰ ἔργα σου, Κύριε
ὁ θεὸς ὁ παντοκράτωρ· δίκαιαι καὶ ἀληθιναὶ αἱ
ὁδοί σου, ὁ βασιλεὺς τῶν ἐθνῶν· ⁴τίς οὐ μὴ 4
φοβηθῇ, Κύριε, καὶ δοξάσει τὸ ὄνομά σου; ὅτι
μόνος ὅσιος, ὅτι πάντα τὰ ἔθνη ἥξουσιν καὶ
προσκυνήσουσιν ἐνώπιόν σου, ὅτι τὰ δικαιώματά
σου ἐφανερώθησαν.

3 *δικαια κ. αληθινα τα εργα* syr^{gw} | *ο βασιλευς*] *βασιλευ* ℵ* 18 29 47 90 98 130 | *εθνων* ℵ$^{c.a}$APQ 1 6 7 8 14 130 186 al$^{plq\,40}$ me arm aeth Ps-Cypr Prim Andr Ar] *αιωνων* ℵ*C 18 95 vg$^{cle\,fu\,dem\,tol\,lipss}$ syrr 4 *ου μη*] *σε ου* ℵ 95 *σε μη* 130 | *φοβηθη*] +*σε* 6 7 8 29 38 186 al^{pl} vg$^{cle\,lipss}$ syrr Ar | om *κυριε* 14 92 130 vg^{dem} arm aeth^{utr} Cyp Prim | *δοξαση* ℵ 1 7 8 29 38 al^{pl} Andr *θαυμαση* 130 | om *οτι μονος οσιος* me | *οσιος* ℵACP 1 28 31 38 79 al vg (*pius*) syr^{gw} Cypr Prim Ar] *αγιος* Q 6 7 8 al$^{plq\,40}$ *sanctus g sanctus et pius f sanctus es et justus* syr *sanctus et dignus adorari* arm + *ει* 10 36 37 (38) (47) 49 95 96 | *παντα τα εθνη*] *παντες* Q 6 7 14 29 43 al^{30} | *ενωπιον σου*] + *κυριε* A 95 130 | *τα δικ. σου*] *δικ. ενωπιον σου* ℵ

new and old. Primasius is right, if his words are taken in a wider sense than he probably intended: "in Moysis autem vetus, in Agni vero cantico novum significatum est testamentum."

3—4. *μεγάλα καὶ θαυμαστὰ τὰ ἔργα σου, Κύριε κτλ.*] The words of the Martyrs' Song are almost wholly from the O.T., as the following brief catena will shew: Ps. cx. (cxi.) 2 μεγάλα τὰ ἔργα Κυρίου, Ps. cxxxviii. (cxxxix.) 14 θαυμάσια τὰ ἔργα σου, Amos iv. 13 Κύριος ὁ θεὸς ὁ παντοκράτωρ, Deut. xxxii. 4 θεός, ἀληθινὰ τὰ ἔργα αὐτοῦ, καὶ πᾶσαι αἱ ὁδοὶ αὐτοῦ κρίσεις, Jer. x. 7, 10 (Q^{mg}) τίς οὐ μὴ φοβηθήσεται, βασιλεῦ ἐθνῶν...ὁ δὲ κύριος θεὸς... ἐστὶ...βασιλεὺς αἰώνιος, Tob. xiii. 10 εὐλόγει τὸν βασιλέα τῶν αἰώνων, Mal. i. 11 τὸ ὄνομά μου δεδόξασται ἐν τοῖς ἔθνεσιν, Deut. xxxii. 4 δίκαιος καὶ ὅσιος (יָשָׁר) Κύριος, Ps. cxliv. (cxlv.) 17 Κύριος...ὅσιος (חָסִיד) ἐν πᾶσιν τοῖς ἔργοις αὐτοῦ, 1 Regn. xii. 7 ἀπαγγελῶ ὑμῖν τὴν πᾶσαν δικαιοσύνην (A, τὰς πάσας δικαιοσύνας) Κυρίου. The thought as well as the phraseology of the Song is strangely Hebraic, and at first sight does not appear to be specially appropriate to the occasion; there is no reference to the martyrs' own conflicts, and none to the victory of the Lamb; it is rather a hymn of praise than a paean, nor does it obviously answer to its description either as the ᾠδὴ Μωυσέως or as the ᾠδὴ τοῦ ἀρνίου. There is perhaps a reason for this. In the Presence of God the martyrs forget themselves; their thoughts are absorbed by the new wonders that surround them; the glory of God, and the mighty scheme of things in which their own sufferings and victory form an infinitesimal part are opening before them; they begin to see the great issue of the world-drama, and we hear the doxology with which they greet their first unclouded vision of God and His works. Their song, though it has little to do with martyrdom or victory, at any rate suits the context, preparing the reader for the judgements which are about to follow; leading him to view them, as they are viewed by the victors, *sub specie aeternitatis.*

For *μεγάλα καὶ θαυμαστά* see *v.* 1, note; for *παντοκράτωρ*, i. 8, note.

5 [5] Καὶ μετὰ ταῦτα εἶδον, καὶ ἠνοίγη ὁ ναὸς τῆς σκηνῆς

5 μετα ταυτα] μετ αυτα C | ειδον ℵP 1 186 min^pl] ιδον ACQ 7 14 92 130 + και ιδου *f* vg me anon^aug Tyc Prim

Ἀληθιναί, cf. iii. 7, 14, notes; the combination δίκαιος καὶ ἀληθινός (or ἀλ. κ. δικ.) occurs again in xvi. 7, xix. 2. With μόνος ὅσιος cf. Rom. xvi. 27 μόνῳ σοφῷ, 1 Tim. vi. 16 ὁ μόνος ἔχων ἀθανασίαν, and the clause in the ὕμνος ἑωθινός (*O.T. in Greek*[3], iii. p. 833), ὅτι σὺ εἶ μόνος ἅγιος. Ὅσιος, *pius*, is used of God in the N.T. only here and in xvi. 5 (in Heb. vii. 26 it refers to the Incarnate Son); it represents God as fulfilling His relation to His creatures, even as He requires them to fulfil theirs towards Himself. Τὰ δικαιώματά σου, 'Thy righteous acts'; a δικαίωμα is a concrete expression of righteousness, whether in the form of a just decree (e.g. Deut. iv. 1 ἄκουε τῶν δικαιωμάτων (הַחֻקִּים), Lc. i. 6 πορευόμενοι ἐν πάσαις ταῖς ἐντολαῖς καὶ δικαιώμασιν τοῦ κυρίου ἄμεμπτοι), or a just act, as here and in xix. 8 τὰ δικαιώματα τῶν ἁγίων: cf. Sanday and Headlam on Rom. i. 17, v. 18, and Westcott on Heb. ix. 1.

It is not easy to choose between the readings τῶν ἐθνῶν and τῶν αἰώνων. For the latter, besides the references given above, see 1 Tim. i. 17 τῷ δὲ βασιλεῖ τῶν αἰώνων, Enoch ix. 4 σὺ εἶ ὁ...βασιλεὺς τῶν αἰώνων· ὁ θρόνος τῆς δόξης σου εἰς πάσας τὰς γενεὰς τοῦ αἰῶνος, καὶ τὸ ὄνομά σου τὸ ἅγιον καὶ μέγα καὶ εὐλογητὸν εἰς πάντας τοὺς αἰῶνας. On the other hand τῶν ἐθνῶν is suggested by the passage in Jeremiah to which the next words refer, and on the whole agrees best with the drift of the canticle. The true Sovereign of the nations is not the Augustus, but their Creator, the Living God, and He will in the end receive their homage (*v.* 4; cf. xxi. 24 f.).

The Martyrs' Song falls readily into parallelisms after the manner of O.T. poetry—a circumstance which, taken with the general tone and the wording, suggests a Jewish source.

5. καὶ μετὰ ταῦτα εἶδον] A formula which usually introduces a new and important vision; cf. iv. 1, note. The Seven plague-laden Angels form the most striking group since the Seven Angels of the Temple (viii. 1).

καὶ ἠνοίγη ὁ ναὸς τῆς σκηνῆς τοῦ μαρτυρίου] See xi. 19 ἠνοίγη ὁ ναὸς τοῦ θεοῦ ὁ ἐν τῷ οὐρανῷ, and cf. iii. 12, vii. 15, xiv. 15, 17, xvi. 1, 17. In these references to the ναός, the writer, as it now appears, alludes not to Solomon's Temple or its successors, but to the Tabernacle in the Wilderness, the 'Tent of Witness' (Num. ix. 15, xvii. 7 (22) f., xviii. 2, אֹהֶל הָעֵדֻת), or 'Tent of Meeting' (Ex. xxvii. 21 *et passim*, אֹהֶל מוֹעֵד), both of which designations the LXX. usually renders by ἡ σκηνὴ τοῦ μαρτυρίου, and the Vg., following the LXX., by *tabernaculum testimonii*; ὁ ναὸς τῆς σκ. τ. μ. is suggested, as Westcott points out (*Hebrews*, p. 234), by the phrase מִשְׁכַּן אֹהֶל מוֹעֵד (Ex. xl. 2, 6, 29) which the LXX. does not distinguish from the shorter form. That the writers of Hebrews and the Apocalypse have chosen the Tabernacle rather than the Temple as the counterpart of the heavenly Presence-Chamber is due to the feeling that the Tabernacle was the archetype of the later Temple, and was itself constructed on a Divinely imparted plan: cf. Ex. xxv. 40 ὅρα ποιήσεις κατὰ τὸν τύπον τὸν δεδειγμένον σοι ἐν τῷ ὄρει, quoted in Heb. viii. 5 with the comment that the priests under the Law consequently ὑποδείγματι καὶ σκιᾷ λατρεύουσιν τῶν ἐπουρανίων.

τοῦ μαρτυρίου ἐν τῷ οὐρανῷ, ⁶καὶ ἐξῆλθον οἱ ἑπτὰ 6
ἄγγελοι οἱ ἔχοντες τὰς ἑπτὰ πληγὰς ἐκ τοῦ ναοῦ,
ἐνδεδυμένοι λίνον καθαρὸν λαμπρὸν καὶ περιεζωσμένοι
περὶ τὰ στήθη ζώνας χρυσᾶς. ⁷καὶ ἓν ἐκ τῶν τεσ- 7

6 *εξηλθαν* C | *οι εχοντες*] om *οι* ℵPQ 1 48 79 161 al | *εκ του ναου*] *εκ του ουρανου* 10 49 91 96 om Q min^{30} | *ενδεδυμενοι*] pr *οι ησαν* Q min$^{plq\,30}$ syr | *λινον* PQ 186 al^{pl} vg^{cle} syrr (nisi forte *λινουν κ.*) arm anon^{aug} Andr Ar] *λινουν* 14 18 (36) 92 97 *g* (*linteamen*) *h* (*linteamina*) *λινους* ℵ *λιθον* AC 38^{mg} 48 90 codd ap Andr vg$^{am\,fu\,dem\,tol\,lipss}$ hiat 130 | *καθαρους* ℵ | *λαμπρον*] *λαμπρους* ℵ pr *και* 32** vg$^{cle\,lipss\,4,6}$ arm aeth Prim | *περι*] *επι* 28 79 om 1 12 31   7 om *εν* ℵ* 1 7 12 16 79 90 arm

6. *καὶ ἐξῆλθον...ἐκ τοῦ ναοῦ κτλ.*] The Sanctuary is not opened here as in xi. *l.c.* for the purpose of revealing the Ark of the Covenant, but to allow the Seven Angels to issue in procession from the Presence-Chamber. The angels of xiv. 15, 17 f., also came forth from the Sanctuary, but singly and with less solemnity; the curtain was not drawn back to let them pass.

Ἐνδεδυμένοι λίνον καθαρὸν λαμπρόν. All the Seven are clad alike in the pure bright raiment of celestial beings. Unfortunately the reading is far from certain. WH. accept ΛΙΘΟΝ, urging that "the bold image expressed by this well-attested reading is justified by Ez. xxviii. 13 *πάντα λίθον χρηστὸν ἐνδέδεσαι*, where *ἐνδέδυσαι* is a various reading" in a few cursives, and that "on the other hand *λίνον* as distinguished from *λινοῦν* never denotes a fabric or garment made of flax except according to Etym. Magn., and possibly in Aesch. *Suppl.* 121." Others have seen in *λίθον* a reference to the High Priest's breastplate, and some support for such a phrase as *ἐνδύεσθαι λίθον* may be found in the imagery of *cc.* iv. 3, xvii. 4, xxi. 11, 18 ff., 21. But when all has been said, the metaphor is intolerable even in the Apocalypse, and we turn to look again at the evidence for ΛΙΝΟΝ. The argument which WH. adduce that the Apocalypse elsewhere uses *βύσσινον* for a garment of linen (xviii. 12, 16, xix. 8 bis, 14), cuts both ways, for the fact would tempt a corrector to change *λίνον*, and if he remembered Ez. *l.c.*, what more obvious remedy than to write Θ for Ν? Nor is the extreme rarity of *λίνον* = *λινοῦν* conclusive, for our writer is apt to use rare forms and even forms for which no other authority can be claimed. Of *λίνον*, however, in this sense there are traces in Homer (*Il.* ix. 661, *Od.* xiii. 73, 118; cf. Eustathius: *λίνον...ὕφασμά τι ἐκ λίνου*) as well as in Aeschylus (*Suppl.* 120, 132), and the revival of the old poetic use in a book such as the Apocalypse need cause no surprise. On the whole therefore it has seemed best to place *λίνον* in the text provisionally, until further light comes.

The Seven Angels, then, are clad in clear glistening white (cf. xix. 8, *ἐδόθη αὐτῇ ἵνα περιβάληται βύσσινον λαμπρὸν καθαρόν*, *ib.* 14 *ἐνδεδυμένοι βύσσινον λευκὸν καθαρόν*), a garb characteristic of celestial beings (Mt. xxviii. 3, Mc. xvi. 5, Lc. ix. 2). Their snow-white linen tunics are girded high (*περὶ τὰ στήθη* = *πρὸς τοῖς μαστοῖς* i. 13) with golden belts, the symbols of royalty or of priestly functions (*l.c.*, note); they are *λειτουργικὰ πνεύματα* (Heb. i. 14), and they are vested for their liturgy.

7. *καὶ ἓν ἐκ τῶν τεσσάρων ζῴων ἔδωκεν κτλ.*] The Seven are now entrusted with power to execute their ministry. This is done by a symbolical *traditio instrumentorum*, which is

σάρων ζῴων ἔδωκεν τοῖς ἑπτὰ ἀγγέλοις ἑπτὰ φιάλας
χρυσᾶς γεμούσας τοῦ θυμοῦ τοῦ θεοῦ τοῦ ζῶντος
8 εἰς τοὺς αἰῶνας τῶν αἰώνων. [8]καὶ ἐγεμίσθη ὁ ναὸς
καπνοῦ ἐκ τῆς δόξης τοῦ θεοῦ καὶ ἐκ τῆς δυνάμεως
αὐτοῦ, καὶ οὐδεὶς ἐδύνατο εἰσελθεῖν εἰς τὸν ναὸν ἄχρι
τελεσθῶσιν αἱ ἑπτὰ πληγαὶ τῶν ἑπτὰ ἀγγέλων.

7 om επτα 2° ℵ vg^fu | om χρυσας arm Prim | των αιωνων] + αμην ℵ 12 28 46 me syr^gw 8 καπνου] pr εκ του Q min^30 syrr | εδυνατο AC 2 6 7 8 26 al^mu] ηδυνατο ℵPQ 1 al^pl | αχρι] αχρις ου C | om επτα 2° P 1 10 12 17 18 38 49 72 91 96 186

fitly committed to one of the four representatives of Nature (see iv. 6 ff., v. 14, vi. 1 f., notes). Control is thus given to them over the forces of Nature, so far as may be necessary for the purpose of giving effect to the Divine purpose; cf. xiv. 18 ὁ ἔχων ἐξουσίαν ἐπὶ τοῦ πυρός, and Ps. lxxvii. (lxxviii.) 49 ἐξαπέστειλεν εἰς αὐτοὺς... ἀποστολὴν δι' ἀγγέλων πονηρῶν. The instruments given to the Angels of the Last Plagues are φιάλαι χρυσαῖ, cf. v. 8, note, and for χρυσαῖ compare 4 Regn. xxv. 15, 1 Chr. xxviii. 17, 2 Chr. iv. 8, 1 Esdr. ii. 13. But whereas the bowls carried by the Elders in *c.* v. were full of the incense of the Saints' prayers, these are full of the wrath of God. Cf. Primasius: "eaedem quippe phialae et suavitates supplicationum et iram suppliciorum continere dicuntur, cum a sanctis pro regni Dei adventu funduntur"; he adds a reference to 2 Cor. ii. 15 f. χριστοῦ εὐωδία ἐσμὲν τῷ θεῷ ἐν τοῖς σωζομένοις καὶ ἐν τοῖς ἀπολλυμένοις, οἷς μὲν ὀσμὴ ἐκ θανάτου εἰς θάνατον, οἷς δὲ ὀσμὴ ἐκ ζωῆς εἰς ζωήν. In xiv. 8, 10 the Wrath of God is a deadly wine which is given men to drink, a cup (ποτήριον) which sinners must drain; here the metaphor is changed, the cup becomes an open incense bowl, pouring out its burning contents upon the earth; cf. viii. 5, where a similar metaphor is used. Schöttgen notes that the Targum on Isa. li. 17, 22, for אֶת כּוֹס substitutes ית פיילי or ית פייל כוס.

Τοῦ ζῶντος κτλ. adds to the terror of the thought; cf. Heb. x. 31 φοβερὸν τὸ ἐμπεσεῖν εἰς χεῖρας θεοῦ ζῶντος; the gods of heathendom are dead or never were alive, and their wrath has no terrors for Christians; the Living God is to be feared indeed. For ὁ ζῶν εἰς τοὺς αἰῶνας τῶν αἰώνων as a title of the Eternal Father see iv. 9, note, 10, x. 6.

8. καὶ ἐγεμίσθη ὁ ναὸς καπνοῦ ἐκ τῆς δόξης κτλ.] The terrors of the imminent judgement are still further emphasized by the smoke which is seen to fill the Sanctuary; cf. Andreas: διὰ δὲ τοῦ καπνοῦ τὸ φοβερὸν καὶ καταπληκτικὸν καὶ κολαστικὸν τῆς θείας ὀργῆς μανθάνομεν. Smoke is an O.T. symbol of the Divine Presence when the aweful majesty of God is to be insisted upon; cf. Exod. xix. 18 τὸ δὲ ὄρος τὸ Σινὰ ἐκαπνίζετο ὅλον διὰ τὸ καταβεβηκέναι ἐπ' αὐτὸ τὸν θεὸν ἐν πυρί, καὶ ἀνέβαινεν ὁ καπνὸς ὡς καπνὸς καμίνου; Ps. xvii. (xviii.) 9 ἀνέβη καπνὸς ἐν ὀργῇ αὐτοῦ; Isa. vi. 5 ὁ οἶκος ἐνεπλήσθη καπνοῦ, lxv. 5 καπνὸς τοῦ θυμοῦ μου. On this occasion the smoke proceeds from (ἐκ) the Divine glory and power, i.e. from the personal character and attributes of God and His boundless resources, two grounds of undying fear to His enemies.

καὶ οὐδεὶς ἐδύνατο εἰσελθεῖν εἰς τὸν ναόν κτλ.] Both the Tabernacle and the Temple supply an illustration here; for the first see Ex. xl. 29 (35) καὶ οὐκ ἠδυνάσθη Μωσῆς εἰσελθεῖν

XVI.

[1] Καὶ ἤκουσα μεγάλης φωνῆς ἐκ τοῦ ναοῦ λεγούσης 1
τοῖς ἑπτὰ ἀγγέλοις Ὑπάγετε καὶ ἐκχέετε τὰς ἑπτὰ
φιάλας τοῦ θυμοῦ τοῦ θεοῦ εἰς τὴν γῆν. [2] καὶ 2
ἀπῆλθεν ὁ πρῶτος καὶ ἐξέχεεν τὴν φιάλην αὐτοῦ εἰς

XVI 1 φωνης μεγαλης ℵP 1 al^pl vg Prim Andr | εκ του ναου] εκ του ουρανου 13 vg^dem tol lips6 me εκ τ. ουρ. εκ τ. ναου aeth om Q min^30 syr Ar | om και 2° 1 7 12 28 36 130 al^fere 10 vg^lips4 me arm | εκχεετε ℵACP 1 12] εκχεατε Q 186 al^pl Andr Ar εχετε 130 | om επτα P 1 28 49 79 91 96 al *h* me aeth　　2 ο πρωτος] + αγγελος 12 28 33 36 79 87 me arm aeth | εις] επι 1 28 49 79 91 96 al me

εἰς τὴν σκηνὴν τοῦ μαρτυρίου, ὅτι ἐπεσκίαζεν ἐπ' αὐτὴν ἡ νεφέλη, καὶ δόξης Κυρίου ἐπλήσθη ἡ σκηνή, and for the second 3 Regn. viii. 11 καὶ οὐκ ἠδύναντο οἱ ἱερεῖς στήκειν λειτουργεῖν ἀπὸ προσώπου τῆς νεφέλης, ὅτι ἔπλησεν δόξα Κυρίου τὸν οἶκον. The Divine judgements are impenetrable until they are past; when the last plague has fulfilled its course, the smoke will vanish, and the Vision of God be seen. Bede: "si fumum abdita iudiciorum Dei interpretaris arcana, mortalibus haec impenetrabilia manent et clausa donec, finitis praesentis saeculi plagis, advenit Dominus."

XVI. 1—21. The pouring out of the Seven Bowls.

1. καὶ ἤκουσα μεγάλης φωνῆς ἐκ τοῦ ναοῦ κτλ.] A great voice from heaven is usually that of an angel, cf. v. 2 εἶδον ἄγγελον ἰσχυρὸν κηρύσσοντα ἐν φωνῇ μεγάλῃ, vii. 2 εἶδον ἄλλον ἄγγελον...καὶ ἔκραξεν φ. μ., x. 3 ἔκραξεν [ἄγγελος ἰσχυρὸς] φ. μ., and similarly xiv. 7, 9, 15, 18. But as this Voice comes from the ναός, which at the time, as we have been told, no creature could enter, the Speaker here must be presumed to be God Himself; cf. Mt. iii. 17, xvii. 5, Jo. xii. 28, 2 Pet. i. 17 f. The Voice is repeated after the seventh Bowl, *v.* 17.

Ὑπάγετε καὶ ἐκχέετε, 'Go your ways (cf. Mc. vi. 38, xiv. 13, xvi. 7, Jac. ii. 16), pour out (for the form ἐκχέετε see W. Schm. p. 115; Blass would correct ἐκχέατε, *Gr.* p. 41) the Seven Bowls of the Wrath of God into (εἰς, as in xiv. 19) the Earth.' Permission to proceed having been given (cf. xiv. 15, 18), the Seven advance one by one, each in his own order (ὁ πρῶτος, ὁ δεύτερος κτλ., as in viii. 7 ff.).

The Seven Plagues that follow have obvious affinities to (1) the Ten Plagues of Egypt, (2) the visitations which accompany the Seven Trumpet-blasts of *cc.* viii.—xi., and especially to the latter; the first, sixth, and ninth of the Egyptian plagues, and the second, third, fifth, sixth, and seventh of the Trumpet plagues are more or less distinctly in view here. Yet the Last Plagues have features peculiar to themselves: the fourth is entirely new, the rest are more or less freshly conceived. On the other hand the differences are deeper and more suggestive. While no personal suffering is inflicted on Man by the first five of the Egyptian plagues or by the first four of the Trumpet-visitations, he is attacked at the very outset of the present cycle. Again, while the first four Trumpet-plagues affect only a third of the earth, the sea, the fresh water supply, and the lights of heaven, no such limitation appears in the account of the Seven Plagues now about to be described. They are not tentative chastisements, but punitive and final.

2. καὶ ἀπῆλθεν ὁ πρῶτος καὶ ἐξέχεεν κτλ.] Ἀπῆλθεν...καί is doubtless to be repeated by the reader's thought

τὴν γῆν· καὶ ἐγένετο ἕλκος κακὸν καὶ πονηρὸν ἐπὶ τοὺς ἀνθρώπους τοὺς ἔχοντας τὸ χάραγμα τοῦ θηρίου
3 καὶ τοὺς προσκυνοῦντας τῇ εἰκόνι αὐτοῦ. [3]καὶ ὁ δεύτερος ἐξέχεεν τὴν φιάλην αὐτοῦ εἰς τὴν θάλασσαν· καὶ ἐγένετο αἷμα ὡς νεκροῦ, καὶ πᾶσα ψυχὴ ζωῆς

2 κακον και πονηρον] om κακον A om κακον και me arm aeth | επι] εις 1 28 49 79 91 96 al vg me | τους προσκυν.] om τους 130   3 δευτερος] + αγγελος Q min^{pl} vg^{cle} me syrr arm Andr Ar | om αυτου 130 | αιμα ως νεκρου] ως νεκρος syr$^{gw\ vid}$ | ως] ωσει ℵ om 1 46 me ante αιμα pon 7 12 39 | ζωης AC 95 syr aeth] ζωσα ℵPQ 1 7 28 36 37 38 39 91 96 130 186 al Ar *f g* vg (*vivens*) syr^{gw} me arm om 6 8 14 al^{30} Prim

in *vv.* 3, 4, 8, 10, 12, 17. The Seven are not conceived as stepping forward, one by one, to discharge their tasks, and then returning to their places in the procession, but rather as going off, each in his order, until all have vanished. Ἐξέχεεν: the metaphor is not inappropriate, cf. Lucian *Calumn.* 23 τὸν θυμὸν ἐξέχεεν.

The result of the first outpouring is to produce a plague on man similar to the sixth Egyptian plague; cf. Ex. ix. 10 ἐγένετο ἕλκη, φλυκτίδες ἀναζέουσαι ἐν τοῖς ἀνθρώποις, and see Deut. xxviii. 27, 35 πατάξαι σε Κύριος ἕλκει Αἰγυπτίῳ... πατάξαι σε Κ. ἐν ἕλκει πονηρῷ (בִּשְׁחִין רָע)...ὥστε μὴ δύνασθαί σε ἰαθῆναι; Job ii. 7 ἐξῆλθεν δὲ ὁ διάβολος ἀπὸ τοῦ κυρίου, καὶ ἔπαισεν τὸν Ἰὼβ ἕλκει πονηρῷ (בִּשְׁחִין רָע). The Egyptian ἕλκη, it is noted, attacked even the magicians, the antagonists of Moses (οὐκ ἠδύναντο οἱ φαρμακοὶ στῆναι ἐναντίον Μωυσῆ διὰ τὰ ἕλκη); is the Seer mindful of this when he represents the first of the Last Plagues as breaking out in sores on the Caesar-worshippers, who were controlled by the magicians of the temples of Rome and the Augusti (cf. xiii. 13 ff., notes)? Κακὸν καὶ πονηρόν, 'bad and malignant'; the lexicons take πονηρόν as = ἐπίπονον 'painful' (Suidas), but the passages quoted above from the LXX. lead us to regard it as the equivalent of רָע, actively mischievous, 'malignant' in the technical sense. Καὶ ἐγένετο... ἐπί = וְהָיָה...עַל (Ex. *l. c.*).

3. καὶ ὁ δεύτερος ἐξέχεεν...εἰς τὴν θάλασσαν κτλ.] The Second Bowl corresponds generally with the Second Trumpet (viii. 8 f.), and both are suggested by the first Egyptian plague (Ex. vii. 14 ff.). In Egypt the Nile alone is smitten; in Patmos the Seer naturally thinks first of the sea. The Aegean, receiving the contents of the second angel's bowl, turns (as he had often seen it turn at sunset) to a blood red—ἐγένετο αἷμα = הָיָה דָם, Ex. vii. 19 —he adds ὡς νεκροῦ, which brings up the picture of a murdered man weltering in his blood; cf. Arethas: νεκροῦ δέ, τοῦ ἐσφαγμένου. The fish in the Nile died (Ex. vii. 21); a third of the living things in the sea perished under the Second Trumpet (*c.* viii. 9); the destruction wrought by the third Bowl is complete—πᾶσα ψυχὴ ζωῆς (כָּל־נֶפֶשׁ הַחַיָּה, Gen. i. 21) ἀπέθανεν, τὰ ἐν τῇ θαλάσσῃ, where τὰ ἐν τ. θ. is in apposition with π. ψ., as τὰ ἔχοντα ψυχάς with τῶν κτισμάτων in viii. 9, and defines it. No burning mountain (viii. 8) is needed here, and no falling star (viii. 10) in the next plague; the deadly work is done by the direct action of the wrath poured out by the angels of the Bowls (xvi. 1).

ἀπέθανεν, τὰ ἐν τῇ θαλάσσῃ. [4]καὶ ὁ τρίτος ἐξέχεεν 4
τὴν φιάλην αὐτοῦ εἰς τοὺς ποταμοὺς καὶ τὰς πηγὰς
τῶν ὑδάτων· καὶ ἐγένετο αἷμα. [5]καὶ ἤκουσα τοῦ 5
ἀγγέλου τῶν ὑδάτων λέγοντος Δίκαιος εἶ, ὁ ὢν καὶ ὁ
ἦν, [ὁ] ὅσιος, ὅτι ταῦτα ἔκρινας· [6]ὅτι αἵμα[τα] ἁγίων 6

3 τα AC] των 95 syr om ℵPQ min^{pl} vg arm Prim Ar | επι της θαλασσης ℵ 4 τριτος] + αγγελος 1 35 36 38 49 79 87 91 96 186 al vg^{lips4} me syr arm Andr | εις] επι ℵ 18 31 186 *super* vg Prim | εγενετο ℵCPQ 1 min^{pl} vg Andr Ar] εγενοντο A 36 95 130 syrr *facta sunt* Prim 5 των υδατων] pr του επι 95 om τ. υ. 1 arm | ο ην] ος ην Q 2 8 14 29 30 40 41 42 43 92 93 98 | ο οσιος ℵP 5 6 11 12 18 27 28 31 35 49 79 91 94 96 186 al$^{plq\,10}$] οσιος ACQ min$^{fere\,35}$ και ο οσιος 1 34 36 και οσιος 95 om ο οσιος me aeth 6 αιματα ℵ 36 39] αιμα ACPQ min$^{fere\,omn}$ syrr Andr Ar

4. *καὶ ὁ τρίτος...εἰς τοὺς ποταμοὺς κτλ.*] As under the Third Trumpet, the smiting of the fresh-water supply follows that of the sea. But the result is different; in viii. 11 the third part of the waters are turned into wormwood; here the whole supply is turned, as in the case of the sea (*v.* 3), into blood. On *αἱ πηγαὶ τῶν ὑδάτων* cf. viii. 10, note. Ἐγένετο *αἷμα*, sc. *τὰ ὕδατα* (*οἱ ποταμοὶ καὶ αἱ πηγαί*). The smiting of the springs prevented any such measures as the Egyptians took for evading the effects of the plague (Ex. vii. 24).

Why the waters are turned to blood is now explained by two voices which the Seer overhears (*v.* 5 ff.).

5. *καὶ ἤκουσα τοῦ ἀγγέλου τῶν ὑδάτων λέγοντος κτλ.*] With *τοῦ ἀγγ. τ. ὑδάτων* cf. vii. 1 *εἶδον τέσσαρας ἀγγέλους...κρατοῦντας τοὺς τέσσαρας ἀνέμους*, ix. 11 *τὸν ἄγγελον τῆς ἀβύσσου*, xiv. 17 *ἄγγελος...ὁ ἔχων ἐξουσίαν ἐπὶ τοῦ πυρός*. See also Enoch lxvi. 2 (ed. Charles, p. 172): "these angels were over the powers of the waters." The Rabbinic writers speak of an angel set over the earth (מלאך הממונה על הארץ), and of another who is prince of the sea (שר של ים); every element, every form of created life, has its angel-counterpart (*Yalkut Ruben*, f. 7. 1 "dicunt sapientes nostri: 'Non est herba quae non habeat angelum suum in supernis'." Similar ideas prevailed among the Persians and find a place in Zoroastrianism: see reff. in note on i. 20. Cf. Andreas: *κἀντεῦθεν δείκνυται τοῖς στοιχείοις ἐπιτετάχθαι ἀγγέλους;* and so Arethas: *οὐ μόνον ἔφοροι τῶν ἐθνῶν κατὰ τὸν νομοθέτην* Μωυσῆν (Deut. xxxii. 8, LXX.) *αἱ θεῖαι δυνάμεις, ἀλλὰ καὶ τῶν κοσμικῶν στοιχείων.* The spirit of the waters is so far from resenting the plague that he bears witness to the justice which inflicts it. His words form a sort of antiphon to the canticle in xv. 3 f.; they illustrate the divine *δικαιοσύνη* and *ὁσιότης* proclaimed in the Song. Ὁ *ὅσιος* is doubtless to be read, notwithstanding the omission of the article by our best MSS.; ο would have easily dropt out before ΟϹΙΟϹ, and on the other hand *ὅσιος* (anarthrous) cannot be taken as a predicate after *ὁ ὢν καὶ ὁ ἦν*, a procedure which the usage of the Apocalypse forbids, and to treat it as in apposition with *δίκαιος* creates an intolerable harshness. It is not equally certain how *ὁ ὅσιος* is to be rendered, whether as in apposition to *ὁ ὢν καὶ ὁ ἦν* (*qui es et fuisti pius*), or as equivalent to a vocative, but the latter is perhaps to be preferred (cf. R.V., "Thou Holy One," and Blass, *Gr.* p. 26 f.). On *ὁ ὢν κ. ὁ ἦν* see i. 4, note; on *ὅσιος* as applied to God, xv. 4, note.

6. *ὅτι αἵματα ἁγίων καὶ προφητῶν ἐξέχεαν κτλ.*] The construction is not

καὶ προφητῶν ἐξέχεαν, καὶ αἷμα αὐτοῖς δέδωκας πεῖν·
7 ἄξιοί εἰσιν. [7]καὶ ἤκουσα τοῦ θυσιαστηρίου λέγοντος
Ναί, Κύριε ὁ θεὸς ὁ παντοκράτωρ, ἀληθιναὶ καὶ δίκαιαι
8 αἱ κρίσεις σου. [8]καὶ ὁ τέταρτος ἐξέχεεν τὴν φιάλην

6 *προφητων κ. αγιων* syr[gw] | *δεδωκας* AC] *εδωκας* ℵPQ min[fere omn vid] *εδωκεν* 130 | *πειν* A (C *πιν*)] *πιειν* ℵPQ rell | *αξιοι*] pr *οπερ* ℵ pr *οτι* (vel + *γαρ*) vg[cle] me syr aeth 7 *του θυσιαστηριου λεγοντος*] pr *εκ* Q 1 *φωνην εκ τ. θ. λεγουσαν* 36 me *alterum ab altari dicentem* vg[cle] *alterum dicens* vg[am lips 5] *alterum angelum dicentem* vg[lipss 4, 6] *aliam vocem dicentem* Prim | om *ο θεος* 130 8 *τεταρτος*] + *αγγελος* ℵ 1 6 28 35 36 130 186 al[mu] vg[cle dem lipss 4, 6] syr[gw] arm Prim Andr

free from ambiguity; the two clauses beginning *ὅτι αἵματα, καὶ αἷμα*, may be parallel, as in xv. 4 *ὅτι μόνος...ὅτι πάντα...*, or the second *ὅτι* clause may be explanatory of the first (cf. R.V. text, Blass, *Gr.* p. 274); or again, the second *ὅτι* may begin a new sentence: "because they poured out the blood of saints and prophets Thou hast given them blood also to drink" (R.V.[mg.]). On the whole the last-named rendering seems preferable; it gives meaning to *καί*, which as a mere copula is somewhat nerveless in such a context. The Seer still has in view the condition of Asia; as the first plague is directed against the Caesar-worshippers, so the second avenges the blood of those who suffered for refusing to offer sacrifice to the Augusti. Here and perhaps also in xviii. 24 *αἵματα*, though read in each place by only one uncial MS., is probably original; it represents the Hebrew דָּמִים, as in 1 Regn. xxv. 33, 2 Regn. xvi. 7, Ps. v. 7, etc. Ἁγίων *καὶ προφητῶν*, loyal Christians and their leaders, the prophetic order; for the combination cf. xi. 18, xviii. 24, and for *προφῆται* (here the Christian prophets exclusively) see Mt. xxiii. 34, Acts xi. 27, xiii. 1 etc., 1 Cor. xii. 28 f., Eph. ii. 20, iii. 5, iv. 11. On *πεῖν* (also *πῖν*) = *πιεῖν* cf. WH.[2], *Notes*, p. 177, Blass, *Gr.* pp. 23, 36, W. Schm., p. 53 f.

Ἄξιοί *εἰσιν* forms a terrible antithesis to the *ἄ. εἰσιν* of iii. 4, and as Alford remarks, the *asyndeton* adds strength to the words. For *ἄξιος* in a bad sense cf. Lc. xii. 48 *ἄξια πληγῶν*, Rom. i. 32 *ἄξιοι θανάτου*, Heb. x. 29 *ἀξιωθήσεται τιμωρίας*.

7. *καὶ ἤκουσα τοῦ θυσιαστηρίου λέγοντος κτλ.*] A response comes to the Angel of the Waters from the Altar in Heaven, whether the Angel of the Altar is meant (cf. xiv. 18) or the Altar itself is personified; cf. ix. 13 *ἤκουσα φωνὴν μίαν ἐκ τῶν κεράτων τοῦ θυσιαστηρίου τοῦ χρυσοῦ*, and see note there. The Altar or its Angel represents the sacrifices and prayers of the Church (xiv. l.c., note), and thus the *ὑπακοή* (*Petr. Ev.* 9) is ultimately that of the Saints and Prophets.

Ναί, *Κύριε ὁ θεός κτλ.* is taken almost verbally from the 'Song of Moses and of the Lamb,' and indeed is an epitome of it. The phrase *ἀληθιναὶ καὶ δίκαιαι αἱ κρίσεις σου*, which is repeated in the *ἐπινίκιον* on the Fall of Babylon (xix. 2), seems to come from Ps. xviii. (xix.) 10.

8 f. *καὶ ὁ τέταρτος ἐξέχεεν ... ἐπὶ τὸν ἥλιον*] The Fourth Bowl, like the Fourth Trumpet, takes effect upon the sun. But the effect is different and nearly opposite; instead of a plague of darkness (viii. 12) there follows a plague of excessive heat. The sun receives power (*ἐδόθη αὐτῷ*, cf. vii. 2, viii. 3, ix. 5, xiii. 7, 15) to scorch mankind with fire (*ἐν πυρί*, cf. xiv. 10), i.e the temperature rises to fire-heat. For *καυματίζειν*, used of the sun's rays, see Mc. iv. 6, note, and for *καῦμα* Dan.

αὐτοῦ ἐπὶ τὸν ἥλιον· καὶ ἐδόθη αὐτῷ καυματίσαι
τοὺς ἀνθρώπους ἐν πυρί. [9]καὶ ἐκαυματίσθησαν οἱ 9
ἄνθρωποι καῦμα μέγα, καὶ ἐβλασφήμησαν τὸ ὄνομα
τοῦ θεοῦ τοῦ ἔχοντος τὴν ἐξουσίαν ἐπὶ τὰς πληγὰς
ταύτας, καὶ οὐ μετενόησαν δοῦναι αὐτῷ δόξαν. [10]καὶ 10
ὁ πέμπτος ἐξέχεεν τὴν φιάλην αὐτοῦ ἐπὶ τὸν θρόνον
τοῦ θηρίου· καὶ ἐγένετο ἡ βασιλεία αὐτοῦ ἐσκοτωμένη, καὶ ἐμασῶντο τὰς γλώσσας αὐτῶν ἐκ τοῦ

9 καυματι μεγαλω 18 28 79 | εβλασφημησαν]+οι ανθρωποι Q min[40] syrr Ar | το ονομα] ενωπιον A | την εξουσιαν ℵAP 10 12 36 37 49 80 91 96] om την CQ 1 al[pl] Ar | ου] ουχι C 10 ο πεμπτος]+αγγελος (1) 35 36 49 79 87 91 96 186 al vg[cle lipss 4, 6] me arm Prim Andr Ar | εσκοτισμενη ℵ[c.c] Q 28 29 | εμασσωντο Q min[pl] | εκ] απο ℵ 186

iii. 66 εὐλογεῖτε πῦρ καὶ καῦμα τὸν κύριον; on καυματίζειν καῦμα see Blass, *Gr.* p. 91 f. Ἐκαυματίσθησαν οἱ ἄνθρωποι: contrast vii. 16 οὐδὲ μὴ πέσῃ ἐπ' αὐτοὺς ὁ ἥλιος οὐδὲ πᾶν καῦμα.

The moral effect of the visitation was doubly disastrous; men blasphemed God as the cause of their sufferings, and they withheld from Him the tribute of penitence which He demanded. The ἀποτομία of God no less than His χρηστότης (Rom. ii. 4, xi. 22) calls to repentance; but like Pharaoh the sufferers were hardened by His judgements. Andreas has a pathetic illustration to offer from his own experience: ὡς καὶ νῦν ὁρᾷν ἔξεστι πολλοὺς τοῖς κυκλώσασιν ἡμᾶς ἐκ βαρβαρικῶν χειρῶν ἀρρήτοις δεινοῖς ἀσχάλλοντας τὴν θείαν αἰτιᾶσθαι ἀγαθότητα, ὅτι τὰς τοσαύτας κακώσεις τῇ ἡμετέρᾳ γενεᾷ τετήρηκεν. For the phrase βλασφημεῖν τὸ ὄνομα τοῦ θεοῦ (=τὸν θεόν, *vv.* 11, 21) see Isa. lii. 5, Jac. ii. 7, Rom. ii. 24, 1 Tim. vi. 1. Οὐ μετενόησαν is repeated at intervals like a refrain, cf. ix. 20 f., xvi. 11; on δοῦναι δόξαν see xi. 13 note.

10 f. καὶ ὁ πέμπτος ἐξέχεεν...ἐπὶ τὸν θρόνον τοῦ θηρίου κτλ.] The Fifth Plague touches the seat of the World-power, and involves it in Egyptian darkness. With θρόνος τοῦ θηρίου compare ii. 13 ὅπου ὁ θρόνος τοῦ σατανᾶ, and xiii. 2 ἔδωκεν αὐτῷ (sc. τῷ θηρίῳ) ὁ δράκων...τὸν θρόνον αὐτοῦ. The commentators quote Tac. *hist.* iv. 2 "nomen sedemque Caesaris Domitianus acceperat." If a particular place is in view, it is doubtless Rome, but the point is that whilst earlier plagues have seized on the subjects of the Empire, the very seat of government is now assailed; the Empire itself, in its heart and centre (ἡ βασιλεία αὐτοῦ) is covered with a pall of darkness which forebodes death; for ἐσκοτωμένη see ix. 2, note. Meanwhile the effects of the earlier plagues continue. The pain (πόνος = ὀδύνη as in Gen. xxxiv. 25, 1 Regn. xv. 23, Bar. ii. 25, cf. *c.* xxi. 4) caused by the scorching heat of the Fourth Plague, and the malignant sores of the first, was such that men chewed their tongues in agony. Μασᾶσθαι, a word used in Aristophanes and by later Greek writers, occurs in the Greek Bible only here and in Job xxx. 4 ῥίζας ξύλων ἐμασῶντο ὑπὸ λιμοῦ μεγάλου; in Sir. xix. 9 μασήσει, the reading of cod. A, is probably a scribe's error. With ἐμασῶντο τὰς γλώσσας αὐτῶν cf. βρυγμὸς τῶν ὀδόντων used as an indication of intolerable pain in Mt. viii. 12 etc.

As in the case of the Fourth Plague

11 πόνου, [11] καὶ ἐβλασφήμησαν τὸν θεὸν τοῦ οὐρανοῦ ἐκ
τῶν πόνων αὐτῶν καὶ ἐκ τῶν ἑλκῶν αὐτῶν, καὶ οὐ
12 μετενόησαν ἐκ τῶν ἔργων αὐτῶν. [12] καὶ ὁ ἕκτος
ἐξέχεεν τὴν φιάλην αὐτοῦ ἐπὶ τὸν ποταμὸν τὸν
μέγαν [τὸν] Εὐφράτην· καὶ ἐξηράνθη τὸ ὕδωρ αὐτοῦ,
¶ P ἵνα ἑτοιμασθῇ ἡ¶ ὁδὸς τῶν βασιλέων τῶν ἀπὸ

11 τον θεον] το ονομα του θεου 91 syr^gw | εκ των πονων] pr και 130 | om και εκ των ελκων αυτων ℵ | om εκ των εργων αυτων ℵ   12 ο εκτος] + αγγελος 28 35 36 49 79 87 91 96 186 al vg^cle dem lipss 4, 6 me arm Tyc Prim Andr Ar | αυτου την φιαλην 6 7 13 14 27 32 38 42 92 97 | τον ποταμον τον μεγαν] τον μεγαν ποταμον 186 | τον Ευφρατην AC 1 14 18 23 34 35 47 51 79 80 87 95 121] om τον ℵPQ 2 6 7 13 29 30 31 32 36 130 al^plq 20 Ar | των βασιλεων] τω βασιλει (*regi*) *g* Prim

the judgement produced no moral change, but drove men to worse sin; they blasphemed, they did not repent. Τὸν θεὸν τοῦ οὐρανοῦ, as in Dan. ii. 44 (אֱלָהּ שְׁמַיָּא), cf. Bevan *ad loc.*; the phrase recalls the pride of the rulers of old Babylon and their vain resistance to the God of Israel. For the use of ἐκ in ἐκ τῶν πόνων, ἐκ τῶν ἑλκῶν, cf. viii. 13 οὐαὶ...ἐκ τῶν λοιπῶν φωνῶν κτλ., and on ἕλκος see *v.* 2, note. On οὐ μετεν. ἐκ τῶν ἔργων αὐτῶν compare ix. 20 f., notes; without the addition of τῶν χειρῶν the phrase is indefinite, and may include both the idolatries and the immoralities of heathendom.

12. καὶ ὁ ἕκτος ἐξέχεεν...ἐπὶ τὸν ποταμὸν...Εὐφράτην] It is significant that the Euphrates is named in connexion with both the Sixth Trumpet and the Sixth Bowl, see ix. 14, note. The Sixth Trumpet loosed the angels who were detained at the river, and who when released set in motion an enormous host (*ib.* 16). The Sixth Bowl drains the bed of the river, and thus opens the way for the advance of the 'Kings from the East,' the *avant-coureurs* of the forces flocking to the last war (*infra, v.* 14). In both cases a barrier which checks for a time the progress of events is at length removed, while in the present instance the mention of the East points to events expected to arise on the eastern frontier of the Empire.

Καὶ ἐξηράνθη τὸ ὕδωρ αὐτοῦ. More than one O.T. miracle and more than one prophecy may be in view. The drying of the Red Sea (Ex. xiv. 21 ἐποίησεν τὴν θάλασσαν ξηράν), and of the Jordan (Jos. iii. 17 διέβαινον διὰ ξηρᾶς) had suggested such prophecies as Isa. xi. 15 ἐρημώσει Κύριος τὴν θάλασσαν Αἰγύπτου καὶ ἐπιβαλεῖ τὴν χεῖρα αὐτοῦ ἐπὶ τὸν ποταμὸν καὶ πατάξει ἑπτὰ φάραγγας· ὥστε διαπορεύεσθαι κτλ., Jer. xxviii. (li.) 36 ἐρημώσω τὴν θάλασσαν αὐτῆς καὶ ξηρανῶ τὴν πηγὴν αὐτῆς, Zech. x. 11 διελεύσονται ἐν θαλάσσῃ στενῇ...καὶ ξηρανθήσεται πάντα τὰ βάθη ποταμῶν, and were probably in the Apocalyptist's thoughts. It is possible that his mind runs also on the story told by Herodotus (i. 191) of the capture of Babylon by Cyrus, who marched into the city across the drained bed of the Euphrates; a new Babylon is to be surprised, and the drying up of the river marks the removal of the last obstacle to its fall.

Ἵνα ἑτοιμασθῇ ἡ ὁδὸς τῶν βασιλέων τῶν ἀπὸ ἀνατολῆς ἡλίου. Prim.: "venienti regi ab oriente sole"; cf. Commodian, *carm. apol.* 9. 5 f.: "siccatur fluvius Euphrates denique totus, | ut via paretur regi cum gentibus illis." The expected invasion of the Empire by the Parthian satraps (or according to

ἀνατολῆς ἡλίου. [13]καὶ εἶδον ἐκ τοῦ στόματος τοῦ 13
δράκοντος καὶ ἐκ τοῦ στόματος τοῦ θηρίου καὶ ἐκ τοῦ

12 ανατολων A 1 6 28 38 49 79 91 96 186 syr^{gw} 13 ειδον C min^{pl}] ιδον AQ 7 14 36 92 130 186 εδοθη ℵ | om εκ του στοματος του δρακοντος και C 9 27 29 aeth om εκ τ. στ. τ. δρακ. κ. εκ τ. στ. του θηριου ℵ* om εκ τ. σ̓τ. του θηριου 36

the reading of Primasius, the Parthian king) was at least present to the writer's thoughts. Until Parthia was reduced by Trajan and his successors, the Arsacidae not only offered a stubborn resistance to the Roman advance but from time to time caused serious alarm, which was increased by the popular legend of Nero's impending return at the head of a Parthian host; cf. *Orac. Sibyll.* iv. 137 sqq. *ἐς δὲ δύσιν τότε νεῖκος ἐγειρόμενον πολέμοιο | ἥξει καὶ Ῥώμης ὁ φυγάς, μέγα ἔγχος ἀείρας, | Εὐφρήτην διαβὰς πολλαῖς ἅμα μυριάδεσσιν*; v. 363 *ἥξει δ' ἐκ περάτων γαίης μητροκτόνος ἀνήρ | ...ὃς πᾶσαν γαῖαν καθελεῖ καὶ πάντα κρατήσει.* The legend supplies at least in part the imagery under which the Seer imagines the gathering of the powers from East and West for the coming struggle.

For *ἑτοιμάζειν τὴν ὁδόν* see Isa. xl. 3 *ἑτοιμάσατε τὴν ὁδὸν Κυρίου* (Mc. i. 3, Lc. i. 76, iii. 4), and for *ἀπὸ ἀνατολῆς ἡλίου* cf. vii. 2, note.

13. *καὶ εἶδον ἐκ τοῦ στόματος τοῦ δράκοντος κτλ.*] The Dragon is doubtless the *δράκων πυρρὸς μέγας* of xii. 3, identified with Satan (*ib.* 9), the Great Adversary who is behind the whole movement about to be described. Similarly the Wild Beast is the Beast of xiii. 1—called *τὸ θηρίον τὸ πρῶτον* in xiii. 12, but thenceforward simply *τὸ θ.* (xiii. 14 ff., xiv. 9, 11, xv. 2, xvi. 2, 10), i.e. the brute force of the World-power represented by the Roman Empire. Of the False Prophet we have not heard before under that name; but his association here and in xix. 20, xx. 10, with the first Wild Beast points to the second Beast of xiii. 11, and the identification is completed by the description in xix. 20 *ὁ ποιήσας τὰ σημεῖα ἐνώπιον αὐτοῦ κτλ.*, compared with xiii. 14 *πλανᾷ τοὺς κατοικοῦντας ἐπὶ τῆς γῆς διὰ τὰ σημεῖα ἃ ἐδόθη αὐτῷ ποιῆσαι ἐνώπιον τοῦ θηρίου.* The *ψευδοπροφήτης*, then, is the false spiritual power which made common cause with the temporal power in doing Satan's work; cf. xiii. 11 ff., notes.

Professor Ramsay (*Letters to the Seven Churches*, pp. 97, 101 ff.) holds that the Second Beast and the False Prophet are to be distinguished, and that the former is "the Province of Asia in its double aspect of civil and religious administration," and the latter "some definite person who exercised most influence in some part of Asia and was the leading spirit in performing the miracles and signs...as real as the prophetess of Thyatira." He suggests the name of Apollonius of Tyana. But (1) the book itself identifies the False Prophet with the Second Beast; (2) an individual could scarcely be placed in the same category with the Dragon and the Beast. On the other hand it is not impossible that such a person as Apollonius was in the mind of the Seer when he described the pagan priesthood and its influence as *ὁ ψευδοπροφήτης*; it was through such men that their power over the people of Asia was secured.

Ψευδοπροφήτης, a LXX. rendering of נָבִיא in Zech. xiii. 2, and frequently in Jeremiah, is used in the N.T. of pretenders to inspiration, or persons Satanically inspired, whether before or after Christ (Mt. vii. 15, Mc. xiii. 22, note, Lc. vi. 26, 2 Pet. ii. 1, 1 Jo. iv. 1; cf. *Didache* xi. 9). The nearest parallel to the Apocalyptic use of the term is found in Acts xiii. 6 *ἄνδρα τινὰ*

στόματος τοῦ ψευδοπροφήτου πνεύματα τρία ἀκά-
¶ C 14 θαρτα¶, ὡς βάτραχοι· [14]εἰσὶν γὰρ πνεύματα δαιμονίων

13 ως βατραχοι] ως (ωσει ℵ*) βατραχους ℵ* 18 36 38 49** 97 Ar ομοια βατραχοις 1** (om 1*) 14 δαιμονων 1 28 36 38 49 79 186 al

μάγον ψευδοπροφήτην Ἰουδαῖον, ᾧ ὄνομα Βαριησοῦς. Ὁ ψευδοπρ., like ὁ ἀντίχριστος (1 Jo. ii. 22, iv. 3, 2 Jo. 7), covers a whole class—magic-vendors, religious impostors, fanatics, whether deceivers or deceived, regarded as persons who falsely interpret the Mind of God. True religion has no worse enemies, and Satan no better allies.

Πνεύματα τρία ἀκάθαρτα, ὡς βάτραχοι. Three unclean spirits come forth out of the mouths of the three evil powers, one from each. The mouth as the organ of speech, the chief source of human influence, is frequently in the Apoc. the instrument of good or evil; cf. i. 16 (xix. 15, 21), ix. 17 f., xi. 5, xii. 15. The metaphor is specially appropriate here in view of the double sense of πνεῦμα (cf. 2 Th. ii. 8 τῷ πνεύματι τοῦ στόματος αὐτοῦ); the three hostile powers breathed forth evil influences. On πνεῦμα ἀκάθαρτον see Mc. i. 23 ff. note, iii. 11, v. 2 ff., Acts v. 16, viii. 7. Christ expelled unclean spirits, but His enemies send them forth, the False Prophet not less than the Dragon or the Beast; cf. Zech. xiii. 2 τοὺς ψευδοπροφήτας καὶ τὸ πνεῦμα τὸ ἀκάθαρτον. Ὡς βάτραχοι: to the Seer the spirits took the form of frogs—a reference perhaps to the Egyptian plague (Ex. viii. 5 (1) ff., Ps. lxxvii. (lxxviii.) 45, civ. (cv.) 30, Sap. xix. 10), with a side glance at the law of clean and unclean animals (Lev. xi. 10 ff.). Cf. Andreas: βατράχους...διὰ τὸ ἰῶδες αὐτῶν καὶ βορβορῶδες καὶ ἀκάθαρτον. Philo explains the frogs of Egypt as 'idle fancies': (*de sacr. Abelis et Caini* 69 ταῖς ἀψύχοις δόξαις, λέγω δὲ βατράχοις, πιεσθεὶς ἦχον καὶ ψόφον ἔρημον καὶ κενὸν πραγμάτων ἀποτελούσαις); to St John they are worse, the symbols of impure impulses. Artemidorus comes nearer to our writer: ii. 15 βάτραχοι δὲ ἄνδρας γόητας καὶ βωμολόχους προσημαίνουσι. The ceaseless, aimless, βρεκεκεκὲξ κοὰξ κοάξ of the frog often referred to by ancient commentators (cf. Aug. *in Ps.* lxxvii. 27 "rana est loquacissima vanitas") seems to be beside the mark in this context. On εἶδον ... πνεύματα ... ὡς βάτραχοι see Benson, *Apocalypse*, p. 145 f.

14. εἰσὶν γὰρ πνεύματα δαιμονίων κτλ.] A parenthesis which justifies ἀκάθαρτα, ὡς βάτραχοι: 'unclean, for they are daemon-spirits'; cf. 1 Tim. iv. 1 προσέχοντες πνεύμασι πλάνοις καὶ διδασκαλίαις δαιμονίων. The sequence is resumed at ποιοῦντα σημεῖα, which is to be taken with πνεύματα τρία, 'I saw three spirits issuing forth...working signs.' Σημεῖον is characteristically though by no means exclusively Johannine, while τέρας is used in this group of writings but once and δύναμις = 'miracle' not at all. The false prophet of the O.T. offered σημεῖα in proof of his mission (Deut. xiii. 1 (2)), and the Church was warned to expect such tokens from latter-day impostors (Mc. xiii. 22, 2 Th. ii. 9). From the magicians who withstood Moses before Pharaoh down to such products of the first century as Simon Magus and Apollonius, pretenders to spiritual powers had claimed to work signs, which the belief of the age attributed, not perhaps wholly without reason, to superhuman influence, though the wonders themselves were due to such causes as sleight of hand: cf. xiii. 13 f., notes.

Ἃ ἐκπορεύεται ἐπὶ τοὺς βασιλεῖς κτλ. While the Kings from the East, represented by the Parthian enemies of Rome, are ready to move westwards

ποιοῦντα σημεῖα, ἃ ἐκπορεύεται ἐπὶ τοὺς βασιλεῖς τῆς οἰκουμένης ὅλης, συναγαγεῖν αὐτοὺς εἰς τὸν πόλεμον τῆς ἡμέρας τῆς μεγάλης τοῦ θεοῦ τοῦ

14 α εκπορευεται] α εκπορευονται Q 7 26 36 39 et om α ℵ^{c.a} 130 vg^{am tol} arm εκπορευεσθαι ℵ* 1* (α εκπορευεσθαι 1**) 43 79 80 81 95 186 om me aeth | επι] εις ℵ 38 | της οικουμενης] pr της γης και 1** | om ολης syr^{gw} | συναγειν 130 | εις τον πολεμον] om ℵAQ min^{plq30} Ar om τον 1 36 43 130 186 al arm Ar | της ημερας] + εκεινης Q 1 130 186 al^{pl} syr^{gw} Prim Ar

as soon as the obstacle to their progress is removed, the other rulers of the world are roused to action by impulses from without—the unclean spirits of the Beast and the False Prophet, the lust of power, and the bitterness of a false religion contending with the true—behind both these motives there is the spirit of the Great Adversary, antagonism to the Divine Will. There have been times when nations have been seized by a passion for war which the historian can but imperfectly explain. Such an epoch the Seer foresees, but, unlike any that has come before it, it will involve the whole world in war. Ἡ *οἰκουμένη ὅλη* (cf. iii. 10, xii. 9) is perhaps wider than the simple *ἡ οἰκουμένη* (Lc. ii. 1, Acts xvii. 6, xix. 27, xxiv. 5)—not the Empire only, but the world, so far as the conception could be grasped at the end of the first century.

συναγαγεῖν αὐτοὺς εἰς τὸν πόλεμον τῆς ἡμέρας κτλ.] The Greek commentators interpret this of an internecine struggle between the kings; cf. Arethas: *πρὸς τὸν κατάλληλον συγκροτῆσαι πόλεμον*—a remark which he justifies by quoting Mc. xiii. 8 *ἐγερθήσεται γὰρ ἔθνος ἐπ' ἔθνος καὶ βασιλεία ἐπὶ βασιλείαν.* On the other hand *συναγαγεῖν* points to Ps. ii. 2 *παρέστησαν οἱ βασιλεῖς τῆς γῆς καὶ οἱ ἄρχοντες συνήχθησαν ἐπὶ τὸ αὐτὸ κατὰ τοῦ κυρίου καὶ κατὰ τοῦ χριστοῦ αὐτοῦ*, and *τῆς ἡμέρας...τοῦ θεοῦ* leads to the same conclusion; the war is directed against Heaven, and it will culminate in the final triumph of God. But if so, is this the battle which is described in xvii. 14 and in xix. 19? Probably it is, for the Sixth Bowl does not open the campaign, but merely marshals the forces and places them on the battlefield. The Seer sees the whole process foreshortened, and he expresses it in the terms of his own age; the expected Parthian invasion takes shape in his mind as the first scene in the drama; a general arming of the nations follows, and the end, which is not yet, will be the breaking of the Day of God.

On *τῆς ἡμέρας τῆς μεγάλης* see vi. 17, note; *ἐκείνης*, if genuine, points back to the O.T. prophecies, e.g. Joel ii. 11 *μεγάλη ἡμέρα τοῦ κυρίου, μεγάλη καὶ ἐπιφανὴς σφόδρα*, iii. 4 *πρὶν ἐλθεῖν ἡμέραν Κυρίου τὴν μεγάλην καὶ ἐπιφανῆ*; *ἡ ἡμέρα ἐκείνη* is a Pauline synonym for the Parousia (2 Th. i. 10, 2 Tim. i. 12, 18, iv. 8), which is also called [*ἡ*] *ἡμέρα* [*τοῦ*] *Κυρίου* [*'Ιησοῦ Χριστοῦ*] (1 Cor. i. 8, 2 Cor. i. 14, Phil. i. 6, ii. 16, 1 Th. v. 2, 2 Th. ii. 2); *ἡ τοῦ θεοῦ ἡμέρα* occurs in 2 Pet. iii. 12. *Τοῦ παντοκράτορος* (i. 8, note) asserts the sovereignty of God, which 'that day' will manifest; or if the writer's mind reverted to the original, he may have thought of the hosts (צְבָאוֹת) which would be ranged on the side of righteousness and truth (cf. xix. 14).

15. *ἰδοὺ ἔρχομαι ὡς κλέπτης κτλ.*] A Voice breaks the thread of the Seer's report: whose voice it is there is no need to explain; cf. iii. 3, note. Its special appositeness in this context

15 παντοκράτορος. [15]ἰδοὺ ἔρχομαι ὡς κλέπτης· μακάριος
ὁ γρηγορῶν καὶ τηρῶν τὰ ἱμάτια αὐτοῦ, ἵνα μὴ
γυμνὸς περιπατῇ καὶ βλέπωσιν τὴν ἀσχημοσύνην
16 αὐτοῦ. [16]καὶ συνήγαγεν αὐτοὺς εἰς τὸν τόπον τὸν

15 ιδου] pr *sic enim dixit dominus* arm | ερχομαι] ερχεται ℵ* (ερχομαι ℵ[1]) 38 47 syr[gw] Prim | περιπατει 130 | βλεπουσιν 130 186 16 συνηγαγεν] συνηγαγον ℵ syr συναξει vg[cle] syr[gw] arm | om τον 1° ℵ 14 92 syr | τοπον] ποταμον A | om τον 2° 14 92 | τον καλ. Εβρ. Αρ Μ.] των ωδων 130

arises from the fact that the Seer has seen the gathering of the forces for the war of the Great Day begin.

Μακάριος ὁ γρηγορῶν is one of seven μακαρισμοί in the Apocalypse; see i. 3, xiv. 13, xix. 9, xx. 6, xxii. 7, 14. On γρηγορεῖν see iii. 2, note, and on τηρεῖν, i. 3, note; the whole saying is based on iii. 3, 18, where see notes. Τὴν ἀσχημοσύνην is euphemistically written for τὴν αἰσχύνην (iii. 18); the former word is repeatedly used in Lev. xviii., xx. for עֶרְוָה, which is rendered by αἰσχύνη in Ez. xvi. 36, 38, xxii. 10, xxiii. 10 (B), 18 (B), 29. With τηρεῖν τὰ ἱμάτια αὐτοῦ cf. Ps.-Clem. '2 Cor.' 8 τηρήσατε τὴν σάρκα ἁγνὴν καὶ τὴν σφραγῖδα ἄσπιλον, ἵνα τὴν ζωὴν ἀπολάβωμεν.

16. καὶ συνήγαγεν αὐτοὺς εἰς...Ἁρ Μαγεδών] The Seer resumes his narrative. They (the daemon-spirits) fulfilled their mission; they (not 'he,' as A.V.) gathered the kings together to the great war, as they were sent to do. The Palestinian writer recognises the battlefield—one familiar to a Galilean and a student of Hebrew history. Ἁρ Μαγεδών is doubtless הַר מְגִדּוֹ: the form Μαγεδών occurs in Jud. i. 27 (A) and 2 Chron. xxxv. 22, and Μαγεδώ in Jud. *l.c.* (B); cf. Cheyne in *Enc. Bibl.* col. 3010. Megiddo, *Lejjun*, "which lay on the route of caravans and military expeditions from the Philistine littoral and from Egypt" (*ib.* 3011; cf. G. A. Smith, *Hist. Geography*, p. 391), was the scene of a series of disasters; there Barak and Deborah overthrew the hosts of the Canaanite king Jabin (Jud. v. 19 τότε ἐπολέμησαν βασιλεῖς Χανάαν, ἐν Θανααχ ἐπὶ ὕδατι Μεγεδδώ); there Ahaziah died of Jehu's arrows (2 Kings ix. 27) and Pharaoh Necho overthrew Josiah (2 Kings xxiii. 29 f., 2 Chr. xxxv. 22; cf. Herod. ii. 159). The last of these events burnt itself into the memory of the Jewish people, and the mourning for Josiah in the valley of Megiddo was long afterwards quoted as a typical instance of national grief (Zech. xii. 11). Thus Megiddo fitly symbolizes the world-wide distress of the nations at the overthrow of their kings in the final war.

But why Ἁρ Μαγεδών? The "water of Megiddo," i.e. probably the Kishon, mentioned as the scene of Sisera's defeat, flows through the plain of Esdraelon; Josiah met his death in the plain (ἐν τῷ πεδίῳ Μ. = בְּבִקְעַת מ׳, 2 Chr., Zech., *ll. cc.*; cf. G. A. Smith, *op. cit.* p. 385); no instance is quoted of הַר מְגִדּוֹ elsewhere. But not to mention that Megiddo itself lay at the base of the hills which terminate in Carmel, the form Har Magedon may have been purposely used to bring the final conflict into connexion with Ez. xxxix. 2, 4 (συνάξω σε...καὶ καταβαλῶ σε ἐπὶ τὰ ὄρη τὰ Ἰσραήλ), which is evidently before the writer's mind in xx. 8 ff. On the proposal to write Ἀρ Μ. = עִר מ׳, i.e. the city of Megiddo, see WH., *Notes*, p. 313, and to the parallels which they produce in support of Ἁρ Μ. add Ἁρ Σιών (Field, *Hexapla*, ii. p. 167). Syr[gw.] has simply

καλούμενον Ἑβραϊστὶ Ἅρ Μαγεδών. [17]καὶ ὁ ἕβδομος 17
ἐξέχεεν τὴν φιάλην αὐτοῦ ἐπὶ τὸν ἀέρα· καὶ ἐξῆλ-
θεν φωνὴ μεγάλη ἐκ τοῦ ναοῦ ἀπὸ τοῦ θρόνου
λέγουσα Γέγονεν. [18]καὶ ἐγένοντο ἀστραπαὶ καὶ 18
φωναὶ καὶ βρονταί, καὶ σεισμὸς ἐγένετο μέγας, οἷος
οὐκ ἐγένετο ἀφ' οὗ ἄνθρωπος ἐγένετο ἐπὶ τῆς γῆς,
τηλικοῦτος σεισμὸς οὕτω μέγας. [19]καὶ ἐγένετο ἡ 19

16 Αρ Μαγεδων ℵA 1 7 35 36 38 47 49 79 87 91 95 186 $al^{sat\ mu}$ Andr Ar] Μαγεδδων (sive -δων) Q (14) (92) vg^{fu} syr^{gw} Tyc Prim 17 ο εβδομος] + αγγελος $ℵ^{c.a}$ 1 28 35 36 49 79 130 186 al $vg^{cle\ dem\ lipss\ 4,6}$ me syr^{gw} arm aeth Prim Andr Ar | επι] εις 1 14 28 31 49 79 91 92 96 186 al *in aerem* vg *in aere* Prim | om μεγαλη A 1 12 46 | εκ] απο Q min^{pl} Ar | ναου] + του ουρανου Q 130 al^{pl} Ar του ουρανου 1 12 28 36 47 79 | om απο του θρονου ℵ 186* 18 αστραπαι κ. φωναι κ. βρονται (ℵ) A (Q) 2 13 28 31 40 79 95 130 al vg arm Prim] αστρ. κ. βρονται κ. φωναι 6 7 8 14 186 $al^{plq\ 25}$ syrr Ar φωναι κ. βρονται κ. αστρ. 1 $al^{vix\ mu}$ | om εγενετο 1° Q $min^{fere\ 25}$ vg^{fu} arm Prim Ar | ανθρωπος εγενετο A 38 me arm aeth] (οι) ανθρωποι εγενοντο (ℵ) (Q) (1) (7) (8) 12 14 17 36 79 92 (95) (130) (186) al^{pl} vg syrr Tyc | om επι της γης 7 14 Tyc

ܡܓܕܘ. The fancy of Gunkel that the reference is not to Megiddo but to an old myth, though accepted by Bousset and by Cheyne (*Enc. Bibl.*, *l.c.*), does not merit serious consideration. On Ἑβραϊστί see ix. 11, note.

17. καὶ ὁ ἕβδομος ἐξέχεεν...ἐπὶ τὸν ἀέρα κτλ.] The air which all men breathe (Sap. vii. 3 τὸν κοινὸν ἀέρα), the 'workshop' of the physical disturbances which affect human health and life, is smitten by the pouring out of the Seventh Bowl—a plague of wider significance than the smiting of the earth (*v.* 2), or sea (*v.* 3), or fresh waters (*v.* 4), or even the sun (*v.* 8). The seventh angel's action is followed by a Great Voice which proceeds out of (ἐκ) the Sanctuary, and from (ἀπὸ) the Throne (iv. 2, note), and proclaims that the end has been reached. Γέγονεν, 'it is done,' 'it has come to pass'; cf. xxi. 6 καὶ εἶπέν μοι Γέγοναν, sc. οὗτοι οἱ λόγοι; here the sing. refers to the whole series of plagues now completed, or to the decree which set it in motion; cf. Lc. xiv. 22 κύριε, γέγονεν ὃ ἐπέταξας. The Voice is specially appropriate in this connexion, since these plagues are "the last" (xv. 1); there remain no further manifestations of this kind.

18. καὶ ἐγένοντο ἀστραπαὶ κτλ.] The usual accompaniments of a great visitation; cf. viii. 5, xi. 19, notes; for σεισμὸς μέγας, see Lc. xxi. 11, Apoc. vi. 12, xi. 13. Writing in a century remarkable for the number and severity of its earthquakes, and to men whose country was specially subject to them, St John is careful to distinguish this final shock from even the greatest hitherto known; it was οἷος οὐκ ἐγένετο ἀφ' οὗ ἄνθρωπος ἐγένετο: cf. Mc. xiii. 19 θλίψις οἵα οὐ γέγονεν τοιαύτη ἀπ' ἀρχῆς κτίσεως...ἕως τοῦ νῦν (see note there). The striking phrase is heightened by the pleonastic τηλικοῦτος (Jac. iii. 4, 2 Cor. i. 10, Heb. ii. 3) σ. οὕτω μέγας. Never had the earth been shaken by such throes as these; cf. Hagg. ii. 6 ἔτι ἅπαξ ἐγὼ σείσω τὸν οὐρανὸν καὶ τὴν γῆν καὶ τὴν θάλασσαν καὶ τὴν ξηράν, with the comment in Heb. xii. 27.

19. καὶ ἐγένετο ἡ πόλις ἡ μεγάλη εἰς τρία μέρη κτλ.] In xi. 13 a tenth part of the city falls; here the whole is

πόλις ἡ μεγάλη εἰς τρία μέρη, καὶ αἱ πόλεις τῶν
ἐθνῶν ἔπεσαν. καὶ Βαβυλὼν ἡ μεγάλη ἐμνήσθη
ἐνώπιον τοῦ θεοῦ, δοῦναι αὐτῇ τὸ ποτήριον τοῦ οἴνου
20 τοῦ θυμοῦ τῆς ὀργῆς αὐτοῦ. [20]καὶ πᾶσα νῆσος
21 ἔφυγεν, καὶ ὄρη οὐχ εὑρέθησαν. [21]καὶ χάλαζα μεγάλη
ὡς ταλαντιαία καταβαίνει ἐκ τοῦ οὐρανοῦ ἐπὶ τοὺς

19 *αι πολεις*] *η πολις* ℵ* syr | *επεσαν* ℵ^{c.a} AQ 7 8 28 38 42 49 96** 97 186] *επεσον* 1 6 14 al^{pl} *επεσεν* ℵ* syr | *δουναι*] pr *του* ℵ 28 79 | *το ποτηριον*] om *το* ℵ 95 | *του οινου*] om *του* ℵ | om *της οργης* 14 92 | om *αυτου* ℵ me 20 om *και* 1° 1 | *ουχ ευρεθησαν*] pr *και* 28 79 21 *καταβαινει*] *εγενετο* syr

torn asunder, great fissures dividing it henceforth into three parts; cf. Zech. xiv. 4 *σχισθήσεται τὸ ὄρος... χάος μέγα σφόδρα*. In the former case it was Jerusalem that suffered (xi. 8, note); now it seems to be Babylon, i.e. Rome (xiv. 8, note). But Rome is not alone in her distress; the effects of the earthquake are felt throughout the Empire and beyond it; everywhere the cities of the heathen (*τῶν ἐθνῶν*, cf. xi. 2) are shaken to their fall; this is no local visitation (Mc. xiii. 8 *κατὰ τόπους*), but world-wide.

καὶ Βαβυλὼν ἡ μεγάλη ἐμνήσθη ἐνώπιον τ. θεοῦ κτλ.] The capital had seemed hitherto to have been overlooked in the meting out of Divine rewards and punishments, but her hour has come at last; cf. Andreas: *ὡς ἐκ λήθης διὰ μακροθυμίας εἰς μνήμην ἐλθοῦσα*; Bede: "impius in memoriam Deo veniet, qui nunc dicit in corde suo Oblitus est Deus." The mills of God, if they grind slowly, are never stopped except by human repentance; cf. Jer. xxxvii. (xxx). 24 *οὐ μὴ ἀποστραφῇ ὀργὴ θυμοῦ Κυρίου ἕως ποιήσῃ*. *Μνησθῆναι*, *μνησθήσεσθαι*, passive, occur in Ezekiel (iii. 20 *οὐ μὴ μνησθῶσιν αἱ δικαιοσύναι αὐτοῦ*, xviii. 22, 24, xxxiii. 16 (A)), and the construction is imitated in Acts x. 31 *αἱ ἐλεημοσύναι σου ἐμνήσθησαν ἐνώπιον τοῦ θεοῦ*; in Sirach, middle and passive are used in consecutive lines (xvi. 17: *μὴ εἴπῃς ὅτι Ἀπὸ Κυρίου κρυβήσομαι· μὴ ἐξ ὕψους τίς μου μνησθήσεται; ἐν λαῷ πλείονι οὐ μὴ μνησθῶ*). Dr Gwynn observes that both the Syriac versions have ܐܬܕܟܪܬ, "a rare use of this form in passive sense," corresponding to the rare *ἐμνήσθη* (passive). With *ἐμνήσθη... δοῦναι*, compare xi. 18 *ἦλθεν...ὁ καιρὸς... δοῦναι τὸν μισθόν*, xvi. 9 *οὐ μετενόησαν δοῦναι αὐτῷ δόξαν*.

It is interesting to find Arethas writing in the tenth century: *Βαβυλῶνα οὐ τὴν Ῥώμην λέγω τὴν παλαιάν... οὐ τὸν ἅπαντα κόσμον.. λείπεται οὖν ἑτέραν ὑπονοεῖν Βαβυλῶνα...καὶ τίς αὕτη; οὐκ ἄλλη ἢ ἡ Κωνσταντίνου*. Each age has its Babylon which seems to call for Divine intervention.

20. *καὶ πᾶσα νῆσος ἔφυγεν κτλ.*] The Seer resumes from *v.* 18 his account of the effects produced by the Seventh Bowl. The words recall vi. 14 *πᾶν ὄρος καὶ νῆσος ἐκ τῶν τόπων αὐτῶν ἐκινήθησαν*, where see note. *Οὐχ εὑρέθησαν* (=לֹא נִמְצָאוּ, cf. 1 Regn. xiii. 22, Ps. xxxvi. (xxxvii.) 36, Jer. xlviii. (xli.) 8); compare *cc.* v. 4, xii. 8, xiv. 5, xviii. 21 ff. For a parallel to the whole verse see *c.* xx. 11 *ἔφυγεν ἡ γῆ καὶ ὁ οὐρανός, καὶ τόπος οὐχ εὑρέθη αὐτοῖς*.

21. *καὶ χάλαζα μεγάλη ὡς ταλαντιαία καταβαίνει κτλ.*] In the seventh Egyptian plague there fell a hail *πολλὴ σφόδρα, ἥτις τοιαύτη οὐ γέγονεν ἐν Αἰγύπτῳ* (Ex. ix. 24). So in the great battle of the Bethhorons a hailstorm decided

ἀνθρώπους· καὶ ἐβλασφήμησαν οἱ ἄνθρωποι τὸν θεὸν ἐκ τῆς πληγῆς τῆς χαλάζης, ὅτι μεγάλη ἐστὶν ἡ πληγὴ αὐτῆς σφόδρα.

[1] Καὶ ἦλθεν εἷς ἐκ τῶν ἑπτὰ §ἀγγέλων τῶν 1 XVII.

21 η πληγη αυτης] om αυτης Q arm η πληγη αυτου 12 29 η πλ. αυτη 7 14 28 31 38 al[10] § P

XVII 1 ηλθεν] εξηλθεν A | om εκ ℵ 28 95

the issue (Jos. x. 11 Κύριος ἐπέρριψεν αὐτοῖς λίθους χαλάζης ἐκ τοῦ οὐρανοῦ... καὶ ἐγένοντο πλείους οἱ ἀποθανόντες διὰ τοὺς λίθους τῆς χ. ἢ οὓς ἀπέκτειναν οἱ υἱοὶ Ἰσραὴλ μαχαίρᾳ). Thus a great hail became the symbol of Divine wrath against the foes of Israel; cf. Isa. xxviii. 2 ἰδοὺ ἰσχυρὸν καὶ σκληρὸν ὁ θυμὸς Κυρίου, ὡς χάλαζα καταφερομένη; Ez. xxxviii. 22 κρινῶ αὐτὸν... λίθοις χαλάζης; Sap. v. 22 ἐκ πετροβόλου θυμοῦ πλήρεις ῥιφήσονται χάλαζαι. A χάλαζα μεγάλη followed the Seventh Trumpet (xi. 19), but that which came with the outpouring of the Seventh Bowl was ὡς ταλαντιαία, *grando ingens talenti ponderis* (Prim.), each stone about the weight of a talent. Τάλαντον in the LXX. almost invariably represents כִּכָּר, a round weight ranging from 108 lbs. or less to 130 (B.D.B., p. 505). A stone weight found at Jerusalem in 1891, supposed to be a talent, weighed about 646,000 grains (*Pal. Expl. Fund Statement*, 1892, p. 289 f., cited in Hastings, iv. p. 906). Josephus (*antt.* iii. 6, 7) speaks of the golden candlestick as weighing μνᾶς ἑκατόν, and adds: Ἑβραῖοι μὲν καλοῦσι κίγχαρες (כִּכָּרִים), εἰς δὲ τὴν Ἑλληνικὴν μεταβαλλόμενον γλῶτταν σημαίνει τάλαντον, which gives 631,150 grains (light standard). The talent was afterwards regarded as = 125 *librae* = 631,665 grains (*Enc. Bibl.* col. 4444). Striking a mean between these estimates we get a talent of 636,271 grains. Ταλαντιαῖος, though ἅπ. λεγ. in the Greek Bible, has good support in the later Greek; cf. e.g. Polybius ix. 41. 8 ἦσαν βελοστάσεις λιθοβόλοις, ὧν ὁ μὲν εἷς ταλαντιαῖος; Josephus, *B. J.* v. 6. 3 ταλαντιαῖοι μὲν γὰρ ἦσαν αἱ βαλλόμεναι πέτραι; a comic author quoted by Pollux (ix. 53) ventured to speak of νοσήματα ταλαντιαῖα.

A hail such as this was clearly a visitation on man; the weight of a single stone was sufficient to kill anyone on whom it fell. Even the Egyptian hailstorm killed the herdsmen in the open country; cf. Diod. Sic. xix. 45 χαλάζης ἀπίστου τὸ μέγεθος, μναααῖαι γὰρ ἔπιπτον, ἔστι δ' ὅτε καὶ μείζους, ὥστε πολλὰς μὲν οἰκιῶν συμπίπτειν διὰ τὸ βάρος, οὐκ ὀλίγους δὲ καὶ τῶν ἀνθρώπων ἀπόλλυσθαι. But the moral effect was no better than under the fourth and fifth plagues (*v.* 9 f.); once more there comes the terrible refrain ἐβλασφήμησαν οἱ ἄνθρωποι τὸν θεόν. Even Pharaoh had shewn signs of repentance under the hail (Ex. ix. 27), though he relapsed into impenitence as soon as it had ceased; but the age of the last plague blasphemed while it suffered. Cf. Andreas: κατὰ τὸν Φαραὼ ἔσονται, μᾶλλον δὲ καὶ τούτου σκληρότεροι· εἴγε ἐκείνου ποσῶς ταῖς θεηλάτοις πληγαῖς μαλασσομένου καὶ τὴν οἰκείαν ὁμολογοῦντος ἀσέβειαν, αὐτοὶ καὶ ἐν τῷ μαστιγοῦσθαι βλασφημοῦσιν.

μεγάλη ἐστὶν ἡ πληγὴ αὐτῆς σφόδρα] For the position of σφόδρα cf. Gen. xiii. 13, Deut. xxx. 14, Jud. xii. 2, 1 Regn. xii. 18 (B), Ps. cxviii. (cxix.) 138, Mt. xix. 25, xxvii. 54, Acts vi. 7, and see B.D.B. *s.v.* מְאֹד.

XVII. 1—6. THE VISION OF BABYLON SEATED ON THE BEAST.

1. καὶ ἦλθεν εἷς ἐκ τῶν ἑπτὰ ἀγγέλων κτλ.] Λέγε μοι (writes Hippolytus,

ἐχόντων τὰς ἑπτὰ φιάλας, καὶ ἐλάλησεν μετ' ἐμοῦ
λέγων Δεῦρο, δείξω σοι τὸ κρίμα τῆς πόρνης τῆς
2 μεγάλης τῆς καθημένης ἐπὶ ὑδάτων πολλῶν, ²μεθ' ἧς
ἐπόρνευσαν οἱ βασιλεῖς τῆς γῆς, καὶ ἐμεθύσθησαν οἱ
κατοικοῦντες τὴν γῆν ἐκ τοῦ οἴνου τῆς πορνείας αὐτῆς.
3 ³καὶ ἀπήνεγκέν με εἰς ἔρημον ἐν πνεύματι. καὶ εἶδον

1 ελαλ. μετ εμου λεγων]+μοι 1 28 79 130 al aeth ελαλ. μοι λεγων Hipp *dixit mihi* Prim | δειξω] pr και 130 | υδατων πολλων ℵAP 1 12 28 33 95 al] των υδατων των π. Q min^pl Ar   2 επορνευσαν] εποιησαν πορνιαν ℵ   3 om εν 2 19 26 29 30 33 40 al | ειδον ℵP min^pl] ιδον Q 7 130 186 ιδα A

de Antichr. 36), μακάριε Ἰωάννη, ἀπόστολε καὶ μαθητὰ τοῦ κυρίου, τί εἶδες καὶ ἤκουσας περὶ Βαβυλῶνος, and the reader of the Apocalypse who has reached this chapter reciprocates the demand. Twice already he has been told that Babylon is doomed (xiv. 8, xvi. 19), but the Seer has given no clue to the meaning of the name, and no description of the city or its downfall. These are to form the subject of a new revelation (xvii.—xviii.) which St John now receives under the guidance of an Angel, one of the Seven who had been charged with the Plague-bowls (τῶν ἐχόντων = οἳ εἶχον; cf. xv. 1, 6, xxi. 9). For ἐλάλησεν μετ' ἐμοῦ see i. 12, and for δείξω σοι, iv. 1; the phrase as a whole is repeated in xxi. 9.

τὸ κρίμα τῆς πόρνης κτλ.] Cf. Jer. xxviii. (li.) 9 ἤγγικεν εἰς οὐρανὸν τὸ κρίμα αὐτῆς (*sc.* τῆς Βαβυλῶνος). St John has heard the sentence pronounced, and is now to see it carried into effect. On τῆς πόρνης see xiv. 8, note; cf. Primasius: "*meretricem* vocans, quia relicto Creatore daemonibus se prostituit"—one reason, doubtless, for the use of the name, but not that which the Apocalyptist has chiefly in view, as the next verse will shew. Τῆς καθημένης ἐπὶ ὑδάτων πολλῶν is borrowed from Jer. xxviii. (li.) 12 f. ποιήσει Κύριος ἃ ἐλάλησεν ἐπὶ τοὺς κατοικοῦντας Βαβυλῶνα, κατασκηνοῦντας (κατασκηνοῦσα, Q) ἐφ' ὕδασι πολλοῖς; the significance of the phrase as applied to the New Babylon appears below, *v.* 15. For καθῆσθαι = κατοικεῖν, κατασκηνοῦν, see xiv. 6, note.

2. μεθ' ἧς ἐπόρνευσαν οἱ βασιλεῖς τῆς γῆς κτλ.] Again the imagery comes from the O.T.; see note on *c.* xiv. 8. The clause is repeated in *c.* xviii. 3; οἱ βασιλεῖς τῆς γῆς or τῆς οἰκουμένης is an Apocalyptic phrase for human rulers in general, as contrasted with the Παντοκράτωρ (i. 5, vi. 15, xvi. 14, xxi. 24), or, as here and in xvii. 18, xviii. 3, 9, xix. 19, with the rulers of territories which had been absorbed into the Empire or were allied to it, and promoted its ends. The πορνεία of which these kings were guilty consisted in purchasing the favour of Rome by accepting her suzerainty and with it her vices and idolatries. Ἐμεθύσθησαν (cf. Jo. ii. 10 ὅταν μεθυσθῶσιν), answers to πεπότικεν in xiv. 8; if Rome was the temptress, the nations and their rulers had shewn themselves ready to comply. Few such kings remained within the Empire; but St John is speaking of the past. He could remember e.g. the princes of the Herod family.

3. καὶ ἀπήνεγκέν με εἰς ἔρημον ἐν πνεύματι] The angel-guide not only invites (δεῦρο), but carries the Seer away, transporting him to the scene of the vision. The verb is used of the ministry of angels at the moment of death (Lc. xvi. 22 ἐγένετο δὲ ἀποθανεῖν τὸν πτωχὸν καὶ ἀπενεχθῆναι αὐτὸν

γυναῖκα καθημένην ἐπὶ θηρίον κόκκινον, γέμοντα ὀνό-

3 κοκκινον] κογκινον Q (item *v.* 4) | γεμοντα ℵ*AP] γεμον Q 1 6 28 31 35 36 130 186 al syr[gw] Hipp Andr Ar

ὑπὸ τῶν ἀγγέλων εἰς τὸν κόλπον Ἀβραάμ), or during an ecstasy (as here and in xxi. 10): for the latter cf. Bel 36 ἐπελάβετο ὁ ἄγγελος Κυρίου τῆς κορυφῆς αὐτοῦ καὶ βαστάσας τῆς κόμης τῆς κεφαλῆς αὐτοῦ ἔθηκεν αὐτὸν εἰς Βαβυλῶνα; *Ev. sec. Hebr.* (ap. Orig. *in Ioann.* t. ii. 6) ἄρτι ἔλαβέ με ἡ μήτηρ μου τὸ ἅγιον πνεῦμα ἐν μιᾷ τῶν τριχῶν μου, καὶ ἀπήνεγκέ με εἰς τὸ ὄρος τὸ μέγα Θαβώρ; and St Paul's ἡρπάγη εἰς τὸν παράδεισον (2 Cor. xii. 4). The Desert into which the Seer is transported is not the retirement and solitude of the inner life (xii. 6, 14, notes), for he would not have found the vision of Babylon there, but the desolation of a life without God (Primasius: "desertum ponit divinitatis absentiam, cuius praesentia paradisus est"). Or possibly it anticipates the time when the busy suburbs and neighbourhood of the city will be left without inhabitant; cf. Isa. xiv. 23 θήσω τὴν Βαβυλωνίαν ἔρημον. Or εἰς ἔρημον may have been suggested by the heading to Isa. xxi. מַשָּׂא מִדְבַּר־יָם, which the LXX. render simply τὸ ὅραμα τῆς ἐρήμου. For the vision of the New Babylon the Seer is carried into a desert; for the vision of the New Jerusalem he ascends a mountain (xxi. 10, note).

The movement took place ἐν πνεύματι, i.e. in the sphere of the Seer's spirit, impelled by the Spirit of God; cf. i. 10, iv. 2, notes. St John does not share St Paul's doubt: εἴτε ἐν σώματι οὐκ οἶδα, εἴτε ἐκτὸς (*v.* 4 χωρίς) τοῦ σώματος οὐκ οἶδα (2 Cor. xii. 2). He probably has in view the frequent ecstasies of Ezekiel; cf. e.g. Ez. iii. 14 f. τὸ πνεῦμα ἐξῆρέν με καὶ ἀνέλαβέν με, καὶ ἐπορεύθην ἐν ὁρμῇ τοῦ πνεύματός μου...καὶ εἰσῆλθον εἰς τὴν αἰχμαλωσίαν μετέωρος, viii. 3 ἀνέλαβέν με πνεῦμα...καὶ ἤγαγέν με εἰς Ἰερουσαλὴμ ἐν ὁράσει θεοῦ, xi. 24 πνεῦμα ἀνέλαβέν με καὶ ἤγαγέν με εἰς γῆν Χαλδαίων...ἐν ὁράσει ἐν πνεύματι θεοῦ.

καὶ εἶδον γυναῖκα καθημένην ἐπὶ θηρίον κόκκινον] The Great Harlot appears riding on a monster which, notwithstanding the absence of the article (cf. ἀρνίῳ in xiii. 11), is doubtless to be identified with the Wild Beast from the Sea (xiii. 1, 14; cf. xix. 20); i.e. the World-power regarded as the enemy of Christ and the Church, and ruling by brute force. On this the Harlot-city reposes; it gives her a proud preeminence, and carries her to victory. The colour of the Beast is now seen to be scarlet, or perhaps crimson. Κόκκινος, dyed with the colouring matter derived from the κόκκος, a parasite of the *ilex coccifera*, represents in the LXX. תּוֹלֵעָה or שָׁנִי, or שְׁנִי תוֹלַעַת, תּוֹלַעַת שָׁנִי (see the lexicons *s.vv.*); the colour was much used for textile materials; cf. Num. iv. 8 ἐπιβαλοῦσιν ἐπ' αὐτὴν (sc. τὴν τράπεζαν τὴν προκειμένην) ἱμάτιον κόκκινον, 2 Regn. i. 24 θυγατέρες Ἰσραήλ... κλαύσατε τὸν ἐνδιδύσκοντα ὑμᾶς κόκκινα, Jer. iv. 30 τί ποιήσεις ἐὰν περιβάλῃ κόκκινον καὶ κοσμήσῃ κόσμῳ χρυσῷ, Mt. xxvii. 28 χλαμύδα κοκκίνην περιέθηκαν αὐτῷ; with it were blended the dark blue known as ὑακίνθινον (Isa. iii. 23; cf. Apoc. ix. 17, note), and the red-blue known as πορφύρα (Ex. xxxix. 13(1), 2 Chr. ii. 7 (6)), while the white of the βύσσος often completed the make-up (2 Chr. iii. 14, Apoc. xviii. 16). A thread or cord dyed with the κόκκος was attached to an object with the view of arresting the eye (Gen. xxxviii. 28, Jos. ii. 18). Thus the epithet conveys the idea of splendour and distinction; the colour it describes enters into the clothing of the woman herself (*v.* 4), while the Beast she rides is completely dyed with it. There is probably no reference to the

ματα βλασφημίας, ἔχον[τα] κεφαλὰς ἑπτὰ καὶ κέρατα
4 *δέκα.* [4]*καὶ ἡ γυνὴ ἦν περιβεβλημένη πορφυροῦν καὶ*
κόκκινον, καὶ κεχρυσωμένη χρυσίῳ καὶ λίθῳ τιμίῳ καὶ

3 *εχοντα* ℵP] *εχων* A 7 28 30 81 94 *εχον* Q 1 130 186 al[pl] | om *κεφ. επτα και* 1 | *κερατα δεκα*] his accessit *v.* 18 ap P 38 (ex Andr comm) 4 *πορφυραν* 1 6 12 28 36 186 al Andr Ar | om *και* 3° PQ min[plq30] syr[gw] (hab ℵA 1 7 18 23 31 36 38 43 al *g* vg me syr arm Cypr Tyc Prim al | *χρυσιω* AQ 130 al[30] Ar] *χρυσω* ℵP 1 28 36 38 49 79 91 95 96 186 al Hipp | *λιθους τιμιους* syrr

blood of the martyrs, or to the fires in which they perished; in either case *πυρρός* would have been more appropriate (cf. vi. 4, xii. 3); rather it is the ostentatious magnificence of the Empire which is represented by the colour of the Beast (cf. Juv. iii. 283 f. "cavet hunc, quem coccina laena | vitari iubet et comitum longissimus ordo"), while its very name indicates its policy of persecution (Andreas: *ὠμότητος γὰρ καὶ ἀγριότητος καὶ φονικῆς γνώμης τό τε θηρίον καὶ τὸ κόκκινον γνώρισμα*).

γέμοντα ὀνόματα βλασφημίας κτλ.] The Seer personifies the Beast and writes *γέμοντα...ἔχοντα* accordingly; *γέμον, ἔχον*, are obviously corrections. *Γέμειν* governs a gen. elsewhere in the Apoc. (iv. 6, 8, v. 8, xv. 7, xxi. 9), in the rest of the N.T. (Mt. xxiii. 27, Lc. xi. 39, Rom. iii. 14, cf. Mt. xxiii. 25 *γέμουσιν ἐξ ἁρπαγῆς*) and in the LXX.; on the acc. here see WM., p. 287, and for the construction in *v.* 4, see below. For *ὀνόματα βλασφ.* cf. xiii. 1, note; there they stand on the Beast's seven heads, here they cover his body. The Empire reeked with the blasphemous worship of the Emperors; not its heads only but the whole body politic did this dishonour to the Living God. It is a first charge against Babylon that she is supported by a system such as this. *Ἔχοντα κεφαλὰς ἑπτὰ καὶ κέρατα δέκα*, as in xiii. 1; for the interpretation see *vv.* 9 f., 12, notes.

4. *καὶ ἡ γυνὴ ἦν περιβεβλημένη πορφυροῦν καὶ κόκκινον κτλ.*] In Babylon's clothing the scarlet or crimson is relieved by purple. The colours were so near to one another that the *χλαμὺς κοκκίνη* of Mt. xxvii. is called *πορφύρα* or *ἱμάτιον πορφυροῦν* in Mc. xv. 17, 20, Jo. xix. 2, 5; here they blend, but are distinct, as in Ex. xxvi. 1 *ποιήσεις δέκα αὐλαίας ἐκ...πορφύρας καὶ κοκκίνου κεκλωσμένου*. On *πορφύρα*, "the colour of clotted blood," see Mayor on Juv. i. 27. Andreas regards it as symbolizing the imperial power of Rome (*κόκκινον δὲ καὶ πορφύραν περιβέβληται ὡς τῆς ἡγεμονίας τῆς κατὰ πάντων σύμβολα*) but mixed with crimson perhaps it rather points to the luxurious living of the metropolis (cf. Lc. xvi. 19) than to its being the seat of empire. St John shares the old Roman dislike of rich attire: cf. Juv. xiv. 187 ff. "peregrina ignotaque nobis | ad scelus atque nefas, quaecumque est, purpura ducit."

The whole passage was used by the Carthaginian Fathers as a persuasive against the love of dress; cf. Tert. *de cult. fem.* ii. 12 "quam maledicta sunt sine quibus non potuit maledicta et prostituta describi"; Cyprian *de hab. virg.* 12 "fugiant castae virgines et pudicae incestarum cultus, habitus impudicarum, lupanarum insignia, ornamenta meretricum."

καὶ κεχρυσωμένη χρυσίῳ κτλ.] Not content with costly and splendid clothing, Babylon wears all her jewellery and even gilds her person (cf. Ex. xxvi. 37 *χρυσώσεις αὐτοὺς χρυσίῳ*); she is *inaurata auro*—a meretricious display which proclaims her vile trade; cf. Juv. vi. 122 f. (quoted in note on

μαργαρίταις, ἔχουσα ποτήριον χρυσοῦν εν τῇ χειρὶ
αὐτῆς γέμον βδελυγμάτων καὶ τὰ ἀκάθαρτα τῆς
πορνείας αὐτῆς· ⁵καὶ ἐπὶ τὸ μέτωπον αὐτῆς ὄνομα 5

4 om εχουσα...της πορνειας αυτης P | γεμον] γεμων ℵ* 7 30 32 94 al^{vid} | πορνειας] πορνιας ℵ πονηριας 130 | αυτης 2° A 1 6 7 28 31* 35 36 38 47 49 79 87 91 95 96 al vg aeth Andr Tyc] της γης Q 130 al^{30} me Hipp Ar *totius terrae* Cypr Prim αυτης και της γης ℵ om arm   5 ονομα]+αυτης 130

v. 5). The commentators compare Ez. xxviii. 12, where it is said of the King of Tyre πᾶν λίθον χρηστὸν ἐνδέδεσαι ... καὶ χρυσίον, but the Apocalyptist more probably reminds himself of the finery of the temple prostitutes of Asia Minor, or recalls the reports which reached the provinces of the gilded vice of the capital. Λίθῳ τιμίῳ (אֶבֶן יְקָרָה) καὶ μαργαρίταις depends by *zeugma* upon κεχρυσωμένη, from which the reader must mentally supply some such participle as κεκοσμημένη (xxi. 2, 19). Λίθος is collective, cf. xviii. 12, 16; λίθῳ τιμίῳ = παντὶ λ. τ. (xxi. 19). On μαργαρῖται see xxi. 21, note.

ἔχουσα ποτήριον χρυσοῦν ἐν τῇ χειρὶ αὐτῆς κτλ.] Adapted from Jer. xxviii. (li.) 7 ποτήριον χρυσοῦν Βαβυλὼν ἐν χειρὶ Κυρίου, μεθύσκον πᾶσαν τὴν γῆν. From one point of view a great centre of heathenism and vice is a cup in the Hand of God, the instrument of His righteous wrath: from another the cup is in the hand of Babylon herself, for it is she that prepares and administers it (xviii. 6 τῷ ποτηρίῳ ᾧ ἐκέρασεν). The cup is of gold—another sign of luxury (cf. Juv. x. 26 f. "illa (*sc.* aconita) time cum pocula sumes | gemmata et lato Setinum ardebit in auro")—but it is full of abominations, as the Beast's scarlet body is covered with "names of blasphemy"; its contents contrast strangely with its external beauty; cf. Mt. xxiii. 25 καθαρίζετε τὸ ἔξωθεν τοῦ ποτηρίου καὶ τῆς παροψίδος, ἔσωθεν δὲ γέμουσιν ἐξ ἁρπαγῆς καὶ ἀκρασίας (Lc. τὸ δὲ ἔσωθεν ὑμῶν γέμει ἁρπαγῆς καὶ πονηρίας). Βδέλυγμα, a rare word in the N.T. (Mc. xiii. 14 = Mt. xxiv. 15,—a quotation from Daniel,—Lc. xvi. 15, Apoc. xvii. 4 f., xxi. 27) is frequent in every part of the LXX., where it usually represents either שֶׁקֶץ or שִׁקּוּץ (e.g. Lev. xi. 10 ff., Dan. ix. 27), or תּוֹעֵבָה (so with few exceptions in Deut., 3, 4 Regn., Prov.), in the sense of ceremonial or moral impurity, or an object of idolatrous worship or an idolatrous rite (cf. 3 Regn. xi. 6 = 5 τῇ Ἀστάρτῃ βδελύγματι Σιδωνίων, 4 Regn. xxiii. 13 τῷ Μολχὸλ βδ. υἱῶν Ἀμμών). Both meanings suit the present context; the βδελύγματα which filled the cup of Rome may include both the cults and the vices of Roman life. Καὶ τὰ ἀκάθαρτα τῆς πορνείας αὐτῆς lays special emphasis on the impurities of Rome's traffic with the nations, the imperial and commercial relations in which she played the πόρνη (xiv. 8, xvii. 1, notes).

A striking parallel to a part of this picture is to be found in Cebes, *tab.*: ὁρᾷς...θρόνον τινὰ κείμενον...ἐφ' οὗ κάθηται γυνή, πεπλασμένη τῷ εἴδει καὶ πιθανὴ φαινομένη, καὶ ἐν τῇ χειρὶ ποτήριόν τι; ὁρῶ, ἀλλὰ τίς ἐστιν αὕτη; ἔφην. Ἀπάτη καλεῖται, φησίν, ἡ πάντας τοὺς ἀνθρώπους πλανῶσα...ποτίζει τῇ ἑαυτῆς δυνάμει...τοῦτο δὲ τί ἐστι τὸ ποτόν; πλάνη ἔφη, καὶ ἄγνοια.

5. καὶ ἐπὶ τὸ μέτωπον αὐτῆς ὄνομα γεγραμμένον] A name written on the forehead may be either that of the person who bears it (cf. xix. 16, where however the name is written ἐπὶ τὸ ἱμάτιον καὶ ἐπὶ τὸν μηρόν), or that of one with whom the bearer stands in a near relation (cf. xiv. 1, xxii. 4).

γεγραμμένον Μυστήριον· Βαβυλὼν ἡ μεγάλη, ἡ
μήτηρ τῶν πορνῶν καὶ τῶν βδελυγμάτων τῆς γῆς.
6 [6]καὶ εἶδα τὴν γυναῖκα μεθύουσαν ἐκ τοῦ αἵματος
τῶν ἁγίων καὶ ἐκ τοῦ αἵματος τῶν μαρτύρων Ἰησοῦ·
καὶ ἐθαύμασα ἰδὼν αὐτὴν θαῦμα μέγα.

5 πορνων] *fornicationum* (quasi πυρνιων) vg Tyc Prim al 6 ειδα ℵA] ειδον P 186 al[pl] ιδον Q (7) 14 92 130 | εκ του αιματος (1°)] του αιματος ℵ[c.a] PQ 2 6 8 9 14 29 130 al[plq 15] Hipp Ar τω αιματι ℵ* 38 | om των αγιων και εκ του αιματος 130 | om και 2° Q 2 8 9 29 al[20] | om εκ 2° 3 11 31 96 al | μαρτυριων A | Ιησου] pr του 95 *Iesu Christi* Prim om 1 36 130

Here the name and style are those of the woman herself, and there is probably an allusion to a custom observed by the Roman πόρναι; cf. Seneca *rhet.* i. 2. 7 "stetisti puella in lupanari...nomen tuum pependit a fronte" [but the meaning is doubtful]; Juv. vi. 122 f. "[Messalina] papillis | constitit auratis, titulum mentita Lyciscae." Cf. Arethas: τὸ δὲ ἐπὶ τὸ μέτωπον γεγράφθαι ὄνομα, τὸ ἀπηρυθριασμένως δηλοῖ πράσσειν τὰ ἀπαίσια.

μυστήριον· Βαβυλὼν ἡ μεγάλη, ἡ μήτηρ κτλ.] The legend borne by the *titulus* on the Harlot's forehead. Μυστήριον, which stands in apposition with Βαβυλὼν κτλ., is used nearly as in i. 20 τὸ μυστήριον τῶν ἑπτὰ ἀστέρων... οἱ ἑπτὰ ἀστέρες ἄγγελοι...εἰσίν, where see note. The Woman on the Beast represents, is the symbol of Babylon the Great, while Babylon itself is a mystical name for the city which is now the mistress of the world. Her gaily attired, jewelled, gilded person, and her cup of abominations proclaim her to be the Mother-Harlot of the Earth. All the πόρναι of all the subject races are her children; all the vices and superstitions of the provinces were suckled at her breasts. The μητρόπολις of the Empire is the source and fountain-head of its impurities, the mother of harlots, even as the Church is the mother of Christ and His Saints (xii. 5, 17). Cf. Andreas: ἡ δὲ μήτηρ [δηλοῖ] τὸ τῆς ψυχικῆς πορνείας εἶναι ταύτην διδάσκαλον ταῖς ἀρχομέναις πόλεσι. The maternal character of Rome was recognized by the provincials themselves as late as the end of the fourth century, but from a different point of view; cf. Libanius, *ep.* 247 οὓς παρειλήφατε παρὰ τῆς μητρός, οὕτω γὰρ εὖ ποιοῦντες καλεῖτε τὴν Ῥώμην.

6. καὶ εἶδα τὴν γυναῖκα μεθύουσαν ἐκ τοῦ αἵματος κτλ.] As the Seer contemplates the Woman, he sees that she is drunken, not with wine (Isa. li. 2 μεθύουσα οὐκ ἀπὸ οἴνου), but with blood. The dreadful conception is familiar to Roman writers; cf. Cic. *Phil.* ii. 29 "gustaras civilem sanguinem vel potius exsorbueras"; Plin. *H.N.* xiv. 22. 28 "[Antonius] ebrius sanguine civium"; Suet. *Tib.* 59 "fastidit vinum, quia iam sitit iste cruorem." Babylon is drunken with the blood of the citizens of the City of God, the Saints and the Witnesses of Jesus; cf. xvi. 6 αἷμα ἁγίων καὶ προφητῶν ἐξέχεαν, xviii. 24 ἐν αὐτῇ αἷμα προφητῶν καὶ ἁγίων εὑρέθη. On μάρτυς in this book see ii. 13 note. The distinction suggested by the repeated ἐκ τοῦ αἵματος is apparent only, for the saints whose blood was shed were by that very circumstance also witnesses to the Faith; but the repetition serves to enhance the guilt of Rome. She had not sinned in ignorance, for testimony had been borne to Christ by more than one generation of saintly sufferers

[7] Καὶ εἶπέν μοι ὁ ἄγγελος Διὰ τί ἐθαύμασας; 7
ἐγὼ ἐρῶ σοι τὸ μυστήριον τῆς γυναικὸς καὶ τοῦ
θηρίου τοῦ βαστάζοντος αὐτήν, τοῦ ἔχοντος τὰς ἑπτὰ
κεφαλὰς καὶ τὰ δέκα κέρατα. [8] τὸ θηρίον ὃ εἶδες ἦν 8
καὶ οὐκ ἔστιν, καὶ μέλλει ἀναβαίνειν ἐκ τῆς ἀβύσσου
καὶ εἰς ἀπώλειαν ὑπάγειν· καὶ θαυμασθήσονται οἱ

7 του εχοντος] pr και 1 38 79 8 ειδες ℵP min^{pl}] ιδες AQ 7 130 | ην] η A | υπαγειν ℵPQ min$^{fere\ omn}$ vg^{vid} me syr aeth Hipp] υπαγει A 12 80 Ir^{int} syr^{gw} Prim Ar | θαυμασθησονται AP syrr] θαυμασονται ℵQ min$^{omn\ vid}$ Andr Ar θαυμασουσιν Hipp

in the presence of high officials of the Empire. For εἶδα see WH.[2], *Notes*, p. 171.

καὶ ἐθαύμασα ἰδὼν αὐτὴν θαῦμα μέγα.] The Seer had been invited to see the downfall of Babylon; the angel offered to shew him her sentence executed. He expected to see a city in ruins. But instead of this there had risen before him on the floor of the desert the picture of a woman gilded, jewelled, splendidly attired, mounted on a scarlet monster, drunk with blood. It was a complete surprise, the greatest marvel of the entire Apocalypse. Who was this woman? what was the meaning of the Beast? The Seer had lost his clue; he was bewildered by a vision so widely different from that for which he looked. An interpreter is needed, and he is at hand in the person of the angel who had undertaken to act as guide; see *v.* 7.

7—18. THE INTERPRETATION OF THE VISION OF BABYLON AND THE BEAST.

7. καὶ εἶπέν μοι ὁ ἄγγελος Διὰ τί ἐθαύμασας; κτλ.] The Angel has read St John's amazement in his face or it has been betrayed by an exclamation; and he proceeds to explain to the Seer the symbolism of the Woman and the Beast. The two belong to the same μυστήριον; hence τὸ μ. τῆς γυναικὸς καὶ τοῦ θηρίου, not τὸ μ. τῆς γυν. καὶ τὸ μ. τοῦ θ. Τοῦ βαστάζοντος αὐτήν: the Harlot-city is a burden which the Beast—the Empire—has to support; cf. 2 Esdr. xxiii. 15 ἐπιγεμίζοντες ἐπὶ τοὺς ὄνους...πᾶν βάσταγμα. Τὰς ἑπτὰ κεφ. καὶ τὰ δέκα κέρατα: the articles point back to xvii. 3, and ultimately to xii. 3.

8. τὸ θηρίον ὃ εἶδες ἦν καὶ οὐκ ἔστιν κτλ.] The interpreter begins with the Beast, for if the Beast is rightly understood, it will not take many words to explain the Woman. Ἦν καὶ οὐκ ἔστιν: cf. Gen. xlii. 36 Ἰωσὴφ οὐκ ἔστιν, Συμεὼν οὐκ ἔστιν (אֵינֶנּוּ); there is perhaps an intentional antithesis to i. 4 ὁ ἦν καὶ ὁ ὤν. The description seems at first to contradict *c.* xiii., where the Beast is said to have recovered from his deadly wound (*vv.* 3, 14 ἡ πληγὴ τοῦ θανάτου αὐτοῦ ἐθεραπεύθη...ἔχει τὴν πληγὴν τῆς μαχαίρης καὶ ἔζησεν). Here the Beast is represented as having died of his wound (οὐκ ἔστιν), and gone down to the abyss (cf. ix. 1 ff., xi. 7), though he is about to return to life (μέλλει ἀναβαίνειν ἐκ τῆς ἀβύσσου = καὶ πάρεσται), before he meets his final doom (εἰς ἀπώλειαν ὑπάγειν, cf. xix. 20). On this apparent inconsistency see below, *v.* 10 f., notes.

καὶ θαυμασθήσονται οἱ κατοικοῦντες κτλ.] Cf. xiii. 3 καὶ ἐθαυμάσθη ὅλη ἡ γῆ ὀπίσω τοῦ θηρίου, and see note there. The Seer had wondered (*v.* 7) with the amazement of a horrible surprise; the world will wonder and admire. Ὧν οὐ γέγραπται τὸ ὄνομα κτλ. recalls xiii. 8 οὗ οὐ γέγραπται τὸ ὄνομα αὐτοῦ

κατοικοῦντες ἐπὶ τῆς γῆς, ὧν οὐ γέγραπται τὸ
ὄνομα ἐπὶ τὸ βιβλίον τῆς ζωῆς ἀπὸ καταβολῆς
κόσμου, βλεπόντων τὸ θηρίον ὅτι ἦν καὶ οὐκ ἔστιν
9 καὶ παρέσται. [9]ὧδε ὁ νοῦς ὁ ἔχων σοφίαν. αἱ
ἑπτὰ κεφαλαὶ ἑπτὰ ὄρη εἰσίν, ὅπου ἡ γυνὴ κάθηται

8 επι της γης] την γην Q min[fere 30] vg Hipp Prim[vid] | ου γεγραπται] ουκ εγεγραπται A ουκ εγεγραπτο 9 | το ονομα] τα ονοματα ℵP 1 al[sat mu] vg syr[gw] arm aeth Prim Andr Ar | επι το βιβλιον ℵAP 1 6 31 36 49 91 186 al Ar] επι του βιβλιου Q 2 7 14 38 al[20] εν βιβλιω 79 Hipp εν τω βιβλιω 95 | βλεποντες 1 36 43 49 91 96 al[vid] Hipp *videntes* vg Prim | οτι ην το θ. Q min[20]. Ar | και (+παλιν ℵ*) παρεσται ℵ* APQ 6 7 14 186 al[fere 40] Hipp Prim Ar] και (οτι) παρεστιν ℵ[c.a] 1 11 12 16 36 47 79 130 *g* syrr *et cecidit* me om vg[vid] aeth: ϛ καιπερ εστιν 9 ωδε ο νους ο εχων σοφιαν cum antecedentibus coniungunt Q (om ωδε) 14 29 93 94 97 98 al[vid] | ο εχων] τω εχοντι syrr | αι επτα κεφ.] om αι 186 Hipp και ε. κεφ. 95 | om επτα 2° 14 92

ἐν τῷ βιβλίῳ τῆς ζωῆς τοῦ ἀρνίου τοῦ ἐσφαγμένου ἀπὸ καταβολῆς κόσμου, omitting the reference to the Lamb (see note *ad loc.*).

βλεπόντων τὸ θηρίον κτλ.] The admiration of mankind for the Beast is due to his vitality, his recuperative power, his power to reassert his authority when they had believed him to be dying or dead. An Empire which could endure the strain upon its resources and the shock to its prestige and authority sustained by Rome during the period between the death of Nero and the accession of Vespasian might well earn the respectful homage of a world which makes success the gauge of strength and right. The Church alone was not deceived, but could foresee the end. Βλεπόντων is probably not a gen. absolute, but follows the case of ὧν by attraction. Πάρεσται, *ventura est*; the Beast, like the Lamb, has a future *Parousia*; cf. 2 Th. ii. 8 f. ἀποκαλυφθήσεται ὁ ἄνομος...οὗ ἐστὶν ἡ παρουσία κατ' ἐνέργειαν τοῦ σατανᾶ. But the Lamb descends from Heaven, the Beast rises from the Abyss; the Lamb comes to celebrate His triumph, the Beast to receive his final doom. The travesty is complete, and it is to the disadvantage of the Beast.

9. ὧδε ὁ νοῦς ὁ ἔχων σοφίαν] Cf. xiii. 18 ὧδε ἡ σοφία ἐστίν· ὁ ἔχων νοῦν κτλ., where see note. What is to follow will put to the proof the spiritual discernment of the hearer or reader. The formula ὧδε ὁ νοῦς is a call to vigilance and close attention, like ὁ ἔχων οὖς ἀκουσάτω (ii. 7, etc.); but whereas ὁ ἔχων κτλ. follows the words which challenge consideration, ὧδε κτλ. precedes them. As Arethas points out, the wisdom which is demanded is a higher gift than ordinary intelligence: πνευματικῶν ὄντων τῶν ἑρμηνευομένων πνευματικῆς σοφίας καὶ οὐ κοσμικῆς χρεία, φησί, πρὸς τὸ νοῆσαι τὰ λεγόμενα.

The interpretation now begins, but (as the reader has been warned) it is itself an enigma, for which more than one solution may be found. In the notes which follow an attempt is made to offer the explanation which on the whole seems to be the best.

αἱ ἑπτὰ κεφαλαὶ ἑπτὰ ὄρη εἰσίν] No reasonable doubt can be entertained as to the meaning of these words. The Seven hills of Rome were a commonplace with the Latin poets; cf. e.g. Vergil, *Aen.* vi. 782 "illa inclyta Roma | imperium terris, animos aequabit Olympo, | septemque una sibi muro circumdabit arces"; Horace, *carm. saec.* 7 "di quibus septem pla-

ἐπ' αὐτῶν. [10]καὶ βασιλεῖς ἑπτά εἰσιν· οἱ πέντε 10
ἔπεσαν, ὁ εἷς ἔστιν, ὁ ἄλλος οὔπω ἦλθεν, καὶ ὅταν
ἔλθῃ ὀλίγον αὐτὸν δεῖ μεῖναι. [11]καὶ τὸ θηρίον ὃ ἦν 11

9 επ] επανω 14 92 10 βασιλεις επτα εισιν] επτα βασ. εισιν ℵ me βασ. εισιν επτα Q min[20] Ar | επεσον 2 7 13 14 120 al[20] Ar | ο εις] pr και 1 al[vid] vg[lips 4] me arm ο δε εις 96 aeth Hipp Prim | ουπω] οπου 130

cuere colles"; Propertius, iii. 10 "septem urbs alta iugis, quae toti praesidet orbi"; Ovid, *trist.* i. 4. 69 "sed quae de septem totum circumspicis orbem | montibus, imperii Roma deumque locus"; Martial, iv. 64 "hinc septem dominos videre montes | et totam licet aestimare Romam"; Cicero, *ad Attic.* vi. 5 ἐξ ἄστεος ἑπταλόφου. The epithet ἑπτάλοφος is freely applied to Rome in the later Sibyllines (ii. 18, xiii. 45, xiv. 108).

ὅπου ἡ γυνὴ κάθηται ἐπ' αὐτῶν] Cf. *v.* 1 τῆς καθημένης ἐπὶ ὑδάτων πολλῶν, *v.* 3 καθημένην ἐπὶ θηρίον. Rome sits mystically on the waters (*v.* 15) and on the Beast, i.e. the subject races and the Empire, which support her; geographically, as the seven heads of the Beast which carries her suggest, she is seated on the seven hills that rise from the banks of the Tiber.

10. καὶ βασιλεῖς ἑπτά εἰσιν.] But the heads of the Beast have a further significance: they are 'kings' (cf. xiii. 3, note). In Dan. vii. 17 the four kings (מַלְכִין) symbolized by the Four Beasts are interpreted both by the LXX. and Th. as τέσσαρες βασιλεῖαι, and this interpretation is supported by *vv.* 23, 24, where the fourth Beast is said to be the fourth Kingdom (מַלְכוּ or מַלְכוּתָה). But in the present passage, where there is but one θηρίον, and the kings are his heads, no such ambiguity can arise; if the Beast is the Roman Empire, his seven heads are Emperors.

οἱ πέντε ἔπεσαν, ὁ εἷς ἔστιν, ὁ ἄλλος οὔπω ἦλθεν κτλ.] Ἔπεσαν, not simply ἀπέθανον, for at death, notwithstanding his apotheosis, each of the five had in fact fallen from his exalted position; for this use of πίπτειν cf. ii. 5. The vision seems to be dated in the reign of the sixth Emperor. Putting aside the name of Julius Caesar, who though he claimed the "praenomen Imperatoris" (Suet. *Jul.* 76) was a Dictator rather than an Imperator in the later sense, the Roman Emperors of the first century are Augustus, Tiberius, Caligula, Claudius, Nero, Galba, Otho, Vitellius, Vespasian, Titus, Domitian, Nerva, Trajan. It is, however, more than doubtful whether a writer living under the Flavian Emperors would reckon Galba, Otho, or Vitellius among the Augusti. If we eliminate these names, the vision belongs to the reign of Vespasian (A.D. 69—79), and probably, as ὁ ἄλλος οὔπω ἦλθεν suggests, to the last years of that reign, when the accession of Titus was already in sight. Titus certainly fulfilled the prediction ὅταν ἔλθῃ κτλ., for he died Sept. 13, 81, "imperii felix brevitate," as Ausonius (*De ord. xii imp.* 11) cynically remarks.

11. καὶ τὸ θηρίον ὃ ἦν καὶ οὐκ ἔστιν, καὶ αὐτὸς ὄγδοος κτλ.] On ὃ ἦν καὶ οὐκ ἔστιν see *v.* 8, note. The eighth in the series of Emperors indicated in the last note is Domitian. But in what sense could he be described as the Beast ὃ ἦν καὶ οὐκ ἔστιν, or be said to be 'of the seven' (cf. Acts xxi. 8)? The 'mystery' reaches its climax here, and is not resolved by placing a full stop after οὐκ ἔστιν, as WH. have done. A more promising key may be found in the circumstances of the age to which the Apocalypse belongs. 'One of the seven' had left

καὶ οὐκ ἔστιν, καὶ αὐτὸς ὄγδοός ἐστιν, καὶ ἐκ τῶν
12 ἑπτά ἐστιν, καὶ εἰς ἀπώλειαν ὑπάγει. [12]καὶ τὰ δέκα
κέρατα ἃ εἶδες δέκα βασιλεῖς εἰσιν, οἵτινες βασιλείαν

11 και ουκ εστιν] om και 95 Hipp | om και 3° ℵ me | αυτος AP 1 al$^{sat\,mu}$ vg syr^{gw} Prim Andr Ar] ουτος ℵQ min^{plq25} | ογδοος pr ο ℵ 32 41 42 12 ειδες ℵAP min^{pl}] ιδες Q 7 130 186 | βασιλεις] βασιλειαι 130

a reputation which even in the last years of the century made his name a terror. Nero was the very impersonation of the Beast, the head (xiii. 9) which seemed to gather into itself all the worst qualities of the body politic. Nero was gone for the time (οὐκ ἔστιν), but he would return as an eighth, the topstone to the heptad, a reincarnation of the Beast, a *Nero redivivus* though not in the sense which popular rumour attached to the phrase (xiii. 3). Even pagan writers recognized the resemblance between Domitian and Nero; cf. Juv. iv. 37 f. "cum iam semianimum laceraret Flavius orbem | ultimus, et calvo serviret Roma Neroni"; Mayor (i. p. 223) compares Pliny, *pan.* 53, where Domitian is "[Neroni] simillimus," and Ausonius, *l.c.* 12 [Titum]...secutus | frater, quem 'calvum' dixit sua Roma 'Neronem.' In Mart. xi. 33 Nero is supposed by some to stand for Domitian. With St John, living under Domitian and unable to refer to him by name, Domitian takes Nero's title, as John the Baptist who came in the spirit and power of Elijah, is called Elijah by our Lord (Mt. xi. 14, Mc. ix. 13). As late as the beginning of the third century the name of Nero stuck to Domitian at least in Christian circles; to Tertullian he is not only "portio Neronis de crudelitate" (*apol.* 5), but a 'sub-Nero' (*De pall.* 4).

One question remains. How can the date which appears to be assigned to this vision by the writer himself be reconciled with the traditional date of the Apocalypse? It may of course be that the Apocalyptist incorporates at this point an older Christian prophecy, or reedits his own earlier work. But it is equally possible that in the vision of the Woman and the Beast he purposely transfers himself in thought to the time of Vespasian, interpreting past events under the form of a prophecy after the manner of apocalyptic writers. Either of these solutions sufficiently accounts for the change of standpoint which is perceptible when the reader compares xvii. 8, 10 f. with xiii. 3, 8; see note on xvii. 8.

Εἰς ἀπωλείαν ὑπάγει received a dramatic fulfilment. Domitian was assassinated (Sept. 18, 96), after a terrible struggle with his murderers. The tyrant's end was a symbol of the end to which the Beast which he personated was hastening.

12. καὶ τὰ δέκα κέρατα ἃ εἶδες δέκα βασιλεῖς εἰσιν κτλ.] Cf. Dan. vii. 24 καὶ τὰ δέκα κέρατα αὐτοῦ (*sc.* τοῦ τετάρτου θηρίου) δέκα βασιλεῖς ἀναστήσονται, where if the Fourth Beast be Alexander's Empire, the ten horns must be explained either as the kingdoms which arose out of it, or the successive kings of one of the kingdoms of the Diadochi, probably the Seleucidae; see Driver, *Daniel*, p. 101 ff. The Apocalyptic Beast from the sea has also ten horns, which are crowned (xiii. 1 ἔχον κέρατα δέκα...καὶ ἐπὶ τῶν κεράτων αὐτοῦ δέκα διαδήματα), i.e., as the writer himself now interprets, ten kings. These have been taken to represent (1) the Parthian satraps, who according to Mommsen were practically independent rulers; or (2) the subordinate potentates of Asia Minor, or (3) unknown future allies of the Roman Empire; or (4) the seven Emperors already referred to, *plus*

οὔπω ἔλαβον, ἀλλὰ ἐξουσίαν ὡς βασιλεῖς μίαν ὥραν
λαμβάνουσιν μετὰ τοῦ θηρίου. [13]οὗτοι μίαν γνώμην 13
ἔχουσιν, καὶ τὴν δύναμιν καὶ ἐξουσίαν αὐτῶν τῷ

12 ουπω] ουκ A vg^{fu} | αλλα] αλλ PQ min^{pl} Hipp Andr Ar 13 την δυναμιν] om την 14 92 | εξουσιαν AQ min^{25} arm Ar] pr την ℵP 1 29 35 36 49 al Hipp | αυτων] εαυτων 1 syr^{gw}

the three who held rule between Nero and Vespasian. The last suggestion is excluded not only by the contrast of κέρατα with κεφαλαί, but by the plain statement that not one of the ten had yet begun his reign; and the same objection holds against (1) and (2), notwithstanding Bousset's plea that βασιλείαν οὔπω ἔλαβον was true of the Parthian satraps regarded from the Roman point of view. Far nearer to the Apocalyptist's words is the comment of Irenaeus (v. 26. 1): "de novissimo tempore, et de his qui sunt in eo decem regibus, in quos dividetur quod nunc regnat imperium, significavit Ioannes"; cf. Arethas: δέκα βασιλεῖς εἶναί φασιν ἐκ τῆς Ῥωμαίων ἀρχῆς ἀναστησομένους ἐν τοῖς ἐσχάτοις καιροῖς. The 'ten kings' belong to a period which in St John's time was still remote; they belong, as the sequel will shew, to the last days of the Roman Empire, and represent the forces which arising out of the Empire itself, like horns from a beast's head, and carrying on many of the worst traditions of the Empire, would turn their arms against Rome and bring about her downfall. It is unnecessary to press the number in this case; it has been suggested by the reference to Daniel (*l.c.*), and it is a well-known symbol of completeness (*Enc. Bibl.* 5437) which leaves the exact figure uncertain, cf. ii. 10, note. With the indefinite οἵτινες... ἔλαβον cf. i. 7, ii. 24, ix. 4, xx. 4, and see Blass, *Gr.* p. 173.

ἀλλὰ ἐξουσίαν ὡς βασιλεῖς κτλ.] The new potentates, though not Emperors, will in some sense succeed to the position of the Caesars, possessing quasi-imperial powers, which they will exert in concert with the Beast and to the detriment of Rome. With ὡς βασιλεῖς cf. i. 10 ὡς σάλπιγγος, iv. 6 ὡς θάλασσα, ix. 7 ὡς στέφανοι, xiii. 3 ὡς ἐσφαγμένην, xiv. 3 ὡς ᾠδὴν καινήν, xvi. 21 ὡς ταλαντιαία; in such contexts ὡς compares without identifying; the ten βασιλεῖς are not βασιλεῖς in the same sense as the seven, but resemble them. Cf. Arethas: ὡς β., διὰ τὸ ἀνέδραστον καὶ σκιῶδες τῆς βασιλείας αὐτῶν φησίν; the remark of Bede, "*tamquam reges* dixit, quia velut in somnis regnant qui Christi regno adversantur," true as it is, misses the Apocalyptist's point. With μίαν ὥραν compare Dan. iv. 16 (19), LXX., ὥραν μίαν ἀποθαυμάσας, Apoc. xviii. 10, 16, 19 μιᾷ ὥρᾳ. Great leaders and even dynasties and empires have a relatively brief existence, as compared with the world-power of the Beast, though for the time they share his authority (cf. xiii. 2).

13. οὗτοι μίαν γνώμην ἔχουσιν κτλ.] The 'ten kings' are of one mind: cf. *v.* 17. Γνώμη, 'purpose,' as in Acts xx. 3 ἐγένετο γνώμης τοῦ ὑποστρέφειν διὰ Μακεδονίας, 1 Cor. i. 10 ἦτε δὲ κατηρτισμένοι ἐν τῷ αὐτῷ νοῒ καὶ ἐν τῇ αὐτῇ γνώμῃ. The unanimity of the ten appears in their support of the Beast, i.e. in their worldly policy and hostile attitude towards Christ. The Seer entertains no illusions on this point; he does not anticipate that the rise of new and unknown forces will bring any immediate improvement; the Beast will remain, and the new powers will be his allies. With the old uncontracted form διδόασιν, cf. τιθέασιν (ἐπι-, περι-) in Mt. v. 15, xxiii. 4, Mc. xv. 17; the contracted present διδῶ occurs in *c.* iii. 9; see

14 θηρίῳ διδόασιν. [14]οὗτοι μετὰ τοῦ ἀρνίου πολεμήσουσιν
καὶ τὸ ἀρνίον νικήσει αὐτούς, ὅτι κύριος κυρίων ἐστὶν
καὶ βασιλεὺς βασιλέων, καὶ οἱ μετ' αὐτοῦ κλητοὶ

13 διδοασιν] δωσουσι 13 79 80 διαδωσουσιν 33 Hipp *tradent* vg[cle fu dem tol lipss] Prim *dabunt* Tyc

W.Schm., pp. 118, 121 f. *Δύναμις* and *ἐξουσία* are combined, as in xiii. 2; the Beast can rely both on the actual fighting power of his allies and on the moral force which belongs to their position.

14. *οὗτοι μετὰ τοῦ ἀρνίου πολεμήσουσιν κτλ.*] The allies of the Beast must be enemies of the Lamb. As in xvi. 13 ff., the Seer sees the kings gathering for battle. That is one certain fact—*πολεμήσουσιν*, and another is the victory of the Lamb—*νικήσει*; He will conquer the hostile coalitions of the future as in the past He has overcome the solid resistance of a great empire. The Seer produces his reason for this assurance: "for the Lamb is Lord of lords and King of kings." The stately phrase, so familiar to us in Christian hymns, goes back to Deut. x. 17 *ὁ γὰρ κύριος ὁ θεὸς ἡμῶν, οὗτος θεὸς τῶν θεῶν καὶ κύριος τῶν κυρίων* (אֲדֹנֵי הָאֲדֹנִים), and is heard again in the post-exilic Psalms (cxxxv. (cxxxvi.) 3 *ἐξομολογεῖσθε τῷ κυρίῳ τῶν κυρίων*, and during the Maccabean struggle (Dan. ii. 47 *ἐπ' ἀληθείας ἐστὶν ὁ θεὸς ὑμῶν θεὸς τῶν θεῶν καὶ κύριος τῶν βασιλέων* (מָרֵא מַלְכִין); cf. 2 Macc. xiii. 4 *ὁ δὲ βασιλεὺς τῶν βασιλέων ἐξήγειρεν τὸν θυμὸν τοῦ Ἀντιόχου*). In the N.T. St Paul (1 Tim. vi. 15) uses *ὁ βασιλεὺς τῶν βασιλευόντων* in reference to the Father. The Apocalypse, in its usual manner, transfers such titles to the Son; He is (i. 5) the *ἄρχων τῶν βασιλέων τῆς γῆς*; He is (here and xix. 16) *κύριος κυρίων* and *βασιλεὺς βασιλέων*. The words have a special appropriateness if written in the time of Domitian; cf. Suet. *Domit.* 13: "adclamari etiam in amphitheatro epuli die libenter audiit 'domino et dominae feliciter'... pari arrogantia cum procuratorum suorum nomine formalem dictaret epistolam sic coepit; 'dominus et deus noster hoc fieri iubet'"; see Mart. v. 8 "edictum domini deique nostri." If the Roman Emperor, a Nero or a Domitian, could be styled *princeps*, *imperator*, *dominus*, the Head of the Church was more—*princeps regum*, *rex regum*, *dominus dominorum*; crowned heads were His subjects and would one day be put under His feet.

καὶ οἱ μετ' αὐτοῦ κλητοὶ καὶ ἐκλεκτοὶ καὶ πιστοί] Sc. *νικήσουσιν* (as R.V., Benson), not *εἰσίν* (as A.V.). The Saints will share the victory of the Lamb, as they have shared His conflict. *Οἱ μετ' αὐτοῦ* suggests a contrast with (*οἱ*) *μετὰ τοῦ θηρίου* (*v.* 12 f.); cf. xiv. 1, 4 *μετ' αὐτοῦ ἑκατὸν τεσσεράκοντα τέσσαρες χιλιάδες...οὗτοι οἱ ἀκολουθοῦντες τῷ ἀρνίῳ ὅπου ἂν ὑπάγει.* They are known by three notes; they are *κλητοί*, *ἐκλεκτοί*, *πιστοί*. The first two are contrasted in Mt. xxii. 14 *πολλοὶ γάρ εἰσιν κλητοὶ ὀλίγοι δὲ ἐκλεκτοί*; *κλητός* stands often in good company (Rom. i. 1—where see note in SH., 1 Cor. i. 2 *κλητὸς ἅγιος*, Rom. viii. 28 *τοῖς κατὰ πρόθεσιν κλητοῖς οὖσιν*, Jude 1 *τοῖς ἐν θεῷ πατρὶ ἠγαπημένοις καὶ Ἰησοῦ Χριστῷ τετηρημένοις κλητοῖς*), yet it falls short of *ἐκλεκτός*; to have been chosen by God is more than to have been called by Him. In order of time *ἐκλογή* precedes *κλῆσις*, "the calling being the outward expression of the antecedent choosing" (Hort on 1 Pet. i. 1), but in the order of moral significance this is reversed, and *κλητός* is followed by *ἐκλεκτός*. Yet neither of these qualifications exhausts St John's description of those who have part in the victory of the Lamb; though on

καὶ ἐκλεκτοὶ καὶ πιστοί. [15]καὶ λέγει μοι Τὰ ὕδατα ἃ 15
εἶδες, οὗ ἡ πόρνη κάθηται, λαοὶ καὶ ὄχλοι εἰσὶν καὶ
ἔθνη καὶ γλῶσσαι. [16]καὶ τὰ δέκα κέρατα ἃ εἶδες καὶ 16
τὸ θηρίον, οὗτοι μισήσουσιν τὴν πόρνην, καὶ ἠρημω-
μένην ποιήσουσιν αὐτὴν καὶ γυμνήν, καὶ τὰς σάρκας

14 και εκλεκτοι και πιστοι] κ. πιστοι κ. εκλεκτοι 35 79 87 και πιστοι 8 οτι εκλεκτοι κ. πιστοι 1 15 om και λεγει μοι aeth^{utr} | λεγει] ειπεν vg me syrr Tyc Prim | τα υδατα] ταυτα ℵ* 130 ταυτα τα υδ. ℵ$^{c.a}$ | ειδες ℵAP] ιδες Q 130 | ου] εφ ων syr^{gw} Prim | η πορνη] om η ℵ$^{*c.a}$ | λαοι] pr και ℵ 16 ειδες ℵAP] ιδες Q 7 26 130 | om και το θηριον vg^{cod} Tyc | και 2°] επι vg$^{cle\ lipss\ 4,6}$ Ar | ερημωμενην Q 1 49 79 97 186 | om και γυμνην Q* 1 2 3 al^{6} | γυμνην] + ποιησουσιν αυτην Q** min^{30} Ar

God's side no failure is to be feared (Rom. viii. 29 f. οὓς προέγνω, καὶ προώρισεν...οὓς δὲ προώρισεν, τούτους καὶ ἐκάλεσεν, καὶ οὓς ἐκάλεσεν, τούτους καὶ ἐδικαίωσεν...καὶ ἐδόξασεν), on man's part there is no such security (2 Pet. i. 10 σπουδάσατε βεβαίαν ὑμῶν τὴν κλῆσιν καὶ ἐκλογὴν ποιεῖσθαι); the climax is only reached when the 'called' and 'chosen' are found 'faithful.' For πιστός cf. ii. 10, 13.

15. καὶ λέγει μοι Τὰ ὕδατα ἃ εἶδες κτλ.] A new point is reached in the interpretation of the vision; cf. *v.* 8 τὸ θηρίον ὃ εἶδες, *v.* 12 τὰ δέκα κέρατα ἃ εἶδες. At a first glance the point to which attention is now called seems to break the thread of the angel's teaching; but in fact it forms a connecting link between *vv.* 14 and 16. Rome's greatest danger lay in the multitudes which were under her sway, and out of which would arise the 'ten kings' who were to be the instruments of her downfall.

The waters on which the Harlot had been seen to dwell (*v.* 1) represented the teeming and mixed populations of the Empire. Cf. Isa. viii. 7 Κύριος ἀνάγει ἐφ' ὑμᾶς τὸ ὕδωρ τοῦ ποταμοῦ τὸ ἰσχυρὸν καὶ τὸ πολύ, τὸν βασιλέα τῶν Ἀσσυρίων καὶ τὴν δόξαν αὐτοῦ; Jer. xxix. (xlvii.) 2 ἰδοὺ ὕδατα ἀναβαίνει ἀπὸ βορρᾶ, καὶ ἔσται εἰς χειμάρρουν κατακλύζοντα κτλ. The Harlot-city sits on the brink of a seething flood (contrast Ps. xxviii. (xxix.) 10)—the polyglott races of the Empire, her support and strength at present, but if they rose, as at some future time they might rise, the instrument of certain and swift destruction. For the phrase λαοί κτλ. see v. 9, vii. 9, x. 11, xi. 9, xiii. 7, xiv. 6; it rests ultimately on Dan. iii. 4, 29, iv. 1, v. 19, vi. 21, vii. 14.

16. καὶ τὰ δέκα κέρατα ἃ εἶδες καὶ τὸ θηρίον κτλ.] The fall of the City is to come from the new powers destined to proceed from the Horns and from the Beast himself, who will turn against the Harlot he has long maintained. Sudden changes from fierce love to bitter hatred, familiar enough in private history (cf. e.g. 2 Sam. xiii. 15), find their parallel in the history of nations, and the Seer foresees that the downfall of Rome will come in this way. Already within his memory the capital had been twice in one year (A.D. 69) the scene of carnage and plunder; and although the Flavian Emperors inaugurated a peace which had lasted more than thirty years, there were ominous signs of fresh trouble; Domitian had no obvious heir, and his life was menaced by conspiracies; at any moment Rome might be sacked again. But St John looks beyond the end of Domitian's reign to a future which he does not attempt to fix. He has a divine

αὐτῆς φάγονται, καὶ αὐτὴν κατακαύσουσιν [ἐν] πυρί.
17 [17]ὁ γὰρ θεὸς ἔδωκεν εἰς τὰς καρδίας αὐτῶν ποιῆσαι
τὴν γνώμην αὐτοῦ, καὶ ποιῆσαι μίαν γνώμην καὶ
δοῦναι τὴν βασιλείαν αὐτῶν τῷ θηρίῳ, ἄχρι τελεσθή-
18 σονται οἱ λόγοι τοῦ θεοῦ. [18]καὶ ἡ γυνὴ ἣν εἶδες ἔστιν

16 κατακαυσουσιν] καυσουσιν 1 12 36 38 | εν πυρι A min^{pl} Hipp Ar] om εν ℵPQ 35 87 al^{vid} 17 αυτων 1°] αυτου ℵ* (-των ℵ$^{c.a}$) | om την γνωμην αυτου και ποιησαι 18 39 arm aeth | αυτου] αυτων ℵ$^{c.a}$ | om και ποιησαι μιαν γνωμην A 79 80 *g* vg Tyc | αυτων 2°] αυτω A αυτου Q 14 92 130 | τελεσθησονται ℵAP 1 10 12 37 46 49 79 91 96 130 186 al Hipp] τελεσθωσιν Q 7 8 14 29 31 38 al^{30} Ar 18 ειδες ℵP min^{pl}] ιδες AQ 7 130 | om εστιν syr^{gw} arm Prim

vision of forces within the Empire taking shape under the leadership of many who, without the Imperial purple, would possess Imperial powers, and would use them for the destruction of Rome. His forecast was verified by the long series of disasters sustained at the hands of Alaric, Genseric, Ricimer, Totila, the representatives of the hordes which overran the West in the 5th and 6th centuries; not to mention later sieges by less barbarous foes. No reader of the *Decline and Fall* can be at a loss for materials which will at once illustrate and justify the general trend of St John's prophecy.

With his description cf. Hos. ii. 3 (5): ἐκδύσω αὐτὴν γυμνὴν...καὶ θήσω αὐτὴν ἔρημον; Ez. xxiii. 29 ποιήσουσιν ἐν σοὶ ἐν μίσει...καὶ ἔσῃ γυμνὴ...καὶ ἡ πορνεία σου ἐποίησεν ταῦτα. The phrase ἠρημωμένην ποιήσουσιν finds a parallel in *c.* xii. 15 ἵνα αὐτὴν ποταμοφόρητον ποιήσῃ. Τὰς σάρκας αὐτῆς φάγονται: for the metaphor cf. Ps. xxvi. (xxvii.) 2 ἐν τῷ ἐγγίζειν ἐπ' ἐμὲ κακοῦντα τοῦ φαγεῖν τὰς σάρκας μου. Mic. iii. 3 κατέφαγον τὰς σάρκας τοῦ λαοῦ μου. The pl. σάρκες denotes, as in classical Greek, portions of flesh, or the muscles that compose the flesh; contrast the use of the sing. in Jo. vi. 53 ff., where the whole nature of man is intended.

Καὶ αὐτὴν κατακαύσουσιν ἐν πυρί: the legal punishment of certain gross sins (Lev. xx. 14, xxi. 9, Jos. vii. 15). Compare Jeremiah's threat, xli. (xxxiv.) 22 ἐπιστρέψω αὐτοὺς (the forces of Nebuchadnezzar) εἰς τὴν γῆν ταύτην, καὶ πολεμήσουσιν ἐπ' αὐτὴν καὶ λήμψονται αὐτὴν...καὶ κατακαύσουσιν αὐτὴν ἐν πυρὶ καὶ τὰς πόλεις Ἰούδα, καὶ δώσω αὐτὰς ἐρήμους ἀπὸ κατοικούντων.

17. ὁ γὰρ θεὸς ἔδωκεν εἰς τὰς καρδίας αὐτῶν κτλ.] The angel anticipates the objection that the success of such a coalition against Rome is incredible; the ten kings will surely fall out among themselves. They will not fall out, for their unanimity is of God, Who has chosen them as instruments of His Will; and it will continue until His words (i.e. those of the prophets speaking in His Name, cf. xix. 9, xxi. 5, xxii. 6) shall be fulfilled. For διδόναι εἰς (נָתַן בְּ) see 1 Th. iv. 8, Heb. viii. 10 (Jer. xxxviii. = xxxi. 33); for μία γνώμη cf. *v.* 13. Τὴν γνώμην αὐτοῦ, His purpose, His royal decree, a sense which the word often bears in 1 and 2 Esdras and Daniel, where reference is made to the edicts of the Persian kings. Τελεσθήσονται, cf. Lc. xviii. 31, xxii. 37, Acts xiii. 29, Apoc. x. 7.

18. καὶ ἡ γυνὴ ἣν εἶδες ἔστιν ἡ πόλις ἡ μεγάλη κτλ.] Lastly, the Harlot herself receives interpretation. The words leave no doubt that Rome is meant, even if doubt could have re-

ἡ πόλις ἡ μεγάλη ἡ ἔχουσα βασιλείαν ἐπὶ τῶν
βασιλέων τῆς γῆς.

[1] Μετὰ ταῦτα εἶδον ἄλλον ἄγγελον καταβαίνοντα 1 XVIII.
ἐκ τοῦ οὐρανοῦ, ἔχοντα ἐξουσίαν μεγάλην, καὶ ἡ γῆ
ἐφωτίσθη ἐκ τῆς δόξης αὐτοῦ. [2] καὶ ἔκραξεν [ἐν] ἰσχυρᾷ 2
φωνῇ λέγων Ἔπεσεν ἔπεσεν Βαβυλὼν ἡ μεγάλη, καὶ

18 η εχουσα] om η ℵ 90 94 95 | βασιλειαν] pr την P | βασιλεων] βασιλειων ℵ | της γης] pr επι Q** pr των επι 16 39 αυτης 130

XVIII 1 μετα ταυτα] pr και 1 7 186 al$^{sat\,mu}$ vg syr^{gw} arm aeth Prim al | ειδον ℵAP min^{pl}] ιδον Q (7) 14 33 36 92 130 186 | om αλλον 1 14 92 2 εκεκραξεν A | om εν ℵQ min^{pl} Hipp Prim^{vid} Ar (hab AP 9 36 37 42 49 79 91 96 130 189 vg$^{cle\,am\,fu\,dem\,lipss\,5,6}$) | ισχυρα φωνη] + μεγαλη 1 2 Hipp + και μεγ. 36 *fortitudine* vg$^{cle\,tol}$ Tyc | om λεγων P | επεσεν semel ℵQ al^{30} me arm^{zoh} aeth^{utr} Prim Ar ter P | Βαβυλων] pr η Q 14 92 Ar

mained after *v.* 9. Babylon is the Imperial City of the world, the seat of the one great Empire which was left (ἡ ἔχουσα βασιλείαν κτλ.). Cf. Tert. *adv. Marc.* iii. 13, *adv. Jud.* 9 (cited in note to xiv. 8); Aug. *de civ. Dei* xvi. 17 "ante conditam Romam veluti alteram in Occidente Babyloniam," xviii. 2 "ipsa Roma quasi secunda Babylonia est." Even in a series of non-Christian inscriptions (Audollent, *Defixionum tabellae*, inscrr. 160, 161) νέα Βαβυλών seems to occur as a synonym for Rome.

But Rome does not, of course, exhaust St John's conception of Babylon. His vision sounds a note of warning which may well be taken to heart by any great metropolis which prostitutes its wealth and influence to base or self-seeking ends. The city of the Caesars was the contemporary representative of Babylon; other ages may witness the rise and fall of other mistresses of the world not less magnificent and depraved.

XVIII. 1—24. THE DOOM OF BABYLON.

1. μετὰ ταῦτα κτλ.] The Vision of Babylon on the Beast is followed by (1) the descent of an angel who repeats and enhances the sentence of xiv. 8 (*vv.* 1—3); (2) a voice from heaven, which passes into a succession of dirges chaunted over the doomed city (*vv.* 4—19); (3) a call to Heaven and the Church to rejoice (*v.* 20); (4) the fall of Babylon, symbolically executed, and its effects described (*vv.* 21—24).

εἶδον ἄλλον ἄγγελον καταβαίνοντα κτλ.] The Angel of the Doom is not the angel who acted as the Seer's guide (xvii. 1, 7, 15). He comes down from heaven expressly charged with this mission (cf. x. 1, xx. 1); he possesses great authority (xiii. 2), to enable him to enforce his sentence; so recently has he come from the Presence that in passing he flings a broad belt of light across the dark Earth—a phrase used of the Vision of God in Ez. xliii. 2 f. (ἰδοὺ δόξα θεοῦ Ἰσραὴλ ἤρχετο κατὰ τὴν ὁδὸν τὴν πρὸς ἀνατολάς...καὶ ἡ γῆ ἐξέλαμπεν (הֵאִירָה) ὡς φέγγος ἀπὸ τῆς δόξης κυκλόθεν). For ἐκ, 'by reason of,' see viii. 13, xvi. 10 f., notes.

2. καὶ ἔκραξεν ἐν ἰσχυρᾷ φωνῇ λέγων κτλ.] A strong voice (cf. Ps. xxviii. (xxix.) 4 φωνὴ Κυρίου ἐν ἰσχύι, Heb. v. 7 μετὰ κραυγῆς ἰσχυρᾶς), like the voice of the spheres which, inaudible to the ear, appeals to the universal conscience (Ps. xix. 3 f.); for the cry itself see *c.* xiv. 8, note. Ἔπεσεν is still anticipatory, for the actual fall is not yet, but in the Seer's thought the purpose of God has been accomplished already.

ἐγένετο κατοικητήριον δαιμονίων καὶ φυλακὴ παντὸς
§ C πνεύματος ἀκαθάρτου καὶ φυλακὴ §παντὸς ὀρνέου
3 ἀκαθάρτου καὶ μεμισημένου· ³ὅτι ἐκ [τοῦ οἴνου] τοῦ

2 *δαιμονων* P min^{pl} Hipp Andr Ar | *ακαθαρτου* 1°] + *και μεμισημενου* AP 1 12 16 31 36 38 48 79 vg^{tol*} Hipp Ar | om *και φυλακη παντος ορνεου ακαθ.* P 1 7 12 14 31 36 38 48 79 92 vg^{tol*} syr^{gw} Hipp Ar | *ορνεου*] *θηριου* A *spiritus* arm | *και μεμισημενου*] *κ. μεμιασμενου* (vel *-μμενου*) 51 130 *et inquinatae* Tyc om 7 14 92 vg$^{am\ fu}$ 3 *του οινου του θυμου της πορνειας* ℵQ min^{pl} vg$^{cle\ dem\ lipss\ 4}$ syr Hipp Tyc Ar] *του θ. του οινου της π.* P 1 35 36 37 47 49 79 87 91 96 186 me arm *του οινου της π. του θ.* C om *του οινου* A vg$^{am\ fu\ tol\ lipss\ 5,\ 6}$ om *του θυμου* 130 syr^{gw} Prim om *της πορνειας* 33

καὶ ἐγένετο κατοικητήριον κτλ.] So Isaiah writes of Babylon (xiii. 21 f. *ἀναπαύσονται ἐκεῖ θηρία...καὶ ἀναπαύσονται ἐκεῖ σειρῆνες καὶ δαιμόνια ἐκεῖ ὀρχήσονται καὶ ὀνοκένταυροι ἐκεῖ κατοικήσουσιν καὶ νοσσοποιήσουσιν ἐχῖνοι ἐν τοῖς οἴκοις αὐτῶν*), and of Edom in the very similar passage xxxiv. 14 f. Cf. Jer. xxvii. (l.) 39 *κατοικήσουσιν ἰνδάλματα ἐν ταῖς νήσοις καὶ κατοικήσουσιν ἐν αὐτῇ θυγατέρες σειρήνων* (of Babylon); Zeph. ii. 14 *νεμήσονται ἐν μέσῳ αὐτῆς ποίμνια καὶ πάντα τὰ θηρία τῆς γῆς, καὶ χαμαιλέοντες καὶ ἐχῖνοι ἐν τοῖς φατνώμασιν αὐτῆς κοιτασθήσονται* (of Nineveh); Baruch iv. 35 *κατοικηθήσεται ὑπὸ δαιμονίων τὸν πλείονα χρόνον* (of the cities of the Exile). The O.T. prophets fill the ruins of cities hostile to Judah with satyrs (שְׂעִירִים) and the *lilith*; the N.T. Apocalyptist, while he takes over both the conception and the word *δαιμόνια*, thinks doubtless of the demon-powers represented by the idols of paganism (cf. ix. 20, xvi. 14) which will haunt the wrecked temples of Rome, the scene of their old magnificence. The resonant *κατοικητήριον* may be purposely chosen; contrast with *κατοικ. δαιμονίων* St Paul's *κατοικ. τοῦ θεοῦ* (Eph. ii. 22). *Φυλακή*, *refugium* (Prim.), *custodia* (Vg.), is here perhaps rather a watch-tower or stronghold (as in Hab. ii. 1 *ἐπὶ τῆς φυλακῆς μου στήσομαι*, Bar. iii. 34 *οἱ δὲ ἄστερες ἔλαμψαν ἐν ταῖς φυλακαῖς αὐτῶν*), than a prison or cage (xx. 7); the evil spirits, watching over fallen Rome like night-birds or harpies that wait for their prey, build their eyries in the broken towers which rise from the ashes of the city. *Μεμισημένου*: Prim., Vg., *odibilis*.

3. **ὅτι ἐκ τοῦ οἴνου τοῦ θυμοῦ τῆς πορνείας αὐτῆς κτλ.**] Cf. xiv. 10, xvi. 19, notes; and on the accumulation of genitives see Blass, *Gr.* p. 99. *Πέπτωκαν* has overwhelming external support, but can scarcely be more than an early and widespread error, due perhaps to the proximity of *ἔπεσεν* (*v.* 2); both the general sense and the prophetic *usus loquendi* (cf. Jer. xxviii. (li.) 7, 39, xxxii. (xxv.) 14 f.) require *πέπωκαν*.

Two classes would be more especially affected by the fate of Babylon. The ruling class had "committed fornication with her," i.e. were deeply and often guiltily involved in the sins of Rome; cf. xvii. 2, note. The mercantile class would suffer yet more severely by the fall of the city, and the rest of the chapter is largely occupied with the effect of the event on commerce and trade. The writer has in view the graphic description of the collapse of the trade of Tyre given by Ezekiel (xxvi.—xxviii.); cf. also Isaiah's reference to Babylon (xlvii. 15). Allusions to trade in the N.T. are fairly frequent (cf. Mt. xiii. 45, xxii. 5, xxv. 14, Jac. iv. 13), but it is only in this passage that we catch

θυμοῦ τῆς πορνείας αὐτῆς πέπωκαν πάντα τὰ ἔθνη, καὶ οἱ βασιλεῖς τῆς γῆς μετ' αὐτῆς ἐπόρνευσαν, καὶ οἱ ἔμποροι τῆς γῆς ἐκ τῆς δυνάμεως τοῦ στρήνους αὐτῆς
ἐπλούτησαν. [4]καὶ ἤκουσα ἄλλην φωνὴν ἐκ τοῦ 4
οὐρανοῦ λέγουσαν Ἐξέλθατε, ὁ λαός μου, ἐξ αὐτῆς,

3 πεπωκαν (P) (1) 8 31 32 37 (38) 39 47 (48) (49) 50 90 93 (97) 98 186 al vg syr arm Hipp Tyc Ar] πεπτωκαν (vel -κασιν) (ℵ) AC(Q) 7 14 92 al[plq 10] me aeth πεπτωκε 130 πεποτικε(ν) 18 36 37 79 syr[gw] | στρηνου C 47 94 4 αλλην φωνην] αλλης φωνης C om αλλης me arm | εξελθατε (-θετε P 1 32 49 91 95 96 130 186)] εξελθε CQ min[plq 25] Cypr (*exi*) Ar

sight of the vast traffic which carried the produce of the East and of Egypt to Italy, and found its centre in Rome. The merchants of the world had grown rich (*ἐπλούτησαν*, cf. iii. 17, note) by reason of (cf. *ἐκ τῆς δόξης*, *v.* 1) the might of her wanton luxury. *Στρῆνος* in 4 Regn. xix. 28 is the self-satisfied, complacent, arrogance (שַׁאֲנָן, cf. Gwynn p. 80) of Sennacherib, while in Isa. lxi. 6 Symm. uses *στρηνιάσετε* for תִּתְאַבָּלוּ; cf. 1 Tim. v. 11, where *καταστρηνιᾶν τοῦ χριστοῦ* means apparently 'to grow restive under the restrictions imposed by Christian discipline.' In the present context *στρηνιᾶν* (*vv.* 7, 9) is probably, as Hesychius says, *διὰ τὸν πλοῦτον ὑβρίζειν*, and *στρῆνος* is little more than 'insolent luxury' (*deliciae*, Prim., Vg.). It was by ministering to the heartless luxury of the capital that the traders of the Empire made their money. On the extravagant expenditure of the Roman Emperors and aristocracy see Dill, *Roman Society from Nero to M. Aurelius*, pp. 20, 32 f., 55 f., 66 ff., 128 ff., 177 f.

4. *ἤκουσα ἄλλην φωνὴν ἐκ τοῦ οὐρανοῦ λέγουσαν κτλ.*] The Angel's cry is followed by another voice which comes from heaven itself (x. 4, 8, xi. 12, xiv. 2, 13), whether the Voice of God, as *ὁ λαός μου* at first sight suggests (cf. xvi. 1), or that of one of the angels of the Presence, as the character of the whole utterance that follows renders more probable. *Ἐξέλθατε κτλ.* is modelled on several passages in the Prophets which relate to Babylon, e.g. Isa. xlviii. 20 *ἔξελθε ἐκ Βαβυλῶνος φεύγων ἀπὸ τῶν Χαλδαίων*; Jer. xxvii. (l.) 8 *ἀπαλλοτριώθητε ἐκ μέσου Βαβυλῶνος καὶ ἀπὸ γῆς Χαλδαίων καὶ ἐξέλθατε*; xxviii. (li.) 6 *φεύγετε ἐκ μέσου Βαβυλῶνος, καὶ ἀνασώζετε ἕκαστος τὴν ψυχὴν αὐτοῦ*; *ib.* 45 *ἐξέλθετε ἐκ μέσου αὐτῆς λαός μου* (the last cited words, however, are not in codd. BℵAQ*). Cf. also Isa. lii. 11 *ἀπόστητε, ἀπόστητε, ἐξέλθατε ἐκεῖθεν, καὶ ἀκαθάρτου μὴ ἅψησθε, ἐξέλθατε ἐκ μέσου αὐτῆς.* But the cry *ἔξελθε, ἐξέλθετε*, rings through the Hebrew history; we hear it in the Call of Abram (Gen. xii. 1) in the rescue of Lot (Gen. xix. 12 ff.), in the Exodus, in the call to depart from the neighbourhood of the tents of Dathan and Abiram (Num. xvi. 26); an echo has been heard in the command of Mc. xiii. 14. In this context the *sauve qui peut* is to be regarded partly as a feature borrowed from the O.T. models cited above, partly as a warning to Christians at Rome and elsewhere to shun entanglement in the sin and punishment of the new Babylon; cf. 2 Cor. vi. 14 *μὴ γίνεσθε ἑτεροζυγοῦντες ἀπίστοις*, Eph. v. 11 *μὴ συγκοινωνεῖτε τοῖς ἔργοις τοῖς ἀκάρποις τοῦ σκότους*, 1 Tim. v. 22 *μηδὲ κοινώνει ἁμαρτίαις ἀλλοτρίαις.* There is no occasion to look for any single fulfilment in history, such as an actual

ἵνα μὴ συνκοινωνήσητε ταῖς ἁμαρτίαις αὐτῆς, καὶ ἐκ
5 τῶν πληγῶν αὐτῆς ἵνα μὴ λάβητε· [5]ὅτι ἐκολλήθησαν
αὐτῆς αἱ ἁμαρτίαι ἄχρι τοῦ οὐρανοῦ, καὶ ἐμνημόνευσεν
6 ὁ θεὸς τὰ ἀδικήματα αὐτῆς. [6]ἀπόδοτε αὐτῇ ὡς καὶ
αὐτὴ ἀπέδωκεν, καὶ διπλώσατε [τὰ] διπλᾶ κατὰ τὰ

4 *συγκοινωνησητε* PQ | om *εκ των πληγων αυτης* P 130 186 *της πληγης g* syr^{gw} | *λαβητε*] *βλαβητε* 79 130 186 *laedamini* Tyc 5 *εκολληθησαν*] *pervenerunt* vg Cypr Prim *adscenderunt* Tyc | *αχρι*] *εως* P Hipp | *εμνημονευσεν*] + *αυτης* 28 29 35 43 49 87 93 al | *τα αδικηματα αυτης* cum seqq coniungunt min^{pl} 6 *απεδωκεν*] + *υμιν* 1 31 91 96 186 al vg$^{cle\ lipss}$ Tyc Ar al + *ημιν* arm | om *και* 2° ℵ | *διπλωσατε*] + *αυτη* P 17 31 91 130 186 syrr | *τα διπλα*] om *τα* APQ 1 7 31 38 130 186 al^{satmu} Andr Ar

exodus of members of the Roman Church: such a precept is sufficiently obeyed by aloofness of spirit maintained in the very heart of the world's traffic. As Augustine writes (*de civ. Dei*, xviii. 18): "quod praeceptum propheticum ita spiritualiter intellegitur ut de huius saeculi civitate... fidei passibus quae per dilectionem operatur in Deum vivum proficiendo fugiamus."

5. *ὅτι ἐκολλήθησαν...ἄχρι τοῦ οὐρανοῦ*] A reminiscence of Jer. xxviii. (li.) 9 *ὅτι ἤγγικεν εἰς οὐρανὸν τὸ κρίμα αὐτῆς, ἐξῆρεν ἕως τῶν ἄστρων*; this conception is already in Hom. *Od.* xv. 329 *ὕβρις τε βίη τε σιδήρεον οὐρανὸν ἥκει*. Ἐκολλήθησαν ἄχρι τ. οὐρ., Vg. *pervenerunt usque ad caelum*; joined one another till they reached heaven, till the ever-growing mass rose sky-high; for a somewhat similar use of *κολλᾶσθαι* cf. Deut. xxviii. 60 *καὶ κολληθήσονται* (וְדָבְקוּ) *ἐν σοὶ* [sc. *πᾶσαι αἱ ὀδύναι Αἰγύπτου*], Bar. i. 20 *ἐκολλήθη εἰς ἡμᾶς τὰ κακὰ καὶ ἡ ἀρά*, Lc. x. 11 *τὸν κονιορτὸν τὸν κολληθέντα ἡμῖν*, Acts ix. 26 *κολλᾶσθαι ταῖς μαθηταῖς*; the exact construction occurs in Zech. xiv. 5, *ἐνκολληθήσεται φάραγξ ὀρέων ἕως Ἰασόδ*.

Καὶ ἐμνημόνευσεν ὁ θεὸς τὰ ἀδικήματα αὐτῆς: cf. xvi. 19 *Βαβυλὼν ἡ μεγάλη ἐμνήσθη ἐνώπιον τοῦ θεοῦ*. For *μνημονεύειν* followed by the acc. see Blass, *Gr.* p. 104.

6. *ἀπόδοτε αὐτῇ ὡς καὶ αὐτὴ ἀπέδωκεν κτλ.*] The command is addressed of course not to the 'people of God,' but to the ministers of Divine justice, the yet untrained and unknown forces which the Seer saw gathering for the work of destruction: cf. xvii. 16 ff. Several O.T. denunciations of Babylon are in view, e.g. Ps. cxxxvi. (cxxxvii.) 8 *θυγάτηρ Βαβυλῶνος, μακάριος ὃς ἀνταποδώσει σοι τὸ ἀνταπόδομά σου ὃ ἀνταπέδωκας ἡμῖν*; Jer. xxvii. (l.) 29 *ἀνταπόδοτε αὐτῇ κατὰ τὰ ἔργα αὐτῆς· κατὰ πάντα ὅσα ἐποίησεν ποιήσατε αὐτῇ*. The principle of a Divine *lex talionis* runs through the O.T., and asserts itself even in the Sermon on the Mount (Mt. vii. 2 *ἐν ᾧ μέτρῳ μετρεῖτε μετρηθήσεται ὑμῖν*). Even for *διπλώσατε τὰ διπλᾶ* there is abundant support; see the legislation of Ex. xxii. 4, 7, 9, and cf. Isa. xl. 2 *ἐδέξατο ἐκ χειρὸς Κυρίου διπλᾶ τὰ ἁμαρτήματα αὐτῆς*; Jer. xvi. 18 *ἀνταποδώσω διπλᾶς* (B*, *διὰ πάσας*) *τὰς κακίας αὐτῶν*. The same thought, that good and evil return upon the doer with interest which may reach an hundredfold, finds a place in Greek poetry; cf. Aesch. *Ag.* 537 *διπλᾶ δ' ἔτισαν Πριαμίδαι θἀμάρτια*. On the vindictive spirit sometimes displayed by Christians under persecution, and its relation to such passages as this, see vi. 10 note.

ἔργα αὐτῆς· ἐν τῷ ποτηρίῳ ᾧ ἐκέρασεν κεράσατε
αὐτῇ διπλοῦν· ⁷ὅσα ἐδόξασεν αὐτὴν καὶ ἐστρηνίασεν, 7
τοσοῦτον δότε αὐτῇ βασανισμὸν καὶ πένθος. ὅτι ἐν
τῇ καρδίᾳ αὐτῆς λέγει ὅτι Κάθημαι βασίλισσα, καὶ
χήρα οὐκ εἰμὶ καὶ πένθος οὐ μὴ ἴδω· ⁸διὰ τοῦτο ἐν 8
μιᾷ ἡμέρᾳ ἥξουσιν αἱ πληγαὶ αὐτῆς, θάνατος καὶ

6 ποτηριω] + αυτης ℵQ 7 8 14 29 38 al$^{plq\,20}$ me | αυτη] αυτην Q 7 αυτην] εαυτην ℵ$^{c.a}$ 1 8 14 al^{pl} Hipp Andr Ar | δοτε] κερασατε 1 | om βασανισμον και arm | om και πενθος 1* 10 12 37 49 91 96 186 | om οτι 1° 186 | om οτι 2° 1 al$^{vix\,mu}$ vg Hipp Cypr Tyc al | καθημαι] καθιω Q 14 92 καθως 28 29 30 43 50 90 93 98 al^{pauc} ειμι καθως 94 | βασιλισσα] βασιλευουσα C | ιδω] ειδω ℵC 8 ημερα] ωρα 14 92 aeth Cypr Prim | θανατου πενθος κ. λιμου Q θανατος πενθος κ. λ. 2 6 8 9 29 30* 35 38 al^{20}

Διπλοῦν διπλᾶ, Vg. *duplicare duplicia*, to pay double, is perhaps unique, but it follows the analogy of καυματίζεσθαι καῦμα (xvi. 9), διπλᾶ being the acc. of content. Ἐν τῷ ποτηρίῳ κτλ.: cf. xiv. 8, 10, notes, and xvii. 4, xviii. 3.

7. ὅσα ἐδόξασεν αὐτὴν καὶ ἐστρηνίασεν κτλ.] Let her share of misery be proportionate to her arrogant self-glorification. Cf. Isa. iii. 16 ff. ἀνθ' ὧν ὑψώθησαν αἱ θυγατέρες Σειὼν...καὶ ταπεινώσει ὁ θεὸς ἀρχούσας θυγατέρας Σειών κτλ. The general principle is affirmed continually, e.g. Prov. xxix. 23 ὕβρις ἄνδρα ταπεινοῖ; Lc. i. 51 διεσκόρπισεν ὑπερηφάνους διανοίᾳ καρδίας αὐτῶν...πλουτοῦντας ἐξαπέστειλεν κενούς, *ib.* xiv. 11 πᾶς ὁ ὑψῶν ἑαυτὸν ταπεινωθήσεται; here the humiliating loss of wealth and place is aggravated by acute suffering (βασανισμός, cf. ix. 5, note) and sorrow; the ease of luxury is exchanged for pain, and its light-hearted laugh for the gloom of bereavement; cf. Lc. vi. 25 οὐαί, οἱ γελῶντες νῦν, ὅτι πενθήσετε; Jac. iv. 9 ὁ γέλως ὑμῶν εἰς πένθος μετατραπήτω. The same sharp contrast is seen in the parable of Lc. xvi. 19 ff.: ἄνθρωπος δέ τις ἦν πλούσιος, καὶ ἐνεδιδύσκετο πορφύραν καὶ βύσσον εὐφραινόμενος καθ' ἡμέραν λαμπρῶς...καὶ ἐν τῷ ᾅδῃ...ὑπάρχων ἐν βασάνοις κτλ.

ὅτι ἐν τῇ καρδίᾳ αὐτῆς λέγει κτλ.] After Isa. xlvii. 7 ff. εἶπας Εἰς τὸν αἰῶνα ἔσομαι ἄρχουσα (גְּבֶרֶת, cf. *v.* 6 גְּבֶרֶת מַמְלָכוֹת)...οὐ καθιῶ χήρα, a passage applied to Rome also in *Orac. Sibyll.* v. 167 ff. αἲ αἲ πάντ' ἀκάθαρτε πόλι Λατινίδος αἴης | ...χήρη καθεδῇ ὑπὲρ ὄχθας | καὶ ποταμὸς Τίβερίς σε κλαύσεται κτλ. A similar boast is ascribed to Tyre by Ezekiel (xxvii. 3). Cf. Andreas: ἔθος γὰρ τοῖς ἐν εὐθυμίᾳ λέγειν (εἰ μὴ θεῖος αὐτοῖς πρόσεστι φόβος) Οὐ μὴ σαλευθῶ εἰς τὸν αἰῶνα.

8. διὰ τοῦτο ἐν μιᾷ ἡμέρᾳ ἥξουσιν αἱ πληγαὶ αὐτῆς κτλ.] The elation and self-confidence induced by luxury would be the direct cause (ὅτι...διὰ τοῦτο) of sudden and utter ruin. The writer still has in mind Isaiah *l.c.*; the prophet proceeds νῦν δὲ ἄκουε ταῦτα, τρυφερά, ἡ καθημένη, ἡ πεποιθυῖα ...ἥξει ἐξέφνης ἐπὶ σὲ [τὰ δύο ταῦτα ἐν ἡμέρᾳ μιᾷ, ἀτεκνία καὶ χηρεία]...καὶ ἥξει ἐπὶ σὲ ἀπώλεια...βόθυνος...ταλαιπωρία. Ἐν μιᾷ ἡμέρᾳ adds to the pathos of the downfall; cf. Seneca, *ep.* 91 "una nox fuit inter urbem maximam et nullam"; cf. Lucret. iii. 911 "omnia ademit | una dies infesta tibi tot praemia vitae." The 'plagues' of Babylon, when they come, will make a dire antithesis to her present condition; death, mourning, dearth will reign where life at its gayest and fullest has

15—2

πένθος καὶ λιμός, καὶ ἐν πυρὶ κατακαυθήσεται· ὅτι
9 ἰσχυρὸς Κύριος ὁ θεὸς ὁ κρίνας αὐτήν. [9]καὶ κλαύ-
σουσιν καὶ κόψονται ἐπ' αὐτὴν οἱ βασιλεῖς τῆς γῆς
οἱ μετ' αὐτῆς πορνεύσαντες καὶ στρηνιάσαντες, ὅταν
10 βλέπωσιν τὸν καπνὸν τῆς πυρώσεως αὐτῆς, [10]ἀπὸ
μακρόθεν ἑστηκότες διὰ τὸν φόβον τοῦ βασανισμοῦ

8 *κυριος ο θεος*] *ο θεος κυριος* ℵ* *ο θεος* A 95 vg aeth^utr *κυριος* syr^gw + *ο παντοκρατωρ* 79 | *κρινων* ℵ^c.a 1 6 31 79 al Ar 9 *κλαυσουσιν* CPQ 130 186 al^fere 40 Ar] *κλαυσονται* ℵA 1 36 al^vix mu Hipp + *αυτην* P 1 79 al^pauc vid syr^gw aeth | *επ αυτην*] *επ αυτη* A 1 36 38 79 95 97 al^vid om 14 92 Prim | *οι βασιλεις*] pr *παντες* 130 | *βλεπωσιν* (-*πουσιν* 186)] *ιδωσιν* ℵ | *πυρωσεως*] *πτωσεως* ℵ* (*πυρ.* ℵ^c.a)

long prevailed. Fire will complete the work of destruction: cf. xvii. 16, note. Incredible as all this may seem, the Seer is assured that it will be realized; Babylon had already been doomed, and the Judge who pronounced the sentence (*ὁ κρίνας*, *qui iudicavit*, Prim.) is strong to execute it; cf. Jer. xxvii. (l.) 34 *ὁ λυτρούμενος αὐτοὺς ἰσχυρός...κρίσιν κρινεῖ πρὸς τοὺς ἀντιδίκους αὐτοῦ*. *Κύριος ὁ θεός* is the O. T. אֲדֹנָי יֱהוִֹה, or the like.

9 f. *καὶ κλαύσουσιν καὶ κόψονται ἐπ' αὐτὴν κτλ.*] The Voice now describes the effects of the great catastrophe, in the form of a series of dirges chanted over the dead city by the kings (9—10), merchants (11—17), and shipowners (17—19) of the world. The whole passage seems to have been suggested by Ezekiel's dirge over Tyre (Ez. xxvii).

The *θρῆνος* is begun by the kings of the earth, i.e. the subordinate and allied princes who had flourished under the protection of Rome: for *οἱ β. τῆς γῆς* see i. 5, vi. 15, and for their relation to the Empire, xvii. 2, 18, xviii. 3, notes. As in Ezekiel Tyre is bewailed by the "princes of the sea" (Ez. xxvi. 16 f. *καταβήσονται ἀπὸ τῶν θρόνων αὐτῶν πάντες οἱ ἄρχοντες ἐκ τῶν ἐθνῶν τῆς θαλάσσης...καὶ λήμψονται ἐπὶ σὲ θρῆνον κτλ.*), so St John represents the vassals of the Empire as assembling themselves to deplore the fate of Rome. With a touch of grim humour he paints them as standing at a safe distance from the conflagration, and contenting themselves with idle lamentations. Rome's subjects and allies have shared her favours and her luxury (*οἱ μετ' αὐτῆς πορνεύσαντες καὶ στρηνιάσαντες*), but cannot help her in the time of need, and are careful not to be drawn into her doom. Their *οὐαὶ οὐαί* is sincere enough, for in Rome they have lost a protectress, but it avails nothing to the dead city.

Κλαύσουσιν is for the Attic *κλαύσονται*, as in Lc. vi. 21, Jo. xvi. 20; cf. *ἀκούσω* Jo. v. 25, *ἁρπ 'σω* Jo. x. 28, *γελάσω* Lc. *l.c.* (W. Schm. p. 107). For the combinations *κλ. καὶ κόψονται* cf. Lc. viii. 52 *ἔκλαιον δὲ πάντες καὶ ἐκόπτοντο αὐτήν*; similarly, xxiii. 27 *ἐκόπτοντο καὶ ἐθρήνουν αὐτόν*. For *πύρωσις* see 1 Pet. iv. 12, and cf. 2 Pet. iii. 12 *οὐρανοὶ πυρούμενοι λυθήσονται*; for *ἀπὸ μακρόθεν*, Mc. v. 6, note. *Ἡ πόλις ἡ ἰσχυρά*, 'that seemed so strong': contrast Isa. xxvi. 1 *ἰδοὺ πόλις ἰσχυρά, καὶ σωτήριον θήσει τὸ τεῖχος καὶ περίτειχος ...πόλεις ὀχυρὰς καταβαλεῖς κτλ.* *Μιᾷ ὥρᾳ*, cf. *v.* 8 *ἐν μιᾷ ἡμέρᾳ*; the thought recurs in *vv.* 16, 19.

αὐτῆς, λέγοντες Οὐαὶ οὐαί, ἡ πόλις ἡ μεγάλη Βαβυ-
λών, ἡ πόλις ἡ ἰσχυρά, ὅτι μιᾷ ὥρᾳ ἦλθεν ἡ κρίσις
σου. [11]καὶ οἱ ἔμποροι τῆς γῆς κλαίουσιν καὶ πενθοῦ- 11
σιν ἐπ' αὐτήν, ὅτι τὸν γόμον αὐτῶν οὐδεὶς ἀγοράζει
οὐκέτι, [12]γόμον χρυσοῦ καὶ ἀργύρου καὶ λίθου τιμίου 12

10 ουαι semel 36 40 arm[zoh] ter 35 87 syr[gw] | Βαβυλων] pr η 35 49 87 | μια ωρα] pr εν 1 38 al arm Ar μιαν ωραν A 95 | om ηλθεν A   11 της γης]+σου ℵ | κλαυσονται κ. πενθησουσιν Q min[35] vg (syr) syr[gw] Hipp Ar | επ αυτην] επ αυτη 6 7 45 49 91 al[mu vid] Ar επ αυτης 35 87 92 εν αυτη A επ αυτους Q εφ (ε)αυτους 36 186 εν εαυτοις 1 79 επι σοι arm | ουκ ετι cum seqq coniungunt ACQ 95 al[mu] Ar   12 χρυσου κ. αργυρου κ. λιθου τιμιου] χρυσουν κ. αργυρουν κ. λιθους τιμιους CP χρυσου κ. αργυρου κ. λιθων τιμιων syr Prim

11. *καὶ οἱ ἔμποροι τῆς γῆς κλαίουσιν κτλ.*] 'The kings of the earth' are succeeded by the 'merchants of the earth,' who take up the dirge, weeping and mourning for their dead mistress; for *κλαίειν καὶ πενθεῖν* cf. 'Mc.' xvi. 10, Lc. vi. 25, Jac. iv. 9, and below, *v.* 15. The second lamentation over Babylon is even more frankly self-interested than the first; the merchants mourn because they have lost their market, and there is no longer any demand for their shiploads of costly wares. *Γόμος* may be used of a load on the back of horse or camel or ass (cf. Ex. xxiii. 5 *τὸ ὑποζύγιον...πεπτωκὸς ὑπὸ τὸν γόμον αὐτοῦ*, but the more usual sense 'ship's burden,' 'cargo' (cf. Acts xxi. 3 *τὸ πλοῖον ἦν ἀποφορτιζόμενον τὸν γόμον*) is in better keeping with the present context. Merchandize came to Rome by sea direct from such ports as Seleucia, Ephesus, Smyrna, Corinth, Alexandria, Carthage, which tapped the resources of the East and of Africa, and on the West from Marseilles and Spain. How vast the traffic was appears from hints dropped by contemporary writers, e.g. Pliny *H. N.* xii. 41 "minima computatione millies centena millia sestertium annis omnibus India et Seres peninsulaque illa imperio nostro adimunt"; Galen, *antid.* 1. 4 *τοῖς...ἐν Ῥώμῃ κατοικοῦσιν...εἰς ἣν τὰ πανταχόθεν ἧκε καλὰ διὰ παντὸς ἔτους*. Aristides, cited by Wetstein: *ὅσα γὰρ παρ' ἑκάστοις φύεται καὶ κατασκευάζεται οὐκ ἔστιν ὡς οὐκ ἐνταῦθα* (at Rome) *ἀεὶ καὶ περισσεύει...πάντα ἐνταῦθα συμπίπτει, ἐμπορίαι, ναυτιλίαι, γεωργίαι, μετάλλων καθάρσια, τέχναι ὁπόσαι εἰσί τε καὶ γεγένηνται...ὅτι δ' ἂν μὴ ἐνταῦθα ἴδοι τις, οὐκ ἔστι τῶν γενομένων ἢ γιγνομένων*. Such words reveal the extent of the loss which the commerce of the world might be expected to suffer from a sudden collapse of its chief market.

12. *γόμον χρυσοῦ καὶ ἀργύρου καὶ λίθου τιμίου κτλ.*] A list of the imports which flowed into the port of Rome—(1) precious metals, marbles and gems, (2) textile materials for costly clothing, (3) choice woods, articles of *vertu*, cosmetics, (4) food stuffs, (5) live stock, from sheep and cattle to slaves and other human ministers to the wants or the vices of the rich.

Only a few of these articles of commerce call for separate notice. *Σιρικόν*, 'Seric fabric,' i.e. silk, is *ἅπ. λεγ.* in Biblical Greek, for שֵׁשׁ in Prov. xxxi. 22 is rendered by *βύσσος*, and מֶשִׁי in Ez. xvi. 10, 13 by *τριχαπτός*; but *σηρικός* is freely used by Greek writers after the Macedonian conquest, when silk found its way to the West; how abundant the material was at Rome in the first century appears from a statement of Josephus (*B. J.* vii. 5. 4) that at the triumph of

καὶ μαργαριτῶν καὶ βυσσίνου καὶ πορφύρας καὶ
σιρικοῦ καὶ κοκκίνου, καὶ πᾶν ξύλον θύϊνον καὶ πᾶν
σκεῦος ἐλεφάντινον καὶ πᾶν σκεῦος ἐκ ξύλου τιμιω-
13 τάτου καὶ χαλκοῦ καὶ σιδήρου καὶ μαρμάρου, [13]καὶ
κιννάμωμον καὶ ἄμωμον καὶ θυμιάματα καὶ μύρον καὶ

12 *μαργαριτων* ℵ 35 87 95 syr Prim] *μαργαριτας* CP *μαργαριταις* A *μαργαριτου* Q min^{pl} vg$^{cle\ am\ dem\ lipss}$ arm aeth Hipp Andr Ar | *βυσσινου*] *βυσσινων* ℵ *βυσσου* 1 36 49 79 91 96 130 186 al | *πορφυρας* ℵCP 7 35 95 Hipp] *πορφυρου* Q 1 6 8 14 29 186 al$^{plq\ 30}$ Ar om A | *σιρικου* ℵACPQ 7 32 130 186 al] *σηρικου* min$^{pl\ vid}$ *συρικου* 31 35 36 94 | om *παν* 1° 130 | *ξυλον*] *σκευος* A *ξυλινον* P | om *εκ* C 18 | *ξυλου*] *λιθου* A vg aeth^{vid} | *τιμιον κ. χαλκον κ. σιδηρον κ. μαρμαρον* syr^{gw} | om *και μαρμαρου* ℵ 1 13 *κινναμωμον* (*κιναμ.* Q* 1 6 14 38 al^{mu} Hipp Ar)] *κινναμωμου* ℵ(Q) min^{25} (Hipp) | om *και αμωμον* ℵ$^{c.a}$ Q 1 al^{pl} vg$^{cle\ dem}$ syr^{gw} Prim Ar | *θυμιαματος* Q 14 92 *θυμιαματων* 94 vg | om *και μυρον* C

Vespasian and Titus τὸ στρατιωτικὸν... χωρὶς ὅπλων ἦσαν ἐν ἐσθήσεσιν σηρικαῖς ἐστεφανωμένοι δάφναις. The form σιρικός (Prim. *sirici*) which is attested here by all the uncials, has some external support; see W.H.[2] *Notes*, p. 158, W. Schm. p. 46. Ξύλον θύϊνον (*lignum citreum*, Prim. *l. thyinum*, Vg.), wood of the tree known to the Greeks as θύον, θύα, or θυΐα and to the Romans as *citrus*, probably the *Thuia articulata* of botany. This wood, which was imported from North Africa, where it grew freely in the neighbourhood of the Atlas, was much prized for its veining, which in the best specimens simulated the eyes of the peacock's tail (Mart. xiv. 85), or the stripes of the tiger and spots of the panther (Plin. *H. N.* xiii. 96), or the seeds of the parsley; the colour also varied in different specimens; hence πᾶν ξ. θύϊνον. At Rome *citrus* wood was much sought after for dining tables: "Seneca, Dio lxi. 10, § 3, ...had 300 tables of citrus wood with ivory feet" (Mayor on Juv. i. 137); but it was also used for veneering, and for small works of art, which were made out of the hard roots of the tree (Theophrast. *H. P.* v. 5 ἐκ ταύτης (sc. τῆς ῥίζης) τὰ σπουδαιότατα ποιεῖται τῶν ἔργων). Ἐλεφάντινον (LXX. = שֵׁן); ivory was used by the Hebrews for boxes (Cant. v. 14), beds (Am. vi. 4), and even in building (3 Regn. xxii. 39 οἶκον ἐλεφάντινον, cf. Ps. xliv. (xlv.) 9, Cant. vii. 4, Am. iii. 15). It is mentioned by Ezekiel (xxvii. 15) among the imports of Tyre. By wealthy Romans under the Empire it was largely used in the decoration of furniture such as beds, couches, tables: thus Juvenal complains (xi. 120 ff.): "cenandi nulla voluptas | ...latos nisi sustinet orbes | grande ebur et magno sublimis pardus hiatu | dentibus ex illis quos mittit porta Syenes"—people cannot enjoy their supper unless their table rests on a leopard carved in ivory.

13. κιννάμωμον (קִנָּמוֹן), according to Herodotus (iii. 111) a word of Phoenician origin, was among the ingredients of the 'holy anointing oil' (Ex. xxx. 24 ff.), and is named with other spices in Prov. vii. 17, Cant. iv. 14, Sir. xxiv. 15. Probably it was not the Ceylon spice now known by that name, but the product of the *Cinnamon cassia* from South China (*Enc. Bibl.* 828 f.). In Roman life it supplied one of the cosmetics of the banquet; Plaut. *Curc.* 1. 2. 6, "tu mihi stacte, tu cinnamomum," Lucan, x. 165, "multumque madenti | infudere comae quod nondum evanuit aura | cinnamon." Ἄμωμον, *amomum* (Theo-

λίβανον καὶ οἶνον καὶ ἔλαιον καὶ σεμίδαλιν καὶ σῖτον
καὶ κτήνη καὶ πρόβατα, καὶ ἵππων καὶ ῥεδῶν καὶ
σωμάτων, καὶ ψυχὰς ἀνθρώπων. [14]καὶ ἡ ὀπώρα σου 14

13 om *και οινον* Q min[fere 20] | *προβατα*] + *και τραγους* Hipp | *ιππους* 95 130 syrr | *ρεδων* (*ραιδων* 2 6 7 31 38 186 al[25] Ar *ρεδιων* 14 43 92)] *ρεδας* syr | *σωματα* syrr
14 *η οπωρα*] om *η* C | om *σου* 1° Q min[pl] vg[cle dem lipss] Hipp Andr Ar

phrast. *H. P.* ix. 7. 2, Plin. *H. N.* xii. 28) is another Eastern perfume familiar to Roman writers: cf. Ovid, *Cydipp.* xxi. 266 "spissaque de nitidis tergit amoma comis"; Martial, viii. 77 "si sapis, Assyrio semper tibi crinis amomo | splendeat." As to its place of origin, Theophrastus (ix. 7) can only say οἱ μὲν ἐκ Μηδείας οἱ δὲ ἐξ Ἰνδῶν; *Enc. Bibl.* 145 suggests that it came from the *cissus vitigena*, a native of Armenia. On θυμιάματα see v. 8, note, on μύρον, Mc. xiv. 3, note; on λίβανος, c. viii. 3, note. Σεμίδαλις (here only in N.T., but frequent in LXX. = סֹלֶת), the fine flour imported for the use of the wealthy: Plin. *H. N.* xiii. 21 "similago ex tritico fit laudatissimo." The wheat supply of Rome (σῖτος) came largely from Egypt and was brought in large cornships from Alexandria; see Blass on Acts xxvii. 6.

Καὶ ἵππων καὶ ῥεδῶν καὶ σωμάτων, sc. γόμον, though it is not easy to see why the construction should at this point revert to that of γόμον χρυσοῦ κτλ., to return almost immediately to the accusative in καὶ ψυχὰς ἀνθρώπων. Mr Anderson Scott suggests that "we should see here additional items which distinguish Rome from her O.T. representative, Tyre"; but Tyre, too, had dealings in horses and human flesh (Ez. xxvii. 13 f.). It would seem as if the writer merely wished to relieve the monotony of the long sentence and perhaps at the same time to throw greater solemnity into the last clause. Ῥέδη according to Isid. *etym.* xx. 12, is a "genus vehiculi quattuor rotarum," and according to Quintilian (i. 5. 5) came from Gaul; it became fashionable at Rome, and in the third century, according to Lampridius, Senators acquired the privilege of plating their *rhedae* with silver. Σωμάτων, *mancipiorum*, slaves, a use which is familiar to the LXX. (Gen. xxxvi. 6 σώματα τοῦ οἴκου, Tob. x. 10 σώματα καὶ κτήνη, Bel 32 δύο σώματα καὶ δύο πρόβατα, 2 Macc. viii. 11 ἐπ' ἀγορασμὸν Ἰουδαίων σωμάτων), who, as the papyri shew (Deissmann, *Bible Studies*, page 160) found it in the Egyptian Greek of the Delta. It was repudiated by the Atticists (e.g. Pollux iii. 78 σώματα δὲ ἁπλῶς οὐκ ἂν εἴποις ἀλλὰ δοῦλα σώματα), but established itself in the later language; the slave merchant was known as a σωματέμπορος (Eustath. in Od. i.), and as late as the end of the fourth century Epiphanius could write: ἡ συνήθεια τοὺς δούλους σώματα εἴωθε καλεῖν. Ψυχαὶ ἀνθρώπων (Prim. strangely, *diversi generis animalia*) is from Ez. xxvii. 13 ἡ Ἑλλάς, καὶ ἡ σύμπασα, καὶ τὰ παρατείνοντα, οὗτοι ἐνεπορεύοντό σοι ἐν ψυχαῖς ἀνθρώπων (בְּנֶפֶשׁ אָדָם). Though in itself this old Hebrew phrase means little more than 'human live stock,' it serves to draw attention to the serious side of the Roman slave trade. The world of St John's day ministered in a thousand ways to the follies and vices of its Babylon, but the climax was reached in the sacrifice of human life which recruited the huge *familiae* of the rich, filled the *lupanaria*, and ministered to the brutal pleasures of the amphitheatre.

14. καὶ ἡ ὀπώρα σου τῆς ἐπιθυμίας κτλ.] 'And the ripe fruit of the desire of thy soul is gone from thee, and all thy rich and bright things

τῆς ἐπιθυμίας τῆς ψυχῆς ἀπῆλθεν ἀπὸ σοῦ, καὶ
πάντα τὰ λιπαρὰ καὶ τὰ λαμπρὰ ἀπώλετο ἀπὸ σοῦ,
15 καὶ οὐκέτι οὐ μὴ αὐτὰ εὑρήσουσιν. [15]οἱ ἔμποροι
τούτων, οἱ πλουτήσαντες ἀπ' αὐτῆς, ἀπὸ μακρόθεν
στήσονται διὰ τὸν φόβον τοῦ βασανισμοῦ αὐτῆς
16 κλαίοντες καὶ πενθοῦντες, [16]λέγοντες Οὐαὶ οὐαί, ἡ

14 *η επιθυμια* syr^{gw} Prim | *της ψυχης*]+*σου* Q 35 87 al^{pl} vg$^{cle\ dem\ lipss}$ syrr Hipp Andr Ar | *τα λαμπρα*] om *τα* ℵC | *απωλετο*] *απωλοντο* ℵ 7 8 10 11 16 35 37 39 49 87 91 96 *απηλθεν* 1 79 130 186 syr^{gw} | *ευρησουσιν*] *ευρης* Q^{txt} min$^{plq\ 30}$ Hipp Ar *ευρησεις* 1 37 49 91 96 (186 -*σης*)+*ουτε ψυχας ανθρωπων του λοιπου εμπορευση* 6 11 31 47 15 *κλαιοντες*] pr *και* Q min^{30} *et flebunt* syr 16 *λεγοντες*] pr *και* P min^{pl} *g* vg syr^{gw} aeth Hipp Prim Ar om *λεγ.* 1 12 16 39 186 | *ουαι* semel Q min^{25} ter 35 87

have perished from thee.' Ὀπώρα is the autumn fruit, ripe for ingathering; see Jer. xlvii. (xl.) 10, 12 *συναγάγετε οἶνον καὶ ὀπώραν καὶ ἔλαιον κτλ.*; and cf. Jude 12 *δένδρα φθινοπωρινὰ ἄκαρπα*, 'trees in late autumn when the fruit is past.' Just when the fruit of the labour of many generations seemed ready to fall into the mouth, it had vanished like a dream; the long desired consummation never came. The first *σου* may be taken with *ἡ ὀπώρα* (Prim. *pomorum tuorum concupiscentia animae*), or with *τῆς ψυχῆς* (Vg. *poma desiderii animae tuae*); its position in the latter case is not necessarily emphatic (WM. p. 193; Blass, *Gr* p. 288). For *λιπαρός*, *nitidus*, in the wider sense see Isa. xxx. 23 *ὁ ἄρτος τοῦ γενήματος τῆς γῆς σου ἔσται πλησμονὴ καὶ λιπαρός* (שָׁמֵן); 2 Esdr. xix. 35 *ἐν τῇ γῇ τῇ πλατείᾳ καὶ λιπαρᾷ* (הַשְּׁמֵנָה) *ᾗ ἔδωκας ἐνώπιον αὐτῶν*. Of the two adjectives to be distinguished here, *τὰ λιπαρά* is perhaps the rich and dainty food, *τὰ λαμπρά* the gay attire and costly furniture, which were the fruits of Roman conquests and policy. The Seer sees them all gone, and gone for ever; another summer, another ingathering, is not to be hoped for; never again will be found (*οὐ μὴ... εὑρήσουσιν*, "nicht mehr wird man finden") in the city on the Tiber the extravagant luxury, the inhuman selfishness, of the age of the Caesars.

15. *οἱ ἔμποροι τούτων, οἱ πλουτήσαντες ἀπ' αὐτῆς κτλ.*] The writer comes back to the merchants' dirge from which he had turned aside in *v.* 11 in order to describe the nature of their traffic with Rome. 'The merchants,' he resumes, 'who deal in these wares (*οἱ ἔμπ. τούτων*, comp. *v.* 23 *οἱ ἔμποροί σου*) and have gotten their wealth from Rome (cf. *v.* 3 *ἐκ τῆς δυνάμεως τοῦ στρήνους αὐτῆς ἐπλούτησαν*) will do as the kings did; they will stand at a safe distance from the city (*v.* 10), and pay their tribute of respect in similar terms.'

16. *λέγοντες Οὐαὶ οὐαί κτλ.*] The second dirge begins as the first did (*v.* 10), and ends similarly (*ὅτι μιᾷ ὥρᾳ κτλ.*). But there is an apposite change in the description of the city; while to the kings Rome is simply *ἡ ἰσχυρά*, the merchants naturally measure her by her opulence and splendour. For *ἡ περιβεβλημένη...καὶ κεχρυσωμένη* see xvii. 4, note; *βύσσινον*, which finds no place in the earlier description, has perhaps been suggested by *v.* 12; it comes in merely as an article used in the attire of the very rich (cf. Lc. xvi. 19), and clearly has not the symbolical significance which it bears in xix. 8, 14.

πόλις ἡ μεγάλη, ἡ περιβεβλημένη βύσσινον καὶ
πορφυροῦν καὶ κόκκινον, καὶ κεχρυσωμένη [ἐν] χρυσίῳ
καὶ λίθῳ τιμίῳ καὶ μαργαρίτῃ, ὅτι μιᾷ ὥρᾳ ἠρημώθη
ὁ τοσοῦτος πλοῦτος. [17]καὶ πᾶς κυβερνήτης καὶ πᾶς 17

16 *η περιβεβλημενη*] om *η* A | *κοκκ. κ. πορφ. κ. βυσσ.* A | *βυσσινον*] *βυσσον* Q min^{25} *bysso* vg$^{\text{cle lipss}}$ | *πορφυραν* P 18 35 36 40 47 87 94 | *και κεχρ.*] om *και* 1 79 152 186 syr^{gw} (cum *κεχρυσωμενα*) | *εν χρυσιω* (*-σω* ℵ 1 14 36 186 al)] om *εν* APQ min^{30} vg Tyc Prim Ar | *λιθοις τιμιοις* syrr | *μαργαριταις* Q min$^{\text{fere omn}}$ vg syrr^{vid} arm Hipp Andr Ar | *ερημωθη* 1 79 186 | *ο τοσουτος*] om *ο* P 95

ὅτι μιᾷ ὥρᾳ ἠρημώθη ὁ τοσοῦτος πλοῦτος] This corresponds to *ὅτι μιᾷ ὥρᾳ ἦλθεν ἡ κρίσις σου* in the dirge of the kings. Ἠρημώθη might be more properly used to describe the condition of the city itself, as in xvii. 16 and below, *v.* 19; cf. Mt. xii. 25 *πᾶσα βασιλεία μερισθεῖσα καθ' ἑαυτῆς ἐρημοῦται.* But the merchants still think of the wealth of Rome; it is Rome's money they miss and deplore, not the city and its people.

17. *καὶ πᾶς κυβερνήτης καὶ πᾶς ὁ ἐπὶ τόπον πλέων κτλ.*] One other class finds its interests gravely affected by the fall of Rome—the shipmasters and seafaring people in general; and from these there comes a third dirge. Compare Ezekiel's lamentation over Tyre, xxvii. 28 f. *πρὸς τὴν κραυγὴν τῆς φωνῆς σου οἱ κυβερνῆταί σου φόβῳ φοβηθήσονται, καὶ καταβήσονται ἀπὸ τῶν πλοίων πάντες οἱ κωπηλάται καὶ οἱ ἐπιβάται, καὶ οἱ πρωρεῖς τῆς θαλάσσης κτλ.* If Rome was not like Tyre a seaport, and had no direct business on the sea, the sea-going population of the shores of the Mediterranean were not less interested in her fate than they had once been in that of Tyre. Ostia was doubtless the destination of most of the merchant vessels of the Empire; cf. Florus i. 4 "Ostiam coloniam posuit, iam tum videlicet praesagiens animo futurum ut totius mundi opes et commeatus illo veluti maritimae urbis hospitio exciperentur."

Κυβερνῆται (Ez. = חֹבְלִים) are shipmasters, in contrast with *ναύκληροι* on the one hand and *ναῦται* on the other; cf. Acts xxvii. 11 *τῷ κυβερνήτῃ καὶ τῷ ναυκλήρῳ μᾶλλον ἐπείθετο*, where Blass cites Plut. *mor.* 807 B *ναύτας μὲν ἐκλέγεται κυβερνήτης καὶ κυβερνήτην ναύκληρος.* It is not quite so clear who is meant by *ὁ ἐπὶ τόπον πλέων.* The rendering of Prim. *omnis super mare navigans* gives some colour to Nestle's ingenious correction *πόντον* (ΠΟ|ΤΟΝ for ΤΟ|ΠΟΝ, an easy change; see *Text. Criticism of N.T.*, p. 168); but it is perhaps unnecessary to depart from the well-attested *τόπον.* 'He who sails for (any) part' is the merchantman who goes with his goods, or the chance passenger (*vector*); if the exact phrase does not occur elsewhere, it is approached in Mc. xiii. 8 *ἔσονται σεισμοὶ κατὰ τόπους*, Acts xxvii. 2 *μέλλοντι πλεῖν εἰς τοὺς κατὰ τὴν Ἀσίαν τόπους*, Strab. iii. 230 B *ἐν κόλπῳ... ὃν οἱ πλέοντες καὶ χρώμενοι τοῖς τόποις Ἀρτάβρων λιμένα προσαγορεύουσιν.* Καὶ *ὅσοι τὴν θάλασσαν ἐργάζονται*, 'and all who make their living by the sea,' not only sea captains and their crews, but the whole *θαλαττουργὸν καὶ ναυτικὸν ἔθνος* (Philostr. *vit. Apoll.* iv. 32); the phrase *ἐργάζεσθαι τὴν θάλασσαν*—the correlative of *ἐργ. τὴν γῆν* (Gen. iii. 5)—is abundantly illustrated by Wetstein, *ad loc.*; on the construction cf. WM., p. 279.

ὁ ἐπὶ τόπον πλέων καὶ ναῦται καὶ ὅσοι τὴν θάλασσαν
18 ἐργάζονται, ἀπὸ μακρόθεν ἔστησαν [18] καὶ ἔκραξαν
βλέποντες τὸν καπνὸν τῆς πυρώσεως αὐτῆς λέγοντες
19 Τίς ὁμοία τῇ πόλει τῇ μεγάλῃ; [19] καὶ ἔβαλαν χοῦν ἐπὶ
τὰς κεφαλὰς αὐτῶν καὶ ἔκραξαν κλαίοντες καὶ πεν-
θοῦντες, λέγοντες Οὐαὶ οὐαί, ἡ πόλις ἡ μεγάλη, ἐν
ᾗ ἐπλούτησαν πάντες οἱ ἔχοντες τὰ πλοῖα ἐν τῇ
θαλάσσῃ ἐκ τῆς τιμιότητος αὐτῆς, ὅτι μιᾷ ὥρᾳ
20 ἠρημώθη. [20] εὐφραίνου ἐπ' αὐτῇ, οὐρανέ, καὶ οἱ ἅγιοι

17 ο επι (+τον Q) τοπον πλεων] (ο) επι των πλοιων πλεων P (6) 12 36 49 (79) al^{10} επι των πλοιων ο ομιλος 1 Hipp | την θαλασσαν] εν τη θαλασση vg^{cle} syr^{gw} 18 εκραξαν] εκραξεν ℵQ 1 130 186 al^{pl} εκραυγαζον 9 13 27 εκλαυσαν αυτην syr^{gw} | βλεποντες] ορωντες 1 | καπνον] τοπον A 10 vg | ομοιος 130 | τη πολει] + ταυτη C *g* vg Prim 19 εβαλον ℵ(C)Q min$^{fere\ omn}$ syrr Hipp Andr Ar] εβαλλον P 29 186 επεβαλον A (95) | τας κεφαλας] της κεφαλης ℵ | αυτων] εαυτων C | εκραξαν AC 35 Hipp] εκραζον ℵPQ min^{pl} Ar | om κλαιοντες και πενθουντες A 1 | λεγοντες] pr και PQ min^{30} vg$^{am\ lipss\ 5,\ 6}$ syr aeth Prim Ar | ουαι semel ℵ 26 29 36 37 40 41 42 95 130 ter 36 87 | τα πλοια] om τα 1 35 79 87^{vid} al 20 ευφραινεσθε syrr Prim | επ αυτη] επ αυτην P 1 35 36 79 186 al εν αυτη A 98

19. *τίς ὁμοία τῇ πόλει τῇ μεγάλῃ;*] In Isa. xlvii. 10 Babylon boasts Ἐγώ εἰμι, καὶ οὐκ ἔστιν ἑτέρα, while in Ez. xxvii. 32 the exact phrase here used occurs in the Heb. though not in the LXX: וְקוֹנְנוּ עָלַיִךְ מִי כְצוֹר. Καὶ ἔβαλον χοῦν ἐπὶ τὴς κεφαλὰς αὐτῶν comes from the preceding verse in Ezekiel (καὶ ἐπιθήσουσιν ἐπὶ τὴν κεφαλὴν αὐτῶν γῆν καὶ σποδὸν στρώσονται); the exact words used by the Apocalyptist occur in Jos. vii. 6 (LXX.). For χοῦς = עָפָר see Gen. ii. 7, Lev. xiv. 41, etc., and in N.T. Mc. vi. 11 ἐκτινάξατε τὸν χοῦν = Mt. x. 14 τὸν κονιορτόν. Ἐκ τῆς τιμιότητος αὐτῆς, 'by reason of her valuableness,' i.e. her great wealth, which gave her unrivalled spending power; the word is ἅπ. λεγ. in LXX. and N.T., but occurs occasionally in the later literary Greek, e.g. Arist. *eth. Nic.* x. 7 διαφέρουσι τιμιότητι αἱ ψυχαί, xx. 7 δυνάμει καὶ τιμιότητι πολὺ μᾶλλον πάντων ὑπερέχει, Lib. *ep.* 1557 προσαγορεύω τὴν τιμιότητά σου. Compare the use of τιμή in 1 Pet. ii. 7 (see Hort's note).

20. *εὐφραίνου ἐπ' αὐτῇ κτλ.*] While the kings and merchants of the earth and its mariners bewail Babylon, Heaven and its friends rejoice over her doom: the reverse of the picture drawn in xi. 10, where upon the death of the Two Witnesses οἱ κατοικοῦντες ἐπὶ τῆς γῆς χαίρουσιν ἐπ' αὐτοῖς καὶ εὐφραίνονται: see notes there. There is perhaps a reference to Deut. xxxii. 43, LXX. (cf. *Intr. to the O.T. in Greek*, p. 243) εὐφράνθητε οὐρανοὶ ἅμα αὐτῷ... εὐφράνθητε ἔθνη μετὰ τοῦ λαοῦ αὐτοῦ ...ὅτι τὸ αἷμα τῶν υἱῶν αὐτοῦ ἐκδικᾶται, καὶ ἐκδικήσει καὶ ἀνταποδώσει δίκην τοῖς ἐχθροῖς; cf. Isa. xliv. 23 εὐφράνθητε, οὐρανοί, ὅτι ἠλέησεν ὁ θεὸς τὸν Ἰσραήλ, and Lc. xv. 7, 10 χαρὰ ἐν τῷ οὐρανῷ ἔσται. Andreas: διὰ τοῦ οὐρανοῦ ἢ τοὺς ἀγγέλους φησίν, ἢ τοὺς ἐν αὐτῷ ἔχοντας ἁγίους τὸ πολίτευμα. Οἱ ἅγιοι καὶ οἱ ἀπόστολοι καὶ οἱ προφῆται, the Church and her two highest ministries (1 Cor. xii. 28 πρῶτον ἀποστόλους, δεύτερον προφήτας);

*καὶ οἱ ἀπόστολοι καὶ οἱ προφῆται, ὅτι ἔκρινεν ὁ θεὸς
τὸ κρίμα ὑμῶν ἐξ αὐτῆς.* [21]*καὶ ἦρεν εἷς ἄγγελος* 21
*ἰσχυρὸς λίθον ὡς μύλινον μέγαν, καὶ ἔβαλεν εἰς τὴν
θάλασσαν λέγων Οὕτως ὁρμήματι βληθήσεται Βα-*

20 *και οι αποστολοι*] om *και οι* C *g* 1 186 al[pauc vid] vg[cle dem tol lipss 5, 6] arm om *οι* 130
21 *ισχυρος λιθον*] *λιθον ισχυρον* ℵ* *ισχυρον λιθον* 40 130 om *ισχυρος* A syr Tyc | *ως μυλινον* (vel *μυλικον*) *μεγαν* A(C) *quasi molarem magnum* vg etc.] *ως μυλον μεγαν* PQ 186 al[pl] syrr Hipp Andr *ως λιθον μεγαν* ℵ (36)

in xvi. 6, xviii. 24, the Prophets alone are mentioned. It is not clear whether in the present passage the Apostles are the College of the Twelve, as in xxi. 14, or whether the word is used in the wider sense (ii. 2, note); but probably the title is inclusive. The absence of any reference to a local ministry is remarkable—contrast Phil. i. 1 *τοῖς ἁγίοις...σὺν ἐπισκόποις καὶ διακόνοις*—but it is characteristic of a book which emanates from prophetic circles and is charismatic throughout.

ὅτι ἔκρινεν ὁ θεὸς τὸ κρίμα ὑμῶν ἐξ αὐτῆς] Κρίμα is here, not as in xvii. 1, a sentence pronounced by a judge, but a case for trial, as in Ex. xviii. 22 *τὰ δὲ βραχέα τῶν κριμάτων κρινοῦσιν αὐτοί*, 1 Cor. vi. 7, *κρίματα ἔχετε*. God has judged the case of Heaven and the Church—*ὑμῶν*, for in this instance their cause is one—against Babylon, with the result which the vision has revealed; the Church is at last avenged upon her enemy. Ἐξ *αὐτῆς*, at her expense; the trial has issued in justice being exacted from her. On the whole verse Andreas well remarks: *οὐχ ὡς χαιρεσίκακοι δὲ τῇ τῶν παιδειῶν ἐπιφορᾷ χαίρουσιν, ἀλλ' ὡς ἐπιθυμίαν διάπυρον περὶ τὴν διακοπὴν τῆς ἁμαρτίας ἔχοντες*. Cf. vi. 10, xviii. 6, notes.

21. *καὶ ἦρεν εἷς ἄγγελος ἰσχυρὸς κτλ.*] In the silence which follows the Voice from Heaven (*vv.* 4—20), a single angel (for *εἷς* cf. viii. 13, ix. 13, xix. 17; the numeral approaches the force of an indefinite article, but has not yet quite lost its proper meaning) represents the fall of Babylon by a symbolical action. He takes what appears to be (*ὡς*) a great millstone and with all his might (*ἰσχυρός*) hurls it into the sea, which in this chapter (*v.* 17) as throughout the book (e.g. vii. 1, viii. 8 f., x. 2 ff., xii. 12, 18, xiii. 1, xvi. 3 f.) belongs to the scenery of the Apocalyptic drama. A *λίθος μύλινος* (cf. *λ. μυλικός*, Lc. xvii. 2; the former adj. lays stress upon the purpose to which the stone is put, the latter upon its fitness for the work) or *μύλος* (Mc. ix. 42) might be one of the stones of a hand-mill such as women could work (Ex. xi. 5 *τῆς θεραπαίνης τῆς παρὰ τὸν μύλον*, Mt. xxiv. 41 *δύο ἀλήθουσαι ἐν τῷ μύλῳ*), or one which needed an ass to turn it (*μύλος ὀνικός*, Mc. *l.c.*); the latter or even a stone of greater weight (*μέγας*) is intended here. The Seer has in his mind Jer. xxviii. (li.) 63 *ἔσται ὅταν παύσῃ τοῦ ἀναγινώσκειν τὸ βιβλίον τοῦτο, καὶ ἐπιδήσεις ἐπ' αὐτὸ λίθον καὶ ῥίψεις αὐτὸ εἰς μέσον τοῦ Εὐφράτου, καὶ ἐρεῖς Οὕτως καταδύσεται Βαβυλών, καὶ οὐ μὴ ἀναστῇ*, and perhaps also an earlier passage, Ex. xv. 5 *κατέδυσαν εἰς βυθὸν ὡσεὶ λίθος* (cf. 2 Esdr. xix. 11). Compare also Herod. i. 165 *μυδρὸν σιδήρεον κατεπόντωσαν καὶ ὤμοσαν μὴ πρὶν ἐς Φωκαίαν ἥξειν, πρὶν ἢ τὸν μυδρὸν τοῦτον ἀναφανῆναι*.

οὕτως ὁρμήματι βληθήσεται Βαβυλών] 'As this stone is flung into the deep, so shall Babylon vanish.' Ὁρμήματι, *impetu*, 'with a rush,' like a stone whizzing through the air; cf. Deut. xxviii. 49 *ὡσεὶ ὅρμημα ἀετοῦ*; Hos. v. 10 *ἐπ' αὐτοὺς ἐκχεῶ ὡς ὕδωρ τὸ ὅρμημά*

22 βυλὼν ἡ μεγάλη πόλις, καὶ οὐ μὴ εὑρεθῇ ἔτι. [22]καὶ
φωνὴ κιθαρῳδῶν καὶ μουσικῶν καὶ αὐλητῶν καὶ
σαλπιστῶν οὐ μὴ ἀκουσθῇ ἐν σοὶ ἔτι, καὶ πᾶς
τεχνίτης [πάσης τέχνης] οὐ μὴ εὑρεθῇ ἐν σοὶ ἔτι, καὶ

21 *ου μη ευρ. ετι*] + *εν αυτη* ℵQ 14 92 22 om *και* 1° ℵ 1 | *σαλπιστων* (-*πιγκτων* Hipp)] *σαλπιγγων* ℵ 35 87 130 *σαλπιγγος* syr[gw] | om *και πας τεχνιτης...εν σοι ετι* 14 92 vg[fu] syr[gw] arm Hipp | om *πασης τεχνης* ℵA me (hab CPQ min[omn vid] vg syr aeth Prim Andr Ar) | om *και φωνη μυλου...εν σοι ετι* ℵ 29 38 40 87 93 98 syr[gw] arm aeth Hipp

μου (Symm. *ὑδροκελίαν ὁρμήματός μου*), 1 Macc. vi. 33 *ἀπῆρεν τὴν παρεμβολὴν ἐν ὁρμήματι αὐτῆς*. The action symbolizes the complete submergence, the final disappearance of pagan Imperial Rome; *οὐ μὴ εὑρεθῇ ἔτι*—she is to vanish, as Babylon had vanished in the time of St John; cf. Strabo, xvi. 1073: *ἡ δὲ* [*Βαβυλὼν*] *ἔρημος ἡ πολλή, ὥστ' ἐπ' αὐτῆς μὴ ἂν ὀκνῆσαί τινα εἰπεῖν ...'Ερημία μεγάλη 'στιν ἡ μεγάλη πόλις*; Lucian, *contempl.* 23 *ἡ Νίνος μὲν...ἀπόλωλεν ἤδη...ἡ Βαβυλὼν δέ σοι...οὐ μετὰ πολὺ καὶ αὐτὴ ζητηθησομένη ὥσπερ ἡ Νῖνος*.

22. *καὶ φωνὴ κιθαρῳδῶν καὶ μουσικῶν κτλ.*] No sounds of rejoicing, or of industrial life or even of domestic work shall be heard in Babylon again. For the first compare what is said of Tyre by Ezekiel (xxvi. 13 *καταλύσει τὸ πλῆθος τῶν μουσικῶν σου* (שִׁירַיִךְ), *καὶ ἡ φωνὴ τῶν ψαλτηρίων σου οὐ μὴ ἀκουσθῇ ἔτι*), and of Jerusalem by Isaiah and Jeremiah (Isa. xxiv. 8 *πέπαυται εὐφροσύνη τυμπάνων...πέπαυται φωνὴ κιθάρας*; Jer. vii. 34 *καταλύσω...φωνὴν εὐφραινομένων καὶ φωνὴν χαιρόντων, φωνὴν νυμφίου καὶ φωνὴν νύμφης*, cf. xxv. 10, xl. (xxxiii.) 9. On *κιθάρα, κιθαρῳδός*, see v. 8, xiv. 2, note; the *αὐλητής* (Mt. ix. 23) is the player on the flute (חָלִיל, *αὐλός*), who performed, often with the *κιθαρῳδός*, at the festivities of Hebrew life (2 Regn. vi. 5, Isa. v. 12, xxx. 29, 32 (A), Sir. xl. 21, 1 Macc. iii. 45. *Σαλπιστής*, a later form of *σαλπιγκτής*, founded on the analogy of *σαλπίσω, ἐσάλπισα* (viii. 6 ff.) is *ἅπ. λεγ.* in Biblical Greek. The trumpet proper (חֲצֹצְרָה) was in Jewish use nearly limited to religious services, but at Rome the *tuba* was heard at the games (Juv. vi. 249) and in the theatre (*ib.* x. 214, with Mayor's note), and even at funerals (Pers. iii. 103). *Μουσικῶν* may be songs (Gen. xxxi. 27, Ez., *l.c.*) or instruments of music (Dan. iii. 5 f. = זְמָרָא), but the analogy of *κιθαρῳδῶν, αὐλητῶν, σαλπιστῶν* is in favour of the masc., and by *μουσικοί* must be intended either 'performers on (other) instruments,' or vocalists, R.V. "minstrels"; cf. 1 Macc. ix. 39, 41, where the same ambiguity exists: *ὁ νυμφίος ἐξῆλθεν...μετὰ τυμπάνων καὶ μουσικῶν...καὶ μετεστράφη...φωνὴ μουσικῶν αὐτῶν εἰς θρῆνον.*

καὶ πᾶς τεχνίτης πάσης τέχνης κτλ.] The industries of the great city will be swept away as well as its festivities. A *τεχνίτης* may be an artist in metal (Deut. xxvii. 15, Cant. vii. 1, Acts xix. 24, 38), in stone (1 Chr. xxii. 15), or even in textile fabrics (Sir. xlv. 11). All the arts of civilized life are at an end in the new Babylon; one will hear no more among its ruins the stroke of the hammer or the whir of the loom; even domestic sounds such as may be heard in the merest hamlet, e.g. the creaking and droning of the upper millstone as it turns upon the lower, are hushed for ever; there is no hope that they will be revived in a restored city. *Μύλος* is here apparently the mill, i.e. the whole apparatus as distinguished

φωνὴ μύλου οὐ μὴ ἀκουσθῇ ἐν σοὶ ἔτι, 23 καὶ φῶς 23
λύχνου οὐ μὴ φάνῃ ἐν σοὶ ἔτι, καὶ φωνὴ νυμφίου καὶ
νύμφης οὐ μὴ ἀκουσθῇ ἐν σοὶ ἔτι. ὅτι οἱ ἔμποροί σου

22 μυλου] μυθου C | ακουσθη] ευρεθη Q φανη 4 6 31 Ar 23 om και φως λυχνου ...εν σοι ετι A 26 vg^codd Hipp | om και 1° Q | om εν 1° C vg^am fu dem lipss syr^gw Prim (*tibi*) | νυμφης] pr φωνη C syr^gw | οτι 1°] om 2 29 30 al^plq 23 ουδε arm | οι εμποροι (ενπ. Q) σου] om οι A 95 om σου 36 79

from the λίθος μύλινος (*v.* 21); cf. Num. xi. 8 ἤληθον αὐτὸ ἐν τῷ μύλῳ, Mt. xxiv. 41. The φωνὴ μύλου is best explained as the sound made by the mill, and not the singing of the women who turn it, though the ᾠδὴ ἐπιμύλιος, as Wetstein shews, was traditional in Greece.

23. καὶ φῶς λύχνου οὐ μὴ φάνῃ ἐν σοὶ ἔτι κτλ.] Whether the streets of Rome were regularly lit after dark is doubtful: Juvenal (iii. 285) speaks of the brilliant lights carried by the rich, contrasting his own dependence on the moon or on the "breve lumen candelae"; at a festival in A.D. 32 the spectators were escorted home by torchlight, provided by an army of slaves; on the other hand Ammianus writes (xiv. 1, § 9): "in urbe...pernoctantium luminum claritudo dierum solet imitari fulgorem"; see Mayor's note on Juv. *l.c.* Certainly the houses of the wealthy were not wanting in means of illumination; *lucernae* and *candelabra* of artistic forms abounded; even bed chambers were provided with lamps (*lucernae cubiculares*) which sometimes were burnt all night (Mart. x. 38, xiv. 39). But in the Seer's forecast the lights of Rome have gone out in utter darkness. Even the occasional flash of the torches carried by bridal processions (Mt. xxv. 1 ff.) is seen no more, and with it has ceased the "voice of the bridegroom and the bride," a phrase which is frequent in Jeremiah (vii. 34, xvi. 9, xxv. 10, xl. (xxxiii.) 11, cf. Bar. ii. 23); for φωνὴ νυμφίου see also Jo. iii. 29.

ὅτι οἱ ἔμποροί σου ἦσαν οἱ μεγιστᾶνες κτλ.] The connexion of thought is difficult. Are the two clauses introduced by ὅτι parallel, or is the second dependent on the first? For other examples of the writer's use of ὅτι... ὅτι see xv. 4, xvi. 6 (note). In the present instance it seems best to take the first ὅτι as controlling the whole sentence, and the second as explaining the first. Babylon has been submerged by her very greatness, for her greatness has been used to bewitch and mislead the world, and not to raise and purify it. Οἱ ἔμποροί σου κτλ. rests upon Isa. xxiii. 8 οἱ ἔμποροι αὐτῆς ἔνδοξοι, ἄρχοντες τῆς γῆς (שָׂרִים... נִכְבַּדֵּי אָרֶץ), and Ez. xxvii. 21 πάντες οἱ ἄρχοντες Κηδάρ, οὗτοι ἔμποροί σου; for μεγιστᾶνες see vi. 15, note. Traders who could make Rome their market rose to the first rank, became merchant princes (*vv.* 3, 15), while Rome on her part acquired a worldwide influence which she used for evil; through their traffic with her all nations had learnt to adopt her false standards of life and worship. On φαρμακία see ix. 21 note. Like Nineveh (Nah. iii. 4 ἡγουμένη φαρμάκων, ἡ πωλοῦσα ἔθνη ἐν τῇ πορνείᾳ αὐτῆς καὶ λαοὺς ἐν τοῖς φαρμάκοις αὐτῆς), and Babylon (Isa. xlvii. 12 στῆθι νῦν ἐν ταῖς ἐπαοιδαῖς σου καὶ τῇ πολλῇ φαρμακίᾳ σου ἃ ἐμάνθανες ἐκ νεότητός σου), Rome was full of professors of the black art; for the authorities see Mayor's note on Juv. iii. 77, and cf. *Orac. Sibyll.* v. 163 ἀλλὰ μενεῖς πανέρημος ὅλους αἰῶνας...σὸν στυγέουσ' ἔδαφος, ὅτι φαρμακίην ἐπόθησας. But the word is

ἦσαν οἱ μεγιστᾶνες τῆς γῆς, ὅτι ἐν τῇ φαρμακίᾳ σου
24 ἐπλανήθησαν πάντα τὰ ἔθνη, ²⁴καὶ ἐν αὐτῇ αἵμα[τα]
προφητῶν καὶ ἁγίων εὑρέθη καὶ πάντων τῶν ἐσφαγ-
μένων ἐπὶ τῆς γῆς.

XIX. 1 ¹Μετὰ ταῦτα ἤκουσα ὡς φωνὴν μεγάλην ὄχλου
πολλοῦ ἐν τῷ οὐρανῷ λεγόντων

23 τη φαρμακια (-κεια Q 1 130 al^{pl} Hipp Ar)] ταις φαρμακειαις latt syr^{gw} | επλανηθησαν] επλανησας 87 syr^{gw} 24 αιματα Q 2 6 7 8 9 14 16 29 31 35 36 95 130 186 al$^{plq\,30}$ Ar] αιμα ℵACP 1 38 79 al^{pauc} Hipp | ευρεθησαν 7 14 39 | εσφαγμενων] εσφραγισμενων 38 γεγραμμενων εν τη γη ζωντος arm^{vid}

XIX 1 μετα ταυτα] pr και 1 36 38 49 79 91 96 186 al syr^{gw} arm aeth | om ως 1 7 12 16 18 38 47 186* syrr arm | om μεγαλην 1 40 79 vg^{clo} | οχλου πολλου] *turbarum multarum* vg$^{fu\,al}$ (*tubarum m.* vg$^{am\,lipss}$) syr^{gw} Prim

probably used by St John in the wider sense of the witchery of gay and luxurious vice and its attendant idolatries, by which the world was fascinated and led astray. See xxi. 8, xxii. 15, notes.

24. καὶ ἐν αὐτῇ αἵματα προφητῶν κτλ.] A further reason for the overthrow of Rome was her bloodguiltiness (ὅτι is to be carried on from *v.* 23). Cf. Jer. xxviii. (li.) 35 τὸ αἷμά μου ἐπὶ τοὺς κατοικοῦντας Χαλδαίους, ἐρεῖ Ἰερουσαλήμ (see also *v.* 49, Heb.); Ez. xxiv. 6 ὦ πόλις αἱμάτων λέβης κτλ. The blood shed by Rome was not simply that of gladiators 'butchered to make a Roman holiday,' many of whom may have deserved their fate (cf. Dill, *Roman Society*, p. 242), but that also of Saints and Prophets: cf. xvi. 6, xvii. 6, notes. The massacre of 64, and recent troubles under Domitian sufficiently explain αἷμα ἁγίων (cf. Clem. *Cor.* 1, 5 ff.); among the προφῆται martyred at Rome may have been such prominent Roman Christians as Andronicus and Junias (Rom. xvi. 7 οἵτινές εἰσιν ἐπίσημοι ἐν τοῖς ἀποστόλοις), or possibly the writer may have in view St Peter and St Paul, who were prophets as well as Apostles. But the responsibility of Rome was not limited to martyrdoms which occurred within the city; the world was under her rule, and the loss of all lives sacrificed (ἐσφαγμένων, cf. v. 9, 12, xiii. 8) throughout the Empire lay at her door. It is remarkable that the same is said of Jerusalem before her fall (Mt. xxiii. 35 ὅπως ἔλθῃ ἐφ' ὑμᾶς πᾶν αἷμα δίκαιον ἐκχυννόμενον ἐπὶ τῆς γῆς). On αἵματα see *c.* xvi. 6, note.

XIX. 1—10. TRIUMPH IN HEAVEN. TWO HALLELUJAH PSALMS; AN ANGELIC MESSAGE.

1. μετὰ ταῦτα ἤκουσα ὡς φωνὴν κτλ.] The triumphant shouts which follow are an answer to the appeal in xviii. 20 εὐφραίνου...οὐρανέ, κτλ. The first (1—8) is the *Te Deum* of Heaven ἐπὶ τῇ δικαιοκρισίᾳ τοῦ θεοῦ, as Arethas expresses it. It comes from a 'great multitude,' which reminds the reader of the multitude of vii. 9, but as the Church is called to add her Hallelujah afterwards (*v.* 5), this first-named ὄχλος πολύς is probably the Angel Host, the μυριάδες ἀγγέλων of Heb. xii. 22, the μυριάδες μυριάδων καὶ χιλιάδες χιλιάδων of Apoc. v. 11. Their paean takes the form of a Hallelujah Psalm.

The liturgical note הַלְלוּיָהּ (ܗܠܠܘܝܐ, ἀλληλουϊά (on η for ϵ see Dalman, *Gr.* p. 152), *alleluia*) occurs

Ἀλληλουϊά· ἡ σωτηρία καὶ ἡ δόξα καὶ ἡ
δύναμις τοῦ θεοῦ ἡμῶν, ²ὅτι ἀληθιναὶ καὶ δίκαιαι 2
αἱ κρίσεις αὐτοῦ· ὅτι ἔκρινεν τὴν πόρνην τὴν
μεγάλην ἥτις ἔφθειρεν τὴν γῆν ἐν τῇ πορνείᾳ
αὐτῆς, καὶ ἐξεδίκησεν τὸ αἷμα τῶν δούλων αὐτοῦ
ἐκ χειρὸς αὐτῆς.

1 και η δοξα και η δυναμις] και η δοξα και η τιμη 1 36 al me κ. η δυν. κ. η δοξα κ. η τιμη syr | του θεου] τω θεω 36 47 vg me syrr arm aeth Tyc Prim κυριω τω θ. 1 2 om ητις εφθ. τ. γην arm | εφθειρεν] διεφθειρεν Q 130 al[plq35] Ar εκρινεν A | πορνεια CPQ min[pl]] πορνια ℵA | χειρων vg syr[gw]

at the beginning of Pss. cv.—cvi., cxi.—cxiii., cxvii.—cxviii., cxxxv., cxlvi.—cl. (Heb.) and of a few other Psalms in the LXX. which are without it in M. T. (cf. *Intr. to O. T. in Greek*, p. 250). The transliteration ἀλληλουϊά must have come into use among the Hellenistic Jews before the Christian era (cf. Tob. xiii. 18 ἐροῦσιν πᾶσαι αἱ ῥῦμαι αὐτῆς (sc. Ἰερουσαλήμ) Ἀλληλουϊά, 3 Macc. vii. 13 ἐπιφωνήσαντες τὸ ἀλληλουϊά), and was taken over by the Apostolic Church from the Hellenistic Synagogue. Like *Hosanna*, this Hebrew word became familiar even to the most unlettered Christians everywhere, rather perhaps through the Easter *Alleluia* than through the influence of the N. T., where it occurs only in this passage; cf. Aug. *enarr. in Pss.* xxi. 24 "his diebus per totum orbem terrarum...dicitur *Amen* et *Alleluia*," and for its early use in these islands see Bede, *H. E.* i. 20, ii. 1. It was hailed as a connecting link between the worship of the Church on earth and the worship of Heaven; cf. Aug. *serm.* cclv. (a paschal sermon): "in hoc quidem tempore peregrinationis nostrae ad solatium viatici dicimus *Alleluia*; modo nobis *Alleluia* canticum est viatoris, tendimus autem per viam laboriosam ad quietam patriam, ubi retractis omnibus actionibus nostris non remanebit nisi *Alleluia*." This view of the word no doubt had its origin in the present passage, where Hallelujah is the keynote of the heavenly hymn of praise.

ἡ σωτηρία καὶ ἡ δόξα καὶ ἡ δύναμις τοῦ θεοῦ ἡμῶν] 'Salvation, Glory, and Power are our God's'; cf. xii. 10 ἄρτι ἐγένετο ἡ σωτηρία...τοῦ θεοῦ ἡμῶν, and the more usual form in vii. 10 (ἡ σ. τῷ θεῷ ἡμῶν); on ἡ σωτηρία see note on vii. 10. A definite reason is given for the present psalm of praise—the execution of judgement upon Babylon (ὅτι ἀληθιναί...ὅτι ἔκρινεν κτλ.). For ἀληθ. καὶ δίκ. αἱ κρίσεις σου cf. xv. 3, xvi. 7. The thought of the coming doom of Babylon has been in view from *c.* xiv. 7; now at length it is seen in its realization.

The second ὅτι, as in xviii. 23 (see note there), justifies the statement introduced by the first. That the Divine judgements are true and just has been shewn anew by His sentence on the Great Harlot (cf. xvii. 1, 5, notes); on ἔκρινεν see xviii. 8, 20. Ἥτις (cf. i. 7 οἵτινες αὐτὸν ἐξεκέντησαν, ii. 24 οἵτινες οὐκ ἔγνωσαν, xii. 13 τὴν γυναῖκα ἥτις ἔτεκεν τὸν ἄρσενα; even in the Apoc. ὅστις and ὅς are not indistinguishable in meaning) ἔφθειρεν τὴν γῆν ἐν τῇ πορνείᾳ αὐτῆς: 'it is just that she who brought moral ruin upon the world should herself lie in ruins.' For the general sense see xiv. 8, xvii. 2, 5, xviii. 3, notes: for ἔφθειρεν τὴν γῆν cf. xi. 18 διαφθεῖ-

3 [3]καὶ δεύτερον εἴρηκαν Ἀλληλουϊά· καὶ ὁ καπνὸς αὐτῆς
4 ἀναβαίνει εἰς τοὺς αἰῶνας τῶν αἰώνων. [4]καὶ ἔπεσαν
οἱ πρεσβύτεροι οἱ εἴκοσι τέσσαρες καὶ τὰ τέσσερα
ζῷα, καὶ προσεκύνησαν τῷ θεῷ τῷ καθημένῳ ἐπὶ τῷ

3 om και 1° 98 syr[gw] | ειρηκαν (-κασιν 14 92 94 95)] ειρηκεν Q 130 al[plq25] me (cum δευτερος) Ar | ανεβη 73 79 syr[gw] 4 επεσον Q** min[pl] Ar | τεσσαρα PQ min[pl] | τω θρονω] των θρονων P του θρονου 1 36 38 49 79 91 96 97

ραι τοὺς διαφθείροντας τὴν γῆν, and notes there; the phrase is perhaps suggested here by Jer. xxviii. (li.) 25, where Babylon is *τὸ ὄρος τὸ διεφθαρμένον, τὸ διαφθεῖρον πᾶσαν τὴν γῆν*. The uncompounded verb is used freely in an ethical sense; cf. 1 Cor. iii. 17, xv. 33, Jude 10.

The grounds on which judgement was pronounced against Babylon are again rehearsed, viz.: (1) *πορνεία*, (2) *αἱματεκχυσία*; cf. xviii. 23 ff. *Τῶν δούλων αὐτοῦ* seems here to include both Saints and Prophets—the Church and her leaders. For *ἐκδικεῖν αἷμα ἔκ τινος* see vi. 10; *ἐκδ. ἐκ χειρός τινος* is less usual, but cf. 4 Regn. ix. 7, which perhaps is in the Seer's mind: *ἐκδικήσεις τὰ αἵματα τῶν δούλων μου τῶν προφητῶν καὶ τὰ αἵματα πάντων τῶν δούλων Κυρίου ἐκ χειρὸς* (מִיַּד) *Ἰεζάβελ καὶ ἐκ χειρὸς ὅλου τοῦ οἴκου Ἀχαάβ*. The phrase seems to be 'pregnant'; written at length it would have run: *ἐρύσατο τοὺς δούλους αὐτοῦ ἐκ τῆς χειρὸς αὐτῆς, ἐκδικήσας ἐξ αὐτῆς τὸ αἷμα αὐτῶν*.

3. *καὶ δεύτερον εἴρηκαν Ἀλληλουϊά*] The shout of praise ends as it began, after the manner of certain of the Hallelujah Psalms (cvi., cxxxv., cxlvi., cl.); compare Miriam's repetition of the first distich of the Song of Moses (Ex. xv. 1, 21). Iteration emphasizes, as in Ps. lxi. (lxii.) 12 *ἅπαξ ἐλάλησεν ὁ θεός, δύο ταῦτα ἤκουσα, ὅτι τὸ κράτος τοῦ θεοῦ*; Job xxxiii. 14 *ἐν γὰρ τῷ ἅπαξ λαλῆσαι ὁ κύριος, ἐν δὲ τῷ δευτέρῳ*. Thus the second Hallelujah is not merely formal, but adds strength to the first, like the *antiphona* with which the later Church learnt to call attention to the leading idea of a psalm or to the thought on which for the time she wished to lay special emphasis. On the termination of *εἴρηκαν* see WH.[2], *Notes*, p. 173, W. Schm., p. 113, note, and cf. xviii. 3 *πέπωκαν*, xxi. 6 *γέγοναν*; and on the perfect see iii. 3, v. 7 (note).

καὶ ὁ καπνὸς αὐτῆς ἀναβαίνει κτλ.] With the offering of praise there goes up, instead of incense (viii. 4 *ἀνέβη ὁ καπνὸς τῶν θυμιαμάτων*), the smoke which rises perpetually from the embers of the city; cf. xiv. 11 *ὁ καπνὸς τοῦ βασανισμοῦ αὐτῶν εἰς αἰῶνας αἰώνων ἀναβαίνει*. The same is said of Edom, regarded as an enemy of Israel, in Isa. xxxiv. 9 f.: *ἔσται ἡ γῆ αὐτῆς ὡς πίσσα καιομένη νυκτὸς καὶ ἡμέρας, καὶ οὐ σβεσθήσεται εἰς τὸν αἰῶνα χρόνον, καὶ ἀναβήσεται ὁ καπνὸς αὐτῆς ἄνω*. The words add a last touch to the description already given (xviii. 21 ff.) of Babylon's utter collapse.

4. *καὶ ἔπεσαν οἱ πρεσβύτεροι κτλ.*] The Elders and the *ζῷα* have not been mentioned since xiv. 3. Now that the worship of Heaven is again visible to the Seer, they are discovered in the act of adoration as before (iv. 9 ff., v. 8, 14). As in v. 14 (*τὰ τέσσαρα ζῷα ἔλεγον Ἀμήν, καὶ οἱ πρεσβύτεροι ἔπεσαν καὶ προσεκύνησαν*), they assent to the Angels' service of praise, saying the Amen to the celestial Eucharist (1 Cor. xiv. 16)—an attitude which agrees with their character as representatives in Heaven of Nature and the Church (*c.* iv. 4, 6, note). For *ἀμήν* in such a connexion see v. 14, vii. 12, and on the word, *c.* i. 7, note.

θρόνῳ λέγοντες Ἀμήν, ἀλληλουϊά. 5καὶ φωνὴ ἀπὸ 5
τοῦ θρόνου ἐξῆλθεν λέγουσα

Αἰνεῖτε τῷ θεῷ ἡμῶν, πάντες οἱ δοῦλοι
αὐτοῦ [καὶ] οἱ φοβούμενοι αὐτόν, οἱ μικροὶ¶ καὶ ¶ C
οἱ μεγάλοι.

6καὶ ἤκουσα ὡς φωνὴν ὄχλου πολλοῦ καὶ ὡς φωνὴν 6

5 *φωναι...εξηλθον λεγουσαι* ℵ* | *απο* ACQ min[25] Ar] *εκ* ℵP 1 31 32 36 47 48 49 79 91 93 96 al[mu] | *θρονου*] *ουρανου* Q 14 92 | *τω θεω*] *τον θεον* 1 7 13 al[pl] Andr Ar | om *και* 2° ℵCP (hab AQ min[omn vid] vg syrr al Prim Andr Ar) 6 *ως* 1°] om 1* 8 12 31 35 87 Prim post *φωνην* ponunt 36 syr[gw] | *οχλων πολλων* syr[gw] Prim | om *ως* 2° A 6 12 94

5. **καὶ φωνὴ ἀπὸ τοῦ θρόνου ἐξῆλθεν λέγουσα Αἰνεῖτε κτλ.**] In *c.* xvi. 17 a voice comes from the Throne, but *ἐκ τοῦ ναοῦ*, which is not added on this occasion. Here the voice cannot be that either of God, or (as Bousset thinks) of the Lamb; in the latter case we should certainly have had *τῷ θεῷ μου*, as in iii. 12, and not *τῷ θ. ἡμῶν*. It remains that one of the Angels of the Presence is the speaker. The voice summons all the Servants of God, i.e. the whole Church, which is now called to add its tribute to that of the Angels, the *ζῷα*, and the representative Elders. The call *αἰνεῖτε κτλ.* comes from the Hallelujah Psalm cxxxiv. (cxxxv.) 1, 20 *αἰνεῖτε* (הַלְלוּ) *τὸ ὄνομα Κυρίου, αἰνεῖτε, δοῦλοι Κυρίου ... οἱ φοβούμενοι τὸν κύριον*. In the original עַבְדֵי יְהוָֹה are the Priests and Levites who ministered in the Temple (cf. 2 *οἱ ἑστῶτες ἐν οἴκῳ Κυρίου*), while the יִרְאֵי יְהוָֹה are the worshipping Israelites in general; but in St John's adaptation of the words their exact sense is less clear. There is a fairly close parallel in *c.* xi. 18 *δοῦναι τὸν μισθὸν τοῖς δούλοις σου τοῖς προφήταις καὶ τοῖς ἁγίοις καὶ τοῖς φοβουμένοις κτλ.*; see note there. Here the *δοῦλοι* probably include the Saints and the Prophets, as in *v.* 2, and if we read *καὶ οἱ φοβ.* the latter may be, as in xi. 18, the unbaptized friends of the Church, catechumens, enquirers, and the like; if on the other hand *καί* is to be omitted, *οἱ φοβ.* is merely a description, somewhat otiose as it may seem, of *οἱ δοῦλοι αὐτοῦ*. *Οἱ μικροὶ καὶ οἱ μεγάλοι*, a phrase characteristic of the book (cf. xi. 18, xix. 18, xx. 12, xxi. 16), but based on the O.T. מִקָּטֹן וְעַד־גָּדוֹל (Gen. xix. 11), and in this connexion perhaps on Ps. cxiii. 21 (cxv. 13) *τοὺς φοβουμένους τὸν κύριον τοὺς μικροὺς μετὰ τῶν μεγάλων*; it seems here to embrace Christians of all intellectual capacities and social grades, and of all stages of progress in the life of Christ, even the *ἐλάχιστοι ἐν τῇ βασιλείᾳ* (Mt. v. 19), and the *ἐξουθενημένοι ἐν τῇ ἐκκλησίᾳ* (1 Cor. vi. 4); all are included in the summons to thanksgiving and are capable of bearing a part in it; cf. Bede: "parvitas non nocet ingenii cuius cor et lingua Domini laude repleta est." *Αἰνεῖν τῷ θεῷ* is an unusual construction; Winer (WM. p.673) compares *διδάσκειν τινί* in *c.* ii. 14, where see note.

6. **καὶ ἤκουσα ὡς φωνὴν ὄχλου πολλοῦ κτλ.**] The voice of a second great multitude is wafted across to the Seer. If the *ὄχλος πολύς* of *v.* 1 is the Angelic Host, that of *v.* 6 is the Universal Church, the innumerable multitude described in Apoc. vii. 9. The sound of the collective praises of the Church

ὑδάτων πολλῶν καὶ ὡς φωνὴν βροντῶν ἰσχυρῶν,
λεγόντων
'Αλληλουϊά, ὅτι ἐβασίλευσεν Κύριος ὁ θεὸς
§ the 7 ἡμῶν ὁ παντοκράτωρ. 7 § χαίρωμεν καὶ ἀγαλ-
λιῶμεν, καὶ δώσωμεν τὴν δόξαν αὐτῷ, ὅτι ἦλθεν

6 λεγοντων AP 6 35 36 38 79 87 95] λεγουσων ℵ λεγοντες Q min$^{plq\,30}$ Tyc λεγοντας 1 186 al Ar | κυριος ο θεος] ο θεος ο κυριος ℵ* om κυριος 1 8 12 36 186 arm^{zoh} om ο θεος syr^{gw} Prim | om ημων A 1 49 95 al me arm aeth 7 αγαλλιωμεν ℵAP 1 12 18 35 36 79 87 95 130] αγαλλιωμεθα Q min^{pl} Ar | δωσωμεν P 11 79 (δωσομεν ℵ$^{c.a}$ A)] δωμεν ℵ* Q 1 6 7 14 35 38 47 48 49 50 130 186 al^{mu} Ar

was in St John's ears like the din of a vast concourse, the roar of a cataract (i. 15, xiv. 2), or the roll of thunder (vi. 1, x. 3 f.): "magna vox canentium magna cordis est devotio" (Bede). The words could be distinguished. They begin with Hallelujah, repeated a fourth time, and thus they are connected with the triumph of Heaven. But when the grounds of the Church's thanksgiving are assigned, an entirely new note is struck. It is not the doom of Babylon for which the Church thanks God, but its sequel—the setting up of the Kingdom of God—ὅτι ἐβασίλευσεν Κύριος: cf. Ps. xcvi. (xcvii.) 1 ὁ κύριος ἐβασίλευσεν (מָלָךְ), ἀγαλλιάσεται ἡ γῆ, and see c. xi. 15, 17, and notes there. The aorist looks back to the fall of Babylon, now *ex hypothesi* past (cf. ἔπεσεν...ἔκρινας), seeing in it the epoch of the entrance of God upon His Reign. The World-power has fallen, in order that the spiritual and eternal may take its place; for the *deus et dominus noster* of the pagan provincials St John substitutes the Κύριος ὁ θεὸς ἡμῶν of the Church throughout the Empire, of the Saints and the Angels on earth and in Heaven. For Κύριος or ὁ κύριος in this book = יְהוָה see i. 8, iv. 8, 11, xi. 17, xv. 3, xvi. 7, xviii. 8, xxi. 22, xxii. 5 f., and for παντοκράτωρ i. 8 (note), iv. 8, xi. 17, xv. 3, xvi. 7, 14. 'Ο θεὸς ἡμῶν is used in *vv.* 1, 5, as well as in 6; it is a title which angels and members of the Church have an equal right to use.

7. χαίρωμεν καὶ ἀγαλλιῶμεν κτλ.] For this combination cf. Mt. v. 12 χαίρετε καὶ ἀγαλλιᾶσθε (Lc. vi. 23 χάρητε ... καὶ σκιρτήσατε), Ps. xcvii. (xcviii.) 4 ᾄσατε καὶ ἀγαλλιᾶσθε καὶ ψάλατε: ἀγαλλιᾶσθαι and εὐφραίνεσθαι are still more frequently found together, e.g. Pss. ix. 3, xv. (xvi.) 9, etc. The active ἀγαλλιᾶν is used only here and in Lc. i. 47 ἠγαλλίασεν τὸ πνεῦμά μου ἐπὶ τῷ θεῷ, with the possible addition of 1 Pet. i. 8 (WH.[2], *Notes*, p. 176). For δοῦναι τὴν δόξαν αὐτῷ cf. xi. 13, xiv. 7, xvi. 9, and for the form δώσωμεν (if that is to be read) see Mc. vi. 37, note, and W. Schm., p. 107.

ὅτι ἦλθεν ὁ γάμος τοῦ ἀρνίου κτλ.] In these words the reason of the Church's exuberant joy appears, and at the same time there is sounded the first note of transition to the final vision of the book. It is the manner of the writer to throw out hints of the next great scene some time before he begins to enter upon it; thus Ἔπεσεν ἔπεσεν Βαβυλών is heard in xiv. 8, though the fall itself does not come into sight before *cc.* xvii.—xviii. Here in like manner the Marriage of the Lamb is announced as imminent (ἦλθεν), though a thousand years are yet to pass before its consummation (xx. 3), and the Bride is not revealed until we reach *c.* xxi.

The conception of a Divine Marriage is deeply rooted in O.T. teaching. God

ὁ γάμος τοῦ ἀρνίου, καὶ ἡ γυνὴ αὐτοῦ ἡτοίμασεν
ἑαυτήν, [8]καὶ ἐδόθη αὐτῇ ἵνα περιβάληται βύσ- 8

7 γυνη (νυμφη ℵ[c.c])] + νυμφη arm

is the Bridegroom of Israel (Hos. ii. 19=21 μνηστεύσομαί σε ἐμαυτῷ εἰς τὸν αἰῶνα; Isa. liv. 6 οὐχ ὡς γυναῖκα καταλελιμμένην καὶ ὀλιγόψυχον κέκληκέν σε ὁ κύριος; cf. Ez. xvi. 1 ff.). In Ps. xliv. (xlv.) "expounded of the Messiah by the Targum and many Jewish scholars, e.g. Kimchi" (Cheyne, *Psalms*, p. 123), the nuptials of the King are depicted at length. All this imagery is taken over by the Gospels, and applied to Christ and the Church; we meet with the νυμφίος (Mc. ii. 19), the νύμφη (Mt. xxv. 1, D), the νυμφών (Mt. xxii. 10), the υἱοὶ τοῦ νυμφῶνος (Mc. *l.c.*), the φίλος τοῦ νυμφίου (Jo. iii. 29), the γάμος made by the King for His Son (Mt. xxii. 2 ff.), the ἔνδυμα γάμου (Mt. xxii. 11)—all in a clearly Messianic sense. Nor has St Paul failed to seize on this group of ideas, cf. 2 Cor. xi. 2 ἡρμοσάμην γὰρ ὑμᾶς ἑνὶ ἀνδρὶ παρθένον ἁγνὴν παραστῆσαι τῷ χριστῷ; Eph. v. 25 ff. οἱ ἄνδρες, ἀγαπᾶτε τὰς γυναῖκας, καθὼς καὶ ὁ χριστὸς ἠγάπησεν τὴν ἐκκλησίαν...τὸ μυστήριον τοῦτο μέγα ἐστίν, ἐγὼ δὲ λέγω εἰς Χριστὸν καὶ εἰς τὴν ἐκκλησίαν. St John, following St Paul, but with a characteristic independence as to detail, adopts so much of this symbolism as lends itself to his purpose; the marriage, the supper, the bride and her attire enter into his vision; cf. iii. 20, xix. 9, xxi. 2, 9, xxii. 17.

The nuptial festivity (γάμος here, as in Mt. xxii. 8 f., Jo. ii. 1 ff.; elsewhere in N.T. γάμοι) is come (ἦλθεν, as in xi. 18, xiv. 7, 15, xvii. 10); the rejoicings in Heaven are the sign of its arrival; the Bride is ready, the Bridegroom is at hand (*v.* 11). Ἡ γυνὴ αὐτοῦ: for ἡ γυνή = ἡ μεμνηστευμένη cf. Gen. xxix. 21, Deut. xxii. 24, Mt. i. 20, Apoc. xxi. 9. Only three female figures appear in the visions of the Apocalypse—the γυνὴ περιβεβλημένη τὸν ἥλιον of *c.* xii. the γ. περιβεβλ. πορφυροῦν καὶ κόκκινον of *c.* xvii. and the γ. περιβεβλ. βύσσινον of *c.* xix.—the Mother, the Harlot, and the Bride; the first and third present the Church under two different aspects of her life, while the second answers to her great rival and enemy. With ἡτοίμασεν ἑαυτήν cf. xxi. 2 ἡτοιμασμένην ὡς νύμφην. In Eph. v. 25 ff. the preparation of the Bride is represented as the act of Christ (ἑαυτὸν παρέδωκεν ὑπὲρ αὐτῆς, ἵνα αὐτὴν ἁγιάσῃ καθαρίσας τῷ λουτρῷ τοῦ ὕδατος ἐν ῥήματι, ἵνα παραστήσῃ αὐτὸς ἑαυτῷ ἔνδοξον τὴν ἐκκλησίαν κτλ.; see Dean Robinson, note *ad loc.*). Here, though no special emphasis is laid on ἑαυτήν, the complementary truth comes into sight; personal effort is demanded, as in 1 Jo. iii. 3 ἁγνίζει ἑαυτόν, Jude 21 ἑαυτοὺς ἐν ἀγάπῃ θεοῦ τηρήσατε, and 2 Cor. vii. 1 καθαρίσωμεν ἑαυτούς... ἐπιτελοῦντες ἁγιωσύνην.

8. καὶ ἐδόθη αὐτῇ ἵνα περιβάληται βύσσινον κτλ.] A Divine gift supplies the Bride with the right or the power to attire herself as she does. Ἐδόθη αὐτῇ (αὐτῷ, αὐτοῖς) is one of the keynotes of this Book, and occurs some twenty times in *cc.* vi—xx. The bridal dress—in sharp contrast with that of the Harlot (xvii. 4, xviii. 16)—is of simple *byssus*, the fine linen of Egypt; cf. the στολὴ βυσσίνη in which Joseph was arrayed by Pharaoh (Gen. xli. 42). For βύσσινον as a noun see Dan. x. 5 (LXX.) ἐνδεδυμένος βύσσινα καὶ τὴν ὀσφὺν περιεζωσμένος βυσσίνῳ, and *ib.* xii. 6 f. Λαμπρὸν καθαρόν: cf. *c.* xv. 6 ἐνδεδυμένοι λίνον καθαρὸν λαμπρόν.

σινον λαμπρὸν καθαρόν· τὸ γὰρ βύσσινον τὰ δικαιώματα τῶν ἁγίων ἐστίν.

9 [9]καὶ λέγει μοι Γράψον Μακάριοι οἱ εἰς τὸ δεῖπνον τοῦ γάμου τοῦ ἀρνίου κεκλημένοι. καὶ λέγει μοι

8 λαμπρον καθαρον] λαμπρ. και καθ. Q min[30] syr καθ. και λαμπρ. 1 36 73 79 152 syr[gw] arm καθ. λαμπρ. 186 9 τον δειπνον Q 16 38 87 98 | om του γαμου ℵ* P 1 16 36 79 *g* | om και λεγει μοι (2°) ℵ* 6 11 36 38 39

τὸ γὰρ βύσσινον τὰ δικαιώματα κτλ.] Γάρ introduces the explanation; 'with fine linen, for this clean, glistering, byssus-made fabric represents the righteous actions of the Saints,' the two are equivalents; cf. 1 Jo. iii. 4 ἡ ἁμαρτία ἐστὶν ἡ ἀνομία: "sin and lawlessness are convertible terms" (Westcott). For δικαίωμα see xv. 4, note; τὰ δικαιώματα τῶν ἁγίων is the sum of the saintly acts of the members of Christ, wrought in them by His Spirit, which are regarded as making up the clothing of His mystical Body. As each guest at the wedding feast has an ἔνδυμα γάμου (Mt. xxii. 11), as the Saints are individually clad in robes made white in the Blood of the Lamb (Apoc. vii. 9, 14); so corporately the whole Church is seen to be attired in the dazzling whiteness of their collective purity.

9. *καὶ λέγει μοι Γράψον Μακάριοι οἱ εἰς τὸ δεῖπνον κτλ.*] The speaker is perhaps the angel-guide of xvii. 1, who now again reveals his presence; for the form γράψον... cf. xiv. 13. Μακάριοι οἱ εἰς τὸ δεῖπνον κτλ. carries the beatitude of xiv. 13 (μακάριοι οἱ νεκροὶ...ἵνα ἀναπαήσονται) a step further; rest has now ripened into high festival. The words are a Christian interpretation of the remark which called forth the parable of the Great Supper: μακάριος ὅστις φάγεται ἄρτον ἐν τῇ βασιλείᾳ τοῦ θεοῦ—an expectation based on such prophecies as Isa. xxv. 6. Cf. Mt. viii. 11 πολλοὶ...ἀνακλιθήσονται μετὰ Ἀβραὰμ καὶ Ἰσαὰκ καὶ Ἰακὼβ ἐν τῇ βασιλείᾳ τῶν οὐρανῶν; xxvi. 29 ὅταν αὐτὸ πίνω μεθ' ὑμῶν καινὸν ἐν τῇ βασιλείᾳ τοῦ πατρός μου; 4 Esdr. ii. 38 "surgite et state et videte numerum signatorum in convivio Domini. qui se de umbra saeculi transtulerunt, splendidas tunicas a Domino acceperunt. recipe, Sion, numerum tuum et conclude candidatos tuos...roga imperium Domini, ut sanctificetur populus tuus, qui vocatus est ab initio." Οἱ εἰς τὸ δεῖπνον κεκλημένοι, cf. Mt. xxii. 3, Lc. xiv. 17; the 'called' here are clearly identical with the κλητοὶ καὶ ἐκλεκτοὶ καὶ πιστοί of xvii. 14 (where see note). Cf. Primasius: "illos videlicet significans qui *secundum propositum* vocati sunt"; Arethas: καὶ δή γε καὶ μετὰ τὴν κλῆσιν ἀπιόντες ὡς δεῖ.

καὶ λέγει μοι Οὗτοι οἱ λόγοι ἀληθινοὶ τοῦ θεοῦ εἰσίν] A second utterance of the angel, setting the seal of Divine truth upon the whole series of revelations now completed (xvii. 1—xix. 9): 'these are God's words, and they are true'; or, reading οἱ ἀληθ., 'these are God's true words.' For οἱ λόγοι τοῦ θεοῦ see xvii. 17, and for the whole phrase xxi. 5, xxii. 6, and the opening words of the Oxyrhynchus Sayings (2nd series, 1904; cf. *Exp. Times*, xv. p. 489 f.).

This solemn claim to veracity does not of course require belief in the literal fulfilment of the details. Apocalyptic prophecy has its own methods and laws of interpretation, and by these the student must be guided. Under a literary form Divine truth expresses and fulfils itself πολυμερῶς καὶ πολυτρόπως; it is only in the Son that it reaches finality.

Οὗτοι οἱ λόγοι ἀληθινοὶ τοῦ θεοῦ εἰσίν. [10]*καὶ ἔπεσα* 10
ἔμπροσθεν τῶν ποδῶν αὐτοῦ προσκυνῆσαι αὐτῷ. καὶ
λέγει μοι Ὅρα μή· σύνδουλός σού εἰμι καὶ τῶν
ἀδελφῶν σου τῶν ἐχόντων τὴν μαρτυρίαν Ἰησοῦ· τῷ

9 *ουτοι οι λογοι*] + *μου* ℵ* syr* | *αληθινοι* (pr *οι* A 4 48 syr^{gw}) *του θεου εισιν* APQ min$^{plq\ 25}$ vg$^{am\ dem}$ me syrr Ar] *αληθ. εισιν του θεου* ℵ* 1 38 49 79 91 186 *του θεου αληθ. εισιν* ℵ$^{c.a}$ 95 98 vg$^{cle\ tol\ lipss}$ 10 *επεσον* Q 6 14 29 31 90 95 130 al$^{sat\ mu}$ Ar | *εμπροσθεν*] *ενωπιον* Q | *προσκυνησαι αυτω* (*αυτον* Q)] *και προσεκυνησα αυτω* P 73 79 syr^{gw} | *ορα μη*] + *ποιησης* 32 95 Cypr Prim | om *σου* 2° ℵ* 6

10. *καὶ ἔπεσα ἔμπροσθεν τῶν ποδῶν αὐτοῦ κτλ.*] The Seer overwhelmed by the greatness of the revelation, and realizing that God Himself has spoken in these words of the Angel, prostrates himself before his guide. It can scarcely be that he mistakes an angel for God or for Christ; rather he is tempted by his sense of reverence to a *θρησκεία τῶν ἀγγέλων* (Col. ii. 18) from which in calmer moments he would have shrunk. A tendency to Angel-worship lingered long in Asia Minor, as Theodoret witnesses (on Col. *l.c.*): *ἔμεινε δὲ τοῦτο τὸ πάθος ἐν τῇ Φρυγίᾳ καὶ Πισιδίᾳ μέχρι πολλοῦ· οὗ δὴ χάριν καὶ συνελθοῦσα σύνοδος ἐν Λαοδικείᾳ τῆς Φρυγίας νόμῳ κεκώλυκε τὸ τοῖς ἀγγέλοις προσεύχεσθαι· καὶ μέχρι δὲ τοῦ νῦν εὐκτήρια τοῦ ἁγίου Μιχαὴλ παρ' ἐκείνοις καὶ τοῖς ὁμόροις ἐκείνων ἐστὶν ἰδεῖν.* St John's repeated reference to his temptation and the Angel's rebuke (cf. xxii. 8 f.) may well be due to his knowledge that such a tendency existed in the Churches to which he wrote.

Some of the Fathers regard this prohibition of Angel worship as a feature of the New Dispensation; see Gregory *mor.* xxvii. 15, and Bede *ad loc.*: "postquam Dominus Iesus hominem assumptum super caelos elevavit, angelus ab homine timuit adorari, super se videlicet adorans hominem Deum; quod ante incarnationem Domini ab hominibus factum, et nequaquam ab angelis prohibitum esse legimus." But this is a refinement which is not likely to have been present to the mind of the Apocalyptist.

καὶ λέγει μοι Ὅρα μή] For *ὁρᾶν μή* see Mc. i. 44 *ὅρα μηδενὶ μηδὲν εἴπῃς*; 1 Th. v. 15 *ὁρᾶτε μή τις...ἀποδῷ*; with regard to the ellipse in *ὅρα μή* (sc. *ποιήσῃς τοῦτο*), as Blass observes (*Gr.* p. 293), it must have been a common one. The Angel disclaims worship on the ground that he is a *σύνδουλος* of the Seer and of his brother-prophets (cf. xxii. 9 *τῶν ἀδελφῶν σου τῶν προφητῶν*). That all Christians are *σύνδουλοι* was taught by the Master (Mt. xviii. 28 ff., xxiv. 49), and realized by the greatest of His servants (Col. i. 7, iv. 7, Apoc. vi. 11). But Angels are servants of the same Lord (Heb. i. 4 ff.), and therefore fellow-servants of the Saints, who will be their equals in the future life (Lc. xx. 35 f. *οἱ δὲ καταξιωθέντες τοῦ αἰῶνος ἐκείνου τυχεῖν...ἰσάγγελοι...εἰσίν*).

τῶν ἐχόντων τὴν μαρτυρίαν Ἰησοῦ κτλ.] For *ἔχειν τὴν μ. Ἰησοῦ* cf. vi. 9, xii. 17; *ἡ μαρτυρία Ἰησοῦ* occurs also in i. 2, 9, xx. 4. The question arises in all these cases whether *Ἰησοῦ* is the genitive of subject or object; in i. 2 the context seems plainly to require the former, and it is natural to make this fact determine the use of the Apocalypse; on the other hand in several of the later examples 'witness to Jesus' seems more apposite. Here the problem becomes acute, for the meaning of the following words (*ἡ γὰρ μαρτυρία κτλ.*) depends on the

θεῷ προσκύνησον. ἡ γὰρ μαρτυρία Ἰησοῦ ἐστὶν τὸ
πνεῦμα τῆς προφητείας.
11 [11] Καὶ εἶδον τὸν οὐρανὸν ἠνεῳγμένον, καὶ ἰδοὺ
ἵππος λευκός, καὶ ὁ καθήμενος ἐπ' αὐτὸν πιστὸς

11 ειδον ℵP min^{pl}] ιδον AQ 7 130 186 om arm | ανεωγμενον Q min^{pl} Or Ar | om καλουμενος AP 1 4 6 12 17* 31 32 48 79 186 vg^{cod} arm^{vid} Hipp Ar (hab ℵ et ante πιστος Q min^{pl} vg me the syrr aeth Ir^{int} Or Cypr Vict Hier Tyc Prim)

answer it receives. Perhaps the true account of the matter is that the writer, starting in i. 2 with the thought of Christ as the supreme *μάρτυς* (i. 5, iii. 14), falls insensibly into that of the Church repeating His witness and thus bearing testimony to Him. While the original sense of *ἡ μαρτυρία Ἰησοῦ* is never wholly out of sight, the latter probably predominates here. 'Those who have the witness of Jesus' are those who carry on His witness in the world. Such, the Angel says, are the Seer and his brethren the prophets.

ἡ γὰρ μαρτυρία Ἰησοῦ ἐστὶν τὸ πνεῦμα τῆς προφητείας] 'For (cf. the explanatory *γάρ* in *v.* 8) the witness of Jesus is the Spirit of prophecy.' *I.e.* the possession of the prophetic Spirit, which makes a true prophet, shews itself in a life of witness to Jesus which perpetuates His witness to the Father and to Himself; the two are in practice identical (cf. *v.* 8, note 2); all true prophets are witnesses of Jesus, and all who have the witness of Jesus in the highest sense are prophets. In 1 Cor. xii. 3 (*οὐδεὶς δύναται εἰπεῖν 'Κύριος Ἰησοῦς' εἰ μὴ ἐν πνεύματι ἁγίῳ*) St Paul states the general law which St John applies to the special inspiration of the Christian Prophets. The Spirit of prophecy is the Spirit of Jesus (Acts xvi. 7), Who must needs testify of Jesus (Jo. xv. 26). In the prophets of the O.T. the Spirit of Christ bore witness of the coming Passion and Glory; see 1 Pet. i. 11, with Dr Hort's note, and cf. Irenaeus i. 10. 1 *καὶ εἰς πνεῦμα ἅγιον, τὸ διὰ τῶν προφητῶν κεκηρυχὸς τὰς οἰκονομίας καὶ τὰς ἐλεύσεις κτλ.* Similarly it is the office of N.T. prophecy to bear witness to the Christ as already come and glorified, and to point men to the future Parousia.

11—16. VISION OF THE CROWNED WARRIOR.

11. *καὶ εἶδον τὸν οὐρανὸν ἠνεῳγμένον, καὶ ἰδού κτλ.*] So Ezekiel begins his prophecy (i. 1 *καὶ ἐγένετο...καὶ ἠνεῴχθησαν οἱ οὐρανοί, καὶ εἶδον ὁράσεις θεοῦ*); and a similar epiphany is described in 3 Macc. vi. 18 *τότε ὁ μεγαλόδοξος θεὸς ...ἠνέῳξεν τὰς οὐρανίους πύλας, ἐξ ὧν δεδοξασμένοι δύο φοβεροειδεῖς ἄγγελοι κατέβησαν.* In the Gospels the heavens are opened to Jesus at His Baptism (Mt. iii. 16, Mc. i. 10 *εἶδεν σχιζομένους τοὺς οὐρανούς*, Lc. iii. 21) and He promises a like vision to His disciples (Jo. i. 51 *ὄψεσθε τὸν οὐρανὸν ἀνεῳγότα*). Early in the Apocalypse a door is opened in heaven (iv. 1), and the Sanctuary itself is opened more than once (xi. 19, xv. 5); angels frequently descend from heaven (x. 1, xiv. 17, xviii. 1). The present revelation is on a larger scale; the heavens themselves open to disclose the glorified Christ. Sounds from heaven have been heard already (xix. 1); the Bride has made herself ready (*v.* 7 f.), the marriage supper of the Lamb is at hand (*v.* 9). But it is neither as the Bridegroom nor as the Lamb that the Christ is now revealed; the parted heavens shew a Figure seated on a white horse, a royal commander, followed by a dazzling retinue.

The words *καὶ ἰδοὺ ἵππος λευκός, καὶ ὁ καθήμενος ἐπ' αὐτόν* are repeated

[καλούμενος] καὶ ἀληθινός, καὶ ἐν δικαιοσύνῃ κρίνει καὶ
πολεμεῖ. [12]οἱ δὲ ὀφθαλμοὶ αὐτοῦ [ὡς] φλὸξ πυρός, 12

12 ως A 35 36 87 91 95 al vg syrr aeth Ir Or Cypr Prim Ar] om ℵPQ 1 al[35] arm Hipp

from *c.* vi. 2, where see note. In both passages the 'white horse' is the emblem of victory, for the allegorical sense which Origen (*in Ioann.* t. i. 42, ii. 4) permits himself to give to the horse in the present passage is more curious than convincing. But the Rider here is not the rider of *c.* vi.; there we see the Roman Imperator, or possibly the Parthian King (cf. Ramsay, *Letters to the Seven Churches*, p. 58), with his bow and wreath (ἔχων τόξον, καὶ ἐδόθη αὐτῷ στέφανος); here the Commander-in-chief of the host of heaven (cf. Jos. v. 14 ἀρχιστράτηγος δυνάμεως Κυρίου), with His sharp sword and many diadems; the superficial resemblance seems to emphasize the points of contrast. In any case no doubt is left as to the personality of the present Rider; He is known as (καλούμενος, cf. Lc. vi. 15 καλούμενον Ζηλωτήν, viii. 2 ἡ καλουμένη Μαγδαληνή, Acts viii. 10 ἡ καλουμένη Μεγάλη) 'Faithful' and 'True' (*verus*, as Prim., not *verax*, as Vg. here). Both epithets are applied to our Lord in the early chapters of the Book, e.g. i. 5 ὁ μάρτυς ὁ πιστός, iii. 7 ὁ ἅγιος, ὁ ἀληθινός, 14 ὁ μάρτυς ὁ πιστὸς καὶ ὁ ἀληθινός; for the sense attached to them in this connexion see notes to those passages.

ἐν δικαιοσύνῃ κρίνει καὶ πολεμεῖ] A principal feature in the Messianic character, cf. Isa. xi. 3 ff. οὐ κατὰ τὴν δόξαν κρινεῖ οὐδὲ κατὰ τὴν λαλιὰν ἐλέγξει...καὶ πατάξει τὴν γῆν τῷ λόγῳ τοῦ στόματος αὐτοῦ...καὶ ἔσται δικαιοσύνῃ ἐζωσμένος τὴν ὀσφὺν αὐτοῦ καὶ ἀληθείᾳ εἰλημένος τὰς πλευράς; see also Ps. Sol. xvii. 23 ff. The Christ who comes is both Judge and Warrior, and He judges first, for in the Divine order judgement precedes victory. His judgements are ἐν δικαιοσύνῃ, for they are God's (cf. xv. 3 δίκαιαι καὶ ἀληθιναὶ αἱ ὁδοί σου, xvi. 5 δίκαιος εἶ...ὅτι ταῦτα ἔκρινας, 7, xix. 2 ἀληθιναὶ καὶ δίκαιαι αἱ κρίσεις σου); the Seer perhaps mentally contrasts them with the corrupt practices of Eastern courts, and the injustice often received at the Proconsul's tribunal. The present tense (κρίνει, πολεμεῖ) is used because the writer is stating the normal character of Divine judgements and wars, or it may possibly imply that Christ's work as Judge and Warrior is already proceeding in the world, though the tribunal is invisible and no ear hears the din of battle.

12. οἱ δὲ ὀφθαλμοὶ αὐτοὶ ὡς φλὸξ πυρός κτλ.] The Seer proceeds from the character of the Rider on the white horse to His person. The 'eyes as a flame of fire' are a reminiscence of the vision in *c.* i.; cf. i. 14, ii. 18, notes. The next feature is new: ἐπὶ τὴν κεφαλὴν αὐτοῦ διαδήματα πολλά. For διάδημα see xii. 3, note, xiii. 1. The Dragon wears a diadem on each of his seven heads; the Wild Beast from the Sea has one on each of his ten horns. As contrasted with the wreath, the fillet was the symbol of Regal power, going with the sceptre (Apul. *met.* 10 "caput stringebat diadema candida; ferebat et sceptrum"), and for this reason it was declined by the earlier *principes*: cf. Suet. *Jul.* 79 "[Julius] cum...quidam e turba statuae eius coronam lauream candida fascia praeligata imposuisset, et tribuni plebis...coronae fasciam (i.q. τὸ διάδημα) detrahi...iussissent, dolens seu parum prospere motam regni mentionem sive, ut ferebat, ereptam sibi gloriam recusandi, tribunos graviter increpitos potestate privavit"; and the somewhat similar story told by Plutarch, *C. Caes.* 61 φέρων διάδημα στεφάνῳ δάφνης περι-

καὶ ἐπὶ τὴν κεφαλὴν αὐτοῦ διαδήματα πολλά, ἔχων
ὄνομα γεγραμμένον ὃ οὐδεὶς οἶδεν εἰ μὴ αὐτός, [13]καὶ 13

12 ονομα γεγραμμενον ο] ονοματα γεγραμμενα α ℵ[c.a] 9 13 16 27 39 aeth ονοματα γεγραμμενα και ονομα γεγραμμενον ο Q 130 al[25] syr

πεπλεγμένον ὤρεξε τῷ Καίσαρι...ἀπωσαμένου δὲ τοῦ Καίσαρος ἅπας ὁ δῆμος ἀνεκρότησεν κτλ. Christ, who refused the diadem when offered to Him by the Tempter (Mt. iv. 9) was crowned on the merit of His victorious Passion, and now appears wearing not one royal crown alone, but many. For πολλά cf. Andreas: τὰ δὲ πολλὰ διαδήματα...τὴν κατὰ πάντων αὐτοῦ βασιλείαν τῶν τε ἐν οὐρανῷ καὶ γῇ αἰνίττονται; compare 1 Macc. xi. 13 καὶ εἰσῆλθεν Πτολεμαῖος εἰς Ἀντιοχίαν, καὶ περιέθετο τὸ διάδημα τῆς Ἀσίας, καὶ περιέθετο δύο διαδήματα περὶ τὴν κεφαλὴν αὐτοῦ, τὸ τῆς Ἀσίας καὶ Αἰγύπτου. Not Asia only and Egypt and Europe belonged to the Lord Christ, but all the provinces of God's Universe; cf. Mt. xxviii. 18, Phil. ii. 9, Apoc. i. 18.

ἔχων ὄνομα γεγραμμένον ὃ οὐδεὶς οἶδεν κτλ.] Besides the title 'Faithful and True,' which reputation gave Him, He bore a name written (? upon His forehead; see xiv. 1, xvii. 5) which was known only to Himself; compare ii. 17 ὄνομα καινὸν γεγραμμένον ὃ οὐδεὶς οἶδεν εἰ μὴ ὁ λαμβάνων; iii. 12 γράψω ἐπ' αὐτὸν...τὸ ὄνομά μου τὸ καινόν. A similar mystery attends the name of the Angel who appears to Jacob on the Jabbok (Gen. xxxii. 29 ἵνα τί σὺ ἐρωτᾷς τὸ ὄνομά μου; and the same answer is made by the Angel to Manoah (Jud. xiii. 18), with the reason added καὶ αὐτό ἐστιν θαυμαστόν. The comment of Andreas seems to be justified: τὸ δὲ ἄγνωστον τοῦ ὀνόματος τὸ τῆς οὐσίας αὐτοῦ σημαίνει ἀκατάληπτον· ταῖς γὰρ οἰκονομίαις ὢν πολυώνυμος, ὡς ἀγαθός, ὡς ποιμήν...καὶ ταῖς ἀποφάσεσιν ὁμοίως, ὡς ἄφθαρτος, ὡς ἀθάνατος...τῇ οὐσίᾳ ἐστὶν ἀνώνυμος καὶ ἀνέφικτος. Notwithstanding the dogmatic helps which the Church offers, the mind fails to grasp the inmost significance of the Person of Christ, which eludes all efforts to bring it within the terms of human knowledge. Only the Son of God can understand the mystery of His own Being. The words εἰ μὴ αὐτός do not contradict but supplement our Lord's own saying in Mt. xi. 27 οὐδεὶς ἐπιγινώσκει τὸν υἱὸν εἰ μὴ ὁ πατήρ. As Primasius rightly says: "cavendum sane est ne...nomen Filii...aut Patri aut Spiritui sancto putetur incognitum." Οὐδείς excludes created beings only, not other Persons internal to the Life of God.

13. καὶ περιβεβλημένος ἱμάτιον ῥεραμμένον αἵματι] Dr Hort well observes (WH.[2] *Notes*, p. 139 f.) that "all the variations [ἐρραμμένον, περιρεραμμένον, ἐρραντισμένον, περιρεραντισμένον, and even βεβαμμένον] are easily accounted for if the form used was ῥεραμμένον"—a fact which, considering the comparative paucity of first-rate authorities for the text of this Book, seems to justify its provisional adoption. It is worthy of notice that non-Septuagintal versions of Isa. lxiii. 3—the passage on which St John's conception appears to be based—rendered יֵזּ by ἐρραντίσθη or ἐρράνθη, and that the use of one of these verbs is pre-supposed by the ordinary Syriac, which has ܐܬܠܚ, and possibly also by Dr Gwynn's version (Gwynn, p. 85). On the form ῥεραμμένον see WH[2]. *Notes*, p. 172.

The Rider's cloak (the ἱμάτιον) is perhaps a χλαμύς (Mt. xxvii. 28, 31) or a *paludamentum*, if a Roman General is in view. It is dyed or sprinkled with blood, after the second Isaiah's conception of the Divine Conqueror from Edom (Isa. lxiii. 1 ff.), a prophecy which the later Jews expected to be fulfilled in Messianic times, cf. *syn.*

περιβεβλημένος ἱμάτιον *ῥεραμμένον* αἵματι, καὶ
κέκληται τὸ ὄνομα αὐτοῦ Ὁ λόγος τοῦ θεοῦ. ¹⁴καὶ 14

13 ρεραμμενον] περιρεραμμενον ℵ* ερραμμενον Or (cf. Ir^{int} Cypr Tyc Prim) περιρεραντισμενον ℵ$^{c.c}$ ρεραντισμενον P 36 ερραντισμενον 32 35 87 95 Hipp Or βεβαμμενον AQ 1 130 186 al^{pl} Ar | αιματι] pr εν 6 31 32 33 48 Ar | κεκληται] κεκλητο ℵ* (Or) καλειται 1 31 36 48 49 79 91 al Andr Ar vg$^{cle\ am\ tol\ lipss\ 5}$ syr^{gw} Ir^{int} Cypr Tyc

Sohar, p. 113. 23 (Schöttgen, i. p. 1134): "futuro tempore Deus...vestimentum vindictae induet contra Edom." In the original context the blood upon the Warrior's dress is that of the conquered enemy, who have been trampled under foot like grapes in the winefat; and this idea is certainly present to St John's mind (cf. *v.* 15). But in applying the figure to Christ, he could hardly have failed to think also of the 'Blood of the Lamb' (i. 5, v. 9, vii. 14, xii. 11) which was shed in the act of treading the enemy under foot. To some extent this probability may be held to justify the old interpretation, that e.g. of Hippolytus (*c. Noet.*, ed. Lagarde p. 53 f.: ὁρᾶτε οὖν, ἀδελφοί, πῶς ἐν συμβόλῳ τὸ ἱμάτιον τὸ ἐρραντισμένον αἵματι τὴν σάρκα διηγήσατο, δι' ἧς καὶ ὑπὸ πάθος ἦλθεν ὁ ἀπαθὴς τοῦ θεοῦ λόγος), Origen (*in Ioann.* t. ii. 4), and Andreas, who writes *ad loc.*: ἱματίον τοῦ θεοῦ λόγου ἡ παναγία σὰρξ αὐτοῦ...ἡ βαφεῖσα ἐν τῷ ἑκουσίῳ πάθει τῷ ἰδίῳ αὐτοῦ αἵματι. But this view, if admitted, must be kept subordinate to the other. In this vision Christ is not presented as the Redeemer, but as the Judge and Warrior.

καὶ κέκληται τὸ ὄνομα αὐτοῦ Ὁ λόγος τοῦ θεοῦ] In the N.T. the idea of a personal Logos seems to be limited to the Johannine writings (for Heb. iv. 12 see Westcott *ad loc.*) and there it is found under three forms—ὁ λόγος τοῦ θεοῦ (here), ὁ λόγος τῆς ζωῆς (1 Jo. i. 1), ὁ λόγος (Jo. i. 1 ff.). Of these the present is probably the earliest; the relative use of the term would naturally precede the absolute, and the relation of the Word to God would be the first to present itself. Ὁ λόγος τοῦ θεοῦ (Κυρίου) is a familiar O.T. phrase for a prophetic utterance, which St Luke and St Paul employ for the teaching of Jesus or for the Gospel (Lc. v. 1, viii. 11, xi. 28, Acts vi. 2, xiii. 5, 44, 1 Cor. xiv. 36, 2 Cor. ii. 17, iv. 2, 1 Th. ii. 13 etc.). Meanwhile, the thought had taken root that Jesus is Himself the final and the only perfect revelation of God to man (Heb. i. 1 f.), and St John gave expression to this belief when he applied the term 'Word of God' to the glorified Christ. How far at this stage he had anticipated the doctrine of the Prologue to the Fourth Gospel cannot be determined; but it is difficult to resist the impression that there is some connexion between the present passage and the teaching of the Alexandrine book of Wisdom; cf. Sap. xviii. 15 ὁ παντοδύναμός σου λόγος ἀπ' οὐρανῶν ἐκ θρόνων βασιλείων | ἀπότομος πολεμιστὴς εἰς μέσον τῆς ὀλεθρίας ἥλατο γῆς, | ξίφος ὀξὺ τὴν ἀνυπόκριτον ἐπιταγήν σου φέρων.

Arethas asks how the giving of this name to Christ is to be reconciled with the statement in *v.* 12: εἰκός ἐστί τινα ἐπαπορῆσαι πῶς ὁ πρὸ μικροῦ ἀνώνυμος χρηματίσας καὶ πᾶσιν ἄγνωστος κατὰ τὸ ὄνομα, νῦν ἐνταῦθα Λόγος ὀνομάζεται. His answer is not very convincing, but Apringius at least strikes the right note: "sicut pro ineffabilitate virtutis eius supra fatetur incognitum omnibus eius nomen...ad professionem nostrae fidei...Verbum Dei esse significat." No Name of our Lord, not even ὁ λόγος, is more than a help to faith and a step towards fuller knowledge; cf. note on *v.* 12.

14. καὶ τὰ στρατεύματα τὰ ἐν τῷ οὐρανῷ κτλ.] The existence of a celes-

τὰ στρατεύματα [τὰ] ἐν τῷ οὐρανῷ ἠκολούθει αὐτῷ
ἐφ' ἵπποις λευκοῖς, ἐνδεδυμένοι βύσσινον λευκὸν καθα-
15 ρόν. [15]καὶ ἐκ τοῦ στόματος αὐτοῦ ἐκπορεύεται

14 τα εν τω ουρανω AP 30 32 47 48 49 50 51 91 95 130 186] om τα ℵQ 1 6 7 11 12 al[fere 10] των ουρανων (vel του ουρανου) 8 (36) syr[gw] | ηκολουθουν 186 | εφ ιπποις λευκοις] επι ιππ. λ. Q min[plq 30] Or Ar εφιπποι πολλοι 186 | ενδεδυμενοις ℵ* 152 Or | βυσσινον λευκον] λευκ. βυσσινον A λευκοβυσσινον 95 | καθαρον] pr και ℵ 1 al[vix mu] *g* vg[cle lipss 4, 6] the syr[gw] Or

tial 'army' is implied in xii. 7 ὁ Μιχαὴλ καὶ οἱ ἄγγελοι αὐτοῦ τοῦ πολεμῆσαι μετὰ τοῦ δράκοντος. In the O.T. צְבָא הַשָּׁמַיִם (צְבָאוֹת) is a constant phrase for (1) the ordered ranks of the heavenly bodies (cf. e.g. 2 Esdr. xix. 6 σοὶ προσκυνοῦσιν αἱ στρατεῖαι τῶν οὐρανῶν), and (2) the angelic bodyguard of the Throne of God; see Driver, art. *Host of Heaven*, in Hastings' *D.B.* ii. p. 429 ff. Here the latter are clearly meant. The angelic hosts were at the service of the Incarnate Son even in the days of His Flesh (cf. Mt. xxvi. 53 δοκεῖς ὅτι οὐ δύναμαι παρακαλέσαι τὸν πατέρα μου, καὶ παραστήσει μοι ἄρτι πλείω δώδεκα λεγιῶνας ἀγγέλων), and in His exaltation they wait upon His pleasure (Heb. i. 6 ff., cf. Mt. xiii. 41, xvi. 27, xxiv. 31, xxv. 31, Apoc. v. 11 f.). Some of the ancient interpreters thought here of the elect from among mankind (e.g. Apringius: "exercitus qui in caelo est ipsa est sponsa"), or of the "martyrum candidatus exercitus"; but though either of these bodies might, consistently with the use of the Apoc., be placed in Heaven and clad in white (cf. vii. 9 ff.), yet the general sense of both O. and N.T. points rather to the angelic orders, and Andreas is doubtless right when he says: τὸ δὲ ἀκολουθεῖν αὐτῷ στρατεύματα τὰ ἐν τῷ οὐρανῷ τὰς οὐρανίας τάξεις σημαίνει. As the Lamb, Christ is followed by the Saints (xiv. 4); but as the Celestial Warrior, coming from Heaven to earth upon a mission of judgement, He brings with Him His Angels.

On στρατεύματα see ix. 16, note. A στράτευμα may be a small body of soldiers, such as Herod's bodyguard (Lc. xxiii. 11), or the garrison of the Antonia (Acts xxiii. 10, 27), or a great host, taken in the aggregate (*v.* 19); in the plural the word = troops, forces, *copiae*. These celestial troops are all cavalry (cf. ix. 16), mounted, like their Captain, on white horses, the symbol and omen of victory. But whereas their Captain is arrayed in a cloak sprinkled with blood, they are clad in pure white *byssus* (cf. *v.* 8, note). He only has had experience of mortal conflict; for them bloodshed and death are impossible.

15. καὶ ἐκ τοῦ στόματος αὐτοῦ ἐκπορεύεται κτλ.] Another feature from the vision of *c.* i.; cf. i. 16, notes. But the sharp sword issuing from the mouth of the Word fulfils a new purpose. The Priest-King, walking in the midst of the churches, uses it to chastise the impenitent members of the Asian congregations (ii. 12, 15 f. μετανόησον οὖν· εἰ δὲ μή,...πολεμήσω μετ' αὐτῶν ἐν τῇ ῥομφαίᾳ τοῦ στόματός μου). Here its work lies beyond the pale of the Church; the Warrior-King comes to smite the pagan nations with it. St John has in view Isa. xi. 3 ff. οὐ κατὰ τὴν δόξαν κρινεῖ...πατάξει γῆν τῷ λόγῳ τοῦ στόματος αὐτοῦ, καὶ ἐν πνεύματι διὰ χειλέων ἀνελεῖ ἀσεβῆ. The Word of God fights with the sword of the word; His weapons are spiritual and not carnal (2 Cor. x. 4); He smites the nations not by judgements only, but by the forces which reduce them to

ῥομφαία ὀξεῖα, ἵνα ἐν αὐτῇ πατάξῃ τὰ ἔθνη· καὶ
αὐτὸς ποιμανεῖ αὐτοὺς ἐν ῥάβδῳ σιδηρᾷ· καὶ αὐτὸς
πατεῖ τὴν ληνὸν τοῦ οἴνου τοῦ θυμοῦ τῆς ὀργῆς τοῦ
θεοῦ τοῦ παντοκράτορος. [16]καὶ ἔχει ἐπὶ τὸ ἱμάτιον 16

15 οξεια] pr διστομος Q min$^{pl\,q\,40}$ vg$^{cle\ tol\ lipss}$ syr* Cypr Tyc Prim Ar | της οργης του θυμου ℵ the Or 16 om επι το ιματιον και A | ιματιον] + αυτου 87 152 syr^{gw}

the obedience of faith; cf. Apringius: "percutere dicitur...liberare, damnare, iustificare, eripere, salvare." The whole course of 'the expansion of Christianity' is here in a figure: the conversion of the Empire; the conversion of the Western nations which rose on the ruins of the Empire; the conversion of the South and the far East, still working itself out in the history of our own time. In all St John would have seen Christ using the Sword of His mouth; the white horse and his Rider, the diadem-crowned head, the invisible armies of Heaven.

καὶ αὐτὸς ποιμανεῖ αὐτοὺς ἐν ῥάβδῳ σιδηρᾷ: an image already familiar to readers of this book (ii. 27, xii. 5, where see notes); the same blending of the metaphor of Isa. xi. and Ps. ii. is to be observed in Ps. Sol. xvii. 26 f.: ἐκτρίψαι ὑπερηφανίαν ἁμαρτωλοῦ ὡς σκεύη κεραμέως· ἐν ῥάβδῳ σιδηρᾷ συντρίψαι πᾶσαν ὑπόστασιν αὐτῶν· ὀλεθρεῦσαι ἔθνη παράνομα ἐν λόγῳ στόματος αὐτοῦ—a coincidence which may be explained by supposing that St John here follows a Jewish tradition already existing in the century before Christ. The sense is clear. The work of the Pastor, the Guide and Ruler of souls (1 Pet. ii. 25), follows that of the Evangelist; the heathen are first to be reduced to obedience, and then brought under the discipline of Christ.

καὶ αὐτὸς πατεῖ τὴν ληνὸν τοῦ οἴνου κτλ.] The repetition of καὶ αὐτός adds solemnity; Christ Himself is in all this movement, by whatever ministry He may work. And His work in the world is not all redemptive or restorative; it has its terrible side. The ληνός of judgement and its wine of wrath have been mentioned already more than once; for the first see xiv. 19 f., notes, and for the second, xiv. 8, 10, xvi. 19; now we learn by Whom the winepress is trodden, though this has already been suggested by *v.* 13, with its reference to Isa. lxiii. 1 ff.

16. καὶ ἔχει ἐπὶ τὸ ἱμάτιον κτλ.] While He is known to Himself by a name which is hidden from all others, and to the Churches as the Word of God, He has a third name which all can read, for it is displayed on His habit where it falls over the thigh. Ἐπὶ τὸ ἱμάτιον καὶ ἐπὶ τὸν μηρὸν αὐτοῦ, 'on the cloak and on that most exposed part of it which covers the thigh,' where it cannot escape notice. Modern commentators quote Cic. *Verr.* iv. 43 "signum Apollinis pulcherrimum, cuius in femore literulis minutis argenteis nomen Myronis erat inscriptum"; Paus. *Eliac.* (Wetstein): ἀνδρὸς εἰκών...ἐλεγεῖον δὲ ἐπ' αὐτὸ γεγραμμένον ἐπὶ τοῦ μηροῦ; the Apocalyptist, perhaps, has in view some equestrian statue at Ephesus similarly inscribed. The allegorical meaning which the ancient interpreters offer (e.g. Primasius: "femore illius posteritas seminis designatur in quo benedicentur omnes gentes") is improbable; nor can we press τὸ ἱμάτιον αὐτοῦ after the manner of Apringius, who writes: "in veste, id est, in sacramento Dominici corporis scriptum legitur nomen eius 'Rex regum'," meaning apparently that the glorified humanity of the Lord sufficiently proclaims His universal Sovereignty.

καὶ ἐπὶ τὸν μηρὸν αὐτοῦ ὄνομα γεγραμμένον Βασιλεὺς
βασιλέων καὶ κύριος κυρίων.
17 [17] Καὶ εἶδον ἕνα ἄγγελον ἑστῶτα ἐν τῷ ἡλίῳ,
καὶ ἔκραξεν [ἐν] φωνῇ μεγάλῃ λέγων πᾶσιν τοῖς

16 om επι 2° ℵ 17 ειδον ℵP min^{pl}] ιδον AQ 7 14 36 92 130 186 | ενα αγγελον] αλλον αγγ. ℵ 36 me the syr^{gw} arm αγγελον Q 130 al$^{fere\,30}$ syr Tyc | εκραξεν] εκραζεν Q 12 95 vg^{tol} | εν φωνη ℵQ 2 14 16 92 al$^{fere\,10}$ (om εν AP min^{pl} vg Andr Ar) | om πασιν 95 syr^{gw}

The title Βασιλεύς κτλ. is given to the Lamb in xvii. 14, where see notes; the changed order can hardly be more than accidental.

"Sic semper Verbum Dei," writes Irenaeus (iv. 20. 11), after quoting the three visions of the exalted Christ in Apoc. i., v., xix., "velut lineamenta rerum futurarum habet, et velut species dispositionum Patris hominibus ostendebat, docens nos quae sunt Dei."

17—21. Overthrow and end of the Beast and the False Prophet.

17 f. καὶ εἶδον ἕνα ἄγγελον ἑστῶτα ἐν τῷ ἡλίῳ κτλ.] As in xviii. 21, a single angel suffices for the task. He takes up a position in the sun, whence he can deliver his message to the great birds of prey that fly high in the zenith (ἐν μεσουρανήματι: cf. viii. 13, xiv. 6, notes); he is sent to summon them to the battlefield which is presently to be strewn with the bodies of the King's enemies. The imagery is borrowed from Ez. xxxix. 17 ff., where the slaughter of Gog is described: εἰπὸν παντὶ ὀρνέῳ πετεινῷ...συνάχθητε ἀπὸ πάντων τῶν περικύκλῳ ἐπὶ τὴν θυσίαν μου, ἣν τέθυκα ὑμῖν θυσίαν μεγάλην...καὶ φάγεσθε κρέα καὶ πίεσθε αἷμα. κρέα γιγάντων (גִּבּוֹרִים) φάγεσθε, καὶ αἷμα ἀρχόντων τῆς γῆς πίεσθε...καὶ ἐμπλησθήσεσθε ἐπὶ τῆς τραπέζης μου ἵππον καὶ ἀναβάτην καὶ γίγαντα καὶ πάντα ἄνδρα πολεμιστήν. The same idea is to be found in Mt. xxiv. 28 ὅπου ἐὰν ᾖ τὸ πτῶμα, ἐκεῖ συναχθήσονται οἱ ἀετοί. Carrion, even a single corpse, has a magnetic attraction for vultures, and here is a field piled with the dead, a great repast spread by the hand of God (τὸ δεῖπνον τὸ μέγα τοῦ θεοῦ); or in Ezekiel's words, a sacrificial feast spread on God's table for all the vultures of the sky. In Ezekiel only the bodies of the great are offered to the birds of prey; in St John's conception all the slain lie together; not only kings and captains (χιλίαρχοι, *tribuni*, cf. vi. 15, note), but the rank and file, and these are made up of all sorts and conditions of men free and bond (vi. 18, xiii. 16), small and great (xi. 13, xiii. 16, xix. 5, xx. 12). The great war between Christ and Antichrist, which is now about to enter upon its final stage, draws its recruits from every class, and in war there is no respect of persons.

Is this battle to be identified with that of Har Magedon (xvi. 16), and with that of Gog and Magog (xx. 8 ff.)? In *c.* xvi. the forces are seen gathering for battle, but the battle is not yet begun; and there seems to be no reason why we should not find its consummation here; see note on xvi. 14. It is more difficult to correlate the present passage with xx. 8 f.; the battle of Gog and Magog follows the thousand years, and *prima facie* is distinct from the battle of *c.* xix., and later; see notes *ad loc.* It may be pointed out, however, (1) that xix. 17 ff. and xx. 8 f. are based on the same passage in Ezekiel, and (2) that in the Apocalypse priority in the order of sequence does not always imply priority in time.

ὀρνέοις τοῖς πετομένοις ἐν μεσουρανήματι Δεῦτε,
συνάχθητε εἰς τὸ δεῖπνον τὸ μέγα τοῦ θεοῦ, [18]ἵνα 18
φάγητε σάρκας βασιλέων¶ καὶ σάρκας χιλιάρχων καὶ ¶ the
σάρκας ἰσχυρῶν καὶ σάρκας ἵππων καὶ τῶν καθημένων
ἐπ' αὐτούς, καὶ σάρκας πάντων ἐλευθέρων τε καὶ
δούλων καὶ μικρῶν καὶ μεγάλων. [19]καὶ εἶδον τὸ 19
θηρίον καὶ τοὺς βασιλεῖς τῆς γῆς καὶ τὰ στρατεύματα
αὐτῶν συνηγμένα ποιῆσαι τὸν πόλεμον μετὰ τοῦ
καθημένου ἐπὶ τοῦ ἵππου καὶ μετὰ τοῦ στρατεύματος

17 πετωμενοις P min^{mu} | om συναχθητε 1 186 Prim | τον δειπνον 4 6 8 16 29 31 32 35 41 42 94 95 96 al | τον μεγαν 6 16 31 32 35 38 39 48 51 55 87 94 του μεγαλου 1 36 49 74 186 vg^{lips6} arm aeth 18 om και σαρκας χιλιαρχων 1 49 arm | επ αυτους A 14 92] επ αυτων PQ min$^{fere\ omn}$ Andr Ar επ αυτοις ℵ | παντων (απ. Q*)] pr των 130 Ar om παντ. 1 152 me syr^{gw} arm | om τε 1 6 al^{pauc} | om και 7° Q 9 14 30 36 al | μικρων]+τε Q min^{plq30} | μεγαλων] pr των ℵ 95 19 ειδον P min^{pl}] ιδον ℵAQ 7 36 92 130 | και τα στρατ.] κατα στρατ. ℵ* κατα τα στρατ. ℵ$^{c.a}$ | αυτων] αυτου A 6 11 31 | τον πολεμον] om τον P 1 6 al$^{sat\ mu}$ Andr

On *σάρκας* see xvii. 16, note.

19. *καὶ εἶδον τὸ θηρίον καὶ τοὺς βασιλεῖς κτλ.*] When the Beast was last seen (xvii. 16 f.), he was in league with the ten kings who were to bring about the destruction of Babylon. It was foreseen by the Seer that the kings would ultimately turn their arms against the Lamb (*ib.* 14). This development has now been reached; Babylon is no more, but the Beast survives, and is allied against Christ with the powers which have risen on the ruins of Rome. They are now called *οἱ βασιλεῖς τῆς γῆς*—the representatives of the מַלְכֵי־אֶרֶץ (Ps. ii. 2) who are the hereditary foes of the Lord's Anointed. In *c.* xvii. the Beast's allies are uncrowned (*v.* 12 *βασιλείαν οὔπω ἔλαβον, ἀλλὰ ἐξουσίαν ὡς βασιλεῖς μίαν ὥραν λαμβάνουσιν μετὰ τοῦ θηρίου*), but St John foresees that they will be succeeded by crowned heads; out of the confusion of the age which saw the fall of Rome there will rise a new order with duly constituted powers. These, however, so far as they lend their authority to the Beast (xvii. 13), i.e. inherit the selfish and worldly policy of the Empire, will be animated by the same spirit, and the Seer sees them in the end banded together, like Herod and Pontius Pilate, to wage the war (*τὸν πόλεμον*) foretold in xvii. 14 and even in Ps. ii.

In what form this prediction will fulfil itself cannot be conjectured. But it seems to point to a last struggle between Society and the Church, or rather between Christ and Antichrist. Those who take note of the tendencies of modern civilization will not find it impossible to conceive that a time may come when throughout Christendom the spirit of Antichrist will, with the support of the State, make a final stand against a Christianity which is loyal to the Person and teaching of Christ.

On *τοῦ στρατεύματος αὐτοῦ* as contrasted with *τὰ στρατεύματα αὐτῶν* Andreas makes the shrewd remark: *τοὺς τῷ χριστῷ ἑπομένους ἑνικῶς στράτευμα προσηγόρευσε διὰ τὸ τῆς γνώμης ἑνιαῖον θέλημα τῆς πρὸς τὸν θεὸν λόγον*

20 αὐτοῦ. ²⁰καὶ ἐπιάσθη τὸ θηρίον καὶ μετ' αὐτοῦ ὁ
ψευδοπροφήτης ὁ ποιήσας τὰ σημεῖα ἐνώπιον αὐτοῦ,
ἐν οἷς ἐπλάνησεν τοὺς λαβόντας τὸ χάραγμα τοῦ
θηρίου καὶ τοὺς προσκυνοῦντας τῇ εἰκόνι αὐτοῦ·
ζῶντες ἐβλήθησαν οἱ δύο εἰς τὴν λίμνην τοῦ πυρὸς

20 *μετ αυτου* ℵP (*ο μετ αυτου ο*) 14 37 38 49** 79 91 96 vg syr^{gw} Prim] *οι μετ αυτου* A 41 me *μετα τουτου* 1 49* al^{vid} *ο μετ αυτου* Q min$^{fere\ 30}$ syr arm Ar | *τη εικονι* ℵ$^{c.a}$ AP min$^{fere\ omn}$ Andr Ar (*την εικονα* ℵ* 38 39)] *το χαραγμα* Q | *ζωντες*] pr *και* 130 | *εβληθησαν*] *βληθησονται* 1 36 38 | om *οι δυο* arm

εὐαρεστήσεως. There is a certain unity which comes from making common cause in evil-doing (xvii. 13, 17), but it has its limits and is apt to break down when personal interests differ; the unity of the heavenly *στρατεύματα*, when engaged in the service of God and of Christ, is indissoluble. Even the Church on earth in its last struggle with Antichrist may be expected to present an unbroken front to the foe; a grave common danger will go far to cancel mutual distrust.

20. *καὶ ἐπιάσθη τὸ θηρίον καὶ μετ' αὐτοῦ ὁ ψευδοπροφήτης*] The imagery of the battlefield is carried on; the course of the battle is not recorded, but its issue is stated. The Beast, who had been the prime mover in the revolt against the King of kings, when the day was manifestly lost, made an effort to escape; but his flight was intercepted, and he was seized. For *πιάζειν*, said to be a Doric form of *πιέζειν* which was perpetuated in Hellenistic Greek, see W. Schm. p. 50; *πιέζειν* occurs in Mic. vi. 15 *πιέσεις ἐλαίαν*, Lc. vi. 38 *μέτρον καλὸν πεπιεσμένον*; for the meaning 'seize,' 'arrest,' cf. Cant. ii. 15, Sir. xxiii. 21, Jo. vii. 30, 32, 44, x. 39, xi. 57, Acts xii. 4, 2 Cor. xi. 32. With the Beast was found his subservient ally, the False Prophet (cf. Tert. *de res. carn.* 25 "bestia antichristus cum suo pseudo-propheta"), i.e. the Second Beast of *c.* xiii. 11 ff.; on this identification see xvi. 13, note. Τὰ *σημεῖα*, not 'miracles' (A.V.), but "the signs" (R.V.), i.e. those described in xiii. 13 ff., where see notes. The Seer still has in view the magic art practised by the priests of the Caesar-temples, but though he can only express himself in the terms of existing conditions, his words may be held to cover all forms of religious or irreligious fanaticism, all the juggling and dishonesties of false cults and creeds, whether pagan or Christian or openly antichristian. When Beatus writes: "pseudo-prophetae sunt praepositi...pseudo-episcopi et sacerdotes eorum similes mali," he is wrong only in limiting his interpretation to Christian false prophets; the world is full of systems which misinterpret God and His relation to the creature, and these are not to be overlooked. On *ἐν οἷς ἐπλάνησεν τοὺς λαβόντας τὸ χάραγμα τοῦ θηρίου κτλ.* see the notes to xiii. 16, xiv. 9 ff., xvi. 2, xx. 4.

ζῶντες ἐβλήθησαν οἱ δύο εἰς τὴν λίμνην τοῦ πυρός κτλ.] As the two had fought together against Christ, so they will ultimately fall together; the day that sees the end of a false statecraft will see also that of a false priestcraft. The punishment of the Beast is suggested by Daniel's account of the fate of his fourth Beast (vii. 11 Th. *ἐθεώρουν...ἕως ἀνῃρέθη τὸ θηρίον καὶ ἀπώλετο, καὶ τὸ σῶμα αὐτοῦ ἐδόθη εἰς καῦσιν πυρός*: the meaning being that the Fourth Empire "is to be utterly brought to an end" (Driver). *Ζῶντες* adds to the horror of the

τῆς καιομένης ἐν θείῳ. [21]καὶ οἱ λοιποὶ ἀπεκτάνθησαν 21
ἐν τῇ ῥομφαίᾳ τοῦ καθημένου ἐπὶ τοῦ ἵππου τῇ

20 της καιομενης ℵAP vg aeth Prim] την καιομενην Q min$^{\text{omn vid}}$ Ar | εν θειω] εν τω θ. 1 35 36 49 79 87 185 al και θειου syr^{gw} arm

picture; cf. Num. xvi. 30 καταβήτωσαν ζῶντες εἰς ᾅδου, repeated in Ps. liv. (lv.) 15; the Greek classical writers use the same figure, e.g. Soph. *Ant.* 920 ζῶσ' εἰς θανόντων ἔρχομαι κατασκαφάς. Λίμνη (*stagnum*, Prim., Vg.) is a comparatively shallow pool or lake; Ps. cvi. (cvii.) 35 (A) ἔθετο ἔρημον εἰς λίμνας ὑδάτων; Cant. vii. 4 ὡς λίμναι ἐν Ἐσεβών; 1 Macc. xi. 35 τὰς τοῦ ἁλὸς λίμνας (salt basins near the Dead Sea); Lc. v. 1 f., viii. 22 f., 33 (the Lake of Gennesaret). Thus the λίμνη τοῦ πυρός stands in marked contrast with the ἄβυσσος (ix. 1 ff., xx. 1 ff.); the Beast and False Prophet are not cast into a bottomless dungeon, to be kept in safe custody, but into a pool of blazing sulphur, where they will be consumed. It is the utter destruction and consumption of the two systems which is in view; like Babylon (xvii. 16, xviii. 8), they are to be burnt with fire; not a vestige of them will be left in the new order. Ἡ λίμνη τ. π. κτλ., or an equivalent phrase, occurs again in xx. 10, 14 f., xxi. 8; the use of the definite article on its first appearance seems to imply that the conception was already familiar to the Asian Churches; compare xi. 7 τὸ θηρίον κτλ., note. Possibly it was a local expression for the γέεννα τοῦ πυρός which was familiar to Palestinian Christians (Mt. v. 22 ff., Mc. ix. 43, note, Jac. iii. 6; cf. *Secrets of Enoch*, x. 2 "a gloomy fire is always burning, and a fiery river goes forth," with Charles's note); καιομένης ἐν θείῳ, however, points rather to the story of Sodom and Gomorrah (Gen. xix. 24; cf. Ez. xxxviii. 22). Τῆς καιομένης, if original, can only be a slip due to hasty writing or dictation; cf. xxi. 8 τῇ λίμνῃ τῇ καιομένῃ. For θεῖον see ix. 17 f., xiv. 10, notes.

21. καὶ οἱ λοιποὶ ἀπεκτάνθησαν κτλ.] The rest of the enemy, the kings and their hosts (*v.* 19), were not cast, like the Beast and the Prophet, into the Lake of Fire, but slain outright by the sword of the Word; contrast *Ascension of Isaiah* iv. 14 (ed. Charles, p. 33), "He will drag Beliar into Gehenna, and also his armies." That this wholesale slaughter is to be understood in a purely spiritual sense is clear from the words τῇ ἐξελθούσῃ ἐκ τοῦ στόματος αὐτοῦ which follow. The sword is that of which St Paul speaks in Eph. vi. 17 τὴν μάχαιραν τοῦ πνεύματος, ὅ ἐστιν ῥῆμα θεοῦ, and the action of the living Word who wields it may be illustrated by Heb. iv. 12 ζῶν γὰρ ὁ λόγος τοῦ θεοῦ καὶ ἐνεργὴς καὶ τομώτερος ὑπὲρ πᾶσαν μάχαιραν δίστομον καὶ διϊκνούμενος ἄχρι μερισμοῦ ψυχῆς καὶ πνεύματος, ἁρμῶν τε καὶ μυελῶν. In interpreting room should probably be allowed for punitive as well as for restorative operations; the Word slays by pronouncing judgement as well as by reducing to the obedience of faith. But it is probably the latter process which is chiefly in view; the slaying of the ἔχθρα εἰς θεόν, of the self which resists Christ; cf. Gal. ii. 19 f., vi. 14, and for the exact figure, though used with a somewhat different reference, Eph. ii. 16 ἀποκτείνας τὴν ἔχθραν. Thus the vision of the victorious Word fulfils itself in any movement which leads to conversions on a great scale, such as that which attended the preaching of Boniface; and may find a more complete accomplishment at a time yet future, when Christ will work through some new

ἐξελθούσῃ ἐκ τοῦ στόματος αὐτοῦ, καὶ πάντα τὰ
¶ P ὄρνεα ἐχορτάσθησαν ἐκ τῶν σαρκῶν αὐτῶν¶.
XX. 1 [1] Καὶ εἶδον ἄγγελον καταβαίνοντα ἐκ τοῦ οὐρανοῦ,
ἔχοντα τὴν κλεῖν τῆς ἀβύσσου καὶ ἅλυσιν μεγάλην
2 ἐπὶ τὴν χεῖρα αὐτοῦ. [2] καὶ ἐκράτησεν τὸν δράκοντα,

21 ορνεα] θηρια A*vid

XX 1 ειδον ℵ min[pl]] ιδον AQ 7 92 130 | αγγελον] pr αλλον ℵ[c.a] (16) 32 (39) syr[gw] arm aeth Tyc | om εκ του ουρ. ℵ* (hab ℵ[c.a]) | κλειν ℵAQ min[35]] κλειδα 1 7 al Ar | επι την χειρα AQ min[pl] Andr Ar] εν τη χειρι ℵ 38 syrr

Apostle of the Gentiles for the ὑπακοὴ ἐθνῶν (Rom. xv. 18).

καὶ πάντα τὰ ὄρνεα ἐχορτάσθησαν ἐκ τῶν σαρκῶν αὐτῶν] See *v.* 17 f., notes. The words belong to the scenery of the context, and need no precise interpretation such as that of Andreas (ὄρνεα δὲ τοὺς ἀγγέλους ὠνόμασεν), or of Primasius ("invitantur spirituales ad caenam"). The number of the slain justified the anticipations of the angel who invited all the vultures of the world to feast upon them. Schöttgen quotes a Rabbinical parallel, *syn. Sohar*, p. 114, n. 25 "illo tempore cum Deus vindictam exercebit pro populo suo Israel, carnibus hostium illorum caenabuntur omnes bestiae mensibus xii, et aves cibum exinde habebunt vii annos."

XX. 1—6. The Thousand Years of Satan's captivity and the Martyrs' reign.

1. καὶ εἶδον ἄγγελον καταβαίνοντα ἐκ τοῦ οὐρανοῦ κτλ.] The formula καὶ εἶδον does not, like μετὰ ταῦτα εἶδον, determine the order of time in which the vision was seen relatively to the visions which precede it, but merely connects it with a series of visions which for whatever purpose the writer has seen fit to bring together in this part of his book; cf. xix. 11, 17, 19, xx. 4, 11, 12, xxi. 1, and contrast μετὰ ταῦτα εἶδον in xviii. 1, and μετὰ τ. ἤκουσα in xix. 1. It must not, therefore, be assumed that the events now to be described chronologically follow the destruction of the Beast and the False Prophet and their army.

In the present vision, as in that of *c.* xviii., an angel descends from heaven, charged with a special mission (xviii. 1, note). He carries the key (on κλεῖν = κλεῖδα see i. 18, note) which unlocks the mouth of the shaft that leads down into the Abyss; cf. ix. 1 ἡ κλεὶς τοῦ φρέατος τῆς ἀβύσσου (note). Ἡ ἄβυσσος stands here in sharp contrast with ἡ λίμνη (xix. 20); the locked dungeon with its black and bottomless depths forms an antithesis to the open, shallow pool of fire.

The angel who is charged with the key of the Abyss carries also a manacle; on ἅλυσις as distinguished from πέδη see Mc. v. 4, note, and Acts xii. 7 ἐξέπεσαν αὐτοῦ αἱ ἁλύσεις ἐκ τῶν χειρῶν; and cf. Lightfoot, *Philippians*, p. 8, note 2. The fetter is of great size, being intended to hold a prisoner of no ordinary strength—one stronger than Samson (Jud. xvi. 6 ff.), stronger than the 'Legion' who tore asunder the chains that secured the Gerasene (Mc. *l.c.*); an ἰσχυρός than whom there is but one stronger (Lc. xi. 21 f.). The great chain lies on the angel's hand (ἐπὶ τὴν χεῖρα = ἐπὶ τῆς χειρός = nearly ἐν τῇ χειρί, cf. i. 16, 20), ready for use as soon as he comes upon the criminal.

2. καὶ ἐκράτησεν τὸν δράκοντα κτλ.] The Dragon, who from the first (xiii. 2, 4, notes) has been behind the revolt led by the Beast and False Prophet,

ὁ ὄφις ὁ ἀρχαῖος, ὅς ἐστιν Διάβολος καὶ ὁ σατανᾶς,
καὶ ἔδησεν αὐτὸν χίλια ἔτη, [3]καὶ ἔβαλεν αὐτὸν εἰς 3
τὴν ἄβυσσον, καὶ ἔκλεισεν καὶ ἐσφράγισεν ἐπάνω
αὐτοῦ, ἵνα μὴ πλανήσῃ ἔτι τὰ ἔθνη, ἄχρι τελεσθῇ τὰ

2 ο οφις ο αρχαιος A] τον οφιν τον αρχαιον ℵQ min$^{\text{omn vid}}$ Andr Ar | os AQ min$^{\text{omn vid}}$] ο ℵ | διαβολος] pr ο ℵ 14 38 79 97 Ar (om AQ min^{pl} Andr) | ο σατανας] om ο 1 130 186 al$^{\text{sat mu}}$ + ο πλανων την οικουμενην ολην Q 186 al$^{\text{fere 35}}$ syr Ar | om χιλια ετη και εβαλεν αυτον ℵ (propter homoeotel.) 3 επανω αυτου] εμμενως αυτον A | πλανηση (-σει ℵ) A 1 79 95] πλανα Q min^{40} Ar | om ετι 1 14 40 me aeth Tyc | τα χιλια] om τα 1 12 79 186

but hitherto has escaped justice, is now seized and chained: on κρατεῖν followed by the acc. see ii. 1, note. Ὁ ὄφις ὁ ἀρχαῖος, ὅς ἐστιν κτλ., a parenthesis (cf. i. 5, ii. 13, notes) borrowed from xii. 9, where see note. For the present the Dragon is not slain or consumed, but only made a prisoner (for ἔδησεν in this sense see ix. 14, and cf. Mt. xxvii. 2, Mc. vi. 17, Lc. xiii. 16, Acts xii. 6, xxii. 5) for a term of a thousand years, i.e. a long period of time, a great epoch in human history; cf. Andreas: χίλια δὲ ἔτη οὐ πάντως τὰ τοσαῦτα τῷ ἀριθμῷ νοεῖν εὔλογον· οὐδὲ γὰρ περὶ ὧν φησὶν ὁ Δαυὶδ...εἰς χιλίας γενεὰς δεκάκις ἑκατὸν ταύτας ἀριθμῆσαι δυνάμεθα, ἀλλὰ τὰς πολλάς; Beatus: "pro eloquendi modo dicit, sicut est illud intellegendum *in mille generationes*, cum non sint mille." For the interpretation of this period see the third note on *v.* 6, below.

3. καὶ ἔβαλεν αὐτὸν εἰς τὴν ἄβυσσον κτλ.] Satan, powerless in the hands of the angel, who exercises Divine power (Andreas: ἵνα δείξῃ καὶ τῶν λειτουργικῶν δυνάμεων τοῦτον ἥττονα κατὰ δύναμιν), and fettered, is flung down the shaft into the Abyss, the mouth of which is at once locked and made secure. The Abyss is the destination to which the 'Legion' looks forward (Lc. viii. 31 παρεκάλουν αὐτὸν ἵνα μὴ ἐπιτάξῃ αὐτοῖς εἰς τὴν ἄβυσσον ἀπελθεῖν), and it is under the charge of the Angel Abaddon (Apollyon) (ix. 11, note), who is by some interpreters identified with Satan himself, and is at least a kindred power. Thus the Dragon's committal is in effect a limitation to his proper sphere of influence; already he has been cast out of Heaven (xii. 9), now he is cast out of the earth, and returns to his own place.

Ἐσφράγισεν ἐπάνω αὐτοῦ—a last precaution taken to prevent escape. Not only is the pit's mouth shut and locked; it is sealed. In *c.* v. 1 seven seals guard the secrets of a papyrus roll; in vii. 2 a seal stamps the Divine impress upon the servants of God. The use of the seal here is parallel to that described in Mt. xxvii. 66 ἠσφαλίσαντο τὸν τάφον σφραγίσαντες τὸν λίθον μετὰ τῆς κουστωδίας; cf. *Ev. Petr.* 8 ἐπέχρισαν ἑπτὰ σφραγῖδας. The purpose of sealing the entrance to a prison was to prevent any attempt at escape or rescue passing unobserved; see Dan. vi. 17, LXX. ὅπως μὴ...ὁ βασιλεὺς αὐτὸν ἀνασπάσῃ ἐκ τοῦ λάκκου, and cf. Bel 11 ff.

ἵνα μὴ πλανήσῃ κτλ.] The confinement of Satan to the Abyss is not so much a punitive as a precautionary measure; so long as he is in the Abyss, he cannot deceive the nations, as he had been used to do. To mislead on a great scale is his business and *raison d'être*; see xii. 9 ὁ πλανῶν τὴν οἰκουμένην ὅλην, and cf. Jo. viii. 44 ὅταν λαλῇ τὸ ψεῦδος, ἐκ τῶν ἰδίων λαλεῖ, ὅτι ψεύστης ἐστὶν καὶ ὁ πατὴρ αὐτοῦ. Now

χίλια ἔτη· μετὰ ταῦτα δεῖ λυθῆναι αὐτὸν μικρὸν
4 χρόνον. [4]καὶ εἶδον θρόνους, καὶ ἐκάθισαν ἐπ' αὐτούς,
καὶ κρίμα ἐδόθη αὐτοῖς, καὶ τὰς ψυχὰς τῶν πεπελε-

3 *μετα ταυτα*] pr *και* 1 al[mu] vg[cle dem lips6] me arm aeth Andr Ar *μετα δε τ.* 29 30 130 syr   4 *ειδον* ℵ 1 186 al[pl]] *ιδον* AQ 7 92 130 | *των πεπελεκισμενων* (*-κημενων* 130)] *τας πεπελεκισμενας* syr *των πεπολεμημενων* A

his activity is checked for a season; the great malefactor is in custody, and there is no fear that he will break his prison while it lasts. Afterwards he must be released for a little while: *μικρόν* is relative, as in Jo. vii. 33, xii. 35, Apoc. vi. 11—the release will be brief in comparison with the captivity. But short or long, it must come; there is a necessity for it (*δεῖ*), founded on some mystery of the Divine Will. This use of *δεῖ*, frequent in the N.T. (Mt. xxiv. 6, xxvi. 54, Mc. viii. 31, ix. 11, xiii. 7, Lc. xxiv. 26, 44, Jo. xii. 34, xx. 9, Acts xvii. 3, xxiii. 11; in this book, i. 1, iv. 1, xi. 5, xiii. 10, xvii. 11) occurs first in the versions of Daniel ii. 28, 45 where *ἃ δεῖ γενέσθαι* = מָה דִּי לֶהֱוֵא. It is in vain to speculate on the grounds of this necessity, but it may be that the Christian nations which have long acquiesced in the faith without conviction will need to be sifted before the end; cf. Lc. xxii. 31 *ἰδοὺ ὁ σατανᾶς ἐξῃτήσατο ὑμᾶς τοῦ σινιάσαι ὡς τὸν σῖτον*. A short exposure to the stress of Satan's *ἐνέργεια πλάνης* (2 Th. ii. 11) may suffice to separate the wheat from the chaff.

4. *καὶ εἶδον θρόνους, καὶ ἐκάθισαν ἐπ' αὐτοὺς κτλ.*] Another vision, which is shewn by the sequel (*v.* 7) to be synchronous with Satan's term of imprisonment. The scene is from Daniel vii. 9 *ἐθεώρουν ἕως ὅτε θρόνοι ἐτέθησαν*; the indefinite *ἐκάθισαν*, which follows here, resembles Dan. viii. 26 *τὸ κριτήριον ἐκάθισεν*, 'the court sat'; the plural is perhaps meant to include Christ and His assessors, the Apostles (Mt. xix. 28) and Saints (1 Cor. vi. 3); cf. Dan. vii. 22 *τὸ κρίμα ἔδωκεν ἁγίοις Ὑψίστου*. To these is given the right of pronouncing sentence (*κρίμα*); they are invested with judicial authority. On *θρόνος* see ii. 13, note; it is here the judge's chair, placed upon the *βῆμα*, where he sits to hear cases and deliver judgement; cf. Jo. xix. 13 *ὁ οὖν Πειλᾶτος... ἐκάθισεν ἐπὶ βήματος*; *Ev. Petr.* 3 *ἐκάθισαν αὐτὸν ἐπὶ καθέδραν κρίσεως*; Acts xxv. 6, 17, 1 Cor. vi. 4 *τούτους καθίζετε*, i.e. 'make judges.' The picture presented to the mind is that of a state of society in which Christian opinion is dominant, and positions of influence and authority are held by believers and not, as in the age of St John, by pagans and persecutors.

καὶ τὰς ψυχὰς τῶν πεπελεκισμένων κτλ.] Sc. *εἶδον*. In vi. 9 the souls of the martyrs were seen under the Altar, crying for vengeance. It has now been awarded (xix. 2 *ἐξεδίκησεν τὸ αἷμα τῶν δούλων αὐτοῦ*), and they appear again, living and reigning with Christ. For *ἐσφαγμένων* (vi. 9, xviii. 24), which associated the martyrs with the Sacrificed Lamb (v. 6, 9, 12, xiii. 8), the Apocalyptist now writes *πεπελεκισμένων*, 'beheaded with the *πέλεκυς* (*securis*),' the traditional instrument of capital punishment in republican Rome, which, though under the Empire superseded by the sword (Acts xii. 2), still lingered in the memory of the provincials; cf. Diod. Sic. xix. 101 *ῥαβδίσας ἐπελέκισε κατὰ τὸ πάτριον ἔθος*; Polyb. i. 7. 12 *μαστιγώσαντες ἅπαντας κατὰ τὸ παρ' αὐτοῖς ἔθος ἐπελέκισαν*. The Seer still has in his mind the martyrs of his own age, the victims of Nero and Domitian. With *διὰ τὴν μαρτυρίαν Ἰησοῦ* cf. i. 9, xii. 17, xix. 10, notes; and for *διὰ τὸν λόγον τοῦ θεοῦ* see i. 9, vi. 9.

κισμένων διὰ τὴν μαρτυρίαν Ἰησοῦ καὶ διὰ τὸν λόγον
τοῦ θεοῦ, καὶ οἵτινες οὐ προσεκύνησαν τὸ θηρίον οὐδὲ
τὴν εἰκόνα αὐτοῦ καὶ οὐκ ἔλαβον τὸ χάραγμα ἐπὶ τὸ
μέτωπον καὶ ἐπὶ τὴν χεῖρα αὐτῶν· καὶ ἔζησαν καὶ
ἐβασίλευσαν μετὰ τοῦ χριστοῦ χίλια ἔτη. [5]οἱ 5
λοιποὶ τῶν νεκρῶν οὐκ ἔζησαν ἄχρι τελεσθῇ τὰ χίλια
ἔτη. αὕτη ἡ ἀνάστασις ἡ πρώτη. [6]μακάριος καὶ 6

4 του θεου] αυτου 130 | και οιτινες] ει τινες ουν ℵ | τω θηριω 1 32 49 90 91 95 al Andr | ουδε] ουτε 1 186 al[permu] Andr | τη εικονι 7 49 91 95 al[mu vid] | το μετωπον] των μετωπων 7 12 16 39 79 94 130 + αυτων 1 49 79 91[vid] al vg[tol lips4] me arm aeth | τας χειρας 94 vg syr[gw] | χιλια ετη] τα χ. ε. Q min[pl] syr Ar χιλιοις ετεσιν 130 5 om οι λοιποι...χ. ετη ℵ 7 8 14 29 92 al[20] syr (propter homoeotel.) | οι λοιποι] pr και Q 1 12 26 31 al[plq 12] vg[dem lips4**] me Andr Ar | τ. νεκρων] τ. ανθρωπων Q 32 34 *eorum* Vict Aug Prim | εζησαν AQ min[fere 20] *vixerunt* vg me Aug Prim Ar] ανεζησαν Vict[vid] (*revixerunt*) ανεστησαν 1 6 om και αγιος 14 92 Or[int]

καὶ οἵτινες οὐ προσεκύνησαν τὸ θηρίον κτλ.] Cf. Cyprian, *ad Fortun.* 12 "vivere omnes dicit et regnare cum Christo, non tantum qui occisi fuerint sed quique in fidei suae firmitate et Dei timore perstantes imaginem bestiae non adoraverint." The triumph of Christ is shared not by the martyrs only but by all who under the sway of the Beast and the False Prophet suffered reproach, boycotting, imprisonment, loss of goods, or other inconveniences, though they did not win the martyr's crown: cf. xiii. 15, xiv. 9 ff., xvi. 2, xix. 20, notes. Καὶ οἵτινες introduces a second class of persons, the confessors (as they were afterwards called) of the age of persecution, with special reference to those who in St John's day were resisting the Caesar-worship.

καὶ ἔζησαν καὶ ἐβασίλευσαν μετὰ τοῦ χριστοῦ χίλια ἔτη] The Christ Who suffered under Tiberius now lives (i. 18) and reigns, as the vision of *c.* xix. has shewn (*vv.* 12, 16), and His life and royalty are to be shared for a thousand years (so far it does not appear that this period is identical with the term of Satan's captivity, but see below, *v.* 7) by the martyrs and confessors of the Church. Ὁ χριστός occurs in the Apocalypse only in xi. 15, xii. 10, xx. 4, 6, and is probably in each instance a reminiscence of Ps. ii. 2. The Lord's Anointed, against Whom the kings of the earth conspired, has triumphed over His enemies, and His victory ensures that of those who have fought on His side.

5. οἱ λοιποὶ τῶν νεκρῶν οὐκ ἔζησαν ἄχρι τελεσθῇ τὰ χίλια ἔτη] To infer from this statement, as many expositors have done, that the ἔζησαν of *v.* 4 must be understood of bodily resuscitation, is to interpret apocalyptic prophecy by methods of exegesis which are proper to ordinary narrative. The Seer merely guards against the impression that he had referred to the General Resurrection, which will follow and not precede the Thousand Years of the Martyrs' reign. On ἔζησαν = ἀνέζησαν see ii. 8, note, and for ἄχρι τελεσθῇ cf. Blass, *Gr.* p. 219.

Αὕτη ἡ ἀνάστασις ἡ πρώτη: this, i.e. the return of the martyrs and confessors to life at the beginning of the Thousand Years, is the First Resurrection. It belongs to the Apocalyptist's view of things to see the great realities of life and death

ἅγιος ὁ ἔχων μέρος ἐν τῇ ἀναστάσει τῇ πρώτῃ· ἐπὶ

arranged in antithetical pairs, in which one of the two facts belongs to the present order, and the other, its greater counterpart, to the future; cf. xxi. 1 ὁ πρῶτος οὐρανός, ἡ πρώτη γῆ, contrasted with οὐρ. καινός, γῆ καινή; ii. 11, xx. 6, 14, xxi. 8 ὁ θάνατος ὁ δεύτερος or ὁ δ. θάνατος, implying a πρῶτος θάνατος, though the latter is not expressly named. So here the First Resurrection is one which takes effect in the present life, in contrast with that which belongs to the new order and is to be introduced by the Parousia. There is nothing analogous in this to 1 Th. iv. 16 οἱ νεκροὶ ἐν Χριστῷ ἀναστήσονται πρῶτον, for πρῶτον is there in antithesis to ἔπειτα ἡμεῖς οἱ ζῶντες κτλ., i.e. the dead in Christ are contrasted with His members who will be living upon earth at the time of His coming. Nor again is 1 Cor. xv. 23 really parallel; there St Paul defines the order in which the Resurrection will take place at the Second Advent, and his words (ἔπειτα οἱ τοῦ χριστοῦ ἐν τῇ παρουσίᾳ αὐτοῦ) are not limited, as St John's are, to the martyrs and confessors, but embrace all loyal members of the Church. Hence Origen's remark (fragm. in Isa. ap. Pamph. *Apol.* 7) is inapplicable here: "considerandum est...ne forte dividi possit omnis resurrectionis ratio in duas partes, id est in eos qui salvandi sunt iustos, et etiam in eos qui cruciandi sunt peccatores." On the probable meaning of St John's First Resurrection see note after *v.* 6.

6. **μακάριος καὶ ἅγιος ὁ ἔχων μέρος κτλ.**] A fifth Apocalyptic beatitude (cf. i. 3, xiv. 13, xvi. 15, xix. 9, xxii. 7, 14), distinguished from the other six by the addition of ἅγιος to μακάριος. He to whom this μακαρισμός belongs is not only happy, but holy; he is in the highest degree worthy of the name of Saint; he is beatified, he is canonized by the voice of the Spirit of Jesus. With ὁ ἔχων μέρος ἐν τ. ἀ. cf. Jo. xiii. 8 οὐκ ἔχεις μέρος μετ' ἐμοῦ, and the use of τὸ μέρος in xxi. 8, xxii. 19.

The grounds of the beatification are added. (1) 'Over these (i.e. ἐπὶ τῶν ἐχόντων μέρος κτλ.) the Second Death (see below, *v.* 14, note) has no control'; the first is past already and for them there remains no other. The words recall Rom. vi. 9 οὐκέτι ἀποθνήσκει, θάνατος αὐτοῦ οὐκέτι κυριεύει, but the reference there is to the first death only. (2) 'On the contrary (ἀλλ') they shall be priests of God and the Christ'; cf. i. 6 ἐποίησεν ἡμᾶς...ἱερεῖς τῷ θεῷ καὶ πατρὶ αὐτοῦ; v. 10 ἐποίησας αὐτοὺς τῷ θεῷ ἡμῶν...ἱερεῖς. The destiny purchased by the Christ for all Christians will be realized in those who partake in the First Resurrection; for them priestly service in the glory of its ideal perfection is an accomplished fact. The inclusion of Christ with God in the Object of Divine service is peculiar to this passage, but it agrees with what has been said in *c.* v. 8 ff. as to the joint worship of God and of the Lamb by heavenly beings, and with the general tendency of the Book to regard Christ as the Equivalent of God. (3) There is yet a third reason for the μακαρισμός of the martyrs and confessors; 'they shall reign with the Christ during the thousand years' (i.e. those mentioned in *v.* 4). Priesthood and royalty are the mutually complementary aspects of the service of God, "cui servire regnare est"; cf. i. 6, v. 10, xxii. 3, 5, notes. It is important to notice that no hint is given as to where this service is to be rendered and this royalty to be exercised; ἐπὶ τῆς γῆς (*c.* v. 10) has no place here either in *v.* 4 or in *v.* 6, and must not be read between the lines.

Any serious attempt to interpret the vision of the Thousand Years

τούτων ὁ δεύτερος θάνατος οὐκ ἔχει ἐξουσίαν, ἀλλ'

6 ο θανατος ο δευτερος 1 49 79 al^{vid} me | αλλα ℵ

must begin with an examination, however cursory, of contemporary Jewish belief upon the subject of the Messianic Reign. (1) While the O.T. represents this Reign as permanent (Dan. ii. 44, vii. 27; cf. Jo. xii. 34), the pseudepigraphic writers of 100 B.C.—100 A.D., whether influenced by Persian eschatology, as Briggs suggests (*Messiah of the Gospels*, p. 15 f.) or by the hopes of an unsettled age, looked for a temporary triumph of righteousness before the consummation of all things; see Charles, *Eschatology*, p. 200 ff. (2) To this golden age varying periods were assigned; thus in *Tanchuma* 7, in answer to the question 'How long are the days of the Messiah?', R. Akiba replies, 'Forty years'; other Rabbinic computations give 100, 600, 1000, 2000, 7000 years (Weber, *Jüd. Theologie*², p. 372 f.; while in 4 Esdr. vii. 28 we read: "revelabitur enim filius meus [Iesus] cum his qui cum eo, et iocundabit qui relicti sunt annis quadringentis"). (3) In Enoch xci. ff. human history is divided into weeks, of which the eighth and ninth witness the victory of righteousness, while the tenth is that of the final judgement, followed by the creation of a new heaven and the beginning of an eternal order. The later Slavonic Enoch (*Secrets of E.* xxxiii. 1 f., ed. Charles, p. 46) makes the duration of the world a single week of seven days, each day consisting of 1000 years, to be succeeded by an eighth day in which there are "neither years nor months nor weeks nor days nor hours," i.e. Eternity. This conception of a week of *millennia* took root in early Christian thought, and support for it was found in an allegorical treatment of Gen. ii. 1 ff. coupled with Ps. lxxxix. (xc.) 4; cf. Barn. *ep.* 15. 4 προσέχετε, τέκνα, τί λέγει τὸ Συνετέλεσεν ἐν ἓξ ἡμέραις· τοῦτο λέγει ὅτι ἐν ἑξακισχιλίοις ἔτεσιν συντελέσει Κύριος τὰ σύμπαντα, ἡ γὰρ ἡμέρα παρ' αὐτῷ (σημαίνει) χίλια ἔτη; Iren. v. 28. 3 ἡ γὰρ ἡμέρα Κυρίου ὡς ͵α ἔτη· ἐν ἓξ οὖν ἡμέραις συντετέλεσται τὰ γεγονότα· φανερὸν οὖν ὅτι ἡ συντέλεια αὐτῶν τὸ ͵ϛ ἔτος ἐστί; Clem. Al. *strom.* iv. 25, § 161 ὁ χρόνος...ὁ διὰ τῶν ἑπτὰ περιόδων τῶν ἀριθμουμένων εἰς τὴν ἀκροτάτην ἀνάπαυσιν ἀποκαθιστάς. The idea existed also in Zoroastrianism (Hastings, *D. B.* iv. 990 *b*), but the Judæo-Christian tradition rests clearly and sufficiently on the O.T.

It can scarcely be doubted that St John's mind is familiar with these conceptions; yet he employs them with considerable reserve. Either from (3), or perhaps from the O.T. itself (Ps. *l.c.*, cf. 2 Pet. iii. 8), he has adopted the symbolical term of 1000 years, whilst (1) has been so far used that he assigns this limit to the reign of the martyrs with Christ. But St John does not commit himself to a reign upon earth. When Dr Charles writes (*Eschatology*, p. 349): "the martyrs...reign with Christ personally on earth for a thousand years (xx. 4—6), with Jerusalem as the centre of the kingdom," he introduces into the eschatology of this passage ideas which are in fact absent from it; for *cc.* v. 10, xx. 9, and xxi. 10 belong to other cycles of thought (see notes there).

Early Christian interpretation fell into the same snare. Thus Justin, in answer to Trypho the Jew, admits (*dial.* 80 f.): ἐγὼ δὲ καὶ εἴ τινές εἰσιν ὀρθογνώμονες κατὰ πάντα Χριστιανοὶ καὶ σαρκὸς ἀνάστασιν γενήσεσθαι ἐπιστάμεθα, καὶ χίλια ἔτη ἐν Ἰερουσαλὴμ οἰκοδομηθείσῃ καὶ κοσμηθείσῃ καὶ πλατυνθείσῃ, ὡς οἱ προφῆται Ἰεζεκιὴλ καὶ Ἠσαίας (lxv. 17 ff.) καὶ οἱ ἄλλοι ὁμολογοῦσι; adding after a little: παρ' ἡμῖν ἀνήρ τις ᾧ ὄνομα

ἔσονται ἱερεῖς τοῦ θεοῦ καὶ τοῦ χριστοῦ, καὶ βασι-

6 του θεου κ. του χριστου] pr και ℵ τω θεω κ. τω χριστω 38 syr[gw] | βασιλευουσιν A

Ἰωάννης, εἷς τῶν ἀποστόλων τοῦ χριστοῦ, ἐν ἀποκαλύψει γενομένῃ αὐτῷ χίλια ἔτη ποιήσειν ἐν Ἰερουσαλὴμ τοὺς τῷ ἡμετέρῳ Χριστῷ πιστεύσαντας προεφήτευσε, where ἐν Ἰερουσαλήμ has been suggested by Isa. *l.c.*, or imported from *c.* xxii. 5, which refers to the final state. The same confusion appears in Tertullian, *adv. Marc.* iii. 24: "confitemur in terra nobis regnum repromissum, sed ante caelum, sed alio statu, utpote post resurrectionem, in mille annos in civitate divini operis Hierusalem caelo delata." Still further from St John's thought is the picture of sensuous bliss derived by Papias (cf. Eus. *H. E.* iii. 39) from an apocryphal source (see Iren. v. 33. 3 f., and Charles's note on *Apoc. Baruch*, xxix. 5), and strangely ascribed to our Lord, and the grosser views attributed to Cerinthus (*ap.* Eus. iii. 28 λέγων μετὰ τὴν ἀνάστασιν ἐπίγειον εἶναι τὸ βασίλειον τοῦ χριστοῦ, καὶ πάλιν ἐπιθυμίαις καὶ ἡδοναῖς ἐν Ἰερουσαλὴμ τὴν σάρκα πολιτευομένην δουλεύειν κτλ.). There were, however, even in Justin's days many Christians who refused to accept the chiliastic interpretation of St John's vision, as Justin himself candidly confesses (*l.c.* πολλοὺς δ' αὖ καὶ τῶν τῆς καθαρᾶς καὶ εὐσεβοῦς ὄντων Χριστιανῶν γνώμης τοῦτο μὴ γνωρίζειν ἐσήμανά σοι). At Alexandria in the third century a materialistic chiliasm was strongly condemned by Origen (*de princ.* ii. 11. 2), and Dionysius (*ap.* Eus. *H. E.* vii. 25; ed. Feltoe, p. 115); but no thorough examination of the vision, with a constructive purpose, seems to have been undertaken by the Alexandrian school. To Augustine the Church owes the first effort to interpret Apoc. xx. on these lines (*de civ. Dei* xx. 7 ff.). He confesses that he had at one time been disposed to adopt a modified chiliasm, in which "deliciae spirituales" were substituted for the sensuous expectations of the early *milliarii*. But a longer study of the subject led him to a different conclusion. He had learned to see in the captivity of Satan nothing else than the binding of the strong man by the Stronger than he which the Lord had foretold (Mc. iii. 27, Lc. xi. 22); in the thousand years, the whole interval between the first Advent and the last conflict; in the reign of the Saints, the entire course of the Kingdom of Heaven; in the judgement given to them, the binding and loosing of sinners; in the first resurrection, the spiritual share in the Resurrection of Christ which belongs to the baptized (Col. iii. 1). This exegesis finds a place in most of the ancient commentators, both Greek and Latin, who wrote after Augustine's time.

There are points at which the Augustinian interpretation forsakes the guidance of St John's words. It overlooks, e.g. the limitation of the first Resurrection to the martyrs and confessors. But on the whole it seems to be on right lines. The symbolism of the Book is opposed to a literal understanding of the Thousand Years, and of the resurrection and reign of the Saints with Christ. It is "the souls" of the martyrs that St John sees alive; the resurrection is clearly spiritual and not corporeal. Augustine's reference to the parable of the Strong Man armed is illuminating in a high degree, even if it is impossible to press it to the precise conclusion which he reached.

Turning back to the vision itself, we observe that it has points both of contact and of contrast with the Vision of the Two Witnesses in *c.* xi. 3 ff. In each a definite time is fixed—in *c.* xi. 1260 days, in *c.* xx.

λεύσουσιν μετ' αὐτοῦ [τὰ] χίλια ἔτη. [7] §καὶ ὅταν 7 § the

6 τα χ. ετη] om τα A 130 186 al^{pl} arm Andr Ar 7 οταν τελεσθη] μετα Q 7 14 29 92 min$^{plq\,20}$ arm Ar

1000 years. If the 1260 days symbolize the duration of the triumph of heathenism (xi. 2 f., notes), the 1000 days as clearly symbolize the duration of the triumph of Christianity. In *c.* xi. 11 ff. the Two Witnesses after their martyrdom rise and ascend to heaven in the sight of their enemies; in *c.* xx. 4 ff. the souls of the martyrs and confessors live and reign with Christ. In both passages we have virtually the same fact symbolized, viz. the victory of the principles for which the martyrs died and the confessors endured hardship and loss. How short the age of persecution would be, when compared with the duration of a dominant Christianity, is shewn by the adoption of a term of 3½ years in the one case and of 1000 years in the other. Blessed and holy, indeed, were those who by their brief resistance unto blood secured for the Church so long a continuance of peaceful service; they would live and reign with Christ as kings and priests in the hearts of all succeeding generations of Christians, while their work bore fruit in the subjection of the civilized world to the obedience of the faith.

If this or some similar interpretation be accepted, the question remains at what epoch the great chapter in history represented by the Thousand Years began. An obvious answer would be, 'With the Conversion of Constantine, or of the Empire.' If, however, the visions are to be regarded as following one another in something like chronological order (but see *v.* 1, note), St John has in view the moment of the overthrow of the Beast and the False Prophet, i.e. the final break up of the Roman world-power and its ally, the pagan system of priestcraft and superstition. But possibly the question, like many another raised by this Book, admits of no precise answer. The Seer of the Apocalypse does not anticipate history; he is content to emphasize and express in apocalyptic language the principles which guide the Divine government of the world. That the age of the Martyrs, however long it might last, would be followed by a far longer period of Christian supremacy during which the faith for which the martyrs died would live and reign, is the essential teaching of the present vision. When, under what circumstances, or by what means this happy result should be attained, St John does not see, and has not attempted to explain. It might have been well if students of his book had always followed the example of this wise reserve.

7—10. AFTER THE THOUSAND YEARS. RELEASE OF SATAN: WAR OF GOG AND MAGOG.

7. καὶ ὅταν τελεσθῇ τὰ χίλια ἔτη, λυθήσεται κτλ.] 'Whensoever the thousand years shall end, Satan shall be released.' The use of the future tense is carried on from *v.* 6 into *vv.* 7, 8, with the result that this part of the vision assumes the form of a prophecy. The δεῖ λυθῆναι αὐτὸν μικρὸν χρόνον of *v.* 3 is at length to be accomplished; the thousand years of the Martyrs' Reign (now identified with the thousand years of Satan's captivity; cf. *vv.* 2—5) being ended, he will be set free from his prison (for this sense of φυλακή see ii. 10, and cf. xviii. 2, note), and troublous times will begin again. As the Seer ascribes the first persecution under Nero to Satan's wrath at his expulsion from Heaven (xii. 13, note), so the final

τελεσθῇ τὰ χίλια ἔτη, λυθήσεται ὁ σατανᾶς ἐκ τῆς
8 φυλακῆς αὐτοῦ, [8]καὶ ἐξελεύσεται πλανῆσαι τὰ ἔθνη
τὰ ἐν ταῖς τέσσαρσιν γωνίαις τῆς γῆς, τὸν Γὼγ καὶ

8 τα εθνη] pr παντα ℵ 79 syr^{gw} | τα εν] om τα ℵ 14 29 35 87 92 130 the syr^{gw} | τεσσαρσιν] τετρασι ℵ

outbreak of hostility against the Church is attributed to his return to the earth after long imprisonment in the Abyss.

8. καὶ ἐξελεύσεται πλανῆσαι τὰ ἔθνη κτλ.] Cf. Bede: "*exibit*...: in apertam persecutionem de latebris erumpet odiorum." A thousand years have wrought no change in Satan's methods; no sooner has he been set free than he is at his old work of deceiving the world (*v.* 3, note), and turning it against the Church; his limitations removed, the ἐνέργεια πλάνης begins again. Τὰ ἐν ταῖς τέσσαρσιν γωνίαις τῆς γῆς (see *c.* vii. 1, note), i.e. all the nations of the world, however remote; cf. Ez. vii. 2 τὸ πέρας ἥκει ἐπὶ τὰς τέσσαρας πτέρυγας τῆς γῆς, i.e. on the whole land. The movement which St John foresees is not dictated by an imperial policy, but is the result of a common impulse which will seize men of all races and nationalities.

τὸν Γὼγ καὶ Μαγώγ] Magog (מָגוֹג) appears first in Gen. x. 2, where see Driver's note; but the immediate reference here is to Ez. xxxviii.—xxxix., where the prophet conceives of a great invasion of the land of Israel by Gog (גּוֹג), whom he connects with the land of Magog (xxxviii. 2 ἐπὶ Γὼγ καὶ τὴν γῆν τοῦ Μαγώγ), and describes as the prince of Rosh Meshach and Tubal—the two last usually identified with tribes inhabiting the S. and S.E. shores of the Euxine. "The expedition imagined by the prophet is no doubt modelled upon the great irruption of the Scythians into Asia (Hdt. i. 104—6) which took place in 630 B.C." (Driver on Gen. *l.c.*); Josephus identifies Magog with the Scythians (*antt.* i. 6. 1 Μαγώγης δὲ τοὺς ἀπ' αὐτοῦ Μαγώγας ὀνομασθέντας ᾤκισεν, Σκύθας δὲ ὑπ' αὐτῶν, *sc.* τῶν Ἑλλήνων, προσαγορευομένους), and the older interpreters of the Apocalypse thought of the Scythians here. But whatever Gog and Magog may have meant to Ezekiel, St John's phrase τὸν Γὼγ καὶ Μαγώγ has no definite geographical associations; it comes in all probability not directly from Ezekiel, but from Jewish apocalyptic sources in which it had assumed a new connotation. In the Rabbinical writings Gog and Magog appear as the enemies of the Messiah; cf. the Jerusalem Targum on Num. xi. 29 "Eldad et Medad (cf. Herm. *vis.* ii. 3, Fabric. *cod. pseud. V. T.* i. p. 801 ff.), ambo isti prophetarunt simul et dixerunt: 'In fine extremitatis dierum Gog et Magog et exercitus eorum adscendent Hierosolyma, et per manus regis Messiae ipsi cadent"; *Aboda Sara* i. f. 36 "quando videbunt bellum Gog et Magog dicet ad eos Messias: 'Ad quid huc venistis?' Respondebunt 'Adversus Dominum et adversus Christum eius'"; for other Rabbinical passages see Wetstein *ad l.*; Schöttgen, *de Mess.* (ii. pp. 68, 227); Weber, *Jüd. Theol.*^{2} p. 386 ff. *et passim*. See also *Orac. Sibyll.* iii. 319 ff. αἶ αἴ σοι, χώρη Γὼγ (cf. *Book of Jubilees*, ed. Charles, p. 74) ἠδὲ Μαγώγ, μέσον οὖσα | Αἰθιόπων ποταμῶν, πόσον αἵματος ἔκχυμα δέξῃ, | καὶ κρίσεως οἴκησις ἐν ἀνθρώποισι κεκλήσῃ; *ib.* 512 ff. αἶ αἴ σοι, Γὼγ ἠδὲ Μαγώγ, καὶ πᾶσιν ἐφεξῆς | ...πᾶσιν γάρ, ὅσα χθόνα ναιετάουσιν, | Ὕψιστος δείνην ἐπιπέμψει ἔθνεσι πληγήν; for the expansion of the legend in the later apocalypses see Bousset, *Der Antichrist*, esp. p. 128 f. Conjecture was busy among Christian

Μαγώγ, συναγαγεῖν αὐτοὺς εἰς τὸν πόλεμον, ὧν ὁ
ἀριθμὸς αὐτῶν ὡς ἡ ἄμμος τῆς θαλάσσης. [9]καὶ 9
ἀνέβησαν ἐπὶ τὸ πλάτος τῆς γῆς, καὶ ἐκύκλευσαν τὴν

8 Μαγωγ] pr τον ℵ[c.a] Q min[pl] | συναγαγειν] pr και ℵ 11 (12) 17 31 32 79 186 vg syr[gw] aeth Aug Prim | τον πολεμον] om τον 1 38 49 79 186 al[mu] the arm Andr | om αυτων 1 38 48 49 79 al[mu] Andr Ar 9 εκυκλευσαν AQ 2 8 29 49 al[20]] εκυκλωσαν ℵ 1 7 31 38 130 186 al[sat mu] Andr Ar

interpreters of the fourth and following centuries as to the identity of Gog and Magog; Eusebius (*dem. ev.* ix. 3) mentions the view that Gog represents the Roman Empire; Ambrose (*de fide* ii. 16) says plainly: "Gog iste Gothus est," while Andreas and Arethas *ad loc.* speak of some who thought that the Huns were intended. Augustine, on the other hand (*de civ. Dei* xx. 11), rightly rejects any such narrowing of the sense: "toto namque orbe terrarum significati sunt isti esse, cum dictum est *nationes quae sunt in iv angulis terrae*." This great uprising of the nations will, he adds, be the final protest of the world against the Church: "haec enim erit novissima persecutio quam sancta ecclesia toto terrarum orbe patietur, universa scilicet civitas Christi ab universa diaboli civitate, quantacumque erit ubique super terram."

συναγαγεῖν αὐτοὺς εἰς τὸν πόλεμον κτλ.] Cf. xvi. 14, where the same words are used of the three froglike spirits arising from the Dragon, the Beast, and the False Prophet, which gathered the Kings to the battle of Har Magedon. A similar war is described in xvii. 14, xix. 19; whether the three passages refer to the same event is not clear, but the war of Gog and Magog appears to be distinguished by its position after the Thousand Years (ὅταν τελεσθῇ τὰ χ. ἔ.) and immediately before the Last Judgement. Other onslaughts upon the Church were preludes to this final worldwide attack.

In ὧν ὁ ἀριθμὸς αὐτῶν ὡς ἡ ἄμμος τῆς θαλάσσης the metaphor carries us back to many O.T. contexts in which a great host is described; cf. e.g. Gen. xxii. 17, Jos. xi. 4, Jud. vii. 12, 1 Regn. xiii. 5, 2 Regn. xvii. 11, Judith ii. 20, 1 Macc. xi. 1.

9. καὶ ἀνέβησαν εἰς τὸ πλάτος τῆς γῆς] For τὸ πλάτος τ. γ. see Sir. i. 3 ὕψος οὐρανοῦ καὶ πλάτος γῆς; Hab. i. 6 (of the Chaldean army) τὸ ἔθνος...τὸ πορευόμενον ἐπὶ τὰ πλάτη (A, τὸ πλάτος) τῆς γῆς = לְמֶרְחֲבֵי אֶרֶץ. The land of Israel is doubtless in the Seer's mind; cf. Ez. xxxviii. 15 f. ἥξεις ἐκ τοῦ τόπου σου...καὶ ἔθνη πολλὰ μετὰ σοῦ...συναγωγὴ μεγάλη καὶ δύναμις πολλή, καὶ ἀναβήσῃ ἐπὶ τὸν λαόν μου Ἰσραὴλ ὡς νεφέλη καλύψαι γῆν· ἐπ' ἐσχάτων τῶν ἡμερῶν ἔσται, καὶ ἀνάξω σε ἐπὶ τὴν γῆν μου; Enoch lvi. 6 (ed. Charles): "they will march up to and tread under foot the land of His elect ones, and the land of His elect ones will be before them a threshing floor and a path." In the aorist ἀνέβησαν the writer slips back into his usual apocalyptic manner (cf. *v.* 7, note); he sees the hosts of the invading army just as they appear on the horizon, mounting up, as it were on the edge of the great plain—perhaps Esdraelon is still in his thoughts (xvi. 16, note). Or ἀναβῆναι may be used with its usual reference to the backbone of central Palestine, and the situation of Jerusalem.

καὶ ἐκύκλευσαν τὴν παρεμβολὴν τῶν ἁγίων κτλ.] Apringius: "nihil caeleste sapiunt, nullam caelestis altitudinis potentiam metuunt." The 'Camp of the Saints' and the 'Beloved City' are two aspects of one body, the Universal Church, which is threatened by Gog and

§ P παρεμβολὴν τῶν ἁγίων καὶ τὴν §πόλιν τὴν ἠγαπη-
μένην. καὶ κατέβη πῦρ ἐκ τοῦ οὐρανοῦ καὶ κατέφαγεν
10 αὐτούς· [10]καὶ ὁ διάβολος ὁ πλανῶν αὐτοὺς ἐβλήθη

9 των αγιων] + και την πολιν των αγιων Q 97 | εκ του ουρανου] + απο του θεου Q min[plq 25] me the arm Vict Aug Tyc Ar απο τ. θ. 130 pr απο τ. θ. ℵ[c.a] P 7 al[mu] vg syrr Hier εκ τ. θ. απο τ. ουρανου 1 17 19 186

Magog. Παρεμβολή, a word which, as Phrynichus says, is δεινῶς Μακεδονικόν, a reminiscence of Macedonian military life, the constant LXX. equivalent of מַחֲנֶה, a camp, or an army on the march (Ex. xiv. 19 f.) or engaged in battle (Heb. xi. 34: see Westcott's note), recalls the picture of Israel marching through the wilderness (Num. ii. 2 ff.), and perhaps also of the brave stand of the Maccabees against Antiochus (1 Macc. v. 40 ff.). On the other hand ἡ πόλις ἡ ἠγαπημένη represents the Church as the New Zion, the *civitas Dei* (Heb. xii. 22), already potentially set up on earth (cf. *c.* xxi. 10). Ἡ ἠγαπημένη looks back to Ps. lxxvii. (lxxviii.) 68 τὸ ὄρος τὸ Σειὼν ἠγάπησεν, Ps. lxxxvi. (lxxxvii.) 2 ἀγαπᾷ Κύριος τὰς πύλας Σειὼν ὑπὲρ πάντα τὰ σκηνώματα Ἰακώβ; Hos. ii. 23 (B) καὶ ἀγαπήσω (וְרִחַמְתִּי) τὴν οὐκ ἠγαπημένην (AQ, κ. ἐλεήσω τ. οὐκ ἠλεημένην; for רִחַם = ἀγαπᾶν cf. Ps. xvii. (xviii.) 2, on which see BDB. *s.v.* and Cheyne, *Psalms*, p. 376). Wetstein compares Aesch. *Eum.* 869 χώρας μετασχεῖν τῆσδε θεοφιλεστάτης. The Beloved City includes of course the Gentile Church, once τὴν οὐκ ἠγαπημένην, but now one with Israel in Christ; see Rom. ix. 25 f. (SH.), 1 Pet. ii. 10 (Hort). Κυκλεύειν = κυκλοῦν occurs also in Jo. x. 24 (B) ἐκύκλευσαν αὐτὸν οἱ Ἰουδαῖοι; WH.[2] (*Notes*, p. 178) compare ζηλεύειν = ζηλοῦν in Apoc. iii. 19, and ἀποδεκατεύειν = ἀποδεκατοῦν in Lc. xviii. 12 (ℵ*B); for κυκλοῦν 'besiege' cf. Lc. xix. 43 παρεμβαλοῦσιν οἱ ἐχθροί σου χάρακά σοι καὶ περικυκλώσουσίν σε, and *ib.* xxi. 20 ὅταν δὲ ἴδητε κυκλουμένην ὑπὸ στρατοπέδων Ἰερουσαλήμ. The spiritual Jerusalem will be surrounded by a greater host, but no ἐρήμωσις awaits her. As to the sense in which she will be besieged, Primasius is doubtless right: "hoc est, in angustiis tribulationis arctabitur, urgebitur, concludetur."

καὶ κατέβη πῦρ ἐκ τοῦ οὐρανοῦ κτλ.] Cf. Ez. xxxviii. 22 καὶ πῦρ καὶ θεῖον βρέξω (Gen. xix. 24) ἐπ' αὐτὸν [*sc.* τὸν Γώγ] καὶ ἐπὶ πάντας τοὺς μετ' αὐτοῦ καὶ ἐπ' ἔθνη πολλὰ μετ' αὐτοῦ; *ib.* xxxix. 6 ἀποστελῶ πῦρ ἐπὶ Γώγ (so B, but Γ follows M.T. with Μαγώρ). There is probably also an allusion to 4 Regn. i. 10, 12 κατέβη πῦρ ἐκ τοῦ οὐρανοῦ καὶ κατέφαγεν αὐτὸν καὶ τοὺς πεντήκοντα αὐτοῦ—an O.T. incident which had impressed itself, as we know (Lc. ix. 54) on the mind of St John. For the future Gog and Magog he foresees a destruction as complete as that which overtook the besiegers of the old city (4 Regn. xix. 35).

10. καὶ ὁ διάβολος ὁ πλανῶν αὐτοὺς ἐβλήθη κτλ.] The Deceiver of the nations (for the pres. part. see Blass, *Gr.* p. 198; Dr Gwynn's Syriac version uses the verbal noun ܡܛܥܝܢܐ = πλάνος, Mt. xxvii. 63, or γόης, 2 Tim. iii. 13, Pesh., Gwynn, p. 87) escapes the general doom only to be reserved for one more terrible. Like the Beast and the False Prophet before him he is flung into the Lake of Fire (cf. xix. 20, note); καὶ θείου answers to τῆς καιομένης ἐν θείῳ there. Thus his third and final punishment is reached (compare xii. 9, xx. 2 f.)—so slowly does the Divine Justice assert itself, though the end has been foreseen from the beginning; see Mt. xxv. 41 τὸ πῦρ τὸ αἰώνιον τὸ ἡτοιμασμένον

εἰς τὴν λίμνην τοῦ πυρὸς καὶ θείου, ὅπου καὶ τὸ θηρίον καὶ ὁ ψευδοπροφήτης, καὶ βασανισθήσονται ἡμέρας καὶ νυκτὸς εἰς τοὺς αἰῶνας τῶν αἰώνων.

11 Καὶ εἶδον θρόνον μέγαν λευκὸν καὶ τὸν καθήμενον 11

10 θειου] pr του ℵ 7 13 16 18 32 95 al | om και 3° ℵ 1 91 al vg$^{fu\ dem\ tol}$ me the syr^{gw} arm aeth | om εις τους αιωνας των αιωνων 1 12 arm 11 ειδον ℵP 186 al^{pl} Ar] ιδον AQ 7 92 130 (item *v.* 12)

τῷ διαβόλῳ καὶ τοῖς ἀγγέλοις αὐτοῦ. Ὅπου καί, *sc.* ἐβλήθησαν; cf. xix. 20. The three ringleaders are now at length involved in the same hopeless ruin, and as was meet, suffer a punishment more severe than those whom they misled; whilst their dupes are at once consumed by fire from heaven, they are immersed in a fiery flood where their torture is increasing and perennial: βασανισθήσονται (ix. 5, note) ἡμέρας καὶ νυκτὸς (iv. 8, vii. 15, xii. 10, xiv. 11) εἰς τοὺς αἰῶνας τῶν αἰώνων (i. 18, xi. 15, xiv. 11, xix. 3, xxii. 5). It is not certain that these terrible words can be pressed into the service of the doctrine of the Last Things; since two of the three subjects of the βασανισμός represent systems and not persons, it is safer to regard them as belonging to the scenery of the vision rather than to its eschatological teaching. But beyond a doubt St John intends at least to teach that the forces, personal or impersonal, which have inspired mankind with false views of life and antagonism to God and to Christ will in the end be completely subjugated, and if not annihilated, will at least be prevented from causing further trouble. From the Lake of Fire there is no release, unless evil itself should be ultimately consumed; and over that possibility there lies a veil which our writer does not help us to lift or pierce.

11—15. Vision of the General Resurrection and the Last Judgement.

11. καὶ εἶδον θρόνον μέγαν λευκόν κτλ.] All is now ready for the last scene connected with the present order. The Great White Throne contrasts with the θρόνοι of xx. 4; in the final judgement there is but one throne, since there is but One judge; cf. Heb. xii. 23 κριτῇ θεῷ πάντων; Jac. iv. 12 εἷς ἐστὶν...κριτής. The absolute purity of this Supreme Court is symbolized by the colour of the Throne; cf. Dan. vii. 9, Th., τὸ ἔνδυμα αὐτοῦ ὡσεὶ χιὼν λευκόν...ὁ θρόνος αὐτοῦ φλὸξ πυρός; Enoch xviii. 8 ὥσπερ θρόνος θεοῦ ἀπὸ λίθου φουκά ("of alabaster," Charles, p. 89); and see Ps. ix. 1 ἐκάθισας ἐπὶ θρόνου, ὁ κρίνων δικαιοσύνην; xcvi. (xcvii.) 2 δικαιοσύνη καὶ κρίμα κατόρθωσις τοῦ θρόνου αὐτοῦ. The Judge is not named, and there is solemnity in this reserve; as Bousset says: "der Name Gottes wird hier wie iv. 2 f. ehrfurchtsvoll umschrieben." But throughout the Book ὁ καθήμενος ἐπὶ τοῦ θρόνου is the Almighty Father (iv. 2 f., 9, v. 1, 7, 13, vi. 16, vii. 10, 15, xix. 4, xxi. 5), as distinguished from the Incarnate Son; cf. 4 Esdr. vii. 33 "revelabitur Altissimus (? Ὕψιστος) super sedem iudicii." That the Father will be the Supreme Judge of mankind is a doctrine which seems to join direct issue with Jo. v. 21 οὐδὲ γὰρ ὁ πατὴρ κρίνει οὐδένα, ἀλλὰ τὴν κρίσιν πᾶσαν δέδωκεν τῷ υἱῷ, and indeed with the whole current of early Christian tradition (cf. Mt. xxv. 31 ff., Acts xvii. 31, 2 Cor. v. 10, 2 Tim. iv. 1); but a reconciliation of the two views may be found in the oneness of the Father and the Son (Jo. x. 30)—when the Son acts, the Father acts with and through Him (Jo. v. 19).

ἐπ᾽ αὐτοῦ, οὗ ἀπὸ τοῦ προσώπου ἔφυγεν ἡ γῆ καὶ ὁ
¶ the 12 οὐρανός, καὶ τόπος¶ οὐχ εὑρέθη αὐτοῖς. [12]καὶ εἶδον
τοὺς νεκρούς, τοὺς μεγάλους καὶ τοὺς μικρούς, ἑστῶτας
ἐνώπιον τοῦ θρόνου, καὶ βιβλία ἠνοίχθησαν· καὶ ἄλλο

11 επ αυτου A 1 95] επ αυτον PQ min$^{fere\ 40}$ επ αυτω 33 35 επανω αυτου ℵ 38 | του προσωπου] om του Q al^{pl} Ephr Andr Ar + αυτου 95 syrr 12 τους μικρους κ. τ. μεγαλους Q 4 26 31 32 48 Ar | ενωπιον] επι ℵ* | θρονου] θεου 1 al | om ηνοιχθ. κ. αλλο βιβλιον ℵ* | ηνοιχθησαν APQ 1 al^{10}] ηνεωχθησαν (ανεωχθ.) 7 (37 38 49 91) al^{mu} ηνοιξαν 2 8 29 30 130 al^{8} ηνοιξε 9 13 16 27 39 | om και αλλο βιβλιον ηνοιχθη 1

Thus St Paul can write in one place (2 Cor. v. 10): *φανερωθῆναι δεῖ ἔμπροσθεν τοῦ βήματος τοῦ χριστοῦ*, and in another (Rom. xiv. 10): *πάντες γὰρ παραστησόμεθα τῷ βήματι τοῦ θεοῦ*. But while this is borne in mind, recognition must be given to the fact that the Apocalypse regards judgement as the prerogative of God (cf. vi. 10, xvi. 7, xix. 2); it belongs, perhaps, to the Jewish-Christian character of the Book that in this supreme act prominence is given to the Person of the Father.

οὗ ἀπὸ τοῦ προσώπου ἔφυγεν ἡ γῆ καὶ ὁ οὐρανός] The non-eternity of the external order is taught in the O.T.; cf. Ps. ci. (cii.) 27 *αὐτοὶ* (sc. *οἱ οὐρανοί*) *ἀπολοῦνται, σὺ δὲ διαμένεις· καὶ πάντες ὡς ἱμάτιον παλαιωθήσονται*; ciii. (civ.) 29, 30; Isa. li. 6 *ὁ οὐρανὸς ὡς καπνὸς ἐστερεώθη* (נִמְלָחוּ), *ἡ δὲ γῆ ὡς ἱμάτιον παλαιωθήσεται*; and the N.T. corroborates this doctrine; cf. Mc. xiii. 31 *ὁ οὐρανὸς καὶ ἡ γῆ παρελεύσονται*; 2 Pet. iii. 10 *οἱ οὐρανοὶ ῥοιζηδὸν παρελεύσονται*. As the ancient Church saw plainly, it is only the external order of the world which is to be changed and not its substance or material; so e.g. Irenaeus, v. 36. 1: *οὐ γὰρ ἡ ὑπόστασις οὐδὲ ἡ οὐσία τῆς κτίσεως ἐξαφανίζεται ...ἀλλὰ τὸ σχῆμα παράγει τοῦ κόσμου τούτου*; Primasius, *ad loc.*: "figura ergo praeterit, non natura"; Arethas: *ἡ φυγὴ τοῦ οὐρανοῦ καὶ τῆς γῆς οὐ τοπικὴν σημαίνει μετανάστασιν,...ἀλλὰ φυγὴν τὴν ἀπὸ τῆς φθορᾶς εἰς ἀφθαρσίαν*.

For the metaphor *ἔφυγεν* cf. xvi. 20 *πᾶσα νῆσος ἔφυγεν, καὶ ὄρη οὐχ εὑρέθησαν*. *Ἀπὸ τοῦ προσώπου κτλ.* is illustrated by Ps. xcvi. (xcvii.) 5 *τὰ ὄρη ἐτάκησαν...ἀπὸ προσώπου Κυρίου*, and for *τόπος οὐχ εὑρέθη αὐτοῖς* see xii. 8, note.

12. *καὶ εἶδον τοὺς νεκρούς κτλ.*] The General Resurrection, described below in *v.* 13, is assumed for the moment. The Great White Throne is not surrounded, like the Throne set in Heaven (iv. 2), with heavenly beings, but with the human dead of all former generations, and the dead of the generation which shall be found alive upon earth; the living (2 Tim. iv. 1) are not mentioned here, partly because they form an insignificant minority, partly perhaps because the keen interest which the first generation had felt in the bearing of the Parousia upon the 'quick' (1 Th. iv. 13 f.) had abated before the end of the century. But all the dead are seen standing (Lc. xxi. 36, Rom. xiv. 10) before the Throne, whatever their condition on earth may have been (*τοὺς μεγάλους κ. τοὺς μικρούς*: cf. xi. 18, xiii. 16, xix. 5, 18), from the Proconsul, as that official was often reminded by Christians who appeared before him, down to the meanest slave.

καὶ βιβλία ἠνοίχθησαν] The sentence of the Judge is not arbitrary; it rests upon written evidence; the books which were opened contained, as it seems, a record of the deeds of every human being who came up for judgement. The conception is based on

βιβλίον ἠνοίχθη, ὅ ἐστιν τῆς ζωῆς· καὶ ἐκρίθησαν οἱ νεκροὶ ἐκ τῶν γεγραμμένων ἐν τοῖς βιβλίοις κατὰ τὰ
ἔργα αὐτῶν. [13]καὶ ἔδωκεν ἡ θάλασσα τοὺς νεκροὺς 13

12 *ηνοιχθη*] *ηνεωχθη* (*ανεωχθ.*) ℵQ 7 31 (37) al[satmu] | *της ζωης*] om *της* 130 + *uniuscuiusque hominum* Aug | *τοις βιβλιοις*] *ταις βιβλοις* ℵ

Dan. vii. 10 *κριτήριον ἐκάθισεν καὶ βίβλοι ἠνοίχθησαν*, and it appears in the Jewish apocalypses, e.g. Enoch xc. 20, "that other took the sealed books and opened them before the Lord of the sheep"; *Apoc. Baruch* xxiv. 1 (ed. Charles, p. 46 f.), "behold the days come and the books will be opened in which are written the sins of all those who have sinned"; 4 Esdr. vi. 20 "libri aperientur ante faciem firmamenti, et omnes videbunt simul." The *Testament of Abraham*, recension A (ed. James, p. 92 f.), knows of two recording angels: *οἱ δὲ δύο ἄγγελοι, ὁ ἐκ δεξιῶν καὶ ὁ ἐξ ἀριστερῶν, οὗτοί εἰσιν οἱ ἀπογραφόμενοι τὰς ἁμαρτίας καὶ τὰς δικαιοσύνας*; in recension B (*ib.* p. 114 f.) the same office is fulfilled by Enoch, who is styled *γραμματεὺς τῆς δικαιοσύνης*. The true interpretation of the 'books' is doubtless that given by Augustine, though, misled by a gloss ("qui est vita *uniuscuiusque*"), he wrongly connects it with the *ἄλλο βιβλίον*: *de civ. Dei* xx. 14 "quaedam igitur vis est intellegenda divina qua fiet ut cuique opera sua vel bona vel mala cuncta in memoriam revocentur et mentis intuitu mira celeritate cernantur, ut accuset vel excuset scientia conscientiam, atque ita simul et omnes et singuli iudicentur."

καὶ ἄλλο βιβλίον ἠνοίχθη κτλ.] For the Book of Life see iii. 5, xiii. 8, notes. It is the roll of living citizens of the New Jerusalem; cf. Andreas: *ἡ δὲ μία βίβλος τῆς ζωῆς ἐστιν ᾗ τὰ τῶν ἁγίων γέγραπται ὀνόματα*; Enoch xlvii. 3 "the books of the living were opened before Him." It is only another and complementary view of this 'book' which Bede offers when he calls it "praescientia Dei," for God's foreknowledge fulfils itself in the lives of the elect. In their case as well as in that of the rest of mankind the sentence is *κατὰ τὰ ἔργα*, as St Paul saw no less clearly than St John (Rom. ii. 5, 2 Cor. v. 10; cf. Apoc. ii. 23, xxii. 12).

13. *καὶ ἔδωκεν ἡ θάλασσα τοὺς νεκρούς κτλ.*] The Resurrection, implied in *v.* 12, is now described. The accidents of death will not prevent any of the dead from appearing before the Judge; sea and land will alike deliver up their tale. The Sea, as ever in this island-drama, is foremost in the writer's thoughts. It has been the grave of thousands whose restingplace could not be marked by *στήλη* or *cippus*, whose ashes no *columbarium* had ever received. Both Greeks and Romans attached great importance to burial and the inviolability of the tomb (cf. Dill, *Roman Society*, p. 496; Ramsay, *Cities* etc., ii. p. 514 ff.), and recoiled with proportionate horror from the thought of death by drowning or even of burial at sea; there were wild tales of the condition of souls whose bodies had been lost at sea, cf. Achilles Tatius, cited by Wetstein: *λέγουσι δὲ καὶ ἐν ὕδασι ψυχὰς ἀνῃρημένας μηδὲ εἰς ᾅδου καταβαίνειν ὅλως, ἀλλ' αὐτοῦ περὶ τὸ ὕδωρ ἔχειν τὴν πλάνην*. It is to the hope inspired by the words of the Seer that we owe the confidence with which the Church now commits the departed to the deep, "looking for the resurrection of the body when the Sea shall give up her dead." So far as the righteous are concerned, however, the hope appears also in the Targum on Ps. lxviii. 31: "reducam iustos qui suffocati sunt in profundis

τοὺς ἐν αὐτῇ, καὶ ὁ θάνατος καὶ ὁ ᾅδης ἔδωκαν τοὺς
νεκροὺς τοὺς ἐν αὐτοῖς, καὶ ἐκρίθησαν ἕκαστος κατὰ
14 τὰ ἔργα αὐτῶν. [14]καὶ ὁ θάνατος καὶ ὁ ᾅδης ἐβλήθη-
σαν εἰς τὴν λίμνην τοῦ πυρός. οὗτος ὁ θάνατος ὁ
15 δεύτερός ἐστιν, ἡ λίμνη τοῦ πυρός. [15]καὶ εἴ τις οὐχ

13 τ. νεκρους τ. εν αυτη] τ. εν αυτη ν. 49 96 130 186 al | εδωκαν] εδωκεν A 2 48 | τ. ν. τ. εν αυτοις] τ. εν αυτοις ν. 1 49 130 186 aeth | εκριθησαν] κατεκριθησαν ℵ | αυτων] αυτου Q 7 14 92 al$^{\text{plq10}}$ 14 om ουτος...εστιν 1 18 31 41 42 94 97 me arm^{zoh} Prim | om ουτος...του πυρος 186 | ο θανατος ο δευτερος] ο δ. θανατος 38 | om η λιμνη του πυρος 1 18 31 41 42 94 al vg$^{\text{clelips6}}$ me arm Prim

maris." Enoch (vii. 32) speaks only of a rising of the dead from the dry land.

καὶ ὁ θάνατος καὶ ὁ ᾅδης ἔδωκαν κτλ.] Death and Hades are an inseparable pair, as in i. 18, vi. 8 (notes), representing the two aspects of Death, the physical fact and its spiritual consequences (ὁ ᾅδης ἠκολούθει). Here they appear as two voracious and insatiable monsters who have swallowed all past generations, but are now forced to disgorge their prey. The 'harrowing of Hell,' which the Gospel of Nicodemus connects with the Lord's Descent into Hades, is thus seen to belong in truth to His Return, when the πάμφαγος καὶ ἀκόρεστος Ἅδης will be emptied by Him Who has the keys of Death. But the primary purpose of the great gaol-delivery is judgement—a judgement which will determine the spiritual condition of each individual man; ἕκαστος adds a feature not noticed in *v.* 12, but belonging to the Christian tradition; see Mt. xvi. 27, Rom. ii. 6, xiv. 12, 1 Cor. iii. 13, 2 Cor. v. 10, 1 Pet. i. 17, and already recognized in this Book (ii. 23).

14. καὶ ὁ θ. καὶ ὁ ᾅδης ἐβλήθησαν εἰς τὴν λίμνην τοῦ πυρός κτλ.] I.e., Death and Hades, the phenomenon and the condition, were both irrevocably destroyed and effaced; cf. Andreas: τὸ μηκέτι ἔσεσθαι θάνατον ἢ φθοράν, ἀλλ' ἀφθαρσίαν καὶ ἀθανασίαν βασιλεύειν σημαίνεται. The immersion of this symbolical pair in the Lake of Fire is parallel to that of the Beast and the False Prophet (xix. 20); it can only mean the annihilation of the forces indicated. St John expresses in the language of symbol what St Paul has said in direct words (1 Cor. xv. 26 ἔσχατος ἐχθρὸς καταργεῖται ὁ θάνατος); and both have probably in view Isa. xxv. 8, Th., κατεπόθη (Aq. καταποντίσει) ὁ θάνατος εἰς νῖκος, and Hos. xiii. 14 ποῦ ἡ δίκη σου, θάνατε; ποῦ τὸ κέντρον σου, ᾅδη; (cf. 1 Cor. xv. 54 f.).

Οὗτος ὁ θ. ὁ δεύτερός ἐστιν κτλ. is quaintly rendered by Benson, "this is Death the Second, the Lake of Fire." Death itself is swallowed up by a greater and final Death. The Second Death (ii. 11, xx. 6) is identified here, and again in xxi. 8, with the Lake of Fire; the latter is in the new order the nearest analogue of Death as we know it here.

15. καὶ εἴ τις οὐχ εὑρέθη ἐν τῇ βίβλῳ τῆς ζωῆς κτλ.] The Second Death is shared by all who are not enrolled among the living; cf. Bede: "id est, qui non est iudicatus a Deo vivus." Here at length (cf. xxi. 8) the Lake of Fire is associated with the future condition of human beings; i.e. it is treated as the counterpart of the Jewish Gehenna, on which see Mc. ix. 43, note. Enoch (xc. 26) has a similar representation of the fate of the reprobate: "I saw at that time how a like abyss was opened in the midst of the earth, full of fire, and those blinded sheep were brought, and

εὑρέθη ἐν τῇ βίβλῳ τῆς ζωῆς γεγραμμένος, ἐβλήθη εἰς τὴν λίμνην τοῦ πυρός.

[1] Καὶ εἶδον οὐρανὸν καινὸν καὶ γῆν καινήν· ὁ γὰρ 1 XXI.

15 ευρεθη] ευρεθησεται ℵ* | τη βιβλω] τω βιβλιω Q 1 al[25] Ar
XXI 1 ειδον ℵP min[pl] Ar] ιδον AQ 7 32 130 (item *v.* 2)

they were all judged and found guilty and cast into that fiery abyss, and they burned." The Apocalyptic Lake is doubtless the πῦρ τὸ αἰώνιον of Mt. xxv. 41, 46,—a κόλασις αἰώνιος which is both the reverse and the alternative of ζωὴ αἰώνιος. It is remarkable that here as in Mt. *l.c.* the qualification for the Second Death is a negative one (οὐχ εὑρέθη, οὐκ ἐποιήσατε). The negation of eternal life is eternal death.

That there will be a resurrection to death as well as to life is taught already in Dan. xii. 2 ἐξεγερθήσονται ...οὗτοι εἰς ὀνειδισμὸν καὶ εἰς αἰσχύνην αἰώνιον. Cf. Jo. v. 29 ἐκπορεύσονται... οἱ τὰ φαῦλα πράξαντες εἰς ἀνάστασιν κρίσεως.

XXI. 1—8. The Vision of a New Heaven and a New Earth.

1. καὶ εἶδον οὐρανὸν καινὸν καὶ γῆν καινήν] All is now ready for a revelation of the bliss of the Saints; cf. Bede: "finito iudicio quo malos vidit damnandos, restat ut etiam de bonis dicat." The passing away of earth and heaven before the Face of the Judge (xx. 11) has prepared the way for the present vision, but the conception of a New Heaven and Earth is not peculiar to St John or even to the N. T.; it occurs in Isa. lxv. 17 ἔσται γὰρ ὁ οὐρανὸς καινὸς καὶ ἡ γῆ καινή (שָׁמַיִם חֲדָשִׁים, אֶרֶץ חֲדָשָׁה), lxvi. 22 ὁ οὐρανὸς καινὸς καὶ ἡ γῆ καινὴ ἃ ἐγὼ ποιῶ μένει ἐνώπιον ἐμοῦ—perhaps also in Isa. li. 16 (see Charles, *Eschatology*, p. 122 f., n. 2)—and in Enoch xlv. 4 f., "I will transform the heaven, and make it an eternal blessing and light. And I will transform the earth and make it a blessing; *ib.* lxxii. 1, "the new creation...which dureth till eternity"; xci. 16 "the first heaven will depart and pass away, and a new heaven will appear, and all the powers of the heavens will shine sevenfold for ever"; the *Apocalypse of Baruch* xxxii. 6 "the Mighty One will renew His Creation"; 4 Esdras vii. 75 "tempora illa in quibus incipies creaturam renovare." Compare the interesting Rabbinical parallel quoted by Schöttgen from *Debarim rabba* 4 f. 262. 4 "cum Moses ante obitum oraret, caelum et terra et omnis ordo creaturarum commotus est. tunc dixerunt: Fortasse adest tempus a Deo praestitutum, quo renovandus est orbis universus" (לחדש את עלמו).

On καινός see ii. 17, note, and cf. iii. 12, v. 9, xiv. 3. As the opposite of παλαιός, it suggests fresh life rising from the decay and wreck of the old world; cf. Heb. viii. 13 ἐν τῷ λέγειν Καινὴν [*sc.* διαθήκην], πεπαλαίωκεν τὴν πρώτην· τὸ δὲ παλαιούμενον καὶ γηράσκον ἐγγὺς ἀφανισμοῦ. What is indicated is in fact a παλινγενεσία of heaven and earth (Mt. xix. 28), or to use another figure an ἀποκατάστασις πάντων (Acts iii. 21). As Irenaeus sees, the New Heaven and Earth correspond to the New Man, whose renovation has now been completed by the Resurrection; v. 36. 1 ἀνανεωθέντος τοῦ ἀνθρώπου, καὶ ἀκμάσαντος πρὸς τὴν ἀφθαρσίαν, ὥστε μηκέτι δύνασθαι πέρα παλαιωθῆναι, ἔσται ὁ οὐρανὸς καινὸς καὶ ἡ γῆ καινή· ἐν τοῖς [? οἷς] καινοῖς ἀναμενεῖ ὁ ἄνθρωπος ἀεὶ καινός, καὶ [? καινὰ] προσομιλῶν τῷ θεῷ.

ὁ γὰρ πρῶτος οὐρανὸς καὶ ἡ πρώτη γῆ

πρῶτος οὐρανὸς καὶ ἡ πρώτη γῆ ἀπῆλθαν, καὶ ἡ

1 om πρωτη 13 29 130 arm Ir[int] Aug Prim | απηλθαν (-λθον) ℵA (Q 8 9 13 29 30 al[fere 20] syrr Ar)] απηλθεν P 2 4 11 31 35 47 87 98 130 παρηλθε(ν) 1 49 79 186 al | η θαλασσα ουκ εστιν ετι] την θαλασσαν ουκ ιδον ετι A

ἀπῆλθαν] Cf. xx. 11, note; like ἔφυγεν, ἀπῆλθαν must not be pressed, and Andreas is not far wrong when he glosses: ἀντὶ τοῦ 'ἠλλάγη.' The writer of 2 Peter conceives of a conflagration of the old order at the Parousia (iii. 12 οὐρανοὶ πυρούμενοι λυθήσονται καὶ στοιχεῖα καυσούμενα τήκεται); but no such phenomena suggest themselves to the Apocalyptist, though fire is a frequent factor in his visions.

καὶ ἡ θάλασσα οὐκ ἔστιν ἔτι] The Sea has fulfilled its last function (xx. 13), and when the Seer looks steadily at the New Earth, he sees that "the waters which are under the firmament" have vanished; no place is left for the Sea in the New Creation; it belonged to the order which has passed. There is no need to suspect with Augustine a reference to the effects of the conflagration (*de civ. Dei* xx. 16 "utrum maximo illo ardore siccetur an et ipsum vertatur in melius non facile dixerim." The Sea has disappeared, because in the mind of the writer it is associated with ideas which are at variance with the character of the New Creation. Cf. Aug. *l.c.* "tunc non erit hoc saeculum vita mortalium turbulentum et procellosum"; Andreas: τὸν ταραχώδη βίον καὶ πολυκύμονα σημαινούσης τῆς θαλάσσης. St John, an exile in seagirt Patmos, regarded with no favour the element which mounted guard over his prison, and parted him from the Churches of Asia. For the ancients generally the Sea possessed none of the attractions which it has for moderns. To undertake a voyage without grave cause was to tempt Providence; Hor. *carm.* i. 3. 21 ff. "nequicquam Deus abscidit | prudens Oceano dissociabili terras, si tamen impiae | non tangenda rates transiliunt vada." It is true that since the time of Horace facilities for travel had greatly increased, and, as Dill remarks (*Roman Society*, p. 205) "until the appearance of railways and steamboats it may be doubted whether there was any age in history in which travelling was easier or more general." At the end of the first century Juvenal could write (xiv. 275 ff.): "aspice portus | et plenum magnis trabibus mare, plus hominum est iam | in pelago, veniet classis quocumque vocarit | spes lucri"; and the Apocalyptist has told practically the same tale in *c.* xviii. 17 ff. Yet how great the risks of a seafaring life still were, the story of St Paul's shipwreck shews: to the Apostolic age the ocean spoke of separation and isolation, rather than of a highway linking shore to shore. For this element of unrest, this fruitful cause of destruction and death, this divider of nations and Churches, there could be no place in a world of social intercourse, deathless life, and unbroken peace.

The disappearance of the Sea from the future order is a feature in other apocalyptic writings; cf. e.g. *Orac. Sibyll.* v. 158 ff. ἥξει δ' οὐρανόθεν ἀστὴρ μέγας εἰς ἅλα δεινὴν | καὶ φλέξει πόντον; *ib.* 447 ἔσται δ' ὑστατίῳ καιρῷ ξηρός ποτε πόντος; *Assumption of Moses* x. 6 "the sea will return into the abyss, and the fulness of waters will fail"; in the Coptic Zephaniah, p. 129 flames break out and dry up the sea (Simcox, *ad l.*), and Bousset quotes from Plutarch, *de Is. et Osir.* 7, a similar belief entertained by the priests of Isis: ὅλως δὲ καὶ τὴν θάλατταν ἐκ πυρὸς ἡγοῦνται καὶ παρωρισμένην; but the Apocalyptist (see above) shews no knowledge of this form of the conception.

θάλασσα οὐκ ἔστιν ἔτι. ²καὶ τὴν πόλιν τὴν ἁγίαν 2
Ἰερουσαλὴμ καινὴν εἶδον καταβαίνουσαν ἐκ τοῦ οὐρανοῦ

2 και] + εγω Ιωαννης vg^{clelipss}

2. καὶ τὴν πόλιν τὴν ἁγίαν Ἰ. καινὴν εἶδον] The New Earth must have a new metropolis, not another Babylon, but another and greater Jerusalem. Of a καινὴ Ἰερουσαλήμ we have read in *c.* iii. 12, from which this verse borrows its description as far as ἀπὸ τοῦ θεοῦ, adding τὴν ἁγίαν, which is here no mere conventional epithet (Mt. iv. 5, xxvii. 53), but one significant of the new holiness, the inner and permanent consecration of the new City of God. The Holy City of the O.T. (2 Esdr. xxi. 1, Dan. ix. 24, Mt. xxvii. 53) had been in ruins for a quarter of a century, and Hadrian's new city was not yet planned. The New Jerusalem of the Seer belongs to another order; it is of heavenly origin, a city 'whose builder and maker is God' (Heb. xi. 10), ἡ μέλλουσα πόλις (*ib.* xiii. 14). Some years before the fall of the old city the thought of a celestial city had been familiar to St Paul and his school; cf. Gal. iv. 26 f. ἡ δὲ ἄνω Ἰερουσαλὴμ ἐλευθέρα ἐστίν, ἥτις ἐστὶν μήτηρ ἡμῶν, Phil. iii. 20 ἡμῶν γὰρ τὸ πολίτευμα ἐν οὐρανοῖς ὑπάρχει, Heb. xii. 22 προσεληλύθατε Σιὼν ὄρει καὶ πόλει θεοῦ ζῶντος, Ἰερουσαλὴμ ἐπουρανίῳ. Jewish literature also is full of the hope of an ideal Jerusalem, based on O.T. prophecy (Isa. liv., lx., Ez. xl., xlviii.); cf. *Apoc. Baruch* iv. 3 ff. (ed. Charles, p. 6 ff.): "it is not this building which is now built in your midst; it is that which will be revealed with Me, that which was prepared beforehand...and now, behold, it is preserved with Me"; 4 Esdr. x. 27 ff. "vidi et ecce amplius mulier non comparebat mihi, sed civitas aedificabatur...haec mulier...est Sion... ingredere et vide splendorem et magnitudinem aedificii"; *Orac. Sibyll.* v. 420 ff. καὶ πόλιν ἣν ἐπόθησε θεός, ταύτην ἐποίησεν | φαιδροτέρην ἄστρων τε καὶ ἡλίου ἠδὲ σελήνης | κτλ.; *Test. xii. patr.*, Dan 5: ἐπὶ τῆς νέας Ἰερουσαλὴμ εὐφρανθήσονται δίκαιοι, ἥτις ἔσται εἰς δόξασμα θεοῦ ἕως τοῦ αἰῶνος. The Rabbinical doctrine of an οὐρανόπολις is worked out by Schöttgen (i. 1208 ff., *de Hierusalem caelesti*); see also Schürer, *Geschichte*³, p. 536 f., Weber, *Jüd. Theologie*, pp. 374, 404. On the Christian Society as the realization of the heavenly Jerusalem see Westcott on Heb. xi. 10 (additional note).

καταβαίνουσαν ἐκ τοῦ οὐρανοῦ ἀπὸ τοῦ θεοῦ] Repeated from *c.* iii. 12 τῆς καινῆς Ἰερουσαλήμ, ἡ καταβαίνουσα ἐκ τοῦ οὐρανοῦ ἀπὸ τοῦ θεοῦ μου, where see notes. It is perhaps unnecessary to think of a future visible fulfilment, such as is suggested by 1 Thess. iv. 14 ὁ θεὸς τοὺς κοιμηθέντας διὰ τοῦ Ἰησοῦ ἄξει σὺν αὐτῷ...ἡμεῖς οἱ ζῶντες...ἅμα σὺν αὐτοῖς ἁρπαγησόμεθα ἐν νεφέλαις. What is primarily intended is doubtless the heavenly origin (ἐκ) of the Church, and her Divine mission (ἀπό); as Primasius says: "de caelo descendere dicitur ista civitas, quoniam caelestis est gratia qua Deus eam fecit." The metaphor appears also in the Rabbinical writings, e.g. *Sohar Gen.* f. 69, col. 271; "Deus...aedificabit Hierosolyma, ut ipsam descendere faciat in medium sui de caelo." In its measure the hope fulfils itself already in the daily experience of the Church. If, as St James says (i. 17), πᾶν δώρημα τέλειον ἄνωθέν ἐστιν, καταβαῖνον ἀπὸ τοῦ πατρός, this is in an especial manner true of the highest form of corporate human life, the *Civitas Dei*.

ἀπὸ τοῦ θεοῦ, ἡτοιμασμένην ὡς νύμφην κεκοσμημένην
3 τῷ ἀνδρὶ αὐτῆς. [3]καὶ ἤκουσα φωνῆς μεγάλης ἐκ τοῦ
θρόνου λεγούσης Ἰδοὺ ἡ σκηνὴ τοῦ θεοῦ μετὰ τῶν ἀνθρώ-

2 *απο του θεου εκ του ουρ.* P 1 49 79 91 96 al arm | om *απο του θεου* Ir^int | *κεκοσμημενην*] pr *και* 130 3 *και ηκουσα...λεγουσης*] *και φωνη μεγαλη...λεγουσα* ℵ* | *εκ τ. θρονου*] *εκ τ. ουρανου* PQ min^fere omn me the syrr arm aeth Tyc Prim Andr Ar

ἡτοιμασμένην ὡς νύμφην κεκοσμημένην κτλ.] In xix. 7 the voice of a multitude proclaimed that the Wife of the Lamb has made herself ready for the nuptials; now at length she is revealed to the Seer in her bridal attire. Over her simple dress of white *byssus* (xix. 8) she wears that ornament usual for women of rank; cf. Judith xii. 15 *ἐκοσμήθη τῷ ἱματισμῷ καὶ παντὶ τῷ κόσμῳ τῷ γυναικείῳ*—in what this consisted appears *ib.* x. 4 *περιέθετο...τὰ ψέλια καὶ τοὺς δακτυλίους καὶ τὰ ἐνώτια καὶ πάντα τὸν κόσμον αὐτῆς*; Ez. xvi. 11 *ἐκόσμησά σε κόσμῳ, καὶ περιέθηκα ψέλια...καὶ κάθεμα...καὶ ἐνώτιον...καὶ τροχίσκους...καὶ στέφανον...καὶ ἐκοσμήθης χρυσίῳ καὶ ἀργυρίῳ*; cf. Isa. iii. 18 ff. For the ethical significance of the Bride's ornaments see 3 Macc. vi. 1 *πάσῃ τῇ κατὰ τὸν βίον ἀρετῇ κεκοσμημένος*; 1 Pet. iii. 3 *οὐχ ὁ ἔξωθεν ἐμπλοκῆς τριχῶν καὶ περιθέσεως χρυσίων ἢ ἐνδύσεως ἱματίων κόσμος, ἀλλ' ὁ κρυπτὸς τῆς καρδίας ἄνθρωπος ἐν τῷ ἀφθάρτῳ τοῦ ἡσυχίου καὶ πραέως πνεύματος*; cf. also 1 Tim. ii. 9 f. On *ὡς νύμφην* see Isa. xlix. 18 *περιθήσεις αὐτοὺς ὡς κόσμον, ὡς νύμφη*; *ib.* lxi. 10 *ὡς νύμφην κατεκόσμησέν με κόσμῳ*; and for *τῷ ἀνδρὶ αὐτῆς* cf. 2 Cor. xi. 2, Eph. v. 23.

Fuller particulars of the bridal array of the New Jerusalem are given below (*v.* 9 ff.), where see notes.

3. *καὶ ἤκουσα φωνῆς μεγάλης ἐκ τοῦ θρόνου κτλ.*] The voice is that of one of the Angels of the Presence, as in xvi. 17, xix. 5 (notes), not of God Himself, Who speaks for the first time in *v.* 5. The present voice interprets the New Creation; it is that condition of humanity in which will be realized at length the long promised life of fellowship with God. The words *ἰδοὺ ἡ σκηνή κτλ.* rest upon a series of O.T. predictions, e.g. Lev. xxvi. 11 f. *θήσω τὴν διαθήκην μου* (F, *τ. σκηνήν μου*) *ἐν ὑμῖν...καὶ ἔσομαι ὑμῖν θεός, καὶ ὑμεῖς ἔσεσθέ μου λαός*; Jer. xxxviii. (xxxi.) 33 *ἔσομαι αὐτοῖς εἰς θεόν, καὶ αὐτοὶ ἔσονταί μοι εἰς λαόν*; Ez. xxxvii. 27 *ἔσται ἡ κατασκήνωσίς μου ἐν αὐτοῖς, καὶ ἔσομαι αὐτοῖς θεός, καὶ αὐτοί μου ἔσονται λαός*; Zech. viii. 8 *κατασκηνώσω ἐν μέσῳ Ἰερουσαλήμ, καὶ ἔσονταί μοι εἰς λαόν, κἀγὼ ἔσομαι αὐτοῖς εἰς θεὸν ἐν ἀληθείᾳ καὶ ἐν δικαιοσύνῃ*. One important and doubtless deliberate change has been made in the terms of these prophecies; our writer has substituted *λαοί* for *λαός*—the many peoples of redeemed humanity for the single elect nation, the world for Israel. Neither in the O.T. prophecies nor in their Apocalyptic echoes does the use of *σκηνή* and its derivatives suggest a merely temporary dwelling of God with man. As in vii. 15, xiii. 6, xv. 5, they carry us back to the original settlement in Canaan, when the Sanctuary was still but a tent; they point to a *σκηνὴ ἀληθινή*, a *μείζων καὶ τελειοτέρα σκηνή* (Heb. viii. 2, ix. 11); perhaps they also suggest by the assonance of *σκηνοῦν* and שָׁכַן the Shekinah, realized in the Incarnation (Jo. i. 14) and in the mystical Body of Christ. Ὁ *θεὸς μετ' αὐτῶν* recalls עִמָּנוּ אֵל (Mt. i. 23), and all that that name holds for both the present and the coming age.

πων, καὶ σκηνώσει μετ' αὐτῶν, καὶ αὐτοὶ λαοὶ αὐτοῦ
ἔσονται, καὶ αὐτὸς ὁ θεὸς μετ' αὐτῶν ἔσται [αὐτῶν θεός],
⁴καὶ ἐξαλείψει πᾶν δάκρυον ἐκ τῶν ὀφθαλμῶν αὐτῶν, 4
καὶ ὁ θάνατος οὐκ ἔσται ἔτι οὔτε πένθος οὔτε κραυγὴ
οὔτε πόνος· οὐκ ἔσται ἔτι· [ὅτι] τὰ πρῶτα ἀπῆλθαν.
⁵καὶ εἶπεν ὁ καθήμενος ἐπὶ τῷ θρόνῳ Ἰδοὺ καινὰ ποιῶ 5
πάντα. καὶ λέγει Γράψον, ὅτι οὗτοι οἱ λόγοι πιστοὶ

3 *σκηνωσει*] *εσκηνωσεν* ℵ* | *λαοι* ℵA 1 79 92 al Ir^int] *λαος* PQ min^35 vg syrr me the syr aeth arm Ambr Aug Tyc Prim Ar | *και αυτος*] om *και* ℵ | *αυτων θεος* A vg (syrr) Ir^int Tyc] *θεος αυτων* P 79 130 186 al om ℵQ rell 4 *εξαλειψει*] + *ο θεος* A 1 al^pauc vid vg Tert Aug Prim Tyc | *δακρυον*] *δρακυ* (sic) ℵ* | *εκ* ℵA 32] *απο* PQ min^fere omn Ir Andr Ar | *ο θανατος*] om *ο* ℵ 38 47 Ir | om *ουτε πονος* ℵ | *ετι* 2° om 1 | *οτι τα πρωτα*] om *οτι* AP 186 (hab ℵQ min^fere omn) *τα γαρ πρωτα* 79 | *απηλθαν* A (-*λθον* P 1 7 al^sat mu)] *απηλθεν* ℵQ min^fere 20 Ir Ar 5 om *και* 1° 2 29 41 50 90 94 97 Ir^int | *ειπεν*] *λεγει* 130 | *επι τω θρονω*] *επι του θρονου* 1 49 al *εν τω θρονω* 35 79 87 | *ιδου*] pr *και* A | *καινα ποιω παντα* ℵAP 35 37 38 49 87 91 96 vg syr^gw Ir Aug Prim al] *καινοποιω παντα* 79 186 *παντα καινα ποιω* 1 al syr | *λεγει*] + *μοι* ℵP 1 186 al^pl vg^cle fu lips* me syr^gw arm Prim Andr Ar | om *οτι* 94 186 syr^gw

4. *καὶ ἐξαλείψει πᾶν δάκρυον κτλ.*] The effect of the Divine indwelling on the circumstances of life is described in negative terms; as to the positive conditions of the future existence, *οὔπω ἐφανερώθη τί ἐσόμεθα* (1 Jo. iii. 2). On *ἐξαλείψει πᾶν δάκρυον* (Isa. xxv. 8) see vii. 17, note; *ὁ θάνατος οὐκ ἔσται ἔτι* renews the assurance of xx. 14; cf. *Shemoth rabba* xv. f. 114. 4, "temporibus Messiae mors cessabit in aeternum." For *οὔτε πένθος κτλ.* cf. Isa. xxxv. 10 *ἀπέδρα ὀδύνη καὶ λύπη καὶ στεναγμός*; *ib.* lxv. 19 *οὐκέτι μὴ ἀκουσθῇ ἐν αὐτῇ φωνὴ κλαυθμοῦ καὶ φωνὴ κραυγῆς*—the exact opposite of what is said of Babylon in *c.* xviii. 22; see also Enoch x. 22. On *πόνος*, 'pain,' cf. *c.* xvi. 10, note. *Τὰ πρῶτα ἀπῆλθαν*: 'the first things are gone by'—not, as in A.V., 'the former things' simply, but the things belonging to the first heaven and the first earth, the whole order of things which existed in the first creation. The thought is remarkably close to that of 2 Cor. v. 17 *εἴ τις ἐν Χριστῷ, καινὴ κτίσις· τὰ ἀρχαῖα παρῆλθεν, ἰδού, γέγονεν καινά*; but the reference is wider, including the Church as a whole, and not only the individual life in Christ.

5. *καὶ εἶπεν ὁ καθήμενος ἐπὶ τῷ θρόνῳ κτλ.*] The Speaker is now, probably for the first time in the Book, God Himself; cf. xx. 11, xxi. 3. The words are suggested by Isa. xliii. 18 f. *μὴ μνημονεύετε τὰ πρῶτα, καὶ τὰ ἀρχαῖα μὴ συλλογίζεσθε· ἰδοὺ ἐγὼ ποιῶ καινά*, but the scope of the old prophecy is enlarged indefinitely by *πάντα*; all the fruits of the New Covenant (cf. ii. 17, note) are included. For *ἐπὶ τῷ θρόνῳ* in this connexion cf. vii. 10, xix. 4: the more usual *ἐπὶ τοῦ θρόνου* occurs in iv. 9 f., v. 1, 7, 13, vi. 16, vii. 15, xx. 12.

Καὶ λέγει, coming between *καὶ εἶπεν* (*v.* 5) and *καὶ εἶπεν* (*v.* 6), indicates a change of speaker. The direction to the Seer to write what he has just heard comes doubtless from an angel, as in xiv. 13, xix. 9 f. He is to write, because the words he has heard are as true as they are tremendous; cf. Arethas: *μὴ νόμιζε, φησίν, ὦ Ἰωάννη,*

6 καὶ ἀληθινοί εἰσιν. 6 καὶ εἶπέν μοι, Γέγοναν. ἐγὼ τὸ
ἄλφα καὶ τὸ ὦ, ἡ ἀρχὴ καὶ τὸ τέλος. ἐγὼ τῷ

5 αληθινοι] + του θεου Q min[fere 25] syr Ar + του θεου εισιν 130 6 ειπεν] λεγει ℵ | γεγοναν ℵ[c.a] A (-νασιν 38) syr[gw] Ir[int]] γεγονα ℵ*PQ 1 130 186 al[plq 35] syr arm Or Andr Ar γεγονε 41 94 *factum est* vg Prim om ℵ[c.c(?)] me aeth Tyc | εγω] + ειμι A 38 39 vg me aeth Cypr Tyc | η αρχη] om η 8 29 32 37 130 al[fere 10] Ar | το τελος] om το 8 29 32 37 130 al[fere 10] Ar | τω διψωντι] om τω P

τῇ τοῦ μεγέθους τῶν καινοποιουμένων ἀλλοιώσει ὡς καθ' ὑπερβολὴν φαντασίας ὑποπεσεῖν ψευδεῖ τινὶ ἐκβάσει τὰ λεγόμενά σοι· τοσοῦτον γὰρ ἀληθῆ ὥστε καὶ γραφῇ καταθέσθαι σε ταῦτα παρεγγυῶμαι εἰς ἀνεπίληστον τοῦ ὅτι γενήσεται. For πιστὸς καὶ ἀληθινός in this Book compare *cc.* iii. 14, xix. 11; λόγος π. καὶ ἀλ. occurs again in xxii. 6 and λόγος ἀλ. in xix. 9. These great sayings which concern the future of humanity and the world must be seen to rest on a secure basis; men need to be assured that they are not only worthy of confidence, but answer to realities which in due time will enter into the experience of life, though for the present they cannot be fully realized or adequately expressed. "Haec credi oportet, non exponi" (Primasius).

6. καὶ εἶπέν μοι Γέγοναν] The Divine Voice speaks again. Not only are these sayings true; they have come to pass (cf. xvi. 17 γέγονεν). They have found a fulfilment already in the regeneration of life and thought which exists within the present Church, and the larger fulfilment which awaits the Parousia is potentially realized in the Divine foreknowledge. The aoristic termination of the perfect (-αν for -ασιν) has perplexed the scribes, and the *vv. ll.* γέγονα, γέγονε, are attempts to evade this difficulty; on γέγοναν see Blass, *Gr.* p. 46, and cf. Rom. xvi. 7.

ἐγὼ τὸ ἄλφα καὶ τὸ ὦ κτλ.] Cf. i. 8, note. Here as there the reference is to the Eternal Father, whilst in xxi. 6 it is equally clear that the Incarnate Son is in view; see note *ad loc.* Ἡ ἀρχὴ καὶ τὸ τέλος reflects a phrase of the second Isaiah (Isa. xliv. 6 אֲנִי רִאשׁוֹן וַאֲנִי אַחֲרוֹן; cf. *ib.* xli. 4, xlviii. 12). Ἀρχή is used in Col. i. 18 in reference to the relation of Christ to the Church, and in Apoc. iii. 14 of His relation to the cosmos; here it represents God as the First Cause, the Source and Origin of all things, a sense already found in Aristotle, by whom the Deity is called a πρώτη καὶ κυριωτάτη ἀρχή. Τέλος, as complementary to ἀρχή, is the end and goal—a meaning of the word which is rare in the N.T., but see 1 Tim. i. 5 τὸ δὲ τέλος τῆς παραγγελίας ἐστὶν ἀγάπη, and perhaps Rom. x. 4 τέλος γὰρ νόμου Χριστός (see, however, SH. *ad loc.*). The full phrase is used in reference to the Divine life by Josephus, *antt.* viii. 11. 2 [ὁ θεὸς] ὅς ἔργον ἐστὶν αὐτοῦ καὶ ἀρχὴ καὶ τέλος τῶν ἁπάντων; *contr. Ap.* ii. 22 ὁ θεὸς ἔχει τὰ σύμπαντα παντελὴς καὶ μακάριος, αὐτὸς αὑτῷ καὶ πᾶσιν αὐτάρκης, ἀρχὴ καὶ μέσα καὶ τέλος οὗτος τῶν πάντων. St Paul expresses the same fundamental belief in other terms, when he writes: ἐξ αὐτοῦ καὶ δι' αὐτοῦ καὶ εἰς αὐτὸν τὰ πάντα (Rom. xi. 36), and speaks of the Father as ὁ ἐπὶ πάντων καὶ διὰ πάντων καὶ ἐν πᾶσιν (Eph. iv. 6). The Infinite Life originates, embraces, and transcends the Universe.

ἐγὼ τῷ διψῶντι δώσω ἐκ τῆς πηγῆς κτλ.] The Source and End of all life is the bountiful Giver of life in its highest perfection. Cf. Jac. i. 5 αἰτείτω παρὰ τοῦ διδόντος θεοῦ πᾶσιν ἁπλῶς καὶ μὴ ὀνειδίζοντος; *ib.* 17 πᾶσα δόσις ἀγαθὴ καὶ πᾶν δώρημα τέλειον

διψῶντι δώσω ἐκ τῆς πηγῆς τοῦ ὕδατος τῆς ζωῆς
δωρεάν. 7 ὁ νικῶν κληρονομήσει ταῦτα, καὶ ἔσομαι 7

6 δωσω] + αυτω Q 2 8 29 31 35 48 87 92 94 97 al[25] aeth Ar | om της πηγης A post του υδατος 130   7 κληρονομησει] δωσω αυτω Q min[30] Ar | ταυτα] παντα 1

ἄνωθέν ἐστιν, καταβαῖνον ἀπὸ τοῦ πατρὸς τῶν φώτων. With the form of this Divine offer cf. *c.* vii. 16 f. οὐδὲ διψήσουσιν ἔτι ..ὁδηγήσει αὐτοὺς ἐπὶ ζωῆς πηγὰς ὑδάτων, where see notes. There, however, the perfect state is anticipated; here, and in xxii. 17, it is to the Church and the world in their present condition that the water of life is promised, as τῷ διψῶντι, ὁ διψῶν, clearly shew. Δωρεάν, 'gratuitously,' as in Mt. x. 8 δ. ἐλάβετε, Rom. iii. 24 δικαιούμενοι δ.; for the sense see Isa. lv. 1 οἱ διψῶντες, πορεύεσθε ἐφ' ὕδωρ...καὶ φάγετε ἄνευ ἀργυρίου καὶ τιμῆς; Jo. iv. 10 εἰ ᾔδεις τὴν δωρεὰν τοῦ θεοῦ...σὺ ἂν ᾔτησας αὐτὸν καὶ ἔδωκεν ἄν σοι ὕδωρ ζῶν; Acts viii. 20 τὴν δωρεὰν τοῦ θεοῦ ἐνόμισας διὰ χρημάτων κτᾶσθαι. That God's gifts are gratuitous is rightly urged as an argument for free Sacraments, but the fact has a far wider significance, and lies at the root of the Pauline doctrine of justification by faith without 'works of law.' In the present case the Gift is one which comes here and now from the very Source (ἐκ τῆς πηγῆς; cf. vii. 17)—a point emphasized here but not repeated in xxii. 17. Cf. Bede, "de hoc fonte irrorat nunc credentes in via quem vincentibus ubertim hauriendum praebet in patria, utrumque autem gratis"; and the experience of the Viennese deacon Sanctus in the fires of persecution, related in the letter of the confessors (Eus. *H. E.* v. 1. 18): παρέμενεν ἀνεπίκαμπτος καὶ ἀνένδοτος, στερρὸς πρὸς τὴν ὁμολογίαν, ὑπὸ τῆς οὐρανίου πηγῆς τοῦ ὕδατος τῆς ζωῆς τοῦ ἐξιόντος ἐκ τῆς νηδύος τοῦ χριστοῦ δροσιζόμενος καὶ ἐνδυναμούμενος).

7. ὁ νικῶν κληρονομήσει ταῦτα] While 'he that is athirst' receives the Gift of the Water of Life, it is 'he that conquers' alone whose heritage it will permanently be. Ὁ νικῶν carries the reader back to the seven promises of *cc.* ii., iii., to which κληρονομήσει ταῦτα adds an eighth promise that completes and in effect embraces the rest. On the pre-Christian history of κληρονομεῖν see Mc. x. 17, note, and cf. Dalman, *Words of Jesus*, E. Tr., p. 125 ff.; in the N.T. the use of this verb and its cognate nouns in reference to the future of man is well distributed, but specially frequent in St Paul, with whose doctrine of the sonship of believers it accords; cf. Rom. viii. 17 εἰ δὲ τέκνα, καὶ κληρονόμοι, Gal. iv. 7 εἰ δὲ υἱός, καὶ κληρονόμος διὰ θεοῦ. That in the solitary instance where it occurs in the Apoc. the word has the same reference is one indication among many of the radical agreement between St John and St Paul.

The heritage of the conquerer wil embrace the contents of this vision (ταῦτα)—the new creation with its immunities from sorrow and death, the indwelling of God, the consciousness of a filial relation with Him, and the Water that quenches the thirst and quickens the life of the human soul. The *v. l.* πάντα, with its larger but vaguer outlook, offers a less really satisfying prospect.

καὶ ἔσομαι αὐτῷ θεὸς καὶ αὐτὸς ἔσται μοι υἱός] The words link themselves on to a catena of O.T. prophecies, e.g. Gen. xvii. 7 f., 2 Regn. vii. 14, Ps. lxxxviii. (lxxxix.) 27; the last of these passages is applied to Christ in Heb. i. 5, but may obviously include, in a laxer sense, His συνκληρονόμοι. Their sonship, even their relationship with God is here regarded as belonging to the future (ἔσομαι, ἔσται), when it will be manifested by the

8 *αὐτῷ θεὸς καὶ αὐτὸς ἔσται μοι υἱός.* [8]*τοῖς δὲ δειλοῖς*

7 *αυτω*] *αυτων* A 1 79 130 arm | *αυτος εσται μοι* (*μου* ℵ 14 98 al^{pauc} syr) *υιος*] om *αυτος* A syr^{gw} *αυτοι εσονται μοι υιοι* 130 186

resurrection; cf. Lc. xx. 36 *υἱοί εἰσιν θεοῦ τῆς ἀναστάσεως υἱοὶ ὄντες*; Rom. viii. 23 *υἱοθεσίαν ἀπεκδεχόμενοι τὴν ἀπολύτρωσιν τοῦ σώματος ἡμῶν*. St John is not unconscious of the present existence of both (1 Jo. iii. 1 *ποταπὴν ἀγάπην δέδωκεν ὁ πατὴρ ἵνα τέκνα θεοῦ κληθῶμεν· καί ἐσμεν...νῦν τέκνα θεοῦ ἐσμέν*), but in this passage he has in view the son who is entering on his full inheritance, and not him to whom but the *ἀρραβών* (Eph. i. 13 f.) has as yet been given.

8. *τοῖς δὲ δειλοῖς καὶ ἀπίστοις κτλ.*] Bede: "blandis semper, ad cautelam insinuandam, austera permiscet"; the doom of the impenitent is placed in sharp contrast with the heritage of the conqueror. First among the condemned are the *δειλοί*—members of the Church who, like soldiers turning their backs upon the enemy, fail under trial; not, as A.V. and R.V., 'the fearful,' but the cowards or craven in Christ's army. Cf. Arethas: *δειλοὺς καλεῖ τοὺς ἑκουσίῳ ἀσθενείᾳ πρὸς τὰ ἀπολαυστικὰ τοῦ παρόντος αἰῶνος ἀποκλίναντας*. When Tertullian writes (*de fuga* 7): "in Apocalypsi non fugam timidis offert sed inter ceteros reprobos particulam in stagno sulphuris et ignis," he is led, partly by his Latin version, partly by his personal tendencies, into undue severity; it is not fear or even flight which incurs the penalty, but the cowardice which in the last resort prefers ease or earthly life to Christ; cf. Mc. viii. 35 ff. Such *δειλία* betrays instability of purpose, lack of any deeper faith or loyalty; cf. Sir. ii. 12 f., and Origen on Ps. xxvi. (xxvii.) 1 f.: *προσκόπτει δὲ ψυχὴ τυφλώττουσα καὶ πάντα φοβεῖται, καὶ τὴν εἰς θεὸν ὁμολογίαν ἀρνήσεται· ἀπὸ θεοῦ δὲ φωτισθεῖσα, πρῶτον μὲν τὸν πρόμαχον αὐτῆς καὶ σωτῆρα ἔστι θεωροῦσα, μετὰ δὲ ταῦτα τῶν αὐτῆς πολεμίων καταθαρρεῖ*. The remedy for *δειλία* is *πίστις*, cf. Jo. xiv. 1, 27 *μὴ ταρασσέσθω ὑμῶν ἡ καρδία· πιστεύετε εἰς τὸν θεόν, καὶ εἰς ἐμὲ πιστεύετε ... μὴ ταρασσέσθω ὑμῶν ἡ καρδία μηδὲ δειλιάτω*. The *ἄπιστος*, in the technical sense which appears in the Pauline Epistles, is the non-Christian, the pagan (cf. 1 Cor. vi. 6, vii. 12 ff., x. 27, xiv. 22 ff., 2 Cor. vi. 14 f.); but here, following immediately after *δειλός*, it is probably not to be limited in this way, or referred to the heathen as such, but means simply 'faithless,' 'unbelieving' (Mc. ix. 19, Lc. xii. 46, Jo. xx. 27, Tit. i. 15; cf. 1 Tim. v. 8), and applies to the Christian who by act or word denies his faith, as well as to the pagan who insults and blasphemes it. The other characters described, though they might be found on the fringe of the Christian brotherhood (cf. ii. 15, 20), are such as heathenism produced on a large scale; see ix. 21 where the heathen are clearly in view, and the list of sins is nearly the same. *Ἐβδελυγμένοι*, not simply *βδελυκτοί*, as in Tit. i. 16, but persons whose very natures have been saturated with the abominations which they practised in their lifetime; the context suggests that in this case the *βδελύγματα* are not simply idolatrous acts (cf. xvii. 4), but the monstrous and unnatural vices of heathendom. *Καὶ φονεῦσι καὶ πόρνοις κτλ.* *Φόνοι* are included among prevalent sins in Mc. vii. 21, Rom. i. 29, Apoc. ix. 21 (cf. Jac. iv. 2, 1 Pet. iv. 15), but perhaps the reference is here chiefly to the violent deaths of Christians whether at the hands of the mob or by order of the courts. *Πόρνοι* abounded in Greek cities—at Corinth, St Paul admits it was impossible to avoid meeting them in society (1 Cor. v. 10 *ἐπεὶ ὠφείλετε ἄρα ἐκ τοῦ κόσμου*

καὶ ἀπίστοις καὶ ἐβδελυγμένοις καὶ φονεῦσι καὶ πόρνοις καὶ φαρμακοῖς καὶ εἰδωλολάτραις καὶ πᾶσι τοῖς ψευδέσιν τὸ μέρος αὐτῶν ἐν τῇ λίμνῃ τῇ καιομένῃ πυρὶ καὶ θείῳ, ὅ ἐστιν ὁ θάνατος ὁ δεύτερος.

[9] Καὶ ἦλθεν εἷς ἐκ τῶν ἑπτὰ ἀγγέλων τῶν 9
ἐχόντων τὰς ἑπτὰ φιάλας, τῶν γεμόντων τῶν ἑπτὰ

8 απιστοις]+και αμαρτωλοις Q 130 min[plq 35] syr aeth Ar | ψευδεσιν] ψευσταις A πυρι] pr εν 130 | ο θανατος ο δευτερος ℵAQ min[plq 25] vg syr arm] θαν. ο δ. min[pauc] Ar ο δ. θαν. 1 49 130 186 al[mu] θανατος P   9 ηλθεν]+προς με vg[lips 4] arm | εις] ο πρωτος 35 36 87 | om εκ 1 35 38 79 87 | των γεμοντων] των γεμουσων ℵ[c.a] τας γεμουσας 1 7 130 al[mu vid] et sine τας Q 8 29 31 38 49 91 92 al[15] syrr[vid] Ar | των επτα πληγων] om των Q min[20]

ἐξελθεῖν)—and they fitly follow φονεῖς; cf. 1 Tim. i. 9 f. ἀνδροφόνοις πόρνοις—the M.T. order of the Decalogue. On φαρμακοί see ix. 21, xviii. 23, notes; in Gal. v. 20 φαρμακία follows εἰδωλολατρία, whilst here φαρμακός precedes εἰδωλολάτρης; for the connexion of sorcery and magic with idolatry in Asian cities see xiii. 13 ff., notes. The list ends with καὶ πᾶσιν τοῖς ψευδέσιν, 'all the false,' i.e., as is explained below in xxii. 15, πᾶσιν τοῖς φιλοῦσιν καὶ ποιοῦσιν ψεῦδος. All the insincerities of heathendom are here—the conscious frauds practised by the pagan priesthood and the dealers in 'magic,' and the support rendered to them by those who 'loved to have it so'; the tricks of trade and deceits of domestic life. But the insincerities of Christians are not of course to be excluded; the baptized liar is the worst of his kind, since he lies to the Holy Ghost (Acts v. 3 f.). Tertullian, indeed, seems to limit the reference of the whole passage to Christians: *de pud.* 19 "non enim de ethnicis videbitur sapere, cum de fidelibus pronuntiarit *Qui vicerint*, etc."; but the inference is too sweeping. A better exposition will be found in *de Antichr.* 38 Hipp. (ed. Lagarde, p. 116).

None such have any part in the inheritance of the Saints (Eph. v. 5); their names are not in the roll-call of the living in the New Jerusalem. The alternative is a part in the Second Death, the Lake of Fire. Exclusion from eternal life burns and consumes like a perpetual fire; whether the function of the fire is to destroy or to punish or to purify is not within the scope of the revelation entrusted to the Seer; cf. xix. 20, xx. 10, 14 f., notes. Contrast the dogmatic tone of the Slavonic Enoch (ed. Charles, p. 10): "this place, Enoch, is prepared for those who do not honour God; who commit evil deeds on earth...witchcraft, enchantments, devilish magic, and who boast of their evil deeds...for all these this place is prepared for an eternal inheritance."

XXI. 9—XXII. 5. THE VISION OF THE NEW JERUSALEM.

9. καὶ ἦλθεν εἷς ἐκ τῶν ἑπτά κτλ.] The announcement of *v.* 2 (καὶ τὴν πόλιν τὴν ἁγίαν Ἰερουσαλὴμ καινὴν εἶδον κτλ.) is here resumed and worked out in detail. The Seer tells us that this nearer view of the City was obtained through the ministry of one of the Angels of the Seven Bowls. Compare *c.* xvii. 1 καὶ ἦλθεν εἷς ἐκ τῶν ἑπτὰ ἀγγέλων τῶν ἐχόντων τὰς ἑπτὰ φιάλας, καὶ ἐλάλησεν μετ' ἐμοῦ λέγων Δεῦρο, δείξω σοι τὸ κρίμα τῆς πόρνης, where the same formula is used to introduce

πληγῶν τῶν ἐσχάτων, καὶ ἐλάλησεν μετ᾽ ἐμοῦ λέγων
Δεῦρο, δείξω σοι τὴν νύμφην τὴν γυναῖκα τοῦ
10 ἀρνίου. [10]καὶ ἀπήνεγκέν με ἐν πνεύματι ἐπὶ ὄρος
μέγα καὶ ὑψηλόν, καὶ ἔδειξέν μοι τὴν πόλιν τὴν

9 την νυμφην την γυν. του αρνιου] την ν. του αρν. την γυν. 1 79 186 vg[lips5] την γυν. την ν. τ. α. Q 7 8 29 31 49 al[25] Ar 10 επι] επ PQ min[pl] | την πολιν] + την μεγαλην 1 31 49 79 91 96 130 186 al Andr | την αγιαν] και αγ. 1 31 79 130 186

the vision of the Harlot City; its repetition here serves to place the *νύμφη* in marked contrast with the *πόρνη*—Jerusalem the Holy with Babylon the Great. For *τῶν ἐχόντων τὰς ἑπτὰ φιάλας*, cf. xv. 1, note. *Τῶν γεμόντων* is unexpected; possibly it is a slip on the part of an early scribe or perhaps of the writer himself for *τὰς γεμούσας* (xv. 7), or it may be meant to suggest that these angels were still full of the great task they had accomplished, and that St John's guide came fresh from the scene of the Last Plagues to this widely different office. Both participles are timeless; the Seven Angels have emptied their bowls, and doubtless have ceased to carry them, but they are still known as *οἱ ἔχοντες τὰς φιάλας τὰς γεμούσας* (or *οἱ γέμοντες*) *τῶν ἑπτὰ πληγῶν*. That one of these Angels of wrath should be deputed to shew the Seer the Holy City is a Divine paradox which has not escaped the ancient commentators; cf. Andreas: *ὁ γὰρ τότε τὴν πληγὴν τοῖς ἀξίοις ἐπάγων, νῦν τὴν μακαριότητα τῆς ἐκκλησίας τῷ ἁγίῳ ὑποδείκνυσι*; Bede: "praedicatores iidem qui plagam septimariam (id est, universalem) irrogant impiis, ecclesiae quoque futura gaudia pandunt."

Τὴν νύμφην τὴν γυναῖκα τοῦ ἀρνίου takes up a thread dropt at *c.* xix. 7 *ἦλθεν ὁ γάμος τοῦ ἀρνίου, καὶ ἡ γυνὴ αὐτοῦ ἡτοίμασεν ἑαυτήν*. The espoused wife (Mt. i. 18, 20) is now the Bride (xxi. 2) of the Lamb; the nuptials have begun; indeed, as Andreas remarks: *ὅτε ὡς ἀμνὸς ἐσφαγιάσθη ὁ Χριστός, τότε αὐτὴν τῷ οἰκείῳ αἵματι ἐνυμφεύσατο...τῇ ἐκχύσει τοῦ ἐκ τῆς πλευρᾶς αἵματος ἡ ἐκκλησία συστᾶσα τῷ τυθέντι δι᾽ ἡμᾶς ἥρμοσται*. The metaphor belongs to the first days of the Gospel, and had been employed by St Paul in a passage which has some affinity with the present; see the note on *c.* xix. 7.

10. *καὶ ἀπήνεγκέν με ἐν πνεύματι ἐπὶ ὄρος κτλ.*] Compare xvii. 3 *ἀπήνεγκέν με εἰς ἔρημον ἐν πνεύματι*. The Harlot City is seen in a wilderness, the Bride City from a mountain. The mountain is not Mount Zion (xiv. 1), for the New Jerusalem is not founded upon it, but is seen from it; the indefinite *ὄρος μέγα καὶ ὑψηλόν* points to no particular height, but rather symbolizes the elevation of spirit (Apringius: "in fidei altitudine elevatur") necessary for one who would see the heavenly vision. Cf. Ez. xl. 2 *ἤγαγέν με ἐν ὁράσει θεοῦ...καὶ ἔθηκέν με ἐπ᾽ ὄρος ὑψηλὸν σφόδρα*; Mt. iv. 8 *παραλαμβάνει αὐτὸν ὁ διάβολος εἰς ὄρος ὑψηλὸν λίαν*. The Seer is carried thither 'in spirit' (cf. i. 10, iv. 2); the Angel's *δεῦρο* is a *sursum cor* to which his spirit under the influence of the 'Spirit of revelation' (Eph. i. 17) at once responds.

καὶ ἔδειξέν μοι τὴν πόλιν τὴν ἁγίαν Ἰερουσαλήμ κτλ.] For *τὴν πόλιν κτλ.* see *v.* 2, note. *Καινήν* is not repeated here, for the City is not now regarded in its relation to the rest of the New Creation, but in its specific character, which is Holiness.

ἁγίαν Ἰερουσαλὴμ καταβαίνουσαν ἐκ τοῦ οὐρανοῦ
ἀπὸ τοῦ θεοῦ, [11]ἔχουσαν τὴν δόξαν τοῦ θεοῦ· ὁ 11
φωστὴρ αὐτῆς ὅμοιος λίθῳ τιμιωτάτῳ, ὡς λίθῳ
ἰάσπιδι κρυσταλλίζοντι· [12]ἔχουσα τεῖχος μέγα καὶ 12

10 εκ] απο 11 31 32 33 35 51 90 | απο] εκ Q min[35] Ar | om απο τ. θεου 92 94 Ambr Cassiod   11 om εχουσαν...του θεου A 98 | του θεου] pr απο ℵ Ir[gr ex Anast] om τ. θεου me | ο φωστηρ] pr και 1 7 al[mu] vg [cle dem lipss 4, 6] syr[gw] arm aeth Prim Ar | τιμιωτατω] τιμιω 94 *g* vg syr[gw] | om ως λιθω 1 7 12 17* 18 38 47 186 syr[gw] | κρυσταλιζοντι PQ min[nonn]   12 εχουσα 1°] εχουσαν (τε) 35 87 al (Ar) εχοντα ℵ

11. ἔχουσαν τὴν δόξαν τοῦ θεοῦ] The Church possesses the Divine Presence, which, with its illuminating and elevating powers, she brings with her from her place of origin, and she is transfigured by it; cf. *v.* 23, xxii. 5. Cf. Isa. lx. 1 ἡ δόξα Κυρίου ἐπὶ σὲ ἀνατέταλκεν. The description belongs even to the present condition of the Christian Society: 2 Cor. iii. 18 ἡμεῖς δὲ πάντες ἀνακεκαλυμμένῳ προσώπῳ τὴν δόξαν Κυρίου κατοπτριζόμενοι (R.V. 'reflecting as in a mirror')...μεταμορφούμεθα ἀπὸ δόξης εἰς δόξαν.

ὁ φωστὴρ αὐτῆς ὅμοιος λίθῳ τιμιωτάτῳ κτλ.] Her luminary resembled a rare crystalloid gem, every facet of which is radiant with a Divine light. For φωστήρ, as distinguished from φῶς, see Gen. i. 3, 14 καὶ εἶπεν ὁ θεός Γενηθήτω φῶς...καὶ εἶπεν ὁ θεός Γενηθήτωσαν φωστῆρες, and cf. Sir. xliii. 7 φωστὴρ μειούμενος ἐπὶ συντελείας. A φωστήρ is "something in which light is concentrated and thence radiates" (Benson)—*luminare* rather than *lumen* (Prim., Vg.), ܢܗܝܪܐ (Syr.) rather than ܢܘܗܪܐ (Syr.[gw.]; see Dr Gwynn's notes here and on iv. 5). Our Lord is represented as having spoken indiscriminately of Himself and His disciples as τὸ φῶς τοῦ κόσμου (Mt. v. 14, Jo. viii. 12), but in the underlying Aramaic there may well have been a distinction such as that between אוֹר and מָאוֹר; the saints are properly φωστῆρες (Dan. xii. 3, LXX. φανοῦσιν ὡς φωστῆρες τοῦ οὐρανοῦ, Phil. ii. 16 φαίνεσθε ὡς φωστῆρες ἐν κόσμῳ), and not τὸ φῶς τὸ ἀληθινόν (Jo. i. 8 f.). The distinction is ignored here by patristic commentators (e.g. Andreas: φωστὴρ τῆς ἐκκλησίας ὁ χριστός), and by some moderns, who point to *v.* 23 ὁ λύχνος αὐτῆς τὸ ἀρνίον. But it is unnecessary to depart from the strict sense of φωστήρ. The light which illuminates the Church is Divine; it is the φωτισμὸς...τῆς δόξης τοῦ θεοῦ ἐν προσώπῳ Χριστοῦ (2 Cor. iv. 6); but it shines in the hearts and lives of men. The 'luminary' of the Holy City is her witness to Christ: her teaching, her sacraments, her whole corporate life—the light of tens of thousands of saintly lives.

On λίθος ἴασπις see iv. 3, note. Κρυσταλλίζοντι (ἅπ. λεγ.) modifies λ. ἰάσπιδι, 'having the effect of rock crystal,' 'crystal-clear' (Benson); cf. xxii. 1 λαμπρὸν ὡς κρύσταλλον. Wetstein quotes Psellus: ἡ ἴασπις φύσει κρυσταλλοειδής. King (*Hist. of Precious Stones*, p. 281) proposes to identify the ἴασπις with the true emerald, green in colour, but lustrous as crystal. There seem to have been two kinds known to the ancients: cf. Dioscor. v. 160 λίθος ἴασπις ὁ μέν τίς ἐστι σμαραγδίζων, ὁ δὲ κρυσταλλώδης. St John combines their qualities.

12. ἔχουσα τεῖχος μέγα καὶ ὑψηλόν] Ἔχουσα carries on the description of the City, which was broken by the parenthetic clause ὁ φωστὴρ αὐτῆς...

ὑψηλόν, ἔχουσα πυλῶνας δώδεκα, καὶ ἐπὶ τοῖς πυλῶ-
σιν ἀγγέλους δώδεκα, καὶ ὀνόματα ἐπιγεγραμμένα
13 ἅ ἐστιν τῶν δώδεκα φυλῶν υἱῶν Ἰσραήλ. [13] ἀπὸ

12 εχουσα 2°] εχουσαν 7 35 87 al vg$^{\text{cle dem tol lipss 4, 6}}$ (*habentem*) Ar εχοντας ℵ* | om επι τ. πυλ. αγγελους δωδεκα A vg^{fu} syr | επι τοις πυλωσιν] επι τους πυλωνας ℵ 18 | αγγελους] *angulos* Prim^{txt} (sed cf. Prim^{comm}) Ambr^{edd} | ονοματα] + αυτων ℵ syr^{gw} + εκαστων arm^{vid} | επιγεγραμμενα] γεγραμμενα ℵ syr^{gw} εγγεγραμμενα 18 | των δωδ. φυλων] pr (τα) ονοματα (A) Q 130 min^{30} *g* vg me syrr Ar (om ℵP min^{pl} Prim) | υιων] om 12 27 47 130 syr^{gw} pr των P 1 7 49 91 96 186 al | Ισραηλ] pr του 130

κρυσταλλίζοντι; in his eagerness to note each detail of the transient picture the Seer forgets that he had written ἔχουσαν in *v.* 11. The wall is, perhaps, a conventional feature, necessary to the description of an ancient city; the earlier commentators, however, regard it as a symbol, but interpret variously; e.g. Primasius, "murus ecclesiae Christus"; Bede, "[murum], id est, inexpugnabilem fidei spei caritatisque firmitatem"; and see note on *v.* 17. Cf. Zech. ii. 5 (9) ἐγὼ ἔσομαι αὐτῇ, λέγει Κύριος, τεῖχος πυρὸς κυκλόθεν; Isa. xxvi. 1 ἰδοὺ πόλις ἰσχυρά, καὶ σωτήριον θήσει τὸ τεῖχος καὶ περίτειχος.

ἔχουσα πυλῶνας δώδεκα κτλ.] Ezekiel's city also has twelve gates (Ez. xlviii. 31 ff.). Πυλών may be either the vestibule of a great house, through which visitors pass from the street into the courtyard (cf. Gen. xliii. 18 ἐλάλησαν αὐτῷ ἐν τῷ πυλῶνι τοῦ οἴκου, Lc. xvi. 20 Λάζαρος ἐβέβλητο πρὸς τὸν πυλῶνα αὐτοῦ, Acts xii. 13 κρούσαντος δὲ αὐτοῦ τὴν θύραν τοῦ πυλῶνος); or, as here, the gate-tower of a city-wall (cf. 3 Regn. xvii. 10 ἐπορεύθη εἰς Σάρεπτα, εἰς τὸν πυλῶνα τῆς πόλεως, Acts xiv. 13 ὅ τε ἱερεὺς τοῦ Διὸς τοῦ ὄντος πρὸ τῆς πόλεως ταύρους καὶ στέμματα ἐπὶ τοὺς πυλῶνας ἐνέγκας... ἤθελεν θύειν). In both cases πυλών is more than πύλη, viz. the whole structure through which admission is gained.

The twelve angels posted at the gateways are apparently there as πυλωροί or φύλακες—a feature suggested perhaps by Isa. lxii. 6 ἐπὶ τῶν τειχῶν σου, Ἰερουσαλήμ, κατέστησα φύλακας ὅλην τὴν ἡμέραν καὶ ὅλην τὴν νύκτα. The city which descends from heaven has celestial gatekeepers; cf. Heb. i. 14, and *Yalkut Shim.* f. 7. 1 "duas portas paradisi statuunt lx myriadibus angelorum munitas."

καὶ ὀνόματα ἐπιγεγραμμένα ἅ ἐστιν τῶν δώδεκα φυλῶν] Again the writer is indebted to Ezekiel (xlviii. 31 ff. αἱ πύλαι τῆς πόλεως ἐπ' ὀνόμασιν φυλῶν τοῦ Ἰσραήλ κτλ.); cf. *syn. Sohar* 115. 27 "in atrio mundi futuri xii portae quarum singulis inscriptum est nomen quoddam e xii tribubus." The O.T. prophet allocates the gates to the several Tribes (N., Reuben, Judah, Levi; E., Joseph, Benjamin, Dan; S., Simeon, Issachar, Zebulun; W., Gad, Asher, Naphtali); but the Christian Apocalyptist does not follow him in this: the enumeration in *c.* vii. suffices. The Seer's object in referring to the Tribes is simply to assert the continuity of the Christian Church with the Church of the O.T. The new Society inherits all that was permanent in the number and order of the Tribes, without their limitations; it is constituted ἐκ πάσης φυλῆς καὶ γλώσσης (v. 9, vii. 9), and the gateways standing open on all sides represent its catholicity (cf. Lc. xiii. 29).

13. ἀπὸ ἀνατολῆς πυλῶνες τρεῖς κτλ.] In Num. ii. 3 ff. the Tribes are marshalled in a square the sides of which look ESWN; the gates of Ezekiel's city which bear their names

ἀνατολῆς πυλῶνες τρεῖς, καὶ ἀπὸ βορρᾶ πυλῶνες
τρεῖς, καὶ ἀπὸ νότου πυλῶνες τρεῖς, καὶ ἀπὸ δυσ-
μῶν πυλῶνες τρεῖς. [14]καὶ τὸ τεῖχος τῆς πόλεως 14
ἔχων θεμελίους δώδεκα, καὶ ἐπ' αὐτῶν δώδεκα ὀνό-

13 ανατολων Q min$^{\text{fere 35}}$ Ar | om και ter 1 186 al vg$^{\text{fu dem tol lips 4}}$ Tyc Prim | βορρα ...νοτου...δυσμων ℵ$^{*\text{c.a}}$ PQ min$^{\text{fere omn}}$ vg$^{\text{exc am}}$ me syrr arm Tyc Prim Andr Ar] βορρα ...δυσμων...νοτου A vg^{am} et cum μεσημβριας pro νοτου 1 δυσμων...βορρα...νοτου 91 aeth νοτου...βορρα...δυσμων 98 14 εχων] εχον ℵ$^{\text{c.a}}$ (om ℵ*) 130 186 min$^{\text{pl vid}}$ Ar | om δωδεκα 1° 7 al^{vid} vg$^{\text{lips 6}}$ me aeth Prim

follow the order NESW. St John's order, ENSW, not only differs from both, but suggests that the Seer after surveying the east and north walls returns to his starting place in order to examine those on the south and west. It is difficult to understand the purpose of this change, yet it seems to be deliberate; see *v.* 19 note.

Ἀπὸ ἀνατολῆς, ἀπὸ βορρᾶ κτλ., 'starting from the east,' 'from the north,' etc.; in Ezekiel the LXX. satisfactorily renders אֶל־פְּאַת קָדִימָה etc. by τὰ πρὸς ἀνατολάς κτλ. Archbp Benson renders ἀπό similarly here, 'facing sunrise,' 'facing north' etc., without explanation.

14. καὶ τὸ τεῖχος τῆς πόλεως ἔχων θεμελίους δώδεκα] As there are twelve gate-towers, so there are also twelve foundation stones. The wall is broken into twelve sections by the twelve gates, and each section is seen to rest on a single θεμέλιος—a vast oblong block of worked and bevelled stone, such as the stones which may still be seen in the lower ranges of the Herodian masonry at Jerusalem. For θεμέλιος see 2 Esdr. v. 16 ἔδωκεν θεμελίους τοῦ οἴκου τοῦ θεοῦ τοῦ εἰς Ἰερουσαλήμ; 1 Cor. iii. 10 ὡς σοφὸς ἀρχιτέκτων θεμέλιον ἔθηκα, Heb. xi. 10 ἐξεδέχετο γὰρ τὴν τοὺς θεμελίους ἔχουσαν πόλιν. It is properly an adjective (sc. λίθος), and in the plural may be either masc. or neuter; τὰ θεμέλια is frequent in the LXX., and occurs in Acts xvi. 26.

καὶ ἐπ' αὐτῶν δώδεκα ὀνόματα τῶν δώδεκα ἀποστόλων κτλ.] Another series of inscribed names; if the gateways bear the names of the Twelve Tribes, the foundation stones are distinguished by those of the Twelve Apostles. On the juxtaposition of these two dodecads see Mt. xix. 28 καθήσεσθε καὶ ὑμεῖς ἐπὶ δώδεκα θρόνους κρίνοντες τὰς δώδεκα φυλὰς τοῦ Ἰσραήλ; in the Apocalypse it has been suggested already by the vision of the 24 Elders (*c.* iv. 4, note). In Eph. ii. 20 the Apostles and Prophets themselves are a θεμέλιος (ἐποικοδομηθέντες ἐπὶ τῷ θεμελίῳ τῶν ἀποστόλων καὶ προφητῶν, ὄντος ἀκρογωνιαίου αὐτοῦ Χριστοῦ Ἰησοῦ)—a train of thought which goes back to our Lord's promise to Peter (Mt. xvi. 18) and, beyond it, to Ps. cxviii. 22, Isa. xxviii. 16; cf. Acts iv. 11, and 1 Pet. ii. 6, with Dr Hort's note on the latter verse. The Apocalyptist, as his wont is, seizes a current idea and adapts it to his own purpose. The λίθος ἀκρογωνιαῖος does not come into sight here; the Prophets are not joined with the Apostles, as by St Paul; the foundation stones are those not of the Holy City, but of the exterior wall, and they are not the Apostles, but only bear their names. As the wall gives form and compactness to the City, so the Apostolic Church is conditioned, through the ages, by the preaching and work of the Apostolate.

The Twelve Apostles are not in-

15 ματα τῶν δώδεκα ἀποστόλων τοῦ ἀρνίου. [15]καὶ ὁ
λαλῶν μετ' ἐμοῦ εἶχεν μέτρον κάλαμον χρυσοῦν,
ἵνα μετρήσῃ τὴν πόλιν καὶ τοὺς πυλῶνας αὐτῆς καὶ
16 τὸ τεῖχος αὐτῆς. [16]καὶ ἡ πόλις τετράγωνος κεῖται,

14 om δωδεκα 3° vg^{am} syr^{gw} Tyc   15 om μετρον 1 79 al^{vid} me arm | μετρησει Q 7 | om και το τειχος αυτης Q 130 186 al$^{\text{fere 50}}$ Ar   16 και η πολις αυτης τετρ. κειται και το μηκος οσον ℵ

dividually named; it is the college of the Apostles as a whole to which reference is made; cf. Mt. xix. 28, Acts vi. 2, 1 Cor. xv. 7. When Renan observes (*l'Antechrist*, p. 479), "Paul ...n'a pas de place parmi les douze apôtres de l'Agneau, seule base de l'Église de Dieu," he overlooks this fact. There is nothing to shew how the number is made up, and it must not be assumed that St Paul is excluded. On the other hand it is certainly probable that St John refers here to the original Apostolate, and does not stop to consider the question raised by the lapse of Judas.

15. *καὶ ὁ λαλῶν μετ' ἐμοῦ εἶχεν μέτρον κάλαμον χρ. κτλ.*] The measuring of the City is here, as in *c.* xi. 1, suggested by Ez. xl. 3 ff. In xi. 1 the earthly city is measured by the Seer himself; to measure the City which is from heaven requires the capacities of an Angel, and it is done by the Angel who had been talking with the Seer about the City (*ὁ λαλῶν μετ' ἐμοῦ*, cf. *v.* 9 *ἐλάλησεν μετ' ἐμοῦ*). The *κάλαμος* which the Angel carries is not, as in the Seer's case, a natural reed, cut perhaps in the Jordan valley (Mt. xi. 7), or in the valley of the Upper Nile (Job xl. 16), but a rod of gold such as befitted an instrument used in the service of God; cf. i. 12, v. 8, viii. 3, ix. 13, xv. 7.

The Angel is commissioned to take the measure of the City, its gate-towers and its walls. The measurements of the City are given in *v.* 16, and those of the wall in *v.* 17; the gate-towers are merely described (*v.* 21).

16. *καὶ ἡ πόλις τετράγωνος κεῖται κτλ.*] That the external walls form a square whose sides face the four winds appears from *v.* 12 f. It is now seen that the City itself is not only an equilateral quadrangle, but a perfect cube (cf. *v.* 17), length, breadth, and height being equal.

The tetragon occurs more than once in the legislation of Exodus. Both the altar of burnt offering and the altar of incense were of this form (Ex. xxvii. 1, xxx. 2), and so was the High Priest's breastplate (*ib.* xxviii. 16, xxxvi. 16 = xxxix. 9); the feature reappears in Ezekiel's new city and temple (Ez. xli. 21, xliii. 16, xlv. 1, xlviii. 20). In Solomon's Temple the Holy of Holies was a perfect cube, 20 cubits each way, cf. 3 Regn. vi. 19 (20) *εἴκοσι πήχεις μῆκος, καὶ εἴκοσι πήχεις πλάτος, καὶ εἴκοσι πήχεις τὸ ὕψος αὐτοῦ*—words which may have suggested St John's *τὸ μῆκος καὶ τὸ πλάτος καὶ τὸ ὕψος αὐτῆς ἴσα ἐστίν*; the New Jerusalem answers as a whole to the *ἅγια ἁγίων* of the old city and therefore assumes its shape. In ancient cities the four-square form was not unusual. Archbishop Benson, fresh from his tour in North Africa, thought of Cirta, the modern Constantine, "située sur un cube rocheux" (Tissot). Of Babylon Herodotus writes (i. 178): *κέεται ἐν πεδίῳ μεγάλῳ, μέγαθος ἐοῦσα μέτωπον ἕκαστον εἴκοσι καὶ ἑκατὸν σταδίων, ἐούσης τετραγώνου*, and a similar account is given of Nineveh by Diodorus

καὶ τὸ μῆκος αὐτῆς ὅσον [καὶ] τὸ πλάτος. καὶ ἐμέτρησεν τὴν πόλιν τῷ καλάμῳ ἐπὶ σταδίων δώδεκα χιλιάδων· τὸ μῆκος καὶ τὸ πλάτος καὶ τὸ ὕψος

16 om *και* 3° ℵPQ min$^{plq\,35}$ Ar (hab A min$^{nonn\,vid}$ vg me syr arm aeth Prim al) | *το πλατος* 1°] + *αυτης* 7 syr^{gw} | *τω καλαμω*] pr *εν* P 1 11 12 31 32 79 | *επι σταδιων* ℵP 1 35 79 al^{pl}] *επι σταδιους* AQ 130 min^{pl} Ar | *χιλιαδων*] pr *και* Q + *δωδεκα* (Q) min$^{plq\,25}$ syr | *το μηκος* 2°] + *αυτης* 73 syr^{gw} pr *και* 38 vg^{cle} syr aeth

Siculus (i. 3). As is well known, the rectangular tetragon was to Greek thinkers a symbol of perfection; see Simonides *ap.* Plat. *Protag.* 339 B *ἄνδρ' ἀγαθὸν μὲν ἀλαθέως γενέσθαι χαλεπόν, χερσί τε καὶ ποσὶ καὶ νόῳ τετράγωνον, ἄνευ ψόγου τετυγμένον*, and cf. Arist. *eth. Nic.* i. 11, *rhet.* iii. 11; similarly Hermas *vis.* 3, 5 *οἱ μὲν οὖν λίθοι οἱ τετράγωνοι... οὗτοί εἰσιν οἱ ἀπόστολοι καὶ ἐπίσκοποι καὶ διδάσκαλοι καὶ διάκονοι οἱ πορευθέντες κατὰ τὴν σεμνότητα τοῦ θεοῦ.* To this the cube adds the suggestion of solidity, stability, and permanence: cf. Andreas: *ἑδραιότητα δὲ δηλοῦν λέγεται* [*ὁ κύβος*]; Primasius sees in the cube-like form of the Holy City the "soliditas veritatis invictae." The early commentators allegorize freely: e.g. the anonymous writer *de monte Sion et Sina*, 10: "dicit Hierusalem Novam civitatem quadratam per quattuor evangelia"; Victorinus: "civitatem... quadratam sanctorum adunatam turbam ostendit, in quibus nullo modo fides fluctuare potuit"; while Bede thinks of the three dimensions as representing the "longitudo fidei," the "latitudo caritatis," and the "altitudo spei." All such speculations must be taken for what they are worth. With regard to the dimensions of the cube, though it is natural to see in them a forecast of the extension, the comprehensiveness, and the elevation of Catholic Christianity, neither this nor any other particular interpretation can safely be pressed; cf. Eph. iii. 18 *τὸ πλάτος καὶ μῆκος καὶ ὕψος καὶ βάθος*, with Dean Robinson's note *ad l.*

καὶ ἐμέτρησεν τὴν πόλιν...ἐπὶ σταδίων δ. χ. κτλ.] Each side of the cube measured 12,000 stades, which, counting a stade as 606¾ feet, gives the stupendous sum of nearly 1500 English miles. Such dimensions defy imagination, and are permissible only in the language of symbolism. Renan (*l'Antechrist*, p. 473) with truth calls the Apocalypse "le parfait antipode du chef-d'œuvre grec," but when he proceeds, "sa Jérusalem céleste est gauche, puérile, impossible," he judges the book by Greek standards, rather than by those of Semitic thought. It must indeed be confessed that these measurements exceed the wildest fancies of Jewish writers; cf. e.g. *Orac. Sibyll.* v. 251 *ἄχρι δὲ καὶ Ἰόπης τεῖχος μέγα κυκλώσαντες | ὑψόσ' ἀείρωνται ἐσάχρις νεφέων ἐρεβεννῶν.* The Rabbinical writers are content to say that Jerusalem will reach to the gates of Damascus, will cover as much ground as the whole land of Israel, and rise to the height of twelve miles (*Shir. R.* 7. 5, *Yalkut Shim.* f. 57. 2, *Baba bathra* f. 75. 2, quoted by Wetstein). But their city was but a glorified Jerusalem; a vastly greater City, expressed in the terms of symbolism, needed greater dimensions in proportion to its magnificence.

Ἐπὶ σταδίων, 'at so many stades'; the variant *ἐ. σταδίους* offers the more usual construction (cf. e.g. Dan. iii. 47 *ἐπὶ πήχεις*).

17 αὐτῆς ἴσα ἐστίν. [17]καὶ ἐμέτρησεν τὸ τεῖχος αὐτῆς
ἑκατὸν τεσσεράκοντα τεσσάρων πηχῶν, μέτρον ἀν-
18 θρώπου, ὅ ἐστιν ἀγγέλου. [18]καὶ ἡ ἐνδώμησις τοῦ

17 om εμετρησεν Q 130 al[fere 30] | τειχος] χιλος (sic) ℵ | εκατον τεσσερακοντα τεσσαρων] δʹ και εκατον τεσσερακοντα A | πηχεων ℵ 18 και η 1° ℵ[c.a] AP syr aeth Tyc] και ην ℵ* και ην η Q min[pl] Andr Ar et ut vid vg Prim | ενδωμησις ℵ[c.a] (εν δωμασι ℵ*) A 38 97 130] ενδομησις PQ 186 al[pl] Andr Ar

17. *καὶ ἐμέτρησεν τὸ τεῖχος αὐτῆς κτλ.*] The wall is found to measure 144 cubits, again a multiple of 12 (cf. vii. 4, xiv. 1), but falling far below the dimensions of the City. It is not clear whether the writer means to give the breadth or the height of the wall; its length, of course, is determined by the cube which it surrounds. Babylon, with a circuit of 480 stades, was encircled by a wall 50 'royal' cubits broad and 200 high (Herod. i. 178): the porch of Solomon's Temple, according to the Chronicler (2 Chr. iii. 4), was 20 cubits wide and 120 high. Judged by these standards, 144 cubits would not be an inordinate breadth for a wall intended to protect such a city as the Apocalyptist has conceived. But he probably intends to give its height—*τὸ ὕψος* immediately precedes—and a wall 144 cubits = 216 feet high, though in itself it might fairly be called *μέγα καὶ ὑψηλόν* (*v.* 12), is insignificant when compared with a cube whose height is over 7,000,000 feet. But this great disproportion may be the very point to which the writer desires to call attention. The walls of the City are not for defence—for there is no enemy at large any more (Isa. liv. 14)—but serve for delimitation, marking the external form of the *civitas Dei*. And the order and organization of the Church, necessary as they are, fall infinitely below the elevation of its spiritual life.

μέτρον ἀνθρώπου ὅ ἐστιν ἀγγέλου] "Man's measure which is angel's measure" (Benson). The measurements taken by angelic hands are such as are in common use among men; no fantastic standards are to be employed by the reader. There is perhaps the further thought that men and angels are *σύνδουλοι* (xix. 10, xxii. 9), and men shall one day be *ἰσάγγελοι*; there is no reason therefore why angelic mensuration should differ from human. Compare the warning in *c.* xiii. 18 *ἀριθμὸς γὰρ ἀνθρώπου ἐστίν*, and see note there.

18. *καὶ ἡ ἐνδώμησις τοῦ τείχους αὐτῆς ἴασπις*] Only one other instance is quoted of the use of *ἐνδώμησις* (or *ἐνδόμησις*—on the spelling see WH.[3], *Notes* p. 159, and cf. app. crit. above). Josephus describing the construction of the great mole at Caesarea writes (*antt.* xv. 9. 6): *ἡ δὲ ἐνδόμησις* (*v.l.* *ἐνδώμησις*) *ὅσον ἦν ἐβάλλετο κατὰ τῆς θαλάσσης διακοσίους πόδας*, where the word appears to mean simply 'structure.' And so Arethas here ('*ἐνδόμησιν*' *τὴν οἰκοδομὴν λέγει*), and the Latin versions, which render the word *aedificatio*; the Syriac versions give ܕܘܒܣܐ (Syr.[gw.]) or ܕܘܒܣܘܬܐ (Syr.). But the verb *ἐνδομεῖν* is properly 'to build into' (cf. Jos. *antt.* xv. 11. 5 *τοίχου κίονας ἔχοντος ἐνδεδομημένους*), and such a sense suits the present passage; *ἡ ἐνδώμησις κτλ.* is apparently the equivalent of *ἐνεδομήθη τῷ τείχει ἴασπις*, i.e. the wall had *ἴασπις* built into it, it was cased with the precious stone, so that it sparkled with its crystalline radiance. On *ἴασπις* see iv. 3, xxi. 11, notes.

τείχους αὐτῆς ἴασπις, καὶ ἡ πόλις χρυσίον καθαρὸν
ὅμοιον ὑάλῳ καθαρῷ. [19] οἱ θεμέλιοι τοῦ τείχους τῆς 19

18 *χρυσιου καθαρου* syr[gw] *ex auro mundo* vg[dem] Prim | *ομοιον*] *ομοια* 1 186 al[pauc vid] | *υελω* 9 10 13 17 19 26 27 (29) 30 35 38 41 42 47 49 90 91 94 96 (97) 98 130 | om *καθαρω* P   19 *οι θεμελιοι*] pr *και* ℵ* 1 7 35 49 79 al[mu] vg[cle tol lipss 4, 5] me syr arm aeth *fundamenta autem* Prim

καὶ ἡ πόλις χρυσίον καθαρὸν ὅμοιον ὑάλῳ καθαρῷ] In contrast with the (? emerald) lustre of the outer wall, the City itself shews like a mass of gold—no gilded toy, but 'pure gold, like pure glass,' i.e. so pure that it seemed to be transparent like the best glass (see iv. 6, note). The same is said in *v.* 21 of the street of the City; here it is the buildings or their towers and roofs, seen high above the walls, that are described. The writer possibly remembers the burnished gold of the Herodian Temple, as he had seen it at sunrise from the neighbourhood of Jerusalem: cf. Jos. *B. J.* v. 5. 6: *οὐδὲν οὔτ' εἰς ψυχῆς οὔτ' εἰς ὀμμάτων ἔκπληξιν ἀπέλειπεν· πλαξὶ γὰρ χρυσοῦ στιβαραῖς κεκαλυμμένος πάντοθεν ὑπὸ τὰς πρώτας ἀνατολὰς πυρωδεστάτην ἀπεπάλλεν αὐγήν...τοῖς γε μὴν ἀφικνουμένοις ξένοις πόρρωθεν ὅμοιος ὄρει χιόνος πλήρει κατεφαίνετο· καὶ γὰρ καθὰ μὴ κεχρύσωτο λευκότατος ἦν.* The symbolism of the double *καθαρός* has been well caught by Bede: "nihil simulatum est et non perspicuum in sanctis ecclesiae"—a remark conspicuously exemplified in the commentator's own life.

19. *οἱ θεμέλιοι τοῦ τείχους τ. π. παντὶ λίθῳ τιμίῳ κεκοσμημένοι*] The eye of the Seer returns to the foundation stones of the outer wall (*v.* 14), and he observes that they are decked (*κεκοσμημένοι*, cf. *v.* 2) with precious stones of every shade of colour, or rather that each stone is itself one vast gem. The idea comes originally from Isa. liv. 11 *ἰδοὺ ἐγὼ ἑτοιμάζω σοι ἄνθρακα τὸν λίθον σου καὶ τὰ θεμέλιά σου σάπφειρον*; cf. Tobit xiii. 16 *ὅτι οἰκοδομηθήσεται Ἰερουσαλὴμ σαπφείρῳ καὶ σμαράγδῳ, καὶ λίθῳ ἐντίμῳ τὰ τείχη σου, ...καὶ αἱ πλατεῖαι Ἰ. βηρύλλῳ καὶ ἄνθρακι καὶ λίθῳ ἐκ Σουφεὶρ* (corr. *ἐξ Ὠφείρ*) *ψηφολογηθήσονται*; for Rabbinical illustrations see Schöttgen *ad l.* But with the general conception of a jewelled city St John combines his recollections of the names and order of the stones set in another sacred *τετράγωνον*, the High Priest's breastplate (Ex. xxviii. 17 ff., xxxvi. 17 ff. = Heb. xxxix. 10 ff.); cf. Ez. xxviii. 13, where the same list is partly used in a description of the dress of the King of Tyre. The twelve stones of the breastplate are disposed in four rows as follows: i. *σάρδιον* (אֹדֶם), *τοπάζιον* (פִּטְדָה), *σμάραγδος* (בָּרֶקֶת); ii. *ἄνθραξ* (נֹפֶךְ), *σάπφειρος* (סַפִּיר), *ἴασπις* (יָהֲלֹם); iii. *λιγύριον* (לֶשֶׁם), *ἀχάτης* (שְׁבוֹ), *ἀμέθυστος* (אַחְלָמָה); iv. *χρυσόλιθος* (תַּרְשִׁישׁ), *βηρύλλιον* (שֹׁהַם), *ὀνύχιον* (יָשְׁפֵה). Comparing these with the foundation stones in the Apocalypse, it will be seen that, while eight of the names are common to both lists, the Apocalyptist omits *ἄνθραξ*, *λιγύριον*, *ἀχάτης*, and *ὀνύχιον*, substituting *χαλκηδών*, *χρυσόπρασος*, *ὑάκινθος* and *σαρδόνυξ*—words unknown to the LXX. as the names of precious stones. In the arrangement of the stones, again, he differs from his model; his third and fourth rows answer roughly to the third and fourth in the breastplate, but his first and second reverse the order of the first and second as given in Exodus (see *Enc. Bibl.*, 4811); in other words he has started as in *v.* 13 from the SE. corner of his city-wall, and after traversing the east and north sides has returned to the same corner to examine the south and the west.

πόλεως παντὶ λίθῳ τιμίῳ κεκοσμημένοι· ὁ θεμέλιος
ὁ πρῶτος ἴασπις, ὁ δεύτερος σάπφειρος, ὁ τρίτος
20 χαλκηδών, ὁ τέταρτος σμάραγδος, [20] ὁ πέμπτος

19 om κεκοσμημενοι 92 arm Tyc Prim | ο πρωτος] ο εις ℵ | ο δευτερος] pr και ℵ syr^{gw} | σαπφιρος PQ σαπφηρος 186 | ο τριτος] pr και ℵ syr^{gw} | χαλκηδων] χαρκηδων 35 68 syr^{gw} χαλκιδων Q 1 29 98 | σμαραγδος] *zmaragdus* vg$^{am\ fu}$

ὁ θεμέλιος ὁ πρῶτος ἴασπις κτλ.] See notes on iv. 3, xxi. 11, 18, and cf. Isa. liv. 12 θήσω τὰς ἐπάλξεις σου ἴασπιν. That the first foundation stone is of the sort with which the whole wall is cased (*v.* 18) shews how little our writer studies effect, even in this great picture of the New Jerusalem. Ὁ δεύτερος σάπφειρος: cf. Isa. liv. 11 ἰδοὺ ἐγὼ ἑτοιμάζω σοι...τὰ θεμέλιά σου σάπφειρον, Tob. xiii. 16 οἰκοδομηθήσεται Ἰερουσαλὴμ σαπφείρῳ, *Shem. rabba* 5 "aedificabit Hierosolyma lapide sapphiri." The σάπφειρος is mentioned several times in the O.T.; the most interesting examples are Ex. xxiv. 10 εἶδον τὸν τόπον οὗ ἱστήκει ὁ θεὸς τοῦ Ἰσραήλ· καὶ τὰ ὑπὸ τοὺς πόδας αὐτοῦ ὡσεὶ ἔργον πλίνθου σαπφείρου, and Ez. i. 26, ix. 2, x. 1. As the margin of R.V. suggests, the ancient 'sapphire' was probably *lapis lazuli*; see Pliny, *H.N.* xxxiii. 21, xxxvii. 39, 54, who describes it as a sky-blue stone, flecked with gold; and cf. Epiphanius *de gemmis* 5 λίθος σάπφειρος πορφυρίζων...πολλὰ δὲ γένη τούτου ὑπάρχουσιν· ἔστι γὰρ ὁ βασιλικὸς χρυσοστιγής. Ὁ τρίτος χαλκηδών. Χαλκ. is ἅπ. λεγ. in Biblical Greek; in Exodus ἄνθραξ occupies the corresponding place. The word is supposed to denote a green silicate of copper found in the mines near Chalcedon. In Pliny *H.N.* xxxvii. 18 "Chalcedonii nescio an in totum exoleverint postquam metalla aeris ibi defecerunt... fuere...colore incerti et virentium in caudis pavonum columbarumque e collo plumis similiter." Ὁ τέταρτος σμάραγδος. Of the σμάραγδος (Ex. *ll. cc.*, Ez. *l. c.*, Tob. xiii. 16, Judith x. 21, Esth. i. 6, Sir. xxxv. 6 (xxxii. 8)) Pliny writes (*H.N.* xxxvii. 16): "Smaragdos vero tanto libentius, quoniam nihil omnino viridius comparatum illis viret." Nero, he adds, used it for the purpose of a field-glass ("gladiatorum pugnas spectabat smaragdo"), doubtless to protect his eyes against the glare of the sun; cf. Epiph. *de gemm.* 3 ὁ μὲν Νερωνιανὸς μικρός ἐστι τῷ εἴδει, σφόδρα χλωρίζων, διειδὴς καὶ διαυγής. In view of this evidence the σμάραγδος of the Apocalypse must be identified with the emerald, or some other green stone, and not with rock crystal (*Encl. Bibl.* 4804 f.). Cf. *c.* iv. 3, note.

20. ὁ πέμπτος σαρδόνυξ κτλ.] The σαρδόνυξ was a variety of onyx in which the white was broken by layers of red or brown. Cf. Pliny, *H.N.* xxxvii. 23 "Sardonyches olim ut ex ipso nomine apparet intellegebantur candore in sarda, hoc est, velut carne ungui hominis imposita, et utroque translucido." The sardonyx was much in request for cameos (King, *Engraved Gems*, pp. 55, 363), and was highly valued; cf. Juvenal xiii. 138 "gemmaque princeps | sardonychum, loculis quae custoditur eburnis." Ὁ ἕκτος σάρδιον: see *c.* iv. 3, note. Ὁ ἕβδομος χρυσόλιθος, Pliny, *H.N.* xxxvii. 42 describes these stones as "aureo fulgore translucentes." In the LXX. the word represents תַּרְשִׁישׁ i.e. the stone of Tarshish (Ez. x. 9) in Ex. xxviii. and xxxvi. and Ez. xxviii., and similarly in Aquila (Ez. i. 26, x. 9, Dan. x. 6). The identification of the ancient chrysolite is uncertain; a yellow beryl or a gold-coloured jasper

σαρδόνυξ, ὁ ἕκτος σάρδιον, ὁ ἕβδομος χρυσόλιθος,

20 σαρδονυξ] σαρδιονυξ A σαρδωνυξ 29 31 48 79 | σαρδιον] σαρδιος 1 7 38 al[sat mu] *sardius* vg[cle demlipss] Tyc Prim *sardinus* vg[am tol] *sardonius* vg[fu]

much used in Egyptian art have been suggested (*Enc. Bibl.* 819, Hastings, *D.B.* iv. 620). Ὁ ὄγδοος βήρυλλος (βηρύλλιον Ex., Ez.; βήρυλλος, Tob.). The beryl, as Pliny points out (*H.N.* xxxvii. 20), has much in common with the emerald, but in colour the best stones are blue or sea green: "probatissimi sunt ex iis qui viriditatem maris puri imitantur": similarly Epiphanius: γλαυκίζων μέν ἐστι, θαλασσοβαφής. Ὁ ἔνατος τοπάζιον: another green stone, highly prized both by the Hebrews and in the West; cf. Ps. cxviii. (cxix.) 127 ἠγάπησα τὰς ἐντολάς σου ὑπὲρ τὸ χρυσίον καὶ τοπάζιον (= פָּז ? τὸ πάζιον, cf. *Enc. Bibl.* 4802), Job xxviii. 19 οὐκ ἰσωθήσεται αὐτῇ τοπάζιον Αἰθιοπίας; Hilary on Ps. *l. c.*: "praestat autem, ut ceteris metallis aurum, ita et aliis lapidibus topazion, est enim ipse rarissimus et speciosissimus omnium"; Pliny *H.N.* xxxvii. 32 "egregia etiamnunc topazio gloria est suo virente genere." The green of the τοπάζιον was of a golden hue: Strabo xvi. 770 λίθος δέ ἐστι διαφανής, χρυσοειδὲς διαλάμπων φέγγος, Diod. Sic. viii. 39 λίθος...ὑέλῳ παρεμφερής, καὶ θαυμαστὴν ἔγχρυσον πρόσοψιν παρεχόμενος. Ὁ δέκατος χρυσόπρασος. The χρυσόπρασος, which is not mentioned in the LXX., but answers to the λιγύριον of Ex., was akin to the beryl, but of a paler green; Pliny, *H.N.* xxxvii. 32 "vicinum genus huic est pallidius, et a quibusdam proprii generis existimatur vocaturque chrysoprasus." According to King (*Precious Stones*, pp. 130, 163) it is to be distinguished from the modern chrysoprase, which is applegreen, an agate coloured by oxide of nickel. Ὁ ἑνδέκατος ὑάκινθος. On the word ὑάκινθος see ix. 17, where ὑακίνθινος is associated with πύρινος and θειώδης, apparently meaning 'of the colour of blue smoke.' In Ex. the corresponding stone is the dark red ἀχάτης (cf. *Enc. Bibl.* 4812), but in the Apocalypse at all events it is safer to follow the account of Pliny ("violaceus," see below), and Epiphanius (ὑποπορφυρίζων); the modern sapphire is said to be the stone intended. Ὁ δωδέκατος ἀμέθυστος: distinguished from the ὑάκινθος by its greater brilliancy; see Pliny *H.N.* xxxvii. 41 "differentia haec, quod ille emicans in amethysto fulgor violaceus dilutus est in hyacintho"; Epiph. *de gemm.* 9 οὗτος κατὰ τὴν αὐτοῦ περιφέρειαν φλογίζων ἐστὶ βαθέως, ἡ δὲ αὐτή ἐστι λευκοτέρα ἐκ τοῦ μέσου οἰνωπὸν ἀποπέμπουσα εἶδος. The Libyan sort ἐστὶν ὑακίνθῳ καθαρῷ παραπλήσιος.

Collecting results, we observe that the stones are in the main of four colours, blue (σάπφειρος, ὑάκινθος, ἀμέθυστος), green (ἴασπις (?), χαλκηδών, σμάραγδος, βήρυλλος, τοπάζιον, χρυσόπρασος), red (σαρδόνυξ, σάρδιον), and yellow (χρυσόλιθος). But the stones of the same general colour vary greatly both in hue and brilliancy, as the descriptions shew. In several cases different shades of the same colour appear to be arranged in groups, e.g. the two reds are placed together (5, 6), and the greens form two sequences (3, 4 and 8, 9, 10); but it is precarious to attach significance to this order, which appears to depend on an arbitrary modification of that of the stones in the High Priest's breastplate. If we ask ourselves what purpose the writer had in this enumeration of precious stones beyond the general design of connecting the New Jerusalem with the symbols of the Twelve Tribes, a key to the most probable answer is supplied by Clement of Alexandria, *paed.* ii. 12, § 119 τὰς δώδεκα τῆς οὐρανοπόλεως

ὁ ὄγδοος βήρυλλος, ὁ ἔνατος τοπάζιον, ὁ δέκατος
χρυσόπρασος, ὁ ἑνδέκατος ὑάκινθος, ὁ δωδέκατος
21 ἀμέθυστος. [21]καὶ οἱ δώδεκα πυλῶνες δώδεκα μαρ-
γαρῖται· ἀνὰ εἷς ἕκαστος τῶν πυλώνων ἦν ἐξ ἑνὸς

20 βηρυλλος ℵ min$^{\text{mu vid}}$] βηριλλος A 29 βιρυλλιος Q βηρυλλιος 7 31 79 92 186 βηριλλιος 1 βηρυλλιον P | εννατος P 29 31 47 48 49 98 130 186 al^{mu} Ar | τοπαζιον] τοπανζιον P τοπαδιον ℵ* *topadius* vg^{am} | χρυσοπρασος] χρυσοπρασιος ℵ$^{\text{c.a}}$ Prim χρυσοπρασινος 13 27 39 χρυσοπρασον A χρυσοπρασσος 7 (vg$^{\text{am fu}}$) χρυσοπασος (-πασσος) 2 29 30* (97) 98 130 χρυσοπαστος 40 50 92 | αμεθυστος] αμεθυστινος ℵ* αμεθυσος ℵ$^{\text{c.a}}$ 1 7 29 31 38 130 186 al^{20} Ar   21 om δωδεκα 2° ℵ* (hab ℵ$^{\text{c.a}}$) Prim | ανα] ινα A 35 om 130 | εις] + και P syr^{gw} | εξ ενος] pr ως PQ 79 92

πύλας τιμίοις ἀπεικασμένας λίθοις τὸ περίοπτον τῆς ἀποστολικῆς φωνῆς αἰνίττεσθαι χάριτος ἐκδεχόμεθα...συμβολικῶς τούτοις εἰκότως τειχίζεται τῶν ἁγίων ἡ πόλις πνευματικῶς οἰκοδομουμένη· πρὸς τὸ ἄνθος οὖν τῶν λίθων τὸ ἀμίμητον, τὸ ἄνθος τὸ πνεύματος, τὸ ἀκήρατον καὶ ἅγιον τῆς οὐσίας νενοήκασιν. He does not pursue the train of thought, but it is easy to do so. The Apostolic College itself was composed of men of greatly varying capacities and characters, and in passing under the hand of the great ἀρχιτέκτων, Who made them foundation stones of the wall of the new City of God, no one of these lost his own individuality. The same is true of the entire building; every colour, every shade of colour, every degree of brilliancy is found among the living stones which make up the ideal City. The πολυποίκιλος σοφία τοῦ θεοῦ (Eph. iii. 10) reflects itself in the Saints, but not wholly in any one Saint. The High Priest alone wears all the colours on His breast; of the rest it is said: διαιρέσεις χαρισμάτων εἰσὶν...διαιρέσεις διακονιῶν... διαιρέσεις ἐνεργημάτων (cf. Bede *ad l.*).

21. καὶ οἱ δώδεκα πυλῶνες δώδεκα μαργαρῖται] From the foundation stones the Seer's eye turns back to the gateways which divide them (*v.* 12 ff.). Of these also each is a gem, not however a precious stone as in Isa. liv. 12 θήσω...τὰς πύλας σου λίθους κρυστάλλου, but a single pearl. The pearl has no place in the O.T. lists of jewels, though a reference to it has been suspected in one or two doubtful passages (see *Enc. Bibl.* ad v.). But in N.T. times the dealer in 'goodly pearls' was not unknown on the great roads of Galilee (Mt. xiii. 46), and the pearl was among the treasured ornaments of the wealthier class (Mt. vii. 6, 1 Tim. ii. 9). The later Jews looked forward to a time when pearls would abound in Israel; *Yalkut Shim.* f. 54. 1 "fore ut limites Israelis repleantur gemmis et margaritis, venturosque Israelitas et inde accepturos quantum lubuerit." There is a remarkable parallel to the present verse in *Baba bathra*, f. 75. 1 "Deus adducet gemmas et margaritas triginta cubitos longas totidemque latas easque excavabit in altitudinem viginti cubitorum et latitudinem decem cubitorum, collocabitque in portis Hierusalem."

Bede finds a spiritual significance in the gates of pearl: "sicut *lux vera* ...sanctis donavit lumen esse mundi, sic et ipse cum sit *margarita singularis*... suos nihilominus margaritarum fulgori comparat."

ἀνὰ εἷς ἕκαστος...ἦν ἐξ ἑνὸς μαργαρίτου] Each gate-tower seemed to have been carved out of a single monstrous pearl. With this use of ἀνά cf. the use of κατά in Mc. xiv. 19 εἷς κατὰ εἷς, note, 'Jo.' viii. 9 εἷς καθ' εἷς, Rom. xii. 5 τὸ δὲ καθ' εἷς, and see Blass, *Gr.*,

μαργαρίτου· καὶ ἡ πλατεῖα τῆς πόλεως χρυσίον
καθαρὸν ὡς ὕαλος διαυγής. [22]καὶ ναὸν οὐκ εἶδον ἐν 22
αὐτῇ· ὁ γὰρ κύριος ὁ θεὸς ὁ παντοκράτωρ ναὸς αὐτῆς
ἐστίν, καὶ τὸ ἀρνίον. [23]καὶ ἡ πόλις οὐ χρείαν ἔχει 23

21 χρυσιου καθαρου syr^{gw} Prim | ως] και 186 | υελος 7 8 13 (29) 35 (38) 39 41 49 91 94 96 (97) 98 130 186 al Ir$^{gr\,ex\,Anast}$ Ar   22 ειδον ℵP 1 7 130 186 al^{pl} Andr Ar] ιδον AQ 92 | ο γαρ κυριος ο θεος] οτι ο κ. ο θ. ℵ* οτι κυριος syr aeth Ir$^{gr\,ex\,Anast}$ | ναος αυτης] pr ο A   23 και η πολις] + αυτη 38 97 syr

p. 179. The punctuation of Syr.$^{gw.}$ shews that the translator had before him εἷς ἀνὰ εἷς in the present place; see Dr Gwynn's note *ad l.*

καὶ ἡ πλατεῖα τῆς πόλεως χρυσίον καθαρόν κτλ.] See *v.* 18, where the same is said of the Holy City as a whole. Διαυγής brings out the special point of καθαρός; the gold was so pure that men seemed to look into and through its clear depths as they walked upon it; the word is unknown to the LXX. and ἅπ. λεγ. in the N.T., but used by Philo, and by Aquila in Prov. xvi. 5, where the LXX. has φανερά; Aq. uses also διαυγάζειν, διαύγασμα. For πλατεῖα see Mc. vi. 56, D, and *c.* xxii. 1; the ideal City has no narrow ῥῦμαι (Lc. xiv. 21), but only the broad thoroughfare of a perfect fellowship—how striking a feature those will understand who have threaded their way through the lanes of an Eastern town; even in Tobit's picture of a restored Jerusalem they are not absent, and he is content to present them in a new light: ἐροῦσιν πᾶσαι αἱ ῥῦμαι αὐτῆς Ἀλληλουϊά (Tob. xiv. 18).

Victorinus allegorizes: "*plateae*... ostendunt corda ab omnibus mundata sordibus.. perspicua luce fulgida ut merito in iis deambulet Dominus."

22. καὶ ναὸν οὐκ εἶδον ἐν αὐτῇ] The City possesses no Sanctuary, for it is itself a Holy of holies, as its cubic form suggests (*v.* 16); cf. 2 Cor. vi. 16 ἡμεῖς γὰρ ναὸς θεοῦ ἐσμὲν ζῶντος, καθὼς εἶπεν ὁ θεὸς ὅτι Ἐνοικήσω ἐν αὐτοῖς. The Eternal Presence (*v.* 3) renders the new Jerusalem one vast ναός. There is therefore no conflict between this verse and *c.* iii. 12 ὁ νικῶν, ποιήσω αὐτὸν στύλον ἐν τῷ ναῷ τοῦ θεοῦ μου, which in the light of the present passage is simply a promise of permanent citizenship in the Holy City. Nor do St John's words here condemn the present use or building of magnificent churches. Material sanctuaries, nevertheless, are a confession that the perfect has not yet come; the ideal Church has no need of them; cf. Andreas: τίς γὰρ χρεία ναοῦ αἰσθητοῦ τῇ ἐχούσῃ τὸν θεὸν φρουρὸν καὶ σκέπην;

ὁ γὰρ κύριος...ναὸς αὐτῆς ἐστίν] The Divine Presence in Itself constitutes a Sanctuary which supersedes material structures; cf. Jo. iv. 21 ἔρχεται ὥρα ὅτε οὔτε ἐν τῷ ὄρει τούτῳ οὔτε ἐν Ἱεροσολύμοις προσκυνήσετε τῷ πατρί. For [ὁ] κύριος ὁ θεὸς ὁ παντοκράτωρ see i. 8, note; it answers to the יְהוָה אֱלֹהֵי צְבָאוֹת of the O.T., Who is here significantly associated with the Lamb; cf. vii. 9 f., xiv. 4, xxii. 1 f. The revelation of the O.T. finds its consummation in the Incarnate Son; the promise of God's Presence with His people is realized in the Person of the sacrificed and exalted Christ.

23. καὶ ἡ πόλις οὐ χρείαν ἔχει τοῦ ἡλίου κτλ.] A second distinction of the Holy City. As it needs no material temple, since it is pervaded by the Presence of God, so it needs no created light, since the same Presence irradiates it unceasingly. Cf. Andreas: ἔνθα γὰρ ὁ τῆς δικαιοσύνης

τοῦ ἡλίου οὐδὲ τῆς σελήνης, ἵνα φαίνωσιν αὐτῇ· ἡ
γὰρ δόξα τοῦ θεοῦ ἐφώτισεν αὐτήν, καὶ ὁ λύχνος
24 αὐτῆς τὸ ἀρνίον. ²⁴καὶ περιπατήσουσιν τὰ ἔθνη διὰ

23 φαινωσιν (φαινουσιν 186)]+εν ℵ$^{\text{c.a}}$ 49 91 96 186 al vg^{excam} (*in ea*) me | αυτη] αυτην 35 79 al | η γαρ ℵAP min^{mu} vg syr^{gw}] οτι η Ir$^{\text{gr ex Anast}}$ γαρ η Q 130 min^{30} | το αρνιον] pr εστιν vg syr^{gw} 24 τα εθνη]+των σωζομενων 1 (ex Andr comm ut vid)

νοητὸς ἥλιος, αἰσθητῶν φωστήρων οὐ χρεία. Sun and moon, the luminaries of the first creation (Gen. i. 14), have no place in the second; cf. Isa. lx. 19 f. *οὐκ ἔσται σοι ἔτι ὁ ἥλιος εἰς φῶς ἡμέρας, οὐδὲ ἀνατολὴ σελήνης φωτιεῖ σοι τὴν νύκτα, ἀλλ' ἔσται σοι Κύριος φῶς αἰώνιον.* The thought recurs in *c.* xxii. 5 *οὐκ ἔχουσιν χρείαν φωτὸς λύχνου καὶ φωτὸς ἡλίου.* No words could more clearly demonstrate the purely spiritual character of St John's conception of the New Jerusalem.

For a Rabbinical parallel see *Yalkut Ruben*, f. 7. 3 "neque in mundo futuro necesse habebunt lumen solis interdiu et lumen lunae noctu."

ἡ γὰρ δόξα τοῦ θεοῦ κτλ.] The Divine Glory, the revelation of the fulness of the Divine attributes, is the Sun of the ideal order—"lumen (as Victorinus eloquently writes) cuius splendorem nullus potuerit sensus cogitare nec lingua proloqui"; cf. Ps. xxxv. (xxxvi.) 10 *ἐν τῷ φωτί σου ὀψόμεθα φῶς.* We expect the writer to proceed, *καὶ ἡ σελήνη αὐτῆς τὸ ἀρνίον*, but for *ἡ σελήνη* he writes *ὁ λύχνος*, perhaps because he shrank from likening Christ to 'the lesser light' (Gen. i. 16 *τὸν φωστῆρα τὸν ἐλάσσω*), perhaps because he wished to contrast the one Lamp which illuminates the ideal Church with the many *λυχνίαι* of the churches on earth (i. 12, 20).

24. *καὶ περιπατήσουσιν τὰ ἔθνη διὰ τοῦ φωτὸς αὐτῆς κτλ.*] Based on Isa. lx. 3 *καὶ πορεύσονται βασιλεῖς τῷ φωτί σου, καὶ ἔθνη τῇ λαμπρότητί σου.* No such world-wide influence was ever the lot of the older Jerusalem. Rome came nearer to the ideal in her relation to the provinces of the Empire, and her influence over the countries where she exercised the rights of suzerain. But the light of Rome was in the end to go out in darkness, as the Seer foresaw (xviii. 23). The Church alone possesses an unfailing source of illumination, which radiates far beyond her borders. Nations not yet Christian, or Christian chiefly in name, reap the benefit of Christian opinion and Christian standards of life. Whatever there is in modern life which promises amelioration of social evils is probably to be ascribed to the influence, direct or indirect, of a dominant Christianity, even where that influence is most stoutly denied. On the other hand Christianity derives certain advantages from contact with the world. From the fourth century the Church has received the tribute of recognition from the State; the kings of the earth—not as some of the Latin commentators suggest, the "reges spirituales" of her own body, but secular princes—have heaped honours upon her. So far history has verified the Seer's forecast, and the fulfilment continues to this day. How it will accomplish itself when the ideals of the Church have been realized must be left to the future to disclose. The words may have reference to the present order, or they may indicate some gracious purpose of God towards humanity which has not yet been revealed: cf. *c.* xxii. 2 *τὰ φύλλα τοῦ ξύλου εἰς θεραπείαν τῶν ἐθνῶν*, and the note there.

τοῦ φωτὸς αὐτῆς, καὶ οἱ βασιλεῖς τῆς γῆς φέρουσιν
τὴν δόξαν αὐτῶν εἰς αὐτήν· [25]καὶ οἱ πυλῶνες αὐτῆς 25
οὐ μὴ κλεισθῶσιν ἡμέρας, νὺξ γὰρ οὐκ ἔσται ἐκεῖ·
[26]καὶ οἴσουσιν τὴν δόξαν καὶ τὴν τιμὴν τῶν ἐθνῶν 26
εἰς αὐτήν. [27]καὶ οὐ μὴ εἰσέλθῃ εἰς αὐτὴν πᾶν κοινὸν 27

24 φερουσιν]+αυτω Q 130 $al^{fere 25}$ | την δοξαν]+και (την) τιμην (Q) min^{nonn} vg syr (Ar) | αυτων] των εθνων Q 130 min^{30} me syr 25 ημερα ℵ* (-ρας $ℵ^{c.a}$) 26 totum versum om 1 | εις αυτην]+ινα εισελθωσιν Q min^{25} Ar 27 εισελθη] εισελθωσιν ℵ

25. *καὶ οἱ πυλῶνες αὐτῆς οὐ μὴ κλεισθῶσιν ἡμέρας κτλ.*] The Seer still follows, and while he follows expands Isaiah (lx. 11 *καὶ ἀνοιχθήσονται αἱ πύλαι σου διὰ παντός, ἡμέρας καὶ νυκτὸς οὐ κλεισθήσονται*). In the ideal City night is unknown, because the sun of the Divine Presence never sets; cf. Isa. lx. 20 *οὐ γὰρ δύσεται ὁ ἥλιός σοι...ἔσται γὰρ Κύριός σου φῶς αἰώνιον.* In the history of nations, as in nature, darkness succeeds to light, civilization is followed by outbursts of barbarism. In the ideal Church no such relapses are possible; the future holds no Dark Ages for the City of God. In *c.* vii. 15 *ἡμέρας καὶ νυκτός* savours of the present condition of the Church, and the vision there is expressed in the terms of the present.

The gates of the New Jerusalem stand open through the Eternal Day to allow of the freest ingress and egress, cf. Jo. x. 9 *δι' ἐμοῦ ἐάν τις εἰσέλθῃ...εἰσελεύσεται καὶ ἐξελεύσεται*; the cry *ἐπάρθητε, πύλαι αἰώνιοι* (Ps. xxiii. (xxiv.) 7, 9) is heard no more at the approach of the King, nor is there any hasty closing of the portals as an enemy is seen to be near. *Ἐκλείσθη ἡ θύρα* (Mt. xxv. 10) has reference to other circumstances, which can never occur in the ideal City.

26. *καὶ οἴσουσιν τὴν δόξαν καὶ τὴν τιμὴν τῶν ἐθνῶν εἰς αὐτήν*] A further presentation of the thought expressed in *v.* 24; cf. Isa. lx. 5 *μεταβαλεῖ εἰς σὲ πλοῦτος θαλάσσης καὶ ἐθνῶν καὶ λαῶν.* As Rome in her time attracted the merchandise of the world (xviii. 11 ff.), so in days to come all that is best in human life will flow into the City of God. The Seer foresees the consecration to the service of Christ, in the coming centuries, of art, literature, and science, of national character and power, of social and civic life.

27. *καὶ οὐ μὴ εἰσέλθῃ εἰς αὐτὴν πᾶν κοινὸν κτλ.*] In the ideal condition of the Church the influx of the nations with their several offerings will not bring with it the elements of evil which hitherto have been associated with wholesale conversions. The open gates of the City of Light exclude the works of darkness; *τίς γὰρ* (Andreas appositely asks) *κοινωνία φωτὶ πρὸς σκότος*; Cf. Isa. xxxv. 8 *οὐ μὴ παρελθῇ ἐκεῖ ἀκάθαρτος*; *ib.* lii. 1 *οὐκέτι προστεθήσεται διελθεῖν διὰ σοῦ ἀπερίτμητος καὶ ἀκάθαρτος*; Ez. xliv. 9. The realization of this vision of purity belongs to the future, but not exclusively so; the remark of Primasius: "futuri temporis circumscribit ecclesiam quando non sicut nunc permixtos cum bonis cohabitantes patitur malos" must be taken with Bede's reservation: "sed et nunc omnis immundus et mendax non est in ecclesia." On *κοινόν* see Mc. vii. 2, note, and cf. Acts x. 14 *πᾶν κοινὸν καὶ ἀκάθαρτον.* Here as in Mc. vii. 20, 23 the word has passed into an ethical meaning; the verdict by which Christ 'cleansed all meats' (*ib.* 19) leaves moral pollution the only true *κοινόν*. *Ὁ ποιῶν βδέλυγμα καὶ ψεῦδος.* Babylon the Great was

καὶ [ὁ] ποιῶν βδέλυγμα καὶ ψεῦδος, εἰ μὴ οἱ γεγραμ-
XXII. 1 *μένοι ἐν τῷ βιβλίῳ τῆς ζωῆς τοῦ ἀρνίου.* [1]*καὶ*
ἔδειξέν μοι ποταμὸν ὕδατος ζωῆς λαμπρὸν ὡς κρύ-

27 *ο ποιων* ℵ* min[fere 20] syrr] *ποιων* ℵ[c.a] A 18 41 68 92 *faciens* vg Ambr Tyc Prim *ποιουν* PQ 1 186 al[sat mu] Andr Ar | *βδελυγμα*] pr *ωσει* ℵ* | *γεγραμμενοι*] *εγγεγραμμενοι* 11 31 | om *της ζωης* syr[gw] Prim | *του αρνιου*] *τ. ουρανου* ℵ om Ir[gr ex Anast]

XXII 1 *ποταμον*] pr *καθαρον* 1 + *καθαρον* 7 26 31 32 35 38 46 49 79 91 96 arm Andr Ar | om *λαμπρον* 38 40 arm

full of *βδελύγματα* (xvii. 4); the New Jerusalem has no place for the *ἐβδελυγμένος* (xxi. 8). Falsehood, the antithesis of *ἡ ἀλήθεια*, is no less absolutely excluded. The Apocalyptist, who had experience of pagan life at Ephesus, loses no opportunity of condemning its insincerity; cf. xiv. 5, xxi. 8, xxii. 15. But as the last passage shews, his exclusion of the insincere from the City of God must be limited to those who are consciously and contentedly insincere; *ὁ ποιῶν ψ.* = *ὁ φιλῶν καὶ ποιῶν*.

εἰ μὴ οἱ γεγραμμένοι κτλ.] 'but only those whose names are inscribed etc.'; cf. Dan. xii. 1. The exception refers not to *ὁ ποιῶν βδ. καὶ ψ.*, but to all who seek to enter, as if the sentence had run *οὐ μὴ εἰσέλθῃ οὐδείς, εἰ μή κτλ.* For the 'Book of Life' see iii. 5, note, xx. 15, and for the qualifying *τοῦ ἀρνίου* cf. xiii. 8, note.

XXII. 1. *καὶ ἔδειξέν μοι ποταμὸν ὕδατος ζωῆς κτλ.*] The Seer is now shewn by the Angel (xxi. 9) the interior of the City. The vision combines that of Ezekiel xlvii. 1—12 with the account of Eden in Gen. ii. 9 ff., adding certain new features. In Gen. *l. c.* the river issues from Eden and is parted into four heads; in Ezekiel a stream issues from its source in the Temple-rock, and running eastwards presently becomes a river too deep to be forded; the river makes its way to the Dead Sea, which it converts into fresh water, and on its banks there grow fruit trees which bear throughout the year. In St John's vision the river issues from the Throne of God and of the Lamb, which has taken the place of the Temple (cf. xxi. 22 with xxii. 3); and it waters not the wilderness but the City itself (cf. Ps. xlv. (xlvi.) 5 *τοῦ ποταμοῦ τὰ ὁρμήματα εὐφραίνουσιν τὴν πόλιν τοῦ θεοῦ*), and the fruit trees which grow on its banks are identified with the Tree of Life which grew in the primaeval Paradise.

For *ὕδωρ ζωῆς* see vii. 17, xxi. 6, xxii. 17, notes. The conception of a river of the water of life appears already in Joel iii. 18 *πηγὴ ἐξ οἴκου Κυρίου ἐξελεύσεται*, Zech. xiv. 8 *καὶ ἐν τῇ ἡμέρᾳ ἐκείνῃ ἐξελεύσεται ὕδωρ ζῶν ἐξ Ἰερουσαλήμ*, and Ez. xlvii. 9 *καὶ ἔσται πᾶσα ψυχὴ τῶν ζῴων τῶν ἐκζεόντων, ἐπὶ πάντα ἐφ' ἃ ἂν ἐπέλθῃ ἐκεῖ ὁ ποταμός, ζήσεται*; cf. *Sanhedr.* f. 100. 1 "Deus producturus est fluvium ex sancto sanctorum iuxta quem omnia genera fructuum delicatorum erunt." See especially Jo. vii. 38 *ὁ πιστεύων εἰς ἐμέ, καθὼς εἶπεν ἡ γραφή, ποταμοὶ ἐκ τῆς κοιλίας αὐτοῦ ῥεύσουσιν ὕδατος ζῶντος.* The explanation which follows *ib.* 39 (*τοῦτο δὲ εἶπεν περὶ τοῦ πνεύματος οὗ ἔμελλον λαμβάνειν οἱ πιστεύσαντες εἰς αὐτόν*) leaves no doubt how the metaphor was understood by the school of St John, and may therefore be taken to interpret the present passage. The River of Life which 'gladdens the City of God' is the gift of the Spirit which followed the Ascension and which, once bestowed, remains with the Church for ever (Jo. xiv. 16).

σταλλον, ἐκπορευόμενον ἐκ τοῦ θρόνου τοῦ θεοῦ καὶ
τοῦ ἀρνίου. ²*ἐν μέσῳ τῆς πλατείας αὐτῆς καὶ τοῦ* 2
ποταμοῦ ἐντεῦθεν καὶ ἐκεῖθεν ξύλον ζωῆς ποιοῦν

1 *του θρονου*] om *του* ℵ   2 *εμμεσω* A | om *αυτης* 186 | *του ποταμου*] pr *επι* syr[gw] | *εντευθεν και εκειθεν* AQ (P hiat post *εκ.*) 130 al[30] me syr arm Ar] *εντευθεν κ. εντευθεν* 1 35 49 79 91 186 al *ενθεν κ. ενθεν* ℵ (*ενθεν* 2° suppl ℵ[c.a]) *ex utraque parte fluminis* vg Hil Ambr Tyc Cassiod al | in *ξυλον ζωης* hiat ℵ | *ποιουν* ℵQ 130 186 min[pl] Andr Ar] *ποιων* A 18

Λαμπρὸν ὡς κρύσταλλον (*v.* 1), sparkling like rock crystal; cf. iv. 6 *θάλασσα... ὁμοία κρυστάλλῳ*. *Ἐκπορευόμενον ἐκ τοῦ θρόνου κτλ.*, the River of the life-giving Spirit issues forth out of the Throne, or, as Andreas explains, *ἐκ τοῦ θεοῦ καὶ πατρὸς ἐκπορευόμενον, καὶ διὰ τοῦ ἀρνίου*. The words, however, cannot be used with any confidence in the *Filioque* controversy, for it is the mission of the Spirit rather than His eternal Procession which is in view here, as indeed it probably is even in Jo. xvi. 26. For the patristic interpretation see *History of the Doctrine of the Procession*, p. 8, note.

Ὁ θρόνος τοῦ θεοῦ καὶ τοῦ ἀρνίου (*vv.* 1, 3) is a startling expression; elsewhere the Lamb is *ἐν μέσῳ* or *ἀνὰ μέσον τοῦ θρόνου* (v. 6, vii. 17), and *ὁ καθήμενος ἐπὶ τοῦ θρόνου* is the Almighty Father as distinguished from the Incarnate Son (v. 13, vi. 16, vii. 10). But cf. iii. 21, where the glorified Christ is represented as the Father's *σύνθρονος*, and see note there.

2. *ἐν μέσῳ τῆς πλατείας αὐτῆς καὶ τοῦ ποταμοῦ κτλ.*] W.H., following Matthaei, connect *ἐν μέσῳ τῆς πλ. αὐτῆς* with *v.* 1 (cf. R.V. "he shewed me a river...in the midst of the street thereof"), and govern *τοῦ ποταμοῦ* by *ἐντεῦθεν καὶ ἐκεῖθεν* (R.V. "on this side of the river and on that"). But if the words *ἐν μέσῳ κτλ.* belonged to *v.* 1, they would more naturally precede *ἔδειξεν* than follow *τοῦ ἀρνίου*. Moreover, though the adverbs *ἐντεῦθεν καὶ ἐκεῖθεν* may have a prepositional force (cf. e.g. Jos. ix. 6 (viii. 33) *ἔνθεν καὶ ἔνθεν* (מִזֶּה וּמִזֶּה) *τῆς κιβωτοῦ*, Dan. xii. 5 Th. *εἷς ἐντεῦθεν τοῦ χείλους τοῦ ποταμοῦ*), yet their position after *τοῦ ποταμοῦ* suggests that they are used adverbially as in Ex. xxvi. 13 *ἐπὶ τὰ πλάγια τῆς σκηνῆς ἔνθεν καὶ ἔνθεν*; Ez. xlvii. 7 (the basis of the present passage) *δένδρα πολλὰ σφόδρα ἔνθεν καὶ ἔνθεν*; *ib.* 12 *ἐπὶ τοῦ χείλους αὐτοῦ ἔνθεν καὶ ἔνθεν*. On the whole, then, the usual punctuation seems preferable, and we may translate "between the street of the City and the river, on this side and on that": for *ἐν μέσῳ* = *ἀνὰ μέσον* cf. *c.* v. 6, note. The picture presented is that of a river flowing through the broad street which intersects the city, a row of trees being on either bank. The precise phrase *ἐντεῦθεν καὶ ἐκεῖθεν* is quoted by Wetstein from Aelian *N.A.* ii. 4, ix. 34, xiii. 23.

ξύλον ζωῆς ποιοῦν καρποὺς δώδεκα κτλ.] Cf. Ez. xlvii. 12 *καὶ ἐπὶ τοῦ χείλους αὐτοῦ ἔνθεν καὶ ἔνθεν· πᾶν ξύλον βρώσιμον...οὐδὲ μὴ ἐκλίπῃ ὁ καρπὸς αὐτοῦ· τῆς καινότητος αὐτοῦ* (*ἄλλος· εἰς τοὺς μῆνας αὐτοῦ*, cf. M.T. לְחֳדָשָׁיו) *πρωτοβολήσει*. Andreas well remarks: *οὐ γὰρ ἁμαρτίας ἔσται χειμὼν ἐκεῖ φύλλων ῥοὴν ἀναγκάζων πάσχειν τὰ τῆς ζωῆς δένδρα, καθὼς ὁρῶμεν σήμερον*. For *ξύλον* = *δένδρον* (*ὑγρὸν ξύλον*, Lc. xxiii. 31) and the phrase *ξ. ζωῆς*, see ii. 7, note; like עֵץ in Gen. i. 11 f., *ξύλον* is here clearly collective, since there are trees on either side of the river. Andreas: *ἔθος δὲ τῇ γραφῇ πολλαχοῦ ἀντὶ ξύλων πολλῶν ἑνικῶς*

καρποὺς δώδεκα, κατὰ μῆνα ἕκαστον ἀποδιδοῦν τὸν
καρπὸν αὐτοῦ, καὶ τὰ φύλλα τοῦ ξύλου εἰς θεραπείαν
3 τῶν ἐθνῶν. ³καὶ πᾶν κατάθεμα οὐκ ἔσται ἔτι. καὶ
ὁ θρόνος τοῦ θεοῦ καὶ τοῦ ἀρνίου ἐν αὐτῇ ἔσται, καὶ

2 κατα] pr και 98 syr^{gw} | μηνα (μηναν A)] + ενα 1 186 al^{pauc} Ar | εκαστον] εκαστω Q 39 40 εκαστος 2 8 16 38 130 al^{10} | αποδιδουν A min^{mu}] αποδιδους ℵQ 130 186 al$^{plq 25}$ Ar αποδιδοντα 1 29 | τον καρπον] τους καρπους ℵ syr^{gw} | του ξυλου] των ξυλων ℵ | εις θεραπειαν] pr καταγγελλεται 11 31 32 33 Ar (ex Andr comm) | των εθνων] om των ℵ 3 καταθεμα ℵ$^{c.a}$ (καταγμα ℵ*) APQ 1 al^{40} Andr Ar] καταναθεμα ς nullo suadente codice ut vid, nulla versione | ετι] om ℵ* me εκει 1 7 38 52 186 syr^{gw} Andr Ar | ο θρονος] om ο ℵ

ξύλον καλεῖν. The twelve fruits, one for each month, are suggested by Ezekiel *l. c.* and familiar to later Jewish writers, e.g. *Shemoth rabba* 15 "tempore futuro...Deus faciet arbores quae quovis mense fructus ferant; homo vero qui de illis comedet sanabitur." It is not clear whether twelve crops of fruit are intended or "twelve manner of fruits" (A.V., R.V.); the latter idea lends itself well to the symbolism of the passage, for the one "fruit of the Spirit" is manifold in its varieties (Gal. v. 22). The fruits of the Tree of Life are doubtless life-supporting (Gen. iii. 22) and intended for the service of the citizens of the New Jerusalem; see *v.* 14, and cf. Ez. xlvii. 12 ἔσται ὁ καρπὸς αὐτῶν εἰς βρῶσιν, Enoch xxv. 5 ὁ καρπὸς αὐτοῦ τοῖς ἐκλεκτοῖς εἰς ζωήν, εἰς βοράν. But the tree is not only "good for food" (Gen. iii. 6); its leaves have therapeutic properties (Ez. *l. c.*); the LXX. rendering ἀνάβασις αὐτῶν εἰς ὑγίειαν is obscure, but our writer has access to another version or to the Heb., and rightly translates וְעָלֵהוּ לִתְרוּפָה by καὶ τὰ φύλλα εἰς θεραπείαν. The therapeutic work of Christ (Lc. ix. 11 τοὺς χρείαν ἔχοντας θεραπείας ἰᾶτο) is continued on its spiritual side by the Church, and may find in a future order opportunities at present unsuspected. As in *c.* xxi. 24, 26, the Seer seems to forecast the presence of ἔθνη, nations not yet included among the citizens of the New Jerusalem, even after the Parousia, but the inference is too uncertain to be used for a dogmatic purpose. He may refer only to the functions of the Church in the present state; so far as she fulfils her true office she is the healer of the diseases of humanity.

3. καὶ πᾶν κατάθεμα οὐκ ἔσται ἔτι] Κατάθεμα is without example in Biblical Greek, though καταθεματίζειν occurs in Mt. xxvi. 74 as the equivalent of Mc.'s ἀναθεματίζειν, and the noun is used in *Did.* 16 σωθήσονται ἀπὸ τοῦ καταθέματος. It is perhaps somewhat stronger than ἀνάθεμα (Andreas: κατ' ἐπίτασιν εἰρῆσθαι νομίζομεν κατάθεμα), an 'execration' and not simply a 'ban.' Ἀνάθεμα may be either the sentence pronounced, as in the phrase ἀναθέματι ἀναθεματίζειν (Deut. xiii. 15 f., Acts xxiii. 14), or the object on which it is laid (Deut. vii. 26 βδελύγματι βδελύξῃ, ὅτι ἀνάθημά ἐστιν), cf. Rom. ix. 3, 1 Cor. xii. 3, xvi. 22, Gal. i. 8 f. Probably the latter is the meaning of κατάθεμα here; no execrated or execrable person or thing shall be found in the Holy City; cf. *v.* 15. The form of the thought is from Zech. xiv. 11 ἀνάθεμα (חֵרֶם) οὐκ ἔσται ἔτι, καὶ κατοικήσει Ἰερουσαλὴμ πεποιθότως. Πᾶν adds to the strength of the negative; nothing of the sort remains in the New Jerusalem; contrast Gen. iii. 19.

καὶ ὁ θρόνος τοῦ θεοῦ κτλ.] The

οἱ δοῦλοι αὐτοῦ λατρεύσουσιν αὐτῷ, ⁴καὶ ὄψονται 4
τὸ πρόσωπον αὐτοῦ, καὶ τὸ ὄνομα αὐτοῦ ἐπὶ τῶν
μετώπων αὐτῶν. ⁵καὶ νὺξ οὐκ ἔσται ἔτι, καὶ οὐκ 5
ἔχουσιν χρείαν φωτὸς λύχνου καὶ φῶς ἡλίου, ὅτι
Κύριος ὁ θεὸς φωτίσει ἐπ' αὐτούς· καὶ βασιλεύσουσιν
εἰς τοὺς αἰῶνας τῶν αἰώνων.

3 *λατρευουσιν* 2 8 12 38 98 130 4 *επι των*] pr *και* ℵ 5 *ουκ εσται ετι*] *ουκ εσται εκει* 1 7 al$^{\text{sat mu}}$ arm syr^{gw} Andr Ar *ουκ εστιν εκει* 186 *ουκ εσται εκει ετι* Ir$^{\text{gr ex Anast}}$ *ουκ εσται* tantum Q 130 min$^{\text{fere 20}}$ | *ουκ εχουσιν χρειαν*] *ουχ εξουσιν χρ.* A vg syrr Ambr Tyc *ου χρεια* Q 7 8 38 130 al^{20} arm *neque opus erit* Prim | *φωτος λυχνου* ℵA 18 (38) 47 (79) vg$^{\text{exc fu}}$ syr aeth Ambr semel Tyc Prim] om *φωτος* PQ (1) 130 186 al^{pl} Ambr^{bis} | *φως* AP 11 12 32 48 79] *φωτος* ℵ 1 31 35 38 49 91 96 al^{mu} vg$^{\text{exc lips 5}}$ me syrr aeth | om *ηλιου* Q 2 7 8 16 30 39 51 92 94 97 98 130 al^{8} | *οτι κυριος ο θεος*] *ο γαρ κ.* Ir$^{\text{gr ex Anast}}$ | *φωτισει* AP 12 42] *φωτιει* ℵQ 1 130 186 al^{30} *φωτιζει* 31 32 48 79 al *g* vg$^{\text{am tol lipss 5, 6}}$ syrr Ar | *επ αυτους*] om *επ* PQ min$^{\text{fere omn}}$ vg syrr Andr Ar (hab ℵA 35 Ir$^{\text{gr ex Anast}}$ Tyc Prim (*super eos*)) | *βασιλευουσιν* Ir$^{\text{gr ex Anast}}$

Throne of God, when first revealed to the Seer, was seen through a door opened in Heaven (iv. 1); now he sees it in the Holy City which is descending to the earth, and on it sits not the Father only but the Incarnate and glorified Son (*v.* 1, note.) In Christ the Church has within her that which makes the chief glory of Heaven, the revealed Presence of God.

3, 4. *καὶ οἱ δοῦλοι αὐτοῦ λατρεύσουσιν αὐτῷ κτλ.*] To the final revelation of God there corresponds a perfected service; where the Throne is always in sight the service must be perpetual: cf. vii. 15 *εἰσὶν ἐνώπιον τοῦ θρόνου τοῦ θεοῦ, καὶ λατρεύουσιν αὐτῷ ἡμέρας καὶ νυκτὸς ἐν τῷ ναῷ αὐτοῦ· καὶ ὁ καθήμενος ἐπὶ τοῦ θρόνου σκηνώσει ἐπ' αὐτούς*—a vision which is now seen to find its fulfilment in the New Jerusalem. On *λατρεύειν* see the note on the passage just quoted. *Ὄψονται τὸ πρόσωπον αὐτοῦ* promises to the Church in her ideal state a privilege denied to the Lawgiver of the O.T.; cf. Ex. xxxiii. 20, 23 *οὐ δυνήσῃ ἰδεῖν μου τὸ πρόσωπον· οὐ γὰρ μὴ ἴδῃ ἄνθρωπος τὸ πρόσωπόν μου καὶ ζήσεται...ὄψῃ τὰ ὀπίσω μου, τὸ δὲ πρόσωπόν μου οὐκ ὀφθήσεταί σοι.* A reversal of this positive bar to complete fellowship with God seems to be foreshadowed in Ps. xvi. (xvii.) 15 *ἐγὼ δὲ ἐν δικαιοσύνῃ ὀφθήσομαι τῷ προσώπῳ σου· χορτασθήσομαι ἐν τῷ ὀφθῆναι τὴν δόξαν σου*, but see Kirkpatrick *ad l.* To see God is the reward of purity, and conversely the sight of God in Christ will perfect the process of purification (Mt. v. 8, 1 Jo. iii. 2 ff.).

Καὶ τὸ ὄνομα αὐτοῦ ἐπὶ τῶν μετώπων αὐτῶν. Cf. Andreas: *ἀντὶ τοῦ χρυσοῦ πετάλου οὗ πάλαι ὁ ἀρχιερεὺς ἐφόρει*; Bede: "confessio nominis sancti, nunc inter hostes servata, tunc victores in patria glorificat." Entire consecration to the service of God is however the leading idea of the metaphor; see *cc.* iii. 12, xiv. 1, notes.

5. *καὶ νὺξ οὐκ ἔσται ἔτι, καὶ οὐκ ἔχουσιν χρείαν κτλ.*] See xxi. 23, 25 notes; the Seer repeats like a refrain the absence of night in the ideal City, and the supersession of light, natural or artificial, by the revelation of the glory of God. The more difficult reading *φῶς ἡλίου* adds force to this refrain: 'they have no need of lamplight, and sunlight they have none.'

Καὶ βασιλεύσουσιν εἰς τοὺς αἰῶνας τῶν

6 [6]Καὶ εἶπέν μοι Οὗτοι οἱ λόγοι πιστοὶ καὶ ἀλη-

6 ειπεν] λεγει Q 130 al[fere 30] arm

αἰώνων contrasts the eternal reign of the Saints with the limited reign of c. xx. 4 ἐβασίλευσαν μετὰ τοῦ χριστοῦ χίλια ἔτη, ib. 6 βασιλεύσουσιν μετ' αὐτοῦ τὰ χίλια ἔτη. Potentially, indeed, they were reigning even in the first century (cf. v. 10 βασιλεύουσιν ἐπὶ τῆς γῆς), but neither the first century nor the fourth witnessed a full or permanent realization of the *Regnum Dei*, which is reserved for the Church in her perfect state. Perfect service will be accompanied by perfect sovereignty—will be perfect sovereignty. The beauty of the sequence λατρεύσουσιν...βασιλεύσουσιν has been finely caught by the Gregorian phrase "cui servire regnare est."

Interpreters of the Apocalypse who recognise its prophetic character differ widely with regard to the reference of this final vision. Does the New Jerusalem belong wholly to the future, or is its fulfilment to be sought in the present life of the Church? Augustine (*de civ. Dei* xx. 17) denounces the latter view in no measured terms: "hoc de isto tempore accipere quo regnat [*sc.* ecclesia] cum rege suo mille annis impudentiae nimiae mihi videtur...quis vero tam sit absurdus et obstinatissima contentione vesanus, qui audeat affirmare in huius mortalitatis aerumnis, non dico populum sanctum, sed unumquemque sanctorum...nullas habentem lacrymas et dolores?...In hoc quoque libro... obscura multa dicuntur...verum in his verbis ubi ait *Absterget Deus omnem lacrymam ab oculis eorum* etc., tanta luce dicta sunt de saeculo futuro...ut nulla debeamus in litteris sacris quaerere vel legere manifesta, si haec putaverimus obscura." Even a stronger case might be made out for a purely 'futurist' view; in its favour may be urged the place which the vision occupies in the order of the Book (but see note on xx. 1); the difficulty of finding an approximately complete counterpart to it in the history of the Christian Society; the writer's use of the future tense in xxi. 24 ff., xxii. 3 ff. On the other hand it cannot be denied that there is much in the picture which fulfils itself to a greater or less extent in the present experience of Christendom, if allowance is made for the idealism which characterizes the thought and language of Apocalyptic prophecy.

Perhaps it is in this last consideration that the solution of the difficulty is to be found. The Holy City which passes before the mind of St John is the Ideal Church as conceived in the purpose of God and to be realized in His own time. So far as this conception is purely spiritual, the powers by which it can be converted into actuality have been in the possession of the Church from the first, and the results are manifest in the moral triumphs of Christianity. Already the many colours of the New Jerusalem and the flashes of its crystal luminary may be seen by those whose eyes are not closed against the heavenly vision; men slake their thirst in the River, and nations find healing in the leaves of the Tree. But as a whole the ideal is still far above us, nor will it be reached until a new age has been inaugurated by the Lord's Return.

XXII. 6—20. EPILOGUE: LAST WORDS OF THE ANGEL, THE SEER, AND THE LORD.

6. καὶ εἶπέν μοι Οὗτοι οἱ λόγοι πιστοί κτλ.] The visions of the Apocalypse are now ended; they have reached their climax in the New Jerusalem. It remains for the Seer to report the parting utterances of some of the

θινοί, καὶ ὁ κύριος ὁ θεὸς τῶν πνευμάτων τῶν
προφητῶν ἀπέστειλεν τὸν ἄγγελον αὐτοῦ δεῖξαι
τοῖς δούλοις αὐτοῦ ἃ δεῖ γενέσθαι ἐν¶ τάχει. [7]καὶ 7 ¶ P

6 ο κυριος ℵA 31 92] om ο PQ 130 min^pl Andr Ar | των πνευματων των προφητων ℵAPQ 130 min^35 vg^excam me syr (cum του πνευματος) Prim Ar] των αγιων προφητων 1 79 al arm Andr^vid των πνευματων τ. αγιων προφ. 35 68 syr^gw | απεστειλεν] + με ℵ* (om ℵ^c.a) syr | om δειξαι τοις δουλοις αυτου 130   7 om και 1 35 38 79 92 al^mu vg^dem me Prim Ar

personae dramatis, and this is done in the disjointed manner which characterizes much of the latter portion of the Book; it is often difficult to distinguish the speakers, or to trace the connexion of the thought.

The first speaker (*vv.* 6 f.) is doubtless the hierophant angel of xxi. 9, 15, xxii. 1. The sayings which he pronounces to be 'faithful and true' (xxi. 5, note) are, as the sequel shews, the teachings of the entire Book, and not only the noble words with which the last of its visions has just ended (*vv.* 3—5). The καί which follows is *quasi*-'epexegetic': these sayings are faithful and true, seeing that they constitute a message which the Almighty Himself has sent through His angel. There is a reference here, as in more than one other phrase in the Epilogue, to the Prologue (i. 1—3); the words δεῖξαι τοῖς δούλοις αὐτοῦ ἃ δεῖ γενέσθαι ἐν τάχει are repeated *verbatim* from i. 1. Ὁ κύριος ὁ θεός is doubtless the Eternal Father, as in i. 8, iv. 8, xi. 17, xv. 3, xvi. 7, xviii. 8, xix. 6, xxi. 22, xxii. 5. Here He is ὁ θεὸς τῶν πνευμάτων τῶν προφητῶν, the God from Whom prophetic inspiration proceeds, Who is the Source of prophetic gifts; cf. Arethas: τοῦτο γὰρ βούλεται παριστᾷν διὰ τοῦ 'Κύριος τῶν πνευμάτων,' ὡσπερεὶ ἔλεγεν 'Κύριος τοῦ προφητικοῦ χαρίσματος.' For πνεύματα in this sense cf. 1 Cor. xii. 10 διακρίσεις πνευμάτων, xiv. 12 ζηλωταί ἐστε πνευμάτων, and *ib.* 32 πνεύματα προφητῶν προφηταῖς ὑποτάσσεται. The πνεύματα προφητῶν are not to be identified with the ἑπτὰ πνεύματα of i. 4, v. 6, which are before the Divine Throne, and are the Eyes of the Lamb; they are the natural faculties of the Prophets, raised and quickened by the Holy Spirit, but still under human control, and standing in a creaturely relation to God. Cf. Num. xvi. 22, xxvii. 16 ὁ θεὸς τῶν πνευμάτων καὶ πάσης (לְכָל) σαρκός, where the phrase is used in reference to human life in general. The Enochic "Lord of the Spirits" (Enoch xxxvii. 2 *et passim*) has quite another meaning; see Charles *ad loc.*, and cf. 2 Macc. iii. 24 ὁ τῶν πνευμάτων καὶ πάσης ἐξουσίας δυναστής.

It is noteworthy that even in the visions of this book, which came to him when he was apparently alone in Patmos, St John associates himself with the whole body of the Christian Prophets. The *esprit de corps* thus revealed is interesting; at the same time it is to be observed that he does not isolate the prophetic order from the rest of the Christian Society; if in the first instance the message comes to the Prophets only, it comes to them for the benefit of the Church at large (see Mc. iv. 21 f., note); it is their duty to communicate it to all the Servants of God. For προφῆται see x. 7, xi. 18, xvi. 6, xviii. 20, 24, xxii. 9; and for δοῦλοι, i. 1, ii. 20, vii. 3, xix. 2, 5, xxii. 3, notes.

7. καὶ ἰδοὺ ἔρχομαι ταχύ κτλ.] The Voice of Christ is heard behind, or speaking through, the voice of His angel. For this parenthetical ἰδοὺ

ἰδοὺ ἔρχομαι ταχύ. μακάριος ὁ τηρῶν τοὺς λόγους
8 τῆς προφητείας τοῦ βιβλίου τούτου. [8]κἀγὼ Ἰωάν-
νης ὁ ἀκούων καὶ βλέπων ταῦτα. καὶ ὅτε ἤκουσα
καὶ ἔβλεψα, ἔπεσα προσκυνῆσαι ἔμπροσθεν τῶν
ποδῶν τοῦ ἀγγέλου τοῦ δεικνύοντός μοι ταῦτα.
9 [9]καὶ λέγει μοι Ὅρα μή· σύνδουλός σού εἰμι καὶ

7 ερχομαι] ερχονται ℵ[c.a] ερχεται 12 | ταχυ] εν ταχει 12 syr[gw] 8 καγω] και εγω 1 al[pl] Ar εγω vg[am fu lips6] me syr[gw] | ο ακουων και βλεπων ταυτα AQ min[fere 40] vg syr arm Prim] ο βλεπων κ. ακουων ταυτα ℵ 31 32 33 48 78 79 152 me syr[gw] (aeth) Dionys Prim Ar | om και οτε ηκ. κ. εβλεψα aeth | εβλεψα] εβλεπον A ειδον 16 35 38 94 98 οτε ιδον (vel ειδον) Q 130 min[plq30] | επεσα ℵA 1 16 30 35 38 68] επεσον Q 130 min[pl] Ar | εμπροσθεν] προ A | των ποδων] om των A | δεικνυοντος (A) Q min[pl] Andr] δεικνυντος ℵ 2 4 7 9 10 26 27 49 50 96 97 al[vid] Ar 9 λεγει] ειπεν vg syrr | ορα μη (ορα· μη...; 68 syrr ορα· μη· 130)] + ποιησης 32 (et ut vid vg Aug Prim) + πεσης εμπροσθεν μου και προσκυνησης arm + προσκυνησης μοι aeth

ἔρχομαι cf. xvi. 15, xxii. 12, 20; ταχύ, suggested here by the Angel's ἐν τάχει, is added in ii. 16, iii. 11, and below *vv.* 12, 20. On ἔρχεσθαι in this Book see vi. 1, note.

The beatitude which follows is here, as in xvi. 15, part of Christ's utterance; it is a repetition in a shorter form of i. 3, so that the Book ends as it began, with a felicitation of its devout students. On ὁ τηρῶν Primasius well observes: "'servare' dicit hic reverenter credere et purioris vitae proposito custodire." Τοῦ βιβλίου τούτου points to the all but completed roll on the Seer's knee; throughout the Apocalypse he has represented himself as writing his impressions at the time (cf. x. 4 ἤμελλον γράφειν), and his task is now nearly ended.

8. κἀγὼ Ἰωάννης ὁ ἀκούων καὶ βλέπων ταῦτα κτλ.] As at the beginning of the Book (i. 1, 4, 9), the author gives his name, without any distinguishing title, as Dionysius of Alexandria had already observed (Eus. *H.E.* vii. 25): ὅτι μὲν οὖν Ἰωάννης ἐστὶν ὁ ταῦτα γράφων, αὐτῷ λέγοντι πιστευτέον· ποῖος δὲ οὗτος ἄδηλον. The writer claims however, to be the Seer himself (ὁ ἀκ. καὶ βλέπων); cf. Dan. xii. 5, 8, LXX. καὶ εἶδον ἐγὼ Δανιὴλ...καὶ ἐγὼ ἤκουσα. Ταῦτα, the things which the Angel had just shewn him (cf. *infr.* τοῦ δεικνύοντός μοι ταῦτα), i.e. the revelation of the New Jerusalem. So astounding was this whole vision, the crowning glory of the Book, that the Seer forgets the warning he has recently received (xix. 10), and again prostrates himself before the Angel. The commentators offer alternative explanations, e.g. Primasius writes: "aut semel factum iteravit...aut magno visionum stupore perculsus adorare se iterum voluisse confitetur." There is nothing in the context to justify the supposition that St John believed himself to be worshipping Christ; though the angel had spoken the words ἰδοὺ ἔρχομαι ταχύ in the person of Christ, yet the Seer knew him to be one of the bearers of the Seven Bowls (xxi. 9). Still less can it be maintained that it is Christ Who refuses the worship; here, as in *c.* xix., it is the cult of angelic beings that the Apocalyptist wishes to discourage by the example of his own repeated lapse; see notes on xix. 10.

τῶν ἀδελφῶν σου τῶν προφητῶν καὶ τῶν τηρούν-
των τοὺς λόγους τοῦ βιβλίου· τούτου· τῷ θεῷ
προσκύνησον. [10]καὶ λέγει μοι Μὴ σφραγίσῃς τοὺς 10
λόγους τῆς προφητείας τοῦ βιβλίου τούτου· ὁ
καιρὸς γὰρ ἐγγύς ἐστιν. [11]ὁ ἀδικῶν ἀδικησάτω ἔτι, 11

9 *και των τηρουντων*] om *και* 1 4 10 11 12 17 31 32* 37 47 48 49 91 94 96 Prim Ar | *τους λογους*] + *της προφητειας* 38 vg^cle lipss 4, 6 me arm Prim 10 *τους λογους*] + *τουτους* ℵ* (corr ipse ℵ¹) | *ο καιρος γαρ*] *ο γαρ καιρος* 2 18 40 79 *οτι ο καιρος* 1 49 91 al aeth Cypr Prim *ο καιρος* tantum 4 16 29 39 48 68 Ar 11 *ο αδικων αδικησατω*] *ο ανομος ανομησατω* ep Vienn ap Eus pr *και* 68 syr^gw Prim

Τῶν τηρούντων κτλ. is repeated from *v.* 7 and answers to *τῶν ἐχόντων τὴν μαρτυρίαν Ἰησοῦ* in xix. 10.

10. *καὶ λέγει μοι Μὴ σφραγίσῃς τοὺς λόγους κτλ.*] The Angel continues; on this *καὶ λέγει* see xix. 9, note. His instruction is exactly the reverse of that which is given to Daniel (viii. 26 וְאַתָּה סְתֹם הֶחָזוֹן כִּי לְיָמִים רַבִּים; cf. xii. 9 סְתֻמִים וַחֲתֻמִים הַדְּבָרִים עַד־עֵת קֵץ; LXX. *κάλυψον τὰ προστάγματα καὶ σφράγισαι τὸ βιβλίον ἕως καιροῦ συντελείας*: cf. *v.* 4). But the circumstances are different—indeed, they are reversed; as Milligan well says, "it was not a time" now "for sealing up, but for breaking seals"; the end was not, as in Daniel's case (see Driver on Dan. *l. c.*), far off, but at hand, almost within sight. Therefore the prophecy of this book is to be left open for all who will to read; nay, the hearing and reading of the book (i. 3, xxii. 7), and so far as may be, the study of its mysteries (xiii. 18, xvii. 9), are to be warmly encouraged. The Incarnation had brought the season for the fulfilment of God's purposes relatively near, even before the end of the first century; cf. i. 3, note. On the practice of sealing books, to keep their contents secret, see *c.* v. 1, note. Only in reference to one detail in this Book is the Seer directed *Σφράγισον...μὴ...γράψῃς* (x. 4); the rest is for the ears and eyes of all Christians.

11. *ὁ ἀδικῶν ἀδικησάτω ἔτι κτλ.*] Daniel is still in view; cf. Dan. xii. 10 יִתְבָּרְרוּ...רַבִּים וְהִרְשִׁיעוּ רְשָׁעִים, LXX. *ἕως ἂν...ἁγιασθῶσι πολλοί, καὶ ἁμάρτωσιν οἱ ἁμαρτωλοί* (Th. *ἀνομήσωσιν ἄνομοι*); perhaps the Apocalyptist has also in mind Ez. iii. 27, *ὁ ἀκούων ἀκουέτω καὶ ὁ ἀπειθῶν ἀπειθείτω.* In Daniel the sense seems to be that the great trial which Antiochus was the means of bringing upon the Jewish people, while it exercised a purifying influence upon the faithful, would but confirm the disloyal in their wickedness; see Driver *ad loc.* While this thought may not be entirely absent from the present passage, another is more prominent. It is not only true that the troubles of the last days will tend to fix the character of each individual according to the habits which he has already formed, but there will come a time when change will be impossible—when no further opportunity will be given for repentance on the one hand or for apostasy on the other. In the imagination of the Seer the moment has been reached when the Master of the house has arisen and shut the door, and those that are without will knock in vain (Mt. xxv. 10, Lc. xiii. 25); men can then no longer recede from the position which they have chosen to take up. Cf. Andreas: *ὡς ἂν εἴποι Ἕκαστος τὸ ἀρέσκον αὐτῷ ποιησάτω· οὐ βιάζω τὴν προαίρεσιν,* and the caution added by Arethas: *οὐ προτροπὴ τοῦτο, ἀλλ' ἔλεγχος τῆς*

καὶ ὁ ῥυπαρὸς ῥυπανθήτω ἔτι, καὶ ὁ δίκαιος δικαιο-
σύνην ποιησάτω ἔτι, καὶ ὁ ἅγιος ἁγιασθήτω ἔτι.
12 [12]ἰδοὺ ἔρχομαι ταχύ, καὶ ὁ μισθός μου μετ' ἐμοῦ,

11 om *και ο ρυπαρος ρυπανθητω ετι* A 1 20 21 33 35 68 97 (hab ℵQ min^{pl} vg syrr) | *ρυπανθητω* ℵ 18* 32 Or] *ρυπαρευθητω* 53^{mg} al$^{plq\,30}$ Ar *ρυπαρωθητω* 13 92 | *δικαιοσυνην ποιησατω*] *δικαιωθητω* 38 79 vg$^{clc\,lipss\,5,6}$ (*iustificetur*) ep Vienn ap Eus *καθαρισθητω* Or (cum *ο καθαρος* pro *ο δικαιος*) 12 *ιδου*] pr *και* 1 aeth

ἑκάστου πρὸς ὅτι καὶ βούλοιτο ὁρμῆς. Ὁ ἀδικῶν, he whose habit it is to do wrong, 'the wrong-doer,' with special reference perhaps to the persecutor —so at least the sufferers in the Viennese troubles understood it; cf. Eus. *H.E.* v. 1: τοῦ ἡγεμόνος καὶ τοῦ δήμου τὸ ὅμοιον εἰς ἡμᾶς ἀδίκως ἐπιδεικνυμένων μῖσος, ἵνα ἡ γραφὴ πληρωθῇ Ὁ ἄνομος ἀνομησάτω ἔτι καὶ ὁ δίκαιος δικαιωθήτω ἔτι. Ὁ ῥυπαρός, the representative of another class, the immoral pagan or reprobate; the ἀδικῶν may be scrupulously moral, the ῥυπαρός disregards purity of life or even common decency; for the word and its cognates see Zech. iii. 3 ἐνδεδυμένος ἱμάτια ῥυπαρά (צוֹאִים); Job xiv. 4 τίς γὰρ καθαρὸς ἔσται ἀπὸ ῥύπου; ἀλλ' οὐθείς; Jac. i. 21 ἀποθέμενοι πᾶσαν ῥυπαρίαν, with Dr Mayor's note. The aorists (ἀδικησάτω, ῥυπανθήτω, not ἀδικείτω, ῥυπαινέσθω) indicate the fixity of the state into which the ἀδικῶν and the ῥυπαρός have entered; there is henceforth no break in the downward course, which is indeed viewed as a single act; cf. Blass, *Gr.* p. 194 f. Fixity in good is in like manner to be attained when the end comes; the just (the opposite character to ὁ ἀδικῶν) and the saint (the opposite to ὁ ῥυπαρός) will enter on a permanent life of righteousness and of holiness. Not of course that the δίκαιος and the ἅγιος can be divorced; the true ἅγιος is always δίκαιος, and the δίκαιος is, in the perfect state at least, ἅγιος; the two qualities were united in the Son of Man (Acts iii. 14 τὸν ἅγιον καὶ δίκαιον), and will be united in all who are finally His; but they are kept apart here for the sake of the antithesis to ὁ ἀδικῶν, ὁ ῥυπαρός. For δικαιοσύνην ποιησάτω the Viennese letter quoted above has δικαιωθήτω, a reading which Zahn (*Gesch. d. NTlichen Kanons*, i. 201) pronounces "gewiss ursprünglich," and which certainly has much to recommend it; if we accept it, the sense will be 'let him be held righteous' (Vulg. *iustificetur*), which corresponds with ἁγιασθήτω, 'let him enter on a state of sanctification.' On the other hand it is perhaps more probable that δικαιοσύνην ποιησάτω, which answers to ἀδικησάτω as ἁγιασθήτω to ῥυπανθήτω, has been changed to δικαιωθήτω in order to balance ἁγιασθήτω. Primasius strangely renders: "iustus autem iustiora faciat, similiter et sanctus sanctiora," although above he rightly gives: "qui perseverant nocere noceant et qui in sordibus est, sordescat adhuc."

12. ἰδοὺ ἔρχομαι ταχύ, καὶ ὁ μισθός μου μετ' ἐμοῦ κτλ.] The Voice of Christ comes in parenthetically, as in *v.* 7; see note there. He speaks as the Steward of the great Μισθαποδότης, Who in the eventide of the world will call the labourers to receive their day's wages (Mt. xx. 8); see xi. 18, note. Though the μισθός is one and the same in all cases, its value to the individual worker varies according to the work he has done—a principle which is steadily maintained throughout Scripture (Ps. lxi. 13, Job xxxiv. 11 f., Isa. xl. 14, lxii. 11 (LXX.), Mc. xiii. 34, Rom. ii. 5, Apoc. ii. 23,

ἀποδοῦναι ἑκάστῳ ὡς τὸ ἔργον ἐστὶν αὐτοῦ. [13]ἐγὼ 13
τὸ ἄλφα καὶ τὸ ὦ, ὁ πρῶτος καὶ ὁ ἔσχατος, ἡ
ἀρχὴ καὶ τὸ τέλος. [14]μακάριοι οἱ πλύνοντες τὰς 14

12 αποδουναι] αποδοθηναι ℵ* | ως το εργον εστιν αυτου ℵA 21 (38) syr] ως το εργ. εσται αυτου (vel αυτου εσται) Q (1) 13 30 35 49 91 92 94 96 97 98 al^{plq 10} (Andr) (Ar) κατα τα εργα (vel το εργον) αυτου 79 vg me syr^{gw} (aeth) Cypr Tyc Prim 13 εγω] + ειμι vg^{cle dem fu* tol lipss} me arm aeth | το αλφα] το α Q 130 min^{pl} | ο πρωτος και ο εσχατος] πρωτος κ. εσχατος A 3 7 8 9 21 22 ο πρ. κ. εσχατος 96 post η αρχ. και το τ. pon 1 31 32 48 49 79 91 al arm Ar om me | η αρχη και το τελος] αρχη κ. τελος 1 al^{mu vid} Ar 14 οι πλυνοντες τας στολας αυτων ℵA (7) 38 vg aeth^{utr} Ath^{vid} Prim Fulg vg^{cle lipss 4, 5} (+ *in sanguine agni*)] οι ποιουντες τας εντολας αυτου Q 130 al^{pl} me syrr arm Tert (*qui ex praeceptis agunt*) Cypr Tyc Prim^{vid} Andr Ar

xx. 12 f.). The use of μισθός to represent the gratuitous (Rom. vi. 23) and spiritual compensations of the future life belongs to the circle of ideas associated with Κύριος, δεσπότης, δοῦλος, ἐργάτης. Ὁ μισθός μου, 'the reward which it belongs to Me to give' (2 Tim. iv. 8); contrast ὁ μ. ὑμῶν, Mt. v. 12 (αὐτῶν, Mt. vi. 2, 5, 16; αὐτοῦ, Mc. ix. 41), 'the reward which ye (they, he) shall receive.' Μετ' ἐμοῦ, cf. Isa. xl. 10 ἰδοὺ κύριος Κύριος μετὰ ἰσχύος ἔρχεται...ἰδοὺ ὁ μισθὸς αὐτοῦ μετ' αὐτοῦ; *ib.* lxii. 11 ἰδοὺ ὁ σωτήρ σοι παραγέγονεν ἔχων τὸν ἑαυτοῦ μισθόν. The inf. ἀποδοῦναι expresses the purpose for which the reward is brought (cf. Blass, *Gr.* p. 223), so that it is nearly equivalent to ἵνα ἀποδῷ; ἑκάστῳ strikes a note often heard in this Book (ii. 23, vi. 11, xxi. 13).

13. ἐγὼ τὸ ἄλφα καὶ τὸ ὦ κτλ.] Cf. xxi. 6 ἐγὼ τὸ ἄλφα καὶ τὸ ὦ, ἡ ἀρχὴ καὶ τὸ τέλος, in which is now inserted from i. 17, ii. 8, ὁ πρῶτος καὶ ὁ ἔσχατος. While ὁ πρῶτος κτλ. is applied only to Christ, this is the only occasion on which He receives the great title τὸ ἄλφα καὶ τὸ ὦ. It is the crowning instance in this Book of the attribution of Divine prerogatives to the Incarnate Son; only ὁ ὢν καὶ ὁ ἦν seems to be withheld from the Son, perhaps because it represents the underived Source of the Divine Life. On the meaning of τὸ ἄλφα καὶ τὸ ὦ as applied to our Lord cf. Tert. *de monog.* 5 (quoted in note on *c.* i. 8). The phrase is applicable in many senses, but perhaps it is used here with special reference to our Lord's place in human history. As creation owed its beginning to the Word of God, so in His incarnate glory He will bring it to its consummation by the Great Award. He is the ἀρχηγὸς καὶ τελειωτής of faith (Heb. xii. 2), and not less truly the ἀρχὴ καὶ τέλος of all life.

14. μακάριοι οἱ πλύνοντες τὰς στολὰς αὐτῶν κτλ.] The reading is not altogether easy to determine. Perhaps it is slightly more probable that ΠΛΥΝΟΝΤΕϹΤΑϹϹΤΟΛΑϹ arose out of ΠΟΙΟΥΝΤΕϹΤΑϹЄ̄ΤΟΛΑϹ, than that the reverse occurred; on the other hand, the documentary evidence is decidedly in favour of the former, and it is against the latter that the use of the Johannine writings all but invariably supports the phrase τηρεῖν τὰς ἐντολάς (so Jo. xiv. 15, 21, xv. 10, 1 Jo. ii. 3 f., iii. 22, 24, v. 3, Apoc. xii. 17, xiv. 12—the sole exception is 1 Jo. v. 2, where ποιεῖν τ. ἐ. occurs); moreover, the prepossessions of the scribes would have favoured ποιοῦντες τὰς ἐντολάς rather than πλύνοντες τὰς στολάς. Upon the whole, then, πλύνοντες κτλ. may with some confidence be preferred; and it yields an admirable sense.

This, the final beatitude of the Apoca-

στολὰς αὐτῶν, ἵνα ἔσται ἡ ἐξουσία αὐτῶν ἐπὶ τὸ
ξύλον τῆς ζωῆς, καὶ τοῖς πυλῶσιν εἰσέλθωσιν εἰς
15 τὴν πόλιν. [15]ἔξω οἱ κύνες καὶ οἱ φαρμακοὶ καὶ οἱ

14 η εξουσια αυτων] + ως δε η εξουσια ℵ* (delevit ℵ[c.a])

lypse, deals with the issues of the higher life. They who wash the robes of the inner life from the ῥυπαρία of the world by faith in the Sacrifice of our Lord (vii. 14, note) shall win the right of access to the Tree of Life and of entrance into the City of God; μακάριοι οἱ πλύνοντες...is but another version of μακάριοι οἱ καθαροὶ τῇ καρδίᾳ, ὅτι αὐτοὶ τὸν θεὸν ὄψονται, interpreted in the light of the Cross. Ἵνα ἔσται...καὶ...εἰσέλθωσιν: 'blessed are they...that the right shall be theirs...and they may enter' (Benson)—a mixture of constructions observed already in *c.* iii. 9; the future after ἵνα is frequent in this Book (vi. 4, 11, ix. 5, 20, xiii. 12, xiv. 13), and if it is to be distinguished in meaning from the conjunctive, it may point to the certainty, the actuality, of the result, while the conjunctive suggests that there are conditions which must be fulfilled first.

On the Tree of Life see *v.* 2, and *c.* ii. 7, notes. The Vision of the New Jerusalem places the Paradise of God in the heart of the City, so that right of access to the Tree implies right of entrance into the City, and the entrance must precede the access. If in this passage the right of access is mentioned first, it is probably with the view of laying the emphasis upon the greater right, which indeed includes all. On τ. πυλῶσιν see xxi. 12: the dative is instrumental, the gate-towers being regarded as the means of entrance.

15. ἔξω οἱ κύνες κτλ.] Benson: 'out, ye dogs'—a bold and impressive rendering, but scarcely admissible in this context; the persons thus characterized have already been cast out. Primasius is more true to the mind of the writer: "foris autem remanebunt canes"; cf. Bede: "cuncta enim rabies improborum et nunc intrinsecus ecclesiam tentat, sed cum intraverit paterfamilias et sanctis secum ad nuptias intrantibus clauserit ostium, tunc incipient foris stare et pulsare ostium." No one who has watched the dogs that prowl in the quarters of an Eastern city (Ps. lviii. (lix.) 7, 15) will wonder at the contempt and disgust which the word suggests to the Oriental mind. For its application to unclean or otherwise offensive persons see Deut. xxiii. 18 (19) οὐ προσοίσεις μίσθωμα πόρνης οὐδὲ ἄλλαγμα κυνὸς (see Driver's note *ad loc.*) εἰς τὸν οἶκον Κυρίου; Ps. xxi. (xxii.) 17 ἐκύκλωσάν με κύνες πολλοί; *ib.* 21 ῥῦσαι...ἐκ χειρὸς κυνὸς τὴν μονογενῆ μου; Mt. vii. 6 μὴ δῶτε τὸ ἅγιον τοῖς κυσίν; Mc. vii. 27 οὐ γάρ ἐστιν καλὸν λαβεῖν τὸν ἄρτον τῶν τέκνων καὶ τοῖς κυναρίοις βαλεῖν; Phil. iii. 3 βλέπετε τοὺς κύνας (see Lightfoot's note). In the last two passages at least reference is made to the use of the term by the Jews to denote the heathen or the Gentiles, of which Schöttgen *ad loc.* quotes a typical example from *Pirke R. Eliezer* 29: "quicumque edit cum idolatra idem est ac si ederet cum cane. quis est canis? qui non circumcisus est." But in the present passage neither Jews nor Gentiles as such are in view; the κύνες (Syr.[gw.] ܛܡ̈ܐܐ = οἱ κοινοί) are the ἐβδελυγμένοι of xxi. 8, i.e. those who had been defiled by long contact with the foul vices which honeycombed pagan society. These were not even in St John's day strictly limited to the heathen (see ii. 14, 20 ff., note, and cf. 2 Cor. xii. 21); and he must have foreseen that as time went on, and the Church grew in numbers, she would lose in purity. Tertullian goes too far

πόρνοι καὶ οἱ φονεῖς καὶ οἱ εἰδωλολάτραι καὶ πᾶς
φιλῶν καὶ ποιῶν ψεῦδος.
[16]Ἐγὼ Ἰησοῦς ἔπεμψα τὸν ἄγγελόν μου μαρ- 16

15 πας]+ο 1 7 30* 31 32 38 79 186 al^{mu} Andr Ar | φιλων και ποιων AQ min^{pl} vg syrr Tyc Prim Fulg] ποιων και φιλων ℵ 11 31 32 33 35 48 Hipp Ath Ar om φιλων και me om και ποιων arm aeth

when he says (*de pud.* 19): "non enim de ethnicis videbitur sapere... illorum est enim foras dari qui intus fuerunt"; but Andreas is doubtless right: κύνες δὲ οὐ μόνον οἱ ἀναιδεῖς καὶ ἄπιστοι...ἀλλὰ καὶ οἱ μετὰ τὸ βάπτισμα ἐπιστρέφοντες εἰς τὸν ἴδιον ἔμετον. On οἱ φαρμακοί κτλ. see xxi. 8, note; πᾶς φιλῶν καὶ ποιῶν ψεῦδος is a welcome interpretation of πᾶσιν τοῖς ψευδέσιν in the earlier list, which xxi. 27 ὁ ποιῶν ψεῦδος has already supplied in part. But ὁ φιλῶν goes deeper than ὁ ποιῶν; he who loves falsehood is in his nature akin to it, and has through his love of it proved his affinity to Satan, who is ὁ πατὴρ αὐτοῦ (Jo. viii. 44); for him, while he is such, there can be no entrance into the City, no access to the Tree of Life; cf. 2 Th. ii. 12 ἵνα κριθῶσιν πάντες οἱ μὴ πιστεύσαντες τῇ ἀληθείᾳ ἀλλὰ εὐδοκήσαντες τῇ ἀδικίᾳ. With ποιεῖν ψεῦδος compare Jer. viii. 10 כֻּלֹּה עֹשֶׂה שָּׁקֶר; 1 Jo. i. 6 ψευδόμεθα καὶ οὐ ποιοῦμεν τὴν ἀλήθειαν. To 'do the truth,' or to 'do falsehood,' to 'act a lie,' are St John's terms for a life which is fundamentally sincere or insincere. The rendering of A.V., R.V. (text), "every one that maketh a lie," misses this point, probably out of regard for the circumstance that ψεῦδος is anarthrous here (contrast Jo. viii. 44, Rom. i. 25, Eph. iv. 25, 2 Th. ii. 11). But τὸ ψεῦδος would not have suited this context, if it was the writer's intention to represent the insincere life as a single act, as if the man's whole existence had been a lie.

16. ἐγὼ Ἰησοῦς ἔπεμψα τὸν ἄγγελόν μου κτλ.] Though the whole Book is an ἀποκάλυψις Ἰησοῦ Χριστοῦ (i. 1), the revelation has hitherto been made through the ministry of angels or in a vision of the glorified Lord, or through the Spirit in the mind of the Seer (ii. 7). Now at length Jesus speaks in His human personal name (ἐγὼ Ἰησοῦς, as ἐγὼ Ἰωάννης in *v.* 8). He attests the *bona fides* of His messenger: 'it was I Who sent him; it is on My behalf that he has spoken; his testimony is Mine.' Ἔπεμψα is used rather than ἀπέστειλα (cf. i. 1 ἐσήμανεν ἀποστείλας διὰ τοῦ ἀγγέλου αὐτοῦ)—'I sent,' without the accessory idea of a special commission (cf. Westcott, Add. Note on John xx. 21); it is enough to say that the angel came from the Lord; by His angel Jesus Himself had borne witness to the members of the Asian Churches (ὑμῖν) and the contents of this Book (ταῦτα) were thus ultimately from Him. These communications, though addressed primarily to the Christians of Asia, had a wider purpose: they were made ἐπὶ ταῖς ἐκκλησίαις, with reference to the needs of Christians generally; cf. the use of ἐπί in x. 11 δεῖ σε πάλιν προφητεῦσαι ἐπὶ λαοῖς καὶ ἔθνεσιν καὶ γλωσσαῖς καὶ βασιλεῦσιν πολλοῖς, 'in reference to peoples,' &c., and see Jo. xii. 16. Αἱ ἐκκλησίαι are not the Seven Churches only, but the Christian societies throughout the world, which in the next generation were known in their aggregate as ἡ καθολικὴ ἐκκλησία (Ign. *Smyrn.* 8. 2; cf. Harnack, *Mission u. Ausbreitung*, p. 293). The Apocalypse does not use ἡ ἐκκλησία of the whole Church, as St Paul does (Col., Eph.; cf. Hort, *Ecclesia*, p. 147 ff.); when St John

τυρῆσαι ὑμῖν ταῦτα ἐπὶ ταῖς ἐκκλησίαις. ἐγώ εἰμι
¶ 1 ἡ ῥίζα καὶ τὸ γένος Δαυείδ¶, ὁ ἀστὴρ ὁ λαμπρὸς
17 ὁ πρωϊνός. [17]καὶ τὸ πνεῦμα καὶ ἡ νύμφη λέγουσιν
"Ἔρχου· καὶ ὁ ἀκούων εἰπάτω "Ἔρχου. καὶ ὁ διψῶν

16 επι ℵQ min^{pl} syrr] εν A 18 21 38 79 vg Ath om 1 4 11 12 31 47 48 186 arm Ar | εκκλησιαις] pr επτα Prim | Δαυειδ] pr του 1 7 al | ο αστηρ] pr και 7 35 49 79 186 syr^{gw} | ο πρωινος] pr και A *g* vg Prim 17 το πνευμα και η νυμφη] πνευμα κ. νυμφη ℵ (ο) νυμφιος κ. (η) νυμφη Bed^{vid} (*sponsus et sponsa*) | λεγουσιν] λεγουσα 130 ελεγον 186 | om και 4° vg^{am} Tyc

wishes to express the ideal unity of Christendom, he does so by means of a symbolical female figure, the Mother (xii. 1 ff.) or the Wife or Bride (xix., xxi., xxii.) of Christ.

ἐγώ εἰμι ἡ ῥίζα καὶ τὸ γένος Δαυείδ] Cf. v. 5 ὁ λέων ὁ ἐκ τῆς φυλῆς Ἰούδα, ἡ ῥίζα Δ.; and see note there. To ἡ ῥίζα the Seer now adds: καὶ τὸ γένος. Γένος does not here mean 'race,' 'family' or 'house,' as in Acts iv. 6 ἐκ γένους ἀρχιερατικοῦ, *ib.* vii. 13 τὸ γένος Ἰωσήφ: but 'offspring,' as in Acts xvii. 28 f. 'τοῦ γὰρ καὶ γένος ἐσμέν'· γένος οὖν ὑπάρχοντες τοῦ θεοῦ κτλ.; cf. the similar use of *genus* in Verg. *Aen.* iv. 12 "genus esse deorum." Jesus is not only the ῥάβδος ἐκ τῆς ῥίζης Ἰεσσαί (Isa. xi. 1), but He is at once the ῥάβδος and the ῥίζα, the Root and the Offshoot, the Beginning and the End of the whole economy associated with the Davidic family. In the Messiah, the latest Scion of the House of David, its earliest ideals and hopes are realized.

ὁ ἀστὴρ ὁ λαμπρὸς ὁ πρωϊνός] Cf. ii. 28 δώσω αὐτῷ τὸν ἀστέρα τὸν πρωϊνόν, a promise which is now interpreted. The Morning Star, the Lord's ultimate gift to the conqueror, is Jesus Himself. Among the stars of the spiritual firmament (i. 16, 20) He is as the ἑωσφόρος (Job iii. 9, xi. 17, xxxviii. 12, xli. 9 (10)) or φωσφόρος (2 Pet. i. 19), the brightest in the whole galaxy, the Light which lightens every man by its coming into the world (Jo. i. 9); the Star of Dawn, Whose coming precedes the sunrise of the Day of God. The metaphor is used by the son of Sirach in reference to Simon the High Priest (Sir. l. 6 ὡς ἀστὴρ ἑωθινὸς ἐν μέσῳ νεφέλης), and of Mordecai in the Targum on Esther ("ipse Mardochai similis fuit Lucifero splendenti inter stellas"); in Isa. xiv. 12 it occurs in a splendid dirge over a fallen King of Babylon: πῶς ἐξέπεσεν ἐκ τοῦ οὐρανοῦ ὁ ἑωσφόρος ὁ πρωὶ ἀνατέλλων. The Morning Star of the Church shines to-day as brightly as in the age of St John; He does not fall or set.

17. καὶ τὸ πνεῦμα καὶ ἡ νύμφη λέγουσιν "Ἔρχου] The answer of the Church to the Voice of Jesus in *v.* 12. Τὸ πνεῦμα is probably not the Spirit regarded as the indwelling life of the Body of Christ, as in Eph. iv. 4 ἓν σῶμα καὶ ἓν πνεῦμα, but rather, in accordance with the general use of the Apocalypse, the Spirit of prophecy, the Spirit in the prophetic order; 'the Spirit and the Bride' is thus practically equivalent to 'the Prophets and the Saints' (xvi. 6, xviii. 24). The Christian Prophets inspired by the Spirit of Jesus, and the whole Church —the Churches considered as an ideal unity—respond as with one voice to the Lord's great announcement. It rouses in all Christians the desire, never long dormant, for His Return. On ἡ νύμφη see xxi. 2, 9, notes; for ἔρχου cf. vi. 1, note; here it is obvious to supply Κύριε Ἰησοῦ from *v.* 20.

καὶ ὁ ἀκούων εἰπάτω "Ἔρχου κτλ.] The call is to be taken up and repeated

ἐρχέσθω· ὁ θέλων λαβέτω ὕδωρ ζωῆς δωρεάν.
18 μαρτυρῶ ἐγὼ παντὶ τῷ ἀκούοντι τοὺς λόγους 18

17 ο θελων] om *g* syr^{gw} pr και 33 46 vg$^{clc\,fu\,lips4}$ syrr arm Prim Ar 18 μαρτυρω] μαρτυρομαι 11 31 34 35 48 Ar | τω ακουοντι] om τω 8 49 79 91 96

by every hearer (i. 3, note) of this Book; not only the Church in her ideal unity, but each individual member of every Christian congregation where the book shall be read is invited to demand the fulfilment of the Lord's promise ἰδοὺ ἔρχομαι ταχύ. In what follows there is a remarkable change of reference; for ὁ διψῶν εἰπάτω Ἔρχου, St John writes ὁ δ. ἐρχέσθω, i.e. instead of being bidden to welcome the coming Christ, he who is athirst is himself bidden to come; he is welcomed to Christ in words which remind us of the Johannine Gospel (Jo. vi. 35 ὁ ἐρχόμενος πρὸς ἐμὲ οὐ μὴ πεινάσῃ, καὶ ὁ πιστεύων εἰς ἐμὲ οὐ μὴ διψήσει πώποτε; vii. 37 εἴ τις διψᾷ, ἐρχέσθω πρὸς μὲ καὶ πινέτω). Ὁ διψῶν contrasts happily with οὐδένα εὗρον διψῶντα in the Oxyrhynchus Sayings, though the latter is doubtless relatively true. Here ὁ δ. is contrasted with ὁ ἀκούων; he that still thirsts, the eager enquirer who is seeking after the salvation which is to be found in the Church, the unbaptized catechumen, cannot yet share in the Church's yearning for the Return of the Lord; he must first come to the Fountain of the Water of Life and drink, before he can welcome Christ Himself. Ἐρχέσθω looks back to Isa. lv. 1 כָּל־צָמֵא לְכוּ לַמַּיִם. Behind the διψῶντες, there is yet another class of non-Christians who are welcomed—οἱ θέλοντες; willingness to receive the truth may exist where as yet there is no thirst for it, and such willingness is of God and a first step towards eternal life: cf. Phil. ii. 13 θεὸς γάρ ἐστιν ὁ ἐνεργῶν ἐν ὑμῖν καὶ τὸ θέλειν καὶ τὸ ἐνεργεῖν; Bede *ad loc.*: "et ipsum enim velle Dei donum est." On λαβέτω ὕδωρ ζωῆς δωρεάν, see xxi. 6, note; λαβέτω suggests that though the supply is gratuitous, the responsibility of accepting and using it rests with the individual; cf. iii. 18, note.

18. μαρτυρῶ ἐγὼ παντὶ τῷ ἀκούοντι κτλ.] The Speaker is still surely Jesus, and not, as many commentators have supposed, St John. Jesus has borne testimony throughout the Book by His angel, and now He bears it in person. His testimony, which is addressed to every hearer of the Book, is a solemn protest against wilful perversions of its teaching. The words are doubtless suggested by the warning of Moses in Deut. iv. 2; οὐ προσθήσεσθε πρὸς τὸ ῥῆμα ὃ ἐγὼ ἐντέλλομαι ὑμῖν, καὶ οὐκ ἀφελεῖτε ἀπ' αὐτοῦ; *ib.* xii. 32 πᾶν ῥῆμα ὃ ἐγὼ ἐντέλλομαι ὑμῖν σήμερον, τοῦτο φυλάξῃ ποιεῖν· οὐ προσθήσεις ἐπ' αὐτό, οὐδὲ ἀφελεῖς ἀπ' αὐτοῦ; Prov. xxiv. 29 (xxx. 6) μὴ προσθῇς τοῖς λόγοις αὐτοῦ, ἵνα μὴ ἐλέγξῃ σε καὶ ψευδὴς γένῃ; cf. the imprecation which Aristeas (ed. Thackeray, § 34) supposes to have been pronounced after the completion of the first Greek version of the Pentateuch, and the boast of Josephus, *c. Ap.* i. 8: δῆλον δ' ἐστὶν ἔργῳ, πῶς ἡμεῖς πρόσιμεν τοῖς ἰδίοις γράμμασι· τοσούτου γὰρ αἰῶνος ἤδη παρῳχηκότος οὔτε προσθεῖναί τις οὐδὲν οὔτε ἀφελεῖν αὐτῶν οὔτε μεταθεῖναι τετόλμηκεν. It was not uncommon for writers to protect their works by adding a solemn adjuration to the scribes to correct the copies carefully, and in no case to mutilate or interpolate the original; cf. e.g. Irenaeus *ap.* Eus. *H. E.* v. 20: ὁρκίζω σε τὸν μεταγραψόμενον τὸ βιβλίον τοῦτο κατὰ τοῦ κυρίου ἡμῶν Ἰησοῦ Χριστοῦ καὶ κατὰ τῆς ἐνδόξου παρουσίας αὐτοῦ ἧς

τῆς προφητείας τοῦ βιβλίου τούτου· Ἐάν τις ἐπιθῇ
ἐπ' αὐτά, ἐπιθήσει ὁ θεὸς ἐπ' αὐτὸν τὰς πληγὰς
19 τὰς γεγραμμένας ἐν τῷ βιβλίῳ τούτῳ· [19]καὶ ἐάν
τις ἀφέλῃ ἀπὸ τῶν λόγων τοῦ βιβλίου τῆς προ-

18 επιθη] επιθησει ℵ (sed transiluit ℵ* ab επιθη ad επιθησει) 79 | επιθησει] επιθησαι 8 13 16 49 51 96 97 98 130 186 al$^{plq\,10}$ *apponat* vg^{lips4} Tyc | om επ αυτον A* | τας πληγας] τ. επτα πληγας Q 31 32 33 37 48 49 91 96 186 Andr Ar 19 εαν] αν ℵ | λογων] + τουτων ℵ | του βιβλιου της προφητειας ταυτης] του βιβλιου τουτου A της προφητειας του βιβλιου τουτου 79 94 vg^{lips4} *prophetiae huius* (sine τ. β.) vg^{am} Ambr

ἔρχεται κρῖναι ζῶντας καὶ νεκρούς, ἵνα ἀντιβάλῃς ὃ μετεγράψω καὶ κατορθώσῃς, Rufinus, *prol. in libros* περὶ ἀρχῶν: "omnem qui hos libros descripturus est vel lecturus in conspectu Dei Patris et Filii et Spiritus sancti contestor...ne addat aliquid scripturae, ne auferat, ne inserat, ne immutet; sed conferat cum exemplaribus unde scripserit," etc. If the solemn warning of the present verse was intended in this sense, it has signally failed; for in no other book of the N.T. is the text so uncertain as in the Apocalypse. But, like its archetype in Deuteronomy, it has a deeper reference; it is no mere *lapsus calami*, no error of judgement or merely intellectual fault which is condemned, but the deliberate falsification or misinterpretation of a Divine message. It is not the letter of the Apocalypse, but its spirit which is thus jealously guarded; and no honest copyist in days before the invention of printing, no honest translator or interpreter of either those times or our own, can incur the terrible penalty. As Bede, with his usual discernment, writes: "haec propter falsatores dixit, non propter eos qui simpliciter quod sentiunt dicunt." Nevertheless the warning, with its danger signal on either hand, ought to give pause to any who would lightly handle the Apocalypse, and suggests to those who venture upon handling it at all Augustine's prayer: "si qua de meo, et Tu ignosce et Tui."

In ἐπιθῇ ἐπ' αὐτά, ἐπιθήσει...ἐπ' αὐτὸν τὰς πληγάς there is a play upon the two meanings of ἐπιτιθέναι and πληγή: 'if any one shall lay (more) on them (add to them), God will lay on him the plagues (blows) described in this Book.' Cf. Acts xvi. 23 πολλὰς δὲ ἐπιθέντες αὐτοῖς πληγάς. Ἀφελεῖ τὸ μέρος αὐτοῦ ἀπὸ τοῦ ξύλου is another way of saying ἀφ. ἀπ' αὐτοῦ τὸ μέρος αὐτοῦ τὸ ἐν τῷ ξύλῳ; the portion which the man had once possessed in the Tree is regarded as taken from it, i.e. he has no longer any rights in it; cf. xxi. 8, and Acts viii. 21 οὐκ ἔστιν σοι μερὶς οὐδὲ κλῆρος ἐν τῷ λόγῳ τούτῳ. Τῶν γεγραμμένων: not as Vg. "et de his quae scripta sunt," but in apposition to τοῦ ξύλου τῆς ζωῆς, τῆς πόλεως τῆς ἁγίας; cf. τὰς πληγὰς τὰς γεγραμμένας (*supra*). Consciously to rob this Book of any part of its essential teaching is to rob oneself of the bliss which it promises: to add to its teaching is to incur the visitations which it threatens. For either act, if deliberate, proclaims a will which is out of harmony with the Will of God and with His ordering of the world; and the rebellious will, while it continues such, cannot receive the things of the Spirit of God here or hereafter. The warning is addressed to Christians who by their attitude towards this Book shew themselves to be unworthy of their inheritance.

20. λέγει ὁ μαρτυρῶν ταῦτα Ναί·

φητείας ταύτης, ἀφελεῖ ὁ θεὸς τὸ μέρος αὐτοῦ ἀπὸ
τοῦ ξύλου τῆς ζωῆς καὶ ἐκ τῆς πόλεως τῆς ἁγίας,
τῶν γεγραμμένων ἐν τῷ βιβλίῳ τούτῳ. [20]Λέγει 20
ὁ μαρτυρῶν ταῦτα Ναί· ἔρχομαι ταχύ. ἀμήν·
ἔρχου, κύριε Ἰησοῦ.

[21]Ἡ χάρις τοῦ κυρίου Ἰησοῦ μετὰ τῶν ἁγίων. 21

19 αφελει] αφελοι 2 8 13 35 38 47 49 91 96 130 | του ξυλου] του βιβλιου vg$^{\text{cle fu lipss 4,5}}$ Ambr Prim | om εκ A 10 38 me　　20 ταυτα] + ειναι ℵ* | om ναι arm Prim | om αμην ℵ me | ερχου] pr ναι (7) 35 38 49 79 91 186 al^{pl} | κυριε Ιησου] + Χριστε ℵ$^{\text{c.a}}$ 4 11 13 20 31 32 38 48 55 79 94 me arm Ar　　21 om totum versum Prim | του κυριου Ιησου] του Χριστου 12 20 31 32 49 Ar + Χριστου Q 130 min^{pl} *g* vg me syrr arm aeth Andr | μετα των αγιων ℵ *g*] μετα παντων A vg^{am} μετα παντων των αγιων Q 130 186 al$^{\text{plq 40}}$ me syrr arm Andr Ar μετα παντων υμων vg$^{\text{cle fu dem lipss}}$ aeth | in fine αμην hab ℵQ min$^{\text{fere omn vid}}$ vg me syr arm aeth (om A 79 vg^{fu} Ar)

ἔρχομαι ταχύ κτλ.] To His solemn testimony in reference to the use of the Book the Lord adds a last word in answer to the call of the Church. The Spirit and the Bride and the loyal hearers of the Book had bidden Him 'come,' and to their Ἔρχου He replies Ναί, ἔρχομαι, 'yea, I am coming, and coming quickly'; on which the Seer, speaking both for the Prophets and for the whole Church, responds, 'Amen, so be it: come, Lord Jesus.' On ναί, ἀμήν see i. 7, note; here ναί expresses the Lord's assent to the call Ἔρχου, and ἀμήν, the absolute faith in His word of the Seer and those whom he represents, and their content with the prospect of His Coming; cf. 2 Tim. iv. 8 πᾶσιν τοῖς ἠγαπηκόσι τὴν ἐπιφάνειαν αὐτοῦ. Κύριος Ἰησοῦς (1 Cor. xii. 3) occurs in this Book only here and in the next verse; it belongs to the language of devotion, which is appropriate to the context.

21. THE FINAL BENEDICTION.

ἡ χάρις τοῦ κυρίου Ἰησοῦ μετὰ τῶν ἁγίων] An ending of this kind is unusual in Apocalypses, as Bousset points out; but it is suitable to an Apocalypse which is also a letter to the Churches (i. 4, note), designed to be read in the congregation. An Apocalypse in its inner character, a prophecy in its purpose, the Book is in its literary form an Epistle, and therefore begins and ends with the epistolary forms familiar to the Asian Churches through the Epistles of St Paul. All the thirteen Epistles of St Paul end with a benediction, constructed on the same general lines, but varying in detail. The Pauline parting benediction begins invariably with ἡ χάρις, which is followed (except in Eph., Col., and the Pastorals) by τοῦ κυρίου [ἡμῶν] Ἰησοῦ [Χριστοῦ]; the ending is either μεθ' ὑμῶν (Rom., 1 Cor., 1 Thess., Col., Pastorals), or μετὰ πάντων ὑμῶν (2 Cor., 2 Th., and in substance, Eph.), or μετὰ τοῦ πνεύματος ὑμῶν (Gal., Phil., Philem.). Hebrews follows the Pauline model with ἡ χάρις μετὰ πάντων ὑμῶν, but no such form appears in the Catholic Epistles; the nearest to it is in 1 Peter, which ends εἰρήνη ὑμῖν πᾶσιν τοῖς ἐν Χριστῷ. St John follows St Paul in the opening words (ἡ χάρις τοῦ κυρίου Ἰησοῦ); in the latter part of the sentence the MSS. offer a choice between μετὰ πάντων and μετὰ τῶν

Subscr αποκαλυψεις ℵ αποκαλυψις Ιωαννου A 130 τελος της αποκαλυψεως του αγιου Ιωαννου του ευαγγελιστου 2 55 τελος της του αγιου Ιωαννου του θεολογου θειας αποκαλυψεως 98 επληρωθη η αποκαλυψις Ιωαννου του ευαγγελιστου και θεολογου 186 nil habent subscriptum Q 7 30 32 38 47 48 49 50 90 91 94 96 97 al[pl] hiant ad fin P 8 14 28 29 87 93 95 al[pl]

ἁγίων, for *μετὰ πάντων τῶν ἁγίων* is a conflation, and *μετὰ πάντων ὑμῶν* a correction from St Paul. On the whole the preference should probably be given to the non-Pauline *μετὰ τῶν ἁγίων*, although it has the support of but one of the uncial MSS. (ℵ); not only is it less likely to have suggested itself to a copyist than *μετὰ πάντων*, but it is in close accordance with the writer's usual phraseology; *οἱ ἅγιοι* is his constant term for the members of the Churches (viii. 3 f., xi. 18, xiii. 7, 10, xiv. 12, xvi. 6, xvii. 6, xviii. 20, 24, xix. 8, xx. 9). The Saints, the men of consecrated lives, are, in the Apocalyptist's view, the men for whose advantage the whole course of human history is being carried to its end; who are destined as a body to survive the wreck of cities and empires, and in the end to dominate a new world. But the grace of the Lord Jesus is the only source of their strength, and the guarantee of their triumph; and the last words of the Apocalypse are at once a reminder of this primary condition of success, and a prayer that it may be realized in the experience of the baptized, both in the cities of Asia and throughout the world.

Subscription. Only two of the Uncials give a subscription to the Book; ℵ repeats Ἀποκάλυψις Ἰωάννου (for Ἀποκαλύψεις surely is both here and at the head of the pages in ℵ a mere itacism), and A, which had Ἀποκάλυψις only in the title, now agrees with ℵ. The forms offered by some cursives and versions add nothing to our knowledge of the Book or its writer.

INDEX OF GREEK WORDS USED IN THE APOCALYPSE OF ST JOHN AS PRINTED IN THIS EDITION.

An asterisk denotes that a word is not used elsewhere in the N.T.; a §, that it is used elsewhere in the N.T. but once, or by but one other writer.

INDEX TO INTRODUCTION AND NOTES.

ADDITIONS AND CORRECTIONS.

PAGE

lv, l. 24. Cf. Hicks, *Inscriptions*, iii *Ephesos*, p. 76: "the temple of Artemis was not merely rich in endowments, and in the accumulated gifts of pilgrims and worshippers; but also, beyond this, the inviolable sanctity of the temple, and the renown of its hierarchy, made it the chief bank of deposit for Asia."

lviii, l. 10. Prof. Reid points out to me that the Augusteum in Smyrna was not dedicated to Tiberius alone; see Tac. *Ann.* iv. 15 "decrevere Asiae urbes templum Tiberio matrique eius et senatui."

lx, l. 6. On this point Prof. Reid writes: "The difficulty which Christians felt in membership of the guilds was by no means confined to the question of the feasts. There was probably no guild which was not devoted to some form of heathen worship. Membership was therefore *ipso facto* bowing down in the house of Rimmon. Direct participation in ceremonies was only incumbent on officials of the guild; but any one possessed of money enough to pay the *summa honoraria* would find it hard to decline office."

lxi. Further illustrations of the life of the Asian cities will be found in *C. I. G.* 3266, 3285, 3415, 3416, 3428, 3460, 3497, 3498, 3508, 3517.

lxxxii, l. 24. I am reminded by Prof. Reid that the assumption of these titles by Domitian was not official. According to Mommsen, *Staatsr.* II. p. 760, the first official use of them was by Aurelian.

ccix, l. 12. Miss Paues informs me that the commentary which accompanies the early English versions of the Norman-French Apocalypse (see p. cxci) shews no tendency to identify Antichrist with the papacy.

9, col. 2, l. 12 ff. On Zech. xii. 10 see Deissmann, *Die Septuaginta-papyri...der Heidelberger Papyrus-sammlung*, p. 66 f.

25, col. 2, l. 2 ff. To *Didache* c. 11, add Hermas *mand.* 11.

27, col. 2, l. 2. But see Ramsay, *Letters to the Seven Churches*, p. 143.

PAGE

49, app. crit., l. 5. *For* γνως ACP *read* γνως CP, *and for* γνωση ℵQ *read* γνωση ℵAQ.

57, col. 2, l. 35 f. *For* THE CHURCH *read* THE ANGEL OF THE CHURCH.

71, col. 1, l. 16. *Add* Abbott, *Johannine Grammar*, §§ 1890, 2281.

78, col. 1, l. 16. *After* ἡμῶν *place a bracket*) .

84, col. 2, l. 22. The bow was the Parthian weapon (Ramsay, *Letters*, p. 58).

ibid. l. 26 ff. Prof. Ramsay, who believes the rider on the white horse to represent the Parthian king, writes (*Letters*, l.c.): "The commentators who try to force a Roman meaning on this figure say that the Roman general, when celebrating a Triumph, rode on a white horse. This is a mistake; the general, when celebrating a Triumph,...was borne like the god, in a four-horse car." But the horses, on occasions at least, were white. See Plutarch, *Camill.* 7: τέθριππον ὑποζευξάμενος λευκόπωλον ἐπέβη, καὶ διεξήλασε τῆς Ῥώμης. He adds, it is true: οὐδενὸς τοῦτο ποιήσαντος ἡγεμόνος πρότερον οὐδ' ὕστερον; but cf. Dion Cassius, *H. R.* xliii. 14 (C. Julius Caesar): τὰ ἐπινίκια τὰ προεψηφισμένα ἐπί τε λευκῶν ἵππων καὶ μετὰ ῥαβδούχων κτλ.

102, col. 2, l. 33. *For* Shechinah *read* Shekinah.

108, app. crit., l. 5. *For* Q* *read* AQ*.

110, col. 1, l. 31. *For W. H. read N. H.*

129, col. 2, l. 9. *For* PREPARATION *read* PREPARATIONS.

133, app. crit., l. 1. *For* θελη 7 *read* θελη A 7.

172, col. 1, l. 25. An ingenious explanation of χιϛ' as = ὁ ἀντίχριστος is offered by Professor Burkitt in the proceedings of the Cambridge Philological Society for March 5, 1896; see *Cambridge University Reporter*, 1895—6, p. 625.

197, app. crit., l. 3. *For* ℵACP *read* ℵCP, *and add* και εκχεετε] απεκχεετε A.

274, col. 1, l. 8. *For* that ornament *read* the ornaments.

288 ff. Prof. Ridgeway writes: "the τοπάζιον is a moss-green variety of olivine, termed *peridot*." He regards the ἴασπις as a green chalcedony, and would identify the χρυσόλιθος of the breastplate with the garnet.

291, col. 1, l. 1. *Add* Abbott, *Johannine Grammar*, §§ 1890, 2281.

CAMBRIDGE: PRINTED BY JOHN CLAY, M.A., AT THE UNIVERSITY PRESS.

1. Ephesus.

ΔΟΜ[ΙΤΙΑ]ΝΟϹ ΚΑΙϹΑΡ
ϹΕΒΑϹΤΟϹ ΓΕΡΜΑΝΙΚΟϹ.
℞. ΑΡΤΕΜΙϹ ΕΦΕϹΙΑ.

2. Smyrna.

[ΔΟΜΙΤΙΑ]ΝΟϹ ΚΑΙ·ϹΕ·
ΓΕΡΜΑΝΙΚΟϹ ΔΟΜΙΤΙΑ
ϹΕΒΑϹΤΗ. ℞. [ΕΠΙ ΔΗΜΟ·
ϹΤΡΑΤΟΥ] ϹΤΡΑΤΗΓΟϹ
ϹΗΙΟϹ ΖΜΥΡΝ·

3. Pergamum.

[ΑϹΚ]ΛΗΠΙΟΥ [ϹΩ]ΤΗΡΟϹ.

4. Pergamum.

ϹΕΒΑϹΤΟΙ ΕΠΙ ΠΕΤΡ[ΩΝΙΟΥ].
℞. ΘΕΟΝ ϹΕΒΑϹΤΟΝ ΠΕΡ-
ΓΑΜΗΝΟΙ·

5. Thyatira.

ΘΥΑΤΕΙΡΑ. ℞. ΘΥΑ-
ΤΕΙΡΗΝΩΝ.

6. Sardis.

ϹΑΡΔΙϹ. ℞. ϹΑΡΔΙΑΝΩΝ
ΝΕΩΚΟΡΩ[Ν].

7. Sardis.

[ΔΡΟΥΣΟΣ] ΚΑΙ ΓΕΡ-
ΜΑΝΙΚΟΣ ΚΑΙΣΑΡΕΣ
ΝΕΟΙ ΘΕΟΙ ΦΙΛΑΔΕΛΦΟΙ.
℞. ΓΑΙΩ ΑΣΙΝΙΩ
ΠΩΛΛΙΩΝΙ ΑΝΘΥΠΑΤΩ.
Within wreath of oak leaves:
ΚΟΙΝΟΥ ΑΣΙΑΣ.

8. Sardis.

ΘΕΑ ΡΩΜΗ. ℞. ϹΑΡΔΙ-
ΑΝΩΝ·Β ΝΕΩΚΟΡΩΝ.

9. Philadelphia.

℞. ΦΙΛΑΔΕΛΦΕΩΝ ΕΡ-
ΜΙΠΠΟϹ ΑΡΧΙΕΡΕΥϹ.

10. Philadelphia.

ΔΗΜΟϹ ΦΙΛΑΔΕΛΦΕΩΝ
ΝΕΩΚ· ℞. ΚΑΙ ϹΜΥΡ-
ΝΑΙΩΝ Γ ΝΕΩΚΟΡΩΝ
ΟΜΟΝΟΙΑ.

11. Laodicea.

ΝΕΡΩΝ ΚΑΙϹΑΡ.
℞. ΓΑΙΟΥ ΠΟϹΤΟΜΟΥ.
ΛΑΟΔΙΚΕΩΝ.